S

S#	SNAME	STATUS	CITY
S1	Smith	20	London
S2	Jones	10	Paris
S3	Blake	30	Paris
S4	Clark	20	London
S5	Adams	30	Athens

P

P#	PNAME	COLOR	WEIGHT	CITY
P1	Nut	Red	12.0	London
P2	Bolt	Green	17.0	Paris
P3	Screw	Blue	17.0	Rome
P4	Screw	Red	14.0	London
P5	Cam	Blue	12.0	Paris
P6	Cog	Red	19.0	London

J

J#	JNAME	CITY
J1	Sorter	Paris
J2	Display	Rome
J3	OCR	Athens
J4	Console	Athens
J5	RAID	London
J6	EDS	Oslo
J7	Tape	London

SPJ

S#	P#	J#	QTY
S1	P1	J1	200
S1	P1	J4	700
S2	P3	J1	400
S2	P3	J2	200
S2	P3	J3	200
S2	P3	J4	500
S2	P3	J5	600
S2	P3	J6	400
S2	P3	J7	800
S2	P5	J2	100
S3	P3	J1	200
S3	P4	J2	500
S4	P6	J3	300
S4	P6	J7	300
S5	P2	J2	200
S5	P2	J4	100
S5	P5	J5	500
S5	P5	J7	100
S5	P6	J2	200
S5	P1	J4	100
S5	P3	J4	200
S5	P4	J4	800
S5	P5	J4	400
S5	P6	J4	500

The suppliers-parts-projects database (sample values)

AN INTRODUCTION TO
Database
Systems

SEVENTH
EDITION

C. J. Date

 ADDISON-WESLEY

An imprint of Addison Wesley Longman, Inc.

Reading, Massachusetts • Menlo Park, California • New York • Harlow, England
Don Mills, Ontario • Sydney • Mexico City • Madrid • Amsterdam

Acquisitions Editor: Maite Suarez-Rivas
Associate Editor: Katherine Harutunian
Production Services: Solar Script, Inc.
Composition: Publishers' Design and Production Services, Inc.
Cover Design: Night & Day Design

Access the latest information about Addison-Wesley titles from our World Wide Web site:
http://www.awlonline.com

Many of the designations used by manufacturers and sellers to distinguish their products are claimed as trademarks. Where those designations appear in this book, and Addison-Wesley was aware of a trademark claim, the designations have been printed in initial caps or all caps.

The programs and applications presented in this book have been included for their instructional value. They have been tested with care but are not guaranteed for any purpose. The publisher does not offer any warranties or representations, nor does it accept any liabilities with respect to the programs or applications.

This book was typeset in Quark XPress 3.3 on a Power Macintosh G3. The font families used were Times Roman and Palatino. It was printed on New Era Matte.

Library of Congress Cataloging-in-Publication Data

Date, C. J.
    An introduction to database systems / by C. J. Date. — 7th ed.
        p.   cm.
    Includes bibliographical references.
    ISBN 0-201-38590-2
    1. Database management. I. Title.
    QA76.9.D3D3659   2000
    005.74—dc21   99-30439
                                                                          CIP

1 2 3 4 5 6 7 8 9 10-CRW-0302010099

This book is dedicated to my wife Lindy
and to the memory of my mother Rene

About the Author

C. J. Date is an independent author, lecturer, researcher, and consultant, specializing in relational database technology. He is based in Healdsburg, California.

In 1967, following several years as a mathematical programmer and programming instructor for Leo Computers Ltd. (London, England), Mr. Date moved to the IBM (UK) Development Laboratories, where he worked on the integration of database functionality into PL/I. In 1974 he transferred to the IBM Systems Development Center in California, where he was responsible for the design of a database language known as the Unified Database Language, UDL, and worked on technical planning and externals design for the IBM products SQL/DS and DB2. He left IBM in May 1983.

Mr. Date has been active in the database field for almost 30 years. He was one of the first people anywhere to recognize the significance of Codd's pioneering work on the relational model. He has lectured widely on technical subjects—principally on database topics, and especially on relational database—throughout North America and also in Europe, Australia, Latin America, and the Far East. In addition to the present book, he is author or coauthor of several other database books, including *Foundation for Object/Relational Databases: The Third Manifesto* (1998), a detailed proposal for the future direction of the field; *Database: A Primer* (1983), which treats database systems from the nonspecialist's point of view; a series of *Relational Database Writings* books (1986, 1990, 1992, 1995, 1998), which deal with various aspects of relational technology in depth; and another series of books on specific systems and languages—*A Guide to DB2* (4th edition, 1993), *A Guide to SYBASE and SQL Server* (1992), *A Guide to SQL/DS* (1988), *A Guide to INGRES* (1987), and *A Guide to the SQL Standard* (4th edition, 1997). His books have been translated into many languages, including Chinese, Dutch, French, German, Greek, Italian, Japanese, Korean, Polish, Portuguese, Russian, Spanish, and Braille.

Mr. Date has also produced over 300 technical articles and research papers and has made a variety of original contributions to database theory. He is a regular columnist for the magazines *Database Programming & Design* and *Intelligent Enterprise*. His professional seminars on database technology (offered both in North America and overseas) are widely considered to be second to none for the quality of the subject matter and the clarity of the exposition.

Mr. Date holds an Honours Degree in Mathematics from Cambridge University, England (BA 1962, MA 1966) and the honorary degree of Doctor of Technology from De Montfort University, England (1994).

Contents

PART III   DATABASE DESIGN   327

PART V   FURTHER TOPICS   503

APPENDIXES   887

Preface to the Seventh Edition

This book is a comprehensive introduction to the now very large field of database systems. It provides a solid grounding in the foundations of database technology and gives some idea of how the field is likely to develop in the future. The book is meant primarily as a textbook, not a work of reference (though I believe it can be useful as a reference also, to some extent); the emphasis throughout is on **insight** and **understanding,** not just on formalisms.

PREREQUISITES

The book as a whole is meant for anyone professionally interested in computing in some way who wants to gain an understanding of what database systems are all about. I assume you have at least a basic knowledge of both:

- The storage and file management capabilities (indexing, etc.) of a modern computer system;
- The features of one or more high-level programming languages (e.g., C, Java, Pascal, PL/I, etc.).

STRUCTURE

The book is divided into six major parts:

I. Basic Concepts
II. The Relational Model
III. Database Design
IV. Transaction Management
V. Further Topics
VI. Object and Object/Relational Databases

Each part in turn is divided into several chapters:

- Part I (four chapters) provides a broad introduction to the concepts of database systems in general and relational systems in particular. It also introduces the standard database language **SQL.**

- Part II (five chapters) consists of a detailed and very careful description of **the relational model,** which is not only the theoretical foundation underlying relational systems, but is in fact the theoretical foundation for the database field as a whole.

- Part III (four chapters) discusses the general question of **database design;** three chapters are devoted to design theory, the fourth considers semantic modeling and the entity/relationship model.

- Part IV (two chapters) is concerned with **transaction management** (i.e., recovery and concurrency controls).

- Part V (eight chapters) is a little bit of a *potpourri.* In general, however, it shows how relational concepts are relevant to a variety of further aspects of database technology—**security, distributed databases, temporal data, decision support,** and so on.

- Finally, Part VI (two chapters) describes the impact of **object technology** on database systems. Chapter 25 in particular, the last in the book, considers the possibility of a *rapprochement* between object and relational technologies and discusses **object/relational** systems.

There are also three appendixes—one giving further details of SQL, one on "SQL3" (a new version of SQL that is likely to be ratified as a standard round about the time this book appears in print), and one that lists some important abbreviations and acronyms.

Note: An online *Instructor's Manual* is also available, giving guidance on how to use the book as a basis for teaching a database course. It consists of a series of notes, hints, and suggestions on each part, each chapter, and each appendix, as well as answers to exercises not answered in the book itself and other supporting material. For instructions on how to access the *Manual*, please contact your local Addison-Wesley sales representative. To locate your local representative, please visit us on the web at *http://hepg.awl.com/rep-locator.*

HOW TO READ THIS BOOK

The book overall is meant to be read in sequence more or less as written, but you can skip later chapters, and later sections within chapters, if you choose. A suggested plan for a first reading would be:

- Read Chapters 1 and 2 "once over lightly";
- Read Chapters 3 and 4 very carefully;
- Read Chapters 5, 6, 8, and 9 carefully, but skip Chapter 7 (except perhaps for Section 7.7);
- Read Chapter 10 "once over lightly";
- Read Chapters 11 and 13 carefully, but skip Chapter 12;
- Read Chapters 14 and 15 carefully;
- Read subsequent chapters selectively, according to taste and interest.

Each chapter opens with an introduction and closes with a summary; in addition, most chapters include a set of exercises, usually with answers (often the answers give additional information about the subject of the exercise). Most chapters also include an extensive list of references, many of them annotated. This structure allows the subject matter to be treated in a multi-level fashion, with the most important concepts and results being presented "in line" in the main body of the text and various subsidiary issues and more complex aspects being deferred to the Exercises or Answers or References section, as appropriate. *Note:* References are identified in the text by two-part numbers in square brackets. For example, the reference "[3.1]" refers to the first item in the list of references at the end of Chapter 3: namely, a paper by E. F. Codd published in *CACM,* Vol. 25, No. 2, in February, 1982. (For an explanation of abbreviations used in references—e.g., "CACM"—see Appendix C.)

COMPARISON WITH EARLIER EDITIONS

The major differences between this edition and its immediate predecessor are summarized below.

- *Part I:* Chapters 1–3 cover roughly the same ground as Chapters 1–3 in the previous edition, but they have been rewritten, and the treatment of several topics has been improved and amplified. Chapter 4 is new (though partly based on the old Chapter 8); it provides an introduction to SQL, covering aspects that do not logically belong anywhere else in the book (in particular, host language bindings and embedded SQL).

- *Part II:* Chapters 5–9 (on the relational model) represent a completely rewritten, considerably expanded, and very much improved version of Chapters 4–7 and 17 from the previous edition. In particular, the sections on types (domains), relation values *vs.* relation variables, integrity, predicates, and views have all been drastically revised.

  Note: Some words of explanation are in order here. Earlier editions used SQL to illustrate relational ideas, in the belief that it is easier on the student to show the concrete before the abstract. Unfortunately, however, the gulf between SQL and the relational model has grown so wide that I now feel it would be actively misleading to use SQL for such a purpose. In fact, SQL in its present form is so far from being a true embodiment of relational principles—it suffers from so many sins of both omission and commission—that I would have preferred to relegate it to an appendix; but the language is so important from a commercial point of view (and every database professional needs to have some familiarity with it) that it would just not be appropriate to treat it in so dismissive a manner. I have therefore settled on a compromise—a chapter on SQL basics in Part I of the book, and individual sections in other chapters (where applicable) describing those aspects of SQL that are specific to the subject of the chapter in question.

- *Part III:* Chapters 10–13 are a significant revision of the old Chapters 9–12, with new material on relation-valued attributes, denormalization, orthogonal design, and alternative approaches to semantic modeling (including "business rules").

  Note: Again, some explanation is in order. Some reviewers of earlier editions complained that database design issues were being treated too late. But it is my feeling that students are not ready to design databases properly or to appreciate design issues fully until they have some understanding of what databases are and how they are used; in other words, I believe it is important to spend some time on the relational model and related matters before exposing the student to design questions. Thus, I still believe Part III is in the right place in the book.

- *Part IV:* The two chapters of this part are slightly revised and extended versions of Chapters 13 and 14 from the previous edition.

- *Part V:* Chapters 19 (on type inheritance), 21 (on decision support), and 22 (on temporal databases) are all new. Chapters 16 (on security), 17 (on optimization), 18 (on missing information), and 20 (on distributed databases) are expanded and significantly revised versions of the old Chapters 15, 18, 20, and 21, respectively. Chapter 23 (on logic-based or deductive databases) is a revised version of the old Appendix C.

- *Part VI:* Chapter 24 is a completely rewritten and much improved version of the old Chapters 22–24. Chapter 25 is mostly new.

Finally, Appendix A is based on part of the old Chapter 8; Appendix B is new; and Appendix C is an updated version of the old Appendix D.

In addition to the changes sketched above, the following topics have been dropped in this edition:

- Storage structures and access methods (old Appendix A);
- Detailed discussion of DB2 (old Appendix B).

WHAT MAKES THIS BOOK DIFFERENT?

Every database book on the market has its own individual strengths and weaknesses, and every writer has his or her own particular ax to grind. One concentrates on transaction management issues; another stresses entity/relationship modeling; yet another looks at everything through an SQL lens; still another takes a pure "object" point of view; still another views the field exclusively in terms of commercial products; and so on. And, of course, I am no exception to this rule—I too have an ax to grind: what might be called the **foundation** ax. I believe very firmly that we must get the foundation right, and understand it properly, before we try to build on that foundation in any way. This belief on my part explains the heavy emphasis in this book on the relational model; in particular, it explains the length of Part II—the most important part of the book—where I present my own understanding of the relational model as carefully as I can. I am interested in foundations, not fads and fashions.

In this connection, I should say too that I am well aware that the overall tone of this book has changed over the years. The first few editions were mostly descriptive in nature; they described the field as it actually was in practice, "warts and all." This edition, by contrast, is much more *pre*scriptive; it talks about the way the field *ought* to be and the way it ought to develop in the future, if we do things right (in other words, it is a textbook with an attitude!). And the first part of that "doing things right" is surely educating oneself as to what those right things actually are. I hope this edition can help in that educational endeavor.

And another (related) point: Some of you might know that, along with my colleague Hugh Darwen, I recently published another "prescriptive" book on database technology, whose title (abbreviated) is *The Third Manifesto* [3.3]. That book builds on the relational model to offer a detailed technical proposal for future database systems (it is the result of many years of teaching and thinking about such matters on the part of both Hugh and myself). And, not surprisingly, the ideas of the *Manifesto* inform the present book throughout. Which is not to say that the *Manifesto* is a prerequisite to the present book—it is not; but it *is* directly relevant to much that is in the present book, and further pertinent information is often to be found therein.

A CLOSING REMARK

I would like to close these prefatory notes with the following edited extract from another preface—Bertrand Russell's own preface to *The Bertrand Russell Dictionary of Mind, Matter and Morals* (ed., Lester E. Denonn), Citadel Press, 1993, reprinted here by permission:

> *I have been accused of a habit of changing my opinions . . . I am not myself in any degree ashamed of [that habit]. What physicist who was already active in 1900 would dream of boasting that his opinions had not changed during the last half century? . . . [The] kind of philosophy that I value and have endeavoured to pursue is scientific, in the sense that there is some definite knowledge to be obtained and that new discoveries can make the admission of former error inevitable to any candid mind. For what I have said, whether early or late, I do not claim the kind of truth which theologians claim for their creeds. I claim only, at best, that the opinion expressed was a sensible one to hold at the time . . . I should be much surprised if subsequent research did not show that it needed to be modified. [Such opinions were not] intended as pontifical pronouncements, but only as the best I could do at the time towards the promotion of clear and accurate thinking. Clarity, above all, has been my aim.*

If you compare earlier editions of this book with this seventh edition, you will find that I too have changed my opinions on many matters (and no doubt I will continue to do so). I hope you will accept the remarks quoted above as adequate justification for this state of affairs. I share Bertrand Russell's perception of what the field of scientific inquiry is all about, but he expresses that perception far more eloquently than I could.

ACKNOWLEDGMENTS

Once again it is a pleasure to acknowledge my debt to the many people involved, directly or indirectly, in the production of this book. First of all, I must thank my friends David Mc-Goveran and Hugh Darwen for their major involvement in this edition: David contributed the first draft of Chapter 21 on decision support, and Hugh contributed the first draft of

Chapter 22 on temporal databases. Hugh also did a very thorough reviewing job on large portions of the manuscript, including in particular all of the relational chapters and the appendix on SQL3. Second, the text has benefited from the comments of students on the seminars I have been teaching over the past several years. It has also benefited enormously from the comments of, and discussion with, numerous friends and reviewers, including Charley Bontempo, Declan Brady, Hugh Darwen (again), Tim Hartley, Adrian Larner, Chung Lee, David Livingstone, Nikos Lorentzos, Huizha Lu, Ramon Mata-Toledo, Nelson Mattos, David McGoveran (again), Fabian Pascal, Sudha Ram, Rick van der Lans, Yongdong Wang, Colin White, and Qiang Zhu. Each of these people reviewed at least some portion of the manuscript or made technical material available or otherwise helped me find answers to my many technical questions, and I am very grateful to all of them. I would also like to thank my wife Lindy for contributing the cover art once again. Finally, I am grateful (as always) to everyone at Addison-Wesley—especially Maite Suarez-Rivas and Katherine Harutunian—for all of their encouragement and support throughout this project, and to my editor Elydia Davis for her usual sterling job.

Healdsburg, California   C. J. Date
1999

PRELIMINARIES

Part I consists of four introductory chapters:

- Chapter 1 sets the scene by explaining what a database is and why database systems are desirable. It also briefly discusses the difference between relational database systems and others.

- Next, Chapter 2 presents a general architecture for database systems, the so-called *ANSI/SPARC architecture*. That architecture serves as a framework on which the rest of the book will build.

- Chapter 3 then presents an overview of relational systems (the aim is to serve as a gentle introduction to the much more comprehensive discussions of the same subject in Part II and later parts of the book). It also introduces and explains the running example, the suppliers and parts database.

- Finally, Chapter 4 introduces the standard relational language SQL.

CHAPTER 1

An Overview of Database Management

1.1 INTRODUCTION

A **database** system is basically just a *computerized record-keeping system.* The **database** itself can be regarded as a kind of electronic filing cabinet; i.e., it is a repository or container for a collection of computerized data files. Users of the system can perform a variety of operations on such files—for example:

- Adding new, empty files to the database;
- Inserting data into existing files;
- Retrieving data from existing files;
- Changing data in existing files;
- Deleting data from existing files;
- Removing existing files from the database.

Fig. 1.1 shows a very small database containing just one file, called CELLAR, which in turn contains data concerning the contents of a wine cellar. Fig. 1.2 shows an example

BIN#	WINE	PRODUCER	YEAR	BOTTLES	READY
2	Chardonnay	Buena Vista	1997	1	1999
3	Chardonnay	Geyser Peak	1997	5	1999
6	Chardonnay	Simi	1996	4	1998
12	Joh. Riesling	Jekel	1998	1	1999
21	Fumé Blanc	Ch. St. Jean	1997	4	1999
22	Fumé Blanc	Robt. Mondavi	1996	2	1998
30	Gewurztraminer	Ch. St. Jean	1998	3	1999
43	Cab. Sauvignon	Windsor	1991	12	2000
45	Cab. Sauvignon	Geyser Peak	1994	12	2002
48	Cab. Sauvignon	Robt. Mondavi	1993	12	2004
50	Pinot Noir	Gary Farrell	1996	3	1999
51	Pinot Noir	Fetzer	1993	3	2000
52	Pinot Noir	Dehlinger	1995	2	1998
58	Merlot	Clos du Bois	1994	9	2000
64	Zinfandel	Cline	1994	9	2003
72	Zinfandel	Rafanelli	1995	2	2003

Fig. 1.1   The wine cellar database (file CELLAR)

```
Retrieval:

SELECT  WINE, BIN#, PRODUCER
FROM    CELLAR
WHERE   READY = 2000 ;
```

```
Result (as shown on, e.g., a display screen):
```

WINE	BIN#	PRODUCER
Cab. Sauvignon	43	Windsor
Pinot Noir	51	Fetzer
Merlot	58	Clos du Bois

Fig. 1.2   Retrieval example

of a **retrieval** operation against that database, together with the data returned by that operation. *Note:* Throughout this book we show database operations, file names, and other such material in upper case for clarity. In practice it is often more convenient to enter such material in lower case. Most systems will accept both.

Fig. 1.3 gives examples, all more or less self-explanatory, of **insert, change,** and **delete** operations on the wine cellar database. Examples of adding and removing entire files will be given later, in Chapters 3, 4, 5, and elsewhere.

```
Inserting new data:

INSERT
INTO    CELLAR ( BIN#, WINE, PRODUCER, YEAR, BOTTLES, READY )
VALUES ( 53, 'Pinot Noir', 'Saintsbury', 1997, 6, 2001 ) ;
```

```
Changing existing data:

UPDATE CELLAR
SET    BOTTLES = 4
WHERE  BIN# = 3 ;
```

```
Deleting existing data:

DELETE
FROM    CELLAR
WHERE   BIN# = 2 ;
```

Fig. 1.3   Insert / change / delete examples

Points arising from these examples:

1. For obvious reasons, computerized files such as CELLAR in Fig. 1.1 are often called **tables** (more precisely, **relational** tables—see Sections 1.3 and 1.6).

2. The **rows** of such a table can be thought of as the records of the file, and the **columns** can be regarded as the fields of those records. In this book, we will use the terminology of records and fields when we are talking about database systems in general (mostly just in the first two chapters); we will use the terminology of rows and columns when we are talking about relational systems in particular (again, see Sections 1.3 and 1.6). *Note:* Actually, when we get to our more formal discussions in later parts of the book, we will switch to more formal terms anyway.

3. For simplicity, we have made a tacit assumption in the example that columns WINE and PRODUCER contain character string data and all other columns contain integer data. We will consider this question of column **data types** in more detail in Chapters 3, 4, and especially 5.

4. Column BIN# constitutes the **primary key** for table CELLAR (meaning no two CELLAR rows ever contain the same BIN# value). We often use *double underlining* to indicate primary key columns, as in Fig. 1.1.

5. The sample operations or "statements" in Figs. 1.2 and 1.3—**SELECT, INSERT, UPDATE, DELETE**—are all expressed in a language called **SQL.** SQL is the standard language for interacting with relational databases, and it is supported by just about every database product on the market today. *Note:* The name "SQL" originally stood for "Structured Query Language" and was pronounced "sequel." Now the language has become a standard, however, the name is just a name—it is not officially an abbreviation for anything at all—and the pendulum has swung in favor of the pronunciation "ess-cue-ell." We will assume this latter pronunciation in this book.

6. Note that SQL uses the keyword UPDATE to mean "change" specifically. This fact can cause confusion, because the term "update" is also used to refer to the three operations INSERT, UPDATE, and DELETE as a group. We will distinguish between the two meanings in this book by using lower case when the generic meaning is intended and upper case to refer to the UPDATE operator specifically.

7. As you probably already know, the vast majority of database systems in use today are in fact relational (or would-be relational, at any rate—see Chapter 4, Section 4.7). Partly for this reason, the emphasis in this book is heavily on such systems.

One last preliminary remark: An understanding of the material in this chapter and the next is fundamental to a full appreciation of the features and capabilities of a modern database system. However, it cannot be denied that the material is somewhat abstract and rather dry in places, and it does tend to involve a large number of concepts and terms that might be new to you. In later parts of the book—especially Chapters 3 and 4—you will find material that is much less abstract and hence more immediately understandable, perhaps. You might therefore prefer just to give these first two chapters a "once over lightly" reading for now, and to reread them more carefully later as they become more directly relevant to the topics at hand.

1.2   WHAT IS A DATABASE SYSTEM?

To repeat from the previous section, a database system is basically a computerized record-keeping system; i.e., it is a computerized system whose overall purpose is to store information and to allow users to retrieve and update that information on demand. The information in question can be anything that is of significance to the individual or organization concerned—anything, in other words, that is needed to assist in the general process of running the business of that individual or organization.

Note: The terms "data" and "information" are treated as synonymous in this book. Some writers prefer to distinguish between the two, using "data" to refer to what is actually stored in the database and "information" to refer to the *meaning* of that data as understood by some user. The distinction is clearly important—so important that it seems preferable to make it explicit, where appropriate, instead of relying on a somewhat arbitrary differentiation between two essentially synonymous terms.

Fig. 1.4 is a simplified picture of a database system. It is meant to show that a database system involves four major components: **data, hardware, software,** and **users.** We con-

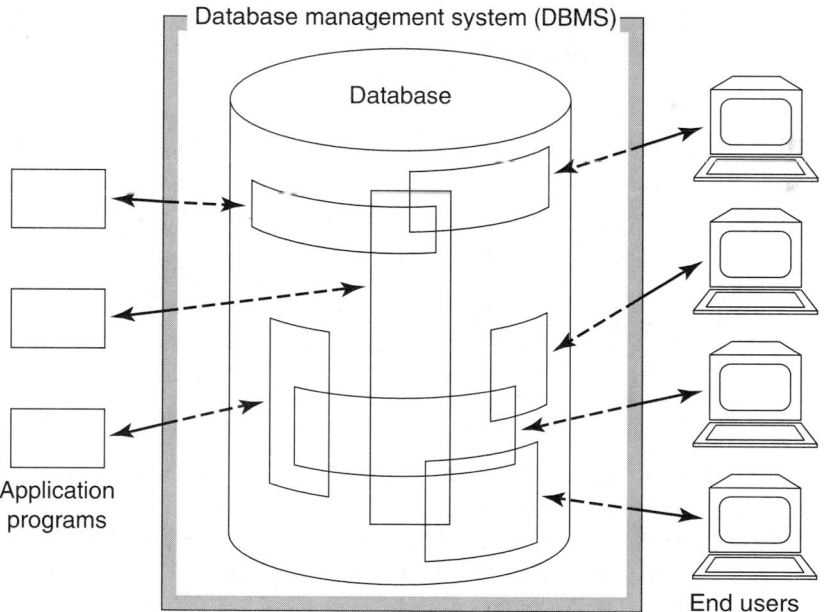

Fig. 1.4   Simplified picture of a database system

sider these four components briefly below. Later, of course, we will discuss each in much more detail (except for the hardware component, details of which are mostly beyond the scope of this book).

Data

Database systems are available on machines that range all the way from the smallest personal computers to the largest mainframes. Needless to say, the facilities provided by any given system are determined to some extent by the size and power of the underlying machine. In particular, systems on large machines ("large systems") tend to be *multi-user,* whereas those on smaller machines ("small systems") tend to be *single-user.* A **single-user system** is a system in which at most one user can access the database at any given time; a **multi-user system** is a system in which many users can access the database at the same time. As Fig. 1.4 suggests, we will normally assume the latter case in this book, for generality, but in fact the distinction is largely irrelevant so far as most users are concerned: A major objective of multi-user systems in general is precisely to allow each user to behave as if he or she were working with a *single*-user system instead. The special problems of multi-user systems are primarily problems that are internal to the system, not ones that are visible to the user (see Part IV of this book, especially Chapter 15).

   Note: It is convenient to assume for the sake of simplicity that the totality of data in the system is all stored in a single database, and we will usually make that assumption in this book (since it does not materially affect any of our other discussions). In practice, however, there might be good reasons, even in a small system, why the data should be split across several distinct databases. We will touch on some of those reasons later, in Chapter 2 and elsewhere.

   In general, then, the data in the database—at least in a large system—will be both *integrated* and *shared.* As we will see in Section 1.4, these two aspects, data integration and data sharing, represent a major advantage of database systems in the "large" environment; and data integration, at least, can be significant in the "small" environment as well. Of course, there are many additional advantages (to be discussed later), even in the small environment. But first let us explain what we mean by the terms *integrated* and *shared.*

- By **integrated,** we mean that the database can be thought of as a unification of several otherwise distinct files, with any redundancy among those files at least partly eliminated. For example, a given database might contain both an EMPLOYEE file, giving employee names, addresses, departments, salaries, etc., and an ENROLLMENT file, representing the enrollment of employees in training courses (refer to Fig. 1.5). Now suppose that, in order to carry out the process of training course administration, it is necessary to know the department for each enrolled student. Then there is clearly no need to include that information redundantly in the ENROLLMENT file, because it can always be discovered by referring to the EMPLOYEE file instead.

- By **shared,** we mean that individual pieces of data in the database can be shared among different users, in the sense that each of those users can have access to the same piece

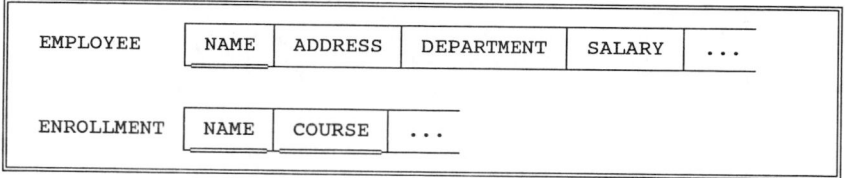

Fig. 1.5   The EMPLOYEE and ENROLLMENT files

of data, possibly for different purposes. As indicated earlier, different users can effectively even access the same piece of data *at the same time* ("concurrent access"). Such sharing, concurrent or otherwise, is partly a consequence of the fact that the database is integrated. In the example cited above, for instance, the department information in the EMPLOYEE file would typically be shared by users in the Personnel Department and users in the Education Department—and, as already suggested, those two classes of users would typically use that information for different purposes. *Note:* If the database is *not* shared, it is sometimes described as "personal" or "application-specific."

Another consequence of the foregoing facts—that the database is integrated and (usually) shared—is that any given user will typically be concerned only with some small portion of the total database; moreover, different users' portions will overlap in various ways. In other words, a given database will be perceived by different users in many different ways. In fact, even when two users share the same portion of the database, their views of that portion might differ considerably at a detailed level. This latter point is discussed more fully in Section 1.5 and Chapters 2, 3, and especially 9.

We will have more to say regarding the nature of the data component of the system in Section 1.3.

Hardware

The hardware components of the system consist of:

- The secondary storage volumes—mostly magnetic disks—that are used to hold the stored data, together with the associated I/O devices (disk drives, etc.), device controllers, I/O channels, and so forth; and

- The hardware processor(s) and associated main memory that are used to support the execution of the database system software (see the next subsection).

This book does not concern itself very much with the hardware aspects of the system, for the following reasons among others: First, those aspects form a major topic in their own right; second, the problems encountered in this area are not peculiar to database systems; and third, those problems have been very thoroughly investigated and described elsewhere.

Software

Between the physical database itself—i.e., the data as physically stored—and the users of the system is a layer of software, known variously as the **database manager** or **database server** or, most commonly, the **database management system** (DBMS). All requests for access to the database are handled by the DBMS; the facilities sketched in Section 1.1 for adding and removing files (or tables), retrieving data from and updating data in such files or tables, and so forth, are all facilities provided by the DBMS. One general function provided by the DBMS is thus *the shielding of database users from hardware-level details* (much as programming language systems shield application programmers from hardware-level details). In other words, the DBMS provides users with a perception of the database that is elevated somewhat above the hardware level, and it supports user operations (such as the SQL operations discussed briefly in Section 1.1) that are expressed in terms of that higher-level perception. We will discuss this function, and other functions of the DBMS, in considerably more detail throughout the body of this book.

A couple of further points:

- The DBMS is easily the most important software component in the overall system, but it is not the only one. Others include utilities, application development tools, design aids, report writers, and (most important) the *transaction manager* or *TP monitor.* See Chapters 2 and 3 and (especially) Part IV for further discussion of these components.

- The term *DBMS* is also used to refer generically to some particular product from some particular vendor—for example, IBM's "DB2 Universal Database" product for OS/390. The term *DBMS instance* is then sometimes used to refer to the particular copy of such a product that happens to be running on some particular computer installation. As you will surely appreciate, sometimes it is necessary to distinguish carefully between these two concepts.

    Note: You should be warned that people in the industry often use the term *database* when they really mean *DBMS* (in either of the foregoing senses). Here is a typical example: "Vendor *X*'s database outperformed vendor *Y*'s database by a ratio of two to one." This usage is sloppy, and deprecated, but very, very common. (The problem is, of course, if we call the DBMS the database, then what do we call the database?) *Caveat lector.*

Users

We consider three broad (and somewhat overlapping) classes of users:

- First, there are **application programmers,** responsible for writing database application programs in some programming language such as COBOL, PL/I, C++, Java, or some higher-level "fourth generation" language (see Chapter 2). Such programs access the database by issuing the appropriate request—typically an SQL statement—to the DBMS. The programs themselves can be conventional batch applications, or they can be **online** applications, whose purpose is to allow an end user (see the next paragraph) to access the database from an online workstation or terminal. Most modern applications are of the online variety.

- The second class of user, then, is **end users,** who interact with the system from online workstations or terminals. A given end user can access the database via one of the online applications mentioned in the previous paragraph, or he or she can use an interface provided as an integral part of the database system software. Such vendor-provided interfaces are also supported by means of online applications, of course, but those applications are **builtin,** not user-written. Most database systems include at least one such builtin application, namely a **query language processor,** by which the user can issue database requests (also known as statements or *commands*) such as SELECT and INSERT to the DBMS interactively. The language SQL mentioned in Section 1.1 is a typical example of a database query language.

    Note: The term "query language," common though it is, is really a misnomer, inasmuch as the natural language verb "to query" suggests *retrieval* only, whereas query languages usually (not always) provide update and other operations as well.

    Most systems also provide additional builtin interfaces in which users do not issue explicit database requests such as SELECT at all, but instead operate by (e.g.) choosing items from a menu or filling in boxes on a form. Such **menu-** or **forms-driven** interfaces tend to be easier to use for people who do not have a formal training in IT (IT = information technology; the abbreviation IS, short for information systems, is also used with much the same meaning). By contrast, **command-driven interfaces**—i.e., query languages—do tend to require a certain amount of professional IT expertise, though perhaps not much (obviously not as much as is needed to write an application program in a language like COBOL). Then again, a command-driven interface is likely to be more flexible than a menu- or forms-driven one, in that query languages typically include certain features that are not supported by those other interfaces.

- The third class of user, not shown in Fig. 1.4, is the **database administrator** or DBA. Discussion of the DBA function—and the associated (very important) **data** administrator function—is deferred to Section 1.4 and Chapter 2 (Section 2.7).

This completes our preliminary description of the major aspects of a database system. We now go on to discuss the ideas in somewhat more detail.

1.3   WHAT IS A DATABASE?

Persistent Data

It is customary to refer to the data in a database as "persistent" (though it might not actually persist for very long!). By *persistent,* we mean, intuitively, that database data differs in kind from other more ephemeral data, such as input data, output data, control statements, work queues, software control blocks, intermediate results, and more generally any data that is transient in nature. More precisely, we say that data in the database "persists" because, once it has been accepted by the DBMS for entry into the database in the first place, *it can subsequently be removed from the database only by some explicit request to the DBMS,* not as a mere side effect of (e.g.) some program completing execution. This notion of persistence thus allows us to give a slightly more precise definition of the term "database":

- A **database** is a collection of persistent data that is used by the application systems of some given enterprise.

The term "enterprise" here is simply a convenient generic term for any reasonably self-contained commercial, scientific, technical, or other organization. An enterprise might be a single individual (with a small personal database), or a complete corporation or similar large body (with a large shared database), or anything in between. Here are some examples:

1. A manufacturing company
2. A bank
3. A hospital
4. A university
5. A government department

Any enterprise must necessarily maintain a lot of data about its operation. Such data is the "persistent data" referred to above. The enterprises just mentioned would typically include the following among their persistent data:

1. Product data
2. Account data
3. Patient data
4. Student data
5. Planning data

Note: The first few editions of this book used the term "operational data" in place of "persistent data." That earlier term reflected the original emphasis in database systems on **operational** or **production** applications—i.e., routine, highly repetitive applications that were executed over and over again to support the day-to-day operation of the enterprise (for example, an application to support the deposit or withdrawal of cash in a banking system). The term **online transaction processing** has come to be used to refer to this kind of environment. However, databases are now increasingly being used for other kinds of applications as well—i.e., **decision support** applications—and the term "operational data" is thus no longer entirely appropriate. Indeed, enterprises nowadays often maintain two separate databases, one containing operational data and one, often called the *data warehouse,* containing decision support data. The data warehouse often includes *summary information* (e.g., totals, averages), where that summary information in turn is extracted from the operational database on a periodic basis—say once a day or once a week. See Chapter 21 for further discussion of decision support databases and applications.

Entities and Relationships

We now consider the example of a manufacturing company ("KnowWare Inc.") in a little more detail. Such an enterprise will typically wish to record information about the *projects* it has on hand; the *parts* used in those projects; the *suppliers* who supply those parts; the *warehouses* in which those parts are stored; the *employees* who work on those projects; and so on. Projects, parts, suppliers, etc., thus constitute the basic **entities** about which KnowWare Inc. needs to record information (the term "entity" is commonly used in database circles to mean any distinguishable object that is to be represented in the database). Refer to Fig. 1.6.

In addition to the basic entities themselves (suppliers, parts, and so on, in the example), there will also be **relationships** linking those basic entities together. Such relationships are represented by diamonds and connecting lines in Fig. 1.6. For example, there is a relationship ("SP") between suppliers and parts: Each supplier supplies certain parts, and conversely each part is supplied by certain suppliers (more accurately, each supplier supplies certain *kinds* of parts, each *kind* of part is supplied by certain suppliers). Similarly, parts are used in projects, and conversely projects use parts (relationship PJ); parts are stored in warehouses, and warehouses store parts (relationship WP); and so on. Note that these relationships are all *bidirectional*—that is, they can be traversed in either direction. For example, relationship SP between suppliers and parts can be used to answer both of the following questions:

- Given a supplier, get the parts supplied by that supplier;
- Given a part, get the suppliers who supply that part.

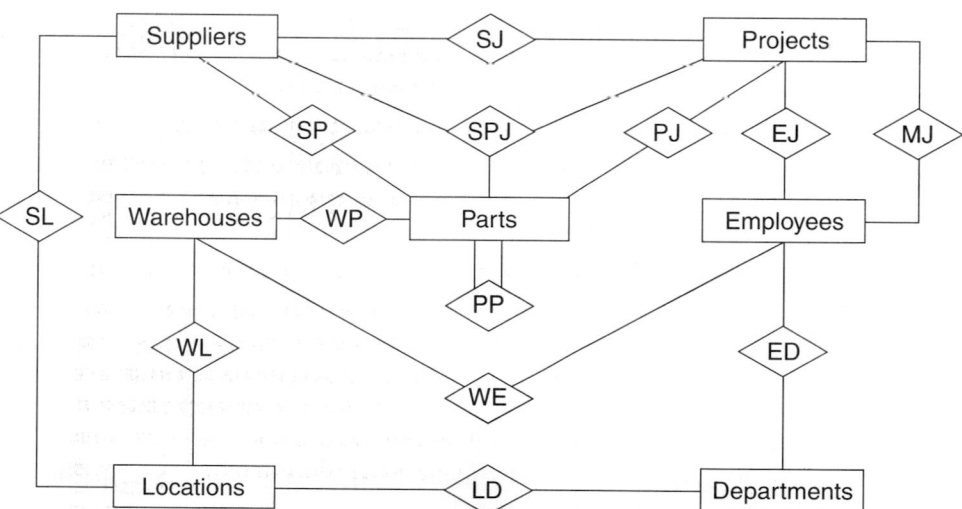

Fig. 1.6 Entity/relationship (E/R) diagram for KnowWare Inc.

The significant point about this relationship (and all of the others illustrated in the figure, of course) is that *they are just as much a part of the data as are the basic entities.* They must therefore be represented in the database, just like the basic entities. *Note:* In a relational system specifically, both the basic entities and the relationships connecting them will be represented by means of tables like the one shown in Fig. 1.1, as we will see in Chapter 3.

We note in passing that Fig. 1.6 is an example of what is called (for obvious reasons) an **entity/relationship diagram** (E/R diagram for short). In Chapter 13 we will consider such diagrams in some detail.

Fig. 1.6 also illustrates a number of other important points:

1. Although most of the relationships in that figure involve *two* entity types—i.e., they are *binary* relationships—it is by no means the case that all relationships must necessarily be binary in this sense. In the example there is one relationship ("SPJ") involving three entity types (suppliers, parts, and projects): a *ternary* relationship. The intended interpretation is that certain suppliers supply certain parts to certain projects. Note carefully that this ternary relationship ("suppliers supply parts to projects") is *not* equivalent, in general, to the combination of the three binary relationships "suppliers supply parts," "parts are used in projects," and "projects are supplied by suppliers." For example, the statement that

   a. Smith supplies monkey wrenches to the Manhattan project

   tells us *more* than the following three statements do:

   b. Smith supplies monkey wrenches,

   c. Monkey wrenches are used in the Manhattan project, and

   d. The Manhattan project is supplied by Smith

   —we cannot (validly!) infer a. knowing only b., c., and d. More precisely, if we know b., c., and d., then we might be able to infer that Smith supplies monkey wrenches to *some* project (say project Jz), that *some* supplier (say supplier Sx) supplies monkey wrenches to the Manhattan project, and that Smith supplies *some* part (say part Py) to the Manhattan project—but we cannot validly infer that Sx is Smith or that Py is monkey wrenches or that Jz is the Manhattan project. False inferences such as these are examples of what is sometimes called **the connection trap.**

2. The figure also shows one relationship (PP) involving just *one* entity type (parts). The relationship here is that certain parts include other parts as immediate components (the so-called **bill-of-materials** relationship)—for example, a screw is a component of a hinge assembly, which is also considered as a part and might in turn be a component of some higher-level part such as a lid. Note that this relationship is still binary; it is just that the two entity types that are linked together, parts and parts, happen to be one and the same.

3. In general, a given set of entity types might be linked together in any number of distinct relationships. In the example in Fig. 1.6, there are two distinct relationships involving projects and employees: One (EJ) represents the fact that employees are assigned to projects, the other (MJ) represents the fact that employees manage projects.

We now observe that *a relationship can be regarded as an entity in its own right.* If we take as our definition of entity "any object about which we wish to record information," then a relationship certainly fits the definition. For instance, "part P4 is stored in warehouse W8" is an entity about which we might well wish to record information—e.g., the corresponding quantity. Moreover, there are definite advantages (beyond the scope of the present chapter) to be obtained by not making any unnecessary distinctions between entities and relationships. In this book, therefore, we will usually treat relationships as just a special kind of entity.

Properties

As just indicated, an entity is any object about which we wish to record information. It follows that entities—relationships included—can be regarded as having **properties,** corresponding to the information we wish to record about them. For example, suppliers have *locations;* parts have *weights;* projects have *priorities;* assignments (of employees to projects) have *start dates;* and so on. Such properties must therefore be represented in the database. For example, the database might include a table called S representing suppliers, and that table might include a column called CITY representing supplier locations.

Properties in general can be as simple or as complex as we please. For example, the "supplier location" property is presumably quite simple, consisting as it does of just a city name, and can be represented in the database by a simple character string. By contrast, a warehouse might have a "floor plan" property, and that property might be quite complex, consisting perhaps of an entire architectural drawing and associated descriptive text. At the time of writing, most database products are only just beginning to be able to deal with complex properties such as drawings and text. We will return to this topic later in this book (especially in Chapter 5 and Part VI); until then, we will mostly assume (where it makes any difference) that properties are "simple" and can be represented by "simple" data types. Examples of such "simple" types include numbers, character strings, dates, times, and so forth.

Data and Data Models

There is another (and important) way of thinking about what data and databases really are. The word *data* derives from the Latin for "to give"; thus, data is really *given facts,* from which additional facts can be inferred. (Inferring additional facts from given facts is exactly what the DBMS is doing when it responds to a user query.) A "given fact" in turn corresponds to what logicians call a *true proposition;** for example, the statement "Supplier S1 is located in London" might be such a true proposition. It follows that a database is really *a collection of such true propositions* [1.2].

---

*A proposition in logic is something that evaluates to either *true* or *false,* unequivocally. For instance, "William Shakespeare wrote *Pride and Prejudice*" is a proposition (a false one, as it happens).

One reason relational database systems have become so dominant—in both the industrial and the academic world, be it noted—is that they support the foregoing interpretation of data and databases very directly (almost trivially, in fact). Relational systems are based on a formal theory called **the relational model of data,** according to which:

- Data is represented by means of rows in tables, and such rows can be directly interpreted as true propositions. For example, the row for BIN# 72 in Fig. 1.1 can be interpreted in an obvious way as the following true proposition:

  "Bin number 72 contains two bottles of 1995 Rafanelli Zinfandel, which will be ready to drink in 2003."

- Operators are provided for operating on rows in tables, and those operators directly support the process of inferring additional true propositions from the given ones. As a simple example, the relational *project* operator (see Section 1.6) allows us to infer, from the true proposition just quoted, the following additional true proposition among others:

  "Some bottles of Zinfandel will be ready to drink in 2003."

  (More precisely: "Some bottles of Zinfandel in some bin, produced by some producer in some year, will be ready to drink in 2003.")

The relational model is not the only data model, however; others do exist (see Section 1.6)—though most of them differ from the relational model in that they are *ad hoc* to a degree, instead of being firmly based on formal logic. Be that as it may, the question arises: What in general *is* a data model? We can define the concept thus:

- **A data model** is an abstract, self-contained, logical definition of the objects, operators, and so forth, that together constitute the *abstract machine* with which users interact. The objects allow us to model the *structure* of data. The operators allow us to model its *behavior.*

We can then usefully distinguish the model from its *implementation:*

- An **implementation** of a given data model is a physical realization on a real machine of the components of the abstract machine that together constitute that model.

In a nutshell: The model is what users have to know about; the implementation is what users do not have to know about.

Note: As you can see, the distinction between model and implementation is really just a special case (a very important special case) of the familiar distinction between *logical* and *physical.* Sadly, however, many of today's database systems—even ones that profess to be relational—do not make these distinctions as clearly as they should. Indeed, there seems to be a fairly widespread lack of understanding of these distinctions and the importance of making them. As a consequence, there is all too often a gap between database *principles* (the way database systems ought to be) and database *practice* (the way they actually are). In this book we are concerned primarily with principles, but it is only fair to warn you that you might therefore be in for a few surprises, mostly of an unpleasant nature, when you start using a commercial product.

In closing this section, we should mention the fact that, actually, the term *data model* is used in the literature with two quite different meanings. The first is as described above. The second is as a model of the persistent data of some *particular enterprise* (e.g., the manufacturing company KnowWare Inc. discussed earlier in this section). The difference between the two meanings can be characterized thus:

- A data model in the first sense is like a *programming language*—albeit one that is somewhat abstract—whose constructs can be used to solve a wide variety of specific problems, but in and of themselves have no direct connection with any such specific problem.

- A data model in the second sense is like a *specific program* written in that language. In other words, a data model in the second sense takes the facilities provided by some model in the first sense and applies them to some specific problem. It can be regarded as *a specific application* of some model in the first sense.

In this book, the term *data model* will be used only in the first sense from this point forward, barring explicit statements to the contrary.

1.4 WHY DATABASE?

Why use a database system? What are the advantages? To some extent the answer to these questions depends on whether the system in question is single- or multi-user (or rather, to be more accurate, there are numerous *additional* advantages in the multi-user case). We consider the single-user case first.

Refer back to the wine cellar example once again (Fig. 1.1), which we can regard as illustrative of the single-user case. Now, that particular database is so small and so simple that the advantages might not be all that obvious. But imagine a similar database for a large restaurant, with a stock of perhaps thousands of bottles and very frequent changes to that stock; or think of a liquor store, with again a very large stock and high turnover on that stock. The advantages of a database system over traditional, paper-based methods of record-keeping are perhaps easier to see in these cases. Here are some of them:

- *Compactness:* There is no need for possibly voluminous paper files.

- *Speed:* The machine can retrieve and update data far faster than a human can. In particular, *ad hoc,* spur-of-the-moment queries (e.g., "Do we have more Zinfandel than Pinot Noir?") can be answered quickly without any need for time-consuming manual or visual searches.

- *Less drudgery:* Much of the sheer tedium of maintaining files by hand is eliminated. Mechanical tasks are always better done by machines.

- *Currency:* Accurate, up-to-date information is available on demand at any time.

The foregoing benefits apply with even more force in a multi-user environment, of course, where the database is likely to be much larger and more complex than in the single-user case. However, there is one overriding additional advantage in such an environment, namely as follows: *The database system provides the enterprise with centralized control of its data* (which, as you should realize by now, is one of its most valuable assets). Such a situation contrasts sharply with that found in an enterprise without a database system, where typically each application has its own private files—quite often its own private tapes and disks, too—so that the data is widely dispersed and difficult to control in any systematic way.

Data Administration and Database Administration

We elaborate briefly on this concept of centralized control. The concept implies that there will be some identifiable person in the enterprise who has this central responsibility for the data. That person is the **data administrator** (DA for short) mentioned briefly at the end of Section 1.2. Given that (to repeat) the data is one of the enterprise's most valuable assets, it is imperative that there should be some person who understands that data, and the needs of the enterprise with respect to that data, *at a senior management level.* The data administrator is that person. Thus, it is the data administrator's job to decide what data should be stored in the database in the first place, and to establish policies for maintaining and dealing with that data once it has been stored. An example of such a policy might be one that dictates who can perform what operations on what data in what circumstances—in other words, a *data security* policy (see the next subsection).

Note carefully that the data administrator is a manager, not a technician (although he or she certainly does need to have some appreciation of the capabilities of database systems at a technical level). The *technical* person responsible for implementing the data administrator's decisions is the **data*base* administrator** (DBA for short). The DBA, unlike the data administrator, is thus an *IT professional.* The job of the DBA is to create the actual database and to implement the technical controls needed to enforce the various policy decisions made by the data administrator. The DBA is also responsible for ensuring that the system operates with adequate performance and for providing a variety of other technical services. The DBA will typically have a staff of system programmers and other technical assistants (i.e., the DBA function will typically be performed in practice by a team of people, not just by one person); for simplicity, however, it is convenient to assume that the DBA is indeed a single individual. We will discuss the DBA function in more detail in Chapter 2.

Benefits of the Database Approach

In this subsection we identify some of the specific advantages that accrue from the foregoing notion of centralized control.

- *The data can be shared*

  We discussed this point in Section 1.2, but for completeness we mention it again here. Sharing means not only that existing applications can share the data in the database, but also that new applications can be developed to operate against that same data. In other words, it might be possible to satisfy the data requirements of new applications without having to add any new data to the database.

- *Redundancy can be reduced*

In nondatabase systems each application has its own private files. This fact can often lead to considerable redundancy in stored data, with resultant waste in storage space. For example, a personnel application and an education records application might both own a file that includes department information for employees. As suggested in Section 1.2, however, those two files can be integrated, and the redundancy eliminated, so long as the data administrator is aware of the data requirements for both applications—i.e., so long as the enterprise has the necessary overall control.

Incidentally, we do not mean to suggest that *all* redundancy can or necessarily should be eliminated. Sometimes there are sound business or technical reasons for maintaining several distinct copies of the same data. However, we do mean to suggest that any such redundancy should be carefully **controlled**; that is, the DBMS should be aware of it, if it exists, and should assume responsibility for "propagating updates" (see the next point below).

- *Inconsistency can be avoided (to some extent)*

This is really a corollary of the previous point. Suppose a given fact about the real world—say the fact that employee E3 works in department D8—is represented by two distinct entries in the database. Suppose also that the DBMS is not aware of this duplication (i.e., the redundancy is not controlled). Then there will necessarily be occasions on which the two entries will not agree: namely, when one of the two has been updated and the other not. At such times the database is said to be *inconsistent*. Clearly, a database that is in an inconsistent state is capable of supplying incorrect or contradictory information to its users.

Of course, if the given fact is represented by a single entry (i.e., if the redundancy is removed), then such an inconsistency cannot occur. Alternatively, if the redundancy is not removed but is *controlled* (by making it known to the DBMS), then the DBMS can guarantee that the database is never inconsistent *as seen by the user,* by ensuring that any change made to either of the two entries is automatically applied to the other one as well. This process is known as **propagating updates.**

- *Transaction support can be provided*

A **transaction** is a logical unit of work, typically involving several database operations (in particular, several update operations). The standard example involves the transfer of a cash amount from one account *A* to another account *B*. Clearly two updates are required here, one to withdraw the cash from account *A* and the other to deposit it to account *B*. If the user has stated that the two updates are part of the same transaction, then the system can effectively guarantee that either both of them are done or neither is—even if, e.g., the system fails (say because of a power outage) halfway through the process.

Note: The transaction *atomicity* feature just illustrated is not the only benefit of transaction support, but unlike some of the others it is one that applies even in the single-user case.* A full description of all of the various advantages of transaction support and how they can be achieved appears in Chapters 14 and 15.

- *Integrity can be maintained*

  The problem of integrity is the problem of ensuring that the data in the database is correct. Inconsistency between two entries that purport to represent the same "fact" is an example of lack of integrity (see the discussion of this point earlier in this subsection); of course, this particular problem can arise only if redundancy exists in the stored data. Even if there is no redundancy, however, the database might still contain incorrect information. For example, an employee might be shown as having worked 400 hours in the week instead of 40, or as belonging to a department that does not exist. Centralized control of the database can help in avoiding such problems—insofar as they can be avoided—by permitting the data administrator to define, and the DBA to implement, **integrity constraints** (also known as *business rules*) to be checked whenever any update operation is performed.

  It is worth pointing out that data integrity is even more important in a database system than it is in a "private files" environment, precisely because the data is shared. For without appropriate controls it would be possible for one user to update the database incorrectly, thereby generating bad data and so "infecting" other innocent users of that data. It should also be mentioned that most database products are currently rather weak in their support for integrity constraints (though there have been some recent improvements in this area). This fact is unfortunate, given that—as we will see in Chapter 8—integrity constraints are both fundamental and crucially important, much more so than is usually realized.

- *Security can be enforced*

  Having complete jurisdiction over the database, the DBA (under appropriate direction from the data administrator, of course) can ensure that the only means of access to the database is through the proper channels, and hence can define **security constraints** or rules to be checked whenever access is attempted to sensitive data. Different constraints can be established for each type of access (retrieve, insert, delete, etc.) to each piece of information in the database. Note, however, that without such constraints the security of the data might actually be more at risk than in a traditional (dispersed) filing system; that is, the centralized nature of a database system in a sense *requires* that a good security system be in place also.

- *Conflicting requirements can be balanced*

  Knowing the overall requirements of the enterprise (as opposed to the requirements of individual users), the DBA—again under the data administrator's direction—can so structure the system as to provide an overall service that is "best for the enterprise." For

---

*On the other hand, single-user systems often do not provide transaction support at all but simply leave the problem on the user's shoulders.

example, a physical representation can be chosen for the data in storage that gives fast access for the most important applications (possibly at the cost of slower access for certain other applications).

■ *Standards can be enforced*

With central control of the database, the DBA (under the direction of the data administrator once again) can ensure that all applicable standards are observed in the representation of the data. Applicable standards might include any or all of the following: departmental, installation, corporate, industry, national, and international standards. Standardizing data representation is particularly desirable as an aid to *data interchange,* or movement of data between systems (this consideration is becoming particularly important with the advent of distributed systems—see Chapters 2 and 20). Likewise, data naming and documentation standards are also very desirable as an aid to data sharing and understandability.

Most of the advantages listed above are probably fairly obvious. However, one further point, which might not be so obvious (although it is in fact implied by several of the others) needs to be added to the list: namely, *the provision of data independence.* (Strictly speaking, this is an *objective* for database systems, rather than an advantage necessarily.) The concept of data independence is so important that we devote a separate section to it.

1.5   DATA INDEPENDENCE

We begin by observing that there are two kinds of data independence, physical and logical [1.3–1.4]; for the time being, however, we will be concerned with the physical kind only. Until further notice, therefore, the unqualified term "data independence" should be understood to mean *physical* data independence specifically; we will discuss logical data independence in Chapters 2, 3, and especially 9. *Note:* We should perhaps say too that the term "data independence" is not very apt (it does not capture very well the essence of what is really going on); however, it is the term traditionally used, and we will stay with it in this book.

Data independence can most easily be understood by first considering its opposite. Applications implemented on older systems—prerelational or even predatabase systems— tend to be *data-dependent.* What this means is that the way the data is physically represented in secondary storage, and the technique used to access it, are both dictated by the requirements of the application under consideration, and moreover that *knowledge of that physical representation and that access technique is built into the application code.*

■ *Example:* Suppose we have an application that uses the EMPLOYEE file of Fig. 1.5, and suppose it is decided, for performance reasons, that the file is to be indexed on its "employee name" field. In an older system, the application in question will typically be aware of the fact that the index exists, and aware also of the record sequence as defined by that index, and the internal structure of the application will be built around that knowledge. In particular, the precise form of the various data access and exception checking routines within the application will depend very heavily on details of the interface presented to the application by the data management software.

We say that an application such as the one in this example is **data-dependent,** because it is impossible to change the physical representation (how the data is physically represented in storage) or access technique (how it is physically accessed) without affecting the application, probably drastically. For instance, it would not be possible to replace the index in the example by a hashing scheme without making major modifications to the application. What is more, the portions of the application requiring alteration in such a situation are precisely those portions that communicate with the data management software; the difficulties involved are quite irrelevant to the problem the application was originally written to solve— i.e., they are difficulties *introduced* by the nature of the data management interface.

In a database system, however, it would be extremely undesirable to allow applications to be data-dependent in the foregoing sense, for at least the following two reasons:

1. Different applications will require different views of the same data. For example, suppose that before the enterprise introduces its integrated database, there are two applications, A and B, each owning a private file that includes the field "customer balance." Suppose, however, that application A stores that field in decimal, whereas application B stores it in binary. It will still be possible to integrate the two files, and to eliminate the redundancy, provided the DBMS is ready and able to perform all necessary conversions between the stored representation chosen (which might be decimal or binary or something else again) and the form in which each application wishes to see it. For example, if it is decided to store the field in decimal, then every access by B will require a conversion to or from binary.

    This is a fairly trivial example of the kind of difference that might exist in a database system between the data as seen by a given application and the data as physically stored. We will consider many other possible differences later in this section.

2. The DBA must have the freedom to change the physical representation or access technique in response to changing requirements, without having to modify existing applications. For example, new kinds of data might be added to the database; new standards might be adopted; application priorities (and therefore relative performance requirements) might change; new storage devices might become available; and so on. If applications are data-dependent, such changes will typically require corresponding changes to programs, thus tying up programmer effort that would otherwise be available for the creation of new applications. It is still not uncommon, even today, to find a significant fraction of the available programming effort devoted to this kind of maintenance (think of the "Year 2000" problem!)—hardly the best use of a scarce and valuable resource.

It follows that the provision of data independence is a major objective for database systems. Data independence can be defined as **the immunity of applications to change in physical representation and access technique**—which implies, of course, that the applications concerned do not depend on any one particular physical representation or access technique. In Chapter 2, we describe an architecture for database systems that provides a basis for achieving this objective. Before then, however, let us consider in more detail some examples of the types of changes that the DBA might wish to make, and that we might therefore wish applications to be immune to.

We start by defining three terms: *stored field, stored record,* and *stored file* (refer to Fig. 1.7).

- A **stored field** is, loosely, the smallest unit of stored data. The database will contain many **occurrences** (or **instances**) of each of several **types** of stored field. For example, a database containing information about different kinds of parts might include a stored field type called "part number," and then there would be one occurrence of that stored field for each kind of part (screw, hinge, lid, etc.).

  Note: In practice it is common to drop the qualifiers "type" and "occurrence" and to rely on context to indicate which is meant. Although there is a slight risk of confu-

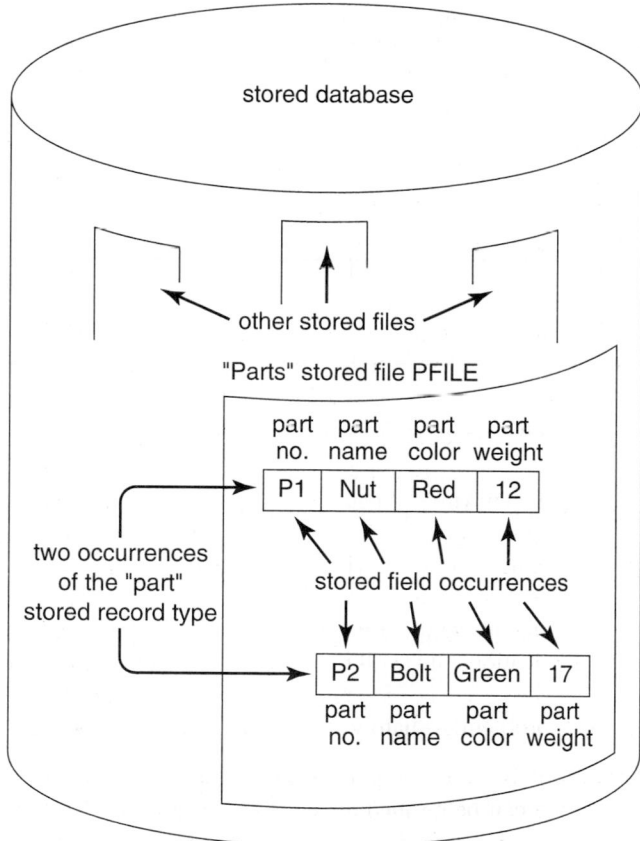

Fig. 1.7:   Stored fields, records, and files

sion, the practice is convenient, and we will adopt it ourselves from time to time in this book. (These remarks apply to stored records as well—see the paragraph immediately following.)

- A **stored record** is a collection of related stored fields. Again we distinguish between type and occurrence. A stored record **occurrence** (or **instance**) consists of a group of related stored field occurrences. For example, a stored record occurrence in the "parts" database might consist of an occurrence of each of the following stored fields: part number, part name, part color, and part weight. We say that the database contains many occurrences of the "part" stored record **type** (again, one occurrence for each kind of part).

- Finally, a **stored file** is the collection of all currently existing occurrences of one type of stored record. *Note:* We assume for simplicity that any given stored file contains just one type of stored record. This simplification does not materially affect any of our subsequent discussions.

Now, in nondatabase systems it is normally the case that any given *logical* record as seen by some application is identical to some corresponding *stored* record. As we have already seen, however, this is not necessarily the case in a database system, because the DBA might need to be able to make changes to the stored representation of data—that is, to the stored fields, records, and files—while the data as seen by applications does *not* change. For example, the DEPARTMENT field in the EMPLOYEE file might be stored in binary to economize on storage space, whereas a given COBOL application might see it as a character string. And later the DBA might decide for some reason to change the stored representation of that field from binary to decimal, say, and yet still allow the COBOL application to see it in character form.

As stated earlier, a difference such as this one, involving data type conversion on some field on each access, is comparatively minor. In general, however, the difference between what the application sees and what is actually stored might be quite considerable. To amplify this remark, we present below a list of aspects of the stored representation that might be subject to change. You should consider in each case what the DBMS would have to do to make applications immune to such change (and indeed whether such immunity can always be achieved).

- *Representation of numeric data*

  A numeric field might be stored in internal arithmetic form (e.g., packed decimal) or as a character string. Either way, the DBA must choose an appropriate base (e.g., binary or decimal), scale (fixed or floating point), mode (real or complex), and precision (number of digits). Any of these aspects might need to be changed to improve performance or to conform to a new standard or for many other reasons.

- *Representation of character data*

  A character string field might be stored using any of several distinct coded character sets—e.g., ASCII, EBCDIC, Unicode.

- *Units for numeric data*

  The units in a numeric field might change—from inches to centimeters, for example, during a process of metrication.

- *Data coding*

  In some situations it might be desirable to represent data in storage by coded values. For example, the "part color" field, which an application sees as a character string ("Red" or "Blue" or "Green" ...), might be stored as a single decimal digit, interpreted according to the coding scheme 1 = "Red," 2 = "Blue," and so on.

- *Data materialization*

  In practice the *logical* field as seen by an application does usually correspond to some specific stored field (although, as we have already seen, there might be differences in data type, coding, and so on). In such a case, the process of materialization—that is, constructing an occurrence of the logical field from the corresponding stored field occurrence and presenting it to the application—can be said to be *direct*. Sometimes, however, a logical field will have no single stored counterpart; instead, its values will be materialized by means of some computation, perhaps on several stored field occurrences. For example, values of the logical field "total quantity" might be materialized by summing a number of individual stored quantities. "Total quantity" here is an example of a **virtual** field, and the materialization process is said to be *indirect*. Note, however, that the user might see a difference between real and virtual fields, inasmuch as it might not be possible to update an occurrence of a virtual field (at least, not directly).

- *Structure of stored records*

  Two existing stored records might be combined into one. For example, the stored records

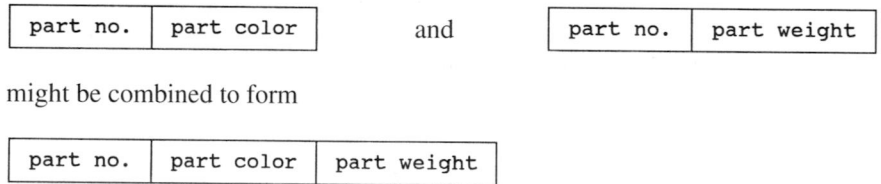

| part no. | part color |

  and

| part no. | part weight |

  might be combined to form

| part no. | part color | part weight |

  Such a change might occur as existing applications are integrated into the database system. It implies that an application's logical record might consist of a proper subset of the corresponding stored record—that is, certain fields in that stored record would be invisible to the application in question.

  Alternatively, a single stored record type might be split into two. Reversing the previous example, the stored record

| part no. | part color | part weight |

might be split into

part no.	part color

and

part no.	part weight

Such a split would allow less frequently used portions of the original record to be stored on a slower device, for example. The implication is that an application's logical record might contain fields from several distinct stored records—that is, it might be a proper superset of any given one of those stored records.

- *Structure of stored files*

  A given stored file can be physically implemented in storage in a wide variety of ways. For example, it might be entirely contained within a single storage volume (e.g., a single disk), or it might be spread across several volumes (possibly on several different device types); it might or might not be physically sequenced according to the values of some stored field; it might or might not be sequenced in one or more additional ways by some other means, e.g., by one or more indexes or one or more embedded pointer chains (or both); it might or might not be accessible via some hashing scheme; the stored records might or might not be physically blocked; and so on. But none of these considerations should affect applications in any way (other than performance, of course).

This concludes our list of aspects of the stored data representation that are subject to possible change. The list implies (among other things) that the database should be able to **grow** without impairing existing applications; indeed, enabling the database to grow without logically impairing existing applications is one of the most important reasons for requiring data independence in the first place. For example, it should be possible to extend an existing stored record by the addition of new stored fields, representing, typically, further information concerning some existing type of entity (e.g., a "unit cost" field might be added to the "part" stored record). Such new fields should simply be invisible to existing applications. Likewise, it should be possible to add entirely new stored record types (and hence new stored files), again without requiring any change to existing applications; such records would typically represent new entity types (e.g., a "supplier" record type could be added to the "parts" database). Again, such additions should be invisible to existing applications.

By now you might have realized that data independence is one of the reasons why separating the data model from its implementation, as discussed near the end of Section 1.3, is so important: To the extent we do not make that separation, we will not achieve data independence. The widespread failure to make the separation properly, in today's SQL systems in particular, is thus particularly distressing. *Note:* We do not mean to suggest by these remarks that today's SQL systems provide no data independence at all, only that they do provide much less than relational systems are theoretically capable of. In other words, data independence is not an absolute (different systems provide it to different degrees, and few if any provide none at all); SQL systems provide more than older systems, but they are still not perfect, as we will see in the chapters to come.

1.6　RELATIONAL SYSTEMS AND OTHERS

As mentioned at the end of Section 1.3, DBMS products that are based on *the relational model of data* ("relational systems") have come to dominate the database marketplace. What is more, the vast majority of database research over the last 30 years has also been based—albeit a little indirectly, in some cases—on that model. In fact, the introduction of the relational model in 1969–70 was undeniably the single most important event in the entire history of the database field. For these reasons, plus the additional reason that the relational model is solidly based on logic and mathematics and therefore provides an ideal vehicle for teaching database principles, the emphasis in this book is (as noted in Section 1.1) heavily on relational systems.

What then exactly is a relational system? It is obviously not possible to answer this question fully at this early point in the book—but it is possible, and desirable, to give a rough and ready answer, which we can make more precise later. Briefly (and loosely), a relational system is one in which:

1. The data is perceived by the user as tables (and nothing but tables); and
2. The operators available to the user (e.g., for retrieval) are operators that generate new tables from old. For example, there is one operator, *restrict,* which extracts a subset of the rows of a given table, and another, *project,* which extracts a subset of the columns—and of course a row subset and a column subset of a table can both in turn be regarded as tables themselves, as we will see in just a moment.

Note: The reason such systems are called "relational" is that the term *relation* is basically just a mathematical term for a *table;* indeed, the terms *relation* and *table* can be taken as synonymous, at least for informal purposes (see Chapters 3 and 5 for further discussion). Perhaps we should add that the reason is definitely *not* that the term *relation* is "basically just a mathematical term for" a *relationship* in the sense of entity/relationship diagrams (see Section 1.3); in fact, there is very little direct connection between relational systems and such diagrams, as we will see in Chapter 13.

To repeat, we will make the foregoing definitions much more precise later, but they will serve for the time being. Fig. 1.8 provides an illustration. The data—see part a. of the figure—consists of a single table, named CELLAR (in fact, it is a scaled down version of the CELLAR table from Fig. 1.1, reduced in size to make it more manageable). Two sample retrievals—one involving a *restriction* or row-subsetting operation and the other a *projection* or column-subsetting operation—are shown in part b. of the figure. *Note:* The two retrievals are expressed in SQL once again.

We can now distinguish between relational and nonrelational systems, as follows. As already stated, the user of a relational system sees the data as tables, and nothing but tables. The user of a nonrelational system, by contrast, sees other data structures, either instead of or in addition to the tables of a relational system. Those other structures, in turn, require other operators to manipulate them. For example, in a **hierarchic** system such as IBM's IMS, the data is represented to the user in the form of a set of tree structures (hierarchies),

```
a. Given table:          CELLAR   ┌──────────────┬───────┬─────────┐
                                  │ WINE         │ YEAR  │ BOTTLES │
                                  ├──────────────┼───────┼─────────┤
                                  │ Chardonnay   │ 1996  │    4    │
                                  │ Fumé Blanc   │ 1996  │    2    │
                                  │ Pinot Noir   │ 1993  │    3    │
                                  │ Zinfandel    │ 1994  │    9    │
                                  └──────────────┴───────┴─────────┘

b. Operators (examples):

1. Restrict:              Result:  ┌──────────────┬───────┬─────────┐
                                   │ WINE         │ YEAR  │ BOTTLES │
   SELECT  WINE, YEAR, BOTTLES     ├──────────────┼───────┼─────────┤
   FROM    CELLAR                  │ Chardonnay   │ 1996  │    4    │
   WHERE   YEAR > 1995 ;           │ Fumé Blanc   │ 1996  │    2    │
                                   └──────────────┴───────┴─────────┘

2. Project:               Result:  ┌──────────────┬─────────┐
                                   │ WINE         │ BOTTLES │
   SELECT  WINE, BOTTLES           ├──────────────┼─────────┤
   FROM    CELLAR ;                │ Chardonnay   │    4    │
                                   │ Fumé Blanc   │    2    │
                                   │ Pinot Noir   │    3    │
                                   │ Zinfandel    │    9    │
                                   └──────────────┴─────────┘
```

Fig. 1.8   Data structure and operators in a relational system (examples)

and the operators provided for manipulating such structures include operators for *traversing pointers—viz.,* the pointers that represent the hierarchic paths up and down the trees. (By contrast, it is an important distinguishing characteristic of relational systems that they involve no such pointers, as we have seen.)

To pursue the issue a little further: Database systems can in fact be conveniently categorized according to the data structures and operators they present to the user. According to this scheme, the oldest (prerelational) systems fall into three broad categories, namely **inverted list, hierarchic,** and **network** systems.* We do not discuss these categories in detail in this book because from a technological point of view, at least, they must be regarded as obsolete. (You can find tutorial descriptions of all three in reference [1.5] if you are interested.) However, we should at least say that the term *network* in this context has nothing to do with a *communications* network!—it refers rather (to repeat) to the kinds of data structures and operators supported by the systems in question.

---

*By analogy with the relational model, earlier editions of this book referred to inverted list, hierarchic, and network *models* (and much of the literature still does). To talk in such terms is rather misleading, however, because, unlike the relational model, the inverted list, hierarchic, and network "models" were all defined *after the fact;* i.e., commercial inverted list, hierarchic, and network products were implemented *first,* and the corresponding "models" were defined *subsequently* by a process of induction—in this context, a polite term for guesswork—from those existing implementations.

Note: Network systems are sometimes called either **CODASYL** systems or **DBTG** systems, after the body that proposed them—namely, the Data Base Task Group (DBTG) of the Conference on Data Systems Languages (CODASYL). Probably the best known example of such a system is IDMS, from Computer Associates International Inc. Like hierarchic systems (but unlike relational ones), all such systems expose pointers to the user (among other things).

The first **relational** products began to appear in the late 1970s and early 1980s. At the time of writing, the vast majority of database systems are relational, and they run on just about every kind of hardware and software platform available. Leading examples include, in alphabetical order, DB2 (various versions) from IBM Corp.; Ingres II from Computer Associates International Inc.; Informix Dynamic Server from Informix Software Inc.; Microsoft SQL Server from Microsoft Corp.; Oracle 8i from Oracle Corp.; and Sybase Adaptive Server from Sybase Inc. *Note:* When we have cause to refer to any of these products later in this book, we will refer to them (as most of the industry does, informally) by the abbreviated names DB2, Ingres (pronounced "ingress"), Informix, SQL Server, Oracle, and Sybase, respectively.

More recently, certain **object** and **object/relational** products have become available.* The object/relational systems represent (for the most part) upward-compatible extensions to certain of the original relational products, as in the case of DB2 and Informix; the object (sometimes *object-oriented*) systems represent attempts to do something entirely different, as in the case of GemStone from GemStone Systems Inc. and Versant ODBMS from Versant Object Technology. We will discuss these newer systems in Part VI of this book.

In addition to the various approaches mentioned above, research has proceeded over the years on a variety of alternative schemes, including the **multi-dimensional** approach and the **logic-based** (also called *deductive* or *expert*) approach. We discuss multi-dimensional systems in Chapter 21 and logic-based systems in Chapter 23.

1.7 SUMMARY

We close this introductory chapter by summarizing the main points discussed. First, a **database system** can be thought of as a computerized record-keeping system. Such a system involves the **data** itself (stored in the **database**), **hardware, software** (in particular the **database management system** or DBMS), and—most important!—**users.** Users in turn can be divided into **application programmers, end users,** and the **database administrator** or DBA. The DBA is responsible for administering the database and database system in accordance with policies established by the **data administrator.**

Databases are **integrated** and (usually) **shared;** they are used to store **persistent data.** Such data can usefully, albeit informally, be considered as representing **entities,** together with **relationships** among those entities—although in fact a relationship is really just a special kind of entity. We very briefly examined the idea of **entity/relationship diagrams.**

---

*The term *object* here has a rather specific meaning, which we will explain in Part VI. Prior to that point, we will use the term in its normal generic sense, barring explicit statements to the contrary.

Database systems provide a number of benefits, of which one of the most important is (physical) **data independence.** Data independence can be defined as the immunity of application programs to changes in the way the data is physically stored and accessed. Among other things, data independence requires that a sharp distinction be made between the **data model** and its **implementation.** (We remind you in passing that the term *data model,* perhaps unfortunately, has two rather different meanings.)

Database systems also usually support **transactions** or logical units of work. One advantage of transactions is that they are guaranteed to be **atomic** (all or nothing), even if the system fails in the middle of their execution.

Finally, database systems can be based on a number of different approaches. Relational systems in particular are based on a formal theory called **the relational model,** according to which data is represented as rows in tables (interpreted as **true propositions**) and operators are provided that directly support the process of **inferring** additional true propositions from the given ones. From both an economic and a theoretical perspective, relational systems are easily the most important (and this state of affairs is not likely to change in the foreseeable future). We have seen a few simple examples of **SQL,** the standard language for dealing with relational systems (in particular, examples of the SQL **SELECT, INSERT, UPDATE,** and **DELETE** statements). This book will be heavily based on relational systems, although—for reasons explained in the preface—not so much on SQL *per se.*

EXERCISES

1.1 Define the following terms:

binary relationship	menu-driven interface
command-driven interface	multi-user system
concurrent access	online application
data administration	persistent data
database	property
database system	query language
data independence	redundancy
DBA	relationship
DBMS	security
entity	sharing
entity/relationship diagram	stored field
forms-driven interface	stored file
integration	stored record
integrity	transaction

1.2 What are the advantages of using a database system?

1.3 What are the disadvantages of using a database system?

1.4 What do you understand by the term *relational system?* Distinguish between relational and nonrelational systems.

1.5 What do you understand by the term *data model?* Explain the difference between a data model and its implementation. Why is the difference important?

1.6 Show the effects of the following SQL retrieval operations on the wine cellar database of Fig. 1.1:

```
a. SELECT WINE, PRODUCER
   FROM   CELLAR
   WHERE  BIN# = 72 ;

b. SELECT WINE, PRODUCER
   FROM   CELLAR
   WHERE  YEAR > 1996 ;

c. SELECT BIN#, WINE, YEAR
   FROM   CELLAR
   WHERE  READY < 1999 ;

d. SELECT WINE, BIN#, YEAR
   FROM   CELLAR
   WHERE  PRODUCER = 'Robt. Mondavi'
   AND    BOTTLES > 6 ;
```

1.7 Give in your own words an interpretation as a true proposition of a typical row from each of your answers to Exercise 1.6.

1.8 Show the effects of the following SQL update operations on the wine cellar database of Fig. 1.1:

```
a. INSERT
   INTO   CELLAR ( BIN#, WINE, PRODUCER, YEAR, BOTTLES, READY )
   VALUES ( 80, 'Syrah', 'Meridian', 1994, 12, 1999 ) ;

b. DELETE
   FROM   CELLAR
   WHERE  READY > 2000 ;

c. UPDATE CELLAR
   SET    BOTTLES = 5
   WHERE  BIN# = 50 ;

d. UPDATE CELLAR
   SET    BOTTLES = BOTTLES + 2
   WHERE  BIN# = 50 ;
```

1.9 Write SQL statements to perform the following operations on the wine cellar database:

a. Get bin number, name of wine, and number of bottles for all Geyser Peak wines.

b. Get bin number and name of wine for all wines for which there are more than five bottles in stock.

c. Get bin number for all red wines.

d. Add three bottles to bin number 30.

e. Remove all Chardonnay from stock.

f. Add an entry for a new case (12 bottles) of Gary Farrell Merlot: bin number 55, year 1996, ready in 2001.

1.10 Suppose you have a classical music collection consisting of CDs and/or LPs and/or audio tapes, and you want to build a database that will let you find which recordings you have for a specific composer (e.g., Sibelius) or conductor (e.g., Simon Rattle) or soloist (e.g., Arthur Grumiaux) or work (e.g., Beethoven's Fifth) or orchestra (e.g., the NYPO) or kind of work (e.g., violin concerto) or chamber group (e.g., the Kronos Quartet). Draw an entity/relationship diagram like that of Fig. 1.6 for this database.

REFERENCES AND BIBLIOGRAPHY

1.1 E. F. Codd: "Data Models in Database Management," Proc. Workshop on Data Abstraction, Databases, and Conceptual Modelling, Pingree Park, Colo. (June 1980): *ACM SIGART Newsletter* No. 74 (January 1981); *ACM SIGMOD Record 11,* No. 2 (February 1981); *ACM SIGPLAN Notices 16,* No. 1 (January 1981).

> Codd was the inventor of the relational model, which he first described in reference [5.1]. Reference [5.1], however, did not in fact define the term *data model* as such!—but the present (much later) paper does. It then addresses the question: What purposes are data models in general, and the relational model in particular, intended to serve? And it goes on to offer evidence to support the claim that, contrary to popular belief, the relational model was actually the first data model to be defined. (In other words, Codd has some claim to being the inventor of the data model concept in general, as well as of the relational data model in particular.)

1.2 Hugh Darwen: "What a Database *Really* Is: Predicates and Propositions," in C. J. Date, Hugh Darwen, and David McGoveran, *Relational Database Writings 1994–1997*. Reading, Mass.: Addison-Wesley (1998).

> This paper gives an informal (but accurate) explanation of the idea, discussed briefly at the end of Section 1.3, that a database is best thought of as a collection of true propositions.

1.3 C. J. Date and P. Hopewell: "Storage Structures and Physical Data Independence," Proc. 1971 ACM SIGFIDET Workshop on Data Definition, Access, and Control, San Diego, California (November 1971).

1.4 C. J. Date and P. Hopewell: "File Definition and Logical Data Independence," Proc. 1971 ACM SIGFIDET Workshop on Data Definition, Access, and Control, San Diego, California (November 1971).

> References [1.3–1.4] were the first papers to define and distinguish between physical and logical data independence.

1.5 C. J. Date: *Relational Database Writings 1991–1994*. Reading, Mass.: Addison-Wesley (1995).

ANSWERS TO SELECTED EXERCISES

1.3 Some disadvantages are as follows:

- Security might be compromised (without good controls);
- Integrity might be compromised (without good controls);
- Additional hardware might be required;
- Performance overhead might be significant;

- Successful operation is crucial (the enterprise might be highly vulnerable to failure);
- The system is likely to be complex (though such complexity should be concealed from the user).

1.6 a.

WINE	PRODUCER
Zinfandel	Rafanelli

b.

WINE	PRODUCER
Chardonnay	Buena Vista
Chardonnay	Geyser Peak
Joh. Riesling	Jekel
Fumé Blanc	Ch. St. Jean
Gewurztraminer	Ch. St. Jean

c.

BIN#	WINE	YEAR
6	Chardonnay	1996
22	Fumé Blanc	1996
52	Pinot Noir	1995

d.

WINE	BIN#	YEAR
Cab. Sauvignon	48	1993

1.7 We give a solution for part a. only: "Rafanelli is a producer of Zinfandel"—or, more precisely, "Some bin contains some bottles of Zinfandel that were produced by Rafanelli in some year, and they will be ready to drink in some year."

1.8 a. A row for bin number 80 is added to the CELLAR table.

b. The rows for bin numbers 45, 48, 64, and 72 are deleted from the CELLAR table.

c. The row for bin number 50 has the number of bottles set to 5.

d. Same as c.

Incidentally, note how convenient it is to be able to refer to rows by their primary key value (the primary key for the CELLAR table is {BIN#}—see Chapter 8).

1.9 a.
```
SELECT BIN#, WINE, BOTTLES
FROM   CELLAR
WHERE  PRODUCER = 'Geyser Peak' ;
```

b.
```
SELECT BIN#, WINE
FROM   CELLAR
WHERE  BOTTLES > 5 ;
```

c.
```
SELECT BIN#
FROM   CELLAR
WHERE  WINE = 'Cab. Sauvignon'
OR     WINE = 'Pinot Noir'
OR     WINE = 'Zinfandel'
OR     WINE = 'Syrah'
OR     ....... ;
```

There is no shortcut answer to this question, because "color of wine" is not explicitly recorded in the database; thus, the DBMS does not know that (e.g.) Pinot Noir is red.

d.
```
UPDATE  CELLAR
SET     BOTTLES = BOTTLES + 3
WHERE   BIN# = 30 ;
```

e.
```
DELETE
FROM    CELLAR
WHERE   WINE = 'Chardonnay' ;
```

f.
```
INSERT
INTO    CELLAR ( BIN#, WINE, PRODUCER, YEAR, BOTTLES, READY )
VALUES ( 55, 'Merlot', 'Gary Farrell', 1996, 12, 2001 ) ;
```

CHAPTER **2**

Database System Architecture

2.1 INTRODUCTION

We are now in a position to present an architecture for a database system. Our aim in presenting this architecture is to provide a framework on which subsequent chapters can build. Such a framework is useful for describing general database concepts and for explaining the structure of specific database systems—but we do not claim that every system can neatly be matched to this particular framework, nor do we mean to suggest that this particular architecture provides the only possible framework. In particular, "small" systems (see Chapter 1) will probably not support all aspects of the architecture. However, the architecture does seem to fit most systems reasonably well; moreover, it is basically identical to the architecture proposed by the ANSI/SPARC Study Group on Data Base Management Systems (the so-called ANSI/SPARC architecture—see references [2.1–2.2]). We choose not to follow the ANSI/SPARC terminology in every detail, however.

Note: This chapter resembles Chapter 1 insofar as, while an understanding of the material it contains is essential to a full appreciation of the structure and capabilities of a modern database system, it is again somewhat abstract and dry. As with Chapter 1, therefore, you might prefer just to give the material a "once over lightly" reading for now and come back to it later as it becomes more directly relevant to the topics at hand.

2.2 THE THREE LEVELS OF THE ARCHITECTURE

The ANSI/SPARC architecture is divided into three levels, known as the internal, conceptual, and external level, respectively (see Fig. 2.1). Broadly speaking:

- The **internal level** (also known as the *physical* level) is the one closest to physical storage—i.e., it is the one concerned with the way the data is physically stored;
- The **external level** (also known as the *user logical* level) is the one closest to the users—i.e., it is the one concerned with the way the data is seen by individual users; and
- The **conceptual level** (also known as the *community logical* level, or sometimes just the *logical* level, unqualified) is a level of indirection between the other two.

Observe that the external level is concerned with *individual* user perceptions, while the conceptual level is concerned with a *community* user perception. In other words, there will be

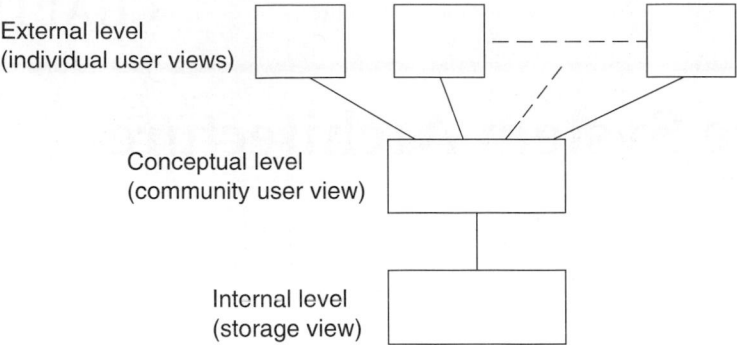

External level
(individual user views)

Conceptual level
(community user view)

Internal level
(storage view)

Fig. 2.1   The three levels of the architecture

many distinct "external views," each consisting of a more or less abstract representation of some portion of the total database, and there will be precisely one "conceptual view," consisting of a similarly abstract representation of the database in its entirety.* (Recall that most users will not be interested in the total database, but only in some restricted portion of it.) Likewise, there will be precisely one "internal view," representing the database as physically stored.

An example will make these ideas clearer. Fig. 2.2 shows the conceptual view, the corresponding internal view, and two corresponding external views (one for a PL/I user and one for a COBOL user), all for a simple personnel database. Of course, the example is completely hypothetical—it is not intended to resemble any real system—and many irrelevant details have deliberately been omitted. *Explanation:*

- At the conceptual level, the database contains information concerning an entity type called EMPLOYEE. Each individual employee has an EMPLOYEE_NUMBER (six characters), a DEPARTMENT_NUMBER (four characters), and a SALARY (five decimal digits).

- At the internal level, employees are represented by a stored record type called STORED_EMP, twenty bytes long. STORED_EMP contains four stored fields: a six-byte prefix (presumably containing control information such as flags or pointers), and three data fields corresponding to the three properties of employees. In addition, STORED_EMP records are indexed on the EMP# field by an index called EMPX, whose definition is not shown.

- The PL/I user has an external view of the database in which each employee is represented by a PL/I record containing two fields (department numbers are of no interest

---

*By *abstract* here, we merely mean that the representation in question involves constructs such as records and fields that are more user-oriented, as opposed to constructs such as bits and bytes that are more machine-oriented.

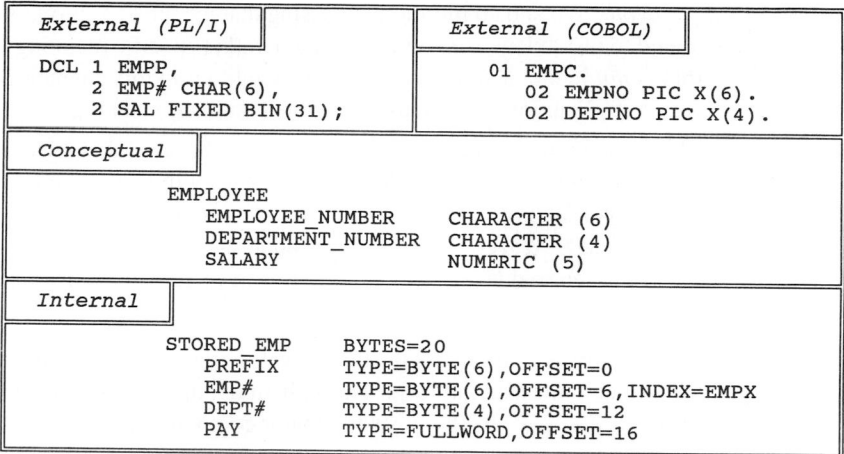

Fig. 2.2   An example of the three levels

to this user and have therefore been omitted). The record type is defined by an ordinary PL/I structure declaration in accordance with the normal PL/I rules.

- Similarly, the COBOL user has an external view in which each employee is represented by a COBOL record containing, again, two fields (this time, salaries have been omitted). The record type is defined by an ordinary COBOL record description in accordance with the normal COBOL rules.

Notice that corresponding data items can have different names at different points. For example, the employee number is called EMP# in the PL/I external view, EMPNO in the COBOL external view, EMPLOYEE_NUMBER in the conceptual view, and EMP# again in the internal view. Of course, the system must be aware of the correspondences; for example, it must be told that the COBOL field EMPNO is derived from the conceptual field EMPLOYEE_NUMBER, which in turn is derived from the stored field EMP# at the internal level. Such correspondences, or **mappings,** are not explicitly shown in Fig. 2.2; refer to Section 2.6 for further discussion.

Now, it makes little difference for the purposes of the present chapter whether the system under consideration is relational or otherwise. However, it might be helpful to indicate briefly how the three levels of the architecture are typically realized in a relational system specifically:

- First, the conceptual level in such a system will definitely be relational, in the sense that the objects visible at that level will be relational tables and the operators will be relational operators (including in particular the *restrict* and *project* operators discussed briefly in Chapter 1).

- Second, a given external view will typically be relational also, or something very close to it; for example, the PL/I and COBOL record declarations of Fig. 2.2 might loosely be regarded as, respectively, the PL/I and COBOL analogs of the declaration of a relational table in a relational system.

Note: We should mention in passing that the term "external view" (usually abbreviated to just "view") unfortunately has a rather specific meaning in relational contexts that is *not* identical to the meaning ascribed to it in this chapter. See Chapters 3 and 9 for an explanation and discussion of the relational meaning.

■ Third, the internal level will *not* be relational, because the objects at that level will not be just (stored) relational tables—instead, they will be the same kinds of objects found at the internal level of any other kind of system (stored records, pointers, indexes, hashes, etc.). In fact, the relational model as such has **nothing whatsoever to say** about the internal level; it is, to repeat from Chapter 1, concerned with how the database looks to the *user*.

We now proceed to discuss the three levels of the architecture in considerably more detail, starting with the external level. Throughout our discussions we will be making repeated references to Fig. 2.3, which shows the major components of the architecture and their interrelationships.

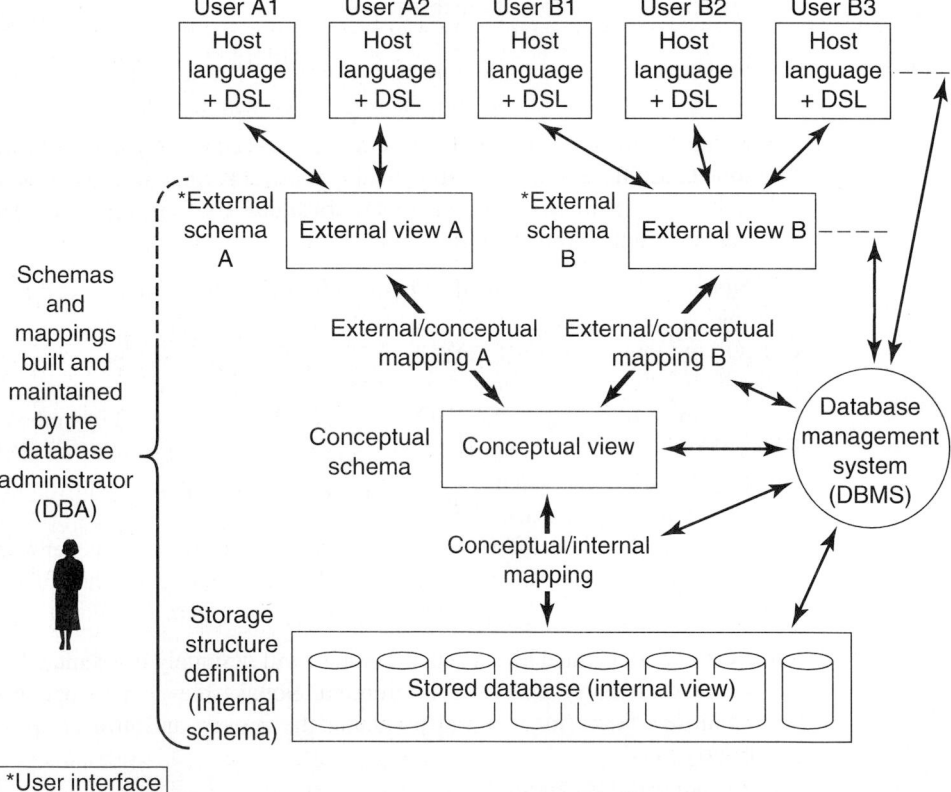

Fig. 2.3 Detailed system architecture

2.3   THE EXTERNAL LEVEL

The external level is the individual user level. As explained in Chapter 1, a given user can be either an application programmer or an end user of any degree of sophistication. (The DBA is an important special case; unlike other users, however, the DBA will need to be interested in the conceptual and internal levels also. See the next two sections.)

Each user has a **language** at his or her disposal:

- For the application programmer, that language will be either a conventional programming language (e.g., PL/I, C++, Java) or else a proprietary language that is specific to the system in question. Such proprietary languages are often called "fourth generation" languages (4GLs), on the—fuzzy!—grounds that (a) machine code, assembler language, and languages such as PL/I can be regarded as three earlier language "generations," and (b) the proprietary languages represent the same kind of improvement over "third generation" languages (3GLs) as those languages did over assembler language and assembler language did over machine code.

- For the end user, the language will be either a query language or some special-purpose language, perhaps forms- or menu-driven, tailored to that user's requirements and supported by some online application program (as explained in Chapter 1).

For our purposes, the important thing about all such languages is that they will include a **data sublanguage**—i.e., a subset of the total language that is concerned specifically with database objects and operations. The data sublanguage (abbreviated DSL in Fig. 2.3) is said to be **embedded** within the corresponding **host language.** The host language is responsible for providing various nondatabase facilities, such as local variables, computational operations, branching logic, and so on. A given system might support any number of host languages and any number of data sublanguages; however, one particular data sublanguage that is supported by almost all current systems is the language SQL discussed briefly in Chapter 1. Most such systems allow SQL to be used both *interactively* as a standalone query language and also *embedded* in other languages such as PL/I or Java (see Chapter 4 for further discussion).

Now, although it is convenient for architectural purposes to distinguish between the data sublanguage and its containing host language, the two might in fact *not* be distinct so far as the user is concerned; indeed, it is probably preferable from the user's perspective if they are not. If they are not distinct, or if they can be distinguished only with difficulty, we say they are **tightly coupled.** If they are clearly and easily separable, we say they are **loosely** coupled. While a few commercial systems (especially object systems—see Chapter 24) do support tight coupling, most do not; SQL systems in particular typically support loose coupling only. (Tight coupling provides a more uniform set of facilities for the user but obviously involves more effort on the part of the system developers, a fact that presumably accounts for the *status quo.*)

In principle, any given data sublanguage is really a combination of at least two subordinate languages—a **data definition language** (DDL), which supports the definition or declaration of database objects, and a **data manipulation language** (DML), which supports the manipulation or processing of such objects. For example, consider the PL/I user of Fig. 2.2 in Section 2.2. The data sublanguage for that user consists of those PL/I features that are used to communicate with the DBMS:

- The DDL portion consists of those declarative constructs of PL/I that are needed to declare database objects—the DECLARE (DCL) statement itself, certain PL/I data types, possibly special extensions to PL/I to support new objects that are not handled by existing PL/I.

- The DML portion consists of those executable statements of PL/I that transfer information to and from the database—again, possibly including special new statements.

Note: In the interests of accuracy, we should say that PL/I in fact does not include any specific database features at all at the time of writing. The "DML" statements in particular are typically just PL/I CALL statements that invoke the DBMS (though those calls might be syntactically disguised in some way to make them a little more user-friendly—see the discussion of embedded SQL in Chapter 4).

To return to the architecture: We have already indicated that an individual user will generally be interested only in some portion of the total database; moreover, that user's view of that portion will generally be somewhat abstract when compared with the way the data is physically stored. The ANSI/SPARC term for an individual user's view is an **external view.** An external view is thus the content of the database as seen by some particular user (that is, to that user the external view *is* the database). For example, a user from the Personnel Department might regard the database as a collection of department and employee record occurrences, and might be quite unaware of the supplier and part record occurrences seen by users in the Purchasing Department.

In general, then, an external view consists of many occurrences of each of many types of **external record** (*not* necessarily the same thing as a stored record).* The user's data sublanguage is defined in terms of external records; for example, a DML *retrieve* operation will retrieve external record occurrences, not stored record occurrences. *Note:* We can now see that the term "logical record" used a couple of times in Chapter 1 actually referred to an external record. From this point forward, in fact, we will generally avoid the term "logical record."

Each external view is defined by means of an **external schema,** which consists basically of definitions of each of the various external record types in that external view (again, refer back to Fig. 2.2 for a couple of simple examples). The external schema is written using the DDL portion of the user's data sublanguage. (That DDL is therefore sometimes referred to as an *external DDL.*) For example, the employee external record type might be defined as a six-character employee number field plus a five-digit (decimal) salary field, and so on.

---

*We are assuming here that all information is represented at the external level in the form of records. However, some systems allow information to be represented in other ways instead of or as well as records. For a system using such alternative methods, the definitions and explanations given in this section will require suitable modification. Analogous remarks apply to the conceptual and internal levels also, *q.v.* Detailed consideration of such matters is beyond the scope of this early part of the book; see Chapters 13 (especially the "References and Bibliography" section) and 24 for further discussion.

In addition, there must be a definition of the *mapping* between the external schema and the underlying *conceptual* schema (see the next section). We will consider that mapping later, in Section 2.6.

2.4   THE CONCEPTUAL LEVEL

The **conceptual view** is a representation of the entire information content of the database, again (as with an external view) in a form that is somewhat abstract in comparison with the way in which the data is physically stored. It will also be quite different, in general, from the way in which the data is viewed by any particular user. Broadly speaking, the conceptual view is intended to be a view of the data "as it really is," rather than as users are forced to see it by the limitations of (for example) the particular language or hardware they might be using.

The conceptual view consists of many occurrences of each of many types of **conceptual record.** For example, it might consist of a collection of department record occurrences plus a collection of employee record occurrences plus a collection of supplier record occurrences plus a collection of part record occurrences (etc., etc.). A conceptual record is not necessarily the same as either an external record on the one hand, or a stored record on the other.

The conceptual view is defined by means of the **conceptual schema,** which includes definitions of each of the various conceptual record types (again, refer to Fig. 2.2 for a simple example). The conceptual schema is written using another data definition language, the *conceptual DDL.* If physical data independence is to be achieved, then those conceptual DDL definitions must not involve any considerations of physical representation or access technique at all—they must be definitions of information content *only.* Thus, there must be no reference in the conceptual schema to stored field representation, stored record sequence, indexes, hashing schemes, pointers, or any other storage and access details. If the conceptual schema is made truly data-independent in this way, then the external schemas, which are defined in terms of the conceptual schema (see Section 2.6), will *a fortiori* be data-independent too.

The conceptual view, then, is a view of the total database content, and the conceptual schema is a definition of that view. However, it would be misleading to suggest that the conceptual schema is nothing more than a set of definitions much like the simple record definitions found in (e.g.) a COBOL program today. The definitions in the conceptual schema are intended to include a great many additional features, such as the security and integrity constraints mentioned in Chapter 1. Some authorities would go so far as to suggest that the ultimate objective of the conceptual schema is to describe the complete enterprise—not just its data *per se,* but also how that data is used: how it flows from point to point within the enterprise, what it is used for at each point, what audit or other controls are to be applied at each point, and so on [2.3]. It must be emphasized, however, that no system today actually supports a conceptual schema of anything approaching this degree of comprehensiveness; in most existing systems, the "conceptual schema" is really little more than a simple union of all of the individual external schemas, plus certain security and integrity constraints. But it is certainly possible that systems of the future will be much more sophisticated in their support of the conceptual level.

2.5   THE INTERNAL LEVEL

The third level of the architecture is the internal level. The **internal view** is a low-level representation of the entire database; it consists of many occurrences of each of many types of **internal record.** "Internal record" is the ANSI/SPARC term for the construct that we have been calling a *stored* record (and we will continue to use this latter term). The internal view is thus still at one remove from the physical level, since it does not deal in terms of *physical* records—also called **blocks** or **pages**—nor with any device-specific considerations such as cylinder or track sizes. In other words, the internal view effectively assumes an infinite linear address space; details of how that address space is mapped to physical storage are highly system-specific and are deliberately omitted from the general architecture. *Note:* The block, or page, is **the unit of I/O**—i.e., it is the amount of data transferred between secondary storage and main memory in a single I/O operation. Typical page sizes are 1K, 2K, or 4K bytes (K = 1024).

The internal view is described by means of the **internal schema,** which not only defines the various stored record types but also specifies what indexes exist, how stored fields are represented, what physical sequence the stored records are in, and so on (once again, see Fig. 2.2 for a simple example). The internal schema is written using yet another data definition language—the *internal DDL. Note:* In this book we will normally use the more intuitive terms "storage structure" or "stored database" in place of "internal view" and "storage structure definition" in place of "internal schema."

In closing, we remark that, in certain exceptional situations, application programs—in particular, applications of a *utility* nature (see Section 2.11)—might be permitted to operate directly at the internal level rather than at the external level. Needless to say, the practice is not recommended; it represents a security risk (since the security constraints are bypassed) and an integrity risk (since the integrity constraints are bypassed likewise), and the program will be data-dependent to boot; but sometimes it might be the only way to obtain the required functionality or performance—just as the user in a high-level programming language system might occasionally need to descend to assembler language in order to satisfy certain functionality or performance objectives today.

2.6   MAPPINGS

In addition to the three levels *per se,* the architecture of Fig. 2.3 involves certain **mappings**—one conceptual/internal mapping and several external/conceptual mappings, in general:

- The *conceptual/internal* mapping defines the correspondence between the conceptual view and the stored database; it specifies how conceptual records and fields are represented at the internal level. If the structure of the stored database is changed—i.e., if a change is made to the storage structure definition—then the conceptual/internal mapping must be changed accordingly, so that the conceptual schema can remain invariant. (It is the responsibility of the DBA to manage such changes, of course.) In other words, the effects of such changes must be isolated below the conceptual level, in order to preserve physical data independence.

- An *external/conceptual* mapping defines the correspondence between a particular external view and the conceptual view. In general, the differences that can exist between these two levels are analogous to those that can exist between the conceptual view and the stored database. For example, fields can have different data types; field and record names can be changed; several conceptual fields can be combined into a single (virtual) external field; and so on. Any number of external views can exist at the same time; any number of users can share a given external view; different external views can overlap.

Note: It should be clear that, just as the conceptual/internal mapping is the key to physical data independence, so the external/conceptual mappings are the key to **logical** data independence. As we saw in Chapter 1, a system provides *physical* data independence [1.3] if users and user programs are immune to changes in the physical structure of the stored database. Analogously, a system provides *logical* data independence [1.4] if users and user programs are also immune to changes in the *logical* structure of the database (meaning changes at the conceptual or "community logical" level). We will have more to say on this important issue in Chapters 3 and 9.

Incidentally, most systems permit the definition of certain external views to be expressed in terms of others (in effect, via *external/external* mappings), rather than always requiring an explicit definition of the mapping to the conceptual level—a useful feature if several external views are rather similar to one another. Relational systems in particular provide such a capability.

2.7 THE DATABASE ADMINISTRATOR

As explained in Chapter 1, the *data* administrator (DA) is the person who makes the strategic and policy decisions regarding the data of the enterprise, and the data*base* administrator (DBA) is the person who provides the necessary technical support for implementing those decisions. Thus, the DBA is responsible for the overall control of the system at a technical level. We can now describe some of the tasks of the DBA in a little more detail. In general, those tasks will include at least all of the following:

- *Defining the conceptual schema*

  It is the data administrator's job to decide exactly what information is to be held in the database—in other words, to identify the entities of interest to the enterprise and to identify the information to be recorded about those entities. This process is usually referred to as **logical**—sometimes *conceptual*—**database design.** Once the data administrator has thus decided the content of the database at an abstract level, the DBA will then create the corresponding conceptual schema, using the conceptual DDL. The object (compiled) form of that schema will be used by the DBMS in responding to access requests. The source (uncompiled) form will act as a reference document for the users of the system.

   Note: In practice, matters might not be as clearcut as the foregoing remarks suggest. In some cases, the data administrator might create the conceptual schema directly. In others, the DBA might do the logical design.

- *Defining the internal schema*

   The DBA must also decide how the data is to be represented in the stored database. This process is usually referred to as **physical** database design.* Having done the physical design, the DBA must then create the corresponding storage structure definition (i.e., the internal schema), using the internal DDL. In addition, he or she must also define the associated conceptual/internal mapping. In practice, either the conceptual DDL or the internal DDL—most likely the former—will probably include the means for defining that mapping, but the two functions (creating the schema, defining the mapping) should be clearly separable. Like the conceptual schema, the internal schema and corresponding mapping will exist in both source and object form.

- *Liaising with users*

   It is the business of the DBA to liaise with users to ensure that the data they need is available and to write (or help the users write) the necessary external schemas, using the applicable external DDL. (As already mentioned, a given system might support several distinct external DDLs.) In addition, the corresponding external/conceptual mappings must also be defined. In practice, the external DDL will probably include the means for specifying those mappings, but once again the schemas and the mappings should be clearly separable. Each external schema and corresponding mapping will exist in both source and object form.

   Other aspects of the user liaison function include consulting on application design; providing technical education; assisting with problem determination and resolution; and similar professional services.

- *Defining security and integrity constraints*

   As already discussed, security and integrity constraints can be regarded as part of the conceptual schema. The conceptual DDL must include facilities for specifying such constraints.

- *Defining dump and reload policies*

   Once an enterprise is committed to a database system, it becomes critically dependent on the successful operation of that system. In the event of damage to any portion of the database—caused by human error, say, or a failure in the hardware or operating system—it is essential to be able to repair the data concerned with the minimum of delay and with as little effect as possible on the rest of the system. For example, the availability of data that has *not* been damaged should ideally not be affected. The DBA must

---

*Observe the sequence: Decide what data you want first, then decide how to represent it in storage. Physical design should always be done *after* logical design.

define and implement an appropriate damage control scheme, typically involving (a) periodic unloading or "dumping" of the database to backup storage and (b) reloading the database when necessary from the most recent dump.

Incidentally, the need for quick data repair is one reason why it might be a good idea to spread the total data collection across several databases, instead of keeping it all in one place; the individual database might very well form the unit for dump and reload purposes. In this connection, note that *terabyte systems**—i.e., commercial database installations that store well over a trillion bytes of data, loosely speaking—already exist, and systems of the future are predicted to be much larger. It goes without saying that such *VLDB* ("very large database") systems require very careful and sophisticated administration, especially if there is a requirement for continuous availability (which there usually is). Nevertheless, we will continue to talk as if there were in fact just a single database, for simplicity.

- *Monitoring performance and responding to changing requirements*

  As indicated in Chapter 1, the DBA is responsible for organizing the system in such a way as to get the performance that is "best for the enterprise," and for making the appropriate adjustments—i.e., **tuning**—as requirements change. For example, it might be necessary to **reorganize** the stored database from time to time to ensure that performance levels remain acceptable. As already mentioned, any change to the physical storage (internal) level of the system must be accompanied by a corresponding change to the definition of the conceptual/internal mapping, so that the conceptual schema can remain constant.

Of course, the foregoing is not an exhaustive list—it is merely intended to give some idea of the extent and nature of the DBA's responsibilities.

2.8   THE DATABASE MANAGEMENT SYSTEM

The **database management system** (DBMS) is the software that handles all access to the database. Conceptually, what happens is the following (refer to Fig. 2.3 once again):

1. A user issues an access request, using some particular data sublanguage (typically SQL).

2. The DBMS intercepts that request and analyzes it.

3. The DBMS inspects, in turn, (the object versions of) the external schema for that user, the corresponding external/conceptual mapping, the conceptual schema, the conceptual/internal mapping, and the storage structure definition.

4. The DBMS executes the necessary operations on the stored database.

---

*1024 bytes = one kilobyte (KB); 1024KB = one megabyte (MB); 1024MB = one gigabyte (GB); 1024GB = one terabyte (TB); 1024TB = one petabyte (PB); 1024PB = one exabyte (EB). Note that a gigabyte is a billion bytes, loosely speaking (the abbreviation BB is sometimes used in place of GB). Incidentally—and contrary to popular belief—*gigabyte* is pronounced with a soft initial *g* ("jigabyte").

By way of an example, consider what is involved in the retrieval of a particular external record occurrence. In general, fields will be required from several conceptual record occurrences, and each conceptual record occurrence in turn will require fields from several stored record occurrences. Conceptually, then, the DBMS must first retrieve all required stored record occurrences, then construct the required conceptual record occurrences, and then construct the required external record occurrence. At each stage, data type or other conversions might be necessary.

Of course, the foregoing description is very much simplified; in particular, it implies that the entire process is interpretive, inasmuch as it suggests that the processes of analyzing the request, inspecting the various schemas, etc., are all done at run time. Interpretation, in turn, often implies poor performance, because of the run-time overhead. In practice, however, it might be possible for access requests to be *compiled* prior to run time (in particular, several of today's SQL products do this—see the annotation to references [4.12] and [4.26] in Chapter 4).

Let us now examine the functions of the DBMS in a little more detail. Those functions will include support for at least all of the following (refer to Fig. 2.4):

- *Data definition*

    The DBMS must be able to accept data definitions (external schemas, the conceptual schema, the internal schema, and all associated mappings) in source form and convert them to the appropriate object form. In other words, the DBMS must include **DDL processor** or **DDL compiler** components for each of the various data definition languages (DDLs). The DBMS must also "understand" the DDL definitions, in the sense that, for example, it "understands" that EMPLOYEE external records include a SALARY field; it must then be able to use this knowledge in analyzing and responding to data manipulation requests (e.g., "Get all employees with salary < $50,000").

- *Data manipulation*

    The DBMS must be able to handle requests to retrieve, update, or delete existing data in the database or to add new data to the database. In other words, the DBMS must include a **DML processor** or **DML compiler** component to deal with the data manipulation language (DML).

- In general, DML requests can be "planned" or "unplanned":

    a. A **planned** request is one for which the need was foreseen well in advance of the time at which the request is executed. The DBA will probably have tuned the physical database design in such a way as to guarantee good performance for planned requests.

    b. An **unplanned** request, by contrast, is an *ad hoc* query, i.e., a request for which the need was not seen in advance, but instead arose in a spur-of-the-moment fashion. The physical database design might or might not be ideally suited for the specific request under consideration.

    To use the terminology introduced in Chapter 1 (Section 1.3), planned requests are characteristic of "operational" or "production" applications, while unplanned requests are characteristic of "decision support" applications. Furthermore, planned requests

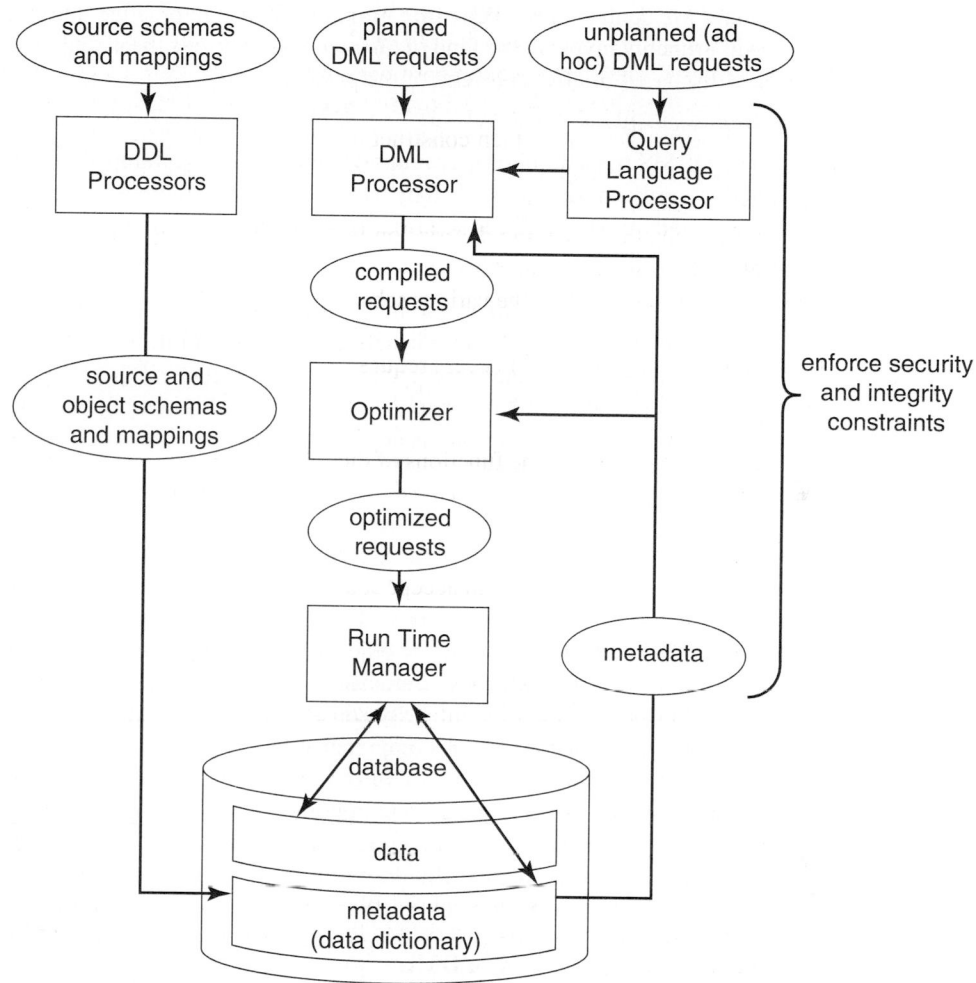

Fig. 2.4   Major DBMS functions and components

will typically be issued from prewritten application programs, whereas unplanned requests, by definition, will be issued interactively via some **query language processor.** *Note:* As we saw in Chapter 1, the query language processor is really a builtin online application, not part of the DBMS *per se;* we include it in Fig. 2.4 for completeness.

■ *Optimization and execution*

DML requests, planned or unplanned, must be processed by the **optimizer** component, whose purpose is to determine an efficient way of implementing the request. Optimization is discussed in detail in Chapter 17. The optimized requests are then executed under the control of the **run-time manager.** *Note:* In practice, the run-time manager will probably invoke some kind of *file manager* to access the stored data. File managers are discussed briefly at the end of the present section.

- *Data security and integrity*

    The DBMS must monitor user requests and reject any attempts to violate the security and integrity constraints defined by the DBA (see the previous section). These tasks can be carried out at compile time or run time or some mixture of the two.

- *Data recovery and concurrency*

    The DBMS—or, more likely, some other related software component, usually called the **transaction manager** or **transaction processing monitor** (TP monitor)—must enforce certain recovery and concurrency controls. Details of these aspects of the system are beyond the scope of this chapter; see Part IV of this book for an indepth discussion. *Note:* The transaction manager is not shown in Fig. 2.4 because it is usually not part of the DBMS *per se.*

- *Data dictionary*

    The DBMS must provide a **data dictionary** function. The data dictionary can be regarded as a database in its own right (but a system database rather than a user database). The dictionary contains "data about the data" (sometimes called *metadata* or *descriptors*)—that is, *definitions* of other objects in the system, instead of just "raw data." In particular, all of the various schemas and mappings (external, conceptual, etc.) and all of the various security and integrity constraints will be stored, in both source and object form, in the dictionary. A comprehensive dictionary will also include much additional information, showing, for instance, which programs use which parts of the database, which users require which reports, and so on. The dictionary might even—in fact, probably should—be integrated into the database it defines and thus include its own definition. Certainly it should be possible to query the dictionary just like any other database, so that, for example, it is possible to tell which programs and/or users are likely to be affected by some proposed change to the system. See Chapter 3 for further discussion.

    Note: We are touching here on an area in which there is much terminological confusion. Some people would refer to what we are calling the dictionary as a *directory* or a *catalog*—with the implication that directories and catalogs are somehow inferior to a true dictionary—and would reserve the term *dictionary* to refer to a specific (important) kind of application development tool. Other terms that are also sometimes used to refer to this latter kind of object are *data repository* (see Chapter 13) and *data encyclopedia.*

- *Performance*

    It goes without saying that the DBMS should perform all of the tasks identified above as efficiently as possible.

We can summarize all of the foregoing by saying that the overall purpose of the DBMS is to provide the **user interface** to the database system. The user interface can be defined as a boundary in the system below which everything is invisible to the user. By definition, therefore, the user interface is at the *external* level. However, as we will see in Chapter 9, there are some situations in which the external view is unlikely to differ very significantly from the relevant portion of the underlying conceptual view, at least in today's commercial SQL products.

We conclude this section by briefly contrasting database management systems as discussed above with **file** management systems (*file managers* or *file servers* for short). Basically, the file manager is that component of the underlying operating system that manages stored files; loosely speaking, therefore, it is "closer to the disk" than the DBMS is. (In fact, the DBMS is typically built on top of some kind of file manager.) Thus, the user of a file management system will be able to create and destroy stored files and perform simple retrieval and update operations on stored records in such files. In contrast to the DBMS, however:

- File managers are not aware of the internal structure of stored records and hence cannot handle requests that rely on a knowledge of that structure.
- They typically provide little or no support for security and integrity constraints.
- They typically provide little or no support for recovery and concurrency controls.
- There is no true data dictionary concept at the file manager level.
- They provide much less data independence than the DBMS does.
- Files are typically not "integrated" or "shared" in the same sense that the database is (they are usually private to some particular user or application).

2.9   THE DATA COMMUNICATIONS MANAGER

In this section, we briefly consider the topic of **data communications.** Database requests from an end user are actually transmitted from the user's workstation—which might be physically remote from the database system itself—to some online application (builtin or otherwise), and thence to the DBMS, in the form of *communication messages.* Likewise, responses back from the DBMS and online application to the user's workstation are also transmitted in the form of such messages. All such message transmissions take place under the control of another software component, the **data communications manager** (DC manager).

The DC manager is not part of the DBMS but is an autonomous system in its own right. However, since it is clearly required to work in harmony with the DBMS, the two are sometimes regarded as equal partners in a higher-level cooperative venture called the **database/data-communications system** (DB/DC system), in which the DBMS looks after the database and the DC manager handles all messages to and from the DBMS, or more accurately to and from applications that use the DBMS. In this book, however, we will have comparatively little to say about message handling as such (it is a large subject in its own right). Section 2.12 does briefly discuss the question of communication *between distinct systems* (i.e., between distinct machines in a communications network, such as the Internet), but that is really a separate topic.

2.10   CLIENT/SERVER ARCHITECTURE

So far in this chapter we have been discussing database systems from the point of view of the so-called ANSI/SPARC architecture. In particular, we gave a simplified picture of that architecture in Fig. 2.3. In this section we take a look at database systems from a slightly different perspective. The overall purpose of such systems, of course, is to support the development and execution of database applications. From a high-level point of view, therefore, a database system can be regarded as having a very simple two-part structure, consisting of a **server** (also called the *backend*) and a set of **clients** (also called *frontends*). Refer to Fig. 2.5. *Explanation:*

- The *server* is just the DBMS itself. It supports all of the basic DBMS functions discussed in Section 2.8—data definition, data manipulation, data security and integrity, and so on. In particular, it provides all of the external, conceptual, and internal level support discussed in Sections 2.3–2.6. Thus, "server" in this context is just another name for the DBMS.

- The *clients* are the various applications that run on top of the DBMS—both user-written applications and builtin applications, i.e., applications provided by the DBMS vendor or by some third party. As far as the server is concerned, of course, there is no difference between user-written and builtin applications—they all use the same interface to the server, namely the external-level interface discussed in Section 2.3.

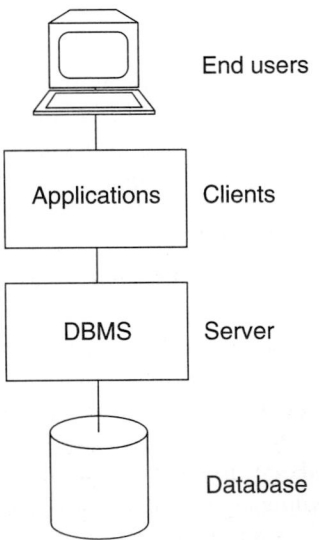

End users

Applications   Clients

DBMS   Server

Database

Fig. 2.5   Client/server architecture

Note: Certain special "utility" applications might constitute an exception to the foregoing, inasmuch as they might sometimes need to operate directly at the *internal* level of the system (as mentioned in Section 2.5). Such utilities are best regarded as integral components of the DBMS, rather than as applications in the usual sense. They are discussed in more detail in the next section.

We elaborate briefly on the question of user-written *vs.* vendor-provided applications:

- *User-written applications* are basically regular application programs, written (typically) either in a conventional 3GL such as C or COBOL or in some proprietary 4GL— though in both cases the language needs to be coupled somehow with an appropriate data sublanguage, as explained in Section 2.3.

- *Vendor-provided applications* (often called **tools**) are applications whose basic purpose is to assist in the creation and execution of other applications! The applications that are created are applications that are tailored to some specific task (they might not look much like applications in the conventional sense; indeed, the whole point of the tools is to allow users, especially end users, to create applications *without* having to write programs in a conventional programming language). For example, one of the vendor-provided tools will be a *report writer,* whose purpose is to allow end users to obtain formatted reports from the system on request. Any given report request can be regarded as a small application program, written in a very high-level (and special purpose) *report writer language.*

    Vendor-provided tools can be divided into several more or less distinct classes:

    a. Query language processors;

    b. Report writers;

    c. Business graphics subsystems;

    d. Spreadsheets;

    e. Natural language processors;

    f. Statistical packages;

    g. Copy management or "data extract" tools;

    h. Application generators (including 4GL processors);

    i. Other application development tools, including computer-aided software engineering (CASE) products;

and many others. Details of most such tools are beyond the scope of this book; however, we remark that since (as stated above) the whole point of a database system is to support the creation and execution of applications, the quality of the available tools is, or should be, a major factor in "the database decision" (i.e., the process of choosing the right database product). In other words, the DBMS *per se* is not the only factor that needs to be taken into account, nor even necessarily the most significant factor.

We close this section with a forward reference. Since the overall system can be so neatly divided into two parts, server and clients, the possibility arises of running the two on *different machines.* In other words, the potential exists for **distributed processing.** Distributed processing means that distinct machines can be connected together into some kind of communications network in such a way that a single data-processing task can be spread across several machines in the network. In fact, so attractive is this possibility—for a variety of reasons, mainly economic—that the term "client/server" has come to apply almost exclusively to the case where client and server are indeed on different machines. We will discuss distributed processing in more detail in Section 2.12.

2.11 UTILITIES

Utilities are programs designed to help the DBA with various administration tasks. As mentioned in the previous section, some utility programs operate at the external level of the system, and thus are effectively nothing more than special-purpose applications; some might not even be provided by the DBMS vendor, but rather by some third party. Other utilities, however, operate directly at the internal level (in other words, they are really part of the server), and hence must be provided by the DBMS vendor.

Here are some examples of the kind of utilities that are typically needed in practice:

- **Load** routines, to create the initial version of the database from one or more operating system files;

- **Unload/reload** routines, to unload the database, or portions thereof, to backup storage and to reload data from such backup copies (of course, the "reload utility" is basically identical to the load utility just mentioned);

- **Reorganization** routines, to rearrange the data in the stored database for various reasons (usually having to do with performance)—e.g., to cluster data together in some particular way on the disk, or to reclaim space occupied by data that has become obsolete;

- **Statistical** routines, to compute various performance statistics such as file sizes or value distributions or I/O counts, etc.;

- **Analysis** routines, to analyze the statistics just mentioned;

and so on. Of course, this list represents just a small sample of the range of functions that utilities typically provide; a wealth of other possibilities exist.

2.12 DISTRIBUTED PROCESSING

To repeat from Section 2.10, the term "distributed processing" means that distinct machines can be connected together into a communications network such as the Internet, such that a single data-processing task can span several machines in the network. (The term "parallel processing" is also sometimes used with essentially the same meaning, except that the distinct machines tend to be physically close together in a "parallel" system and need not be so in a "distributed" system—e.g., they might be geographically dispersed in the latter case.) Communication among the various machines is handled by some kind of network management software—possibly an extension of the DC manager discussed in Section 2.9, more likely a separate software component.

Many levels or varieties of distributed processing are possible. To repeat from Section 2.10, one simple case involves running the DBMS backend (the server) on one machine and the application frontends (the clients) on another. Refer to Fig. 2.6.

As mentioned at the end of Section 2.10, "client/server," though strictly speaking a purely architectural term, has come to be almost synonymous with the arrangement illustrated in Fig. 2.6, in which client and server run on different machines. Indeed, there are many arguments in favor of such a scheme:

- The first is basically just the usual parallel-processing argument: namely, many processing units are now being applied to the overall task, and server (database) and client (application) processing are being done in parallel. Response time and throughput should thus be improved.

- Furthermore, the server machine might be a custom-built machine that is tailored to the DBMS function (a "database machine") and might thus provide better DBMS performance.

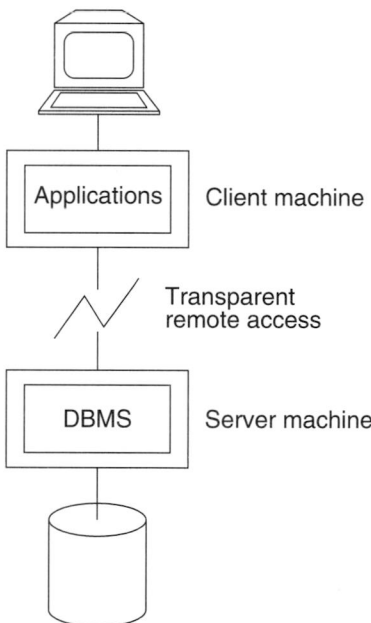

Fig. 2.6   Client(s) and server running on different machines

- Likewise, the client machine might be a personal workstation, tailored to the needs of the end user and thus able to provide better interfaces, high availability, faster responses, and overall improved ease of use to the user.
- Several different client machines might be able (in fact, typically will be able) to access the same server machine. Thus, a single database might be shared across several distinct client systems (see Fig. 2.7).

In addition to the foregoing arguments, there is also the point that running the client(s) and the server on separate machines matches the way enterprises actually operate. It is quite common for a single enterprise—a bank, for example—to operate many computers, such that the data for one portion of the enterprise is stored on one computer and the data for another portion is stored on another. It is also quite common for users on one computer to need at least occasional access to data stored on another. To pursue the banking example for a moment, it is very likely that users at one branch office will occasionally need access to data stored at another. Note, therefore, that the client machines might have stored data of their own, and the server machine might have applications of its own. In general, therefore, each machine will act as a server for some users and a client for others (see Fig. 2.8); in other words, each machine will support *an entire database system,* in the sense of earlier sections of this chapter.

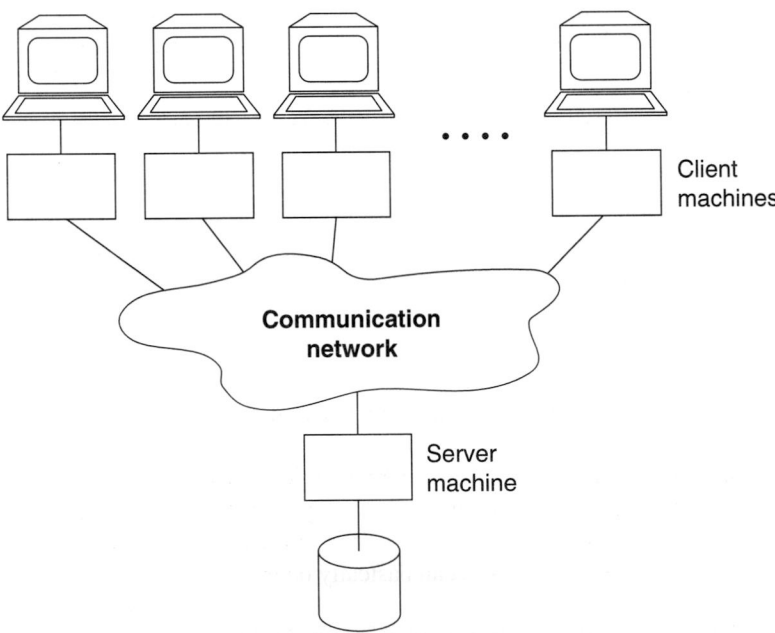

Fig. 2.7   One server machine, many client machines

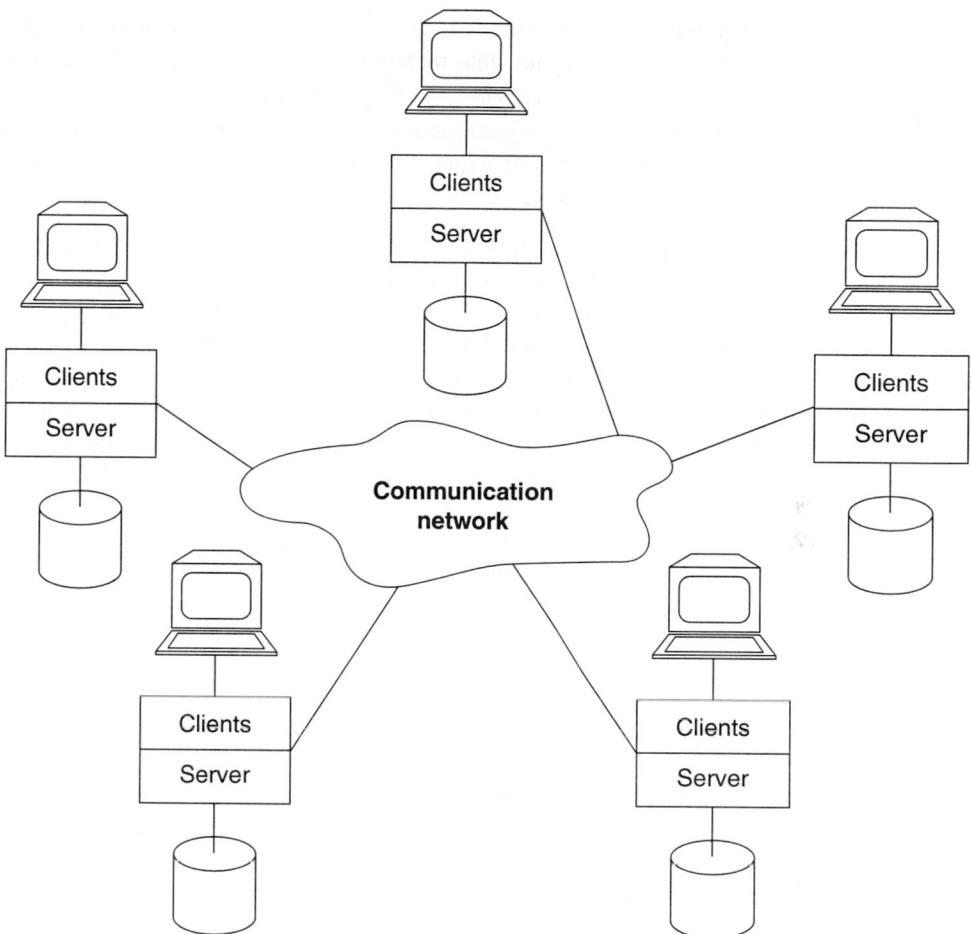

Fig. 2.8   Each machine runs both client(s) and server

The final point is that a single client machine might be able to access several different server machines (the converse of the case illustrated in Fig. 2.7). This capability is desirable because, as mentioned above, enterprises do typically operate in such a manner that the totality of their data is not stored on one single machine but rather is spread across many distinct machines, and applications will sometimes need the ability to access data from more than one machine. Such access can basically be provided in two different ways:

- A given client might be able to access any number of servers, but only one at a time (i.e., each individual database request must be directed to just one server). In such a system it is not possible, within a single request, to combine data from two or more different servers. Furthermore, the user in such a system has to know which particular machine holds which pieces of data.

■ The client might be able to access many servers simultaneously (i.e., a single database request might be able to combine data from several servers). In this case, the servers look to the client—from a logical point of view—as if they were really a single server, and the user does not have to know which machines hold which pieces of data.

This latter case constitutes what is usually called a **distributed database system.** Distributed database is a big topic in its own right; carried to its logical conclusion, full distributed database support implies that a single application should be able to operate "transparently" on data that is spread across a variety of different databases, managed by a variety of different DBMSs, running on a variety of different machines, supported by a variety of different operating systems, and connected together by a variety of different communication networks—where "transparently" means that the application operates from a logical point of view as if the data were all managed by a single DBMS running on a single machine. Such a capability might sound like a pretty tall order!—but it is highly desirable from a practical perspective, and vendors are working hard to make such systems a reality. We will discuss such systems in detail in Chapter 20.

2.13   SUMMARY

In this chapter we have looked at database systems from an architectural point of view. First, we described the **ANSI/SPARC architecture,** which divides a database system into three levels, as follows: The **internal** level is the one closest to physical storage (i.e., it is the one concerned with the way the data is physically stored); the **external** level is the one closest to the users (i.e., it is the one concerned with the way the data is viewed by individual users); and the **conceptual** level is a level of indirection between the other two (it provides a *community view* of the data). The data as perceived at each level is described by a **schema** (or several schemas, in the case of the external level). **Mappings** define the correspondence between (a) a given external schema and the conceptual schema, and (b) the conceptual schema and the internal schema. Those mappings are the key to the provision of **logical** and **physical data independence,** respectively.

Users—i.e., end users and application programmers, both of whom operate at the external level—interact with the data by means of a **data sublanguage,** which divides into at least two components, a **data definition language** (DDL) and a **data manipulation language** (DML). The data sublanguage is embedded in a **host language.** *Note:* The boundaries between the host language and the data sublanguage and between the DDL and the DML are primarily conceptual in nature; ideally they should be "transparent to the user."

We also took a closer look at the functions of the **DBA** and the **DBMS.** Among other things, the DBA is responsible for creating the internal schema (**physical database design**);

by contrast, creating the conceptual schema (**logical** or **conceptual database design**) is the responsibility of the *data* administrator. And the DBMS is responsible, among other things, for implementing DDL and DML requests from the user. The DBMS is also responsible for providing some kind of **data dictionary** function.

Database systems can also be conveniently thought of as consisting of a **server** (the DBMS itself) and a set of **clients** (the applications). Client and server can and often will run on separate machines, thus providing one simple kind of **distributed processing.** In general, each server can serve many clients, and each client can access many servers. If the system provides total "transparency"—meaning that each client can behave as if it were dealing with a single server on a single machine, regardless of the overall physical state of affairs—then we have a true **distributed database system.**

EXERCISES

2.1 Draw a diagram of the database system architecture presented in this chapter (the ANSI/SPARC architecture).

2.2 Define the following terms:

backend	frontend
client	host language
conceptual DDL, schema, view	load
conceptual/internal mapping	logical database design
data definition language	internal DDL, schema, view
data dictionary	physical database design
data manipulation language	planned request
data sublanguage	reorganization
DB/DC system	server
DC manager	storage structure definition
distributed database	unload/reload
distributed processing	unplanned request
external DDL, schema, view	user interface
external/conceptual mapping	utility

2.3 Explain the sequence of steps involved in retrieving a particular external record occurrence.

2.4 List the major functions performed by the DBMS.

2.5 Distinguish between logical and physical data independence.

2.6 What do you understand by the term *metadata?*

2.7 List the major functions performed by the DBA.

2.8 Distinguish between the DBMS and a file management system.

2.9 Give some examples of vendor-provided tools.

2.10 Give some examples of database utilities.

2.11 Examine any database system that might be available to you. Try to map that system to the ANSI/SPARC architecture as described in this chapter. Does it cleanly support the three levels of the architecture? How are the mappings between levels defined? What do the various DDLs (external, conceptual, internal) look like? What data sublanguage(s) does the system support? What host languages? Who performs the DBA function? Are there any security or integrity facilities? Is there a dictionary? Is it self-describing? What vendor-provided applications does the system support? What utilities? Is there a separate DC manager? Are there any distributed processing capabilities?

REFERENCES AND BIBLIOGRAPHY

The following references are all fairly old by now (with the exception of the last one), but they are still relevant to the concepts introduced in the present chapter.

2.1 ANSI/X3/SPARC Study Group on Data Base Management Systems: Interim Report, *FDT* (bulletin of ACM SIGMOD) *7,* No. 2 (1975).

2.2 Dionysios C. Tsichritzis and Anthony Klug (eds.): "The ANSI/X3/SPARC DBMS Framework: Report of the Study Group on Data Base Management Systems," *Information Systems 3* (1978).

> References [2.1–2.2] are the Interim and Final Report, respectively, of the so-called ANSI/SPARC Study Group. The ANSI/X3/SPARC Study Group on Data Base Management Systems (to give it its full title) was established in late 1972 by the Standards Planning and Requirements Committee (SPARC) of the American National Standards Institute (ANSI) Committee on Computers and Information Processing (X3). (Some 25 years later, the name X3 was changed to NCITS—National Committee on Information Technology Standards.) The objectives of the Study Group were to determine which areas, if any, of database technology were appropriate for standardization, and to produce a set of recommendations for action in each such area. In working to meet these objectives, the Study Group took the position that *interfaces* were the only aspect of a database system that could possibly be suitable for standardization, and accordingly defined a generalized database system architecture, or framework, that emphasized the role of such interfaces. The Final Report provides a detailed description of that architecture and of some of the 42 (!) identified interfaces. The Interim Report is an earlier working document that is still of some interest; in some areas it provides additional detail.

2.3 J. J. van Griethuysen (ed.): "Concepts and Terminology for the Conceptual Schema and the Information Base," International Organization for Standardization (ISO) Technical Report ISO/TR 9007:1987(E) (March 1982; revised July 1987).

> This document is the report of an ISO Working Group whose objectives included "the definition of concepts for conceptual schema languages." It includes an introduction to three competing candidates (more accurately, three *sets* of candidates) for an appropriate set of formalisms, and applies each of the three to a common example involving the activities of a hypothetical car registration authority. The three sets of contenders are (1) "entity-attribute-relationship" schemes, (2) "binary relationship" schemes, and (3) "interpreted predicate logic" schemes. The report also includes a discussion of the fundamental concepts underlying the notion of the conceptual schema, and suggests some principles as a basis for implementation of a system that properly

supports that notion. Heavy going in places, but an important document for anyone seriously interested in the conceptual level of the system.

2.4 William Kent: *Data and Reality.* Amsterdam, Netherlands: North-Holland / New York, N.Y.: Elsevier Science (1978).

A stimulating and thought-provoking discussion of the nature of information, and in particular of the conceptual schema. "This book projects a philosophy that life and reality are at bottom amorphous, disordered, contradictory, inconsistent, nonrational, and nonobjective" (excerpt from the final chapter). The book can be regarded in large part as a compendium of real-world problems that (it is suggested) existing database formalisms—in particular, formalisms that are based on conventional record-like structures, which includes the relational model—have difficulty in dealing with. Recommended.

2.5 Odysseas G. Tsatalos, Marvin H. Solomon, and Yannis E. Ioannidis: "The GMAP: A Versatile Tool for Physical Data Independence," Proc. 20th Int. Conf. on Very Large Data Bases, Santiago, Chile (September 1994).

GMAP stands for *Generalized Multi-Level Access Path.* The authors of the paper note correctly that today's database products "force users to frame their queries in terms of a logical schema that is directly tied to physical structures," and hence are rather weak on physical data independence. In their paper, therefore, they propose a conceptual/internal mapping language (to use the terminology of the present chapter) that can be used to specify far more kinds of mappings than are typically supported in products today. Given a particular "logical schema," the language (which is based on relational algebra—see Chapter 6—and is therefore declarative, not procedural, in nature) allows the specification of numerous different physical schemas, all of them formally derived from that logical schema. Among other things, those physical schemas can include vertical and horizontal partitioning (see Chapter 20), any number of physical access paths, clustering, and controlled redundancy.

The paper also gives an algorithm for transforming user operations against the logical schema into equivalent operations against the physical schema. A prototype implementation shows that the DBA can tune the physical schema to "achieve significantly better performance than is possible with conventional techniques."

CHAPTER 3

An Introduction
to Relational Databases

3.1 INTRODUCTION

As explained in Chapter 1, the emphasis in this book is very much on relational systems. In particular, Part II covers the theoretical foundations of such systems (the relational model) in considerable depth. The purpose of the present chapter is just to give a preliminary, intuitive, and very informal introduction to the material to be addressed in Part II (and to some extent in subsequent parts too), in order to pave the way for a better understanding of those later parts of the book. Most of the topics mentioned will be discussed more formally, and in much more detail, in those later chapters.

3.2 AN INFORMAL LOOK AT
THE RELATIONAL MODEL

We have already said several times that relational systems are based on a formal foundation, or theory, called *the relational model of data.* Intuitively, what this statement means (among other things) is that in such a system:

1. **Structural aspect:** The data in the database is perceived by the user as tables, and nothing but tables;

2. **Integrity aspect:** Those tables satisfy certain integrity constraints (to be discussed toward the end of this section);

3. **Manipulative aspect:** The operators available to the user for manipulating those tables—e.g., for purposes of data retrieval—are operators that derive tables from tables. Of those operators, three particularly important ones are *restrict, project,* and *join.*

A simple relational database, the departments and employees database, is shown in Fig. 3.1. As you can see, that database is indeed "perceived as tables" (and the meanings of those tables are intended to be self-evident).

DEPT	DEPT#	DNAME	BUDGET
	D1	Marketing	10M
	D2	Development	12M
	D3	Research	5M

EMP	EMP#	ENAME	DEPT#	SALARY
	E1	Lopez	D1	40K
	E2	Cheng	D1	42K
	E3	Finzi	D2	30K
	E4	Saito	D2	35K

Fig. 3.1   The departments and employees database (sample values)

Fig. 3.2 shows some sample restrict, project, and join operations against the database of Fig. 3.1. Here are (very loose!) definitions of those operations:

- The **restrict** operation (also known as select) extracts specified rows from a table.
- The **project** operation extracts specified columns from a table.
- The **join** operation joins two tables together on the basis of common values in a common column.

Restrict: *Result:*

DEPTs where BUDGET > 8M

DEPT#	DNAME	BUDGET
D1	Marketing	10M
D2	Development	12M

Project: *Result:*

DEPTs over DEPT#, BUDGET

DEPT#	BUDGET
D1	10M
D2	12M
D3	5M

Join:

DEPTs and EMPs over DEPT#

Result:

DEPT#	DNAME	BUDGET	EMP#	ENAME	SALARY
D1	Marketing	10M	E1	Lopez	40K
D1	Marketing	10M	E2	Cheng	42K
D2	Development	12M	E3	Finzi	30K
D2	Development	12M	E4	Saito	35K

Fig. 3.2   Restrict, project, and join (examples)

Of the three examples, the only one that seems to need any further explanation is the last one, the join example. Observe first that the two tables DEPT and EMP do indeed have a common column, DEPT#, so they can be joined together on the basis of common values in that column. A given row from table DEPT will join to a given row in table EMP (to yield a row of the result table) if and only if the two rows in question have a common DEPT# value. For example, the DEPT and EMP rows

DEPT#	DNAME	BUDGET
D1	Marketing	10M

EMP#	ENAME	DEPT#	SALARY
E1	Lopez	D1	40K

(column names shown for explicitness) join together to produce the result row

DEPT#	DNAME	BUDGET	EMP#	ENAME	SALARY
D1	Marketing	10M	E1	Lopez	40K

because they have the same value, D1, in the common column. Note that the common value appears once, not twice, in the result row. The overall result of the join contains all possible rows that can be obtained in this manner (and no other rows). Note in particular that since no EMP row has a DEPT# value of D3 (i.e., no employee is currently assigned to that department), no row for D3 appears in the result, even though there *is* a row for D3 in table DEPT.

Now, one point that Fig. 3.2 clearly shows is that *the result of each of the three operations is another table* (in other words, the operators are indeed "operators that derive tables from tables," as previously stated). This is the **closure** property of relational systems, and it is very important. Basically, because the output of any operation is the same kind of object as the input—they are all tables—so *the output from one operation can become input to another.* Thus it is possible, e.g., to take a projection of a join, or a join of two restrictions, or a restriction of a projection, etc., etc. In other words, it is possible to write *nested expressions*—i.e., expressions in which the operands themselves are represented by general expressions, instead of just by simple table names. This fact in turn has numerous important consequences, as we will see later (both in this chapter and in many subsequent ones).

By the way, when we say that the output from each operation is another table, it is important to understand that we are talking *from a conceptual point of view.* We do not mean to imply that the system actually has to materialize the result of every individual operation in its entirety. For example, suppose we are trying to compute a restriction of a join. Then, as soon as a given row of the join is formed, the system can immediately test that row against the specified restriction condition to see whether it belongs in the final result, and immediately discard it if not. In other words, the intermediate result that is the output from the join might never exist as a fully materialized table in its own right at all. As a general rule, in fact, the system tries very hard *not* to materialize intermediate results in their entirety, for obvious performance reasons. *Note:* If intermediate results are fully materialized, the overall expression evaluation strategy is called (unsurprisingly) *materialized evaluation;* if intermediate results are passed piecemeal to subsequent operations, it is called *pipelined* evaluation.

Another point that Fig. 3.2 also clearly illustrates is that the operations are all **set-at-a-time,** not row-at-a-time; that is, the operands and results are whole tables, not just single rows, and tables contain *sets* of rows. (A table containing a set of just one row is legal, of course; so too is an *empty* table, i.e., one containing no rows at all.) For example, the join in Fig. 3.2 operates on two tables of three and four rows respectively, and returns a result table of four rows. By contrast, the operations in nonrelational systems are typically at the row- or record-at-a-time level; thus, this *set-processing capability* is a major distinguishing characteristic of relational systems (see further discussion in Section 3.5 below).

Let us return to Fig. 3.1 for a moment. There are a couple of additional points to be made in connection with the sample database of that figure:

- First, note that relational systems require only that the database be *perceived by the user* as tables. Tables are the **logical** structure in a relational system, not the physical structure. At the physical level, in fact, the system is free to store the data any way it likes— using sequential files, indexing, hashing, pointer chains, compression, etc.—provided only that it can map that stored representation to tables at the logical level. Another way of saying the same thing is that tables represent an *abstraction* of the way the data is physically stored—an abstraction in which numerous storage-level details, such as stored record placement, stored record sequence, stored data value representations, stored record prefixes, stored access structures such as indexes, and so forth, are all *hidden from the user.*

  Incidentally, the term "logical structure" in the foregoing paragraph is intended to encompass both the conceptual and external levels, in ANSI/SPARC terms. The point is that—as explained in Chapter 2—the conceptual and external levels in a relational system will both be relational, but the internal or physical level will not be. In fact, relational theory as such has nothing to say about the internal level at all; it is, to repeat, concerned with how the database looks to the *user.** The only requirement is that, to repeat, whatever physical structure is chosen must fully implement the logical structure.

- Second, relational databases abide by a very nice principle, called ***The Information Principle:*** *The entire information content of the database is represented in one and only one way, namely as explicit values in column positions in rows in tables.* This method of representation is the *only* method available (at the logical level, of course) in a relational system. In particular, **there are no *pointers*** connecting one table to another. In Fig. 3.1, for example, there is a connection between the D1 row of table DEPT and the E1 row of table EMP, because employee E1 works in department D1; but that

---

*It is an unfortunate fact that most of today's SQL products do not support this aspect of the theory properly. To be more specific, they typically support only rather restrictive conceptual/internal mappings (typically, they map one logical table directly to one stored file). As a consequence, they do not provide nearly as much physical data independence as relational technology is theoretically capable of.

connection is represented, not by a pointer, but by the appearance of the value D1 in the DEPT# position of the EMP row for E1. In nonrelational systems, by contrast (e.g. IMS or IDMS), such information is typically represented—as mentioned in Chapter 1—by some kind of *pointer* that is explicitly visible to the user.

Note: When we say there are no pointers in a relational database, we do not mean there cannot be pointers at the *physical level*—on the contrary, there certainly can, and indeed there almost certainly will. But, to repeat, all such physical storage details are concealed from the user in a relational system.

So much for the structural and manipulative aspects of the relational model; now we turn to the integrity aspect. Consider the departments and employees database of Fig. 3.1 once again. In practice, that database might be required to satisfy any number of integrity constraints—for example, employee salaries might have to be in the range 25K to 95K (say), department budgets might have to be in the range 1M to 15M (say), and so on. Certain of those constraints are of such major pragmatic importance, however, that they enjoy some special nomenclature. To be specific:

1. Each row in table DEPT must include a unique DEPT# value; likewise, each row in table EMP must include a unique EMP# value. We say, loosely, that columns DEPT# in table DEPT and EMP# in table EMP are the **primary keys** for their respective tables. (Recall from Chapter 1 that we indicate primary keys in our figures by double underlining.)

2. Each DEPT# value in table EMP must exist as a DEPT# value in table DEPT, to reflect the fact that every employee must be assigned to an existing department. We say, loosely, that column DEPT# in table EMP is a **foreign** key, referencing the primary key of table DEPT.

We close this section with a definition of the relational model, for purposes of subsequent reference (despite the fact that the definition is quite abstract and will not be very comprehensible at this stage). Briefly, **the relational model** consists of the following five components:

1. An open-ended collection of **scalar types** (including in particular the type *boolean* or *truth value*);

2. A **relation type generator** and an intended interpretation for such generated relation types;

3. Facilities for defining **relation variables** of such generated relation types;

4. A **relational assignment** operation for assigning relation values to such relation variables;

5. An open-ended collection of generic **relational operators** for deriving relation values from other relation values.

As you can see, the relational model is very much more than just "tables plus restrict, project, and join," though it is often characterized in such a manner informally.

Note: You might be surprised to see no explicit mention of integrity constraints in the foregoing definition. The fact is, however, such constraints represent just one application (albeit a very important one) of the relational operators; that is, such constraints are formulated—conceptually, at any rate—in terms of those operators, as we will see in Chapter 8.

3.3 RELATIONS AND RELVARS

If it is true that a relational database is basically just a database in which the data is perceived as tables—and of course it *is* true—then a good question to ask is: Why exactly do we call such a database relational? The answer is simple (in fact, we mentioned it in Chapter 1): "Relation" is just a mathematical term for a table—to be precise, a table of a certain specific kind (details to be discussed in Chapter 5). Thus, for example, we can say that the departments and employees database of Fig. 3.1 contains two *relations*.

Now, in informal contexts it is usual to treat the terms "relation" and "table" as if they were synonymous; informally, indeed, the term "table" is used much more often than the term "relation." But it is worth taking a moment to understand why the term "relation" was introduced in the first place. Briefly, the explanation is as follows:

- As we have seen, relational systems are based on the relational model. The relational model in turn is an abstract theory of data that is based on certain aspects of mathematics (mainly set theory and predicate logic).

- The principles of the relational model were originally laid down in 1969–70 by E. F. Codd, at that time a researcher in IBM. It was late in 1968 that Codd, a mathematician by training, first realized that the discipline of mathematics could be used to inject some solid principles and rigor into a field—database management—that, prior to that time, was all too deficient in any such qualities. Codd's ideas were first widely disseminated in a now classic paper, "A Relational Model of Data for Large Shared Data Banks" (see reference [5.1] in Chapter 5).

- Since that time, those ideas—by now almost universally accepted—have had a wide-ranging influence on just about every aspect of database technology, and indeed on other fields as well, such as the fields of artificial intelligence, natural-language processing, and hardware system design.

Now, the relational model as originally formulated by Codd very deliberately made use of certain terms, such as the term "relation" itself, that were not familiar in IT circles at that time (even though the concepts in some cases were). The trouble was, many of the more familiar terms were very *fuzzy*—they lacked the precision necessary to a formal theory of the kind that Codd was proposing. For example, consider the term "record." At different times and in different contexts that single term can mean either a record *occurrence* or a record *type;* a *logical* record or a *physical* record; a *stored* record or a *virtual* record; and perhaps other things as well. The relational model therefore does not use the term "record" at all; instead, it uses the term "tuple" (rhymes with "couple"), which can be given a very precise definition. We do not give that definition here; for present purposes, it is sufficient to say that the term "tuple" corresponds approximately to the notion of a row (just as the term "relation" corresponds approximately to the notion of a table). When we move on to study the more formal aspects of relational systems in Part II, we will make use of the formal terminology, but in this chapter we are not trying to be so formal (for the most part, at any rate), and we will mostly stick to terms such as "row" and "column" that are reasonably familiar. However, one formal term we *will* use a lot from this point forward is the term "relation" itself.

We return to the departments and employees database of Fig. 3.1 once again in order to make another important point. The fact is, DEPT and EMP in that database are really relation *variables*—variables, that is, whose values are relation *values* (different relation values at different times). For example, suppose EMP currently has the value—the *relation value*, that is—shown in Fig. 3.1, and suppose we delete the row for Saito (employee number E4):

```
DELETE EMP WHERE EMP# = 'E4' ;
```

The result is shown in Fig. 3.3.

EMP	EMP#	ENAME	DEPT#	SALARY
	E1	Lopez	D1	40K
	E2	Cheng	D1	42K
	E3	Finzi	D2	30K

Fig. 3.3   Relation variable EMP after deleting E4 row

Conceptually, what has happened here is that the *old relation value of EMP has been replaced* en bloc *by an entirely new relation value.* Of course, the old value (with four rows) and the new one (with three) are very similar, but conceptually they *are* different values. Indeed, the delete operation in question is basically just shorthand for a certain **relational assignment** operation that might look something like this:

```
EMP  :=  EMP MINUS ( EMP WHERE EMP# = 'E4' ) ;
```

(*Note:* Both the original DELETE and the equivalent assignment statement are expressed in a language called **Tutorial D** [3.3]. MINUS is the **Tutorial D** keyword for the relational *difference* operation—see Chapter 6.) As in all assignments, what is happening here, conceptually speaking, is that (a) the expression on the right-hand side is evaluated, and then (b) the result of that evaluation is assigned to the variable on the left-hand side (by definition, of course, that left-hand side must identify a *variable* specifically). As already stated, the net effect is thus to replace the "old" EMP value by a "new" one.

In analogous fashion, of course, relational INSERT and UPDATE operations are also basically shorthand for certain relational assignments.

Now, it is an unfortunate fact that much of the literature uses the term *relation* when what it really means is a relation *variable* (as well as when it means a relation *per se*—i.e., a relation *value*). Historically, however, this practice has certainly led to some confusion. Throughout this book, therefore, we will distinguish very carefully between relation variables and relations *per se;* following reference [3.3], in fact, we will use the term **relvar** as a convenient shorthand for *relation variable,* and we will take care to phrase our remarks in terms of relvars, not relations, when it really is relvars that we mean.

Note: We should warn you that the term *relvar* is not in common usage—but it should be! We really do feel it is important to be clear about the distinction between relations *per se* (i.e., relation values) and relation variables, even though earlier editions of this book failed to do so, and most of the current database literature still fails in this respect.

3.4 WHAT RELATIONS MEAN

In Chapter 1, we mentioned the fact that columns in relations have associated **data types.***
And at the end of Section 3.2, we said that the relational model includes "an open-ended set of [data] types." What this means (among other things) is that **users will be able to define their own types** (as well as being able to use system-defined or *builtin* types, of course). For example, we might define types as follows (**Tutorial D** syntax again; the ellipses "..." stand for portions of the definitions that are not germane to the present discussion):

```
TYPE EMP# ... ;
TYPE NAME ... ;
TYPE DEPT# ... ;
TYPE MONEY ... ;
```

Type EMP#, for example, can be regarded (among other things) as *the set of all possible employee numbers;* type NAME as *the set of all possible names;* and so on.

Now consider Fig. 3.4, which is basically the EMP portion of Fig. 3.1 expanded to show the column data types. As the figure indicates, every relation—to be more precise, every relation *value*—has two parts, a set of column-name:type-name pairs (the **heading**), together with a set of rows that conform to that heading (the **body**). *Note:* In practice we often ignore the type-name components of the heading, as indeed we have done in all of our examples prior to this point, but you should understand that, conceptually, they are always there.

Now, there is a very important (though perhaps unusual) way of thinking about relations, and that is as follows:

---

*The more usual relational term for data types is domains, as we will see in Chapter 5.

EMP						
EMP#	: EMP#	ENAME	: NAME	DEPT#	: DEPT#	SALARY : MONEY
E1		Lopez		D1		40K
E2		Cheng		D1		42K
E3		Finzi		D2		30K
E4		Saito		D2		35K

Fig. 3.4   Sample EMP relation value, with column types shown

- First, given a relation *r*, the heading of *r* denotes a certain **predicate** or truth-valued function;
- Second, as mentioned briefly in Chapter 1, each row in the body of *r* denotes a certain **true proposition,** obtained from the predicate by substituting certain *argument* values of the appropriate type for the *placeholders* or *parameters* of that predicate ("instantiating the predicate").

In the case of Fig. 3.4, for example, the predicate looks something like this:

Employee EMP# is named ENAME, works in department DEPT#, and earns salary SALARY

(the parameters are EMP#, ENAME, DEPT#, and SALARY, corresponding of course to the four EMP columns). And the corresponding true propositions are:

Employee E1 is named Lopez, works in department D1, and earns salary 40K

(obtained by substituting the EMP# value E1, the NAME value Lopez, the DEPT# value D1, and the MONEY value 40K for the appropriate parameters);

Employee E2 is named Cheng, works in department D1, and earns salary 42K

(obtained by substituting the EMP# value E2, the NAME value Cheng, the DEPT# value D1, and the MONEY value 42K for the appropriate parameters); and so on. In a nutshell, therefore:

- *Types* **are (sets of) things we can talk about;**
- *Relations* **are (sets of) things we say about the things we can talk about.**

(There is a nice analogy here that might help you appreciate and remember these important points: *Types are to relations as nouns are to sentences.*) Thus, in the example, the things we can talk about are employee numbers, names, department numbers, and money values, and the things we say are true utterances of the form "The employee with the specified employee number has the specified name, works in the specified department, and earns the specified salary."

It follows from all of the foregoing that:

- First, types and relations are both *necessary* (without types, we have nothing to talk about; without relations, we cannot say anything).
- Second, types and relations are *sufficient,* as well as necessary—i.e., we do not need anything else, logically speaking.

Note: It also follows that *types and relations are not the same thing.* It is an unfortunate fact that certain commercial products—not relational ones, by definition!—are confused over this very point. We will touch on this confusion in Chapter 25 (Section 25.2).

By the way, it is important to understand that *every* relation has an associated predicate, including relations that are derived from others by means of relational operators such as join. For example, the DEPT relation of Fig. 3.1 and the three result relations of Fig. 3.2 have predicates as follows:

- *DEPT:* "Department DEPT# is named DNAME and has budget BUDGET."
- *Restriction of DEPT where BUDGET > 8M:* "Department DEPT# is named DNAME and has budget BUDGET, which is greater than eight million dollars."
- *Projection of DEPT over DEPT# and BUDGET:* "Department DEPT# has some name and has budget BUDGET."
- *Join of DEPT and EMP over DEPT#:* "Department DEPT# is named DNAME and has budget BUDGET and employee EMP# is named ENAME, works in department DEPT#, and earns salary SALARY." Note that this predicate has six parameters, not seven—the two references to DEPT# denote the same parameter.

3.5   OPTIMIZATION

As explained in Section 3.2, relational operations such as restrict, project, and join are all *set-level* operations. As a consequence, relational languages are often said to be *nonprocedural,* on the grounds that users specify *what,* not *how*—i.e., they say what they want, without specifying a procedure for getting it. The process of "navigating" around the stored data in order to satisfy the user's request is performed automatically by the system, not manually by the user. For this reason, relational systems are sometimes said to perform **automatic navigation.** In nonrelational systems, by contrast, navigation is generally the responsibility of the user. A striking illustration of the benefits of automatic navigation is shown in Fig. 3.5, which contrasts a certain SQL INSERT statement with the "manual navigation" code the user might have to write to achieve an equivalent effect in a nonrelational system (actually a CODASYL network system; the example is taken from the chapter on network databases in reference [1.5]). *Note:* The database is the well-known suppliers and parts database. Refer to Section 3.9 for further explanation.

Despite the remarks of the previous paragraph, it has to be said that *nonprocedural* is not a very satisfactory term, common though it is, because procedurality and nonprocedurality are

```
INSERT INTO SP ( S#, P#, QTY )
       VALUES ( 'S4', 'P3', 1000 ) ;

MOVE 'S4' TO S# IN S
FIND CALC S
ACCEPT S-SP-ADDR FROM S-SP CURRENCY
FIND LAST SP WITHIN S-SP
while SP found PERFORM
   ACCEPT S-SP-ADDR FROM S-SP CURRENCY
   FIND OWNER WITHIN P-SP
   GET P
   IF P# IN P < 'P3'
      leave loop
   END-IF
   FIND PRIOR SP WITHIN S-SP
END-PERFORM
MOVE 'P3' TO P# IN P
FIND CALC P
ACCEPT P-SP-ADDR FROM P-SP CURRENCY
FIND LAST SP WITHIN P-SP
while SP found PERFORM
   ACCEPT P-SP-ADDR FROM P-SP CURRENCY
   FIND OWNER WITHIN S-SP
   GET S
   IF S# IN S < 'S4'
      leave loop
   END-IF
   FIND PRIOR SP WITHIN P-SP
END-PERFORM
MOVE 1000 TO QTY IN SP
FIND DB-KEY IS S-SP-ADDR
FIND DB-KEY IS P-SP-ADDR
STORE SP
CONNECT SP TO S-SP
CONNECT SP TO P-SP
```

Fig. 3.5 Automatic *vs.* manual navigation

not absolutes. The best that can be said is that some language *A* is either more or less procedural than some other language *B*. Perhaps a better way of putting matters would be to say that languages such as SQL are at *a higher level of abstraction* than languages such as C++ and COBOL (or data sublanguages such as are typically found in nonrelational DBMSs, come to that, as Fig. 3.5 shows). Fundamentally, it is this raising of the level of abstraction that is responsible for the increased productivity that relational systems can provide.

Deciding just how to perform the automatic navigation referred to above is the responsibility of a very important DBMS component called the **optimizer** (we mentioned this component briefly in Chapter 2). In other words, for each relational request from the user, it is the job of the optimizer to choose an efficient way to implement that request. By way of an example, let us suppose the user issues the following request (**Tutorial D** once again):

```
RESULT  :=  ( EMP WHERE EMP# = 'E4' ) { SALARY } ;
```

Explanation: The expression in parentheses ("EMP WHERE ...") denotes a restriction of the current value of relvar EMP to just the row where EMP# is E4. The column name in braces ("SALARY") then causes the result of that restriction to be projected over the SALARY column. Finally, the assignment operation (":=") causes the result of that projection to be assigned to relvar RESULT. After that assignment, RESULT contains a single-column, single-row relation that contains employee E4's salary. (Incidentally, note that we are implicitly making use of the relational *closure* property in this example—we have written a nested relational expression on the right-hand side, in which the input to the projection is the output from the restriction.)

Now, even in this very simple example, there are probably at least two ways of performing the necessary data access:

1. By doing a physical sequential scan of (the stored version of) relvar EMP until the required data is found;

2. If there is an index on (the stored version of) the EMP# column—which in practice there probably will be, because EMP# values are supposed to be unique, and many systems in fact *require* an index in order to enforce uniqueness—then by using that index and thus going directly to the required data.

The optimizer will choose which of these two strategies to adopt. More generally, given any particular request, the optimizer will make its choice of strategy for implementing that request on the basis of considerations such as the following:

- Which relvars are referenced in the request;
- How big those relvars currently are;
- What indexes exist;
- How selective those indexes are;
- How the data is physically clustered on the disk;
- What relational operations are involved;

and so on. To repeat, therefore: Users specify only what data they want, not how to get to that data; the access strategy for getting to the data is chosen by the optimizer ("automatic navigation"). Users and user programs are thus independent of such access strategies, which is of course essential if physical data independence is to be achieved.

We will have a lot more to say about the optimizer in Chapter 17.

3.6   THE CATALOG

As explained in Chapter 2, every DBMS must provide a **catalog** or **dictionary** function. The catalog is the place where—among other things—all of the various schemas (external, conceptual, internal) and all of the corresponding mappings (external/conceptual, conceptual/internal) are kept. In other words, the catalog contains detailed information (sometimes called **descriptor information** or **metadata**) regarding the various objects that are of interest to the system itself. Examples of such objects are relvars, indexes, users, integrity constraints, security constraints, and so on and so forth. Descriptor information is essential if the system is to do its job properly. For example, the optimizer uses catalog information about indexes and other physical storage structures, as well as much other information, to help it decide how to implement user requests. Likewise, the security subsystem uses catalog information about users and security constraints (see Chapter 16) to grant or deny such requests in the first place.

Now, one of the nice features of relational systems is that, in such a system, *the catalog itself consists of relvars* (more precisely, *system* relvars, so called to distinguish them from ordinary user ones). As a result, users can interrogate the catalog in exactly the same way they interrogate their own data. For example, the catalog will typically include two system relvars called TABLE and COLUMN, the purpose of which is to describe the tables (i.e., relvars) in the database and the columns in those tables. (We say "typically" because the catalog is not the same in every system; the differences arise because the catalog for a particular system necessarily contains a good deal of information that is specific to that system.) For the departments and employees database of Fig. 3.1, the TABLE and COLUMN relvars might look—in outline—as shown in Fig. 3.6.*

Note: As mentioned in Chapter 2, the catalog should normally be self-describing—i.e., it should include entries describing the catalog relvars themselves. No such entries are shown in Fig. 3.6, however. See Exercise 3.3 at the end of the chapter.

TABLE	TABNAME	COLCOUNT	ROWCOUNT	. . . . .
	DEPT	3	3	. . . . .
	EMP	4	4	. . . . .
	. . . .	. . . .	. . . .	. . . . .

COLUMN	TABNAME	COLNAME	. . . . .
	DEPT	DEPT#	. . . . .
	DEPT	DNAME	. . . . .
	DEPT	BUDGET	. . . . .
	EMP	EMP#	. . . . .
	EMP	ENAME	. . . . .
	EMP	DEPT#	. . . . .
	EMP	SALARY	. . . . .
	. . . .	. . . .	. . . . .

Fig. 3.6 Catalog for the departments and employees database (in outline)

---

*Note that the presence of a ROWCOUNT column in the figure suggests that INSERT and DELETE operations on the database will cause an update to the catalog as a side effect. In practice, ROWCOUNT might be updated only on request (e.g., when some utility is run), meaning the values might not always be current.

Now suppose some user of the departments and employees database wants to know exactly what columns relvar DEPT contains (obviously we are assuming that for some reason the user does not already have this information). Then the expression

```
( COLUMN WHERE TABNAME = 'DEPT' ) { COLNAME }
```

does the job. *Note:* If we had wanted to keep the result of this query in some more permanent fashion, we could have assigned the value of the expression to some other relvar, as in the example in the previous section. We will omit this final assignment step from most of our remaining examples (both here and in subsequent chapters).

Here is another example: "Which relvars include a column called EMP#?"

```
( COLUMN WHERE COLNAME = 'EMP#' ) { TABNAME }
```

Exercise: What does the following do?

```
( ( TABLE JOIN COLUMN )
        WHERE COLCOUNT < 5 ) { TABNAME, COLNAME }
```

3.7 BASE RELVARS AND VIEWS

We have seen that, starting with a set of relvars such as DEPT and EMP, together with a set of relation values for those relvars, relational expressions allow us to obtain further relation values from those given ones—e.g., by joining two of the given ones together. It is time to introduce a little more terminology. The original (given) relvars are called **base relvars,** and their relation values are called **base relations;** a relation that is or can be obtained from those base relations by means of some relational expression is called a **derived** or **derivable** relation. *Note:* Base relvars are called *real* relvars in reference [3.3].

Now, relational systems obviously have to provide a means for creating the base relvars in the first place. In SQL, for example, this task is performed by the CREATE TABLE statement ("TABLE" here meaning, very specifically, a base relvar). And base relvars obviously have to be *named*—for example:

```
CREATE TABLE EMP ... ;
```

However, relational systems usually support another kind of named relvar also, called a **view,** whose value at any given time is a *derived* relation (and so a view can be thought of, loosely, as a **derived relvar**). The value of a given view at a given time is whatever results from evaluating a certain relational expression at that time; the relational expression in question is specified at the time the view in question is created. For example, the statement

```
CREATE VIEW TOPEMP AS
      ( EMP WHERE SALARY > 33K ) { EMP#, ENAME, SALARY } ;
```

might be used to define a view called TOPEMP. *Note:* For reasons that are unimportant at this juncture, this example is expressed in a mixture of SQL and **Tutorial D.**

When this statement is executed, the relational expression following the AS—the **view-defining expression**—is not evaluated but is merely "remembered" by the system in some way (actually by saving it in the catalog, under the specified name TOPEMP). To the user, however, it is now as if there really were a relvar in the database called TOPEMP, with current value as indicated in the unshaded portions (only) of Fig. 3.7 below. And the user should be able to operate on that view just as if it were a base relvar. *Note:* If (as suggested above) DEPT and EMP are thought of as *real* relvars, then TOPEMP might be thought of as a *virtual* relvar—i.e., a relvar that apparently exists in its own right, but in fact does not (its value at any given time depends on the value(s) of certain other relvar(s)).

TOPEMP	EMP#	ENAME	DEPT#	SALARY
	E1	Lopez	D1	40K
	E2	Cheng	D1	42K
	E3	Finzi	D2	30K
	E4	Saito	D2	35K

Fig. 3.7   TOPEMP as a view of EMP (unshaded portions)

Note carefully, however, that although we say that the value of TOPEMP is the relation that would result if the view-defining expression were evaluated, we do not mean to suggest that we now have *a separate copy* of the data; i.e., we do not mean to suggest that the view-defining expression actually *is* evaluated. On the contrary, the view is effectively just a *window* into the underlying base relvar EMP. As a consequence, any changes to that underlying relvar will be automatically and instantaneously visible through that window (assuming they lie within the unshaded portion, of course). Likewise, changes to TOPEMP will automatically and instantaneously be applied to relvar EMP, and hence be visible through the window (see later for an example).

Here is a sample retrieval operation against view TOPEMP:

```
( TOPEMP WHERE SALARY < 42K ) { EMP#, SALARY }
```

Given the sample data of Fig. 3.7, the result will look like this:

EMP#	SALARY
E1	40K
E4	35K

Conceptually, operations against a view like the retrieval operation just shown are handled by replacing references to the view name by the view-defining expression (i.e., the expression that was saved in the catalog). In the example, therefore, the original expression

```
( TOPEMP WHERE SALARY < 42K ) { EMP#, SALARY }
```

is modified by the system to become

```
( ( EMP WHERE SALARY > 33K ) { EMP#, ENAME, SALARY } )
     WHERE SALARY < 42K ) { EMP#, SALARY }
```

(we have italicized the view name in the original expression and the replacement text in the modified version). The modified expression can then be simplified to just

```
( EMP WHERE SALARY > 33K AND SALARY < 42K ) { EMP#, SALARY }
```

(see Chapter 17), which when evaluated yields the result shown earlier. In other words, the original operation against the view is effectively converted into an equivalent operation against the underlying base relvar, and that equivalent operation is then executed in the normal way (more accurately, *optimized and* executed in the normal way).

By way of another example, consider the following DELETE operation:

```
DELETE TOPEMP WHERE SALARY < 42K ;
```

The DELETE that is actually executed looks something like this:

```
DELETE EMP WHERE SALARY > 33K AND SALARY < 42K ;
```

Now, the view TOPEMP is very simple, consisting as it does just of a row and column subset of a single underlying base relvar (loosely speaking). In principle, however, a view definition, since it is essentially just a named relational expression, can be *of arbitrary complexity* (it can even refer to other views). For example, here is a view whose definition involves a join of two underlying base relvars:

```
CREATE VIEW JOINEX AS
    ( ( EMP JOIN DEPT ) WHERE BUDGET > 7M ) { EMP#, DEPT# } ;
```

We will return to the whole question of view definition and view processing in Chapter 9.

Incidentally, we can now explain the remark in Chapter 2, near the end of Section 2.2, to the effect that the term "view" has a rather specific meaning in relational contexts that is not identical to the meaning ascribed to it in the ANSI/SPARC architecture. At the external level of that architecture, the database is perceived as an "external view," defined by an external schema (and different users can have different external views). In relational systems, by contrast, a view (as explained above) is, specifically, a *named, derived, virtual relvar.* Thus, the relational analog of an ANSI/SPARC "external view" is (typically) a collection of several relvars, each of which is a view in the relational sense, and the "external schema" consists of definitions of those views. (It follows that views in the relational sense are the relational model's way of providing **logical data independence,** though once again it has to be said that today's commercial products are seriously deficient in this regard. See Chapter 9.)

Now, the ANSI/SPARC architecture is quite general and allows for arbitrary variability between the external and conceptual levels. In principle, even the *types* of data structures supported at the two levels could be different—for example, the conceptual level could be relational, while a given user could have an external view that was hierarchic. In practice, however, most systems use the same type of structure as the basis for both levels, and relational products are no exception to this rule—views are still relvars, just like the base relvars are. And since the same type of object is supported at both levels, the same data sublanguage (usually SQL) applies at both levels. Indeed, the fact that a view is a relvar is precisely one of the strengths of relational systems; it is important in just the same way that the fact that a subset is a set is important in mathematics. *Note:* SQL products and the SQL standard (see Chapter 4) often seem to miss this point, however, inasmuch as they refer repeatedly to "tables and views" (with the implication that a view is not a table). You are strongly advised *not* to fall into this common trap of taking "tables" (or "relvars") to mean, specifically, *base* tables (or relvars) only.

There is one final point that needs to be made on the subject of base relvars *vs.* views, as follows. The base relvar *vs.* view distinction is frequently characterized thus:

- Base relvars "really exist," in the sense that they represent data that is actually stored in the database;
- Views, by contrast, do not "really exist" but merely provide different ways of looking at "the real data."

However, this characterization, though perhaps useful in an informal sense, does not accurately reflect the true state of affairs. It is true that users can *think* of base relvars as if they were physically stored; in a way, in fact, the whole point of relational systems is to allow users to think of base relvars as physically existing, while not having to concern themselves with how those relvars are actually represented in storage. But—and it is a big but!—this way of thinking should not be construed as meaning that a base relvar is physically stored in any kind of direct way (e.g., as a single stored file).* As explained in Section 3.2, base relvars are best thought of as an *abstraction* of some collection of stored data—an abstraction in which all storage-level details are concealed. In principle, there can be an arbitrary degree of differentiation between a base relvar and its stored counterpart.

A simple example might help to clarify this point. Consider the departments and employees database once again. Most of today's relational systems would probably implement that database with two stored files, one for each of the two base relvars. But there is ab-

---

*The following quote from a recent book displays several of the confusions being discussed here, as well as others discussed in Section 3.3 earlier: "[It] is important to make a distinction between stored relations, which are *tables,* and virtual relations, which are *views* . . . [We] shall use *relation* only where a table or a view could be used. When we want to emphasize that a relation is stored, rather than a view, we shall sometimes use the term *base relation* or *base table.*" The quote is, regrettably, not at all atypical.

solutely no logical reason why there should not be just one stored file of *hierarchic* stored records, each consisting of (a) the department number, name, and budget for some given department, together with (b) the employee number, name, and salary for each employee who happens to be in that department. In other words, the data can be physically stored in whatever way seems appropriate, but it always looks the same at the logical level.

3.8   TRANSACTIONS

Note: The topic of this section is not peculiar to relational systems. We cover it here nevertheless, because an understanding of the basic idea is needed in order to appreciate certain aspects of the material to come in Part II. However, our coverage at this point is deliberately not very deep.

In Chapter 1 we said that a transaction is a *logical unit of work,* typically involving several database operations. We also indicated that the user needs to be able to inform the system when distinct operations are part of the same transaction. The BEGIN TRANSACTION, COMMIT, and ROLLBACK operations are provided for this purpose. Basically, a transaction begins when a BEGIN TRANSACTION operation is executed, and terminates when a corresponding COMMIT or ROLLBACK operation is executed. For example (pseudocode):

```
BEGIN TRANSACTION ; /* move $$$ from account A to account B */
UPDATE account A ;                      /* withdrawal   */
UPDATE account B ;                      /* deposit      */
IF everything worked fine
   THEN COMMIT ;                        /* normal end   */
   ELSE ROLLBACK ;                      /* abnormal end */
END IF ;
```

Points arising:

1. Transactions are guaranteed to be **atomic**—i.e., they are guaranteed (from a logical point of view) either to execute in their entirety or not to execute at all, even if (say) the system fails halfway through the process.

2. Transactions are also guaranteed to be **durable,** in the sense that once a transaction successfully executes COMMIT, its updates are guaranteed to be applied to the database, even if the system subsequently fails at any point. *Note:* Fundamentally, it is this durability property of transactions that makes the data in the database *persistent,* in the sense of Chapter 1.

3. Transactions are also guaranteed to be **isolated** from one another, in the sense that database updates made by a given transaction *T1* are not made visible to any distinct transaction *T2* until and unless *T1* successfully executes COMMIT. COMMIT causes updates made by the transaction to become visible to other transactions; such updates are said to be *committed,* and are guaranteed never to be canceled. If the transaction executes ROLLBACK instead, all updates made by the transaction are canceled (*rolled back*). In this latter case, the effect is as if the transaction never ran in the first place.

4. The interleaved execution of a set of concurrent transactions is (usually) guaranteed to be **serializable,** in the sense that it produces the same result as executing those same transactions one at a time in some unspecified serial order.

Refer to Chapters 14–15 for an extended discussion of all of the foregoing points and much else besides.

3.9   THE SUPPLIERS AND PARTS DATABASE

Our running example throughout most of this book is the well-known **suppliers and parts** database (maintained, as we saw in Chapter 1, by a fictitious company called KnowWare Inc.). The purpose of this section is to explain that database, in order to serve as a point of reference for later chapters. Fig. 3.8 shows a set of sample data values; subsequent examples will actually assume these specific values, where it makes any difference. Fig. 3.9 shows the database definition, expressed in (a slight variation on) **Tutorial D** once again. Note the primary and foreign key specifications in particular. Note too that (a) several columns have data types of the same name as the column in question; (b) the STATUS column and the two CITY columns are defined in terms of builtin types—INTEGER (integers) and CHAR (character strings of arbitrary length)—instead of user-defined ones. Note finally that there is an important point to be made regarding the column values as shown in Fig. 3.8, but we are not yet in a position to make that point; we will come back to it in Chapter 5, Section 5.2, in the subsection entitled "Possible Representations."

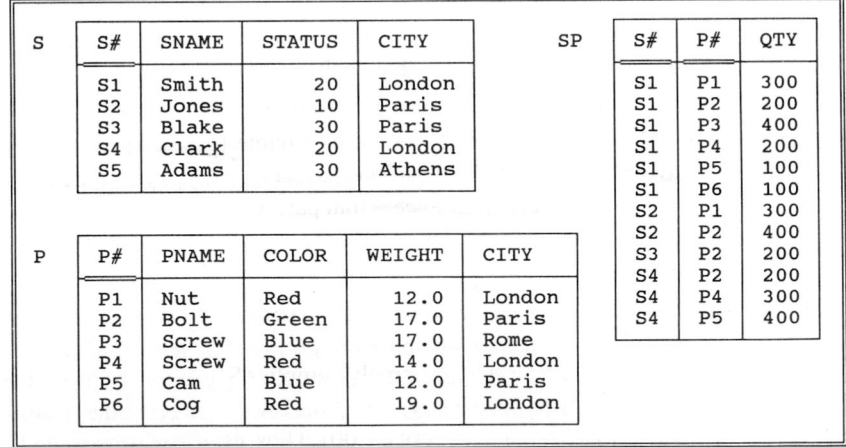

Fig. 3.8   The suppliers and parts database (sample values)

```
TYPE S# ... ;
TYPE NAME ... ;
TYPE P# ... ;
TYPE COLOR ... ;
TYPE WEIGHT ... ;
TYPE QTY ... ;

VAR S BASE RELATION
    { S#       S#,
      SNAME    NAME,
      STATUS   INTEGER,
      CITY     CHAR }
    PRIMARY KEY { S# } ;

VAR P BASE RELATION
    { P#       P#,
      PNAME    NAME,
      COLOR    COLOR,
      WEIGHT   WEIGHT,
      CITY     CHAR }
    PRIMARY KEY { P# } ;

VAR SP BASE RELATION
    { S#       S#,
      P#       P#,
      QTY      QTY }
    PRIMARY KEY { S#, P# }
    FOREIGN KEY { S# } REFERENCES S
    FOREIGN KEY { P# } REFERENCES P ;
```

Fig. 3.9   The suppliers and parts database (data definition)

The database is meant to be understood as follows:

- Relvar S represents *suppliers*. Each supplier has a supplier number (S#), unique to that supplier; a supplier name (SNAME), not necessarily unique (though the SNAME values do happen to be unique in Fig. 3.8); a rating or status value (STATUS); and a location (CITY). We assume that each supplier is located in exactly one city.

- Relvar P represents *parts* (more accurately, *kinds* of parts). Each kind of part has a part number (P#), which is unique; a part name (PNAME); a color (COLOR); a weight (WEIGHT); and a location where parts of that type are stored (CITY). We assume—where it makes any difference—that part weights are given in pounds. We also assume that each kind of part comes in exactly one color and is stored in a warehouse in exactly one city.

- Relvar SP represents *shipments*. It serves in a sense to link the other two relvars together, logically speaking. For example, the first row in SP as shown in Fig. 3.8 links a specific supplier from S (namely, supplier S1) to a specific part from P (namely, part P1)—in other words, it represents a shipment of parts of kind P1 by the supplier called S1 (and the shipment quantity is 300). Thus, each shipment has a supplier number (S#), a part number (P#), and a quantity (QTY). We assume there can be at most one shipment at any given time for a given supplier and a given part; for a given shipment, therefore, the combination of S# value and P# value is unique with respect to the set of shipments currently appearing in SP. *Note:* The sample values in Fig. 3.8 deliberately include one supplier, supplier S5, with no matching shipments at all.

We remark that (as already pointed out in Chapter 1, Section 1.3) suppliers and parts can be regarded as **entities,** and a shipment can be regarded as a **relationship** between a particular supplier and a particular part. As also pointed out in that section, however, a relationship is best regarded as just a special case of an entity. One advantage of relational databases is precisely that all entities, regardless of whether they are in fact relationships, are represented in the same uniform way—namely, by means of rows in relations, as the example indicates.

A couple of final remarks:

- First, the suppliers and parts database is of course extremely simple, much simpler than any real database is likely to be; most real databases will involve many more entities and relationships (and many more *kinds* of entities and relationships) than this one does. Nevertheless, it is at least adequate to illustrate most of the points that we need to make in the rest of the book, and (as already stated) we will use it as the basis for most—not all—of our examples in the next few chapters.

- Second, there is (of course) nothing wrong with using more descriptive names such as SUPPLIERS, PARTS, and SHIPMENTS in place of the rather terse names S, P, and SP used above; indeed, descriptive names are generally to be recommended in practice. But in the case of suppliers and parts specifically, the relvars are referenced so frequently in the chapters that follow that very short names seemed desirable. Long names tend to become irksome with much repetition.

3.10 SUMMARY

This brings us to the end of our short overview of relational technology. Obviously we have barely scratched the surface of what by now has become a very extensive subject, but the whole point of the chapter has been to serve as a gentle introduction to the much more comprehensive discussions to come. Even so, we have managed to cover quite a lot of ground. Here is a summary of the major topics we have discussed.

A **relational database** is a database that is perceived by its users as a collection of **relation variables**—i.e., *relvars*—or, more informally, **tables.** A **relational system** is a system that supports relational databases and operations on such databases, including in particular the operations **restrict, project,** and **join.** These operations, and others like them, are all **set-level.** The **closure** property of relational systems means that the output from every operation is the same kind of object as the input (they are all relations), which means we can write **nested relational expressions.** Relvars can be updated by means of the **relational assignment** operation; the familiar update operations **INSERT, UPDATE,** and **DELETE** can be regarded as shorthands for certain common relational assignments.

The formal theory underlying relational systems is called **the relational model of data.** The relational model is concerned with logical matters only, not physical matters. It addresses three principal aspects of data—data **structure,** data **integrity,** and data **manipulation.** The *structural* aspect has to do with relations *per se;* the *integrity* aspect has to do with (among other things) **primary and foreign keys;** and the *manipulative* aspect has to do with the operators (restrict, project, join, etc.). *The Information Principle* states that the entire information content of a relational database is represented in one and only one way, namely as explicit values in column positions in rows in relations.

Every relation has a **heading** and a **body;** the heading is a set of column-name:type-name pairs, the body is a set of rows that conform to the heading. The heading of a given relation can be regarded as a **predicate,** and each row in the body denotes a certain **true proposition,** obtained by substituting certain **argument** values of the appropriate type for the *placeholders* or **parameters** of the predicate. In other words, *types* are (sets of) things we can talk about, and *relations* are (sets of) things we say about the things we can talk about. Together, types and relations are **necessary** and **sufficient** to represent any data we like (at the logical level, that is).

The **optimizer** is the system component that determines how to implement user requests (which are concerned with *what,* not *how*). Since relational systems therefore assume responsibility for navigating around the stored database to locate the desired data, they are sometimes described as **automatic navigation** systems. Optimization and automatic navigation are prerequisites for **physical data independence.**

The **catalog** is a set of system relvars that contain **descriptors** for the various items that are of interest to the system (base relvars, views, indexes, users, etc.). Users can interrogate the catalog in exactly the same way they interrogate their own data.

The original relvars in a given database are called **base relvars,** and their values are called **base relations;** a relation that is obtained from those base relations by means of some relational expression is called a **derived** relation (collectively, base and derived relations are sometimes referred to as **expressible** relations). A **view** is a relvar whose value at any given time is such a derived relation (loosely, it can be thought of as a **derived relvar**); the value of such a relvar at any given time is whatever results from evaluating the associated **view-defining expression.** Note, therefore, that base relvars have *independent existence,* but views do not—they depend on the applicable base relvars. (Another way of saying the same thing is that base relvars are **autonomous,** but views are not.) Users can operate on views in exactly the same way as they operate on base relvars (at least in theory). The system implements operations on views by replacing references to the name of the view by the view-defining expression, thereby converting the operation into an equivalent operation on the underlying base relvar(s).

A **transaction** is a *logical unit of work,* typically involving several database operations. A transaction begins when **BEGIN TRANSACTION** is executed and terminates when **COMMIT** (normal termination) or **ROLLBACK** (abnormal termination) is executed. Transactions are **atomic, durable,** and **isolated** from one another. The interleaved execution of a set of concurrent transactions is (usually) guaranteed to be **serializable.**

Finally, the base example for most of the book is **the suppliers and parts database.** It is worth taking the time to familiarize yourself with that example now, if you have not already done so; that is, you should at least know which relvars have which columns and what the primary and foreign keys are (it is not so important to know exactly what the sample data values are!).

EXERCISES

3.1 Define the following terms:

automatic navigation	primary key
base relvar	projection
catalog	proposition
closure	relational database
commit	relational DBMS
derived relvar	relational model
foreign key	restriction
join	rollback
optimization	set-level operation
predicate	view

3.2 Sketch the contents of the catalog relvars TABLE and COLUMN for the suppliers and parts database.

3.3 As explained in Section 3.6, the catalog is self-describing—i.e., it includes entries for the catalog relvars themselves. Extend Fig. 3.6 to include the necessary entries for the TABLE and COLUMN relvars themselves.

3.4 Here is a query on the suppliers and parts database. What does it do?

```
RESULT  :=  ( ( S JOIN SP ) WHERE P# = 'P2' ) { S#, CITY } ;
```

Note: Actually there is a slight problem with this query, having to do with the data type of the P# column. We will come back to this point in Chapter 5, Section 5.2 (subsection "Type Conversions"). Analogous remarks apply to the next exercise also.

3.5 Suppose the expression on the right-hand side of the assignment in Exercise 3.4 is used in a view definition:

```
CREATE VIEW V AS
   ( ( S JOIN SP ) WHERE P# = 'P2' ) { S#, CITY } ;
```

Now consider the query

```
RESULT  :=  ( V WHERE CITY = 'London' ) { S# } ;
```

What does this query do? Show what is involved on the part of the DBMS in processing this query.

3.6 What do you understand by the terms (transaction) atomicity, durability, isolation, and serializability?

REFERENCES AND BIBLIOGRAPHY

3.1 E. F. Codd: "Relational Database: A Practical Foundation for Productivity," *CACM 25,* No. 2 (February 1982). Republished in Robert L. Ashenhurst (ed.), *ACM Turing Award Lectures: The First Twenty Years 1966–1985.* Reading, Mass.: Addison-Wesley (*ACM Press Anthology Series,* 1987).

This is the paper Codd presented on the occasion of his receiving the 1981 ACM Turing Award for his work on the relational model. It discusses the well-known *application backlog* problem. To paraphrase: "The demand for computer applications is growing fast—so fast that information systems departments (whose responsibility it is to provide those applications) are lagging further and further behind in their ability to meet that demand." There are two complementary ways of attacking this problem:

1. Provide IT professionals with new tools to increase their productivity;

2. Allow end users to interact directly with the database, thus bypassing the IT professional entirely.

Both approaches are needed, and in this paper Codd gives evidence to suggest that the necessary foundation for both is provided by relational technology.

3.2 C. J. Date: "Why Relational?", in *Relational Database Writings 1985–1989.* Reading, Mass.: Addison-Wesley (1990).

An attempt to provide a succinct yet reasonably comprehensive summary of the major advantages of relational systems. The following observation from the paper is worth repeating here: Among all the numerous advantages of "going relational," there is one in particular that cannot be overemphasized, and that is *the existence of a sound theoretical base.* To quote:

"... relational really is different. It is different because it is not *ad hoc.* Older systems, by contrast, were *ad hoc;* they may have provided solutions to certain important problems of their day, but they did not rest on any solid theoretical base. Relational systems, by contrast, do rest on such a base ... which means [they] are *rock solid.*

"Thanks to this solid foundation, relational systems behave in well-defined ways; and (possibly without realizing the fact) users have a simple model of that behavior in their mind, one that enables them to predict with confidence what the system will do in any given situation. There are (or should be) no surprises. This predictability means that user interfaces are easy to understand, document, teach, learn, use, and remember."

3.3 C. J. Date and Hugh Darwen: *Foundation for Object/Relational Databases: The Third Manifesto.* Reading, Mass.: Addison-Wesley (1998). See also the introductory overview paper "*The Third Manifesto:* Foundation for Object/Relational Databases," in C. J. Date, Hugh Darwen, and David McGoveran, *Relational Database Writings 1994–1997.* Reading, Mass.: Addison-Wesley (1998).

The Third Manifesto is a detailed, formal, and rigorous proposal for the future direction of databases and DBMSs. It can be seen as an abstract blueprint for the design of a DBMS and the language interface to such a DBMS. It is based on the classical core concepts **type, value, variable,** and **operator.** For example, we might have a type INTEGER; the integer "3" might be a value of that type; N might be a variable of that type, whose value at any given time is some integer value (i.e., some value of that type); and "+" might be an operator that applies to integer values (i.e., to values of that type).

ANSWERS TO SELECTED EXERCISES

3.3 Fig. 3.10 below shows the entries for the TABLE and COLUMN relvars (only—the entries for the user's own relvars are omitted). It is obviously not possible to give precise COLCOUNT and ROWCOUNT values.

3.4 The query retrieves supplier number and city for suppliers who supply part P2.

3.5 The meaning of the query is "Get supplier numbers for London suppliers who supply part P2." The first step in processing the query is to replace the name V by the expression that defines V, giving:

```
( ( ( ( S JOIN SP ) WHERE P# = 'P2' ) { S#, CITY } )
                          WHERE CITY = 'London' ) { S# }
```

This simplifies to:

```
( ( S WHERE CITY = 'London' ) JOIN
                    ( SP WHERE P# = 'P2' ) ) { S# }
```

For further discussion and explanation, see Chapters 9 and 17.

TABLE	TABNAME	COLCOUNT	ROWCOUNT	. . . . .
	TABLE	(>3)	(>2)	. . . . .
	COLUMN	(>2)	(>5)	. . . . .
	. . . .	. . . .	. . . .	. . . . .

COLUMN	TABNAME	COLNAME	. . . . .
	TABLE	TABNAME	. . . . .
	TABLE	COLCOUNT	. . . . .
	TABLE	ROWCOUNT	. . . . .
	COLUMN	TABNAME	. . . . .
	COLUMN	COLNAME	. . . . .
	. . . .	. . . .	. . . . .

Fig. 3.10   Catalog entries for TABLE and COLUMN themselves (in outline)

CHAPTER 4

An Introduction to SQL

4.1 INTRODUCTION

As noted in Chapter 1, SQL is the standard language for dealing with relational databases, and it is supported by just about every product on the market. SQL was originally developed in IBM Research in the early 1970s (see references [4.8–4.9] and [4.28]; it was first implemented on a large scale in an IBM prototype called System R (see references [4.1–4.3] and [4.11–4.13]), and subsequently reimplemented in numerous commercial products from IBM (see reference [4.20]) and many other vendors. In this chapter we present an introduction to the SQL language; additional aspects, having to do with such matters as integrity, security, etc., are described in subsequent chapters devoted to those topics. All of our discussions are based (except where otherwise indicated) on the current version of the standard known informally as **SQL/92,** also as *SQL–92* or just *SQL2* [4.22–4.23]; the official name is **International Standard Database Language SQL (1992).**

Note: We should immediately add that work is nearing completion on **SQL3,** the proposed follow-on to the current standard; ratification is expected in late 1999. By the time this book appears in print, therefore, the current standard might possibly be "SQL/99," not SQL/92. However, we felt it would be too confusing to base our discussions on SQL3, since—fairly obviously—no product yet supports it; we therefore decided to discuss SQL3 separately in an appendix (Appendix B). In any case, we should also point out that no product today supports even SQL/92 in its entirety;* instead, products typically support what might be called "a superset of a subset" of SQL/92 (i.e., most of them fail to support certain aspects of the standard and yet go beyond the standard in certain other respects). For example, IBM's DB2 product does not currently support all of the SQL/92 integrity features, but it does go beyond SQL/92 in its rules regarding the updating of views.

A few additional preliminary remarks:

- SQL was originally intended to be a "data sublanguage" specifically. With the incorporation of the *Persistent Stored Modules* feature (PSM) into the standard in late 1996, however, SQL became computationally complete (it now includes statements such as

---

*In fact no product possibly could support SQL/92 in its entirety, because SQL/92 as currently specified contains numerous gaps, mistakes, and inconsistencies. See reference [4.19] for a detailed discussion of this point.

CALL, RETURN, SET, CASE, IF, LOOP, LEAVE, WHILE, and REPEAT, as well as several related features such as variables and exception handlers). As a consequence, there is no longer any need to combine SQL with some distinct "host" language in order to develop a complete application. However, we choose not to discuss PSM in any detail in this book.

■ You will not be surprised to learn that SQL uses the term **table** in place of both of the terms *relation* and *relvar* (see Chapter 3). For consistency with the SQL standard and SQL products, therefore, we will do likewise in this chapter (and elsewhere in this book whenever we are concerned with SQL specifically). Also, SQL does not use the terms *heading* and *body* (of a table or relation).

■ SQL is an enormous language. The standard document [4.22] itself is well over 600 pages long (and the SQL3 specifications are over twice that size). As a consequence, it is not possible in a book of this nature to treat the subject exhaustively; all we can hope to do is describe major aspects in a reasonably comprehensive manner, but you are warned that our discussions are necessarily superficial. In particular, we have not hesitated to omit material that is irrelevant to the purpose at hand, nor to make simplifications in the interest of brevity. More complete (but still tutorial) descriptions can be found in references [4.4], [4.19], and [4.27].

■ Finally, it has to be said that (as indicated at various points in Chapters 1–3) SQL is very far from being the perfect relational language—it suffers from sins of both omission and commission. Nevertheless, it is the standard, it is supported by just about every product on the market, and every database professional needs to know something about it. Hence the coverage in this book.

4.2 OVERVIEW

SQL includes both data definition operations and data manipulation operations. We consider **definitional** operations first. Fig. 4.1 gives an SQL definition for the suppliers and parts database (compare and contrast Fig. 3.9 in Chapter 3). As you can see, the definition includes one **CREATE TABLE** statement for each of the three base tables (as noted in Chapter 3, the keyword TABLE in CREATE TABLE means a base table specifically). Each such CREATE TABLE statement specifies the name of the base table to be created, the names and data types of the columns of that table, and the primary key and any foreign keys in that table (possibly some additional information also, not illustrated in Fig. 4.1). A couple of syntactic points arising:

■ Note that we often make use of the "#" character in (e.g.) names of columns, but in fact that character is not legal in SQL/92.

■ We use the semicolon ";" as a statement terminator. Whether SQL/92 actually uses such terminators depends on the context. The specifics are beyond the scope of this book.

```
CREATE TABLE S
    ( S#        CHAR(5),
      SNAME     CHAR(20),
      STATUS    NUMERIC(5),
      CITY      CHAR(15),
    PRIMARY KEY ( S# ) ) ;

CREATE TABLE P
    ( P#        CHAR(6),
      PNAME     CHAR(20),
      COLOR     CHAR(6),
      WEIGHT    NUMERIC(5,1),
      CITY      CHAR(15),
    PRIMARY KEY ( P# ) ) ;

CREATE TABLE SP
    ( S#        CHAR(5),
      P#        CHAR(6),
      QTY       NUMERIC(9),
    PRIMARY KEY ( S#, P# ),
    FOREIGN KEY ( S# ) REFERENCES S,
    FOREIGN KEY ( P# ) REFERENCES P ;
```

Fig. 4.1   The suppliers and parts database (SQL definition)

One important difference between Fig. 4.1 and its counterpart (Fig. 3.9) in Chapter 3 is that Fig. 4.1 includes nothing corresponding to the type definitions (i.e., TYPE statements) of Fig. 3.9. The reason is, of course, that SQL does not permit users to define their own types;* thus, columns must be defined in terms of *builtin* (system-defined) types only. SQL supports the following more or less self-explanatory builtin types:

```
CHARACTER [ VARYING ] (n)     INTEGER        DATE
BIT [ VARYING ] (n)           SMALLINT       TIME
NUMERIC (p,q)                 FLOAT (p)      TIMESTAMP
DECIMAL (p,q)                                INTERVAL
```

A number of defaults, abbreviations, and alternative spellings—e.g., CHAR for CHAR-ACTER—are also supported; we omit the details here. Also, the square brackets "[" and "]" on CHARACTER and BIT are meant to signify that the material they enclose is optional (as is normal with BNF notation, of course). Observe finally that SQL requires certain *lengths* or *precisions* to be stated for certain types (e.g., CHAR), as our hypothetical syntax of Chapter 3 did not. In fact, SQL apparently regards those lengths and precisions as part of the type (implying that, e.g., CHAR(3) and CHAR(4) are different types); we believe it is better to regard them as *integrity constraints* (and so we do—see Chapter 8, especially Exercise 8.4).

Having defined the database, we can now start operating on it by means of the SQL **manipulative** operations SELECT, INSERT, UPDATE, and DELETE. In particular, we

---

*It does permit them to define what it calls *domains,* but those "domains" are not really domains—i.e., types—in the relational sense (see Chapter 5). *Note:* User-defined types are supported in SQL3, however (see Appendix B).

can perform relational restrict, project, and join operations on the data, in each case by using the SQL data manipulation statement **SELECT.** Fig. 4.2 shows how certain restrict, project, and join operations might be formulated in SQL. *Note:* The join example in that figure illustrates the point that **qualified names** (e.g., S.S#, SP.S#) are sometimes necessary in SQL to "disambiguate" column references. The broad rule is that qualified names are always acceptable, but unqualified names are also acceptable so long as they cause no ambiguity.

We remark that SQL also supports a shorthand form of the SELECT clause as illustrated by the following example:

```
SELECT *    -- or "SELECT S.*" (i.e., the "*" can be qualified)
FROM   S ;
```

The result is a copy of the entire S table; the star or asterisk is shorthand for a comma-separated list of all column names in the table(s) referenced in the FROM clause, in the left-to-right order in which those column(s) are defined within those table(s). Notice the **comment** in this example, incidentally (introduced with a double hyphen and terminated with a newline character). *Note:* The expression SELECT * FROM *T,* where *T* is a table name, can be further abbreviated to just TABLE *T.*

The SELECT statement is discussed at much greater length in Chapter 7 (Section 7.7).

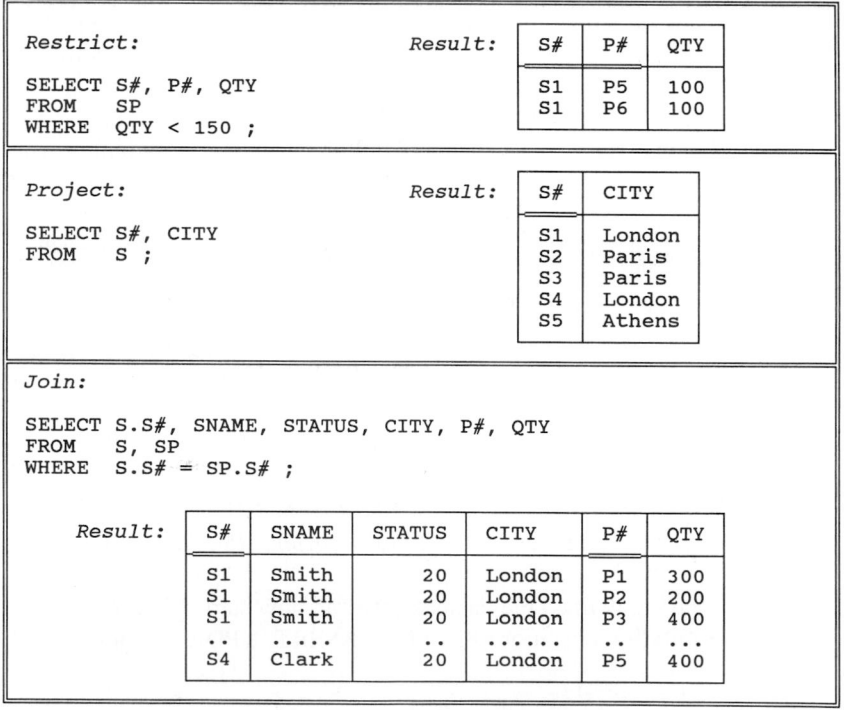

Fig. 4.2   Restrict, project, and join examples in SQL

Turning now to **update** operations: Examples of the SQL INSERT, UPDATE, and DELETE statements have already been given in Chapter 1, but those examples deliberately involved single-row operations only. Like SELECT, however, **INSERT, UPDATE,** and **DELETE** are all *set-level* operations, in general (and some of the exercises and answers in Chapter 1 did in fact illustrate this point). Here are some set-level update examples for the suppliers and parts database:

```
INSERT
INTO    TEMP ( P#, WEIGHT )
        SELECT P#, WEIGHT
        FROM    P
        WHERE   COLOR = 'Red' ;
```

This example assumes that we have already created another table TEMP with two columns, P# and WEIGHT. The INSERT statement inserts into that table part numbers and corresponding weights for all red parts.

```
UPDATE S
SET     STATUS = STATUS * 2
WHERE   CITY = 'Paris' ;
```

This UPDATE statement doubles the status for all suppliers in Paris.

```
DELETE
FROM    SP
WHERE   P# = '
```

This DELETE statement deletes all shipments for part P2.

Note: SQL does not include a direct analog of the **relational assignment** operation. However, we can simulate that operation by first deleting all rows from the target table and then performing an INSERT ... SELECT ... (as in the first example above) into that table.

4.3 THE CATALOG

The SQL standard does include specifications for a standard catalog called the **Information Schema.** In fact, the conventional terms "catalog" and "schema" are both used in SQL, but with highly SQL-specific meanings; loosely speaking, an SQL **catalog** consists of the descriptors for an individual database,* and an SQL **schema** consists of the descriptors for that portion of that database that belongs to some individual user. In other words, there can be any number of catalogs (one per database), each divided up into any number of schemas. However, each catalog is required to include exactly one schema called INFORMATION _SCHEMA, and from the user's perspective it is that schema (as already indicated) that performs the normal catalog function.

---

*In the interests of accuracy, we should mention that there is actually no such thing as a "database" in the SQL standard! Exactly what the collection of data is called that is described by a catalog is implementation-defined. However, it is not unreasonable to think of it as a database.

The Information Schema thus consists of a set of SQL tables whose contents effectively echo, in a precisely defined way, all of the definitions from all of the other schemas in the catalog in question. More precisely, the Information Schema is defined to contain a set of views of a hypothetical "Definition Schema." The implementation is not required to support the Definition Schema as such, but it is required (a) to support *some* kind of "Definition Schema," and (b) to support views of that "Definition Schema" that do look like those of the Information Schema. Points arising:

1. The rationale for stating the requirement in terms of two separate pieces (a) and (b) as just described is as follows. First, existing products certainly do support something akin to the "Definition Schema." However, those "Definition Schemas" vary widely from one product to another (even when the products in question come from the same vendor). Hence the idea of requiring only that the implementation support certain predefined views of its "Definition Schema" does make sense.

2. We should really say "an" (not "the") Information Schema, since as we have seen there is one such schema in every catalog. In general, therefore, the totality of data available to a given user will *not* be described by a single Information Schema. For simplicity, however, we will continue to talk as if there were just one.

It is not worth going into great detail on the content of the Information Schema here; instead, we simply list some of the more important Information Schema views, in the hope that their names alone will be sufficient to give some idea of what those views contain. We should say, however, that the TABLES view contains information for *all* named tables, views as well as base tables, while the VIEWS view contains information for views only.

```
SCHEMATA                   REFERENTIAL_CONSTRAINTS
DOMAINS                    CHECK_CONSTRAINTS
TABLES                     KEY_COLUMN_USAGE
VIEWS                      ASSERTIONS
COLUMNS                    VIEW_TABLE_USAGE
TABLE_PRIVILEGES           VIEW_COLUMN_USAGE
COLUMN_PRIVILEGES          CONSTRAINT_TABLE_USAGE
USAGE_PRIVILEGES           CONSTRAINT_COLUMN_USAGE
DOMAIN_CONSTRAINTS         CONSTRAINT_DOMAIN_USAGE
TABLE_CONSTRAINTS
```

Reference [4.19] gives more details; in particular, it shows how to formulate queries against the Information Schema (the process is not as straightforward as you might expect).

4.4   VIEWS

Here is an example of an SQL view definition:

```
CREATE VIEW GOOD_SUPPLIER
     AS SELECT S#, STATUS, CITY
        FROM   S
        WHERE  STATUS > 15 ;
```

And here is an example of an SQL query against this view:

```
SELECT  S#, STATUS
FROM    GOOD_SUPPLIER
WHERE   CITY = 'London' ;
```

Substituting the view definition for the reference to the view name, we obtain an expression that looks something like this (note the **nested subquery** in the FROM clause):

```
SELECT  GOOD_SUPPLIER.S#, GOOD_SUPPLIER.STATUS
FROM  ( SELECT S#, STATUS, CITY
        FROM    S
        WHERE   STATUS > 15 ) AS GOOD_SUPPLIER
WHERE   GOOD_SUPPLIER.CITY = 'London' ;
```

And this expression can then be simplified to something like this:

```
SELECT  S#, STATUS
FROM    S
WHERE   STATUS > 15
AND     CITY = 'London' ;
```

This latter is the query that is actually executed.

By way of another example, consider the following DELETE operation:

```
DELETE
FROM    GOOD_SUPPLIER
WHERE   CITY = 'London' ;
```

The DELETE that is actually executed looks something like this:

```
DELETE
FROM    S
WHERE   STATUS > 15
AND     CITY = 'London' ;
```

4.5 TRANSACTIONS

SQL's analogs of our COMMIT and ROLLBACK statements are called **COMMIT WORK** and **ROLLBACK WORK,** respectively (the keyword WORK is optional in both cases). However, SQL does not include any explicit BEGIN TRANSACTION statement. Instead, a transaction is begun implicitly whenever the program executes a **"transaction-initiating"** statement and does not already have a transaction in progress. Details of exactly which SQL statements are transaction-initiating would be out of place here; suffice it to say that all of the statements discussed in this chapter are transaction-initiating (except for COMMIT and ROLLBACK themselves, of course).

4.6 EMBEDDED SQL

Most SQL products allow SQL statements to be executed both **directly** (i.e., interactively from an online terminal) and as part of an application program (i.e., the SQL statements can be **embedded,** meaning they can be intermixed with the programming language statements of such a program). In the embedded case, moreover, the application program can typically be written in a variety of host languages—COBOL, Java, PL/I, etc.* In this section we consider the embedded case specifically.

The fundamental principle underlying embedded SQL, which we refer to as **the dual-mode principle,** is that *any SQL statement that can be used interactively can also be used in an application program.* Of course, there are various differences of detail between a given interactive SQL statement and its embedded counterpart, and retrieval operations in particular require significantly extended treatment in a host program environment (see later in this section), but the principle is nevertheless broadly true. (Its converse is not, by the way—several embedded SQL statements cannot be used interactively, as we will see.)

Before we can discuss the actual statements of embedded SQL, it is necessary to cover a number of preliminary details. Most of those details are illustrated by the program fragment shown in Fig. 4.3. (To fix our ideas we assume the host language is PL/I. Most of the ideas translate into other host languages with only minor changes.) Points arising:

1. Embedded SQL statements are prefixed by **EXEC SQL,** to distinguish them from statements of the host language, and are terminated by a special **terminator** symbol (a semicolon for PL/I).

2. An *executable* SQL statement (for the rest of this section we will mostly drop the "embedded" qualifier) can appear wherever an executable host statement can appear. Note that "executable," by the way: Unlike interactive SQL, embedded SQL includes some statements that are purely declarative, not executable. For example, DECLARE CURSOR is not an executable statement (see the subsection "Operations Involving

```
EXEC SQL BEGIN DECLARE SECTION ;

    DCL SQLSTATE CHAR(5) ;
    DCL P#        CHAR(6) ;
    DCL WEIGHT    FIXED DECIMAL(5,1);

EXEC SQL END DECLARE SECTION ;

P# = 'P2' ;                      /* for example              */
EXEC SQL SELECT P.WEIGHT
         INTO   :WEIGHT
         FROM   P
         WHERE  P.P# = :P# ;
IF SQLSTATE = '00000'
THEN ... ;                       /* WEIGHT = retrieved value */
ELSE ... ;                       /* some exception occurred  */
```

Fig. 4.3   Fragment of a PL/I program with embedded SQL

---

*The SQL standard [4.22] currently supports Ada, C, COBOL, Fortran, M (previously called MUMPS), Pascal, and PL/I. Java support is not included at the time of writing, but it is due to be added soon (see reference [4.6], also Appendix B), and some products already support it.

Cursors" later), nor are BEGIN and END DECLARE SECTION (see paragraph 5 below), and nor is WHENEVER (see paragraph 9 below).

3. SQL statements can include references to **host variables;** such references must include a **colon prefix** to distinguish them from SQL column names. Host variables can appear in embedded SQL wherever a literal can appear in interactive SQL. They can also appear in an INTO clause on SELECT (see paragraph 4 below) or FETCH (again, see the subsection "Operations Involving Cursors" later) to designate targets for retrieval operations.

4. Notice the **INTO** clause on the SELECT statement in Fig. 4.3. The purpose of that clause is (as just indicated) to specify the target variables into which values are to be retrieved; the ith target variable mentioned in the INTO clause corresponds to the ith value to be retrieved, as specified by the SELECT clause.

5. All host variables referenced in SQL statements must be declared (DCL in PL/I) within an **embedded SQL declare section,** which is delimited by the **BEGIN** and **END DECLARE SECTION** statements.

6. Every program containing embedded SQL statements must include a host variable called **SQLSTATE.** After any SQL statement has been executed, a status code is returned to the program in that variable; in particular, a status code of 00000 means the statement executed successfully, and a value of 02000 means the statement did execute but no data was found to satisfy the request. In principle, therefore, every SQL statement in the program should be followed by a test on SQLSTATE, and appropriate action taken if the value is not what was expected. In practice, however, such testing can often be implicit (see paragraph 9 below).

7. Host variables must have a **data type** appropriate to the uses to which they are put. In particular, a host variable that is to be used as a target (e.g., on SELECT) must have a data type that is compatible with that of the expression that provides the value to be assigned to that target; likewise, a host variable that is to be used as a source (e.g., on INSERT) must have a data type that is compatible with that of the SQL column to which values of that source are to be assigned. Similar remarks apply to a host variable that is to be used in a comparison, or indeed in any kind of operation. For details of exactly what it means for data types to be compatible in the foregoing sense, see reference [4.22].

8. Host variables and SQL columns can have the same name.

9. As already mentioned, every SQL statement should in principle be followed by a test of the returned SQLSTATE value. The **WHENEVER** statement is provided to simplify this process. The WHENEVER statement takes the form

```
EXEC SQL WHENEVER <condition> <action> ;
```

Here *<condition>* is either SQLERROR or NOT FOUND, and *<action>* is either CONTINUE or a GO TO statement. WHENEVER is not an executable statement; rather, it is a directive to the SQL compiler. "WHENEVER *<condition>* GO TO *<label>*" causes the compiler to insert a statement of the form "IF *<condition>* GO TO *<label>* END IF" after each executable SQL statement it encounters; "WHENEVER

<condition> CONTINUE" causes it not to insert any such statements, the implication being that the programmer will insert such statements by hand. The two *<condition>*s are defined as follows:

NOT FOUND	*means*	no data was found
		— SQLSTATE = 02000 (usually)
SQLERROR	*means*	an error occurred
		— see reference [4.22] for SQLSTATE

Each WHENEVER statement the SQL compiler encounters on its sequential scan through the program text (for a particular condition) overrides the previous one it found (for that condition).

10. Note finally that—to use the terminology of Chapter 2—embedded SQL constitutes a *loose coupling* between SQL and the host language.

So much for the preliminaries. In the rest of this section we concentrate on data manipulation operations specifically. As already indicated, most of those operations can be handled in a fairly straightforward fashion (i.e., with only minor changes to their syntax). Retrieval operations require special treatment, however. The problem is that such operations retrieve many rows (in general), not just one, and host languages are generally not equipped to handle the retrieval of more than one row at a time. It is therefore necessary to provide some kind of bridge between the set-level retrieval capabilities of SQL and the row-level retrieval capabilities of the host, and **cursors** provide such a bridge. A cursor is a special kind of SQL object that applies to embedded SQL only (because interactive SQL has no need of it). It consists essentially of a kind of *(logical) pointer* that can be used to run through a collection of rows, pointing to each of the rows in turn and thereby providing addressability to those rows one at a time. However, we defer detailed discussion of cursors to a later subsection, and consider first those statements that have no need of them.

Operations Not Involving Cursors

The data manipulation statements that do not need cursors are as follows:

- Singleton SELECT
- INSERT
- UPDATE (except the CURRENT form—see later)
- DELETE (again, except the CURRENT form—see later)

We give examples of each of these statements in turn.

Singleton SELECT: Get status and city for the supplier whose supplier number is given by the host variable GIVENS#.

```
EXEC SQL SELECT STATUS, CITY
         INTO   :RANK, :CITY
         FROM   S
         WHERE  S# = :GIVENS# ;
```

We use the term *singleton SELECT* to mean a SELECT expression that evaluates to a table containing at most one row. In the example, if there is exactly one row in table S satisfying the condition in the WHERE clause, then the STATUS and CITY values from that row will be assigned to the host variables RANK and CITY as requested, and SQLSTATE will be set to 00000; if no S row satisfies the WHERE condition, SQLSTATE will be set to 02000; and if more than one does, the program is in error, and SQLSTATE will be set to an error code.

INSERT: Insert a new part (part number, name, and weight given by host variables P#, PNAME, PWT, respectively; color and city unknown) into table P.

```
EXEC SQL INSERT
         INTO    P ( P#, PNAME, WEIGHT )
         VALUES ( :P#, :PNAME, :PWT ) ;
```

The COLOR and CITY values for the new part will be set to the applicable **default values.** See Chapter 5, Section 5.5, for a discussion of SQL default values.

UPDATE: Increase the status of all London suppliers by the amount given by the host variable RAISE.

```
EXEC SQL UPDATE S
         SET     STATUS = STATUS + :RAISE
         WHERE   CITY = 'London' ;
```

If no supplier rows satisfy the WHERE condition, SQLSTATE will be set to 02000.

DELETE: Delete all shipments for suppliers whose city is given by the host variable CITY.

```
EXEC SQL DELETE
         FROM    SP
         WHERE   :CITY =
               ( SELECT CITY
                 FROM    S
                 WHERE   S.S# = SP.S# ) ;
```

Again SQLSTATE will be set to 02000 if no SP rows satisfy the WHERE condition. Again, note the **nested subquery** (in the WHERE clause this time).

Operations Involving Cursors

Now we turn to the question of set-level retrieval—i.e., retrieval of a set containing an arbitrary number of rows, instead of at most one row as in the singleton SELECT case. As explained earlier, what is needed here is a mechanism for accessing the rows in the set one by one, and **cursors** provide such a mechanism. The process is illustrated in outline by the example of Fig. 4.4 (overleaf), which is intended to retrieve supplier details (S#, SNAME, and STATUS) for all suppliers in the city given by the host variable Y.

Explanation: The statement "DECLARE X CURSOR ..." defines a cursor called X, with an associated *table expression* (i.e., an expression that evaluates to a table), specified by the SELECT that forms part of that DECLARE. That table expression is not evaluated at this point; DECLARE CURSOR is a purely declarative statement. The expression is eval-

```
EXEC SQL  DECLARE X CURSOR FOR        /* define the cursor   */
          SELECT S.S#, S.SNAME, S.STATUS
          FROM   S
          WHERE  S.CITY = :Y
          ORDER  BY S# ASC ;

EXEC SQL  OPEN X ;                     /* execute the query   */
          DO for all S rows accessible via X ;
             EXEC SQL FETCH X INTO :S#, :SNAME, :STATUS ;
                                       /* fetch next supplier */
             .........
          END ;
EXEC SQL  CLOSE X ;                    /* deactivate cursor X */
```

Fig. 4.4 Multi-row retrieval example

uated when the cursor is opened ("OPEN X"). The statement "FETCH X INTO ..." is then used to retrieve rows one at a time from the resulting set, assigning retrieved values to host variables in accordance with the specifications of the INTO clause in that statement. (For simplicity we have given the host variables the same names as the corresponding database columns. Notice that the SELECT in the cursor declaration does not have an INTO clause of its own.) Since there will be many rows in the result set, the FETCH will normally appear within a loop; the loop will be repeated so long as there are more rows still to come in that result set. On exit from the loop, cursor X is closed ("CLOSE X").

Now we consider cursors and cursor operations in more detail. First of all, a cursor is declared by means of a **DECLARE CURSOR** statement, which takes the general form

```
EXEC SQL DECLARE <cursor name> CURSOR
         FOR <table expression> [ <ordering> ] ;
```

(we are ignoring a few optional specifications in the interests of brevity). For a complete explanation of *<table expression>,* see Appendix A. The optional *<ordering>* takes the form

```
ORDER BY <order item commalist>
```

where (a) the commalist of *<order item>*s must not be empty—see the paragraph immediately following—and (b) each individual *<order item>* consists of a column name (*un*-qualified, please note), optionally followed by ASC (ascending) or DESC (descending), and ASC is the default.

Note: We define the term *commalist* as follows. Let *<xyz>* denote an arbitrary syntactic category (i.e., anything that appears on the left-hand side of some BNF production rule). Then the expression *<xyz commalist>* denotes a sequence of zero or more *<xyz>*s in which each pair of adjacent *<xyz>*s is separated by a comma (and possibly one or more blanks). Please note that we will make extensive use of the commalist shorthand in future syntax rules (all syntax rules, that is, not just SQL ones).

As previously stated, the DECLARE CURSOR statement is declarative, not executable; it declares a cursor with the specified name and having the specified table expression and ordering permanently associated with it. The table expression can include host variable references. A program can include any number of DECLARE CURSOR statements, each of which must (of course) be for a different cursor.

Three executable statements are provided to operate on cursors: **OPEN, FETCH,** and **CLOSE.**

- The statement

```
EXEC SQL OPEN <cursor name> ;
```

opens or *activates* the specified cursor (which must not currently be open). In effect, the table expression associated with the cursor is evaluated (using the current values for any host variables referenced within that expression); a set of rows is thus identified and becomes the current **active set** for the cursor. The cursor also identifies a *position* within that active set, namely the position just before the first row. (Active sets are always considered to have an ordering, so the concept of position has meaning.* The ordering is either that defined by the ORDER BY clause, or a system-determined ordering in the absence of such a clause.)

- The statement

```
EXEC SQL FETCH <cursor name>
         INTO <host variable reference commalist> ;
```

advances the specified cursor (which must be open) to the next row in the active set and then assigns the *i*th value from that row to the *i*th host variable referenced in the INTO clause. If there is no next row when FETCH is executed, SQLSTATE is set to 02000 and no data is retrieved.

- The statement

```
EXEC SQL CLOSE <cursor name> ;
```

closes or *deactivates* the specified cursor (which must currently be open). The cursor now has no current active set. However, it can subsequently be opened again, in which case it will acquire another active set—probably not exactly the same set as before, especially if the values of any host variables referenced in the cursor declaration have changed in the meantime. Note that changing the values of those host variables while the cursor is open has no effect on the current active set.

Two further statements can include references to cursors, namely the **CURRENT** forms of **UPDATE** and **DELETE.** If a cursor, X say, is currently positioned on a particu-

---

*Sets *per se* do not have an ordering, of course (see Chapter 5), so an "active set" is not really a set, as such, at all. It would be better to think of it as an *ordered list* or *array* (of rows).

lar row, then it is possible to UPDATE or DELETE "the current of X," i.e., the row on which X is positioned. For example:

```
EXEC SQL UPDATE S
         SET     STATUS = STATUS + :RAISE
         WHERE   CURRENT OF X ;
```

Note: The CURRENT forms of UPDATE and DELETE are not permitted if the table expression in the cursor declaration would define a nonupdatable view if it were part of a CREATE VIEW statement (see Chapter 9, Section 9.6).

Dynamic SQL

Dynamic SQL consists of a set of embedded SQL facilities that are intended to support the construction of generalized, online, and possibly interactive applications. (Recall from Chapter 1 that an online application is an application that supports access to the database from an online terminal.) Consider what a typical online application has to do. In outline, the steps it must go through are as follows.

1. Accept a command from the terminal.
2. Analyze that command.
3. Execute appropriate SQL statements on the database.
4. Return a message and/or results to the terminal.

If the set of commands the program can accept in Step 1 is fairly small, as in the case of (perhaps) a program handling airline reservations, then the set of possible SQL statements to be executed will probably also be small and can be "hardwired" into the program. In this case, Steps 2 and 3 above will consist simply of logic to examine the input command and then branch to the part of the program that issues the predefined SQL statement(s). On the other hand, if there can be great variability in the input, then it might not be practicable to predefine and "hardwire" SQL statements for every possible command. Instead, it is probably much more convenient to construct the necessary SQL statements dynamically, and then to compile and execute those constructed statements dynamically. The facilities of dynamic SQL are provided to assist in this process.

The two principal dynamic statements are PREPARE and EXECUTE. Their use is illustrated in the following (unrealistically simple but accurate) example.

```
DCL SQLSOURCE CHAR VARYING (65000) ;

SQLSOURCE = 'DELETE FROM SP WHERE QTY < 300' ;
EXEC SQL PREPARE SQLPREPPED FROM :SQLSOURCE ;
EXEC SQL EXECUTE SQLPREPPED ;
```

Explanation:

1. The name SQLSOURCE identifies a PL/I varying-length character string variable in which the program will somehow construct the source form (i.e., character string representation) of some SQL statement—a DELETE statement, in our particular example.

2. The name SQLPREPPED, by contrast, identifies an *SQL* variable, not a PL/I variable, that will be used (conceptually) to hold the compiled form of the SQL statement whose source form is given in SQLSOURCE. (The names SQLSOURCE and SQLPREPPED are arbitrary, of course.)

3. The PL/I assignment statement "SQLSOURCE = ... ;" assigns to SQLSOURCE the source form of an SQL DELETE statement. In practice, of course, the process of constructing such a source statement is likely to be much more complex—perhaps involving the input and analysis of some request from the end user, expressed in natural language or some other form more user-friendly than SQL.

4. The PREPARE statement then takes that source statement and "prepares" (i.e., compiles) it to produce an executable version, which it stores in SQLPREPPED.

5. Finally, the EXECUTE statement executes that SQLPREPPED version and thus causes the actual DELETE to occur. SQLSTATE information from the DELETE is returned exactly as if the DELETE had been executed directly in the normal way.

Note that since it denotes an SQL variable, not a PL/I variable, the name SQLPREPPED does not have a colon prefix when it is referenced in the PREPARE and EXECUTE statements. Note too that such SQL variables do not have to be explicitly declared.

Incidentally, the process just described is exactly what happens when SQL statements themselves are entered interactively. Most systems provide some kind of interactive SQL query processor. That query processor is in fact just a particular kind of generalized online application; it is ready to accept an extremely wide variety of input, *viz.* any valid (or invalid!) SQL statement. It uses the facilities of dynamic SQL to construct suitable SQL statements corresponding to its input, to compile and execute those constructed statements, and to return messages and results back to the terminal.

We conclude this subsection (and this section) with a brief mention of a more recent (1995) addition to the standard known as the **SQL Call-Level Interface** ("SQL/CLI," *CLI* for short). CLI is heavily based on Microsoft's *Open Database Connectivity* interface, ODBC. CLI permits an application written in one of the usual host languages to issue database requests by invoking certain vendor-provided *CLI routines*. Those routines, which must have been linked to the application in question, then use dynamic SQL to perform the requested database operations on the application's behalf. (From the DBMS's point of view, in other words, the CLI routines can be thought of as just another application.)

As you can see, SQL/CLI (and ODBC too, come to that) both address the same general problem as dynamic SQL does: They both allow applications to be written for which the exact SQL statements to be executed are not known until run time. However, they actually represent a better approach to the problem than dynamic SQL does. There are two principal reasons for this state of affairs:

- First, dynamic SQL is a *source code* standard. Any application using dynamic SQL thus requires the services of some kind of SQL compiler in order to process the operations—PREPARE, EXECUTE, etc.—prescribed by that standard. CLI, by contrast, merely standardizes the details of certain *routine invocations* (i.e., subroutine calls, basically); no special compiler services are needed, only the regular services of the standard host language compiler. As a result, applications can be distributed (perhaps by third-party software vendors) in "shrink-wrapped" *object code* form.

- Second, those applications can be *DBMS-independent;* that is, CLI includes features that permit the creation (again, perhaps by third-party software vendors) of generic applications that can be used with several different DBMSs, instead of having to be specific to some particular DBMS.

Interfaces such as CLI, ODBC, and JDBC (a Java variant of ODBC) are becoming increasingly important in practice, for reasons to be discussed (in part) in Chapter 20.

4.7   SQL IS NOT PERFECT

As stated in the introduction to this chapter, SQL is very far from being the "perfect" relational language—it suffers from numerous sins of both omission and commission. Specific criticisms will be offered at appropriate points in subsequent chapters, but the overriding issue is simply that SQL fails in all too many ways to support the relational model properly. As a consequence, it is not at all clear that today's SQL products really deserve the label "relational" at all! Indeed, so far as this writer is aware, *there is no product on the market today that supports every detail of the relational model.* This is not to say that some parts of the model are unimportant; on the contrary, *every detail* of the model is important, and important, moreover, for genuinely practical reasons. Indeed, the point cannot be stressed too strongly that the purpose of relational theory is not just "theory for its own sake"; rather, the purpose is to provide a base on which to build systems that are *100 percent practical.* But the sad fact is that the vendors have not yet really stepped up to the challenge of implementing the theory in its entirety. As a consequence, the "relational" products of today all fail, in one way or another, to deliver on the full promise of relational technology.

4.8   SUMMARY

This concludes our introduction to some of the major features of the SQL standard ("SQL/92"). We emphasized the fact that SQL is very important from a commercial perspective, though it is unfortunately somewhat deficient from a pure relational point of view.

SQL includes both a **data definition** language (DDL) component and a **data manipulation** language (DML) component. The SQL DML can operate at both the external level (on views) and the conceptual level (on base tables). Likewise, the SQL DDL can be used to define objects at the external level (views), the conceptual level (base tables), and even—in most commercial systems, though not in the standard *per se*—the internal level as well (i.e., indexes and other physical storage structures). Moreover, SQL also provides certain *data control* facilities—i.e., facilities that cannot really be classified as belonging to either the DDL or the DML. An example of such a facility is the GRANT statement, which allows users to grant *access privileges* to each other (see Chapter 16).

We showed how SQL can be used to create base tables, using the **CREATE TABLE** statement. We then gave some examples of the **SELECT, INSERT, UPDATE,** and **DELETE** statements, showing in particular how SELECT can be used to express the relational restrict, project, and join operations. We also briefly described the **Information Schema,** which consists of a set of prescribed views of a hypothetical "Definition Schema," and we took a look at the SQL facilities for dealing with **views** and **transactions.**

A large part of the chapter was concerned with **embedded SQL.** The basic idea behind embedded SQL is **the dual-mode principle,** i.e., the principle that (insofar as possible) *any SQL statement that can be used interactively can also be used in an application program.* The major exception to this principle arises in connection with **multi-row retrieval operations,** which require the use of a **cursor** to bridge the gap between the set-level retrieval capabilities of SQL and the row-level retrieval capabilities of host languages such as PL/I.

Following a number of necessary (though mostly syntactic) preliminaries—including in particular a brief explanation of **SQLSTATE**—we considered those operations, namely **singleton SELECT, INSERT, UPDATE,** and **DELETE,** that have no need for cursors. Then we turned to the operations that *do* need cursors, and discussed **DECLARE CURSOR, OPEN, FETCH, CLOSE,** and the **CURRENT** forms of **UPDATE** and **DELETE.** (The standard refers to the CURRENT forms of these operators as *positioned* UPDATE and DELETE, and uses the term *searched* UPDATE and DELETE for the non-CURRENT or "out of the blue" forms.) Finally, we gave a very brief introduction to the concept of **dynamic SQL,** describing the **PREPARE** and **EXECUTE** statements in particular, and we also mentioned the **SQL Call-Level Interface,** CLI.

EXERCISES

4.1 Fig. 4.5 (overleaf) shows some sample data values for an extended form of the suppliers and parts database called the suppliers-parts-projects database. Suppliers (S), parts (P), and projects (J) are uniquely identified by supplier number (S#), part number (P#), and project number (J#), respectively. The significance of an SPJ (shipment) row is that the specified supplier supplies the specified part to the specified project in the specified quantity (and the combination S#-P#-J# uniquely identifies such a row). Write an appropriate set of SQL definitions for this database. *Note:* This database will be used as the basis for numerous exercises in subsequent chapters.

4.2 In Section 4.2 we described the CREATE TABLE statement as defined by the SQL standard *per se.* Many commercial SQL products support additional options on that statement, however, typically having to do with indexes, disk space allocation, and other implementation matters (thereby undermining the objectives of physical data independence and intersystem compatibility). Investigate any SQL product that might be available to you. Do the foregoing criticisms apply to that product? Specifically, what additional CREATE TABLE options does that product support?

4.3 Once again, investigate any SQL product that might be available to you. Does that product support the Information Schema? If not, what *does* its catalog support look like?

4.4 Give SQL formulations for the following updates to the suppliers-parts-projects database:

a. Insert a new supplier S10 into table S. The name and city are Smith and New York, respectively; the status is not yet known.

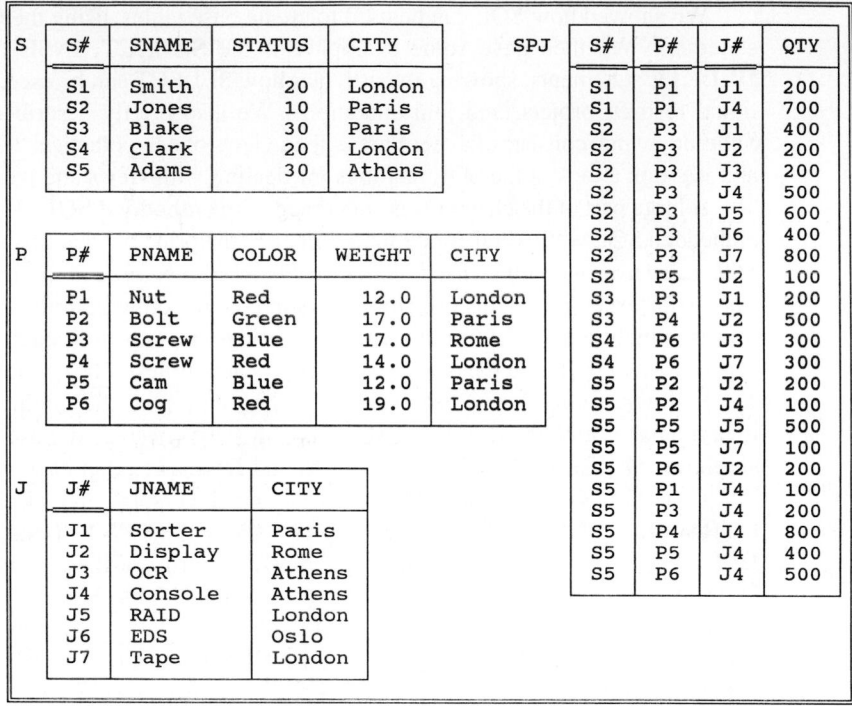

Fig. 4.5   The suppliers-parts-projects database (sample values)

b. Change the color of all red parts to orange.

c. Delete all projects for which there are no shipments.

4.5   Again using the suppliers-parts-projects database, write a program with embedded SQL statements to list all supplier rows, in supplier number order. Each supplier row should be immediately followed in the listing by all project rows for projects supplied by that supplier, in project number order.

4.6   Let tables PART and PART_STRUCTURE be defined as follows:

```
CREATE TABLE PART
    ( P# ... , DESCRIPTION ... ,
    PRIMARY KEY ( P# ) ) ;

CREATE TABLE PART_STRUCTURE
    ( MAJOR_P# ... , MINOR_P# ... , QTY ... ,
    PRIMARY KEY ( MAJOR_P#, MINOR_P# ),
    FOREIGN KEY ( MAJOR_P# ) REFERENCES PART,
    FOREIGN KEY ( MINOR_P# ) REFERENCES PART ) ;
```

Table PART_STRUCTURE shows which parts (MAJOR_P#) contain which other parts (MINOR_P#) as first-level components. Write an SQL program to list all component parts of a given

PART_STRUCTURE	MAJOR_P#	MINOR_P#	QTY
	P1	P2	2
	P1	P3	4
	P2	P3	1
	P2	P4	3
	P3	P5	9
	P4	P5	8
	P5	P6	3

Fig. 4.6   Table PART_STRUCTURE (sample value)

part, to all levels (the **part explosion** problem). *Note:* The sample data shown in Fig. 4.6 might help you visualize this problem. We remark that table PART_STRUCTURE shows how *bill-of-materials* data—see Chapter 1, Section 1.3, subsection "Entities and Relationships"—is typically represented in a relational system.

REFERENCES AND BIBLIOGRAPHY

4.1 M. M. Astrahan and R. A. Lorie: "SEQUEL-XRM: A Relational System," Proc. ACM Pacific Regional Conf., San Francisco, Calif. (April 1975).

Describes the first prototype implementation of SEQUEL, the earliest version of SQL [4.8]. See also references [4.2–4.3], which perform an analogous function for System R.

4.2 M. M. Astrahan *et al.*: "System R: Relational Approach to Database Management," *ACM TODS 1,* No. 2 (June 1976).

System R was the major prototype implementation of the SEQUEL/2 (later SQL) language [4.8]. This paper describes the architecture of System R as originally planned. See also reference [4.3].

4.3 M. W. Blasgen *et al.*: "System R: An Architectural Overview," *IBM Sys. J. 20,* No. 1 (February 1981).

Describes the architecture of System R as it became by the time the system was fully implemented (compare and contrast reference [4.2]).

4.4 Stephen Cannan and Gerard Otten: *SQL—The Standard Handbook.* Maidenhead, UK: McGraw-Hill International (1993).

"[Our] objective . . . is to provide a reference work explaining and describing [SQL/92 as originally defined] in a much less formal and very much more readable way than the standard itself" (from the book's introduction).

4.5 Joe Celko: *SQL for Smarties: Advanced SQL Programming.* San Francisco, Calif.: Morgan Kaufmann (1995).

"This is the first advanced SQL book available that provides a comprehensive presentation of the techniques necessary to support your progress from casual user of SQL to expert programmer" (from the book's own cover).

4.6 Andrew Eisenberg and Jim Melton: "SQLJ Part 0, Now Known as SQL/OLB (Object Language Bindings)," *ACM SIGMOD Record 27,* No. 4 (December 1998). See also Gray Clossman *et al.*: "Java and Relational Databases: SQLJ," Proc. 1998 ACM SIGMOD Int. Conf. on Management of Data, Seattle, Wash. (June 1998).

4.7 Don Chamberlin: *Using the New DB2.* San Francisco, Calif.: Morgan Kaufmann (1996).

A readable and comprehensive description of a state-of-the-art commercial SQL product, by one of the two principal designers of the original SQL language [4.8].

Note: The book also discusses "some controversial decisions" that were made in the design of SQL—primarily (a) the decision to support nulls and (b) the decision to permit duplicate rows. "My [i.e., Chamberlin's] purpose . . . is historical rather than persuasive—I recognize that nulls and duplicates are religious issues . . . For the most part, the designers of [SQL] were practical people rather than theoreticians, and this orientation was reflected in many [design] decisions." This position is very different from that of the present writer! Nulls and duplicates are *scientific* issues, not religious ones; they are discussed, scientifically, in this book in Chapters 18 and 5, respectively. As for "practical . . . rather than [theoretical]," we categorically reject the suggestion that theory is not practical; we have already stated (in Section 4.5) our position that relational theory, at least, is very practical indeed.

4.8 Donald D. Chamberlin and Raymond F. Boyce: "SEQUEL: A Structured English Query Language," Proc. 1974 ACM SIGMOD Workshop on Data Description, Access, and Control, Ann Arbor, Mich. (May 1974).

The paper that first introduced the SQL language (or SEQUEL, as it was originally called; the name was subsequently changed for legal reasons).

4.9 Donald D. Chamberlin *et al.*: "SEQUEL/2: A Unified Approach to Data Definition, Manipulation, and Control," *IBM J. R&D. 20,* No. 6 (November 1976). See also the errata in *IBM J. R&D. 21,* No. 1 (January 1977).

Experience from the early prototype implementation of SEQUEL discussed in reference [4.1] and results from the usability tests reported in reference [4.28] led to the design of a revised version of the language called SEQUEL/2. The language supported by System R [4.2–4.3] was basically SEQUEL/2 (with the conspicuous absence of the so-called "assertion" and "trigger" facilities—see Chapter 8), plus certain extensions suggested by early user experience [4.10].

4.10 Donald D. Chamberlin: "A Summary of User Experience with the SQL Data Sublanguage," Proc. Int. Conf. on Databases, Aberdeen, Scotland (July 1980). Also available as IBM Research Report RJ2767 (April 1980).

Discusses early user experience with System R and proposes some extensions to the SQL language in the light of that experience. Certain of those extensions—EXISTS, LIKE, PREPARE, and EXECUTE—were in fact implemented in the final version of System R. *Note:* See Chapter 7 and Appendix A for a discussion of EXISTS and LIKE, respectively.

4.11 Donald D. Chamberlin *et al.*: "Support for Repetitive Transactions and *Ad Hoc* Queries in System R," *ACM TODS 6,* No. 1 (March 1981).

Gives some measurements of System R performance in both the *ad hoc* query and "canned transaction" environments. (A "canned transaction" is a simple application that accesses only a small part of the database and is compiled prior to execution time. It corresponds to what we called a *planned request* in Chapter 2, Section 2.8.) The measurements were taken on an IBM System

370 Model 158, running System R under the VM operating system. They are described as "preliminary"; with this caveat, however, the paper shows, among other things, that (a) compilation is almost always superior to interpretation, even for *ad hoc* queries, and (b) a system like System R is capable of processing several canned transactions a second, provided appropriate indexes exist in the database.

The paper is notable because it was one of the first to give the lie to the claim, frequently heard at the time, that "relational systems will never perform." Since it was first published, of course, commercial relational products have achieved transaction rates in the hundreds and even thousands of transactions per second.

4.12 Donald D. Chamberlin *et al.*: "A History and Evaluation of System R," CACM 24, No. 10 (October 1981).

Describes the three principal phases of the System R project (preliminary prototype, multi-user prototype, evaluation), with emphasis on the technologies of compilation and optimization that were pioneered in System R. There is some overlap between this paper and reference [4.13].

4.13 Donald D. Chamberlin, Arthur M. Gilbert, and Robert A. Yost: "A History of System R and SQL / Data System," Proc. 7th Int. Conf. on Very Large Data Bases, Cannes, France (September 1981).

Discusses the lessons learned from the System R prototype and describes the evolution of that prototype into the first of IBM's DB2 product family, SQL/DS (subsequently renamed "DB2 for VM and VSE").

4.14 C. J. Date: "A Critique of the SQL Database Language," *ACM SIGMOD Record 14,* No. 3 (November 1984). Republished in *Relational Database: Selected Writings.* Reading, Mass.: Addison-Wesley (1986).

As noted in the body of the chapter, SQL is not perfect. This paper presents a critical analysis of a number of the language's principal shortcomings (mainly from the standpoint of formal computer languages in general rather than database languages specifically). *Note:* Certain of this paper's criticisms do not apply to SQL/92.

4.15 C. J. Date: "What's Wrong with SQL?", in *Relational Database Writings 1985–1989.* Reading, Mass.: Addison-Wesley (1990).

Discusses some additional shortcomings of SQL, over and above those identified in reference [4.14], under the headings "What's Wrong with SQL *per se,*" "What's Wrong with the SQL Standard," and "Application Portability." *Note:* Again, certain of this paper's criticisms do not apply to SQL/92.

4.16 C. J. Date: "SQL Dos and Don'ts," in *Relational Database Writings 1985–1989.* Reading, Mass.: Addison-Wesley (1990).

This paper offers some practical advice on how to use SQL in such a way as (a) to avoid some of the potential pitfalls arising from the problems discussed in references [4.14–4.15] and [4.18] and (b) to realize the maximum possible benefits in terms of productivity, portability, connectivity, and so forth.

4.17 C. J. Date: "How We Missed the Relational Boat," in *Relational Database Writings 1991–1994.* Reading, Mass.: Addison-Wesley (1995).

A succinct summary of SQL's shortcomings with respect to its support (or lack thereof) for the structural, integrity, and manipulative aspects of the relational model.

4.18 C. J. Date: "Grievous Bodily Harm" (in two parts), *DBP&D 11,* No. 5 (May 1998) and *11,* No. 6 (June 1998); "Fifty Ways to Quote Your Query," on the *DBP&D* website *www.dbpd.com* (July 1998).

SQL is an extremely redundant language, in the sense that all but the most trivial of queries can be expressed in many different ways. These papers illustrate this point and discuss some of its implications. In particular, they show that the GROUP BY clause, the HAVING clause, and range variables could all be dropped from the language with effectively no loss of functionality (and the same is also true of the "IN *subquery*" construct). *Note:* All of these SQL constructs are explained in Chapter 7 (Section 7.7) and/or Appendix A.

4.19 C. J. Date and Hugh Darwen: *A Guide to the SQL Standard* (4th edition). Reading, Mass.: Addison-Wesley (1997).

A comprehensive tutorial on SQL/92, including CLI and PSM. In particular, the book contains an appendix, Appendix D, that documents "many aspects of the standard that appear to be inadequately defined, or even incorrectly defined, at this time." *Note:* References [4.4] and [4.27] are also SQL/92 tutorials.

4.20 C. J. Date and Colin J. White: *A Guide to DB2* (4th edition). Reading, Mass.: Addison-Wesley (1993).

Provides an extensive and thorough overview of IBM's original DB2 product (as of 1993) and some of its companion products. DB2, like SQL/DS [4.13], was based on System R.

4.21 Neal Fishman: "SQL *du Jour,*" *DBP&D 10,* No. 10 (October 1997).

A depressing survey of some of the incompatibilities to be found among SQL products that all claim to "support the SQL standard."

4.22 International Organization for Standardization (ISO): *Database Language SQL,* Document ISO/IEC 9075:1992. Also available as American National Standards Institute (ANSI) Document ANSI X3.135-1992.

The original ISO/ANSI SQL/92 definition (known to the cognoscenti as *ISO/IEC 9075,* or sometimes just *ISO 9075*). The original single-part document has since been expanded into an open-ended series of separate parts, under the general title *Information Technology—Database Languages—SQL.* At the time of writing, the following parts have been defined (though certainly not all completed):

Part 1: Framework (SQL/Framework)
Part 2: Foundation (SQL/Foundation)
Part 3: Call-Level Interface (SQL/CLI)
Part 4: Persistent Stored Modules (SQL/PSM)
Part 5: Host Language Bindings (SQL/Bindings)
Part 6: XA Specialization (SQL/Transaction)
Part 7: Temporal (SQL/Temporal)
Part 8: *There is no Part 8*
Part 9: Management of External Data (SQL/MED)
Part 10: Object Language Bindings (SQL/OLB)

The SQL3 proposals that are expected to be ratified in 1999 logically belong in Parts 1, 2, 4, and 5. Working drafts describing those proposals can be found on the World Wide Web at *ftp://jerry.ece.umassd.edu/isowg3/dbl/BASEdocs/public.*

Note: The point is worth mentioning that, although SQL is widely recognized as the international "relational" database standard, the standard document does not describe itself as such;

in fact, it never actually uses the term "relation" at all! (As mentioned in an earlier footnote, it does not mention the term "database" either, come to that.)

4.23 International Organization for Standardization (ISO): *Information Technology—Database Languages—SQL—Technical Corrigendum 2,* Document ISO/IEC 9075:1992/Cor.2:1996(E).

Contains a large number of revisions and corrections to the original version of reference [4.22]. Unfortunately, those revisions and corrections fix almost none of the problems identified in reference [4.19].

4.24 Raymond A. Lorie and Jean-Jacques Daudenarde: *SQL and Its Applications.* Englewood Cliffs, N.J.: Prentice-Hall (1991).

An SQL "how to" book (almost half the book consists of a detailed series of case studies involving realistic applications).

4.25 Raymond A. Lorie and J. F. Nilsson: "An Access Specification Language for a Relational Data Base System," *IBM J. R&D. 23,* No. 3 (May 1979).

Gives more details on one particular aspect of the System R compilation mechanism [4.11,4.25–4.26]. For any given SQL statement, the System R optimizer generates a program in an internal language called ASL (Access Specification Language). That language serves as the interface between the optimizer and the *code generator.* (The code generator, as its name implies, converts an ASL program into machine code.) ASL consists of operators such as "scan" and "insert" on objects such as indexes and stored files. The purpose of ASL was to make the overall translation process more manageable, by breaking it down into a set of well-defined subprocesses.

4.26 Raymond A. Lorie and Bradford W. Wade: "The Compilation of a High-Level Data Language," IBM Research Report RJ2598 (August 1979).

System R pioneered a scheme for compiling queries ahead of run time and then automatically recompiling them if the physical database structure had changed significantly in the interim. This paper describes the System R compilation and recompilation mechanism in some detail, without however getting into questions of optimization (see reference [17.34] for information on this latter topic).

4.27 Jim Melton and Alan R. Simon: *Understanding the New SQL: A Complete Guide.* San Mateo, Calif.: Morgan Kaufmann (1993).

A tutorial on SQL/92 (as originally defined). Melton was the editor of the original SQL/92 specification [4.22].

4.28 Phyllis Reisner, Raymond F. Boyce, and Donald D. Chamberlin: "Human Factors Evaluation of Two Data Base Query Languages: SQUARE and SEQUEL," Proc. NCC 44, Anaheim, Calif. Montvale, N.J.: AFIPS Press (May 1975).

SQL's predecessor SEQUEL [4.8] was based on an earlier language called SQUARE. The two languages were fundamentally the same, in fact, but SQUARE used a rather mathematical syntax whereas SEQUEL was based on English keywords such as SELECT, FROM, WHERE, etc. The present paper reports on a set of experiments that were carried out on the usability of the two languages, using college students as subjects. A number of revisions were made to SEQUEL as a result of that work [4.9].

4.29 David Rozenshtein, Anatoly Abramovich, and Eugene Birger: *Optimizing Transact-SQL: Advanced Programming Techniques.* Fremont, Calif.: SQL Forum Press (1995).

Transact-SQL is the dialect of SQL supported by the Sybase and SQL Server products. This book presents a series of programming techniques for Transact-SQL based on the use of *characteris-*

tic functions (defined by the authors as "devices that allow programmers to encode conditional logic as . . . expressions within SELECT, WHERE, GROUP BY, and SET clauses"). Although expressed in terms of Transact-SQL specifically, the ideas are actually of wider applicability. *Note:* We should perhaps add that the "optimizing" mentioned in the book's title refers not to the DBMS optimizer component, but rather to "optimizations" that can be done by users themselves, by hand.

ANSWERS TO SELECTED EXERCISES

4.1
```
CREATE  TABLE  S
      ( S#      CHAR(5),
        SNAME   CHAR(20),
        STATUS  NUMERIC(5),
        CITY    CHAR(15),
      PRIMARY  KEY ( S# ) ) ;

CREATE  TABLE  P
      ( P#      CHAR(6),
        PNAME   CHAR(20),
        COLOR   CHAR(6),
        WEIGHT  NUMERIC(5,1),
        CITY    CHAR(15),
      PRIMARY  KEY ( P# ) ) ;

CREATE  TABLE  J
      ( J#      CHAR(4),
        JNAME   CHAR(20),
        CITY    CHAR(15),
      PRIMARY  KEY ( J# ) ) ;

CREATE  TABLE  SPJ
      ( S#      CHAR(5),
        P#      CHAR(6),
        J#      CHAR(4),
        QTY     NUMERIC(9),
      PRIMARY  KEY ( S#, P#, J# ),
      FOREIGN  KEY ( S# ) REFERENCES S,
      FOREIGN  KEY ( P# ) REFERENCES P,
      FOREIGN  KEY ( J# ) REFERENCES J ) ;
```

4.4 a.
```
INSERT  INTO  S ( S#, SNAME, CITY )
        VALUES ( 'S10', 'Smith', 'New York' ) ;
```

STATUS here is set to the applicable default value.

b.
```
UPDATE  P
SET     COLOR = 'Orange'
WHERE   COLOR = 'Red' ;
```

c.
```
DELETE
FROM    J
WHERE   J# NOT IN
      ( SELECT J#
        FROM   SPJ ) ;
```

Note the nested subquery and the **IN** operator (actually, the *negated* IN operator) in the solution to part c. here. See Chapter 7 for further explanation.

4.5 Note that there might be some suppliers who supply no projects at all; the following solution deals with such suppliers satisfactorily (how, exactly?). First we define two cursors, CS and CJ, as follows:

```
EXEC SQL DECLARE CS CURSOR FOR
         SELECT S.S#, S.SNAME, S.STATUS, S.CITY
         FROM    S
         ORDER   BY S# ;

EXEC SQL DECLARE CJ CURSOR FOR
         SELECT J.J#, J.JNAME, J.CITY
         FROM    J
         WHERE   J.J# IN
               ( SELECT SPJ.J#
                 FROM    SPJ
                 WHERE   SPJ.S# = :CS_S# )
         ORDER   BY J# ;
```

(Note the nested subquery and the IN operator once again.)

When cursor CJ is opened, host variable CS_S# will contain a supplier number value, fetched via cursor CS. The procedural logic is essentially as follows:

```
EXEC SQL OPEN CS ;
DO for all S rows accessible via CS ;
   EXEC SQL FETCH CS INTO :CS_S#, :CS_SN, :CS_ST, :CS_SC;
   print CS_S#, CS_SN, CS_ST, CS_SC ;
   EXEC SQL OPEN CJ ;
   DO for all J rows accessible via CJ ;
      EXEC SQL FETCH CJ INTO :CJ_J#, :CJ_JN, :CJ_JC ;
      print CJ_J#, CJ_JN, CJ_JC ;
   END DO ;
   EXEC SQL CLOSE CJ ;
END DO ;
EXEC SQL CLOSE CS ;
```

4.6 This is a good example of a problem that SQL/92 does not handle well. The basic difficulty is as follows: We need to "explode" the given part to *n* levels, where the value of *n* is unknown at the time of writing the program. A comparatively straightforward way of performing such an *n*-level "explosion"—if it were possible—would be by means of a recursive program, in which each recursive invocation creates a new cursor, as follows:

```
CALL RECURSION ( GIVENP# ) ;

RECURSION: PROC ( UPPER_P# ) RECURSIVE ;
   DCL UPPER_P# ... ;
   DCL LOWER_P# ... ;
   EXEC SQL DECLARE C "reopenable" CURSOR FOR
            SELECT MINOR_P#
            FROM    PART_STRUCTURE
            WHERE   MAJOR_P# = :UPPER_P# ;

   print UPPER_P# ;
   EXEC SQL OPEN C ;
   DO for all PART_STRUCTURE rows accessible via C ;
      EXEC SQL FETCH C INTO :LOWER_P# ;
      CALL RECURSION ( LOWER_P# ) ;
   END DO ;
   EXEC SQL CLOSE C ;
END PROC ;
```

We have assumed here that the (fictitious) specification "reopenable" on DECLARE CURSOR means that it is legal to OPEN that cursor even if it is already open, and that the effect of such an OPEN is to create a new *instance* of the cursor for the specified table expression (using the current values of any host variables referenced in that expression). We have assumed further that references to such a cursor in FETCH (etc.) are references to the "current" instance, and that CLOSE destroys that instance and reinstates the previous instance as "current." In other words, we have assumed that a reopenable cursor forms a *stack,* with OPEN and CLOSE serving as the "push" and "pop" operators for that stack.

Unfortunately, these assumptions are purely hypothetical today. There is no such thing as a reopenable cursor in SQL today (indeed, an attempt to OPEN a cursor that is already open will fail). The foregoing code is illegal. But the example makes it clear that "reopenable cursors" would be a very desirable extension.

Since the foregoing approach does not work, we give a sketch of a possible (but very inefficient) approach that does.

```
CALL RECURSION ( GIVENP# ) ;
RECURSION: PROC ( UPPER_P# ) RECURSIVE ;
   DCL UPPER_P# ... ;
   DCL LOWER_P# ... INITIAL ( '        ' ) ;
   EXEC SQL DECLARE C CURSOR FOR
                    SELECT MINOR_P#
                    FROM   PART_STRUCTURE
                    WHERE  MAJOR_P# = :UPPER_P#
                    AND    MINOR_P# > :LOWER_P#
                    ORDER  BY MINOR_P# ;

   print UPPER_P# ;
   DO "forever" ;
      EXEC SQL OPEN C ;
      EXEC SQL FETCH C INTO :LOWER_P# ;
      EXEC SQL CLOSE C ;
      IF no "lower P#" retrieved THEN RETURN ; END IF ;
      IF "lower P#" retrieved THEN
         CALL RECURSION ( LOWER_P# ) ; END IF ;
   END DO ;
END PROC ;
```

Observe in this solution that the same cursor is used on every invocation of RECURSION. (By contrast, new instances of UPPER_P# and LOWER_P# are created dynamically each time RECURSION is invoked; those instances are destroyed at completion of that invocation.) Because of this fact, we have to use a trick—

```
... AND MINOR_P# > :LOWER_P# ORDER BY MINOR_P#
```

—so that, on each invocation of RECURSION, we ignore all immediate components (LOWER_P#s) of the current UPPER_P# that have already been processed.

See (a) references [4.5] and [4.7] for a discussion of some alternative SQL-style approaches to this problem, (b) Chapter 6 (end of Section 6.7) for a description of a pertinent relational operator called *transitive closure,* and (c) Appendix B for an overview of some relevant SQL3 facilities.

PART II

THE RELATIONAL MODEL

The foundation of modern database technology is without question the relational model; it is that foundation that makes the field a science. Thus, any book on the fundamentals of database technology that does not include thorough coverage of the relational model is by definition shallow. Likewise, any claim to expertise in the database field can hardly be justified if the claimant does not understand the relational model in depth. Not that the material is at all "difficult," we hasten to add—it certainly is not—but, to repeat, it *is* the foundation, and will remain so for as far out as anyone can see.

As explained in Chapter 3, the relational model is concerned with three principal aspects of data: data *structure,* data *manipulation,* and data *integrity.* In this part of the book, we consider each of these aspects in turn: Chapter 5 discusses structure, Chapters 6 and 7 discuss manipulation, and Chapter 8 discusses integrity. (There are two chapters on manipulation because the manipulative part of the model can be realized in two distinct but equivalent forms, known as the *relational algebra* and the *relational calculus,* respectively.) Finally, Chapter 9 discusses the important topic of *views.*

Now, it is important to understand that the relational model is not a static thing—it has evolved and expanded over the years, and it continues to do so.* The text that follows reflects the current thinking of the present writer and other workers in this field (in particular, as mentioned in the preface, it is informed throughout by the ideas of *The Third Manifesto* [3.3]). The treatment is meant to be fairly complete, even definitive (as of the time of writing), though of course it is pedagogic in style; however, you should not take what follows as the last word on the subject.

To say it again, the relational model is not hard to understand—but it is a theory, and most theories come equipped with their own special terminology, and (for reasons already explained in Section 3.3) the relational model is no exception in this regard. And, of course, we will be using that special terminology in this part of the book. However, it cannot be denied that the terminology can be a little bewildering at first, and indeed can serve as a barrier to understanding (this latter fact is particularly unfortunate, given that the underlying ideas are not difficult at all). So if you are having trouble in understanding some of the material that follows, please have patience: You will probably find that the concepts do become very straightforward, once you have become familiar with the terminology.

---

*It resembles mathematics in this respect (mathematics also is not static but grows over time). In fact, the relational model itself can be regarded as a small branch of mathematics.

As you will soon see, the five chapters that follow are very long (this part of the book is almost a book in its own right). But the length reflects the importance of the subject matter. It would be quite possible to provide an overview of the topic in just one or two pages; indeed, it is a major strength of the relational model that its basic ideas can be explained and understood very easily. However, a one- or two-page treatment cannot do justice to the subject, nor illustrate its wide range of applicability. The considerable length of this part of the book should thus be seen, not as a comment on the model's complexity, but as a tribute to its importance and its success as a foundation for numerous far-reaching developments.

Finally, a word regarding SQL. We have already explained in Part I of this book that SQL is the standard "relational" database language, and just about every database product on the market supports it (or, more accurately, some dialect of it [4.21]). As a consequence, no modern database book would be complete without extensive coverage of SQL. The chapters that follow on various aspects of the relational model therefore do also discuss the relevant SQL facilities where applicable (they build on Chapter 4, which covers basic SQL concepts).

Domains, Relations, and Base Relvars

5.1 INTRODUCTION

As explained in Chapter 3, the relational model can be regarded as having three principal parts, having to do with *data structure, data integrity,* and *data manipulation,* respectively. Each part has its own special terminology. The most important **structural** terms are illustrated in Fig. 5.1 (which as you can see is based on the sample suppliers relation from the suppliers and parts database of Fig. 3.8, expanded to show the applicable data types or domains). The terms in question are *relation* itself (of course), *tuple, cardinality, attribute, degree, domain,* and *primary key.*

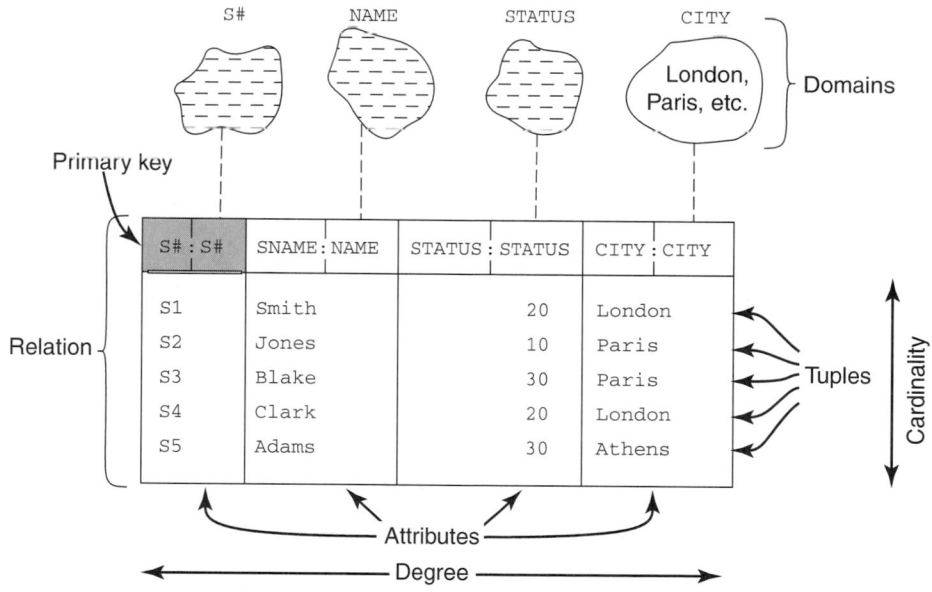

Fig. 5.1 Structural terminology

Of these terms, *relation* and *primary key,* at least, should be reasonably familiar to you from Chapter 3; we explain the other terms informally here, then go on to give more formal definitions in subsequent sections. Briefly, if we think of a relation as a table, then a **tuple** corresponds to a row of such a table and an **attribute** to a column; the number of tuples is called the **cardinality** and the number of attributes is called the **degree;** and a **domain** is a pool of values, from which the values of specific attributes of specific relations are taken. The domain labeled S# in Fig. 5.1, for example, is the set of all possible supplier numbers, and every S# value appearing in the suppliers relation is some value from that set (likewise, every S# value appearing in the shipments relation—see Fig. 3.8—is also some value from that set).

Fig. 5.2 presents a summary of the foregoing. Please understand, however, that the "equivalences" shown in that figure are all only approximate (the formal relational terms have precise definitions, while the informal "equivalents" have only rough and ready definitions). Thus, e.g., a relation and a table are not really the same thing, although—as we saw in Part I of this book—it is common in practice to pretend that they are.

Now we proceed with our formal treatment.

Formal relational term	Informal equivalents
relation	table
tuple	row or record
cardinality	number of rows
attribute	column or field
degree	number of columns
primary key	unique identifier
domain	pool of legal values

Fig. 5.2   Structural terminology (summary)

5.2 DOMAINS

A domain is nothing more nor less than a **data type** (*type* for short)—possibly a simple **system-defined** type like INTEGER or CHAR, more generally a **user-defined** type like S# or P# or WEIGHT or QTY in the suppliers and parts database. Indeed, we can use the terms *type* and *domain* interchangeably, and we will do so in this book (though we prefer the term *type;* when we use the term *domain,* we do so mainly for historical reasons).

So what is a type? Among other things, it is **a set of values**—*all possible* values of the type in question. The type INTEGER, for example, is the set of all possible integers; the type S# is the set of all possible supplier numbers; and so on. Also, along with the notion of a given type is the associated notion of the valid **operators** that can legally be applied to values of that type; i.e., values of that type can be operated upon *solely* by means of the operators defined for that type. For example, in the case of type INTEGER (which we assume for simplicity is system-defined):

- The system provides operators "=", "<", and so on, for comparing integers;
- It also provides operators "+", "*", and so on, for performing arithmetic on integers;
- It does *not* provide operators "$||$" (concatenate), SUBSTR (substring), and so on, for performing string operations on integers. In other words, string operations on integers are not supported.

And in a system that provided proper type support, we would be able to define our own types: type S#, for example. And we would probably define operators "=", "<", and so on, for comparing supplier numbers. However, we would probably *not* define operators "+", "*", and so on, which would mean that arithmetic on supplier numbers would not be supported for this type (why would we ever want to add or multiply two supplier numbers together?).

Observe, therefore, that we distinguish very carefully between a **type** *per se,* on the one hand, and the **physical representation** of values of that type inside the system, on the other.* (In fact, types are a *model* issue, while physical representations are an *implementation* issue.) For example, supplier numbers might be physically represented as character strings, but it does not follow that we can perform character string operations on supplier numbers; rather, we can perform such operations only if appropriate operators have been defined for the type. And, of course, the operators we define for a given type will depend on the intended *meaning* or *semantics* of the type in question, not on the way values of that type happen to be physically represented—indeed, those physical representations should be *hidden* so far as the user is concerned.

By now, you might have realized that what we are talking about is what is known in programming language circles as **strong typing.** Different writers have slightly different definitions for this term; as we use it, however, it means, among other things, that (a) every value *has* a type, and (b) whenever we try to perform an operation, the system checks that the operands are of the right types for the operation in question. For example, consider the following expressions:

```
P.WEIGHT + SP.QTY    /* part weight plus shipment quantity */

P.WEIGHT * SP.QTY    /* part weight times shipment quantity */
```

The first of these makes no sense, and the system should reject it. The second, on the other hand, does make sense—it denotes the total weight for all parts involved in the shipment.

---

*Types are sometimes called **abstract** data types (ADTs) in the literature, to stress the point that types must be distinguished from their implementation. We do not use this term ourselves, however, because it suggests there might be some types that are not "abstract" in this sense, whereas we believe a distinction should *always* be drawn between a type and its implementation.

So the operators we would define for weights and quantities (in combination) would presumably include "∗" but not "+".

Here are some more examples, involving comparison operations this time (actually equality comparisons):

```
P.WEIGHT = SP.QTY

P.CITY = S.CITY
```

Again the first does not make sense but the second does. So the operators we would define for weights and quantities (in combination) presumably would not include "=", but those for cities presumably would.* (As a matter of fact, we follow reference [3.3] in insisting, reasonably enough, that the equality comparison operator "=" be defined for *every* type; it must always be possible to test whether two values of the same type are in fact the same value.)

Observe now that so far we have said nothing at all about the nature of the values that constitute a type. In fact, they can be **of any kind at all.** We tend to think of them as being very simple—numbers, strings, and so forth—but there is absolutely nothing in the relational model that requires them to be limited to such simple forms. Thus, we can have domains of audio recordings, domains of maps, domains of video recordings, domains of engineering drawings, domains of architectural blueprints, domains of geometric points (etc., etc.). The only requirement is that, to repeat, the values in the domain must be manipulable *solely* by means of the operators defined for the domain in question (the physical representation must be hidden).

The foregoing message is so important—and so widely misunderstood—that we state it again in different terms:

> **The question as to what data types are supported is orthogonal to the question of support for the relational model**

Values Are Typed

Every value has a type. In other words, if *v* is a value, then *v* can be thought of as carrying around with it a kind of flag that announces "I am an integer" or "I am a supplier number" or "I am a geometric point" (etc., etc.). Note that, by definition, any given value will always be of exactly one type,[†] and can never change its type. (It follows that distinct types are always *disjoint,* meaning they have no values in common.)

---

*Incidentally, with respect to this question of deciding which operators are legal for which types, we note that historically much of the database literature—the first few editions of this book included—considered only comparison operators such as "=" and ">" and ignored other operators such as "+" and "∗".

†Except possibly if type inheritance is supported. We ignore this possibility until Chapter 19.

A given type can be either *scalar* or *nonscalar*. A **nonscalar** type is a type that is explicitly defined to have user-visible components. In particular, *relation* types are nonscalar in this sense; for example, the relation shown in Fig. 5.1 is of a certain relation type, and that relation type certainly does have user-visible components (namely, the S#, SNAME, STATUS, and CITY attributes). **Scalar** types, by contrast, are types that have no user-visible components. Points arising:

1. For the remainder of this section, all of the types we will be dealing with will be scalar types specifically, and we will therefore take the unqualified term *type* to mean a scalar type specifically.

2. Of course, the *physical* representation of a given scalar value—that is, a given value of a given scalar type—can be arbitrarily complex. In particular, it can have components (but those components will not be user-visible). For example, a given scalar value might have a physical representation consisting of an array of stacks of lists of character strings, in appropriate circumstances.

3. Given that they have no user-visible components, scalar types are sometimes said to be **encapsulated.** They are also sometimes said to be **atomic.** We prefer not to use either of these terms, however, because they have led to too much confusion in the past (on our own part as much as anyone else's, we hasten to add). To be specific, they have caused confusion over the distinctions between model and implementation and between type and representation (and they often still do).

4. As we will see in a few moments, scalar types do have what are called *possible representations,* and those possible representations in turn do have user-visible components. Do not let yourself be misled by this fact: The components in question are *not* components of the type, they are components of the possible representation. The type itself is still scalar in the sense defined above.

Type Definition

Throughout this book, we will use the language **Tutorial D** (or, rather, a slight variation on that language) first mentioned in Chapter 3 to illustrate the ideas we are discussing. **Tutorial D** might be characterized, loosely, as a Pascal-like language. We will introduce it feature by feature as we go. Clearly, the first thing we need is a way for users to define their own types:

```
TYPE <type name> <possible representation> ... ;
```

By way of example, here are the type definitions (repeated from Fig. 3.9) for the suppliers and parts database:

```
TYPE S#      POSSREP ( CHAR ) ;
TYPE NAME    POSSREP ( CHAR ) ;
TYPE P#      POSSREP ( CHAR ) ;
TYPE COLOR   POSSREP ( CHAR ) ;
TYPE WEIGHT  POSSREP ( RATIONAL ) ;
TYPE QTY     POSSREP ( INTEGER ) ;
```

Explanation:

1. Recall first from Chapter 3 that the supplier STATUS attribute and the supplier and part CITY attributes are defined in terms of builtin types instead of user-defined ones, so no type definitions are shown corresponding to these attributes.

2. As we have already seen, *physical* representations are hidden from the user. Type definitions therefore say nothing about any such physical representations. Instead, such representations must be specified as part of the conceptual/internal mapping (see Chapter 2, Section 2.6).

   We do require, however, that every type have at least one associated **possible** representation, for reasons to be discussed in the next subsection. In the example, values of type S#, NAME, P#, and COLOR might possibly be represented as character strings (of whatever length is necessary), values of type QTY might possibly be represented as integers, and values of type WEIGHT might possibly be represented as rational numbers. *Note:* Throughout this book (following reference [3.3]), we prefer the more accurate RATIONAL over the more familiar REAL.

3. We adopt the obvious syntax conventions that (a) unnamed possible representations inherit the name of the relevant type; (b) unnamed possible representation components inherit the name of the relevant possible representation. Thus, for example, the sole possible representation defined for type QTY is also called QTY, and so is the sole component of that possible representation.

4. Defining a new type causes the system to make an entry in the catalog to describe that new type (refer back to Chapter 3, Section 3.6, if you need to refresh your memory regarding the catalog). Analogous remarks apply to operator definitions also (see the next two subsections).

5. You might have noticed that the one thing the TYPE definitions shown above do *not* do is specify the actual values that make up the types in question! That function is performed by the associated type *constraints* (indicated in the syntax above by an ellipsis "…"), which we will discuss in Chapter 8.

   Of course, it must also be possible to get rid of a type if we have no further use for it:

```
DROP TYPE <type name> ;
```

The *<type name>* must identify a user-defined type, not a builtin one. The operation causes the catalog entry describing the type to be deleted, meaning the type in question is no longer known to the system. *Note:* For simplicity, we assume that DROP TYPE will fail if the type in question is still being used somewhere—in particular, if some attribute of some relation somewhere is defined on it.

Possible Representations

In order to illustrate the significance of the "possible representation" concept, we consider a slightly more complicated example:

```
TYPE POINT /* geometric points */
    POSSREP CARTESIAN ( X RATIONAL, Y RATIONAL )
    POSSREP POLAR ( R RATIONAL, THETA RATIONAL ) ;
```

Observe first that type POINT has two distinct possible representations, CARTESIAN and POLAR, reflecting the fact that geometric points can indeed be represented by either Cartesian or polar coordinates. (Of course, the *physical* representation in the particular system at hand might be Cartesian coordinates, or polar coordinates, or something else entirely.) Each possible representation in turn has two components. Note in particular that this example differs from previous ones in that, this time, the possible representations and their components have all been given explicit names.

Every possible representation declaration causes automatic* definition of the following more or less self-explanatory operators:

- A **selector** operator (with the same name as the possible representation), which allows the user to specify or select a value of the type in question by supplying a value for each component of the possible representation;

- A set of **THE_** operators (one for each component of the possible representation), which allow the user to access the corresponding possible representation components of values of the type in question.

For example, here are some sample selector and THE_ operator invocations for type POINT:

```
CARTESIAN ( 5.0, 2.5 )
/* denotes the point with x = 5.0, y = 2.5 */

CARTESIAN ( XXX, YYY )
/* denotes the point with x = XXX, y = YYY -- */
/* XXX and YYY are variables of type RATIONAL */

POLAR ( 2.7, 1.0 )
/* denotes the point with r = 2.7, theta = 1.0 */

THE_X ( P )
/* returns the x coordinate of point P */
/* -- P is a variable of type POINT    */

THE_R ( P )
/* returns the r coordinate of point P */
```

Note: As you can see, selectors (or, rather, selector invocations) are a generalization of the familiar concept of a *literal*.

To see how the foregoing could work in practice, suppose the physical representation of points is in fact Cartesian coordinates (though there is no need, in general, for a physical representation to be identical to any of the stated possible ones). Then the system will

---

*By "automatic" here, we mean that (a) whatever agency—possibly the system, possibly some human user—is responsible for defining the possible representation in question is also responsible for defining the corresponding operators, and further that (b) until those operators have been defined, the process of defining that possible representation is not complete.

provide certain highly protected operators—denoted in what follows by *italic pseudo-code*—that effectively expose that physical representation, and the *type definer* will then use those operators to implement the necessary CARTESIAN and POLAR selectors.* For example:

```
OPERATOR CARTESIAN ( X RATIONAL, Y RATIONAL )
                                  RETURNS ( POINT ) ;
   BEGIN ;
      VAR P POINT ;
      X component of physical representation of P  :=  X ;
      Y component of physical representation of P  :=  Y ;
      RETURN ( P ) ;
   END ;
END OPERATOR ;

OPERATOR POLAR ( R RATIONAL, THETA RATIONAL )
                                  RETURNS ( POINT ) ;
   RETURN ( CARTESIAN ( R * COS ( THETA ),
                        R * SIN ( THETA ) ) ) ;
END OPERATOR ;
```

Observe that the POLAR definition makes use of the CARTESIAN selector, as well as the (presumably builtin) operators SIN and COS. Alternatively, the POLAR definition could be expressed directly in terms of the protected operators, as follows:

```
OPERATOR POLAR ( R RATIONAL, THETA RATIONAL )
                                  RETURNS ( POINT ) ;
   BEGIN ;
      VAR P POINT ;
      X component of physical representation of P
                              :=  R * COS ( THETA ) ;
      Y component of physical representation of P  :=  Y ;
                              :=  R * SIN ( THETA ) ;
      RETURN ( P ) ;
   END ;
END OPERATOR ;
```

The type definer will also use those protected operators to implement the necessary THE_ operators, thus:

```
OPERATOR THE_X ( P POINT ) RETURNS ( RATIONAL ) ;
   RETURN ( X component of physical representation of P ) ;
END OPERATOR ;

OPERATOR THE_Y ( P POINT ) RETURNS ( RATIONAL ) ;
   RETURN ( Y component of physical representation of P ) ;
END OPERATOR ;

OPERATOR THE_R ( P POINT ) RETURNS ( RATIONAL ) ;
   RETURN ( SQRT ( THE_X ( P ) ** 2 + THE_Y ( P ) ** 2 ) ) ;
END OPERATOR ;

OPERATOR THE_THETA ( P POINT ) RETURNS ( RATIONAL ) ;
   RETURN ( ARCTAN ( THE_Y ( P ) / THE_X ( P ) ) ) ;
END OPERATOR ;
```

---

*Obviously the type definer is—in fact, must be—an exception to the general rule that users are not aware of physical representations.

Observe that the definitions of THE_R and THE_THETA make use of THE_X and THE_Y, as well as the (presumably builtin) operators SQRT and ARCTAN. Alternatively, THE_R and THE_THETA could be defined directly in terms of the protected operators (details left as an exercise).

So much for the POINT example. However, it is important to understand that all of the concepts discussed apply to simpler types as well—for example, type QTY. Here are some sample selector invocations for that type:

```
QTY ( 100 )
QTY ( Q )
QTY ( ( Q1 - Q2 ) * 2 )
```

And here are some sample THE_ operator invocations:

```
THE_QTY ( Q )
THE_QTY ( ( Q1 - Q2 ) * 2 )
```

Note in particular that since values are always typed, it is strictly incorrect to say that (e.g.) the quantity for a certain shipment is 100. A quantity is a value of type QTY, not a value of type INTEGER! For the shipment under discussion, therefore, we should more properly say the quantity is QTY(100), not just 100. In informal contexts, however, we often do not bother to be quite so precise, thus using (e.g.) 100 as a convenient shorthand for QTY(100).* In particular, we have used such shorthands in Fig. 3.8 (the suppliers and parts database) and Fig. 4.5 (the suppliers-parts-projects database).

We give one final type definition example, LINESEG (line segments):

```
TYPE LINESEG POSSREP ( BEGIN POINT, END POINT ) ;
```

A given possible representation can of course be defined in terms of *user-defined* types, as here, not just system-defined types as in all of our previous examples.

Operator Definition

Now we take a closer look at the business of defining operators. Here are some more examples. The first is a user-defined operator for the builtin type RATIONAL:

```
OPERATOR ABS ( Z RATIONAL ) RETURNS ( RATIONAL ) ;
   RETURN ( CASE
              WHEN Z ≥ 0.0 THEN +Z
              WHEN Z < 0.0 THEN −Z
           END CASE ) ;
END OPERATOR ;
```

---

*We do the same thing in SQL contexts too, but for a different reason: namely, because SQL does not (yet) support user-defined types. See Appendix B.

The operator ABS ("absolute value") is defined in terms of just one parameter, Z, of type RATIONAL, and returns a result of that same type. (In other words, an invocation of ABS—e.g., ABS (AMT1 – AMT2)—is an expression of type RATIONAL.)

The next example, DIST ("distance between"), involves some user-defined types:

```
OPERATOR DIST ( P1 POINT, P2 POINT ) RETURNS ( LENGTH ) ;
    RETURN ( WITH THE_X ( P1 ) AS X1 ,
                  THE_X ( P2 ) AS X2 ,
                  THE_Y ( P1 ) AS Y1 ,
                  THE_Y ( P2 ) AS Y2 :
            LENGTH ( SQRT ( ( X1 - X2 ) ** 2
                          + ( Y1 - Y2 ) ** 2 ) ) ) ;
END OPERATOR ;
```

We are assuming here that LENGTH is a user-defined type with a RATIONAL possible representation. Note the use of a WITH clause to introduce shorthand names for certain expressions.

The next example is the required "=" comparison operator for type POINT:

```
OPERATOR EQ ( P1 POINT, P2 POINT ) RETURNS ( BOOLEAN ) ;
    RETURN ( THE_X ( P1 ) = THE_X ( P2 ) AND
             THE_Y ( P1 ) = THE_Y ( P2 ) ) ;
END OPERATOR ;
```

Observe that the expression in the RETURN statement here makes use of the *builtin* "=" operator for type RATIONAL. For simplicity, we will assume from this point forward that the usual infix notation "=" can be used for the equality operator (for all types, that is, including type POINT in particular); we omit consideration of how such an infix notation might be specified in practice, since it is basically just a matter of syntax.

Here is the "<" operator for type QTY:

```
OPERATOR LT ( Q1 QTY, Q2 QTY ) RETURNS ( BOOLEAN ) ;
    RETURN ( THE_QTY ( Q1 ) < THE_QTY ( Q2 ) ) ;
END OPERATOR ;
```

The expression in the RETURN statement here makes use of the builtin "<" operator for type INTEGER. Again, we will assume from this point forward that the usual infix notation can be used for this operator—for all "ordered types," that is, not just type QTY. (In fact, an **ordered type** is, by definition, a type to which "<" applies. A simple example of a type that is definitely not ordered in this sense is type POINT.)

Here finally is an example of an *update* operator definition (all previous examples have been of *read-only* operators).* As you can see, the definition involves an UPDATES specification instead of a RETURNS specification; update operators do not return a value and must be invoked by explicit CALLs [3.3].

```
OPERATOR REFLECT ( P POINT ) UPDATES ( P ) ;
    BEGIN ;
        THE_X ( P )   :=   - THE_X ( P ) ;
        THE_Y ( P )   :=   - THE_Y ( P ) ;
        RETURN ;
    END ;
END OPERATOR ;
```

---

*Read-only and update operators are also known as *observers* and *mutators*, respectively, especially in object systems (see Part VI of this book).

The REFLECT operator effectively moves the point with Cartesian coordinates (x,y) to the inverse position $(-x,-y)$; it does this by updating its point argument appropriately. Note the use of THE_ **pseudovariables** in this example. A THE_ pseudovariable is an invocation of a THE operator in a target position (in particular, on the left-hand side of an assignment). Such an invocation actually *designates*—rather than just returning the value of—the specified component of (the applicable possible representation of) its argument. Within the REFLECT definition, for instance, the assignment

```
THE_X ( P )  :=  ... ;
```

actually assigns a value to the X component of (the Cartesian possible representation of) the argument variable corresponding to the parameter P. Of course, any argument to be updated by an update operator—by assignment to a THE_ pseudovariable in particular—must be specified as a variable specifically, not as some more general expression.

Pseudovariables can be nested, as here:

```
VAR LS LINESEG ;

THE_X ( THE_BEGIN ( LS ) )  :=  6.5 ;
```

Finally, of course, it must be possible to get rid of an operator if we have no further use for it. For example:

```
DROP OPERATOR REFLECT ;
```

The specified operator must be user-defined, not builtin.

Type Conversion

Consider the following type definition once again:

```
TYPE S# POSSREP ( CHAR ) ;
```

By default, the possible representation here has the inherited name S#, and hence the corresponding selector operator does, too. Thus the following is a valid selector invocation:

```
S# ( 'S1' )
```

(it returns a certain supplier number). Note, therefore, that the S# selector might be regarded, loosely, as a **type conversion** operator that converts character strings to supplier numbers. Analogously, the P# selector might be regarded as a conversion operator that converts character strings to part numbers; the QTY selector might be regarded as a conversion operator that converts integers to quantities; and so on.

Now, in Chapter 3 we gave several examples in which a comparison was performed between (e.g.) a part number and a character string. For example, Exercise 3.4 included the following WHERE clause:

```
... WHERE P# = 'P2'
```

The left comparand here is of type P# and the right comparand is of type CHAR; on the face of it, therefore, the comparison should fail on a **type error** (a *compile-time* type error, in fact). Conceptually, however, what happens is that the system realizes that it can use the P# "conversion operator" to convert the CHAR comparand to type P#, so it effectively rewrites the comparison as follows:

```
... WHERE P# = P# ( 'P2' )
```

The comparison is now legal.

Invoking a conversion operator implicitly in this way is known as **coercion,** and we made heavy, albeit tacit, use of it throughout Chapter 3. However, it is well known in practice that coercion can lead to program bugs. For that reason, we will adopt the conservative position from this point forward that no coercions are permitted—operands must always be of the appropriate types, not merely coercible to those types. In particular, we will insist that:

- The comparands for "=", "<", and ">" must be of the same type;
- The left- and right-hand sides of an assignment (":=") must be of the same type.

Of course, we do allow what are usually called "CAST" operators to be defined and explicitly invoked for converting between types, where necessary—for example:

```
CAST_AS_RATIONAL ( 5 )
```

As we have already pointed out, selectors—at least, those that take just one argument—can also be thought of as explicit conversion operators (of a kind).

Concluding Remarks

Complete support for types along the lines sketched in the present section has a number of significant implications, which we briefly summarize here:

- First, and most important, it means the system will know (a) exactly **which expressions are legal,** and (b) the **type of the result** for each such legal expression.
- It also means that the total collection of types for a given database will be a **closed set**—that is, the type of the result of every legal expression will be a type that is known to the system. Observe in particular that this closed set of types *must* include the type *boolean* or *truth value,* if comparisons are to be legal expressions!
- In particular, the fact that the system knows the type of the result of every legal expression means it knows which **assignments** are legal, and also which **comparisons.**

We close this section with an important forward reference. We have claimed that domains are data types, system- or user-defined, of arbitrary internal complexity, whose values are manipulable solely by means of the operators defined for the type in question (and whose internal representation is therefore hidden from the user). Now, if we turn our attention for a moment to **object** systems, we find that the most fundamental object concept, the *object class,* is a data type, system- or user-defined, of arbitrary internal complexity, whose values are manipulable solely by means of the operators defined for the type in question (and whose internal representation is therefore hidden from the user) . . . In other words, domains and object classes are *the same thing!*—and so we have here the key to marrying the two technologies (relations and objects) together. We will elaborate on this important issue in Chapter 25.

5.3 RELATION VALUES

Recall from Chapter 3 that it is necessary to distinguish carefully between relations *per se* (i.e., relation *values*), on the one hand, and relation *variables* (i.e., variables whose values are relation values), on the other. We discuss relation values (relations for short) in this section and relation variables in the next. First of all, then, here is a precise definition of the term *relation:*

- Given a collection of n types or domains Ti ($i = 1, 2, \ldots, n$), not necessarily all distinct, r is a **relation** on those types if it consists of two parts, a *heading* and a *body,** where:

  a. The **heading** is a set of n **attributes** of the form $Ai:Ti$, where the Ai (which must all be distinct) are the *attribute names* of r and the Ti are the corresponding *type names* ($i = 1, 2, \ldots, n$);

  b. The **body** is a set of m **tuples** $t,$ where t in turn is a set of components of the form $Ai:vi$ in which vi is a value of type Ti—the *attribute value* for attribute Ai of tuple t ($i = 1, 2, \ldots, n$).

  The values m and n are called the **cardinality** and the **degree,** respectively, of relation r.

Points arising from this definition:

1. In terms of the tabular representation of a relation, of course, the heading is the row of column names and corresponding type names, the body is the set of data rows (see further discussion below).

2. Attribute Ai is said to be *of* type Ti or (sometimes) *defined* on type Ti. Note that any number of distinct attributes, in the same relation or in distinct relations or both, can be of the same type (see Fig. 3.8 in Chapter 3, also Figs. 4.5 and 4.6 in Chapter 4, for several illustrations of this point).

3. At any given time there will typically be values of a given type that do not currently appear in the database as a value for any of the attributes that are of that type. For example, P8 might be a valid part number, even though there is no "part P8" in Fig. 3.8.

4. As stated in the definition, the value n—the number of attributes in the relation—is called the **degree** (sometimes the **arity**). A relation of degree one is said to be *unary,* a relation of degree two *binary,* a relation of degree three *ternary,* . . . , and a relation of

---

*The heading is also referred to in the literature as a (relation) **schema,** or sometimes **scheme.** It is also referred to as the **intension** (note the spelling), in which case the body is then called the **extension.**

degree *n n-ary*. The relational model is thus concerned with *n*-ary relations, in general, for arbitrary nonnegative integer *n*.

5. The term *n-tuple* is sometimes used in place of *tuple* (and so we speak of, e.g., 4-tuples, 5-tuples, and so on). However, it is usual to drop the "*n-*" prefix.

6. To say that relation *r* has heading *H* is to say, precisely, that relation *r* is of type RELATION{*H*} (and the name of that type is, precisely, RELATION{H}). See Section 5.4 for further discussion.

By way of example, let us examine the table in Fig. 5.1 (we deliberately do not call it a relation, for the moment) to see how it measures up to the foregoing definition.

- First, that table does have four underlying types, namely supplier numbers (S#), names (NAME), status values (STATUS), and city names (CITY). *Note:* It is true that when we draw a relation as a table on paper we often do not bother to mention the underlying types (as we saw in Chapter 3), but we must understand that, at least conceptually, they are always there.

- Next, the table certainly does have two parts—it has a row of column names and it has a set of data rows. We consider the row of column names first:

```
( S#, SNAME, STATUS, CITY )
```

What this row really represents is the following *set of ordered pairs:*

```
{ S#     : S#     ,
  SNAME  : NAME   ,
  STATUS : STATUS ,
  CITY   : CITY   }
```

The first component in each pair is an attribute name, the second is the corresponding type name. Thus, we can agree that the row of column headings does indeed represent a *heading* in the sense of the definition. *Note:* As already indicated, it is common in practice to think of a heading as consisting just of a set of attribute names (i.e., the type names are often omitted), except when precision is particularly important. This practice is sloppy but convenient, and we will frequently adopt it ourselves in what follows.

- As for the rest of the table, it certainly does consist of a *set,* namely a set of data rows. Let us concentrate on just one of the rows in that set, say the row:

```
( S1, Smith, 20, London )
```

What this row really represents is the following *set of ordered pairs:*

```
{ S#     :  S# ( 'S1' )      ,
  SNAME  :  NAME ( 'Smith' ) ,
  STATUS :  20               ,
  CITY   :  'London'         }
```

The first component in each pair is an attribute name, the second is the corresponding attribute value. Now, we usually omit the attribute names in informal contexts, because we have a convention that says that each individual value in the table is actually a value of the attribute whose name appears at the top of the relevant column; furthermore, that value is indeed a value of the relevant underlying type, namely the type of the attribute in question. For example, the value S1—more properly, S#('S1')—is a value of the S# attribute, and it is indeed a value of the relevant type, namely the type "supplier numbers" (which is also called S#). So we can agree that each row does indeed represent a *tuple,* in the sense of the definition.

It follows from all of the above that we can agree that the table in Fig. 5.1 can indeed be regarded as a picture of a relation in the sense of the definition—*provided* we can agree on how to "read" such a picture (i.e., *provided* we can agree on certain **rules of interpretation** for such pictures). In other words, we have to agree that yes, there are some underlying types; yes, each column corresponds to exactly one of those types; yes, each row represents a tuple; yes, each attribute value is a value of the relevant type; and so on. If we can agree on all of these "rules of interpretation," then—*and only then*—we can agree that a "table" is a reasonable picture of a relation.

So we can now see that a table and a relation are indeed not quite the same thing (even though we pretended in earlier chapters that they were). Rather, a **relation** is what the definition says it is, namely a rather abstract kind of object, and a **table** is a concrete picture (typically on paper) of such an abstract object. They are not (to repeat) quite the same. Of course, they are very similar . . . and in informal contexts, at least, it is usual, and perfectly acceptable, to say they are the same. But when we are trying to be more precise (and right now, of course, we *are* trying to be more precise), then we do have to recognize that the two concepts are not exactly identical.

Note: If you are having difficulty with this idea that there are some differences between a relation and a table, the following might help. First, it is undeniably a major advantage of the relational model that its basic abstract object, the relation, does have such a simple representation on paper; it is that simple representation that makes relational systems easy to use and easy to understand, and makes it easy to reason about the way relational systems behave. However, it is unfortunately also the case that the tabular representation *suggests some things that are not true.* For example, it clearly suggests that the rows of the table—i.e., the tuples of the relation—are in a certain top-to-bottom order, but they are not (see the next subsection).

Properties of Relations

Relations possess certain properties, all of them immediate consequences of the definition of *relation* given in the previous subsection, and all of them very important. We first briefly state the properties, then discuss them in detail. They are as follows. Within any given relation:

- There are no duplicate tuples;
- Tuples are unordered, top to bottom;

- Attributes are unordered, left to right;
- Each tuple contains exactly one value for each attribute.

1. *There are no duplicate tuples*

This property follows from the fact that the body of the relation is a mathematical set (of tuples); sets in mathematics do not include duplicate elements.

Note: In fact, it should be obvious that the concept of "duplicate tuples" makes no sense. Consider a relation with attributes S# and CITY (meaning "supplier S# is located in city CITY"). Suppose the relation contains a tuple showing that it is a "true fact" that supplier S1 is located in London. Then if the relation contained a duplicate of that tuple (if that were possible), it would simply be telling us that same "true fact" a second time. But if something is true, saying it twice does not make it *more* true!

Incidentally, this first property serves right away to illustrate the point that a relation and a table (in general) are not the same thing, because a table (in general) might contain duplicate rows—in the absence of any discipline to prevent such a thing—whereas a relation *cannot* contain any duplicate tuples. (For if a "relation" does contain duplicate tuples, then *it is not a relation!*—by definition.) It is very unfortunately the case that SQL does permit tables to contain duplicate rows. This is not the place to go into all of the reasons why such duplicates are a mistake (see references [5.3] and [5.6] for a comprehensive discussion); for present purposes, we content ourselves with observing that the relational model does not recognize duplicates, and hence that in this book we will take care to ensure that they never occur. (This remark applies primarily to our discussions of SQL. So far as the relational model itself is concerned, of course, no special care is necessary.)

2. *Tuples are unordered, top to bottom*

This property also follows from the fact that the body of the relation is a mathematical set; sets in mathematics are not ordered. In Fig. 5.1, for example, the tuples could just as well have been shown in reverse sequence—it would still have been the same relation. Thus, there is no such thing as "the fifth tuple" or "the 97th tuple" or "the first tuple" of a relation, and there is no such thing as "the next tuple"; in other words, there is no concept of positional addressing, and there is no concept of "nextness." Reference [5.6], already mentioned above in connection with the "no duplicate tuples" property, shows why the "no tuple ordering" property is important too (indeed, the two properties are interrelated).

Note: It is true that some concept of "nextness" is required in the interface between the database and a host language such as C or COBOL (see the discussion of SQL cursors and ORDER BY in Chapter 4). But it is the host language, not the relational model, that imposes that requirement. In effect, the host language requires *unordered* sets to be converted into *ordered* lists or arrays (of tuples), so that operations such as "fetch next tuple" can have a meaning. Note too that such facilities form part of the application programming interface only—they are not exposed to end users.

As mentioned earlier in this section, this second property also serves to illustrate the point that a relation and a table are not the same thing, because the rows of a table obviously do have a top-to-bottom ordering, whereas the tuples of a relation do not.

3. *Attributes are unordered, left to right*

This property follows from the fact that the heading of a relation is also a set (of attributes). In Fig. 5.1, for example, the attributes could just as well have been shown in the order (say) SNAME, CITY, STATUS, S#—it would still have been the same relation, at least so far as the relational model is concerned.* Thus, there is no such thing as "the first attribute" or "the second attribute" (etc.), and there is no "next attribute" (again, there is no concept of "nextness"); in other words, attributes are always referenced by name, never by position. As a result, the scope for errors and obscure programming is reduced. For example, there is, or should be, no way to subvert the system by somehow "flopping over" from one attribute into another. This situation contrasts with that found in many programming systems, where it often is possible to exploit the physical adjacency of logically discrete items, deliberately or otherwise, in a variety of subversive ways.

Observe that this question of attribute ordering is yet another area where the concrete representation of a relation as a table suggests something that is not true: The columns of a table obviously do have a left-to-right ordering, but the attributes of a relation do not.

4. *Each tuple contains exactly one value for each attribute*

This property follows immediately from the definition of a tuple—a tuple is a set of n components or ordered pairs of the form $Ai{:}vi$ ($i = 1, 2, ..., n$). A relation that satisfies this fourth property is said to be **normalized,** or equivalently to be in **first normal form.**

Note: This particular property might seem very obvious, and indeed so it is—especially since (as you might have already realized) *all* relations are normalized according to the definition! Nevertheless, the property does have some important consequences. See (a) the annotation to reference [5.10], (b) Chapter 18 on missing information, (c) the subsection immediately following.

Relation-Valued Attributes

In Section 5.2, we said the values that make up a type can be **of any kind at all.** In particular, therefore, we can have a type whose values are *relations*—and therefore we can have relations with attributes whose values are relations in turn. In other words, we can have relations that have other relations nested inside themselves. An example, relation S_SP, is shown in Fig. 5.3; attribute PQ of that relation is relation-valued. Observe in particular that the empty set of parts supplied by supplier S5 is represented by an empty set (more precisely, by an empty relation).

Our main reason for explicitly mentioning the possibility of relation-valued attributes here is that, historically, most relational database publications—earlier editions of this book included—have asserted that such a possibility is illegal (and most of them still do). For

---

*Mathematical relations, unlike their counterparts in the relational model, do have a left-to-right order to their attributes.

S_SP	S#	SNAME	STATUS	CITY	PQ	

	S1	Smith	20	London	P#	QTY
					P1	300
					P2	200
					..	...
					P6	100
	S2	Jones	10	Paris	P#	QTY
					P1	300
					P2	400
	..	.....	..	......	....	
	S5	Adams	30	Athens	P#	QTY

Fig. 5.3   A relation with a relation-valued attribute

example, the following is a lightly edited excerpt from the previous edition of the present book:

> Note that *all column values are atomic* ... That is, at every row and column position in every table there is always exactly one data value, never a group of several values. Thus, for example, in table EMP, we have

DEPT#	EMP#
D1	E1
D1	E2
..	..

instead of

DEPT#	EMP#
D1	E1,E2
..	..

Column EMP# in the second version of this table is an example of what is usually called a **repeating group.** A repeating group is a column ... that contains several values in each row (different numbers of values in different rows, in general). *Relational databases do not allow repeating groups;* the second version of the table above would not be permitted in a relational system.

And later in the same book:

> [Domains] contain atomic values only . . . [Therefore,] *relations do not contain repeating groups.* A relation satisfying this condition is said to be normalized, or equivalently to be in first normal form . . . The term *relation* is always taken to mean a normalized relation in the context of the relational model.

These remarks are not correct, however (at least not in their entirety): They arose from a misunderstanding on this writer's part of the true nature of types and predicates. For reasons to be discussed in Chapter 11 (Section 11.6), it is unlikely that this mistake will have caused any very serious errors in practice; nevertheless, apologies are still due to anyone who might have been misled. At least the previous edition was correct when it said that relations in the relational model were always normalized! Again, see Chapter 11 for further discussion.

Relations and Their Interpretation

We conclude this section with a reminder to the effect that, as explained in Chapter 3, Section 3.4, (a) the heading of any given relation can be regarded as a *predicate,* and (b) the tuples of that relation can be regarded as *true propositions,* obtained from the predicate by substituting values of the appropriate type for the *parameters* or *placeholders* of that predicate ("instantiating the predicate"). In fact, the **Closed World Assumption** (also known as the **Closed World Interpretation**) says that if an otherwise valid tuple—i.e., one conforming to the relation heading—does *not* appear in the body of the relation, then we can assume the corresponding proposition is *false.* That is, the body of the relation contains *all* and *only* the tuples that correspond to true propositions.

5.4 RELATION VARIABLES

Recall from Chapter 3 that relation variables—*relvars* for short—come in two varieties, base relvars and views (also called real and virtual relvars, respectively). In this section, we consider base relvars only; views are discussed in Chapter 9.

Base Relvar Definition

Here is the syntax for defining a base relvar:

```
VAR <relvar name> BASE <relation type>
              <candidate key definition list>
            [ <foreign key definition list> ] ;
```

The *<relation type>* takes the form

```
RELATION { <attribute commalist> }
```

where each *<attribute>* in turn is an ordered pair of the form

```
<attribute name> <type name>
```

Regarding the *<candidate key definition list>* and optional *<foreign key definition list>*, see below.

Note: The term *commalist* was defined in Chapter 4 (Section 4.6). The term *list* is defined analogously, thus: Let *<xyz>* denote an arbitrary syntactic category (i.e., anything that appears on the left-hand side of some BNF production rule). Then the expression *<xyz list>* denotes a sequence of zero or more *<xyz>*s in which each pair of adjacent *<xyz>*s is separated by one or more blanks.

Here by way of example are the base relvar definitions for the suppliers and parts database (repeated from Fig. 3.9):

```
VAR S BASE RELATION
    { S#       S#,
      SNAME    NAME,
      STATUS   INTEGER,
      CITY     CHAR }
    PRIMARY KEY { S# } ;

VAR P BASE RELATION
    { P#       P#,
      PNAME    NAME,
      COLOR    COLOR,
      WEIGHT   WEIGHT,
      CITY     CHAR }
    PRIMARY KEY { P# } ;

VAR SP BASE RELATION
    { S#       S#,
      P#       P#,
      QTY      QTY }
    PRIMARY KEY { S#, P# }
    FOREIGN KEY { S# } REFERENCES S
    FOREIGN KEY { P# } REFERENCES P ;
```

Explanation:

1. The (relation) **types** of these three base relvars are as follows:

```
RELATION { S# S#, SNAME NAME, STATUS INTEGER, CITY CHAR }

RELATION { P# P#, PNAME NAME, COLOR COLOR,
                            WEIGHT WEIGHT, CITY CHAR }

RELATION { S# S#, P# P#, QTY QTY }
```

Note that each of these relation types is indeed a type and can be used in all of the usual ways—in particular, as the type for some attribute in some relation. (In fact, RELATION is a **type generator** that allows us to define as many specific relation types as we like, much as, e.g., "array" is a type generator in conventional programming languages.)

2. All possible relation values of any given relvar, base or otherwise, are of the same relation type (namely, the relation type specified, directly or indirectly, in the relvar de-

finition) and therefore have the same heading. In particular, the initial value of any given base relvar is an empty relation of the appropriate type.

3. The terms *heading, body, attribute, tuple, cardinality,* and *degree,* already defined for relation values, are all interpreted in the obvious way to apply to relvars as well (all relvars, that is, not just base ones).

4. Defining a new base relvar causes the system to make entries in the catalog to describe that relvar.

5. Candidate key definitions are explained in detail in Chapter 8. Prior to that point, we will simply assume that each base relvar definition includes exactly one such definition, of the following particular form:

```
PRIMARY KEY { <attribute name commalist> }
```

6. Foreign key definitions are also explained in Chapter 8.

Finally, here is the syntax for dropping an existing base relvar:

```
DROP VAR <relvar name> ;
```

This operation sets the value of the specified base relvar to an empty relation (i.e., it deletes all tuples in the relvar, loosely speaking), and then deletes all catalog entries for that relvar. The relvar will now no longer be known to the system. *Note:* For simplicity, we assume the DROP will fail if the relvar in question is still being used somewhere—for example, if it is referenced in some view definition somewhere. See Chapter 9 for further discussion.

Updating Relvars

The relational model includes a **relational assignment** operation for assigning values to— i.e., *updating*—relvars (base relvars in particular). Here is the **Tutorial D** syntax:

```
<relvar name>  :=  <relational expression> ;
```

The *<relational expression>* is evaluated and the relation resulting from that evaluation is assigned to the relvar identified by *<relvar name>*, replacing the previous value of that relvar. Of course, the relvar and relation in question must be of the same type (i.e., have the same heading).

By way of example, suppose we are given another relvar R of the same type as the suppliers relvar S:

```
VAR R BASE RELATION
    { S# S#, SNAME NAME, STATUS INTEGER, CITY CHAR } ... ;
```

Here then are some legal relational assignments:

- ■ ```
  R   :=   S ;
  ```

- ■ ```
  R   :=   S WHERE CITY = 'London' ;
  ```

- ■ ```
  R   :=   S MINUS (S WHERE CITY = 'Paris') ;
  ```

Note that each of these examples can be regarded as both (a) *retrieving* the relation specified on the right-hand side and (b) *updating* the relvar specified on the left-hand side.

Now suppose we change the second and third examples by replacing relvar R on the left-hand side by relvar S in each case:

- ■ ```
  S   :=   S WHERE CITY = 'London' ;
  ```

- ■ ```
  S   :=   S MINUS (S WHERE CITY = 'Paris') ;
  ```

Observe that these two assignments are both effectively *updates to relvar S*—one effectively deletes all suppliers not in London, the other effectively deletes all suppliers in Paris. For convenience **Tutorial D** does support explicit INSERT, DELETE, and UPDATE operations, but each of these operations is defined to be shorthand for a certain relational assignment. Here are some examples:*

- ■ ```
  INSERT INTO S
     RELATION { TUPLE { S# S# ( 'S6' ),
                        SNAME NAME ( 'Smith' ),
                        STATUS 50,
                        CITY 'Rome' } } ;
  ```

Assignment equivalent:

```
S   :=   S UNION
         RELATION { TUPLE { S# S# ( 'S6' ),
                            SNAME NAME ( 'Smith' ),
                            STATUS 50,
                            CITY 'Rome' } } ;
```

Note, incidentally, that this assignment will succeed if the specified tuple for supplier S6 already appears in relvar S. In practice, we might wish to extend the assignment analog of INSERT to ensure that such is not the case; for simplicity, however, we ignore this refinement here. Analogous remarks apply to DELETE and UPDATE also, of course.

- ■ ```
  DELETE S WHERE CITY = 'Paris' ;
  ```

Assignment equivalent:

```
S   :=   S MINUS ( S WHERE CITY = 'Paris' ) ;
```

---

*The expression RELATION {…} in the INSERT example is a *relation selector invocation* (and as a matter of fact, the expression inside those braces, TUPLE {…}, is a *tuple* selector invocation in turn, and the expressions inside those inner braces are *scalar* selector invocations). See Chapter 6, Sections 6.3 and 6.4.
```

```
■  UPDATE S WHERE CITY = 'Paris'
                 STATUS := 2 * STATUS,
                 CITY   := 'Rome' ;
```

The assignment equivalent is a little complicated in the UPDATE case, and we omit the details here. See reference [3.3].

For purposes of reference, here is a slightly simplified summary of the syntax of INSERT, DELETE, and UPDATE:

■ `INSERT INTO <relvar name> <relational expression> ;`

■ `DELETE <relvar name> [ WHERE <boolean expression> ] ;`

■ `UPDATE <relvar name> [ WHERE <boolean expression> ]`
   `                       <attribute update commalist> ;`

An *<attribute update>* in turn takes the form:

```
<attribute name> := <expression>
```

The syntax of *<boolean expression>* we take to be more or less self-explanatory, though further details are given in Chapter 6.

We close this subsection by stressing the point that relational assignment, and hence INSERT, UPDATE, and DELETE, are all **set-level** operations. UPDATE, for example, updates a *set* of tuples in the target relvar, loosely speaking. Informally, we often talk of (e.g.) updating some individual tuple, but it must be clearly understood that:

1. We are really talking about updating a *set* of tuples, a set that just happens to have cardinality one; and

2. Sometimes updating a set of tuples of cardinality one is impossible!

Suppose, for example, that the suppliers relvar is subject to the integrity constraint (see Chapter 8) that suppliers S1 and S4 must have the same status. Then any "single-tuple" UPDATE that tries to change the status of just one of those two suppliers must necessarily fail. Instead, both must be updated simultaneously, as here:

```
UPDATE S WHERE S# = S# ( 'S1' ) OR S# = S# ( 'S4' )
         STATUS := some value ;
```

To pursue the foregoing point a moment longer, we should now add that to talk, as we have just been doing, of "updating a tuple" (or set of tuples) is really rather sloppy. Tuples, like relations, are *values* and *cannot* be updated (by definition, the one thing you cannot do to *any* value is change it). In order to be able to "update tuples," we would need some notion of a tuple *variable* or "tuplevar"—a notion that is not part of the relational model at all! Thus, what we really mean when we talk of "updating tuple *t* to *t'*," for example, is that we are **replacing** the tuple *t* (the tuple *value t,* that is) by another tuple *t'* (which is, again, a tuple *value*). Analogous remarks apply to phrases such as "updating attribute *A*" (in some tuple). In this book, we will continue to talk in terms of "updating tuples" or "updating attributes of tuples"—the practice is convenient—but it must be understood that such usage is only shorthand, and rather sloppy shorthand at that.

5.5 SQL FACILITIES

The SQL statements most relevant to the material discussed in the foregoing sections are:

```
CREATE DOMAIN    CREATE TABLE    INSERT
ALTER DOMAIN     ALTER TABLE     UPDATE
DROP DOMAIN      DROP TABLE      DELETE
```

The INSERT, UPDATE, and DELETE statements have already been discussed in Chapter 4. We consider the other statements below.

Domains

As noted in Chapter 4, SQL's "domains" are unfortunately a long way from being true relational domains (i.e., types); in fact, the two concepts are so far apart that it would have been preferable to use some other name for the SQL construct. The primary purpose of domains in SQL is simply to allow a builtin type to be given a name that can be used as a shorthand by several columns in several base table definitions. Here are some examples:

```
CREATE DOMAIN S# CHAR(5) ;
CREATE DOMAIN P# CHAR(6) ;

CREATE TABLE S  ( S# S#, ... ) ;
CREATE TABLE P  ( P# P#, ... ) ;
CREATE TABLE SP ( S# S#, P# P#, ... ) ;
```

For purposes of reference, we list below some differences between true domains and the SQL construct:

- As already indicated, SQL domains are really just a syntactic shorthand; they are not really data types (as such) at all, and they are certainly not full *user-defined* types.

- Values in SQL domains certainly cannot be "of arbitrary internal complexity" but are limited to the complexity—what complexity there is—of the builtin types.

- An SQL domain must be defined in terms of one of the builtin types, not another user-defined domain.

- In fact, an SQL domain must be defined in terms of *exactly one* builtin type. Thus, for example, it is not possible to define SQL domains analogous to the POINT and LINESEG types in Section 5.2.

- An SQL domain cannot have more than one "possible" representation. In fact, SQL domains do not properly distinguish between types and (physical) representations. For example, the SQL domains S# and P# are defined in terms of type CHAR, and so SQL will allow us to perform (e.g.) string concatenation operations on supplier numbers and part numbers.

■ It follows that there is no strong typing, and very little true type checking. Given the S# and P# definitions shown above, for example, the following SQL operation will *not* fail on a type check, though logically it should:

```
SELECT  *
FROM    SP
WHERE   S# = P# ;
```

Note: Perhaps a more polite way of saying the same thing is to say that SQL supports exactly eight true relational domains, namely the following eight "basic types":

- numbers
- character strings
- bit strings
- dates
- times
- timestamps
- year/month intervals
- day/time intervals

We could then say that type checking is performed, but only on the basis of these eight types. Thus, for example, an attempt to compare a number and a bit string is illegal, but an attempt to compare two numbers is legal, even if those numbers have different representations—one as INTEGER and one as FLOAT, say.

■ SQL does not allow users to define the operators that apply to a given domain. Instead, the operators that apply are, precisely, those builtin operators that apply to the corresponding *representation*.

Here then is the syntax for the SQL **CREATE DOMAIN** statement:

```
CREATE DOMAIN <domain name> <builtin type name>
          [ <default spec> ]
          [ <constraints> ] ;
```

Explanation:

1. See Chapter 4, Section 4.2, for a list of legal *<builtin type name>*s.

2. The optional *<default spec>* specifies a default value that applies to every column defined on the domain that does not have an explicit default value of its own (see the next subsection). It takes the form "DEFAULT *<default>*"—where *<default>* in turn is a literal, a niladic builtin operator name, or NULL.* *Note:* A niladic operator is one that takes no operands (CURRENT_DATE is an example).

3. The optional *<constraint>*s specify certain integrity constraints that apply to the domain in question. We defer discussion of constraints to Chapter 8.

---

*We defer detailed discussion of SQL's support for "nulls" to Chapter 18. Passing references prior to that point are unavoidable, however.

An existing SQL domain can also be *altered* at any time in a variety of ways by means of the statement **ALTER DOMAIN.** Specifically, ALTER DOMAIN allows a new *<default spec>* to be defined for an existing domain or an existing one to be deleted. It also allows a new integrity constraint to be defined for an existing domain or an existing one to be deleted. The details of these options are surprisingly complex, however, and beyond the scope of this book; see reference [4.19] for the specifics.

Finally, an existing SQL domain can be *dropped* by means of the statement **DROP DOMAIN**—syntax:

```
DROP DOMAIN <domain name> <option> ;
```

where *<option>* is either RESTRICT or CASCADE. The general idea is as follows:

- If RESTRICT is specified, the DROP will fail if the domain is referenced anywhere;
- If CASCADE is specified, the DROP will succeed and will "cascade" in various ways. For example, columns that were previously defined on the domain will now be considered to be directly defined on the domain's underlying data type instead.

Once again the details are quite complex, and we omit them here. See reference [4.19] for further information.

Base Tables

Before we get into the details of base tables specifically, there are a couple of points to be made on the topic of SQL tables in general:

- First, SQL tables are allowed to include **duplicate rows.** They therefore do not necessarily have a primary key (or, more fundamentally, any candidate keys).
- Second, SQL tables are considered to have a **left-to-right column ordering.** In the suppliers table S, for example, column S# might be the first column, column SNAME might be the second column, and so on.

Turning now to base tables specifically: Base tables are defined by means of the **CREATE TABLE** statement (note, therefore, that the keyword TABLE here refers to a base table specifically; the same is true of ALTER TABLE and DROP TABLE, *q.v.*). The syntax is as follows:

```
CREATE TABLE <base table name>
        ( <base table element commalist> ) ;
```

where each *<base table element>* is either a *<column definition>* or a *<constraint>*. The *<constraint>*s specify certain integrity constraints that apply to the base table in question; we defer detailed discussion of such constraints to Chapter 8. The *<column definition>*s— there must be at least one—take the following general form:

```
<column name> <type or domain name> [ <default spec> ]
```

Here *<type or domain name>* is either a builtin type name or a domain name, and the optional *<default spec>* specifies a default value for the column, overriding any default value specified at the domain level, if applicable. *Note:* A *<default spec>* defines the *default value,* or simply *default,* that is to be placed in the applicable column if the user does not provide an explicit value on INSERT. See Chapter 4, Section 4.6, subsection "Operations Not Involving Cursors," for an illustration. If a given column does not have an explicit default of its own and does not inherit one from an underlying domain, it is implicitly assumed to have a default of NULL—i.e., NULL is the "default default."

For some examples of CREATE TABLE, see, e.g., Fig. 4.1 in Chapter 4.

Next, an existing base table can be *altered* at any time by means of the **ALTER TABLE** statement. The following "alterations" are supported:

- A new column can be added;
- A new default can be defined for an existing column (replacing the previous one, if any);
- An existing column default can be deleted;
- An existing column can be deleted;
- A new integrity constraint can be specified;
- An existing integrity constraint can be deleted.

We give an example of the first case only:

```
ALTER TABLE S ADD COLUMN DISCOUNT INTEGER DEFAULT -1 ;
```

This statement adds a DISCOUNT column (of type INTEGER) to the suppliers base table. All existing rows in that table are extended from four columns to five; the initial value of the new fifth column is –1 in every case.

Finally, an existing base table can be dropped by means of **DROP TABLE**—syntax:

```
DROP TABLE <base table name> <option> ;
```

where (as with DROP DOMAIN) *<option>* is either RESTRICT or CASCADE. If RESTRICT is specified and the base table is referenced in any view definition or integrity constraint, the DROP will fail; if CASCADE is specified, the DROP will succeed (dropping the table and deleting all of its rows), and any referencing view definitions and integrity constraints will be dropped also.

5.6 SUMMARY

In this chapter we have taken a comprehensive look at the **structural** part of the relational model. A **domain** is just a **data type** (possibly builtin or system-defined, more generally user- defined); it provides (a) a set of **values** (all possible values of the type in question), from which various attributes in various relations take their actual values, and (b) a set of **operators** (both *read-only* and *update* operators) for operating on values and variables of the type in question. Values of a given type can be **of any kind at all**—numbers, strings, dates, times, audio recordings, maps, video recordings, geometric points, etc., etc., etc. Types **constrain operations,** inasmuch as the operands to a given operation are required to of the appropriate types for that operation (*strong typing*). Strong typing is a good idea because it allows certain logical errors to be caught, and caught moreover at compile time instead of run time. Note that strong typing has important implications for the *relational* operations in particular (join, union, etc.), as we will see in the next chapter.

Types are either **scalar** or **nonscalar.** A scalar type is one that has no user-visible components. The most important *non*scalar types in the relational model are *relation* types (see the next paragraph below), which are defined by means of the **RELATION type generator.** We distinguish carefully between a type and its physical **representation** (types are a *model* issue, physical representations are an *implementation* issue). However, we do require that each scalar type have at least one declared **possible** representation. Each such possible representation causes automatic definition of (a) one **selector** operator and (b) for each component of that possible representation, one **THE_** operator (including a THE_ **pseudovariable**). We support explicit type **conversions** but no implicit type **coercions.** We also support the definition of any number of additional operators for scalar types, and we require that an **equality** operator be defined for every type (with prescribed semantics!).

Turning now to relations: We distinguish between relation **values** ("relations") and relation **variables** ("relvars"). A **relation** has two parts, a **heading** and a **body;** the heading is a set of **attributes,** the body is a set of **tuples** that conform to the heading. The number of attributes in the heading is called the **degree** and the number of tuples in the body is called the **cardinality.** A relation has a **relation type:** to be specific, the type RELATION{H}, where H is the applicable heading. A relation can be thought of as a **table,** with the columns representing the attributes and the rows representing the tuples, but that representation is only approximate. Also, all relations satisfy four very important properties:

- They do not contain any duplicate tuples;
- There is no ordering to the tuples, top to bottom;
- There is no ordering to the attributes, left to right;
- Each tuple contains exactly one value for each attribute (i.e., all relations are **normalized,** or equivalently in **first normal form**).

As we saw in Chapter 3, the heading of a given relation can be regarded as a **predicate** and the tuples of that relation can be regarded as **true propositions,** obtained from the predicate by substituting argument values of the appropriate type for the placeholders or parameters of the predicate. The **Closed World Assumption** says we can assume that if an otherwise valid tuple—i.e., one conforming to the relation heading—does *not* appear in the body of the relation, then the corresponding proposition is *false.*

Since values of a given type can be of any kind at all, relations with **relation-valued attributes** are legal (and indeed useful, as we will see in Chapters 6 and 11).

Relvars come in two varieties, **base** relvars and **views.** We saw how to define base relvars (and also how to define types for the attributes of such relvars) in **Tutorial D,** a language that we will be using for illustrative purposes throughout this book.

Note: You might have noticed that we discussed the question of user-defined operators for scalar types but not for relation types. The reason is that most of the relational operators we need—restrict, project, join, relational assignment, and so forth—are in fact built into the model itself and do not require any "user definition." (What is more, those operations are *generic,* in that they apply to relations of all types, loosely speaking.) However, there is no reason why those builtin operations should not be augmented with a set of user-defined operations, if the system provided a means for defining them.

Finally, we sketched the SQL facilities for defining (SQL- style) "domains" and base tables. In particular, we pointed out that:

- SQL-style "domains" are not types;
- SQL-style tables (base or otherwise) are not relations, because—among other things—(a) they allow duplicate rows and (b) they have a left-to-right ordering to their columns. In fact, they can even have two or more columns with the same name (though this remark does not apply to named SQL tables, i.e., to base tables or views). By way of example, consider the table that is returned by the following SQL query:

```
SELECT  *
FROM    S, P ;
```

EXERCISES

5.1 Given the outline catalog structure for the departments and employees database shown in Fig. 3.6 in Chapter 3:

a. Rename the various components of that catalog in accordance with the formal relational terms introduced in this chapter.

b. How could the structure of that catalog be extended to take account of types (domains)?

c. Write a query against that extended catalog to get names of all relvars that have an attribute of type EMP#.

d. How would you handle part c. of this exercise in an SQL system with no user-defined data type support?

5.2 What domains are the catalog relvars themselves defined on?

5.3 Given the base relvar PART_STRUCTURE (see Fig. 4.6 in Chapter 4 for a sample value):

a. Use the **Tutorial D** facilities sketched in this chapter to write a relvar definition and appropriate set of type definitions.

b. Assuming this relvar is included in the departments and employees database of Exercise 5.1, show the updates the system must make to the catalog to reflect your answer to part a.

c. Write an appropriate set of **Tutorial D** DROP operations to cause the catalog updates of part b. to be undone.

5.4 Again using the **Tutorial D** facilities sketched in this chapter, write an appropriate set of definitions for the suppliers-parts-projects database of Fig. 4.5 (see the exercises in Chapter 4).

5.5 We pointed out in Section 5.2 that it is strictly incorrect to say that (e.g.) the quantity for a certain shipment is 100 ("a quantity is a value of type QTY, not a value of type INTEGER"). As a consequence, Fig. 4.5 (for example) is rather sloppy, inasmuch as it pretends that it *is* correct to think of, e.g., quantities as integers. Given your answer to Exercise 5.4, show the correct way of referring to the various scalar values in Fig. 4.5.

5.6 Given your answer to Exercise 5.4, which of the following scalar expressions are legal? For the legal ones, state the type of the result; for the others, show a legal expression that will achieve what appears to be the desired effect.

a. `J.CITY = P.CITY`

b. `JNAME || PNAME`

c. `QTY * 100`

d. `QTY + 100`

e. `STATUS + 5`

f. `J.CITY < S.CITY`

g. `COLOR = P.CITY`

h. `J.CITY = P.CITY || 'burg'`

5.7 Give a plausible type definition for a scalar type called CIRCLE. What selectors and THE_ operators apply to this type? Also:

a. Define a set of read-only operators to compute the diameter, circumference, and area of a given circle.

b. Define an update operator to double the radius of a given circle (more precisely, to update a given CIRCLE variable in such a way that its circle value is unchanged except that the radius is twice what it was before).

5.8 It is sometimes suggested that domains or types are really variables too, like relvars. For example, legal employee numbers might grow from three digits to four as a business expands, so we might need to update "the set of all possible employee numbers." Discuss.

5.9 A relation is defined to have a *set* of attributes and a *set* of tuples. Now, in mathematics the empty set is a perfectly respectable set; indeed, it is usually desirable that results, theorems, etc., that hold true for a set of *n* elements should continue to hold true if *n* = 0. Can a relation have an empty set of tuples? Or an empty set of attributes?

5.10 It is sometimes suggested that a relvar is really just a traditional computer file, with "tuples" instead of records and "attributes" instead of fields. Discuss.

5.11 As we have seen, data definition operations cause updates to be made to the catalog. But the catalog is only a collection of relvars, just like the rest of the database; so could we not use the regular update operations INSERT, UPDATE, and DELETE to update the catalog appropriately? Discuss.

5.12 Write a sequence of **Tutorial D** DROP operations that will have the effect of destroying all user-created information in the suppliers-parts-projects database.

REFERENCES AND BIBLIOGRAPHY

Most of the following references are applicable to all aspects of the relational model, not just the structural aspect.

5.1 E. F. Codd: "A Relational Model of Data for Large Shared Data Banks," *CACM 13,* No. 6 (June 1970). Republished in *Milestones of Research—Selected Papers 1958–1982 (CACM 25th Anniversary Issue), CACM 26,* No. 1 (January 1983). See also the earlier version "Derivability, Redundancy, and Consistency of Relations Stored in Large Data Banks," IBM Research Report RJ599 (August 19th, 1969). *Note:* That earlier version was Codd's very first publication on the relational model.

The paper that started it all. Although now some 30 years old, it stands up remarkably well to repeated rereading. Of course, many of the ideas have been refined somewhat since the paper was first published, but by and large the changes have been evolutionary, not revolutionary, in nature. Indeed, there are some ideas in the paper whose implications have still not been fully explored.

We remark on a small matter of terminology. In his paper, Codd uses the term "time-varying relations" in place of our preferred "relation variables" (relvars). But "time-varying relations" is really not a very good term. First, relations as such are *values* and simply do not "vary with time" (there is no notion in mathematics of a relation having different values at different times). Second, if we say in some programming language, e.g.,

```
DECLARE N INTEGER ;
```

we do not call N a "time-varying integer," we call it an *integer variable.* In this book, therefore, we will stay with our "relation variable" terminology, not the "time-varying" terminology; however, you should at least be aware of the existence of this latter terminology.

5.2 E. F. Codd: *The Relational Model for Database Management Version 2.* Reading, Mass.: Addison-Wesley (1990).

Codd spent much of the late 1980s revising and extending his original model (which he now refers to as "the Relational Model Version 1" or RM/V1), and this book is the result. It describes "the Relational Model Version 2" (RM/V2). The essential difference between RM/V1 and RM/V2 is as follows: Whereas RM/V1 was intended as an abstract blueprint for one particular aspect of the total database problem (essentially the foundational aspect), RM/V2 is intended as an abstract blueprint for *the entire system.* Thus, where RM/V1 contained just three parts—structure, integrity, and manipulation—RM/V2 contains 18; and those 18 parts include not only the original three (of course), but also parts having to do with the catalog, authorization, naming, distributed database, and various other aspects of database management. For purposes of reference, here is a complete list of the 18 parts:

A	Authorization	M	Manipulation
B	Basic operators	N	Naming
C	Catalog	P	Protection
D	Principles of DBMS design	Q	Qualifiers
E	Commands for the DBA	S	Structure
F	Functions	T	Data types
I	Integrity	V	Views
J	Indicators	X	Distributed database
L	Principles of language design	Z	Advanced operators

The ideas promulgated in this book are by no means universally accepted, however [5.7–5.8]. We comment on one particular issue here. As we saw in the body of the chapter, domains constrain comparisons. In the case of suppliers and parts, for instance, the comparison S.S# = SP.P# is not valid, because the comparands are of different types; hence, an attempt to join suppliers and shipments over matching supplier and part numbers will fail. Codd therefore proposes **"domain check override"** (DCO) versions of certain of the relational algebra operations, which allow the operations in question to be performed even if they involve a comparison between values of different types. A DCO version of the join just mentioned, for example, will cause the join to be done even though attributes S.S# and SP.P# are of different types (presumably the join is done on the basis of matching *representations* instead of matching *types*).

But therein lies the problem, of course. *The whole DCO idea is based on a confusion between types and representations.* Recognizing domains for what they are (i.e., types)—with all that such recognition entails—gives us the domain checking that we want *and* gives us something like the DCO capability as well. For example, the following expression constitutes a possible representation-level comparison between a supplier number and a part number:

`THE_S# ( S# ) = THE_P# ( P# )`

(both comparands here are of type CHAR). Thus, it is our claim that the kind of mechanism discussed in Section 5.2 gives us the all the facilities we want, but does so in a manner that is clean, systematic (i.e., not *ad hoc*), and fully orthogonal. In particular, there is now no need to clutter up the relational model with new operators such as "DCO join" (etc.).

5.3 Hugh Darwen: "The Duplicity of Duplicate Rows," in C. J. Date and Hugh Darwen, *Relational Database Writings 1989–1991*. Reading, Mass.: Addison-Wesley (1992).

This paper was written as further support for the arguments previously presented in reference [5.6] in support of the prohibition against duplicate rows. The paper not only offers novel versions of some of those same arguments, it also manages to come up with some additional ones. In particular, it stresses the fundamental point that, in order to discuss in any intelligent manner the question of whether two objects are duplicates, it is essential to have a clear *criterion of equality* (called a criterion of *identity* in the paper) for the class of objects under consideration. In other words, what does it mean for two objects, be they rows in a table or anything else, to be "the same"?

5.4 Hugh Darwen: "Relation-Valued Attributes," in C. J. Date and Hugh Darwen, *Relational Database Writings 1989–1991*. Reading, Mass.: Addison-Wesley (1992).

5.5 Hugh Darwen: "The Nullologist in Relationland," in C. J. Date and Hugh Darwen, *Relational Database Writings 1989–1991*. Reading, Mass.: Addison-Wesley (1992).

Nullology is, as Darwen puts it, "the study of nothing at all"—or, in other words, the study of the empty set. Sets are ubiquitous in relational theory, and the question of what happens if such a set happens to be empty is far from a frivolous one. In fact, it turns out that very often the empty-set case turns out to be absolutely fundamental.

So far as the present chapter is concerned, the most immediately applicable portions of this paper are Section 2 ("Tables with No Rows") and Section 3 ("Tables with No Columns"). See also the answer to Exercise 5.9.

5.6 C. J. Date: "Why Duplicate Rows Are Prohibited," in *Relational Database Writings 1985–1989*. Reading, Mass.: Addison-Wesley (1990).

Presents an extensive series of arguments, with examples, in support of the prohibition against duplicate rows. In particular, the paper shows that duplicate rows constitute a major *optimization inhibitor* (see Chapter 17). See also reference [5.3].

5.7 C. J. Date: "Notes Toward a Reconstituted Definition of the Relational Model Version 1 (RM/V1)," in C. J. Date and Hugh Darwen, *Relational Database Writings 1989–1991*. Reading, Mass.: Addison-Wesley (1992).

> Summarizes and criticizes Codd's "RM/V1" [5.2] and offers an alternative definition. The assumption is that it is crucially important to get "Version 1" right before we can even think about moving on to some "Version 2." *Note:* The version of the relational model described in the present book is based on the "reconstituted" version as sketched in this paper (and further clarified and described in reference [3.3]).

5.8 C. J. Date: "A Critical Review of the Relational Model Version 2 (RM/V2)," in C. J. Date and Hugh Darwen, *Relational Database Writings 1989–1991*. Reading, Mass.: Addison-Wesley (1992).

> Summarizes and criticizes Codd's "RM/V2" [5.2].

5.9 C. J. Date: "30 Years of Relational" (series of twelve articles), *Intelligent Enterprise 1*, Nos. 1–3 and *2*, Nos. 1–9 (October 1998 onward). *Note:* Most installments after the first are published in the online portion of the magazine at *www.intelligententerprise.com*.

> These articles are offered as a careful, unbiased, retrospective review and assessment of Codd's relational contribution as documented in his 1970s publications. To be specific, they examine the following papers in detail (as well as touching on several others in passing):
>
> - Derivability, Redundancy, and Consistency of Relations Stored in Large Data Banks (the first version of reference [5.1]);
> - A Relational Model of Data for Large Shared Data Banks [5.1];
> - Relational Completeness of Data Base Sublanguages [6.1];
> - A Data Base Sublanguage Founded on the Relational Calculus [7.1];
> - Further Normalization of the Data Base Relational Model [10.4];
> - Extending the Relational Database Model to Capture More Meaning [13.6];
> - Interactive Support for Nonprogrammers: The Relational and Network Approaches [25.8].

5.10 Mark A. Roth, Henry F. Korth, and Abraham Silberschatz: "Extended Algebra and Calculus for Nested Relational Databases," *ACM TODS 13,* No. 4 (December 1988).

> Over the years, several researchers have proposed what are called "NF^2 relations," where NF^2 = NFNF = "non first normal form." Actually there is some confusion over exactly what the term NF^2 means, but the interpretation that seems to make the most sense is this: Let *nr* be an "NF^2 relation" and let "attribute" *A* of *nr* be of type *T*. Then a given "tuple" *t* of *nr* can include any number of values (possibly even none at all?) for "attribute" *A*, and different "tuples" can contain different numbers of such *A* values.* (Attribute *A* is thus a **repeating group** attribute—see the remarks on this topic from the previous edition of this book, quoted in Section 5.3 of the present chapter.) Note carefully, therefore, that "relation" *nr* is quite definitely *not* normalized (it does not contain exactly one value for each attribute in each tuple); in fact, it is not a relation at all so far as the relational model is concerned. Be that as it may, this paper discusses one version of the NF^2 idea. Specifically, it defines a calculus and an algebra (see Chapters 6 and 7) for "NF^2 relations" and proves their equivalence. It also gives references to a considerable body of other work on the subject.

---

*Some writers would reject this definition and define an "NF^2 relation" to be any relation with at least one attribute that is relation-valued. We have our own reasons for arguing that such a relation in fact is in first normal form.

ANSWERS TO SELECTED EXERCISES

5.1

a. The obvious changes are summarized below:

Replace TABLE   *by*   RELVAR
          COLUMN   ATTRIBUTE
          TABNAME   RVNAME
          COLCOUNT   DEGREE
          ROWCOUNT   CARDINALITY (abbreviated CARD)
          COLNAME   ATTRNAME

Also, the TABLE (now RELVAR) relvar needs another attribute (RVKIND) whose values indicate whether the corresponding relvar is a base relvar or a view. The catalog structure thus now looks something like this:

RELVAR	RVNAME	DEGREE	CARD	RVKIND	. . .

ATTRIBUTE	RVNAME	ATTRNAME	. . . . .

b. We need a new catalog relvar (TYPE) containing an entry for each type, and a new attribute (TYPENAME) in the ATTRIBUTE relvar giving the type of each attribute of each relvar. The catalog structure thus now looks something like this:

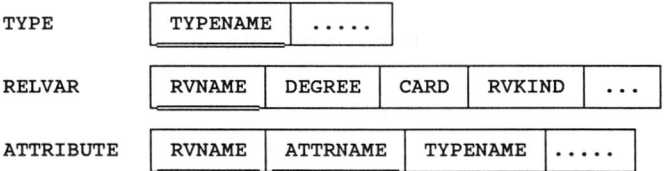

TYPE	TYPENAME	. . . . .

RELVAR	RVNAME	DEGREE	CARD	RVKIND	. . .

ATTRIBUTE	RVNAME	ATTRNAME	TYPENAME	. . . . .

As a subsidiary exercise, you might like to consider what further extensions to the catalog would be needed to represent information regarding primary and foreign keys.

c. (ATTRIBUTE WHERE TYPENAME = NAME ('EMP#')) { RVNAME }

Note the NAME selector invocation here (see the answer to Exercise 5.2 below).

d. In a system that does not support user-defined types, it is obviously not possible to query the catalog regarding such types!—it is only possible to query it regarding *attributes*. Generally speaking, however, it is a good idea if attributes are given the same name as the corresponding type where possible (even if the system has no knowledge of such types), or at least include that type name as (say) the trailing portion of their own name. If the database definer has followed some such naming convention, then such an attribute query might possibly solve the problem.

5.2 It is obviously not possible to give a definitive answer to this exercise. Here are some reasonable suggestions:

TYPENAME   *is defined on domain*   NAME
RVNAME   NAME
ATTRNAME   NAME

DEGREE	NONNEG_INTEGER
CARD	NONNEG_INTEGER
RVKIND	RVKIND

These domains in turn are assumed to be defined as follows:

- NAME is the set of all legal names.

- NONNEG_INTEGER is the set of all nonnegative integers less than some implementation-defined upper limit.

- RVKIND is (loosely) the set { "Base", "View" }.

Note that we have (partly) violated our own principle in the foregoing!—the principle, that is, that each attribute should have the same name as the corresponding type if possible. The exercise illustrates the point that such violations will tend to occur if relvars are designed before the underlying types have been properly pinned down (an observation that applies to all relvars, of course, not just to catalog ones).

5.3

a.
```
TYPE P#  POSSREP ( CHAR ) ;
TYPE QTY POSSREP ( INTEGER ) ;

VAR PART_STRUCTURE BASE RELATION
    { MAJOR_P# P#,
      MINOR_P# P#,
      QTY      QTY }
    PRIMARY KEY { MAJOR_P#, MINOR_P# } ;
```

b. We show the new catalog entries only (see Fig. 5.4). Note that the CARD value in the RELVAR relvar for RELVAR itself will also need to be incremented by one. Also, we have shown the cardinality for PART_STRUCTURE as 0, not 7 (despite the fact that Fig. 4.6 shows it as containing seven tuples), because the relvar will presumably be empty when it is first created.

c.
```
DROP VAR PART_STRUCTURE ;
DROP TYPE QTY ;
DROP TYPE P# ;
```

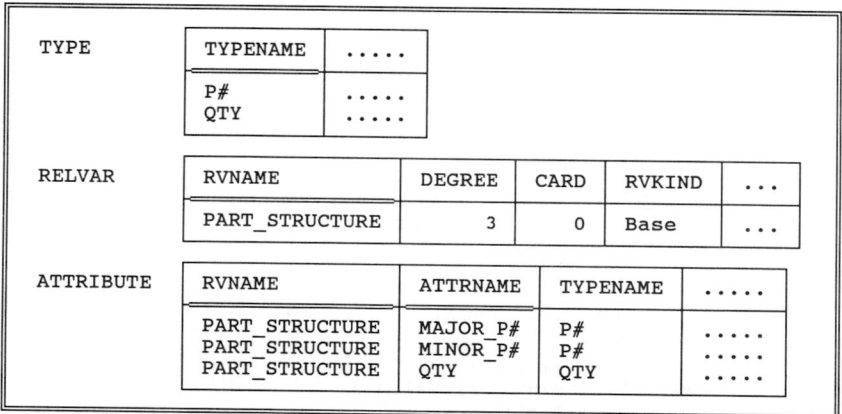

Fig. 5.4　Catalog entries for relvar PART_STRUCTURE

```
5.4   TYPE S#       POSSREP ( CHAR ) ;
      TYPE NAME     POSSREP ( CHAR ) ;
      TYPE P#       POSSREP ( CHAR ) ;
      TYPE COLOR    POSSREP ( CHAR ) ;
      TYPE WEIGHT   POSSREP ( RATIONAL ) ;
      TYPE J#       POSSREP ( CHAR ) ;
      TYPE QTY      POSSREP ( INTEGER ) ;

      VAR S BASE RELATION
          { S#       S#,
            SNAME    NAME,
            STATUS   INTEGER,
            CITY     CHAR }
          PRIMARY KEY { S# } ;

      VAR P BASE RELATION
          { P#       P#,
            PNAME    NAME,
            COLOR    COLOR,
            WEIGHT   WEIGHT,
            CITY     CHAR }
          PRIMARY KEY { P# } ;

      VAR J BASE RELATION
          { J#       J#,
            JNAME    NAME,
            CITY     CHAR }
          PRIMARY KEY { J# } ;

      VAR SPJ BASE RELATION
          { S#       S#,
            P#       P#,
            J#       J#,
            QTY      QTY }
          PRIMARY KEY { S#, P#, J# }
          FOREIGN KEY { S# } REFERENCES S
          FOREIGN KEY { P# } REFERENCES P
          FOREIGN KEY { J# } REFERENCES J ;
```

5.5   We show a typical value for each attribute. First, relvar S:

```
      S#       :  S# ( 'S1' )
      SNAME    :  NAME ( 'Smith' )
      STATUS   :  20
      CITY     :  'London'
```

Relvar P:

```
      P#       :  P# ( 'P1' )
      PNAME    :  NAME ( 'Nut' )
      COLOR    :  COLOR ( 'Red' )
      WEIGHT   :  WEIGHT ( 12.0 )
      CITY     :  'London'
```

Relvar J:

```
      J#       :  J# ( 'J1' )
      JNAME    :  NAME ( 'Sorter' )
      CITY     :  'Paris'
```

5.6

a. Legal; BOOLEAN.

b. Illegal; NAME (THE_NAME(JNAME) ‖ THE_NAME(PNAME)). *Note:* The idea here is to concatenate the (possible) *character string representations* and then "convert" the result of that concatenation back to type NAME. Of course, that conversion itself will fail on a type error, if the result of the concatenation cannot be converted to a legal name.

c. Legal; QTY.

d. Illegal; QTY + QTY(100).

e. Legal; STATUS.

f. Legal; BOOLEAN.

g. Illegal; THE_COLOR(COLOR) = P.CITY.

h. Legal.

5.7
```
TYPE LENGTH POSSREP ( RATIONAL ) ;
TYPE POINT  POSSREP ( X RATIONAL, Y RATIONAL ) ;
TYPE CIRCLE POSSREP ( R LENGTH, CTR POINT ) ;
          /* R is (the length of) the radius of the circle */
          /* and CTR is the center                         */
```

The sole selector that applies to type CIRCLE is as follows:

```
CIRCLE ( r, ctr )
/* returns the circle with radius r and center ctr */
```

The THE_ operators are:

```
THE_R ( c )
/* returns the length of the radius of circle c */

THE_CTR ( c )
/* returns the point that is the center of circle c */
```

a.
```
OPERATOR DIAMETER ( C CIRCLE ) RETURNS ( LENGTH ) ;
    RETURN ( 2 * THE_R ( C ) ) ;
END OPERATOR ;

OPERATOR CIRCUMFERENCE ( C CIRCLE ) RETURNS ( LENGTH ) ;
    RETURN ( 3.14159 * DIAMETER ( C ) ) ;
END OPERATOR ;

OPERATOR AREA ( C CIRCLE ) RETURNS ( AREA ) ;
    RETURN ( 3.14159 * ( THE_R ( C ) ** 2 ) ) ;
END OPERATOR ;
```

We are assuming that (a) multiplying a length by an integer or a rational returns a length and (b) multiplying a length by a length returns an area (where AREA is another user-defined type).

b.
```
OPERATOR DOUBLE_R ( C CIRCLE ) UPDATES ( C ) ;
    BEGIN ;
        THE_R ( C )  :=  2 * THE_R ( C ) ;
        RETURN ;
    END ;
END OPERATOR ;
```

5.8   The following observations are pertinent. First, the operation of defining a type does not actually create the corresponding set of values; conceptually, those values already exist, and always will exist (think of type INTEGER, for example). Thus, all that the "define type" operation—i.e., the TYPE statement, in **Tutorial D**—really does is introduce a *name* by which that set of values can be referenced. Likewise, the DROP TYPE statement does not actually drop the corresponding values, it merely drops the name that was introduced by the corresponding TYPE statement. It follows that "updating an existing type" really means dropping the existing type *name* and then redefining that same name to refer to a different set of values. Of course, there is nothing to preclude the use of some kind of "alter type" shorthand to simplify such an operation.

5.9   A relation with an empty set of tuples is perfectly reasonable, and indeed common (it is analogous to a file with no records). In particular, of course, every base relvar has such a relation as its initial value, as noted in Section 5.4. It is usual, though perhaps a trifle imprecise, to refer to such a relation as *an empty relation.*

What is perhaps less immediately obvious is that a relation with an empty set of attributes is perfectly reasonable too! In fact, such relations turn out to be of *crucial importance*—much as empty sets are crucially important in general set theory, or zero is important in ordinary arithmetic.

In order to examine this notion in slightly more detail, we first have to consider the question of whether a relation with no attributes can contain any tuples. In fact, such a relation can contain *at most one* tuple, namely the 0-tuple (i.e., the tuple with no components); it cannot contain more than one, because all 0-tuples are duplicates of one another. There are thus precisely two relations of degree zero, one that contains just one tuple and one that contains no tuples at all. So important are these two relations that, following Darwen [5.5], we have pet names for them: We call the first TABLE_DEE and the other TABLE_DUM, or DEE and DUM for short (DEE is the one with one tuple, DUM is the empty one).

It is not appropriate here to go into too much detail on this subject; suffice it to say that one reason these relations are so important is that DEE corresponds to *true* (or *yes*) and DUM corresponds to *false* (or *no*). The exercises and answers in Chapters 6 and 8 offer a little more insight. For further discussion, see reference [5.5].

5.10   We might agree that a tuple does resemble a *record* (occurrence, not type) and an attribute a *field* (type, not occurrence). These correspondences are only approximate, however. A relvar should not be regarded as "just a file," but rather as a *disciplined* file (see the subsection "Properties of Relations" in Section 5.3). The discipline in question is one that results in a considerable simplification in the structure of the data as seen by the user, and hence in a corresponding simplification in the operators needed to deal with that data, and indeed in the user interface in general.

5.11   In principle, the answer is yes, it *might* be possible to update the catalog by means of regular INSERT, UPDATE, and DELETE operations. However, allowing such operations would potentially be very dangerous, because it would be all too easy to destroy (inadvertently or otherwise) catalog information that the system needs in order to be able to function correctly. Suppose, for example, that the DELETE operation

```
DELETE RELVAR WHERE RVNAME = NAME ( 'EMP' ) ;
```

were allowed on the departments and employees catalog. Its effect would be to remove the tuple describing relvar EMP from the RELVAR relvar. *As far as the system is concerned, relvar EMP would now no longer exist*—i.e., the system would no longer have any knowledge of that relvar. Thus, all subsequent attempts to access that relvar would fail.

In most real products, therefore, UPDATE, DELETE, and INSERT operations on the catalog *either* (a) are not permitted at all (the usual case) or (b) are permitted only to very highly authorized users (perhaps only to the DBA); instead, catalog updates are performed by means of *data definition* statements. For example, defining relvar EMP causes (a) an entry to be made for EMP in the RELVAR relvar and (b) a set of four entries, one for each of the four attributes of EMP, to be made in the ATTRIBUTE relvar. (It also causes a number of other things to happen that, however, are of no concern to us here.) Thus, defining a new object—e.g., a new type or a new base relvar—is in some ways the analog of INSERT for the catalog. Likewise, DROP is the analog of DELETE; and in SQL, which provides a variety of ALTER statements—e.g., ALTER (base) TABLE—for changing catalog entries in various ways, ALTER is the analog of UPDATE.

Note: The catalog also includes entries for the catalog relvars themselves, as we have seen. However, those entries are not created by explicit data definition operations. Instead, they are created automatically by the system itself as part of the system installation process. In effect, they are "hard-wired" into the system.

5.12 `DROP VAR SPJ, S, P, J ;`

   `DROP TYPE S#, NAME, P#, COLOR, WEIGHT, J#, QTY ;`

We have assumed an obvious extended form of DROP VAR and DROP TYPE that allows several variables or types to be dropped in a single operation.

CHAPTER **6**

Relational Algebra

6.1 INTRODUCTION

The manipulative part of the relational model has evolved considerably since the publication of Codd's original papers on the subject [5.1,6.1]. However, it is still the case that the principal component of that manipulative part is what is called the **relational algebra,** which is basically just a set of operators that take relations as their operands and return a relation as their result. In Chapter 3 we discussed three such operators—*restrict, project,* and *join*—very briefly; in the present chapter we examine those operators, and several others, in depth.

In reference [6.1], Codd defined what is usually regarded as the "original" algebra, *viz.* the set of eight operators shown symbolically in Fig. 6.1. Now, Codd had a very specific purpose in mind, which we will examine in the next chapter, for defining precisely those eight. But you must understand that those eight are not the end of the story; in fact, any number of operators could be defined that satisfy the simple requirement of "relations in, relations out," and many such operators have been defined, by many different writers (see, e.g., reference [6.10]). In this chapter we will first discuss Codd's original operators (or at least our version of them), and use them as the basis for discussing a variety of algebraic ideas; we will then go on to consider ways in which that original set of eight might usefully be expanded.

An Overview of the Original Algebra

To repeat, the original algebra [6.1] consisted of eight operators, two groups of four each:

1. The traditional set operators *union, intersection, difference,* and *Cartesian product* (all of them modified somewhat to take account of the fact that their operands are, specifically, relations instead of arbitrary sets);
2. The special relational operators *restrict* (also known as *select*), *project, join,* and *divide.*

Here are simplified definitions of these eight operators (refer to Fig. 6.1):

Restrict: Returns a relation containing all tuples from a specified relation that satisfy a specified condition.

Project: Returns a relation containing all (sub)tuples that remain in a specified relation after specified attributes have been removed.

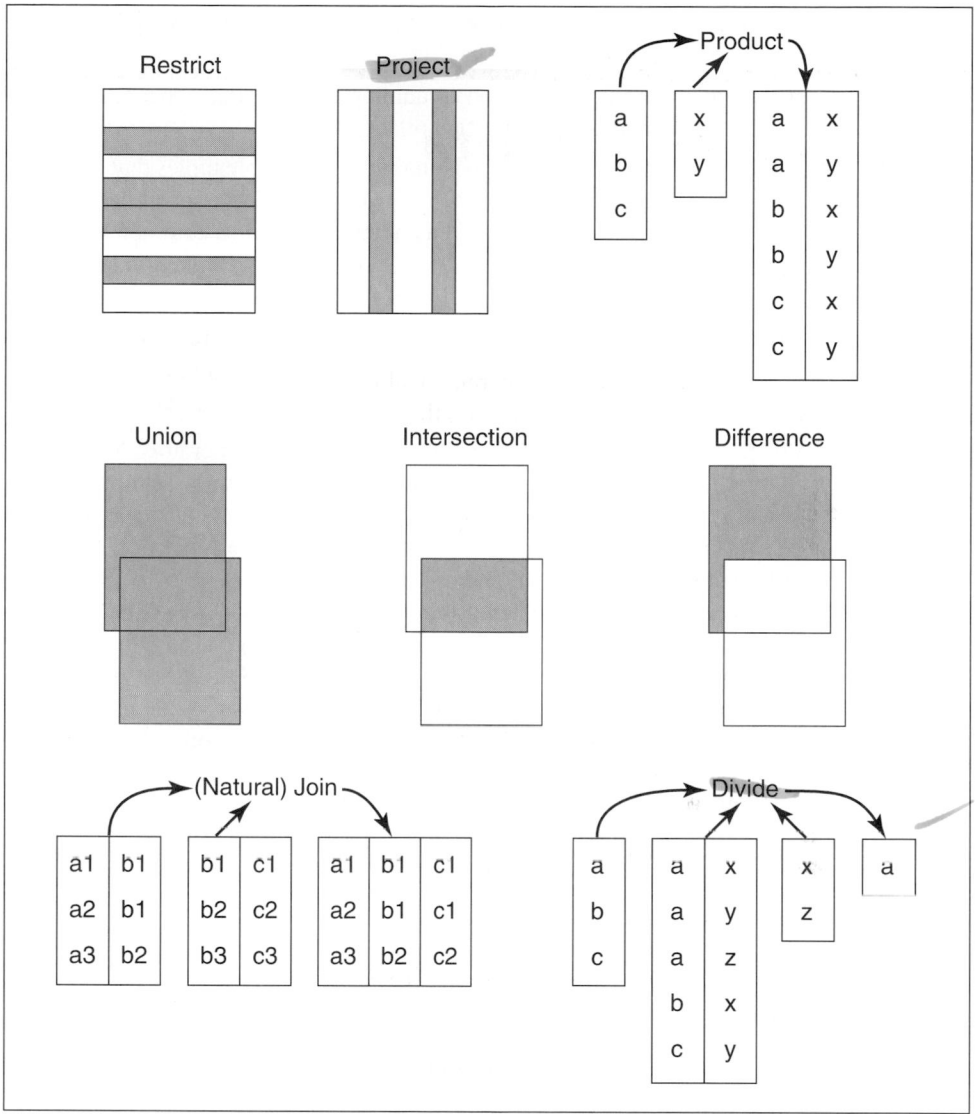

Fig. 6.1   The original eight operators (overview)

Product: Returns a relation containing all possible tuples that are a combination of two tuples, one from each of two specified relations.

Union: Returns a relation containing all tuples that appear in either or both of two specified relations.

Intersect: Returns a relation containing all tuples that appear in both of two specified relations.

Difference: Returns a relation containing all tuples that appear in the first and not the second of two specified relations.

Join: Returns a relation containing all possible tuples that are a combination of two tuples, one from each of two specified relations, such that the two tuples contributing to any given combination have a common value for the common attributes of the two relations (and that common value appears just once, not twice, in the result tuple).

Divide: Takes two unary relations and one binary relation and returns a relation containing all tuples from one unary relation that appear in the binary relation matched with all tuples in the other unary relation.

So much for our quick overview of the original operators. The plan of the rest of the chapter is as follows. Following this introductory section, Section 6.2 discusses the question of relational closure once again and elaborates on it considerably. Sections 6.3 and 6.4 then discuss Codd's original eight operators in detail, and Section 6.5 gives some examples of how those operators can be used to formulate queries. Next, Section 6.6 considers the more general question of what the algebra is for. Then Section 6.7 describes a number of useful extensions to Codd's original algebra, including in particular the important EXTEND and SUMMARIZE operators. Section 6.8 discusses operators for mapping between relations involving relation-valued attributes and relations involving only scalar attributes. Section 6.9 then considers relational comparisons. Finally, Section 6.10 offers a brief summary.

Two final preliminary remarks:

■ For obvious reasons, we often say things like "*X* is a restriction of *R*" (where *R* is, specifically, a *relvar*) when what we should more correctly be saying is "*X* is a restriction of the relation that is the current value of relvar *R*," or even "*X* is a variable whose current value is a restriction of the relation that is the current value of relvar *R*." We trust these slightly sloppy shorthands will not cause any confusion.

■ We defer discussion of the SQL analogs of the relational algebra operators to Chapter 7, for reasons to be explained in that chapter.

6.2   CLOSURE REVISITED

As we saw in Chapter 3, the fact that the output from any given relational operation is another relation is referred to as the relational **closure** property. To recap briefly, closure means we can write **nested relational expressions**—i.e., relational expressions in which the operands are themselves represented by relational expressions in turn, of potentially arbitrary complexity. (There is an obvious analogy between the ability to nest relational expressions in the relational algebra and the ability to nest arithmetic expressions in ordinary arithmetic; indeed, the fact that relations are closed under the algebra is important for exactly the same kinds of reasons that the fact that numbers are closed under ordinary arithmetic is important.)

Now, when we discussed closure in Chapter 3, there was one very significant point that we deliberately glossed over. Recall that every relation has two parts, a **heading** and a **body;** loosely speaking, the heading is the attributes and the body is the tuples. Now, the heading for a *base* relation—i.e., the value of a base relvar—is obviously well understood and known to the system, because it is specified as part of the relevant base relvar definition. But what about *derived* relations? For example, consider the expression

    S JOIN P

(which represents the join of suppliers and parts over matching cities, CITY being the only attribute common to the two relations). We know what the body of the result looks like—but what about the heading? Closure dictates that it must *have* a heading, and the system needs to know what it is (in fact, of course, the user does too, as we will see in a moment). In other words, that result must—of course!—be of a well-defined **relation type.** If we are to take closure seriously, therefore, clearly we must define the relational operations in such a way as to guarantee that every operation produces a result with a proper relation type—in particular, with proper attribute names.*

One reason we require every result relation to have proper attribute names is, of course, to allow us to *refer* to those attribute names in subsequent operations—in particular, in operations appearing elsewhere within the overall nested expression. For example, we could not sensibly even *write* an expression such as

    (S JOIN P) WHERE CITY = 'Athens'

if we did not know that the result of evaluating the expression S JOIN P had an attribute called CITY.

What we need, therefore, is a set of (relation) **type inference rules** built into the algebra, such that if we know the (relation) type(s) of the input relation(s) for any given relational operation, we can infer the (relation) type of the output from that operation. Given such rules, it will follow that an arbitrary relational *expression,* no matter how complex, will produce a result that also has a well-defined (relation) type, and in particular a well-defined set of attribute names.

As a preparatory step to achieving this goal, we introduce a new operator, RENAME, whose purpose is (loosely) to rename attributes within a specified relation. More precisely, the RENAME operator takes a given relation and returns another that is identical to the given one except that at least one of its attributes has a different name. (The given relation

---

*We remark that this aspect of the algebra has been much overlooked in the literature (and also, regrettably, in the SQL language and hence in SQL products)—with the notable exception of the treatment found in Hall *et al.* [6.10] and Darwen [6.2]. The version of the algebra presented in this chapter is very much influenced by these two references.

is specified by means of a relational expression, of course, possibly involving other relational operations.) For example, we might write:

```
S RENAME CITY AS SCITY
```

This expression—please note that it *is* an expression, not a "command" or statement, and hence that it can be nested within other expressions—yields a relation having the same heading and body as relation S, except that the city attribute is named SCITY instead of CITY:

S#	SNAME	STATUS	SCITY
S1	Smith	20	London
S2	Jones	10	Paris
S3	Blake	30	Paris
S4	Clark	20	London
S5	Adams	30	Athens

Important: Please note that this RENAME expression has *not* changed the suppliers relvar in the database—it is just an expression, just as (e.g.) S JOIN SP is, and like any other expression it merely produces a certain result (a result that, in this particular case, happens to look very much like the current value of the suppliers relvar).

Here is another example (a "multiple renaming" this time):

```
P RENAME PNAME AS PN, WEIGHT AS WT
```

The result looks like this:

P#	PN	COLOR	WT	CITY
P1	Nut	Red	12.0	London
P2	Bolt	Green	17.0	Paris
P3	Screw	Blue	17.0	Rome
P4	Screw	Red	14.0	London
P5	Cam	Blue	12.0	Paris
P6	Cog	Red	19.0	London

It is worth pointing out explicitly that the availability of RENAME means that (unlike SQL) the relational algebra has no need for qualified attribute names such as S.S#.

6.3 SYNTAX

In this section, we present a concrete syntax (basically the syntax of **Tutorial D**) for relational algebra expressions. *Note:* Most database texts use a somewhat mathematical or "Greek" notation for the relational operators, typically using σ for restriction, π for projection, $\cap$ for intersection, $\bowtie$ ("bow tie") for join, and so on. As you will already have noticed, we prefer to use keywords such as JOIN and WHERE. Keywords make for lengthier expressions, of course, but we think they also make for more user-friendly ones.

```
<relational expression>
    ::=   RELATION { <tuple expression commalist> }
        | <relvar name>
        | <relational operation>
        | ( <relational expression> )
```

A *<relational expression>* is an expression that denotes a relation (meaning a relation *value,* of course). The first format is a *relation selector invocation* (it includes relation literals as a special case); we do not spell out the syntax of *<tuple expression>* in detail here, hoping that examples will prove sufficient to illustrate the general idea. The other formats are meant to be self-explanatory.

```
<relational operation>
    ::=   <project> | <nonproject>
```

We distinguish *<project>*s from *<nonproject>*s in the syntax merely for operator precedence reasons (it is convenient to assign a high precedence to projection).

```
<project>
    ::=   <relational expression>
                  { [ ALL BUT ] <attribute name commalist
```

The *<relational expression>* must not be a *<nonproject>*.

```
<nonproject>
    ::=   <rename>
        | <union> | <intersect> | <minus> | <times>
        | <restrict> | <join> | <divide>

<rename>
    ::=   <relational expression>
                  RENAME <renaming commalist>
```

The *<relational expression>* must not be a *<nonproject>*. For the syntax of *<renaming>*, see the examples in the previous section.

```
<union>
    ::=   <relational expression>
                  UNION <relational expression>
```

The *<relational expression>*s must not be *<nonproject>*s, except that either or both can be another *<union>*.

```
<intersect>
    ::=   <relational expression>
                  INTERSECT <relational expression>
```

The *<relational expression>*s must not be *<nonproject>*s, except that either or both can be another *<intersect>*.

```
<minus>
    ::=   <relational expression>
                  MINUS <relational expression>
```

The *<relational expression>*s must not be *<nonproject>*s.

```
<times>
    ::=    <relational expression>
                   TIMES <relational expression>
```

The *<relational expression>*s must not be *<nonproject>*s, except that either or both can be another *<times>*.

```
<restrict>
    ::=    <relational expression> WHERE <boolean expression>
```

The *<relational expression>* must not be a *<nonproject>*. *Note:* The *<boolean expression>* can include a reference to an attribute of the relation denoted by the *<relational expression>* wherever a selector invocation is allowed (thus, e.g., S WHERE CITY = 'London' is a legal *<restrict>*).

```
<join>
    ::=    <relational expression>
                   JOIN <relational expression>
```

The *<relational expression>*s must not be *<nonproject>*s, except that either or both can be another *<join>*.

```
<divide>
    ::=    <relational expression>
                   DIVIDEBY <relational expression> PER <per>
```

The *<relational expression>*s must not be *<nonproject>*s.

```
<per>
    ::=    <relational expression>
         | ( <relational expression>, <relational expression> )
```

The *<relational expression>*s must not be *<nonproject>*s.

6.4 SEMANTICS

In this section we explain the syntax of Section 6.3, with examples. We consider the operators in the sequence *union, intersection, difference, product, restrict, project, join,* and *divide* (*rename* was covered in Section 6.2).

Union

In mathematics, the union of two sets is the set of all elements belonging to either or both of the original sets. Since a relation is (or, rather, contains) a set, namely a set of tuples, it is obviously possible to construct the union of two such sets; the result will be a set consisting of all tuples appearing in either or both of the original relations. For example, the union of the set of supplier tuples currently appearing in relvar S and the set of part tuples currently appearing in relvar P is certainly a set.

However, although that result is a set, *it is not a relation;* relations cannot contain a mixture of different kinds of tuples, they must be "tuple-homogeneous." And, of course, we do want the result to be a relation, because we want to preserve the closure property. Therefore, the union in the relational algebra is not the usual mathematical union; rather, it is a special kind of union, in which we require the two input relations to be **of the same type**— meaning, for example, that they both contain supplier tuples, or both part tuples, but not a mixture of the two. If the two relations are of the same (relation) type, then we can take their union, and the result will also be a relation of the same (relation) type; in other words, the closure property will be preserved.*

Here then is a definition of the relational union operator: Given two relations *A* and *B* of the same type, the **union** of those two relations, *A* UNION *B,* is a relation of the same type, with body consisting of all tuples *t* such that *t* appears in *A* or in *B* or in both.

Example: Let relations *A* and *B* be as shown in Fig. 6.2 (both are derived from the suppliers relvar S; *A* is the suppliers in London, and *B* is the suppliers who supply part P1, intuitively speaking). Then *A* UNION *B*—see part a. of the figure—is the suppliers who either are located in London or supply part P1 (or both). Notice that the result has three tuples, not four; duplicate tuples are eliminated, by definition. We remark in passing that the only other operation for which this question of duplicate elimination arises is projection (see later in this section).

Intersect

Like union, and for essentially the same reason, the relational intersection operator requires its operands to be of the same type. Given two relations *A* and *B* of the same type, then, the **intersection** of those two relations, *A* INTERSECT *B,* is a relation of the same type, with body consisting of all tuples *t* such that *t* appears in both *A* and *B.*

Example: Again, let *A* and *B* be as shown in Fig. 6.2. Then *A* INTERSECT *B*—see part b. of the figure—is the suppliers who are located in London and supply part P1.

Difference

Like union and intersection, the relational difference operator also requires its operands to be of the same type. Given two relations *A* and *B* of the same type, then, the **difference** between those two relations, *A* MINUS *B* (in that order), is a relation of the same type, with body consisting of all tuples *t* such that *t* appears in *A* and not in *B.*

---

*Historically, most of the database literature (earlier editions of this book included) used the term **union-compatibility** to refer to the notion that the two relations must be of the same type. This term is not very apt, however, for a variety of reasons, the most obvious of which is that the notion does not apply just to union.

A				B			
S#	SNAME	STATUS	CITY	S#	SNAME	STATUS	CITY
S1	Smith	20	London	S1	Smith	20	London
S4	Clark	20	London	S2	Jones	10	Paris

a. *Union*
   (A UNION B)

S#	SNAME	STATUS	CITY
S1	Smith	20	London
S4	Clark	20	London
S2	Jones	10	Paris

b. *Intersection*
   (A INTERSECT B)

S#	SNAME	STATUS	CITY
S1	Smith	20	London

c. *Difference*
   (A MINUS B)

d. *Difference*
   (B MINUS A)

S#	SNAME	STATUS	CITY	S#	SNAME	STATUS	CITY
S4	Clark	20	London	S2	Jones	10	Paris

Fig. 6.2   Union, intersection, and difference examples

Example: Let *A* and *B* again be as shown in Fig. 6.2. Then *A* MINUS *B*—see part c. of the figure—is the suppliers who are located in London and do not supply part P1, and *B* MINUS *A*—see part d. of the figure—is the suppliers who supply part P1 and are not located in London. Observe that MINUS has a directionality to it, just as subtraction does in ordinary arithmetic (e.g., "5 – 2" and "2 – 5" are not the same thing).

Product

In mathematics, the Cartesian product (product for short) of two sets is the set of all ordered pairs such that, in each pair, the first element comes from the first set and the second element comes from the second set. Thus, the Cartesian product of two relations would be a set of ordered pairs of *tuples,* loosely speaking. But again we want to preserve the closure property; in other words, we want the result to contain tuples *per se,* not *ordered pairs* of tuples. Therefore, the relational version of Cartesian product is an *extended form* of the operation, in which each ordered pair of tuples is replaced by the single tuple that is the *union* of the two tuples in question (using "union" in its normal set theory sense, not its special relational sense). That is, given the tuples

    { A1:a1, A2:a2, ..., Am:am }

and

```
{ B1:b1, B2:b2, ..., Bn:bn }
```

the union of the two is the single tuple

```
{ A1:a1, A2:a2, ..., Am:am, B1:b1, B2:b2, ..., Bn:bn }
```

Another problem that occurs in connection with Cartesian product is that (of course) we require the result relation to have a well-formed heading (i.e., to be of a proper relation type). Now, clearly the heading of the result consists of all of the attributes from both of the two input relations. A problem will therefore arise if those two headings have any attribute names in common; if the operation were permitted, the result heading would have two attributes with the same name and would thus not be "well-formed." If we need to construct the Cartesian product of two relations that do have any such common attribute names, therefore, we must use the RENAME operator first to rename attributes appropriately.

We therefore define the (relational) **Cartesian product** of two relations *A* and *B*, *A* TIMES *B*, where *A* and *B* have no common attribute names, to be a relation with a heading that is the (set theory) union of the headings of *A* and *B* and with a body consisting of the set of all tuples *t* such that *t* is the (set theory) union of a tuple appearing in *A* and a tuple appearing in *B*. Note that the cardinality of the result is the product of the cardinalities of *A* and *B*, and the degree of the result is the sum of their degrees.

Example: Let relations *A* and *B* be as shown in Fig. 6.3 (*A* is all current supplier numbers and *B* is all current part numbers, intuitively speaking). Then *A* TIMES *B*—see the lower part of the figure—is all current supplier-number/part-number pairs.

A

S#
S1
S2
S3
S4
S5

B

P#
P1
P2
P3
P4
P5
P6

Cartesian product (A TIMES B)

S#	P#
S1	P1
S1	P2
S1	P3
S1	P4
S1	P5
S1	P6
..	..
..	..
S2	P1
S2	P2
S2	P3
S2	P4
S2	P5
S2	P6
..	..
..	..
S3	P1
S3	P2
S3	P3
S3	P4
S3	P5
S3	P6
..	..
..	..
S4	P1
S4	P2
S4	P3
S4	P4
S4	P5
S4	P6
..	..
..	..
S5	P1
S5	P2
S5	P3
S5	P4
S5	P5
S5	P6

Fig. 6.3 Cartesian product example

Restrict

Let relation *A* have attributes *X* and *Y* (and possibly others), and let Θ be an operator—typically "=", ">", etc.—such that the **condition** *X* Θ *Y* is well defined and, given particular values for *X* and *Y,* evaluates to a truth value (*true* or *false*). Then the Θ-**restriction** of relation *A* on attributes *X* and *Y* (in that order)—

```
S WHERE CITY = 'London'
```

—is a relation with the same heading as *A* and with body consisting of all tuples *t* of *A* such that the condition *X* Θ *Y* evaluates to *true* for that tuple *t*.

Points arising:

1. A selector invocation (in particular, a literal) can appear in the condition in place of either *X* or *Y* (or both); indeed, such is the normal case. However, we should explain that this "normal case" is really just shorthand. For example, the restriction

```
S WHERE CITY = 'London'
```

is really shorthand for an expression of the form

```
( EXTEND S ADD 'London' AS TEMP ) WHERE CITY = TEMP
```

(where the name TEMP is arbitrary). See the discussion of EXTEND in Section 6.7.

2. A condition of the form *b* (where *b* is a boolean selector invocation) is also legal.

3. Restriction as we have defined it permits only a single condition in the WHERE clause. By virtue of the closure property, however, it is possible to extend it unambiguously to a form in which the expression in the WHERE clause consists of an arbitrary boolean combination of such conditions, thanks to the following equivalences:

```
A WHERE c1 AND c2  ≡  ( A WHERE c1 ) INTERSECT ( A WHERE c2 )

A WHERE c1 OR c2   ≡  ( A WHERE c1 ) UNION ( A WHERE c2 )

A WHERE NOT c      ≡  A MINUS ( A WHERE c )
```

Henceforth, therefore, we will assume that the *<boolean expression>* in the WHERE clause of a restriction consists of such an arbitrary combination of conditions (with parentheses if necessary in order to indicate a desired order of evaluation), where each condition in turn involves only attributes of the pertinent relation or selector invocations or both. Note that such a *<boolean expression>* can be established as *true* or *false* for a given tuple by examining just that tuple in isolation. Such a *<boolean expression>* is said to be a **restriction condition.**

The restriction operator effectively yields a "horizontal" subset of a given relation— that is, that subset of the tuples of the given relation for which some specified restriction condition is satisfied. Some examples are given in Fig. 6.4.

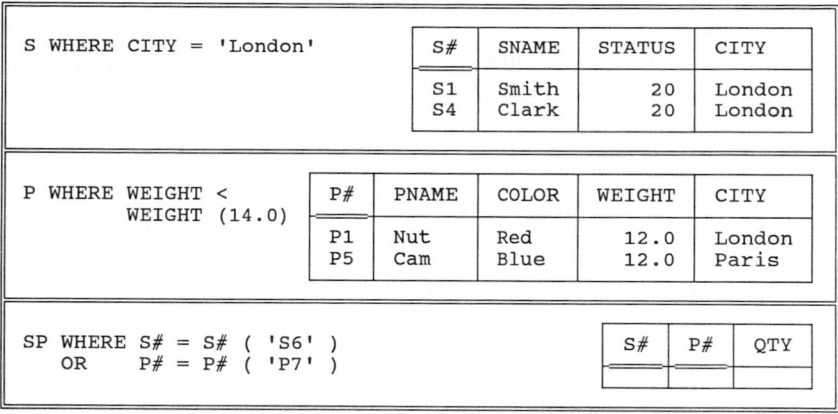

S WHERE CITY = 'London'	S#	SNAME	STATUS	CITY
	S1	Smith	20	London
	S4	Clark	20	London

P WHERE WEIGHT < WEIGHT (14.0)	P#	PNAME	COLOR	WEIGHT	CITY
	P1	Nut	Red	12.0	London
	P5	Cam	Blue	12.0	Paris

SP WHERE S# = S# ('S6') OR P# = P# ('P7')	S#	P#	QTY

Fig. 6.4   Restriction examples

Project

Let relation *A* have attributes *X, Y, ..., Z* (and possibly others). Then the **projection** of relation *A* on *X, Y, ..., Z*—

```
A { X, Y, ..., Z }
```

—is a relation with:

- A heading derived from the heading of *A* by removing all attributes not mentioned in the set {*X,Y,...,Z*}, and
- A body consisting of all tuples {*X:x,Y:y,...,Z:z*} such that a tuple appears in *A* with *X* value *x*, *Y* value *y*, ..., and *Z* value *z*.

The projection operator thus effectively yields a "vertical" subset of a given relation—that is, that subset obtained by removing all attributes not mentioned in the specified commalist of attribute names and then eliminating duplicate (sub)tuples from what is left.

Points arising:

1. No attribute can be mentioned more than once in the attribute name commalist (why not?).
2. If the attribute name commalist mentions all of the attributes of *A*, the projection is an *identity* projection.
3. A projection of the form *A*{ }—i.e., one in which the attribute name commalist is empty—is legal. It represents a *nullary* projection. See Exercises 6.8–6.10 at the end of the chapter.

Some examples of projection are given in Fig. 6.5. Notice in the first example (the projection of suppliers over CITY) that, although relvar S currently contains five tuples and

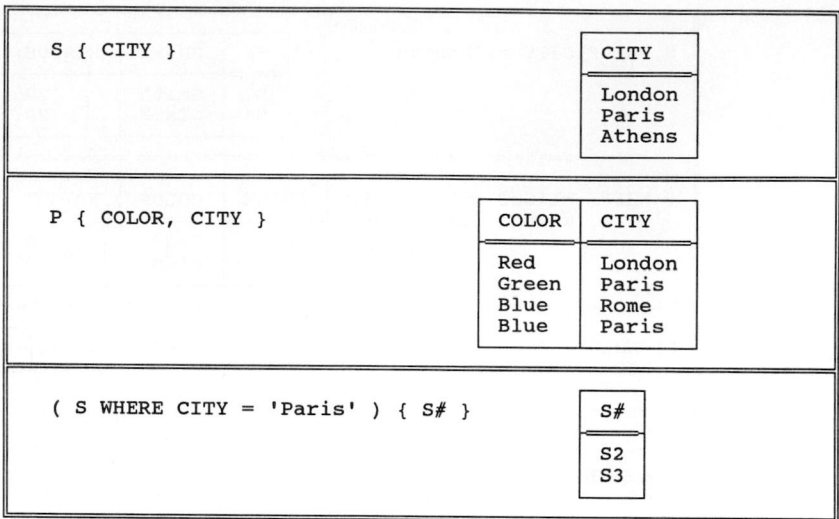

Fig. 6.5   Projection examples

hence five cities, there are only three cities in the result—duplicates (duplicates *tuples,* that is) are eliminated. Analogous remarks apply to the other examples also, of course.

In practice, it is often convenient to be able to specify, not the attributes over which the projection is to be taken, but rather the ones that are to be "projected away" (i.e., removed). Instead of saying "project relation P over the P#, PNAME, COLOR, and CITY attributes," for example, we might say "project the WEIGHT attribute away from relation P," as here:

```
P { ALL BUT WEIGHT }
```

Join

Joins come in several different varieties. Easily the most important, however, is the so-called *natural* join—so much so, in fact, that the unqualified term *join* is invariably taken to mean the natural join specifically, and we adopt that usage in this book. Here then is the definition (it is a little abstract, but you should already be familiar with natural join at an intuitive level from our discussions in Chapter 3). Let relations A and B have headings

```
{ X1, X2, ..., Xm, Y1, Y2, ..., Yn }
```

and

```
{ Y1, Y2, ..., Yn, Z1, Z2, ..., Zp }
```

respectively; i.e., the Y attributes $Y1, Y2, \ldots, Yn$ (only) are common to the two relations, the X attributes $X1, X2, \ldots, Xm$ are the other attributes of A, and the Z attributes $Z1, Z2, \ldots, Zp$ are the other attributes of *B*. Now consider $\{X1,X2,\ldots,Xm\}$, $\{Y1,Y2,\ldots,Yn\}$, and $\{Z1,Z2,\ldots,Zp\}$ as three composite attributes *X, Y,* and *Z,* respectively. Then the **natural join** of *A* and *B*—

```
A JOIN B
```

—is a relation with heading $\{X,Y,Z\}$ and body consisting of the set of all tuples $\{X{:}x,Y{:}y,Z{:}z\}$ such that a tuple appears in *A* with *X* value *x* and *Y* value *y* and a tuple appears in *B* with *Y* value *y* and *Z* value *z*.

An example of a natural join (the natural join S JOIN P, over the common attribute CITY) is given in Fig. 6.6.

S#	SNAME	STATUS	CITY	P#	PNAME	COLOR	WEIGHT
S1	Smith	20	London	P1	Nut	Red	12.0
S1	Smith	20	London	P4	Screw	Red	14.0
S1	Smith	20	London	P6	Cog	Red	19.0
S2	Jones	10	Paris	P2	Bolt	Green	17.0
S2	Jones	10	Paris	P5	Cam	Blue	12.0
S3	Blake	30	Paris	P2	Bolt	Green	17.0
S3	Blake	30	Paris	P5	Cam	Blue	12.0
S4	Clark	20	London	P1	Nut	Red	12.0
S4	Clark	20	London	P4	Screw	Red	14.0
S4	Clark	20	London	P6	Cog	Red	19.0

Fig. 6.6   The natural join S JOIN P

Note: We have illustrated the point several times—indeed, it is illustrated by Fig. 6.6—but it is still worth stating explicitly that joins are *not* always between a foreign key and a matching primary key, even though such joins are a very common and important special case.

Now we turn to the Θ-*join* operation. This operation is intended for those occasions (comparatively rare, but by no means unknown) where we need to join two relations together on the basis of some comparison operator other than equality. Let relations *A* and *B* satisfy the requirements for Cartesian product (i.e., they have no attribute names in common); let *A* have an attribute *X* and let *B* have an attribute *Y*, and let *X, Y,* and Θ satisfy the requirements for restriction. Then the Θ-**join** of relation *A* on attribute *X* with relation *B* on attribute *Y* is defined to be the result of evaluating the expression

```
( A TIMES B ) WHERE X θ Y
```

In other words, it is a relation with the same heading as the Cartesian product of *A* and *B*, and with a body consisting of the set of all tuples *t* such that *t* appears in that Cartesian product and the condition "$X \Theta Y$" evaluates to *true* for that tuple *t*.

By way of example, suppose we wish to compute the *greater-than join* of relation S on CITY with relation P on CITY (so Θ here is ">"; we assume that ">" makes sense for cities, and interpret it to mean simply "greater in alphabetic ordering"). An appropriate relational expression is as follows:

```
( ( S RENAME CITY AS SCITY ) TIMES
  ( P RENAME CITY AS PCITY ) )
                 WHERE SCITY > PCITY
```

Note the attribute renaming in this example. (Of course, it would be sufficient to rename just one of the two CITY attributes; the only reason for renaming both is symmetry.) The result of the overall expression is shown in Fig. 6.7.

If Θ is "=", the Θ-join is called an **equijoin.** It follows from the definition that the result of an equijoin must include two attributes with the property that the values of those two attributes are equal in every tuple in the relation. If one of those two attributes is projected away and the other renamed appropriately (if necessary), the result is the natural join! For example, the expression representing the natural join of suppliers and parts (over cities)—

```
S JOIN P
```

—is equivalent to the following more complex expression:

```
( ( S TIMES ( P RENAME CITY AS PCITY ) )
               WHERE CITY = PCITY )
                            { ALL BUT PCITY }
```

Note: **Tutorial D** does not include direct support for the Θ-join operator because (a) it is not needed very often in practice, and in any case (b) it is not a primitive operator, as we have seen.

S#	SNAME	STATUS	SCITY	P#	PNAME	COLOR	WEIGHT	PCITY
S2	Jones	10	Paris	P1	Nut	Red	12.0	London
S2	Jones	10	Paris	P4	Screw	Red	14.0	London
S2	Jones	10	Paris	P6	Cog	Red	19.0	London
S3	Blake	30	Paris	P1	Nut	Red	12.0	London
S3	Blake	30	Paris	P4	Screw	Red	14.0	London
S3	Blake	30	Paris	P6	Cog	Red	19.0	London

Fig. 6.7   Greater-than join of suppliers and parts on cities

Divide

Reference [6.3] defines two distinct "divide" operators that it calls the Small Divide and the Great Divide, respectively. In **Tutorial D**, a *<divide>* in which the *<per>* consists of just one *<relational expression>* is a Small Divide, a *<divide>* in which it consists of a parenthesized commalist of two *<relational expression>*s is a Great Divide. The description that follows applies to the Small Divide only, and only to a particular limited form of the Small Divide at that. See reference [6.3] for a discussion of the Great Divide and for further details regarding the Small Divide as well.

We should say too that the version of the Small Divide as discussed here is not the same as Codd's original operator—in fact, it is an improved version that overcomes certain difficulties that arose with that original operator in connection with empty relations. It is also not the same as the version discussed in the first few editions of this book.

Here then is the definition. Let relations *A* and *B* have headings

```
{ X1, X2, ..., Xm }
```

and

```
{ Y1, Y2, ..., Yn }
```

respectively (i.e., *A* and *B* have disjoint headings), and let relation *C* have heading

```
{ X1, X2, ..., Xm, Y1, Y2, ..., Yn }
```

(i.e., *C* has a heading that is the union of the headings of *A* and *B*). Let us now regard $\{X1,X2,...,Xm\}$ and $\{Y1,Y2,...,Yn\}$ as *composite* attributes *X* and *Y,* respectively. Then the **division** of *A* by *B* per *C* (where *A* is the dividend, *B* is the divisor, and *C* is the "mediator")—

```
A DIVIDEBY B PER C
```

—is a relation with heading $\{X\}$ and body consisting of all tuples $\{X:x\}$ such that a tuple $\{X:x,Y:y\}$ appears in *C* for all tuples $\{Y:y\}$ appearing in *B*. In other words, the result consists of those *X* values from *A* whose corresponding *Y* values in *C* include all *Y* values from *B,* loosely speaking.

Fig. 6.8 (overleaf) shows some simple examples of division. The dividend (DEND) in each case is the projection of the current value of relvar S over S#; the mediator (MED) in each case is the projection of the current value of relvar SP over S# and P#; the three divisors (DOR) are as indicated in the figure. Notice the last example in particular, in which the divisor is a relation containing part numbers for all currently known parts; the result (obviously) shows supplier numbers for suppliers who supply all of those parts. As this example suggests, the DIVIDEBY operator is intended for queries of this same general nature; in fact, whenever the natural language version of the query contains the word "all" ("Get suppliers who supply *all* parts"), it is a strong possibility that division will be involved.* However, it is worth pointing out that such queries are often more readily expressed in terms of relational comparisons anyway (see Section 6.9).

Associativity and Commutativity

It is easy to verify that UNION is **associative**—that is, if *A, B,* and *C* are arbitrary relational expressions yielding relations of the same type, then the expressions

```
( A UNION B ) UNION C
```

---

*Indeed, division was specifically intended by Codd to be an algebraic counterpart to the *universal quantifier*—see Chapter 7—much as projection was intended to be an algebraic counterpart to the *existential* quantifier.

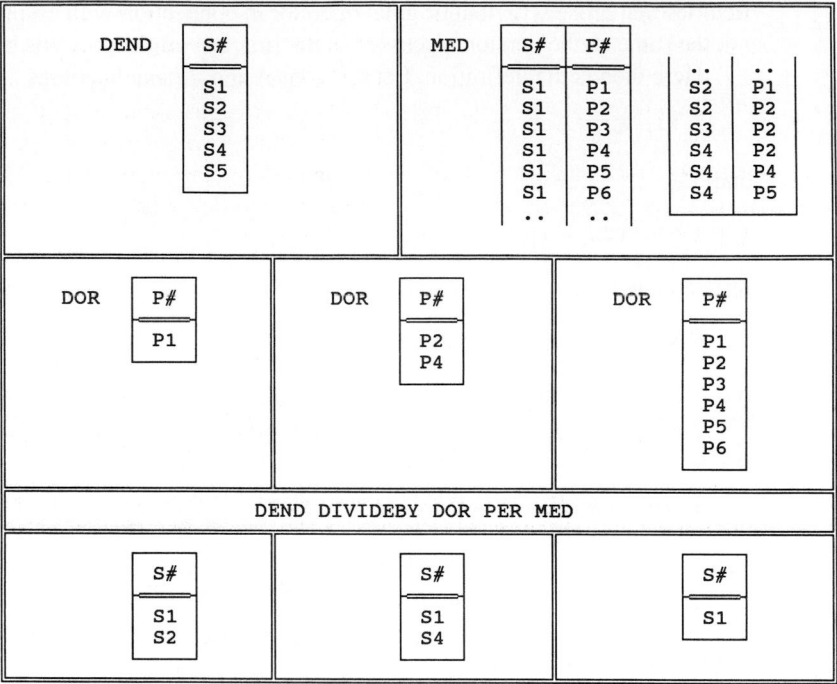

Fig. 6.8 Division examples

and

```
A UNION ( B UNION C )
```

are logically equivalent. For convenience, therefore, we allow a sequence of UNIONs to be written without any embedded parentheses; i.e., each of the foregoing expressions can be unambiguously simplified to just

```
A UNION B UNION C
```

Analogous remarks apply to INTERSECT, TIMES, and JOIN (but not to MINUS).

We remark too that UNION, INTERSECT, TIMES, and JOIN (but not MINUS) are also **commutative**—that is, the expressions

```
A UNION B
```

and

```
B UNION A
```

are also logically equivalent, and similarly for INTERSECT, TIMES, and JOIN. *Note:* We will revisit the whole question of associativity and commutativity in Chapter 17. Regarding TIMES, incidentally, we note that the Cartesian product operation of set theory is neither associative nor commutative, but (as we have just seen) the relational version is both.

Finally, we remark that if *A* and *B* have no attribute names in common, then *A* JOIN *B* is equivalent to *A* TIMES *B* [5.5]—i.e., natural join degenerates to Cartesian product in this case. Indeed, the version of **Tutorial D** defined in reference [3.3] includes no direct support for the TIMES operator for this very reason.

6.5 EXAMPLES

In this section we present a few examples of the use of relational algebra expressions in formulating queries. We recommend that you check these examples against the sample data of Fig. 3.8.

6.5.1 Get supplier names for suppliers who supply part P2.

```
( ( SP JOIN S ) WHERE P# = P# ( 'P2' ) ) { SNAME }
```

Explanation: First the natural join of relations SP and S over supplier numbers is constructed, which has the effect—conceptually—of extending each SP tuple with the corresponding supplier information (i.e., the appropriate SNAME, STATUS, and CITY values). That join is then restricted to just those tuples for part P2. Finally, that restriction is projected over SNAME. The final result has just one attribute, called SNAME.

6.5.2 Get supplier names for suppliers who supply at least one red part.

```
( ( ( P WHERE COLOR = COLOR ( 'Red' ) )
              JOIN SP ) { S# } JOIN S ) { SNAME }
```

The sole attribute of the result is SNAME again.

Here, by the way, is a different formulation of the same query:

```
( ( ( P WHERE COLOR = COLOR ( 'Red' ) ) { P# }
              JOIN SP ) JOIN S ) { SNAME }
```

The example thus illustrates the important point that there will often be several different ways of formulating any given query. See Chapter 17 for a discussion of some of the implications of this point.

6.5.3 Get supplier names for suppliers who supply all parts.

```
( ( S { S# } DIVIDEBY P { P# } PER SP { S#, P# } )
                              JOIN S ) { SNAME }
```

Once again the result has a sole attribute called SNAME.

6.5.4 Get supplier numbers for suppliers who supply at least all those parts supplied by supplier S2.

```
S { S# } DIVIDEBY ( SP WHERE S# = S# ( 'S2' ) ) { P# }
                                       PER SP { S#, P# }
```

The result has a sole attribute called S#.

6.5.5 Get all pairs of supplier numbers such that the two suppliers concerned are "colocated" (i.e., located in the same city).

```
( ( ( S RENAME S# AS SA ) { SA, CITY } JOIN
    ( S RENAME S# AS SB ) { SB, CITY } )
        WHERE SA < SB ) { SA, SB }
```

The result has two attributes, called SA and SB (of course, it would be sufficient to rename just one of the two S# attributes; we have renamed both for symmetry). *Note:* We have assumed that the operator "<" has been defined for type S#. The purpose of the condition SA < SB is twofold:

- It eliminates pairs of supplier numbers of the form (x,x);
- It guarantees that the pairs (x,y) and (y,x) will not both appear.

We show another formulation of this query in order to illustrate the use of *WITH* to introduce shorthand names for expressions and thereby to simplify the business of writing lengthy queries. (In fact, we did illustrate WITH once before, in Chapter 5, Section 5.2—subsection "Operator Definition.")

```
WITH ( S RENAME S# AS SA ) { SA, CITY } AS T1,
     ( S RENAME S# AS SB ) { SB, CITY } AS T2,
     T1 JOIN T2 AS T3,
     T3 WHERE SA < SB AS T4 :
     T4 { SA, SB }
```

WITH allows us to think about large, complicated expressions in a step-at-a-time fashion, and yet it does not in any way violate the nonprocedurality of the relational algebra. We will elaborate on this point in the discussion following the next example.

6.5.6 Get supplier names for suppliers who do not supply part P2.

```
( ( S { S# } MINUS ( SP WHERE P# = P# ( 'P2' ) ) { S# } )
                                      JOIN S ) { SNAME }
```

The result has a sole attribute called SNAME.

As promised, we elaborate on this example in order to illustrate another point. It is not always easy to see immediately how to formulate a given query as a single nested expression. Nor should it be necessary to do so, either. Here is a step-at-a-time formulation of Example 6.5.6:

```
WITH S { S# } AS T1,
     SP WHERE P# = P# ( 'P2' ) AS T2,
     T2 { S# } AS T3,
     T1 MINUS T3 AS T4,
     T4 JOIN S AS T5,
     T5 { SNAME } AS T6 :
     T6
```

T6 denotes the desired result. *Explanation:* Names introduced by a WITH clause—i.e., names of the form Ti, in the example—are assumed to be local to the statement containing that clause. Now, if the system supports "lazy evaluation" (as, for example, the PRTV system did [6.9]), then breaking the overall query down into a sequence of steps in this fashion need have *no* undesirable performance implications. Instead, the query can be processed as follows:

- The expressions preceding the colon require no immediate evaluation by the system—all the system has to do is remember them, along with the names introduced by the corresponding AS clauses.

- The expression following the colon denotes the final result of the query (in the example, that expression is just "T6"). When it reaches this point, the system cannot delay evaluation any longer but instead must somehow compute the desired value (i.e., the value of T6).

- In order to evaluate T6, which is the projection of T5 over SNAME, the system must first evaluate T5; in order to evaluate T5, which is the join of T4 and S, the system must first evaluate T4; and so on. In other words, the system effectively has to evaluate the original nested expression, exactly as if the user had written that nested expression in the first place.

See the next section for a brief discussion of the general question of evaluating such nested expressions, also Chapter 17 for an extended treatment of the same topic.

6.6   WHAT IS THE ALGEBRA FOR?

To summarize this chapter so far: We have defined a *relational algebra,* i.e., a collection of operations on relations. The operations in question are union, intersect, difference, product, restrict, project, join, and divide, plus an attribute renaming operator, RENAME (this is essentially the set that Codd originally defined in reference [6.1], except for RENAME). We have also presented a syntax for those operations, and used that syntax as a basis for a number of examples and illustrations.

As our discussions have implied, however, Codd's eight operators do not constitute a *minimal* set (nor were they ever meant to), because some of them are not primitive—they can be defined in terms of the others. For example, the three operators join, intersect, and divide can be defined in terms of the other five (see Exercise 6.2). Since none of those other five—restrict, project, product, union, and difference*—can be defined in terms of the remaining four (see Exercise 6.4), we can regard them as a **primitive** or minimal set (not necessarily the only one, of course). In practice, however, the other three operators (especially join) are so useful that a good case can be made for supporting them directly.

We are now in a position to clarify an important point. Although we never said as much explicitly, the body of the chapter up to now has certainly suggested that the primary purpose of the algebra is merely *data retrieval.* Such is not the case, however. The fundamental intent of the algebra is to allow **the writing of relational expressions.** Those expressions in turn are intended to serve a variety of purposes, including retrieval of course, but not limited to that purpose alone. The following list—which is not meant to be exhaustive—indicates some possible applications for such expressions:

- Defining a scope for **retrieval**—i.e., defining the data to be fetched in some retrieval operation (as already discussed at length);

- Defining a scope for **update**—i.e., defining the data to be inserted, changed, or deleted in some update operation (see Chapter 5);

- Defining **integrity constraints**—i.e., defining some constraint that the database must satisfy (see Chapter 8);

- Defining **derived relvars**—i.e., defining the data to be included in a view or snapshot (see Chapter 9);

- Defining **stability requirements**—i.e., defining the data that is to be the scope of some concurrency control operation (see Chapter 15);

- Defining **security constraints**—i.e., defining the data over which authorization of some kind is to be granted (see Chapter 16).

In general, in fact, the expressions serve as *a high-level, symbolic representation of the user's intent* (with regard to some particular query, for example). And precisely because they are high-level and symbolic, they can be manipulated in accordance with a variety of high-level, symbolic **transformation rules.** For example, the expression

```
( ( SP JOIN S ) WHERE P# = P# ( 'P2' ) ) { SNAME }
```

("names of suppliers who supply part P2"—Example 6.5.1) can be transformed into the logically equivalent, but probably more efficient, expression

```
( ( SP WHERE P# = P# ( 'P2' ) ) JOIN S ) { SNAME }
```

(*Exercise:* In what sense is the second expression probably more efficient? Why only "probably"?)

---

*Since (as we have seen) product is a special case of join, we could replace product by join in this list of primitives. What is more, we really need to add RENAME to the list as well, because our algebra (unlike that defined in reference [6.1]) relies on attribute naming instead of ordinal position.

The algebra thus serves as a convenient basis for **optimization** (refer back to Chapter 3, Section 3.5, if you need to refresh your memory regarding the concept of optimization). That is, even if the user states the query in the first of the two forms shown above, the optimizer should convert it into the second form before executing it (ideally, the performance of a given query should *not* depend on the particular form in which the user happens to state it). See Chapter 17 for further discussion.

We conclude this section by noting that, precisely because of its fundamental nature, the algebra is often used as a kind of *yardstick* against which the expressive power of some given language can be measured. Basically, a language is said to be **relationally complete** [6.1] if it is at least as powerful as the algebra—i.e., if its expressions permit the definition of every relation that can be defined by means of expressions of the algebra (the *original* algebra, that is, as described in previous sections). We will discuss this notion of relational completeness in more detail in the next chapter.

6.7 ADDITIONAL OPERATORS

Numerous writers have proposed new algebraic operators since Codd defined his original eight. In this section we examine a few such operators—SEMIJOIN, SEMIMINUS, EXTEND, SUMMARIZE, and TCLOSE—in some detail. In terms of our **Tutorial D** syntax, these operators involve five new forms of *<nonproject>*, with specifics as follows:

```
<semijoin>
     ::=    <relational expression>
                      SEMIJOIN <relational expression>

<semiminus>
     ::=    <relational expression>
                      SEMIMINUS <relational expression>

<extend>
     ::=    EXTEND <relational expression>
                ADD <extend add commalist>

<extend add>
     ::=    <expression> AS <attribute name>

<summarize>
     ::=    SUMMARIZE <relational expression>
                PER <relational expression>
                ADD <summarize add commalist>

<summarize add>
     ::=    <summary type> [ ( <scalar expression> ) ]
                                  AS <attribute name>

<summary type>
     ::=    COUNT   | SUM  | AVG  | MAX | MIN | ALL | ANY
          | COUNTD  | SUMD | AVGD

<tclose>
     ::=    TCLOSE <relational expression>
```

The various <*relational expression*>s mentioned in the foregoing BNF production rules must not be <*nonproject*>s.

Semijoin

Let *A, B, X, Y,* and *Z* be as defined in the subsection "Join" in Section 6.4. Then the **semijoin** of *A* with *B* (in that order), *A* SEMIJOIN *B,* is defined to be equivalent to

```
( A JOIN B ) { X, Y }
```

In other words, the semijoin of *A* with *B* is the join of *A* and *B,* projected over the attributes of *A.* The body of the result is thus (loosely) the tuples of *A* that have a counterpart in *B.*

   Example: Get S#, SNAME, STATUS, and CITY for suppliers who supply part P2:

```
S SEMIJOIN ( SP WHERE P# = P# ( 'P2' ) )
```

Semidifference

Again, let *A, B, X, Y,* and *Z* be as defined in the subsection "Join" in Section 6.4. Then the **semidifference** between *A* and *B* (in that order), *A* SEMIMINUS *B,* is defined to be equivalent to

```
A MINUS ( A SEMIJOIN B )
```

The body of the result is thus (loosely) the tuples of *A* that have no counterpart in *B.*

   Example: Get S#, SNAME, STATUS, and CITY for suppliers who do not supply part P2:

```
S SEMIMINUS ( SP WHERE P# = P# ( 'P2' ) )
```

Extend

You might have noticed that the algebra as described so far has no computational capabilities (as that term is conventionally understood). In practice, however, such capabilities are obviously desirable. For example, we would like to be able to retrieve the value of an arithmetic expression such as WEIGHT * 454, or to refer to such a value in a WHERE clause (recall that part weights are given in pounds; the expression WEIGHT * 454 will convert such a weight to grams*). The purpose of the **extend** operation is to support such capabilities. More precisely, EXTEND takes a relation and returns another that is identical to the given one except that it includes an additional attribute, values of which are

---

We assume for the sake of the example that "" is a legal operation between weights and integers. What is the type of the result of such an operation?

obtained by evaluating some specified computational expression. For example, we might write:

```
EXTEND P ADD ( WEIGHT * 454 ) AS GMWT
```

This expression—please note that it *is* an expression, not a "command" or statement, and hence can be nested within other expressions—yields a relation with the same heading as P, except that it additionally includes an attribute called GMWT. Each tuple of that relation is the same as the corresponding tuple of P, except that it additionally includes a GMWT value, computed in accordance with the specified arithmetic expression. See Fig. 6.9.

P#	PNAME	COLOR	WEIGHT	CITY	GMWT
P1	Nut	Red	12.0	London	5448.0
P2	Bolt	Green	17.0	Paris	7718.0
P3	Screw	Blue	17.0	Rome	7718.0
P4	Screw	Red	14.0	London	6356.0
P5	Cam	Blue	12.0	Paris	5448.0
P6	Cog	Red	19.0	London	8626.0

Fig. 6.9   An example of EXTEND

Important: Please note that this EXTEND expression has *not* changed the parts relvar in the database; it is just an expression, just as (e.g.) S JOIN SP is, and like any other expression it merely produces a certain result—a result that, in this particular case, happens to look rather like the current value of the parts relvar. (In other words, EXTEND is *not* a relational algebra analog of SQL's ALTER TABLE.)

Now we can use attribute GMWT in projections, restrictions, etc. For example:

```
( ( EXTEND P ADD ( WEIGHT * 454 ) AS GMWT )
        WHERE GMWT > WEIGHT ( 10000.0 ) ) { ALL BUT GMWT }
```

Note: Of course, a more user-friendly language would allow the computational expression to appear directly in the WHERE clause, as here:

```
P WHERE ( WEIGHT * 454 ) > WEIGHT ( 10000.0 )
```

However, such a capability is really just syntactic sugar.

In general, then, the value of the expression

```
EXTEND A ADD exp AS Z
```

is defined to be a relation (a) with heading equal to the heading of *A* extended with the new attribute *Z* and (b) with body consisting of all tuples *t* such that *t* is a tuple of *A* extended with a value for the new attribute *Z* that is computed by evaluating the expression *exp* on that tuple of *A*. Relation *A* must not have an attribute called *Z,* and exp must not refer to *Z.*

Observe that the result has cardinality equal to that of *A* and degree equal to that of *A* plus one. The type of *Z* in that result is the type of *exp*.

Here are some more examples:

1. `EXTEND S ADD 'Supplier' AS TAG`

   This expression effectively tags each tuple of the current value of relvar S with the character string value "Supplier" (a literal—or, more generally, a selector invocation— is a special case of a computational expression, of course).

2. `EXTEND ( P JOIN SP ) ADD ( WEIGHT * QTY ) AS SHIPWT`

   This example illustrates the application of EXTEND to the result of a relational expression that is more complicated than just a simple relvar name.

3. `( EXTEND S ADD CITY AS SCITY ) { ALL BUT CITY }`

   An attribute name such as CITY is also a legal computational expression. Observe that this particular example is equivalent to

   `S RENAME CITY AS SCITY`

   In other words, RENAME is not primitive!—it can be defined in terms of EXTEND (and project). We would not want to discard our familiar RENAME operator, of course, for usability reasons, but it is at least interesting to note that it is really just shorthand.

4. `EXTEND P ADD WEIGHT * 454 AS GMWT, WEIGHT * 16 AS OZWT`

   This example illustrates a "multiple EXTEND."

5. `EXTEND S`
   `ADD COUNT ( ( SP RENAME S# AS X ) WHERE X = S# )`
   `AS NP`

   The result of this expression is shown in Fig. 6.10 (opposite). *Explanation:*

   ■ For a given supplier tuple in the current value of relvar S, the expression

   `( ( SP RENAME S# AS X ) WHERE X = S# )`

   yields the set of shipment tuples corresponding to that supplier tuple in the current value of relvar SP.

   ■ The **aggregate operator** COUNT is then applied to that set of shipment tuples and returns the corresponding cardinality (which is a scalar value, of course).

Attribute NP in the result thus represents the number of parts supplied by the supplier identified by the corresponding S# value. Notice the NP value for supplier S5 in particular; the set of SP tuples for supplier S5 is empty, of course, and so the COUNT invocation returns zero.

We elaborate briefly on this question of aggregate operators. The purpose of such an operator, in general, is to derive a single scalar value from the values appearing in some specified attribute of some specified relation. Typical examples are COUNT,

S#	SNAME	STATUS	CITY	NP
S1	Smith	20	London	6
S2	Jones	10	Paris	2
S3	Blake	30	Paris	1
S4	Clark	20	London	3
S5	Adams	30	Athens	0

Fig. 6.10   Another EXTEND example

SUM, AVG, MAX, MIN, ALL, and ANY. In **Tutorial D,** an *<aggregate operator invocation>*—which, since it returns a scalar value, is a special case of a *<scalar expression>*—takes the general form

```
<op name> ( <relational expression> [, <attribute name> ] )
```

If the *<op name>* is COUNT, the *<attribute name>* is irrelevant and must be omitted; otherwise, it can be omitted if and only if the *<relational expression>* denotes a relation of degree one, in which case the sole attribute of the result of that *<relational expression>* is assumed by default. Here are a couple of examples:

```
SUM ( SP WHERE S# = S# ( 'S1' ), QTY )
SUM ( ( SP WHERE S# = S# ( 'S1' ) ) { QTY } )
```

Note the difference between these two—the first gives the total of all shipment quantities for supplier S1, the second gives the total of all *distinct* shipment quantities for supplier S1.

If the argument to an aggregate operator happens to be an empty set, COUNT (as we have seen) returns zero, and so does SUM; MAX and MIN return, respectively, the lowest and the highest value in the relevant domain; ALL and ANY return *true* and *false,* respectively; and AVG raises an exception.

Summarize

We should begin this subsection by saying that the version of SUMMARIZE discussed here is not the same as that discussed in earlier editions of this book—in fact, it is an improved version that overcomes certain difficulties that arose with that earlier version in connection with empty relations.

As we have seen, the *extend* operator provides a way of incorporating "horizontal" or "row-wise" computations into the relational algebra. The **summarize** operator performs the analogous function for "vertical" or "column-wise" computations. For example, the expression

```
SUMMARIZE SP PER SP { P# } ADD SUM ( QTY ) AS TOTQTY
```

P#	TOTQTY
P1	600
P2	1000
P3	400
P4	500
P5	500
P6	100

Fig. 6.11   An example of SUMMARIZE

evaluates to a relation with heading {P#,TOTQTY}, in which there is one tuple for each P# value in the projection SP{P#}, containing that P# value and the corresponding total quantity (see Fig. 6.11). In other words, relation SP is conceptually grouped into *sets* of tuples, one set for each P# value in P{P#}, and then each group is used to generate one result tuple.

In general, the value of the expression

```
SUMMARIZE A PER B ADD summary AS Z
```

is defined as follows:

- First, *B* must be of the same type as some projection of *A;* i.e., every attribute of *B* must be an attribute of *A.* Let the attributes of that projection (equivalently, of *B*) be *A1, A2, …, An.*

- The heading of the result consists of the attributes *A1, A2, …, An* plus the new attribute *Z.*

- The body of the result consists of all tuples *t* such that *t* is a tuple of *B* extended with a value for the new attribute *Z.* That new *Z* value is computed by evaluating *summary* over all tuples of *A* that have the same values for *A1, A2, …, An* as does tuple *t.* (Of course, if no tuples of *A* have the same values for *A1, A2, …, An* as tuple *t* does, *summary* will be evaluated over an empty set.) Relation *B* must not have an attribute called *Z,* and *summary* must not refer to *Z.* Observe that the result has cardinality equal to that of *B* and degree equal to that of *B* plus one. The type of *Z* in that result is the type of *summary.*

Here is another example:

```
SUMMARIZE ( P JOIN SP ) PER P { CITY } ADD COUNT AS NSP
```

The result looks like this:

CITY	NSP
London	5
Paris	6
Rome	1

In other words, the result contains one tuple for each of the three part cities (London, Paris, and Rome), showing in each case the number of shipments of parts stored in that city.

Points arising:

1. Our syntax allows "multiple SUMMARIZEs." For example:

```
SUMMARIZE SP PER P { P# } ADD SUM ( QTY ) AS TOTQTY,
                            AVG ( QTY ) AS AVGQTY
```

2. The general form of *<summarize>* (to repeat) is as follows:

```
SUMMARIZE <relational expression>
        PER <relational expression>
                ADD <summarize add commalist>
```

Each *<summarize add>* in turn takes the form:

```
<summary type> [ ( <scalar expression> ) ] AS <attribute name>
```

Typical legal *<summary type>*s are COUNT, SUM, AVG, MAX, MIN, ALL, ANY, COUNTD, SUMD, and AVGD. The "D" ("distinct") in COUNTD, SUMD, and AVGD means "eliminate redundant duplicate values before performing the summary." The *<scalar expression>* can include references to attributes of the relation denoted by the *<relational expression>* immediately following the keyword SUMMARIZE. *Note:* The *<scalar expression>* (and enclosing parentheses) can be omitted only if the *<summary type>* is COUNT.

Incidentally, please note that a *<summarize add>* is *not* the same thing as an *<aggregate operator invocation>*. An *<aggregate operator invocation>* is a scalar expression and can appear wherever a scalar selector invocation—in particular, a scalar literal—can appear. A *<summarize add>*, by contrast, is merely a SUMMARIZE operand; it is not a scalar expression, it has no meaning outside the context of SUMMARIZE, and in fact cannot appear outside that context.

3. As you might have already realized, SUMMARIZE is not a primitive operator—it can be simulated by means of EXTEND. For example, the expression

```
SUMMARIZE SP PER S { S# } ADD COUNT AS NP
```

is defined to be shorthand for the following:

```
( EXTEND S { S# }
        ADD ( ( SP RENAME S# AS X ) WHERE X = S# ) AS Y,
            COUNT ( Y ) AS NP )
{ S#, NP }
```

Or equivalently:

```
WITH ( S { S# } ) AS T1,
    ( SP RENAME S# AS X ) AS T2,
    ( EXTEND T1 ADD ( T2 WHERE X = S# ) AS Y ) AS T3,
    ( EXTEND T3 ADD COUNT ( Y ) AS NP ) AS T4 :
T4 { S#, NP }
```

4. Consider the following example:

```
SUMMARIZE SP PER SP { } ADD SUM ( QTY ) AS GRANDTOTAL
```

In this example, the grouping and summarization are done "per" *a relation that has no attributes at all.* Let *sp* be the current value of relvar SP, and assume for the moment that relation *sp* does contain at least one tuple. Then all of those *sp* tuples have the same value for no attributes at all—namely, the 0-tuple [5.5]; hence there is just one group, and so just one tuple in the overall result. In other words, the aggregate computation is performed precisely once for the entire relation *sp.* The SUMMARIZE thus evaluates to a relation with one attribute and one tuple; the attribute is called GRANDTOTAL, and the single scalar value in the single result tuple is the total of all QTY values in the original relation *sp.*

If on the other hand the original relation *sp* has no tuples at all, then there are no groups, and hence no result tuples—i.e., the result relation is empty too. By contrast, the following expression*—

```
SUMMARIZE SP PER RELATION { TUPLE { } }
              ADD SUM ( QTY ) AS GRANDTOTAL
```

—will "work" (i.e., it will return the "correct" answer, namely zero) even if *sp* is empty. More precisely, it will return a relation with one attribute, called GRAND-TOTAL, and one tuple, containing a GRANDTOTAL value of zero. We therefore suggest that it should be possible to omit the PER clause in SUMMARIZE, as here:

```
SUMMARIZE SP ADD SUM ( QTY ) AS GRANDTOTAL
```

Omitting the PER clause is defined to be equivalent to specifying a PER clause of the form

```
PER RELATION { TUPLE { } }
```

Tclose

"Tclose" stands for *transitive closure.* We mention it here mainly for completeness; detailed discussion is beyond the scope of this chapter. However, we do at least define the operation, as follows. Let *A* be a binary relation with attributes *X* and *Y*, both of the same type *T*. Then the **transitive closure** of *A*, TCLOSE *A*, is a relation A^+ with heading the same as that of *A* and body a superset of that of *A*, defined as follows: The tuple

```
{ X:x , Y:y }
```

appears in A^+ if and only if it appears in *A* or there exists a sequence of values $z1, z2, …, zn$, all of type *T*, such that the tuples

```
{ X:x, Y:z1 }, { X:z1, Y:z2 }, ..., { X:zn, Y:y }
```

---

*The expression RELATION { TUPLE { } } in the PER clause in this example denotes a relation—in fact, the *only* relation—with no attributes but one tuple (namely, the 0-tuple). It can be abbreviated to TABLE_DEE (see references [3.3], [5.5], and [6.2]).

all appear in *A*. (In other words, the "(*x,y*)" tuple appears only if there is a path in the graph that is represented by relation *A* from node *x* to node *y*, loosely speaking. Note that the body of A^+ necessarily includes the body of *A* as a subset.)

For further discussion of this topic, see Chapter 23.

6.8 GROUPING AND UNGROUPING

The fact that we can have relations with attributes whose values are relations in turn leads to the desirability of certain additional relational operators, which we call *group* and *ungroup*, respectively [3.3]. Here first is an example of *group:*

```
SP GROUP ( P#, QTY ) AS PQ
```

Given our usual sample data, this expression yields the result shown in Fig. 6.12. *Note:* You will probably find it helpful to use that figure to check the explanations that follow, since they are—regrettably but unavoidably—a little abstract.

S#	PQ	
S1	**P#**	**QTY**
	P1	300
	P2	200
	P3	400
	P4	200
	P5	100
	P6	100
S2	**P#**	**QTY**
	P1	300
	P2	400
S3	**P#**	**QTY**
	P2	200
S4	**P#**	**QTY**
	P2	200
	P4	300
	P5	400

Fig. 6.12 Grouping SP by S#

We begin by observing that the original expression

```
SP GROUP ( P#, QTY ) AS PQ
```

might be read as "group SP by S#," since S# is the sole attribute of SP *not* mentioned in the GROUP clause. The result is a relation defined as follows. First, the heading looks like this:

```
{ S# S#, PQ RELATION { P# P#, QTY QTY } }
```

In other words, it consists of a relation-valued attribute PQ (where PQ in turn has attributes P# and QTY), together with all of the other attributes of SP (of course, "all of the other attributes of SP" here means just attribute S#). Second, the body contains exactly one tuple for each distinct S# value in SP (and no other tuples). Each tuple in that body consists of the applicable S# value (*s*, say), together with a PQ value (*pq*, say) obtained as follows:

- Each SP tuple is conceptually replaced by a tuple (*x*, say) in which the P# and QTY components have been "wrapped" into a tuple-valued component (*y*, say).

- The *y* components of all such tuples *x* in which the S# value is equal to *s* are "grouped" into a relation, *pq*, and a result tuple with S# value equal to *s* and PQ value equal to *pq* is thereby generated.

The overall result is thus indeed as shown in Fig. 6.12. ■

Now we turn to *ungroup*. Let SPQ be the relation shown in Fig. 6.12. Then the expression

```
SPQ UNGROUP PQ
```

(perhaps unsurprisingly) gives us back our usual sample SP relation. To be more specific, it yields a relation defined as follows. First, the heading looks like this:

```
{ S# S#, P# P#, QTY QTY }
```

In other words, the heading consists of attributes P# and QTY (derived from attribute PQ), together with all of the other attributes of SPQ (i.e., just attribute S#, in the example). Second, the body contains exactly one tuple for each combination of a tuple in SPQ and a tuple in the PQ value within that SPQ tuple (and no other tuples). Each tuple in that body consists of the applicable S# value (*s*, say), together with P# and QTY values (*p* and *q*, say) obtained as follows:

- Each SPQ tuple is conceptually replaced by a set of tuples, one such tuple (*x*, say) for each tuple in the PQ value in that SPQ tuple. Each such tuple *x* contains an S# component (*s*, say) equal to the S# component from the SPQ tuple in question and a tuple-valued component (*y*, say) equal to some tuple from the PQ component from the SPQ tuple in question.

- The *y* components of each such tuple *x* in which the S# value is equal to *s* are "unwrapped" into separate P# and QTY components (*p* and *q*, say), and a result tuple with S# value equal to *s*, P# value equal to *p*, and QTY value equal to *q* is thereby generated.

The overall result is thus, as claimed, our usual sample SP relation.   ■

As you can see, GROUP and UNGROUP together provide what are more usually referred to as relation "nest" and "unnest" capabilities. We prefer our group/ungroup terminology, however, because the nest/unnest terminology is strongly associated with the concept of NF^2 relations, a concept we find somewhat confused to begin with and do not endorse.

For completeness, we close this section with some remarks concerning the *reversibility* of the GROUP and UNGROUP operations (though we realize our remarks might not be fully comprehensible on a first reading). If we group some relation *r* in some way, there is always an inverse ungrouping that will take us back to *r* again. However, if we ungroup some relation *r* in some way, an inverse grouping to take us back to *r* again might or might not exist. Here is an example (based on one given in reference [5.4]). Suppose we start with relation TWO (see Fig. 6.13) and ungroup it to obtain THREE. If we now group THREE by A (and name the resulting relation-valued attribute RVX once again), we obtain not TWO but ONE.

Note that, in ONE, RVX is (necessarily) *functionally dependent* on A, which thus constitutes a candidate key (see Chapters 8 and 10). If we now ungroup ONE, we return to THREE, and we have already seen that THREE can be grouped to give ONE; thus, the group and ungroup operations are indeed inverses of each other for this particular pair of relations. In general, it is the functional dependency that is crucial in determining whether or not a given ungrouping is reversible. In fact, if relation *r* has a relation-valued attribute *RVX*, then *r* is reversibly ungroupable (with respect to *RVX*) if and only if the following are both true:

- No tuple of *r* has an empty relation as its *RVX* value.

- *RVX* is functionally dependent on the combination of all other attributes of *r*. Another way of saying the same thing is that there must be some candidate key of *r* that does not include *RVX* as a component.

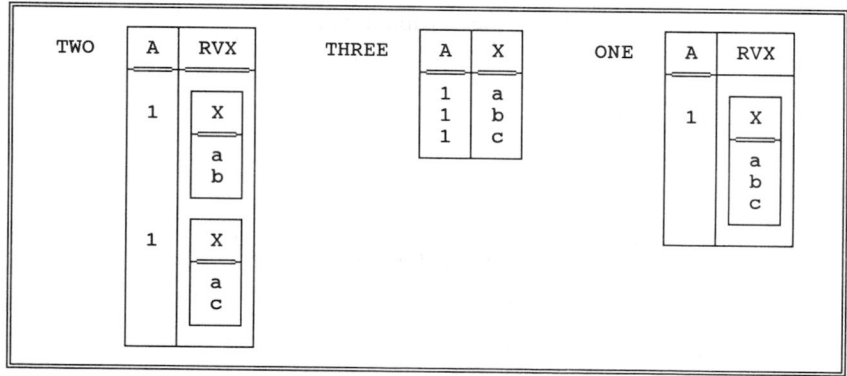

Fig. 6.13   Ungrouping and (re)grouping are not necessarily reversible

6.9 RELATIONAL COMPARISONS

The relational algebra as originally defined did not include any direct way of comparing two relations—e.g., testing them for equality, or testing whether every tuple appearing in one relation also appeared in another (i.e., testing whether one relation was a subset of another, loosely speaking). One consequence of this omission was that certain queries were extremely hard to express (see Exercise 6.48 at the end of this chapter for an example). However, the omission is easily repaired. First of all, we define a new kind of *condition,* a **relational comparison,** with syntax as follows:

```
<relational expression>  θ  <relational expression>
```

The relations denoted by the two *<relational expressions>* must be of the same type. The comparison operator Θ can be any of the following:

= (equals)

≠ (not equals)

≤ (subset of)

< (proper subset of)

≥ (superset of)

> (proper superset of)

Note: The choice of operator symbols is perhaps a little unwise, since, e.g., the negation of "*A* is a proper subset of *B*" is certainly not "*A* is a superset of *B*" (i.e., "<" and "≥" are not inverses of each other). However, we will stay with those symbols for the purposes of this book, for typographical reasons.

Here then are a couple of examples:

1. `S { CITY } = P { CITY }`

   Meaning: Is the projection of suppliers over CITY the same as the projection of parts over CITY?

2. `S { S# } > SP { S# }`

   Meaning (considerably paraphrased): Are there any suppliers who supply no parts at all?

Next, we permit this new kind of condition to be used at appropriate points within relational expressions. For example:

```
S WHERE ( ( SP RENAME S# AS X ) WHERE X = S# ) { P# } = P { P# }
```

This expression evaluates to a relation containing supplier tuples for suppliers who supply all parts. *Explanation:*

■ For a given supplier, the expression

```
( ( SP RENAME S# AS X ) WHERE X = S# ) { P# }
```

yields the set of part numbers for parts supplied by that supplier.

■ That set of part numbers is then compared with the set of *all* part numbers. If the two sets are equal, the corresponding supplier tuple appears in the result.

Of course, we already know how to formulate this particular query in terms of DIVIDEBY:

```
S JOIN ( S { S# } DIVIDEBY P { P# } PER SP { S#, P# } )
```

However, you might feel that the relational comparison version is conceptually easier to deal with. But there is one point we must make clear: Relational comparisons are not *restriction conditions* as that term was defined in Section 6.4, and the example shown above involving such a comparison is not a genuine restriction! Rather, it is shorthand for something like the following:

```
WITH ( EXTEND S
       ADD ( ( SP RENAME S# AS X ) WHERE X = S# ) { P# }
       AS A ) AS T1,
     ( EXTEND T1
       ADD P { P# }
       AS B ) AS T2 :
T2 WHERE A = B
```

A and B here are relation-valued attributes, and the final expression, T2 WHERE A = B, *is* now a genuine restriction after all. *Note:* Incidentally, it follows from the foregoing that—conceptually speaking, at least—support for relational comparisons requires support for relation-valued attributes.

One particular relational comparison that is needed very often in practice is a test to see whether a given relation is empty (i.e., contains no tuples). Once again it seems worthwhile to introduce a shorthand. We therefore define a truth-valued operator of the form

```
IS_EMPTY ( <relational expression> )
```

which returns *true* if the relation denoted by the *<relational expression>* is empty and *false* otherwise.

Another common requirement is to be able to test whether a given tuple *t* appears within a given relation *r*. The following relational comparison will suffice:

```
RELATION { t } ≤ r
```

However, the following shorthand—which will be very familiar if you know SQL—is a little more user-friendly:

```
t IN r
```

IN here is really the **set membership** operator, usually represented as ∈.

6.10 SUMMARY

We have discussed the **relational algebra.** We began by reemphasizing the importance of **closure** and **nested relational expressions,** and explained that if we are going to take closure seriously, then we need a set of **relation type inference rules** (and our version of the algebra does include such rules, of course).

The original algebra consisted of eight operators—the traditional set operators **union, intersect, difference,** and **product** (all of them modified somewhat to take account of the fact that their operands are very specifically relations, not arbitrary sets), and the special relational operators **restrict, project, join,** and **divide.** To this original set we added **RENAME, SEMIJOIN, SEMIMINUS, EXTEND,** and **SUMMARIZE** (and we also mentioned **TCLOSE** and briefly discussed **GROUP** and **UNGROUP**). For certain of these operators the two relation operands are required to be of the same type (previously called "union-compatible"). We also pointed out that these operators are not all **primitive**—several of them can be defined in terms of others. We showed how the operators can be combined into expressions that serve a variety of purposes: **retrieval, update,** and several others. We also very briefly discussed the idea of **transforming** such expressions for **optimization** purposes (but we will discuss this idea in much more detail in Chapter 17). And we considered the possibility of using a **step-at-a-time** approach to deal with complex queries, using **WITH** to introduce names for expressions. Finally, we discussed the idea of **relational comparisons,** which make certain kinds of queries—typically ones that would otherwise require DIVIDEBY—somewhat easier to express.

EXERCISES

6.1 In the body of the chapter we claimed that union, intersection, product, and (natural) join are all both commutative and associative. Verify these claims.

6.2 Of Codd's original set of eight operators, union, difference, product, restrict, and project can be considered as primitives. Give definitions of natural join, intersect, and (harder!) divide in terms of those primitives.

6.3 Consider the expression *A* JOIN *B*. If *A* and *B* have disjoint headings (i.e., have no common attributes), this expression is equivalent to *A* TIMES *B*. Verify this assertion. What is the expression equivalent to if instead *A* and *B* have *identical* headings?

6.4 Show that the five primitive operators mentioned in Exercise 6.2 truly are primitive, in the sense that none of them can be expressed in terms of the other four.

6.5 In ordinary arithmetic, multiplication and division are inverse operations. Are TIMES and DIVIDEBY inverse operations in the relational algebra?

6.6 Given the usual suppliers and parts database, what is the value of the expression S JOIN SP JOIN P? *Warning:* There is a trap here.

6.7 Let *A* be a relation of degree *n*. How many different projections of *A* are there?

6.8 In ordinary arithmetic there is a special number, 1, with the property that

```
n * 1 = 1 * n = n
```

for all numbers *n*. We say that 1 is the **identity** with respect to multiplication. Is there any relation that plays an analogous role in the relational algebra? If so, what is it?

6.9   In ordinary arithmetic there is another special number, 0, with the property that

```
n * 0  =  0 * n  =  0
```

for all numbers *n*. Is there any relation that plays an analogous role in the relational algebra? If so, what is it?

6.10   Investigate the effect of the algebraic operations discussed in this chapter on the relations that are the answers to the two previous exercises.

6.11   In Section 6.2, we said that the relational closure property was important for the same kind of reason that the arithmetic closure property was important. In arithmetic, however, there is one unpleasant situation where the closure property breaks down—namely, division by zero. Is there any analogous situation in the relational algebra?

6.12   The operators union, intersect, product, and join were all defined originally as *dyadic* operators (i.e., each of them took exactly two operands). In this chapter, however, we have shown how they could be unambiguously extended to become *n*-adic operators for arbitrary *n* > 1; e.g., the expression *A* UNION *B* UNION *C* could be unambiguously regarded as the *triadic* union of *A, B,* and *C*. But what about *n* = 1? Or *n* = 0?

Query Exercises

The remaining exercises are all based on the suppliers-parts-projects database (see Fig. 4.5 in the "Exercises" section in Chapter 4 and the answer to Exercise 5.4 in Chapter 5). In each case you are asked to write a relational algebra expression for the indicated query. (By way of an interesting variation, you might like to try looking at some of the answers first and stating what the given expression means in natural language.) For convenience we show the structure of the database (in outline) below:

```
S     { S#, SNAME, STATUS, CITY }
      PRIMARY KEY { S# }
P     { P#, PNAME, COLOR, WEIGHT, CITY }
      PRIMARY KEY { P# }
J     { J#, JNAME, CITY }
      PRIMARY KEY { J# }
SPJ   { S#, P#, J#, QTY }
      PRIMARY KEY { S#, P#, J# }
      FOREIGN KEY { S# } REFERENCES S
      FOREIGN KEY { P# } REFERENCES P
      FOREIGN KEY { J# } REFERENCES J
```

6.13   Get full details of all projects.

6.14   Get full details of all projects in London.

6.15   Get supplier numbers for suppliers who supply project J1.

6.16   Get all shipments where the quantity is in the range 300 to 750 inclusive.

6.17   Get all part-color/part-city combinations. *Note:* Here and subsequently, the term "all" is to be taken to mean "all currently represented in the database," not "all possible."

6.18   Get all supplier-number/part-number/project-number triples such that the indicated supplier, part, and project are all colocated (i.e., all in the same city).

6.19 Get all supplier-number/part-number/project-number triples such that the indicated supplier, part, and project are not all colocated.

6.20 Get all supplier-number/part-number/project-number triples such that no two of the indicated supplier, part, and project are colocated.

6.21 Get full details for parts supplied by a supplier in London.

6.22 Get part numbers for parts supplied by a supplier in London to a project in London.

6.23 Get all pairs of city names such that a supplier in the first city supplies a project in the second city.

6.24 Get part numbers for parts supplied to any project by a supplier in the same city as that project.

6.25 Get project numbers for projects supplied by at least one supplier not in the same city.

6.26 Get all pairs of part numbers such that some supplier supplies both the indicated parts.

6.27 Get the total number of projects supplied by supplier S1.

6.28 Get the total quantity of part P1 supplied by supplier S1.

6.29 For each part being supplied to a project, get the part number, the project number, and the corresponding total quantity.

6.30 Get part numbers of parts supplied to some project in an average quantity of more than 350.

6.31 Get project names for projects supplied by supplier S1.

6.32 Get colors of parts supplied by supplier S1.

6.33 Get part numbers for parts supplied to any project in London.

6.34 Get project numbers for projects using at least one part available from supplier S1.

6.35 Get supplier numbers for suppliers supplying at least one part supplied by at least one supplier who supplies at least one red part.

6.36 Get supplier numbers for suppliers with a status lower than that of supplier S1.

6.37 Get project numbers for projects whose city is first in the alphabetic list of such cities.

6.38 Get project numbers for projects supplied with part P1 in an average quantity greater than the greatest quantity in which any part is supplied to project J1.

6.39 Get supplier numbers for suppliers supplying some project with part P1 in a quantity greater than the average shipment quantity of part P1 for that project.

6.40 Get project numbers for projects not supplied with any red part by any London supplier.

6.41 Get project numbers for projects supplied entirely by supplier S1.

6.42 Get part numbers for parts supplied to all projects in London.

6.43 Get supplier numbers for suppliers who supply the same part to all projects.

6.44 Get project numbers for projects supplied with at least all parts available from supplier S1.

6.45 Get all cities in which at least one supplier, part, or project is located.

6.46 Get part numbers for parts that are supplied either by a London supplier or to a London project.

6.47 Get supplier-number/part-number pairs such that the indicated supplier does not supply the indicated part.

6.48 Get all pairs of supplier numbers, S*x* and S*y* say, such that S*x* and S*y* supply exactly the same set of parts each. (Thanks to a correspondent, Fatma Mili of Oakland University, Rochester, Michigan, for this problem. For simplicity, you might want to use the original suppliers and parts database for this exercise, instead of the expanded suppliers-parts-projects database.)

6.49 Get a "grouped" version of all shipments showing, for each supplier-number/part-number pair, the corresponding project numbers and quantities in the form of a binary relation.

6.50 Get an "ungrouped" version of the relation produced in Exercise 6.49.

REFERENCES AND BIBLIOGRAPHY

6.1 E. F. Codd: "Relational Completeness of Data Base Sublanguages," in Randall J. Rustin (ed.), *Data Base Systems, Courant Computer Science Symposia Series 6*. Englewood Cliffs, N.J.: Prentice-Hall (1972).

> This is the paper in which Codd first *formally* defined the original algebraic operators (definitions did appear in reference [5.1] also, of course, but they were somewhat less formal, or at least less complete).
>
> One perhaps unfortunate aspect of the paper is that it assumes "for notational and expository convenience" that the attributes of a relation have a left-to-right ordering and hence can be identified by their ordinal position (though Codd does say too that "names rather than position numbers [should] be used . . . when actually storing or retrieving information"—and of course he had previously said much the same thing in reference [5.1]). The paper therefore does not mention an attribute RENAME operator, and it does not consider the question of result type inference. Possibly as a consequence of these omissions, the same criticisms can still be leveled today at many discussions of the algebra in the literature, at today's SQL products, and (to a slightly lesser extent) at the SQL standard as well.
>
> Additional commentary on this paper appears in Chapter 7, especially in Section 7.4. *Note:* Reference [3.3] describes a kind of "reduced instruction set" algebra called **A** that allows the systematic definition of more powerful operators in terms of suitable combinations of a very small number of primitives. In fact, reference [3.3] shows that the entire functionality of Codd's algebra as originally defined can be achieved with just two primitives called *remove* and *nor*.

6.2 Hugh Darwen (writing as Andrew Warden): "Adventures in Relationland," in C. J. Date, *Relational Database Writings 1985–1989*. Reading, Mass.: Addison-Wesley (1990).

> A series of short papers that examine various aspects of the relational model and relational DBMSs in an original, entertaining, and informative style. The papers have the following titles:
>
> 1. The Naming of Columns
> 2. In Praise of Marriage
> 3. The Keys of the Kingdom
> 4. Chivalry
> 5. A Constant Friend
> 6. Table_Dee and Table_Dum
> 7. Into the Unknown

6.3 Hugh Darwen and C. J. Date: "Into the Great Divide," in C. J. Date and Hugh Darwen, *Relational Database Writings 1989–1991*. Reading, Mass.: Addison-Wesley (1992).

> This paper analyzes both (a) Codd's original divide as defined in reference [6.1] and (b) a generalization of that operator due to Hall, Hitchcock, and Todd [6.10] that—unlike Codd's

original divide—allowed any relation to be divided by any relation (Codd's original divide was defined only for dividend and divisor relations such that the heading of the divisor was a subset of the heading of the dividend). The paper shows that both operators get into difficulties over empty relations, with the result that neither of them quite solves the problem it was originally intended to solve (i.e., neither of them is quite the counterpart of the universal quantifier that it was meant to be). Revised versions of both operators (the "Small Divide" and the "Great Divide," respectively) are proposed to overcome these problems. *Note:* As the **Tutorial D** syntax for these two operators suggests, they really are two different operators; that is, the Great Divide is (unfortunately) *not* quite an upward-compatible extension of the Small Divide. The paper also suggests that the revised operators no longer merit the name "divide"! In connection with this last point, see Exercise 6.5.

For purposes of reference, we give here a definition of Codd's original divide. Let relations *A* and *B* have headings $\{X,Y\}$ and $\{Y\}$, respectively (where *X* and *Y* can be composite). Then the expression *A* DIVIDEBY *B* gives a relation with heading $\{X\}$ and body consisting of all tuples $\{X:x\}$ such that a tuple $\{X:x,Y:y\}$ appears in *A* for *all* tuples $\{Y:y\}$ appearing in *B*. In other words, loosely speaking, the result consists of those *X* values from *A* whose corresponding *Y* values (in *A*) include all *Y* values from *B*.

6.4 C. J. Date: "Quota Queries" (in three parts), in C. J. Date, Hugh Darwen, and David McGoveran, *Relational Database Writings 1994–1997*. Reading, Mass.: Addison-Wesley (1998).

A *quota query* is a query that specifies a desired limit on the cardinality of the result—for example, the query "Get the three heaviest parts." Here is a possible **Tutorial D** formulation of this example:

```
P QUOTA ( 3, DESC WEIGHT )
```

This expression is defined to be shorthand for the following:

```
( ( EXTEND P
    ADD COUNT ( ( P RENAME WEIGHT AS WT ) WHERE WT > WEIGHT )
    AS #_HEAVIER )
  WHERE #_HEAVIER < 3 ) { ALL BUT #_HEAVIER }
```

(where the names WX, WY, and #_HEAVIER are arbitrary). Given our usual sample data, the result consists of parts P2, P3, and P6.

The present three-part paper [6.4] analyzes the quota query requirement in depth and proposes several syntactic shorthands for dealing with it and related matters.

6.5 Michael J. Carey and Donald Kossmann: "On Saying 'Enough Already!' in SQL," Proc. 1997 Int. Conf. on Management of Data, Tucson, Ariz. (May 1997).

Another paper on quota queries. Unlike reference [6.4], it focuses on implementation matters rather than model issues. The query "Get the three heaviest parts" in the proposals of this paper would look like this:

```
SELECT  *
FROM    P
ORDER   BY WEIGHT DESC
STOP    AFTER 3 ;
```

One problem with this approach is that the STOP AFTER applies to the result of the ORDER BY, which (as we saw in Chapter 5, Section 5.3, subsection "Properties of Relations") is not a relation at all but an array or a list; hence, the overall result is presumably not a relation either, and the relational closure property has been violated. The paper does not discuss this issue.

Of course, the result could perhaps be converted back into a relation—but then we run into another problem, which is that the result of the STOP AFTER is, in general, unpredictable. Given our usual sample data values, for example, if we replace STOP AFTER 3 by STOP AFTER 2 in the foregoing SQL query, then the result is not well defined.

The STOP AFTER clause has been implemented in an IBM research prototype and might thus find its way into IBM products, and possibly from there into the SQL standard—though not, one hopes, before the problems identified above have been satisfactorily resolved.

6.6 R. C. Goldstein and A. J. Strnad: "The MacAIMS Data Management System," Proc. 1970 ACM SICFIDET Workshop on Data Description and Access (November 1970).

See the annotation to reference [6.7] immediately following.

6.7 A. J. Strnad: "The Relational Approach to the Management of Data Bases," Proc. IFIP Congress, Ljubljana, Yugoslavia (August 1971).

We mention MacAIMS [6.6–6.7] primarily for reasons of historical interest; it seems to have been the earliest example of a system supporting *n*-ary relations and an algebraic language. The interesting thing about it is that it was developed in parallel with, and at least partly independently of, Codd's work on the relational model. Unlike Codd's work, however, the MacAIMS effort apparently did not lead to any significant follow-on activities.

6.8 M. G. Notley: "The Peterlee IS/1 System," IBM UK Scientific Centre Report UKSC-0018 (March 1972).

See the annotation to reference [6.9].

6.9 S. J. P. Todd: "The Peterlee Relational Test Vehicle—A System Overview," *IBM Sys. J. 15,* No. 4 (1976).

The Peterlee Relational Test Vehicle PRTV was an experimental system developed at the IBM UK Scientific Centre in Peterlee, England. It was based on an earlier prototype—possibly the very first implementation of Codd's ideas—called IS/1 [6.8]. It supported *n*-ary relations and a version of the algebra called ISBL (Information System Base Language), which was based on proposals documented in reference [6.10]. The ideas discussed in the present chapter regarding relation type inference can be traced back to ISBL and the proposals of reference [6.10].

Significant aspects of PRTV included the following:

- It supported RENAME, EXTEND, and SUMMARIZE.

- It incorporated some sophisticated expression transformation techniques (see Chapter 17).

- It included a lazy evaluation feature, which was important both for optimization and for view support (see the discussion of WITH in the body of this chapter).

- It provided "function extensibility"—i.e., the ability for users to define their own operators.

6.10 P. A. V. Hall, P. Hitchcock, and S. J. P. Todd: "An Algebra of Relations for Machine Computation," Conf. Record of the 2nd ACM Symposium on Principles of Programming Languages, Palo Alto, Calif. (January 1975).

6.11 Patrick A. V. Hall: "Relational Algebras, Logic, and Functional Programming," Proc. 1984 ACM SIGMOD Int. Conf. on Management of Data, Boston, Mass. (June 1984).

Presents a functional programming interpretation of the relational algebra, with the aims (paraphrasing from the paper) of (a) providing a theoretical basis for the so-called "4GLs" (see

Chapter 2), and (b) integrating functional, logic-based (see Chapter 23), and relational languages so that they can share implementation technology. The author claims that, whereas logic programming and databases have been moving toward each other for some time, at the time of writing the functional or applicative languages have paid little heed to database issues. The paper is therefore presented principally as a contribution toward a *rapprochement* between the latter two.

6.12 Anthony Klug: "Equivalence of Relational Algebra and Relational Calculus Query Languages Having Aggregate Functions," *JACM 29,* No. 3 (July 1982).

Defines extensions to both the original relational algebra and the original relational calculus (see Chapter 7) to support aggregate operators, and demonstrates the equivalence of the two extended formalisms.

ANSWERS TO SELECTED EXERCISES

Note: The answers given for Exercises 6.13–6.50 are not the only ones possible.

6.2 JOIN is discussed in Section 6.4. INTERSECT can be defined as follows:

```
A INTERSECT B  ≡  A MINUS ( A MINUS B )
```

or (equally well)

```
A INTERSECT B  ≡  B MINUS ( B MINUS A )
```

These equivalences, though valid, are slightly unsatisfactory, since A INTERSECT B is symmetric in A and B and the other two expressions are not. Here by contrast is a symmetric equivalent:

```
( A MINUS ( A MINUS B ) ) UNION ( B MINUS ( B MINUS A ) )
```

Note: Given that A and B must be of the same type, we also have:

```
A INTERSECT B  ≡  A JOIN B
```

As for DIVIDEBY, we have:

```
A DIVIDEBY B PER C  ≡  A { X }
                       MINUS ( ( A { X } TIMES B { Y } )
                                     MINUS C { X, Y } ) { X }
```

Here *X* is the set of attributes common to *A* and *C* and *Y* is the set of attributes common to *B* and *C*.
Note: DIVIDEBY as just defined is actually a generalization of the version defined in the body of the chapter—though it is still a Small Divide [6.3]—inasmuch we assumed previously that *A* had no attributes apart from *X, B* had no attributes apart from *Y,* and *C* had no attributes apart from *X* and *Y.* The foregoing generalization would allow us to express, e.g., the query "Get supplier numbers for suppliers who supply all parts" more simply as just

```
S DIVIDEBY P PER SP
```

instead of as

```
S { S# } DIVIDEBY P { P# } PER SP { S#, P# }
```

6.3 *A* INTERSECT *B* (see the answer to Exercise 6.2 above). *Note:* We remark that since TIMES is a special case of JOIN, we could regard JOIN as a primitive operator instead of TIMES—a preferable alternative, in fact, precisely because it is more general.

6.4 We give an informal (*very* informal) sketch of a "proof" only.

- Product is the only operator that can increase the number of attributes, so it cannot be simulated by any combination of the other operators. Therefore product is primitive.

- Project is the only operator that can reduce the number of attributes, so it cannot be simulated by any combination of the other operators. Therefore project is primitive.

- Union is the only operator that can increase the number of tuples, apart from product, and product usually increases the number of attributes as well. Let the two relations to be "unioned" be *A* and *B*. Note that *A* and *B* must be of the same type, and their union has exactly the same attributes as each of them. If we form "the *product of A and B*" by (say) first renaming all of the attributes of *B* and then applying the product operator, and then use projection to reduce the set of attributes in the result to just the set of attributes in *A,* we simply get back to the original relation *A* again:

```
( A TIMES B ) { all attributes of A } ≡ A
```

(unless *B* happens to be empty; we ignore this case for simplicity). Therefore product cannot be used to simulate union, and union is primitive.

- Difference cannot be simulated via union (because union never reduces the number of tuples) or product (likewise, usually) or projection (because project reduces the number of attributes, usually). Nor can it be simulated by restrict, because difference is sensitive to the values appearing in the second relation, whereas restrict cannot be (by virtue of the nature of a restriction condition). Therefore difference is primitive.

- Restrict is the only operator that allows attribute values to be compared with each other. Therefore restrict is primitive.

6.5 The short answer is no. Codd's original DIVIDEBY did satisfy the property that

```
( A TIMES B ) DIVIDEBY B = A
```

However:

- Codd's DIVIDEBY was a dyadic operator; our DIVIDEBY is triadic, and hence cannot possibly satisfy a similar property.

- In any case, even with Codd's DIVIDEBY, dividing *A* by *B* and then forming the Cartesian product of the result with *B* will yield a relation that *might* be identical to *A,* but is more likely to be some proper subset of *A:*

```
( A DIVIDEBY B ) TIMES B ≤ A
```

Codd's DIVIDEBY is thus more analogous to integer division in ordinary arithmetic (i.e., it ignores the remainder).

6.6   The trap is that the join involves the CITY attributes as well as the S# and P# attributes. The result looks like this:

S#	SNAME	STATUS	CITY	P#	QTY	PNAME	COLOR	WEIGHT
S1	Smith	20	London	P1	300	Nut	Red	12.0
S1	Smith	20	London	P4	200	Screw	Red	14.0
S1	Smith	20	London	P6	100	Cog	Red	19.0
S2	Jones	10	Paris	P2	400	Bolt	Green	17.0
S3	Blake	30	Paris	P2	200	Bolt	Green	17.0
S4	Clark	20	London	P4	200	Screw	Red	14.0

6.7 2^n. This count includes the *identity* projection (i.e., the projection over all n attributes), which yields a result that is identical to the original relation *A,* and the *nullary* projection (i.e., the projection over no attributes at all), which yields TABLE_DUM if the original relation *A* is empty and TABLE_DEE otherwise [5.5].

6.8   Yes, there is such a relation, namely TABLE_DEE. TABLE_DEE (DEE for short) is the analog of 1 with respect to multiplication in ordinary arithmetic because

    R TIMES DEE ≡ DEE TIMES R ≡ R

for all relations *R*. In other words, DEE is the **identity** with respect to TIMES (and, more generally, with respect to JOIN).

6.9   There is no relation that behaves with respect to TIMES in a way that is *exactly* analogous to the way that 0 behaves with respect to multiplication. However, the behavior of TABLE_DUM (DUM for short) is somewhat reminiscent of the behavior of 0, inasmuch as

    R TIMES DUM ≡ DUM TIMES R ≡ an empty relation with
                                          the same heading as R

for all relations *R*.

6.10   First, note that the only relations that are of the same type as DEE and DUM are DEE and DUM themselves. We have:

UNION	DEE DUM
DEE	DEE DEE
DUM	DEE DUM

INTERSECT	DEE DUM
DEE	DEE DUM
DUM	DUM DUM

MINUS	DEE DUM
DEE	DUM DEE
DUM	DUM DUM

In the case of difference, the first operand is shown at the left and the second at the top (for the other operators, of course, the operands are interchangeable). Notice how reminiscent these tables are of the truth tables for OR, AND, and AND NOT, respectively; of course, the resemblance is not a coincidence.

Turning now to restrict and project, we have:

- Any restriction of DEE yields DEE if the restriction condition is *true,* DUM if it is *false.*
- Any restriction of DUM yields DUM.
- Projection of any relation over no attributes yields DUM if the original relation is empty, DEE otherwise. In particular, projection of DEE or DUM, necessarily over no attributes at all, returns its input.

For extend and summarize, we have:

- Extending DEE or DUM to add a new attribute yields a relation of degree one and the same cardinality as its input.

- Summarizing DEE or DUM (necessarily per no attributes at all) yields a relation of degree one and the same cardinality as its input.

Note: We omit consideration of DIVIDEBY, SEMIJOIN, and SEMIMINUS because they are not primitive. TCLOSE is irrelevant (it applies to binary relations only). We also omit consideration of GROUP and UNGROUP for obvious reasons.

6.11 No!

6.12 We can (and do) reasonably define the union or the intersection or the product or the join of a single relation *R* to be just *R* itself. As for the zero case, let *RT* be some relation type. Then:

- The union of no relations at all of type *RT* is the empty relation of type *RT*. Note that there must be some way of specifying *RT* as an operand to the union.

- The intersection of no relations at all of type *RT* is the "universal" relation of type *RT*, where by the term "universal relation of type *RT*" we mean that relation of type *RT* whose body contains all possible tuples that conform to the heading of that relation (again there must be some way of specifying *RT* as an operand to the operation). Note that the term "universal relation" is more frequently used in the literature with a very different meaning!—see, e.g., reference [12.19].

- The product and join of no relations at all are both TABLE_DEE.

6.13 J

6.14 J WHERE CITY = 'London'

6.15 (SPJ WHERE J# = J# ('J1')) { S# }

6.16 SPJ WHERE QTY ≥ QTY (300) AND QTY ≤ QTY (750)

6.17 P { COLOR, CITY }

6.18 (S JOIN P JOIN J) { S#, P#, J# }

6.19
```
( ( ( S RENAME CITY AS SCITY ) TIMES
    ( P RENAME CITY AS PCITY ) TIMES
    ( J RENAME CITY AS JCITY ) )
WHERE SCITY ≠ PCITY
OR    PCITY ≠ JCITY
OR    JCITY ≠ SCITY ) { S#, P#, J# }
```

6.20
```
( ( ( S RENAME CITY AS SCITY ) TIMES
    ( P RENAME CITY AS PCITY ) TIMES
    ( J RENAME CITY AS JCITY ) )
WHERE SCITY ≠ PCITY
AND   PCITY ≠ JCITY
AND   JCITY ≠ SCITY ) { S#, P#, J# }
```

6.21 P SEMIJOIN (SPJ SEMIJOIN (S WHERE CITY = 'London'))

6.22 Just to remind you of the possibility, we show a step-at-a-time solution to this exercise:

```
WITH ( S WHERE CITY = 'London' ) AS T1,
     ( J WHERE CITY = 'London' ) AS T2,
     ( SPJ JOIN T1 ) AS T3,
     T3 { P#, J# } AS T4,
     ( T4 JOIN T2 ) AS T5 :
     T5 { P# }
```

Here is the same query without using WITH:

```
( ( SPJ JOIN ( S WHERE CITY = 'London' ) ) { P#, J# }
            JOIN ( J WHERE CITY = 'London' ) ) { P# }
```

We will give a mixture of solutions (some using WITH, some not) to the remaining exercises.

6.23 ((S RENAME CITY AS SCITY) JOIN SPJ JOIN
         (J RENAME CITY AS JCITY)) { SCITY, JCITY }

6.24 (J JOIN SPJ JOIN S) { P# }

6.25 (((J RENAME CITY AS JCITY) JOIN SPJ JOIN
         (S RENAME CITY AS SCITY))
                        WHERE JCITY ≠ SCITY) { J# }

6.26 WITH (SPJ { S#, P# } RENAME S# AS XS#, P# AS XP#) AS T1,
         (SPJ { S#, P# } RENAME S# AS YS#, P# AS YP#) AS T2,
         (T1 TIMES T2) AS T3,
         (T3 WHERE XS# = YS# AND XP# < YP#) AS T4 :
         T4 { XP#, YP# }

6.27 (SUMMARIZE SPJ { S#, J# }
       PER RELATION { TUPLE { S# S# ('S1') } }
       ADD COUNT AS N) { N }
```

We remind you that the expression in the PER clause here is a relation selector invocation (in fact, it is a relation literal).

```
6.28 (SUMMARIZE SPJ { S#, P#, QTY }
       PER RELATION { TUPLE { S# S# ('S1'), P# P# ('P1') } }
       ADD SUM (QTY) AS Q) { Q }

6.29 SUMMARIZE SPJ PER SPJ { P#, J# } ADD SUM (QTY) AS Q

6.30 WITH (SUMMARIZE SPJ PER SPJ { P#, J# }
                        ADD AVG (QTY) AS Q) AS T1,
         (T1 WHERE Q > QTY (350)) AS T2 :
         T2 { P# }

6.31 (J JOIN (SPJ WHERE S# = S# ('S1'))) { JNAME }

6.32 (P JOIN (SPJ WHERE S# = S# ('S1'))) { COLOR }

6.33 (SPJ JOIN (J WHERE CITY = 'London')) { P# }

6.34 (SPJ JOIN (SPJ WHERE S# = S# ('S1')) { P# }) { J# }

6.35 (((SPJ JOIN
           (P WHERE COLOR = COLOR ('Red')) { P# }) { S# }
                        JOIN SPJ) { P# } JOIN SPJ) { S# }
```
```

```
6.36  WITH ( S { S#, STATUS } RENAME S# AS XS#,
                                    STATUS AS XSTATUS ) AS T1,
           ( S { S#, STATUS } RENAME S# AS YS#,
                                    STATUS AS YSTATUS ) AS T2,
           ( T1 TIMES T2 ) AS T3,
           ( T3 WHERE XS# = S# ( 'S1' ) AND
                      XSTATUS > YSTATUS ) AS T4 :
           T4 { YS# }

6.37  ( ( EXTEND J ADD MIN ( J, CITY ) AS FIRST )
                              WHERE CITY = FIRST ) { J# }
```

What does this query return if relvar J is empty?

```
6.38  WITH ( SPJ RENAME J# AS ZJ# ) AS T1,
           ( T1 WHERE ZJ# = J# AND P# = P# ( 'P1' ) ) AS T2,
           ( SPJ WHERE P# = P# ( 'P1' ) ) AS T3,
           ( EXTEND T3 ADD AVG ( T2, QTY ) AS QX ) AS T4,
           T4 { J#, QX } AS T5,
           ( SPJ WHERE J# = J# ( 'J1' ) ) AS T6,
           ( EXTEND T6 ADD MAX ( T6, QTY ) AS QY ) AS T7,
           ( T5 TIMES T7 { QY } ) AS T8,
           ( T8 WHERE QX > QY ) AS T9 :
           T9 { J# }

6.39  WITH ( SPJ WHERE P# = P# ( 'P1' ) ) AS T1,
           T1 { S#, J#, QTY } AS T2,
           ( T2 RENAME J# AS XJ#, QTY AS XQ ) AS T3,
           ( SUMMARIZE T1 PER SPJ { J# }
                       ADD AVG ( QTY ) AS Q ) AS T4,
           ( T3 TIMES T4 ) AS T5,
           ( T5 WHERE XJ# = J# AND XQ > Q ) AS T6 :
           T6 { S# }

6.40  WITH ( S WHERE CITY = 'London' ) { S# } AS T1,
           ( P WHERE COLOR = COLOR ( 'Red' ) ) AS T2,
           ( T1 JOIN SPJ JOIN T2 ) AS T3 :
           J { J# } MINUS T3 { J# }

6.41  J { J# } MINUS ( SPJ WHERE S# ≠ S# ( 'S1' ) ) { J# }

6.42  WITH ( ( SPJ RENAME P# AS X ) WHERE X = P# ) { J# } AS T1,
           ( J WHERE CITY = 'London' ) { J# } AS T2,
           ( P WHERE T1 ≥ T2 ) AS T3 :
           T3 { P# }

6.43  S { S#, P# } DIVIDEBY J { J# } PER SPJ { S#, P#, J# }

6.44  ( J WHERE
            ( ( SPJ RENAME J# AS Y ) WHERE Y = J# ) { P# } ≥
            ( SPJ WHERE S# = S# ( 'S1' ) ) { P# } ) { J# }

6.45  S { CITY } UNION P { CITY } UNION J { CITY }

6.46  ( SPJ JOIN ( S WHERE CITY = 'London' ) ) { P# }
      UNION
      ( SPJ JOIN ( J WHERE CITY = 'London' ) ) { P# }

6.47  ( S TIMES P ) { S#, P# } MINUS SP { S#, P# }
```

6.48 We show two solutions to this problem. The first, which is due to Hugh Darwen, uses only the operators of Sections 6.2–6.3:

```
WITH ( SP RENAME S# AS SA ) { SA, P# } AS T1,
      /* T1 {SA,P#} : SA supplies part P# */

      ( SP RENAME S# AS SB ) { SB, P# } AS T2,
      /* T2 {SB,P#} : SB supplies part P# */

      T1 { SA } AS T3,
      /* T3 {SA} : SA supplies some part */

      T2 { SB } AS T4,
      /* T4 {SB} : SB supplies some part */

      ( T1 TIMES T4 ) AS T5,
      /* T5 {SA,SB,P#} : SA supplies some part and
                         SB supplies part P# */

      ( T2 TIMES T3 ) AS T6,
      /* T6 {SA,SB,P#} : SB supplies some part and
                         SA supplies part P# */

      ( T1 JOIN T2 ) AS T7,
      /* T7 {SA,SB,P#} : SA and SB both supply part P# */

      ( T3 TIMES T4 ) AS T8,
      /* T8 {SA,SB} : SA supplies some part and
                      SB supplies some part */

      SP { P# } AS T9,
      /* T9 {P#} : part P# is supplied by some supplier */

      ( T8 TIMES T9 ) AS T10,
      /* T10 {SA,SB,P#} :
         SA supplies some part,
         SB supplies some part, and
         part P# is supplied by some supplier */

      ( T10 MINUS T7 ) AS T11,
      /* T11 {SA,SB,P#} : part P# is supplied,
                          but not by both SA and SB */

      ( T6 INTERSECT T11 ) AS T12,
      /* T12 {SA,SB,P#} : part P# is supplied by SA
                          but not by SB */

      ( T5 INTERSECT T11 ) AS T13,
      /* T13 {SA,SB,P#} : part P# is supplied by SB
                          but not by SA */

      T12 { SA, SB } AS T14,
      /* T14 {SA,SB} :
         SA supplies some part not supplied by SB */

      T13 { SA, SB } AS T15,
      /* T15 {SA,SB} :
         SB supplies some part not supplied by SA */

      ( T14 UNION T15 ) AS T16,
      /* T16 {SA,SB} : some part is supplied by SA or SB
                       but not both */
```

```
T7 { SA, SB } AS T17,
/* T17 {SA,SB} :
     some part is supplied by both SA and SB */

( T17 MINUS T16 ) AS T18,
/* T18 {SA,SB} :
     some part is supplied by both SA and SB,
     and no part supplied by SA is not supplied by SB,
     and no part supplied by SB is not supplied by SA
     -- so SA and SB each supply exactly the same parts */

( T18 WHERE SA < SB ) AS T19 :
/* tidy-up step */

    T19
```

The second solution—which is much more straightforward!—makes use of the relational comparisons introduced in Section 6.9.

```
WITH ( S RENAME S# AS SA ) { SA } AS RA ,
     ( S RENAME S# AS SB ) { SB } AS RB :
     ( RA TIMES RB )
          WHERE ( SP WHERE S# = SA ) { P# } =
                ( SP WHERE S# = SB ) { P# }
          AND   SA < SB
```

6.49 `SPJ GROUP ( J#, QTY ) AS JQ`

6.50 Let SPQ denote the result of the expression shown in the answer to Exercise 6.49. Then:

```
SPQ UNGROUP JQ
```

Relational Calculus

7.1 INTRODUCTION

In Chapter 6 we said the manipulative part of the relational model was based on the relational algebra; however, we might equally well have said it was based on the relational *calculus* instead. In other words, the algebra and the calculus are alternatives to each other. The principal distinction between them is as follows: Whereas the algebra provides a collection of explicit operators—join, union, project, etc.—that can be used to tell the system how to *construct* some desired relation from given relations, the calculus merely provides a notation for stating the *definition* of that desired relation in terms of those given relations. For example, consider the query "Get supplier numbers and cities for suppliers who supply part P2." An algebraic formulation of that query might specify operations as follows (we deliberately do not use the formal syntax of Chapter 6):

- First, join supplier and shipment tuples over S#;
- Next, restrict the result of that join to tuples for part P2;
- Finally, project the result of that restriction over S# and CITY.

A calculus formulation, by contrast, might state simply:

- Get S# and CITY for suppliers such that there exists a shipment SP with the same S# value and with P# value P2.

In this latter formulation, the user has merely stated the defining characteristics of the desired result, and has left it to the system to decide exactly what joins, restrictions, etc., must be executed in order to construct that result.

Thus, we might say that—at least superficially—the calculus formulation is *descriptive,* while the algebraic one is *prescriptive:* The calculus simply describes what the problem *is,* the algebra prescribes a procedure for *solving* that problem. Or, *very* informally: The algebra is procedural (admittedly high-level, but still procedural); the calculus is nonprocedural.

However, we stress the point that the foregoing distinctions are only superficial. The fact is, *the algebra and the calculus are logically equivalent:* For every algebraic expression there is an equivalent calculus one, for every calculus expression there is an equivalent algebraic one. There is a one-to-one correspondence between the two. Thus, the difference between them is really just a difference of *style:* The calculus is arguably closer to natural language, the algebra is perhaps more like a programming language. But, to repeat, such distinctions are more apparent than real; in particular, neither approach is genuinely more nonprocedural than the other. We will examine this equivalence question in detail in Section 7.4.

Relational calculus is based on a branch of mathematical logic called the **predicate** calculus. The idea of using predicate calculus as the basis for a query language appears to have originated in a paper by Kuhns [7.6]. The concept of a relational calculus—i.e., an applied predicate calculus specifically tailored to relational databases—was first proposed by Codd in reference [6.1]; a language explicitly based on that calculus called *Data Sublanguage ALPHA* was also presented by Codd in another paper [7.1]. ALPHA itself was never implemented, but a language called QUEL [7.5,7.10–7.12]—which certainly was implemented and for some time was a serious competitor to SQL—was very similar to it; indeed, the design of QUEL was much influenced by ALPHA.

Range variables are a fundamental feature of the calculus. Briefly, a range variable is a variable that "ranges over" some specified relation—i.e., a variable whose permitted values are tuples of that relation. Thus, if range variable V ranges over relation r, then, at any given time, the expression "V" denotes some tuple t of r. For example, the query "Get supplier numbers for suppliers in London" might be expressed in QUEL as follows:

```
RANGE OF SX IS S ;
RETRIEVE ( SX.S# ) WHERE SX.CITY = "London" ;
```

The range variable here is SX, and it ranges over whatever relation is the current value of relvar S (the RANGE statement is a *definition* of that range variable). The RETRIEVE statement can thus be paraphrased: "For each possible value of variable SX, retrieve the S# component of that value, if and only if the CITY component has the value London."

Because of its reliance on range variables whose values are tuples (and to distinguish it from the *domain* calculus—see the next paragraph), the original relational calculus has come to be known as the **tuple** calculus. The tuple calculus is described in detail in Section 7.2. *Note:* For simplicity, we adopt the convention throughout this book that the terms *calculus* and *relational calculus,* without a "tuple" or "domain" qualifier, refer to the tuple calculus specifically (where it makes any difference).

In reference [7.7], Lacroix and Pirotte proposed an alternative version of the calculus called the **domain** calculus, in which the range variables range over domains instead of relations.* Various domain calculus languages have been proposed in the literature; probably the best known is Query-By-Example, QBE [7.14] (though QBE is really something of a hybrid—it incorporates elements of the tuple calculus as well). Several commercial implementations of QBE exist. We sketch the domain calculus in Section 7.6; QBE is discussed briefly in the annotation to reference [7.14].

---

*The terminology is illogical: If the domain calculus is so called for the reason given (which it is), then the tuple calculus ought by rights to be called the *relation* calculus.

Note: We deliberately omit discussion of the calculus analogs of certain topics from Chapter 6, *viz.,* transitive closure, grouping and ungrouping, and relational comparisons. We also omit consideration of calculus versions of the relational update operators. You can find a brief discussion of such matters in reference [3.3].

7.2   TUPLE CALCULUS

As with our discussions of the algebra in Chapter 6, we first introduce a concrete syntax—patterned after, though deliberately not quite identical to, the calculus version of **Tutorial D** defined in reference [3.3]—and then go on to discuss semantics. The subsection immediately following discusses syntax, the remaining subsections consider semantics.

Syntax

Note: Many of the syntax rules given in prose form in this subsection will not make much sense until you have studied some of the semantic material that comes later, but we gather them all here in this one place for purposes of subsequent reference.

It is convenient to begin by repeating the syntax of *<relational expression>*s from Chapter 6:

```
<relational expression>
    ::=    RELATION { <tuple expression commalist> }
         | <relvar name>
         | <relational operation>
         | ( <relational expression> )
```

In other words, the syntax of *<relational expression>*s is the same as before, but one of the most important cases, *<relational operation>*, now has a very different definition (see later).

```
<range var definition>
    ::=    RANGEVAR <range var name>
           RANGES OVER <relational expression commalist> ;
```

A *<range var name>* can be used as a *<tuple expression>*,* but only in certain contexts—namely:

- Preceding the dot qualifier in a *<range attribute reference>;*
- Immediately following the quantifier in a *<quantified boolean expression>;*
- As an operand within a *<boolean expression>;*
- As a *<proto tuple>* or as (an operand within) an *<expression>* within a *<proto tuple>.*

---

*As in Chapter 6, we do not spell out all of the details of *<tuple expression>*s here, trusting that examples will prove sufficient to illustrate the general idea.

```
<range attribute reference>
   ::=   <range var name> . <attribute reference>
                               [ AS <attribute name> ]
```

A *<range attribute reference>* can be used as an *<expression>*, but only in certain contexts—namely:

- As an operand within a *<boolean expression>;*
- As a *<proto tuple>* or as (an operand within) an *<expression>* within a *<proto tuple>*.

```
<boolean expression>
   ::=   ... all the usual possibilities, together with:
      | <quantified boolean expression>
```

References to range variables within a *<boolean expression>* can be free within that *<boolean expression>* only if the following are both true:

- The *<boolean expression>* appears immediately within a *<relational operation>* (i.e., the *<boolean expression>* immediately follows the keyword WHERE), and
- A reference (necessarily free) to that very same range variable appears immediately within the *<proto tuple>* immediately contained within that very same *<relational operation>* (i.e., the *<proto tuple>* immediately precedes the keyword WHERE).

A point of terminology: In the context of the relational calculus (tuple or domain version), boolean expressions are often called **well-formed formulas** or WFFs (pronounced "weffs"). We will use this terminology ourselves in much of what follows.

```
<quantified boolean expression>
   ::=   EXISTS <range var name> ( <boolean expression> )
      | FORALL <range var name> ( <boolean expression> )

<relational operation>
   ::=   <proto tuple> [ WHERE <boolean expression> ]
```

As in the algebra of Chapter 6, a *<relational operation>* is one form of *<relational expression>*, but (as noted earlier) we are giving it a different definition here. The other forms of *<relational expression>*—basically relvar names and relation selector invocations—are still legal, as before.

```
<proto tuple>
   ::=   <tuple expression>
```

All references to range variables appearing immediately within a *<proto tuple>* must be free within that *<proto tuple>*. *Note:* "Proto tuple" stands for "prototype tuple"; the term is apt but not standard.

Range Variables

Here are some sample range variable definitions (expressed as usual in terms of suppliers and parts):

```
RANGEVAR SX   RANGES OVER S ;
RANGEVAR SY   RANGES OVER S ;
RANGEVAR SPX  RANGES OVER SP ;
RANGEVAR SPY  RANGES OVER SP ;
RANGEVAR PX   RANGES OVER P ;

RANGEVAR SU RANGES OVER
          ( SX WHERE SX.CITY = 'London' ) ,
          ( SX WHERE EXISTS SPX ( SPX.S# = SX.S# AND
                                  SPX.P# SPX = P# ('P1') ) ) ;
```

Range variable SU in this last example is defined to range over the *union* of the set of supplier tuples for suppliers who are located in London and the set of supplier tuples for suppliers who supply part P1. Note that the definition of range variable SU makes use of the range variables SX and SPX. Note too that in such "union-style" definitions, the relations to be "unioned" must (of course) all be of the same type.

Note: Range variables are not variables in the usual programming language sense, they are variables in the sense of logic. In fact, they are analogous, somewhat, to the predicate *placeholders* or *parameters* discussed in Chapter 3 (the difference is that the placeholders of Chapter 3 stood for domain values, while range variables in the tuple calculus stand for tuples).

Throughout the rest of this chapter, we will assume that the range variable definitions shown above are in effect. We note that in a real language there would have to be some rules regarding the scope of such definitions. We ignore such matters in the present chapter.

Free and Bound Variable References

Every reference to a range variable is either **free** or **bound** (in some context—in particular, within some WFF). We explain this notion in purely syntactic terms first, then go on to discuss its significance afterwards.

Let V be a range variable. Then:

- References to V in the WFF "NOT p" are free or bound within that WFF according as they are free or bound in p. References to V in the WFFs "(p AND q)" and "(p OR q)" are free or bound in those WFFs according as they are free or bound in p or q, as applicable.

- References to V that are free in the WFF "p" are bound in the WFFs "EXISTS V (p)" and "FORALL V (p)." Other references to range variables in "p" are free or bound in the WFFs "EXISTS V (p)" and "FORALL V (p)" according as they are free or bound in "p".

For completeness, we need to add the following:

- The sole reference to V in the *<range var name>* "V" is free within that *<range var name>*.

- The sole reference to V in the *<range attribute reference>* "$V.A$" is free within that *<range attribute reference>*.

- If a reference to *V* is free in some expression *exp,* that reference is also free in any expression *exp′* that immediately contains *exp* as a subexpression, unless *exp′* introduces a quantifier that makes the reference bound instead.

Here then are some examples of WFFs containing range variable references:

- *Simple comparisons:*

```
SX.S# = S# ( 'S1' )

SX.S# = SPX.S#

SPX.P# ≠ PX.P#
```

All references to SX, PX, and SPX are free in these examples.

- *Boolean combinations of simple comparisons:*

```
PX.WEIGHT < WEIGHT ( 15.5 ) OR PX.CITY = 'Rome'

NOT ( SX.CITY = 'London' )

SX.S# = SPX.S# AND SPX.P# ≠ PX.P#

PX.COLOR = COLOR ( 'Red' ) OR PX.CITY = 'London'
```

Again, all references to SX, PX, and SPX here are free.

- *Quantified WFFs:*

```
EXISTS SPX ( SPX.S# = SX.S# AND SPX.P# = P# ( 'P2' ) )

FORALL PX ( PX.COLOR = COLOR ( 'Red' ) )
```

The references to SPX and PX in these two examples are bound, the reference to SX is free. See the subsection immediately following.

Quantifiers

There are two quantifiers, EXISTS and FORALL; EXISTS is the **existential** quantifier, FORALL is the **universal** quantifier. Basically, if *p* is a WFF in which *V* is free, then

```
EXISTS V ( p )
```

and

```
FORALL V ( p )
```

are both legal WFFs, and *V* is bound in both of them. The first means: **There exists at least one value** of *V* that makes *p* evaluate to *true.* The second means: **For all values** of *V, p* evaluates to *true.* For example, suppose the variable *V* ranges over the set "Members of the US Senate in 1999," and suppose *p* is the WFF "*V* is female" (of course, we are not trying to use our formal syntax here!). Then "EXISTS *V* (*p*)" and "FORALL *V* (*p*)" are both legal WFFs, and they evaluate to *true* and *false,* respectively.

Look again at the EXISTS example from the end of the previous subsection:

```
EXISTS SPX ( SPX.S# = SX.S# AND SPX.P# = P# ( 'P2' ) )
```

It follows from the foregoing that we can read this WFF as follows:

> *There exists a tuple SPX, say, in the current value of relvar SP such that the S# value in that tuple SPX is equal to the value of SX.S#—whatever that is—and the P# value in that tuple SPX is P2.*

Each reference to SPX here is bound. The single reference to SX is free.

We define EXISTS formally as **an iterated OR.** In other words, if (a) *r* is a relation with tuples *t1, t2, …, tm,* (b) *V* is a range variable that ranges over *r,* and (c) *p(V)* is a WFF in which *V* occurs as a free variable, then the WFF

```
EXISTS V ( p ( V ) )
```

is defined to be equivalent to the WFF

```
false OR p ( t1 ) OR ... OR p ( tm )
```

Observe in particular that this expression evaluates to false if *R* is empty (i.e., if *m* is zero).

By way of example, suppose relation *r* contains exactly the following tuples:

```
( 1, 2, 3 )
( 1, 2, 4 )
( 1, 3, 4 )
```

For simplicity, assume that (a) the three attributes, in left-to-right order as shown, are called *A, B,* and *C,* respectively; (b) every attribute is of type INTEGER. Then the following WFFs have the indicated values:

```
EXISTS V ( V.C > 1 )              :   true
EXISTS V ( V.B > 3 )              :   false
EXISTS V ( V.A > 1 OR V.C = 4 )   :   true
```

We turn now to FORALL. Here to repeat is the FORALL example from the end of the previous subsection:

```
FORALL PX ( PX.COLOR = COLOR ( 'Red' ) )
```

We can read this WFF as follows:

> For all tuples PX, say, in the current value of relvar P, the COLOR value in that tuple PX is Red.

The two references to PX here are both bound.

Just as we define EXISTS as an iterated OR, so we define FORALL as **an iterated AND.** In other words, if *r, V,* and *p(V)* are as in our discussion of EXISTS above, then the WFF

```
FORALL V ( p ( V ) )
```

is defined to be equivalent to the WFF

```
true AND p ( t1 ) AND ... AND p ( tm )
```

Observe in particular that this expression evaluates to *true* if *R* is empty (i.e., if *m* is zero).

By way of example, let relation *r* contain the same tuples as before. Then the following WFFs have the indicated values:

```
FORALL V ( V.A > 1 )              :  false
FORALL V ( V.B > 1 )              :  true
FORALL V ( V.A = 1 AND V.C > 2 )  :  true
```

Note: FORALL is included purely for convenience (it is not essential). To be specific, the identity

```
FORALL V ( p )  ≡  NOT EXISTS V ( NOT p )
```

(loosely, "all *V*'s satisfy *p*" is the same as "no *V*'s do not satisfy *p*") shows that any WFF involving FORALL can always be replaced by an equivalent WFF involving EXISTS instead. For example, the (true) statement

For all integers *x*, there exists an integer *y* such that $y > x$

(i.e., every integer has a greater integer) is equivalent to the statement

There does not exist an integer *x* such that there does not exist an integer *y* such that $y > x$

(i.e., there is no greatest integer). But it is usually easier to think in terms of FORALL than in terms of EXISTS and a double negative. In other words, it is desirable in practice to support both quantifiers.

Free and Bound Variable References Revisited

Suppose *x* ranges over the set of all integers, and consider the WFF

```
EXISTS x ( x > 3 )
```

Observe that *x* here is a kind of *dummy*—it serves only to link the boolean expression inside the parentheses to the quantifier outside. The WFF simply states that there exists some integer, *x* say, that is greater than three. *Note, therefore, that the meaning of this WFF would remain totally unchanged if all references to* x *were replaced by references to some other variable* y. In other words, the WFF

```
EXISTS y ( y > 3 )
```

is semantically identical to the one above.

Now consider the WFF

```
EXISTS x ( x > 3 ) AND x < 0
```

Here there are three references to *x, denoting two different variables.* The first two references are bound, and could be replaced by references to some other variable *y* without changing the overall meaning. The third reference is free, and *cannot* be replaced with impunity. Thus, of the two WFFs shown below, the first is equivalent to the one just given and the second is not:

```
EXISTS y ( y > 3 ) AND x < 0

EXISTS y ( y > 3 ) AND y < 0
```

Note, moreover, that the truth value of the original WFF cannot be determined without knowing the value denoted by the free variable reference *x.* By contrast, a WFF in which all variable references are bound is *true* or *false,* unequivocally. *More terminology:* A WFF in which all variable references are bound is called a **closed WFF** (in fact, it is a *proposition*). An **open WFF** is a WFF that is not closed, i.e., one that contains at least one free variable reference.

Relational Operations

The term *<relational operation>* is perhaps not very apt in a calculus context—*<relational definition>* might be more appropriate—but we use it for consistency with Chapter 6. Here to remind you is the syntax:

```
<relational operation>
     ::=     <proto tuple> [ WHERE <boolean expression> ]

<proto tuple>
     ::=     <tuple expression>
```

We remind you also of the following syntax rules, now slightly simplified:

- First, all references to range variables in the "proto tuple" must be free within that "proto tuple."

- Second, a reference to a range variable in the WHERE clause can be free only if a reference to that very same range variable (necessarily free) appears in the corresponding "proto tuple."

For example, the following is a legal *<relational operation>* ("Get supplier numbers for suppliers in London"):

```
SX.S# WHERE SX.CITY = 'London'
```

The reference to SX in the proto tuple here is free. The reference to SX in the WHERE clause is also free, a state of affairs that is legal because a reference (necessarily free) to the very same range variable also appears in the *proto tuple. Note:* From now on, we will no longer place the term *proto tuple* in quotation marks.

Here is another example ("Get supplier names for suppliers who supply part P2"—see the discussion of EXISTS in the subsection on quantifiers, earlier):

```
SX.SNAME WHERE EXISTS SPX ( SPX.S# = SX.S# AND
                            SPX.P# = P# ( 'P2' ) )
```

The references to SX are all free; the references to SPX (in the WHERE clause) are all bound, as they must be, because there are no references to that same range variable in the proto tuple.

Intuitively, a given *<relational operation>* evaluates to a relation containing every possible value of the *<proto tuple>* for which the *<boolean expression>* specified in the WHERE clause evaluates to *true* (and omitting the WHERE clause is equivalent to specifying "WHERE *true*"). To be more specific:

- First of all, a proto tuple is a possibly parenthesized commalist of items, in which each item is either a range attribute reference (possibly including an AS clause to introduce a new attribute name) or a simple range variable name.* However:

  a. A range variable name in this context is basically just shorthand for a commalist of range attribute references, one such for each attribute of the relation the range variable ranges over;

  b. A range attribute reference without an AS clause is basically just shorthand for one that includes such a clause in which the new attribute name is the same as the old one.

  Without loss of generality, therefore, we can regard a proto tuple as a commalist of range attribute references of the form *Vi.Aj* AS *Bj*. Note that the *Vi*'s and the *Aj*'s need not all be distinct, but the *Bj*'s must be.

- Let the distinct range variables mentioned in the proto tuple be *V1, V2, ..., Vm*. Let the relations over which these variables range be *r1, r2, ..., rm*, respectively. Let the corresponding relations after application of the attribute renamings specified in the AS clauses be *r1', r2', ..., rm'*, respectively. Let *r'* be the Cartesian product of *r1', r2', ..., rm'*.

- Let *r* be that restriction of *r'* that satisfies the WFF in the WHERE clause. *Note:* We assume for the sake of this explanation that the renamings in the previous step are applied to attributes mentioned in the WHERE clause also—for otherwise the WFF in that WHERE clause might not make sense. In fact, however, our concrete syntax does not rely on this assumption but instead relies on dot qualification to handle any necessary "disambiguation," as we will see in the next section.

- The overall value of the *<relational operation>* is defined to be the projection of *r* over all of the *Bj*'s.

For some examples, see the section immediately following.

---

*Typically, at any rate (for the time being we limit our attention to these two possibilities only).

7.3 EXAMPLES

We present a few examples of the use of the calculus in formulating queries. As an exercise, you might like to try giving algebraic solutions as well, for "compare and contrast" purposes.

7.3.1 Get supplier numbers and status for suppliers in Paris with status > 20.

```
( SX.S#, SX.STATUS )
WHERE SX.CITY = 'Paris' AND SX.STATUS > 20
```

7.3.2 Get all pairs of supplier numbers such that the two suppliers are colocated (i.e., located in the same city).

```
( SX.S# AS SA, SY.S# AS SB )
               WHERE SX.CITY = SY.CITY AND SX.S# < SY.S#
```

Note that the AS clauses in the proto tuple give names to attributes of the *result;* those names are thus not available for use in the WHERE clause, which is why the second comparison in that WHERE clause is "SX.S# < SY.S#," not "SA < SB."

7.3.3 Get full supplier information for suppliers who supply part P2.

```
SX
WHERE EXISTS SPX ( SPX.S# = SX.S# AND SPX.P# = P# ( 'P2' ) )
```

Note the use of a range variable name in the proto tuple here. The example is shorthand for the following:

```
( SX.S#, SX.SNAME, SX.STATUS, SX.CITY )
WHERE EXISTS SPX ( SPX.S# = SX.S# AND SPX.P# = P# ( 'P2' ) )
```

7.3.4 Get supplier names for suppliers who supply at least one red part.

```
SX.SNAME
WHERE EXISTS SPX ( SX.S# = SPX.S# AND
                  EXISTS PX ( PX.P# = SPX.P# AND
                              PX.COLOR = COLOR ( 'Red' ) ) )
```

Or equivalently (but in **prenex normal form,** in which all quantifiers appear at the front of the WFF):

```
SX.SNAME
WHERE EXISTS SPX ( EXISTS PX ( SX.S# = SPX.S# AND
                              SPX.P# = PX.P# AND
                              PX.COLOR = COLOR ( 'Red' ) ) )
```

Prenex normal form is not inherently more or less correct than any other form, but with a little practice it does tend to become the most natural formulation in many cases. Furthermore, it introduces the possibility of reducing the number of parentheses, as follows. The WFF

```
quant1 vble1 ( quant2 vble2 ( wff ) )
```

(where each of *quant1* and *quant2* is either EXISTS or FORALL) can optionally, and unambiguously, be abbreviated to just

```
quant1 vble1 quant2 vble2 ( wff )
```

Thus we can simplify the calculus expression shown above to just

```
SX.SNAME
WHERE EXISTS SPX EXISTS PX ( SX.S# = SPX.S# AND
                             SPX.P# = PX.P# AND
                             PX.COLOR = COLOR ( 'Red' ) )
```

For clarity, however, we will continue to show all parentheses explicitly in this section.

7.3.5 Get supplier names for suppliers who supply at least one part supplied by supplier S2.

```
SX.SNAME
WHERE EXISTS SPX ( EXISTS SPY ( SX.S# = SPX.S# AND
                                SPX.P# = SPY.P# AND
                                SPY.S# = S# ( 'S2' ) ) )
```

7.3.6 Get supplier names for suppliers who supply all parts.

```
SX.SNAME WHERE FORALL PX ( EXISTS SPX ( SPX.S# = SX.S# AND
                                        SPX.P# = PX.P# ) )
```

Or equivalently, but without using FORALL:

```
SX.SNAME WHERE NOT EXISTS PX ( NOT EXISTS SPX
                                 ( SPX.S# = SX.S# AND
                                   SPX.P# = PX.P# ) )
```

7.3.7 Get supplier names for suppliers who do not supply part P2.

```
SX.SNAME WHERE NOT EXISTS SPX
                 ( SPX.S# = SX.S# AND SPX.P# = P# ( 'P2' ) )
```

Notice how easily this solution is derived from the solution to Example 7.3.3 above.

7.3.8 Get supplier numbers for suppliers who supply at least all those parts supplied by supplier S2.

```
SX.S# WHERE FORALL SPX ( SPX.S# ≠ S# ( 'S2' ) OR
                         EXISTS SPY ( SPY.S# = SX.S# AND
                                      SPY.P# = SPX.P# ) )
```

Paraphrasing: "Get supplier numbers for suppliers SX such that, for all shipments SPX, either that shipment is not from supplier S2, or if it is, then there exists a shipment SPY of the SPX part from supplier SX."

We introduce another syntactic shorthand to help with complex queries such as this one, namely an explicit syntactic form for the **logical implication** operator. If *p* and *q* are WFFs, then the logical implication expression

```
IF p THEN q END IF
```

is also a WFF, with semantics identical to those of the WFF

```
( NOT p ) OR q
```

The example can thus be reformulated as follows:

```
SX.S# WHERE FORALL SPX ( IF SPX.S# = S# ( 'S2' ) THEN
                            EXISTS SPY ( SPY.S# = SX.S# AND
                                         SPY.P# = SPX.P# )
                 END IF )
```

Paraphrasing: "Get supplier numbers for suppliers SX such that, for all shipments SPX, if that shipment SPX is from supplier S2, then there exists a shipment SPY of the SPX part from supplier SX."

7.3.9 Get part numbers for parts that either weigh more than 16 pounds or are supplied by supplier S2, or both.

```
RANGEVAR PU RANGES OVER
        ( PX.P# WHERE PX.WEIGHT > WEIGHT ( 16.0 ) ),
        ( SPX.P# WHERE SPX.S# = S# ( 'S2' ) ) ;

PU.P#
```

The relational algebra analog here would involve an explicit union.

For interest, we show an alternative formulation of this query. However, this second formulation relies on the fact that every part number in relvar SP also appears in relvar P, which the "union-style" formulation does not.

```
PX.P# WHERE PX.WEIGHT > WEIGHT ( 16.0 )
      OR    EXISTS SPX ( SPX.P# = PX.P# AND
                         SPX.S# = S# ( 'S2' ) )
```

7.4   CALCULUS *VS.* ALGEBRA

We claimed in the introduction to this chapter that the algebra and the calculus are fundamentally equivalent. We now examine that claim in more detail. First, Codd showed in reference [6.1] that the algebra is at least as powerful as the calculus. He did this by giving an algorithm—"Codd's reduction algorithm"—by which an arbitrary expression of the calculus could be reduced to a semantically equivalent expression of the algebra. We do not present Codd's algorithm in detail here, but content ourselves with a reasonably complex example that illustrates in broad terms how that algorithm works.*

---

*Actually, the algorithm presented in reference [6.1] had a slight flaw in it [7.2]. Furthermore, the version of the calculus defined in that paper did not include a full counterpart to the union operator, so in fact Codd's calculus was strictly less powerful than Codd's algebra. The claim that the algebra and the calculus, enhanced to include a full union counterpart, are equivalent is nevertheless true, however, as several writers have demonstrated; see, e.g., Klug [6.12].

As a basis for our example we use, not the familiar suppliers and parts database, but the extended suppliers-parts-projects version from the exercises in Chapter 4 and elsewhere. For convenience we show in Fig. 7.1 a set of sample values for that database (repeated from Fig. 4.5 in Chapter 4).

Now consider the query "Get names and cities for suppliers who supply at least one Athens project with at least 50 of every part." A calculus expression for this query is:

```
( SX.SNAME, SX.CITY ) WHERE EXISTS JX FORALL PX EXISTS SPJX
                      ( JX.CITY = 'Athens' AND
                        JX.J# = SPJX.J# AND
                        PX.P# = SPJX.P# AND
                        SX.S# = SPJX.S# AND
                        SPJX.QTY ≥ QTY ( 50 ) )
```

where SX, PX, JX, and SPJX are range variables ranging over S, P, J, and SPJ, respectively. We now show how this expression can be evaluated to yield the desired result.

Step 1: For each range variable, retrieve the range (i.e., the set of possible values for that variable), restricted if possible. By "restricted if possible," we mean that there might be a restriction condition embedded within the WHERE clause that can be used right away

S	S#	SNAME	STATUS	CITY
	S1	Smith	20	London
	S2	Jones	10	Paris
	S3	Blake	30	Paris
	S4	Clark	20	London
	S5	Adams	30	Athens

P	P#	PNAME	COLOR	WEIGHT	CITY
	P1	Nut	Red	12.0	London
	P2	Bolt	Green	17.0	Paris
	P3	Screw	Blue	17.0	Rome
	P4	Screw	Red	14.0	London
	P5	Cam	Blue	12.0	Paris
	P6	Cog	Red	19.0	London

J	J#	JNAME	CITY
	J1	Sorter	Paris
	J2	Display	Rome
	J3	OCR	Athens
	J4	Console	Athens
	J5	RAID	London
	J6	EDS	Oslo
	J7	Tape	London

SPJ	S#	P#	J#	QTY
	S1	P1	J1	200
	S1	P1	J4	700
	S2	P3	J1	400
	S2	P3	J2	200
	S2	P3	J3	200
	S2	P3	J4	500
	S2	P3	J5	600
	S2	P3	J6	400
	S2	P3	J7	800
	S2	P5	J2	100
	S3	P3	J1	200
	S3	P4	J2	500
	S4	P6	J3	300
	S4	P6	J7	300
	S5	P2	J2	200
	S5	P2	J4	100
	S5	P5	J5	500
	S5	P5	J7	100
	S5	P6	J2	200
	S5	P1	J4	100
	S5	P3	J4	200
	S5	P4	J4	800
	S5	P5	J4	400
	S5	P6	J4	500

Fig. 7.1   The suppliers-parts-projects database (sample values)

to eliminate certain tuples from all further consideration. In the case at hand, the sets of tuples retrieved are as follows:

SX	:	All tuples of S	5 tuples
PX	:	All tuples of P	6 tuples
JX	:	Tuples of J where CITY = 'Athens'	2 tuples
SPJX	:	Tuples of SPJ where QTY ≥ QTY (50)	24 tuples

Step 2: Construct the Cartesian product of the ranges retrieved in Step 1, to yield:

S#	SN	STATUS	CITY	P#	PN	COLOR	WEIGHT	CITY	J#	JN	CITY	S#	P#	J#	QTY
S1	Sm	20	Lon	P1	Nt	Red	12.0	Lon	J3	OR	Ath	S1	P1	J1	200
S1	Sm	20	Lon	P1	Nt	Red	12.0	Lon	J3	OR	Ath	S1	P1	J4	700
..	..	..	...	..	..	...	..	...	..	..	...	..	..	..	...
..	..	..	...	..	..	...	..	...	..	..	...	..	..	..	...
..	..	..	...	..	..	...	..	...	..	..	...	..	..	..	...

(etc., etc.). The complete product contains 5 ∗ 6 ∗ 2 ∗ 24 = 1440 tuples. *Note:* We have made a number of obvious abbreviations here in the interests of space. Also, we have not bothered to rename attributes (as we really ought to have done, to avoid ambiguity), but instead are relying on ordinal position to show (e.g.) which "S#" comes from S and which from SPJ. This unorthodox trick is adopted purely to shorten the exposition.

Step 3: Restrict the Cartesian product constructed in Step 2 in accordance with the "join portion" of the WHERE clause. In the example, that portion is

```
JX.J# = SPJX.J# AND PX.P# = SPJX.P# AND SX.S# = SPJX.S#
```

We therefore eliminate tuples from the product for which the supplier S# value is not equal to the shipment S# value or the part P# value is not equal to the shipment P# value or the project J# value is not equal to the shipment J# value, to yield a subset of the Cartesian product consisting (as it happens) of just ten tuples:

S#	SN	STATUS	CITY	P#	PN	COLOR	WEIGHT	CITY	J#	JN	CITY	S#	P#	J#	QTY
S1	Sm	20	Lon	P1	Nt	Red	12.0	Lon	J4	Cn	Ath	S1	P1	J4	700
S2	Jo	10	Par	P3	Sc	Blue	17.0	Rom	J3	OR	Ath	S2	P3	J3	200
S2	Jo	10	Par	P3	Sc	Blue	17.0	Rom	J4	Cn	Ath	S2	P3	J4	200
S4	Cl	20	Lon	P6	Cg	Red	19.0	Lon	J3	OR	Ath	S4	P6	J3	300
S5	Ad	30	Ath	P2	Bt	Green	17.0	Par	J4	Cn	Ath	S5	P2	J4	100
S5	Ad	30	Ath	P1	Nt	Red	12.0	Lon	J4	Cn	Ath	S5	P1	J4	100
S5	Ad	30	Ath	P3	Sc	Blue	17.0	Rom	J4	Cn	Ath	S5	P3	J4	200
S5	Ad	30	Ath	P4	Sc	Red	14.0	Lon	J4	Cn	Ath	S5	P4	J4	800
S5	Ad	30	Ath	P5	Cm	Blue	12.0	Par	J4	Cn	Ath	S5	P5	J4	400
S5	Ad	30	Ath	P6	Cg	Red	19.0	Lon	J4	Cn	Ath	S5	P6	J4	500

(This relation is the pertinent equijoin, of course.)

Step 4: Apply the quantifiers from right to left, as follows.

- For the quantifier "EXISTS *RX*" (where *RX* is a range variable that ranges over some relation *r*), *project* the current intermediate result to eliminate all attributes of relation *r*.

■ For the quantifier "FORALL *RX*," *divide* the current intermediate result by the "restricted range" relation associated with *RX* as retrieved in Step 1. This operation will also have the effect of eliminating all attributes of relation *R*. *Note:* "Divide" here means Codd's original divide operation (see the annotation to reference [6.3]).

In the example, the quantifiers are:

```
EXISTS JX FORALL PX EXISTS SPJX
```

Hence:

1. *(EXISTS SPJX)* Project away the attributes of SPJ—*viz.*, SPJ.S#, SPJ.P#, SPJ.J#, and SPJ.QTY. *Result:*

S#	SN	STATUS	CITY	P#	PN	COLOR	WEIGHT	CITY	J#	JN	CITY
S1	Sm	20	Lon	P1	Nt	Red	12.0	Lon	J4	Cn	Ath
S2	Jo	10	Par	P3	Sc	Blue	17.0	Rom	J3	OR	Ath
S2	Jo	10	Par	P3	Sc	Blue	17.0	Rom	J4	Cn	Ath
S4	Cl	20	Lon	P6	Cg	Red	19.0	Lon	J3	OR	Ath
S5	Ad	30	Ath	P2	Bt	Green	17.0	Par	J4	Cn	Ath
S5	Ad	30	Ath	P1	Nt	Red	12.0	Lon	J4	Cn	Ath
S5	Ad	30	Ath	P3	Sc	Blue	17.0	Rom	J4	Cn	Ath
S5	Ad	30	Ath	P4	Sc	Red	14.0	Lon	J4	Cn	Ath
S5	Ad	30	Ath	P5	Cm	Blue	12.0	Par	J4	Cn	Ath
S5	Ad	30	Ath	P6	Cg	Red	19.0	Lon	J4	Cn	Ath

2. *(FORALL PX)* Divide by P. *Result:*

S#	SNAME	STATUS	CITY	J#	JNAME	CITY
S5	Adams	30	Athens	J4	Console	Athens

(We now have room to show the result without any abbreviations.)

3. *(EXISTS JX)* Project away the attributes of J—*viz.*, J.J#, J.JNAME, and J.CITY. *Result:*

S#	SNAME	STATUS	CITY
S5	Adams	30	Athens

Step 5: Project the result of Step 4 in accordance with the specifications in the proto tuple. In our example, the proto tuple is:

```
( SX.SNAME, SX.CITY )
```

Hence the final result is:

SNAME	CITY
Adams	Athens

It follows from all of the foregoing that the original calculus expression is semantically equivalent to a certain nested algebraic expression—to be precise, a projection of a projection of a division of a projection of a restriction of a product of four restrictions (!).

This concludes the example. Of course, many improvements to the algorithm are possible (see Chapter 17, in particular reference [17.5], for some ideas for such improvements), and many details have been glossed over in our explanation; nevertheless, the example should be adequate to give the general idea of how the reduction works.

Incidentally, we are now able to explain one of the reasons (not the only one) why Codd defined precisely the eight algebraic operators he did: Those eight operators provided a convenient **target language** as a vehicle for a possible implementation of the calculus. In other words, given a language such as QUEL that is founded on the calculus, one possible approach to implementing that language would be to take the query as submitted by the user—which is basically just a calculus expression—and apply the reduction algorithm to it, thereby obtaining an equivalent algebraic expression. That algebraic expression of course consists of a set of algebraic operators, which are by definition inherently implementable. (The next step is to go on to *optimize* that algebraic expression—see Chapter 17.)

Another point to note is that Codd's eight algebraic operators also provide a *yardstick* for measuring the expressive power of any given database language. We mentioned this issue briefly in Chapter 6, at the end of Section 6.6; we now examine it in a little more depth.

First, a language is said to be **relationally complete** if it is at least as powerful as the calculus—that is, if any relation definable by some expression of the calculus is also definable by some expression of the language in question [6.1]. (In Chapter 6 we said that "relationally complete" meant as powerful as the *algebra,* not the calculus, but it comes to the same thing, as we will see in a moment. Note that it follows immediately from the existence of Codd's reduction algorithm that the algebra is relationally complete.)

Relational completeness can be regarded as a basic measure of expressive power for database languages in general. In particular, since the calculus and the algebra are both relationally complete, they both provide a basis for designing languages that provide this power of expressiveness *without having to resort to the use of loops*—a particularly important consideration in the case of a language that is intended for end users, though it is significant for application programmers as well.

Next, since the algebra is relationally complete, it follows that, to show that any given language *L* is also complete, it is sufficient to show (a) that *L* includes analogs of each of the eight algebraic operators (indeed, it is sufficient to show that it includes analogs of the five *primitive* algebraic operators), and (b) that the operands of any operator in *L* can be arbitrary *L* expressions. SQL is an example of a language that can be shown to be relationally complete in this manner—see Exercise 7.9—and QUEL is another. Indeed, it is often easier in practice to show that a given language has equivalents of the algebraic operators than it is to show that it has equivalents of the expressions of the calculus. This is why we typically define relational completeness in algebraic rather than calculus terms.

Incidentally, please understand that relational completeness does not necessarily imply any other kind of completeness. For example, it is desirable that a language provide "computational completeness" also—i.e., it should be capable of computing all computable functions. Computational completeness was one of the motivations for the EXTEND and SUM-MARIZE operators that we added to the algebra in Chapter 6. In the next section, we will consider calculus analogs of those operators.

To return to the question of the equivalence of the algebra and the calculus: We have shown by example that any calculus expression can be reduced to an algebraic equivalent, and hence that the algebra is at least as powerful as the calculus. Conversely, it is possible to show that any algebraic expression can be reduced to a calculus equivalent, and hence that the calculus is at least as powerful as the algebra; for proof, see, e.g., Ullman [7.13]. It follows that the two are logically equivalent.

7.5 COMPUTATIONAL CAPABILITIES

We did not call the point out explicitly earlier, but in fact the calculus as we have defined it already includes analogs of the algebraic EXTEND and SUMMARIZE operators, because:

- One possible form of proto tuple is a *<tuple selector invocation>,* and the components of a *<tuple selector invocation>* can be arbitrary *<expression>*s.

- The comparands in a comparison in a *<boolean expression>* can also be arbitrary *<expression>*s.

- The first or only argument to an *<aggregate operator invocation>* is a *<relational operation>*.

Note: We are appealing here to the full definition of **Tutorial D** as given in reference [3.3].

It is not worth going into all of the applicable syntactic and semantic details here. We content ourselves with giving a few examples merely (and those examples themselves are slightly simplified in certain respects).

7.5.1 Get the part number and the weight in grams for each part with weight > 10000 grams.

```
( PX.P#, PX.WEIGHT * 454 AS GMWT )
                WHERE PX.WEIGHT * 454 > WEIGHT ( 10000.0 )
```

Observe that the specification "AS GMWT" in the proto tuple gives a name to the applicable attribute of the *result.* That name is thus not available for use in the WHERE clause, which is why the expression "PX.WEIGHT * 454" appears twice.

7.5.2 Get all suppliers and tag each one with the literal value "Supplier."

```
( SX, 'Supplier' AS TAG )
```

7.5.3 For each shipment, get full shipment details, including total shipment weight.

```
( SPX, PX.WEIGHT * SPX.QTY ) AS SHIPWT WHERE PX.P# = SPX.P#
```

7.5.4 For each part, get the part number and the total shipment quantity.

```
( PX.P#, SUM ( SPX WHERE SPX.P# = PX.P#, QTY ) AS TOTQTY )
```

7.5.5 Get the total shipment quantity.

```
SUM ( SPX, QTY ) AS GRANDTOTAL
```

7.5.6 For each supplier, get the supplier number and the total number of parts supplied.

```
( SX.S#, COUNT ( SPX WHERE SPX.S# = SX.S# ) AS #_OF_PARTS )
```

7.5.7 Get part cities that store more than five red parts.

```
RANGEVAR PY RANGES OVER P ;

PX.CITY
WHERE COUNT ( PY WHERE PY.CITY = PX.CITY
                  AND   PY.COLOR = COLOR ( 'Red' ) ) > 5
```

7.6   DOMAIN CALCULUS

As indicated in Section 7.1, the domain calculus differs from the tuple calculus in that its range variables range over *domains* instead of relations. We discuss the domain calculus only rather briefly in this book. From a practical standpoint, the most immediately obvious syntax difference is that the domain calculus supports an additional form of *<boolean expression>*, which we will refer to as a **membership condition.** A membership condition takes the form

```
R ( pair, pair, ... )
```

where *R* is a relvar name, and each *pair* is of the form *A:v,* where *A* is an attribute of *R* and *v* is either the name of a range variable of the domain calculus or a selector invocation (usually a literal). The condition evaluates to *true* if and only if there exists a tuple in whatever relation is the current value of *R* having the specified values for the specified attributes. For example, the expression

```
SP ( S#:S#('S1'), P#:P#('P1') )
```

is a membership condition that evaluates to *true* if and only if there currently exists a shipment tuple with S# value S1 and P# value P1. Likewise, the membership condition

```
SP ( S#:SX, P#:PX )
```

evaluates to *true* if and only if there currently exists a shipment tuple with S# value equal to the current value of range variable SX (whatever that might be) and P# value equal to the current value of range variable PX (again, whatever that might be).

For the remainder of this section we assume the existence of domain calculus range variables as follows:

Domain:	*Range variables:*
S#	SX, SY, ...
P#	PX, PY, ...
NAME	NAMEX, NAMEY, ...
COLOR	COLORX, COLORY, ...
WEIGHT	WEIGHTX, WEIGHTY, ...
QTY	QTYX, QTYY, ...
CHAR	CITYX, CITYY, ...
INTEGER	STATUSX, STATUSY, ...

Here then are some examples of domain calculus expressions:

```
SX

SX WHERE S ( S#:SX )

SX WHERE S ( S#:SX, CITY:'London' )

( SX, CITYX ) WHERE S ( S#:SX, CITY:CITYX )
             AND   SP ( S#:SX, P#:P#('P2') )

( SX, PX ) WHERE S ( S#:SX, CITY:CITYX )
           AND   P ( P#:PX, CITY:CITYY )
           AND   CITYX ≠ CITYY
```

Loosely speaking, the first of these expressions denotes the set of all supplier numbers; the second denotes the set of all supplier numbers in relvar S; the third denotes that subset of those supplier numbers for which the city is London. The next is a domain calculus representation of the query "Get supplier numbers and cities for suppliers who supply part P2" (note that the tuple calculus version of this query required an existential quantifier). The last is a domain calculus representation of the query "Get supplier-number/part-number pairs such that the supplier and part are not colocated."

We give domain calculus versions of some of the examples from Section 7.3 (some of them slightly modified).

7.6.1 Get supplier numbers for suppliers in Paris with status > 20.

```
SX WHERE EXISTS STATUSX
       ( STATUSX > 20 AND
         S ( S#:SX, STATUS:STATUSX, CITY:'Paris' ) )
```

This first example is somewhat clumsier than its tuple calculus counterpart (observe in particular that quantifiers are still needed). On the other hand, there are also cases where the reverse is true; see especially some of the more complex examples later in this section.

7.6.2 Get all pairs of supplier numbers such that the two suppliers are colocated.

```
( SX AS SA, SY AS SB ) WHERE EXISTS CITYZ
                           ( S ( S#:SX, CITY:CITYZ ) AND
                             S ( S#:SY, CITY:CITYZ ) AND
                             SX < SY )
```

7.6.3 Get supplier names for suppliers who supply at least one red part.

```
NAMEX WHERE EXISTS SX EXISTS PX
           ( S ( S#:SX, SNAME:NAMEX )
             AND SP ( S#:SX, P#:PX )
             AND P ( P#:PX, COLOR:COLOR('Red') ) )
```

7.6.4 Get supplier names for suppliers who supply at least one part supplied by supplier S2.

```
NAMEX WHERE EXISTS SX EXISTS PX
           ( S ( S#:SX, SNAME:NAMEX )
             AND SP ( S#:SX, P#:PX )
             AND SP ( S#:S#('S2'), P#:PX ) )
```

7.6.5 Get supplier names for suppliers who supply all parts.

```
NAMEX WHERE EXISTS SX ( S ( S#:SX, SNAME:NAMEX )
           AND FORALL PX ( IF P ( P#:PX )
                           THEN SP ( S#:SX, P#:PX )
                           END IF )
```

7.6.6 Get supplier names for suppliers who do not supply part P2.

```
NAMEX WHERE EXISTS SX ( S ( S#:SX, SNAME:NAMEX )
           AND NOT SP ( S#:SX, P#:P#('P2') ) )
```

7.6.7 Get supplier numbers for suppliers who supply at least all those parts supplied by supplier S2.

```
SX WHERE FORALL PX ( IF SP ( S#:S#('S2'), P#:PX )
                     THEN SP ( S#:SX, P#:PX )
                     END IF )
```

7.6.8 Get part numbers for parts that either weigh more than 16 pounds or are supplied by supplier S2, or both.

```
PX WHERE EXISTS WEIGHTX
           ( P ( P#:PX, WEIGHT:WEIGHTX )
             AND WEIGHTX > WEIGHT ( 16.0 ) )
           OR SP ( S#:S#('S2'), P#:PX )
```

The domain calculus, like the tuple calculus, is formally equivalent to the relational algebra (i.e., it is relationally complete). For proof see, e.g., Ullman [7.13].

7.7   SQL FACILITIES

We said in Section 7.4 that a given relational language could be based on either the relational algebra or the relational calculus. So which is SQL based on? The answer, regrettably, is partly both and partly *neither . . .* When it was first designed, SQL was specifically intended to be different from both the algebra and the calculus [4.8]; indeed, such a goal was the motivation for the introduction of the "IN *<subquery>*" construct (see Example 7.7.10

later in this section). As time went by, however, it turned out that certain features of both the algebra and the calculus were needed after all, and the language grew to accommodate them.* The situation today is thus that some aspects of SQL are "algebra-like," some are "calculus-like," and some are neither. This state of affairs explains why we said in Chapter 6 that we would defer discussion of the SQL data manipulative facilities to the present chapter. (We leave it as an exercise to figure out which portions of SQL are based on the algebra, which on the calculus, and which on neither.)

An SQL query is formulated as a **table expression,** of potentially considerable complexity. We do not get into all of that complexity here; rather, we simply present a set of examples, in the hope that those examples will highlight the most important points. The examples are based on the SQL table definitions for suppliers and parts shown in Chapter 4 (Fig. 4.1). Recall in particular that there are no user-defined data types in the SQL version of that database; instead, all columns are defined in terms of one of the SQL builtin types. *Note:* A more complete and more formal treatment of SQL expressions in general, and SQL table expressions in particular, appears in Appendix A.

7.7.1 Get color and city for "nonParis" parts with weight greater than ten pounds.

```
SELECT  PX.COLOR, PX.CITY
FROM    P AS PX
WHERE   PX.CITY <> 'Paris'
AND     PX.WEIGHT > 10.0 ;
```

Points arising:

1. Note the use of the comparison operator "<>" (not equals) in this example. The usual scalar comparison operators are written as follows in SQL: =, <>, <, >, <=, >=.

2. Note also the specification "P AS PX" in the FROM clause. That specification effectively constitutes the definition of a (tuple-calculus-style) range variable called PX, with range the current value of table P. The scope of that definition is, loosely, the table expression in which it appears. *Note:* SQL calls PX a *correlation name.*

3. SQL also supports the notion of *implicit* range variables, according to which the query at hand might equally well have been expressed as follows:

```
SELECT  P.COLOR, P.CITY
FROM    P
WHERE   P.CITY <> 'Paris'
AND     P.WEIGHT > 10.0 ;
```

The basic idea is to allow a table name to be used to denote an implicit range variable that ranges over the table in question (provided of course that no ambiguity results). In

---

*One consequence of that growth is that—as noted in the annotation to reference [4.18], *q.v.*—the entire "IN *<subquery>*" construct could now be removed from the language with no loss of functionality! This fact is ironic, since it was that construct that the "Structured" in the original name "Structured Query Language" referred to; indeed, it was that construct that was the original justification for adopting SQL rather than the algebra or the calculus in the first place.

the example, the FROM clause FROM P can be regarded as shorthand for a FROM clause that reads FROM P AS P. In other words, it has to be clearly understood that the "P" in (e.g.) "P.COLOR" in the SELECT and WHERE clauses here does *not* stand for table P—it stands for a *range variable* called P that ranges over the table with the same name.

4. As noted in Chapter 4, we could have used unqualified column names throughout this example, thereby writing:

```
SELECT  COLOR, CITY
FROM    P
WHERE   CITY <> 'Paris'
AND     WEIGHT > 10.0 ;
```

The general rule is that unqualified names are acceptable if they cause no ambiguity. In our examples, however, we will generally include all qualifiers, even when they are technically redundant. Unfortunately, however, there are certain contexts in which column names are explicitly required *not* to be qualified! The ORDER BY clause is a case in point—see the example immediately following.

5. The **ORDER BY** clause, mentioned in connection with DECLARE CURSOR in Chapter 4, can also be used in interactive SQL queries. For example:

```
SELECT  P.COLOR, P.CITY
FROM    P
WHERE   P.CITY <> 'Paris'
AND     P.WEIGHT > 10.0
ORDER   BY CITY DESC ;
```

6. We remind you of the "SELECT *" shorthand, also mentioned in Chapter 4. For example:

```
SELECT  *
FROM    P
WHERE   P.CITY <> 'Paris'
AND     P.WEIGHT > 10.0 ;
```

The star in "SELECT *" is shorthand for a commalist of all column names in the table(s) referenced in the FROM clause, in the left-to-right order in which those column(s) are defined within those table(s). We remark that the star notation is convenient for interactive queries, since it saves keystrokes. However, it is potentially dangerous in embedded SQL—i.e., SQL embedded in an application program—because the meaning of the "*" might change (e.g., if a column is added to or dropped from some table, via ALTER TABLE).

7. *(Much more important than the previous points!)* Note that, given our usual sample data, the query under discussion will return *four* rows, not two, even though three of those four rows are identical. SQL does not eliminate redundant duplicate rows from a query result unless the user explicitly requests it to do so via the keyword **DISTINCT,** as here:

```
SELECT DISTINCT P.COLOR, P.CITY
FROM    P
WHERE   P.CITY <> 'Paris'
AND     P.WEIGHT > 10.0 ;
```

This query will return two rows only, not four.

It follows that *the fundamental data object in SQL is not a relation*—it is, rather, a table, and SQL-style tables contain (in general) not sets but *bags* of rows. (A "bag"— also called a *multi-set*—is like a set but permits duplicates.) SQL thus violates *The Information Principle* (see Chapter 3, Section 3.2). One consequence is that the fundamental operators in SQL are not true relational operators but bag analogs of those operators; another is that results and theorems that hold true in the relational model—regarding the transformation of expressions, for example [5.6]—do not necessarily hold true in SQL.

7.7.2 For all parts, get the part number and the weight of that part in grams.

```
SELECT P.P#, P.WEIGHT * 454 AS GMWT
FROM   P ;
```

The specification AS GMWT introduces an appropriate result column name for the "computed column." The two columns of the result table are thus called P# and GMWT, respectively. If the AS clause had been omitted, the corresponding result column would effectively have been unnamed. Observe, therefore, that SQL does not actually require the user to provide a result column name in such circumstances, but we will always do so in our examples.

7.7.3 Get all combinations of supplier and part information such that the supplier and part in question are colocated. SQL provides many different ways of formulating this query. We give three of the simplest here.

```
1. SELECT S.*, P.P#, P.PNAME, P.COLOR, P.WEIGHT
   FROM   S, P
   WHERE  S.CITY = P.CITY ;
```

```
2. S JOIN P USING CITY ;
```

```
3. S NATURAL JOIN P ;
```

The result in each case is the **natural join** of tables S and P (on cities).

The first of the foregoing formulations—which is the only one that would have been valid in SQL as originally defined (explicit JOIN support was added in SQL/92)—merits further discussion. Conceptually, we can think of that version of the query as being implemented as follows:

- First, the FROM clause is executed, to yield the **Cartesian product** S TIMES SP. (Strictly, we should worry here about renaming columns before we compute the product. We ignore this issue for simplicity. Also, recall that—as we saw in Exercise 6.12 in Chapter 6—the "Cartesian product" of a single table *T* can be regarded as just *T* itself.)

- Next, the WHERE clause is executed, to yield a **restriction** of that product in which the two CITY values in each row are equal (in other words, we have now computed the *equijoin* of suppliers and parts over cities).

- Finally, the SELECT clause is executed, to yield a **projection** of that restriction over the columns specified in the SELECT clause. The final result is the natural join.

Loosely speaking, therefore, FROM in SQL corresponds to Cartesian product, WHERE to restrict, and SELECT to project, and the SQL SELECT–FROM–WHERE represents a projection of a restriction of a product. See Appendix A for further discussion.

7.7.4 Get all pairs of city names such that a supplier located in the first city supplies a part stored in the second city.

```
SELECT DISTINCT S.CITY AS SCITY, P.CITY AS PCITY
FROM    S JOIN SP USING S# JOIN P USING P# ;
```

Notice that the following is *not* correct (because it includes CITY as a joining column in the second join):

```
SELECT DISTINCT S.CITY AS SCITY, P.CITY AS PCITY
FROM    S NATURAL JOIN SP NATURAL JOIN P ;
```

7.7.5 Get all pairs of supplier numbers such that the two suppliers concerned are colocated.

```
SELECT A.S# AS SA, B.S# AS SB
FROM   S AS A, S AS B
WHERE  A.CITY = B.CITY
AND    A.S# < B.S# ;
```

Explicit range variables are clearly required in this example. Note that the introduced column names SA and SB refer to columns of the *result table,* and so cannot be used in the WHERE clause.

7.7.6 Get the total number of suppliers.

```
SELECT COUNT(*) AS N
FROM    S ;
```

The result here is a table with one column, called N, and one row, containing the value 5. SQL supports the usual aggregate operators **COUNT, SUM, AVG, MAX,** and **MIN,** but there are a few SQL-specific points the user needs to be aware of:

- In general, the argument can optionally be preceded by the keyword DISTINCT—as in, e.g., SUM (DISTINCT QTY)—to indicate that duplicates are to be eliminated before the aggregation is applied. For MAX and MIN, however, DISTINCT is irrelevant and has no effect.

- The special operator COUNT(∗)—DISTINCT not allowed—is provided to count all rows in a table without any duplicate elimination.

- Any nulls in the argument column (see Chapter 18) are eliminated before the aggregation is done, regardless of whether DISTINCT is specified, except for the case of COUNT(∗), where nulls behave as if they were values.

- If the argument happens to be an empty set, COUNT returns zero; the other operators all return null. (This latter behavior is logically incorrect—see reference [3.3]—but it is the way SQL is defined.)

7.7.7 Get the maximum and minimum quantity for part P2.

```
SELECT  MAX ( SP.QTY ) AS MAXQ, MIN ( SP.QTY ) AS MINQ
FROM    SP
WHERE   SP.P# = 'P2' ;
```

Observe that the FROM and WHERE clauses here both effectively provide part of the argument to the two aggregate operators. They should therefore logically appear within the argument-enclosing parentheses. Nevertheless, the query is indeed written as shown. This unorthodox approach to syntax has significant negative repercussions on the structure, usability, and orthogonality* of the SQL language. For instance, one immediate consequence is that aggregate operators cannot be nested, with the result that a query such as "Get the average total-part-quantity" cannot be formulated without cumbersome circumlocutions. To be specific, the following query is *** *ILLEGAL* ***:

```
SELECT  AVG ( SUM ( SP.QTY ) )            -- Warning! Illegal!
FROM    SP ;
```

Instead, it has to be formulated something like this:

```
SELECT  AVG ( X )
FROM  ( SELECT SUM ( SP.QTY ) AS X
        FROM    SP
        GROUP  BY SP.S# ) AS POINTLESS ;
```

See the example immediately following for an explanation of GROUP BY, and several subsequent examples for an explanation of "nested subqueries." It is worth noting that the ability to nest a subquery inside the FROM clause, as here, was new with SQL/92 and is still not widely implemented. *Note:* The specification AS *POINTLESS* is pointless but is required by SQL's syntax rules (see Appendix A).

7.7.8 For each part supplied, get the part number and the total shipment quantity.

```
SELECT  SP.P#, SUM ( SP.QTY ) AS TOTQTY
FROM    SP
GROUP  BY SP.P# ;
```

---

*__Orthogonality__ means *independence*. A language is orthogonal if independent concepts are kept independent, not mixed together in confusing ways. Orthogonality is desirable because the less orthogonal a language is, the more complicated it is and—paradoxically but simultaneously—the less powerful it is.

The foregoing is the SQL analog of the relational algebra expression

```
SUMMARIZE SP PER SP { P# } ADD SUM ( QTY ) AS TOTQTY
```

or the tuple calculus expression

```
( SPX.P#, SUM ( SPY WHERE SPY.P# = SPX.P#, QTY ) AS TOTQTY )
```

Observe in particular that if the GROUP BY clause is specified, expressions in the SELECT clause must be **single-valued per group.**

Here is an alternative (actually preferable) formulation of the same query:

```
SELECT P.P#, ( SELECT SUM ( SP.QTY )
               FROM   SP
               WHERE  SP.P# = P.P# ) AS TOTQTY
FROM   P ;
```

The ability to use nested subqueries to represent scalar values (e.g., within the SELECT clause, as here) was added in SQL/92 and represents a major improvement over SQL as originally defined. In the example, it allows us to generate a result that includes rows for parts that are not supplied at all, which the previous formulation (using GROUP BY) does not. (The TOTQTY value for such parts will unfortunately be given as null, however, not zero.)

7.7.9 Get part numbers for parts supplied by more than one supplier.

```
SELECT SP.P#
FROM   SP
GROUP  BY SP.P#
HAVING COUNT ( SP.S# ) > 1 ;
```

The HAVING clause is to groups what the WHERE clause is to rows; in other words, HAVING is used to eliminate groups, just as WHERE is used to eliminate rows. Expressions in a HAVING clause must be single-valued per group.

7.7.10 Get supplier names for suppliers who supply part P2.

```
SELECT DISTINCT S.SNAME
FROM   S
WHERE  S.S# IN
    ( SELECT SP.S#
      FROM   SP
      WHERE  SP.P# = 'P2' ) ;
```

Explanation: This example makes use of a subquery in the WHERE clause. Loosely speaking, a **subquery** is a SELECT–FROM–WHERE–GROUP BY–HAVING expression that is nested somewhere inside another such expression. Subqueries are used among other things to represent the set of values to be searched via an **IN condition,** as the example illustrates. The system evaluates the overall query by evaluating the subquery first (at least conceptually). That subquery returns the set of supplier *numbers* for suppliers who supply part P2, namely the set {S1,S2,S3,S4}. The original expression is thus equivalent to the following simpler one:

```
SELECT DISTINCT S.SNAME
FROM     S
WHERE    S.S# IN ( 'S1', 'S2', 'S3', 'S4' ) ;
```

It is worth pointing out that the original problem—"Get supplier names for suppliers who supply part P2"—can equally well be formulated by means of a *join,* e.g., as follows:

```
SELECT DISTINCT S.SNAME
FROM     S, SP
WHERE    S.S# = SP.S#
AND      SP.P# = 'P2' ;
```

7.7.11 Get supplier names for suppliers who supply at least one red part.

```
SELECT DISTINCT S.SNAME
FROM     S
WHERE    S.S# IN
       ( SELECT SP.S#
         FROM     SP
         WHERE    SP.P# IN
                ( SELECT P.P#
                  FROM     P
                  WHERE    P.COLOR = 'Red' ) ) ;
```

Subqueries can be nested to any depth. *Exercise:* Give some equivalent join formulations of this query.

7.7.12 Get supplier numbers for suppliers with status less than the current maximum status in the S table.

```
SELECT S.S#
FROM     S
WHERE    S.STATUS <
       ( SELECT MAX ( S.STATUS )
         FROM     S ) ;
```

This example involves *two distinct implicit range variables,* both denoted by the same symbol "S" and both ranging over the S table.

7.7.13 Get supplier names for suppliers who supply part P2. *Note:* This example is the same as Example 7.7.10; we show a different solution, in order to introduce another SQL feature.

```
SELECT DISTINCT S.SNAME
FROM     S
WHERE    EXISTS
       ( SELECT *
         FROM     SP
         WHERE    SP.S# = S.S#
         AND      SP.P# = 'P2' ) ;
```

Explanation: The SQL expression "EXISTS (SELECT … FROM …)" evaluates to *true* if and only if the result of evaluating the "SELECT … FROM …" is not empty. In other words, the SQL **EXISTS** *operator* corresponds to the *existential quantifier* of the tuple calculus (but see reference [18.6]). *Note:* SQL refers to the subquery in this particular example as a *correlated* subquery, since it includes references to a range variable—namely, the implicit range variable S—that is defined in the outer query. Refer back to the "preferable formulation" of Example 7.7.8 for another example of a correlated subquery.

7.7.14 Get supplier names for suppliers who do not supply part P2.

```
SELECT  DISTINCT S.SNAME
FROM    S
WHERE   NOT EXISTS
      ( SELECT *
        FROM    SP
        WHERE   SP.S# = S.S#
        AND     SP.P# = 'P2' ) ;
```

Alternatively:

```
SELECT  DISTINCT S.SNAME
FROM    S
WHERE   S.S# NOT IN
      ( SELECT SP.S#
        FROM    SP
        WHERE   SP.P# = 'P2' ) ;
```

7.7.15 Get supplier names for suppliers who supply all parts.

```
SELECT  DISTINCT S.SNAME
FROM    S
WHERE   NOT EXISTS
      ( SELECT *
        FROM    P
        WHERE   NOT EXISTS
              ( SELECT *
                FROM    SP
                WHERE   SP.S# = S.S#
                AND     SP.P# = P.P# ) ) ;
```

SQL does not include any direct support for the universal quantifier FORALL; hence, "FORALL" queries typically have to be expressed in terms of existential quantifiers and double negation, as in this example.

By the way, it is worth pointing out that expressions such as the one just shown, daunting though they might appear at first glance, are easily constructed by a user who is familiar with relational calculus, as explained in reference [7.4]. Alternatively—if they are still thought too daunting—then there are several "workaround" approaches that can be used that avoid the need for negated quantifiers. In the example, for instance, we might write:

```
SELECT  DISTINCT S.SNAME
FROM    S
WHERE   ( SELECT COUNT ( SP.P# )
          FROM    SP
          WHERE   SP.S# = S.S# ) =
        ( SELECT COUNT ( P.P# )
          FROM    P ) ;
```

("Get names of suppliers where the count of the parts they supply is equal to the count of all parts"). Note, however, that:

- First, this latter formulation relies—as the NOT EXISTS formulation did not—on the fact that every shipment part number is the number of some existing part. In other words, the two formulations are equivalent (and the second is correct) only because a certain *integrity constraint* is in effect (see the next chapter).

- Second, the technique used in the second formulation to compare the two counts (subqueries on both sides of the equals sign) was not supported in SQL as originally defined but was added in SQL/92. It is still not supported in many products.

- We remark too that what we would really like to do is to compare two *tables* (see the discussion of relational comparisons in Chapter 6), thereby expressing the query as follows:

```
SELECT  DISTINCT S.SNAME
FROM    S
WHERE   ( SELECT  SP.P#
          FROM    SP
          WHERE   SP.S# = S.S# ) =
        ( SELECT  P.P#
          FROM    P ) ;
```

SQL does not directly support comparisons between tables, however, and so we have to resort to the trick of comparing table *cardinalities* instead (relying on our own external knowledge to ensure that if the cardinalities are the same then the tables are the same too, at least in the situation at hand). See Exercise 7.11 at the end of the chapter.

7.7.16 Get part numbers for parts that either weigh more than 16 pounds or are supplied by supplier S2, or both.

```
SELECT  P.P#
FROM    P
WHERE   P.WEIGHT > 16.0

UNION

SELECT  SP.P#
FROM    SP
WHERE   SP.S# = 'S2' ;
```

Redundant duplicate rows are always eliminated from the result of an unqualified **UNION, INTERSECT,** or **EXCEPT** (EXCEPT is the SQL analog of our MINUS). However, SQL also provides the qualified variants **UNION ALL, INTERSECT ALL,** and **EXCEPT ALL,** where duplicates (if any) are retained. We deliberately omit examples of these variants.

This brings us to the end of our list of retrieval examples. The list is rather long; nevertheless, there are numerous SQL features that we have not even mentioned. The fact is, SQL is an extremely *redundant* language [4.18], in the sense that it almost always provides numerous different ways of formulating the same query, and space simply does not permit us to describe all possible formulations and all possible options, even for the comparatively small number of examples we have discussed in this section.

7.8 SUMMARY

We have briefly considered the **relational calculus,** an alternative to the relational algebra. Superficially, the two look very different—the calculus is **descriptive** where the algebra is **prescriptive**—but at a deep level they are the same thing, because any expression of the calculus can be converted into a semantically equivalent expression of the algebra, and *vice versa.*

The calculus comes in two versions, tuple calculus and **domain** calculus. The key difference between them is that the range variables of the tuple calculus range over relations, while the range variables of the domain calculus range over domains.

An expression of the tuple calculus consists of a **proto tuple** and an optional WHERE clause containing a boolean expression or **WFF** ("well-formed formula"). That WFF is allowed to contain **quantifiers** (EXISTS and FORALL), **free** and **bound variable references,** boolean operators (AND, OR, NOT, etc.), and so on. Every free variable mentioned in the WFF must also be mentioned in the proto tuple. *Note:* We did not explicitly discuss the point in the body of the chapter, but expressions of the calculus are intended to serve essentially the same purposes as expressions of the algebra (see Chapter 6, Section 6.6).

We showed by example how Codd's **reduction algorithm** can be used to convert an arbitrary expression of the calculus to an equivalent expression of the algebra, thus paving the way for a possible implementation strategy for the calculus. And we mentioned once again the issue of **relational completeness,** and discussed briefly what is involved in proving that some given language L is complete in this sense.

We also considered the question of including **computational** capabilities (analogous to the capabilities provided by EXTEND and SUMMARIZE in the algebra) in the tuple calculus. We then presented a brief introduction to the **domain** calculus, and claimed (without attempting to prove as much) that it too was relationally complete. Thus, the tuple calculus, the domain calculus, and the algebra are all equivalent to one another.

Finally, we presented an overview of the relevant features of **SQL.** SQL is a kind of hybrid of the algebra and the (tuple) calculus; for example, it includes direct support for the JOIN and UNION operators of the algebra, but it also uses the range variables and the existential quantifier of the calculus. An SQL query consists of a **table expression.** Usually such an operation consists of a single **select expression,** but various kinds of explicit **JOIN** expressions are also supported, and join expressions and select expressions can be combined together in various ways using the **UNION, INTERSECT,** and **EXCEPT** operators. We also mentioned the use of **ORDER BY** to impose an order on the table resulting from a table expression (of any kind).

Regarding **select expressions** in particular, we described:

- The basic **SELECT clause** itself, including the use of **DISTINCT,** scalar expressions, the introduction of result column names, and "SELECT *";
- The **FROM clause,** including the use of **range variables;**
- The **WHERE clause,** including the use of the **EXISTS** operator;

- The **GROUP BY** and **HAVING clauses,** including the use of the **aggregate operators** COUNT, SUM, AVG, MAX, and MIN;
- The use of **subqueries** in (e.g.) the SELECT, FROM, and WHERE clauses.

We also gave a **conceptual evaluation algorithm**—i.e., an outline of a formal definition—for select expressions.

EXERCISES

7.1 Let $p(x)$ and q be arbitrary WFFs in which x does and does not appear, respectively, as a free variable. Which of the following statements are valid? (The symbol "$\Rightarrow$" means "implies"; the symbol "$\equiv$" means "is equivalent to." Note that "$A \Rightarrow B$" and "$B \Rightarrow A$" are together the same as "$A \equiv B$.")

a. `EXISTS x ( q )` $\equiv$ `q`

b. `FORALL x ( q )` $\equiv$ `q`

c. `EXISTS x ( p(x) AND q )` $\equiv$ `EXISTS x ( p(x) ) AND q`

d. `FORALL x ( p(x) AND q )` $\equiv$ `FORALL x ( p(x) ) AND q`

e. `FORALL x ( p(x) )` $\Rightarrow$ `EXISTS x ( p(x) )`

7.2 Let $p(x,y)$ be an arbitrary WFF with free variables x and y. Which of the following statements are valid?

a. `EXISTS x EXISTS y ( p(x,y) )` $\equiv$ `EXISTS y EXISTS x ( p(x,y) )`

b. `FORALL x FORALL y ( p(x,y) )` $\equiv$ `FORALL y FORALL x ( p(x,y) )`

c. `FORALL x ( p(x,y) )` $\equiv$ `NOT EXISTS x ( NOT p(x,y) )`

d. `EXISTS x ( p(x,y) )` $\equiv$ `NOT FORALL x ( NOT p(x,y) )`

e. `EXISTS x FORALL y ( p(x,y) )` $\equiv$ `FORALL y EXISTS x ( p(x,y) )`

f. `EXISTS y FORALL x ( p(x,y) )` $\Rightarrow$ `FORALL x EXISTS y ( p(x,y) )`

7.3 Let $p(x)$ and $q(y)$ be arbitrary WFFs with free variables x and y, respectively. Which of the following statements are valid?

a. `EXISTS x ( p(x) ) AND EXISTS y ( q(y) )` $\equiv$
   `EXISTS x EXISTS y ( p(x) AND q(y) )`

b. `EXISTS x ( IF p(x) THEN q(x) END IF )` $\equiv$
   `IF FORALL x ( p(x) ) THEN EXISTS x ( q(x) ) END IF`

7.4 Consider once again Example 7.3.8—"Get supplier numbers for suppliers who supply at least all those parts supplied by supplier S2"—for which a possible tuple calculus formulation is

```
SX.S# WHERE FORALL SPY ( IF SPY.S# = S# ( 'S2' ) THEN
                               EXISTS SPZ ( SPZ.S# = SX.S# AND
                                            SPZ.P# = SPY.P# )
                         END IF )
```

(SPZ here is another range variable that ranges over shipments.) What will this query return if supplier S2 currently supplies no parts at all? What difference would it make if we replaced SX by SPX throughout?

7.5   Here is a sample query against the suppliers-parts-projects database (the usual conventions apply regarding range variable names):

```
( PX.PNAME, PX.CITY ) WHERE FORALL SX FORALL JX EXISTS SPJX
                            ( SX.CITY = 'London' AND
                              JX.CITY = 'Paris' AND
                              SPJX.S# = SX.S# AND
                              SPJX.P# = PX.P# AND
                              SPJX.J# = JX.J# AND
                              SPJX.QTY < QTY ( 500 ) )
```

a.   Translate this query into natural language.

b.   Play DBMS and "execute" Codd's reduction algorithm on this query. Can you see any improvements that might be made to that algorithm?

7.6   Give a tuple calculus formulation of the query "Get the three heaviest parts."

7.7   Consider the *bill-of-materials* relvar PART_STRUCTURE of Chapter 4 (an SQL definition is given in the answer to Exercise 4.6 and a sample relation value is given in Fig. 4.6). The well-known **part explosion** query "Get part numbers for all parts that are components, *at any level,* of some given part, say part P1"—the result of which, PART_BILL say, is certainly a relation that can be derived from PART_STRUCTURE—cannot be formulated as a single expression of the original relational calculus (or algebra). In other words, PART_BILL is a derivable relation that nevertheless *cannot* be derived by means of a single expression of the original calculus (or algebra). Why is this?

7.8   Suppose the suppliers relvar S were to be replaced by a set of relvars LS, PS, AS, … (one for each distinct supplier city; the LS relvar, for example, contains just the supplier tuples for the suppliers in London). Suppose too that we are unaware of exactly what supplier cities exist, and are therefore unaware of exactly how many such relvars there are. Consider the query "Is supplier S1 represented in the database?" Can this query be expressed in the calculus (or the algebra)? Justify your answer.

7.9   Show that SQL is relationally complete.

7.10   Does SQL have equivalents of the relational EXTEND and SUMMARIZE operators?

7.11   Does SQL have equivalents of the relational comparison operators?

7.12   Give as many different SQL formulations as you can think of for the query "Get supplier names for suppliers who supply part P2."

Query Exercises

The remaining exercises are all based on the suppliers-parts-projects database (see Fig. 4.5 in the "Exercises" section in Chapter 4 and the answer to Exercise 5.4 in Chapter 5). In each case you are asked to write an expression for the indicated query. (By way of an interesting variation, you might like to try looking at some of the answers first and stating what the given expression means in natural language.)

7.13 Give tuple calculus solutions to Exercises 6.13–6.50.

7.14 Give domain calculus solutions to Exercises 6.13–6.50.

7.15 Give SQL solutions to Exercises 6.13–6.50.

REFERENCES AND BIBLIOGRAPHY

In addition to the following, see also reference [4.7], which includes a description of some extensions to SQL for dealing with transitive closure and similar issues. Extensions very similar to those in question are included in SQL3 and are described briefly in Appendix B. Regarding the incorporation of such facilities into the relational calculus *per se,* see Chapter 23.

7.1 E. F. Codd: "A Data Base Sublanguage Founded on the Relational Calculus," Proc. 1971 ACM SIGFIDET Workshop on Data Description, Access and Control, San Diego, Calif. (November 1971).

7.2 C. J. Date: "A Note on the Relational Calculus," *ACM SIGMOD Record 18,* No. 4 (December 1989). Republished as "An Anomaly in Codd's Reduction Algorithm" in C. J. Date and Hugh Darwen, *Relational Database Writings 1989–1991.* Reading, Mass.: Addison-Wesley (1992).

7.3 C. J. Date: "Why Quantifier Order Is Important," in C. J. Date and Hugh Darwen, *Relational Database Writings 1989–1991.* Reading, Mass.: Addison-Wesley (1992).

7.4 C. J. Date: "Relational Calculus as an Aid to Effective Query Formulation," in C. J. Date and Hugh Darwen, *Relational Database Writings 1989–1991.* Reading, Mass.: Addison-Wesley (1992).

Just about every relational product on the market currently supports SQL, not the relational calculus or the relational algebra. This paper nevertheless advocates (and illustrates) the use of relational calculus as an intermediate step in the construction of "complex" SQL queries.

7.5 G. D. Held, M. R. Stonebraker, and E. Wong: "INGRES—A Relational Data Base System," Proc. NCC *44,* Anaheim, Calif. Montvale, N.J.: AFIPS Press (May 1975).

There were two major relational prototypes under development in the mid to late 1970s: System R at IBM, and Ingres (originally INGRES, all upper case) at the University of California at Berkeley. Both of those projects became extremely influential in the research world, and both subsequently led to commercial systems, including DB2 in the case of System R and the commercial Ingres product in the case of Ingres. *Note:* The Ingres prototype is sometimes referred to as "University Ingres" [7.11] in order to distinguish it from "Commercial Ingres," the commercial version of the system. A tutorial overview of the commercial version can be found in reference [1.5].

Ingres was not originally an SQL system; instead, it supported a language called QUEL ("Query Language"), which in many respects was technically superior to SQL. Indeed, QUEL still forms the basis of a certain amount of current database research, and examples expressed in QUEL still appear in the research literature. This paper, which was the first to describe the Ingres prototype, includes a preliminary definition of QUEL. See also references [7.10–7.12].

7.6 J. L. Kuhns: "Answering Questions by Computer: A Logical Study," Report RM-5428-PR, Rand Corp., Santa Monica, Calif. (1967).

7.7 M. Lacroix and A. Pirotte: "Domain-Oriented Relational Languages," Proc. 3rd Int. Conf. on Very Large Data Bases, Tokyo, Japan (October 1977).

7.8 T. H. Merrett: "The Extended Relational Algebra, A Basis for Query Languages," in B. Shneiderman (ed.), *Databases: Improving Usability and Responsiveness.* New York, N.Y.: Academic Press (1978).

Proposes the introduction of quantifiers into the algebra [*sic*]—not just the existential and universal quantifiers of the calculus, but the more general quantifiers "the number of" and "the proportion of" (e.g., "at least three of," "not more than half of," "an odd number of," etc.).

7.9 M. Negri, G. Pelagatti, and L. Sbattella: "Formal Semantics of SQL Queries," *ACM TODS 16*, No. 3 (September 1991).

To quote from the abstract: "The semantics of SQL queries are formally defined by stating a set of rules that determine a syntax-driven translation of an SQL query to a formal model called Extended Three-Valued Predicate Calculus (E3VPC), which is largely based on well-known mathematical concepts. Rules for transforming a general E3VPC expression to a canonical form are also given; [in addition,] problems like equivalence analysis of SQL queries are completely solved." Note, however, that the SQL dialect considered is only the first version of the standard ("SQL/86"), not SQL/92.

7.10 Michael Stonebraker (ed.): *The INGRES Papers: The Anatomy of a Relational Database Management System.* Reading, Mass.: Addison-Wesley (1986).

A collection of some of the major papers from the University Ingres project, edited and annotated by one of the original Ingres designers. (References [7.11–7.12] below are included in the collection.) To this writer's knowledge, this is the only book available that describes the design and implementation of a full-scale relational DBMS in detail. Essential reading for the serious student.

7.11 Michael Stonebraker, Eugene Wong, Peter Kreps, and Gerald Held: "The Design and Implementation of INGRES," *ACM TODS 1,* No. 3 (September 1976). Republished in reference [7.10].

A detailed description of the University Ingres prototype.

7.12 Michael Stonebraker: "Retrospection on a Data Base System," *ACM TODS 5,* No. 2 (June 1980). Republished in reference [7.10].

An account of the history of the Ingres prototype project (to January 1979). The emphasis is on mistakes and lessons learned rather than on successes.

7.13 Jeffrey D. Ullman: *Principles of Database and Knowledge-Base Systems: Volume I.* Rockville, Md.: Computer Science Press (1988).

Ullman's book includes a more formal treatment of relational calculus and related matters than the present book does. In particular, it discusses the concept of **safety** of calculus expressions. This topic is of concern if we adopt a slightly different version of the calculus, one in which range variables are not defined by separate statements but instead are bound to their range by means of explicit expressions within the WHERE clause. In such a version of the calculus, the query "Get suppliers in London" (for example) might look something like this—

```
SX WHERE SX ∈ S AND SX.CITY = 'London'
```

One problem (not the only one) with this version of the calculus is that it would apparently permit a query such as

```
SX WHERE NOT ( SX ∈ S )
```

Such an expression is said to be "unsafe," because it does not return a finite answer (the set of all things that are not tuples of S is infinite). As a consequence, certain rules must be imposed to guarantee that all legal expressions are safe. Such rules are described in Ullman's book (for both tuple and domain calculus). We note that Codd's original calculus did effectively include such rules.

7.14 Moshé M. Zloof: "Query-By-Example," Proc. NCC *44,* Anaheim, Calif. (May 1975). Montvale, N.J.: AFIPS Press (1977).

The relational language **Query-By-Example** (QBE) incorporates elements of both the tuple and the domain calculus (with the emphasis on the latter). Its syntax, which is attractive and intuitively very simple, is based on the idea of making entries in "skeleton tables." For example, a QBE formulation of the query "Get supplier names for suppliers who supply at least one part supplied by supplier S2" (a fairly complex query) might look like this:

S	S#	SNAME
	_SX	P._NX

SP	S#	P#
	_SX	_PX

SP	S#	P#
	S2	_PX

Explanation: The user asks the system to display three skeleton tables on the screen, one for suppliers and two for shipments, and makes entries in them as shown. Entries beginning with a leading underscore are "examples" (i.e., domain calculus range variables); other entries are literal values. The user is asking the system to "present" ("P.") supplier name values (_NX) such that, if the supplier is _SX, then _SX supplies some part _PX, and part _PX in turn is also supplied by supplier S2. Notice that the existential quantifiers are all implicit (as they are also in QUEL, incidentally)—another reason why the syntax is intuitively easy to understand.

Here is another example: "Get pairs of supplier numbers such that the suppliers concerned are colocated."

S	S#	CITY
	_SX	_CZ
	_SY	_CZ

P.	_SX	_SY

Unfortunately QBE is not relationally complete. To be specific, it does not properly support the negated existential quantifier (NOT EXISTS). As a result, certain queries (e.g., "Get names of suppliers who supply all parts") cannot be expressed in QBE. (Actually QBE did originally "support" NOT EXISTS, at least implicitly, but the construct was always somewhat troublesome. The basic problem was that there was no way to specify the order in which the various implicit quantifiers were to be applied, and unfortunately the order is significant—see reference [7.3] or the answer to Exercise 7.2. As a result, certain QBE query formulations were ambiguous [7.3].)

Zloof was the original inventor and designer of QBE. This paper was the first of many by Zloof on the subject.

ANSWERS TO SELECTED EXERCISES

7.1 a. Valid. b. Valid. c. Valid. d. Valid. e. Not valid. *Note:* The reason e. is not valid is that FORALL applied to an empty set yields *true,* while EXISTS applied to an empty set yields *false.* Thus, e.g., the fact that the statement "All purple parts weigh over 100 pounds" is *true* (i.e., is a true proposition) does not necessarily mean any purple parts actually exist.

We remark that the (valid!) equivalences and implications can be used as a basis for a set of calculus expression transformation rules, much like the algebraic expression transformation rules mentioned in Chapter 6 and discussed in detail in Chapter 17. An analogous remark applies to the answers to Exercises 7.2 and 7.3 as well.

7.2 a. Valid. b. Valid. c. Valid (this one was discussed in the body of the chapter). d. Valid (hence each of the quantifiers can be defined in terms of the other). e. Not valid. f. Valid. Observe that (as a. and b. show) a sequence of **like** quantifiers can be written in any order without changing the meaning, whereas (as e. shows) for **unlike** quantifiers the order is significant. By way of illustration of this latter point, let x and y range over the set of integers and let p be the WFF "$y > x$". It should be clear that the WFF

```
FORALL x EXISTS y ( y > x )
```

("For all integers x, there exists a larger integer y") evaluates to *true,* whereas the WFF

```
EXISTS y FORALL x ( y > x )
```

("There exists an integer x that is larger than every integer y") evaluates to *false.* Hence interchanging unlike quantifiers changes the meaning. In a calculus-based query language, therefore, interchanging unlike quantifiers in a WHERE clause will change the meaning of the query. See reference [7.3].

7.3 a. Valid. b. Valid.

7.4 If supplier S2 currently supplies no parts, the original query will return all supplier numbers currently appearing in S (including in particular S2, who presumably appears in S but not in SP). If we replace SX by SPX throughout, it will return all supplier numbers currently appearing in SP. The difference between the two formulations is thus as follows: The first means "Get supplier numbers for suppliers who supply at least all those parts supplied by supplier S2" (as required). The second means "Get supplier numbers for suppliers who *supply at least one part and* supply at least all those parts supplied by supplier S2."

7.5 a. Get part name and city for parts supplied to every project in Paris by every supplier in London in a quantity less than 500. b. The result of this query is empty.

7.6 This exercise is very difficult!—especially when we take into account the fact that part weights are not unique. (If they were unique, we could paraphrase the query as "Get all parts such that the count of heavier parts is less than three.") The exercise is so difficult, in fact, that we do not attempt to give a pure calculus solution here. It illustrates very well the point that relational completeness is only a *basic* measure of expressive power, not necessarily a sufficient one. (The next two exercises also illustrate this point.) See reference [6.4] for an extended discussion of queries of this type.

7.7 Let PSA, PSB, PSC, …, PSn be range variables ranging over (the current value of) relvar PART_STRUCTURE, and suppose the given part is part P1. Then:

a. A calculus expression for the query "Get part numbers for all parts that are components, at the *first* level, of part P1" is:

```
PSA.MINOR_P# WHERE PSA.MAJOR_P# = P# ( 'P1' )
```

b. A calculus expression for the query "Get part numbers for all parts that are components, at the *second* level, of part P1" is:

```
PSB.MINOR_P# WHERE EXISTS PSA
             ( PSA.MAJOR_P# = P# ( 'P1' ) AND
               PSB.MAJOR_P# = PSA.MINOR_P# )
```

c. A calculus expression for the query "Get part numbers for all parts that are components, at the *third* level, of part P1" is:

```
PSC.MINOR_P# WHERE EXISTS PSA EXISTS PSB
             ( PSA.MAJOR_P# = P# ( 'P1' ) AND
               PSB.MAJOR_P# = PSA.MINOR_P# AND
               PSC.MAJOR_P# = PSB.MINOR_P# )
```

And so on. A calculus expression for the query "Get part numbers for all parts that are components, at the *nth* level, of part P1" is:

```
PSn.MINOR_P# WHERE EXISTS PSA EXISTS PSB ... EXISTS PS(n-1)
             ( PSA.MAJOR_P# = P# ( 'P1' ) AND
               PSB.MAJOR_P# = PSA.MINOR_P# AND
               PSC.MAJOR_P# = PSB.MINOR_P# AND
               ..................     AND
               PSn.MAJOR_P# = PS(n-1).MINOR_P# )
```

All of these result relations a., b., c., ... then need to be "unioned" together to construct the PART_BILL result.

The problem is, of course, that there is no way to write n such expressions if the value of n is unknown. In fact, the part explosion query is a classic illustration of a problem that cannot be formulated by means of a single expression in a language that is only relationally complete—i.e., a language that is no more powerful than the original calculus (or algebra). We therefore need another extension to the original calculus (and algebra). The TCLOSE operator discussed briefly in Chapter 6 is part of the solution to this problem (but only part). Further details are beyond the scope of this book.

Note: Although this problem is usually referred to as "bill-of-materials" or "part explosion," it is actually of much wider applicability than those names might suggest. In fact, the kind of relationship typified by the "parts contain parts" structure occurs in a very wide range of applications. Other examples include management hierarchies, family trees, authorization graphs, communication networks, software module invocation structures, transportation networks, etc., etc.

7.8 This query cannot be expressed in either the calculus or the algebra. For example, to express it in the calculus, we would basically need to be able to say something like the following:

Does there exist a relation r such that there exists a tuple t in r such that $t.S\# = S\#('S1')$?

In other words, we would need to be able to quantify over *relations* instead of tuples, and we would therefore need a new kind of range variable, one that denoted relations instead of tuples. The query therefore cannot be expressed in the relational calculus as currently defined.

Note, incidentally, that the query under discussion is a "yes/no" query (the desired answer is basically a truth value). You might be tempted to think, therefore, that the reason the query cannot be handled in the calculus or the algebra is that calculus and algebra expressions are relation-valued, not truth-valued. However, yes/no queries can be handled in the calculus and algebra if properly implemented! The crux of the matter is to recognize that yes and no (equivalently, *true* and *false*) are representable as relations. The relations in question are TABLE_DEE and TABLE_DUM, respectively [5.5].

7.9 In order to show that SQL is relationally complete, we have to show first that there exist SQL expressions for each of the five primitive (algebraic) operators restrict, project, product, union, and difference, and then that the operands to those SQL expressions can be arbitrary SQL expressions in turn.

We begin by observing that SQL effectively does support the relational algebra RENAME operator, thanks to the introduction in SQL/92 of the optional "AS *<column name>*" specification on items in the SELECT clause. We can therefore ensure that all tables do have proper column names, and in particular that the operands to product, union, and difference satisfy the requirements of (our version of) the algebra with respect to column naming. Furthermore—provided those operand column-naming requirements are indeed satisfied—the SQL column-name inheritance rules in fact coincide with those of the algebra as described (under the name *relation type inference*) in Chapter 6.

Here then are SQL expressions corresponding to the five primitive operators:

Algebra	*SQL*
`A WHERE p`	`SELECT * FROM A WHERE p`
`A {x,y,...,z}`	`SELECT DISTINCT x,y,...,z FROM A`
`A TIMES B`	`A CROSS JOIN B`
`A UNION B`	`SELECT * FROM A UNION SELECT * FROM B`
`A MINUS B`	`SELECT * FROM A EXCEPT SELECT * FROM B`

Referring to the grammar for SQL table expressions given in Appendix A, we see that each of *A* and *B* in the SQL expressions shown above is in fact a *<table reference>*. We also see that if we take any of the five SQL expressions shown and enclose it in parentheses, what results is in turn a *<table reference>*.* It follows that SQL is indeed relationally complete.

Note: Actually there is a glitch in the foregoing—SQL does not support *projection over no columns at all* (because it does not support empty SELECT clauses). As a consequence, it does not support TABLE_DEE or TABLE_DUM [5.5].

7.10 SQL supports EXTEND but not SUMMARIZE (at least, not very directly). Regarding EXTEND, the relational algebra expression

```
EXTEND A ADD exp AS Z
```

can be represented in SQL as

```
SELECT A.*, exp' AS Z
FROM   ( A ) AS A
```

The expression *exp'* in the SELECT clause is the SQL counterpart of the EXTEND operand *exp*. The parenthesized *A* in the FROM clause is a *<table reference>* of arbitrary complexity (corresponding to the EXTEND operand *A*); the other *A* in the FROM clause is a range variable name.

Regarding SUMMARIZE, the basic problem is that the relational algebra expression

```
SUMMARIZE A PER B ...
```

---

*We choose to overlook the point that SQL would in fact require such a *<table reference>* to include a pointless range variable definition (see Appendix A).

yields a result with cardinality equal to that of *B,* while the SQL "equivalent"

```
SELECT ...
FROM    A
GROUP  BY C ;
```

yields a result with cardinality equal to that of the projection of *A* over *C.*

7.11 SQL does not support relational comparisons directly. However, such operations can be simulated, albeit only in a very cumbersome manner. For example, the comparison

```
A = B
```

(where *A* and *B* are relvars) can be simulated by the SQL expression

```
NOT EXISTS ( SELECT * FROM A
                WHERE NOT EXISTS ( SELECT * FROM B
                                    WHERE A-row = B-row ) )
```

(where *A-row* and *B-row* are <*row constructor*>s—see Appendix A—representing an entire row of *A* and an entire row of *B,* respectively).

7.12 Here are a few such formulations. Note that the following list is not even close to being exhaustive [4.18]. Note too that this is a very simple query!

```
SELECT DISTINCT S.SNAME
FROM    S
WHERE   S.S# IN
        ( SELECT SP.S#
          FROM    SP
          WHERE   SP.P# = 'P2' ) ;

SELECT DISTINCT T.SNAME
FROM ( S NATURAL JOIN SP ) AS T
WHERE   T.P# = 'P2' ;

SELECT DISTINCT T.SNAME
FROM ( S JOIN SP ON S.S# = SP.P# AND SP.P# = 'P2' ) AS T ;

SELECT DISTINCT T.SNAME
FROM ( S JOIN SP USING S# ) AS T
WHERE   T.P# = 'P2' ;

SELECT DISTINCT S.SNAME
FROM    S
WHERE   EXISTS
        ( SELECT *
          FROM    SP
          WHERE   SP.S# = S.S#
          AND     SP.P# = 'P2' ) ;

SELECT DISTINCT S.SNAME
FROM    S, SP
WHERE   S.S# = SP.S#
AND     SP.P# = 'P2' ;

SELECT DISTINCT S.SNAME
FROM    S
WHERE   0 <
        ( SELECT COUNT(*)
          FROM    SP
          WHERE   SP.S# = S.S#
          AND     SP.P# = 'P2' ) ;
```

```
SELECT DISTINCT S.SNAME
FROM    S
WHERE   'P2' IN
      ( SELECT SP.P#
        FROM    SP
        WHERE   SP.S# = S.S# ) ;

SELECT S.SNAME
FROM   S, SP
WHERE  S.S# = SP.S#
AND    SP.P# = 'P2'
GROUP  BY S.SNAME ;
```

Subsidiary question: What are the implications of the foregoing?

7.13 We have numbered the following solutions as 7.13.*n,* where 6.*n* is the number of the original exercise in Chapter 6. We assume that SX, SY, PX, PY, JX, JY, SPJX, SPJY (etc.) are range variables ranging over suppliers, parts, projects, and shipments, respectively; definitions of those range variables are not shown.

7.13.13 JX

7.13.14 JX WHERE JX.CITY = 'London'

7.13.15 SPJX.S# WHERE SPJX.J# = J# ('J1')

7.13.16 SPJX WHERE SPJX.QTY ≥ QTY (300) AND
                 SPJX.QTY ≤ QTY (750)

7.13.17 (PX.COLOR, PX.CITY)

7.13.18 (SX.S#, PX.P#, JX.J#) WHERE SX.CITY = PX.CITY
                             AND   PX.CITY = JX.CITY
                             AND   JX.CITY = SX.CITY

7.13.19 (SX.S#, PX.P#, JX.J#) WHERE SX.CITY ≠ PX.CITY
                             OR   PX.CITY ≠ JX.CITY
                             OR   JX.CITY ≠ SX.CITY

7.13.20 (SX.S#, PX.P#, JX.J#) WHERE SX.CITY ≠ PX.CITY
                             AND   PX.CITY ≠ JX.CITY
                             AND   JX.CITY ≠ SX.CITY

7.13.21 SPJX.P# WHERE EXISTS SX (SX.S# = SPJX.S# AND
                                 SX.CITY = 'London')

7.13.22 SPJX.P# WHERE EXISTS SX EXISTS JX
              (SX.S# = SPJX.S# AND SX.CITY = 'London' AND
                JX.J# = SPJX.J# AND JX.CITY = 'London')

7.13.23 (SX.CITY AS SCITY, JX.CITY AS JCITY)
      WHERE EXISTS SPJX (SPJX.S# = SX.S# AND SPJX.J# = JX.J#)

7.13.24 SPJX.P# WHERE EXISTS SX EXISTS JX
                    (SX.CITY = JX.CITY AND
                    SPJX.S# = SX.S# AND
                    SPJX.J# = JX.J#)

7.13.25 `SPJX.J# WHERE EXISTS SX EXISTS JX`
`                 ( SX.CITY ≠ JX.CITY AND`
`                 SPJX.S# = SX.S# AND`
`                 SPJX.J# = JX.J# )`

7.13.26 `( SPJX.P# AS XP#, SPJY.P# AS YP# )`
`        WHERE SPJX.S# = SPJY.S# AND SPJX.P# < SPJY.P#`

7.13.27 `COUNT ( SPJX.J# WHERE SPJX.S# = S# ( 'S1' ) ) AS N`

7.13.28 `SUM ( SPJX WHERE SPJX.S# = S# ( 'S1' )`
`                 AND SPJX.P# = P# ( 'P1' ), QTY ) AS Q`

Note: The following "solution" is *not* correct (why not?):

`        SUM ( SPJX.QTY WHERE SPJX.S# = S# ( 'S1' )`
`                     AND SPJX.P# = P# ( 'P1' ) ) AS Q`

Answer: Because duplicate QTY values will now be eliminated before the sum is computed.

7.13.29 `( SPJX.P#, SPJX.J#,`
`        SUM ( SPJY WHERE SPJY.P# = SPJX.P#`
`                 AND   SPJY.J# = SPJX.J#, QTY ) AS Q )`

7.13.30 `SPJX.P# WHERE`
`        AVG ( SPJY WHERE SPJY.P# = SPJX.P#`
`                 AND   SPJY.J# = SPJX.J#, QTY ) > QTY ( 350 )`

7.13.31 `JX.JNAME WHERE EXISTS SPJX ( SPJX.J# = JX.J# AND`
`                                 SPJX.S# = S# ( 'S1' ) )`

7.13.32 `PX.COLOR WHERE EXISTS SPJX ( SPJX.P# = PX.P# AND`
`                                 SPJX.S# = S# ( 'S1' ) )`

7.13.33 `SPJX.P# WHERE EXISTS JX ( JX.CITY = 'London' AND`
`                             JX.J# = SPJX.J# )`

7.13.34 `SPJX.J# WHERE EXISTS SPJY ( SPJX.P# = SPJY.P# AND`
`                               SPJY.S# = S# ( 'S1' ) )`

7.13.35 `SPJX.S# WHERE EXISTS SPJY EXISTS SPJZ EXISTS PX`
`                 ( SPJX.P# = SPJY.P# AND`
`                 SPJY.S# = SPJZ.S# AND`
`                 SPJZ.P# = PX.P# AND`
`                 PX.COLOR = COLOR ( 'Red' ) )`

7.13.36 `SX.S# WHERE EXISTS SY ( SY.S# = S# ( 'S1' ) AND`
`                           SX.STATUS < SY.STATUS )`

7.13.37 `JX.J# WHERE FORALL JY ( JY.CITY ≥ JX.CITY )`

Or: `JX.J# WHERE JX.CITY = MIN ( JY.CITY )`

7.13.38 `SPJX.J# WHERE SPJX.P# = P# ( 'P1' ) AND`
`                 AVG ( SPJY WHERE SPJY.P# = P# ( 'P1' )`
`                         AND   SPJY.J# = SPJX.J#, QTY ) >`
`                 MAX ( SPJZ.QTY WHERE SPJZ.J# = J# ( 'J1' ) )`

7.13.39 SPJX.S# WHERE SPJX.P# = P# ('P1')
         AND   SPJX.QTY >
                AVG (SPJY
                      WHERE SPJY.P# = P# ('P1')
                      AND   SPJY.J# = SPJX.J#, QTY)

7.13.40 JX.J# WHERE NOT EXISTS SPJX EXISTS SX EXISTS PX
             (SX.CITY = 'London' AND
               PX.COLOR = COLOR ('Red') AND
               SPJX.S# = SX.S# AND
               SPJX.P# = PX.P# AND
               SPJX.J# = JX.J#)

7.13.41 JX.J# WHERE FORALL SPJY (IF SPJY.J# = JX.J#
                                THEN SPJY.S# = S# ('S1')
                                END IF)

7.13.42 PX.P# WHERE FORALL JX
             (IF JX.CITY = 'London' THEN
               EXISTS SPJY (SPJY.P# = PX.P# AND
                             SPJY.J# = JX.J#)
               END IF)

7.13.43 SX.S# WHERE EXISTS PX FORALL JX EXISTS SPJY
             (SPJY.S# = SX.S# AND
               SPJY.P# = PX.P# AND
               SPJY.J# = JX.J#)

7.13.44 JX.J# WHERE FORALL SPJY (IF SPJY.S# = S# ('S1') THEN
                                EXISTS SPJZ
                                (SPJZ.J# = JX.J# AND
                                  SPJZ.P# = SPJY.P#)
                                END IF)

7.13.45 RANGEVAR VX RANGES OVER
             (SX.CITY), (PX.CITY), (JX.CITY) ;

         VX.CITY

7.13.46 SPJX.P# WHERE EXISTS SX (SX.S# = SPJX.S# AND
                               SX.CITY = 'London')
             OR   EXISTS JX (JX.J# = SPJX.J# AND
                                JX.CITY = 'London')

7.13.47 (SX.S#, PX.P#)
         WHERE NOT EXISTS SPJX (SPJX.S# = SX.S# AND
                                 SPJX.P# = PX.P#)

7.13.48 (SX.S# AS XS#, SY.S# AS YS#)
         WHERE FORALL PZ
             ((IF   EXISTS SPJX (SPJX.S# = SX.S# AND
                                    SPJX.P# = PZ.P#)
                 THEN EXISTS SPJY (SPJY.S# = SY.S# AND
                                    SPJY.P# = PZ.P#)
                 END IF)
             AND
               (IF   EXISTS SPJY (SPJY.S# = SY.S# AND
                                    SPJY.P# = PZ.P#)
                 THEN EXISTS SPJX (SPJX.S# = SX.S# AND
                                    SPJX.P# = PZ.P#)
                 END IF))

7.13.49 (SPJX.S#, SPJX.P#, (SPJY.J#, SPJY.QTY WHERE
SPJY.S# = SPJX.S# AND
SPJY.P# = SPJX.P#) AS JQ)

7.13.50 Let R denote the result of evaluating the expression shown in the previous solution. Then:

RANGEVAR RX RANGES OVER R ,
RANGEVAR RY RANGES OVER RX.JQ ;

(RX.S#, RX.P#, RY.J#, RY.QTY)

We are extending the syntax and semantics of *<range var definition>* slightly. The idea is that the definition of RY depends on that of RX (note that the two definitions are separated by a comma, not a semicolon, and are thereby bundled into a single operation). See reference [3.3] for further discussion.

7.14 We have numbered the following solutions as 7.14.*n*, where 6.*n* is the number of the original exercise in Chapter 6. We follow the same conventions as in Section 7.6 regarding the definition and naming of range variables.

7.14.13 (JX, NAMEX, CITYX)
WHERE J (J#:JX, JNAME:NAMEX, CITY:CITYX)

7.14.14 (JX, NAMEX, 'London' AS CITY)
WHERE J (J#:JX, JNAME:NAMEX, CITY:'London')

7.14.15 SX WHERE SPJ (S#:SX, J#:J#('J1'))

7.14.16 (SX, PX, JX, QTYX)
WHERE SPJ (S#:SX, P#:PX, J#:JX, QTY:QTYX)
AND   QTYX ≥ QTY (300) AND QTYX ≤ QTY (750)

7.14.17 (COLORX, CITYX WHERE P (COLOR:COLORX, CITY:CITYX)

7.14.18 (SX, PX, JX) WHERE EXISTS CITYX
(S (S#:SX, CITY:CITYX) AND
P (P#:PX, CITY:CITYX) AND
J (J#:JX, CITY:CITYX))

7.14.19 (SX, PX, JX)
WHERE EXISTS CITYX EXISTS CITYY EXISTS CITYZ
(S (S#:SX, CITY:CITYX) AND
P (P#:PX, CITY:CITYY) AND
J (J#:JX, CITY:CITYZ)
AND (CITYX ≠ CITYY OR
CITYY ≠ CITYZ OR
CITYZ ≠ CITYX))

7.14.20 (SX, PX, JX)
WHERE EXISTS CITYX EXISTS CITYY EXISTS CITYZ
(S (S#:SX, CITY:CITYX) AND
P (P#:PX, CITY:CITYY) AND
J (J#:JX, CITY:CITYZ)
AND (CITYX ≠ CITYY AND
CITYY ≠ CITYZ AND
CITYZ ≠ CITYX))

7.14.21 PX WHERE EXISTS SX (SPJ (P#:PX, S#:SX) AND
S (S#:SX, CITY:'London')

7.14.22 PX WHERE EXISTS SX EXISTS JX
           (SPJ (S#:SX, P#:PX, J#:JX)
             AND S (S#:SX, CITY:'London')
             AND J (J#:JX, CITY:'London')

7.14.23 (CITYX AS SCITY, CITYY AS JCITY)
             WHERE EXISTS SX EXISTS JY
                (S (S#:SX, CITY:CITYX)
                  AND J (J#:JY, CITY:CITYY)
                  AND SPJ (S#:SX, J#:JY))

7.14.24 PX WHERE EXISTS SX EXISTS JX EXISTS CITYX
           (S (S#:SX, CITY:CITYX)
             AND J (J#:JX, CITY:CITYX)
             AND SPJ (S#:SX, P#:PX, J#:JX))

7.14.25 JY WHERE EXISTS SX EXISTS CITYX EXISTS CITYY
           (SPJ (S#:SX, J#:JY)
             AND S (S#:SX, CITY:CITYX)
             AND J (J#:JY, CITY:CITYY)
             AND CITYX ≠ CITYY)

7.14.26 (PX AS XP#, PY AS YP#) WHERE EXISTS SX
                          (SPJ (S#:SX, P#:PX)
                            AND SPJ (S#:SX, P#:PY)
                            AND PX < PY)

7.14.27–7.14.30 Solutions omitted.

7.14.31 NAMEX WHERE EXISTS JX
              (J (J#:JX, JNAME:NAMEX)
                AND SPJ (S#:S#('S1'), J#:JX))

7.14.32 COLORX WHERE EXISTS PX
              (P (P#:PX, COLOR:COLORX) AND
                SPJ (S#:S#('S1'), P#:PX))

7.14.33 PX WHERE EXISTS JX
              (SPJ (P#:PX, J#:JX) AND
                J (J#:JX, CITY:'London'))

7.14.34 JX WHERE EXISTS PX
              (SPJ (P#:PX, J#:JX) AND
                SPJ (P#:PX, S#:S#('S1')))

7.14.35 SX WHERE EXISTS PX EXISTS SY EXISTS PY
              (SPJ (S#:SX, P#:PX) AND
                SPJ (P#:PX, S#:SY) AND
                SPJ (S#:SY, P#:PY) AND
                P (P#:PY, COLOR:COLOR('Red')))

7.14.36 SX WHERE EXISTS STATUSX EXISTS STATUSY
              (S (S#:SX, STATUS:STATUSX) AND
                S (S#:S#('S1'), STATUS:STATUSY) AND
                STATUSX < STATUSY)

7.14.37 JX WHERE EXISTS CITYX
               (J (J#:JX, CITY:CITYX) AND
                 FORALL CITYY (IF J (CITY:CITYY)
                                THEN CITYY ≥ CITYX
                                END IF)

7.14.38–7.14.39 Solutions omitted.

7.14.40 JX WHERE J (J#:JX) AND
               NOT EXISTS SX EXISTS PX
                 (SPJ (S#:SX, P#:PX, J#:JX) AND
                   S (S#:SX, CITY:'London') AND
                   P (P#:PX, COLOR:COLOR('Red')))

7.14.41 JX WHERE J (J#:JX)
           AND   FORALL SX (IF SPJ (S#:SX, J#:JX)
                             THEN SX = S#('S1')
                             END IF)

7.14.42 PX WHERE P (P#:PX)
           AND   FORALL JX (IF J (J#:JX, CITY:'London')
                             THEN SPJ (P#:PX, J#:JX)
                             END IF)

7.14.43 SX WHERE S (S#:SX)
           AND   EXISTS PX FORALL JX
               (SPJ (S#:SX, P#:PX, J#:JX))

7.14.44 JX WHERE J (J#:JX)
           AND   FORALL PX (IF SPJ (S#:S#('S1'), P#:PX)
                             THEN SPJ (P#:PX, J#:JX)
                             END IF)

7.14.45 CITYX WHERE S (CITY:CITYX)
             OR   P (CITY:CITYX)
             OR   J (CITY:CITYX)

7.14.46 PX WHERE EXISTS SX (SPJ (S#:SX, P#:PX) AND
                               S (S#:SX, CITY:'London'))
             OR   EXISTS JX (SPJ (J#:JX, P#:PX) AND
                               J (J#:JX, CITY:'London'))

7.14.47 (SX, PX) WHERE S (S#:SX) AND P (P#:PX)
                           AND NOT SPJ (S#:SX, P#:PX)

7.14.48 (SX AS XS#, SY AS YS#)
           WHERE S (S#:SX) AND S (S#:SY) AND FORALL PZ
             ((IF SPJ (S#:SX, P#:PZ) THEN SPJ (S#:SY, P#:PZ)
                 END IF)
               AND
               (IF SPJ (S#:SY, P#:PZ) THEN SPJ (S#:SX, P#:PZ)
                 END IF))

7.14.49–7.14.50 Solutions omitted.

7.15 We have numbered the following solutions as 7.15.*n,* where 6.*n* is the number of the original exercise in Chapter 6.

7.15.13 `SELECT *`
       `FROM   J ;`

Or simply:

      `TABLE J ;`

7.15.14 `SELECT J.*`
       `FROM   J`
       `WHERE  J.CITY = 'London' ;`

7.15.15 `SELECT DISTINCT SPJ.S#`
       `FROM   SPJ`
       `WHERE  SPJ.J# = 'J1' ;`

7.15.16 `SELECT SPJ.*`
       `FROM   SPJ`
       `WHERE  SPJ.QTY >= 300`
       `AND    SPJ.QTY <= 750 ;`

7.15.17 `SELECT DISTINCT P.COLOR, P.CITY`
       `FROM   P ;`

7.15.18 `SELECT S.S#, P.P#, J.J#`
       `FROM   S, P, J`
       `WHERE  S.CITY = P.CITY`
       `AND    P.CITY = J.CITY ;`

7.15.19 `SELECT S.S#, P.P#, J.J#`
       `FROM   S, P, J`
       `WHERE  NOT ( S.CITY = P.CITY AND`
       `             P.CITY = J.CITY ) ;`

7.15.20 `SELECT S.S#, P.P#, J.J#`
       `FROM   S, P, J`
       `WHERE  S.CITY <> P.CITY`
       `AND    P.CITY <> J.CITY`
       `AND    J.CITY <> P.CITY ;`

7.15.21 `SELECT DISTINCT SPJ.P#`
       `FROM   SPJ`
       `WHERE  ( SELECT S.CITY`
       `           FROM   S`
       `           WHERE  S.S# = SPJ.S# ) = 'London' ;`

7.15.22 `SELECT DISTINCT SPJ.P#`
       `FROM   SPJ`
       `WHERE  ( SELECT S.CITY`
       `           FROM   S`
       `           WHERE  S.S# = SPJ.S# ) = 'London'`
       `AND    ( SELECT J.CITY`
       `           FROM   J`
       `           WHERE  J.J# = SPJ.J# ) = 'London' ;`

7.15.23
```
SELECT DISTINCT S.CITY AS SCITY, J.CITY AS JCITY
FROM   S, J
WHERE  EXISTS
       ( SELECT *
         FROM    SPJ
         WHERE   SPJ.S# = S.S#
         AND     SPJ.J# = J.J# ) ;
```

7.15.24
```
SELECT DISTINCT SPJ.P#
FROM   SPJ
WHERE  ( SELECT S.CITY
         FROM    S
         WHERE   S.S# = SPJ.S# ) =
       ( SELECT J.CITY
         FROM    J
         WHERE   J.J# = SPJ.J# ) ;
```

7.15.25
```
SELECT DISTINCT SPJ.J#
FROM   SPJ
WHERE  ( SELECT S.CITY
         FROM    S
         WHERE   S.S# = SPJ.S# ) <>
       ( SELECT J.CITY
         FROM    J
         WHERE   J.J# = SPJ.J# ) ;
```

7.15.26
```
SELECT DISTINCT SPJX.P# AS PA, SPJY.P# AS PB
FROM   SPJ AS SPJX, SPJ AS SPJY
WHERE  SPJX.S# = SPJY.S#
AND    SPJX.P# < SPJY.P# ;
```

7.15.27
```
SELECT COUNT ( DISTINCT SPJ.J# ) AS N
FROM   SPJ
WHERE  SPJ.S# = 'S1' ;
```

7.15.28
```
SELECT SUM ( SPJ.QTY ) AS X
FROM   SPJ
WHERE  SPJ.S# = 'S1'
AND    SPJ.P# = 'P1' ;
```

7.15.29
```
SELECT SPJ.P#, SPJ.J#, SUM ( SPJ.QTY ) AS Y
FROM   SPJ
GROUP  BY SPJ.P#, SPJ.J# ;
```

7.15.30
```
SELECT DISTINCT SPJ.P#
FROM   SPJ
GROUP  BY SPJ.P#, SPJ.J#
HAVING AVG ( SPJ.QTY ) > 350 ;
```

7.15.31
```
SELECT DISTINCT J.JNAME
FROM   J, SPJ
WHERE  J.J# = SPJ.J#
AND    SPJ.S# = 'S1' ;
```

7.15.32
```
SELECT DISTINCT P.COLOR
FROM   P, SPJ
WHERE  P.P# = SPJ.P#
AND    SPJ.S# = 'S1' ;
```

```
7.15.33   SELECT DISTINCT SPJ.P#
          FROM     SPJ, J
          WHERE    SPJ.J# = J.J#
          AND      J.CITY = 'London' ;

7.15.34   SELECT DISTINCT SPJX.J#
          FROM     SPJ AS SPJX, SPJ AS SPJY
          WHERE    SPJX.P# = SPJY.P#
          AND      SPJY.S# = 'S1' ;

7.15.35   SELECT DISTINCT SPJX.S#
          FROM     SPJ AS SPJX, SPJ AS SPJY, SPJ AS SPJZ
          WHERE    SPJX.P# = SPJY.P#
          AND      SPJY.S# = SPJZ.S#
          AND    ( SELECT P.COLOR
                   FROM    P
                   WHERE   P.P# = SPJZ.P# ) = 'Red' ;

7.15.36   SELECT S.S#
          FROM     S
          WHERE    S.STATUS < ( SELECT S.STATUS
                                FROM    S
                                WHERE   S.S# = 'S1' ) ;

7.15.37   SELECT J.J#
          FROM     J
          WHERE    J.CITY = ( SELECT MIN ( J.CITY )
                              FROM    J ) ;

7.15.38   SELECT DISTINCT SPJX.J#
          FROM     SPJ AS SPJX
          WHERE    SPJX.P# = 'P1'
          AND    ( SELECT AVG ( SPJY.QTY )
                   FROM    SPJ AS SPJY
                   WHERE   SPJY.J# = SPJX.J#
                   AND     SPJY.P# = 'P1' ) >
                 ( SELECT MAX ( SPJZ.QTY )
                   FROM    SPJ AS SPJZ
                   WHERE   SPJZ.J# = 'J1' ) ;

7.15.39   SELECT DISTINCT SPJX.S#
          FROM     SPJ AS SPJX
          WHERE    SPJX.P# = 'P1'
          AND      SPJX.QTY > ( SELECT AVG ( SPJY.QTY )
                                FROM    SPJ AS SPJY
                                WHERE   SPJY.P# = 'P1'
                                AND     SPJY.J# = SPJX.J# ) ;

7.15.40   SELECT J.J#
          FROM     J
          WHERE    NOT EXISTS
                 ( SELECT *
                   FROM    SPJ, P, S
                   WHERE   SPJ.J# = J.J#
                   AND     SPJ.P# = P.P#
                   AND     SPJ.S# = S.S#
                   AND     P.COLOR = 'Red'
                   AND     S.CITY = 'London' ) ;
```

```
7.15.41  SELECT  J.J#
         FROM    J
         WHERE   NOT EXISTS
               ( SELECT  *
                 FROM    SPJ
                 WHERE   SPJ.J# = J.J#
                 AND     NOT ( SPJ.S# = 'S1' ) ) ;


7.15.42  SELECT  P.P#
         FROM    P
         WHERE   NOT EXISTS
               ( SELECT  *
                 FROM    J
                 WHERE   J.CITY = 'London'
                 AND     NOT EXISTS
                       ( SELECT  *
                         FROM    SPJ
                         WHERE   SPJ.P# = P.P#
                         AND     SPJ.J# = J.J# ) ) ;


7.15.43  SELECT  S.S#
         FROM    S
         WHERE   EXISTS
               ( SELECT  *
                 FROM    P
                 WHERE   NOT EXISTS
                       ( SELECT  *
                         FROM    J
                         WHERE   NOT EXISTS
                               ( SELECT  *
                                 FROM    SPJ
                                 WHERE   SPJ.S# = S.S#
                                 AND     SPJ.P# = P.P#
                                 AND     SPJ.J# = J.J# ) ) ) ;


7.15.44  SELECT  J.J#
         FROM    J
         WHERE   NOT EXISTS
               ( SELECT  *
                 FROM    SPJ AS SPJX
                 WHERE   SPJX.S# = 'S1'
                 AND     NOT EXISTS
                       ( SELECT  *
                         FROM    SPJ AS SPJY
                         WHERE   SPJY.P# = SPJX.P#
                         AND     SPJY.J# = J.J# ) ) ;


7.15.45  SELECT  S.CITY FROM S
         UNION
         SELECT  P.CITY FROM P
         UNION
         SELECT  J.CITY FROM J ;


7.15.46  SELECT  DISTINCT SPJ.P#
         FROM    SPJ
         WHERE   ( SELECT  S.CITY
                   FROM    S
                   WHERE   S.S# = SPJ.S# ) = 'London'
         OR      ( SELECT  J.CITY
                   FROM    J
                   WHERE   J.J# = SPJ.J# ) = 'London' ;
```

7.15.47
```
SELECT S.S#, P.P#
FROM   S, P
EXCEPT
SELECT SPJ.S#, SPJ.P#
FROM   SPJ ;
```

7.15.48 Solution omitted.

7.15.49–7.15.50 Cannot be done.

Integrity

8.1 INTRODUCTION

The term **integrity** refers to the *accuracy* or *correctness* of data in the database. As noted in Chapter 3, a given database might be subject to any number of integrity constraints, of (in general) arbitrary complexity. In the case of suppliers and parts, for example, supplier numbers might have to be of the form S*nnnn* (*nnnn* = up to four decimal digits) and unique; status values might have to be in the range 1 to 100; London suppliers might have to have status 20; shipment quantities might have to be a multiple of 50; red parts might have to be stored in London; and so on. In general, therefore, the DBMS needs to be informed of such constraints, and of course needs to enforce them somehow (basically by rejecting any update that would otherwise violate them). For example (**Tutorial D** once again):

```
CONSTRAINT SC3
     IS_EMPTY ( S WHERE STATUS < 1 OR STATUS > 100 ) ;
```

("status values must be in the range 1 to 100"). Note the constraint *name* SC3 ("suppliers constraint three"); the constraint will be registered in the system catalog under that name, and that name will appear in any diagnostic messages produced by the system in response to an attempt to violate the constraint. The constraint itself is specified as a boolean expression that is required not to evaluate to *false*.

Note: We assume the algebraic version of **Tutorial D** for definiteness; as a consequence, the boolean expression will often—though not invariably—take the form IS_EMPTY (…), meaning there is no data in the database that violates the constraint in question (see Chapter 6, Section 6.9). A calculus analog of the example just shown might look like this:*

```
CONSTRAINT SC3
     FORALL SX ( SX.STATUS ≥ 1 AND SX.STATUS ≤ 100 ) ;
```

(where SX is a range variable ranging over suppliers, of course).

---

*In practice it often seems to be easier to formulate constraints (especially complicated ones) in terms of the calculus rather than the algebra. We focus on the algebra in this chapter for consistency with our discussions elsewhere in the book, but you might like to try the exercise of converting some of the examples that follow into calculus form.

As an aside, we remark that the boolean expression in a calculus constraint must be a *closed WFF* (see Chapter 7, Section 7.2) and will often—though not invariably—take the form FORALL x (...). Note, therefore, that the example specifies that *all* supplier status values must be in the indicated range. In practice, of course, it is sufficient for the system to check just the supplier that has been newly inserted or updated, not all suppliers.

When a new constraint is declared, the system must first make sure the database currently satisfies it. If it does not, the new constraint is rejected; otherwise it is accepted (i.e., saved in the catalog) and enforced from that point forward. Enforcement in the example at hand requires the DBMS to monitor all operations that would insert a new supplier or change an existing supplier's status.

Of course, we also need a way of getting rid of existing constraints:

```
DROP CONSTRAINT <constraint name> ;
```

For example:

```
DROP CONSTRAINT SC3 ;
```

Note: As the foregoing discussion indicates, we are concerned very specifically with **declarative** integrity support. Regrettably, few products today provide much in the way of such support. While the situation is slowly improving in this regard, it is still the case that some products (especially nonrelational ones) quite specifically emphasize the opposite approach—i.e., *procedural* support, using **stored** or **triggered procedures.*** But it has been suggested that if the DBMS did in fact provide declarative support, then as much as 90 percent of a typical database definition would consist of constraints; thus, a system that provided such support would relieve application programmers of a considerable burden and would allow them to become significantly more productive. Declarative integrity support is important.

Before we go any further, we should say that the integrity part of the relational model is probably the part that has changed the most over the years (perhaps we should say *evolved* rather than *changed*). As mentioned in Chapter 3, the original emphasis was on primary and foreign keys specifically ("keys" for short). Gradually, however, the importance—indeed, the **crucial** importance!—of integrity constraints in general has begun to be better understood and more widely appreciated; at the same time, certain awkward questions regarding keys in particular have begun to be raised. The structure of this chapter reflects this shift in emphasis, inasmuch as it deals with integrity constraints in general first (at some length), and then discusses keys—which do continue to be of major pragmatic importance—subsequently.

---

*Stored and triggered procedures are precompiled procedures that can be invoked from application programs. Examples might include the user-defined operators ABS, DIST, REFLECT, etc., discussed in Section 5.2 (subsection "Operator Definition"). Such procedures can logically be regarded as an extension to the DBMS (in a client/server system they will often be kept and executed at the server site). We will have a little more to say regarding such procedures in Section 8.8 and in the annotation to some of the references at the end of this chapter, also in Chapter 20.

A Constraint Classification Scheme

Following reference [3.3], we classify integrity constraints in general into four broad categories: type (domain), attribute, relvar, and database constraints. Basically:

- A *type* constraint specifies the legal values for a given type. *Note:* Throughout this chapter, we take "type" to mean a *scalar* type specifically. Relation types are subject to type constraints too, of course, but those constraints are basically just a logical consequence of the type constraints that apply to the scalar types in terms of which those relation types are (ultimately) defined.
- An *attribute* constraint specifies the legal values for a given attribute.
- A *relvar* constraint specifies the legal values for a given relvar.
- A *database* constraint specifies the legal values for a given database.

The four cases are discussed in detail in Sections 8.2–8.5, respectively.

8.2 TYPE CONSTRAINTS

Essentially, a type constraint is (or is logically equivalent to) just an enumeration of the legal values of the type. Here is a simple example, the type constraint for type WEIGHT:

```
TYPE WEIGHT POSSREP ( RATIONAL )
    CONSTRAINT THE_WEIGHT ( WEIGHT ) > 0.0 ;
```

We adopt an obvious convention by which a type constraint is allowed to make use of the applicable *type name* to denote an arbitrary value of the type in question; thus, this example constrains weights to be such that they can be represented by a rational number that is greater than zero. Any expression that is supposed to evaluate to a weight but does not in fact yield a value that satisfies this constraint will fail. *Note:* Refer to Chapter 5 if you need to refresh your memory regarding POSSREP specifications and THE_ operators.

To repeat, a type constraint is basically just a specification of the values that make up the type in question. In **Tutorial D,** therefore, we bundle such constraints with the definition of the applicable type, and we identify them by means of the applicable type name. (It follows that a type constraint can be dropped only by dropping the type itself.)

Now, it should be clear that, ultimately, the only way *any* expression can yield a value of type WEIGHT is by means of some WEIGHT selector invocation. Hence, the only way any such expression can violate the WEIGHT type constraint is if the selector invocation in question does so. It follows that *type constraints can always be thought of, at least conceptually, as being checked during the execution of some selector invocation.* As a consequence, we can say that type constraints are checked *immediately,* and hence that no relvar can ever acquire a value for any attribute in any tuple that is not of the appropriate type (in a system that supports type constraints properly, of course!).

Here is another example of a type constraint:

```
TYPE POINT POSSREP CARTESIAN ( X RATIONAL, Y RATIONAL )
     CONSTRAINT ABS ( THE_X ( POINT ) ) ≤ 100.0 AND
                ABS ( THE_Y ( POINT ) ) ≤ 100.0 ;
```

The type checking here is done, conceptually, during execution of invocations of the CARTESIAN selector. Note the use of the user-defined operator ABS (see Chapter 5, Section 5.2).

Here is a third example:

```
TYPE ELLIPSE POSSREP ( A LENGTH, B LENGTH, CTR POINT )
     CONSTRAINT THE_A ( ELLIPSE ) > THE_B ( ELLIPSE ) ;
```

The possible representation components here, namely A, B, and CTR, represent, respectively, the major semiaxis length *a,* the minor semiaxis length *b,* and the center point *ctr* of the ellipse in question. Suppose scalar variable E is declared to be of type ELLIPSE, and its current value has a major semiaxis of length five and a minor semiaxis of length four. Now consider the assignment:

```
THE_B ( E )  :=  LENGTH ( 6.0 ) ;
```

Note: We base this example on a *scalar* variable and scalar assignment specifically for reasons of simplicity, but we could easily have based it on a *relation* variable (relvar) and relational assignment instead.

The assignment as shown will fail, of course, but it is not the assignment *per se* that is in error. Instead, the error occurs inside a selector invocation once again (even though no such invocation is directly visible in the assignment), because in fact the assignment shown is really shorthand for the following:*

```
E  :=  ELLIPSE ( THE_A ( E ), LENGTH ( 6.0 ), THE_CTR ( E ) ) ;
```

And it is the selector invocation on the right-hand side here that fails.

8.3 ATTRIBUTE CONSTRAINTS

An attribute constraint is basically just a declaration to the effect that a specified attribute is of a specified type. For example, consider the suppliers relvar definition once again:

```
VAR S BASE RELATION
    { S#       S#,
      SNAME    NAME,
      STATUS   INTEGER,
      CITY     CHAR } ... ;
```

---

*In other words—and despite the fact that we did not mention the point explicitly in Chapter 5—THE_ pseudovariables are logically unnecessary! That is, any assignment to a THE_ pseudovariable is always logically equivalent to (and is in fact defined to be shorthand for) assigning the result of a certain selector invocation to a regular variable instead.

In this relvar, values of attributes S#, SNAME, STATUS, and CITY are constrained to be of types S#, NAME, INTEGER, and CHAR, respectively. In other words, attribute constraints are part of the definition of the attribute in question, and they can be identified by means of the corresponding attribute name. It follows that an attribute constraint can be dropped only by dropping the attribute itself (which in practice will usually mean dropping the containing relvar).

Note: In principle, any attempt to introduce an attribute value into the database that is not a value of the relevant type will simply be rejected. In practice, however, such a situation should never arise, so long as the system in fact enforces the type constraints described in the previous section.

8.4 RELVAR CONSTRAINTS

A relvar constraint is a constraint on an individual relvar (it is expressed in terms of the relvar in question only, though in other respects it can be arbitrarily complex). Here are some examples:

```
CONSTRAINT SC5
    IS_EMPTY ( S WHERE CITY = 'London' AND STATUS ≠ 20 ) ;
```

("suppliers in London must have status 20").

```
CONSTRAINT PC4
    IS_EMPTY ( P WHERE COLOR = COLOR ( 'Red' ) )
                AND CITY ≠ 'London' ) ;
```

("red parts must be stored in London").

```
CONSTRAINT SCK
    COUNT ( S ) = COUNT ( S { S# } ) ;
```

("supplier numbers are unique," or, more formally, "{S#} is a candidate key for suppliers"—see Section 8.8).

```
CONSTRAINT PC7
    IF NOT ( IS_EMPTY ( P ) ) THEN
        COUNT ( P WHERE COLOR = COLOR ( 'Red' ) ) > 0
    END IF ;
```

("if there are any parts at all, at least one of them must be red"). Note, incidentally, that this example differs from all of the others we have seen, inasmuch as DELETE operations have the potential for violating the constraint too.

Relvar constraints are always checked immediately (in effect, as part of the execution of any statement that might cause them to be violated). Thus, any statement that attempts to assign a value to a given relvar that violates any relvar constraint for that relvar will effectively just be rejected.

8.5   DATABASE CONSTRAINTS

A database constraint is a constraint that interrelates two or more distinct relvars. Here are some examples:

```
CONSTRAINT DBC1
    IS_EMPTY ( ( S JOIN SP )
                WHERE STATUS < 20 AND QTY > QTY ( 500 ) ) ;
```

("no supplier with status less than 20 can supply any part in a quantity greater than 500"). *Exercise:* What update operations does the DBMS have to monitor in order to enforce constraint DBC1?

```
CONSTRAINT DBC2 SP { S# } ≤ S { S# } ;
```

("every supplier number in the shipments relvar also exists in the suppliers relvar"; recall from Chapter 6 that we use "≤" to mean "subset of"). Since attribute S# in relvar S constitutes a candidate key for suppliers, this constraint is basically the necessary *referential* constraint from shipments to suppliers (i.e., {S#} in relvar SP is a foreign key for shipments that refers to suppliers). See Section 8.8 for further discussion.

```
CONSTRAINT DBC3 SP { P# } = P { P# } ;
```

("every part must have at least one shipment"). *Note:* Of course, it is also the case that every shipment must have exactly one part, by virtue of the fact that {P#} in relvar P is a candidate key for parts and there is a referential constraint from shipments to parts; we have not bothered to show this latter constraint here. Again, see Section 8.8 for further discussion.

These last two examples serve to illustrate the point that (in general) database constraint checking cannot be done immediately, but must be *deferred* to end-of-transaction— i.e., to COMMIT time (refer to Chapter 3 if you need to refresh your memory regarding COMMIT). For suppose, contrariwise, that the checking is immediate, and suppose there are currently no parts or shipments at all. Then inserting a part will fail, because it violates constraint DBC3; likewise, inserting a shipment will fail, because it violates constraint DBC2.*

If a database constraint is violated at COMMIT time, the transaction is rolled back.

8.6   THE GOLDEN RULE

Note: The material of this section is of fundamental importance. Unfortunately, however, it is not very widely supported in practice, nor even much understood, even though in principle it is quite straightforward. Caveat lector.

---

*Actually, reference [3.3] proposes a *multiple* form of assignment that would allow parts and shipments to be inserted in a single operation. If such assignments were supported, database constraints could be checked immediately.

In Chapter 3, Section 3.4, we explained how any given relation had an associated *predicate* and how tuples of that relation denoted *true propositions* derived from that predicate. And in Chapter 5, Section 5.3, we mentioned the *Closed World Assumption,* which says, in effect, that if a certain tuple does not appear in a certain relation, then we are entitled to assume that the corresponding proposition is *false.*

Now, we did not stress the point before, but it should be clear that a *relvar* too has a predicate: namely, the predicate that is common to all of the possible relations that are legal values of the relvar in question. Consider the suppliers relvar S, for example. The predicate for that relvar looks something like this:

> *The supplier with the specified supplier number (S#) has the specified name (SNAME) and the specified status value (STATUS), and is located in the specified city (CITY); moreover, no two suppliers have the same supplier number at the same time.*

This statement is neither precise nor complete, but it will serve for present purposes.

It should be clear also that, fundamentally, the predicate for a given relvar serves as the **criterion for acceptability of updates** on the relvar in question—it dictates whether a particular INSERT or UPDATE or DELETE operation on that relvar should be allowed to succeed. For example, an attempt to insert a new supplier with supplier number the same as that of some existing supplier must surely be rejected.

Ideally, therefore, the DBMS would know and understand the predicate for every relvar, so that it could deal correctly with all possible attempts to update the database. But of course this goal is unachievable. For example, there is no way the DBMS can know what it means for a certain supplier to be "in" a certain city. And there is no way the DBMS can know *a priori* that the predicate for suppliers is such that (e.g.) the tuple

```
{ S#      :  S# ( 'S1' )        ,
  SNAME   :  NAME ( 'Smith' ) ,
  STATUS  :  20                 ,
  CITY    :  'London'          }
```

satisfies it, while the tuple

```
{ S#      :  S# ( 'S6' )        ,
  SNAME   :  NAME ( 'Smith' ) ,
  STATUS  :  50                 ,
  CITY    :  'Rome'            }
```

does not. Indeed, if the end user presents this latter tuple for insertion, all the system can do is make sure that it does not violate any known integrity constraint. Assuming it does not, the system will then accept the tuple for insertion *and treat it as a true proposition from that point forward.*

To repeat, therefore: The system does not (and cannot) know and understand the suppliers predicate 100 percent. *But it does know a good approximation to that predicate;* to be specific, it knows the integrity constraints that apply to suppliers. We therefore *define* the **relvar predicate** for the suppliers relvar (or, more generally, any relvar) to be the logical AND of all relvar constraints that apply to that relvar. For example, the relvar predicate for relvar S looks something like this:

```
( IS_EMPTY ( S WHERE STATUS < 1 OR STATUS > 100 ) ) AND
( IS_EMPTY ( S WHERE CITY = 'London' AND STATUS ≠ 20 ) ) AND
( COUNT ( S ) = COUNT ( S { S# } ) )
```

(In addition, of course, the system knows that attributes S#, SNAME, STATUS, and CITY are of types S#, NAME, INTEGER, and CHAR, respectively.)

Note, therefore, that there are effectively two predicates associated with any given relvar: the informal or **external** predicate, which is understood by users but not by the system, and the formal or **internal** predicate, which is understood by both users *and* the system. And, of course, it is the internal predicate that we mean by the term "relvar predicate," and it is the internal predicate that the system will check whenever updates are attempted on the relvar in question. Indeed, from now on we will take the term *predicate* (when used in connection with some relvar) to mean that relvar's internal predicate specifically, barring explicit statements to the contrary.

Given the foregoing definitions, we can now state **The Golden Rule** (at least, the first version of that rule):

> *No update operation must ever be allowed to leave any relvar in a state that violates its own predicate.*

We should stress the point too that "relvar" here does not necessarily mean a base relvar—*The Golden Rule* applies to *all* relvars, derived as well as base. We will return to this point in the next chapter.

We close this section by pointing out that, just as every relvar has an associated predicate, so every database has an associated predicate too—the **database predicate** for that database, which we define as the logical AND of all database and relvar constraints that apply to the database in question. And so we can extend *The Golden Rule* thus:*

> *No update operation must ever be allowed to leave any relvar in a state that violates its own predicate. Likewise, no update transaction must ever be allowed to leave the database in a state that violates its own predicate.*

8.7 STATE *VS.* TRANSITION CONSTRAINTS

All of the constraints discussed in this chapter so far have been **state** constraints: They were concerned with correct *states* of the database. Sometimes, however, it is necessary to consider **transition** constraints as well—i.e., constraints on legal transitions from one correct state to another. In a database concerning people, for example, there might be a series of transition constraints having to do with changes of marital status. For instance, the following transitions are all valid—

---

*If multiple assignments were supported (a possibility noted in an earlier footnote), we could perhaps leave *The Golden Rule* in its original and simpler form.

- Never married to married
- Married to widowed
- Married to divorced
- Widowed to married

(etc., etc.), whereas the following are not—

- Never married to widowed
- Never married to divorced
- Widowed to divorced
- Divorced to widowed

(etc., etc.). Reverting to the suppliers and parts database, here is another example ("no supplier's status must ever decrease"):

```
CONSTRAINT TRC1 IS_EMPTY
    ( ( ( S' { S#, STATUS } RENAME STATUS AS STATUS' )
        JOIN S { S#, STATUS } )
      WHERE STATUS' > STATUS ) ;
```

Explanation: We introduce the convention that a primed relvar name, such as S′ in the example, is understood to refer to the corresponding relvar as it was *prior to the update under consideration.* The constraint in the example can thus be understood as follows: If (a) we join together (over supplier numbers) the relation that is the value of relvar S before the update and the relation that is the value afterwards, and (b) we pick out the tuples in that join for which the old status value is greater than the new one, then (c) the final result must be empty. (Since the join is over supplier numbers, any tuple in the result of the join for which the old status value is greater than the new one would represent a supplier whose status had decreased.)

Note: Constraint TRC1 is a *relvar* transition constraint (it applies to just a single relvar, *viz.* suppliers), and the checking is therefore immediate. Here by contrast is an example of a *database* transition constraint ("the total quantity of any given part, taken over all suppliers, can never decrease"):

```
CONSTRAINT TRC2 IS_EMPTY
    ( ( ( SUMMARIZE SP' PER S'{ S# } ADD SUM ( QTY ) AS SQ' )
        JOIN
        ( SUMMARIZE SP  PER S { S# } ADD SUM ( QTY ) AS SQ  ) )
      WHERE SQ' > SQ ) ;
```

Constraint TRC2 is a database transition constraint (it involves two distinct relvars, suppliers and shipments); the checking is therefore deferred to COMMIT time, and the primed relvar names S′ and SP′ are taken to mean relvars S and SP as they were at BEGIN TRANSACTION.

The concept of state *vs.* transition constraints has no meaning for type or attribute constraints.

8.8 KEYS

The relational model has always stressed the concept of keys, though as we have seen they are really just a special case—albeit an important one—of a more general phenomenon. In this section, we turn our attention to keys specifically.

Note: Although the basic ideas here are quite simple, there is unfortunately one significant complicating factor: *nulls.* The possibility that (e.g.) a given foreign key might permit nulls muddies the picture considerably. However, nulls form a large topic in their own right, one that it would be inappropriate to discuss in detail at this juncture. For pedagogic reasons, therefore, we ignore nulls almost totally in the present section; we will come back to discuss the impact of nulls on keys when we discuss nulls in general, in Chapter 18. (In fact, it is our very strong opinion that nulls are a mistake and should never have been introduced at all, but it would be wrong in a book of this nature to ignore them entirely.)

Candidate Keys

Let *R* be a relvar. By definition, the set of all attributes of *R* has the **uniqueness** property, meaning that, at any given time, no two tuples in the value of *R* at that time are duplicates of one another. In practice, it is often the case that some proper subset of the set of all attributes of *R* also has the uniqueness property; in the case of the suppliers relvar *S,* for example, the subset containing just attribute S# has that property. These facts constitute the intuition behind the definition of *candidate key:*

- Let *K* be a set of attributes of relvar *R.* Then *K* is a **candidate key** for *R* if and only if it possesses both of the following properties:*

  a. **Uniqueness:** No legal value of *R* ever contains two distinct tuples with the same value for *K.*

  b. **Irreducibility:** No proper subset of *K* has the uniqueness property.

Note that every relvar does have at least one candidate key. The uniqueness property of such keys is self-explanatory. As for the irreducibility property, the point is that if we were to specify a "candidate key" that was *not* irreducible, the system would not be aware of the true state of affairs, and would thus not be able to enforce the associated integrity constraint properly. For example, suppose we were to define the combination {S#,CITY}—instead of just {S#} alone—as a candidate key for suppliers. Then the system will not enforce the constraint that supplier numbers are "globally" unique; instead, it will enforce only the weaker constraint that supplier numbers are "locally" unique within city. For this reason among others, we require candidate keys not to include any attributes that are irrelevant for unique identification purposes.[†]

---

*Observe that the definition applies to *relation variables* (relvars) specifically. An analogous notion can be defined for relation *values* also [3.3], but relvars are the important case.

[†]Another good reason why candidate keys are required to be irreducible has to do with matching *foreign* keys. Any foreign key that referenced a "reducible" candidate key (if such a thing were possible) would be "reducible" too, and the relvar containing it would thus almost certainly be in violation of the principles of further normalization (see Chapter 11).

Incidentally, irreducibility in the foregoing sense is referred to as *minimality* in much of the literature (including earlier editions of this book). However, "minimality" is really not the *mot juste,* because to say that candidate key *K1* is "minimal" does not mean that another candidate key *K2* cannot be found that has fewer components; it is entirely possible that (e.g.) *K1* has four components and *K2* only two. We will stay with the term "irreducible."

In **Tutorial D,** we use the syntax

```
KEY { <attribute name commalist > }
```

within a relvar definition to specify a candidate key for the relvar in question. Here are some examples:

```
■ VAR S BASE RELATION
      { S#      S#,
        SNAME   NAME,
        STATUS  INTEGER,
        CITY    CHAR }
      KEY { S# } ;
```

Note: In previous chapters, we have shown this definition with a PRIMARY KEY clause, not a KEY clause. See the subsection "Primary and Alternate Keys," later in this section, for further discussion and explanation.

```
■ VAR SP BASE RELATION
      { S#      S#,
        P#      P#,
        QTY     QTY }
      KEY { S#, P# } ... ;
```

This example shows a relvar with a **composite** candidate key (i.e., a candidate key involving more than one attribute). A **simple** candidate key is one that is not composite.

```
■ VAR ELEMENT BASE RELATION { NAME    NAME,
                              SYMBOL  CHAR,
                              ATOMIC# INTEGER }
                      KEY { NAME }
                      KEY { SYMBOL }
                      KEY { ATOMIC# } ;
```

This example shows a relvar with several distinct (simple) candidate keys.

```
■ VAR MARRIAGE BASE RELATION { HUSBAND              NAME,
                               WIFE                 NAME,
                               DATE /* of marriage */ DATE }
   /* assume no polyandry, no polygyny, and no husband and */
   /* wife marry each other more than once ...            */
                       KEY { HUSBAND, DATE }
                       KEY { DATE, WIFE }
                       KEY { WIFE, HUSBAND } ;
```

This example shows a relvar with several distinct composite (and overlapping) candidate keys.

Of course, as pointed out in Section 8.4, a candidate key definition is really just shorthand for a certain relvar constraint. The shorthand is useful because the candidate key concept is so important from a pragmatic point of view. To be specific, candidate keys provide the basic **tuple-level addressing mechanism** in the relational model—meaning that the only system-guaranteed way of pinpointing some specific tuple is by some candidate key value. For example, the expression

```
S WHERE S# = S# ( 'S3' )
```

is guaranteed to yield at most one tuple (more precisely, it yields a *relation* that contains at most one tuple). By contrast, the expression

```
S WHERE CITY = 'Paris'
```

yields an unpredictable number of tuples, in general. It follows that *candidate keys are just as fundamental to the successful operation of a relational system as main memory addresses are to the successful operation of the underlying machine.* As a consequence:

1. "Relvars" that do not have a candidate key—i.e., "relvars" that permit duplicate tuples—are bound to display strange and anomalous behavior in some circumstances.

2. A system that has no knowledge of candidate keys is bound to display behavior on occasion that is not "truly relational," even if the relvars it deals with are indeed true relvars and do not permit duplicate tuples.

The behavior referred to above as "strange and anomalous" and "not truly relational" has to do with such matters as *view updating* and *optimization* (see Chapters 9 and 17, respectively).

A few final points to close out this subsection:

- A superset of a candidate key is a **superkey.** For example, the set of attributes {S#,CITY} is a superkey for relvar S. A superkey has the uniqueness property but not necessarily the irreducibility property (of course, a candidate key is a special case of a superkey).

- If *SK* is a superkey for relvar *R* and *A* is an attribute of *R,* then the **functional dependency** *SK* → *A* necessarily holds true in *R* (this important concept is discussed in depth in Chapter 10). In fact, we can *define* a superkey to be a subset *SK* of the attributes of *R* such that the functional dependency *SK* → *A* holds true for all attributes *A* of *R*.

- Finally, please note that the logical notion of a candidate key should not be confused with the physical notion of a "unique index" (even though the latter is very often used to implement the former). In other words, there is no implication that there must be an index (or any other special physical access path, come to that) on a candidate key. In practice, there probably *will* be some such special access path, but whether there is or not is beyond the scope of the relational model as such.

Primary Keys and Alternate Keys

We have seen that it is possible for a given relvar to have more than one candidate key. In such a case, the relational model has historically required—at least in the case of *base* relvars—that exactly one of those keys be chosen as the **primary** key, and the others are then called

alternate keys. In the ELEMENT example, for instance, we might choose {SYMBOL} as the primary key; {NAME} and {ATOMIC#} would then be alternate keys. And in the case where there is only one candidate key anyway, the relational model has again historically required that that candidate key be designated the primary key for the base relvar in question. Hence every base relvar has always had a primary key.

Now, choosing one candidate key (in those cases where there is a choice) as primary might be a good idea in many cases—possibly even in most cases—but it cannot be justified in *all* cases, unequivocally. Detailed arguments in support of this position are given in reference [8.13]; here we just note one such, which is that the choice of which candidate key is primary is essentially arbitrary (to quote Codd [8.8], "the normal basis [for making the choice] is simplicity, but this aspect is outside the scope of the relational model"). In our own examples, we will sometimes define a primary key and sometimes not (we will, of course, always define at least one *candidate* key).

Foreign Keys

Loosely speaking, a *foreign key* is a set of attributes of one relvar $R2$ whose values are required to match values of some candidate key of some relvar $R1$. For example, consider the set of attributes {S#} of relvar SP (a set that contains just one attribute, of course). It should be clear that a given value for {S#} should be allowed to appear in relvar SP only if that same value also appears as a value of the sole candidate key {S#} for relvar S (we cannot have a shipment for a nonexistent supplier). Likewise, a given value for the set of attributes {P#} should be allowed to appear in relvar SP only if the same value also appears as a value of the sole candidate key {P#} for relvar P (we cannot have a shipment for a nonexistent part either). These examples serve to motivate the following definition:

- Let $R2$ be a relvar. Then a **foreign key** in $R2$ is a set of attributes of $R2$, say FK, such that:

  a. There exists a relvar $R1$ ($R1$ and $R2$ not necessarily distinct) with a candidate key CK, and

  b. For all time, each value of FK in the current value of $R2$ is identical to the value of CK in some tuple in the current value of $R1$.

Points arising:

1. The definition requires every value of a given foreign key to appear as a value of the matching candidate key (which is usually but not invariably a primary key specifically). Note, however, that the converse is *not* a requirement; that is, the candidate key corresponding to some given foreign key might contain a value that does not currently appear as a value of that foreign key. In the case of suppliers and parts, for example (sample values as shown in Fig. 3.8), the supplier number S5 appears in relvar S but not in relvar SP, because supplier S5 does not currently supply any parts.

2. A foreign key is **simple** or **composite** according as the candidate key it matches is simple or composite.

3. Each attribute of a given foreign key must have the same name and type as the corresponding component of the matching candidate key.

4. *Terminology:* A foreign key value represents a **reference** to the tuple containing the matching candidate key value (the **referenced tuple**). The problem of ensuring that the database does not include any invalid foreign key values is therefore known as the **referential integrity** problem. The constraint that values of a given foreign key must match values of the corresponding candidate key is known as a **referential constraint.** We refer to the relvar that contains the foreign key as the **referencing** relvar and the relvar that contains the corresponding candidate key as the **referenced** relvar.

5. *Referential diagrams:* Consider suppliers and parts once again. We can represent the referential constraints that exist in that database by means of the following **referential diagram:**

$$S \longleftarrow SP \longrightarrow P$$

Each arrow means there is a foreign key in the relvar from which the arrow emerges that refers to some candidate key in the relvar to which the arrow points. *Note:* For clarity, it is sometimes a good idea to label each arrow in a referential diagram with the name(s) of the attribute(s) that constitute the relevant foreign key.* For instance:

$$S \overset{S\#}{\longleftarrow} SP \overset{P\#}{\longrightarrow} P$$

In this book, however, we will show such labels only when omitting them might lead to confusion or ambiguity.

6. A given relvar can of course be both referenced and referencing, as in the case of *R2* here:

$$R3 \longrightarrow R2 \longrightarrow R1$$

It is convenient to introduce the term *referential path.* Let relations *Rn, R(n-1), ..., R2, R1* be such that there is a referential constraint from *Rn* to *R(n-1),* a referential constraint from *R(n-1)* to *R(n-2), ...,* and a referential constraint from *R2* to *R1:*

$$Rn \longrightarrow R(n-1) \longrightarrow R(n-2) \longrightarrow \; \cdots \; \longrightarrow R2 \longrightarrow R1$$

Then the chain of arrows from *Rn* to *R1* represents a **referential path** from *Rn* to *R1.*

7. Note that relvars *R1* and *R2* in the foreign key definition are *not necessarily distinct.* That is, a relvar might include a foreign key whose values are required to match the values of some candidate key in that same relvar. By way of example, consider the following relvar definition (we will explain the syntax in just a moment, but in any case it should be fairly self-explanatory):

```
VAR EMP BASE RELATION
      { EMP# EMP#, ..., MGR_EMP# EMP#, ... }
   PRIMARY KEY { EMP# }
   FOREIGN KEY { RENAME MGR_EMP# AS EMP# } REFERENCES EMP ;
```

---

*Alternatively (and perhaps preferably) we could *name* the foreign keys and then use those names to label the arrows.

Here attribute MGR_EMP# represents the employee number of the manager of the employee identified by EMP#; for example, the tuple for employee E4 might include a MGR_EMP# value of E3, which represents a reference to the EMP tuple for employee E3. (Note the need to rename an attribute of the foreign key in this example in order to conform with the requirements of paragraph 3 above.) Such a relvar is sometimes said to be **self-referencing.** *Exercise:* Invent some sample data for this example.

8. Self-referencing relvars such as EMP above actually represent a special case of a more general situation—namely, there can exist *referential cycles.* Relvars *Rn, R(n-1), R(n-2), ..., R2, R1* form a **referential cycle** if *Rn* includes a foreign key referring to *R(n-1), R(n-1)* includes a foreign key referring to *R(n-2), ...,* and so on, and finally *R1* includes a foreign key referring back to *Rn* again. More succinctly, a referential cycle exists if there is a referential path from some relvar *Rn* to itself:

$$Rn \longrightarrow R(n\text{-}1) \longrightarrow R(n\text{-}2) \longrightarrow \cdots \longrightarrow R2 \longrightarrow R1 \longrightarrow Rn$$

9. Foreign-to-candidate-key matches are sometimes said to be the "glue" that holds the database together. Another way of saying the same thing is that such matches represent certain *relationships* between tuples. Note carefully, however, that not all such relationships are represented by keys in this way. For example, there is a relationship ("colocation") between suppliers and parts, represented by the CITY attributes of relations S and P; a given supplier and a given part are colocated if they are located in the same city. However, this relationship is not represented by keys.

10. Historically, the foreign key concept has been defined for base relvars only, a fact that raises some questions in itself (see the discussion of *The Interchangeability Principle* in Chapter 9, Section 9.2). We do not impose such a restriction here; however, we do limit our discussions to base relvars only (where it makes any difference), for reasons of simplicity.

11. The relational model originally required that foreign keys reference, very specifically, *primary* keys, not just candidate keys (see, e.g., reference [8.8] once again). We reject that limitation as unnecessary and undesirable in general, though it might often constitute good discipline in practice [8.13]. We will usually follow that discipline in our own examples.

12. Along with the foreign key concept, the relational model includes the following rule (the *referential integrity* rule):

   ■ **Referential integrity:** The database must not contain any unmatched foreign key values.*

---

*The referential integrity rule can be regarded as a *metaconstraint:* It implies that any given database must be subject to certain integrity constraints, specific to the database in question, that together guarantee that the rule is not violated by that database. We note in passing that the relational model is usually considered to include another such "metaconstraint," the *entity* integrity rule; this latter rule has to do with nulls, however, and we therefore defer discussion of it to Chapter 18.

The term "unmatched foreign key value" here simply means a foreign key value in some referencing relvar for which there does not exist a matching value of the relevant candidate key in the relevant referenced relvar. In other words, the constraint simply says: If *B* references *A,* then *A* must exist.

Here then is the syntax for defining a foreign key:

```
FOREIGN KEY { <item commalist > } REFERENCES <relvar name>
```

This clause appears within a referencing relvar definition. Note that:

- Each *<item>* is either an *<attribute name>* of the referencing relvar or an expression of the form

  ```
  RENAME <attribute name> AS <attribute name>
  ```

  (see the self-referencing relvar EMP above for an example of the RENAME case).
- The *<relvar name>* identifies the referenced relvar.

Examples have already been given at many earlier points in the book (see, e.g., Fig. 3.9 in Chapter 3). *Note:* Of course, as pointed out in Section 8.5, a foreign key definition is really just shorthand for a certain database constraint (or a certain relvar constraint, in the case of a self-referencing relvar)—*unless* the foreign key definition is extended to include certain "referential actions," in which case it becomes more than just an integrity constraint *per se.* See the two subsections immediately following.

Referential Actions

Consider the following statement:

```
DELETE S WHERE S# = S# ( 'S1' ) ;
```

Assume this DELETE does exactly what it says—i.e., it deletes the supplier tuple for supplier S1, no more and no less. Assume too that (a) the database does include some shipments for supplier S1, as in Fig. 3.8, and (b) the application does not go on to delete those shipments. When the system checks the referential constraint from shipments to suppliers, then, it will find a violation, and an error will occur.

Note: Since the referential constraint here is a *database* constraint, the checking will be done at COMMIT time—at least conceptually (the system might in fact check the constraint as soon as the DELETE is executed, but a violation at that time is not necessarily an error; it just means that the system will have to do the check again at COMMIT time).

However, an alternative approach does exist, one that might be preferable in some cases, and that is for the system to perform an appropriate *compensating action* that will guarantee that the overall result does still satisfy the constraint. In the example, the obvious compensating action would be for the system to delete the shipments for supplier S1 "automatically." We can achieve this effect by extending the foreign key definition as follows:

```
VAR SP BASE RELATION { ... } ...
    FOREIGN KEY { S# } REFERENCES S
                    ON DELETE CASCADE ;
```

The specification ON DELETE CASCADE defines a *DELETE rule* for this particular foreign key, and the specification CASCADE is the *referential action* for that DELETE rule. The meaning of these specifications is that a DELETE operation on the suppliers relvar should "cascade" to delete matching tuples in the shipments relvar as well.

Another common referential action is RESTRICT (nothing to do with the *restrict* operator of the relational algebra). In the case at hand, RESTRICT would mean that DELETE operations are "restricted" to the case where there are no matching shipments (they are rejected otherwise). Omitting a referential action for a particular foreign key is equivalent to specifying the "action" NO ACTION, which means what it says—the DELETE is performed exactly as requested, no more and no less. (If NO ACTION is specified in the case at hand, of course, and a supplier that has matching shipments is deleted, we will subsequently get a referential integrity violation.) Points arising:

1. DELETE is not the only operation for which referential actions make sense. For example, what should happen if we try to update the supplier number for a supplier for which there exists at least one matching shipment? Clearly, we need an *UPDATE* rule as well as a DELETE rule. In general, there are the same possibilities for UPDATE as there are for DELETE:

   ■ CASCADE—The UPDATE cascades to update the foreign key in those matching shipments also;

   ■ RESTRICT—The UPDATE is restricted to the case where there are no such matching shipments (it is rejected otherwise);

   ■ NO ACTION—The UPDATE is performed exactly as requested.

2. Of course, CASCADE, RESTRICT, and NO ACTION are not the only possible referential actions—they are merely ones that are commonly required in practice. In principle, however, there could be an arbitrary number of possible responses to, e.g., an attempt to delete a particular supplier. For example:

   ■ Information could be written to some archive database;

   ■ The shipments for the supplier in question could be transferred to some other supplier;

   and so on. It will never be feasible to provide declarative syntax for all conceivable responses. In general, therefore, it should be possible to specify a referential action of the form "CALL *proc*(...)," where *proc* is a user-defined procedure.

   Note: The execution of that procedure must be considered part of the execution of the transaction that caused the integrity check to be done. Furthermore, that integrity check must be performed again after that procedure has executed (the procedure must obviously not leave the database in a state that violates the constraint).

3. Let *R2* and *R1* be, respectively, a referencing relvar and the corresponding referenced relvar:

   R2 ——▶ R1

Let the applicable DELETE rule specify CASCADE. Then a DELETE on a given tuple of *R1* will imply a DELETE on certain tuples of relvar *R2* (in general). Now suppose relvar *R2* in turn is referenced by some other relvar *R3:*

$$R3 \longrightarrow R2 \longrightarrow R1$$

Then the effect of the implied DELETE on tuples of *R2* is defined to be exactly as if an attempt had been made to delete those tuples directly; i.e., it depends on the DELETE rule specified for the referential constraint from *R3* to *R2*. If that implied DELETE fails (because of the DELETE rule from *R3* to *R2* or for any other reason), then the entire operation fails and the database remains unchanged. And so on, recursively, to any number of levels.

Analogous remarks apply to the CASCADE UPDATE rule also, *mutatis mutandis,* if the foreign key in relvar *R2* has any attributes in common with the candidate key of that relvar that is referenced by the foreign key in *R3*.

4. It follows from the foregoing that, from a logical point of view, database updates are always atomic (all or nothing), even if under the covers they involve several updates on several relvars because of, e.g., a CASCADE referential action.

Triggered Procedures

As you might already have realized (and indeed as the remark in the foregoing subsection regarding user-defined procedures should have suggested), the whole concept of referential actions takes us beyond integrity constraints as such and into the realm of *triggered procedures.* A **triggered procedure** (usually just called a *trigger* in the literature) is a procedure that is invoked "automatically" on the occurrence of some specified event or *trigger condition.* The trigger condition is typically the execution of some database update operation, but might be, e.g., the occurrence of a specified exception (in particular, the violation of a specified integrity constraint) or the passage of a specified interval of time. CASCADE referential actions provide a simple example of a triggered procedure (declaratively specified, please note!).

In general, triggered procedures are applicable to a much wider variety of problems than just the integrity question that is the topic of the present chapter (a good list of such applications can be found in reference [8.1]). However, they represent a large subject in their own right, one that is beyond the scope of this chapter (see reference [8.22] for further discussion). Here we would just like to say that, while triggered procedures are certainly useful for many purposes, they are usually *not* a good approach to the problem of database integrity specifically, for obvious reasons (declarative approaches, if such are possible, are always to be preferred). *Note:* These remarks are not meant to suggest that referential actions are a bad idea. While it is true that referential actions do cause certain procedures to be invoked, they are at least (as already noted) specified declaratively.

8.9   SQL FACILITIES

SQL's integrity constraint classification scheme is very different from the one described in Sections 8.1–8.5. First of all, it classifies constraints into three broad categories, as follows:

- Domain constraints
- Base table constraints
- General constraints ("assertions")

However, "domain constraints" are not the same as our type constraints, "base table constraints" are not the same as our relvar constraints, and "assertions" are not the same as our database constraints. In fact:

- SQL does not really support type constraints at all (because, of course, it does not really support *types* at all, other than a handful of builtin ones).
- SQL's "domain" constraints are an undesirably generalized form of our attribute constraints (recall that SQL-style domains are not really domains at all in the relational sense).
- SQL's base table constraints and assertions (which are effectively interchangeable) are loosely equivalent to our relvar and database constraints taken together.

We note too that SQL has no support at all for transition constraints. Nor does it currently support triggered procedures, though some such support is included in SQL3 (see Appendix B).

Domain Constraints

An SQL-style domain constraint is a constraint that applies to every column defined on the domain in question. Here is an example:

```
CREATE DOMAIN COLOR CHAR(6) DEFAULT '???'
    CONSTRAINT VALID_COLORS
        CHECK ( VALUE IN
                ( 'Red', 'Yellow', 'Blue', 'Green', '???' ) ) ;
```

Suppose the CREATE TABLE for base table P looks like this:

```
CREATE TABLE P ( ... , COLOR COLOR, ... ) ;
```

Then if the user inserts a part row and does not provide a COLOR value for that row, the value "???" will be placed in that position by default. Alternatively, if the user *does* provide a COLOR value but it is not one of the legal set, the operation will fail, and the system will produce a suitable diagnostic that mentions the constraint VALID_COLORS by name.

Now, we saw in Section 8.2 that a domain constraint is—or, rather, should be—conceptually nothing more than an enumeration of the values that make up that domain, and the VALID_COLORS example indeed abides by this definition. In general, however, SQL allows a domain constraint to involve a boolean expression of *arbitrary complexity;* thus, e.g., the legal values for some domain *D* might depend on the values currently appearing in some table *T*. You might care to meditate on some of the implications of this unwarranted permissiveness.

Base Table Constraints

An SQL base table constraint is any of the following:

- a candidate key definition
- a foreign key definition
- a "check constraint" definition

We discuss each case in detail below. *Note:* Any of these definitions can optionally be preceded by the phrase "CONSTRAINT *<constraint name>*," thereby providing a name for the new constraint (the same is true for domain constraints, as we saw in the VALID_COLORS example earlier). For brevity, we ignore this option below.

Candidate keys: A candidate key definition takes the form

```
UNIQUE ( <column name commalist> )
```

or the form

```
PRIMARY KEY ( <column name commalist> )
```

The *<column name commalist>* must not be empty in either case. A given base table can have at most one PRIMARY KEY specification but any number of UNIQUE specifications. In the case of PRIMARY KEY, each specified column is additionally assumed to be NOT NULL, even if NOT NULL is not specified explicitly (see the discussion of check constraints below).

Foreign keys: A foreign key definition takes the form

```
FOREIGN KEY ( <column name commalist> )
    REFERENCES <base table name> [ ( <column name commalist> ) ]
  [ ON DELETE <referential action> ]
  [ ON UPDATE <referential action> ]
```

where *<referential action>* is NO ACTION (the default) or CASCADE or SET DEFAULT or SET NULL. We defer discussion of SET DEFAULT and SET NULL to Chapter 18. The second *<column name commalist>* is required if the foreign key references a candidate key that is not a primary key. *Note:* The foreign-to-candidate-key matching is done on the basis not of column names but of column *position* (left to right) within the commalists.

Check constraints: A "check constraint definition" takes the form

```
CHECK ( <conditional expression> )
```

An attempt to create a row *r* within base table *T* is considered to violate a check constraint for *T* if the conditional expression specified within that constraint evaluates to *false* for *r*. *Note:* Conditional expressions are the SQL analog of what we have elsewhere been calling *boolean* expressions. They are explained in detail in Appendix A. Note in particular that (in the context at hand) the conditional expression can be arbitrarily complex—it is explicitly *not* limited to a condition that refers just to *T*, but can instead refer to anything in the database. Again, you might care to meditate on some of the implications of this unwarranted permissiveness.

Here then is an example of CREATE TABLE involving base table constraints of all three kinds:

```
CREATE TABLE SP
     ( S# S# NOT NULL, P# P# NOT NULL, QTY QTY NOT NULL,
       PRIMARY KEY ( S#, P# ),
       FOREIGN KEY ( S# ) REFERENCES S
                          ON DELETE CASCADE
                          ON UPDATE CASCADE,
       FOREIGN KEY ( P# ) REFERENCES P
                          ON DELETE CASCADE
                          ON UPDATE CASCADE,
       CHECK ( QTY > 0 AND QTY < 5001 ) ) ;
```

We are assuming here that (a) domains S#, P#, and QTY have already been defined, and (b) S# and P# have been explicitly defined to be the primary keys for tables S and P, respectively. Also, we have deliberately made use of the shorthand by which a check constraint of the form

```
CHECK ( <column name> IS NOT NULL )
```

can be replaced by a simple NOT NULL specification in the definition of the column in question. In the example, we have thus replaced three slightly cumbersome check constraints by three simple NOT NULLs.

We close this subsection with a remark on one slight oddity, namely as follows: An SQL base table constraint is *always* considered to be satisfied if the base table in question happens to be empty—even if the constraint is of the form "this table must not be empty"!

Assertions

For the remainder of this section, we concentrate on the third case, general constraints or "assertions." General constraints are defined by means of **CREATE ASSERTION**—syntax:

```
CREATE ASSERTION <constraint name>
       CHECK ( <conditional expression> ) ;
```

And here is the syntax of **DROP ASSERTION:**

```
DROP ASSERTION <constraint name> ;
```

Note that, unlike all other forms of the SQL DROP operator discussed in this book (DROP DOMAIN, DROP TABLE, DROP VIEW), DROP ASSERTION does not offer a RESTRICT *vs.* CASCADE option.

Here are some examples of CREATE ASSERTION:

1. Every supplier has status at least five:

```
CREATE ASSERTION IC13 CHECK
        ( ( SELECT MIN ( S.STATUS ) FROM S ) > 4 ) ;
```

2. Every part has a positive weight:

```
CREATE ASSERTION IC18 CHECK
        ( NOT EXISTS ( SELECT * FROM P
                       WHERE  NOT ( P.WEIGHT > 0.0 ) ) ) ;
```

3. All red parts must be stored in London:

```
CREATE ASSERTION IC99 CHECK
        ( NOT EXISTS ( SELECT * FROM P
                       WHERE P.COLOR = 'Red'
                       AND   P.CITY <> 'London' ) ) ;
```

4. No shipment has a total weight (part weight times shipment quantity) greater than 20,000:

```
CREATE ASSERTION IC46 CHECK
        ( NOT EXISTS ( SELECT * FROM P, SP
                       WHERE P.P# = SP.P#
                       AND ( P.WEIGHT * SP.QTY ) > 20000.0 ) ) ;
```

5. No supplier with status less than 20 can supply any part in a quantity greater than 500:

```
CREATE ASSERTION IC95 CHECK
        ( NOT EXISTS ( SELECT * FROM S, SP
                       WHERE S.STATUS < 20
                       AND   S.S# = SP.S#
                       AND   SP.QTY > 500 ) ) ;
```

Deferred Checking

SQL's integrity constraint classification scheme also differs from ours with respect to the question of when the checking is done. In our scheme, database constraints are checked at COMMIT time, others are checked "immediately." In SQL, by contrast, constraints can be defined to be DEFERRABLE or NOT DEFERRABLE; if a given constraint is DEFERRABLE, it can further be defined to be INITIALLY DEFERRED or INITIALLY IMMEDIATE, which defines its state at the beginning of each transaction. NOT DEFERRABLE constraints are always checked immediately, but DEFERRABLE constraints can be dynamically switched on and off by means of the statement

```
SET CONSTRAINTS <constraint name commalist> <option> ;
```

where *<option>* is either IMMEDIATE or DEFERRED. Here is an example:

```
SET CONSTRAINTS IC46, IC95 DEFERRED ;
```

DEFERRABLE constraints are checked only when they are in the IMMEDIATE state. Setting a DEFERRABLE constraint into the IMMEDIATE state causes that constraint to be immediately checked, of course; if the check fails, the SET IMMEDIATE fails. COMMIT forces a SET IMMEDIATE for all DEFERRABLE constraints; if any integrity check then fails, the transaction is rolled back.

8.10 SUMMARY

In this chapter we have discussed the crucial concept of **integrity.** The integrity problem is the problem of ensuring that the data in the database is *accurate* or *correct* (and, of course, we are interested in **declarative** solutions to that problem). In fact, as you should have realized by now, "integrity" in this context really means **semantics:** It is the integrity constraints (in particular, the relvar and database predicates—see below) that represent the **meaning** of the data. And that is why, as we claimed in Section 8.6, integrity is *crucially important.*

We divide integrity constraints into four categories:

- A **type** constraint specifies the legal values for a given type (or domain), and is checked during invocations of the corresponding **selector.**

- An **attribute** constraint specifies the legal values for a given attribute, and should never be violated (assuming type constraints are checked).

- A **relvar** constraint specifies the legal values for a given relvar, and is checked when the relvar in question is **updated.**

- A **database** constraint specifies the legal values for a given database, and is checked at **COMMIT time.**

The logical AND of all relvar constraints for a given relvar is the (internal) **relvar predicate** for that relvar. The relvar predicate is the system-understood meaning of the relvar, and is the **criterion for acceptability of updates** on that relvar. *The Golden Rule* states that *no update operation is ever allowed to leave any relvar in a state that violates its own predicate.* The overall database in turn is subject to a **database predicate,** and no transaction is ever allowed to leave the database in a state that violates that predicate, either.

Next, we briefly sketched the basic idea of **transition** constraints (other constraints are **state** constraints). Then we moved on to discuss the pragmatically important special cases of **candidate, primary, alternate,** and **foreign** keys. Candidate keys satisfy the **uniqueness** and **irreducibility** properties, and every relvar has at least one (no exceptions!). The constraint that values of a given foreign key must match values of the corresponding candidate key is a **referential constraint;** we explored several implications of the referential integrity idea, including in particular the notion of **referential actions** (especially **CASCADE**). This latter discussion led us on a brief foray into the realm of **triggered procedures.**

We concluded our discussions with a look at the relevant aspects of **SQL.** SQL supports "domain" constraints, base table constraints, and "assertions" (general constraints), and its base table constraint support includes special case support for keys.

EXERCISES

8.1 Using the syntax introduced in Sections 8.2–8.5, write integrity constraints for the suppliers-parts-projects database as follows:

a. The only legal cities are London, Paris, Rome, Athens, Oslo, Stockholm, Madrid, and Amsterdam.

b. The only legal supplier numbers are ones that can be represented by a character string of at least two characters, of which the first is an "S" and the remainder denote a decimal integer in the range 0 to 9999.

c. All red parts must weigh less than 50 pounds.

d. No two projects can be located in the same city.

e. At most one supplier can be located in Athens at any one time.

f. No shipment can have a quantity more than double the average of all such quantities.

g. The highest status supplier must not be located in the same city as the lowest status supplier.

h. Every project must be located in a city in which there is at least one supplier.

i. Every project must be located in a city in which there is at least one supplier of that project.

j. There must exist at least one red part.

k. The average supplier status must be greater than 18.

l. Every London supplier must supply part P2.

m. At least one red part must weigh less than 50 pounds.

n. Suppliers in London must supply more different kinds of parts than suppliers in Paris.

o. Suppliers in London must supply more parts in total than suppliers in Paris.

p. No shipment quantity can be reduced (in a single update) to less than half its current value.

q. Suppliers in Athens can move only to London or Paris, and suppliers in London can move only to Paris.

8.2 For each of your answers to Exercise 8.1, state whether the constraint is a relvar constraint or a database constraint.

8.3 For each of your answers to Exercise 8.1, state the operations that might cause the applicable constraint to be violated.

8.4 Let CHAR(5) and CHAR(3) denote character strings of length five and three characters, respectively. How many types are there here—one or two?

8.5 Let *A* and *B* be two relvars. State the candidate key(s) for each of the following:

a. `A WHERE ...`

b. `A {...}`

c. *A* TIMES *B*

d. *A* UNION *B*

e. *A* INTERSECT *B*

f. *A* MINUS *B*

g. *A* JOIN *B*

h. EXTEND *A* ADD *exp* AS *Z*

i. SUMMARIZE *A* PER *B* ADD *exp* AS *Z*

j. *A* SEMIJOIN *B*

k. *A* SEMIMINUS *B*

Assume in each case that *A* and *B* meet the requirements for the operation in question (e.g., they are of the same type, in the case of UNION).

8.6 Let *R* be a relvar of degree *n*. What is the maximum number of candidate keys *R* might possess?

8.7 Let *R* be a relvar whose sole legal values are the special (and very important) degree-0 relations DEE and DUM. What candidate key(s) does *R* have?

8.8 The body of the chapter discussed foreign key DELETE and UPDATE rules, but it did not mention any foreign key "INSERT rule." Why not?

8.9 Using the sample suppliers-parts-projects data values from Fig. 4.5, say what the effect of each of the following operations is:

a. UPDATE project J7, setting CITY to New York;

b. UPDATE part P5, setting P# to P4;

c. UPDATE supplier S5, setting S# to S8, if the applicable referential action is RESTRICT;

d. DELETE supplier S3, if the applicable referential action is CASCADE;

e. DELETE part P2, if the applicable referential action is RESTRICT;

f. DELETE project J4, if the applicable referential action is CASCADE;

g. UPDATE shipment S1-P1-J1, setting S# to S2;

h. UPDATE shipment S5-P5-J5, setting J# to J7;

i. UPDATE shipment S5-P5-J5, setting J# to J8;

j. INSERT shipment S5-P6-J7;

k. INSERT shipment S4-P7-J6;

l. INSERT shipment S1-P2-*jjj* (where *jjj* stands for a default project number).

8.10 An education database contains information about an inhouse company education training scheme. For each training course, the database contains details of all prerequisite courses for that course and all offerings for that course; for each offering, it contains details of all teachers and all student enrollments for that offering. The database also contains information about employees. The relevant relvars are as follows, in outline:

```
COURSE        { COURSE#, TITLE }
PREREQ        { SUP_COURSE#, SUB_COURSE# }
OFFERING      { COURSE#, OFF#, OFFDATE, LOCATION }
TEACHER       { COURSE#, OFF#, EMP# }
ENROLLMENT    { COURSE#, OFF#, EMP#, GRADE }
EMPLOYEE      { EMP#, ENAME, JOB }
```

The meaning of the PREREQ relvar is that the superior course (SUP_COURSE#) has the subordinate course (SUB_COURSE#) as an immediate prerequisite; the others should be self-explanatory. Draw a referential diagram for this database. Also give the corresponding database definition (i.e., write an appropriate set of type and relvar definitions).

8.11 The following two relvars represent a database containing information about departments and employees:

```
DEPT   { DEPT#, ..., MGR_EMP#, ... }
EMP    { EMP#, ..., DEPT#, ... }
```

Every department has a manager (MGR_EMP#); every employee has a department (DEPT#). Again, draw a referential diagram and write a database definition for this database.

8.12 The following two relvars represent a database containing information about employees and programmers:

```
EMP    { EMP#, ..., JOB, ... }
PGMR   { EMP#, ..., LANG, ... }
```

Every programmer is an employee, but the converse is not the case. Once again, draw a referential diagram and write a suitable database definition.

8.13 One issue we did not discuss in the body of the chapter is the question of what should happen if the user attempts to drop some relvar or type and some existing constraint refers to that relvar or type. What *should* happen in such a situation?

8.14 Give SQL solutions to Exercise 8.1.

8.15 Compare and contrast SQL's integrity support with the integrity mechanism described in the body of this chapter.

REFERENCES AND BIBLIOGRAPHY

8.1 Alexander Aiken, Joseph M. Hellerstein, and Jennifer Widom: "Static Analysis Techniques for Predicting the Behavior of Active Database Rules," *ACM TODS 20,* No. 1 (March 1995).

This paper continues the work of references [8.2] and [8.5], *q.v.,* on "expert database systems" (here called *active* database systems). In particular, it describes the rule system of the IBM Starburst prototype (see references [17.50], [25.14], [25.17], and [25.21–25.22], also reference [8.22]).

8.2 Elena Baralis and Jennifer Widom: "An Algebraic Approach to Rule Analysis in Expert Database Systems," Proc. 20th Int. Conf. on Very Large Data Bases, Santiago, Chile (September 1994).

According to this paper, an "expert database system" is a database system that supports "condition/action rules" (in our terminology, the condition here is a *trigger condition* and the action is the corresponding *triggered procedure*). One problem with such systems is that their behavior is inherently difficult to predict or understand. This paper presents methods for determining prior to execution time whether a given set of rules possesses the properties of *termination* and *confluence*. *Termination* means that rule processing is guaranteed not to go on forever. *Confluence* means the final database state is independent of the order in which the rules are executed.

8.3 Philip A. Bernstein, Barbara T. Blaustein, and Edmund M. Clarke: "Fast Maintenance of Semantic Integrity Assertions Using Redundant Aggregate Data," Proc. 6th Int. Conf. on Very Large Data Bases, Montreal, Canada (October 1980).

Presents an efficient method of enforcement for integrity constraints of a certain special kind. An example is "every value in set *A* must be less than every value in set *B*." The enforcement technique is based on the observation that (e.g.) the constraint just given is logically equivalent to the constraint "the *maximum* value in *A* must be less than the *minimum* value in *B*." By recognizing this class of constraint and automatically keeping the relevant maximum and minimum values in hidden variables, the system can reduce the number of comparisons involved in enforcing the constraint on a given update from something on the order of the cardinality of either *A* or *B* (depending which set the update applies to) to *one*—at the cost, of course, of having to maintain the hidden variables.

8.4 O. Peter Buneman and Erik K. Clemons: "Efficiently Monitoring Relational Databases," *ACM TODS 4,* No. 3 (September 1979).

This paper is concerned with the efficient implementation of triggered procedures (here called *alerters*)—in particular, with the problem of deciding when the trigger condition is satisfied, without necessarily evaluating that condition. It gives a method (an *avoidance* algorithm) for detecting updates that cannot possibly satisfy a given trigger condition; it also discusses a technique for reducing the processing overhead in the case where the avoidance algorithm fails, by evaluating the trigger condition for some small subset (a *filter*) of the total set of relevant tuples.

8.5 Stefano Ceri and Jennifer Widom: "Deriving Production Rules for Constraint Maintenance," Proc. 16th Int. Conf. on Very Large Data Bases, Brisbane, Australia (August 1990).

Describes an SQL-based language for defining constraints and gives an algorithm for identifying all of the operations that might violate a given constraint. (A preliminary outline of such an algorithm was given earlier in reference [8.11]. The existence of that algorithm means there is no need to tell the DBMS explicitly when a given constraint needs to be checked, and of course the scheme described in the body of this chapter provides no way for the user to do so.) The paper also addresses questions of optimization and correctness.

8.6 Stefano Ceri, Piero Fraternali, Stefano Paraboschi, and Letizia Tanca: "Automatic Generation of Production Rules for Integrity Maintenance," *ACM TODS 19,* 3 (September 1994).

This paper, which builds on the work of reference [8.5], introduces the possibility of *automatically repairing* damage done by a constraint violation. Constraints are compiled into *production rules* with the following components:

1. A list of operations that can violate the constraint;
2. A boolean expression that will evaluate to *true* if the constraint is violated (basically just the negation of the original constraint);
3. An SQL repair procedure.

The paper also includes a good survey of related work.

8.7 Roberta Cochrane, Hamid Pirahesh, and Nelson Mattos: "Integrating Triggers and Declarative Constraints in SQL Database Systems," Proc. 22nd Int. Conf. on Very Large Data Bases, Mumbai (Bombay), India (September 1996).

To quote: "The semantics of the interaction of triggers and declarative constraints must be carefully defined to avoid inconsistent execution and to provide users [with] a comprehensive model for understanding such interactions. This [paper] defines such a model." The model in question has been implemented in DB2 and is "accepted as the model for the emerging SQL standard (SQL3)" (see Appendix B).

8.8 E. F. Codd: "Domains, Keys, and Referential Integrity in Relational Databases," *InfoDB 3,* No. 1 (Spring 1988).

A discussion of the domain, primary key, and foreign key concepts. The paper is obviously authoritative, since Codd was the inventor of all three concepts; in this writer's opinion, however, it still leaves too many issues unresolved or unexplained. Incidentally, it gives the following argument in favor of the discipline of requiring one candidate key to be selected as primary: "Failure to support this discipline is something like trying to use a computer with an addressing scheme . . . that changes radix whenever a particular kind of event occurs (for example, encountering an address that happens to be a prime number)." But if we accept this argument, why not take it to its logical conclusion and use an identical addressing scheme for *everything?* Is it not awkward to have to "address" suppliers by supplier numbers and parts by part numbers?— not to mention shipments, which involve "addresses" that are *composite.* (In fact, there is much to be said for this idea of a globally uniform addressing scheme. See the discussion of *surrogates* in the annotation to reference [13.16] in Chapter 13.)

8.9 C. J. Date: "Referential Integrity," Proc. 7th Int. Conf. on Very Large Data Bases, Cannes, France (September 1981). Republished in revised form in *Relational Database: Selected Writings.* Reading, Mass: Addison-Wesley (1986).

The paper that introduced the referential actions (principally CASCADE and RESTRICT) discussed in Section 8.8 of the present chapter. *Note:* The main difference between the original (VLDB 1981) version of the paper and the revised version is that the original version, following reference [13.6], permitted a given foreign key to reference any number of relvars, whereas— for reasons explained in detail in reference [8.10]—the revised version backed off from that excessively general position.

8.10 C. J. Date: "Referential Integrity and Foreign Keys" (in two parts), in *Relational Database Writings 1985–1989.* Reading, Mass: Addison-Wesley (1990).

Part I of this paper discusses the history of the referential integrity concept and offers a preferred set of basic definitions (with rationale). Part II provides further arguments in favor of those preferred definitions and gives some specific practical recommendations; in particular, it discusses problems caused by (a) overlapping foreign keys, (b) composite foreign key values that are partly null, and (c) *conterminous* referential paths (i.e., distinct referential paths that have the same start point and the same end point). *Note:* Certain of the positions of this paper are slightly (but not very seriously) undermined by the arguments of reference [8.13].

8.11 C. J. Date: "A Contribution to the Study of Database Integrity," in *Relational Database Writings 1985–1989.* Reading, Mass.: Addison-Wesley (1990).

To quote from the abstract: "This paper attempts to impose some structure on the [integrity] problem by (a) proposing a classification scheme for integrity constraints, (b) using that scheme to clarify the principal underlying concepts of data integrity, (c) sketching an approach to a concrete language for formulating integrity constraints, and (d) pinpointing some specific areas for further research." Portions of the present chapter are based on this earlier paper, but the classification scheme itself should be regarded as superseded by the revised version described in Sections 8.2–8.5 of the present chapter.

8.12 C. J. Date: "Integrity," Chapter 11 of C. J. Date and Colin J. White, *A Guide to DB2* (4th edition) [4.20]. Reading, Mass: Addison-Wesley (1993).

IBM's DB2 product does provide declarative primary and foreign key support (in fact, it was one of the first to do so, if not *the* first). As this reference explains, however, that support does suffer from certain implementation restrictions, the general purpose of which is *to guarantee predictable behavior*. We give a simple example here. Suppose relvar *R* currently contains just two tuples, with primary key values 1 and 2 respectively, and consider the update request "Double every primary key value in *R*." The correct result is that the tuples should now have primary key values 2 and 4, respectively. If the system updates the "2" first (replacing it by "4") and then updates the "1" second (replacing it by "2"), the request will succeed. If, on the other hand, the system updates—or, rather, tries to update—the "1" first (replacing it by "2"), it will run into a uniqueness violation, and the request will fail (the database will remain unchanged). In other words, *the result of the request is unpredictable*. In order to avoid such unpredictability, DB2 simply outlaws situations in which it might otherwise occur. Unfortunately, however, some of the resulting restrictions are quite severe [8.17].

Note that, as the foregoing example suggests, DB2 typically does do "inflight checking"— i.e., it applies integrity checks to each individual tuple *as it updates that tuple*. Such inflight checking is logically incorrect (see the discussion of update operations at the end of Section 5.4 in Chapter 5); it is done for performance reasons.

8.13 C. J. Date: "The Primacy of Primary Keys: An Investigation," in *Relational Database Writings 1991–1994*. Reading, Mass.: Addison-Wesley (1995).

Presents arguments in support of the position that sometimes it is not a good idea to make one candidate key "more equal than others."

8.14 M. M. Hammer and S. K. Sarin: "Efficient Monitoring of Database Assertions," Proc. 1978 ACM SIGMOD Int. Conf. on Management of Data, Austin, Texas (May/June 1978).

An algorithm is sketched for generating integrity checking procedures that are more efficient than the obvious "brute force" method of simply evaluating constraints after an update has been performed. The checks are incorporated into application object code at compile time. In some cases it is possible to detect that no run-time checks are needed at all. Even when they are needed, it is frequently possible to reduce the number of database accesses significantly in a variety of different ways.

8.15 Bruce M. Horowitz: "A Run-Time Execution Model for Referential Integrity Maintenance," Proc. 8th IEEE Int. Conf. on Data Engineering, Phoenix, Ariz. (February 1992).

It is well known that certain combinations of

1. Referential structures (i.e., collections of relvars that are interrelated via referential constraints),

2. Foreign key DELETE and UPDATE rules, and

3. Actual data values in the database,

can together lead to certain conflict situations and can potentially cause unpredictable behavior on the part of the implementation (see, e.g., reference [8.10] for further explanation). There are three broad approaches to dealing with this problem:

a. Leave it to the user;

b. Have the system detect and reject attempts to define structures that might potentially lead to conflicts at run time; or

c. Have the system detect and reject *actual* conflicts at run time.

Option a. is a nonstarter and option b. tends to be excessively cautious [8.12,8.17]; Horowitz therefore proposes option c. The paper gives a set of rules for such run-time actions and proves their correctness. Note, however, that the question of performance overhead of such run-time checking is not considered.

Horowitz was an active member of the committee that defined SQL/92, and the referential integrity portions of that standard effectively imply that the proposals of this paper must be supported.

8.16 Victor M. Markowitz: "Referential Integrity Revisited: An Object-Oriented Perspective," Proc. 16th Int. Conf. on Very Large Data Bases, Brisbane, Australia (August 1990).

The "object-oriented perspective" of this paper's title reflects the author's opening position statement that "referential integrity underlies the relational representation of object-oriented structures." The paper is not, however, really about object orientation at all. Rather, it presents an algorithm that, starting from an entity/relationship diagram (see Chapter 13), will generate a relational database definition in which certain of the problem situations identified in reference [8.10] (e.g., overlapping keys) are guaranteed not to occur.

The paper also discusses three commercial products (DB2, Sybase, and Ingres, as of around 1990) from a referential integrity viewpoint. DB2, which provides *declarative* support, is shown to be unduly restrictive; Sybase and Ingres, which provide *procedural* support (via "triggers" and "rules," respectively), are shown to be less restrictive than DB2 but cumbersome and difficult to use (though the Ingres support is said to be "technically superior" to that of Sybase).

8.17 Victor M. Markowitz: "Safe Referential Integrity Structures in Relational Databases," Proc. 17th Int. Conf. on Very Large Data Bases, Barcelona, Spain (September 1991).

Proposes two formal "safeness conditions" that guarantee that certain of the problem situations discussed in (e.g.) references [8.10] and [8.15] cannot occur. The paper also considers what is involved in satisfying those conditions in DB2, Sybase, and Ingres (again, as of around 1990). Regarding DB2, it is shown that some of the implementation restrictions imposed in the interests of safety [8.12] are logically unnecessary, while at the same time others are inadequate (i.e., DB2 still permits certain unsafe situations). Regarding Sybase and Ingres, it is claimed that the procedural support found in those products does not provide for the detection of unsafe—or even incorrect!—referential specifications.

8.18 Ronald G. Ross: *The Business Rule Book: Classifying, Defining, and Modeling Rules* (Version 3.0). Boston, Mass.: Database Research Group (1994).

See the annotation to reference [8.19].

8.19 Ronald G. Ross: *Business Rule Concepts*. Houston, Tx.: Business Rule Solutions Inc. (1998).

A groundswell of support for **business rules** has been building in the commercial world over the last few years; some industry figures have begun to suggest that they might be a better basis for designing and building databases and database applications (better, that is, than more established techniques such as "entity/relationship modeling," "object modeling," "semantic modeling," and others). And we agree, because "business rules" are essentially nothing more than a more user-friendly (i.e., less academic and less formal) way of talking about predicates, propositions, and all of the other aspects of integrity discussed in the present chapter. Ross is one of the foremost advocates of the business rules approach, and his books are recommended to the serious practitioner. Reference [8.18] is exhaustive, reference [8.19] is a short tutorial.

8.20 M. R. Stonebraker and E. Wong: "Access Control in a Relational Data Base Management System by Query Modification," Proc. ACM National Conf. (1974).

The University Ingres prototype [7.11] pioneered an interesting approach to integrity constraints (and security constraints also—see Chapter 16), based on *request modification.* Integrity constraints were defined by means of the DEFINE INTEGRITY statement—syntax:

```
DEFINE INTEGRITY ON <relvar name> IS <boolean expression>
```

For example:

```
DEFINE INTEGRITY ON S IS S.STATUS > 0
```

Suppose user *U* attempts the following QUEL REPLACE operation:

```
REPLACE S ( STATUS = S.STATUS - 10 )
WHERE    S.CITY = "London"
```

Then Ingres automatically modifies the REPLACE to:

```
REPLACE S ( STATUS = S.STATUS - 10 )
WHERE    S.CITY = "London"
AND      ( S.STATUS - 10 ) > 0
```

And of course this modified operation cannot possibly violate the integrity constraint.

One disadvantage of this approach is that not all constraints can be enforced in this simple way; as a matter of fact, QUEL supported only constraints in which the boolean expression was a simple restriction condition. However, even that limited support represented more than was found in most systems at the time.

8.21 A. Walker and S. C. Salveter: "Automatic Modification of Transactions to Preserve Data Base Integrity Without Undoing Updates," State University of New York, Stony Brook, N.Y.: Technical Report 81/026 (June 1981).

Describes a technique for automatically modifying any "transaction template" (i.e., transaction source code) into a corresponding *safe* template—safe, in the sense that no transaction instance conforming to that modified template can possibly violate any declared integrity constraints. The method works by adding queries and tests to the original template to ensure *before* any updating is done that no constraints will be violated. At run time, if any of those tests fails, the transaction is rejected and an error message is generated.

8.22 Jennifer Widom and Stefano Ceri (eds.): *Active Database Systems: Triggers and Rules for Advanced Database Processing.* San Francisco, Calif.: Morgan Kaufmann (1996).

A useful compendium of research and tutorial papers on "active database systems" (i.e., database systems that automatically carry out specified actions in response to specified events—in other words, database systems with triggered procedures). Descriptions are included of several prototype systems, including in particular Starburst from IBM Research (see references [17.50], [25.14], [25.17], and [25.21–25.22]) and Postgres from the University of California at Berkeley (see references [25.26], [25.30], and [25.32]). The book also summarizes the relevant aspects of SQL/92, (an early version of) SQL3, and certain commercial products (Oracle, Informix, and Ingres among them). An extensive bibliography is also included.

ANSWERS TO SELECTED EXERCISES

8.1

a.
```
TYPE CITY POSSREP ( CHAR )
CONSTRAINT THE_CITY ( CITY ) = 'London'
      OR THE_CITY ( CITY ) = 'Paris'
      OR THE_CITY ( CITY ) = 'Rome'
      OR THE_CITY ( CITY ) = 'Athens'
      OR THE_CITY ( CITY ) = 'Oslo'
      OR THE_CITY ( CITY ) = 'Stockholm'
      OR THE_CITY ( CITY ) = 'Madrid'
      OR THE_CITY ( CITY ) = 'Amsterdam' ;
```

An obvious shorthand would be:

a.
```
TYPE CITY POSSREP ( CHAR )
CONSTRAINT THE_CITY ( CITY ) IN { 'London' , 'Paris'     ,
                                  'Rome'   , 'Athens'    ,
                                  'Oslo'   , 'Stockholm' ,
                                  'Madrid' , 'Amsterdam' } ;
```

b.
```
TYPE S# POSSREP ( CHAR ) CONSTRAINT
      SUBSTR ( THE_S# ( S# ), 1, 1 ) = 'S' AND
      CAST_AS_INTEGER ( SUBSTR ( THE_S# ( S# ), 2 ) ≥ 0 AND
      CAST_AS_INTEGER ( SUBSTR ( THE_S# ( S# ), 2 ) ≤ 9999 ;
```

We assume here that the substring operator SUBSTR and the explicit conversion operator CAST_AS_INTEGER are both available.

c.
```
CONSTRAINT C IS_EMPTY ( P WHERE WEIGHT ≥ WEIGHT ( 50.0 ) ) ;
```

d.
```
CONSTRAINT D COUNT ( J ) = COUNT ( J { CITY } ) ;
```

e.
```
CONSTRAINT E COUNT ( S WHERE CITY = 'Athens' ) ≤ 1 ;
```

f.
```
CONSTRAINT F
      IS_EMPTY ( ( EXTEND SPJ ADD 2 * AVG ( SPJ, QTY )
                              AS X ) WHERE QTY > X ) ;
```

g.
```
CONSTRAINT G
      IS_EMPTY ( ( S WHERE STATUS = MIN ( S { STATUS } ) ) JOIN
                 ( S WHERE STATUS = MAX ( S { STATUS } ) ) ) ;
```

Actually, the terms "highest status supplier" and "lowest status supplier" are not well defined, since status values are not unique. We have interpreted the requirement to be that if *Sx* and *Sy* are *any* suppliers with "highest status" and "lowest status," respectively, then *Sx* and *Sy* must not be colocated. Note that the constraint will necessarily be violated if the "highest" and "lowest" status are equal!—in particular, it will be violated if there is just one supplier.

h.
```
CONSTRAINT H IS_EMPTY ( J { CITY } MINUS S { CITY } ) ;
```

i.
```
CONSTRAINT I IS_EMPTY ( J WHERE NOT ( TUPLE { CITY CITY } IN
                        ( J { J# } JOIN SPJ JOIN S ) { CITY } ) ) ;
```

j.
```
CONSTRAINT J NOT ( IS_EMPTY
                     ( P WHERE COLOR = COLOR ( 'Red' ) ) ) ;
```

This constraint will be violated if there are no parts at all. A better formulation would be:

```
CONSTRAINT J IS_EMPTY ( P ) OR NOT ( IS_EMPTY
                  ( P WHERE COLOR = COLOR ( 'Red' ) ) ) ;
```

k.
```
CONSTRAINT K IF NOT ( IS_EMPTY ( S ) )
            THEN AVG ( S, STATUS ) > 18
            END IF ;
```

The IF test here is to avoid the error that would otherwise occur if the system tried to check the constraint when there were no suppliers at all.

l.
```
CONSTRAINT L IS_EMPTY
          ( ( S WHERE CITY = 'London' ) { S# } MINUS
            ( SPJ WHERE P# = P# ( 'P2' ) ) { S# } ) ;
```

m.
```
CONSTRAINT M IS_EMPTY ( P ) OR NOT
          ( IS_EMPTY ( P WHERE WEIGHT < WEIGHT ( 50.0 ) ) ) ;
```

n.
```
CONSTRAINT N
COUNT ( ( ( S WHERE CITY = 'London') JOIN SPJ ) { P# } ) >
COUNT ( ( ( S WHERE CITY = 'Paris' ) JOIN SPJ ) { P# } ) ;
```

o.
```
CONSTRAINT O
    SUM ( ( ( S WHERE CITY = 'London') JOIN SPJ ), QTY ) >
    SUM ( ( ( S WHERE CITY = 'Paris' ) JOIN SPJ ), QTY ) ;
```

p.
```
CONSTRAINT P IS_EMPTY
          ( ( SPJ JOIN ( SPJ' RENAME QTY AS QTY' ) )
            WHERE QTY > 0.5 * QTY' ) ;
```

q.
```
CONSTRAINT Q IS_EMPTY (
  ( S JOIN ( S' WHERE CITY = 'Athens' ) ) WHERE
    CITY ≠ 'Athens' AND CITY ≠ 'London' AND CITY ='Paris' )
        AND IS_EMPTY (
  ( S JOIN ( S' WHERE CITY = 'London' ) ) WHERE
    CITY ≠ 'London' AND CITY ='Paris' ) ;
```

As a subsidiary exercise, you could try formulating the foregoing constraints in a calculus style instead of an algebraic style.

8.2 The first two are type constraints, of course. Of the others, constraints C, D, E, F, G, J, K, M, P, and Q are relvar constraints, the rest are database constraints.

8.3

a. CITY selector invocation.

b. S# selector invocation.

c. INSERT on P, UPDATE on part WEIGHT.

d. INSERT on J, UPDATE on project CITY.

e. INSERT on S, UPDATE on supplier CITY.

f. INSERT or DELETE on SPJ, UPDATE on shipment QTY.

g. INSERT or DELETE on S, UPDATE on supplier STATUS.

h. INSERT on J, DELETE on S, UPDATE on supplier or project CITY.

i. INSERT on J, DELETE on or SPJ, UPDATE on supplier or project

j. INSERT or DELETE on P, UPDATE on part CITY.

k. INSERT or DELETE on S, UPDATE on supplier STATUS.

l. INSERT on S, DELETE on SPJ, UPDATE on supplier CITY or shipment S# or P#.

m. INSERT or DELETE on P, UPDATE on part WEIGHT.

n. INSERT or DELETE on S or SPJ, UPDATE on supplier CITY or shipment S# or P#.

o. INSERT or DELETE on S or SPJ, UPDATE on supplier CITY or shipment S# or P# or QTY.

p. UPDATE on shipment QTY.

q. UPDATE on supplier CITY.

8.4 One. The specifications "(5)" and "(3)" are best seen as *integrity constraints*. As noted in reference [3.3], one desirable consequence of this approach is that if variables X and Y are defined as, say, CHAR(5) and CHAR(3), respectively, then comparisons between X and Y are legal—i.e., they do not violate the requirement that the comparands must be of the same type.

8.5 We offer the following as a "first cut" set of answers (but see the note at the end).

a. Any restriction of *A* inherits all of the candidate keys of *A*.

b. If the projection includes any candidate key *K* of *A,* then *K* is a candidate key for the projection. Otherwise the only candidate key is the combination of all attributes of the projection (in general).

c. Every combination *K* of a candidate key *KA* of *A* and a candidate key *KB* of *B* is a candidate key for the product *A* TIMES *B*.

d. The only candidate key for the union *A* UNION *B* is the combination of all attributes (in general).

e. Left as an exercise (intersection is not a primitive).

f. Every candidate key of *A* is a candidate key for the difference *A* MINUS *B*.

g. We leave the general case as an exercise (natural join is not a primitive). However, we remark that in the special case where the joining attribute in A is a candidate key of *A,* every candidate key of *B* is a candidate key for the join.

h. The candidate keys for an arbitrary extension of *A* are the same as the candidate keys of *A*.

i. The candidate keys for an arbitrary summarization of *A* "per *B*" are the candidate keys of *B*.

j. Every candidate key of *A* is a candidate key for the semijoin *A* SEMIJOIN *B*.

k. Every candidate key of *A* is a candidate key for the semidifference *A* SEMIMINUS *B*.

However, many of the foregoing statements can be refined somewhat in certain situations. For example:

- The combination {S#,P#,J#} is not a candidate key for the restriction SPJ WHERE S# = S#('S1')—rather, the combination {P#,J#} is;
- If *A* has heading {X,Y,Z} and sole candidate key *X* and satisfies the functional dependency $Y \to Z$ (see Chapter 10), then *Y* is a candidate key for the projection of *A* over *Y* and *Z;*
- If *A* and *B* are both restrictions of *C,* then every candidate key of *C* is a candidate key of *A* UNION *B;*

and so on. This whole question of *candidate key inference* is discussed in some detail in reference [10.6].

8.6 Let m be the largest integer greater than or equal to $n/2$. R will have the maximum possible number of candidate keys if either (a) every distinct set of m attributes is a candidate key or (b) n is odd and every distinct set of m-1 attributes is a candidate key. Either way, it follows that the maximum number of candidate keys in R is $n! / (m! * (n-m)!)$. *Note:* Relvars ELEMENT and MARRIAGE in Section 8.8 are both examples of relvars with the maximum possible number of candidate keys.

8.7 R has exactly one candidate key, namely the empty set of attributes { } (sometimes written ϕ). *Note:* The concept of an empty (or *nullary*) candidate key is worth some slight elaboration. A relvar such as R whose sole legal values are DEE and DUM must necessarily have no attributes, and thus it is "obvious" that its sole candidate key has no attributes either. But it is not just relvars with no attributes that can have such a candidate key. However, if ϕ is a candidate key for some relvar R, then:

- It must be the *only* candidate key for R, because any other set of attributes of R would be a proper superset of ϕ, thus violating the irreducibility requirement for candidate keys. (It is therefore in fact the *primary* key, if a primary key must be chosen.)

- R is constrained to contain at most one tuple, because every tuple has the same value (namely, the 0-tuple) for the empty set of attributes.

Note that our syntax certainly does permit the declaration of such a relvar—for example:

```
VAR R BASE RELATION { ... }
    PRIMARY KEY { } ;
```

It also permits the declaration of a relvar with no attributes at all—i.e., a relvar whose only possible values are DEE and DUM:

```
VAR R BASE RELATION { }
    PRIMARY KEY { } ;
```

To revert to the question of empty candidate keys: Of course, if a candidate key can be empty, then so can a matching foreign key. Reference [5.5] discusses this possibility in some detail.

8.8 There is no explicit foreign key "INSERT rule," because INSERTs on the referencing relvar (also UPDATEs on the foreign key in the referencing relvar) are governed by the basic referential integrity rule itself, i.e., the requirement that there be no unmatched foreign key values. In other words, taking suppliers and parts as a concrete example:

- An attempt to INSERT a shipment (SP) tuple will succeed only if (a) the supplier number in that tuple exists as a supplier number in S, *and* (b) the part number in that tuple exists as a part number in P.

- An attempt to UPDATE a shipment (SP) tuple will succeed only if (a) the supplier number in the updated tuple exists as a supplier number in S, *and* (b) the part number in the updated tuple exists as a part number in P.

Note carefully also that the foregoing remarks apply to the *referencing* relvar, whereas the (explicit) DELETE and UPDATE rules apply to the *referenced* relvar. Thus, to talk about an "INSERT rule," as if that rule were somehow similar to the existing DELETE and UPDATE rules, is really a rather confusing thing to do. This fact provides additional justification for not including any explicit "INSERT rule" support in the concrete syntax.

8.9

a. Accepted.

b. Rejected (candidate key uniqueness violation).

    c. Rejected (violates RESTRICT specification).

    d. Accepted (supplier S3 and all shipments for supplier S3 are deleted).

    e. Rejected (violates RESTRICT specification).

    f. Accepted (project J4 and all shipments for project J4 are deleted).

    g. Accepted.

    h. Rejected (candidate key uniqueness violation).

    i. Rejected (referential integrity violation).

    j. Accepted.

    k. Rejected (referential integrity violation).

    l. Rejected (referential integrity violation—the default project number *jjj* does not exist in relvar J).

8.10 The referential diagram is shown in Fig. 8.1. A possible database definition follows. For simplicity, we have not bothered to define any type constraints—except inasmuch as the POSSREP specification on a given type definition serves as an *a priori* constraint on the type, of course.

```
TYPE COURSE# POSSREP ( CHAR ) ;
TYPE TITLE   POSSREP ( CHAR ) ;
TYPE OFF#    POSSREP ( CHAR ) ;
TYPE OFFDATE POSSREP ( DATE ) ;
TYPE CITY    POSSREP ( CHAR ) ;
TYPE EMP#    POSSREP ( CHAR ) ;
TYPE NAME    POSSREP ( NAME ) ;
TYPE JOB     POSSREP ( CHAR ) ;
TYPE GRADE   POSSREP ( CHAR ) ;

VAR COURSE BASE RELATION
    { COURSE# COURSE#,
      TITLE   TITLE }
    PRIMARY KEY { COURSE# } ;

VAR PREREQ BASE RELATION
    { SUP_COURSE# COURSE#,
      SUB_COURSE# COURSE# }
    PRIMARY KEY { SUP_COURSE#, SUB_COURSE# }
    FOREIGN KEY { RENAME SUP_COURSE# AS COURSE# }
                                    REFERENCES COURSE
                                    ON DELETE CASCADE
                                    ON UPDATE CASCADE
    FOREIGN KEY { RENAME SUB_COURSE# AS COURSE# }
                                    REFERENCES COURSE
                                    ON DELETE CASCADE
                                    ON UPDATE CASCADE ;

VAR OFFERING BASE RELATION
    { COURSE#  COURSE#,
      OFF#     OFF#,
      OFFDATE  OFFDATE,
      LOCATION CITY }
    PRIMARY KEY { COURSE#, OFF# }
    FOREIGN KEY { COURSE# } REFERENCES COURSE
                            ON DELETE CASCADE
                            ON UPDATE CASCADE ;

VAR EMPLOYEE BASE RELATION
    { EMP#  EMP#,
      ENAME NAME,
      JOB   JOB }
    PRIMARY KEY { EMP# } ;
```

```
VAR TEACHER BASE RELATION
     { COURSE#  COURSE#,
       OFF#     OFF#,
       EMP#     EMP# }
     PRIMARY KEY { COURSE#, OFF#, EMP# }
     FOREIGN KEY { COURSE#, OFF# } REFERENCES OFFERING
                                   ON DELETE CASCADE
                                   ON UPDATE CASCADE
     FOREIGN KEY { EMP# } REFERENCES EMPLOYEE
                         ON DELETE CASCADE
                         ON UPDATE CASCADE ;

VAR ENROLLMENT BASE RELATION ENROLLMENT
     { COURSE#  COURSE#,
       OFF#     OFF#,
       EMP#     EMP#,
       GRADE    GRADE }
     PRIMARY KEY { COURSE#, OFF#, EMP# }
     FOREIGN KEY { COURSE#, OFF# } REFERENCES OFFERING
                                   ON DELETE CASCADE
                                   ON UPDATE CASCADE
     FOREIGN KEY { EMP# } REFERENCES EMPLOYEE
                         ON DELETE CASCADE
                         ON UPDATE CASCADE ;
```

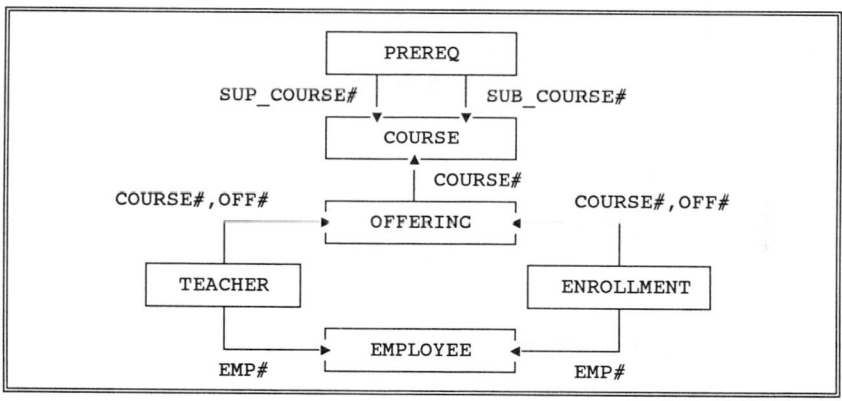

Fig. 8.1   Referential diagram for the education database

Points arising:

1. The (singleton) attribute sets {COURSE#} in TEACHER and {COURSE#} in ENROLLMENT could also be regarded as foreign keys, both of them referring to COURSE. However, if the referential constraints from TEACHER to OFFERING, ENROLLMENT to OFFERING, and OFFERING to COURSE are all properly maintained, the referential constraints from TEACHER to COURSE and ENROLLMENT to COURSE will be maintained automatically. See reference [8.10] for further discussion.

2. OFFERING is an example of a relvar that is simultaneously both referenced and referencing: There is a referential constraint to OFFERING from ENROLLMENT (also from TEACHER, as a matter of fact), and a referential constraint from OFFERING to COURSE:

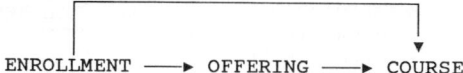

3. Note that there are two distinct referential paths from ENROLLMENT to COURSE—one direct (foreign key {COURSE#} in ENROLLMENT), and the other indirect via OFFERING (foreign keys {COURSE#,OFF#} in ENROLLMENT and {COURSE#} in OFFERING):

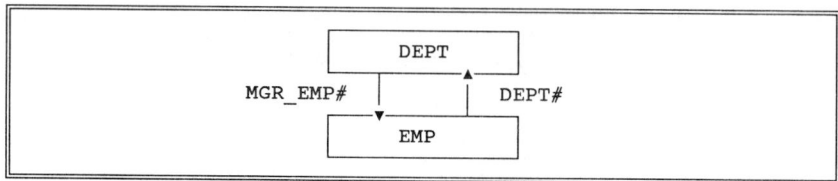

However, the two paths are not truly independent of one another (the upper path is implied by the combination of the lower two). For further discussion of this point, see reference [8.10] once again.

4. There are also two distinct referential paths from PREREQ to COURSE, but this time the two paths *are* truly independent (they have totally separate meanings). See reference [8.10] yet again.

8.11 The referential diagram is shown in Fig. 8.2. Note that the database involves a referential cycle (there is a referential path from each of the two relvars to itself). Apart from this consideration, the database definition is essentially straightforward. We omit the details.

```
            DEPT
          ┌──────┐
MGR_EMP#  │      │  DEPT#
          └──────┘
            EMP
```

Fig. 8.2 Referential diagram involving a cycle

8.12 We show just the relvar definitions (and those only in outline):

```
VAR EMP BASE RELATION
      { EMP# ... ,
        ...... ,
        JOB  ... }
      PRIMARY KEY { EMP# } ;

VAR PGMR BASE RELATION
      { EMP# ... ,
        ...... ,
        LANG ... }
      PRIMARY KEY { EMP# }
      FOREIGN KEY { EMP# } REFERENCES EMP
            ON DELETE CASCADE
            ON UPDATE CASCADE ;
```

Points arising:

1. This example illustrates the point that a foreign key can also be a candidate key of its containing relvar. Relvar EMP contains all employees, and relvar PGMR contains just those employees

that are programmers; thus, every employee number appearing in PGMR must also appear in EMP (but the converse is not true). The primary key of PGMR is also a foreign key, referring to the primary key of EMP.

2. Note that there is another constraint that needs to be maintained in this example—namely, the constraint that a given employee will appear in PGMR if and only if the value of JOB for that employee is "Programmer." This constraint is not a *referential* constraint, of course.

8.14 Note that solutions a. and b. below are only approximations to their counterparts shown in the answer to Exercise 8.1.

a.
```
CREATE DOMAIN CITY CHAR(15) VARYING
    CONSTRAINT VALID_CITIES
        CHECK ( VALUE IN ( 'London', 'Paris', 'Rome',
                           'Athens', 'Oslo', 'Stockholm',
                           'Madrid', 'Amsterdam' ) ) ;
```

b.
```
CREATE DOMAIN S# CHAR(5) VARYING
    CONSTRAINT VALID_S# CHECK
        ( SUBSTRING ( VALUE FROM 1 FOR 1 ) = 'S' AND
    CAST ( SUBSTRING ( VALUE FROM 2 ) AS INTEGER ) >= 0 AND
    CAST ( SUBSTRING ( VALUE FROM 2 ) AS INTEGER ) <= 9999 ) ;
```

c.
```
CREATE ASSERTION SQL_C CHECK
        ( P.COLOR <> 'Red' OR P.WEIGHT < 50.0 ) ;
```

d.
```
CREATE ASSERTION SQL_D CHECK
        ( NOT EXISTS ( SELECT * FROM J JX WHERE
            EXISTS ( SELECT * FROM J JY WHERE
                ( JX.J# <> JY.J# AND
                  JX.CITY = JY.CITY ) ) ) ) ;
```

e.
```
CREATE ASSERTION SQL_E CHECK
        ( ( SELECT COUNT(*) FROM S
            WHERE  S.CITY = 'Athens' ) < 2 ) ;
```

f.
```
CREATE ASSERTION SQL_F CHECK
        ( NOT EXISTS ( SELECT *
                       FROM   SPJ SPJX
                       WHERE  SPJX.QTY > 2 *
                           ( SELECT AVG ( SPJY.QTY )
                             FROM   SPJ SPJY ) ) ) ;
```

g.
```
CREATE ASSERTION SQL_G CHECK
        ( NOT EXISTS ( SELECT * FROM S SX WHERE
            EXISTS ( SELECT * FROM S SY WHERE
                SX.STATUS = ( SELECT MAX ( S.STATUS )
                              FROM    S ) AND
                SY.STATUS = ( SELECT MIN ( S.STATUS )
                              FROM    S ) AND
                SX.STATUS <> SY.STATUS AND
                SX.CITY = SY.CITY ) ) ) ;
```

h.
```
CREATE ASSERTION SQL_H CHECK
        ( NOT EXISTS ( SELECT * FROM J WHERE
            NOT EXISTS ( SELECT * FROM S WHERE
                S.CITY = J.CITY ) ) ) ;
```

```
i.  CREATE ASSERTION SQL_I CHECK
            ( NOT EXISTS ( SELECT * FROM J WHERE
              NOT EXISTS ( SELECT * FROM S WHERE
                           S.CITY = J.CITY AND
                           EXISTS ( SELECT * FROM SPJ
                                    WHERE  SPJ.S# = S.S#
                                    AND    SPJ.J# = J.J# ) ) ) )

j.  CREATE ASSERTION SQL_J CHECK
            ( NOT EXISTS ( SELECT * FROM P )
              OR EXISTS ( SELECT * FROM P
                          WHERE  P.COLOR = 'Red' ) ) ;

k.  CREATE ASSERTION SQL_K CHECK
            ( ( SELECT AVG ( S.STATUS ) FROM S ) > 10 ) ;
```

If the suppliers table is empty, the SQL AVG operator will (incorrectly!) return a null, the conditional expression will evaluate to *unknown,* and the constraint will *not* be regarded as violated. See Chapter 18 for further explanation.

```
l.  CREATE ASSERTION SQL_L CHECK
            ( NOT EXISTS ( SELECT * FROM S
                           WHERE   S.CITY = 'London'
                           AND     NOT EXISTS
                                   ( SELECT * FROM SPJ
                                     WHERE  SPJ.S# = S.S#
                                     AND    SPJ.P# = 'P2' ) ) ) ;

m.  CREATE ASSERTION SQL_M CHECK
            ( NOT EXISTS ( SELECT * FROM P
                           WHERE  P.COLOR = 'Red' )
              OR EXISTS ( SELECT * FROM P
                          WHERE  P.COLOR = 'Red'
                          AND    P.WEIGHT < 50.0 ) ) ;

n.  CREATE ASSERTION SQL_N CHECK
            ( ( SELECT COUNT(*) FROM P
                WHERE   EXISTS ( SELECT * FROM SPJ WHERE
                        EXISTS ( SELECT * FROM S WHERE
                                 ( P.P# = SPJ.P# AND
                                 SPJ.S# = S.S# AND
                                 S.CITY = 'London' ) ) ) ) >
              ( SELECT COUNT(*) FROM P
                WHERE   EXISTS ( SELECT * FROM SPJ WHERE
                        EXISTS ( SELECT * FROM S WHERE
                                 ( P.P# = SPJ.P# AND
                                 SPJ.S# = S.S# AND
                                 S.CITY = 'Paris' ) ) ) ) ) ;

o.  CREATE ASSERTION SQL_O CHECK
            ( ( SELECT SUM ( SPJ.QTY ) FROM SPJ
                WHERE   ( SELECT S.CITY FROM S
                          WHERE  S.S# = SPJ.S# ) = 'London' ) >
              ( SELECT SUM ( SPJ.QTY ) FROM SPJ
                WHERE   ( SELECT S.CITY FROM S
                          WHERE  S.S# = SPJ.S# ) = 'Paris' ) ) ;
```

p. Cannot be done.

q. Cannot be done.

Views

9.1 INTRODUCTION

As explained in Chapter 3, a **view** is essentially just a named expression of the relational algebra (or something equivalent to the relational algebra). For example:

```
VAR GOOD_SUPPLIER VIEW
   ( S WHERE STATUS > 15 ) { S#, STATUS, CITY } ;
```

When this statement is executed, the relational algebra expression (i.e., the **view-defining expression**) is not evaluated but is merely "remembered" by the system—actually by saving it in the catalog, under the specified name GOOD_SUPPLIER. To the user, however, it is now as if there really were a relvar in the database called GOOD_SUPPLIER, with tuples and attributes as shown in the unshaded portions of Fig. 9.1 (we assume our usual sample data values, of course). In other words, the name GOOD_SUPPLIER denotes a **derived** (and **virtual**) relvar, whose value at any time is the relation that would result if the view-defining expression were in fact evaluated at that time.

We also explained in Chapter 3 that a view such as GOOD_SUPPLIER is effectively just a *window* into the underlying data: Any updates to that underlying data will be automatically and instantaneously visible through that window (so long as they lie within the scope of the view, of course); likewise, any updates to the view will automatically and instantaneously be applied to the underlying data, and hence be visible through the window.

Now, depending on circumstances, the user might or might not realize that GOOD_SUPPLIER really is a view; some users might be aware of that fact and might

GOOD_SUPPLIER	S#	SNAME	STATUS	CITY
	S1	Smith	20	London
	S2	Jones	10	Paris
	S3	Blake	30	Paris
	S4	Clark	20	London
	S5	Adams	30	Athens

Fig. 9.1 GOOD_SUPPLIER as a view of base relvar S (unshaded portions)

understand that there is a "real" relvar S underneath, others might genuinely believe that GOOD_SUPPLIER is a "real" relvar in its own right. Either way, it makes little difference: The point is, users can operate on GOOD_SUPPLIER just as if it *were* a real relvar. For instance, here is an example of a query against GOOD_SUPPLIER:

```
GOOD_SUPPLIER WHERE CITY ≠ 'London'
```

Given the sample data of Fig. 9.1, the result is:

S#	STATUS	CITY
S3	30	Paris
S5	30	Athens

This query certainly looks just like a regular query on a regular "real" relvar. And, as we saw in Chapter 3, the system handles such a query by converting it into an equivalent query on the underlying base relvar (or base relvars, plural). It does this by effectively replacing each appearance in the query of the *name* of the view by the expression that *defines* the view. In the example, this **substitution procedure** gives

```
( ( S WHERE STATUS > 15 ) { S#, STATUS, CITY } )
                         WHERE CITY ≠ 'London'
```

which is readily seen to be equivalent to the simpler form

```
( S WHERE STATUS > 15 AND CITY ≠ 'London' )
                         { S#, STATUS, CITY }
```

And this query produces the result shown earlier.

Incidentally, it is worth pointing out that the substitution process just outlined—i.e., the process of substituting the view-defining expression for the view name—*works precisely because of the relational closure property.* Closure implies, among many other things, that wherever a simple relvar name *R* can appear within an expression, a relational expression of arbitrary complexity can appear instead (just so long as it evaluates to a relation of the same type as *R*). In other words, views work precisely because of the fact that relations are closed under the relational algebra—yet another illustration of the fundamental importance of the closure property.

Update operations are treated in a similar manner. For example, the operation

```
UPDATE GOOD_SUPPLIER WHERE CITY = 'Paris'
       STATUS := STATUS + 10 ;
```

is effectively converted into

```
UPDATE S WHERE STATUS > 15 AND CITY = 'Paris'
       STATUS := STATUS + 10 ;
```

INSERT and DELETE operations are handled analogously.

Further Examples

In this subsection we present a number of further examples, for purposes of subsequent reference.

1. ```
   VAR REDPART VIEW
         ( ( P WHERE COLOR = COLOR ( 'Red' ) ) { ALL BUT COLOR } )
                                          RENAME WEIGHT AS WT ;
   ```

   View REDPART has attributes P#, PNAME, WT, and CITY, and contains tuples for red parts only.

2. ```
   VAR PQ VIEW
         SUMMARIZE SP PER P { P# } ADD SUM ( QTY ) AS TOTQTY ;
   ```

   Unlike GOOD_SUPPLIER and REDPART, view PQ is not just a simple subset—i.e., a restriction and/or projection—of some underlying base relvar. It can be regarded instead as a kind of *statistical summary* or *compression* of that underlying relvar.

3. ```
   VAR CITY_PAIR VIEW
         ( ( S RENAME CITY AS SCITY ) JOIN SP JOIN
           ( P RENAME CITY AS PCITY ) ) { SCITY, PCITY } ;
   ```

   Loosely speaking, a pair of city names (x,y) appears in view CITY_PAIR if and only if a supplier located in city x supplies a part stored in city y. For example, supplier S1 supplies part P1; supplier S1 is located in London and part P1 is stored in London; and so the pair (London,London) appears in the view.

4. ```
   VAR HEAVY_REDPART VIEW
         REDPART WHERE WT > WEIGHT ( 12.0 ) ;
   ```

   This example shows one view defined in terms of another.

Defining and Dropping Views

Here then is the syntax for defining a view:

```
VAR <relvar name> VIEW <relational expression>
                  <candidate key definition list> ;
```

The *<candidate key definition list>* is allowed to be empty, because the system should be able to *infer* candidate keys for views [10.6]. In the case of GOOD_SUPPLIER, for example, the system should be aware that the sole candidate key is {S#}, inherited from the underlying base relvar S.

We remark that—to use the ANSI/SPARC terminology of Chapter 2—view definitions combine (a) the *external schema* function and (b) the *external/conceptual mapping* function, because they specify both (a) what the external object (i.e., the view) looks like and (b) how that object maps to the conceptual level (i.e., to the underlying base relvar(s)). *Note:* Some view definitions specify, not the external/conceptual mapping as such, but rather an *external/external* mapping. View HEAVY_REDPART from the previous subsection is a case in point.

The syntax for dropping a view is

```
DROP VAR <relvar name> ;
```

where, of course, the *<relvar name>* refers to a view specifically. Now, in Chapter 5 we assumed that an attempt to drop a base relvar would fail if any view definition currently referred to that base relvar. Analogously, we assume that an attempt to drop a view will also fail if some other view definition currently refers to that view. Alternatively (and by analogy with referential constraints), we might consider extending the view definition statement to include some kind of "RESTRICT *vs.* CASCADE" option; RESTRICT (the default) would mean that an attempt to drop any relvar referenced in the view definition should fail, CASCADE would mean that such an attempt should succeed and should "cascade" to drop the referencing view as well. *Note:* SQL does support such an option, but puts it on the DROP statement instead of on the view definition. There is no default—the required option must be stated explicitly (see Section 9.6).

9.2   WHAT ARE VIEWS FOR?

There are many reasons why view support is desirable. Here are some of them:

■ *Views provide automatic security for hidden data*

"Hidden data" refers to data not visible through some given view (e.g., supplier names, in the case of view GOOD_SUPPLIER). Such data is clearly secure from access (retrieval access, at least) through that particular view. Thus, forcing users to access the database through views constitutes a simple but effective **security** mechanism. We will have more to say on this particular use of views in Chapter 16.

■ *Views provide a shorthand or "macro" capability*

Consider the query "Get cities that store parts that are available from some supplier in London." Given view CITY_PAIR from the subsection "Further Examples" in the previous section, the following formulation suffices:

```
( CITY_PAIR WHERE SCITY = 'London' ) { PCITY }
```

Without the view, by contrast, the query is much more complex:

```
( ( ( S RENAME CITY AS SCITY )
      JOIN SP
      JOIN ( P RENAME CITY AS PCITY ) )
            WHERE SCITY = 'London' ) { PCITY }
```

While the user *could* use this second formulation directly—security constraints permitting, of course—the first is obviously simpler. (Of course, the first is really just shorthand for the second; the system's view processing mechanism will effectively expand the first formulation into the second before it is executed.)

There is a strong analogy here with **macros** in a programming language system. In principle, a user in a programming language system *could* write out the expanded form of a given macro directly in his or her source code—but it is much more convenient (for a variety of well-understood reasons) not to do so, but rather to use the macro shorthand and let the system's macro processor do the expansion in the user's behalf. Analogous remarks apply to views. Thus, views in a database system play a role somewhat analogous to that of macros in a programming language system, and the well-known advantages and benefits of macros apply directly to views as well, *mutatis mutandis.* Note in particular that (as with macros) no run-time performance overhead attaches to the use of views—there is only a small overhead at view-processing time (analogous to macro-expansion time).

■ *Views allow the same data to be seen by different users in different ways at the same time*

Views effectively allow users to focus on—and perhaps logically restructure—just that portion of the database that is of concern to them and to ignore the rest. This consideration is obviously important when there are many different users, with many different requirements, all interacting simultaneously with a single integrated database.

■ *Views can provide logical data independence*

This is one of the most important points of all. See the subsection immediately following.

Logical Data Independence

We remind you that logical data independence can be defined as *the immunity of users and user programs to changes in the logical structure of the database* (where by *logical structure* we mean the conceptual or "community logical" level—see Chapter 2). And, of course, views are the means by which logical data independence is achieved in a relational system. There are two aspects to such logical data independence, namely **growth** and **restructuring.** *Note:* We discuss *growth* here mainly for completeness; it is important, but it has little to do with views as such.

■ *Growth*

As the database grows to incorporate new kinds of information, the definition of the database must obviously grow accordingly. There are two possible kinds of growth that can occur:

1. The expansion of an existing base relvar to include a new attribute, corresponding to the addition of new information concerning some existing type of object—for example, the addition of a DISCOUNT attribute to the suppliers base relvar.

2. The inclusion of a new base relvar, corresponding to the addition of a new type of object—for example, the addition of project information to the suppliers and parts database.

Neither of these changes should have any effect on existing users or user programs at all, at least in principle (but see Example 7.7.1 in Chapter 7 for a warning regarding SQL specifically).

■ *Restructuring*

Occasionally it might become necessary to restructure the database in some way such that, although the overall information content remains the same, the *logical placement* of information changes—i.e., the allocation of attributes to base relvars is altered in some way. We consider just one simple example here. Suppose that for some reason (the precise reason is not important for present purposes) we wish to replace base relvar S by the following two base relvars:

```
VAR SNC BASE RELATION { S# S#, SNAME NAME, CITY CHAR }
   PRIMARY KEY { S# } ;

VAR ST BASE RELATION { S# S#, STATUS INTEGER }
   PRIMARY KEY { S# } ;
```

The crucial point to note here is that *the old relvar S is the join of the two new relvars SNC and ST* (and SNC and ST are both *projections* of that old relvar S). So we create a view that is exactly that join, and we name it S:

```
VAR S VIEW
   SNC JOIN ST ;
```

Any application program or interactive operation that previously referred to base relvar S will now refer to view S instead. Hence—*provided the system supports data manipulation operations on views correctly*—users and user programs will indeed be logically immune to this particular restructuring of the database.*

As an aside, we remark that the replacement of the original suppliers relvar S by its two projections SNC and ST is not a totally trivial matter. In particular, observe that something must be done about the shipments relvar SP, since that relvar has a foreign key that references the original suppliers relvar. See Exercise 9.13 at the end of the chapter.

To revert to the main thread of the discussion: Of course, it does not follow from the SNC-ST example that logical data independence can be achieved in the face of *all possible* restructurings. The critical issue is whether there exists an unambiguous mapping from the restructured version of the database back to the previous version (i.e., whether the restructuring is reversible), or in other words whether the two versions are **information-equivalent.** If not, logical data independence is clearly not achievable.

---

*In principle! Sadly, today's SQL products (and the SQL standard) do *not* support data manipulation operations on views correctly, for the most part, and hence do not provide the desired degree of immunity to changes like the one in the example. To be more specific, some products (not all) do support view retrievals correctly, but no product—to this writer's knowledge—supports view updates 100 percent correctly. Thus, some products do provide full logical data independence for retrieval operations, but none currently does so for update operations.

Two Important Principles

The foregoing discussion of logical data independence raises another point. The fact is, views really serve two rather different purposes:

- A user who actually *defines* a view *V* is, obviously, aware of the corresponding view-defining expression *X;* that user can use the name *V* wherever the expression *X* is intended, but (as we have already seen) such uses are basically just shorthand.

- A user who is merely informed that view *V* exists and is available for use, on the other hand, is typically *not* aware of the view-defining expression *X;* to that user, in fact, view *V* should look and behave exactly like a base relvar.

Following on from the foregoing, we now stress the point that the question as to which relvars are base and which derived (i.e., views) is to a large extent arbitrary! Take the case of relvars S, SNC, and ST from the "restructuring" discussion in the previous subsection. It should be clear that we could *either* (a) define S to be a base relvar and SNC and ST to be projection views of that base relvar, *or* (b) define SNC and ST to be base relvars and S to be a join view of those two base relvars.* *It follows that there must be no arbitrary and unnecessary distinctions between base and derived relvars.* We refer to this fact as ***The Principle of Interchangeability*** (of base and derived relvars). Note in particular that this principle implies that we *must* be able to update views—the updatability of the database must not depend on the essentially arbitrary decision as to which relvars we decide should be base ones and which we decide should be views. See Section 9.4 for further discussion.

Let us agree for the moment to refer to the set of all base relvars as the "real" database. But a typical user interacts (in general) not with that real database *per se* but with what might be called an "expressible" database, consisting (again in general) of some mixture of base relvars and views. Now, we can assume that none of the relvars in that expressible database can be derived from the rest (because such a relvar could be dropped without loss of information).† Hence, *from the user's point of view,* those relvars are all base relvars, by definition!—certainly they are all independent of one another (i.e., all autonomous, to use the terminology of Chapter 3). And likewise for the database itself—i.e., the choice of which database is the "real" one is arbitrary, just so long as the choices are all information-equivalent. We refer to this fact as ***The Principle of Database Relativity.***

9.3 VIEW RETRIEVALS

We have already explained in outline how a retrieval operation on a view is converted into an equivalent operation on the underlying base relvar(s). We now make our explanation slightly more formal, as follows.

---

*See the discussion of *nonloss decomposition* in Chapter 11, Section 11.2.
† We ignore here any views that are defined by the user in question, which as we have already seen are really just shorthands.

First, note that any given relational expression can be regarded as a relation-valued **function:** Given values for the various relvars mentioned in the expression (representing the arguments to this particular invocation of the function), the expression yields another relation. Now let D be a database (which for present purposes we regard as just a set of base relvars) and let V be a view on D, i.e., a view whose defining expression X is some function on D:

```
V  =  X ( D )
```

Let R be a retrieval operation on V; R is of course another relation-valued function, and the result of the retrieval is

```
R ( V )  =  R ( X ( D ) )
```

Thus, the result of the retrieval is defined to be equal to the result of applying X to D— i.e., **materializing** a copy of the relation that is the current value of view V—and then applying R to that materialized copy. Now, it is almost certainly more efficient in practice to use the **substitution** procedure instead, as discussed in Section 9.1 (and we can now see that that procedure is equivalent to forming the function C that is the *composition* $R(X)$ of the functions X and R, in that order, and then applying C directly to D). Nevertheless, it is convenient, at least conceptually, to define the semantics of view retrieval in terms of materialization rather than substitution; in other words, substitution is valid so long as it is guaranteed to produce the same result as would be produced if materialization were used instead (and of course it *is* so guaranteed).

Now, you should basically be familiar with the foregoing explanation already from our earlier discussions. We make it explicit here for the following reasons:

- First, it lays the groundwork for a similar (but more searching) discussion of update operations in Section 9.4 below.

- Second, it makes it clear that materialization is a perfectly legitimate view implementation technique (albeit one that is likely to be rather inefficient)—at least for retrieval operations. But it cannot be used for update operations, of course, because the whole point of updating a view is precisely to apply the updates to the underlying base relvar(s), not just to some temporarily materialized *copy* of the data. Again, see Section 9.4 below.

- Third, although the substitution procedure is quite straightforward and works perfectly well in theory in 100 percent of cases, the sad fact is that (at the time of writing) there are some SQL products for which it does *not* work in practice!—that is, there are some SQL products in which some retrievals on some views fail in surprising ways. It also does not work in practice for versions of the SQL standard prior to SQL/92. And the reason for the failures is precisely that the products in question, and earlier versions of the SQL standard, do not fully support the relational closure property. See Exercise 9.14, part a., at the end of the chapter.

9.4 VIEW UPDATES

The view update problem can be stated thus: Given a particular update on a particular view, what updates need to be applied to what underlying base relvar(s) in order to implement the original view update? More precisely, let D be a database, and let V be a view on D, i.e., a view whose definition X is a function on D:

$$V \;=\; X \; (\; D \;)$$

(as in Section 9.3). Now let U be an update operation on V; U can be regarded as an operation that has the effect of changing its argument, yielding

$$U \; (\; V \;) \;\;=\;\; U \; (\; X \; (\; D \;) \;)$$

The problem of view update is then the problem of finding an update operation U' on D such that

$$U \; (\; X \; (\; D \;) \;) \;\;=\;\; X \; (\; U' \; (\; D \;) \;)$$

because, of course, D is the only thing that "really exists" (views are virtual), and so updates cannot be directly implemented in terms of views *per se*.

Before going any further, we must emphasize the point that the view update problem has been the subject of considerable research over the years, and many different approaches have been proposed to its solution (by the present writer among others); see, e.g., references [9.7], [9.10–9.13], [9.15], and in particular Codd's proposals for RM/V2 [5.2]. In this chapter we describe a comparatively new approach [9.9], one that is less *ad hoc* than previous proposals but does have the virtue of being upward-compatible with the best aspects of those proposals. It also has the virtue of treating as updatable a much wider class of views than earlier approaches do; in fact, it treats *all* views as potentially updatable, barring integrity constraint violations.

The Golden Rule Revisited

Recall *The Golden Rule* from the previous chapter:

> *No update operation must ever be allowed to leave any relvar in a state that violates its own predicate.*

When we first introduced this rule, we stressed the point that it applies to *all* relvars, derived as well as base. In other words, derived relvars have predicates too—as indeed they must, by virtue of *The Principle of Interchangeability*—and the system needs to know what those predicates are in order to perform view updates correctly. So what does the predicate for a view look like? Clearly, what we need is a set of **predicate inference rules,** such that if we know the predicate(s) for the input(s) to any relational operation, we can infer the predicate for the output from that operation. Given such a set of rules, we will be able to infer the predicate for a view from the predicate(s) for the base relvar(s) in terms of which that view is directly or indirectly defined. (Of course, the predicates for those base relvars are already known: They are the logical AND of whatever relvar constraints—e.g., candidate key constraints—have been declared for the base relvar in question.)

It is in fact very easy to find such a set of rules—they follow immediately from the definitions of the relational operators. For example, if *A* and *B* are any two relvars of the same type and their respective predicates are *PA* and *PB,* and if view *C* is defined as *A* INTERSECT *B,* then the predicate *PC* for that view is obviously (*PA*) AND (*PB*); that is, a given tuple will appear in *C* if and only if it makes *PA* and *PB* both *true.* We will consider the other relational operators later in this section.

Note: Derived relvars thus automatically "inherit" certain constraints from the relvars from which they are derived. But it is possible that a given derived relvar will be subject to certain additional constraints, over and above the inherited ones. Thus, it is desirable to be able to state constraints explicitly for derived relvars (an example might be a candidate key definition for a view), and **Tutorial D** does in fact support such a possibility. For simplicity, however, we will mostly ignore this possibility in what follows.

Toward a View Updating Mechanism

There are a number of important principles that must be satisfied by any systematic approach to the view updating problem (*The Golden Rule* is the overriding one, of course, but it is not the only one). The principles in question are as follows:

1. View updatability is a semantic issue, not a syntactic one—i.e., it must not depend on the particular syntactic form in which the view definition in question happens to be stated. For example, the following two definitions are semantically identical:

   ```
   VAR V VIEW
       S WHERE STATUS > 25 OR CITY  = 'Paris' ;

   VAR V VIEW
     ( S WHERE STATUS > 25 ) UNION ( S WHERE CITY = 'Paris' ) ;
   ```

   Obviously, these two views should either both be updatable or both not be (in fact, of course, they should both be updatable). By contrast, the SQL standard, and most of today's SQL products, adopt the *ad hoc* position that the first is updatable and the second is not (see Section 9.6).

2. It follows from the previous point that the view updating mechanism must work correctly in the special case when the "view" is in fact a base relvar—because any base relvar *B* is semantically indistinguishable from a view *V* that is defined as *B* UNION *B,* or *B* INTERSECT *B,* or *B* WHERE *true,* or any of several other expressions that are identically equivalent to just *B.* Thus, for example, the rules for updating a union view, when applied to the view *V* = *B* UNION *B,* must yield exactly the same result as if the update in question had been applied directly to the base relvar *B.* In other words, the subject of this section, though advertised as "view updating," is really "*relvar* updating" in general; we will be describing a theory of updating that works for *all* relvars, not just for views.

3. The updating rules must preserve symmetry where applicable. For example, the DELETE rule for an intersection view $V = A$ INTERSECT B must not arbitrarily cause a tuple to be deleted from A and not from B, even though such a one-sided delete would certainly have the effect of deleting the tuple from the view. Instead, the tuple must be deleted from both A and B. (In other words, there should be *no ambiguity*—there should always be exactly one way of implementing a given update, a way that works in all cases. In particular, there should be no logical difference between a view defined as A INTERSECT B and one defined as B INTERSECT A.)

4. The updating rules must take into account any applicable triggered procedures, including in particular referential actions such as cascade DELETE.

5. For reasons of simplicity among others, it is desirable to regard UPDATE as shorthand for a DELETE-INSERT sequence (i.e., just as syntactic sugar), and we will so regard it. This shorthand is acceptable *provided* it is understood that:

   - No checking of relvar predicates is done "in the middle of" any given update; that is, the expansion of UPDATE is DELETE-INSERT-check, not DELETE-check-INSERT-check. The reason is, of course, that the DELETE might temporarily violate the relvar predicate while the UPDATE overall does not; e.g., suppose relvar R contains exactly 10 tuples, and consider the effect of "UPDATE tuple t" on R if R's relvar predicate says that R must contain at least 10 tuples.

   - Triggered procedures are likewise never performed "in the middle of" any given update (in fact they are done at the end, immediately prior to the relvar predicate checking).

   - The shorthand requires some slight refinement in the case of projection views (see later in this section).

6. All updates on views must be implemented by the same kind of updates on the underlying relvars. That is, INSERTs map to INSERTs and DELETEs to DELETEs (we can ignore UPDATEs, thanks to the previous point). For suppose, contrariwise, that there is some kind of view—say a union view—for which (say) INSERTs map to DELETEs. Then it must follow that INSERTs *on a base relvar* must also sometimes map to DELETEs! This conclusion follows because (as already observed under point 2 above) the base relvar B is semantically identical to the union view $V = B$ UNION B. An analogous argument applies to every other kind of view also (restriction, projection, intersection, etc.). The idea that an INSERT on a base relvar might really be a DELETE we take to be self-evidently absurd; hence our position that (to repeat) INSERTs map to INSERTs and DELETEs to DELETEs.

7. In general, the updating rules when applied to a given view V will specify the operations to be applied to the relvar(s) in terms of which V is defined. And those rules must work correctly even when those underlying relvars are themselves views in turn. In other words, the rules must be capable of *recursive application*. Of course, if an attempt to update an underlying relvar fails for some reason, the original update will fail also; i.e., updates on views are all or nothing, just as updates on base relvars are.

8. The rules cannot assume that the database is well designed (e.g., fully normalized—see Chapters 11 and 12). However, they might on occasion produce a slightly surprising result if the database is *not* well designed—a fact that can be seen in itself as an additional argument in support of good design. We will give an example of such a "slightly surprising result" in the next subsection.

9. There should be no *prima facie* reason for permitting some updates but not others (e.g., DELETEs but not INSERTs) on a given view.

10. INSERT and DELETE should be inverses of each other, insofar as possible.

We remind you of one other important point. As explained in Chapter 5, relational operations—relational updates in particular—are always **set-level;** a set containing a single tuple is merely a special case. What is more, multi-tuple updates are sometimes *required* (i.e., some updates cannot be simulated by a series of single-tuple operations). And this remark is true of both base relvars and views, in general. For reasons of simplicity, we will for the most part present our updating rules in terms of single-tuple operations, but do not lose sight of the fact that considering single-tuple operations only is a simplification, and indeed an oversimplification in certain cases.

We now consider the operators of the relational algebra one by one, starting with union, intersection, and difference. *Note:* In these first three cases in particular, we assume we are dealing with a view whose defining expression is of the form *A* UNION *B* or *A* INTERSECT *B* or *A* MINUS *B* (as appropriate), where *A* and *B* are in turn relational expressions (i.e., they do not necessarily denote base relvars). The relations denoted by *A* and *B* must be of the same relation type. The corresponding relvar predicates are *PA* and *PB,* respectively.

Union

Here is the INSERT rule for A UNION B:

■ **INSERT:** The new tuple must satisfy *PA* or *PB* or both. If it satisfies *PA,* it is inserted into *A;* note that this INSERT might have the side effect of inserting the tuple into *B* also.* If it satisfies *PB,* it is inserted into *B,* unless it was inserted into *B* already as a side effect of inserting it into *A.*

Note: The specific procedural manner in which this rule is stated ("insert into *A,* then insert into *B*") should be understood purely as a pedagogic simplification; it does not mean that the DBMS must actually perform the INSERTs in sequence as stated. Indeed, the principle of symmetry—Principle No. 3 from the immediately preceding subsection—implies as much, because neither *A* nor *B* has precedence over the other. Analogous remarks apply to many of the rules to be discussed in what follows.

---

*Several of the rules and examples discussed in what follows refer to the possibility of side effects. Now, it is well known that side effects are usually undesirable; the point is, however, that side effects might be unavoidable if *A* and *B* happen to represent overlapping subsets of the same underlying relvar, as will frequently be the case with union, intersection, and difference views. What is more, the side effects in question are (for once) desirable, not undesirable.

Explanation: The new tuple must satisfy at least one of *PA* and *PB,* because otherwise it would not qualify for inclusion in *A* UNION *B*—i.e., it would not satisfy the relvar predicate, viz. (*PA*) OR (*PB*), for *A* UNION *B*. (We assume too, though in fact the assumption is not strictly necessary, that the new tuple must not currently appear in either *A* or *B*, because otherwise we would be trying to insert a tuple that already exists.) Assuming the foregoing requirements are satisfied, the new tuple is inserted into whichever of *A* or *B* it logically belongs to (possibly both).

Examples: Let view UV be defined as follows:

```
VAR UV VIEW
   ( S WHERE STATUS > 25 ) UNION ( S WHERE CITY = 'Paris' ) ;
```

Fig. 9.2 shows a possible value for this view, corresponding to our usual sample data values.

UV	S#	SNAME	STATUS	CITY
	S2	Jones	10	Paris
	S3	Blake	30	Paris
	S5	Adams	30	Athens

Fig. 9.2   View UV (sample values)

- Let the tuple to be inserted be (S6,Smith,50,Rome).* This tuple satisfies the predicate for S WHERE STATUS > 25 but not the predicate for S WHERE CITY = 'Paris'. It is therefore inserted into S WHERE STATUS > 25. Because of the rules regarding INSERT on a restriction (which are fairly obvious—see later in this section), the effect is to insert the new tuple into the suppliers base relvar, and hence to make the tuple appear in the view as desired.

- Now let the tuple to be inserted be (S7,Jones,50,Paris). This tuple satisfies the predicate for S WHERE STATUS > 25 and the predicate for S WHERE CITY = 'Paris'. It is therefore logically inserted into both of these two restrictions. However, inserting it into either one has the side effect of inserting it into the other anyway, so there is no need to perform the second INSERT explicitly.

Now suppose SA and SB are two distinct *base* relvars, SA representing suppliers with status > 25 and SB representing suppliers in Paris (see Fig. 9.3); suppose view UV is defined as SA UNION SB, and consider again the two sample INSERTs previously discussed. Inserting the tuple (S6,Smith,50,Rome) into view UV will cause that tuple to be inserted into base relvar SA, presumably as required. However, inserting the tuple (S7,Jones,50,Paris) into view UV will cause that tuple to be inserted into *both* base relvars!

---

*We adopt this simplified notation for tuples throughout this section for readability reasons.

SA					SB			
S#	SNAME	STATUS	CITY		S#	SNAME	STATUS	CITY
S3	Blake	30	Paris		S2	Jones	10	Paris
S5	Adams	30	Athens		S3	Blake	30	Paris

Fig. 9.3   Base relvars SA and SB (sample values)

This result is logically correct, although arguably counterintuitive (it is an example of what we called a "slightly surprising result" in the previous subsection). *It is our position that such surprises can occur only if the database is badly designed.* In particular, it is our position that a design that permits the very same tuple to appear in—i.e., to satisfy the predicate for—two distinct base relvars is by definition a bad design. This perhaps controversial position is elaborated in Chapter 12, Section 12.6.

We turn now to the DELETE rule for *A* UNION *B:*

- **DELETE:** If the tuple to be deleted appears in *A,* it is deleted from *A* (note that this DELETE might have the side effect of deleting the tuple from *B* also). If it (still) appears in *B,* it is deleted from *B.*

Examples to illustrate this rule are left as an exercise. Note that deleting a tuple from *A* or *B* might cause a cascade DELETE or some other triggered procedure to be performed. Finally, the UPDATE rule:

- **UPDATE:** The tuple to be updated must be such that the updated version satisfies *PA* or *PB* or both. If the tuple to be updated appears in *A,* it is deleted from *A without* performing any triggered procedures (cascade DELETE, etc.) that such a DELETE would normally cause, and likewise without checking the relvar predicate for *A.* Note that this DELETE might have the side effect of deleting the tuple from *B* also. If the tuple (still) appears in *B,* it is deleted from *B* (again without performing any triggered procedures or relvar predicate checks). Next, if the updated version of the tuple satisfies *PA,* it is inserted into *A* (note that this INSERT might have the side effect of inserting the tuple into *B* also). Finally, if the updated version satisfies *PB,* it is inserted into *B,* unless it was inserted into *B* already as a side effect of inserting it into *A.*

This UPDATE rule essentially consists of the DELETE rule followed by the INSERT rule, except that—as indicated—no triggered procedures or predicate checks are performed after the DELETE (any triggered procedures associated with the UPDATE are conceptually performed after all deletions and insertions have been done, just prior to the predicate checks).

It is worth pointing out that one important consequence of treating UPDATEs in this fashion is that a given UPDATE can cause a tuple to *migrate* from one relvar to another, loosely speaking. Given the database of Fig. 9.3, for example, updating the tuple

(S5,Adams,30,Athens) in view UV to (S5,Adams,15,Paris) will delete the old tuple for S5 from SA and insert the new tuple for S5 into SB.

Intersect

Here now are the rules for updating *A* INTERSECT *B*. This time we simply state the rules without further discussion (they follow the same general pattern as the union rules), except to note that the predicate for *A* INTERSECT *B* is (*PA*) AND (*PB*). Examples to illustrate the various cases are left as an exercise.

- **INSERT:** The new tuple must satisfy both *PA* and *PB*. If it does not currently appear in *A*, it is inserted into *A* (note that this INSERT might have the side effect of inserting the tuple into *B* also). If it (still) does not appear in *B*, it is inserted into *B*.

- **DELETE:** The tuple to be deleted is deleted from *A* (note that this DELETE might have the side effect of deleting the tuple from *B* also). If it (still) appears in *B*, it is deleted from *B*.

- **UPDATE:** The tuple to be updated must be such that the updated version satisfies both *PA* and *PB*. The tuple is deleted from *A* without performing any triggered procedures or predicate checks (note that this DELETE might have the side effect of deleting it from *B* also); if it (still) appears in *B*, it is deleted from *B*, again without performing any triggered procedures or predicate checks. Next, if the updated version of the tuple does not currently appear in *A*, it is inserted into *A* (note that this INSERT might have the side effect of inserting the tuple into *B* also). If it (still) does not appear in *B*, it is inserted into *B*.

Difference

Here are the rules for updating *A* MINUS *B* (the relvar predicate is (*PA*) AND NOT (*PB*)):

- **INSERT:** The new tuple must satisfy *PA* and not *PB*. It is inserted into *A*.
- **DELETE:** The tuple to be deleted is deleted from *A*.
- **UPDATE:** The tuple to be updated must be such that the updated version satisfies *PA* and not *PB*. The tuple is deleted from *A* without performing any triggered procedures or relvar predicate checks; the updated version is then inserted into *A*.

Restrict

Let the defining expression for view *V* be *A* WHERE *p*, and let the predicate for *A* be *PA*. Then the predicate for *V* is (*PA*) AND (*p*). For example, the predicate for the restriction S WHERE CITY = 'London' is (PS) AND (CITY = 'London'), where PS is the predicate for suppliers. Here then are the rules for updating *A* WHERE *p*:

- **INSERT:** The new tuple must satisfy both *PA* and *p*. It is inserted into *A*.
- **DELETE:** The tuple to be deleted is deleted from *A*.

■ **UPDATE:** The tuple to be updated must be such that the updated version satisfies both *PA* and *p*. The tuple is deleted from *A* without performing any triggered procedures or predicate checks. The updated version is then inserted into *A*.

Examples: Let view LS be defined as

```
VAR LS VIEW
    S WHERE CITY = 'London' ;
```

Fig. 9.4 shows a sample value for this view.

LS	S#	SNAME	STATUS	CITY
	S1	Smith	20	London
	S4	Clark	20	London

Fig. 9.4   View LS (sample values)

■ An attempt to insert the tuple (S6,Green,20,London) into LS will succeed. The new tuple will be inserted into relvar S, and will therefore effectively be inserted into view LS as well.

■ An attempt to insert the tuple (S1,Green,20,London) into LS will fail, because it violates the relvar predicate for relvar S (and hence for LS too)—specifically, it violates the uniqueness constraint on candidate key {S#}.

■ An attempt to insert the tuple (S6,Green,20,Athens) into LS will fail, because it violates the constraint CITY = 'London'.

■ An attempt to delete the LS tuple (S1,Smith,20,London) will succeed. The tuple will be deleted from relvar S, and will therefore effectively be deleted from view LS as well.

■ An attempt to update the LS tuple (S1,Smith,20,London) to (S6,Green,20,London) will succeed. An attempt to update that same tuple (S1,Smith,20,London) to either (S2,Smith,20,London) or (S1,Smith,20,Athens) will fail (why, exactly, in each case?).

Project

Again we begin with a discussion of the relevant predicate. Let the attributes of relvar *A* (with predicate *PA*) be partitioned into two disjoint groups, *X* and *Y* say. Regard each of *X* and *Y* as a single *composite* attribute, and consider the projection of *A* over *X*, *A{X}*. Let {*X:x*} be a tuple of that projection. Then it should be clear that the predicate for that projection is basically "There exists some value *y* from the domain of *Y* values such that the tuple {*X:x,Y:y*} satisfies *PA*." For example, consider the projection of relvar S over S#, SNAME, and CITY. Every tuple (*s,n,c*) appearing in that projection is such that there exists a status value *t* such that the tuple (*s,n,t,c*) satisfies the predicate for relvar S.

Here then are the rules for updating $A\{X\}$:

- **INSERT:** Let the tuple to be inserted be (x). Let the default value of Y be y (it is an error if no such default value exists, i.e., if Y has "defaults not allowed").* The tuple (x,y) (which must satisfy PA) is inserted into A.

  Note: Candidate key attributes will usually, though not invariably, have no default (see Chapter 18). As a consequence, a projection that does not include all candidate keys of the underlying relvar will usually not permit INSERTs.

- **DELETE:** All tuples of A with the same X value as the tuple to be deleted from $A\{X\}$ are deleted from A.

  Note: In practice, it will usually be desirable that X include at least one candidate key of A, so that the tuple to be deleted from $A\{X\}$ corresponds to exactly one tuple of A. However, there is no logical reason to make this a hard requirement. Analogous remarks apply in the case of UPDATE also—see below.

- **UPDATE:** Let the tuple to be updated be (x) and let the updated version be (x'). Let a be a tuple of A with the same X value x, and let the value of Y in a be y. All such tuples a are deleted from A without performing any triggered procedures or relvar predicate checks. Then, for each such value y, the tuple (x',y) (which must satisfy PA) is inserted into A.

  Note: It is here that the "slight refinement" regarding projection mentioned in Principle No. 5 in the subsection "Toward a View Updating Mechanism" shows itself. Specifically, observe that the final "INSERT" step in the UPDATE rule reinstates the previous Y value in each inserted tuple—it does *not* replace it by the applicable default value, as a standalone INSERT would.

Examples: Let view SC be defined as

```
SC { S#, CITY }
```

Fig. 9.5 shows a sample value for this view.

SC	S#	CITY
	S1	London
	S2	Paris
	S3	Paris
	S4	London
	S5	Athens

Fig. 9.5 View SC (sample values)

---

*As this sentence implies, we are assuming here that (as in SQL) a means is available for specifying default values for attributes of base relvars. Suitable **Tutorial D** syntax might take the form of a new clause on the base relvar definition, DEFAULT (*<default spec commalist>*) say, where each *<default spec>* takes the form *<attribute name> <default>*. For example, we might specify DEFAULT (STATUS 0, CITY ' ') in the definition of the suppliers relvar S.

- An attempt to insert the tuple (S6,Athens) into SC will succeed, and will have the effect of inserting the tuple (S6,*n*,*t*,London) into relvar S, where *n* and *t* are the default values for attributes SNAME and STATUS respectively.

- An attempt to insert the tuple (S1,Athens) into SC will fail, because it violates the relvar predicate for relvar S (and hence for SC too)—specifically, it violates the uniqueness constraint on candidate key {S#}.

- An attempt to delete the tuple (S1,London) from SC will succeed. The tuple for S1 will be deleted from relvar S.

- An attempt to update the SC tuple (S1,London) to (S1,Athens) will succeed; the effect will be to update the tuple (S1,Smith,20,London) in relvar S to (S1,Smith,20,Athens)—*not* to (S1,*n*,*t*,Athens), please observe, where *n* and *t* are the applicable defaults.

- An attempt to update that same SC tuple (S1,London) to (S2,London) will fail (why, exactly?).

Consideration of the case in which the projection does not include a candidate key of the underlying relvar—for example, the projection of relvar S over STATUS and CITY—is left as an exercise.

Extend

Let the defining expression for view *V* be

```
EXTEND A ADD exp AS X
```

(where as usual the predicate for *A* is *PA*). Then the predicate *PE* for *V* is

```
PA ( a ) AND e.X = exp ( a )
```

Here *e* is a tuple of *V* and *a* is the tuple that remains when *e*'s *X* component is removed (i.e., *a* is the projection of *e* over all attributes of *A,* loosely speaking). In (stilted) natural language:

> Every tuple *e* in the extension is such that (1) the tuple *a* that is derived from *e* by projecting away the *X* component satisfies *PA,* and (2) that *X* component has a value equal to the result of applying the expression *exp* to that tuple *a*.

Here then are the update rules:

- **INSERT:** Let the tuple to be inserted be *e; e* must satisfy *PE*. The tuple *a* that is derived from *e* by projecting away the *X* component is inserted into *A*.

- **DELETE:** Let the tuple to be deleted be *e*. The tuple *a* that is derived from *e* by projecting away the *X* component is deleted from *A*.

- **UPDATE:** Let the tuple to be updated be *e* and let the updated version be *e'; e'* must satisfy *PE*. The tuple *a* that is derived from *e* by projecting away the *X* component is deleted from *A* without performing any triggered procedures or relvar predicate checks. The tuple *a'* that is derived from *e'* by projecting away the *X* component is inserted into *A*.

Examples: Let view VPX be defined as

```
EXTEND P ADD ( WEIGHT * 454 ) AS GMWT
```

Fig. 9.6 shows a sample value for this view.

VPX	P#	PNAME	COLOR	WEIGHT	CITY	GMWT
	P1	Nut	Red	12.0	London	5448.0
	P2	Bolt	Green	17.0	Paris	7718.0
	P3	Screw	Blue	17.0	Rome	7718.0
	P4	Screw	Red	14.0	London	6356.0
	P5	Cam	Blue	12.0	Paris	5448.0
	P6	Cog	Red	19.0	London	8626.0

Fig. 9.6   View VPX (sample values)

- An attempt to insert the tuple (P7,Cog,Red,12,Paris,5448) will succeed, and will have the effect of inserting the tuple (P7,Cog,Red,12,Paris) into relvar P.
- An attempt to insert the tuple (P7,Cog,Red,12,Paris,5449) will fail (why?).
- An attempt to insert the tuple (P1,Cog,Red,12,Paris,5448) will fail (why?).
- An attempt to delete the tuple for P1 will succeed, and will have the effect of deleting the tuple for P1 from relvar P.
- An attempt to update the tuple for P1 to (P1,Nut,Red,10,Paris,4540) will succeed; the effect will be to update the tuple (P1,Nut,Red,12,London) in relvar P to (P1,Nut,Red,10,Paris).
- An attempt to update that same tuple to one for P2 (with all other values unchanged) or to one in which the GMWT value is not equal to 454 times the WEIGHT value will fail (in each case, why?).

Join

Most previous treatments of the view update problem—including those in the first five editions of this book and in other books by the present author—have argued that the updatability or otherwise of a given join depends, at least in part, on whether the join is one-to-one, one-to-many, or many-to-many. In contrast to those previous treatments, we now contend that joins are *always* updatable. Moreover, the rules are identical in all three cases, and are essentially quite straightforward. What makes this claim plausible—startling though it might seem at first sight—is the new perspective on the problem afforded by adoption of *The Golden Rule,* as we now explain.

Broadly speaking, the goal of view support has always been to make views look as much like base relvars as possible, and this goal is indeed a laudable one. However:

- It is usually assumed (implicitly) that it is always possible to update an individual tuple of a base relvar independently of all other tuples in that base relvar.

- At the same time, it is realized (explicitly) that it is manifestly *not* always possible to update an individual tuple of a view independently of all other tuples in that view.

For example, Codd shows in reference [11.2] that it is not possible to delete just one tuple from a certain join, because the effect would be to leave a relation that "is not the join of any two relations whatsoever" (which means that the result could not possibly satisfy the relvar predicate for the view). And the approach to such view updates historically has always been to reject them altogether, on the grounds that it is impossible to make them look completely like base relvar updates.

Our approach is rather different. To be specific, we recognize that even with a base relvar, it is not always possible to update individual tuples independently of all the rest. Typically, therefore, we accept those view updates that have historically been rejected, interpreting them in an obvious and logically correct way to apply to the underlying relvar(s); we accept them, moreover, in full recognition of the fact that updating those underlying relvars might have side effects on the view—*side effects that are, however, required in order to avoid the possibility that the view might violate its own predicate.*

With that preamble out of the way, let us now get down to specifics. In what follows, we first define our terms. Then we present the rules for updating join views. Then we consider the implications of those rules for each of the three cases (one-to-one, one-to-many, many-to-many) in turn.

Consider the join $J = A$ JOIN B, where (as in Chapter 6, Section 6.4) relvars A, B, and J have headings $\{X,Y\}$, $\{Y,Z\}$, and $\{X,Y,Z\}$, respectively. Let the relvar predicates for A and B be PA and PB, respectively. Then the relvar predicate PJ for J is

```
PA ( a ) AND PB ( b )
```

where for a given tuple j of the join, a is "the A portion" of j (i.e., the tuple that is derived from j by projecting away the Z component) and b is "the B portion" of j (i.e., the tuple that is derived from j by projecting away the X component). In other words:

Every tuple in the join is such that the A portion satisfies PA and the B portion satisfies PB.

For example, the predicate for the join of relvars S and SP over S# is as follows:

Every tuple (s,n,t,c,p,q) in the join is such that the tuple (s,n,t,c) satisfies the predicate for S and the tuple (s,p,q) satisfies the predicate for SP.

Here then are the update rules:

- **INSERT:** The new tuple *j* must satisfy *PJ*. If the *A* portion of *j* does not appear in *A*, it is inserted into *A*.* If the *B* portion of *j* does not appear in *B*, it is inserted into *B*.

- **DELETE:** The *A* portion of the tuple to be deleted is deleted from *A* and the *B* portion is deleted from *B*.

- **UPDATE:** The tuple to be updated must be such that the updated version satisfies *PJ*. The *A* portion is deleted from *A*, without performing any triggered procedures or relvar predicate checks, and the *B* portion is deleted from *B*, again without performing any triggered procedures or relvar predicate checks. Then, if the *A* portion of the updated version of the tuple does not appear in *A*, it is inserted into *A;* if the *B* portion does not appear in *B*, it is inserted into *B*.

Let us now examine the implications of these rules for the three different cases.

Case 1 (one-to-one): Note first that the term "one-to-one" here would more accurately be "(zero-or-one)-to-(zero-or-one)." In other words, there is an integrity constraint in effect that guarantees that for each tuple of *A* there is at most one matching tuple in *B* and *vice versa*—implying that the set of attributes *Y* over which the join is performed must be a *superkey* for both of *A* and *B*. (Refer to Chapter 8, Section 8.8, if you need to refresh your memory regarding superkeys.)

Examples:

- For a first example, you are invited to consider the effect of the foregoing rules on the join of the suppliers relvar S to itself over supplier numbers (only).

- By way of a second example, suppose we have another base relvar SR with attributes S# and REST, where S# identifies a supplier and REST identifies that supplier's favorite restaurant. Assume that not all suppliers in S appear in SR. Consider the effect of the join update rules on S JOIN SR. What difference would it make if some supplier could appear in SR and not in S?

Case 2 (one-to-many): The term "one-to-many" here would more accurately be "(zero-or-one)-to-(zero-or-more)." In other words, there is an integrity constraint in effect that guarantees that for each tuple of *B* there is at most one matching tuple in *A*. Typically, what this means is that the set of attributes *Y* over which the join is performed must include a set *K*, say, such that *K* is a candidate key for *A* and a matching foreign key for *B*. *Note:* If the foregoing is in fact the case, we can replace the phrase "zero-or-one" by "exactly one."

Examples: Let view SSP be defined as

```
S JOIN SP
```

(this is a foreign-to-matching-candidate-key join, of course). Sample values are shown in Fig. 9.7.

---

*Note that this INSERT might have the side effect of inserting the *B* portion into *B* also, as in the case of the union, intersection, and difference views discussed earlier. Analogous remarks apply to the DELETE and UPDATE rules also; for brevity, we do not bother to spell out this possibility in detail in every case.

SSP	S#	SNAME	STATUS	CITY	P#	QTY
	S1	Smith	20	London	P1	300
	S1	Smith	20	London	P2	200
	S1	Smith	20	London	P3	400
	S1	Smith	20	London	P4	200
	S1	Smith	20	London	P5	100
	S1	Smith	20	London	P6	100
	S2	Jones	10	Paris	P1	300
	S2	Jones	10	Paris	P2	400
	S3	Blake	30	Paris	P2	200
	S4	Clark	20	London	P2	200
	S4	Clark	20	London	P4	300
	S4	Clark	20	London	P5	400

Fig. 9.7   View SSP (sample values)

- An attempt to insert the tuple (S4,Clark,20,London,P6,100) into SSP will succeed, and will have the effect of inserting the tuple (S4,P6,100) into relvar SP (thereby adding a tuple to the view).

- An attempt to insert the tuple (S5,Adams,30,Athens,P6,100) into SSP will succeed, and will have the effect of inserting the tuple (S5,P6,100) into relvar SP (thereby adding a tuple to the view).

- An attempt to insert the tuple (S6,Green,20,London,P6,100) into SSP will succeed, and will have the effect of inserting the tuple (S6,Green,20,London) into relvar S and the tuple (S6,P6,100) into relvar SP (thereby adding a tuple to the view).

   Note: Suppose for the moment that it is possible for SP tuples to exist without a corresponding S tuple. Suppose moreover that relvar SP already includes some tuples with supplier number S6, but not one with supplier number S6 and part number P1. Then the INSERT in the example just discussed will have the effect of inserting some additional tuples into the view—namely, the join of the tuple (S6,Green,20,London) and those previously existing SP tuples for supplier S6.

- An attempt to insert the tuple (S4,Clark,20,Athens,P6,100) into SSP will fail (why?).

- An attempt to insert the tuple (S1,Smith,20,London,P1,400) into SSP will fail (why?).

- An attempt to delete the tuple (S3,Blake,30,Paris,P2,200) from SSP will succeed, and will have the effect of deleting the tuple (S3,Blake,30,Paris) from relvar S and the tuple (S3,P2,200) from relvar SP.

- An attempt to delete the tuple (S1,Smith,20,London,P1,300) from SSP will "succeed"—see the note below—and will have the effect of deleting the tuple (S1,Smith,20,London) from relvar S and the tuple (S1,P1,300) from relvar SP.

   Note: Actually the overall effect of this attempted DELETE will depend on the foreign key DELETE rule from shipments to suppliers. If the rule specifies RESTRICT the overall operation will fail. If it specifies CASCADE it will have the side effect of deleting all other SP tuples (and hence SSP tuples) for supplier S1 as well.

■ An attempt to update the SSP tuple (S1,Smith,20,London,P1,300) to (S1,Smith, 20,London,P1,400) will succeed, and will have the effect of updating the SP tuple (S1,P1,300) to (S1,P1,400).

■ An attempt to update the SSP tuple (S1,Smith,20,London,P1,300) to (S1,Smith, 20,Athens,P1,400) will succeed, and will have the effect of updating the S tuple (S1,Smith,20,London) to (S1,Smith,20,Athens) and the SP tuple (S1,P1,300) to (S1,P1,400).

■ An attempt to update the SSP tuple (S1,Smith,20,London,P1,300) to (S6,Smith, 20,London,P1,300) will "succeed"—see the note below—and will have the effect of updating the S tuple (S1,Smith,20,London) to (S6,Smith,20,London) and the SP tuple (S1,P1,300) to (S6,P1,300).

Note: Actually, the overall effect of this attempted update will depend on the foreign key UPDATE rule from shipments to suppliers. The details are left as an exercise.

Case 3 (many-to-many): The term "many-to-many" here would more accurately be "(zero-or-more)-to-(zero-or-more)." In other words, there is no integrity constraint in effect that guarantees that we are really dealing with a Case 1 or Case 2 situation instead.

Examples: Suppose we have a view defined as

    S JOIN P

(join of S and P over CITY—a many-to-many join). Sample values are shown in Fig. 9.8.

■ Inserting the tuple (S7,Bruce,15,Oslo,P8,Wheel,White,25) will succeed, and will have the effect of inserting the tuple (S7,Bruce,15,Oslo) into relvar S and the tuple (P8,Wheel,White,25,Oslo) into relvar P (thereby adding the specified tuple to the view).

S#	SNAME	STATUS	CITY	P#	PNAME	COLOR	WEIGHT
S1	Smith	20	London	P1	Nut	Red	12.0
S1	Smith	20	London	P4	Screw	Red	14.0
S1	Smith	20	London	P6	Cog	Red	19.0
S2	Jones	10	Paris	P2	Bolt	Green	17.0
S2	Jones	10	Paris	P5	Cam	Blue	12.0
S3	Blake	30	Paris	P2	Bolt	Green	17.0
S3	Blake	30	Paris	P5	Cam	Blue	12.0
S4	Clark	20	London	P1	Nut	Red	12.0
S4	Clark	20	London	P4	Screw	Red	14.0
S4	Clark	20	London	P6	Cog	Red	19.0

Fig. 9.8 The join of S and P over CITY

- Inserting the tuple (S1,Smith,20,London,P7,Washer,Red,5) will succeed, and will have the effect of inserting the tuple (P7,Washer,Red,5,London) into relvar P (thereby adding *two* tuples to the view—the tuple (S1,Smith,20,London,P7,Washer,Red,5), as specified, and also the tuple (S4,Clark,20,London,P7,Washer,Red,5)).

- Inserting the tuple (S6,Green,20,London,P7,Washer,Red,5) will succeed, and will have the effect of inserting the tuple (S6,Green,20,London) into relvar S and the tuple (P7,Washer,Red,5,London) into relvar P (thereby adding *six* tuples to the view).

- Deleting the tuple (S1,Smith,20,London,P1,Nut,Red,12) will succeed, and will have the effect of deleting the tuple (S1,Smith,20,London) from relvar S and the tuple (P1,Nut,Red,12,London) from relvar P (thereby deleting *four* tuples from the view).

Further examples are left as an exercise.

Other Operators

Finally, we briefly consider the remaining operators of the algebra. We note first that Θ-join, semijoin, semidifference, and divide are not primitive, so the rules for these operators can be derived from those for the operators in terms of which they are defined. As for the others:

- *Rename:* Trivial.

- *Cartesian product:* As noted at the very end of Section 6.4 in Chapter 6, Cartesian product is a special case of natural join (*A* JOIN *B* degenerates to *A* TIMES *B* if *A* and *B* have no attributes in common). As a consequence, the rules for *A* TIMES *B* are just a special case of the rules for *A* JOIN *B* (as are the rules for *A* INTERSECT *B* also, of course).

- *Summarize:* Summarize is also not primitive—it is defined in terms of extend, and so the updating rules can be derived from those for extend. *Note:* It is true that most updates on most SUMMARIZE views will fail in practice. However, the failures occur not because such views are *inherently* nonupdatable, but rather because attempts to update them usually fall foul of some integrity constraint. For example, let the view-defining expression be:

```
SUMMARIZE SP PER SP { S# } ADD SUM ( QTY ) AS TOTQTY
```

Then an attempt to delete, say, the tuple for supplier S1 will succeed. However, an attempt to insert, say, the tuple (S5,500) will fail, because it violates the constraint that the TOTQTY value must be equal to the sum of all applicable individual QTY values. An attempt to insert the tuple (S5,0) will also fail, but for a different reason (why, exactly?).

- *Group and ungroup:* Remarks analogous to those for summarize apply here also.

- *Tclose:* Somewhat analogous remarks apply once again.

9.5 SNAPSHOTS (A DIGRESSION)

In this section we digress briefly to discuss **snapshots** [9.2]. Snapshots do have some points in common with views,* but they are not the same thing. Like views, snapshots are derived relvars; unlike views, however, they are real, not virtual—i.e., they are represented not just by their definition in terms of other relvars, but also (at least conceptually) by their own separately materialized copy of the data. For example:

```
VAR P2SC SNAPSHOT
    ( ( S JOIN SP ) WHERE P# = P# ( 'P2' ) ) { S#, CITY }
        REFRESH EVERY DAY ;
```

Defining a snapshot is much like executing a query, except that:

a. The result of the query is kept in the database under the specified name (P2SC in the example) as a *read-only relvar* (read-only, that is, apart from the periodic refresh—see point b.);

b. Periodically (EVERY DAY in the example) the snapshot is **refreshed**—i.e., its current value is discarded, the query is executed again, and the result of that new execution becomes the new snapshot value.

Thus, snapshot P2SC represents the relevant data as it was at most 24 hours ago (so what is the predicate?).

The point of snapshots is that many applications—perhaps even most—can tolerate, or might even require, data "as of" some particular point in time. Reporting and accounting applications are a case in point; such applications typically require the data to be frozen at an appropriate moment (e.g., the end of an accounting period), and snapshots allow such freezing to occur without preventing other transactions from performing updates on the data in question (that is, on "the real data"). Similarly, it might be desirable to freeze large amounts of data for a complex query or read-only application, again without locking out updates. *Note:* This idea becomes particularly attractive in a distributed database or decision support environment—see Chapters 20 and 21, respectively. We remark that snapshots represent an important special case of *controlled redundancy* (see Chapter 1), and "snapshot refresh" is the corresponding *update propagation* process (again, see Chapter 1).

In general, then, a snapshot definition will look something like this:

```
VAR <relvar name> SNAPSHOT <relational expression>
    <candidate key definition list>
    REFRESH EVERY <now and then> ;
```

---

*Indeed, they are sometimes called **materialized views** (see, e.g., references [9.1], [9.3], [9.6], [9.14], and [9.16]). This terminology is unfortunate, however, and indeed deprecated, since whether views are materialized or not is an implementation issue, not a model issue; as far as the model is concerned, in fact, views are *not* materialized, and a "materialized view" is a contradiction in terms.

where *<now and then>* is, e.g., MONTH or WEEK or DAY or HOUR or *n* MINUTES or MONDAY or WEEKDAY ... (etc.). (In particular, a specification of the form REFRESH [ON] EVERY UPDATE might be used to keep the snapshot permanently in synch with the relvar(s) from which it is derived.) And here is the syntax of the corresponding DROP:

```
DROP VAR <relvar name> ;
```

where, of course, the *<relvar name>* refers to a snapshot specifically. *Note:* We assume that an attempt to drop a snapshot will fail if some other relvar definition currently refers to it. Alternatively, we might consider extending the snapshot definition to include some kind of "RESTRICT *vs.* CASCADE" option once again. We do not consider this latter possibility further here.

9.6   SQL FACILITIES

In this section we summarize SQL's support for views (only—SQL does not support snapshots at all at the time of writing). First, the syntax of **CREATE VIEW** is:

```
CREATE VIEW <view name> AS <table expression>
     [ WITH [ <qualifier> ] CHECK OPTION ] ;
```

where the *<qualifier>* is either CASCADED or LOCAL, and CASCADED is the default (and indeed the only sensible option, as explained in detail in reference [4.19]; we omit further discussion of LOCAL here for this reason). *Explanation:*

1. The *<table expression>* is the view-defining expression. See Appendix A for a detailed explanation of SQL table expressions.

2. WITH CHECK OPTION, if specified, means that INSERTs and UPDATEs on the view will be rejected if they violate any integrity constraint implied by the view-defining expression. Observe, therefore, that such operations will fail *only* if WITH CHECK OPTION is specified—i.e., by default, they will *not* fail. You will realize from Section 9.4 that we regard such behavior as logically incorrect; we would therefore strongly recommend that WITH CHECK OPTION *always* be specified in practice* (see reference [9.8]).

Examples:

1. ```
   CREATE VIEW GOOD_SUPPLIER
        AS SELECT S.S#, S.STATUS, S.CITY
           FROM   S
           WHERE  S.STATUS > 15
        WITH CHECK OPTION ;
   ```

---

*If the view is updatable, that is. As we will see later, views in SQL are often not updatable, and WITH CHECK OPTION is illegal if the view is not updatable according to SQL.
   ```

```
2.  CREATE VIEW REDPART
         AS SELECT P.P#, P.PNAME, P.WEIGHT AS WT, P.CITY
            FROM    P
            WHERE   P.COLOR = 'Red'
         WITH CHECK OPTION ;

3.  CREATE VIEW PQ
         AS SELECT SP.P#, SUM ( SP.QTY ) AS TOTQTY
            FROM    SP
            GROUP   BY SP.P# ;
```

Unlike its counterpart in Section 9.1 (subsection "Further Examples"), this view will not include rows for parts not supplied by any supplier. See the discussion of Example 7.7.8 in Chapter 7.

```
4.  CREATE VIEW CITY_PAIR
         AS SELECT DISTINCT S.CITY AS SCITY, P.CITY AS PCITY
            FROM    S, SP, P
            WHERE   S.S# = SP.S#
            AND     SP.P# = P.P# ;

5.  CREATE VIEW HEAVY_REDPART
         AS SELECT RP.P#, RP.PNAME, RP.WT, RP.CITY
            FROM    REDPART AS RP
            WHERE   RP.WT > 12.0
         WITH CHECK OPTION ;
```

An existing view can be dropped by means of **DROP VIEW**—syntax:

```
DROP VIEW <view name> <option> ;
```

where (as with DROP TABLE and DROP DOMAIN) *<option>* is either RESTRICT or CASCADE. If RESTRICT is specified and the view is referenced in any other view definition or in an integrity constraint, the DROP will fail; if CASCADE is specified, the DROP will succeed, and any referencing view definitions and integrity constraints will be dropped also.

View Retrievals

As indicated in Section 9.3, all retrievals against all views are guaranteed to work correctly in the current version of the SQL standard (SQL/92). The same is unfortunately not true for certain current products, nor for earlier versions of the standard. See Exercise 9.14, part a., at the end of this chapter.

View Updates

The SQL/92 support for view updating is very limited. Basically, the only views that are considered to be updatable are views that are derived from a single base table via some combination of restrict and project operations. Furthermore, even this simple case is treated incorrectly, owing to SQL's lack of understanding of relvar predicates, and in particular to the fact that SQL tables permit duplicate rows.

Here is a more precise statement of the SQL/92 view updatability rules (this list is taken from reference [4.19] but is slightly simplified here). In SQL, a view is updatable if all of the following conditions 1–8 apply:

1. The table expression that defines the scope of the view is a select expression; that is, it does not immediately contain any of the keywords JOIN, UNION, INTERSECT, or EXCEPT.

2. The SELECT clause of that select expression does not directly contain the keyword DISTINCT.

3. Every select item in that SELECT clause (after any necessary expansion of "asterisk-style" select items) consists of a possibly qualified column name (optionally accompanied by an AS clause), representing a simple reference to a column of the underlying table (see paragraph 5 below).

4. The FROM clause of that select expression contains exactly one table reference.

5. That table reference identifies either a base table or an updatable view. *Note:* The table identified by that table reference is the (single) underlying table for the updatable view in question (see paragraph 3 above).

6. That select expression does not include a WHERE clause that includes a subquery that includes a FROM clause that includes a reference to the same table as is referenced in the FROM clause mentioned in paragraph 4 above.

7. That select expression does not include a GROUP BY clause.

8. That select expression does not include a HAVING clause.

Points arising:

1. Updatability in SQL is "all or nothing," in the sense that *either* all three of INSERT, UPDATE, or DELETE can be applied to a given view or none of them can—it is not possible for (e.g.) DELETE to be applicable but INSERT not (although some commercial products do support such a capability).

2. In SQL, the UPDATE operation either *can* or *cannot* be applied to a given view—it is not possible to have some columns updatable and others not within the same view (although, again, some commercial products do go beyond the standard in this respect).

9.7 SUMMARY

A **view** is essentially a named relational expression; it can be regarded as a **derived, virtual relvar.** Operations against a view are normally implemented by a process of **substitution;** that is, references to the *name* of the view are replaced by the expression that *defines* the view—and this substitution process works precisely because of **closure.** For **retrieval** operations, the substitution process works 100 percent of the time (at least in theory, though not necessarily in current products). For **update** operations, it also works 100 percent of the time* (again in theory, though definitely not in current products); in the case of some views, however (e.g., views defined in terms of **summarize**), updates will usually fail because of integrity constraint violations. We also presented an extensive set of **principles** that the updating scheme must satisfy, and we showed in detail how the updating scheme worked for views defined in terms of the **union, intersection, difference, restrict, project, join,** and **extend** operators. For each of these operators, we described the corresponding (relvar) **predicate inference rules.**

We also examined the question of views and **logical data independence.** There are two aspects to such independence, **growth** and **restructuring.** Other benefits of views include (a) their ability to hide data and thereby provide a certain measure of **security,** and (b) their ability to act as a shorthand and thereby make life easier for the user. We went on to explain two important principles, *The Principle of Interchangeability* (which implies among other things that we must be able to update views), and *The Principle of Database Relativity.*

We also digressed for a moment to give a brief discussion of **snapshots.** Finally, we described the relevant aspects of SQL (in outline).

EXERCISES

9.1 Give calculus-based analogs of the algebraic view definitions in Section 9.1, subsection "Further Examples."

9.2 Define a view consisting of supplier numbers and part numbers for suppliers and parts that are not colocated.

9.3 Define a view for suppliers in London.

9.4 Define relvar SP of the suppliers and parts database as a view of relvar SPJ of the suppliers-parts-projects database.

9.5 Define a view over the suppliers-parts-projects database consisting of all projects (project number and city attributes only) that are supplied by supplier S1 and use part P1.

9.6 Given the view definition—

```
VAR HEAVYWEIGHT VIEW
   ( ( P RENAME WEIGHT AS WT, COLOR AS COL )
       WHERE WT > WEIGHT ( 14.0 ) ) { P#, WT, COL } ;
```

—show the converted form after the substitution procedure has been applied for each of the following statements:

a. `RA := HEAVYWEIGHT WHERE COL = COLOR ( 'Green' ) ;`

b. `RB := ( EXTEND HEAVYWEIGHT ADD WT + WEIGHT ( 5.3 ) AS WTP )`
    `                                          { P#, WTP } ;`

---

*This is why we regard views as *relvars,* or in other words *variables;* variables are always updatable, by definition.

c. `UPDATE HEAVYWEIGHT WHERE WT = WEIGHT ( 18.0 ) COL := 'White' ;`

d. `DELETE HEAVYWEIGHT WHERE WT < WEIGHT ( 10.0 ) ;`

e.
```
INSERT INTO HEAVYWEIGHT
    RELATION { TUPLE { P# P# ( 'P99' ),
                       WT WEIGHT ( 12.0 ),
                       COL COLOR ( 'Purple' ) } } ;
```

9.7 Suppose the HEAVYWEIGHT view definition from Exercise 9.6 is revised as follows:

```
VAR HEAVYWEIGHT VIEW
( ( ( EXTEND P ADD WEIGHT * 454 AS WT ) RENAME COLOR AS COL )
    WHERE WT > WEIGHT ( 14.0 ) ) { P#, WT, COL } ;
```

(i.e., attribute WT now denotes weights in grams rather than pounds). Now repeat Exercise 9.6.

9.8 In Chapter 8 we suggested that it might sometimes be desirable to be able to declare candidate keys—or possibly a primary key—for a view. Why might such a facility be desirable?

9.9 What extensions to the system catalog as described in Chapters 3 and 5 are needed to support views? What about snapshots?

9.10 Suppose a given base relvar R is replaced by two restrictions A and B such that A UNION B is always equal to R and A INTERSECT B is always empty. Is logical data independence achievable?

9.11

a. The intersection A INTERSECT B is equivalent to the join A JOIN B (this join is one-to-one, but not *strictly* so, because there might exist tuples in A without counterparts in B and *vice versa*). Are the updatability rules given in Section 9.4 for intersection and join views consistent with this equivalence?

b. A INTERSECT B is also equivalent to A MINUS (A MINUS B) and to B MINUS (B MINUS A). Are the updatability rules given in Section 9.4 for intersection and difference views consistent with these equivalences?

9.12 One of the principles we laid down in Section 9.4 was that INSERT and DELETE should be inverses of each other, insofar as possible. Do the rules given in that section for updating union, intersection, and difference views abide by this principle?

9.13 In Section 9.2 (in our discussion of logical data independence), we discussed the possibility of restructuring the suppliers and parts database by replacing base relvar S by two of its projections SNC and ST. We also observed that such a restructuring was not a totally trivial matter. What are the implications?

9.14 Investigate any SQL product that might be available to you.

a. Can you find any examples of view retrievals that fail in that product?

b. What are the rules regarding view updates in that product? (They are probably less stringent than those given in Section 9.6.)

9.15 Consider the suppliers and parts database, but ignore the parts relvar for simplicity. Here in outline are two possible designs for suppliers and shipments:

a.
```
S  { S#, SNAME, STATUS, CITY }
SP { S#, P#, QTY }
```

b.
```
SSP { S#, SNAME, STATUS, CITY, P#, QTY }
XSS { S#, SNAME, STATUS, CITY }
```

Design a. is as usual. In Design b., by contrast, relvar SSP contains a tuple for every shipment, giving the applicable part number and quantity and full supplier details, and relvar XSS contains supplier details for suppliers who supply no parts at all. (Note that the two designs are information-equivalent and that the two designs therefore illustrate *The Principle of Interchangeability.*) Write view definitions to express Design b. as views of Design a. and *vice versa.* Also, show the applicable *database constraints* for each design (see Chapter 8 if you need to refresh your memory regarding database constraints). Does either design have any obvious advantages over the other? If so, what are they?

9.16 Give SQL solutions to Exercises 9.2–9.5.

9.17 As the final (important!) exercise in this part of the book, revisit the definition of the relational model as given at the end of Section 3.2 in Chapter 3 and make sure you now understand it thoroughly.

REFERENCES AND BIBLIOGRAPHY

9.1 Brad Adelberg, Hector Garcia-Molina, and Jennifer Widom: "The STRIP Rule System for Efficiently Maintaining Derived Data," Proc. 1997 ACM SIGMOD Int. Conf. on Management of Data, Tucson, Ariz. (May 1997).

STRIP is an acronym for STanford Real-time Information Processor. It uses "rules"—i.e., triggered procedures, in effect (see, e.g., reference [8.22])—to update snapshots (here called *derived data*) whenever changes occur to the underlying base data. The problem with such systems in general is that if the base data changes very frequently, the computation overhead in executing the rules can be excessive. This paper describes the STRIP techniques for reducing that overhead.

9.2 Michel Adiba: "Derived Relations: A Unified Mechanism for Views, Snapshots, and Distributed Data," Proc. 1981 Int. Conf. on Very Large Data Bases, Cannes, France (September 1981). See also the earlier version "Database Snapshots," by Michel E. Adiba and Bruce G. Lindsay, IBM Research Report RJ2772 (March 7th, 1980).

The paper that first proposed the snapshot concept. Semantics and implementation are both discussed. Regarding implementation, note in particular that various kinds of "differential refresh" or *incremental maintenance* are possible under the covers—it is not always necessary for the system to reexecute the original query in its entirety at refresh time.

9.3 D. Agrawal, A. El Abbadi, A. Singh, and T. Yurek: "Efficient View Maintenance at Data Warehouses," Proc. 1997 ACM SIGMOD Int. Conf. on Management of Data, Tucson, Ariz. (May 1997).

Recall from Chapter 1 that a *data warehouse* is a database that contains decision support data—i.e., snapshots, to use the terminology of the present chapter (and the "views" of this paper's title are not views at all but snapshots). As noted in the annotation to reference [9.2], snapshots can be maintained incrementally, and such incremental maintenance is desirable for performance reasons. However, incremental maintenance can lead to problems if the snapshots are derived from several distinct databases that are all being updated at the same time. This paper offers a solution to this problem.

9.4 H. W. Buff: "Why Codd's Rule No. 6 Must Be Reformulated," *ACM SIGMOD Record 17,* No. 4 (December 1988).

In 1985, Codd published a set of twelve rules to be used as "part of a test to determine whether a product that is claimed to be fully relational is actually so" [9.5]. His Rule No. 6 required that all views that are theoretically updatable also be updatable by the system. In this short note, Buff claims that the general view updatability problem is undecidable—i.e., no general algorithm exists to determine the updatability (in Codd's sense) or otherwise of an arbitrary view. Note, however, that the definition of view updatability adopted in the present chapter is somewhat different from Codd's, in that it explicitly pays attention to the applicable relvar predicates.

9.5 E. F. Codd: "Is Your DBMS Really Relational?" and "Does Your DBMS Run by the Rules?", *Computerworld* (October 14th and 21st, 1985).

9.6 Latha S. Colby *et al.*: "Supporting Multiple View Maintenance Policies," Proc. 1997 ACM SIGMOD Int. Conf. on Management of Data, Tucson, Ariz. (May 1997).

The "views" of this paper's title are not views but snapshots. There are three broad approaches to snapshot maintenance:

1. *Immediate:* Every update to any underlying relvar immediately triggers a corresponding update to the snapshot.
2. *Deferred:* The snapshot is refreshed only when it is queried.
3. *Periodic:* The snapshot is refreshed at specified intervals (e.g., every day).

The purpose of snapshots in general is to improve query performance at the expense of update performance, and the three maintenance policies represent a spectrum of tradeoffs between the two. This paper investigates issues relating to the support of different policies on different snapshots in the same system at the same time.

9.7 Donald D. Chamberlin, James N. Gray, and Irving L. Traiger: "Views, Authorization, and Locking in a Relational Data Base System," Proc. NCC *44,* Anaheim, Calif. Montvale, N.J.: AFIPS Press (May 1975).

Includes a brief rationale for the approach adopted to view updating in the System R prototype (and hence in SQL/DS, DB2, the SQL standard, etc.). See also reference [9.15], which performs the same function for the University Ingres prototype.

9.8 Hugh Darwen: "Without Check Option," in C. J. Date and Hugh Darwen, *Relational Database Writings 1989–1991*. Reading, Mass.: Addison-Wesley (1992).

9.9 C. J. Date and David McGoveran: "Updating Union, Intersection, and Difference Views" and "Updating Joins and Other Views," in C. J. Date, *Relational Database Writings 1991–1994*. Reading, Mass.: Addison-Wesley (1995). *Note:* A formal version of these papers is in preparation at the time of writing.

9.10 Umeshwar Dayal and Philip A. Bernstein: "On the Correct Translation of Update Operations on Relational Views," *ACM TODS 7,* No. 3 (September 1982).

An early formal treatment of the view update problem (for restriction, projection, and join views only). Relvar predicates are not considered, however.

9.11 Antonio L. Furtado and Marco A. Casanova: "Updating Relational Views," in reference [17.1].

There are two broad approaches to the view update problem. One (the only one discussed in any detail in the present book) attempts to provide a general mechanism that works regardless of the specific database involved; it is driven purely by the definitions of the views in question. The other, less ambitious, approach requires the DBA to specify, for each view, exactly what updates are allowed and what their semantics are, by (in effect) writing the procedural code to implement those updates in terms of the underlying base relvars. This paper surveys work on each of the two approaches (as of 1985). An extensive set of references to earlier work is included.

9.12 Nathan Goodman: "View Update Is Practical," *InfoDB 5,* No. 2 (Summer 1990).

A very informal discussion of the problem of view updating. Here is a slightly paraphrased excerpt from the introduction: "Dayal and Bernstein [9.10] have proved that essentially no interesting views can be updated; Buff [9.4] has proved that no algorithm exists that can decide whether an arbitrary view is updatable. There seems little reason for hope. [However,] nothing could be further from the truth. The fact is, view update is both possible and practical." And the paper goes on to give a variety of *ad hoc* view update techniques. However, the crucial notion of *relvar predicates* is not mentioned.

9.13 Arthur M. Keller: "Algorithms for Translating View Updates to Database Updates for Views Involving Selections, Projections, and Joins," Proc. 4th ACM SIGACT-SIGMOD Symposium on Principles of Database Systems, Portland, Ore. (March 1985).

Proposes a set of five criteria that should be satisfied by view updating algorithms—no side effects, one-step changes only, no unnecessary changes, no simpler replacements possible, and no DELETE-INSERT pairs instead of UPDATEs—and presents algorithms that satisfy those criteria. Among other things, the algorithms permit the implementation of one kind of update by another; for example, a DELETE on a view might translate into an UPDATE on the underlying base relvar (e.g., a supplier could be deleted from the "London suppliers" view by changing the CITY value to Paris). As another example (beyond the scope of Keller's paper, however), a DELETE on *V* (where *V* is defined as the difference *A* MINUS *B*) might be implemented by means of an INSERT on *B* instead of a DELETE on *A*. Note that we explicitly rejected such possibilities in the body of this chapter, by virtue of our Principle No. 6.

9.14 Dallan Quass and Jennifer Widom: "On-Line Warehouse View Maintenance," Proc. 1997 ACM SIGMOD Int. Conf. on Management of Data, Tucson, Ariz. (May 1997).

The "views" of this paper's title are not views but snapshots. The paper presents an algorithm for snapshot maintenance that allows the maintenance transactions to run simultaneously with queries against the snapshots.

9.15 M. R. Stonebraker: "Implementation of Views and Integrity Constraints by Query Modification," Proc. ACM SIGMOD Int. Conf. on Management of Data, San Jose, Calif. (May 1975).

See the annotation to reference [9.7].

9.16 Yue Zhuge, Hector Garcia-Molina, Joachim Hammer, and Jennifer Widom: "View Maintenance in a Warehousing Environment," Proc. 1995 ACM SIGMOD Int. Conf. on Management of Data, San Jose, Calif. (May 1995).

The "views" of this paper's title are not views but snapshots. When it is informed of an update to some underlying data, the data warehouse site might need to issue a query to the base data site before it can carry out the necessary snapshot maintenance, and the time lag between such a query and the original base data update can lead to anomalies. This paper presents an algorithm for dealing with such anomalies.

ANSWERS TO SELECTED EXERCISES

9.1 We have numbered the following solutions as 9.1.*n,* where *n* is the number of the original example in Section 9.1. We make our usual assumptions regarding range variables.

9.1.1
```
VAR REDPART VIEW
    ( PX.P#, PX.PNAME, PX.WEIGHT AS WT, PX.CITY )
    WHERE PX.COLOR = COLOR ( 'Red' ) ;
```

```
9.1.2 VAR FQ VIEW
      ( PX.P#,
        SUM ( SPX WHERE SPX.P# = PX.P#, QTY ) AS TOTQTY ) ;

9.1.3 VAR CITY_PAIR VIEW
      ( SX.CITY AS SCITY, PX.CITY AS PCITY )
        WHERE EXISTS SPX ( SPX.S# = SX.S# AND
                           SPX.P# = PX.P# ) ;

9.1.4 VAR HEAVY_REDPART VIEW
          RPX WHERE RPX.WT > WEIGHT ( 12.0 ) ;
```

RPX here is a range variable that ranges over REDPART.

```
9.2   VAR NON_COLOCATED VIEW
      ( S TIMES P ) { S#, P# } MINUS
      ( S JOIN  P ) { S#, P# } ;

9.3   VAR LONDON_SUPPLIER VIEW
      ( S WHERE CITY = 'London' ) { ALL BUT CITY } ;
```

Note: We omit the CITY attribute here because we know its value must be London for every supplier in the view. Observe, however, that this omission means that any INSERT on the view will necessarily fail (unless the default value for attribute CITY in the underlying suppliers relvar happens to be London). In other words, a view like this one probably cannot support INSERT operations at all. (Alternatively, we might consider the possibility of defining the default value for CITY *for tuples inserted via this view* to be London. This idea of **view-specific defaults** requires more study.)

9.4 The question here is: How should attribute QTY be defined in the SP view? The sensible answer seems to be that, for a given S#-P# pair, it should be the *sum* of all SPJ.QTY values, taken over all J#'s for that S#-P# pair:

```
VAR SP VIEW
    SUMMARIZE SPJ PER SPJ { S#, P# }
                   ADD SUM ( QTY ) AS QTY ;

9.5   VAR JC VIEW
      ( ( SPJ WHERE S# = S# ( 'S1' ) ) { J# } JOIN
        ( SPJ WHERE P# = P# ( 'P1' ) ) { J# } ) JOIN
                                      J { J#, CITY } ;
```

9.6 We do not show the converted forms. However, we remark that e. will fail, because the tuple presented for insertion does not satisfy the predicate for the view.

9.7 Again e. fails, though for a slightly different reason this time. First, the DBMS will provide a default WEIGHT value, w say, since the user has not provided a "real" WEIGHT value (and cannot do so, of course). Second, it is extremely unlikely that whatever WT value the user does provide will be equal to $w * 454$—even if (as is not the case in the INSERT shown) that particular WT value happens to be greater than 14.0. Thus, the tuple presented for insertion again does not satisfy the predicate for the view.

Note: It could be argued that the WEIGHT value in the new tuple should properly be set to the specified WT value *divided* by 454. This possibility requires more study.

9.8 The following list of reasons is taken from reference [5.7]:

- If users are to interact with views instead of base relvars, then it is clear that those views should look to the user as much like base relvars as possible. Ideally, in fact, the user should not even have to know they are views, but should be able to treat them as if they actually were base relvars, thanks to *The Principle of Database Relativity*. And just as the user of a base relvar needs to know what candidate keys that base relvar has (in general), so the user of a view needs to know what candidate keys that view has (again, in general). Explicitly declaring those keys is the obvious way to make that information available.

- The DBMS might not be able to deduce candidate keys for itself (such is certainly the case with every DBMS on the market today). Explicit declarations are thus likely to be the only means available (to the DBA, that is) of informing the DBMS—as well as the user—of the existence of such keys.

- Even if the DBMS were able to deduce candidate keys for itself, explicit declarations would at least enable the system to check that its deductions and the DBA's explicit specifications were not inconsistent.

- The DBA might have some knowledge that the DBMS does not, and might thus be able to improve on the DBMS's deductions. Reference [5.7] gives an example of this possibility.

And reference [11.3] offers another reason, which is essentially that such a facility would provide a simple and convenient way of stating certain important integrity constraints that otherwise could be stated only in a very circumlocutory fashion.

9.9 It is obviously impossible to provide a definitive answer to this question. We offer the following observations.

- Each view and each snapshot will have an entry in the catalog relvar RELVAR, with a RVKIND value of "View" or "Snapshot" as appropriate.

- Each view will also have an entry in a new catalog relvar, which we might as well call VIEW. That entry should include the relevant view-defining expression.

- Similarly, each snapshot will also have an entry in a new catalog relvar (SNAPSHOT). That entry should include the relevant defining expression. It should also include information regarding the snapshot refresh interval.

- Yet another catalog relvar will show which views and snapshots are defined in terms of which other relvars. Note that the structure of this relvar is somewhat similar to that of the PART_STRUCTURE relvar (see Fig. 4.6 in Chapter 4): Just as parts can contain other parts, so views and snapshots can be defined in terms of other views and snapshots. Note, therefore, that the points discussed in the answer to Exercise 7.7 in Chapter 7 are relevant here.

9.10 Yes!—but note the following. Suppose we replace the suppliers relvar S by two restrictions, SA and SB say, where SA is the suppliers in London and SB is the suppliers not in London. We can now define the union of SA and SB as a view called S. If we now try (through this view) to UPDATE a London supplier's city to something other than London, or a "nonLondon" supplier's city to London, the implementation must map that UPDATE to a DELETE on one of the two restrictions and an INSERT on the other. Now, the rules given in Section 9.4 do handle this case correctly—in fact, we (deliberately) *defined* UPDATE as a DELETE followed by an INSERT; however, there was a tacit assumption that the implementation would actually use an UPDATE, for efficiency reasons. This example shows that sometimes mapping an UPDATE to an UPDATE does not work; in fact, determining those cases in which it does work can be regarded as an optimization.

9.11 a. Yes!   b. Yes!

9.12 INSERT and DELETE will always be inverses of each other so long as (a) the database is designed in accordance with *The Principle of Orthogonal Design* (see Section 12.6 in Chapter 12) *and* (b) the DBMS supports relvar predicates properly. If these conditions are not satisfied, however, then it is possible that they might not be inverses of each other after all. For instance, if A and B are distinct base relvars, inserting tuple *t* into *V = A* INTERSECT *B* might cause *t* to be inserted into A only (because it is already present in B); subsequently deleting *t* from *V* will now cause *t* to be deleted from both A and B. (On the other hand, deleting *t* and then reinserting it will always preserve the *status quo*.) However, note carefully that such an asymmetry can arise only if *t* satisfies the predicate for A and yet is not present in A in the first place.

9.13 We offer the following comments. First, the replacement process itself involves several steps, which might be summarized as follows. (This sequence of operations will be refined in a moment.)

```
/* define the new base relvars */

VAR SNC BASE RELATION
      { S# S#, SNAME NAME, CITY CHAR }
        PRIMARY KEY { S# } ;

VAR ST BASE RELATION
      { S# S#, STATUS INTEGER }
        PRIMARY KEY { S# } ;

/* copy the data to the new base relvars */

INSERT INTO SNC S { S#, SNAME, CITY } ;

INSERT INTO ST  S { S#, STATUS } ;

/* drop the old relvar */

DROP VAR S ;
```

Now we can create the desired view:

```
VAR S VIEW
      SNC JOIN ST ;
```

We now observe that each of the two S# attributes (in SNC and ST) constitutes a foreign key that references the other. Indeed, there is a strict one-to-one relationship between relvars SNC and ST, and so we run into a variety of "one-to-one" difficulties that have been discussed in some detail by this writer elsewhere [13.7].

Note also that we must do something about the foreign key in relvar SP that references the old base relvar S. It would be nice if that foreign key could now be taken as referring to the view S instead; if this is not possible (as indeed it is typically not in today's products), then it would be better to add a third projection of base relvar S to the database, as follows:

```
VAR SS BASE RELATION
      { S# S# } PRIMARY KEY { S# } ;

INSERT INTO SS S { S# } ;
```

(In fact, this design is recommended in reference [8.10] for other reasons anyway.) We now change the definition of view S thus:

```
VAR S VIEW S
      SS JOIN SNC JOIN ST ;
```

We also add the following foreign key specification to the definitions of relvars SNC and ST:

```
FOREIGN KEY { S# } REFERENCES SS
               ON DELETE CASCADE
               ON UPDATE CASCADE
```

Finally, we must change the specification for the foreign key {S#} in relvar SP to refer to SS instead of S.

Note: The idea of allowing a foreign key to reference a view instead of a base relvar requires further study.

9.14 Regarding part a. of this exercise, here is one example of a view retrieval that certainly does fail in certain SQL products at the time of writing. Consider the following SQL view definition (Example 3 from Section 9.6):

```
CREATE VIEW PQ AS
       SELECT SP.P#, SUM ( SP.QTY ) AS TOTQTY
       FROM   SP
       GROUP  BY SP.P# ;
```

Consider also the following attempted query:

```
SELECT AVG ( PQ.TOTQTY ) AS PT
FROM   PQ ;
```

If we follow the simple substitution process explained in the body of the chapter (i.e., we try to replace references to the view name by the expression that defines the view), we obtain something like the following:

```
SELECT AVG ( SUM ( SP.QTY ) ) AS PT
FROM   SP
GROUP  BY SP.P# ;
```

And this is not a valid SELECT statement, because (as noted in the discussion following Example 7.7.7 in Chapter 7) SQL does not allow aggregate operators to be nested in this fashion.

Here is another example of a query against the same view PQ that also fails in certain products for much the same reason:

```
SELECT PQ.P#
FROM   PQ
WHERE  PQ.TOTQTY > 500 ;
```

Precisely because of the problem illustrated by these examples, incidentally, certain products—IBM's DB2 is a case in point—sometimes physically materialize the view (instead of applying the more usual substitution procedure) and then execute the query against that materialized version. This technique will always work, of course, but it is liable to incur a performance penalty. Moreover, in the case of DB2 in particular, it is still the case that some retrievals on some views do not work; i.e., DB2 does not *always* use materialization if substitution does not work, nor is it easy to say exactly which cases work and which do not. For instance, the second of the two examples given above still fails in DB2 at the time of writing. See reference [4.20] for further discussion.

9.15 First, here is a definition of Design b. in terms of Design a.:

```
VAR SSP VIEW
    S JOIN SP ;

VAR XSS VIEW
    S MINUS ( S JOIN SP ) { S#, SNAME, STATUS, CITY } ;
```

And here is a definition of Design a. in terms of Design b.:

```
VAR S VIEW
    XSS UNION SSP { S#, SNAME, STATUS, CITY } ;

VAR SP VIEW
    SSP { S#, P#, QTY } ;
```

The applicable database constraints for the two designs can be stated as follows:

```
CONSTRAINT DESIGN_A
    IS_EMPTY ( SP { S# } MINUS S { S# } ) ;

CONSTRAINT DESIGN_B
    IS_EMPTY ( SSP { S# } INTERSECT XSS { S# } ) ;
```

(Observe that constraint DESIGN_A here exemplifies another way of formulating a referential constraint.)

Design a. is clearly superior, for reasons discussed in detail in Chapter 11.

9.16 We have numbered the following solutions as 9.16.*n,* where *n* is the number of the original exercise.

9.16.2 CREATE VIEW NON_COLOCATED
```
        AS SELECT S.S#, P.P#
           FROM   S, P
           WHERE  S.CITY <> P.CITY ;
```

9.16.3 CREATE VIEW LONDON_SUPPLIER
```
        AS SELECT S.S#, S.SNAME, S.STATUS
           FROM   S
           WHERE  S.CITY = 'London' ;
```

9.16.4 CREATE VIEW SP
```
        AS SELECT SPJ.S#, SPJ.P#, SUM ( SPJ.QTY ) AS QTY
           FROM   SPJ
           GROUP  BY SPJ.S#, SPJ.P# ;
```

9.16.5 CREATE VIEW JC
```
        AS SELECT J.J#, J.CITY
           FROM   J
           WHERE  J.J# IN ( SELECT SPJ.J#
                            FROM    SPJ
                            WHERE   SPJ.S# = 'S1' )
           AND    J.J# IN ( SELECT SPJ.J#
                            FROM    SPJ
                            WHERE   SPJ.P# = 'P1' ) ;
```

DATABASE DESIGN

This part of the book is concerned with the general subject of database design (more specifically, *relational* database design). The database design problem can be stated very simply: Given some body of data to be represented in a database, how do we decide on a suitable logical structure for that data?—in other words, how do we decide what relvars should exist and what attributes they should have? The practical significance of this problem is obvious.

Before we start getting into details, a number of preliminary remarks are in order:

- First, note that we are concerned here with *logical* (or *conceptual*) design only, not physical design. Of course, we are not suggesting that physical design is not important—on the contrary, physical design is very important. However:

  a. Physical design can be treated as a separate, follow-on activity. In other words, the "right" way to do database design is to do a clean logical (i.e., relational) design first, and then, as a separate and subsequent step, to map that logical design into whatever physical structures the target DBMS happens to support. (In other words, as noted in Chapter 2, the physical design should be derived from the logical design, not the other way around.)

  b. Physical design, by definition, tends to be somewhat DBMS-specific, and as a topic is thus not appropriate for a general textbook such as this one. Logical design, by contrast, is or should be quite DBMS-independent, and there are some solid theoretical principles that can be applied to the problem. And, of course, such principles definitely do have a place in a book of this nature.

Unfortunately we live in an imperfect world, and in practice it might be the case that design decisions made at the physical level will have an impact back on the logical level (precisely because of the point, noted several times in this book already, that today's DBMS products typically support only rather simple mappings between the logical and physical levels). In other words, several iterations might have to be made over the "logical-then-physical" design cycle, and compromises might have to be made. Nevertheless, we stand by our original contention that the right way to do database design is to get the logical design right first, without paying any attention whatsoever to that stage to physical—i.e., performance—considerations. Thus, this part of the book is primarily concerned with what is involved in "getting the logical design right first."

- Although (as already stated) we are concerned primarily with *relational* design, it is our firm belief that the ideas to be discussed are relevant to the design of nonrelational databases also. In other words, we believe the right way to do database design in a nonrelational system is to do a clean relational design first, and then, as a separate and subsequent step, to map that relational design into whatever nonrelational structures (e.g., hierarchies) the target DBMS happens to support.

- Having said all of the above, we must now also say that database design is still very much an art, not a science. There *are* (to repeat) some scientific principles that can be brought to bear on the problem, and those principles are the subject of the next three chapters; however, there are many, many design issues that those principles simply do not address at all. As a consequence, numerous database theoreticians and practitioners have proposed design methodologies*—some of them fairly rigorous, others less so, but all of them *ad hoc* to a degree—that can be used as an attack on what at the time of writing is still a rather intractable problem, *viz.,* the problem of finding "the" logical design that is incontestably the right one. Since those methodologies are mostly *ad hoc* to some degree, there can be few objective criteria for preferring any given approach over all the rest; nevertheless, we present in Chapter 13 a well-known approach that does at least have the merit of being widely used in practice. We also briefly consider a number of other commercially supported approaches in that chapter.

- We should also state explicitly a couple of assumptions that underlie most of the discussions in this part of the book:

  a. Database design is not just a question of getting the data structures right—data integrity is a (perhaps *the*) key ingredient too. This remark will be repeated and amplified at many points in the chapters that follow.

  b. We will be concerned for the most part with what might be termed *application-independent* design. In other words, we are primarily concerned with what the data *is,* rather than how it will be *used.* Application independence in this sense is desirable for the very good reason that it is normally—perhaps always—the case that not all uses to which the data will be put are known at design time; thus, we want a design that will be *robust,* in the sense that it will not be invalidated by the advent of application requirements that were not foreseen at the time of the original design. To put this another way (and to use the terminology of Chapter 2), what we are trying to do, primarily, is *get the conceptual schema right;* i.e., we are interested in producing a hardware-independent, operating-system-independent, DBMS-independent, language-independent, user-independent—etc., etc.—abstract logical design. In particular, we are *not* interested in making compromises for performance reasons, as already explained.

---

*The term *methodology* originally meant the *study of methods,* but has come to be used to mean "a system of methods and rules applicable to research or work in a given science or art" (*Chambers Twentieth Century Dictionary*).

■ We stated above that the problem of database design is the problem of deciding what relvars should exist and what attributes they should have. In fact, of course, it involves the problem of deciding what *domains* or *types* should be defined too. We will have little to say on this topic, however, since little relevant work seems to have been done on it at the time of writing (references [13.11] and [13.39] are exceptions).

The structure of this part is as follows. Chapter 10 lays some theoretical groundwork. Chapters 11 and 12 are concerned with the ideas of *further normalization,* which build directly on that groundwork to give formal meaning to informal claims to the effect that certain designs are "better" than others in certain ways. Chapter 13 then discusses *semantic modeling;* in particular, it describes the concepts of "entity/relationship" modeling, and shows how those concepts can be used to tackle the design problem from the top down (starting with real-world entities and ending up with a formal relational design).

Functional Dependencies

10.1 INTRODUCTION

In this chapter, we examine a concept that has been characterized as "not quite fundamental, but very nearly so" [10.7]—*viz.,* the concept of **functional dependence.** This concept turns out to be crucially important to a number of issues to be discussed in later chapters, including in particular the database design theory described in Chapter 11.

Basically, a functional dependency (FD for short) is *a many-to-one relationship* from one set of attributes to another within a given relvar. In the case of the shipments relvar SP, for example, there is a functional dependency from the set of attributes {S#,P#} to the set of attributes {QTY}. What this means is that within any relation that happens to be a legal value for relvar SP:

a. For any given value for the pair of attributes S# and P#, there is just one corresponding value of attribute QTY, but

b. Many distinct values of the pair of attributes S# and P# can have the same corresponding value for attribute QTY (in general).

Note that our usual sample SP value (see Fig. 3.8) does satisfy both of these properties.

In Section 10.2, we define the concept of functional dependence more precisely, distinguishing carefully between those FDs that happen to be satisfied by a given relvar at some particular time and those that must be satisfied by that relvar at *all* times. As already mentioned, it turns out that FDs provide a basis for a scientific attack on a number of practical problems. And the reason they do so is because they possess a rich set of interesting formal properties, which make it possible to treat the problems in question in a formal and rigorous manner. Sections 10.3–10.6 explore some of those formal properties in detail and explain some of their practical consequences. Section 10.7 then presents a brief summary.

Note: You might like to skip portions of this chapter on a first reading. Indeed, most of what you need in order to understand the material of the next three chapters is covered in Sections 10.2 and 10.3. You might therefore prefer to give the remaining sections a "once over lightly" reading for now, and come back to them later when you have assimilated the material of the next three chapters.

A small point regarding terminology: The terms functional **dependence** and functional **dependency** are used interchangeably in the literature. Normal English usage would suggest that the term "dependence" be used for the FD concept *per se* and would reserve the term "dependency" for "the object that depends." But we very frequently need to refer to FDs in the plural, and "dependencies" seems to trip off the tongue more readily than "dependences"; hence our use of both terms.

10.2   BASIC DEFINITIONS

In order to illustrate the ideas of the present section, we make use of a slightly revised version of the shipments relvar, one that includes, in addition to the usual attributes S#, P#, and QTY, an attribute CITY, representing the city for the relevant supplier. We will refer to this revised relvar as SCP to avoid confusion. A possible value for relvar SCP is shown in Fig. 10.1.

SCP	S#	CITY	P#	QTY
	S1	London	P1	100
	S1	London	P2	100
	S2	Paris	P1	200
	S2	Paris	P2	200
	S3	Paris	P2	300
	S4	London	P2	400
	S4	London	P4	400
	S4	London	P5	400

Fig. 10.1   Sample value for relvar SCP

Now, it is very important in this area—as in so many others!—to distinguish clearly between (a) the value of a given relvar at a given point in time and (b) the *set of all possible values* that the given relvar might assume at different times. In what follows, we will first define the concept of functional dependence as it applies to Case (a), and then extend it to apply to Case (b). Here then is the definition for Case (a):

- Let r be a relation, and let X and Y be arbitrary subsets of the set of attributes of r. Then we say that Y is **functionally dependent** on X—in symbols,

$$X \rightarrow Y$$

(read "X **functionally determines** Y," or simply "X arrow Y")—if and only if each X value in r has associated with it precisely one Y value in r. In other words, whenever two tuples of r agree on their X value, they also agree on their Y value.

For example, the relation shown in Fig. 10.1 satisfies the FD

$$\{ S\# \} \rightarrow \{ CITY \}$$

because every tuple of that relation with a given S# value also has the same CITY value. Indeed, it also satisfies several more FDs, the following among them:

```
{ S#, P# } → { QTY }
{ S#, P# } → { CITY }
{ S#, P# } → { CITY, QTY }
{ S#, P# } → { S# }
{ S#, P# } → { S#, P#, CITY, QTY }
{ S# }     → { QTY }
{ QTY }    → { S# }
```

(*Exercise:* Check these.)

The left- and right-hand sides of an FD are sometimes called the **determinant** and the **dependent,** respectively. As the definition indicates, the determinant and dependent are both *sets* of attributes. When such a set contains just one attribute, however—i.e., when it is a **singleton set**—we often drop the set braces and write just, e.g.,

```
S# → CITY
```

As already explained, the foregoing definitions apply to "Case (a)"—i.e., to individual relation *values.* However, when we consider relation *variables* (i.e., relvars)—in particular, when we consider *base* relvars—we are usually interested not so much in the FDs that happen to hold for the particular value that the relvar happens to have at some particular time, but rather in those FDs that hold for *all possible values* of that relvar. In the case of SCP, for example, the FD

```
S# → CITY
```

holds for all possible values of SCP, because, at any given time, a given supplier has precisely one corresponding city, and so any two tuples appearing in SCP at the same time with the same supplier number must necessarily have the same city as well. Indeed, the fact that this FD holds "for all time" (i.e., for all possible values of SCP) is an *integrity constraint* on relvar SCP—it places limits on the values that relvar SCP can legitimately assume. Here is a formulation of that constraint using the syntax of Chapter 8:

```
CONSTRAINT S#_CITY_FD
   COUNT ( SCP { S# } ) = COUNT ( SCP { S#, CITY } ) ;
```

The syntax S# → CITY can be regarded as shorthand for this longer formulation.

Here then is the "Case (b)" definition of functional dependence (the extensions over the Case (a) definition are shown in **boldface**):

- Let *R* be a relation **variable,** and let *X* and *Y* be arbitrary subsets of the set of attributes of *R.* Then we say that *Y* is functionally dependent on *X*—in symbols,

```
X → Y
```

(read "*X* functionally determines *Y,*" or simply "*X* arrow *Y*")—if and only if, **in every possible legal value of *R*,** each *X* value has associated with it precisely one *Y* value. In other words, **in every possible legal value of *R*,** whenever two tuples agree on their *X* value, they also agree on their *Y* value.

Henceforth, we will use the term "functional dependence" in this latter, more demanding, and *time-independent* sense, barring explicit statements to the contrary.

Here then are some (time-independent) FDs that apply to relvar SCP:

```
{ S#, P# }  →  QTY
{ S#, P# }  →  CITY
{ S#, P# }  →  { CITY, QTY }
{ S#, P# }  →  S#
{ S#, P# }  →  { S#, P#, CITY, QTY }
{ S# }      →  CITY
```

Notice in particular that the following FDs, which do happen to hold for the relation value shown in Fig. 10.1, do *not* hold "for all time" for relvar SCP:

```
S#   →  QTY
QTY  →  S#
```

In other words, the statement that (e.g.) "every shipment for a given supplier has the same quantity" does happen to be true for the particular SCP relation value shown in Fig. 10.1, but it is not true for all possible legal values of the SCP relvar.

We now observe that if *X* is a candidate key of relvar *R,* then all attributes *Y* of relvar *R* must be functionally dependent on *X.* (We mentioned this fact in passing in Section 8.8. It follows from the definition of candidate key.) For the parts relvar P, for example, we necessarily have:

```
P#  →  { P#, PNAME, COLOR, WEIGHT, CITY }
```

In fact, if relvar *R* satisfies the FD *A → B* and *A* is *not* a candidate key,* then *R* will involve some **redundancy.** In the case of relvar SCP, for example, the FD S# → CITY implies that the fact that a given supplier is located in a given city will appear many times, in general (see Fig. 10.1 for an illustration). We will take up this point and discuss it in detail in the next chapter.

Now, even if we restrict our attention to FDs that hold for all time, the complete set of FDs for a given relvar can still be very large, as the SCP example suggests. (*Exercise:* State the complete set of FDs satisfied by relvar SCP.) What we would like is to find some way of reducing that set to a manageable size—and, indeed, most of the remainder of this chapter is concerned with exactly this issue.

Why is this objective desirable? One reason is that (as already stated) FDs represent integrity constraints, and the DBMS thus needs to enforce them. Given a particular set *S* of FDs, therefore, it is desirable to find some other set *T* that is (ideally) much smaller than *S* and has the property that every FD in *S* is implied by the FDs in *T.* If such a set *T* can be found, it is sufficient that the DBMS enforce just the FDs in *T,* and the FDs in *S* will then be enforced automatically. The problem of finding such a set *T* is thus of considerable practical interest.

---

*And the FD is not *trivial* (see Section 10.3) and *A* is not a *superkey* (see Section 10.5) and *R* contains at least two tuples.

10.3   TRIVIAL AND NONTRIVIAL DEPENDENCIES

Note: In the remainder of this chapter, we will occasionally abbreviate "functional depen-dency" to just "dependency." Similarly for "functionally dependent on," "functionally de-termines," etc.

One obvious way to reduce the size of the set of FDs we need to deal with is to elimi-nate the *trivial* dependencies. A dependency is "trivial" if it cannot possibly not be satis-fied. Just one of the FDs shown for relvar SCP in the previous section was trivial in this sense, *viz.* the FD

```
{ S#, P# } → S#
```

In fact, an FD is **trivial** if and only if the right-hand side is a subset (not necessarily a proper subset) of the left-hand side.

As the name implies, trivial dependencies are not very interesting in practice; we are usually more interested in practice in **nontrivial** dependencies (which are, of course, pre-cisely the ones that are not trivial), because they are the ones that correspond to "genuine" integrity constraints. When we are dealing with the formal theory, however, we have to ac-count for *all* dependencies, trivial as well as nontrivial.

10.4   CLOSURE OF A SET OF DEPENDENCIES

We have already suggested that some FDs might imply others. As a simple example, the FD

```
{ S#, P# } → { CITY, QTY }
```

implies both of the following:

```
{ S#, P# } → CITY
{ S#, P# } → QTY
```

As a more complex example, suppose we have a relvar R with three attributes A, B, and C, such that the FDs $A \rightarrow B$ and $B \rightarrow C$ both hold for R. Then it is easy to see that the FD $A \rightarrow C$ also holds for R. The FD $A \rightarrow C$ here is an example of a **transitive** FD—C is said to depend on A *transitively*, via B.

The set of all FDs that are implied by a given set S of FDs is called the **closure** of S, written S^+. Clearly we need an algorithm that (at least in principle) will allow us to com-pute S^+ from S. The first attack on this problem appeared in a paper by Armstrong [10.1], which gave a set of **inference rules** (more usually called **Armstrong's axioms**) by which new FDs can be inferred from given ones. Those rules can be stated in a variety of equiva-lent ways, of which one of the simplest is as follows. Let A, B, and C be arbitrary subsets of the set of attributes of the given relvar R, and let us agree to write (e.g.) AB to mean the union of A and B. Then:

1. **Reflexivity:** If B is a subset of A, then $A \rightarrow B$.
2. **Augmentation:** If $A \rightarrow B$, then $AC \rightarrow BC$.
3. **Transitivity:** If $A \rightarrow B$ and $B \rightarrow C$, then $A \rightarrow C$.

Each of these three rules can be directly proved from the definition of functional dependency (the first is just the definition of a **trivial** dependency, of course). Moreover, the rules are **complete,** in the sense that, given a set S of FDs, all FDs implied by S can be derived from S using the rules. They are also **sound,** in the sense that no additional FDs (i.e., FDs not implied by S) can be so derived. In other words, the rules can be used to derive precisely the closure S^+.

Several further rules can be derived from the three given above, the following among them. These additional rules can be used to simplify the practical task of computing S^+ from S. (In what follows, D is another arbitrary subset of the set of attributes of R.)

4. **Self-determination:** $A \rightarrow A$.
5. **Decomposition:** If $A \rightarrow BC$, then $A \rightarrow B$ and $A \rightarrow C$.
6. **Union:** If $A \rightarrow B$ and $A \rightarrow C$, then $A \rightarrow BC$.
7. **Composition:** If $A \rightarrow B$ and $C \rightarrow D$, then $AC \rightarrow BD$.

And in reference [10.6], Darwen proves the following rule, which he calls the *General Unification Theorem:*

8. If $A \rightarrow B$ and $C \rightarrow D$, then $A \cup (C - B) \rightarrow BD$ (where "$\cup$" is union and "$-$" is set difference).

The name "General Unification Theorem" refers to the fact that several of the earlier rules can be seen as special cases [10.6].

Example: Suppose we are given relvar R with attributes A, B, C, D, E, F, and the FDs

```
A  → BC
B  → E
CD → EF
```

Observe that we are extending our notation slightly, though not incompatibly, by writing, e.g., BC for the set consisting of attributes B and C (previously BC would have meant the *union* of B and C, where B and C were *sets* of attributes). *Note:* If you would prefer a more concrete example, take A as employee number, B as department number, C as manager's employee number, D as project number for a project directed by that manager (unique within manager), E as department name, and F as percentage of time allocated by the specified manager to the specified project.

We now show that the FD $AD \rightarrow F$ holds for R and is thus a member of the closure of the given set:

1. $A \rightarrow BC$ (given)
2. $A \rightarrow C$ (1, decomposition)
3. $AD \rightarrow CD$ (2, augmentation)
4. $CD \rightarrow EF$ (given)
5. $AD \rightarrow EF$ (3 and 4, transitivity)
6. $AD \rightarrow F$ (5, decomposition)   ∎

10.5 CLOSURE OF A SET OF ATTRIBUTES

In principle, we can compute the closure S^+ of a given set S of FDs by means of an algorithm that says "Repeatedly apply the rules from the previous section until they stop producing new FDs." In practice, there is little need to compute the closure *per se* (which is just as well, because the algorithm just mentioned is hardly very efficient). In this section, however, we will show how to compute a certain subset of the closure: namely, that subset consisting of all FDs with a certain (specified) set Z of attributes as the left-hand side. More precisely, we will show how, given a relvar R, a set Z of attributes of R, and a set S of FDs that hold for R, we can determine the set of all attributes of R that are functionally dependent on Z—the so-called **closure Z^+ of Z under S.*** A simple algorithm for computing that closure is given in Fig. 10.2. *Exercise:* Prove that algorithm is correct.

```
CLOSURE[Z,S] := Z ;
do "forever" ;
    for each FD X → Y in S
        do ;
            if X ≤ CLOSURE[Z,S]              /* ≤ = "subset of" */
            then CLOSURE[Z,S] := CLOSURE[Z,S] ∪ Y ;
        end ;
    if CLOSURE[Z,S] did not change on this iteration
    then leave loop ;               /* computation complete */
end ;
```

Fig. 10.2   Computing the closure Z^+ of Z under S

Example: Suppose we are given relvar R with attributes A, B, C, D, E, F, and FDs

$$
\begin{aligned}
A &\rightarrow BC \\
E &\rightarrow CF \\
B &\rightarrow E \\
CD &\rightarrow EF
\end{aligned}
$$

---

*The set of FDs with Z as the left-hand side is the set consisting of all FDs of the form $Z \rightarrow Z'$, where Z' is some subset of Z^+. The closure S^+ of the original set S is then the union of all such sets of FDs, taken over all possible attribute sets Z.

We now compute the closure $\{A,B\}^+$ of the set of attributes $\{A,B\}$ under this set of FDs.

1. We initialize the result CLOSURE[Z,S] to $\{A,B\}$.

2. We now go round the inner loop four times, once for each of the given FDs. On the first iteration (for the FD $A \rightarrow BC$), we find that the left-hand side is indeed a subset of CLOSURE[Z,S] as computed so far, so we add attributes (B and) C to the result. CLOSURE[Z,S] is now the set $\{A,B,C\}$.

3. On the second iteration (for the FD $E \rightarrow CF$), we find that the left-hand side is *not* a subset of the result as computed so far, which thus remains unchanged.

4. On the third iteration (for the FD $B \rightarrow E$), we add E to to CLOSURE[Z,S], which now has the value $\{A,B,C,E\}$.

5. On the fourth iteration (for the FD $CD \rightarrow EF$), CLOSURE[Z,S] remains unchanged.

6. Now we go round the inner loop four times again. On the first iteration, the result does not change; on the second, it expands to $\{A,B,C,E,F\}$; on the third and fourth, it does not change.

7. Now we go round the inner loop four times again. CLOSURE[Z,S] does not change, and so the whole process terminates, with $\{A,B\}^+ = \{A,B,C,E,F\}$. ∎

An important corollary of the foregoing is as follows: Given a set S of FDs, we can easily tell whether a specific FD $X \rightarrow Y$ follows from S, because that FD will follow if and only if Y is a subset of the closure X^+ of X under S. In other words, we now have a simple way of determining whether a given FD $X \rightarrow Y$ is in the closure S^+ of S, without actually having to compute that closure S^+.

Another important corollary is the following. Recall from Chapter 8 that a **superkey** for a relvar R is a set of attributes of R that includes some candidate key of R as a subset—not necessarily a proper subset, of course. Now, it follows immediately from the definition that the superkeys for a given relvar R are precisely those subsets K of the attributes of R such that the FD

$K \rightarrow A$

holds true for every attribute A of R. In other words, K is a superkey if and only if the closure K^+ of K—under the given set of FDs—is precisely the set of all attributes of R (and K is a *candidate* key if and only if it is an irreducible superkey).

10.6 IRREDUCIBLE SETS OF DEPENDENCIES

Let $S1$ and $S2$ be two sets of FDs. If every FD implied by $S1$ is implied by $S2$—i.e., if $S1^+$ is a subset of $S2^+$—we say that $S2$ is a **cover** for $S1$.* What this means is that if the DBMS enforces the FDs in $S2$, then it will automatically be enforcing the FDs in $S1$.

---

*Some writers use the term "cover" to mean what we will be calling (in just a moment) an *equivalent* set.

Next, if S2 is a cover for *S1* and *S1* is a cover for S2—i.e., if $S1^+ = S2^+$—we say that *S1* and *S2* are **equivalent.** Clearly, if *S1* and *S2* are equivalent, then if the DBMS enforces the FDs in S2 it will automatically be enforcing the FDs in *S1,* and *vice versa.*

Now we define a set *S* of FDs to be **irreducible*** if and only if it satisfies the following three properties:

1. The right-hand side (the dependent) of every FD in *S* involves just one attribute (i.e., it is a singleton set).

2. The left-hand side (the determinant) of every FD in *S* is irreducible in turn—meaning that no attribute can be discarded from the determinant without changing the closure S^+ (i.e., without converting *S* into some set not equivalent to *S*). We will say that such an FD is **left-irreducible.**

3. No FD in *S* can be discarded from *S* without changing the closure S^+ (i.e., without converting *S* into some set not equivalent to *S*).

With regard to points 2 and 3 here, by the way, note carefully that it is not necessary to know exactly what the closure S^+ *is* in order to tell whether it will be changed if something is discarded. For example, consider the familiar parts relvar P. The following FDs (among others) hold for that relvar:

```
P# → PNAME
P# → COLOR
P# → WEIGHT
P# → CITY
```

This set of FDs is easily seen to be irreducible: The right-hand side is a single attribute in each case, the left-hand side is obviously irreducible in turn, and none of the FDs can be discarded without changing the closure (i.e., without *losing some information*). By contrast, the following sets of FDs are not irreducible:

1. ```
   P# → { PNAME, COLOR }
   P# → WEIGHT
   P# → CITY
   ```
   : The right-hand side of the first FD here is not a singleton set

2. ```
   { P#, PNAME } → COLOR
   P# → PNAME
   P# → WEIGHT
   P# → CITY
   ```
   : The first FD here can be simplified by dropping PNAME from the left-hand side without changing the closure (i.e., it is not left-irreducible)

3. ```
   P# → P#
   P# → PNAME
   P# → COLOR
   P# → WEIGHT
   P# → CITY
   ```
   : The first FD here can be discarded without changing the closure

---

*Usually called *minimal* in the literature.
   ```

We now claim that for every set of FDs, there exists at least one equivalent set that is irreducible. In fact, this is easy to see. Let the original set of FDs be *S*. Thanks to the decomposition rule, we can assume without loss of generality that every FD in *S* has a singleton right-hand side. Next, for each FD *f* in *S*, we examine each attribute *A* in the left-hand side of *f*; if deleting *A* from the left-hand side of *f* has no effect on the closure S^+, we delete *A* from the left-hand side of *f*. Then, for each FD *f* remaining in *S*, if deleting *f* from *S* has no effect on the closure S^+, we delete *f* from *S*. The final set *S* is irreducible and is equivalent to the original set *S*.

Example: Suppose we are given relvar *R* with attributes *A, B, C, D,* and FDs

```
A  → BC
B  → C
A  → B
AB → C
AC → D
```

We now compute an irreducible set of FDs that is equivalent to this given set.

1. The first step is to rewrite the FDs such that each has a singleton right-hand side:

```
A  → B
A  → C
B  → C
A  → B
AB → C
AC → D
```

   We observe immediately that the FD $A \rightarrow B$ occurs twice, so one occurrence can be eliminated.

2. Next, attribute *C* can be eliminated from the left-hand side of the FD $AC \rightarrow D$, because we have $A \rightarrow C$, so $A \rightarrow AC$ by augmentation, and we are given $AC \rightarrow D$, so $A \rightarrow D$ by transitivity; thus the *C* on the left-hand side of $AC \rightarrow D$ is redundant.

3. Next, we observe that the FD $AB \rightarrow C$ can be eliminated, because again we have $A \rightarrow C$, so $AB \rightarrow CB$ by augmentation, so $AB \rightarrow C$ by decomposition.

4. Finally, the FD $A \rightarrow C$ is implied by the FDs $A \rightarrow B$ and $B \rightarrow C$, so it can also be eliminated. We are left with:

```
A → B
B → C
A → D
```

   This set is irreducible.   ■

A set *I* of FDs that is irreducible and equivalent to some other set *S* of FDs is said to be an **irreducible equivalent** to *S*. Thus, given some particular set *S* of FDs that need to be enforced, it is sufficient for the system to find and enforce the FDs in an irreducible equivalent *I* instead (and, to repeat, there is no need to compute the closure S^+ in order to compute an irreducible equivalent *I*). We should make it clear, however, that a given set of FDs does not necessarily have a *unique* irreducible equivalent (see Exercise 10.12).

10.7 SUMMARY

A **functional dependency** (FD) is a many-to-one relationship between two sets of attributes of a given relvar. Given a relvar R, the FD $A \rightarrow B$ (where A and B are subsets of the set of attributes of R) is said to hold for R if and only if, whenever two tuples of R have the same value for A, they also have the same value for B. Every relvar necessarily satisfies certain **trivial** FDs; an FD is trivial if and only if the right-hand side (the **dependent**) is a subset of the left-hand side (the **determinant**).

Certain FDs imply others. Given a set S of FDs, the **closure** S^+ of that set is the set of all FDs implied by the FDs in S. S^+ is necessarily a superset of S. **Armstrong's inference rules** provide a **sound** and **complete** basis for computing S^+ from S (usually, however, we do not actually perform that computation). Several other useful rules can easily be derived from Armstrong's rules.

Given a subset Z of the set of attributes of relvar R and a set S of FDs that hold for R, the **closure** Z^+ of Z under S is the set of all attributes A of R such that the FD $Z \rightarrow A$ is a member of S^+. If Z^+ consists of all attributes of R, Z is said to be a **superkey** for R (and a **candidate key** is an irreducible superkey). We gave a simple algorithm for computing Z^+ from Z and S, and hence a simple way of determining whether a given FD $X \rightarrow Y$ is a member of S^+ ($X \rightarrow Y$ is a member of S^+ if and only if Y is a subset of X^+).

Two sets of FDs $S1$ and $S2$ are **equivalent** if and only if they are **covers** for each other, i.e., if and only if $S1^+ = S2^+$. Every set of FDs is equivalent to at least one **irreducible** set. A set of FDs is irreducible if (a) every FD in the set has a singleton right-hand side, (b) no FD in the set can be discarded without changing the closure of the set, and (c) no attribute can be discarded from the left-hand side of any FD in the set without changing the closure of the set. If I is an irreducible set equivalent to S, enforcing the FDs in I will automatically enforce the FDs in S.

In conclusion, we note that many of the foregoing ideas can be extended to integrity constraints in general, not just to FDs. For example, it is true in general that:

- Certain constraints are trivial;
- Certain constraints imply others;
- The set of all constraints implied by a given set can be regarded as the closure of the given set;
- The question of whether a specific constraint is in a certain closure—i.e., whether the specific constraint is implied by certain given constraints—is an interesting practical problem;
- The question of finding an irreducible equivalent for a given set of constraints is an interesting practical problem.

What makes FDs in particular much more tractable than integrity constraints in general is the existence of a sound and complete set of inference rules for FDs. The "References and Bibliography" sections in this chapter and in Chapter 12 give references to papers describing several other specific kinds of constraints—"MVDs," "JDs," and "INDs"—for which such sets of inference rules also exist. In this book, however, we choose not to give those other kinds of constraints so extensive and so formal a treatment as we have just given FDs.

EXERCISES

10.1 Let *R* be a relvar of degree *n*. What is the maximum number of functional dependencies *R* can possibly satisfy (trivial as well as nontrivial)?

10.2 What does it mean to say that Armstrong's inference rules are sound? Complete?

10.3 Prove the *reflexivity, augmentation,* and *transitivity* rules, assuming only the basic definition of functional dependence.

10.4 Prove that the three rules of the previous exercise imply the *self-determination, decomposition, union,* and *composition* rules.

10.5 Prove Darwen's "General Unification Theorem." Which of the rules of the previous two exercises did you use? Which rules can be derived as special cases of the theorem?

10.6 Define (a) the closure of a set of FDs; (b) the closure of a set of attributes under a set of FDs.

10.7 List all of the FDs satisfied by the shipments relvar SP.

10.8 Relvar $R\{A,B,C,D,E,F,G\}$ satisfies the following FDs:

```
A    → B
BC   → DE
AEF  → G
```

Compute the closure $\{A,C\}^+$ under this set of FDs. Is the FD $ACF \rightarrow DG$ implied by this set?

10.9 What does it mean to say that two sets *S1* and *S2* of FDs are equivalent?

10.10 What does it mean to say that a set of FDs is irreducible?

10.11 Here are two sets of FDs for a relvar $R\{A,B,C,D,E\}$. Are they equivalent?

```
1.  A → B     AB → C     D → AC     D → E
2.  A → BC    D → AE
```

10.12 Relvar $R\{A,B,C,D,E,F\}$ satisfies the following FDs:

```
AB   → C
C    → A
BC   → D
ACD  → B
BE   → C
CE   → FA
CF   → BD
D    → EF
```

Find an irreducible equivalent for this set of FDs.

10.13 A relvar TIMETABLE is defined with the following attributes:

D   Day of the week (1 to 5)
P   Period within day (1 to 8)
C   Classroom number

T   Teacher name

L   Lesson name

The tuple $\{D:d,P:p,C:c,T:t,L:l\}$ appears in this relvar if and only if at time $\{D:d,P:p\}$ lesson l is taught by teacher t in classroom c. You can assume that lessons are one period in duration and that every lesson has a name that is unique with respect to all lessons taught in the week. What functional dependencies hold in this relvar? What are the candidate keys?

10.14 A relvar NADDR is defined with attributes NAME (unique), STREET, CITY, STATE, and ZIP. For any given zipcode, there is just one city and state. Also, for any given street, city, and state, there is just one zipcode. Give an irreducible set of FDs for this relvar. What are the candidate keys?

10.15 Relvar $R\{A,B,C,D,E,F,G,H,I,J\}$ satisfies the following FDs:

$$ABD \rightarrow E$$
$$AB \rightarrow G$$
$$B \rightarrow F$$
$$C \rightarrow J$$
$$CJ \rightarrow I$$
$$G \rightarrow H$$

Is this an irreducible set? What are the candidate keys?

REFERENCES AND BIBLIOGRAPHY

10.1 W. W. Armstrong: "Dependency Structures of Data Base Relationships," Proc. IFIP Congress, Stockholm, Sweden (1974).

> The paper that first formalized the theory of FDs (it is the source of "Armstrong's axioms"). The paper also gives a precise characterization of candidate keys.

10.2 Marco A. Casanova, Ronald Fagin, and Christos H. Papadimitriou: "Inclusion Dependencies and Their Interaction with Functional Dependencies," Proc. 1st ACM SIGACT-SIGMOD Symposium on Principles of Database Systems, Los Angeles, Calif. (March 1982).

> **Inclusion dependencies** (INDs) can be regarded as a generalization of referential constraints. For example, the IND
>
> `SP.S# ─► S.S#`
>
> (not the notation used in the paper) states that the set of values appearing in attribute S# of relvar SP must be a subset of the set of values appearing in attribute S# of relvar S. This particular example in fact *is* a referential constraint, of course; in general, however, there is no requirement for an IND that the left-hand side be a foreign key or the right-hand side a candidate key. *Note:* INDs do have some points in common with FDs, since both represent many-to-one relationships; however, INDs usually span relvars, while FDs do not.
>
>   The paper provides a sound and complete set of inference rules for INDs, which we may state (a little loosely) as follows:
>
> 1. A ─► A.
> 2. If AB ─► CD, then A ─► C and B ─► D.
> 3. If A ─► B and B ─► C, then A ─► C.

10.3 R. G. Casey and C. Delobel: "Decomposition of a Data Base and the Theory of Boolean Switching Functions," *IBM J. R&D 17,* No. 5 (September 1973).

This paper shows that for any given relvar, the set of FDs (called *functional relations* in this paper) satisfied by that relvar can be represented by a "boolean switching function." Moreover, that function is unique in the following sense: The original FDs can be specified in many superficially different (but actually equivalent) ways, each giving rise to a superficially different boolean function—but all such functions can be reduced by the laws of boolean algebra to the same canonical form. The problem of *decomposing* the original relvar (i.e., in a nonloss way—see Chapter 11) is then shown to be logically equivalent to the well-understood boolean algebra problem of finding "a covering set of prime implicants" for the boolean function corresponding to that relvar together with its FDs. Hence the original problem can be transformed into an equivalent problem in boolean algebra, and well-known techniques can be brought to bear on it.

This paper was the first of several to draw parallels between dependency theory and other disciplines. See, for example, reference [10.8] below, also several of the references in Chapter 12.

10.4 E. F. Codd: "Further Normalization of the Data Base Relational Model," in Randall J. Rustin (ed.), *Data Base Systems, Courant Computer Science Symposia Series 6.* Englewood Cliffs, N.J.: Prentice-Hall (1972).

The paper that first introduced the concept of functional dependence (apart from an early IBM internal memo). The "further normalization" of the title refers to the specific database design discipline discussed in Chapter 11; the purpose of the paper was, very specifically, to show the applicability of the ideas of functional dependence to the database design problem. (Indeed, FDs represented the first scientific attack on that problem.) However, the functional dependency idea has since shown itself to be of much wider applicability.

10.5 E. F. Codd: "Normalized Data Base Structure: A Brief Tutorial," Proc. 1971 ACM SIGFIDET Workshop on Data Description, Access, and Control, San Diego, Calif. (November 1971).

A tutorial introduction to the ideas of reference [10.4].

10.6 Hugh Darwen: "The Role of Functional Dependence in Query Decomposition," in C. J. Date and Hugh Darwen, *Relational Database Writings 1989–1991.* Reading, Mass.: Addison-Wesley (1992).

This paper gives a set of inference rules by which FDs holding for an arbitrary derived relvar can be inferred from those holding for the relvar(s) from which the relvar in question is derived. The set of FDs thus inferred can then be inspected to determine candidate keys for the derived relvar, thus providing the *candidate key* inference rules mentioned in passing (very briefly) in Chapters 8 and 9. The paper shows how these various rules can be used to provide significant improvements in DBMS performance, functionality, and usability.

10.7 Hugh Darwen: "OObservations [*sic*] of a Relational Bigot," presentation to BCS Special Interest Group on Formal Aspects of Computing Science, London, UK (December 21st, 1990).

10.8 R. Fagin: "Functional Dependencies in a Relational Database and Propositional Logic," *IBM J. R&D 21,* No. 6 (November 1977).

Shows that "Armstrong's axioms" [10.1] are strictly equivalent to the system of implicational statements in propositional logic. In other words, the paper defines a mapping between FDs and propositional statements, and then shows that a given FD *f* is a consequence of a given set S of FDs if and only if the proposition corresponding to *f* is a logical consequence of the set of propositions corresponding to *S*.

10.9 Claudio L. Lucchesi and Sylvia L. Osborn: "Candidate Keys for Relations," *J. Comp. and Sys. Sciences 17,* No. 2 (1978).

Presents an algorithm for finding all candidate keys for a given relvar, given the set of FDs that hold in that relvar.

ANSWERS TO SELECTED EXERCISES

10.1 An FD is basically a statement of the form $A \rightarrow B$ where A and B are each subsets of the set of attributes of R. Since a set of n elements has 2^n possible subsets, each of A and B has 2^n possible values, and hence an upper limit on the number of possible FDs is 2^{2n}.

10.5

1.	$A \rightarrow B$	(given)
2.	$C \rightarrow D$	(given)
3.	$A \rightarrow B \cap C$	(joint dependence, 1)
4.	$C - B \rightarrow C - B$	(self-determination)
5.	$A \cup (C - B) \rightarrow (B \cap C) \cup (C - B)$	(composition, 3, 4)
6.	$A \cup (C - B) \rightarrow C$	(simplifying 5)
7.	$A \cup (C - B) \rightarrow D$	(transitivity, 6, 2)
8.	$A \cup (C - B) \rightarrow B \cup D$	(composition, 1, 7)

This completes the proof. ■

The rules used in the proof are as indicated in the comments above. The following are all special cases of Darwen's theorem: union, transitivity, composition, and augmentation. So too is the following useful rule:

- If $A \rightarrow B$ and $AB \rightarrow C$, then $A \rightarrow C$.

10.7 The complete set of FDs—i.e., the closure—for relvar SP is as follows:

```
{ S#, P#, QTY } → { S#, P#, QTY }
{ S#, P#, QTY } → { S#, P# }
{ S#, P#, QTY } → { P#, QTY }
{ S#, P#, QTY } → { S#, QTY }
{ S#, P#, QTY } → { S# }
{ S#, P#, QTY } → { P# }
{ S#, P#, QTY } → { QTY }
{ S#, P#, QTY } → { }

{ S#, P# }      → { S#, P#, QTY }
{ S#, P# }      → { S#, P# }
{ S#, P# }      → { P#, QTY }
{ S#, P# }      → { S#, QTY }
{ S#, P# }      → { S# }
{ S#, P# }      → { P# }
{ S#, P# }      → { QTY }
{ S#, P# }      → { }
```

```
{ P#, QTY }        → { P#, QTY }
{ P#, QTY }        → { P# }
{ P#, QTY }        → { QTY }
{ P#, QTY }        → { }

{ S#, QTY }        → { S#, QTY }
{ S#, QTY }        → { S# }
{ S#, QTY }        → { QTY }
{ S#, QTY }        → { }

{ S# }             → { S# }
{ S# }             → { }

{ P# }             → { P# }
{ P# }             → { }

{ QTY }            → { QTY }
{ QTY }            → { }

{ }                → { }
```

10.8 $\{A,C\}^+ = \{A,B,C,D,E\}$. The answer to the second part of the question is yes.

10.11 They are equivalent. Let us number the FDs of the first set as follows:

1. $A \rightarrow B$
2. $AB \rightarrow C$
3. $D \rightarrow AC$
4. $D \rightarrow E$

First, 3 can be replaced by:

3. $D \rightarrow A$ and $D \rightarrow C$

Next, 1 and 2 together imply that 2 can be replaced by:

2. $A \rightarrow C$

But now we have $D \rightarrow A$ and $A \rightarrow C$, so $D \rightarrow C$ is implied (by transitivity) and so can be dropped, leaving:

3. $D \rightarrow A$

The first set of FDs is thus equivalent to the following irreducible set:

$A \rightarrow B$
$A \rightarrow C$
$D \rightarrow A$
$D \rightarrow E$

The second given set of FDs

$A \rightarrow BC$
$D \rightarrow AE$

is clearly also equivalent to this irreducible set. Thus, the two given sets are equivalent. ▮

10.12 The first step is to rewrite the given set such that every FD has a singleton right-hand side:

1. $AB \rightarrow C$
2. $C \rightarrow A$
3. $BC \rightarrow D$
4. $ACD \rightarrow B$
5. $BE \rightarrow C$
6. $CE \rightarrow A$
7. $CE \rightarrow F$
8. $CF \rightarrow B$
9. $CF \rightarrow D$
10. $D \rightarrow E$
11. $D \rightarrow F$

Now:

- 2 implies 6, so we can drop 6.
- 8 implies $CF \rightarrow BC$ (by augmentation), which with 3 implies $CF \rightarrow D$ (by transitivity), so we can drop 10.
- 8 implies $ACF \rightarrow AB$ (by augmentation), and 11 implies $ACD \rightarrow ACF$ (by augmentation), and so $ACD \rightarrow AB$ (by transitivity), and so $ACD \rightarrow B$ (by decomposition), so we can drop 4.

No further reductions are possible, and so we are left with the following irreducible set:

$$
\begin{aligned}
AB &\rightarrow C \\
C &\rightarrow A \\
BC &\rightarrow D \\
BE &\rightarrow C \\
CE &\rightarrow F \\
CF &\rightarrow B \\
D &\rightarrow E \\
D &\rightarrow F
\end{aligned}
$$

Alternatively:

- 2 implies $CD \rightarrow ACD$ (by composition), which with 4 implies $CD \rightarrow B$ (by transitivity), so we can replace 4 by $CD \rightarrow B$.
- 2 implies 6, so we can drop 6 (as before).
- 2 and 10 imply $CF \rightarrow AD$ (by composition), which implies $CF \rightarrow ADC$ (by augmentation), which with (the original) 4 implies $CF \rightarrow B$ (by transitivity), so we can drop 8.

No further reductions are possible, and so we are left with the following irreducible set:

$$
\begin{aligned}
AB &\rightarrow C \\
C &\rightarrow A \\
BC &\rightarrow D \\
CD &\rightarrow B \\
BE &\rightarrow C \\
CE &\rightarrow F \\
CF &\rightarrow D \\
D &\rightarrow E \\
D &\rightarrow F
\end{aligned}
$$

Observe, therefore, that there are two distinct irreducible equivalents for the original set of FDs.

10.13 The candidate keys are *L, DPC,* and *DPT.*

10.14 Abbreviating NAME, STREET, CITY, STATE, and ZIP to *N, R, C, T,* and *Z,* respectively, we have:

$$N \rightarrow RCT \qquad RCT \rightarrow Z \qquad Z \rightarrow CT$$

An obviously equivalent irreducible set is:

$$N \rightarrow R \quad N \rightarrow C \quad N \rightarrow T \quad RCT \rightarrow Z \quad Z \rightarrow C \quad Z \rightarrow T$$

The only candidate key is *N.*

10.15 We do not give a full answer to this exercise, but content ourselves with the following observations. First, the set is clearly not irreducible, since $C \rightarrow J$ and $CJ \rightarrow I$ together imply $C \rightarrow I$. Second, an obvious *superkey* is $\{A,B,C,D,G,J\}$ (i.e., the set of all attributes mentioned on the left-hand sides of the given FDs). We can eliminate *J* from this set because $C \rightarrow J$, and we can eliminate *G* because $AB \rightarrow G$. Since none of *A, B, C, D* appears on the right-hand side of any of the given FDs, it follows that $\{A,B,C,D\}$ is a candidate key.

Further Normalization I:
1NF, 2NF, 3NF, BCNF

11.1 INTRODUCTION

Throughout this book so far we have made use of the suppliers and parts database as a running example, with logical design as follows (in outline):

```
S  { S#, SNAME, STATUS, CITY }
   PRIMARY KEY { S# }

P  { P#, PNAME, COLOR, WEIGHT, CITY }
   PRIMARY KEY { P# }

SP { S#, P#, QTY }
   PRIMARY KEY { S#, P# }
   FOREIGN KEY { S# } REFERENCES S
   FOREIGN KEY { P# } REFERENCES P
```

Now, this design does have a feeling of rightness about it: It is "obvious" that three relvars S, P, and SP are necessary; it is also "obvious" that the supplier CITY attribute belongs in relvar S, the part COLOR attribute belongs in relvar P, the shipment QTY attribute belongs in relvar SP, and so on. But what is it that tells us these things are so? Some insight into this question can be gained by seeing what happens if the design is changed in some way. Suppose, for example, that the supplier CITY attribute is moved out of the suppliers relvar and into the shipments relvar (intuitively the wrong place for it, since "supplier city" obviously concerns suppliers, not shipments). Fig. 11.1 (opposite), a variation on Fig. 10.1 from Chapter 10, shows a sample value for this revised shipments relvar. *Note:* In order to avoid confusion with our usual shipments relvar SP, we will refer to this revised version as SCP, as we did in Chapter 10.

A glance at the figure is sufficient to show what is wrong with this design: **redundancy.** To be specific, every SCP tuple for supplier S1 tells us S1 is located in London, every SCP tuple for supplier S2 tells us S2 is located in Paris, and so on. More generally, the fact that a given supplier is located in a given city is stated as many times as there are shipments for that supplier. This redundancy in turn leads to several further problems. For example, after an update, supplier S1 might be shown as being located in London accord-

SCP	S#	CITY	P#	QTY
	S1	London	P1	300
	S1	London	P2	200
	S1	London	P3	400
	S1	London	P4	200
	S1	London	P5	100
	S1	London	P6	100
	S2	Paris	P1	300
	S2	Paris	P2	400
	S3	Paris	P2	200
	S4	London	P2	200
	S4	London	P4	300
	S4	London	P5	400

Fig. 11.1 Sample value for relvar SCP

ing to one tuple and in Amsterdam according to another.* So perhaps a good design principle is "one fact in one place" (i.e., avoid redundancy). *The subject of further normalization is essentially just a formalization of simple ideas like this one*—a formalization, however, that does have very practical application to the problem of database design.

Of course, *relations* are always normalized so far as the relational model is concerned, as we saw in Chapter 5. As for *relvars,* we can say that they are normalized too so long as their legal values are normalized relations; thus, relvars are always normalized too so far as the relational model is concerned. Equivalently, we can say that relvars (and relations) are always in **first normal form** (abbreviated 1NF). In other words, "normalized" and "1NF" mean *exactly the same thing*—though you should be aware that the term "normalized" is often used to mean one of the higher levels of normalization (typically *third* normal form, 3NF); this latter usage is sloppy but very common.

Now, a given relvar might be normalized in the foregoing sense and yet still possess certain undesirable properties. Relvar SCP is a case in point (see Fig. 11.1). The principles of further normalization allow us to recognize such cases and to replace such relvars by ones that are more desirable in some way. In the case of relvar SCP, for example, those principles would tell us precisely what is wrong with that relvar, and they would tell us how to replace it by two "more desirable" relvars, one with heading {S#,CITY} and one with heading {S#,P#,QTY}.

---

*Throughout this chapter and the next, it is necessary to assume (realistically enough!) that relvar predicates are not being fully enforced—for if they were, problems such as this one could not possibly arise (it would not be possible to update the city for supplier S1 in some tuples and not in others). In fact, one way to think about the normalization discipline is as follows: It helps us structure the database in such a way as to make more single-tuple updates logically acceptable than would otherwise be the case (i.e., if the design were not fully normalized). This goal is achieved because the relvar predicates are simpler with a fully normalized design.

Normal Forms

The process of further normalization—hereinafter abbreviated to just *normalization*—is built around the concept of **normal forms.** A relvar is said to be in a particular normal form if it satisfies a certain prescribed set of conditions. For example, a relvar is said to be in **second normal form** (2NF) if and only if it is in 1NF and also satisfies another condition, to be discussed in Section 11.3.

Many normal forms have been defined (see Fig. 11.2). The first three (1NF, 2NF, 3NF) were defined by Codd in reference [10.4]. As Fig. 11.2 suggests, all normalized relvars are in 1NF; some 1NF relvars are also in 2NF; and some 2NF relvars are also in 3NF. The motivation behind Codd's definitions was that 2NF was "more desirable" (in a sense to be explained) than 1NF, and 3NF in turn was more desirable than 2NF. Thus, the database designer should generally aim for a design involving relvars in 3NF, not ones that are merely in 2NF or 1NF.

Reference [10.4] also introduced the idea of a procedure, the so-called **normalization procedure,** by which a relvar that happens to be in some given normal form, say 2NF, can be replaced by a set of relvars in some more desirable form, say 3NF. (The procedure as originally defined only went as far as 3NF, of course, but it was subsequently extended all the way to 5NF, as we will see in the next chapter.) We can characterize that procedure as *the successive reduction of a given collection of relvars to some more desirable form.* Note that the procedure is **reversible;** that is, it is always possible to take the output from the procedure (say the set of 3NF relvars) and map it back to the input (say the original 2NF relvar). Reversibility is important, of course, because it means the normalization process is *information-preserving.*

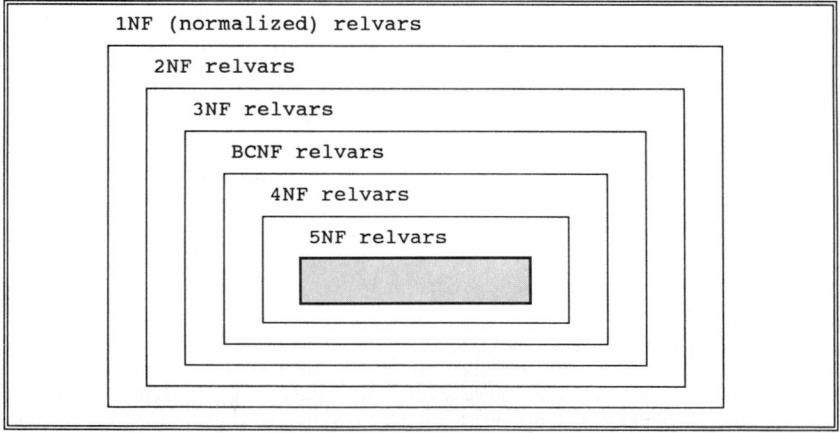

Fig. 11.2   Levels of normalization

To return to the topic of normal forms *per se:* Codd's original definition of 3NF [10.4] turned out to suffer from certain inadequacies, as we will see in Section 11.5. A revised and stronger definition, due to Boyce and Codd, was given in reference [11.2]—stronger, in the sense that any relvar that was in 3NF by the new definition was certainly in 3NF by the old, but a relvar could be in 3NF by the old definition and not by the new. The new 3NF is now usually referred to as **Boyce/Codd normal form** (BCNF) in order to distinguish it from the old form.

Subsequently, Fagin [11.8] defined a new **"fourth"** normal form (4NF—"fourth" because at that time BCNF was still being called "third"). And in reference [11.9], Fagin defined yet another normal form which he called **projection-join normal form** (PJ/NF, also known as **"fifth"** normal form or 5NF). As Fig. 11.2 shows, some BCNF relvars are also in 4NF, and some 4NF relvars are also in 5NF.

By now you might well be wondering whether there is any end to this progression, and whether there might be a 6NF, a 7NF, and so on *ad infinitum.* Although this is a good question to ask, we are obviously not yet in a position to give it detailed consideration. We content ourselves with the rather equivocal statement that there are indeed additional normal forms not shown in Fig. 11.2, but 5NF is the "final" normal form in a special (but important) sense. We will return to this question in Chapter 12.

Structure of the Chapter

The aim of this chapter is to examine the concepts of further normalization, up to and including Boyce/Codd normal form (we leave the other two to Chapter 12). The plan of the chapter is as follows. Following this rather lengthy introduction, Section 11.2 discusses the basic concept of **nonloss decomposition,** and demonstrates the crucial importance of **functional dependence** to this concept (indeed, functional dependence forms the basis for Codd's original three normal forms, as well as BCNF). Section 11.3 then describes the original three normal forms, showing by example how a given relvar can be carried through the normalization procedure as far as 3NF. Section 11.4 digresses slightly to consider the question of **alternative decompositions**—that is, the question of choosing the "best" decomposition of a given relvar, when there is a choice. Next, Section 11.5 discusses BCNF. Finally, Section 11.6 provides a summary and offers a few concluding remarks.

You are warned that we make little attempt at rigor in what follows; rather, we rely to a considerable extent on plain intuition. Indeed, part of the point is that concepts such as nonloss decomposition, BCNF, etc., despite the somewhat esoteric terminology, are essentially very simple and commonsense ideas. Most of the references treat the material in a much more formal and rigorous manner. A good tutorial can be found in reference [11.5].

Two final introductory remarks:

1. As already suggested, the general idea of normalization is that the database designer should aim for relvars in the "ultimate" normal form (5NF). However, this recommendation should not be construed as law; occasionally—*very* occasionally!—there might be good reasons for flouting the principles of normalization (see, e.g., Exercise

11.7 at the end of the chapter). Indeed, this is as good a place as any to make the point that database design can be an extremely complex task (at least in a "large database" environment; the design of "small" databases is—usually—comparatively straightforward). Normalization is a useful aid in the process, but it is not a panacea; thus, anyone designing a database is certainly advised to be familiar with normalization principles, but we do not mean to suggest that the design should necessarily be based on those principles alone. Chapter 13 discusses a number of other aspects of design that have little or nothing to do with normalization as such.

2. As indicated above, we will be using the normalization procedure as a basis for introducing and discussing the various normal forms. However, we do not mean to suggest that database design is actually done by applying that procedure in practice; in fact, it probably is not—it is much more likely that some top-down scheme such as the one described in Chapter 13 will be used instead. The ideas of normalization can then be used to *verify* that the resulting design does not unintentionally violate any of the normalization principles. Nevertheless, the normalization procedure does provide a convenient framework in which to describe those principles. For the purposes of this chapter, therefore, we adopt the useful fiction that we are indeed carrying out the design process by applying that procedure.

11.2 NONLOSS DECOMPOSITION AND FUNCTIONAL DEPENDENCIES

Before we can get into the specifics of the normalization procedure, we need to examine one crucial aspect of that procedure more closely, namely the concept of **nonloss** (also called **lossless**) **decomposition.** We have seen that the normalization procedure involves breaking down or *decomposing* a given relvar into other relvars, and moreover that the decomposition is required to be *reversible,* so that no information is lost in the process; in other words, the only decompositions we are interested in are ones that are indeed nonloss. As we will see, the question of whether a given decomposition is nonloss is intimately bound up with the concept of functional dependence.

By way of example, consider the familiar suppliers relvar S, with heading {S#, STATUS,CITY} (we ignore SNAME for simplicity). Fig. 11.3 (opposite) shows a sample value for this relvar and—in the parts of the figure labeled (a) and (b)—two possible decompositions corresponding to that sample value.

Examining the two decompositions, we observe that:

1. In Case (a), no information is lost; the SST and SC values still tell us that supplier S3 has status 30 and city Paris, and supplier S5 has status 30 and city Athens. In other words, this first decomposition is indeed nonloss.

2. In Case (b), by contrast, information definitely is lost; we can still tell that both suppliers have status 30, but we cannot tell which supplier has which city. In other words, the second decomposition is not nonloss but **lossy.**

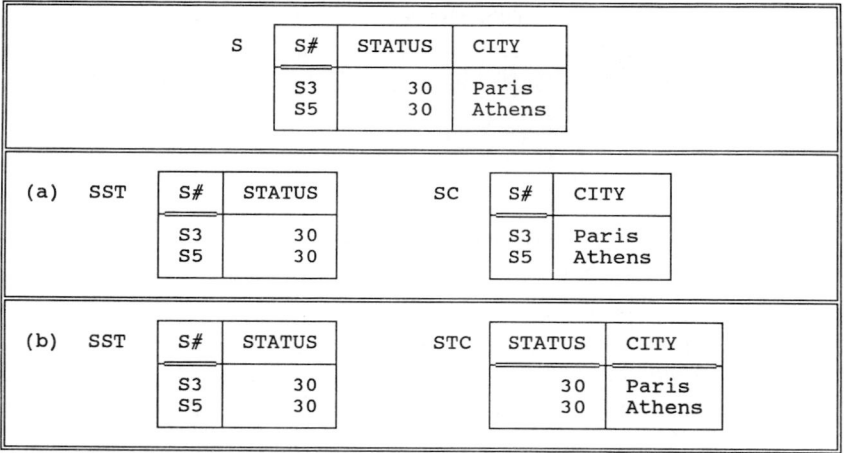

Fig. 11.3 Sample value for relvar S and two corresponding decompositions

What exactly is it here that makes the first decomposition nonloss and the other lossy? Well, observe first that the process we have been referring to as "decomposition" is really a process of **projection;** SST, SC, and STC in the figure are each projections of the original relvar S. So the decomposition operator in the normalization procedure is in fact *projection. Note:* As in Part II of this book, we often say things like "SST is a projection of relvar S" when what we should more correctly say is "SST is a relvar whose value at any given time is a projection of the relation that is the value of relvar S at that time." We hope these shorthands will not cause any confusion.

Observe next that when we say in Case (a) that no information is lost, what we really mean is that *if we join SST and SC back together again, we get back to the original S.* In Case (b), by contrast, if we join SST and SC together again, we do *not* get back the original S, and so we have lost information.* In other words, "reversibility" means, precisely, that *the original relvar is equal to the join of its projections.* Thus, just as the decomposition operator for normalization purposes is projection, so the *re*composition operator is **join.**

So the interesting question is this: If *R1* and *R2* are projections of some relvar *R,* and *R1* and *R2* between them include all of the attributes of *R,* what conditions have to be satisfied in order to guarantee that joining *R1* and *R2* back together takes us back to the original *R?* And this is where functional dependencies come in. Returning to our example, observe that relvar S satisfies the irreducible set of FDs

```
S# → STATUS
S# → CITY
```

---

*More precisely, we get back all of the tuples in the original S, together with some additional "spurious" tuples; we can never get back anything *less* than the original S. (*Exercise:* Prove this statement.) Since we have no way in general of knowing which tuples are spurious and which genuine, we have indeed lost information.

Given the fact that it satisfies these FDs, it surely cannot be coincidence that relvar S is equal to the join of its projections on {S#,STATUS} and {S#,CITY}. And of course it is not. In fact, we have the following *theorem* (due to Heath [11.4]):

- **Heath's theorem:** Let $R\{A,B,C\}$ be a relvar, where *A, B,* and *C* are sets of attributes. If *R* satisfies the FD $A \rightarrow B$, then *R* is equal to the join of its projections on $\{A,B\}$ and $\{A,C\}$.

Taking *A* as S#, *B* as STATUS, and *C* as CITY, this theorem confirms what we have already observed, namely that relvar S can be nonloss-decomposed into its projections on {S#,STATUS} and {S#,CITY}.

At the same time, we also know that relvar S *cannot* be nonloss-decomposed into its projections on {S#,STATUS} and {STATUS,CITY}. Heath's theorem does not explain why this is so;* intuitively, however, we can see that the problem is that *one of the FDs is lost in this latter decomposition.* Specifically, the FD S# $\rightarrow$ STATUS is still represented (by the projection on {S#,STATUS}), but the FD S# $\rightarrow$ CITY has been lost.

More on Functional Dependencies

We conclude this section with a few additional remarks concerning FDs.

1. **Left-irreducible FDs:** Recall from Chapter 10 that an FD is said to be *left-irreducible* if its left-hand side is "not too big." For example, consider relvar SCP once again from Section 11.1. That relvar satisfies the FD

   ```
   { S#, P# } → CITY
   ```

   However, attribute P# on the left-hand side here is redundant for functional dependency purposes; that is, we also have the FD

   ```
   S# → CITY
   ```

   (i.e., CITY is also functionally dependent on S# alone). This latter FD is left-irreducible, but the previous one is not; equivalently, CITY is *irreducibly dependent* on S#, but not irreducibly dependent on {S#,P#}.†

   Left-irreducible FDs and irreducible dependencies will turn out to be important in the definition of second and third normal form (see Section 11.3).

2. **FD diagrams:** Let *R* be a relvar and let *I* be some irreducible set of FDs that apply to *R* (again, refer to Chapter 10 if you need to refresh your memory regarding irreducible

---

*It does not do so because it is of the form "if ... then ...," not "if *and only if* ... then ..." (see Exercise 11.1 at the end of the chapter). We will be discussing a stronger form of Heath's theorem in the next chapter (in Section 12.2).

†"Left-irreducible FD" and "irreducibly dependent" are our preferred terms for what are more usually called "**full** FD" and "**fully** dependent" in the literature (and were so called in the first few editions of this book). These latter terms have the merit of brevity but are less descriptive and less apt.

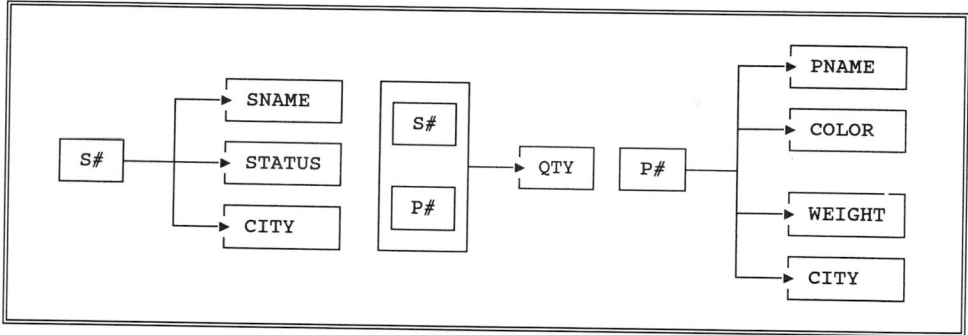

Fig. 11.4   FD diagrams for relvars S, SP, and P

sets of FDs). It is convenient to represent the set *I* by means of a *functional dependency diagram* (FD diagram). FD diagrams for relvars S, SP, and P—which should be self-explanatory—are given in Fig. 11.4. We will make frequent use of such diagrams throughout the rest of this chapter.

Now, you will observe that every arrow in Fig. 11.4 is an *arrow out of a candidate key* (actually the primary key) of the relevant relvar. By definition, there will always be arrows out of each candidate key,* because, for one value of each candidate key, there is always one value of everything else; those arrows can never be eliminated. *It is if there are any other arrows that difficulties arise.* Thus, the normalization procedure can be characterized, very informally, as a procedure for eliminating arrows that are not arrows out of candidate keys.

3. **FDs are a semantic notion:** FDs are, of course, a special kind of integrity constraint. As such, they are definitely a *semantic* notion. Recognizing the FDs is part of the process of understanding what the data *means;* the fact that relvar S satisfies the FD S# → CITY, for example, means that each supplier is located in precisely one city. To look at this another way:

- There is a constraint in the real world that the database represents, namely that each supplier is located in precisely one city;

- Since it is part of the semantics of the situation, that constraint must somehow be observed in the database;

- The way to ensure that it is so observed is to specify it in the database definition, so that the DBMS can enforce it;

- The way to specify it in the database definition is to declare the FD.

---

*More precisely, there will always be arrows out of *superkeys*. If the set of FDs is irreducible as stated, however, all FDs (or "arrows") will be left-irreducible.

And we will see later that the concepts of normalization lead to a very simple means of declaring FDs.

11.3   FIRST, SECOND, AND THIRD NORMAL FORMS

Caveat: Throughout this section, we assume for simplicity that each relvar has exactly one candidate key, which we further assume is the primary key. These assumptions are reflected in our definitions, which (we repeat) are not very rigorous. The case of a relvar having more than one candidate key is discussed in Section 11.5.

We are now in a position to describe Codd's original three normal forms. We present a preliminary, very informal, definition of 3NF first in order to give some idea of the point we are aiming for. We then consider the process of reducing an arbitrary relvar to an equivalent collection of 3NF relvars, giving somewhat more precise definitions of the three forms as we go. However, we note at the outset that 1NF, 2NF, and 3NF are not very significant in themselves except as stepping stones to BCNF (and beyond).

Here then is our preliminary 3NF definition:

- **Third normal form** *(very informal definition):* A relvar is in 3NF if and only if the nonkey attributes (if any) are
    a. Mutually independent, and
    b. Irreducibly dependent on the primary key.

We explain the terms "nonkey attribute" and "mutually independent" (loosely) as follows:

- A *nonkey attribute* is any attribute that does not participate in the primary key of the relvar concerned.

- Two or more attributes are *mutually independent* if none of them is functionally dependent on any combination of the others. Such independence implies that each such attribute can be updated independently of all the rest.

By way of example, the parts relvar P is in 3NF according to the foregoing definition: Attributes PNAME, COLOR, WEIGHT, and CITY are all independent of one another (it is possible to change, e.g., the color of a part without simultaneously having to change its weight), and they are all irreducibly dependent on the primary key {P#}.

The foregoing informal definition of 3NF can be interpreted, even more informally, as follows:

- **Third normal form** *(even more informal definition):* A relvar is in third normal form (3NF) if and only if, for all time, each tuple consists of a primary key value that identifies some entity, together with a set of zero or more mutually independent attribute values that describe that entity in some way.

Again, relvar P fits the definition: Each tuple of P consists of a primary key value (a part number) that identifies some part in the real world, together with four additional values (part name, part color, part weight, and part city), each of which serves to describe that part, and each of which is independent of all the rest.

Now we turn to the normalization procedure. We begin with a definition of first normal form.

- **First normal form:** A relvar is in 1NF if and only if, in every legal value of that relvar, every tuple contains exactly one value for each attribute.

This definition merely states that relvars are always in 1NF, which is of course correct. However, a relvar that is *only* in first normal form (that is, a 1NF relvar that is not also in 2NF, and therefore not in 3NF either) has a structure that is undesirable for a number of reasons. To illustrate the point, let us suppose that information concerning suppliers and shipments, rather than being split into the two relvars S and SP, is lumped together into a single relvar as follows:

```
FIRST { S#, STATUS, CITY, P#, QTY }
       PRIMARY KEY { S#, P# }
```

This relvar is an extended version of SCP from Section 11.1. The attributes have their usual meanings, except that for the sake of the example we introduce an additional constraint:

```
CITY → STATUS
```

(STATUS is functionally dependent on CITY; the meaning of this constraint is that a supplier's status is determined by the location of that supplier—e.g., all London suppliers *must* have a status of 20). Also, we ignore SNAME for simplicity. The primary key of FIRST is the combination {S#,P#}; the FD diagram is shown in Fig. 11.5 below.

Observe that this FD diagram is, informally, "more complex" than the FD diagram for a 3NF relvar. As indicated in the previous section, a 3NF diagram has arrows out of candidate keys *only,* whereas a non3NF diagram such as that for FIRST has arrows out of candidate keys *together with certain additional arrows*—and it is those additional arrows that cause the trouble. In fact, relvar FIRST violates both conditions a. and b. in the 3NF definition above: The nonkey attributes are not all mutually independent, because STATUS depends on CITY (one additional arrow), and they are not all irreducibly dependent on the primary key, because STATUS and CITY are each dependent on S# alone (two more additional arrows).

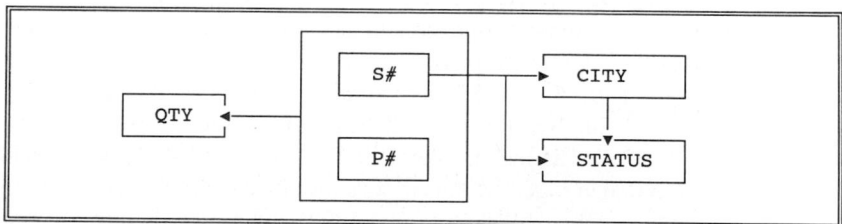

Fig. 11.5   FDs for relvar FIRST

As a basis for illustrating some of the difficulties that arise from those additional arrows, Fig. 11.6 shows a sample value for relvar FIRST. The attribute values are basically as usual, except that the status of supplier S3 has been changed from 30 to 10 to be consistent with the new constraint that CITY determines STATUS. The redundancies are obvious. For example, every tuple for supplier S1 shows the city as London; likewise, every tuple for city London shows the status as 20.

FIRST	S#	STATUS	CITY	P#	QTY
	S1	20	London	P1	300
	S1	20	London	P2	200
	S1	20	London	P3	400
	S1	20	London	P4	200
	S1	20	London	P5	100
	S1	20	London	P6	100
	S2	10	Paris	P1	300
	S2	10	Paris	P2	400
	S3	10	Paris	P2	200
	S4	20	London	P2	200
	S4	20	London	P4	300
	S4	20	London	P5	400

Fig. 11.6   Sample value for relvar FIRST

The redundancies in relvar FIRST lead to a variety of what for historical reasons are usually called **update anomalies**—that is, difficulties with the update operations INSERT, DELETE, and UPDATE. To fix our ideas we concentrate first on the supplier-city redundancy, corresponding to the FD S# → CITY. Problems occur with each of the three operations:

- **INSERT:** We cannot insert the fact that a particular supplier is located in a particular city until that supplier supplies at least one part. Indeed, Fig. 11.6 does not show that supplier S5 is located in Athens. The reason is that, until S5 supplies some part, we have no appropriate primary key value. (As in Chapter 9, Section 9.4, we assume throughout this chapter—reasonably enough—that primary key attributes have no default value. See Chapter 18.)

- **DELETE:** If we delete the sole FIRST tuple for a particular supplier, we delete not only the shipment connecting that supplier to a particular part but also the information that the supplier is located in a particular city. For example, if we delete the FIRST tuple with S# value S3 and P# value P2, we lose the information that S3 is located in Paris. (The INSERT and DELETE problems are really two sides of the same coin.)

   Note: The real problem here is that relvar FIRST contains too much information all bundled together; hence, when we delete a tuple, *we delete too much.* To be more precise, relvar FIRST contains information regarding shipments and information regarding suppliers, and so deleting a shipment causes supplier information to be deleted as well. The solution to this problem, of course, is to "unbundle"—that is, to place shipment information in one relvar and supplier information in another (and this is exactly what we will do in just a moment). Thus, another informal way of characterizing the normalization procedure is as an *unbundling* procedure: Place logically separate information into separate relvars.

■ **UPDATE:** The city value for a given supplier appears in FIRST many times, in general. This redundancy causes update problems. For example, if supplier S1 moves from London to Amsterdam, we are faced with *either* the problem of searching FIRST to find every tuple connecting S1 and London (and changing it) *or* the possibility of producing an inconsistent result (the city for S1 might be given as Amsterdam in one tuple and London in another).

The solution to these problems, as already suggested, is to replace relvar FIRST by the two relvars

```
SECOND { S#, STATUS, CITY }
```

and

```
SP { S#, P#, QTY }
```

The FD diagrams for these two relvars are given in Fig. 11.7; sample values are given in Fig. 11.8. Observe that information for supplier S5 has now been included (in relvar SECOND but not in relvar SP). Relvar SP is now in fact exactly our usual shipments relvar.

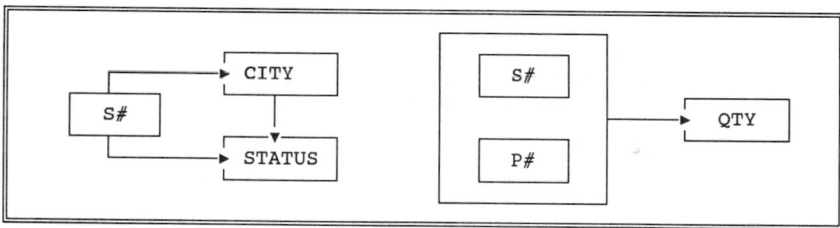

Fig. 11.7   FDs for relvars SECOND and SP

SECOND	S#	STATUS	CITY	SP	S#	P#	QTY
	S1	20	London		S1	P1	300
	S2	10	Paris		S1	P2	200
	S3	10	Paris		S1	P3	400
	S4	20	London		S1	P4	200
	S5	30	Athens		S1	P5	100
					S1	P6	100
					S2	P1	300
					S2	P2	400
					S3	P2	200
					S4	P2	200
					S4	P4	300
					S4	P5	400

Fig. 11.8   Sample values for relvars SECOND and SP

It should be clear that this revised structure overcomes all the problems with update operations sketched earlier:

- **INSERT:** We can insert the information that S5 is located in Athens, even though S5 does not currently supply any parts, by simply inserting the appropriate tuple into SECOND.

- **DELETE:** We can delete the shipment connecting S3 and P2 by deleting the appropriate tuple from SP; we do not lose the information that S3 is located in Paris.

- **UPDATE:** In the revised structure, the city for a given supplier appears once, not many times, because there is precisely one tuple for a given supplier in relvar SECOND (the primary key for that relvar is {S#}); in other words, the S#-CITY redundancy has been eliminated. Thus, we can change the city for S1 from London to Amsterdam by changing it once and for all in the relevant SECOND tuple.

Comparing Figs. 11.7 and 11.5, we see that the effect of the decomposition of FIRST into SECOND and SP has been to eliminate the dependencies that were not irreducible, and it is that elimination that has resolved the difficulties. Intuitively, we can say that in relvar FIRST the attribute CITY did not describe the entity identified by the primary key, namely a shipment; instead it described the *supplier* involved in that shipment (and likewise for attribute STATUS, of course). Mixing the two kinds of information in the same relvar was what caused the problems in the first place.

We now give a definition of second normal form:*

- **Second normal form** *(definition assuming only one candidate key, which we assume is the primary key):* A relvar is in 2NF if and only if it is in 1NF and every nonkey attribute is irreducibly dependent on the primary key.

Relvars SECOND and SP are both in 2NF (the primary keys are {S#} and the combination {S#,P#}, respectively). Relvar FIRST is not in 2NF. A relvar that is in first normal form and not in second can always be reduced to an equivalent collection of 2NF relvars. The reduction process consists of replacing the 1NF relvar by suitable projections; the collection of projections so obtained is equivalent to the original relvar, in the sense that the original relvar can always be recovered by joining those projections back together again. In our example, SECOND and SP are projections of FIRST,[†] and FIRST is the join of SECOND and SP over S#.

---

*Strictly speaking, 2NF can be defined only *with respect to a specified set of dependencies,* but it is usual to ignore this point in informal contexts. Analogous remarks apply to all of the normal forms (other than first, of course).

[†]Except for the fact that SECOND can include tuples, such as the tuple for supplier S5 in Fig. 11.8, that have no counterpart in FIRST. In other words, the new structure can represent information that could not be represented in the previous one. In this sense, the new structure can be regarded as a slightly more faithful representation of the real world.

To summarize, the first step in the normalization procedure is to take projections to eliminate "nonirreducible" functional dependencies. Thus, given relvar *R* as follows—

```
R { A, B, C, D }
   PRIMARY KEY { A, B }
   /* assume A → D holds */
```

—the normalization discipline recommends replacing *R* by its two projections *R1* and *R2*, as follows:

```
R1 { A, D }
   PRIMARY KEY { A }

R2 { A, B, C }
   PRIMARY KEY { A, B }
   FOREIGN KEY { A } REFERENCES R1
```

R can be recovered by taking the foreign-to-matching-primary-key join of *R2* and *R1*.

To return to the example: The SECOND-SP structure still causes problems, however. Relvar SP is satisfactory; as a matter of fact, relvar SP is now in 3NF, and we will ignore it for the remainder of this section. Relvar SECOND, on the other hand, still suffers from a lack of mutual independence among its nonkey attributes. The FD diagram for SECOND is still "more complex" than a 3NF diagram. To be specific, the dependency of STATUS on S#, though it *is* functional, and indeed irreducible, is **transitive** (via CITY): Each S# value determines a CITY value, and that CITY value in turn determines the STATUS value. More generally, whenever the FDs $A \rightarrow B$ and $B \rightarrow C$ both hold, then it is a logical consequence that the transitive FD $A \rightarrow C$ holds also, as explained in Chapter 10. And transitive dependencies lead, once again, to update anomalies. (We now concentrate on the city-status redundancy, corresponding to the FD CITY $\rightarrow$ STATUS.)

- **INSERT:** We cannot insert the fact that a particular city has a particular status—e.g., we cannot state that any supplier in Rome must have a status of 50—until we have some supplier actually located in that city.

- **DELETE:** If we delete the sole SECOND tuple for a particular city, we delete not only the information for the supplier concerned but also the information that that city has that particular status. For example, if we delete the SECOND tuple for S5, we lose the information that the status for Athens is 30. (Again, the INSERT and DELETE problems are really two sides of the same coin.)

    Note: The problem is bundling again, of course: Relvar SECOND contains information regarding suppliers *and* information regarding cities. And again, of course, the solution is to "unbundle"—i.e., to place supplier information in one relvar and city information in another.

- **UPDATE:** The status for a given city appears in SECOND many times, in general (the relvar still contains some redundancy). Thus, if we need to change the status for London from 20 to 30, we are faced with *either* the problem of searching SECOND to find every tuple for London (and changing it) *or* the possibility of producing an inconsistent result (the status for London might be given as 20 in one tuple and 30 in another).

Again the solution to the problems is to replace the original relvar (SECOND, in this case) by two projections, namely the projections

```
SC { S#, CITY }
```

and

```
CS { CITY, STATUS }
```

The FD diagrams for these two relvars are given in Fig. 11.9; sample values are given in Fig. 11.10. Observe that status information for Rome has been included in relvar CS. The reduction is reversible once again, since SECOND is the join of SC and CS over CITY.

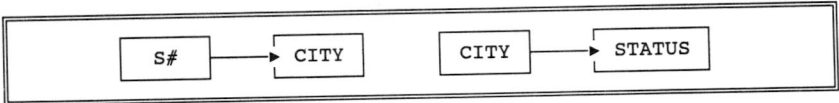

Fig. 11.9   FDs for relvars SC and CS

SC	S#	CITY		CS	CITY	STATUS
	S1	London			Athens	30
	S2	Paris			London	20
	S3	Paris			Paris	10
	S4	London			Rome	50
	S5	Athens				

Fig. 11.10   Sample values for relvars SC and CS

It should be clear, again, that this revised structure overcomes all the problems with update operations sketched earlier. Detailed consideration of those problems is left as an exercise. Comparing Figs. 11.9 and 11.7, we see that the effect of the further decomposition is to eliminate the transitive dependence of STATUS on S#, and again it is that elimination that has resolved the difficulties. Intuitively, we can say that in relvar SECOND the attribute STATUS did not describe the entity identified by the primary key, namely a supplier; instead it described the city in which that supplier happened to be located. Once again, mixing the two kinds of information in the same relvar was what caused the problems.

We now give a definition of third normal form:

- **Third normal form** *(definition assuming only one candidate key, which we further assume is the primary key):* A relvar is in 3NF if and only if it is in 2NF and every nonkey attribute is nontransitively dependent on the primary key. *Note:* "No transitive dependencies" implies no *mutual* dependencies, in the sense of that term explained near the beginning of this section.

Relvars SC and CS are both in 3NF (the primary keys are {S#} and {CITY}, respectively). Relvar SECOND is not in 3NF. A relvar that is in second normal form and not in third can always be reduced to an equivalent collection of 3NF relvars. We have already indicated that the process is reversible, and hence that no information is lost in the reduction; however, the 3NF collection can contain information, such as the fact that the status for Rome is 50, that could not be represented in the original 2NF relvar.*

To summarize, the second step in the normalization procedure is to take projections to eliminate transitive dependencies. In other words, given relvar *R* as follows—

```
R { A, B, C }
   PRIMARY KEY { A }
   /* assume B → C holds */
```

—the normalization discipline recommends replacing *R* by its two projections *R1* and *R2*, as follows:

```
R1 { B, C }
   PRIMARY KEY { B }

R2 { A, B }
   PRIMARY KEY { A }
   FOREIGN KEY { B } REFERENCES R1
```

R can be recovered by taking the foreign-to-matching-primary-key join of *R2* and *R1*.

We conclude this section by stressing the point that the level of normalization of a given relvar is a matter of semantics, not merely a matter of the value that relvar happens to have at some particular time. In other words, it is not possible just to look at the value at a given time and to say whether the relvar is in (say) 3NF—it is also necessary to know the meaning of the data, i.e., the dependencies, before such a judgment can be made. Note too that even knowing the dependencies, it is never possible to *prove* by examining a given value that the relvar is in 3NF. The best that can be done is to show that the value in question does not violate any of the dependencies; assuming it does not, then the value is *consistent with the hypothesis* that the relvar is in 3NF, but of course that fact does not guarantee that the hypothesis is valid.

11.4 DEPENDENCY PRESERVATION

During the reduction process it is frequently the case that a given relvar can be nonloss-decomposed in a variety of different ways. Consider the relvar SECOND from Section 11.3 once again, with FDs S# → CITY and CITY → STATUS and therefore also, by transitivity, S# → STATUS (refer to Fig. 11.11, in which the transitive FD is shown as a broken

---

*It follows that, just as the SECOND-SP combination was a slightly better representation of the real world than the 1NF relvar FIRST, so the SC-CS combination is a slightly better representation than the 2NF relvar SECOND.

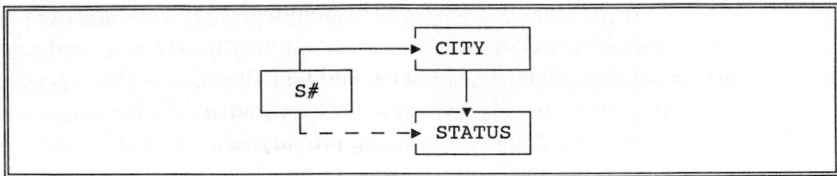

Fig. 11.11   FDs for relvar SECOND

arrow). We showed in Section 11.3 that the update anomalies encountered with SECOND could be overcome by replacing it by its decomposition into the two 3NF projections

```
SC { S#, CITY }
CS { CITY, STATUS }
```

Let us refer to this decomposition as "decomposition *A*." Here by contrast is an alternative decomposition ("decomposition *B*"):

```
SC { S#, CITY }
SS { S#, STATUS }
```

(projection SC is the same in both cases). Decomposition *B* is also nonloss, and the two projections are again both in 3NF. But decomposition *B* is less satisfactory than decomposition *A* for a number of reasons. For example, it is still not possible in *B* to insert the information that a particular city has a particular status unless some supplier is located in that city.

Let us examine this example a little more closely. First, note that the projections in decomposition *A* correspond to the *solid* arrows in Fig. 11.11, whereas one of the projections in decomposition *B* corresponds to the *broken* arrow. In decomposition *A*, in fact, the two projections are **independent** of one another, in the following sense: Updates can be made to either one without regard for the other.* Provided only that such an update is legal within the context of the projection concerned—which means only that it must not violate the primary key uniqueness constraint for that projection—then *the join of the two projections after the update will always be a valid SECOND* (i.e., the join cannot possibly violate the FD constraints on SECOND). In decomposition *B*, by contrast, updates to either of the two projections must be monitored to ensure that the FD CITY → STATUS is not violated (if two suppliers have the same city, then they must have the same status; consider, for example, what is involved in decomposition *B* in moving supplier S1 from London to Paris). In other words, the two projections are not independent of one another in decomposition *B*.

The basic problem is that, in decomposition *B*, the FD CITY → STATUS has become—to use the terminology of Chapter 8—a *database constraint* that spans two relvars (implying, incidentally, that in many products today it will have to be maintained by pro-

---

*Except for the referential constraint from SC to CS, of course.

cedural code). In decomposition *A*, by contrast, it is the *transitive* FD S# → STATUS that has become the database constraint, and that constraint will be enforced automatically if the two *relvar* constraints S# → CITY and CITY → STATUS are enforced. And enforcing these two latter constraints is very simple, of course, involving as it does nothing more than the enforcement of the corresponding primary key uniqueness constraints.

The concept of independent projections thus provides a guideline for choosing a particular decomposition when there is more than one possibility. Specifically, a decomposition in which the projections are independent in the sense described above is generally preferable to one in which they are not. Rissanen [11.6] shows that projections *R1* and *R2* of a relvar *R* are independent in the foregoing sense if and only if:

- Every FD in *R* is a logical consequence of those in *R1* and *R2,* and
- The common attributes of *R1* and *R2* form a candidate key for at least one of the pair.

Consider decompositions *A* and *B* as defined earlier. In *A* the two projections are independent, because their common attribute CITY constitutes the primary key for CS, and every FD in SECOND either appears in one of the two projections or is a logical consequence of those that do. In *B*, by contrast, the two projections are not independent, because the FD CITY → STATUS cannot be deduced from the FDs for those projections—although it is true that their common attribute, S#, does constitute a candidate key for both. *Note:* The third possibility, replacing SECOND by its two projections on {S#,STATUS} and {CITY, STATUS}, is not a valid decomposition, because it is not nonloss. *Exercise:* Prove this statement.

A relvar that cannot be decomposed into independent projections is said to be **atomic** [11.6]. Note carefully, however, that the fact that some given relvar is not atomic in this sense should not necessarily be taken to mean that it should be decomposed into atomic components. For example, relvars S and P of the suppliers and parts database are not atomic, but there seems little point in decomposing them further. Relvar SP, by contrast, *is* atomic.

The idea that the normalization procedure should decompose relvars into projections that are independent in Rissanen's sense has come to be known as **dependency preservation.** We close this section by explaining this concept more precisely.

1. Suppose we are given some relvar *R*, which—after we have applied all steps of the normalization procedure—we replace by a set of relvars *R1, R2, ..., Rn* (all of them projections of *R*, of course).

2. Let the set of given FDs for the original relvar *R* be *S*, and let the sets of FDs that apply to relvars *R1, R2, ..., Rn* be *S1, S2, ..., Sn*, respectively.

3. Each FD in the set *Si* will refer to attributes of *Ri* only ($i = 1, 2, ..., n$). Enforcing the constraints (FDs) in any given set *Si* is thus a simple matter. But what we need to do is to enforce the constraints in the original set *S*. We would therefore like the decomposition into *R1, R2, ..., Rn* to be such that enforcing the constraints in *S1, S2, ..., Sn* individually is together equivalent to enforcing the constraints in the original set *S*—in other words, we would like the decomposition to be *dependency-preserving.*

4. Let S' be the union of $S1, S2, ..., Sn$. Note that it is *not* the case that $S' = S$, in general; in order for the decomposition to be dependency-preserving, however, it is sufficient that the *closures* of S and S' be equal (refer back to Section 10.4 if you need to refresh your memory regarding the notion of the closure of a set of FDs).

5. There is no efficient way of computing the closure S^+ of a set of FDs, in general, so actually computing the two closures and testing them for equality is infeasible. Nevertheless, there is an efficient way of testing whether a given decomposition is dependency-preserving. Details of the algorithm are beyond the scope of this chapter; see, e.g., Ullman's book [7.13] for the specifics.

Note: The answer to Exercise 11.3 at the end of the chapter gives an algorithm by which an arbitrary relvar can be nonloss-decomposed (in a dependency-preserving way) into a set of 3NF projections.

11.5 BOYCE/CODD NORMAL FORM

In this section we drop our simplifying assumption that every relvar has just one candidate key and consider what happens in the general case. The fact is, Codd's original definition of 3NF [10.4] did not treat the general case satisfactorily. To be precise, it did not adequately deal with the case of a relvar that

1. Had two or more candidate keys, such that
2. The candidate keys were composite, and
3. They overlapped (i.e., had at least one attribute in common).

The original definition of 3NF was therefore subsequently replaced by a stronger definition, due to Boyce and Codd, that catered for this case also [11.2]. However, since that new definition actually defines a normal form that is strictly stronger than the old 3NF, it is better to introduce a new name for it, instead of just continuing to call it 3NF; hence the name *Boyce/Codd normal form* (BCNF).* *Note:* The combination of conditions 1, 2, and 3 might not occur very often in practice. For a relvar where it does not, 3NF and BCNF are equivalent.

In order to explain BCNF, we first remind you of the term **determinant,** introduced in Chapter 10 to refer to the left-hand side of an FD. We also remind you of the term **trivial FD,** which is an FD in which the left-hand side is a superset of the right-hand side. Now we can define BCNF:

- **Boyce/Codd normal form:** A relvar is in BCNF if and only if every nontrivial, left-irreducible FD has a candidate key as its determinant.

---

*A definition of "third" normal form that was in fact equivalent to the BCNF definition was first given by Heath in 1971 [11.4]; "Heath normal form" might thus have been a more appropriate name.

Or, less formally:

- **Boyce/Codd normal form** *(informal definition):* A relvar is in BCNF if and only if the only determinants are candidate keys.

In other words, the only arrows in the FD diagram are arrows out of candidate keys. We have already explained that there will always be arrows out of candidate keys; the BCNF definition says *there are no others,* meaning there are no arrows that can be eliminated by the normalization procedure. *Note:* The difference between the two BCNF definitions is that we tacitly assume in the informal case (a) that determinants are "not too big" and (b) that all FDs are nontrivial. In the interests of simplicity, we will continue to make these same assumptions throughout the rest of this chapter, except where otherwise indicated.

It is worth pointing out that the BCNF definition is conceptually simpler than the old 3NF definition, in that it makes no explicit reference to first and second normal forms as such, nor to the concept of transitive dependence. Furthermore, although (as already stated) BCNF is strictly stronger than 3NF, it is still the case that any given relvar can be nonloss-decomposed into an equivalent collection of BCNF relvars.

Before considering some examples involving more than one candidate key, let us convince ourselves that relvars FIRST and SECOND, which were not in 3NF, are not in BCNF either; also that relvars SP, SC, and CS, which were in 3NF, are also in BCNF. Relvar FIRST contains three determinants, namely {S#}, {CITY}, and {S#,P#}; of these, only {S#,P#} is a candidate key, so FIRST is not in BCNF. Similarly, SECOND is not in BCNF either, because the determinant {CITY} is not a candidate key. Relvars SP, SC, and CS, on the other hand, are each in BCNF, because in each case the sole candidate key is the only determinant in the relvar.

We now consider an example involving two disjoint—i.e., nonoverlapping—candidate keys. Suppose that in the usual suppliers relvar S{S#,SNAME,STATUS,CITY}, {S#} and {SNAME} are both candidate keys (i.e., for all time, it is the case that every supplier has a unique supplier number and also a unique supplier name). Assume, however (as elsewhere in this book), that attributes STATUS and CITY are mutually independent—i.e., the FD CITY → STATUS, which we introduced purely for the purposes of Section 11.3, no longer holds. Then the FD diagram is as shown in Fig. 11.12.

Relvar S is in BCNF. Although the FD diagram does look "more complex" than a 3NF diagram, it is nevertheless still the case that the only determinants are candidate keys; i.e.,

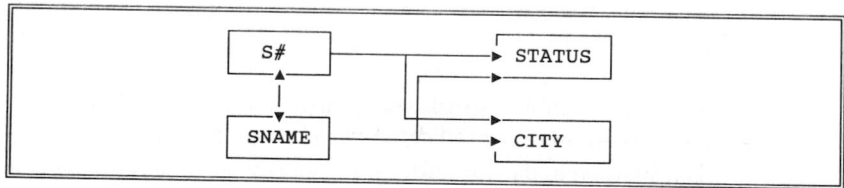

Fig. 11.12 FDs for relvar S if {SNAME} is a candidate key (and CITY → STATUS does not hold)

the only arrows are arrows out of candidate keys. So the message of this first example is just that having more than one candidate key is not necessarily bad. (Of course, it is desirable to specify both candidate keys in the database definition, so that the DBMS can enforce both required uniqueness constraints.)

Now we present some examples in which the candidate keys overlap. Two candidate keys *overlap* if they involve two or more attributes each and have at least one attribute in common. *Note:* In accordance with our discussions on this subject in Chapter 8, we will not attempt to choose one of the candidate keys as the primary key in any of the examples that follow. We will therefore also not mark any columns with double underlining in our figures in this section.

For our first example, we suppose again that supplier names are unique, and we consider the relvar

```
SSP { S#, SNAME, P#, QTY }
```

The candidate keys are {S#,P#} and {SNAME,P#}. Is this relvar in BCNF? The answer is no, because it contains two determinants, S# and SNAME, that are not candidate keys for the relvar ({S#} and {SNAME} are both determinants because each determines the other). A sample value for this relvar is shown in Fig. 11.13.

SSP	S#	SNAME	P#	QTY
	S1	Smith	P1	300
	S1	Smith	P2	200
	S1	Smith	P3	400
	S1	Smith	P4	200
	..	.....	..	...

Fig. 11.13   Sample value (partial) for relvar SSP

As the figure shows, relvar SSP involves the same kind of redundancies as did relvars FIRST and SECOND of Section 11.3 (and relvar SCP of Section 11.1), and hence is subject to the same kind of update anomalies. For example, changing the name of supplier S1 from Smith to Robinson leads, once again, either to search problems or to possibly inconsistent results. Yet SSP *is* in 3NF by the old definition, because that definition did not require an attribute to be irreducibly dependent on each candidate key if it was itself a component of some candidate key of the relvar, and so the fact that SNAME is not irreducibly dependent on {S#,P#} was ignored. *Note:* By "3NF" here we mean 3NF as originally defined in reference [10.4], not the simplified form we defined in Section 11.3.

The solution to the SSP problems is, of course, to break the relvar down into two projections, in this case the projections

```
SS { S#, SNAME }
SP { S#, P#, QTY }
```

—or alternatively the projections

```
SS { S#, SNAME }
SP { SNAME, P#, QTY }
```

(there are two equally valid decompositions in this example). All of these projections are in BCNF.

At this point, we should probably stop for a moment and reflect on what is "really" going on here. The original design, consisting of the single relvar SSP, is *clearly* bad; the problems with it are intuitively obvious, and it is unlikely that any competent database designer would ever seriously propose it, even if he or she had no exposure to the ideas of BCNF etc. at all. Common sense would tell the designer that the SS-SP design is better. But what do we mean by "common sense"? What are the *principles* (inside the designer's brain) that the designer is applying when he or she chooses the SS-SP design over the SSP design?

The answer is, of course, that they are exactly the principles of functional dependency and Boyce/Codd normal form. In other words, those concepts (FD, BCNF, and all the other formal ideas discussed in this chapter and the next) are nothing more nor less than *formalized common sense*. The whole point of the theory underlying this area is to try to identify such common sense principles and formalize them—which, of course, is not an easy thing to do! But if it can be done, then we can *mechanize* those principles; in other words, we can write a program and get the machine to do the work. Critics of normalization usually miss this point; they claim (quite rightly) that the ideas are all basically common sense, but they typically do not realize that it is a significant achievement to state what "common sense" means in a precise and formal way.

To return to the main thread of our discussion: As a second example of overlapping candidate keys—an example that we should warn you some people might consider pathological—we consider a relvar SJT with attributes S, J, and T, standing for student, subject, and teacher, respectively. The meaning of an SJT tuple {S:*s*,J:*j*,T:*t*} is that student *s* is taught subject *j* by teacher *t*. The following constraints apply:

- For each subject, each student of that subject is taught by only one teacher.
- Each teacher teaches only one subject (but each subject is taught by several teachers).

A sample SJT value is given in Fig. 11.14.

SJT	S	J	T
	Smith	Math	Prof. White
	Smith	Physics	Prof. Green
	Jones	Math	Prof. White
	Jones	Physics	Prof. Brown

Fig. 11.14 Sample value for relvar SJT

What are the FDs for relvar SJT? From the first constraint, we have the FD {S,J} → T. From the second constraint, we have the FD T → J. Finally, the fact that each subject is taught by several teachers tells us that the FD J → T does *not* hold. So the FD diagram is as shown in Fig. 11.15.

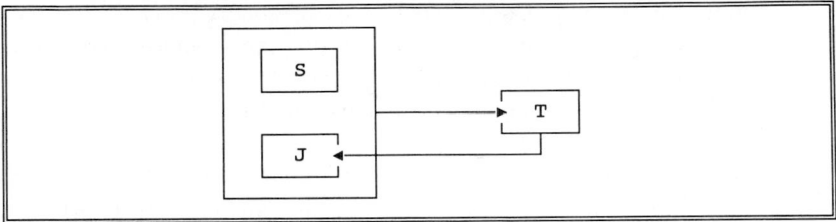

Fig. 11.15   FDs for relvar SJT

Again we have two overlapping candidate keys, namely {S,J} and {S,T}. Once again the relvar is in 3NF and not BCNF, and once again the relvar suffers from certain update anomalies—for example, if we wish to delete the information that Jones is studying physics, we cannot do so without at the same time losing the information that Professor Brown teaches physics. Such difficulties are caused by the fact that attribute T is a determinant but not a candidate key. Again we can get over the problems by replacing the original relvar by two BCNF projections, in this case the projections

```
ST { S, T }
TJ { T, J }
```

It is left as an exercise to show the values of these two relvars corresponding to the data of Fig. 11.14, to draw a corresponding FD diagram, to prove that the two projections are indeed in BCNF (what are the candidate keys?), and to check that the decomposition does in fact avoid the anomalies.

There is another problem, however. The fact is, although the decomposition into ST and TJ does avoid certain anomalies, it unfortunately introduces others! The trouble is, the two projections are not *independent,* in Rissanen's sense (see Section 11.4). To be specific, the FD

```
{ S, J } → T
```

cannot be deduced from the FD

```
T → J
```

(which is the only FD represented in the two projections). As a result, the two projections cannot be independently updated. For example, an attempt to insert a tuple for Smith and Prof. Brown into relvar ST must be rejected, because Prof. Brown teaches physics and Smith is already being taught physics by Prof. Green; yet the system cannot detect this fact without examining relvar TJ. We are forced to the unpleasant conclusion that the two objectives of (a) decomposing a relvar into *BCNF* components, and (b) decomposing it into *independent* components, can occasionally be in conflict; that is, it is not always possible to satisfy both objectives simultaneously.

Note: In fact, relvar SJT is *atomic* (see Section 11.4), even though it is not in BCNF. Observe, therefore, that the fact that an atomic relvar cannot be decomposed into independent components does not mean it cannot be decomposed at all (where by "decomposed," of course, we mean decomposed in a nonloss way). Intuitively speaking, therefore, "atomicity" is not a very good term, since it is neither necessary nor sufficient for good database design.

Our third and final example of overlapping candidate keys concerns a relvar EXAM with attributes S (student), J (subject), and P (position). The meaning of an EXAM tuple {S:*s*,J:*j*,P:*p*} is that student *s* was examined in subject *j* and achieved position *p* in the class list. For the purposes of the example, we assume that the following constraint holds:

- There are no ties; that is, no two students obtained the same position in the same subject.

Then the FDs are as shown in Fig. 11.16.

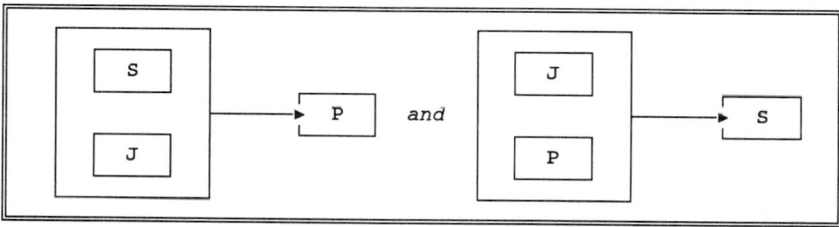

Fig. 11.16 FDs for relvar EXAM

Again we have two overlapping candidate keys, namely {S,J} and {J,P}, because (a) if we are given a student and a subject, then there is exactly one corresponding position, and equally (b) if we are given a subject and a position, there is exactly one corresponding student. However, the relvar is in BCNF, because those candidate keys are the only determinants, and update anomalies such as those discussed earlier in this chapter do not occur with this relvar. (*Exercise:* Check this claim.) Thus, overlapping candidate keys do not *necessarily* lead to problems of the kind we have been discussing.

In conclusion, we see that the concept of BCNF eliminates certain additional problem cases that could occur under the old definition of 3NF. Also, BCNF is conceptually simpler than 3NF, in that it makes no overt reference to the concepts of 1NF, 2NF, primary key, or transitive dependence. What is more, the reference it does make to candidate keys could be replaced by a reference to the more fundamental notion of functional dependence (the definition given in reference [11.2] in fact makes this replacement). On the other hand, the concepts of primary key, transitive dependence, etc., are useful in practice, since they give some idea of the actual step-by-step process the designer might go through in order to reduce an arbitrary relvar to an equivalent collection of BCNF relvars.

We remark finally that the answer to Exercise 11.3 at the end of the chapter includes an algorithm by which an arbitrary relvar can be nonloss-decomposed into a set of BCNF projections.

11.6   A NOTE ON RELATION-VALUED ATTRIBUTES

In Chapter 5, we saw that it is possible for a relation to include an attribute whose values are relations in turn (an example is shown in Fig. 11.17). As a result, of course, relvars can have relation-valued attributes too. From the point of view of database design, however, such relvars are usually contraindicated because they tend to be *asymmetric**—not to mention the fact that their predicates tend to be rather complicated!—and such asymmetry can lead to various practical problems. In the case of Fig. 11.17, for example, suppliers and parts are treated asymmetrically. As a consequence, the (symmetric) queries—

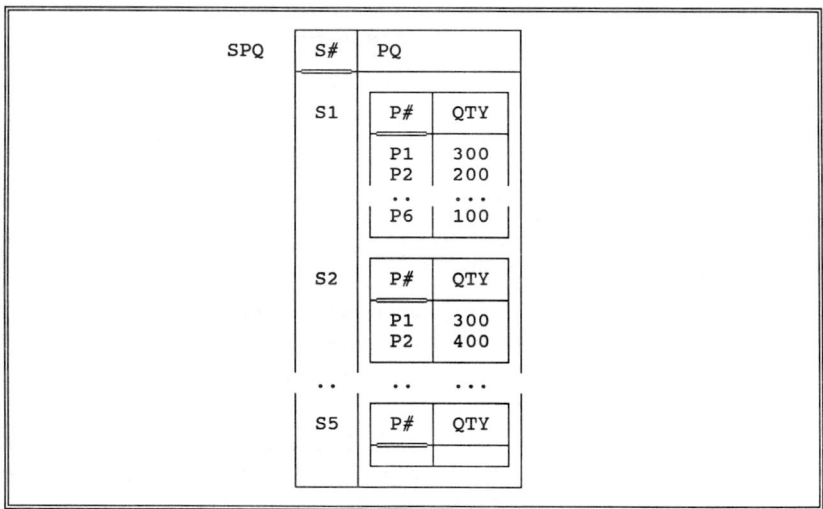

Fig. 11.17   A relation with a relation-valued attribute

---

*Historically, in fact, such relvars were not even legal—they were said to be *unnormalized,* meaning they were not even regarded as being in 1NF [10.4]. See Chapter 5.

1. Get S# for suppliers who supply part P1

2. Get P# for parts supplied by supplier S1

—have very different formulations:

1. (SPQ WHERE P# ('P1') IN PQ { P# }) { S# }

2. ((SPQ WHERE S# = S# ('S1')) { PQ }) { P# }

SPQ here is assumed to be a relvar whose values are relations of the form indicated by Fig. 11.17.

Matters are even worse for update operations. For example, consider the following two updates:

1. Create a new shipment for supplier S6, part P5, quantity 500

2. Create a new shipment for supplier S2, part P5, quantity 500

With our usual shipments relvar SP, there is no qualitative difference between these two updates—both involve the insertion of a single tuple into the relvar. With relvar SPQ, by contrast, the two updates differ in kind significantly (not to mention the fact that they are *both* much more complicated than their SP counterpart):

```
1. INSERT INTO SPQ RELATION
        { TUPLE { S# S# ( 'S6' ),
                  PQ RELATION { TUPLE { P# ( 'P5' ),
                                        QTY QTY ( 500 ) } } } } ;

2. UPDATE SPQ WHERE S# = S# ( 'S2' )
        INSERT INTO PQ RELATION { TUPLE { P# ( 'P5' ),
                                          QTY QTY ( 500 ) } } ;
```

Relvars—at least, base relvars—without relation-valued attributes are thus usually to be preferred, because the fact that they have a simpler logical structure leads to corresponding simplifications in the operations we need to perform on them. Please understand, however, that this position should be seen as a guideline only, not as an inviolable law. In practice, there might well be cases where a relation-valued attribute does make sense, even for a base relvar. For example, Fig. 11.18 (overleaf) shows (part of) a possible value for a *catalog* relvar RVK that lists the relvars in the database and their candidate keys. Attribute CK in that relvar is relation-valued. It is also a component of the sole candidate key for RVK! A **Tutorial D** definition for RVK might thus look something like this:

```
VAR RVK BASE RELATION
        { RVNAME NAME, CK RELATION { ATTRNAME NAME } }
        KEY { RVNAME, CK } ;
```

_____

*And is possible! Note that it is *not* possible in the case of RVK, at least not directly (i.e., without the introduction of some kind of CKNAME—"candidate key name"—attribute).

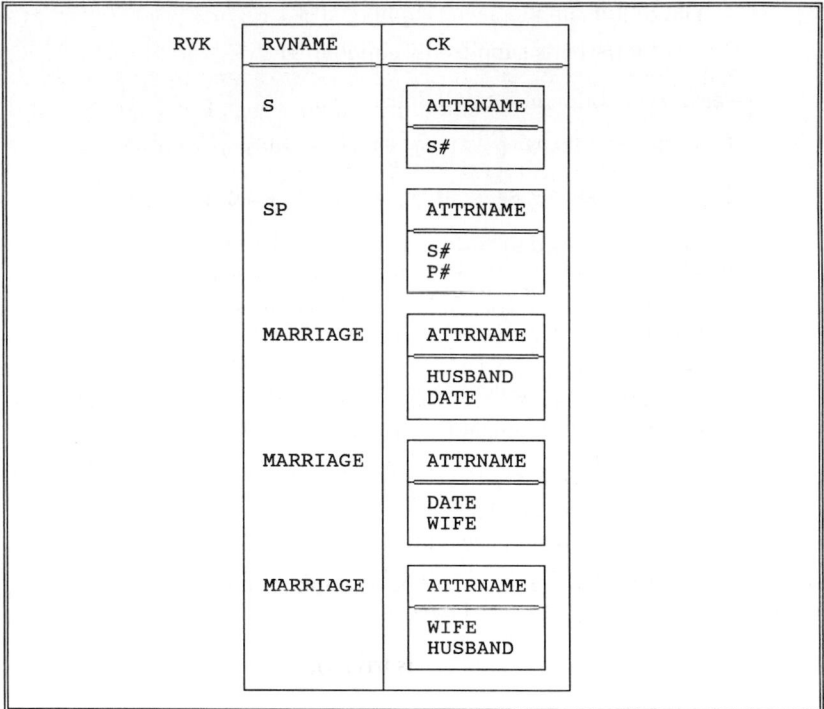

Fig. 11.18   Sample value for catalog relvar RVK

Note: The answer to Exercise 11.3 at the end of the chapter shows how to eliminate relation-valued attributes, if such elimination is considered desirable (as it usually is).* See also the discussion of the UNGROUP operator in Chapter 6 (Section 6.8).

11.7   SUMMARY

This brings us to the end of the first of our two chapters on further normalization. We have discussed the concepts of **first, second, third,** and **Boyce/Codd normal form.** The various normal forms (including fourth and fifth, to be discussed in the next chapter) constitute a *total ordering,* in the sense that every relvar at a given level of normalization is automatically at all lower levels also, whereas the converse is not true—there exist relvars at each level that are not at any higher level. Furthermore, reduction to BCNF (and indeed to 5NF) is always possible; that is, any given relvar can always be replaced by an equivalent set of relvars in BCNF (or 5NF). And the purpose of such reduction is to **avoid redundancy,** and hence to avoid certain **update anomalies.**

_____

*And is possible! Note that it is *not* possible in the case of RVK, at least not directly (i.e., without the introduction of some kind of CKNAME—"candidate key name"—attribute).

The reduction process consists of replacing the given relvar by certain **projections,** in such a way that **joining** those projections back together again gives us back the original relvar; in other words, the process is **reversible** (equivalently, the decomposition is **nonloss**). We also saw the crucial role that **functional dependencies** play in the process; in fact, **Heath's theorem** tells us that if a certain FD is satisfied, then a certain decomposition is nonloss. This state of affairs can be seen as further confirmation of the claim made in Chapter 10 to the effect that FDs are "not quite fundamental, but very nearly so."

We also discussed Rissanen's concept of **independent projections,** and suggested that it is better to decompose into such projections rather than into projections that are not independent, when there is a choice. A decomposition into such independent projections is said to be **dependency-preserving.** Unfortunately, we also saw that the two objectives of (a) nonloss decomposition to BCNF and (b) dependency preservation can occasionally conflict with one another.

We conclude this chapter with a very elegant (and fully accurate) pair of definitions, due to Zaniolo [11.7], of the concepts of 3NF and BCNF. First, 3NF:

- **Third normal form** *(Zaniolo's definition):* Let R be a relvar, let X be any subset of the attributes of R, and let A be any single attribute of R. Then R is in 3NF if and only if, for every FD $X \rightarrow A$ in R, at least one of the following is true:

   1. X contains A (so the FD is trivial);
   2. X is a superkey;
   3. A is contained in a candidate key of R.

The definition of **Boyce/Codd normal form** is obtained from the 3NF definition by simply dropping possibility number 3 (a fact that shows clearly that BCNF is strictly stronger than 3NF). Incidentally, possibility number 3 is precisely the cause of the "inadequacy" in Codd's original 3NF definition [10.4] that we referred to in the introduction to this chapter.

EXERCISES

11.1 Prove Heath's theorem. Is the converse of that theorem valid?

11.2 It is sometimes claimed that every binary relvar is necessarily in BCNF. Is this claim valid?

11.3 Fig. 11.19 shows the information to be recorded in a company personnel database, represented as it would be in a *hierarchic* system such as IBM's Information Management System, IMS (see Chapter 1). The figure is read as follows:

- The company has a set of departments.
- Each department has a set of employees, a set of projects, and a set of offices.
- Each employee has a job history (set of jobs the employee has held). For each such job, the employee also has a salary history (set of salaries received while employed on that job).
- Each office has a set of phones.

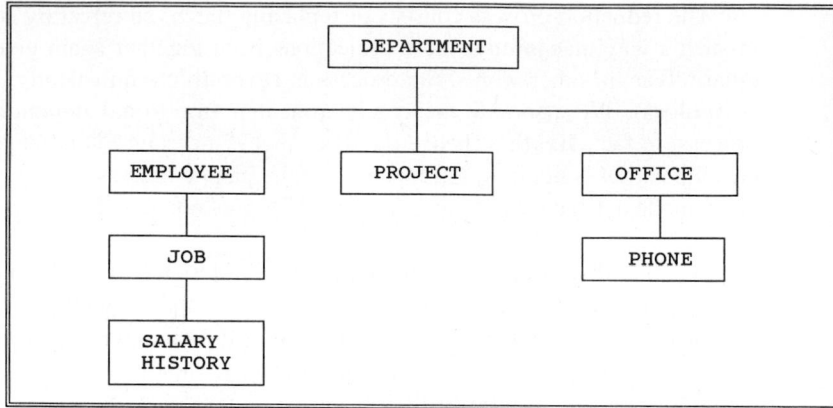

Fig. 11.19   A company database (hierarchic view)

The database is to contain the following information:

- For each department: department number (unique), budget, and the department manager's employee number (unique);
- For each employee: employee number (unique), current project number, office number, and phone number; also, title of each job the employee has held, plus date and salary for each distinct salary received in that job;
- For each project: project number (unique) and budget;
- For each office: office number (unique), floor area, and phone numbers (unique) for all phones in that office.

Design an appropriate set of relvars to represent this information. State any assumptions you make regarding functional dependencies.   .

11.4 A database used in an order/entry system is to contain information about customers, items, and orders. The following information is to be included.

- For each customer:
    Customer number (unique)
    "Ship-to" addresses (several per customer)
    Balance
    Credit limit
    Discount
- For each order:
    Heading information: customer number
                          ship-to address
                          date of order
    Detail lines (several per order):   item number
                                        quantity ordered
- For each item:
    Item number (unique)

> Manufacturing plants
> Quantity on hand at each plant
> Stock danger level for each plant
> Item description

Also, for internal processing reasons, a "quantity outstanding" value is associated with each detail lin of each order; this value is initially set equal to the quantity of the item ordered and is (progressively) reduced to zero as (partial) shipments are made. Again, design a database for this data. As in the previous question, state any assumptions you make regarding dependencies.

11.5 Suppose that in Exercise 11.4 only a very small number of customers, say one percent or less, actually have more than one ship-to address. (This is typical of real-life situations, in which it is frequently the case that just a few exceptions—often rather important ones—fail to conform to some general pattern.) Can you see any drawbacks to your solution to Exercise 11.4? Can you think of any improvements?

11.6 *(Modified version of Exercise 10.13)* Relvar TIMETABLE has the following attributes:

> D Day of the week (1 to 5)
> P Period within day (1 to 8)
> C Classroom number
> T Teacher name
> S Student name
> L Lesson name

The tuple $\{D:d,P:p,C:c,T:t,S:s,L:l\}$ appears in this relvar if and only if at time $\{D:d,P:p\}$ student s is attending lesson l, which is being taught by teacher t in classroom c. You can assume that lessons are one period in duration and that every lesson has a name that is unique with respect to all lessons taught in the week. Reduce TIMETABLE to a more desirable structure.

11.7 *(Modified version of Exercise 10.14)* Relvar NADDR has attributes NAME (unique), STREET, CITY, STATE, and ZIP. For any given zipcode, there is just one city and state. Also, for any given street, city, and state, there is just one zipcode. Is NADDR in BCNF? 3NF? 2NF? Can you think of a better design?

REFERENCES AND BIBLIOGRAPHY

In addition to the following, see also the references in Chapter 10, especially Codd's original papers on 1NF, 2NF, and 3NF [10.4–10.5].

11.1 Philip A. Bernstein: "Synthesizing Third Normal Form Relations from Functional Dependencies," *ACM TODS 1*, No. 4 (December 1976).

> In this chapter we have discussed techniques for decomposing "large" relvars into "smaller" ones (i.e., ones of lower degree). In this paper, Bernstein considers the inverse problem of using "small" relvars to construct "larger" ones (i.e., ones of higher degree). The problem is not actually characterized in this way in the paper; rather, it is described as the problem of *synthesizing* relvars given a set of attributes and a set of corresponding FDs, with the constraint that the synthesized relvars must be in 3NF. However, since attributes and FDs have no meaning outside the context of some containing relvar, it would be more accurate to regard the primitive construct as a binary relvar involving an FD, rather than as a pair of attributes plus an FD.
>   *Note:* It would equally well be possible to regard the given set of attributes and FDs as defining a **universal relvar**—see, e.g., reference [12.9]—that satisfies a given set of FDs, in which

case the "synthesis" process can alternatively be perceived as a process of *decomposing* that universal relvar into 3NF projections. But we stay with the original "synthesis" interpretation for the purposes of the present discussion.

The synthesis process, then, is one of constructing *n*-ary relvars from binary relvars, given a set of FDs that apply to those binary relvars, and given the objective that all constructed relvars be in 3NF (BCNF had not been defined when this work was done). Algorithms are presented for performing this task.

One objection to the approach (recognized by Bernstein) is that the manipulations performed by the synthesis algorithm are purely syntactic in nature and take no account of semantics. For instance, given the FDs—

$A \rightarrow B$ (for relvar $R\{A, B\}$)
$B \rightarrow C$ (for relvar $S\{B, C\}$)
$A \rightarrow C$ (for relvar $T\{A, C\}$)

—the third might or might not be redundant (i.e., implied by the first and second), depending on the meanings of *R, S,* and *T.* As an example of where it is not so implied, take *A* as employee number, *B* as office number, *C* as department number; take *R* as "office of employee," *S* as "department owning office," *T* as "department of employee"; and consider the case of an employee working in an office belonging to a department not the employee's own. The synthesis algorithm simply assumes that, e.g., the two *C* attributes are one and the same (in fact, it does not recognize relvar names at all); it thus relies on the existence of some external mechanism—i.e., human intervention—for avoiding semantically invalid manipulations. In the case at hand, it would be the responsibility of the person defining the original FDs to use distinct attribute names *C1* and *C2* (say) in the two relvars *S* and *T.*

11.2 E. F. Codd: "Recent Investigations into Relational Data Base Systems," Proc. IFIP Congress, Stockholm, Sweden (1974), and elsewhere.

This paper covers a somewhat mixed bag of topics. In particular, however, it gives "an improved definition of third normal form," where "third normal form" in fact refers to what is now known as *Boyce/Codd* normal form. Other topics discussed include *views and view updating, data sublanguages, data exchange,* and *needed investigations* (all as of 1974).

11.3 C. J. Date: "A Normalization Problem," in *Relational Database Writings 1991–1994.* Reading, Mass.: Addison-Wesley (1995).

To quote the abstract, this paper "examines a simple problem of normalization and uses it to make some observations on the subject of database design and explicit integrity constraint declaration." The problem involves a simple airline application and the following FDs:

```
{ FLIGHT } → DESTINATION
{ FLIGHT } → HOUR
{ DAY, FLIGHT } → GATE
{ DAY, FLIGHT } → PILOT
{ DAY, HOUR, GATE } → DESTINATION
{ DAY, HOUR, GATE } → FLIGHT
{ DAY, HOUR, GATE } → PILOT
{ DAY, HOUR, PILOT } → DESTINATION
{ DAY, HOUR, PILOT } → FLIGHT
{ DAY, HOUR, PILOT } → GATE
```

Among other things, this example serves as a good illustration of the point that the "right" database design can rarely be decided on the basis of normalization principles alone.

11.4 I. J. Heath: "Unacceptable File Operations in a Relational Database," Proc. 1971 ACM SIG-FIDET Workshop on Data Description, Access, and Control, San Diego, Calif. (November 1971).

This paper gives a definition of "3NF" that was in fact the first published definition of *BCNF*. It also includes a proof of what we referred to in Section 11.2 as *Heath's theorem*. Note that the three steps in the normalization procedure as discussed in the body of this chapter are all applications of that theorem.

11.5 William Kent: "A Simple Guide to Five Normal Forms in Relational Database Theory," *CACM* *26,* No. 2 (February 1983).

The source of the following intuitively attractive characterization of "3NF" (more accurately, BCNF): **Each attribute must represent a fact about the key, the whole key, and nothing but the key** (slightly paraphrased).

11.6 Jorma Rissanen: "Independent Components of Relations," *ACM TODS 2,* No. 4 (December 1977).

11.7 Carlo Zaniolo: "A New Normal Form for the Design of Relational Database Schemata," *ACM TODS 7,* No. 3 (September 1982).

The source of the elegant definitions of 3NF and BCNF mentioned in Section 11.7. The principal purpose of the paper is to define another normal form, *elementary key normal form* (EKNF), which lies between 3NF and BCNF and "captures the salient qualities of both" while avoiding the problems of both (namely, that 3NF is "too forgiving" and BCNF is "prone to computational complexity"). The paper also shows that Bernstein's algorithm [11.1] in fact generates relvars that are in EKNF, not just 3NF.

ANSWERS TO SELECTED EXERCISES

11.1 Heath's theorem states that if $R\{A,B,C\}$ satisfies the FD $A \rightarrow B$ (where A, B, and C are sets of attributes), then R is equal to the join of its projections $R1$ on $\{A,B\}$ and $R2$ on $\{A,C\}$. In the following proof of this theorem, we adopt our usual informal shorthand for tuples, writing, e.g., (a,b,c) for $\{A:a,B:b,C:c\}$.

First we show that no tuple of R is lost by taking the projections and then joining those projections back together again. Let $(a,b,c) \in R$. Then $(a,b) \in R1$ and $(a,c) \in R2$, and so $(a,b,c) \in R1$ JOIN $R2$. ∎

Next we show that every tuple of the join is indeed a tuple of R (i.e., the join does not generate any "spurious" tuples). Let $(a,b,c) \in R1$ JOIN $R2$. In order to generate such a tuple in the join, we must have $(a,b) \in R1$ and $(a,c) \in R2$. Hence there must exist a tuple $(a,b',c) \in R$ for some b', in order to generate the tuple $(a,c) \in R2$. We therefore must have $(a,b') \in R1$. Now we have $(a,b) \in R1$ and $(a,b') \in R1$; hence we must have $b = b'$, because $A \rightarrow B$. Hence $(a,b,c) \in R$. ∎

The converse of Heath's theorem would state that if $R\{A,B,C\}$ is equal to the join of its projections on $\{A,B\}$ and on $\{A,C\}$, then R satisfies the FD $A \rightarrow B$. This statement is false. For example, Fig. 12.2 in the next chapter shows a relation that is certainly equal to the join of two of its projections and yet does not satisfy any (nontrivial) FDs at all.

11.2 The claim is almost but not quite valid. The following pathological counterexample is taken from reference [5.5]. Consider the relvar USA {COUNTRY,STATE}, interpreted as "STATE is a member of COUNTRY," where COUNTRY is the United States of America in every tuple. Then the FD

```
{ } → COUNTRY
```

holds in this relvar, and yet the empty set { } is not a candidate key. So USA is not in BCNF (it can be nonloss-decomposed into its two unary projections—though whether it actually should be further normalized in this way could be the subject of debate).

Note, incidentally, that it is quite possible in general to have a candidate key that *is* the empty set! See the answer to Exercise 8.7 in Chapter 8 for further discussion.

11.3 Fig. 11.20 shows the most important functional dependencies, both those implied by the wording of the exercise and those corresponding to reasonable semantic assumptions (stated explicitly below). The attribute names are intended to be self-explanatory.

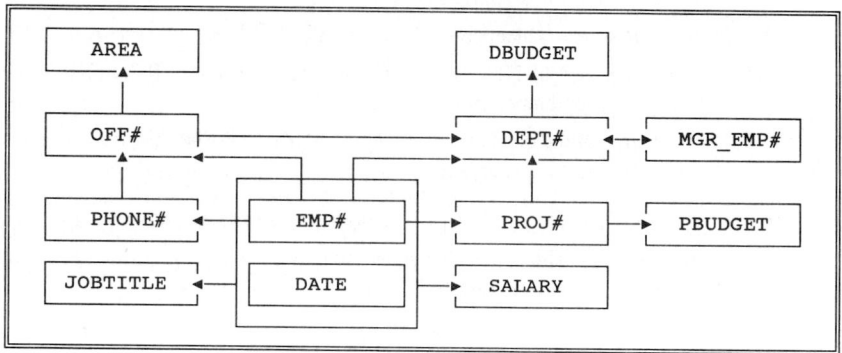

Fig. 11.20   FD diagram for Exercise 11.3

Semantic assumptions:

- No employee is the manager of more than one department at a time.
- No employee works in more than one department at a time.
- No employee works on more than one project at a time.
- No employee has more than one office at a time.
- No employee has more than one phone at a time.
- No employee has more than one job at a time.
- No project is assigned to more than one department at a time.
- No office is assigned to more than one department at a time.
- Department numbers, employee numbers, project numbers, office numbers, and phone numbers are all "globally" unique.

Step 0: Establish initial relvar structure

Observe first that the original hierarchic structure can be regarded as a relvar DEPT0 with *relation-valued attributes:*

```
DEPT0 { DEPT#, DBUDGET, MGR_EMP#, XEMP0, XPROJ0, XOFFICE0 }
      KEY { DEPT# }
      KEY { MGR_EMP# }
```

Attributes DEPT#, DBUDGET, and MGR_EMP# are self-explanatory, but attributes XEMP0, XPROJ0, and XOFFICE0 are relation-valued and do require a little more explanation:

- The XPROJ0 value within a given DEPT0 tuple is a relation with attributes PROJ# and PBUDGET.

- Likewise, the XOFFICE0 value within a given DEPT0 tuple is a relation with attributes OFF#, AREA, and (say) XPHONE0, where XPHONE0 is relation-valued in turn. XPHONE0 relations have just one attribute, PHONE#.

- Finally, the XEMP0 value within a given DEPT0 tuple is a relation with attributes EMP#, PROJ#, OFF#, PHONE#, and (say) XJOB0, where XJOB0 is relation-valued in turn. XJOB0 relations have attributes JOBTITLE and (say) XSALHIST0, where XSALHIST0 is once again relation-valued (XSALHIST0 relations have attributes DATE and SALARY).

Thus the complete hierarchy can be represented by the following nested structure:

```
DEPT0 { DEPT#, DBUDGET, MGR_EMP#,
        XEMP0 { EMP#, PROJ#, OFF#, PHONE#,
                XJOB0 { JOBTITLE,
                        XSALHIST0 { DATE, SALARY } } },
        XPROJ0 { PROJ#, PBUDGET },
        XOFFICE0 { OFF#, AREA, XPHONE0 { PHONE# } } }
```

Note: Instead of attempting to show candidate keys, we have used *italics* here to indicate attributes that are at least "unique within parent" (in fact, DEPT#, EMP#, PROJ#, OFF#, and PHONE# are, according to our stated assumptions, all *globally* unique).

Step 1: Eliminate relation-valued attributes

Now let us assume for simplicity that we wish every relvar to have a *primary* key specifically—i.e., we will always designate one candidate key as primary for some reason (the reason is not important here). In the case of DEPT0 in particular, let us choose {DEPT#} as the primary key (and so {MGR_EMP#} becomes an alternate key).

We now proceed to get rid of all of the relation-valued attributes in DEPT0, since as noted in Section 11.6 such attributes are usually undesirable:*

- For each relation-valued attribute in DEPT0—i.e., attributes XEMP0, XPROJ0, and XOFFICE0—form a new relvar with attributes consisting of the attributes of the applicable relations together with the primary key of DEPT0. The primary key of each such relvar is the combination of the attribute that previously gave "uniqueness within parent," together with the primary key of DEPT0. (Note, however, that many of those "primary keys" will include attributes that are redundant for unique identification purposes and will be eliminated later.) Remove attributes XEMP0, XPROJ0, and XOFFICE0 from DEPT0.

---

*We remark that the procedure given here for eliminating relation-valued attributes amounts to repeatedly executing the UNGROUP operator (see Chapter 6, Section 6.8) until the desired result is obtained. Incidentally, the procedure as described also guarantees that any multi-valued dependencies (MVDs) that are not FDs are eliminated too; as a consequence, the relvars we eventually wind up with are in fact in 4NF, not just BCNF (see Chapter 12).

- If any relvar *R* still includes any relation-valued attributes, perform an analogous sequence of operations on *R*.

We obtain the following collection of relvars, with (as indicated) all relation-valued attributes eliminated. Note, however, that while the resulting relvars are in 1NF (of course), they are not necessarily in any higher normal form.

```
DEPT1 { DEPT#, DBUDGET, MGR_EMP# }
    PRIMARY KEY { DEPT# }
    ALTERNATE KEY { MGR_EMP# }

EMP1 { DEPT#, EMP#, PROJ#, OFF#, PHONE# }
    PRIMARY KEY { DEPT#, EMP# }

JOB1 { DEPT#, EMP#, JOBTITLE }
    PRIMARY KEY { DEPT#, EMP#, JOBTITLE }

SALHIST1 { DEPT#, EMP#, JOBTITLE, DATE, SALARY }
        PRIMARY KEY { DEPT#, EMP#, JOBTITLE, DATE }

PROJ1 { DEPT#, PROJ#, PBUDGET }
    PRIMARY KEY { DEPT#, PROJ# }

OFFICE1 { DEPT#, OFF#, AREA }
        PRIMARY KEY { DEPT#, OFF# }

PHONE1 { DEPT#, OFF#, PHONE# }
        PRIMARY KEY { DEPT#, OFF#, PHONE# }
```

Step 2: Reduce to 2NF

We now reduce the relvars produced in Step 1 to an equivalent collection of relvars in 2NF by eliminating any FDs that are not irreducible. We consider the relvars one by one.

DEPT1: This relvar is already in 2NF.

EMP1: First observe that DEPT# is actually redundant as a component of the primary key for this relvar. We can take {EMP#} alone as the primary key, in which case the relvar is in 2NF as it stands.

JOB1: Again, DEPT# is not required as a component of the primary key. Since DEPT# is functionally dependent on EMP#, we have a nonkey attribute (DEPT#) that is not irreducibly dependent on the primary key (the combination {EMP#,JOBTITLE}), and hence JOB1 is not in 2NF. We can replace it by

```
JOB2A { EMP#, JOBTITLE }
    PRIMARY KEY { EMP#, JOBTITLE }
```

and

```
JOB2B { EMP#, DEPT# }
    PRIMARY KEY { EMP# }
```

However, JOB2A is a projection of SALHIST2 (see below), and JOB2B is a projection of EMP1 (renamed as EMP2 below), so both of these relvars can be discarded.

SALHIST1: As with JOB1, we can project away DEPT# entirely. Moreover, JOBTITLE is not required as a component of the primary key; we can take the combination {EMP#,DATE} as the primary key, to obtain the 2NF relvar

```
            SALHIST2 { EMP#, DATE, JOBTITLE, SALARY }
                    PRIMARY KEY { EMP#, DATE }
```

PROJ1:   As with EMP1, we can consider DEPT# as a nonkey attribute; the relvar is then in 2NF as it stands.

OFFICE1:   Similar remarks apply.

PHONE1:   We can project away DEPT# entirely, since the relvar (DEPT#,OFF#) is a projection of OFFICE1 (renamed as OFFICE2 below). Also, OFF# is functionally dependent on PHONE#, so we can take {PHONE#} alone as the primary key, to obtain the 2NF relvar

```
            PHONE2 { PHONE#, OFF# }
                   PRIMARY KEY { PHONE# }
```

Note that this relvar is not necessarily a projection of EMP2 (phones or offices might exist without being assigned to employees), so we cannot discard this relvar.

Hence our collection of 2NF relvars is

```
DEPT2 { DEPT#, DBUDGET, MGR_EMP# }
     PRIMARY KEY { DEPT# }
     ALTERNATE KEY { MGR_EMP# }

EMP2 { EMP#, DEPT#, PROJ#, OFF#, PHONE# }
     PRIMARY KEY { EMP# }

SALHIST2 { EMP#, DATE, JOBTITLE, SALARY }
        PRIMARY KEY { EMP#, DATE }

PROJ2 { PROJ#, DEPT#, PBUDGET }
     PRIMARY KEY { PROJ# }

OFFICE2 { OFF#, DEPT#, AREA }
        PRIMARY KEY { OFF# }

PHONE2 { PHONE#, OFF# }
        PRIMARY KEY { PHONE# }
```

Step 3: Reduce to 3NF

Now we reduce the 2NF relvars to an equivalent 3NF set by eliminating transitive dependencies. The only 2NF relvar not already in 3NF is the relvar EMP2, in which OFF# and DEPT# are both transitively dependent on the primary key {EMP#}—OFF# via PHONE#, and DEPT# via PROJ# and also via OFF# (and hence via PHONE#). The 3NF relvars (projections) corresponding to EMP2 are

```
EMP3 { EMP#, PROJ#, PHONE# }
     PRIMARY KEY { EMP# }

X { PHONE#, OFF# }
   PRIMARY KEY { PHONE# }

Y { PROJ#, DEPT# }
   PRIMARY KEY { PROJ# }

Z { OFF#, DEPT# }
   PRIMARY KEY { OFF# }
```

However, X is PHONE2, Y is a projection of PROJ2, and Z is a projection of OFFICE2. Hence our collection of 3NF relvars is simply

```
DEPT3 { DEPT#, DBUDGET, MGR_EMP# }
       PRIMARY KEY { DEPT# }
       ALTERNATE KEY { MGR_EMP# }

EMP3 { EMP#, PROJ#, PHONE# }
     PRIMARY KEY { EMP# }

SALHIST3 { EMP#, DATE, JOBTITLE, SALARY }
          PRIMARY KEY { EMP#, DATE }

PROJ3 { PROJ#, DEPT#, PBUDGET }
       PRIMARY KEY { PROJ# }

OFFICE3 { OFF#, DEPT#, AREA }
         PRIMARY KEY { OFF# }

PHONE3 { PHONE#, OFF# }
        PRIMARY KEY { PHONE# }
```

Finally, it is easy to see that each of these 3NF relvars is in fact in BCNF. ▮

Note that, given certain (reasonable) additional semantic constraints, this collection of BCNF relvars is **strongly redundant** [5.1], in that the projection of relvar PROJ3 over {PROJ#,DEPT#} is at all times equal to a projection of the join of EMP3 and PHONE3 and OFFICE3.

Observe finally that it is possible to "spot" the BCNF relvars from the FD diagram (how?). *Note:* We do not claim that it is *always* possible to "spot" a BCNF decomposition—only that it is often possible to do so in practical cases. A more precise statement is the following. Given a relvar *R* satisfying a set of FDs *S*, the algorithm below (Steps 0 to 8) is guaranteed to produce a decomposition *D* of *R* into 3NF (not BCNF) relvars that is both nonloss and dependency-preserving:

0. Initialize *D* to the empty set.

1. Let *I* be an irreducible cover for *S*.

2. Let *X* be a set of attributes appearing on the left-hand side of some FD $X \to Y$ in *I*.

3. Let the complete set of FDs in *I* with left-hand side *X* be $X \to Y1$, $X \to Y2$, ... $X \to Yn$.

4. Let the union of *Y1*, *Y2*, ..., *Yn* be *Z*.

5. Replace *D* by the union of *D* and the projection of *R* over *X* and *Z*.

6. Repeat Steps 3 through 5 for each distinct *X*.

7. Let *A1*, *A2*, ..., *An* be those attributes of *R* (if any) still unaccounted for (i.e., still not included in any relvar in *D*). Replace *D* by the union of *D* and the projection of *R* over *A1*, *A2*, ..., *An*.

8. If no relvar in *D* includes a candidate key of *R*, replace *D* by the union of *D* and the projection of *R* over some candidate key of *R*.

And the following algorithm (Steps 0 to 3) is guaranteed to produce a decomposition *D* of *R* into BCNF relvars that is nonloss but not necessarily dependency-preserving:

0. Initialize *D* to contain just *R*.

1. For each nonBCNF relvar *T* in *D*, execute Steps 2 and 3.

2. Let $X \to Y$ be an FD for *T* that violates the requirements for BCNF.

3. Replace *T* in *D* by two of its projections, viz. that over *X* and *Y* and that over all attributes except those in *Y*.

To revert to the company database example: As a subsidiary exercise—not much to do with normalization as such, but very relevant to database design in general—try extending the foregoing design to incorporate the necessary *foreign key* specifications as well.

11.4 Fig. 11.21 shows the most important FDs for this exercise. The semantic assumptions are as follows:

- No two customers have the same ship-to address.
- Each order is identified by a unique order number.
- Each detail line within an order is identified by a line number, unique within the order.

An appropriate set of BCNF relvars is as follows:

```
CUST { CUST#, BAL, CREDLIM, DISCOUNT }
    KEY { CUST# }

SHIPTO { ADDRESS, CUST# }
      KEY { ADDRESS }

ORDHEAD { ORD#, ADDRESS, DATE }
      KEY { ORD# }

ORDLINE { ORD#, LINE#, ITEM#, QTYORD, QTYOUT }
        KEY { ORD#, LINE# }

ITEM { ITEM#, DESCN }
    KEY { ITEM# }

IP { ITEM#, PLANT#, QTYOH, DANGER }
  KEY { ITEM#, PLANT# }
```

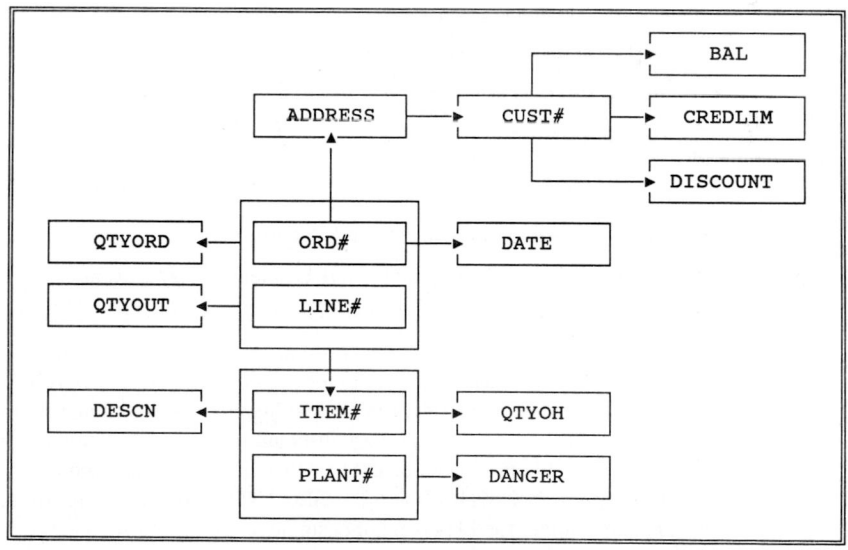

Fig. 11.21   FD diagram for Exercise 11.4

11.5 Consider the processing that must be performed by a program handling orders. We assume that the input order specifies customer number, ship-to address, and details of the items ordered (item numbers and quantities).

```
RETRIEVE CUST WHERE CUST# = input CUST# ;
check balance, credit limit, etc. ;
RETRIEVE SHIPTO WHERE ADDRESS = input ADDRESS
                AND   CUST#   = input CUST#
/* this checks the ship-to address */ ;
IF everything is OK THEN process the order ; END IF ;
```

If 99 percent of customers actually have only one ship-to address, it would be rather inefficient to put that address in a relvar other than CUST (if we consider only that 99 percent, ADDRESS is in fact functionally dependent on CUST#). We can improve matters as follows. For each customer we designate one valid ship-to address as that customer's *primary* address. For the 99 percent, of course, the primary address is the only address. Any other addresses we refer to as *secondary*. Relvar CUST can then be redefined as

```
CUST { CUST#, ADDRESS, BAL, CREDLIM, DISCOUNT }
    KEY { CUST# }
```

and relvar SHIPTO can be replaced by

```
SECOND { ADDRESS, CUST# }
     KEY { ADDRESS }
```

Here CUST contains the primary address, and SECOND contains all secondary addresses (and corresponding customer numbers). These relvars are both in BCNF. The order processing program now looks like this:

```
RETRIEVE CUST WHERE CUST# = input CUST# ;
check balance, credit limit, etc. ;
IF retrieved ADDRESS ≠ input ADDRESS THEN
   RETRIEVE SECOND WHERE ADDRESS = input ADDRESS
                   AND   CUST#   = input CUST#
   /* this checks the ship-to address */ ;
END IF :
IF everything is OK THEN process the order ; END IF ;
```

The advantages of this approach include the following:

- Processing is simpler (and possibly more efficient) for 99 percent of customers.

- If the ship-to address is omitted from the input order, the primary address could be used by default.

- Suppose that the customer can have a different discount for each ship-to address. With the original approach (shown as the answer to the previous exercise), the DISCOUNT attribute would have to be moved to the SHIPTO relvar, making processing still more complicated. With the revised approach, however, the primary discount (corresponding to the primary address) can be represented by an appearance of DISCOUNT in CUST, and secondary discounts by a corresponding appearance of DISCOUNT in SECOND. Both relvars are still in BCNF, and processing is again simpler for 99 percent of customers.

To sum up: Isolating exceptional cases seems to be a valuable technique for obtaining the best of both worlds—i.e., combining the advantages of BCNF with the simplification in retrieval that can occur if the restrictions of BCNF are violated.

11.6 Fig. 11.22 shows the most important functional dependencies. A possible collection of relvars is:

```
SCHED { L, T, C, D, P }
      KEY { L }
      KEY { T, D, P }
      KEY { C, D, P }

STUDY { S, L }
      KEY { S, L }
```

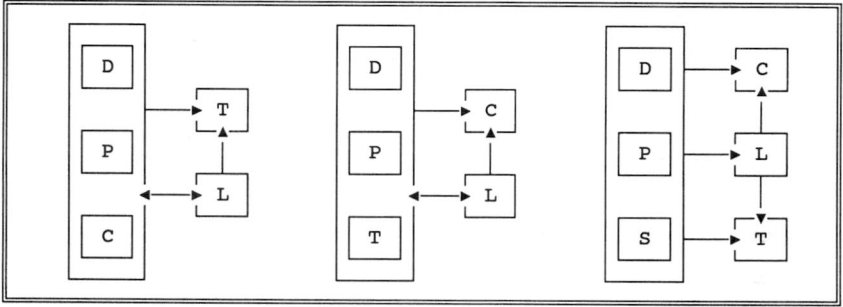

Fig. 11.22   FD diagram for Exercise 11.6

11.7 NADDR is in 2NF but not 3NF (and hence not BCNF). A better design might be:

```
NSZ { NAME, STREET, ZIP }
    KEY { NAME }

ZCS { ZIP, CITY, STATE }
    KEY { ZIP }
```

These two relvars are both in BCNF. Note, however, that:

- Since STREET, CITY, and STATE are almost invariably required together (think of printing a mailing list), and since zipcodes do not change very often, it might be argued that such a decomposition is hardly worthwhile. (In other words, normalization should generally be carried out with respect to *relevant* dependencies—not necessarily *all* dependencies.)

- Observe in particular that retrieving the full address for a given NAME now requires a join (although that join could be concealed from the user by defining NADDR as a view of NSZ and ZCS). Hence, it might be argued that normalization to BCNF is *good for update but bad for retrieval*—i.e., the redundancy that occurs in the absence of full normalization certainly causes problems with update but might help with retrieval.* Redundancy causes difficulties if it is *uncontrolled;* but *controlled* redundancy (i.e., redundancy that is declared to the DBMS, and managed by the DBMS) might be acceptable in some situations.

---

*On the other hand, such redundancy can actually hinder certain retrievals (i.e., it can make the corresponding queries more awkward to formulate), as we will see in Section 12.5 in the next chapter.

- The FD {STREET,CITY,STATE} $\rightarrow$ ZIP is not directly represented by this design; instead, it will have to be maintained separately, either declaratively (if the DBMS supports a declarative integrity language along the lines of the one sketched in Chapter 8), or procedurally otherwise. In fact, of course, relvars NSZ and ZCS are not *independent* in Rissanen's sense [11.6].

Further Normalization II: Higher Normal Forms

12.1 INTRODUCTION

In the previous chapter we discussed the ideas of further normalization up to and including Boyce/Codd normal form (which is as far as the functional dependency concept can carry us). Now we complete our discussions by examining **fourth** and **fifth** normal forms (4NF and 5NF). As we will see, the definition of fourth normal form makes use of a new kind of dependency, called a **multi-valued** dependency (MVD); MVDs are a generalization of FDs. Likewise, the definition of fifth normal form makes use of another new kind of dependency, called a **join** dependency (JD); JDs in turn are a generalization of MVDs. Section 12.2 discusses MVDs and 4NF, Section 12.3 discusses JDs and 5NF (and explains why 5NF is, in a certain special sense, the *final* normal form). Note that our discussions of MVDs and JDs are deliberately less formal and complete than our discussions of FDs in Chapter 10; we leave the formal treatment to the research papers (see the "References and Bibliography" section).

Section 12.4 then reviews the entire normalization procedure and makes some additional comments on it. Section 12.5 briefly discusses the notion of *de*normalization. Section 12.6 describes another important design principle called **orthogonal design.** Finally, Section 12.7 briefly examines some possible directions for future research in the normalization field, and Section 12.8 presents a summary.

12.2 MULTI-VALUED DEPENDENCIES AND FOURTH NORMAL FORM

Suppose we are given a relvar HCTX (H for "hierarchic") containing information about courses, teachers, and texts, in which the attributes corresponding to teachers and texts are *relation-valued* (see Fig. 12.1 overleaf for a sample HCTX value). As you can see, each HCTX tuple consists of a course name, plus a relation containing teacher names, plus a relation containing text names (two such tuples are shown in the figure). The intended meaning of such a tuple is that the specified course can be taught by any of the specified teachers and uses all of the specified texts as references. We assume that, for a given course, there

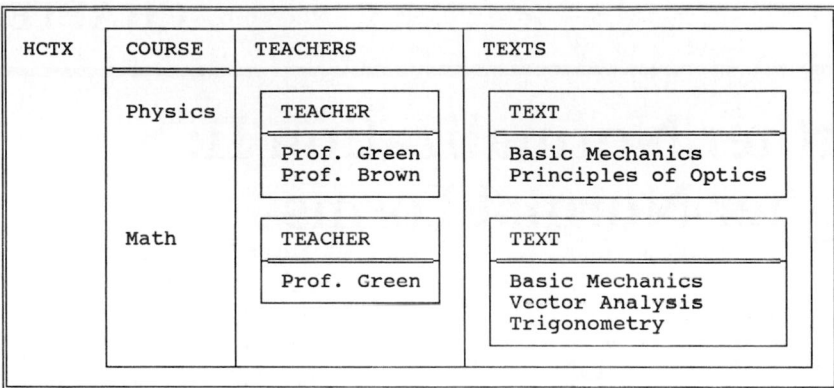

Fig. 12.1   Sample value for relvar HCTX

can exist any number of corresponding teachers and any number of corresponding texts. Moreover, we also assume—perhaps not very realistically!—that teachers and texts are quite independent of one another; that is, no matter who actually teaches any particular offering of a given course, the same texts are used. Finally, we also assume that a given teacher or a given text can be associated with any number of courses.

Now suppose that (as in Section 11.6 in the previous chapter) we want to eliminate the relation-valued attributes. One way to do this—not the way described in the answer to Exercise 11.3, however (a point we will return to at the end of this section)—is simply to replace relvar HCTX by a relvar CTX with three *scalar* attributes COURSE, TEACHER, and TEXT as indicated in Fig. 12.2. As you can see from the figure, each tuple of HCTX gives rise to $m * n$ tuples in CTX, where m and n are the cardinalities of the TEACHERS and TEXTS relations in that HCTX tuple. Note that the resulting relvar CTX is "all key" (the sole candidate key for HCTX, by contrast, was just {COURSE}).

CTX	COURSE	TEACHER	TEXT
	Physics	Prof. Green	Basic Mechanics
	Physics	Prof. Green	Principles of Optics
	Physics	Prof. Brown	Basic Mechanics
	Physics	Prof. Brown	Principles of Optics
	Math	Prof. Green	Basic Mechanics
	Math	Prof. Green	Vector Analysis
	Math	Prof. Green	Trigonometry

Fig. 12.2   Value for relvar CTX corresponding to the HCTX value in Fig. 12.1

The meaning of relvar CTX is basically as follows: A tuple {COURSE:c,TEACHER:t, TEXT:x} appears in CTX if and only if course c can be taught by teacher t and uses text x as a reference. Observe that, for a given course, all possible combinations of teacher and text appear; that is, CTX satisfies the (relvar) constraint

if   tuples $(c,t1,x1)$, $(c,t2,x2)$ both appear

then   tuples $(c,t1,x2)$, $(c,t2,x1)$ both appear also

(using our usual shorthand for tuples once again).

Now, it should be apparent that relvar CTX involves a good deal of **redundancy,** leading as usual to certain **update anomalies.** For example, to add the information that the physics course can be taught by a new teacher, it is necessary to insert *two* new tuples, one for each of the two texts. Can we avoid such problems? Well, it is easy to see that:

1. The problems in question are caused by the fact that teachers and texts are *completely independent of one another;*

2. Matters would be much improved if CTX were decomposed into its two projections—call them CT and CX—on {COURSE,TEACHER} and {COURSE,TEXT}, respectively (see Fig. 12.3).

To add the information that the physics course can be taught by a new teacher, all we have to do now is insert a single tuple into relvar CT. (Note too that relvar CTX can be recovered by joining CT and CX back together again, so the decomposition is nonloss.) Thus, it does seem reasonable to suggest that there should be a way of "further normalizing" a relvar like CTX.

Note: At this point, you might object that the redundancy in CTX was unnecessary in the first place, and hence that the corresponding update anomalies were unnecessary too. More specifically, you might suggest that CTX need not include all possible teacher/text combinations for a given course; for example, two tuples are obviously sufficient to show that the physics course has two teachers and two texts. The problem is, *which* two tuples? Any particular choice leads to a relvar having a very unobvious interpretation and very strange update behavior (try stating the predicate for such a relvar!—i.e., try stating the

CT		CX	
COURSE	TEACHER	COURSE	TEXT
Physics	Prof. Green	Physics	Basic Mechanics
Physics	Prof. Brown	Physics	Principles of Optics
Math	Prof. Green	Math	Basic Mechanics
		Math	Vector Analysis
		Math	Trigonometry

Fig. 12.3   Values for relvars CT and CX corresponding to the CTX value in Fig. 12.2

criteria for deciding whether or not some given update is an acceptable operation on that relvar).

Informally, therefore, it is obvious that the design of CTX is bad and the decomposition into CT and CX is better. The trouble is, however, these facts are not *formally* obvious. Note in particular that CTX satisfies no functional dependencies at all (apart from trivial ones such as COURSE → COURSE); in fact, CTX is in BCNF, since as already noted it is all key—any "all key" relvar must necessarily be in BCNF. (Note that the two projections CT and CX are also all key and hence in BCNF.) The ideas of the previous chapter are therefore of no help with the problem at hand.

The existence of "problem" BCNF relvars like CTX was recognized very early on, and the way to deal with them was also soon understood, at least intuitively. However, it was not until 1977 that these intuitive ideas were put on a sound theoretical footing by Fagin's introduction of the notion of **multi-valued dependencies,** MVDs [12.13]. Multi-valued dependencies are a generalization of functional dependencies, in the sense that every FD is an MVD, but the converse is not true (i.e., there exist MVDs that are not FDs). In the case of relvar CTX there are two MVDs that hold:

```
COURSE  ↠  TEACHER
COURSE  ↠  TEXT
```

Note the double arrows; the MVD $A \rightarrow\rightarrow B$ is read as "*B* is **multi-dependent** on *A*," or, equivalently, "*A* **multi-determines** *B*." Let us concentrate on the first MVD, COURSE →→ TEACHER. Intuitively, what this MVD means is that, although a course does not have a *single* corresponding teacher—i.e., the *functional* dependence COURSE → TEACHER does *not* hold—nevertheless, each course does have a well-defined *set* of corresponding teachers. By "well-defined" here we mean, more precisely, that for a given course *c* and a given text *x*, the set of teachers *t* matching the pair (*c,x*) in CTX depends on the value *c* alone—it makes no difference which particular value of *x* we choose. The second MVD, COURSE →→ TEXT, is interpreted analogously.

Here then is the formal definition:

- **Multi-valued dependence:** Let *R* be a relvar, and let *A, B,* and *C* be subsets of the attributes of *R*. Then we say that *B* is **multi-dependent** on *A*—in symbols,

$$A \twoheadrightarrow B$$

(read "A multi-determines B," or simply "A double arrow B")—if and only if, in every possible legal value of *R*, the set of *B* values matching a given (*A* value, *C* value) pair depends only on the *A* value and is independent of the *C* value.

It is easy to show—see Fagin [12.13]—that, given the relvar *R*{*A,B,C*}, the MVD *A* →→ *B* holds if and only if the MVD *A* →→ *C* also holds. MVDs always go together in pairs in this way. For this reason it is common to represent them both in one statement, thus:

$$A \twoheadrightarrow B \mid C$$

For example:

COURSE →→ TEACHER | TEXT

Now, we stated above that multi-valued dependencies are a generalization of functional dependencies, in the sense that every FD is an MVD. More precisely, an FD is an MVD in which the set of dependent (right-hand side) values matching a given determinant (left-hand side) value is always a singleton set. Thus, if $A \rightarrow B$, then certainly A →→ B.

Returning to our original CTX problem, we can now see that the trouble with relvars such as CTX is that they involve MVDs that are not also FDs. (In case it is not obvious, we point out that it is precisely the existence of those MVDs that leads to the necessity of—for example—inserting *two* tuples to add another physics teacher. Those two tuples are needed in order to maintain the integrity constraint that is represented by the MVD.) The two projections CT and CX do not involve any such MVDs, which is why they represent an improvement over the original design. We would therefore like to replace CTX by those two projections, and an important theorem proved by Fagin in reference [12.13] allows us to make exactly that replacement:

- **Theorem** (Fagin): Let $R\{A,B,C\}$ be a relvar, where A, B, and C are sets of attributes. Then R is equal to the join of its projections on $\{A,B\}$ and $\{A,C\}$ if and only if R satisfies the MVDs $A \rightarrow\rightarrow B \mid C$.

(Notice that this is a stronger version of Heath's theorem as defined in Chapter 11.) Following Fagin [12.13], we can now define *fourth normal form* (so called because—as noted in Chapter 11—BCNF was still being called *third* normal form at the time):

- **Fourth normal form:** Relvar R is in 4NF if and only if, whenever there exist subsets A and B of the attributes of R such that the nontrivial* MVD $A \rightarrow\rightarrow B$ is satisfied, then all attributes of R are also *functionally* dependent on A.

In other words, the only nontrivial dependencies (FDs or MVDs) in R are of the form $K \rightarrow X$ (i.e., a *functional* dependency from a superkey K to some other attribute X). Equivalently: R is in 4NF if it is in BCNF and all MVDs in R are in fact "FDs out of keys." Note in particular, therefore, that 4NF implies BCNF.

Relvar CTX is not in 4NF, since it involves an MVD that is not an FD at all, let alone an FD "out of a key." The two projections CT and CX are both in 4NF, however. Thus 4NF is an improvement over BCNF, in that it eliminates another form of undesirable dependency. What is more, Fagin shows in reference [12.13] that 4NF is always achievable; that is, any relvar can be nonloss-decomposed into an equivalent collection of 4NF relvars— though our discussion of the SJT example in Section 11.5 shows that in some cases it might not be desirable to carry the decomposition that far (or even as far as BCNF).

---

*An MVD $A \rightarrow\rightarrow B$ is **trivial** if either A is a superset of B or the union of A and B is the entire heading.

Note: We remark that Rissanen's work on independent projections [11.6], though couched in terms of FDs, is applicable to MVDs also. Recall that a relvar $R\{A,B,C\}$ satisfying the FDs $A \rightarrow B$ and $B \rightarrow C$ is better decomposed into its projections on $\{A,B\}$ and $\{B,C\}$ rather than into those on $\{A,B\}$ and $\{A,C\}$. The same holds true if we replace the FDs by the MVDs $A \rightarrow\rightarrow B$ and $B \rightarrow\rightarrow C$.

We conclude this section by returning, as promised, to the question of eliminating relation-valued attributes (RVAs for short)—in particular, to the procedure for performing that elimination as described in the answer to Exercise 11.3 in the previous chapter. The point is this: All we need to do in practice to achieve 4NF is *recognize that if we start with a relvar involving two or more independent RVAs, the first thing to do is to separate those RVAs.* Not only does this rule make intuitive sense, it was exactly what we did in our answer to Exercise 11.3! In the case of relvar HCTX, for example, the first thing to do is replace the original relvar by its two projections HCT {COURSE,TEACHERS} and HCX {COURSE,TEXTS} (where TEACHERS and TEXTS are still RVAs). The RVAs in those two projections can then be eliminated (and the projections reduced to BCNF) in the usual way, and the "problem" BCNF relvar CTX will simply never arise. But the theory of MVDs and 4NF gives us a formal basis for what would otherwise be a mere rule of thumb.

12.3   JOIN DEPENDENCIES AND FIFTH NORMAL FORM

So far in this chapter (and throughout the previous chapter) we have tacitly assumed that the sole operation necessary or available in the further normalization process is the replacement of a relvar in a nonloss way by *exactly two* of its projections. This assumption has successfully carried us as far as 4NF. It comes perhaps as a surprise, therefore, to discover that there exist relvars that cannot be nonloss-decomposed into two projections but *can* be nonloss-decomposed into three (or more). To coin an ugly but convenient term, we will describe such a relvar as "n-decomposable" (for some $n > 2$)—meaning that the relvar in question can be nonloss-decomposed into n projections but not into m for any $m < n$. A relvar that can be nonloss-decomposed into two projections we will call "2-decomposable." *Note:* The phenomenon of n-decomposability for $n > 2$ was first noted by Aho, Beeri, and Ullman [12.1]. The particular case $n = 3$ was also studied by Nicolas [12.25].

Consider relvar SPJ from the suppliers-parts-projects database (but ignore attribute QTY for simplicity); a sample value is shown at the top of Fig. 12.4. Note that relvar SPJ is all key and involves no nontrivial FDs or MVDs at all, and is therefore in 4NF. Note too that Fig. 12.4 also shows:

a. The three binary projections SP, PJ, and JS corresponding to the SPJ relation value shown at the top of the figure;

b. The effect of joining the SP and PJ projections (over P#);

c. The effect of joining that result and the JS projection (over J# and S#).

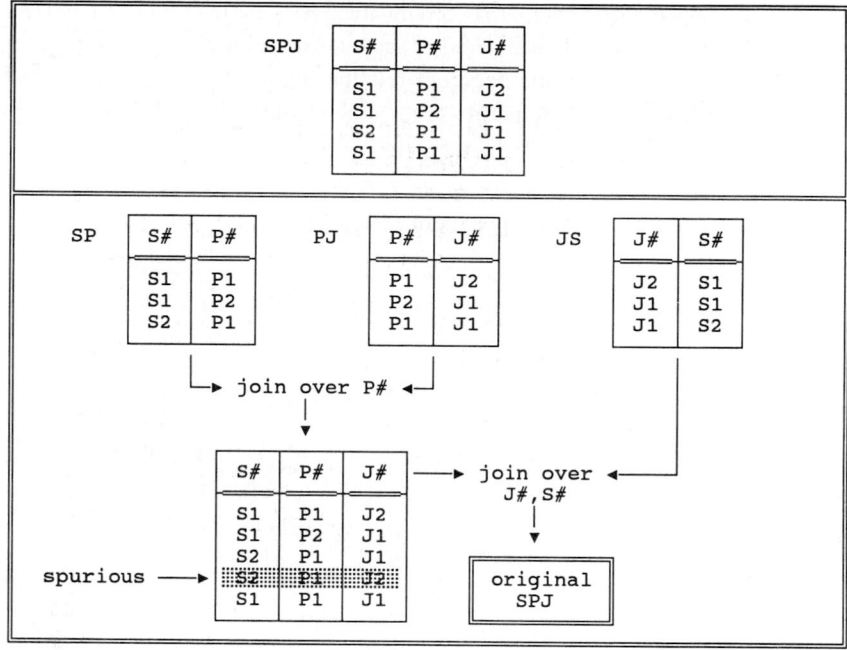

Fig. 12.4   Relation SPJ is the join of all three of its binary projections but not of any two

Observe that the result of the first join is to produce a copy of the original SPJ relation plus one additional (spurious) tuple, and the effect of the second join is then to eliminate that spurious tuple, thereby bringing us back to the original SPJ relation. In other words, the original SPJ relation is 3-decomposable. *Note:* The net result is the same whatever pair of projections we choose for the first join, though the intermediate result is different in each case. *Exercise:* Check this claim.

Now, the example of Fig. 12.4 is of course expressed in terms of *relations,* not *relvars.* However, the 3-decomposability of SPJ could be a more fundamental, time-independent property—i.e., a property satisfied by all legal values of the relvar—*if* the relvar satisfies a certain time-independent integrity constraint. To understand what that constraint must be, observe first that the statement "SPJ is equal to the join of its three projections SP, PJ, and JS" is precisely equivalent to the following statement:

if   the pair $(s1,p1)$ appears in SP
and   the pair $(p1,j1)$ appears in PJ
and   the pair $(j1,s1)$ appears in JS
then   the triple $(s1,p1,j1)$ appears in SPJ

because the triple (*s1,p1,j1*) obviously appears in the join of SP, PJ, and JS. (The converse of this statement, that if (*s1,p1,j1*) appears in SPJ then (*s1,p1*) appears in projection SP, etc., is clearly true for any degree-3 relation SPJ.) Since (*s1,p1*) appears in SP if and only if (*s1,p1,j2*) appears in SPJ for some *j2,* and similarly for (*p1,j1*) and (*j1,s1*), we can rewrite the statement above as a constraint on SPJ:

> **if**   (*s1,p1,j2*), (*s2,p1,j1*), (*s1,p2,j1*) appear in SPJ
> **then**   (*s1,p1,j1*) appears in SPJ also

And if this statement is true for all time—i.e., for all possible legal values of relvar SPJ—then we do have a time-independent constraint on the relvar (albeit a rather bizarre one). Notice the **cyclic nature** of that constraint ("if *s1* is linked to *p1* and *p1* is linked to *j1* and *j1* is linked back to *s1* again, then *s1* and *p1* and *j1* must all coexist in the same tuple"). *A relvar will be n-decomposable for some n > 2 if and only if it satisfies some such (n-way) cyclic constraint.*

Suppose then that relvar SPJ does in fact satisfy that time-independent constraint (the sample values in Fig. 12.4 are consistent with this hypothesis). For brevity, let us agree to refer to that constraint as *Constraint 3D* (3D for 3-decomposable). What does Constraint 3D mean in real-world terms? Let us try to make it a little more concrete by giving an example. The constraint says that, in the portion of the real world that relvar SPJ is supposed to represent, it is a fact that, *if* (for example)

a. Smith supplies monkey wrenches, and

b. Monkey wrenches are used in the Manhattan project, and

c. Smith supplies the Manhattan project,

then

d. Smith supplies monkey wrenches to the Manhattan project.

Note that (as pointed out in Chapter 1, Section 1.3), a., b., and c. together normally do *not* imply d.; indeed, exactly this example was held up in Chapter 1 as an illustration of "the connection trap." In the case at hand, however, we are saying *there is no trap*—because there is an additional real-world constraint in effect, namely Constraint 3D, that makes the inference of d. from a., b., and c. valid in this particular case.

To return to the main topic of discussion: Because Constraint 3D is satisfied if and only if the relvar concerned is equal to the join of certain of its projections, we refer to that constraint as a **join dependency** (JD). A JD is a constraint on the relvar concerned, just as an MVD or an FD is a constraint on the relvar concerned. Here is the definition:

- **Join dependency:** Let *R* be a relvar, and let *A, B, ..., Z* be subsets of the attributes of *R*. Then we say that *R* satisfies the JD

  ```
  * { A, B, ..., Z }
  ```

  (read "star *A, B, ..., Z*") if and only if every possible legal value of *R* is equal to the join of its projections on *A, B, ..., Z*.

For example, if we agree to use SP to mean the subset {S#,P#} of the set of attributes of SPJ, and similarly for PJ and JS, then relvar SPJ satisfies the JD ✳{SP,PJ,JS}.

We have seen, then, that relvar SPJ, with its JD ✳{SP,PJ,JS}, can be 3-decomposed. The question is, *should* it be? And the answer is "Probably yes." Relvar SPJ (with its JD) suffers from a number of problems over update operations, problems that are removed when it is 3-decomposed. Some examples of such problems are illustrated in Fig. 12.5. Consideration of what happens after 3-decomposition is left as an exercise.

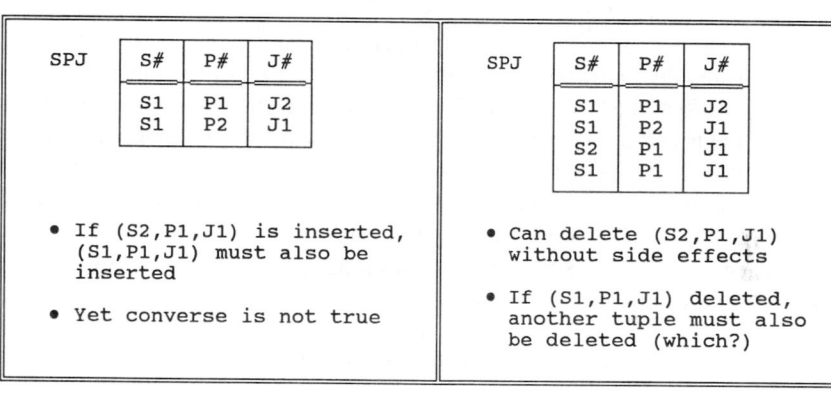

Fig. 12.5   Sample update problems in SPJ

Fagin's theorem (discussed in Section 12.2), to the effect that $R\{A,B,C\}$ can be non-loss-decomposed into its projections on $\{A,B\}$ and $\{A,C\}$ if and only if the MVDs $A \rightarrow\rightarrow B$ and $A \rightarrow\rightarrow C$ hold in R, can now be restated as follows:

- $R\{A,B,C\}$ satisfies the JD ✳$\{AB,AC\}$ if and only if it satisfies the MVDs $A \rightarrow\rightarrow B \mid C$.

Since this theorem can be taken as a *definition* of multi-valued dependency, it follows that an MVD is just a special case of a JD, or (equivalently) that JDs are a generalization of MVDs.

Formally, we have

```
A  ↠  B  |  C  ≡  ✳ { AB,  AC }
```

Note: It is immediate from the definition that join dependencies are **the most general form of dependency possible** (using, of course, the term "dependency" in a very special sense). That is, there does not exist a still higher form of dependency such that JDs are merely a special case of that higher form—so long as we restrict our attention to dependencies that deal with a relvar being decomposed via projection and recomposed via join. (However, if we permit other decomposition and recomposition operators, then other types of dependencies might come into play. We discuss this possibility very briefly in Section 12.7.)

Returning now to our example, we can see that the problem with relvar SPJ is that it involves a JD that is not an MVD, and hence not an FD either. (*Exercise: Why* is this a problem, exactly?) We have also seen that it is possible, and probably desirable, to decompose such a relvar into smaller components—namely, into the projections specified by the join dependency. That decomposition process can be repeated until all resulting relvars are in *fifth normal form,* which we now define:

- **Fifth normal form:** A relvar *R* is in 5NF—also called **projection-join normal form** (PJ/NF)—if and only if every nontrivial* join dependency that holds for *R* is implied by the candidate keys of *R*.

Note: We explain below what it means for a JD to be "implied by candidate keys."

Relvar SPJ is not in 5NF; it satisfies a certain join dependency, namely Constraint 3D, that is certainly not implied by its sole candidate key (that key being the combination of all of its attributes). To state this differently, relvar SPJ is not in 5NF, because (a) it *can* be 3-decomposed and (b) that 3-decomposability is not implied by the fact that the combination {S#,P#,J#} is a candidate key. By contrast, after 3-decomposition, the three projections SP, PJ, and JS are each in 5NF, since they do not involve any (nontrivial) JDs at all.

Although it might not yet be obvious—because we have not yet explained what it means for a JD to be implied by candidate keys—it is a fact that any relvar in 5NF is automatically in 4NF also, because (as we have seen) an MVD is a special case of a JD. In fact, Fagin shows in reference [12.14] that any MVD that is implied by a candidate key must in fact be an FD in which that candidate key is the determinant. Fagin also shows in that same reference [12.14] that any given relvar can be nonloss-decomposed into an equivalent collection of 5NF relvars; that is, 5NF is always achievable.

We now explain what it means for a JD to be implied by candidate keys. First we consider a simple example. Suppose once again (as we did in Chapter 11, Section 11.5) that the familiar suppliers relvar S has two candidate keys, {S#} and {SNAME}. Then that relvar satisfies several join dependencies—for example, it satisfies the JD

```
* { { S#, SNAME, STATUS }, { S#, CITY } }
```

That is, relvar S is equal to the join of its projections on {S#,SNAME,STATUS} and {S#,CITY}, and hence can be nonloss-decomposed into those projections. (This fact does not mean that it *should* be so decomposed, of course, only that it *could* be.) This JD is implied by the fact that {S#} is a candidate key (in fact it is implied by Heath's theorem [11.4]). Likewise, relvar S also satisfies the JD

```
* { { S#, SNAME }, { S#, STATUS }, { SNAME, CITY } }
```

This JD is implied by the fact that {S#} and {SNAME} are *both* candidate keys.

As the foregoing examples suggest, a given JD ∗ {*A,B,...,Z*} is implied by candidate keys *if and only if each of A, B, ..., Z is in fact a superkey for the relvar in question.* Thus,

---

*The JD ∗ {*A,B,...,Z*} is **trivial** if and only if one of the projections *A, B, ..., Z* is the identity projection of *R* (i.e., the projection over all attributes of *R*).

given a relvar *R,* we can tell if *R* is in 5NF so long as we know all candidate keys **and all JDs** in *R*. However, discovering all the JDs might itself be a nontrivial operation. That is, whereas it is relatively easy to identify FDs and MVDs (because they have a fairly straightforward real-world interpretation), the same cannot be said for JDs—JDs, that is, that are not MVDs and not FDs—because the intuitive meaning of JDs might not be obvious. Hence the process of determining when a given relvar is in 4NF but not 5NF, and so could probably be decomposed to advantage, is *still unclear.* Experience suggests that such relvars are pathological cases and likely to be rare in practice.

In conclusion, we note that it follows from the definition that 5NF is the **ultimate normal form** with respect to projection and join (which accounts for its alternative name, *projection-join* normal form). That is, a relvar in 5NF is **guaranteed to be free of anomalies** that can be eliminated by taking projections.* For if a relvar is in 5NF, the only join dependencies are those that are implied by candidate keys, and so the only valid decompositions are ones that are based on those candidate keys. (Each projection in such a decomposition will consist of one or more of those candidate keys, plus zero or more additional attributes.) For example, the suppliers relvar S is in 5NF. It *can* be further decomposed in several nonloss ways, as we saw earlier, but every projection in any such decomposition will still include one of the original candidate keys, and hence there does not seem to be any particular advantage in that further reduction.

12.4 THE NORMALIZATION PROCEDURE SUMMARIZED

Up to this point in this chapter (and throughout the previous chapter), we have been concerned with the technique of *nonloss decomposition* as an aid to database design. The basic idea is as follows: Given some 1NF relvar *R* and some set of FDs, MVDs, and JDs that apply to *R*, we systematically reduce *R* to a collection of "smaller" (i.e., lower-degree) relvars that are equivalent to *R* in a certain well-defined sense but are also in some way more desirable. (The original relvar *R* might have been obtained by first eliminating certain relation-valued attributes, as in Section 12.2 or—better—the answer to Exercise 11.3.) Each step of the reduction process consists of taking projections of the relvars resulting from the preceding step. The given constraints are used at each step to guide the choice of which projections to take next. The overall process can be stated informally as a set of rules, thus:

1. Take projections of the original 1NF relvar to eliminate any FDs that are not irreducible. This step will produce a collection of 2NF relvars.

2. Take projections of those 2NF relvars to eliminate any transitive FDs. This step will produce a collection of 3NF relvars.

3. Take projections of those 3NF relvars to eliminate any remaining FDs in which the determinant is not a candidate key. This step will produce a collection of BCNF relvars.

---

*Of course, this remark does not mean it is free of all possible anomalies; it just means (to repeat) that it is free of anomalies that can be removed by taking projections.

Note: Rules 1–3 can be condensed into the single guideline "Take projections of the original relvar to eliminate all FDs in which the determinant is not a candidate key."

4. Take projections of those BCNF relvars to eliminate any MVDs that are not also FDs. This step will produce a collection of 4NF relvars. *Note:* In practice it is usual—by "separating independent RVAs," as explained in our discussion of the CTX example in Section 12.2—to eliminate such MVDs *before* applying Rules 1–3 above.

5. Take projections of those 4NF relvars to eliminate any JDs that are not implied by the candidate keys—though perhaps we should add "if you can find them." This step will produce a collection of relvars in 5NF.

Several points arise from the foregoing summary:

1. First of all, the process of taking projections at each step must of course be done in a nonloss way, and preferably in a dependency-preserving way as well.

2. Observe that (as was first noted by Fagin in reference [12.14]) there is a very attractive parallelism among the definitions of BCNF, 4NF, and 5NF, *viz.*:

   ■ A relvar R is in BCNF if and only if every FD satisfied by R is implied by the candidate keys of R;

   ■ A relvar R is in 4NF if and only if every MVD satisfied by R is implied by the candidate keys of R;

   ■ A relvar R is in 5NF if and only if every JD satisfied by R is implied by the candidate keys of R.

   The update anomalies discussed in Chapter 11 and in earlier sections of the present chapter are precisely anomalies that are caused by FDs or MVDs or JDs that are not implied by candidate keys.

3. The overall objectives of the normalization process are as follows:

   ■ To eliminate certain kinds of redundancy;

   ■ To avoid certain update anomalies;

   ■ To produce a design that is a "good" representation of the real world—one that is intuitively easy to understand and a good base for future growth;

   ■ To simplify the enforcement of certain integrity constraints.

   We elaborate a little on the last item in this list. The general point is that (as mentioned in Chapters 8, 10, and elsewhere in this book) *some integrity constraints imply others.* As a trivial example, the constraint that salaries must be greater than $10,000 certainly implies the constraint that they must be greater than zero. Now, if constraint *A* implies constraint *B*, then *enforcing A will enforce B automatically* (it will not even be necessary to state *B* explicitly, except perhaps in the form of a comment). And normalization to 5NF gives us a simple way of enforcing certain important and commonly occurring constraints; basically, all we have to do is enforce uniqueness of candidate keys, and then all JDs (and all MVDs and all FDs) will be enforced automatically—

because, of course, all of those JDs (and MVDs and FDs) will be implied by the candidate keys.

4. Once again, we stress the point that the normalization guidelines are only guidelines, and occasionally there might be good reasons for not normalizing "all the way." The classic example of a case where complete normalization *might* not be a good idea is provided by the name and address relvar NADDR (see Exercise 11.7 in Chapter 11)—though, to be frank, that example is not very convincing . . . As a rule of thumb, *not* normalizing all the way is usually a bad idea.

5. We also repeat the point from Chapter 11 that the notions of dependency and further normalization are *semantic* in nature—in other words, they are concerned with what the data *means*. By contrast, the relational algebra and relational calculus, and languages such as SQL that are based on those formalisms, are concerned only with actual data values; they do not and cannot require any particular level of normalization other than first. The further normalization guidelines should be regarded primarily as a discipline to help the database designer (and hence the user)—a discipline by which the designer can capture a part, albeit a small part, of the semantics of the real world in a simple and straightforward manner.

6. Following on from the previous point: The ideas of normalization are useful in database design, but they are not a panacea. Here are some of the reasons why not (this list is elaborated in reference [12.9]):

   - It is true that normalization can help to enforce certain integrity constraints very simply, but (as we know from Chapter 8) JDs and MVDs and FDs are not the only kinds of constraints that can arise in practice.

   - The decomposition might not be unique (usually, in fact, there will be many ways of reducing a given collection of relvars to 5NF), and there are few objective criteria by which to choose among alternative decompositions.

   - The BCNF and dependency preservation objectives can be in conflict, as explained in Section 11.5 ("the SJT problem").

   - The normalization procedure eliminates redundancies by taking projections, but not all redundancies can be eliminated in this manner ("the CTXD problem"—see the annotation to reference [12.13]).

   We should also mention the point that good top-down design methodologies tend to generate fully normalized designs anyway (see Chapter 13).

12.5   A NOTE ON DENORMALIZATION

Up to this point in this chapter (and throughout the previous chapter), we have taken it for granted that full normalization all the way to 5NF is desirable. In practice, however, it is often claimed that "denormalization" is necessary to achieve good performance. The argument goes something like this:

1. Full normalization means lots of logically separate relvars (and we assume here that the relvars in question are base relvars specifically);

2. Lots of logically separate relvars means lots of physically separate stored files;

3. Lots of physically separate stored files means lots of I/O.

Strictly speaking, this argument is invalid, of course, because (as stated elsewhere in this book) the relational model nowhere stipulates that base relvars must map one for one to stored files. *Denormalization, if necessary, should be done at the level of stored files, not at the level of base relvars.* But the argument is valid, somewhat, for today's SQL products, precisely because of the inadequate degree of separation between those two levels found in those products. In this section, therefore, we take a closer look at the notion of "denormalization." *Note:* The discussion that follows is heavily based on material from reference [12.6].

What Is Denormalization?

To review briefly, **normalizing** a relvar R means replacing R by a set of projections $R1, ..., Rn$ (say), such that for all possible values r of relvar R, if the corresponding values $r1, ..., rn$ of projections $R1, ..., Rn$ are joined back together again, then the result of that join is guaranteed to be equal to r. The overall objective is to *reduce redundancy*, by making sure that each of the projections $R1, ..., Rn$ is at the highest possible level of normalization (i.e., 5NF).

Now we can define denormalization, as follows. Let $R1, ..., Rn$ be a set of relvars. Then **denormalizing** those relvars means replacing them by their join R (say), such that for all possible values $r1, ..., rn$ of $R1, ..., Rn$, projecting the corresponding value r of R over the attributes of Ri is guaranteed to yield ri again ($i = 1, ..., n$). The overall objective is to *increase redundancy*, by ensuring that R is at a lower level of normalization than the relvars $R1, ..., Rn$. More specifically, the objective is to reduce the number of joins that need to be done at run time by (in effect) doing some of those joins ahead of time, as part of the database design.

By way of an example, we might consider denormalizing parts and shipments to produce a relvar PSQ as indicated in Fig. 12.6 (opposite).* Observe that relvar PSQ is in 1NF but not in 2NF.

Some Problems

The concept of denormalization suffers from a number of well-known problems. One obvious one is that once we start denormalizing, it is not clear where we should stop . . . With normalization, there are clear logical reasons for continuing until we reach the highest possible normal form; do we then conclude that with denormalization we should proceed until

---

*There is a problem with denormalizing *suppliers* and shipments, given our usual sample data, because supplier S5 is lost in the join. For such reasons, some people might argue that we should use "outer" joins in the denormalization process. But outer joins have problems of their own, as we will see Chapter 18.

PSQ	P#	PNAME	COLOR	WEIGHT	CITY	S#	QTY
	P1	Nut	Red	12.0	London	S1	300
	P1	Nut	Red	12.0	London	S2	300
	P2	Bolt	Green	17.0	Paris	S1	200
	..	.....	.....	......	......	..	...
	P6	Cog	Red	19.0	London	S1	100

Fig. 12.6 Denormalizing parts and shipments

we reach the *lowest* possible normal form? Surely not; yet there are no *logical* criteria for deciding exactly where to stop. In choosing to denormalize, in other words, we are backing off from a position that does at least have some solid science and logical theory behind it, and replaced it by one that is purely pragmatic in nature, and subjective.

The second obvious point is that there are redundancy and update problems, precisely because we are dealing once again with relvars that are less than fully normalized. We have already discussed these issues at length. What is less obvious, however, is that there can be *retrieval* problems too; that is, denormalization can actually make certain queries more difficult to express. For example, consider the query "For each part color, get the average weight." Given our usual normalized design, a suitable formulation is:

```
SUMMARIZE P PER P { COLOR } ADD AVG ( WEIGHT ) AS AVWT
```

Given the denormalized design of Fig. 12.6, however, the formulation is a little trickier (not to mention the fact that it relies on the—generally invalid!—assumption that every part does have at least one shipment):

```
SUMMARIZE PSQ { P#, COLOR, WEIGHT } PER PSQ { COLOR }
                       ADD AVG ( WEIGHT ) AS AVWT
```

(Note that the latter formulation is likely to perform worse, too.) In other words, the common perception that denormalization is "good for retrieval but bad for update" is incorrect, in general, for both usability and performance reasons.

A third, and major, problem is as follows (and this point applies to "proper" denormalization—i.e., denormalization that is done at the physical level only—as well as to the kind of denormalization that sometimes has to be done in today's SQL products): When we say that denormalization is "good for performance," we really mean it is good for *the performance of specific applications*. Any given physical design is, of necessity, good for some applications but bad for others (in terms of performance, that is). For example, assume that each base relvar does map to one physically stored file, and assume too that each stored file consists of a physically contiguous collection of stored records, one for each tuple in the corresponding relvar. Then:

- Suppose we represent the join of suppliers, shipments, and parts as one base relvar and hence one stored file. Then the query "Get supplier details for suppliers who supply red parts" will presumably perform well against this physical structure.

- However, the query "Get supplier details for London suppliers" will perform *worse* against this physical structure than it would if we had stayed with three base relvars and mapped them to three physically separate stored files. The reason is that, with the latter design, all supplier stored records will be physically contiguous, whereas in the former design they will be physically spread over a wider area, and will therefore require more I/O.

  Analogous remarks apply to any other query that accesses suppliers only, or parts only, or shipments only, instead of performing some kind of join.

12.6 ORTHOGONAL DESIGN (A DIGRESSION)

In this section we briefly examine another database design principle, one that is not part of further normalization *per se* but does resemble normalization in that it is *scientific.* It is called ***The Principle of Orthogonal Design.*** Consider Fig. 12.7, which shows an obviously bad but possible design for suppliers; relvar SA in that design corresponds to suppliers who are located in Paris, relvar SB corresponds to suppliers who are either not located in Paris or have status greater than 30 (i.e., these are the relvar predicates, loosely speaking). As the figure indicates, the design leads to certain *redundancies;* to be specific, the tuple for supplier S3 appears twice, once in each relvar.

/* suppliers in Paris */

SA

S#	SNAME	STATUS	CITY
S2	Jones	10	Paris
S3	Blake	30	Paris

SB

S#	SNAME	STATUS	CITY
S1	Smith	20	London
S3	Blake	30	Paris
S4	Clark	20	London
S5	Adams	30	Athens

/* suppliers not in Paris or with status 30 */

??? ??? redundancy

Fig. 12.7 A bad but possible design for suppliers

Note, incidentally, that the tuple *must* appear in both places. For suppose, contrariwise, that it were to appear in SB (say) but not SA. Applying the Closed World Assumption to SA would then tell us that it is not the case that supplier S3 is located in Paris. However, SB tells us that it *is* the case that supplier S3 is located in Paris. In other words, we would have a contradiction on our hands, and the database would be inconsistent.

The problem with the design of Fig. 12.7 is obvious, of course: It is precisely the fact that it is possible for the very same tuple to appear in two distinct relvars. In other words, the two relvars have *overlapping meanings,* in the sense that it is possible for the very same tuple to satisfy the relvar predicates for both. So an obvious rule is:

- **The Principle of Orthogonal Design** *(initial version):* Within a given database, no two base relvars should have overlapping meanings.

Points arising:

1. Recall from Chapter 9 that, from the user's point of view, *all* relvars are base relvars (apart from views that are defined as mere shorthands). In other words, the principle applies to the design of all "expressible" databases, not just to the "real" database—*The Principle of Database Relativity* at work once again. (Of course, analogous remarks apply to the principles of normalization also.)

2. Note that, two relvars cannot possibly have overlapping meanings unless they are of the same type (i.e., unless they have the same heading).

3. Adherence to the orthogonal design principle implies that (e.g.) when we insert a tuple, we can regard the operation as inserting a tuple *into the database,* rather than into some specific relvar—because there will be at most one relvar whose predicate the new tuple satisfies.

   Now, it is true that when we insert a tuple, we do typically specify the name of the relvar *R* into which that tuple is to be inserted. But this fact does not invalidate the foregoing point. The fact is, that name *R* is really just *shorthand for the corresponding predicate, PR* say; we are really saying "INSERT tuple *t*—and by the way, *t* is required to satisfy predicate *PR*." Furthermore, of course, *R* might be a view, perhaps defined by means of an expression of the form *A* UNION *B*—and, as we saw in Chapter 9, it is very desirable that the system know whether the new tuple is to go into *A* or *B* or both.

   In fact, remarks analogous to the foregoing apply to all operations, not just to INSERTs; in all cases, relvar names are really just shorthand for relvar predicates. *The point cannot be emphasized too strongly that it is predicates, not names, that represent data semantics.*

We have not yet finished with the orthogonal design principle—there is an important refinement that needs to be addressed. Consider Fig. 12.8, which shows another obviously bad but possible design for suppliers. Here the two relvars *per se* do not have overlapping meanings, but their projections on {S#,SNAME} certainly do (in fact, the meanings of those

SX	S#	SNAME	STATUS		SY	S#	SNAME	CITY
	S1	Smith	20			S1	Smith	London
	S2	Jones	10			S2	Jones	Paris
	S3	Blake	30			S3	Blake	Paris
	S4	Clark	20			S4	Clark	London
	S5	Adams	30			S5	Adams	Athens

Fig. 12.8 Another bad but possible design for suppliers

two projections are identical). As a consequence, an attempt to insert, say, the tuple (S6,Lopez) into a view defined as the union of those two projections will cause the tuple (S6,Lopez,*t*) to be inserted into SX and the tuple (S6,Lopez,*c*) to be inserted into SY (where *t* and *c* are the applicable default values). Clearly, we need to extend the orthogonal design principle to take care of problems like that of Fig. 12.8:

- ■ ***The Principle of Orthogonal Design*** *(final version):* Let *A* and *B* be any two base relvars in the database. Then there must not exist nonloss decompositions of *A* and *B* into *A1*, ..., *Am* and *B1*, ..., *Bn* (respectively) such that some projection *Ai* in the set *A1*, ..., *Am* and some projection *Bj* in the set *B1*, ..., *Bn* have overlapping meanings.

Points arising:

1. The term "nonloss decomposition" here means exactly what it always means—*viz.,* decomposition into a set of projections such that:
   - ■ The given relvar can be reconstructed by joining the projections back together;
   - ■ None of those projections is redundant in that reconstruction process.
2. This version of the principle subsumes the original version, because one nonloss decomposition that always exists for relvar *R* is the identity projection of *R* (i.e., the projection over all attributes).

Remarks

1. Suppose we start with the usual suppliers relvar S, but decide for design purposes to break that relvar down into a set of restrictions. Then the orthogonal design principle tells us that the restrictions in that breakdown should all be disjoint, in the sense that no supplier tuple can ever appear in more than one of them. We refer to such a breakdown as an *orthogonal decomposition. Note:* The term *orthogonality* derives from the fact that what the design principle effectively means is that base relvars should be mutually independent (no overlapping meanings). The principle is common sense, of course, but *formalized* common sense (like the principles of normalization).
2. The overall objective of orthogonal design is to reduce redundancy and thereby to avoid update anomalies (again like normalization). In fact, it complements normalization, in the sense that—loosely speaking—normalization reduces redundancy *within* relvars, while orthogonality reduces redundancy *across* relvars.
3. Orthogonality might be common sense, but it is often flouted in practice (indeed, such flouting is sometimes even recommended). Designs like the following one, from a financial database, are all too common:

```
ACTIVITIES_1997 { ENTRY#, DESCRIPTION, AMOUNT, NEW_BAL }
ACTIVITIES_1998 { ENTRY#, DESCRIPTION, AMOUNT, NEW_BAL }
ACTIVITIES_1999 { ENTRY#, DESCRIPTION, AMOUNT, NEW_BAL }
ACTIVITIES_2000 { ENTRY#, DESCRIPTION, AMOUNT, NEW_BAL }
ACTIVITIES_2001 { ENTRY#, DESCRIPTION, AMOUNT, NEW_BAL }
```

In fact, encoding meaning into names—of relvars or anything else—violates *The Information Principle,* which states (to remind you) that all information in the database must be cast explicitly in terms of values and in no other way.

4. If *A* and *B* are base relvars of the same type, adherence to the orthogonal design principle implies that:

`A UNION B`	is always a disjoint union;
`A INTERSECT B`	is always empty;
`A MINUS B`	is always equal to *A*.

12.7 OTHER NORMAL FORMS

Back to normalization *per se.* Recall from the introduction to Chapter 11 that there do exist other normal forms, over and above those discussed in these two chapters so far. The fact is, the theory of normalization and related topics—now usually known as **dependency theory**—has grown into a considerable field in its own right, with a very extensive literature. Research in the area is continuing, and indeed flourishing. It is beyond the scope of this chapter to discuss that research in any depth; a good survey of the field (as of the mid 1980s) can be found in reference [12.17]. Here we just mention a couple of specific issues.

1. **Domain-key normal form:** Domain-key normal form (DK/NF) was proposed by Fagin in reference [12.15]. DK/NF—unlike the normal forms we have been discussing—is not defined in terms of FDs, MVDs, or JDs at all. Instead, a relvar *R* is said to be in DK/NF if and only if every constraint on *R* is a logical consequence of the *domain constraints* and *key constraints* that apply to *R:*

   ■ A *domain constraint*—as the term is used here—is a constraint to the effect that values of a given attribute are taken from some prescribed domain. (In the terminology of Chapter 8, such a constraint is really an *attribute* constraint, not a domain constraint.)

   ■ A *key constraint* is a constraint to the effect that a certain attribute or attribute combination constitutes a candidate key.

   Enforcing constraints on a DK/NF relvar is thus conceptually simple, since it is sufficient to enforce just the "domain" and key constraints and all other constraints will then be enforced automatically. Note carefully too that "all other constraints" here means more than just FDs and MVDs and JDs—in fact, it means the entire relvar predicate.

   Fagin shows in reference [12.15] that any DK/NF relvar is necessarily in 5NF (and therefore in 4NF, etc.), and indeed in (3,3)NF also (see below). However, DK/NF is not always achievable, nor has the question "Exactly when *can* it be achieved?" been answered.

2. **"Restriction-union" normal form:** Consider the suppliers relvar S once again. Normalization theory as we have described it tells us that relvar S is in a "good" normal

form; indeed, it is in 5NF, and is therefore guaranteed to be free of anomalies that can be eliminated by taking projections. But why keep all suppliers in a single relvar? What about a design in which London suppliers are kept in one relvar (LS, say), Paris suppliers in another (PS, say), and so on? In other words, what about the possibility of decomposing the original suppliers relvar via **restriction** instead of projection? Would the resulting structure be a good design or a bad one? (In fact it would almost certainly be bad—see Exercise 7.8 in Chapter 7—but the point is that classical normalization theory as such has absolutely nothing to say in answer to such questions.)

Another direction for normalization research therefore consists of examining the implications of decomposing relvars by some operation other than projection. In the example, the decomposition operator is, as already mentioned, (disjoint) *restriction;* the corresponding recomposition operator is (disjoint) **union.** Thus, it might be possible to construct a "restriction-union" normalization theory, analogous but orthogonal once again to the projection-join normalization theory we have been discussing.* To this writer's knowledge no such theory has ever been worked out in detail, but some initial ideas can be found in a paper by Smith [12.31], where a new normal form called **"(3,3)NF"** is defined. (3,3)NF implies BCNF; however, a (3,3)NF relvar need not be in 4NF, nor need a 4NF relvar be in (3,3)NF, so that (as suggested above) reduction to (3,3)NF is orthogonal to reduction to 4NF (and 5NF). Further ideas on this topic appear in references [12.14] and [12.22].

12.8 SUMMARY

In this chapter we have completed our discussion (begun in Chapter 11) of **further normalization.** We have discussed **multi-valued dependencies** (MVDs), which are a generalization of functional dependencies, and **join dependencies** (JDs), which are a generalization of multi-valued dependencies. Loosely speaking:

- A relvar $R\{A,B,C\}$ satisfies the MVDs $A \rightarrow\rightarrow B \mid C$ if and only if the set of B values matching a given (A,C) pair depends only on the A value, and similarly for the set of C values matching a given (A,B) pair. Such a relvar can be nonloss-decomposed into its projections on $\{A,B\}$ and $\{A,C\}$; in fact, the MVDs are a necessary and sufficient condition for this decomposition to be valid (Fagin's theorem).

- A relvar $R\{A,B,...,Z\}$ satisfies the JD $\ast\{A,B,...,Z\}$ if and only if it is equal to the join of its projections on $A, B, ... Z$. Such a relvar can (obviously) be nonloss-decomposed into those projections.

---

*Indeed, Fagin [12.14] originally called 5NF *projection-join* normal form precisely because it was **the** normal form with respect to the projection and join operators.

A relvar is in 4NF if the only MVDs it satisfies are in fact FDs out of superkeys. A relvar is in 5NF—also called **projection-join** normal form, PJ/NF—if and only if the only JDs it satisfies are in fact FDs out of superkeys (meaning that if the JD is ⋇ {$A,B,...,Z$}, then each of A, B, ..., Z is a superkey). 5NF (which is always achievable) is the *ultimate normal form* with respect to projection and join.

We also summarized the **normalization procedure,** presenting it as an informal sequence of steps and offering a few relevant comments. We then described ***The Principle of Orthogonal Design:*** Loosely, no two relvars should have projections with overlapping meanings. Finally, we briefly mentioned some *additional normal forms.*

In conclusion, we should perhaps point out that research into issues such as those we have been discussing is very much a worthwhile activity. The reason is that the field of "further normalization," or rather **dependency theory** as it is now more usually called, does represent a piece of *science* in a field—database design—that is, regrettably, still far too much of an artistic endeavor (i.e., it is far too subjective and lacking in solid principles and guidelines). Thus, any further successes in dependency theory research are very much to be welcomed.

EXERCISES

12.1 Relvars CTX and SPJ as discussed in the body of the chapter—see Figs. 12.2 and 12.4 for some sample values—satisfied a certain MVD and a certain JD, respectively, that was not implied by the candidate keys of the relvar in question. Express that MVD and that JD in the syntax of Chapter 8.

12.2 Let C be a certain club, and let relvar $R\{A,B\}$ be such that the tuple (a,b) appears in R if and only if a and b are both members of C. What FDs, MVDs, and JDs does R satisfy? What normal form is it in?

12.3 A database is to contain information concerning sales representatives, sales areas, and products. Each representative is responsible for sales in one or more areas; each area has one or more responsible representatives. Similarly, each representative is responsible for sales of one or more products, and each product has one or more responsible representatives. Every product is sold in every area; however, no two representatives sell the same product in the same area. Every representative sells the same set of products in every area for which that representative is responsible. Design a suitable set of relvars for this data.

12.4 In the answer to Exercise 11.3 in Chapter 11, we gave an algorithm for nonloss decomposition of an arbitrary relvar R into a set of BCNF relvars. Revise that algorithm so that it yields 4NF relvars instead.

12.5 *(Modified version of Exercise 12.3)* A database is to contain information concerning sales representatives, sales areas, and products. Each representative is responsible for sales in one or more areas; each area has one or more responsible representatives. Similarly, each representative is responsible for sales of one or more products, and each product has one or more responsible representatives. Finally, each product is sold in one or more areas, and each area has one or more products sold in it. Moreover, if representative R is responsible for area A, and product P is sold in area A, and representative R is responsible for product P, then R sells P in A. Design a suitable set of relvars for this data.

REFERENCES AND BIBLIOGRAPHY

12.1 A. V. Aho, C. Beeri, and J. D. Ullman: "The Theory of Joins in Relational Databases," *ACM TODS 4,* No. 3 (September 1979). First published in Proc. 19th IEEE Symp. on Foundations of Computer Science (October 1977).

> The paper that first pointed out that relvars could exist that were not equal to the join of any two of their projections, but were equal to the join of three or more. The major objective of the paper was to present an algorithm, now generally called the **chase,** for determining whether or not a given JD is a logical consequence of a given set of FDs (an example of the **implication problem**—see reference [12.17]). This problem is equivalent to the problem of determining whether a given decomposition is nonloss, given a certain set of FDs. The paper also discusses the question of extending the algorithm to deal with the case where the given dependencies are not FDs but MVDs.

12.2 Catriel Beeri, Ronald Fagin, and John H. Howard: "A Complete Axiomatization for Functional and Multi-Valued Dependencies," Proc. 1977 ACM SIGMOD Int. Conf. on Management of Data, Toronto, Canada (August 1977).

> Extends the work of Armstrong [10.1] to include MVDs as well as FDs. In particular, it gives the following set of sound and complete inference rules for MVDs:
>
> 1. **Complementation:** If A, B, and C together include all attributes of the relvar and A is a superset of $B \cap C$, then $A \rightarrow\rightarrow B$ if and only if $A \rightarrow\rightarrow C$.
>
> 2. **Reflexivity:** If B is a subset of A then $A \rightarrow\rightarrow B$.
>
> 3. **Augmentation:** If $A \rightarrow\rightarrow B$ and C is a subset of D then $AD \rightarrow\rightarrow BC$.
>
> 4. **Transitivity:** If $A \rightarrow\rightarrow B$ and $B \rightarrow\rightarrow C$ then $A \rightarrow\rightarrow C - B$.
>
> The following additional (and useful) inference rules can be derived from those given above:
>
> 5. **Pseudotransitivity:** If $A \rightarrow\rightarrow B$ and $BC \rightarrow\rightarrow D$ then $AC \rightarrow\rightarrow D - BC$.
>
> 6. **Union:** If $A \rightarrow\rightarrow B$ and $A \rightarrow\rightarrow C$ then $A \rightarrow\rightarrow BC$.
>
> 7. **Decomposition:** If $A \rightarrow\rightarrow BC$ then $A \rightarrow\rightarrow B \cap C$, $A \rightarrow\rightarrow B - C$, and $A \rightarrow\rightarrow C - B$.
>
> The paper then goes on to give two further rules by which certain FDs can be inferred from certain combinations of FDs and MVDs:
>
> 8. **Replication:** If $A \rightarrow B$ then $A \rightarrow\rightarrow B$.
>
> 9. **Coalescence:** If $A \rightarrow\rightarrow B$ and $C \rightarrow D$ and D is a subset of B and $B \cap C$ is empty, then $A \rightarrow D$.
>
> Armstrong's rules (see Chapter 10) plus rules 1–4 and 8–9 above form a sound and complete set of inference rules for FDs and MVDs taken together.
>
> The paper also derives one more useful rule relating FDs and MVDs:
>
> 10. If $A \rightarrow\rightarrow B$ and $AB \rightarrow C$ then $A \rightarrow C - B$.

12.3 Volkert Brosda and Gottfried Vossen: "Update and Retrieval Through a Universal Schema Interface," *ACM TODS 13,* No. 4 (December 1988).

> Previous attempts at providing a "universal relation" interface (see reference [12.19]) deal with retrieval operations only. This paper proposes an approach for dealing with update operations also.

12.4 C. Robert Carlson and Robert S. Kaplan: "A Generalized Access Path Model and Its Application to a Relational Data Base System," Proc. 1976 ACM SIGMOD Int. Conf. on Management of Data, Washington, DC (June 1976).

See the annotation to reference [12.19].

12.5 C. J. Date: "Will the Real Fourth Normal Form Please Stand Up?", in C. J. Date and Hugh Darwen, *Relational Database Writings 1989–1991*. Reading, Mass.: Addison-Wesley (1992).

To paraphrase from the abstract: "There are several distinct notions in the database design world all laying claim to the title of *fourth normal form* (4NF). The purpose of this paper is to try to set the record straight." Perhaps we should add that (of course) the notion referred to as 4NF in the body of this chapter is the only true 4NF . . . Accept no substitutes!

12.6 C. J. Date: "The Normal Is So . . . Interesting" (in two parts), *DBP&D 10,* Nos. 11–12 (November–December 1997).

The denormalization discussion in Section 12.5 is taken from this paper. The following additional points are worth making:

- Even in a read-only database, it is still necessary to state the integrity constraints, since they define the meaning of the data, and (as noted in Section 12.4) *not* denormalizing provides a simple way of stating certain important constraints. And if the database is *not* read-only, then not denormalizing provides a simple way of *enforcing* those constraints also.

- Denormalization implies increased redundancy—but (contrary to popular opinion) increased redundancy does not necessarily imply denormalization! Many writers have fallen into this trap, and some continue to do so.

- As a general rule, denormalization (denormalization at the logical level, that is) should be tried as a performance tactic "only if all else fails" [4.16].

12.7 C. J. Date: "The Final Normal Form!" (in two parts), *DBP&D 11,* Nos. 1–2 (January–February 1998).

A tutorial on JDs and 5NF.

12.8 C. J. Date: "What's Normal, Anyway?", *DBP&D 11,* No. 3 (March 1998).

A survey of certain "pathological" normalization examples, such as the USA example from Exercise 11.2 in Chapter 11.

12.9 C. J. Date: "Normalization Is No Panacea," *DBP&D 11,* No. 4 (April 1998).

A survey of some database design issues *not* helped by the theory of normalization. The paper is not meant as an attack.

12.10 C. J. Date and Ronald Fagin: "Simple Conditions for Guaranteeing Higher Normal Forms in Relational Databases," in C. J. Date and Hugh Darwen, *Relational Database Writings 1989–1991*. Reading, Mass.: Addison-Wesley (1992). Also published in *ACM TODS 17,* No. 3 (September 1992).

Shows that if (a) relvar R is in 3NF and (b) all candidate keys of R are simple, then R is automatically in 5NF. In other words, there is no need to worry in the case of such a relvar about the comparatively complicated topics—MVDs, JDs, 4NF, 5NF—discussed in the present chapter. *Note:* The paper also proves another result, namely that if (a) R is in BCNF and (b) at least one of its candidate keys is simple, then R is automatically in 4NF, but not necessarily 5NF.

12.11 C. J. Date and David McGoveran: "A New Database Design Principle," in C. J. Date, *Relational Database Writings 1991–1994*. Reading, Mass.: Addison-Wesley (1995).

12.12 C. Delobel and D. S. Parker: "Functional and Multi-Valued Dependencies in a Relational Database and the Theory of Boolean Switching Functions," Tech. Report No. 142, Dept. Maths. Appl. et Informatique, Univ. de Grenoble, France (November 1978).

Extends the results of reference [10.3] to include MVDs as well as FDs.

12.13 Ronald Fagin: "Multi-Valued Dependencies and a New Normal Form for Relational Databases," *ACM TODS 2,* No. 3 (September 1977).

The new normal form was 4NF.

We add a note here on **embedded** multi-valued dependencies. Suppose we extend relvar CTX of Section 12.2 to include an additional attribute DAYS, representing the number of days spent with the indicated TEXT by the indicated TEACHER on the indicated COURSE. Let us refer to this relvar as CTXD. Here is a sample value:

CTXD	COURSE	TEACHER	TEXT	DAYS
	Physics	Prof. Green	Basic Mechanics	5
	Physics	Prof. Green	Principles of Optics	5
	Physics	Prof. Brown	Basic Mechanics	6
	Physics	Prof. Brown	Principles of Optics	4
	Math	Prof. Green	Basic Mechanics	3
	Math	Prof. Green	Vector Analysis	3
	Math	Prof. Green	Trigonometry	4

The combination {COURSE,TEACHER,TEXT} is a candidate key, and we have the FD:

```
{ COURSE, TEACHER, TEXT } → DAYS
```

Observe that the relvar is in fourth normal form; it does not involve any MVDs that are not also FDs. However, it does include two *embedded* MVDs (of TEACHER on COURSE and TEXT on COURSE). The embedded MVD of B on A is said to hold in relvar R if the "regular" MVD $A \rightarrow\rightarrow B$ holds in some projection of R. A regular MVD is a special case of an embedded MVD, but not all embedded MVDs are regular MVDs.

As the example illustrates, embedded MVDs imply redundancy, just like regular MVDs; however, that redundancy cannot (in general) be eliminated by taking projections. The relvar shown above cannot be nonloss-decomposed into projections at all (in fact, it is in fifth normal form as well as fourth), because DAYS depends on all three of COURSE, TEACHER, and TEXT and so cannot appear in a relvar with anything less than all three. Instead, therefore, the two embedded MVDs would have to be stated as additional, explicit constraints on the relvar. The details are left as an exercise.

12.14 Ronald Fagin: "Normal Forms and Relational Database Operators," Proc. 1979 ACM SIG-MOD Int. Conf. on Management of Data, Boston, Mass. (May/June 1979).

This is the paper that introduced the concept of projection-join normal form (PJ/NF, or 5NF). However, it is also much more than that. It can be regarded as the definitive statement of what might be called "classical" normalization theory—i.e., the theory of nonloss decomposition based on projection as the decomposition operator and natural join as the corresponding recomposition operator.

12.15 Ronald Fagin: "A Normal Form for Relational Databases that Is Based on Domains and Keys," *ACM TODS 6,* No. 3 (September 1981).

12.16 Ronald Fagin: "Acyclic Database Schemes (of Various Degrees): A Painless Introduction," IBM Research Report RJ3800 (April 1983). Republished in G. Ausiello and M. Protasi (eds.), *Proc. CAAP83 8th Colloquium on Trees in Algebra and Programming* (Springer Verlag Lecture Notes in *Computer Science 159*). New York, N.Y.: Springer Verlag (1983).

> Section 12.3 of the present chapter showed how a certain ternary relvar SPJ that satisfied a certain cyclic constraint could be nonloss-decomposed into its three binary projections. The resulting database structure (i.e., schema, called *scheme* in this paper) is said to be **cyclic,** because each of the three relvars has an attribute in common with each of the other two. (If the structure is depicted as a *hypergraph,* in which edges represent individual relvars and the node that is the intersection of two edges corresponds precisely to the attributes in common to those two edges, then it should be clear why the term "cyclic" is used.) By contrast, most structures that arise in practice are acyclic. Acyclic structures enjoy a number of formal properties that do not apply to cyclic structures. In this paper, Fagin presents and explains a list of such properties.
>
> A helpful way to think about acyclicity is the following: Just as the theory of normalization can help in determining when *a single relvar* should be restructured in some way, so the theory of acyclicity can help in determining when a *collection* of relvars should be restructured in some way.

12.17 R. Fagin and M. Y. Vardi: "The Theory of Data Dependencies—A Survey," IBM Research Report RJ4321 (June 1984). Republished in *Mathematics of Information Processing: Proc. Symposia in Applied Mathematics 34,* American Mathematical Society (1986).

> Provides a brief history of the subject of dependency theory as of the mid 1980s (note that "dependency" here does *not* refer to FDs only). In particular, the paper summarizes the major achievements in three specific areas within the overall field, and in so doing provides a good selected list of relevant references. The three areas are (1) the implication problem, (2) the "universal relation" model, and (3) acyclic schemas. The **implication problem** is the problem of determining, given a set of dependencies D and some specific dependency d, whether d is a logical consequence of D (see Section 10.7). The **universal relation model** and **acyclic schemas** (also known as acyclic *schemes*) are discussed, briefly, in the annotation to references [12.19] and [12.16], respectively.

12.18 Ronald Fagin, Alberto O. Mendelzon, and Jeffrey D. Ullman: "A Simplified Universal Relation Assumption and Its Properties," *ACM TODS 7,* No. 3 (September 1982).

> Conjectures that the real world can always be represented by means of a "universal relation" [12.19]—or universal relvar, rather—that satisfies precisely one join dependency plus a set of functional dependencies, and explores some of the consequences of that conjecture.

12.19 W. Kent: "Consequences of Assuming a Universal Relation," *ACM TODS 6,* No. 4 (December 1981).

> The concept of the **universal relation** manifests itself in several different ways. First of all, the normalization discipline described in the last two chapters tacitly assumed that it is possible to define an initial universal *relation*—or, more correctly, a universal relvar—that includes all of the attributes relevant to the database under consideration, and then showed how that relvar can be replaced by successively "smaller" (lower-degree) projections until some "good" structure is reached. But is that initial assumption realistic or justifiable? Reference [12.19] suggests not, on both practical and theoretical grounds. Reference [12.32] is a reply to reference [12.19], and reference [12.20] is a reply to that reply.

The second, and more pragmatically significant, manifestation of the universal relvar concept is as a *user interface*. The basic idea here is quite straightforward, and indeed (from an intuitive standpoint) quite appealing: Users should be able to frame their database requests, not in terms of relvars and joins among those relvars, but rather in terms of attributes alone. For example:

```
STATUS WHERE COLOR = COLOR ( 'Red' )
```

("Get status for suppliers who supply some red part"). At this point the idea forks into two more or less distinct interpretations:

1. One possibility is that the system should somehow determine for itself what logical access paths to follow (in particular, what joins to perform) in order to answer the query. This is the approach suggested in reference [12.4] (which seems to have been the first paper to discuss the possibility of a "universal relation" interface, though it did not use the term). This approach is critically dependent on proper naming of attributes. Thus, for example, the two supplier number attributes (in relvars S and SP respectively) *must* be given the same name; conversely, the supplier city and part city attributes (in relvars S and P respectively) must *not* be given the same name. If either of these two rules is violated, there will be certain queries that the system will be unable to handle properly.

2. The other, less ambitious, approach is simply to regard all queries as being formulated in terms of a *predefined* set of joins—in effect, a predefined view consisting of "the" join of all relvars in the database.

While there is no question that either approach would greatly simplify the expression of many queries arising in practice—and indeed some such approach is essential to the support of any natural-language frontend—it is also clear that the system must support the ability to specify (logical) access paths explicitly as well, in general. To see that this must be so, consider the query

```
STATUS WHERE COLOR ≠ COLOR ( 'Red' )
```

Does this query mean "Get status of suppliers who supply a part that is not red" or "Get status of suppliers who do not supply a red part"? Whichever it is, there has to be some way of formulating the other. (Come to that, the first example above is also susceptible to an alternative interpretation: "Get status for suppliers who supply *only* red parts.") And here is a third example: "Get pairs of suppliers who are colocated." Here again it is clear that an explicit join will be necessary (because the problem involves a join of relvar S with itself, loosely speaking).

12.20 William Kent: "The Universal Relation Revisited," *ACM TODS 8,* No. 4 (December 1983).

12.21 Henry F. Korth *et al.:* "System/U: A Database System Based on the Universal Relation Assumption," *ACM TODS 9,* No. 3 (September 1984).

Describes the theory, DDL, DML, and implementation of an experimental "universal relation" system built at Stanford University.

12.22 David Maier and Jeffrey D. Ullman: "Fragments of Relations," Proc. 1983 SIGMOD Int. Conf. on Management of Data, San Jose, Calif. (May 1983).

12.23 David Maier, Jeffrey D. Ullman, and Moshe Y. Vardi: "On the Foundations of the Universal Relation Model," *ACM TODS 9,* No. 2 (June 1984). An earlier version of this paper, under the title

"The Revenge of the JD," appeared in Proc. 2nd ACM SIGACT-SIGMOD Symposium on Principles of Database Systems, Atlanta, Ga. (March 1983).

12.24 David Maier and Jeffrey D. Ullman: "Maximal Objects and the Semantics of Universal Relation Databases," *ACM TODS 8,* No. 1 (March 1983).

Maximal objects represent an approach to the ambiguity problem that arises in "universal relation" systems when the underlying structure is not acyclic (see reference [12.16]). A maximal object corresponds to a predeclared subset of the totality of attributes for which the underlying structure *is* acyclic. Such objects are then used to guide the interpretation of queries that would otherwise be ambiguous.

12.25 J.-M. Nicolas: "Mutual Dependencies and Some Results on Undecomposable Relations," Proc. 4th Int. Conf. on Very Large Data Bases, Berlin, Federal German Republic (September 1978).

Introduces the concept of "mutual dependency." A mutual dependency is actually a special case of the general join dependency—i.e., a JD that is not an MVD or FD—that happens to involve exactly three projections (like the JD example given in Section 12.3). It has nothing to do with the concept of mutual dependence discussed in Chapter 11.

12.26 Sylvia L. Osborn: "Towards a Universal Relation Interface," Proc. 5th Int. Conf. on Very Large Data Bases, Rio de Janeiro, Brazil (October 1979).

The proposals of this paper assume that if there are two or more sequences of joins in a "universal relation" system that will generate a candidate answer to a given query, then the desired response is the union of all such candidates. Algorithms are given for generating all such sequences of joins.

12.27 D. Stott Parker and Claude Delobel: "Algorithmic Applications for a New Result on Multi-Valued Dependencies," Proc. 5th Int. Conf. on Very Large Data Bases, Rio de Janeiro, Brazil (October 1979).

Applies the results of reference [12.12] to various problems, such as the problem of testing for a nonloss decomposition.

12.28 Y. Sagiv, C. Delobel, D. S. Parker, and R. Fagin: "An Equivalence between Relational Database Dependencies and a Subclass of Propositional Logic," *JACM 28,* No. 3 (June 1981).

Combines references [10.8] and [12.29].

12.29 Y. Sagiv and R. Fagin: "An Equivalence between Relational Database Dependencies and a Subclass of Propositional Logic," IBM Research Report RJ2500 (March 1979).

Extends the results of reference [10.8] to include MVDs as well as FDs.

12.30 E. Sciore: "A Complete Axiomatization of Full Join Dependencies," *JACM 29,* No. 2 (April 1982).

Extends the work of reference [12.2] to include JDs as well as FDs and MVDs.

12.31 J. M. Smith: "A Normal Form for Abstract Syntax," Proc. 4th Int. Conf. on Very Large Data Bases, Berlin, Federal German Republic (September 1978).

The paper that introduced (3,3)NF.

12.32 Jeffrey D. Ullman: "On Kent's 'Consequences of Assuming a Universal Relation,'" *ACM TODS 8,* No. 4 (December 1983).

12.33 Jeffrey D. Ullman: "The U.R. Strikes Back," Proc. 1st ACM SIGACT-SIGMOD Symposium on Principles of Database Systems, Los Angeles, Calif. (March 1982).

ANSWERS TO SELECTED EXERCISES

12.1 Here first is the MVD for relvar CTX:

```
CONSTRAINT CTX_MVD
   WITH
     ( CTX RENAME COURSE AS C, TEACHER AS T, TEXT AS X )
                                       AS T1,
     ( EXTEND T1
       ADD ( CTX WHERE COURSE = C ) { T } AS A )
                                       AS T2,
     ( EXTEND T2
       ADD ( CTX WHERE COURSE = C AND TEXT = X ) { T } AS B )
                                       AS T3,
     ( T3 WHERE A ≠ B ) AS T4 :
     IS_EMPTY ( T4 ) ;
```

Of course, a much simpler formulation exists also:

```
CONSTRAINT CTX_MVD CTX = CTX { COURSE, TEACHER } JOIN
                         CTX { COURSE, TEXT } ;
```

And here is the JD for relvar SPJ:

```
CONSTRAINT SPJ_JD SPJ = SPJ { S#, P# } JOIN
                        SPJ { P#, J# } JOIN
                        SPJ { J#, S# } ;
```

12.2 Note first that R contains every possible A value paired with every possible B value, and further that the set of all A values, S say, is the same as the set of all B values. The body of R is thus equal to the Cartesian product of set S with itself; equivalently, R is equal to the Cartesian product of its projections $R\{A\}$ and $R\{B\}$. R thus satisfies the following MVDs (which are not trivial, please note, since they are certainly not satisfied by all binary relvars):

$$\{ \ \} \twoheadrightarrow A \mid B$$

Equivalently, R satisfies the *JD* $\bowtie \{A,B\}$ (remember that join degenerates to Cartesian product when there are no common attributes). It follows that R is not in 4NF, and it can be nonloss-decomposed into its projections on A and B (those projections have identical bodies, of course). R is, however, in BCNF (it is all key), and it satisfies no nontrivial FDs.

Note: R also satisfies the MVDs

$$A \twoheadrightarrow B \mid \{ \ \}$$

and

$$B \twoheadrightarrow A \mid \{ \ \}$$

However, these MVDs *are* trivial, since they are satisfied by every binary relvar with attributes A and B.

12.3 First we introduce three relvars

```
REP      { REP#, ... }
         KEY { REP# }

AREA     { AREA#, ... }
         KEY { AREA# }

PRODUCT  { PROD#, ... }
         KEY { PROD# }
```

with the obvious interpretation. Second, we can represent the relationship between sales representatives and sales areas by a relvar

```
RA { REP#, AREA# }
   KEY { REP#, AREA# }
```

and the relationship between sales representatives and products by a relvar

```
RP { REP#, PROD# }
   KEY { REP#, PROD# }
```

(both of these relationships are many-to-many).

Next, we are told that every product is sold in every area. So if we introduce a relvar

```
AP { AREA#, PROD# }
   KEY { AREA#, PROD# }
```

to represent the relationship between areas and products, then we have the constraint (let us call it C) that

```
AP = AREA { AREA# } TIMES PRODUCT { PROD# }
```

Notice that constraint C implies that relvar AP is not in 4NF (see Exercise 12.2). In fact, relvar AP does not give us any information that cannot be obtained from the other relvars; to be precise, we have

```
AP { AREA# } = AREA { AREA# }
```

and

```
AP { PROD# } = PRODUCT { PROD# }
```

Nevertheless, let us assume for the moment that relvar AP *is* included in our design anyway.

No two representatives sell the same product in the same area. In other words, given an {AREA#,PROD#} combination, there is exactly one responsible sales representative (REP#), so we can introduce a relvar

```
APR { AREA#, PROD#, REP# }
   KEY { AREA#, PROD# }
```

in which (to make the FD explicit)

```
{ AREA#, PROD# } → REP#
```

(of course, specification of the combination {AREA#,PROD#} as a candidate key is sufficient to express this FD). Now, however, relvars RA, RP, and AP are all redundant, since they are all projections of APR; they can therefore all be dropped. In place of constraint C, we now need constraint C1:

```
APR { AREA#, PROD# } = AREA { AREA# } TIMES PRODUCT { PROD# }
```

This constraint must be stated separately and explicitly (it is not "implied by candidate keys").

Also, since every representative sells all of that representative's products in all of that representative's areas, we have the additional constraint C2 on relvar APR:

```
REP# →→ AREA# | PROD#
```

(a nontrivial MVD; relvar APR is not in 4NF). Again the constraint must be stated separately and explicitly. Thus the final design consists of the relvars REP, AREA, PRODUCT, and APR, together with the explicit constraints C1 and C2. ▪

This exercise illustrates very clearly the point that, in general, the normalization discipline is adequate to represent some semantic aspects of a given problem (basically, dependencies that are implied by candidate keys, where by "dependencies" we mean FDs, MVDs, or JDs), but that explicit statement of additional dependencies might also be needed for other aspects, and some aspects cannot be represented in terms of such dependencies at all. It also illustrates the point (once again) that it is not always desirable to normalize "all the way" (relvar APR is in BCNF but not in 4NF).

12.4 The revision is straightforward—all that is necessary is to replace the references to FDs and BCNF by analogous references to MVDs and 4NF, thus:

0. Initialize D to contain just *R*.

1. For each non4NF relvar *T* in *D*, execute Steps 2 and 3.

2. Let $X \rightarrow\rightarrow Y$ be an MVD for *T* that violates the requirements for 4NF.

3. Replace *T* in *D* by two of its projections, *viz.* that over *X* and *Y* and that over all attributes except those in *Y*.

12.5 This is a "cyclic constraint" example. The following design is suitable:

```
REP       { REP#, ... }
          KEY { REP# }

AREA      { AREA#, ... }
          KEY { AREA# }

PRODUCT { PROD#, ... }
          KEY { PROD# }

RA { REP#, AREA# }
   KEY { REP#, AREA# }

AP { AREA#, PROD# }
   KEY { AREA#, PROD# }

PR { PROD#, REP# }
   KEY { PROD#, REP# }
```

Also, the user needs to be informed that the join of RA, AP, and PR does *not* involve any "connection trap":

```
( RA JOIN AP JOIN PR ) { REP#, AREA# }  = RA AND
( RA JOIN AP JOIN PR ) { AREA#, PROD# } = AP AND
( RA JOIN AP JOIN PR ) { PROD#, REP# }  = PR
```

CHAPTER 13

Semantic Modeling

13.1 INTRODUCTION

Semantic modeling has been a subject of research ever since the late 1970s. The general motivation for that research—i.e., the problem the researchers have been trying to solve—is this: Database systems typically have only a very limited understanding of what the data in the database *means;* they typically "understand" certain simple data values, and perhaps certain simple constraints that apply to those values, but very little else (any more sophisticated interpretation is left to the human user). And it would be nice if systems understood a little more,* so that they could respond a little more intelligently to user interactions, and perhaps support more sophisticated (higher-level) user interfaces. For example, it would be nice if SQL understood that part weights and shipment quantities, though obviously both numeric values, are different in kind—i.e., *semantically* different—so that (e.g.) a request to join parts and shipments on the basis of matching weights and quantities could at least be questioned, if not rejected out of hand.

Of course, the notion of *domains* (or types) is very relevant to this particular example—which serves to illustrate the important point that current data models are not totally devoid of semantic features. For instance, domains, candidate keys, and foreign keys are all semantic features of the relational model as originally defined. To put this another way, the various "extended" data models that have been developed over the years to address the semantics issue are only slightly more semantic than earlier models; to paraphrase Codd [13.6], capturing the meaning of the data is a never-ending task, and we can expect (or hope!) to see continuing developments in this area as our understanding continues to evolve. The term **semantic model,** often used to refer to one or other of the "extended" models, is thus not particularly apt, because it tends to suggest that the model in question has somehow managed to capture *all* of the semantics of the situation under consideration. On the other hand, "semantic modeling" *is* an appropriate label for the overall activity of attempting to represent

---

*Needless to say, it is our position that a system that supported **relvar and database predicates** as discussed in Chapter 8 *would* "understand a little more"; that is, we would argue that such predicate support is the right and proper foundation for semantic modeling. Sadly, however, most semantic modeling schemes are not based on any such solid foundation but are *ad hoc* to a degree (the proposals of references [13.17–13.19] are an exception). This state of affairs might change, though, thanks to the increasing awareness in the commercial world of the importance of **business rules** [8.18–8.19]; the predicates of Chapter 8 are basically just "business rules" in this sense.

meaning. In this chapter we first present a short introduction to some of the ideas underlying that activity; we then examine one particular approach, the *entity/relationship* approach (the one most commonly used in practice), in some depth.

We remark that semantic modeling is known by many names, including *data* modeling, *entity/relationship* modeling, *entity* modeling, and *object* modeling. We prefer *semantic* modeling for the following reasons:

- We dislike "data modeling" because (a) it clashes with our previously established use of the term "data model" to mean a formal system with structural, integrity, and manipulative aspects, and (b) it tends to reinforce the popular misconception that a data model (in our sense) involves data structure *only*. *Note:* It is relevant to remind you of the point made in Chapter 1, Section 1.3, to the effect that the term *data model* is used in the literature with two quite different meanings. The first is as a model of *data in general* (the relational model is a data model in this sense). The second is as a model of the persistent data of *some given enterprise in particular*. We do not use the term in this latter sense ourselves, but you should be aware that many writers do.

- We also dislike "entity/relationship modeling" because it tends to suggest that there is just one specific approach to the problem, whereas, of course, many different approaches are possible in practice. However, the term "entity/relationship modeling" is well established, and indeed very popular and commonly encountered.

- We have no deep objections to "entity modeling," except that it seems a little more specific as a label than "semantic modeling," and thus might suggest an emphasis that is not intended or appropriate.

- As for "object modeling," the problem here is that the term "object" is clearly a synonym for "entity" in this context, whereas it is used with a completely different meaning in other contexts (in other *database* contexts in particular—see Part VI of this book). Indeed, it seems to us that exactly this fact (that the term has two different meanings) is responsible for what we have elsewhere termed **The First Great Blunder** [3.3]. See Chapter 25 for further elaboration of this point.

Let us get back to the main thread of the discussion. Our reason for including this material in this part of the book is as follows: *Semantic modeling ideas can be useful as an aid in database design, even in the absence of direct DBMS support for those ideas.* Thus, just as the ideas of the original relational model were used as a primitive database design aid well before there were any commercial implementations of that model, so the ideas of some "extended" model might be useful as a design aid even if there are no commercial implementations of those ideas. At the time of writing, in fact, it is probably fair to say that the *major* impact of semantic modeling ideas has been in the area of database design—several design methodologies have been proposed that are based on one semantic modeling approach or another. For this reason, the major emphasis of this chapter is on the application of semantic modeling ideas to the issue of database design specifically.

The plan of the chapter is as follows. Following this introductory section, Section 13.2 explains in general terms what is involved in semantic modeling. Section 13.3 then introduces the best known of the extended models, Chen's *entity/relationship* (E/R) model, and Sections 13.4 and 13.5 consider the application of that model to database design. (Other models are discussed briefly in the annotation to some of the references in the "References and Bibliography" section.) Finally, Section 13.6 offers a brief analysis of certain aspects of the E/R model, and Section 13.7 gives a summary.

13.2   THE OVERALL APPROACH

We can characterize the overall approach to the semantic modeling problem in terms of the following four steps.

1. First, we attempt to identify a set of *semantic* concepts that seem to be useful in talking informally about the real world. For example:

   - We might agree that the world is made up of **entities.** (Despite the fact that we cannot state with any precision exactly what an entity is, the entity concept does seem to be useful in talking about the world, at least intuitively.)

   - We might go further and agree that entities can usefully be classified into **entity types.** For example, we might agree that all individual employees are **instances** of the generic EMPLOYEE entity **type.** The advantage of such classification is that all entities of a given type will have certain **properties** in common—e.g., all employees have a salary—and hence that it can lead to some (fairly obvious) *economies of representation.* In relational terms, for example, the commonality can be factored up into a relvar heading.

   - We might go still further and agree that every entity has a special property that serves to *identify* that entity—i.e., every entity has an **identity.**

   - We might go further again and agree that any entity can be related to other entities by means of **relationships.**

   And so on. But note carefully that all of these terms (entity instance, entity type, property, relationship, etc.) are *not* precisely or formally defined—they are "real-world" concepts, not formal ones. Step 1 is not a formal step. Steps 2–4 below, by contrast, are formal.

2. Next, we try to devise a set of corresponding *symbolic* (i.e., formal) **objects** that can be used to represent the foregoing semantic concepts. (*Note:* We are not using the term *object* here in any loaded sense!) For example, the *extended relational model* RM/T [13.6] provides some special kinds of relations called *E-* and *P-relations.* Roughly speaking, E-relations represent entities and P-relations represent properties; however, E- and P-relations of course have formal definitions, whereas, as explained above, entities and properties do not.

3. We also devise a set of formal, general **integrity rules** (or "metaconstraints," to use the terminology of Chapter 8) to go along with those formal objects. For example, RM/T includes a rule called *property integrity,* which says that every entry in a P-relation must have a corresponding entry in an E-relation (to reflect the fact that every property in the database must be a property of some entity).

4. Finally, we also develop a set of formal **operators** for manipulating those formal objects. For example, RM/T provides a *PROPERTY* operator, which can be used to join together an E-relation and all of its corresponding P-relations, regardless of how many there are and what their names are, thus allowing us to collect together all of the properties for an arbitrary entity.

The objects, rules, and operators of Steps 2–4 above together constitute an extended data model—"extended," that is, if those constructs are truly a superset of those of one of the basic models, such as the basic relational model; but there is not really a clear distinction in this context between what is extended and what is basic. Please note carefully that *the rules and operators are just as much part of the model as the objects are* (just as they are in the basic relational model, of course). On the other hand, it is probably fair to say that the operators are less important than the objects and rules from the point of view of database design; the emphasis in the rest of this chapter is therefore on objects and rules rather than on operators, though we will offer a few comments regarding operators on occasion.

Step 1, to repeat, involves an attempt to identify a set of semantic concepts that seem to be useful in talking about the world. A few such concepts—entity, property, relationship, subtype—are shown in Fig. 13.1, along with informal definitions and a few examples. Note that the examples are deliberately chosen to illustrate the point that the very same object in the real world might legitimately be regarded as an entity by some people, as a property by others, and as a relationship by still others. (This point shows why it is impossible to give terms such as "entity" a precise definition, by the way.) It is a goal of semantic modeling—by no means fully achieved—to support such *flexibility of interpretation.*

By the way, note that there are likely to be clashes between (a) terms such as those illustrated in Fig. 13.1 that are used at the semantic level, and (b) terms used in some underlying formalism such as the relational model. For example, many semantic modeling schemes use the term *attribute* in place of our *property*—but it does not necessarily follow that such an attribute is the same thing as, or maps to, an attribute at the relational level. As another (important!) example, the *entity type* concept as used in (e.g.) the E/R model is not at all the same thing as the *type* concept discussed in Chapter 5. To be more specific, such entity types will probably map to *relvars* in a relational design, so they certainly do not correspond to relational *attribute* types (domains). But they do not fully correspond to *relation* types either, because:

1. Some base relation types will probably correspond to relationship types, not entity types, at the semantic level, and

2. Derived relation types might not correspond to anything at all at the semantic level (speaking a trifle loosely).

Concept	Informal definition	Examples
ENTITY	A distinguishable object	Supplier, Part, Shipment Employee, Department Person Composition, Concerto Orchestra, Conductor Purchase order, Order line
PROPERTY	A piece of information that describes an entity	Supplier number Shipment quantity Employee department Person height Concerto type Purchase order date
RELATIONSHIP	An entity that serves to interconnect two or more other entities	Shipment (supplier-part) Assignment (employee-department) Recording (composition-orchestra-conductor)
SUBTYPE	Entity type Y is a subtype of entity type X if and only if every Y is necessarily an X	Employee is a subtype of Person Concerto is a subtype of Composition

Fig. 13.1 Some useful semantic concepts

Confusion over levels—in particular, confusion arising from such terminological conflicts—has led to some expensive mistakes in the past, and continues to do so to this day (see Chapter 25, Section 25.2).

One final remark to close this section: We pointed out in Chapter 1 that relationships are best regarded as entities in their own right and that we would generally treat them that way in this book. We also pointed out in Chapter 3 that one advantage of the relational model was precisely that it represented all entities, including relationships, in the same uniform way—namely, by means of relvars. Nevertheless, the relationship concept (like the entity concept) does seem to be *intuitively* useful in talking about the world; moreover, the approach to database design to be discussed in Sections 13.3–13.5 does rely heavily on the entity *vs.* relationship distinction. We therefore adopt the relationship terminology for the purposes of the next few sections. However, we will have more to say on this issue in Section 13.6.

13.3   THE E/R MODEL

As indicated in Section 13.1, one of the best-known semantic modeling approaches—certainly one of the most widely used—is the so-called **entity/relationship** (E/R) approach, based on the "entity/relationship model" introduced by Chen in 1976 [13.5], and refined in various ways by Chen and numerous others since that time (see, e.g., references [13.13] and [13.40–13.42]). The bulk of this chapter is therefore devoted to a discussion of the E/R approach. (We should stress, however, that the E/R model is very far from being the only "extended" model—many, many others have been proposed. See, e.g., references [13.5], [13.13], [13.25], and particularly [13.19] for introductions to several others, also references [13.22] and [13.31] for tutorial surveys of the field.)

The E/R model includes analogs of all of the semantic objects listed in Fig. 13.1. We will examine them one by one. First, however, we should note that reference [13.5] not only introduced the E/R model *per se,* it also introduced a corresponding **diagramming technique** ("E/R diagrams"). We will discuss E/R diagrams in some detail in the next section, but a simple example of such a diagram, based on a figure from reference [13.5], is shown in Fig. 13.2, and you might find it helpful to study that example in conjunction with the discussions of the present section. The example represents the data for a simple manufacturing company (it is an extended version of the E/R diagram given for the company "KnowWare Inc." in Fig. 1.6 in Chapter 1).

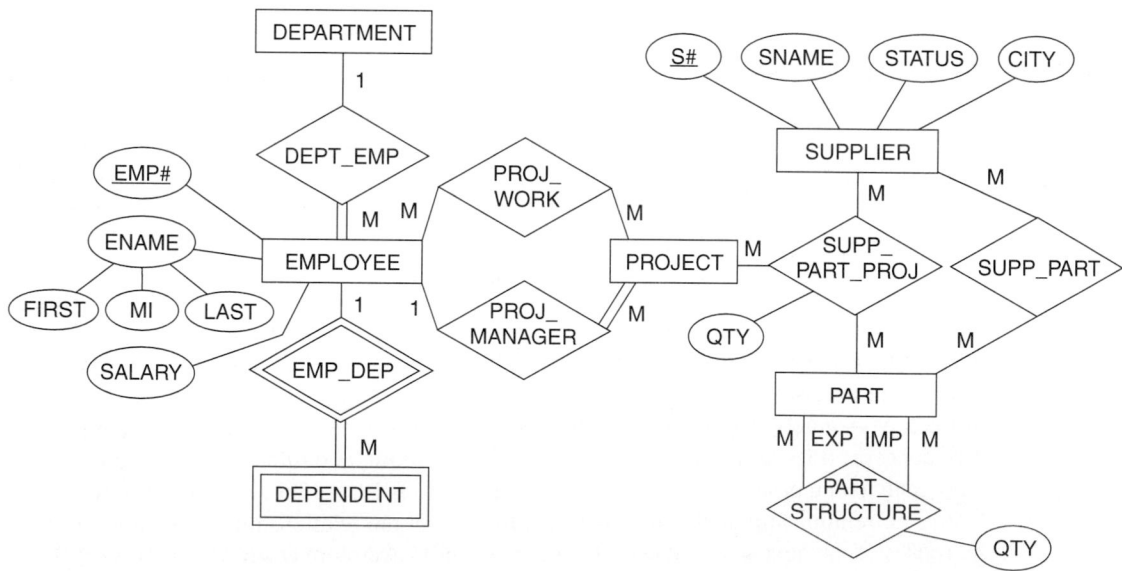

Fig. 13.2   Entity/relationship diagram (example, incomplete)

Note: Most of the ideas to be discussed in the following subsections will be fairly familiar to anyone who knows the relational model. However, there are certain differences in terminology, as you will soon see.

Entities

Reference [13.5] begins by defining an **entity** as "a thing which can be distinctly identified." It then goes on to classify entities into **regular entities** and **weak entities.** A weak entity is an entity that is existence-dependent on some other entity, in the sense that it cannot exist if that other entity does not also exist. For example, referring to Fig. 13.2, an employee's dependents might be weak entities—they cannot exist (so far as the database is concerned) if the relevant employee does not exist. In particular, if a given employee is deleted, all dependents of that employee must be deleted too. A regular entity, by contrast, is an entity that is not weak; e.g., employees might be regular entities. *Note:* Some writers use the term "strong entity" instead of "regular entity."

Properties

Entities—and also relationships, *q.v.*—have **properties.** All entities or relationships of a given type have certain kinds of properties in common; for example, all employees have an employee number, a name, a salary, and so on. (*Note:* We deliberately do not mention "department number" as an employee property here. See the discussion of relationships below.) Each kind of property draws its values from a corresponding **value set** (i.e., domain, in relational terms). Furthermore, properties can be:

- **Simple** or **composite:** For example, the composite property "employee name" might be made up of the simple properties "first name," "middle initial," and "last name."

- **Key** (i.e., unique, possibly within some context): For example, a dependent's name might be unique within the context of a given employee.

- **Single-** or **multi-valued** (in other words, repeating groups are permitted): All properties shown in Fig. 13.2 are single-valued, but if, e.g., a given supplier could have several distinct supplier locations, then "supplier city" might be a multi-valued property.

- **Missing** (e.g., "unknown" or "not applicable"): This concept is not illustrated in Fig. 13.2. Refer to Chapter 18 for a detailed discussion.

- **Base** or **derived:** For example, "total quantity" for a given part might be derived as the sum of the individual shipment quantities for that part. Again, this concept is not illustrated in Fig. 13.2.

Note: Some writers use the term "attribute" instead of "property" in an E/R context.

Relationships

Reference [13.5] defines a **relationship** as "an association among entities." For example, there is a relationship called DEPT_EMP between departments and employees, representing the fact that certain departments employ certain employees. As with entities (see Chapter 1), it is necessary in principle to distinguish between relationship types and relationship instances, but it is common to ignore such refinements in informal discussion, and we will often do so ourselves in what follows.

The entities involved in a given relationship are said to be **participants** in that relationship. The number of participants in a given relationship is called the **degree** of that relationship. (Note, therefore, that this term does not mean the same thing as it does in the relational model.)

Let R be a relationship type that involves entity type E as a participant. If every instance of E participates in at least one instance of R, then the participation of E in R is said to be **total,** otherwise it is said to be **partial.** For example, if every employee must belong to a department, then the participation of employees in DEPT_EMP is total; if it is possible for a given department to have no employees at all, then the participation of departments in DEPT_EMP is partial.

An E/R relationship can be **one-to-one, one-to-many** (also known as **many-to-one**), or **many-to-many** (we assume for simplicity that all relationships are binary, i.e., degree two; extending the concepts, and the terminology, to relationships of higher degree is essentially straightforward, of course). Now, if you are familiar with the relational model, you might be tempted to think of the many-to-many case as the only one that is a genuine relationship, since that case is the only one that demands representation by means of a separate relvar—one-to-one and one-to-many relationships can always be represented by means of a foreign key in one of the participant relvars. However, there are good reasons to treat the one-to-one and one-to-many cases just like the many-to-many case, at least if there is any possibility that they could ever evolve and become many-to-many over time. Only if there is no such possibility is it safe to treat them differently. Of course, sometimes there *is* no such possibility; for example, it will always be true that a circle has exactly one point as its center.

Entity Subtypes and Supertypes

Note: The ideas discussed in this subsection were not included in the original E/R model [13.5] but were added later. See, e.g., Teorey, Yang, and Fry [13.41].

Any given entity is of at least one entity type, but an entity can be of several types simultaneously. For example, if some employees are programmers (and all programmers are employees), then we might say that entity type PROGRAMMER is a **subtype** of entity type EMPLOYEE (or, equivalently, that entity type EMPLOYEE is a **supertype** of entity type PROGRAMMER). All properties of employees apply automatically to programmers, but the converse is not true (e.g., programmers might have a property "programming language skill," which does not apply to employees in general). Likewise, programmers automatically participate in all relationships in which employees participate, but the converse is not true (e.g., programmers might belong to some professional computer society, while employees in general do not). We say that properties and relationships that apply to the supertype are **inherited** by the subtype.

Note further that some programmers might be application programmers and others might be system programmers; thus we might say that the entity types APPLICATION_PROGRAMMER and SYSTEM_PROGRAMMER are both subtypes of

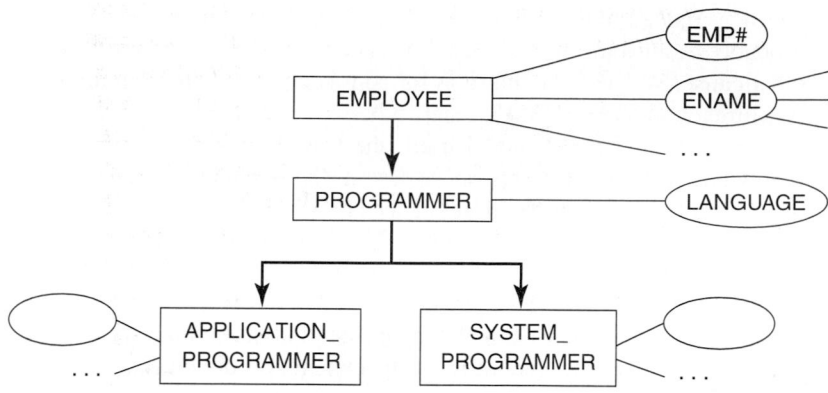

Fig. 13.3   Example of an entity type hierarchy

the PROGRAMMER supertype (and so on). In other words, an entity subtype is still an entity type and can therefore have subtypes of its own. A given entity type and its immediate subtypes, their immediate subtypes, and so on, together constitute an **entity type hierarchy** (see Fig. 13.3).

Points arising:

1. We will discuss type hierarchies and type inheritance in depth in Chapter 19. We should immediately warn you, however, that in that chapter we will use the term *type* to mean exactly what it meant in Chapter 5—it will *not* mean an "entity type" in the sense of the present chapter.

2. If you happen to be familiar with IMS (or some other database system that supports a hierarchic data structure), you should note that type hierarchies are *not* like IMS-style hierarchies. In Fig. 13.3, for example, there is no suggestion that for one EMPLOYEE there are many corresponding PROGRAMMERs (as there would be if the figure was meant to represent an IMS-style hierarchy); on the contrary, for one instance of EMPLOYEE there is *at most one* corresponding PROGRAMMER, representing that same EMPLOYEE in his or her PROGRAMMER role.

This brings us to the end of our brief discussion of the major structural features of the E/R model. Now we turn our attention to E/R diagrams.

13.4   E/R DIAGRAMS

As explained in the previous section, reference [13.5] not only introduced the E/R model *per se,* it also introduced the concept of **entity/relationship diagrams** (E/R diagrams). E/R diagrams constitute a technique for representing the logical structure of a database in a pictorial manner. As such, they provide a simple and readily understood means of communicating the salient features of the design of any given database ("a picture is worth a thousand words"). Indeed, the popularity of the E/R model as an approach to database design can probably be attributed more to the existence of the E/R diagramming technique than to any other cause. We describe the rules for constructing an E/R diagram in terms of the examples already given in Figs. 13.2 and 13.3.

Note: Like the E/R model itself, the E/R diagramming technique has also evolved somewhat over time. The version we describe here differs in certain important respects from the one originally described in reference [13.5].

Entities

Each entity type is shown as a rectangle containing the name of the entity type in question. For a weak entity type, the border of the rectangle is doubled.

> *Examples* (see Fig. 13.2):

- Regular entities:
  DEPARTMENT
  EMPLOYEE
  SUPPLIER
  PART
  PROJECT
- Weak entity:
  DEPENDENT

Properties

Properties are shown as ellipses containing the name of the property in question and attached to the relevant entity or relationship by means of a solid line. The ellipse border is dotted or dashed if the property is derived and doubled if it is multi-valued. If the property is composite, its component properties are shown as further ellipses, connected to the ellipse for the composite property in question by means of further solid lines. Key properties are underlined. The value sets corresponding to properties are not shown.

> *Examples* (see Fig. 13.2):

- For EMPLOYEE:
  EMP# (key)
  ENAME (composite, consisting of FIRST, MI, and LAST)
  SALARY
- For SUPPLIER:
  S# (key)
  SNAME
  STATUS
  CITY

- For SUPP_PART_PROJ:

  QTY

- For PART_STRUCTURE:

  QTY

All other properties are omitted from Fig. 13.2 for reasons of space.

Relationships

Each relationship type is shown as a diamond containing the name of the relationship type in question. The diamond border is doubled if the relationship in question is that between a weak entity type and the entity type on which its existence depends. The participants in each relationship are connected to the relevant relationship by means of solid lines; each such line is labeled "1" or "M" to indicate whether the relationship is one-to-one, many-to-one, etc. The line is doubled if the participation is total.

Examples (see Fig. 13.2):

- DEPT_EMP (one-to-many relationship between DEPARTMENT and EMPLOYEE)
- EMP_DEP (one-to-many relationship between EMPLOYEE and DEPENDENT, a weak entity type)
- PROJ_WORK and PROJ_MANAGER (many-to-many relationship and one-to-many relationship, respectively, between EMPLOYEE and PROJECT)
- SUPP_PART_PROJ (many-to-many-to-many relationship involving SUPPLIER, PART, and PROJECT)
- SUPP_PART (many-to-many relationship between SUPPLIER and PART)
- PART_STRUCTURE (many-to-many relationship between PART and PART)

Observe in the last example here that the two lines from PART to PART_STRUCTURE are distinguished by labeling them with two distinct **role** names (EXP and IMP, for "part explosion" and "part implosion," respectively). PART_STRUCTURE is an example of what is sometimes called a **recursive relationship.**

Entity Subtypes and Supertypes

Let entity type *Y* be a subtype of entity type *X*. Then we draw a solid line from the *X* rectangle to the *Y* rectangle, marked with an arrowhead at the *Y* end. The line denotes what is sometimes called "the *isa* relationship" (because every *Y* "is a" *X*—equivalently, the set of all *Y*'s is a subset of the set of all *X*'s).

Examples (see Fig. 13.3):

- PROGRAMMER is a subtype of EMPLOYEE
- APPLICATION_PROGRAMMER and SYSTEM_PROGRAMMER are subtypes of PROGRAMMER

13.5   DATABASE DESIGN WITH THE E/R MODEL

In a sense, an E/R diagram constructed in accordance with the rules sketched in the previous section *is* a database design. If we attempt to map such a design into the formalisms of a specific DBMS,* however, we will soon discover that the E/R diagram is still very imprecise in certain respects and leaves a number of details unspecified (especially details of integrity constraints). To illustrate the point, we consider what is involved in mapping the design of Fig. 13.2 into a relational database definition.

Regular Entities

To repeat, the regular entities in Fig. 13.2 are as follows:

> DEPARTMENT
> EMPLOYEE
> SUPPLIER
> PART
> PROJECT

Each regular entity type maps into a base relvar. The database will thus contain five base relvars, say DEPT, EMP, S, P, and J, corresponding to these five entity types. Furthermore, each of those five base relvars will have a candidate key—represented by attributes DEPT#, EMP#, S#, P#, and J#, say—corresponding to the "keys" identified in the E/R diagram. For definiteness, let us agree to give every relvar a *primary* key specifically. Then the definition of the DEPT relvar (for example) might start out looking something like this:

```
VAR DEPT BASE RELATION
      { DEPT# ..., ... }
      PRIMARY KEY { DEPT# } ;
```

The other four relvars are left as an exercise. *Note:* The domains or "value sets" need to be pinned down too, of course. We omit detailed discussion of this aspect here, since as already mentioned value sets are not included in the E/R diagram.

Many-to-Many Relationships

The many-to-many (or many-to-many-to-many, etc.) relationships in the example are as follows:

> PROJ_WORK (involving employees and projects)
> SUPP_PART (involving suppliers and parts)
> SUPP_PART_PROJ (involving suppliers, parts, and projects)
> PART_STRUCTURE (involving parts and parts)

Each such relationship also maps into a base relvar. We therefore introduce four more base relvars corresponding to these four relationships. Let us focus on the SUPP_PART relation-

---

*Many tools now exist that can help in that mapping process (e.g., by using the E/R diagram to generate SQL CREATE TABLE statements and the like).

ship. Let the relvar for that relationship be SP (the usual shipments relvar). Let us defer for a moment the question of the primary key for this relvar, and concentrate instead on the matter of the *foreign* keys that are necessary in order to identify the participants in the relationship:

```
VAR SP BASE RELATION SP
    { S# ... , P# ... , ... }
    .....
    FOREIGN KEY { S# } REFERENCES S
    FOREIGN KEY { P# } REFERENCES P ;
```

Clearly, the relvar must include two foreign keys (S# and P#) corresponding to the two participants (suppliers and parts), and those foreign keys must reference the corresponding participant relvars S and P. Furthermore, an appropriate set of *foreign key rules*—i.e., a DELETE rule and an UPDATE rule—must be specified for each of those foreign keys (refer to Chapter 8 if you need to refresh your memory regarding such rules). In the case of relvar SP, we might specify rules as follows. (The specific rules shown are only by way of illustration, of course; note in particular that they are *not* derivable from or specified by the E/R diagram.)

```
VAR SP BASE RELATION SP
    { S# ... , P# ... , ... }
    .....
    FOREIGN KEY { S# } REFERENCES S
            ON DELETE RESTRICT
            ON UPDATE CASCADE
    FOREIGN KEY { P# } REFERENCES P
            ON DELETE RESTRICT
            ON UPDATE CASCADE ;
```

What about the primary key for this relvar? One possibility would be to take the combination of the participant-identifying foreign keys (S# and P#, in the case of SP)—*if* (a) that combination has a unique value for each instance of the relationship (which might or might not be the case, but usually is), and *if* (b) the designer has no objection to composite primary keys (which might or might not be the case). Alternatively, a new noncomposite *surrogate* attribute, "shipment number" say, could be introduced to serve as the primary key (see references [13.10] and [13.16]). For the sake of the example, we will go with the first of these two possibilities, and so add the clause

```
PRIMARY KEY { S#, P# }
```

to the definition of base relvar SP.

Consideration of the PROJ_WORK, PART_STRUCTURE, and SUPP_PART_PROJ relationships is left as an exercise.

Many-to-One Relationships

There are three many-to-one relationships in the example:

PROJ_MANAGER (from projects to managers)

DEPT_EMP (from employees to departments)

EMP_DEP (from dependents to employees)

Of these three, the last involves a weak entity type (DEPENDENT), the other two involve only regular entity types. We will discuss the weak entity case in just a moment; for now, let us concentrate on the other two cases. Consider the DEPT_EMP example. This example does *not* cause the introduction of any new relvars.* Instead, we simply introduce a foreign key in the relvar on the "many" side of the relationship (EMP) that references the relvar on the "one" side (DEPT), thus:

```
VAR EMP BASE RELATION
     { EMP# ..., DEPT# ..., ... }
     PRIMARY KEY { EMP# }
     FOREIGN KEY ( DEPT# ) REFERENCES DEPT
             ON DELETE ...
             ON UPDATE ... ;
```

The DELETE and UPDATE rule possibilities here are exactly the same as those for a foreign key that represents a participant in a many-to-many relationship (in general). Observe once again that they are not specified by the E/R diagram.

Note: For the sake of the present exposition, we assume that one-to-one relationships (which in any case are not all that common in practice) are treated in exactly the same way as many-to-one relationships. Reference [13.7] contains an extended discussion of the special problems of the one-to-one case.

Weak Entities

The relationship from a weak entity type to the entity type on which it depends is of course a many-to-one relationship, as indicated in the previous subsection. However, the DELETE and UPDATE rules for that relationship *must* be as follows:

```
ON DELETE CASCADE
ON UPDATE CASCADE
```

These specifications together capture and reflect the necessary existence dependence. Here is an example:

```
VAR DEPENDENT BASE RELATION
   { EMP# ..., ... }
     .....
   FOREIGN KEY ( EMP# ) REFERENCES EMP
           ON DELETE CASCADE
           ON UPDATE CASCADE ;
```

What is the primary key for such a relvar? As with the case of many-to-many relationships, it turns out we have a choice. One possibility is to take the combination of the foreign key and the weak entity "key" from the E/R diagram—*if* (once again) the database designer has no objection to composite primary keys. Alternatively, we could introduce a new (noncomposite) surrogate attribute to serve as the primary key (again, see references

---

*Though it could; as mentioned in Section 13.3, there are sometimes good reasons to treat a many-to-one relationship as if it were in fact many-to-many. See, e.g., the final part of reference [18.20] for more discussion.

[13.10] and [13.16]). For the sake of the example again, we will go with the first of the two possibilities, and so add the clause

```
PRIMARY KEY { EMP#, DEP_NAME }
```

(where DEP_NAME is the name of the employee's dependent) to the definition of base relvar DEPENDENT.

Properties

Each property shown in the E/R diagram maps into an attribute in the appropriate relvar—except that, if the property is multi-valued, we would usually create a new relvar for it in accordance with the principles of normalization as discussed in Chapter 11 (especially Section 11.6). Domains are created for value sets in the obvious way (though deciding the value sets in the first place might not be quite so obvious!). Details of these steps are straightforward and are omitted here.

Entity Subtypes and Supertypes

Since Fig. 13.2 does not involve any subtypes and supertypes, let us switch to the example of Fig. 13.3, which does. Let us concentrate for the moment on entity types EMPLOYEE and PROGRAMMER. Assume for simplicity that programmers have just one programming language skill (i.e., the property LANG is single-valued). Then:*

- The supertype EMPLOYEE maps into a base relvar, EMP say, in the usual way (i.e., as already discussed).

- The subtype PROGRAMMER maps into another base relvar, PGMR say, with primary key the same as the supertype relvar and with other attributes corresponding to the properties that apply only to employees who are programmers (i.e., just LANG, in the example):

```
VAR PGMR BASE RELATION
  { EMP# ..., LANG ... }
  PRIMARY KEY { EMP# } ... ;
```

Furthermore, the PGMR primary key is also a *foreign* key, referring back to the EMP relvar. We therefore need to extend the definition accordingly (note the DELETE and UPDATE rules in particular):

```
VAR PGMR BASE RELATION
  { EMP# ..., LANG ... }
  PRIMARY KEY { EMP# }
  FOREIGN KEY { EMP# } REFERENCES EMP
          ON DELETE CASCADE
          ON UPDATE CASCADE ;
```

---

*Observe in particular that what we do *not* do in what follows is map employees and programmers into some kind of "supertable" and "subtable" constructs. There is a conceptual difficulty, or at least a trap, here: Just because entity type *Y* is a subtype of entity type *X* in the E/R diagram, it does not follow that the relational analog of *Y* is a "sub" *anything* of the relational analog of *X*—and indeed it is not. See reference [13.12] for further discussion.

- We also need a *view*, EMP_PGMR say, that is the join of the supertype and subtype relvars:

```
VAR EMP_PGMR VIEW
    EMP JOIN PGMR ;
```

Note that this join is (zero-or-one)-to-one—it is over a candidate key and a matching foreign key, and that foreign key is itself a candidate key. The view thus contains just those employees who are programmers, loosely speaking.

Given this design:

- We can access properties that apply to all employees (e.g., for retrieval purposes) by using base relvar EMP.

- We can access properties that apply only to programmers by using base relvar PGMR.

- We can access *all* properties that apply to programmers by using view EMP_PGMR.

- We can insert employees who are not programmers by using base relvar EMP.

- We can insert employees who are programmers by using view EMP_PGMR.

- We can delete employees, programmers or otherwise, by using base relvar EMP or (for programmers only) view EMP_PGMR.

- We can update properties that apply to all employees by using base relvar EMP or (for programmers only) view EMP_PGMR.

- We can update properties that apply only to programmers by using base relvar PGMR.

- We can make an existing nonprogrammer into a programmer by inserting the employee into either base relvar PGMR or view EMP_PGMR.

- We can make an existing programmer into a nonprogrammer by deleting the programmer from base relvar PGMR.

Consideration of the other entity types in Fig. 13.3 (APPLICATION_PROGRAMMER and SYSTEM_PROGRAMMER) is left as an exercise.

13.6   A BRIEF ANALYSIS

In this section we briefly examine certain aspects of the E/R model in a little more depth. The discussions that follow are taken in part from an extended examination of the same topics by the present writer in reference [13.8]. Additional analysis and commentary can be found in the annotation to many of the references in the "References and Bibliography" section at the end of the chapter.

The E/R Model as a Foundation for the Relational Model?

We begin by considering the E/R approach from a slightly different perspective. It is probably obvious to you that the ideas of the E/R approach, or something very close to those ideas, must have been the *informal* underpinnings in Codd's mind when he first developed the *formal* relational model. As explained in Section 13.2, the overall approach to developing an "extended" model involves four broad steps, as follows:

1. Identify useful semantic concepts
2. Devise formal objects
3. Devise formal integrity rules ("metaconstraints")
4. Devise formal operators

But these same four steps are applicable to the design of the *basic* relational model also (and indeed to any formal data model), not just to "extended" models such as the E/R model. In other words, in order for Codd to have constructed the (formal) basic relational model in the first place, he must have had some (informal) "useful semantic concepts" in his mind, and those concepts must basically have been those of the E/R model, or something very like them. Indeed, Codd's own writings support this contention. In his very first paper on the relational model (the earlier version of reference [5.1]), we find the following:

> The set of entities of a given entity type can be viewed as a relation, and we shall call such a relation an *entity type relation* . . . The remaining relations . . . are between entity types and are . . . called *inter-entity relations* . . . An essential property of every inter-entity relation is that [it includes at least two foreign keys that] either refer to distinct entity types or refer to a common entity type serving distinct roles.

Here Codd is clearly proposing that relations be used to represent both "entities" and "relationships." But—and it is a very big but—the point is that *relations are formal objects, and the relational model is a formal system.* The essence of Codd's contribution was that he found a good *formal* model for certain aspects of the real world.

In contrast to the foregoing, the entity/relationship model is *not* (or, at least, not primarily) a formal model. Instead, it consists primarily of a set of *in*formal concepts, corresponding to Step 1 (only) of the four steps mentioned above. (Furthermore, what formal aspects it does possess do not seem to be significantly different from the corresponding aspects of the basic relational model—see the further discussion of this point in the next subsection below.) And while it is unquestionably useful to have an armory of "Step 1" concepts at one's disposal for database design purposes (among others), the fact remains that database designs cannot be completed without the formal objects and rules of Steps 2 and 3, and numerous other tasks cannot be carried out at all without the formal operators of Step 4.

Please note that the foregoing remarks are not intended to suggest that the E/R model is not useful. It is. But it is not the whole story. Moreover, it is a little strange to realize that the first published description of the *in*formal E/R model appeared several years after the first published description of the *formal* relational model, given that (as we have seen) the latter was originally founded on some rather E/R-like ideas.

Is the E/R Model a Data Model?

In light of the discussions above, it is not even clear that the E/R "model" is truly a data model at all, at least in the sense in which we have been using that term in this book so far (i.e., as a formal system involving structural, integrity, and manipulative aspects). Certainly the term "E/R modeling" is usually taken to mean the process of deciding the *structure* (only) of the database, although we did briefly consider certain integrity aspects also (mostly having to do with primary and foreign keys) in our discussions in Sections 13.3–13.5.* However, a charitable reading of reference [13.5] would suggest that the E/R model is indeed a data model, but one that is essentially just *a thin layer on top of the basic relational model* (it is certainly not a candidate for replacing the relational model, as some people have suggested). We justify this claim as follows:

- First, the fundamental E/R data object—that is, the fundamental *formal* object, as opposed to the informal objects "entity," "relationship," etc.—is the *n*-ary relation.

- The E/R operators are basically the operators of the relational algebra. (Actually, reference [13.5] is not very clear on this point, but it seems to propose a set of operators that are strictly less powerful than those of the relational algebra; for example, there is apparently no union and no explicit join.)

- It is in the area of integrity that the E/R model has some (minor) functionality that the relational model does not: The E/R model includes a set of *builtin* integrity rules, corresponding to some but not all of the foreign key rules discussed in the present book. Thus, where a "pure" relational system would require the user to formulate certain foreign key rules explicitly, an E/R system would require only that the user state that a given relvar represents a certain kind of relationship, and certain foreign key rules would then be understood.

Entities *vs.* Relationships

We have indicated several times already in this book that "relationships" are best regarded merely as a special kind of entity. By contrast, it is a *sine qua non* of the E/R approach that the two concepts be distinguished somehow. In this writer's opinion, any approach that insists on making such a distinction is seriously flawed, because (as mentioned in Section 13.2) *the very same object* can quite legitimately be regarded as an entity by some users and a relationship by others. Consider the case of a marriage, for example:

- From one perspective, a marriage is clearly a relationship between two people (sample query: "Who was Elizabeth Taylor married to in 1975?").

- From another perspective, a marriage is equally clearly an entity in its own right (sample query: "How many marriages have been performed in this church since April?").

---

*There is a major weakness right here, of course: The E/R model is *completely incapable* of dealing with integrity constraints or "business rules," except for a few special cases (admittedly important ones). Here is a typical quote: "Declarative rules are too complex to be captured as part of the business model and must be defined separately by the analyst/developer" [13.27]. And yet there is a strong argument that database design should be, precisely, a process of pinning down the applicable constraints (see references [8.18–8.19] and [13.17–13.19]).

If the design methodology insists on distinguishing between entities and relationships, then (at best) the two interpretations will be treated asymmetrically (i.e., "entity" queries and "relationship" queries will take different forms); at worst, one interpretation will not be supported at all (i.e., one class of query will be impossible to formulate).

As a further illustration of the point, consider the following statement from a tutorial on the E/R approach in reference [13.17]:

> It is common *initially* to represent some relationships as attributes [meaning, specifically, foreign keys] during conceptual schema design and then to convert these attributes into relationships as the design progresses and is better understood.

But what happens if an attribute *becomes* a foreign key at some later time?—i.e., if the database evolves after it has already been in existence for some time? If we take this argument to its logical conclusion, database designs should involve only relationships, no attributes at all. (In fact, there is some merit to this position. See the annotation to reference [13.18] at the end of the chapter.)

A Final Observation

There are many other semantic modeling schemes in addition to the specific one, E/R modeling, that we have been describing in this chapter. However, most of those schemes do bear a strong family resemblance to one another; in particular, most of them can be characterized as simply providing a graphic notation for representing certain foreign key constraints, plus a few other bits and pieces. Such graphical representations can be useful in a "big picture" kind of way, of course, but they are far too simplistic to do the whole design job.* In particular, as noted earlier, they typically cannot deal with general integrity constraints. For example, how would you represent a join dependency in an E/R diagram?

13.7 SUMMARY

We opened this chapter by presenting a brief introduction to the general idea of **semantic modeling.** There are four broad steps involved, of which the first is informal and the rest are formal:

1. Identify useful semantic concepts
2. Devise corresponding symbolic objects
3. Devise corresponding integrity rules ("metaconstraints")
4. Devise corresponding operators

---

*It is a sad comment on the state of the industry that simple solutions are popular even when they are *too* simple. On such matters, we agree with Einstein, who once said: "Everything should be made as simple as possible—*but no simpler.*"

Some useful semantic concepts are **entity, property, relationship,** and **subtype.** *Note:* We also stressed the points that (a) there will very likely be **terminological conflicts** between the (informal) semantic modeling level and the underlying (formal) support system level, and (b) such conflicts can cause confusion! *Caveat lector.*

The ultimate objective of semantic modeling research is to make database systems a little more intelligent. A more immediate objective is to provide a basis for a systematic attack on the problem of **database design.** We described the application of one particular "semantic" model, Chen's **entity/relationship (E/R) model,** to the design problem.

In connection with the foregoing, the point is worth repeating that the original E/R paper [13.5] actually contained two distinct, and more or less independent, proposals: It proposed the E/R model *per se,* and it also proposed **the E/R diagramming technique.** As stated in Section 13.4, the popularity of the E/R model can probably be attributed more to the existence of that diagramming technique than to any other cause. But the point is, it is not necessary to adopt all of the ideas of the *model* in order to use the *diagrams;* it is quite possible to use E/R diagrams as a basis for *any* design methodology—perhaps an RM/T-based methodology, for example [13.6]. Arguments regarding the relative suitability of E/R modeling and some other approach as a basis for database design often seem to miss this point.

Let us also contrast the ideas of semantic modeling (and of the E/R model in particular) with the normalization discipline as described in Chapters 11 and 12. The normalization discipline involves reducing large relvars to smaller ones; it assumes that we have some small number of large relvars as input, and it manipulates that input to produce a large number of small relvars as output—i.e., it maps large relvars into small ones (we are speaking *very* loosely here, of course!). But the normalization discipline has absolutely nothing to say about how we arrive at those large relvars in the first place. Top-down methodologies such as the one described in the present chapter, by contrast, address exactly that problem; they map the real world into large relvars. In other words, the two approaches (top-down design and normalization) *complement each other.* The overall design procedure thus goes something like this:

1. Use the E/R approach (or something analogous*) to generate "large" relvars representing regular entities, weak entities, etc., and then

2. Use the ideas of further normalization to break those "large" relvars down into "small" ones.

However, you will have realized from the quality of the discussions in the body of this chapter that semantic modeling in general is not nearly so rigorous or clearcut as the further normalization discipline discussed in Chapters 11 and 12. The reason for this state of affairs is that (as indicated in the introduction to this part of the book) database design is still very much a subjective exercise, not an objective one; there is comparatively little by

---

*Our own preferred approach would be *to write down the predicates* that describe the enterprise and then map those predicates (straightforwardly) into database and relvar constraints as described in Chapter 8.

way of really solid principles that can be brought to bear on the problem (the few principles that do exist being, of course, basically the principles discussed in the previous two chapters). The ideas of the present chapter can be regarded as more in the way of rules of thumb, albeit ones that do seem to work reasonably well in practical situations.

There is one final point that is worth calling out explicitly. Although the whole field is still somewhat subjective, there is one specific area in which semantic modeling ideas can be very relevant and useful today—namely, the **data dictionary** area. The data dictionary can be regarded in some respects as "the database designer's database"; it is after all a database in which database design decisions are recorded, among other things [13.2]. The study of semantic modeling can thus be useful in the design of the dictionary system, because it identifies the kinds of objects the dictionary itself needs to support and "understand"—for example, entity categories (such as the E/R model's regular and weak entities), integrity rules (such as the E/R model's notion of total *vs.* partial participation in a relationship), entity supertypes and subtypes, and so forth.

EXERCISES

13.1 What do you understand by the term "semantic modeling"?

13.2 Identify the four broad steps involved in defining an "extended" model such as the E/R model.

13.3 Define the following E/R terms:

entity	relationship
inheritance	supertype, subtype
key property	type hierarchy
property	value set
regular entity	weak entity

13.4 Give examples of:

a. A many-to-many relationship in which one of the participants is a weak entity;

b. A many-to-many relationship in which one of the participants is another relationship;

c. A many-to-many relationship that has a subtype;

d. A subtype that has an associated weak entity that does not apply to the supertype.

13.5 Draw an E/R diagram for the education database from Exercise 8.10 in Chapter 8.

13.6 Draw an E/R diagram for the company personnel database from Exercise 11.3 in Chapter 11. Use that diagram to derive an appropriate set of base relvar definitions.

13.7 Draw an E/R diagram for the order/entry database from Exercise 11.4 in Chapter 11. Use that diagram to derive an appropriate set of base relvar definitions.

13.8 Draw an E/R diagram for the sales database from Exercise 12.3 in Chapter 12. Use that diagram to derive an appropriate set of base relvar definitions.

13.9 Draw an E/R diagram for the revised sales database from Exercise 12.5 in Chapter 12. Use that diagram to derive an appropriate set of base relvar definitions.

REFERENCES AND BIBLIOGRAPHY

The length of the following list of references is due, in large part, to the number of competing design methodologies currently to be found in the database world, both in industry and in academia. There is very little consensus in this field; the E/R scheme discussed in the body of the chapter is certainly the most widely used approach, but not everyone agrees with it (or likes it). In fact, the point should be made that the best-*known* approaches are not necessarily the *best* approaches. We remark too that many of the commercially available products are more than just database design tools; rather, what they do is generate entire applications—frontend screens, application logic, triggered procedures, etc., as well as database definitions (schemas) in particular.

Some other references that are relevant to the material of the present chapter are the ISO report on the conceptual schema [2.3]; Kent's book *Data and Reality* [2.4]; and Ross's books on business rules [8.18–8.19].

13.1 J. R. Abrial: "Data Semantics," in J. W. Klimbie and K. L. Koffeman (eds.), *Data Base Management.* Amsterdam, Netherlands: North-Holland / New York, N.Y.: Elsevier Science (1974).

One of the very earliest proposals in the semantic modeling area. The following quote nicely captures the general flavor of the paper (some might say of the subject as a whole): "Hint for the reader: If you are looking for a definition of the term *semantics,* stop reading because there is no such definition in this paper."

13.2 Philip A. Bernstein: "The Repository: A Modern Vision," *Database Programming and Design 9,* No. 12 (December 1996).

There seems to be a move afoot at the time of writing to replace the term *dictionary* by the term *repository.* A repository system is a DBMS that is specialized to the management of metadata—metadata not just for DBMSs but for all kinds of software tools: "tools for the design, development, and deployment of software, as well as tools for managing electronic designs, mechanical designs, websites, and many other kinds of formal documents related to engineering activities," to quote Bernstein. This paper is a tutorial on repository concepts.

13.3 Michael Blaha and William Premerlani: *Object-Oriented Modeling and Design for Database Applications.* Upper Saddle River, N.J.: Prentice-Hall (1998).

Describes a design methodology called Object Modeling Technique (OMT) in depth. OMT can be regarded as a variation on the E/R model—its *objects* are basically E/R's *entities*—but it covers much more than just *database* design specifically. See also the annotation to reference [13.32].

13.4 Grady Booch: *Object-Oriented Design with Applications.* Redwood City, Calif.: Benjamin/ Cummings (1991).

See the annotation to reference [13.32].

13.5 Peter Pin-Shan Chen: "The Entity-Relationship Model—Toward a Unified View of Data," *ACM TODS 1,* No. 1 (March 1976). Republished in Michael Stonebraker (ed.), *Readings in Database Systems.* San Mateo, Calif.: Morgan Kaufmann (1988).

The paper that introduced the E/R model and E/R diagrams. As mentioned in the body of this chapter, the model has been revised and refined considerably over time; certainly the explanations and definitions given in this first paper were quite imprecise, so such refinements were definitely needed. (One of the criticisms of the E/R model has always been that the terms do not seem to have a single, well-defined meaning but are instead interpreted in many different ways. Of course, it is true that the whole database field is bedeviled by inaccurate and conflicting terminology, but this particular area is worse than most.) To illustrate:

- As stated in Section 13.3, an entity is defined as "a thing which can be distinctly identified" and a relationship as "an association among entities." The first question that arises, then, is the following: Is a relationship an entity? A relationship is clearly "a thing which can be distinctly identified," but later sections of the paper seem to reserve the term "entity" to mean something that is definitely *not* a relationship. Presumably this latter is the intended interpretation, for otherwise why the term "entity/relationship" model? But the paper really is not clear.

- Entities and relationships can have *attributes* (we used the term "property" in the body of the chapter). Again, the paper is ambivalent as to the meaning of the term—at first it defines an attribute to be a property that is not the primary key, nor any component thereof (contrast the relational definition), but later it uses the term in the relational sense.

- The primary key for a relationship is assumed to be the combination of the foreign keys that identify the entities involved in the relationship (the term "foreign key" is not used, however). This assumption is appropriate only for many-to-many relationships, and not always then. For example, consider a relvar SPD {S#,P#,DATE,QTY} , which represents shipments of certain parts by certain suppliers on certain dates; assume that the same supplier can ship the same part more than once, but not more than once on the same date. Then the primary key (or, at least, the sole candidate key) is the combination {S#,P#,DATE} ; yet we might choose to regard suppliers and parts as entities but dates not.

13.6 E. F. Codd: "Extending the Database Relational Model to Capture More Meaning," *ACM TODS 4*, No. 4 (December 1979).

In this paper, Codd introduced an "extended" version of the relational model, which he called RM/T. RM/T addresses some of the same issues as the E/R model does but is rather more carefully defined. Some immediate differences between the two are as follows. First, RM/T makes no unnecessary distinctions between entities and relationships (a relationship is regarded merely as a special kind of entity). Second, the structural and integrity aspects of RM/T are more extensive, and more precisely defined, than those of the E/R model. Third, RM/T includes its own special operators, over and above the operators of the basic relational model (though much additional work remains to be done in this last area).

In outline, RM/T works as follows:

- First, entities (including "relationships") are represented by *E-* and *P-relations*,* both of which are special forms of the general *n*-ary relation. E-relations are used to record the fact that certain entities exist, and P-relations are used to record certain properties of those entities.

- Second, a variety of relationships can exist among entities—for example, entity types *A* and *B* might be linked together in an **association** (RM/T's term for a many-to-many relationship), or entity type *Y* might be a **subtype** of entity type *X*. RM/T includes a formal **catalog** structure by which such relationships can be made known to the system; the system is thus

---

*Or, rather, E- and P-*relvars.*

capable of enforcing the various **integrity constraints** that are implied by the existence of such relationships.

- Third, a number of high-level **operators** are provided to facilitate the manipulation of the various RM/T objects (E-relations, P-relations, catalog relations, etc.).

Like the E/R model, RM/T includes analogs of all of the constructs (entity, property, relationship, subtype) listed in Fig. 13.1. Specifically, it provides an **entity classification scheme** (which in many respects constitutes the most significant aspect—or, at least, the most immediately visible aspect—of the entire model), according to which entities are divided into three categories, namely *kernels, characteristics,* and *associations:*

- **Kernels:** Kernel entities are entities that have *independent existence;* they are "what the database is really all about." In other words, kernels are entities that are neither characteristic nor associative (see below).

- **Characteristics:** A characteristic entity is an entity whose primary purpose is to describe or "characterize" some other entity. Characteristics are *existence-dependent* on the entity they describe. The entity described can be kernel, characteristic, or associative.

- **Associations:** An associative entity is an entity that represents a *many-to-many* (or many-to-many-to-many, etc.) *relationship* among two or more other entities. The entities associated can each be kernel, characteristic, or associative.

In addition:

- Entities (regardless of their classification) can also have **properties.**

- In particular, any **entity** (again, regardless of its classification) can have a property that **designates** some other related entity. A designation represents a many-to-one relationship between two entities. *Note:* Designations were not discussed in the original paper [13.6] but were added later.

- Entity **supertypes** and **subtypes** are supported. If *Y* is a subtype of *X,* then *Y* is a kernel, a characteristic, or an association depending on whether *X* is a kernel, a characteristic, or an association.

We can relate the foregoing concepts to their E/R analogs (somewhat loosely) as follows: A kernel corresponds to an E/R "regular entity," a characteristic to an E/R "weak entity," and an association to an E/R "relationship" (many-to-many variety only).

Note: Another term occasionally encountered in the literature, *primary domain,* was also first defined in this paper. A **primary domain** is a domain on which at least one single-attribute (i.e., noncomposite) primary key is defined. In the case of suppliers and parts, for example, the primary domains are S# and P#.

In addition to the aspects discussed briefly above, RM/T also includes support for (a) *surrogates* (see reference [13.16]), (b) the *time* dimension (see Chapter 22), and (c) various kinds of *data aggregation* (see references [13.35–13.36]).

13.7 C. J. Date: "A Note on One-to-One Relationships," in *Relational Database Writings 1985–1989.* Reading, Mass.: Addison-Wesley (1990).

An extensive discussion of the problem of one-to-one relationships, which turn out to be rather more complicated than they might appear at first sight.

13.8 C. J. Date: "Entity/Relationship Modeling and the Relational Model," in C. J. Date and Hugh Darwen, *Relational Database Writings 1989–1991*. Reading, Mass.: Addison-Wesley (1992).

13.9 C. J. Date: "Don't Encode Information into Primary Keys!", in C. J. Date and Hugh Darwen, *Relational Database Writings 1989–1991*. Reading, Mass.: Addison-Wesley (1992).

Presents a series of informal arguments against what are sometimes called "intelligent keys." See also reference [13.10] for some related recommendations regarding foreign keys.

13.10 C. J. Date: "Composite Keys," in C. J. Date and Hugh Darwen, *Relational Database Writings 1989–1991*. Reading, Mass.: Addison-Wesley (1992).

To quote from the abstract: "Arguments for and against the inclusion of composite [keys] in the design of a relational database are summarized and some . . . recommendations offered." In particular, the paper shows that surrogate keys [13.16] are not *always* a good idea.

13.11 C. J. Date: "A Database Design Dilemma?", on the *DBP&D* website *www.dbpd.com* (January 1999). See also Appendix B of reference [3.3].

On the face of it, a given entity type—employees, say—could be represented in a relational system either by an employees *type* (i.e., a domain) or by an employees *relvar*. This short paper gives guidance on how to choose between the two options.

13.12 C. J. Date: "Subtables and Supertables" (in two parts), on the *DBP&D* website *www.dbpd.com* (to appear late 2000 or early 2001). See also Appendix D of reference [3.3].

It is often thought that entity type inheritance should be dealt with in a relational context by means of what are called "subtables and supertables"—the entity subtype mapping to a "subtable" and the entity supertype mapping to a "supertable." For example, SQL3 supports such an approach at the time of writing (see Appendix B), and so do certain products. This paper argues against this idea, strongly.

13.13 Ramez Elmasri and Shamkant B. Navathe: *Fundamentals of Database Systems* (2nd edition). Redwood City, Calif.: Benjamin/Cummings (1994).

This general textbook on database management includes two full chapters (out of a total of 25) on the use of E/R techniques for database design.

13.14 David W. Embley: *Object Database Development: Concepts and Principles*. Reading, Mass.: Addison-Wesley (1998).

Presents a design methodology based on OSM (Object-oriented Systems Model). Parts of OSM resemble ORM [13.17–13.19].

13.15 Candace C. Fleming and Barbara von Hallé: *Handbook of Relational Database Design*. Reading, Mass.: Addison-Wesley (1989).

A good pragmatic guide to database design in a relational system, with specific examples based on IBM's DB2 product and the Teradata (now NCR) DBC/1012 product. Both logical and physical design issues are addressed—though the book uses the term "logical design" to mean what we would call "relational design," and the term "relational design" to include at least some aspects of what we would call "physical design"!

13.16 P. Hall, J. Owlett, and S. J. P. Todd: "Relations and Entities," in G. M. Nijssen (ed.), *Modelling in Data Base Management Systems*. Amsterdam, Netherlands: North-Holland / New York, N.Y.: Elsevier Science (1975).

The first paper to treat the concept of **surrogate keys** in detail (the concept was later incorporated into RM/T [13.6]). Surrogate keys are keys in the usual relational sense but have the following specific properties:

- They always involve exactly one attribute.

- Their values serve *solely* as surrogates (hence the name) for the entities they stand for. In other words, such values serve merely to represent the fact that the corresponding entities exists—they carry no additional information or meaning whatsoever.

- When a new entity is inserted into the database, it is given a surrogate key value that has never been used before and will never be used again, even if the entity in question is subsequently deleted.

Ideally, surrogate key values would be system-generated, but whether they are system- or user-generated has nothing to do with the basic idea of surrogate keys as such.

It is worth emphasizing that surrogates are *not* (as some writers seem to think) the same thing as "tuple IDs." For one thing—to state the obvious—tuple IDs identify tuples and surrogates identify entities, and there is certainly nothing like a one-to-one correspondence between tuples and entities (think of tuple IDs for derived tuples in particular). Furthermore, tuple IDs have performance connotations, while surrogates do not; access to a tuple via its tuple ID is usually assumed to be fast (we are assuming here that tuples—at least, tuples in base relations—map fairly directly to physical storage, as is in fact the case in most of today's products). Also, tuple IDs are usually concealed from the user, while surrogates must not be (because of *The Information Principle*); in other words, it is not possible to store a tuple ID as an attribute value, while it certainly is possible to store a surrogate as an attribute value.

In a nutshell: Surrogates are a logical concept; tuple IDs are a physical concept.

13.17 Terry Halpin: *Conceptual Schema and Relational Database Design* (2nd edition). Sydney, Australia: Prentice-Hall of Australia Pty., Ltd. (1995).

A detailed treatment of ORM (see the annotation to the next two references below).

13.18 Terry Halpin: "Business Rules and Object-Role Modeling," *DBP&D 9,* No. 10 (October 1996).

An excellent introduction to **object-role modeling,** ORM [13.17]. Halpin begins by observing that "[unlike] E/R modeling, which has dozens of different dialects, ORM has only a few dialects with only minor differences." (*Note:* One of those dialects is NIAM [13.29].) ORM is also known as *fact-based* modeling, because what the designer does is write down—either in natural language or in a special graphical notation—a series of *elementary* facts (or fact *types,* rather) that together characterize the enterprise to be modeled. Examples of such fact types might be:

- Each Employee has at most one Empname.

- Each Employee reports to at most one Employee.

- If Employee *e1* reports to Employee *e2,* then it cannot be that Employee *e2* reports to Employee *e1.*

- No Employee can direct and assess the same Project.

As you can see, fact types are really *predicates* or business rules; as the title of Halpin's paper suggests, ORM is very much in the spirit of the approach to database design that is preferred by the "business rules" advocates [8.18–8.19], and indeed by the present writer. In general, facts specify *roles* played by *objects* in relationships (hence the name "object-role modeling," of course). Note that (a) "objects" here really means entities, not objects in the special sense described in Part VI of this book, and (b) relationships are not necessarily binary. However, facts are *elementary*—they cannot be decomposed into smaller facts. *Note:* The idea that the database should contain only elementary (or *irreducible*) facts at the conceptual level was proposed earlier by Hall, Owlett, and Todd [13.16].

Observe that ORM has no concept of "attributes." As a consequence, ORM designs are conceptually simpler and more robust than their E/R counterparts, as the paper shows (in this connection, see also the annotation to reference [13.19]). However, attributes can and do appear in E/R or SQL designs that are generated (automatically) from an ORM design.

ORM also emphasizes the use of "sample facts" (i.e., sample fact *instances*—what we would call *propositions*) as a way of allowing the end user to validate the design. The claim is that such an approach is straightforward with fact-based modeling, much less so with E/R modeling.

There are, of course, many logically equivalent ways of describing a given enterprise, and hence many logically equivalent ORM schemas. ORM therefore includes a set of *transformation rules* that allow logically equivalent schemas to be transformed into one another, so an ORM tool can perform some optimization on the design as specified by the human designer. It can also, as previously mentioned, generate an E/R or an SQL schema from an ORM schema, and it can reverse-engineer an ORM schema from an existing E/R or SQL schema. Depending on the target DBMS, a generated SQL schema can include (SQL/92-style) declarative constraints, or those constraints can be implemented via stored or triggered procedures. Regarding constraints, incidentally, note that—unlike the E/R model—ORM *by definition* includes "a rich language for expressing constraints." (However, Halpin does admit in reference [13.19] that not all business rules can be expressed in the ORM *graphical* notation—text is still needed for this purpose.)

Finally, an ORM schema can (of course) be regarded as a high-level, abstract view of the database (in fact, we would argue that it is rather close to a pure, perhaps somewhat disciplined, *relational* view). As such, it can be **directly queried.** See the annotation to reference [13.19] immediately following.

13.19 Terry Halpin: "Conceptual Queries," *Data Base Newsletter 26,* No. 3 (March/April 1998).

To quote the abstract: "Formulating nontrivial queries in relational languages such as SQL or QBE can prove daunting to end users. *ConQuer,* a new conceptual query language based on object-role modeling (ORM), enables users to pose queries in a readily understandable way . . . This article highlights the advantages of [such a language] over traditional query languages for specifying queries and business rules."

Among other things, the article discusses a ConQuer query somewhat along the following lines:

✓Employee

    +− drives Car

    +− works for ✓Branch

("Get employee and branch for employees who drive cars"). If employees can drive any number of cars but work for just one branch, the underlying SQL design will involve two tables, and the generated SQL code will look something like this:

```
SELECT DISTINCT X1.EMP#, X1.BRANCH#
FROM   EMPLOYEE AS X1, DRIVES AS X2
WHERE  X1.EMP# = X2.EMP# ;
```

Now suppose it becomes possible for employees to work for several branches at the same time. Then the underlying SQL design will have to change to involve three tables instead of two, and the generated SQL code will have to change as well:

```
SELECT  DISTINCT X1.EMP#, X3.BRANCH#
FROM    EMPLOYEE AS X1, DRIVES AS X2, WORKS_FOR AS X3
WHERE   X1.EMP# = X2.EMP# AND X1.EMP# = X3.EMP# ;
```

The ConQuer formulation remains unchanged, however.

As the foregoing example illustrates, a language like ConQuer can be regarded as providing a particularly strong form of logical data independence. In order to explain this remark, however, we first need to refine the ANSI/SPARC architecture [2.1–2.2] somewhat. We said in Chapter 2 that logical data independence meant independence of changes to the conceptual schema—but the whole point of the foregoing example is that changes to the conceptual schema do not occur! The trouble is, today's SQL products do not properly support a conceptual schema, they support an *SQL* schema instead. And that SQL schema can be regarded as lying at an intermediate level between the true conceptual level and the internal or physical level. If an ORM tool allows us to define a true conceptual schema and then map it to an SQL schema, then ConQuer can provide independence of changes to that SQL schema (by making appropriate changes to the mapping, of course).

It is not clear from the paper what limits there might be on ConQuer's expressive power. Halpin does not address this question directly; however, he does say (slightly worryingly) that "the language should ideally allow you to formulate any question relevant to your application; in practice, something less than this ideal is acceptable" (slightly reworded). He also states that ConQuer's "most powerful feature . . . is its ability to perform correlations of arbitrary complexity," and gives the following as an example:

✓ Employee1

    +–lives in City1

    +– was born in Country1

    +– supervises Employee2

        +– lives in City1

        +– was born in Country2 <> Country1

("Get employees who supervise an employee living in the same city as the supervisor but born in a different country from the supervisor"). As Halpin says: "Try this in SQL!"

Finally, regarding ConQuer and business rules, Halpin has this to say: "Although ORM's graphical notation can capture more business rules than [E/R approaches], it still needs to be supplemented by a textual language [for expressing certain constraints]. Research is currently under way to adapt ConQuer for this purpose."

13.20 M. M. Hammer and D. J. McLeod: "The Semantic Data Model: A Modelling Mechanism for Database Applications," Proc. 1978 ACM SIGMOD Int. Conf. on Management of Data, Austin, Texas (May/June 1978).

The Semantic Data Model (SDM) represents another proposal for a database design formalism. Like the E/R model, it concentrates on structural and (to some extent) integrity aspects, and has little or nothing to say regarding manipulative aspects. See also references [13.21] and [13.24].

13.21 Michael Hammer and Dennis McLeod: "Database Description with SDM: A Semantic Database Model," *ACM TODS 6,* No. 3 (September 1981).

See the annotation to reference [13.20].

13.22 Richard Hull and Roger King: "Semantic Database Modeling: Survey, Applications, and Research Issues," *ACM Comp. Surv. 19,* No. 3 (September 1987).

A comprehensive tutorial on the semantic modeling field and related matters as of the late 1980s. This paper is a good place to start a deeper investigation into the issues and research problems surrounding semantic modeling activities. See also reference [13.31].

13.23 Ivar Jacobson *et al.: Object-Oriented Software Engineering* (revised printing). Reading, Mass.: Addison-Wesley (1994).

Describes a design methodology called Object-Oriented Software Engineering (OOSE). Like OMT [13.3], the database portions, at least, of OOSE can be regarded as a variation on the E/R model (as with OMT, OOSE's *objects* are basically E/R's *entities*). The following quote is worthy of note: "Most of the methods used in the industry today, for both information and technical system development, are based on a functional and/or data-driven decomposition of the system. These approaches differ in many ways from the approach taken by object-oriented methods where data and functions are highly integrated." It seems to us that here Jacobson puts his finger on a significant mismatch between object and database thinking. Databases—at least, general-purpose, shared databases, which are the primary focus of the database community at large—are *supposed* to be divorced from "functions"; they are *supposed* to be designed separately from the applications that use them. Thus, it seems to us that the term "database" as used in the object community really means a database that is *application-specific,* not one that is shared and general-purpose.

See also (a) the annotation to reference [13.32] and (b) the discussion of object databases in Chapter 24.

13.24 D. Jagannathan *et al.*: "SIM: A Database System Based on the Semantic Data Model," Proc. 1988 ACM SIGMOD Int. Conf. on Management of Data, Chicago, Ill. (June 1988).

Describes a commercial DBMS product based on "a semantic data model similar to" the Semantic Data Model proposed by Hammer and McLeod in reference [13.20].

13.25 Warren Keuffel: "Battle of the Modeling Techniques: A Look at the Three Most Popular Modeling Notations for Distilling the Essence of Data," *DBMS 9,* No. 9 (August 1996).

The "three most popular notations" are said to be E/R modeling, Nijssen's Natural-Language Information Analysis Method, NIAM [13.29], and Semantic Object Modeling, SOM. Keuffel asserts that E/R modeling is the "grandfather" of the other two, but he is critical of its lack of a formal foundation; as he says, entities, relationships, and attributes (i.e., properties) are all "described without reference to how they are discovered." NIAM is much more rigorous; when its rules are followed faithfully, the resulting conceptual designs "possess much more integrity" than designs produced using other methodologies, although "some developers find the rigor of NIAM too confining" (!). As for SOM, it "resembles E/R modeling . . . with [its similarly] vaguely articulated definitions of entities, attributes, and relationships"; it differs from E/R modeling, however, in that it supports *group attributes* (i.e., repeating groups, in effect), which allow one "object" (i.e., entity) to contain others. (E/R modeling allows entities to contain repeating groups of *attributes* but not of other *entities.*)

13.26 Heikki Mannila and Kari-Jouko Räihä: *The Design of Relational Databases*. Reading, Mass.: Addison-Wesley (1992).

To quote from the preface, this book is "a graduate level textbook and reference on the design of relational databases." It covers both dependency theory and normalization on the one hand, and the E/R approach on the other, in each case from a fairly formal perspective. The following (incomplete) list of chapter titles gives some idea of the book's scope:

- Design Principles
- Integrity Constraints and Dependencies
- Properties of Relational Schemas
- Axiomatizations for Dependencies
- Algorithms for Design Problems
- Mappings between E/R Diagrams and Relational Database Schemas
- Schema Transformations
- Use of Example Databases in Design

The techniques described in the book have been implemented by the authors in the form of a commercially available tool called Design By Example.

13.27 Terry Moriarty: *Enterprise View* (regular column), *DBP&D 10,* No. 8 (August 1997).

Describes a commercial application design and development tool called Usoft (*www.usoft.com*) that allows business rules to be defined using an SQL-like syntax and uses those rules to generate the application (including the database definition).

13.28 G. M. Nijssen, D. J. Duke, and S. M. Twine: "The Entity-Relationship Data Model Considered Harmful," Proc. 6th Symposium on Empirical Foundations of Information and Software Sciences, Atlanta, Ga. (October 1988).

"The E/R model considered harmful?" Well, it does seem that it has a lot to answer for, including:

- Confusion over types and relvars (see the discussion of **The First Great Blunder** in Chapter 25);
- The strange business of "subtables and supertables" [13.12];
- A widespread failure to appreciate *The Principle of Database Relativity* (see Chapter 9);
- Confusion over entities and relationships themselves, as discussed in the present chapter.

    Reference [13.28] adds to the foregoing litany. To be more specific, it claims that the E/R model:

- Provides too many overlapping ways of representing data structure, thereby complicating the design process unduly;
- Provides no guidance on how to choose between alternative representations, and in fact can require existing designs to be changed unnecessarily if circumstances change;
- Provides too few ways of representing data integrity, thereby making certain aspects of the design process impossible ("[it is true that] constraints can be formally expressed in a more general notation [such as] predicate logic, [but] saying that this is a reasonable excuse for omitting [constraints] from the data model itself is like saying that a programming language is ad-

equate [even though] it forces you to call assembly language routines to implement all those things you can't express in the language itself!");

- Contrary to popular opinion, does not serve as a good vehicle for communication between end users and database professionals; and

- Violates **The Conceptualization Principle:** "A conceptual schema should . . . include [only] conceptually relevant aspects, both static and dynamic, of the universe of discourse, thus excluding all aspects of (external or internal) data representation, physical data organization and access, [and] all aspects of particular external user representation such as message formats, data structures, etc." [2.3]. In fact, the authors suggest that the E/R model is "essentially just a reincarnation" of the old CODASYL network model (see Chapter 1). "Could this strong bias toward implementation structures be the major reason that the E/R model has received such wide acceptance in the professional [database] community?"

The paper also identifies numerous additional weaknesses of the E/R model at the detail level. It then proposes the alternative methodology NIAM [13.29] as the way forward. In particular, it stresses the point that NIAM does not include the unnecessary E/R distinction between attributes and relationships.

13.29 T. W. Olle, H. G. Sol, and A. A. Verrijn-Stuart (eds.): *Information Systems Design Methodologies: A Comparative Review.* Amsterdam, Netherlands: North-Holland / New York, N.Y.: Elsevier Science (1982).

The proceedings of an IFIP Working Group 8.1 conference. Some 13 different methodologies are described and applied to a standard benchmark problem. One of the methodologies included is NIAM (see reference [13.28]); the paper in question must be one of the earliest on the NIAM approach. The book also includes reviews of some of the proposed approaches, again including NIAM in particular.

13.30 M. P. Papazoglou: "Unraveling the Semantics of Conceptual Schemas," *CACM 38,* No. 9 (September 1995).

This paper proposes an approach to what might be called *metadata queries*—i.e., queries regarding the meaning (as opposed to the values) of the data in the database, or in other words queries regarding the conceptual schema itself. An example of such a query might be "What is a permanent employee?"

13.31 Joan Peckham and Fred Maryanski: "Semantic Data Models," *ACM Comp. Surv. 20,* No. 3 (September 1988).

Another tutorial survey (see also reference [13.22]).

13.32 Paul Reed: "The Unified Modeling Language Takes Shape," *DBMS 11,* No. 8 (July 1998).

The Unified Modeling Language, UML, is yet another graphical notation to support the task of application design and development (in other words, it lets you develop applications by drawing pictures). It can also be used to develop SQL schemas. *Note:* UML is likely to become commercially significant, partly because it has been adopted as a standard by the Object Management Group, OMG (it does have a strong object flavor overall). It is already supported by a number of commercial products.

UML supports the modeling of both data and processes (it goes beyond E/R modeling in this regard), but it does not seem to have much to say concerning integrity constraints. (The section of reference [13.32] entitled "From Models to Code: Business Rules" does not mention the term *declarative* at all! Rather, it concentrates on the generation of *procedural application code* to implement "processes." Here is a direct quote: "The UML formalizes what object practitioners have known for years: Real-world objects are best modeled as self-contained entities that contain both data and functionality." And elsewhere: "It is evident from a historical perspective that the formal separation of data and function has rendered much of our software development efforts fragile at best." These remarks might be valid from an application perspective, but it is not at all clear that they are valid from a database perspective. See, e.g., reference [24.29].)

UML grew out of earlier work by Booch on "Booch method" [13.4], Rumbaugh on OMT [13.3], and Jacobson on OOSE [13.23]. Booch, Rumbaugh, and Jacobson have recently produced a series of books on UML, which will doubtless become the definitive references: *The Unified Modeling Language User Guide, The Unified Modeling Language Reference Manual,* and *The Unified Software Development Process,* all of them published by Addison-Wesley in 1999.

13.33 H. A. Schmid and J. R. Swenson: "On the Semantics of the Relational Data Base Model," Proc. 1975 ACM SIGMOD Int. Conf. on Management of Data, San Jose, Calif. (May 1975).

This paper proposed a "basic semantic model" that predated Chen's work on the E/R model [13.5] but in fact was very similar to that model (except in terminology, of course; Schmid and Swenson use *independent object, dependent object,* and *association* in place of Chen's terms *regular entity, weak entity,* and *relationship,* respectively).

13.34 J. F. Sowa: *Conceptual Structures: Information Processing in Mind and Machine.* Reading, Mass.: Addison-Wesley (1984).

This book is not about database systems specifically but rather about the general problem of knowledge representation and processing. However, portions of it are directly relevant to the topic of the present chapter. (The remarks that follow are based on a live presentation by Sowa in or around 1990 on the application of "conceptual structures" to semantic modeling.) A major problem with E/R diagrams and similar formalisms is that they are strictly less powerful than formal logic. As a consequence, they are incapable of dealing with certain important design features—in particular, anything involving quantifiers, which includes most integrity constraints—that formal logic *can* handle. (The quantifiers were invented by Frege in 1879, which makes E/R diagrams "a pre-1879 kind of logic"!) But formal logic tends to be hard to read; as Sowa says, "predicate calculus is the assembly language of knowledge representation." *Conceptual graphs* are a readable, rigorous, graphical notation that can represent the whole of logic. They are therefore (Sowa claims) much better suited to the activity of semantic modeling than E/R diagrams and the like.

13.35 J. M. Smith and D. C. P. Smith: "Database Abstractions: Aggregation," *CACM 20,* No. 6 (June 1977).

See reference [13.36] immediately following.

13.36 J. M. Smith and D. C. P. Smith: "Database Abstractions: Aggregation and Generalization," *ACM TODS 2,* No. 2 (June 1977).

The proposals of these two papers [13.35–13.36] had a significant influence on RM/T [13.6], especially in the area of entity subtypes and supertypes.

13.37 Veda C. Storey: "Understanding Semantic Relationships," *The VLDB Journal 2,* No. 4 (October 1993).

To quote from the abstract: "Semantic data models have been developed [in the database community] using abstractions such as [subtyping], aggregation, and association. Besides these well-known relationships, a number of additional semantic relationships have been identified by researchers in other disciplines such as linguistics, logic, and cognitive psychology. This article explores some of [these latter] relationships and discusses . . . their impact on database design."

13.38 B. Sundgren: "The Infological Approach to Data Bases," in J. W. Klimbie and K. L. Koffeman (eds.), *Data Base Management.* Amsterdam, Netherlands: North-Holland / New York, N.Y.: Elsevier Science (1974).

The "infological approach" was one of the earliest semantic modeling schemes to be developed. It has been successfully used for database design for many years in Scandinavia.

13.39 Dan Tasker: *Fourth Generation Data: A Guide to Data Analysis for New and Old Systems.* Sydney, Australia: Prentice-Hall of Australia Pty., Ltd. (1989).

A good pragmatic guide to database design, with the emphasis on individual data items (i.e., on *domains,* in effect). Data items are divided into three basic kinds: label, quantity, and description. *Label* items stand for entities; in relational terms, they correspond to primary and foreign keys. *Quantity* items represent amounts or measures or positions on a scale (possibly a timeline scale), and are subject to the usual arithmetic manipulations. *Description* items are all the rest. (Of course, there is much more to the classification scheme than this brief sketch can suggest.) The book goes on to deal with each kind in considerable detail. The discussions are not always "relationally pure"—for example, Tasker's use of the term "domain" does not fully coincide with the relational use of that term—but the book does contain a great deal of sound practical advice.

13.40 Toby J. Teorey and James P. Fry: *Design of Database Structures.* Englewood Cliffs, N.J.: Prentice-Hall (1982).

A textbook on all aspects of database design. The book is divided into five parts: Introduction, Conceptual Design, Implementation Design (i.e., mapping the conceptual design to constructs that a specific DBMS can understand), Physical Design, and Special Design Issues.

13.41 Toby J. Teorey, Dongqing Yang, and James P. Fry: "A Logical Design Methodology for Relational Databases Using the Extended Entity-Relationship Model," *ACM Comp. Surv. 18,* No. 2 (June 1986).

The "extended E/R model" of this paper's title adds support for emtity type hierarchies, nulls (see Chapter 18), and relationships involving more than two participants.

13.42 Toby J. Teorey: *Database Modeling and Design: The Entity-Relationship Approach* (3rd edition). San Francisco, Calif.: Morgan Kaufmann (1998).

A more recent textbook on the application of E/R and "extended" E/R concepts [13.41] to database design.

PART IV

TRANSACTION MANAGEMENT

This part of the book consists of two chapters. The topics of those chapters, recovery and concurrency, are very much interrelated, both of them being aspects of the broader topic of *transaction management;* for pedagogic reasons, however, it is desirable to treat them separately as far as possible.

Recovery and concurrency—or, rather, recovery and concurrency *controls*—are both concerned with the general business of **data protection:** that is, protecting the data in the database against loss or damage. In particular, they are concerned with problems such as the following:

- The system might crash in the middle of executing some program, thereby leaving the database in an unknown state;
- Or two programs executing at the same time ("concurrently") might interfere with each other and hence produce incorrect results, either inside the database or in the outside world.

Chapter 14 considers recovery and Chapter 15 concurrency. *Note:* Portions of these chapters originally appeared, in somewhat different form, in *An Introduction to Database Systems: Volume II* (Addison-Wesley, 1983).

Recovery

14.1 INTRODUCTION

As noted in the introduction to this part of the book, the topics of this chapter and the next, recovery and concurrency, are very much intertwined, since they are both part of the more general topic of *transaction management.* In order to simplify the presentation, however, it is desirable to keep them separate as much as possible (at least until we have finished describing some of the basic concepts); our primary focus in the present chapter is therefore on recovery specifically, and we leave concurrency to Chapter 15. Nevertheless, a few references to concurrency will inevitably creep into this chapter from time to time.

Recovery in a database system means, primarily, recovering the database itself: that is, restoring the database to a state that is known to be correct (or, rather, consistent*) after some failure has rendered the current state inconsistent, or at least suspect. And the underlying principles on which such recovery is based are quite simple, and can be summed up in one word: **redundancy.** (Redundancy, that is, at the physical level; for reasons discussed in depth in Part III of this book, we usually do not want such redundancy to show through to the logical level.) In other words, the way to make sure the database is indeed recoverable is to make sure that any piece of information it contains can be reconstructed from some other information stored, redundantly, somewhere else in the system.

Before we go any further, we should make it clear that the ideas of recovery—indeed, the ideas of transaction processing in general—are somewhat independent of whether the underlying system is relational or something else. (On the other hand, we should also say that most of the theoretical work on transaction processing historically has been done, and continues to be done, in a specifically relational context.) We should also make it clear that this is an enormous subject!—all we can hope to do here is introduce you to some of the most important and basic ideas. See the "References and Bibliography" section, especially reference [14.12], for some suggestions for further reading, also the exercises and answers for some brief discussions of additional topics.

The plan of the chapter is as follows. Following this brief introduction, Sections 14.2 and 14.3 explain the fundamental notion of a *transaction* and the associated idea of *transaction*

---

*Consistent here means "satisfying all known integrity constraints." Observe, therefore, that *consistent* does not necessarily mean *correct;* a correct state must necessarily be consistent, but a consistent state might still be incorrect, in the sense that it does not accurately reflect the true state of affairs in the real world. "Consistent" might be defined as "correct as far as the system is concerned."

recovery (i.e., recovering the database after some individual transaction has failed for some reason). Section 14.4 then goes on to expand the foregoing ideas into the broader sphere of *system* recovery (i.e., recovering after some kind of system crash has caused all current transactions to fail simultaneously). Section 14.5 takes a slight detour into the question of *media* recovery (i.e., recovering after the database has been physically damaged in some way, e.g., by a head crash on the disk). Section 14.6 then introduces the crucially important concept of *two-phase commit.* Section 14.7 describes the relevant facilities of SQL. Finally, Section 14.8 presents a summary and a few concluding remarks.

One last preliminary note: We assume throughout this chapter that we are in a "large" (shared, multi-user) database environment. "Small" (nonshared, single-user) DBMSs typically provide little or no recovery support—instead, recovery is regarded as the user's responsibility (implying that the user has to make periodic backup copies of the database and redo work manually if a failure occurs).

14.2 TRANSACTIONS

As indicated in Section 14.1, we begin our discussions by examining the fundamental notion of a **transaction.** A transaction is a **logical unit of work.** Consider the following example. Suppose the parts relvar P includes an additional attribute TOTQTY, representing the total shipment quantity for the part in question; in other words, the value of TOTQTY for any given part is supposed to be equal to the sum of all QTY values, taken over all shipments for that part (in the terminology of Chapter 8, this is a *database constraint*). Now consider the pseudocode procedure shown in Fig. 14.1, the intent of which is to add a new shipment

```
    BEGIN TRANSACTION ;

    INSERT INTO SP
          RELATION { TUPLE { S#  S#  ( 'S5' ),
                             P#  P#  ( 'P1' ),
                             QTY QTY ( 1000 ) } } ;
    IF any error occurred THEN GO TO UNDO ; END IF ;

    UPDATE P WHERE P# = P# ( 'P1' )
          TOTQTY := TOTQTY + QTY ( 1000 ) ;
    IF any error occurred THEN GO TO UNDO ; END IF ;

    COMMIT ;
    GO TO FINISH ;

UNDO :
    ROLLBACK ;

FINISH :
    RETURN ;
```

Fig. 14.1   A sample transaction (pseudocode)

for supplier S5 and part P1, with quantity 1000, to the database (the INSERT inserts the new shipment, the UPDATE updates the TOTQTY value for part P1 accordingly).

The point of the example is that what is presumably intended to be a single atomic operation—"add a new shipment"—in fact involves *two* updates to the database, one INSERT operation and one UPDATE operation. What is more, the database is not even consistent between those two updates; it temporarily violates the constraint that the value of TOTQTY for part P1 is supposed to be equal to the sum of all QTY values for part P1. Thus, a logical unit of work (i.e., a transaction) is not necessarily just a single database operation; rather, it is a *sequence* of several such operations, in general, that transforms a consistent state of the database into another consistent state, without necessarily preserving consistency at all intermediate points.

Now, it is clear that what must *not* be allowed to happen in the example is for one of the updates to be executed and the other not, because that would leave the database in an inconsistent state. Ideally, of course, we would like a cast-iron guarantee that both updates will be executed. Unfortunately, it is impossible to provide such a guarantee—there is always a chance that things will go wrong, and go wrong moreover at the worst possible moment. For example, a system crash might occur between the INSERT and the UPDATE, or an arithmetic overflow might occur on the UPDATE, etc.* But a system that supports **transaction management** does provide the next best thing to such a guarantee. Specifically, it guarantees that if the transaction executes some updates and then a failure occurs (for whatever reason) before the transaction reaches its planned termination, *then those updates will be undone*. Thus the transaction *either* executes in its entirety or is totally canceled (i.e., made as if it never executed at all). In this way, a sequence of operations that is fundamentally not atomic can be made to look as if it were atomic from an external point of view.

The system component that provides this atomicity—or semblance of atomicity—is known as the **transaction manager** (also known as the **transaction processing monitor** or **TP monitor**), and the COMMIT and ROLLBACK operations are the key to the way it works:

- The **COMMIT** operation signals *successful* end-of-transaction: It tells the transaction manager that a logical unit of work has been successfully completed, the database is (or should be) in a consistent state again, and all of the updates made by that unit of work can now be "committed" or made permanent.

- By contrast, the **ROLLBACK** operation signals *unsuccessful* end-of-transaction: It tells the transaction manager that something has gone wrong, the database might be in an inconsistent state, and all of the updates made by the logical unit of work so far must be "rolled back" or undone.

In the example, therefore, we issue a COMMIT if we get through the two updates successfully, which will commit the changes in the database and make them permanent. If anything goes wrong, however—i.e., if either update raises an error condition—then we

---

*System crash is also known as a *global* or *system* failure; an individual program failure such as overflow is also known as a *local* failure. See Sections 14.3 and 14.4.

issue a ROLLBACK instead, to undo any changes made so far. *Note:* Even if we issued a COMMIT instead, the system should in principle check the database integrity constraint, detect the fact that the database is inconsistent, and force a ROLLBACK anyway. However, we (realistically!) do not assume that the system is aware of all pertinent constraints, and so the user-issued ROLLBACK is necessary. Commercial DBMSs do not do very much COMMIT-time integrity checking at the time of writing.

Incidentally, we should point out that a realistic application will not only update the database (or attempt to), but will also send some kind of message back to the end user indicating what has happened. In the example, we might send the message "Shipment added" if the COMMIT is reached, or the message "Error—shipment not added" otherwise. Message handling, in turn, has additional implications for recovery. See reference [14.12] for further discussion.

Note: At this juncture, you might be wondering how it is possible to undo an update. The answer, of course, is that the system maintains a **log** or **journal** on tape or (more commonly) disk, on which details of all updates—in particular, before- and after-images of the updated object—are recorded. Thus, if it becomes necessary to undo some particular update, the system can use the corresponding log entry to restore the updated object to its previous value.

(Actually the foregoing paragraph is somewhat oversimplified. In practice, the log will consist of two portions, an *active* or online portion and an *archive* or offline portion. The online portion is the portion used during normal system operation to record details of updates as they are performed, and is normally held on disk. When the online portion becomes full, its contents are transferred to the offline portion, which—because it is always processed sequentially—can be held on tape.)

One further important point: The system must guarantee that individual statements are themselves atomic (all or nothing). This consideration becomes particularly significant in a relational system, where statements are set-level and typically operate on many tuples at a time; it must not be possible for such a statement to fail in the middle and leave the database in an inconsistent state (e.g., with some tuples updated and some not). In other words, if an error does occur in the middle of such a statement, then the database must remain totally unchanged. Moreover, as explained in Chapters 8 and 9, the same is true even if the statement causes additional operations to occur under the covers because of, e.g., a foreign key DELETE rule that specifies a CASCADE referential action.

14.3 TRANSACTION RECOVERY

A transaction begins with successful execution of a BEGIN TRANSACTION statement, and it ends with successful execution of either a COMMIT or a ROLLBACK statement. COMMIT establishes what is called, among many other things, a **commit point** (also—especially in commercial products—known as a **synchpoint**). A commit point thus corresponds to the end of a logical unit of work, and hence to a point at which the database is or should be in a consistent state. ROLLBACK, by contrast, rolls the database back to the state it was in at BEGIN TRANSACTION, which effectively means back to the previous commit point. (The phrase "the previous commit point" is still accurate, even in the case of the first transaction in the program, if we agree to think of the first BEGIN TRANSACTION in the program as tacitly establishing an initial "commit point.")

Note: Throughout this section, the term "database" really means just that portion of the database being accessed by the transaction under consideration. Other transactions might be executing in parallel with that transaction and making changes to their own portions, and so "the total database" might *not* be in a fully consistent state at a commit point. As explained in Section 14.1, however, we are ignoring the possibility of concurrent transactions in the present chapter (so far as possible). This simplification does not materially affect the issue at hand, of course.

When a commit point is established:

1. All updates made by the executing program since the previous commit point are committed; that is, they are **made permanent.** Prior to the commit point, all such updates should be regarded as *tentative only*—tentative in the sense that they might subsequently be undone (i.e., rolled back). Once committed, an update is guaranteed never to be undone (this is the definition of "committed").

2. All database positioning is lost and all tuple locks are released. "Database positioning" here refers to the idea that at any given time an executing program will typically have addressability to certain tuples (e.g., via certain *cursors* in the case of SQL, as explained in Chapter 4); this addressability is lost at a commit point. "Tuple locks" are explained in the next chapter. *Note:* Some systems do provide an option by which the program in fact might be able to retain addressability to certain tuples (and therefore retain certain tuple locks) from one transaction to the next. See Section 14.7 for further discussion.

Paragraph 2 here—excluding the remark about possibly retaining some addressability and hence possibly retaining certain tuple locks—also applies if a transaction terminates with ROLLBACK instead of COMMIT. Paragraph 1, of course, does not.

Note carefully that COMMIT and ROLLBACK terminate the *transaction,* not the program. In general, a single program execution will consist of a *sequence* of several transactions running one after another, as illustrated in Fig. 14.2.

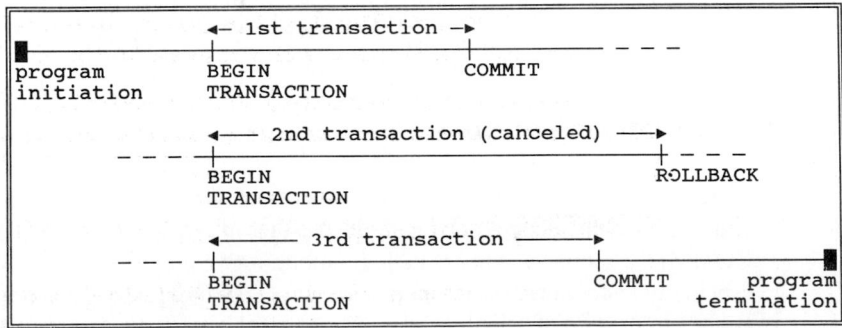

Fig. 14.2 Program execution is a sequence of transactions

Now let us return to the example of the previous section (Fig. 14.1). In that example, we included explicit tests for errors, and issued an explicit ROLLBACK if any error was detected. But, of course, the system cannot assume that application programs will always include explicit tests for all possible errors. Therefore, the system will issue an *implicit* ROLLBACK for any transaction that fails for any reason to reach its planned termination (where "planned termination" means either an explicit COMMIT or an explicit ROLLBACK).

We can now see, therefore, that transactions are not only the unit of work but also the unit of **recovery.** For if a transaction successfully commits, then the system will guarantee that its updates will be permanently installed in the database, even if the system crashes the very next moment. It is quite possible, for instance, that the system might crash after the COMMIT has been honored but before the updates have been physically written to the database—they might still be waiting in a main memory buffer and so be lost at the time of the crash. Even if that happens, the system's restart procedure will still install those updates in the database; it is able to discover the values to be written by examining the relevant entries in the log. (It follows that the log must be physically written before COMMIT processing can complete—the **write-ahead log rule.**) Thus, the restart procedure will recover any transactions that completed successfully but did not manage to get their updates physically written prior to the crash; hence, as stated earlier, transactions are indeed the unit of recovery. *Note:* In the next chapter we will see that they are the unit of *concurrency* also. Further, since they are supposed to transform a consistent state of the database into another consistent state, they can also be regarded as a unit of (database) *integrity*—see Chapter 8.

The ACID Properties

Following reference [14.14], we can summarize this section and the previous one by saying that transactions have four important properties—*atomicity, consistency, isolation,* and *durability* (referred to colloquially as "the ACID properties"):

- **Atomicity:** Transactions are atomic (all or nothing).

- **Consistency:** Transactions preserve database consistency. That is, a transaction transforms a consistent state of the database into another consistent state, without necessarily preserving consistency at all intermediate points.

- **Isolation:** Transactions are isolated from one another. That is, even though in general there will be many transactions running concurrently, any given transaction's updates are concealed from all the rest, until that transaction commits. Another way of saying the same thing is that, for any two distinct transactions *T1* and *T2, T1* might see *T2*'s updates (after *T2* has committed) or *T2* might see *T1*'s updates (after *T1* has committed), but certainly not both. See Chapter 15 for further discussion.

- **Durability:** Once a transaction commits, its updates survive in the database, even if there is a subsequent system crash.

14.4 SYSTEM RECOVERY

The system must be prepared to recover, not only from purely local failures such as the occurrence of an overflow condition within an individual transaction, but also from "global" failures such as a power outage. A local failure, by definition, affects only the transaction in which the failure has actually occurred; such failures have already been discussed in Sections 14.2 and 14.3. A global failure, by contrast, affects all of the transactions in progress at the time of the failure, and hence has significant system-wide implications. In this section and the next, we briefly consider what is involved in recovering from a global failure. Such failures fall into two broad categories:

- **System failures** (e.g., power outage), which affect all transactions currently in progress but do not physically damage the database. A system failure is sometimes called a *soft crash*.
- **Media failures** (e.g., head crash on the disk), which do cause damage to the database, or to some portion of it, and affect at least those transactions currently using that portion. A media failure is sometimes called a *hard crash*.

System failures are discussed below, media failures are discussed in Section 14.5.

The key point regarding system failure is that *the contents of main memory are lost* (in particular, the database buffers are lost). The precise state of any transaction that was in progress at the time of the failure is therefore no longer known; such a transaction can therefore never be successfully completed, and so must be *undone*—i.e., rolled back—when the system restarts.

Furthermore, it might also be necessary (as suggested in Section 14.3) to *redo* certain transactions at restart time that did successfully complete prior to the crash but did not manage to get their updates transferred from the database buffers to the physical database.

The obvious question therefore arises: How does the system know at restart time which transactions to undo and which to redo? The answer is as follows. At certain prescribed intervals—typically whenever some prescribed number of entries have been written to the log—the system automatically **takes a checkpoint.** Taking a checkpoint involves (a) physically writing ("force-writing") the contents of the database buffers out to the physical database, and (b) physically writing a special **checkpoint record** out to the physical log. The checkpoint record gives a list of all transactions that were in progress at the time the checkpoint was taken. To see how this information is used, consider Fig. 14.3, which is read as follows (note that time in the figure flows from left to right):

- A system failure has occurred at time *tf*.
- The most recent checkpoint prior to time *tf* was taken at time *tc*.
- Transactions of type *T1* completed (successfully) prior to time *tc*.
- Transactions of type *T2* started prior to time *tc* and completed (successfully) after time *tc* and before time *tf*.
- Transactions of type *T3* also started prior to time *tc* but did not complete by time *tf*.
- Transactions of type *T4* started after time *tc* and completed (successfully) before time *tf*.
- Finally, transactions of type *T5* also started after time *tc* but did not complete by time *tf*.

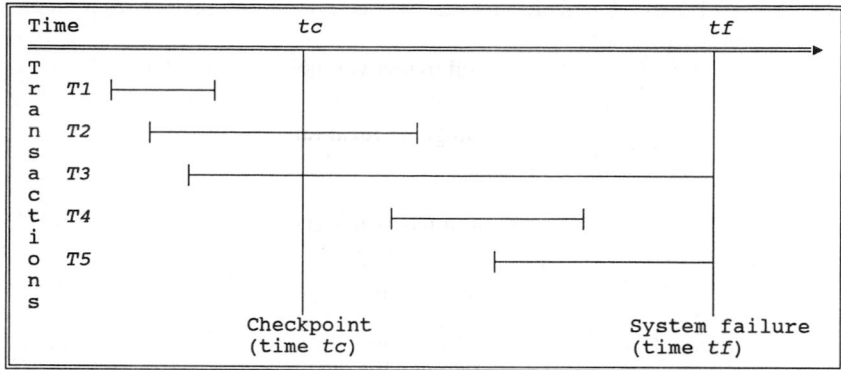

Fig. 14.3 Five transaction categories

It should be clear that, when the system is restarted, transactions of types *T3* and *T5* must be undone, and transactions of types *T2* and *T4* must be redone. Note, however, that transactions of type *T1* do not enter into the restart process at all, because their updates were forced to the database at time *tc* as part of the checkpoint process. Note too that transactions that completed unsuccessfully (i.e., with a rollback) before time *tf* also do not enter into the restart process at all (why not?).

At restart time, therefore, the system first goes through the following procedure in order to identify all transactions of types *T2–T5:*

1. Start with two lists of transactions, the UNDO list and the REDO list. Set the UNDO list equal to the list of all transactions given in the most recent checkpoint record; set the REDO list to empty.

2. Search forward through the log, starting from the checkpoint record.

3. If a BEGIN TRANSACTION log entry is found for transaction *T,* add *T* to the UNDO list.

4. If a COMMIT log entry is found for transaction *T,* move *T* from the UNDO list to the REDO list.

5. When the end of the log is reached, the UNDO and REDO lists identify, respectively, transactions of types *T3* and *T5* and transactions of types *T2* and *T4*.

The system now works backward through the log, undoing the transactions in the UNDO list; then it works forward again, redoing the transactions in the REDO list.* *Note:* Restoring the database to a consistent state by undoing work is sometimes called *backward recovery.* Similarly, restoring it to a consistent state by redoing work is sometimes called *forward* recovery.

---

*You will realize that our description of the system recovery provedure is very much simplified. In particular, it shows the system performing "undo" operations first and "redo" operations second. Early systems did in fact work that way, but for efficiency reasons modern systems typically do things the other way around (see, e.g., references [4.17] and [4.19]).

Finally, when all such recovery activity is complete, then (and only then) the system is ready to accept new work.

14.5   MEDIA RECOVERY

Note: The topic of media recovery is somewhat different in kind from the topics of transaction and system recovery. We include it here for completeness.

To repeat from Section 14.4, a media failure is a failure such as a disk head crash, or a disk controller failure, in which some portion of the database has been physically destroyed. Recovery from such a failure basically involves reloading (or *restoring*) the database from a backup copy (or *dump*), and then using the log—both active and archive portions, in general—to redo all transactions that completed since that backup copy was taken. There is no need to undo transactions that were still in progress at the time of the failure, since by definition all updates of such transactions have been "undone" (actually lost) anyway.

The need to be able to perform media recovery implies the need for a *dump/restore* (or *unload/reload*) *utility*. The dump portion of that utility is used to make backup copies of the database on demand. (Such copies can be kept on tape or other archival storage; it is not necessary that they be on direct access media.) After a media failure, the restore portion of the utility is used to recreate the database from a specified backup copy.

14.6   TWO-PHASE COMMIT

In this section we briefly discuss a very important elaboration on the basic commit/rollback concept called **two-phase commit.** Two-phase commit is important whenever a given transaction can interact with several independent "resource managers," each managing its own set of recoverable resources and maintaining its own recovery log.*
For example, consider a transaction running on an IBM mainframe that updates both an IMS database and a DB2 database (such a transaction is perfectly legal, by the way). If the transaction completes successfully, then *all* of its updates, to both IMS data and DB2 data, must be committed; conversely, if it fails, then *all* of its updates must be rolled back. In other words, it must not be possible for the IMS updates to be committed and the DB2 updates rolled back, or *vice versa*—for then the transaction would no longer be atomic.

It follows that it does not make sense for the transaction to issue, say, a COMMIT to IMS and a ROLLBACK to DB2; and even if it issued the same instruction to both, the system could

---

*In particular, it is important in the context of distributed database systems, and for that reason is discussed in more detail in Chapter 20.

still crash in between the two, with unfortunate results. Instead, therefore, the transaction issues a single **system-wide** COMMIT (or ROLLBACK). That "global" COMMIT or ROLLBACK is handled by a system component called the **coordinator,** whose task it is to guarantee that both resource managers (i.e., IMS and DB2 in the example) commit or roll back the updates they are responsible for *in unison*—and furthermore to provide that guarantee *even if the system fails in the middle of the process.* And it is the two-phase commit protocol that enables the coordinator to provide such a guarantee.

Here is how it works. Assume for simplicity that the transaction has completed its database processing successfully, so that the system-wide instruction it issues is COMMIT, not ROLLBACK. On receiving that COMMIT request, the coordinator goes through the following two-phase process:

1. First, it instructs all resource managers to get ready to "go either way" on the transaction. In practice, this means that each **participant** in the process—i.e., each resource manager involved—must force all log entries for local resources used by the transaction out to its own physical log (i.e., out to nonvolatile storage; whatever happens thereafter, the resource manager will now have a *permanent record* of the work it did on behalf of the transaction, and so will be able to commit its updates or roll them back, as necessary). Assuming the forced write is successful, the resource manager now replies "OK" to the coordinator, otherwise it replies "Not OK."

2. When the coordinator has received replies from all participants, it forces an entry to its own physical log, recording its decision regarding the transaction. If all replies were "OK," that decision is "commit"; if any reply was "Not OK," the decision is "rollback." Either way, the coordinator then informs each participant of its decision, and *each participant must then commit or roll back the transaction locally, as instructed.* Note that each participant *must* do what it is told by the coordinator in Phase 2—that is the protocol. Note too that it is the appearance of the decision record in the coordinator's physical log that marks the transition from Phase 1 to Phase 2.

Now, if the system fails at some point during the overall process, the restart procedure will look for the decision record in the coordinator's log. If it finds it, then the two-phase commit process can pick up where it left off. If it does not find it, then it assumes that the decision was "rollback," and again the process can complete appropriately. *Note:* It is worth pointing out that if the coordinator and the participants are executing on different machines, as they might be in a distributed system (see Chapter 20), then a failure on the part of the coordinator might keep some participant waiting a long time for the coordinator's decision—and, so long as it *is* waiting, any updates made by the transaction via that participant must be kept hidden from other transactions (i.e., those updates will probably have to be kept *locked,* as discussed in the next chapter).

We remark that the data communications manager (DC manager—see Chapter 2) can also be regarded as a resource manager in the sense described above. That is, messages too can be regarded as a recoverable resource, just like databases, and the DC manager needs to be able to participate in the two-phase commit process. For further discussion of this point, and of the whole idea of two-phase commit in general, see reference [14.12].

14.7   SQL FACILITIES

SQL's support for transactions, and hence for transaction-based recovery, follows the general outline described in the foregoing sections. In particular, SQL does support the usual **COMMIT** and **ROLLBACK** statements (with an optional extra keyword WORK in both cases, as we saw in Chapter 4); these statements force a CLOSE for every open cursor, thereby causing all database positioning to be lost. *Note:* Some SQL implementations provide a way to prevent this automatic CLOSE and loss of positioning on COMMIT (but not ROLLBACK). DB2, for example, supports a WITH HOLD option on a cursor declaration; COMMIT does not close such a cursor but leaves it open, positioned such that the next FETCH will move it to the next row in sequence. The possibly complex repositioning code that might otherwise be needed on the next OPEN is thus no longer required. Such a feature is currently included in SQL3 (see Appendix B).

One difference between SQL's support for transactions and the general concepts outlined in this chapter is that SQL does not include any explicit BEGIN TRANSACTION statement. Instead, a transaction is begun implicitly whenever the program executes a **"transaction-initiating"** statement and does not already have a transaction in progress. (As with the "cursor hold" option discussed above, it is likely that support for an explicit BEGIN TRANSACTION statement will be added to the standard in some future release; such a statement is currently included in SQL3.) Details of exactly which SQL statements are "transaction-initiating" are beyond the scope of this book—suffice it to say that all of the executable statements discussed in previous chapters *are* transaction-initiating, while COMMIT and ROLLBACK themselves are obviously not. A special statement called **SET TRANSACTION** is used to define certain characteristics of the next transaction to be initiated (SET TRANSACTION can be executed only when no transaction is in progress, and is not itself transaction-initiating). The only such characteristics we discuss here are the *access mode* and the *isolation level.* The syntax is:

```
SET TRANSACTION <option commalist> ;
```

where the *<option commalist>* specifies an access mode, an isolation level, or both.

- The **access mode** is either READ ONLY or READ WRITE. If neither is specified, READ WRITE is assumed, unless READ UNCOMMITTED isolation level is specified, in which case READ ONLY is assumed. If READ WRITE is specified, the isolation level must not be READ UNCOMMITTED.

- The **isolation level** takes the form ISOLATION LEVEL *<isolation>*, where *<isolation>* is READ UNCOMMITTED, READ COMMITTED, REPEATABLE READ, or SERIALIZABLE. For further explanation, see Chapter 15.

14.8 SUMMARY

In this chapter we have presented a necessarily brief introduction to the topic of **transaction management.** A transaction is a **logical unit of work,** also a **unit of recovery** (and a unit of concurrency and a unit of integrity—see Chapters 15 and 8, respectively). Transactions possess the **ACID properties** of **atomicity, consistency, isolation,** and **durability. Transaction management** is the task of supervising the execution of transactions in such a way that they can indeed be guaranteed to possess these important properties. In fact, the overall purpose of the system might well be defined as **the reliable execution of transactions.**

Transactions are initiated by **BEGIN TRANSACTION** and terminated either by **COMMIT** (*successful* termination) or by **ROLLBACK** (*unsuccessful* termination). COMMIT establishes a **commit point** (updates are made permanent), ROLLBACK rolls the database back to the previous commit point (updates are undone). If a transaction does not reach its planned termination, the system *forces* a ROLLBACK for it (**transaction recovery**). In order to be able to undo (or redo) updates, the system maintains a recovery **log.** Moreover, the log records for a given transaction must be written to the physical log before COMMIT processing for that transaction can complete (the **write-ahead log rule**).

The system also guarantees the ACID properties of transactions in the face of a system crash. To provide such a guarantee, the system must (a) **redo** all work done by transactions that completed successfully prior to the crash, and (b) **undo** all work done by transactions that started but did not complete prior to the crash. This **system recovery** activity is carried out as part of the system's **restart** procedure (sometimes known as the *restart/recovery* procedure). The system discovers what work has to be redone and what undone by examining the most recent **checkpoint record.** Checkpoint records are written to the log at prescribed intervals.

The system also provides **media recovery** by restoring the database from a previous **dump** and then—using the log—redoing the work completed since that dump was taken. Dump/restore **utilities** are needed to support media recovery.

Systems that permit transactions to interact with two or more distinct **resource managers**—for example, two different DBMSs, or a DBMS and a DC manager—must use a protocol called **two-phase commit** if they are to maintain the transaction atomicity property. The two phases are (a) the **prepare** phase, in which the **coordinator** instructs all **participants** to "get ready to go either way," and (b) the **commit** phase, in which—assuming all participants responded satisfactorily during the prepare phase—the coordinator then instructs all participants to perform the actual commit (or the actual rollback otherwise).

Regarding support for recovery in the SQL standard, SQL does provide explicit **COMMIT** and **ROLLBACK** statements (but no explicit BEGIN TRANSACTION statement). It also supports a **SET TRANSACTION** statement, which allows the user to specify the **access mode** and **level of isolation** for the next transaction to begin.

One last point: We have tacitly been assuming an application programming environment throughout this chapter. However, all of the concepts discussed apply equally to the end user environment also (though they might be somewhat more concealed at that level).

For example, SQL products typically allow the user to enter SQL statements interactively from a terminal. Usually each such interactive SQL statement is treated as a transaction in its own right; the system will typically issue an automatic COMMIT on the user's behalf after the SQL statement has been executed (or an automatic ROLLBACK if it failed, of course). However, some systems do allow the user to inhibit those automatic COMMITs, and instead to execute a whole series of SQL statements (followed by an explicit COMMIT or ROLLBACK) as a single transaction. The practice is not generally recommended, however, since it might cause portions of the database to remain locked, and therefore inaccessible to other users, for excessive periods of time (see Chapter 15). In such an environment, moreover, it is possible for end users to *deadlock* with one another, which is another good argument for prohibiting the practice (again, see Chapter 15).

EXERCISES

14.1 Systems do not allow a given transaction to commit changes to databases (or relvars or . . .) on an individual basis, i.e., without simultaneously committing changes to all other databases (or relvars or . . .). Why not?

14.2 Transactions cannot be nested inside one another. Why not?

14.3 State the write-ahead log rule. Why is the rule necessary?

14.4 What are the recovery implications of:

a. Forcing buffers to the database at COMMIT?

b. Never physically writing buffers to the database prior to COMMIT?

14.5 State the two-phase commit protocol, and discuss the implications of a failure on the part of (a) the coordinator, (b) a participant, during each of the two phases.

14.6 Using the suppliers and parts database, write an SQL program to read and print all parts in part number order, deleting every tenth one as you go, and beginning a new transaction after every tenth row. You can assume that the foreign key DELETE rule from parts to shipments specifies CASCADE (i.e., you can ignore shipments for the purposes of this exercise). *Note:* We specifically ask for an *SQL* solution here so that you can use the SQL cursor mechanism in your answer.

REFERENCES AND BIBLIOGRAPHY

14.1 Philip A. Bernstein: "Transaction Processing Monitors," *CACM 33,* No. 11 (November 1990).

To quote: "A *TP system* is an integrated set of products that . . . include both hardware, such as processors, memories, disks, and communications controllers, and software, such as operating systems, database management systems, computer networks, and TP monitors. Much of the integration of these products is provided by TP monitors." The article serves as a good informal introduction to the structure and functionality of TP monitors.

14.2 Philip A. Bernstein, Vassos Hadzilacos, and Nathan Goodman: *Concurrency Control and Recovery in Database Systems.* Reading, Mass.: Addison-Wesley (1987).

A textbook, covering (as the title indicates) not just recovery but the whole of transaction management, from a much more formal perspective than the present chapter.

14.3 A. Bilris *et al.*: "ASSET: A System for Supporting Extended Transactions," Proc. 1994 ACM SIGMOD Int. Conf. on Management of Data, Minneapolis, Minn. (May 1994).

The basic transaction notions as described in the body of this chapter and the next are widely regarded as being too rigid for certain newer kinds of applications (especially highly interactive applications), and a variety of "extended transaction models" have therefore been proposed to address this issue (see reference [14.15]). At the time of writing, however, none of those proposals has been clearly shown to be superior to all the rest; as a consequence, "database vendors [have been reluctant] to incorporate any one model into a product."

The focus of ASSET is rather different. Instead of proposing yet another new transaction model, it provides a set of primitive operators—including the usual COMMIT and so forth, but certain new ones as well—that can be used "to define customized transaction models suitable for specific applications." In particular, the paper shows how ASSET can be used to specify "nested transactions, split transactions, sagas, and other extended transaction models described in the literature."

14.4 L. A. Bjork: "Recovery Scenario for a DB/DC System," Proc. ACM National Conf., Atlanta, Ga. (August 1973).

This paper and its companion paper by Davies [14.7] represent probably the earliest theoretical work in the area of recovery.

14.5 R. A. Crus: "Data Recovery in IBM DATABASE 2," *IBM Sys. J. 23,* No. 2 (1984).

Describes the DB2 recovery mechanism in detail, and in so doing provides a good description of recovery techniques in general. In particular, the paper explains how DB2 recovers from a system crash during the recovery process itself, while some transaction is in the middle of a rollback. This problem requires special care to ensure that uncommitted updates from the transaction being rolled back are in fact undone (the opposite of the lost update problem, in a sense—see Chapter 15).

14.6 C. J. Date: "Distributed Database: A Closer Look," in C. J. Date and Hugh Darwen, *Relational Database Writings 1989–1991.* Reading, Mass.: Addison-Wesley (1992).

Section 14.6 of the present chapter describes what might be called the *basic* two-phase commit protocol. Several improvements on that basic protocol are possible. For example, if participant *P* responds to the coordinator *C* in Phase 1 that it did no updates for the transaction under consideration (i.e., it was *read-only*), then *C* can simply ignore *P* in Phase 2. Further, if all participants respond *read-only* in Phase 1, then Phase 2 can be omitted entirely.

Other improvements and refinements are possible. This paper [14.6] includes a tutorial description of some of them. Specifically, it discusses the *presumed commit* and *presumed rollback* protocols (improved versions of the basic protocol), the *tree of processes* model (when a participant needs to serve as the coordinator for certain portions of a transaction), and what happens if a *communication failure* occurs during the acknowledgment process from a participant to the coordinator. *Note:* Although the discussions are presented in the context of a distributed system, most of the concepts are actually of wider applicability. Refer to Chapter 20 for an extended discussion of some of these issues.

14.7 C. T. Davies, Jr.: "Recovery Semantics for a DB/DC System," Proc. ACM National Conf., Atlanta, Ga. (August 1973).

See the annotation to reference [14.4].

14.8 C. T. Davies, Jr.: "Data Processing Spheres of Control," *IBM Sys. J. 17,* No. 2 (1978).

Spheres of control were the first attempt to investigate and formalize what later became the discipline of transaction management. A sphere of control is an abstraction that represents a piece of work that (from the outside) can be viewed as atomic. Unlike transactions as supported in most systems today, however, spheres of control can be nested inside one another, to arbitrary depth (see the answer to Exercise 14.2).

14.9 Hector Garcia-Molina and Kenneth Salem: "Sagas," Proc. 1987 ACM SIGMOD Int. Conf. on Management of Data, San Francisco, Calif. (May 1987).

A major problem with transactions as described in the body of this chapter is that they are tacitly assumed to be very short in duration (milliseconds or even microseconds). If a transaction lasts a long time (hours, days, weeks), then (a) if it has to be rolled back, a very great deal of work has to be undone, and (b) even if it succeeds, it still has to hold on to system resources (database data, etc.) for an inordinately long time, thereby locking other users out (see Chapter 15). Unfortunately, many "real-world" transactions tend to be long in duration, especially in some of the newer application areas such as hardware and software engineering.

Sagas are an attack on this problem. A saga is a sequence of short transactions (in the usual sense of the term) with the property that the system guarantees that *either* (a) all the transactions in the sequence execute successfully, *or* (b) certain **compensating transactions** are executed in order to cancel the effects of successfully completed transactions in an overall incomplete execution of the saga (thereby making it as if the saga had never executed in the first place). In a banking system, for example, we might have the transaction "Add $100 to account *A*"; the compensating transaction would obviously be "Subtract $100 from account *A*." An extension to the COMMIT statement allows the user to inform the system of the compensating transaction to be run should it later be necessary to cancel the effects of the now completed transaction. Note that a compensating transaction should ideally never terminate with rollback!

14.10 James Gray: "Notes on Data Base Operating Systems," in R. Bayer, R. M. Graham, and G. Seegmuller (eds.), *Operating Systems: An Advanced Course* (Springer Verlag *Lecture Notes in Computer Science 60*). New York, N.Y.: Springer Verlag (1978). Also available as IBM Research Report RJ 2188 (February 1978).

One of the earliest—certainly one of the most approachable—sources for material on transaction management. It contains the first generally available description of the two-phase commit protocol. It is obviously not as comprehensive as the more recent reference [14.12], but is nevertheless still recommended.

14.11 Jim Gray: "The Transaction Concept: Virtues and Limitations," Proc. 7th Int. Conf. on Very Large Data Bases, Cannes, France (September 1981).

A concise statement of various transaction-related concepts and problems, including a variety of implementation issues. One particular problem addressed is the following: Transactions as usually understood cannot be nested inside one another (see the answer to Exercise 14.2). Is there nevertheless some way of allowing transactions to be broken down into smaller "subtransactions"? The answer is a limited "Yes"—it is possible for a transaction to establish intermediate **savepoints** while it is executing, and subsequently to roll back to a previously established savepoint (if required) instead of having to roll back all the way to the beginning. In fact, a savepoint facility along such lines has been incorporated into several implemented systems, including (e.g.) Ingres—the commercial product, not the prototype—and System R (although not DB2). Such a concept seems a little closer to the notion of transactions as that term is usually understood in the real world. But note that establishing a savepoint is not the same as performing a COMMIT; updates made by the transaction are still not visible to other transactions until (successful) end-of-transaction.

Note: The "sagas" of reference [14.9]—which in some respects address the same problem as savepoints—were proposed after Gray first wrote this paper.

14.12 Jim Gray and Andreas Reuter: *Transaction Processing: Concepts and Techniques.* San Mateo, Calif.: Morgan Kaufmann (1993).

If any computer science text ever deserved the epithet "instant classic," it is surely this one. Its size might be a little daunting at first (?), but the authors display an enviable lightness of touch that makes even the driest aspects of the subject enjoyable reading. In their preface, they state their intent as being "to help . . . solve real problems"; the book is "pragmatic, covering basic transaction issues in considerable detail"; and the presentation "is full of code fragments showing . . . basic algorithms and data structures" and is not "encyclopedic." Despite this last claim, the book is (not surprisingly) comprehensive, and is surely destined to become the standard work. Strongly recommended.

14.13 Jim Gray *et al.*: "The Recovery Manager of the System R Data Manager," *ACM Comp. Surv. 13,* No. 2 (June 1981).

References [14.13] and [14.18] are both concerned with the recovery features of System R (which was something of a pioneer in this field). Reference [14.13] provides an overview of the entire recovery subsystem; reference [14.18] describes a specific aspect, called the *shadow page* mechanism, in detail (see the annotation to this latter reference below).

14.14 Theo Härder and Andreas Reuter: "Principles of Transaction-Oriented Database Recovery," *ACM Comp. Surv. 15,* No. 4 (December 1983).

The source of the ACID acronym, this paper gives a very clear and careful tutorial presentation of the principles of recovery. It also provides a consistent terminological framework for describing a wide variety of recovery schemes and logging techniques in a uniform way, and classifies and describes a number of existing systems in accordance with that framework.

The paper includes some interesting empirical figures regarding frequency of occurrence and typical (acceptable) recovery times for the three kinds of failures (local, system, media) in a typical large system:

Type of failure	Frequency of occurrence	Recovery time
Local	10-100 per minute	Same as transaction execution time
System	Several per week	Few minutes
Media	Once or twice per year	1-2 hours

14.15 Henry F. Korth: "The Double Life of the Abstraction Concept: Fundamental Principle and Evolving System Concept" (invited talk), Proc. 21st Int. Conf. on Very Large Data Bases, Zurich, Switzerland (September 1995).

A good brief overview of ways in which the transaction concept needs to evolve in order to support new application requirements.

14.16 Henry F. Korth, Eliezer Levy, and Abraham Silberschatz: "A Formal Approach to Recovery by Compensating Transactions," Proc. 16th Int. Conf. on Very Large Data Bases, Brisbane, Australia (August 1990).

Formalizes the notion of **compensating transactions,** which are used in sagas [14.9] and elsewhere for "undoing" committed (as well as uncommitted) transactions.

14.17 David Lomet and Mark R. Tuttle: "Redo Recovery after System Crashes," Proc. 21st Int. Conf. on Very Large Data Bases, Zurich, Switzerland (September 1995).

A precise and careful analysis of redo recovery (i.e., forward recovery). "[Although] redo recovery is just one form of recovery, it is . . . important [because it is a crucial part of the overall recovery process and it] must solve the hardest [problems]." (In this connection, note that—in contrast to the algorithm sketched in Section 14.4—ARIES [14.19] "suggests understanding recovery . . . as performing redo recovery followed by undo recovery.") The authors claim that their analysis leads to a better understanding of existing implementations and the potential for significantly improved recovery systems.

14.18 Raymond A. Lorie: "Physical Integrity in a Large Segmented Database," *ACM TODS 2,* No. 1 (March 1977).

As explained in the annotation to reference [14.13], this paper is concerned with a specific aspect of the System R recovery subsystem, called the *shadow page* mechanism. (Note, incidentally, that the term "integrity" as used in the title of this paper has very little to do with the notion of integrity as discussed in Chapter 8.) The basic idea is simple: When an (uncommitted) update is first written to the database, the system does not overwrite the existing page but stores a new page somewhere else on the disk. The old page is then the "shadow" for the new one. Committing the update involves updating various pointers to point to the new page and discarding the shadow; rolling back the update, on the other hand, involves reinstating the shadow page and discarding the new one.

Although conceptually simple, the shadow page scheme suffers from the serious drawback that it destroys any physical clustering that might previously have existed in the data. For this reason the scheme was not picked up from System R for use in DB2 [14.5], though it *was* used in SQL/DS [4.13].

14.19 C. Mohan, Don Haderle, Bruce Lindsay, Hamid Pirahesh, and Peter Schwartz: "ARIES: A Transaction Recovery Method Supporting Fine-Granularity Locking and Partial Rollbacks Using Write Ahead Logging," *ACM TODS 17,* No. 1 (March 1992).

ARIES stands for "Algorithm for Recovery and Isolation Exploiting Semantics." ARIES has been implemented ("to varying degrees") in several commercial and experimental systems, including in particular DB2. To quote from the paper: "Solutions to [the transaction management problem] may be judged using several metrics: degree of concurrency supported within a page and across pages, complexity of the resulting logic, space overhead on nonvolatile storage and in memory for data and the log, overhead in terms of the number of synchronous and asynchronous I/O's required during restart/recovery and normal processing, kinds of functionality supported (partial transaction rollbacks, etc.), amount of processing performed during restart/ recovery, degree of concurrent processing supported during restart/recovery, extent of system-induced transaction rollbacks caused by deadlocks, restrictions placed on stored data (e.g., requiring unique keys for all records, restricting maximum size of objects to the page size, etc.), ability to support novel lock modes that allow the concurrent execution—based on commutativity and other properties—of operations like increment/decrement on the same data by different transactions, and so on.

[ARIES] fares very well with respect to all these metrics." (Very slightly reworded.)

Since ARIES was first designed, numerous refinements and specialized versions have been developed and described in the literature: ARIES/CS (for client/server systems), ARIES/IM (for index management), ARIES/NT (for nested transactions), and so on.

ANSWERS TO SELECTED EXERCISES

14.1 Such a feature would conflict with the objective of transaction atomicity. If a transaction could commit some but not all of its updates, then the uncommitted ones might subsequently be rolled back, whereas the committed ones of course could not be. Thus, the transaction would no longer be "all or nothing."

14.2 Such a feature would conflict with the objective of transaction atomicity. For consider what would happen if transaction *B* were nested inside transaction *A* and the following sequence of events occurred (once again we assume for simplicity that it makes sense to talk about "updating a tuple"):

```
BEGIN TRANSACTION (transaction A) ;
   ...
   BEGIN TRANSACTION (transaction B) ;
   transaction B updates tuple t ;
   COMMIT (transaction B) ;
   ...
ROLLBACK (transaction A) ;
```

If tuple *t* is restored to its pre-*A* value at this point, then *B*'s COMMIT was not in fact a COMMIT at all. Conversely, if *B*'s COMMIT was genuine, then tuple *t* cannot be restored to its pre-*A* value, and hence *A*'s ROLLBACK cannot be honored.

Observe that to say that transactions cannot be nested is to say that a program can execute a BEGIN TRANSACTION operation only when it has no transaction currently running.

Actually, many writers (beginning with Davies in reference [14.7]) have proposed the ability to nest transactions by dropping the requirement for *durability* (the "D" property in ACID) on the part of an inner transaction. What this means is that COMMIT by an inner transaction will commit that transaction's updates, *but only to the next outer level*. If that outer level then terminates with rollback, the inner transaction will be rolled back too. In the example, *B*'s COMMIT would thus be a COMMIT to *A* only, not to the outside world, and it might indeed subsequently be revoked.

It is worth taking a moment to elaborate on the foregoing ideas briefly. Nested transactions can be thought of as a generalization of savepoints [14.11]. Savepoints allow a transaction to be organized as a *sequence* of actions (and rollback can occur at any time to the start of any earlier action in the sequence); nesting, by contrast, allows a transaction to be organized, recursively, as a *hierarchy* of such actions (see Fig. 14.4). In other words:

- BEGIN TRANSACTION is extended to support subtransactions (i.e., if BEGIN TRANSACTION is issued when a transaction is already running, it starts a *child* transaction);

- COMMIT "commits" but only within the *parent scope* (if this transaction is a child);

- ROLLBACK undoes work, but only back to the start of this particular transaction (including child, grandchild, etc., transactions but *not* including the parent transaction, if any).

We remark that nested transactions will be awkward to implement—from a purely syntactic point of view!—in a language like SQL that lacks an explicit BEGIN TRANSACTION (there has to

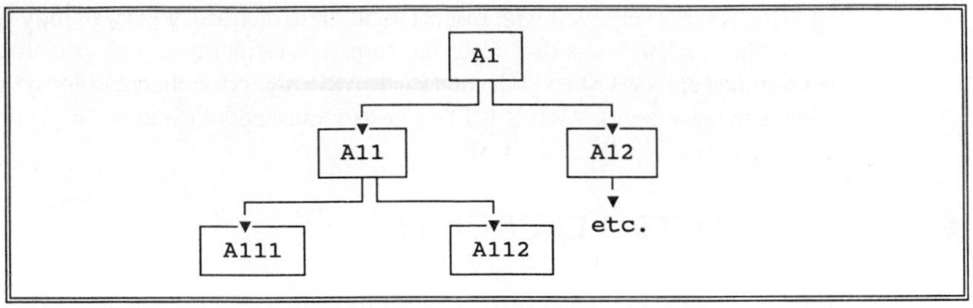

Fig. 14.4   Typical nested transaction

be *some* explicit way of indicating that an inner transaction is to be started, and marking the point to roll back to if that inner transaction fails).

14.4

a. Redo is never necessary following system failure.

b. Physical undo is never necessary, and hence undo log records are also unnecessary.

14.6 This exercise is typical of a wide class of applications, and the following outline solution is typical too.

```
EXEC SQL DECLARE CP CURSOR FOR
        SELECT P.P#, P.PNAME, P.COLOR, P.WEIGHT, P.CITY
        FROM   P
        WHERE  P.P# > previous_P#
        ORDER  BY P# ;
previous_P# := '        ' ;
eof := false ;
DO WHILE ( eof = false ) ;
EXEC SQL OPEN CP ;
    DO count := 1 TO 10 ;
        EXEC SQL FETCH CP INTO :P#, ... ;
        IF SQLSTATE = '02000' THEN
            DO ;
                EXEC SQL CLOSE CP ;
                EXEC SQL COMMIT ;
                eof := true ;
            END DO ;
        ELSE print P#, ... ;
        END IF ;
    END DO ;
    EXEC SQL DELETE FROM P WHERE P.P# = :P# ;
    EXEC SQL CLOSE CP ;
    EXEC SQL COMMIT ;
    previous_P# := P# ;
END DO ;
```

Observe that we lose position within the parts table P at the end of each transaction (even if we did not close cursor CP explicitly, the COMMIT would close it automatically anyway). The foregoing code will therefore not be particularly efficient, because each new transaction requires a search on the parts table in order to reestablish position. Matters might be improved somewhat if there happens to be an index on the P# column—as in fact there probably will be, since {P#} is the primary key—and the optimizer chooses that index as the access path for the table.

Concurrency

15.1 INTRODUCTION

As explained in the introduction to Chapter 14 on recovery, the topics of concurrency and recovery go hand in hand, both being part of the more general topic of *transaction management*. Now we turn our attention to concurrency specifically. The term **concurrency** refers to the fact that DBMSs typically allow many transactions to access the same database at the same time—and in such a system, as is well known, some kind of **concurrency control mechanism** is needed to ensure that concurrent transactions do not interfere with each other. Examples of the kinds of interference that can occur (in the absence of suitable controls, that is) are given later, in Section 15.2.

The structure of the chapter is as follows:

- As just indicated, Section 15.2 explains some of the problems that can arise if proper concurrency control is not provided.

- Section 15.3 introduces the conventional mechanism for dealing with such problems, namely **locking.** *Note:* Locking is not the only possible approach to the concurrency control problem, but it is far and away the one most commonly encountered in practice. Some other approaches are described in the annotation to references [15.1], [15.3], [15.6–15.7], and [15.14–15.15].

- Section 15.4 then shows how locking can be used to solve the problems described in Section 15.2.

- Locking unfortunately introduces problems of its own, of which one of the best known is **deadlock.** Section 15.5 discusses this issue.

- Section 15.6 describes the concept of **serializability,** which is generally recognized as the formal criterion of correctness for the execution of a set of concurrent transactions.

- Sections 15.7 and 15.8 then go on to consider some important refinements on the basic idea of locking, namely **levels of isolation** and **intent locking.**

- Section 15.9 describes the relevant facilities of SQL.

- Finally, Section 15.10 presents a summary and a few concluding observations.

Note: A couple of the general remarks from the introduction to Chapter 14 are applicable again here:

- First, the ideas of concurrency, like those of recovery, are fairly independent of whether the underlying system is relational or something else. However, it is significant that—as with recovery—most of the early theoretical work in the area was done in a specifically relational context "for definiteness" [15.5].

- Second, concurrency, like recovery, is a very large subject, and all we can hope to do in this chapter is introduce some of the most important and basic ideas. The exercises, answers, and annotation to the references at the end of the chapter include some discussion of certain more advanced aspects of the subject.

15.2   THREE CONCURRENCY PROBLEMS

We begin by considering some of the problems that any concurrency control mechanism must address. There are essentially three ways in which things can go wrong—three ways, that is, in which a transaction, though correct in itself, can nevertheless produce the wrong answer if some other transaction interferes with it in some way. Note that the interfering transaction might also be correct in itself; it is the uncontrolled *interleaving* of operations from the two correct transactions that produces the overall incorrect result. (As for the notion of a transaction being "correct in itself," all we mean by this is that the transaction does not violate *The Golden Rule*—see Chapter 8.) The three problems are:

- The *lost update* problem;
- The uncommitted dependency problem; and
- The inconsistent analysis problem.

We consider each in turn.

The Lost Update Problem

Consider the situation illustrated in Fig. 15.1. That figure is meant to be read as follows: Transaction *A* retrieves some tuple *t* at time *t1;* transaction *B* retrieves that same tuple *t* at

Transaction A	*time*	*Transaction B*
–		–
–		–
RETRIEVE *t*	*t1*	–
–		–
–	*t2*	RETRIEVE *t*
–		–
UPDATE *t*	*t3*	–
–		–
–	*t4*	UPDATE *t*
–		–

Fig. 15.1   Transaction *A* loses an update at time *t4*

time *t2;* transaction *A* updates the tuple (on the basis of the values seen at time *t1*) at time *t3;* and transaction *B* updates the same tuple (on the basis of the values seen at time *t2,* which are the same as those seen at time *t1*) at time *t4.* Transaction *A*'s update is lost at time *t4,* because transaction *B* overwrites it without even looking at it. *Note:* Here and throughout this chapter we adopt the convenient fiction yet again that it makes sense to talk about "updating a tuple."

The Uncommitted Dependency Problem

The uncommitted dependency problem arises if one transaction is allowed to retrieve—or, worse, update—a tuple that has been updated by another transaction but not yet committed by that other transaction. For if it has not yet been committed, there is always a possibility that it never will be committed but will be rolled back instead—in which case the first transaction will have seen some data that now no longer exists (and in a sense never did exist). Consider Figs. 15.2 and 15.3.

In the first example (Fig. 15.2), transaction *A* sees an *uncommitted update* (also called an *uncommitted change*) at time *t2.* That update is then undone at time *t3.* Transaction *A* is

Transaction A	*time*	*Transaction B*
-		-
-		-
-	t1	UPDATE t
-		-
RETRIEVE t	t2	-
-		-
-	t3	ROLLBACK
-		

Fig. 15.2 Transaction *A* becomes dependent on an uncommitted change at time *t2*

Transaction A	*time*	*Transaction B*
-		-
-		-
-	t1	UPDATE t
-		-
UPDATE t	t2	-
-		-
-	t3	ROLLBACK
-		

Fig. 15.3 Transaction *A* updates an uncommitted change at time *t2,* and loses that update at time *t3*

therefore operating on a false assumption—namely, the assumption that tuple *t* has the value seen at time *t2,* whereas in fact it has whatever value it had prior to time *t1.* As a result, transaction *A* might well produce incorrect output. Note, by the way, that the rollback of transaction *B* might be due to no fault of *B*'s—it might, for example, be the result of a system crash. (And transaction *A* might already have terminated by that time, in which case the crash would not cause a rollback to be issued for *A* also.)

The second example (Fig. 15.3) is even worse. Not only does transaction *A* become dependent on an uncommitted change at time *t2,* but it actually loses an update at time *t3*—because the rollback at time *t3* causes tuple *t* to be restored to its value prior to time *t1.* This is another version of the lost update problem.

The Inconsistent Analysis Problem

Consider Fig. 15.4, which shows two transactions *A* and *B* operating on account (ACC) tuples: Transaction *A* is summing account balances, transaction *B* is transferring an amount 10 from account 3 to account 1. The result produced by *A,* 110, is obviously incorrect; if *A* were to go on to write that result back into the database, it would actually

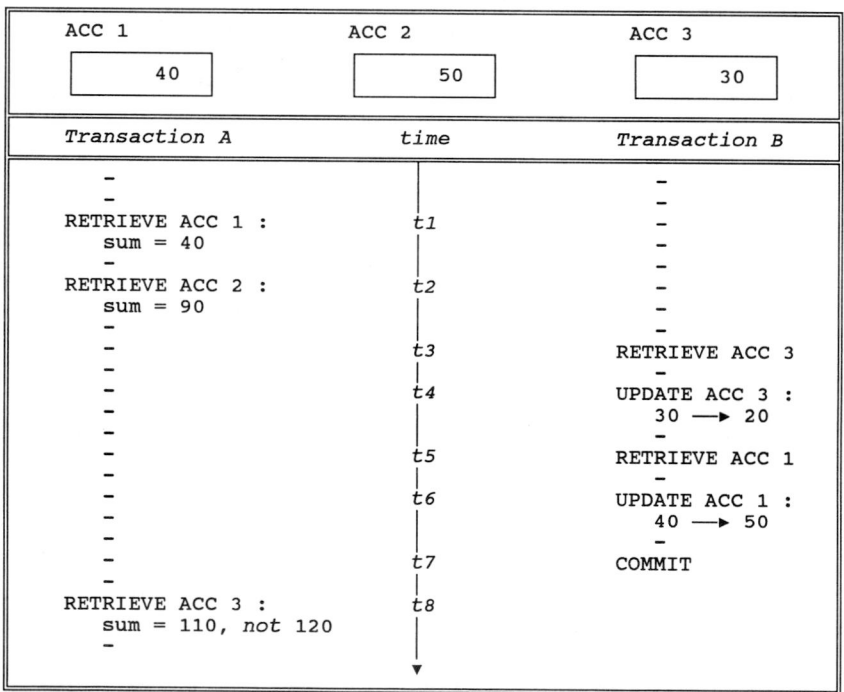

Fig. 15.4   Transaction *A* performs an inconsistent analysis

leave the database in an inconsistent state.* We say that *A* has seen an inconsistent state of the database and has therefore performed an inconsistent analysis. Note the difference between this example and the previous one: There is no question here of *A* being dependent on an uncommitted change, since *B* commits all of its updates before *A* sees ACC 3.

15.3   LOCKING

As indicated in Section 15.1, the problems of Section 15.2 can all be solved by means of a concurrency control technique called **locking.** The basic idea is simple: When a transaction needs an assurance that some object it is interested in—typically a database tuple—will not change in some manner while its back is turned (as it were), it **acquires a lock** on that object. The effect of the lock is to "lock other transactions out of" the object in question, and thus in particular to prevent them from changing it. The first transaction is therefore able to carry out its processing in the certain knowledge that the object in question will remain in a stable state for as long as that transaction wishes it to.

We now give a more detailed explanation of the way locking works:

1. First, we assume the system supports two kinds of locks, **exclusive locks** (X locks) and **shared locks** (S locks), defined as indicated in the next two paragraphs. *Note:* X and S locks are sometimes called **write locks** and **read locks,** respectively. We assume until further notice that X and S locks are the only kinds available; see Section 15.8 for examples of other kinds. We also assume until further notice that tuples are the only kind of "lockable object"; again, see Section 15.8 for other possibilities.

2. If transaction *A* holds an exclusive (X) lock on tuple *t*, then a request from some distinct transaction *B* for a lock of either type on *t* will be denied.

3. If transaction *A* holds a shared (S) lock on tuple *t*, then:

    - A request from some distinct transaction *B* for an X lock on *t* will be denied;

    - A request from some distinct transaction *B* for an S lock on *t* will be granted (that is, *B* will now also hold an S lock on *t*).

These rules can conveniently be summarized by means of a *lock type compatibility matrix* (Fig. 15.5). That matrix is interpreted as follows: Consider some tuple *t;* suppose transaction *A* currently holds a lock on *t* as indicated by the entries in the column headings (dash = no lock); and suppose some distinct transaction *B* issues a request for a lock on *t* as indicated by the entries down the left-hand side (for completeness we again include the "no lock" case). An "N" indicates a *conflict* (*B*'s request cannot be satisfied and *B* goes into a **wait state**), a "Y" indicates compatibility (*B*'s request is satisfied). The matrix is obviously symmetric.

---

*Regarding this possibility (i.e., writing the result back into the database), it is of course necessary to assume that there is no integrity constraint in effect to prevent such a write.

	X	S	-
X	N	N	Y
S	N	Y	Y
-	Y	Y	Y

Fig. 15.5   Compatibility matrix for lock types X and S

Next, we introduce a **data access protocol** (or **locking protocol**) that makes use of X and S locks as just defined to guarantee that problems such as those described in Section 15.2 cannot occur: *

1. A transaction that wishes to retrieve a tuple must first acquire an S lock on that tuple.
2. A transaction that wishes to update a tuple must first acquire an X lock on that tuple. Alternatively, if it already holds an S lock on the tuple (as it will in a RETRIEVE-UPDATE sequence), then it must *promote* that S lock to X level.

Note: Transaction requests for tuple locks are normally implicit; a "tuple retrieve" request is an implicit request for an S lock, and a "tuple update" request is an implicit request for an X lock, on the relevant tuple. Also, of course (as always), we take the term "update" to include INSERTs and DELETEs as well as UPDATEs *per se,* but the rules requires some minor refinement to take care of INSERTs and DELETEs. We omit the details here.

To continue with the protocol:

3. If a lock request from transaction *B* is denied because it conflicts with a lock already held by transaction *A,* transaction *B* goes into a wait state. *B* will wait until *A*'s lock is released. *Note:* The system must guarantee that *B* does not wait forever (a possibility sometimes referred to as **livelock**). A simple way to provide such a guarantee is to service all lock requests on a "first-come, first-served" basis.
4. X locks are held until end-of-transaction (COMMIT or ROLLBACK). S locks are normally held until that time also (but see Section 15.7).

15.4   THE THREE CONCURRENCY PROBLEMS REVISITED

Now we are in a position to see how the foregoing scheme solves the three problems described in Section 15.2. Again we consider them one at a time.

---

*The protocol described is an example of *two-phase locking* (discussed in detail in Section 15.6).

The Lost Update Problem

Fig. 15.6 is a modified version of Fig. 15.1, showing what would happen to the interleaved execution of that figure under the locking protocol described in Section 15.3. Transaction A's UPDATE at time *t3* is not accepted, because it is an implicit request for an X lock on *t,* and such a request conflicts with the S lock already held by transaction *B;* so *A* goes into a wait state. For analogous reasons, *B* goes into a wait state at time *t4.* Now both transactions are unable to proceed, so there is no question of any update being lost. Locking thus solves the lost update problem by reducing it to another problem!— but at least it does solve the original problem. The new problem is called **deadlock**. It is discussed in Section 15.5.

```
┌─────────────────────────────────────────────────────────────────┐
│    Transaction A            time        Transaction B             │
├─────────────────────────────────────────────────────────────────┤
│          -                   │                 -                  │
│          -                   │                 -                  │
│    RETRIEVE t               t1                 -                  │
│    (acquire S lock on t)     │                 -                  │
│          -                   │                 -                  │
│          -                  t2          RETRIEVE t                │
│          -                   │          (acquire S lock on t)     │
│          -                   │                 -                  │
│    UPDATE t                 t3                 -                  │
│    (request X lock on t)     │                 -                  │
│      wait                    │                 -                  │
│      wait                   t4          UPDATE t                  │
│      wait                    │          (request X lock on t)     │
│      wait                    │            wait                    │
│      wait                    │            wait                    │
│      wait                    ▼            wait                    │
└─────────────────────────────────────────────────────────────────┘
```

Fig. 15.6   No update is lost, but deadlock occurs at time *t4*

The Uncommitted Dependency Problem

Figs. 15.7 and 15.8 (overleaf) are, respectively, modified versions of Figs. 15.2 and 15.3, showing what would happen to the interleaved executions of those figures under the locking protocol of Section 15.3. Transaction A's operation at time *t2* (RETRIEVE in Fig. 15.7, UPDATE in Fig. 15.8) is not accepted in either case, because it is an implicit request for a lock on *t,* and such a request conflicts with the X lock already held by *B;* so *A* goes into a wait state. It remains in that wait state until *B* reaches its termination (either COMMIT or ROLLBACK), when *B*'s lock is released and *A* is able to proceed; and at that point *A* sees a *committed* value (either the pre-*B* value, if *B* terminates with rollback, or the post-*B* value otherwise). Either way, *A* is no longer dependent on an uncommitted update.

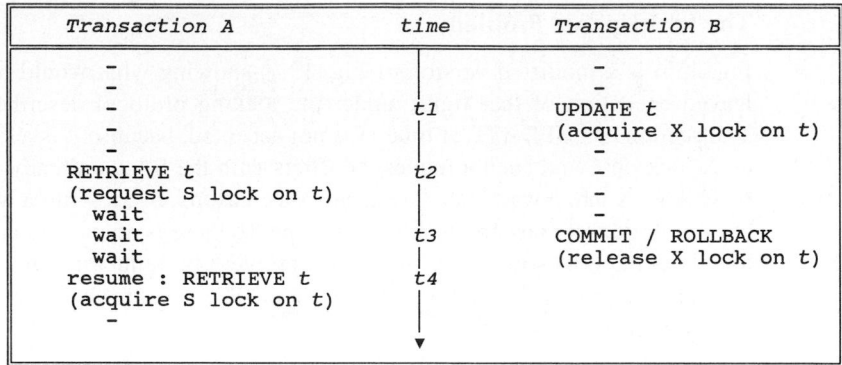

Fig. 15.7   Transaction *A* is prevented from seeing an uncommitted change at time *t2*

```
┌─────────────────────────────────────────────────────────────────────┐
│  Transaction A          time        Transaction B                    │
├─────────────────────────────────────────────────────────────────────┤
│        -                  │                -                          │
│        -                  │                -                          │
│        -                 t1          UPDATE t                         │
│        -                  │          (acquire X lock on t)            │
│        -                  │                -                          │
│  UPDATE t                t2                -                          │
│  (request X lock on t)    │                -                          │
│     wait                  │                -                          │
│     wait                 t3          COMMIT / ROLLBACK                 │
│     wait                  │          (release X lock on t)            │
│  resume : UPDATE t       t4                                           │
│  (acquire X lock on t)    │                                           │
│        -                  ▼                                           │
└─────────────────────────────────────────────────────────────────────┘
```

Fig. 15.8   Transaction *A* is prevented from updating an uncommitted change at time *t2*

The Inconsistent Analysis Problem

Fig. 15.9 is a modified version of Fig. 15.4, showing what would happen to the interleaved execution of that figure under the locking protocol of Section 15.3. Transaction *B*'s UPDATE at time *t6* is not accepted, because it is an implicit request for an X lock on ACC 1, and such a request conflicts with the S lock already held by *A;* so *B* goes into a wait state. Likewise, transaction *A*'s RETRIEVE at time *t7* is also not accepted, because it is an implicit request for an S lock on ACC 3, and such a request conflicts with the X lock already held by *B;* so *A* goes into a wait state also. Again, therefore, locking solves the original problem (the inconsistent analysis problem, in this case) by forcing a deadlock. Again, see Section 15.5.

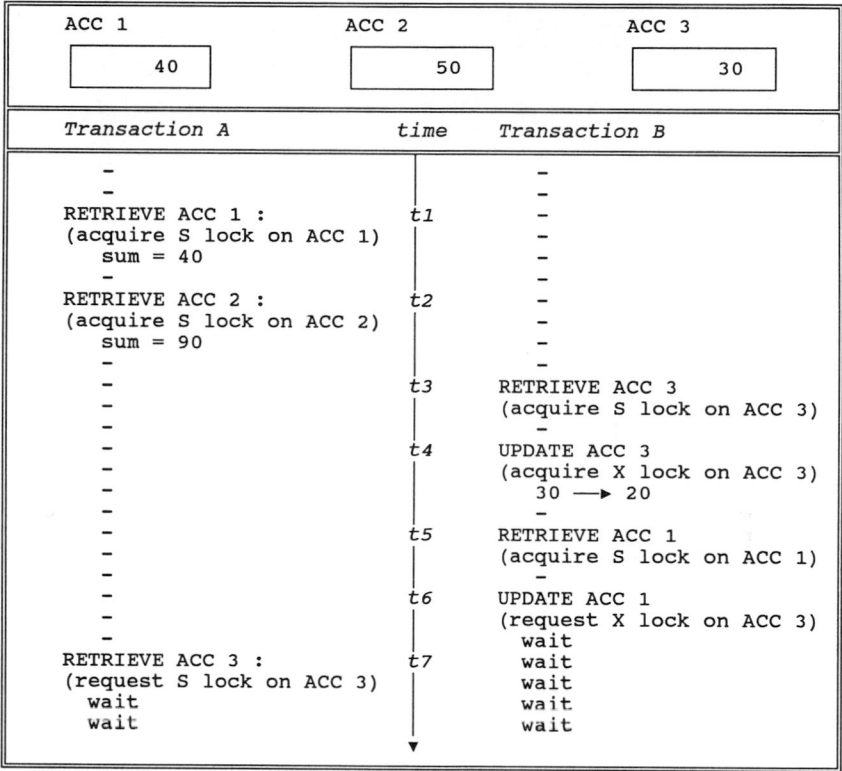

Fig. 15.9 Inconsistent analysis is prevented, but deadlock occurs at time *t7*

15.5 DEADLOCK

We have now seen how locking can be used to solve the three basic problems of concurrency. Unfortunately, however, we have also seen that locking can introduce problems of its own, principally the problem of **deadlock.** Two examples of deadlock were given in the previous section. Fig. 15.10 (overleaf) shows a slightly more general version of the problem; *r1* and *r2* in that figure (*r* for "resource") are intended to represent any lockable objects, not necessarily just database tuples (see Section 15.8), and the "LOCK ... EXCLUSIVE" statements are intended to represent any operations that acquire (exclusive) locks, either explicitly or implicitly.

Deadlock is a situation in which two or more transactions are in a simultaneous wait state, each of them waiting for one of the others to release a lock before it can proceed.*

---

*Deadlock is also referred to in the literature, somewhat colorfully, as *deadly embrace*.

Transaction A	time	Transaction B
-		-
-		-
LOCK *r1* EXCLUSIVE	*t1*	-
-		-
-	*t2*	LOCK *r2* EXCLUSIVE
-		-
LOCK *r2* EXCLUSIVE	*t3*	-
wait		-
wait	*t4*	LOCK *r1* EXCLUSIVE
wait		wait
wait		wait

Fig. 15.10 An example of deadlock

Fig. 15.10 shows a deadlock involving two transactions, but deadlocks involving three, four, . . . transactions are also possible, at least in principle; we remark, however, that experiments with System R seemed to show that in practice deadlocks almost never do involve more than two transactions [15.8],

If a deadlock occurs, it is desirable that the system detect it and break it. Detecting the deadlock involves detecting a cycle in the **Wait-For Graph** (i.e., the graph of "who is waiting for whom"—see Exercise 15.4). Breaking the deadlock involves choosing one of the deadlocked transactions—i.e., one of the transactions in the cycle in the graph—as the **victim** and rolling it back, thereby releasing its locks and so allowing some other transaction to proceed. *Note:* In practice, not all systems do in fact detect deadlocks; some just use a timeout mechanism and simply assume that a transaction that has done no work for some prescribed period of time is deadlocked.

Observe, incidentally, that the victim has "failed" and been rolled back *through no fault of its own*. Some systems will automatically restart such a transaction from the beginning, on the assumption that the conditions that caused the deadlock in the first place will probably not arise again. Other systems simply send a "deadlock victim" exception code back to the application; it is then up to the program to deal with the situation in some graceful manner. The first of these two approaches is clearly preferable from the application programmer's point of view. But even if the programmer does sometimes have to get involved, it is *always* desirable to conceal the problem from the end user, for obvious reasons.

15.6 SERIALIZABILITY

We have now laid the groundwork for explaining the crucial notion of **serializability.** Serializability is the generally accepted **criterion for correctness** for the execution of a given set of transactions. More precisely, a given execution of a set of transactions is considered to be correct if it is serializable—i.e., if it produces the same result as some *serial* execution of the same transactions, running them one at a time. Here is the justification for this claim:

1. Individual transactions are assumed to be correct—i.e., they are assumed to transform a correct state of the database into another correct state.

2. Running the transactions one at a time in any serial order is therefore also correct—"any" serial order because individual transactions are assumed to be independent of one another.

3. An *interleaved* execution is therefore correct if it is equivalent to some serial execution—i.e., if it is serializable.

Referring back to the examples of Section 15.2 (Figs. 15.1–15.4), we can see that the problem in every case was that the interleaved execution was *not* serializable—that is, the interleaved execution was never equivalent to running either *A*-then-*B* or *B*-then-*A*. And the effect of the locking scheme discussed in Section 15.3 was precisely to *force* serializability in every case. In Figs. 15.7 and 15.8, the interleaved execution was equivalent to *B*-then-*A*. In Figs. 15.6 and 15.9, a deadlock occurred, implying that one of the two transactions would be rolled back and—presumably—run again later. If *A* is the one rolled back, then the interleaved execution again becomes equivalent to *B*-then-*A*.

Terminology: Given a set of transactions, any execution of those transactions, interleaved or otherwise, is called a **schedule.** Executing the transactions one at a time, with no interleaving, constitutes a **serial** schedule; a schedule that is not serial is an **interleaved** schedule (or simply a nonserial schedule). Two schedules are said to be **equivalent** if they are guaranteed to produce the same result, independent of the initial state of the database. Thus, a schedule is correct (i.e., serializable) if it is equivalent to some serial schedule.

The point is worth emphasizing that two different serial schedules involving the same set of transactions might well produce different results, and hence that two different interleaved schedules involving those transactions might also produce different results and yet both be considered correct. For example, suppose transaction *A* is of the form "Add 1 to *x*" and transaction *B* is of the form "Double *x*" (where *x* is some item in the database). Suppose also that the initial value of *x* is 10. Then the serial schedule *A*-then-*B* gives $x = 22$, whereas the serial schedule *B*-then-*A* gives $x = 21$. These two results are equally correct, and any schedule that is guaranteed to be equivalent to either *A*-then-*B* or *B*-then-*A* is likewise correct. See Exercise 15.3 at the end of the chapter.

The concept of serializability was first introduced (although not by that name) by Eswaran *et al.* in reference [15.5]. That same paper also proved an important theorem, called the **two-phase locking theorem,** which we state briefly as follows:*

> If all transactions obey the "two-phase locking protocol," then all possible interleaved schedules are serializable.

The **two-phase locking protocol,** in turn, is as follows:

1. Before operating on any object (e.g., a database tuple), a transaction must acquire a lock on that object;

2. After releasing a lock, a transaction must never go on to acquire any more locks.

---

*Two-phase locking has nothing to do with two-phase commit—they just have similar names.

A transaction that obeys this protocol thus has two phases, a lock acquisition or "growing" phase and a lock releasing or "shrinking" phase. *Note:* In practice the shrinking phase is often compressed into the single operation of COMMIT (or ROLLBACK) at end-of-transaction. In fact, the data access protocol we discussed in Section 15.3 can be regarded as a strong form of the two-phase locking protocol.

The notion of serializability is a great aid to clear thinking in this potentially confusing area, and we therefore offer a few additional observations on it here. Let *I* be an interleaved schedule involving some set of transactions *T1, T2, ..., Tn*. If *I* is serializable, then there exists some serial schedule *S* involving *T1, T2, ..., Tn* such that *I* is equivalent to *S*. *S* is said to be a **serialization** of *I*. As we have already seen, *S* is not necessarily unique—i.e., a given interleaved schedule can have more than one serialization.

Now let *Ti* and *Tj* be any two transactions in the set *T1, T2, ..., Tn*. Assume without loss of generality that *Ti* precedes *Tj* in the serialization *S*. In the interleaved schedule *I*, therefore, the effect must be as if *Ti* really did execute before *Tj*. In other words, an informal—but very helpful—characterization of serializability is that, if *A* and *B* are any two transactions involved in some serializable schedule, then either *A* logically precedes *B* or *B* logically precedes *A* in that schedule; that is, **either *B* can see *A*'s output or *A* can see *B*'s**. (If *A* updates resources *r, s, ..., t*, and if *B* sees any of these resources as input, then *B* sees them *either* all as they are after being updated by *A or* all as they were before being updated by *A*—not a mixture of the two.) Conversely, if the effect is not as if either *A* ran before *B* or *B* ran before *A*, then the schedule is not serializable and not correct.

In conclusion, the point is worth stressing that if some transaction *A* is not two-phase (i.e., does not obey the two-phase locking protocol), then it is *always* possible to construct some other transaction *B* that can run interleaved with *A* in such a way as to produce an overall schedule that is not serializable and not correct. Now, in the interests of reducing resource contention and thereby improving performance and throughput, real systems typically do allow the construction of transactions that are not two-phase—i.e., transactions that "release locks early" (prior to COMMIT) and then go on to acquire more locks. However, it should be clear that such transactions are a risky proposition; in effect, allowing a given transaction *A* to be non-two-phase amounts to a gamble that no interfering transaction *B* will ever coexist in the system with *A* (for if it does, then the system will potentially produce wrong answers).

15.7 ISOLATION LEVELS

The term **isolation level** is used to refer to what might loosely be described as *the degree of interference* that a given transaction is prepared to tolerate on the part of concurrent transactions. Now, if serializability is to be guaranteed, the only amount of interference that can possibly be acceptable is none at all!—in other words, the isolation level should be the maximum possible. As indicated at the end of the previous section, however, real systems typically do permit transactions to operate at isolation levels that are less than this maximum, for a variety of pragmatic reasons.

Note: As the foregoing paragraph suggests, isolation level is generally regarded as a property of a *transaction.* Actually there is no reason why a given transaction should not operate at different levels at the same time on different parts of the database, at least in principle. For simplicity, however, we will continue to think of isolation level as a transaction-wide property.

At least five different isolation levels can be defined; reference [15.9] and the SQL standard each define only four, however, while DB2 currently supports just two. Generally speaking, the higher the isolation level, the less the interference (and the lower the concurrency); the lower the isolation level, the more the interference (and the higher the concurrency). By way of example, we consider the two levels supported by DB2, which are called **cursor stability** and **repeatable read,** respectively. *Repeatable read* (RR) is the maximum level; if all transactions operate at this level, all schedules are serializable (the explanations in Section 15.3 and 15.4 were tacitly assuming this isolation level). Under *cursor stability* (CS), by contrast, if a transaction *T1*

- Obtains addressability to some tuple *t,** and thus

- Acquires a lock on *t,* and then

- Relinquishes its addressability to *t* without updating it, and so

- Does not promote its lock to X level, then

- That lock can be released without having to wait for end-of-transaction.

But note that some other transaction *T2* can now update *t* and commit the change. If transaction *T1* subsequently comes back and looks at *t* again, it will see that change, and so might (in effect) see an inconsistent state of the database. Under repeatable read (RR), by contrast, *all* tuple locks—not just X locks—are held until end-of-transaction, and the problem just mentioned therefore cannot occur.

Points arising:

1. The foregoing problem is *not* the only problem that can occur under CS—it just happens to be the easiest one to explain. But it unfortunately suggests that RR is needed only in the comparatively unlikely case that a given transaction needs to look at the same tuple twice. On the contrary, there are arguments to suggest that RR is *always* a better choice than CS; a transaction running under CS is non-two-phase, and so (as explained in the previous section) serializability can no longer be guaranteed. The counterargument, of course, is that CS gives more concurrency than RR (probably but not necessarily).

2. An implementation that supports any isolation level lower than the maximum will normally provide some explicit concurrency control facilities—typically explicit

---

*It does this by setting a *cursor* to point to the tuple, as explained in Chapter 4—hence the name "cursor stability." In the interests of accuracy, we should mention that the lock *T1* acquires on *t* in DB2 is an "update" (U) lock, not an S lock (see reference [4.20]).

LOCK statements—in order to allow users to write their applications in such a way as to guarantee safety in the absence of such a guarantee from the system itself. For example, DB2 provides an explicit LOCK TABLE statement, which allows users operating at level CS to acquire explicit locks, over and above the ones that DB2 acquires automatically to enforce that level. (Note, however, that the SQL standard includes no such explicit concurrency control mechanisms—see Section 15.9.)

In closing this section, we note that the foregoing characterization of RR as the maximum isolation level refers to repeatable read as implemented in DB2. Unfortunately, the SQL standard uses the same term "repeatable read" to mean an isolation level that is strictly lower than the maximum level (again, see Section 15.9).

15.8   INTENT LOCKING

Up to this point we have been assuming that the unit for locking purposes is the individual tuple. In principle, however, there is no reason why locks should not be applied to larger or smaller units of data—an entire relation variable (relvar), or even the entire database, or (going to the opposite extreme) a specific component within a specific tuple. We speak of **locking granularity** [15.9–15.10]. As usual, there is a tradeoff: The finer the granularity, the greater the concurrency; the coarser, the fewer locks need to be set and tested and the lower the overhead. For example, if a transaction has an X lock on an entire relvar, there is no need to set X locks on individual tuples within that relvar; on the other hand, no concurrent transaction will be able to obtain any locks on that relvar, or on tuples within that relvar, at all.

Suppose some transaction *T* does in fact request an X lock on some relvar *R*. On receipt of *T*'s request, the system must be able to tell whether any other transaction already has a lock on any tuple of *R*—for if it does, then *T*'s request cannot be granted at this time. How can the system detect such a conflict? It is obviously undesirable to have to examine every tuple in *R* to see whether any of them is locked by any other transaction, or to have to examine every existing lock to see whether any of them is for a tuple in *R*. Instead, we introduce another protocol, the **intent locking protocol,** according to which no transaction is allowed to acquire a lock on a tuple before first acquiring a lock—probably an *intent* lock (see below)—on the relvar that contains it. Conflict detection in the example then becomes a comparatively simple matter of seeing whether any transaction has a conflicting lock *at the relvar level.*

Now, we have already implied that X and S locks make sense for whole relvars as well as for individual tuples. Following references [15.9–15.10], we now introduce three new kinds of locks, called **intent locks,** that also make sense for relvars, but not for individual tuples. The new kinds of locks are called **intent shared** (IS), **intent exclusive** (IX), and **shared intent exclusive** (SIX) locks, respectively. They can be defined informally as follows (we suppose that transaction *T* has requested a lock of the indicated type on relvar *R;* for completeness, we include definitions for types X and S as well):

- **IS:** *T* intends to set S locks on individual tuples in *R,* in order to guarantee the stability of those tuples while they are being processed.

- **IX:** Same as IS, *plus T* might update individual tuples in *R* and will therefore set X locks on those tuples.

- **S:** *T* can tolerate concurrent readers, but not concurrent updaters, in *R. T* itself will not update any tuples in *R*.

- **SIX:** Combines S and IX; i.e., *T* can tolerate concurrent readers, but not concurrent updaters, in *R, plus T* might update individual tuples in *R* and will therefore set X locks on those tuples.

- **X:** *T* cannot tolerate any concurrent access to *R* at all; *T* itself might or might not update individual tuples in *R*.

The formal definitions of these five lock types are given by an extended version of the lock type compatibility matrix first discussed in Section 15.3. See Fig. 15.11.

	X	SIX	IX	S	IS	–
X	N	N	N	N	N	Y
SIX	N	N	N	N	Y	Y
IX	N	N	Y	N	Y	Y
S	N	N	N	Y	Y	Y
IS	N	Y	Y	Y	Y	Y
–	Y	Y	Y	Y	Y	Y

Fig. 15.11   Compatibility matrix extended to include intent locks

Here now is a more precise statement of the intent locking protocol:

1. Before a given transaction can acquire an S lock on a given tuple, it must first acquire an IS or stronger lock (see below) on the relvar containing that tuple;

2. Before a given transaction can acquire an X lock on a given tuple, it must first acquire an IX or stronger lock (see below) on the relvar containing that tuple.

(Note, however, that this is still not a complete definition. See the annotation to reference [15.9].)

The notion, mentioned in the foregoing protocol, of *relative lock strength* can be explained as follows. Refer to the **precedence graph** in Fig. 15.12. We say that lock type *L2* is stronger—i.e., higher in the graph—than lock type *L1* if and only if, whenever there is an "N" (conflict) in *L1*'s column in the compatibility matrix for a given row, there is also an "N" in *L2*'s column for that same row (see Fig. 15.11). Note that a lock request that fails for a given lock type will certainly fail for a stronger lock type (and this fact implies that it

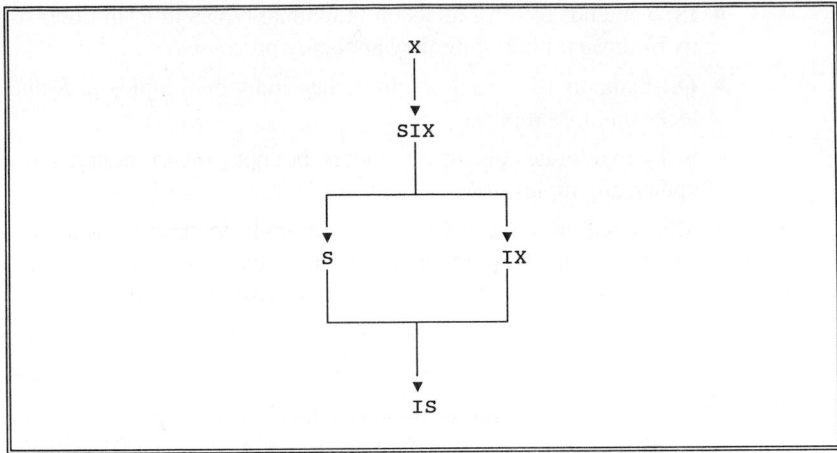

Fig. 15.12   Lock type precedence graph

is always safe to use a lock type that is stronger than strictly necessary). Note too that neither of S and IX is stronger than the other.

It is worth pointing out that, in practice, the relvar level locks required by the intent locking protocol will usually be acquired implicitly. For a read-only transaction, for example, the system will probably acquire an IS lock implicitly on every relvar the transaction accesses. For an update transaction, it will probably acquire IX locks instead. But the system will probably also have to provide an explicit LOCK statement of some kind in order to allow transactions to acquire S, X, or SIX locks at the relvar level if they want them. Such a statement is supported by DB2, for example (though for S and X locks only, not SIX locks).

We close this section with a remark on **lock escalation,** which is implemented in many systems and represents an attempt to balance the conflicting requirements of high concurrency and low lock management overhead. The basic idea is that when the system reaches some predefined threshold, it automatically replaces a set of fine-granularity locks by a single coarse-granularity lock—for example, by trading in a set of individual tuple level S locks and converting the IS lock on the containing relvar to an S lock. This technique seems to work well in practice.

15.9   SQL FACILITIES

The SQL standard does not provide any explicit locking capabilities (in fact, it does not mention locking, as such, at all). However, it does require the implementation to provide the usual guarantees regarding interference, or rather lack thereof, among concurrently executing transactions. Specifically, it requires that updates made by a given transaction *T1* not be made visible to any distinct transaction *T2* until and unless transaction *T1* terminates with commit. Termination with commit causes all updates made by the transaction to become visible to other transactions. Termination with rollback causes all updates made by the transaction to be canceled.

Note: The foregoing assumes that all transactions execute at isolation level READ COMMITTED, REPEATABLE READ, or SERIALIZABLE (see the subsection immediately following). Special considerations apply to transactions executing at the READ UNCOMMITTED level, which (a) are allowed to perform "dirty reads"—again, see the subsection immediately following—but (b) must be defined to be READ ONLY (as noted in Chapter 14).

Isolation Levels

Recall from Chapter 14 that SQL includes a statement called SET TRANSACTION that is used to define certain characteristics of the next transaction to be initiated. One of those characteristics is *isolation level*. The possible levels are **READ UNCOMMITTED, READ COMMITTED, REPEATABLE READ,** or **SERIALIZABLE**.* The default is SERIALIZABLE; if any of the other three is specified, the implementation is free to assign some higher level, where "higher" is defined in terms of the ordering SERIALIZABLE > REPEATABLE READ > READ COMMITTED > READ UNCOMMITTED.

If all transactions execute at isolation level SERIALIZABLE (the default), then the interleaved execution of any set of concurrent transactions is guaranteed to be serializable. However, if any transaction executes at a lesser isolation level, then serializability can be violated in a variety of different ways. The standard defines three specific ways in which serializability might be violated, namely *dirty read, nonrepeatable read,* and *phantoms:*

- **Dirty read:** Suppose transaction *T1* performs an update on some row, transaction *T2* then retrieves that row, and transaction *T1* then terminates with rollback. Transaction *T2* has then seen a row that no longer exists, and in a sense never did exist (because transaction *T1* effectively never ran).

- **Nonrepeatable read:** Suppose transaction *T1* retrieves a row, transaction *T2* then updates that row, and transaction *T1* then retrieves the "same" row again. Transaction *T1* has now retrieved the "same" row twice but seen two different values for it.

- **Phantoms:** Suppose transaction *T1* retrieves the set of all rows that satisfy some condition (e.g., all supplier rows satisfying the condition that the city is Paris). Suppose that transaction *T2* then inserts a new row satisfying that same condition. If transaction *T1* now repeats its retrieval request, it will see a row that did not previously exist—a "phantom."

---

*SERIALIZABLE is not a good keyword here, since it is *schedules* that are supposed to be serializable, not *transactions*. A better term might be just TWO PHASE, meaning the transaction will obey (or will be forced to obey) the two-phase locking protocol.

The various isolation levels are defined in terms of which of the foregoing violations of serializability they permit. They are summarized in Fig. 15.13 ("Y" means the indicated violation can occur, "N" means it cannot).

isolation level	dirty read	nonrepeatable read	phantom
READ UNCOMMITTED	Y	Y	Y
READ COMMITTED	N	Y	Y
REPEATABLE READ	N	N	Y
SERIALIZABLE	N	N	N

Fig. 15.13   SQL isolation levels

An obvious question that arises is: How can the system prevent "phantoms" from occurring? The answer is that it must lock the *access path* used to get to the data under consideration. In the example mentioned above regarding Paris suppliers, for instance, if that access path happens to be an index on supplier cities, then the system must lock the Paris entry in that index. Such a lock will prevent the creation of phantoms, because such creation would require the access path (the index entry, in our example) to be updated. See reference [14.12] for further discussion.

We close this section by repeating the point that the REPEATABLE READ of SQL and the "repeatable read" (RR) of DB2 are not the same thing. In fact, DB2's RR is the same as SQL's SERIALIZABLE.

15.10 SUMMARY

We have examined the question of **concurrency control.** We began by looking at three problems that can arise in an interleaved execution of concurrent transactions if no such control is in place—the **lost update** problem, the **uncommitted dependency** problem, and the **inconsistent analysis** problem. All of these problems arise from schedules that are not **serializable**—i.e., not equivalent to some serial schedule involving the same transactions.

The most widespread technique for dealing with such problems is **locking.** There are two basic types of locks, **shared** (S) and **exclusive** (X). If a transaction has an S lock on an object, other transactions can also acquire an S lock on that object, but not an X lock; if a transaction has an X lock on an object, no other transaction can acquire a lock on the object at all, of either type. Then we introduce a protocol for the use of these locks to ensure that the lost update (etc.) problems cannot occur: Acquire an S lock on everything retrieved, acquire an X lock on everything updated, and keep all locks until end-of-transaction. This protocol enforces serializability.

The protocol just described is a strong (but common) form of the **two-phase locking protocol.** It can be shown that if all transactions obey this protocol, then all schedules are serializable—the **two-phase locking theorem.** A serializable schedule implies that if *A* and *B* are any two transactions involved in that schedule, then either *A* can see *B*'s output or *B* can see *A*'s. Unfortunately, the two-phase locking protocol can lead to **deadlocks.** Deadlocks are resolved by choosing one of the deadlocked transactions as the **victim** and rolling it back (thereby releasing all of its locks).

Anything less than full serializability cannot be guaranteed to be safe (in general). However, systems typically allow transactions to operate at a **level of isolation** that is indeed unsafe, with the aim of reducing resource contention and increasing transaction throughput. We described one such "unsafe" level, *viz.* **cursor stability** (this is the DB2 term; the SQL term is READ COMMITTED).

Next we briefly considered the question of **lock granularity** and the associated idea of **intent locking.** Basically, before a transaction can acquire a lock of any kind on some object, say a database tuple, it must first acquire an appropriate intent lock (at least) on the "parent" of that object (i.e., the containing relvar, in the case of a tuple). In practice, such intent locks will usually be acquired implicitly, just as S and X locks on tuples are usually acquired implicitly. However, **explicit LOCK statements** of some kind should be provided in order to allow a transaction to acquire stronger locks (when needed) than the ones acquired implicitly.

Finally, we outlined SQL's concurrency control support. Basically, SQL does not provide any explicit locking capabilities at all. However, it does support various isolation levels—**READ UNCOMMITTED, READ COMMITTED, REPEATABLE READ,** and **SERIALIZABLE**—which the DBMS will probably implement by means of locking behind the scenes.

We conclude this part of the book with another brief comment on the importance of integrity. When we say, loosely, that the database is **correct,** what we mean is that it does not violate any known integrity constraint. Clearly, therefore, a system that does not provide much in the way of integrity support will have only a very weak sense of what it means for the database to be "correct." Since we said in Chapter 14 that *recovery* meant recovery to a previously known "correct state," and in the present chapter that *concurrency*—or, rather, concurrency *control*—meant that a serializable schedule transforms "a correct state" of the database into another "correct state," you can see that integrity is really a much more fundamental issue than either recovery or concurrency. Indeed, integrity is an issue even in a single-user system.

EXERCISES

15.1 Define *serializability.*

15.2 State:

  a. The two-phase locking protocol;

  b. The two-phase locking theorem.

15.3 Let transactions *T1, T2,* and *T3* be defined to perform the following operations:

    T1: Add one to *A*
    T2: Double *A*
    T3: Display *A* on the screen and then set *A* to one

(where *A* is some item in the database).

a. Suppose transactions *T1, T2, T3* are allowed to execute concurrently. If *A* has initial value zero, how many possible correct results are there? Enumerate them.

b. Suppose the internal structure of *T1, T2, T3* is as indicated below. If the transactions execute *without* any locking, how many possible schedules are there?

T1	*T2*	*T3*
R1: RETRIEVE A INTO *t1* ; *t1* := *t1* + 1 ; U1: UPDATE A FROM *t1* ;	R2: RETRIEVE A INTO *t2* ; *t2* := *t2* * 2 ; U2: UPDATE A FROM *t2* ;	R3: RETRIEVE A INTO *t3* ; display *t3* ; U3: UPDATE A FROM 1 ;

c. With the given initial value for *A* (zero), are there any interleaved schedules that in fact produce a "correct" result and yet are not serializable?

d. Are there any schedules that are in fact serializable but could not be produced if all three transactions obeyed the two-phase locking protocol?

15.4 The following represents the sequence of events in a schedule involving transactions *T1, T2, ..., T12. A, B, ..., H* are items in the database.

```
time t0      ..........
time t1   (T1)  : RETRIEVE A ;
time t2   (T2)  : RETRIEVE B ;
  -       (T1)  : RETRIEVE C ;
  -       (T4)  : RETRIEVE D ;
  -       (T5)  : RETRIEVE A ;
  -       (T2)  : RETRIEVE E ;
  -       (T2)  : UPDATE E ;
  -       (T3)  : RETRIEVE F ;
  -       (T2)  : RETRIEVE F ;
  -       (T5)  : UPDATE A ;
  -       (T1)  : COMMIT ;
  -       (T6)  : RETRIEVE A ;
  -       (T5)  : ROLLBACK ;
  -       (T6)  : RETRIEVE C ;
  -       (T6)  : UPDATE C ;
  -       (T7)  : RETRIEVE G ;
  -       (T8)  : RETRIEVE H ;
  -       (T9)  : RETRIEVE G ;
  -       (T9)  : UPDATE G ;
  -       (T8)  : RETRIEVE E ;
  -       (T7)  : COMMIT ;
  -       (T9)  : RETRIEVE H ;
  -       (T3)  : RETRIEVE G ;
  -       (T10) : RETRIEVE A ;
  -       (T9)  : UPDATE H ;
  -       (T6)  : COMMIT ;
  -       (T11) : RETRIEVE C ;
  -       (T12) : RETRIEVE D ;
  -       (T12) : RETRIEVE C ;
  -       (T2)  : UPDATE F ;
  -       (T11) : UPDATE C ;
  -       (T12) : RETRIEVE A ;
  -       (T10) : UPDATE A ;
  -       (T12) : UPDATE D ;
  -       (T4)  : RETRIEVE G ;
time tn      ..........
```

Assume that "RETRIEVE *R*" (if successful) acquires an S lock on *R,* and "UPDATE *R*" (if successful) promotes that lock to X level. Assume also that all locks are held until end-of-transaction. Are there any deadlocks at time *tn?*

15.5 Consider the concurrency problems illustrated in Figs. 15.1–15.4 once again. What would happen in each case if all transactions were executing under isolation level CS instead of RR?

15.6 Give both informal and formal definitions of lock types X, S, IX, IS, SIX.

15.7 Define the notion of relative lock strength and give the corresponding precedence graph.

15.8 Define the intent locking protocol. What is the purpose of that protocol?

15.9 SQL defines three concurrency problems: *dirty read, nonrepeatable read,* and *phantoms.* How do these relate to the three concurrency problems identified in Section 15.2?

15.10 Sketch an implementation mechanism for the multi-version concurrency control protocols described briefly in the annotation to reference [15.1].

REFERENCES AND BIBLIOGRAPHY

In addition to the following, see also references [14.2], [14.10], and (especially) [14.12] in Chapter 14.

15.1 R. Bayer, M. Heller, and A. Reiser: "Parallelism and Recovery in Database Systems," *ACM TODS 5,* No. 2 (June 1980).

As noted in Chapter 14, newer application areas (e.g., hardware and software engineering) often involve complex processing requirements for which the classical transaction management controls as described in the body of this chapter and its predecessor are not well suited. The basic problem is that complex transactions might last for hours or days, instead of for just a few milliseconds at most as in traditional systems. As a consequence:

1. Rolling back a transaction all the way to the beginning might cause the loss of an unacceptably large amount of work;

2. The use of conventional locking might cause unacceptably long delays (waiting for locks to be released).

The present paper is one of several to address such concerns (other include references [15.7], [15.11–15.13], and [15.17]). It proposes a concurrency control technique known as **multi-version locking** (also called **multi-version read,** and now implemented in several commercial products). The biggest advantage of the technique is that read operations never have to wait—any number of readers *and one writer* can operate on the same logical object simultaneously. To be more specific:

- Reads are never delayed (as just stated);

- Reads never delay updates;

- It is never necessary to roll back a read-only transaction;

- Deadlock is possible only between update transactions.

These advantages are particularly significant in distributed systems—see Chapter 20—where updates can take a long time and read-only queries might therefore otherwise be unduly delayed (and *vice versa*). The basic idea is as follows:

- If transaction *T2* asks to read an object that transaction *T1* currently has update access to, transaction *T2* is given access to a *previously committed* version of that object. Such a version must exist anyway in the system somewhere—probably in the log—for recovery purposes.

- If transaction *T2* asks to update an object that transaction *T1* currently has read access to, transaction *T2* is given access to that object, while transaction *T1* retains access to its own version of the object (which is now really the previous version).

- If transaction *T2* asks to update an object that transaction *T1* currently has update access to, transaction *T2* goes into a wait state* (deadlock and forced rollback are thus still possible, as noted earlier).

Of course, the approach includes appropriate controls to ensure that each transaction always sees a consistent state of the database.

15.2 Hal Berenson *et al.*: "A Critique of ANSI SQL Isolation Levels," Proc. 1995 ACM SIGMOD Int. Conf. on Management of Data, San Jose, Calif. (May 1995).

This paper is critical of the SQL standard's attempt to characterize isolation levels in terms of serializability violations (see Section 15.9): "[The] definitions fail to properly characterize several popular isolation levels, including the standard locking implementations of the levels covered." The paper goes on to point out in particular that the standard fails to prohibit **dirty writes** (defined as the possibility that two transactions *T1* and *T2* might both perform an update on the same row before either transaction terminates).

It does seem to be true that the standard does not prohibit dirty writes explicitly. What it actually says is the following (slightly reworded):

- "The execution of concurrent transactions at isolation level SERIALIZABLE is guaranteed to be serializable." In other words, if all transactions operate at isolation level SERIALIZABLE, the implementation is *required* to prohibit dirty writes, since dirty writes would certainly violate serializability.

- "The four isolation levels guarantee that . . . no updates will be lost." This claim is just wishful thinking; the definitions of the four isolation levels by themselves do not provide any such guarantee. However, it does indicate that the standard definers *intended* to prohibit dirty writes.

- "Changes made by one transaction cannot be perceived by other transactions [except those with isolation level READ UNCOMMITTED] until the original transaction terminates with commit." The question here is, what exactly does *perceived* mean? Would it be possible for a transaction to update a piece of "dirty data" without "perceiving" it?

Note: The foregoing comments are taken from reference [4.19].

15.3 Philip A. Bernstein and Nathan Goodman: "Timestamp-Based Algorithms for Concurrency Control in Distributed Database Systems," Proc. 6th Int. Conf. on Very Large Data Bases, Montreal, Canada (October 1980).

Discusses a collection of approaches to concurrency control based not on locking but on **time-stamping.** The basic idea is that if transaction *A* starts execution before transaction *B,* then the system should behave as if *A* actually executed in its entirety before *B* started (as in a genuine serial schedule). Thus *A* should never be allowed to see any of *B*'s updates; likewise, *A* should never be allowed to update anything that *B* has already seen. Such controls can be enforced as

---

*In other words, update/update conflicts can still occur, and we assume here that locking is used to resolve such conflicts. Other techniques (e.g., timestamping [15.3]) might perhaps be used instead.

follows. For any given database request, the system compares the timestamp of the requesting transaction with the timestamp of the transaction that last retrieved or updated the requested tuple. If there is a conflict, then the requesting transaction can simply be restarted with a new timestamp (as in the so-called *optimistic* methods [15.14]).

As the title of the paper suggests, timestamping was originally introduced in the context of a distributed system (where it was felt that locking imposed intolerable overheads, because of the messages needed to test and set locks, etc.). It is almost certainly not appropriate in a nondistributed system. Indeed, there is considerable skepticism as to its practicality in distributed systems also. One obvious problem is that each tuple has to carry the timestamp of the transaction that last *retrieved* it (as well as the timestamp of the transaction that last updated it), which implies that every read becomes a write! In fact, reference [14.12] claims that timestamping schemes are really just a degenerate case of optimistic concurrency control schemes [15.14], which in turn suffer from problems of their own.

15.4 M. W. Blasgen, J. N. Gray, M. Mitoma, and T. G. Price: "The Convoy Phenomenon," *ACM Operating Systems Review 13,* No. 2 (April 1979).

The **convoy phenomenon** is a problem encountered with high-traffic locks, such as the lock needed to write a record to the log, in systems with *preemptive scheduling. Note:* "Scheduling" here refers to the problem of allocating machine cycles to transactions, not to the interleaving of database operations from different transactions as discussed in the body of this chapter.

The problem is as follows. If a transaction *T* is holding a high-traffic lock and is preempted by the system scheduler—i.e., forced into a wait state, perhaps because its timeslice has expired—then a *convoy* of transactions will form, all waiting for their turn at the high-traffic lock. When *T* comes out of its wait state, it will soon release the lock, but (precisely because the lock is high-traffic) *T* itself will probably rejoin the convoy before the next transaction has finished with the resource, will therefore not be able to continue processing, and so will go into a wait state again.

The root of the problem is that in most cases (not all) the scheduler is part of the underlying operating system, not the DBMS, and is therefore designed on the basis of different assumptions. As the authors observe, a convoy, once established, tends to be stable; the system is in a state of "lock thrashing," most of the machine cycles are devoted to process switching, and not much useful work is being done. A suggested solution—barring the possibility of replacing the scheduler—is to grant the lock not on a first-come, first-served basis but instead in random order.

15.5 K. P. Eswaran, J. N. Gray, R. A. Lorie, and I. L. Traiger: "The Notions of Consistency and Predicate Locks in a Data Base System," *CACM 19,* No. 11 (November 1976).

The paper that first put the subject of concurrency control on a sound theoretical footing.

15.6 Peter Franaszek and John T. Robinson: "Limitations on Concurrency in Transaction Processing," *ACM TODS 10,* No. 1 (March 1985).

See the annotation to reference [15.14].

15.7 Peter A. Franaszek, John T. Robinson, and Alexander Thomasian: "Concurrency Control for High Contention Environments," *ACM TODS 17,* No. 2 (June 1992).

This paper claims that, for a variety of reasons, future transaction processing systems are likely to involve a significantly greater degree of concurrency than the systems of today, and that there is therefore likely to be substantially more data contention in such systems. The authors then present "a number of [nonlocking] concurrency control concepts and transaction scheduling techniques that are applicable to high-contention environments" that—it is claimed, on the basis of experiments with simulation models—"can offer substantial benefits" in such environments.

15.8 J. N. Gray: "Experience with the System R Lock Manager," IBM San Jose Research Laboratory internal memo (Spring 1980).

This reference is really just a set of notes, not a finished paper, and its findings might be a little out of date by now. Nevertheless, it does contain some interesting claims, the following among them:

- Locking imposes about ten percent overhead on online transactions, about one percent on batch transactions.

- It is desirable to support a variety of lock granularities.

- Automatic lock escalation works well.

- Deadlocks are rare in practice and never involve more than two transactions. Almost all deadlocks (97 percent) could be avoided by supporting U locks, as DB2 does but System R did not. (U locks are defined to be compatible with S locks but not with other U locks—and certainly not with X locks, of course. For further details, see reference [4.20].)

- Repeatable read (RR) is more efficient, as well as safer, than cursor stability (CS).

15.9 J. N. Gray, R. A. Lorie, and G. R. Putzolu: "Granularity of Locks in a Large Shared Data Base," Proc. 1st Int. Conf. on Very Large Data Bases, Framingham, Mass. (September 1975).

The paper that introduced the concept of **intent locking.** As explained in Section 15.8, the term "granularity" refers to the size of the objects that can be locked. Since different transactions obviously have different characteristics and different requirements, it is desirable that the system provide a range of different locking granularities (as indeed many systems do). This paper presents an implementation mechanism for such a multi-granularity system, based on intent locking.

We elaborate here on the **intent locking protocol,** since the explanations given in the body of the chapter were deliberately somewhat simplified. First of all, the lockable object types need not be limited to just relvars and tuples, as we were assuming previously. Second, those lockable object types need not even form a strict hierarchy; the presence of indexes and other access structures means they should be regarded rather as a *directed acyclic graph*. For example, the suppliers and parts database might contain both (a stored form of) the parts relvar P and an index, XP say, on the P# attribute. To get to the tuples of relvar P, we must start with the overall database, and then *either* go straight to the relvar and do a sequential scan *or* go to index XP and thence to the required P tuples. So the tuples of P have two "parents" in the graph, P and XP, both of which have the database as a "parent" in turn.

We can now state the protocol in its most general form.

- Acquiring an X lock on a given object implicitly acquires an X lock on all children of that object.

- Acquiring an S or SIX lock on a given object implicitly acquires an S lock on all children of that object.

- Before a transaction can acquire an S or IS lock on a given object, it must first acquire an IS (or stronger) lock on at least one parent of that object.

- Before a transaction can acquire an X, IX, or SIX lock on a given object, it must first acquire an IX (or stronger) lock on all parents of that object.

- Before a transaction can release a lock on a given object, it must first release all locks it holds on all children of that object.

In practice, the protocol does not impose as much run-time overhead as might be thought, because at any given moment the transaction will probably already have most of the locks it needs. For example, an IX lock, say, will probably be acquired on the entire database just once, at program initiation time. That lock will then be held throughout all transactions executed during the lifetime of the program.

15.10 J. N. Gray, R. A. Lorie, G. R. Putzolu, and I. L. Traiger: "Granularity of Locks and Degrees of Consistency in a Shared Data Base," in G. M. Nijssen (ed.), *Proc. IFIP TC-2 Working Conf. on Modelling in Data Base Management Systems.* Amsterdam, Netherlands: North-Holland / New York, N.Y.: Elsevier Science (1976).

The paper that introduced the concept of isolation level (under the name *degrees of consistency*).

15.11 Theo Härder and Kurt Rothermel: "Concurrency Control Issues in Nested Transactions," *The VLDB Journal 2,* No. 1 (January 1993).

As explained in Chapter 14, several writers have suggested the idea of **nested transactions.** This paper proposes an appropriate set of locking protocols for such transactions.

15.12 J. R. Jordan, J. Banerjee, and R. B. Batman: "Precision Locks," Proc. 1981 ACM SIGMOD Int. Conf. on Management of Data, Ann Arbor, Mich. (April/May 1981).

Precision locking is a tuple-level locking scheme that guarantees that only those tuples that need to be locked (in order to achieve serializability) are actually locked, phantoms included. It is in fact a form of what is elsewhere called *predicate* locking [15.5]. It works by (a) checking update requests to see whether a tuple to be inserted or deleted satisfies an earlier retrieval request by some concurrent transaction, and (b) checking retrieval requests to see whether a tuple that has already been inserted or deleted by some concurrent transaction satisfies the retrieval request in question. Not only is the scheme quite elegant, the authors claim that it actually performs better than conventional techniques (which typically lock too much anyway).

15.13 Henry F. Korth and Greg Speegle: "Formal Aspects of Concurrency Control in Long-Duration Transaction Systems Using the NT/PV Model," *ACM TODS 19,* No. 3 (September 1994).

As noted elsewhere (see, e.g., references [14.3], [14.9], and [14.15–14.16]), serializability is often considered too demanding a condition to impose on certain kinds of transaction processing systems, especially in newer application areas that involve human interaction and hence transactions of long duration. This paper presents a new transaction model called NT/PV ("nested transactions with predicates and views") that addresses such concerns. Among other things, it shows that the standard model of transactions with serializability is a special case; it defines "new and more useful correctness classes"; and it claims that the new model provides "an appropriate framework for solving long-duration transaction problems."

15.14 H. T. Kung and John T. Robinson: "On Optimistic Methods for Concurrency Control," *ACM TODS 6,* No. 2 (June 1981).

Locking schemes can be described as *pessimistic,* inasmuch as they make the worst-case assumption that every piece of data accessed by a given transaction might be needed by some concurrent transaction and had therefore better be locked. By contrast, **optimistic** schemes—also known as *certification* or *validation* schemes—make the opposite assumption that conflicts are likely to be quite rare in practice. Thus, they operate by allowing transactions to run to completion completely unhindered, and then checking at COMMIT time to see whether a conflict did in fact occur. If it did, the offending transaction is simply started again from the beginning. No updates are ever written to the database prior to successful completion of commit processing, so such restarts do not require any updates to be undone.

A subsequent paper [15.6] showed that under certain reasonable assumptions, optimistic methods enjoy certain inherent advantages over traditional locking methods in terms of the expected level of concurrency (i.e., number of simultaneous transactions) they can support, suggesting that optimistic methods might become the technique of choice in systems with large numbers of parallel processors. (Reference [14.12], by contrast, claims that optimistic methods in general are actually *worse* than locking in "hotspot" situations—where a hotspot is a data item that is updated very frequently, by many distinct transactions. See the annotation to reference [15.15] for a discussion of a technique that works well on hotspots.)

15.15 Patrick E. O'Neil: "The Escrow Transactional Method," *ACM TODS 11,* No. 4 (December 1986).

Consider the following simple example. Suppose the database contains a data item *TC* representing "total cash on hand," and suppose almost every transaction in the system updates *TC,* decrementing it by some amount (corresponding to some cash withdrawal, say). Then *TC* is an example of a "hotspot," i.e., an item in the database that is accessed by a significant percentage of the transactions running in the system. Under traditional locking, a hotspot can very quickly become a bottleneck (to mix metaphors horribly). But using traditional locking on a data item like *TC* is really overkill. If *TC* initially has a value of ten million dollars, and each individual transaction decrements it (on average) by only ten dollars, then we could run 1,000,000 such transactions, *and furthermore apply the 1,000,000 corresponding decrements in any order,* before running into trouble. There is thus no need to apply a traditional lock to *TC* at all; instead, all that is necessary is to make sure that the current value is large enough to permit the required decrement, and then do the update. (If the transaction subsequently fails, the amount of the decrement must be added back in again, of course.)

The **escrow** method applies to situations such as the one just described—i.e., situations in which the updates are of a certain special form, instead of being completely arbitrary. The system must provide a special new kind of update statement (e.g., "decrement by *x,* if and only if the current value is greater than *y*"). It can then perform the update by placing the decrement amount *x* "in escrow," taking it out of escrow at end-of-transaction (and committing the change if end-of-transaction is COMMIT, or adding the amount back into the original total if end-of-transaction is ROLLBACK).

The paper describes a number of cases in which the escrow method can be used. One example of a commercial product that supports the technique is the Fast Path version of IMS, from IBM. We remark that the technique might be regarded as a special case of optimistic concurrency control [15.14] (note, however, that the "special-case" aspect—the provision of the special update statements—is critical).

15.16 Christos Papadimitriou: *The Theory of Database Concurrency Control.* Rockville, Md.: Computer Science Press (1986).

A textbook, with the emphasis on formal theory.

15.17 Kenneth Salem, Hector Garcia-Molina, and Jeannie Shands: "Altruistic Locking," *ACM TODS 19,* No. 1 (March 1994).

Proposes an extension to two-phase locking according to which a transaction *T1* that has finished with some locked piece of data but cannot unlock it (because of the two-phase locking protocol) can nevertheless "donate" the data back to the system, thereby allowing some other transaction *T2* to acquire a lock on it. *T2* is then said to be "in the wake of" *T1.* Protocols are defined to prevent, e.g., a transaction from seeing any updates by transactions in its wake. Altruistic locking (the term derives from the fact that "donating" data benefits other transactions, not the donor transaction) is shown to provide more concurrency than conventional two-phase locking, especially when some of the transactions are of long duration.

ANSWERS TO SELECTED EXERCISES

15.3

a. There are six possible correct results, corresponding to the six possible serial schedules:

```
Initially : A = 0
T1-T2-T3  : A = 1
T1-T3-T2  : A = 2
T2-T1-T3  : A = 1
T2-T3-T1  : A = 2
T3-T1-T2  : A = 4
T3-T2-T1  : A = 3
```

Of course, the six possible correct results are not all distinct. As a matter of fact, it so happens in this particular example that the possible correct results are all independent of the initial state of the database, owing to the nature of transaction *T3*.

b. There are 90 possible distinct schedules. We can represent the possibilities as follows. (*Ri, Rj, Rk* stand for the three RETRIEVE operations *R1, R2, R3,* not necessarily in that order; similarly, *Up, Uq, Ur* stand for the three UPDATE operations *U1, U2, U3,* again not necessarily in that order.)

```
Ri-Rj-Rk-Up-Uq-Ur : 3 * 2 * 1 * 3 * 2 * 1 = 36 possibilities
Ri-Rj-Up-Rk-Uq-Ur : 3 * 2 * 2 * 1 * 2 * 1 = 24 possibilities
Ri-Rj-Up-Uq-Rk-Ur : 3 * 2 * 2 * 1 * 1 * 1 = 12 possibilities
Ri-Up-Rj-Rk-Uq-Ur : 3 * 1 * 2 * 1 * 2 * 1 = 12 possibilities
Ri-Up-Rj-Uq-Rk-Ur : 3 * 1 * 2 * 1 * 1 * 1 =  6 possibilities
                                            _____
                               TOTAL = 90 combinations
```

c. Yes. For example, the schedule *R1-R2-R3-U3-U2-U1* produces the same result (one) as two of the six possible serial schedules (*Exercise:* Check this statement), and thus happens to be "correct" for the given initial value of zero. But it must be clearly understood that this "correctness" is a mere fluke, and results purely from the fact that the initial data value happened to be zero and not something else. As a counterexample, consider what would happen if the initial value of *A* were ten instead of zero. Would the schedule *R1-R2-R3-U3-U2-U1* shown above still produce one of the genuinely correct results? (What *are* the genuinely correct results in this case?) If not, then that schedule is not serializable.

d. Yes. For example, the schedule *R1-R3-U1-U3-R2-U2* is serializable (it is equivalent to the serial schedule *T1-T3-T2*), but it cannot be produced if *T1, T2,* and *T3* all obey the two-phase locking protocol. For, under that protocol, operation *R3* will acquire an S lock on *A* on behalf of transaction *T3;* operation *U1* in transaction *T1* will thus not be able to proceed until that lock has been released, and that will not happen until transaction *T3* terminates (in fact, transactions *T3* and *T1* will deadlock when operation *U3* is reached).

This exercise illustrates very clearly the following important point. Given a set of transactions and an initial state of the database, (a) let ALL be the set of all possible schedules involving those transactions; (b) let "CORRECT" be the set of all schedules that are guaranteed to produce a correct final state or at least happen to do so from the given initial state; (c) let SERIALIZABLE be the set of all serializable schedules; and (d) let PRODUCIBLE be the set of all schedules producible under the two-phase locking protocol. Then, in general,

```
PRODUCIBLE ≤ SERIALIZABLE ≤ "CORRECT" ≤ ALL
```

(using "≤" to mean "is a subset of").

15.4 At time *tn* no transactions are doing any useful work at all! There is one deadlock, involving transactions *T2, T3, T9,* and *T8;* in addition, *T4* is waiting for *T9, T12* is waiting for *T4,* and *T10* and *T11* are both waiting for *T12.* We can represent the situation by means of a graph (the **Wait-For Graph**), in which the nodes represent transactions and a directed edge from node *Ti* to node *Tj* indicates that *Ti* is waiting for *Tj* (see Fig. 15.14). Edges are labeled with the name of the database item and level of lock they are waiting for.

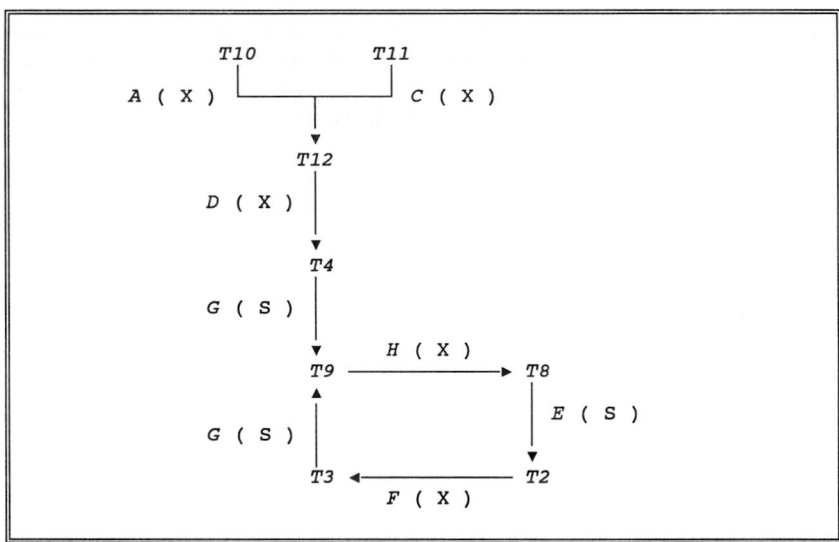

Fig. 15.14   The Wait-For Graph for Exercise 15.4

15.5 Isolation level CS has the same effect as isolation level RR on the problems of Figs. 15.1–15.3. (Note, however, that this statement does *not* apply to CS as implemented in DB2, thanks to DB2's use of U locks in place of S locks [4.20].) As for the inconsistent analysis problem (Fig. 15.4): Isolation level CS does not solve this problem; transaction *A* must execute under RR in order to retain its locks until end-of-transaction, for otherwise it will still produce the wrong answer. (Alternatively, of course, *A* could lock the entire accounts relvar via some explicit lock request, if the system supports such an operation. This solution would work under both CS and RR isolation levels.)

15.6 See Section 15.8. Note in particular that the *formal* definitions are given by the lock type compatibility matrix (Fig. 15.11).

15.9 The three concurrency problems identified in Section 15.2 were *lost update, uncommitted dependency,* and *inconsistent analysis.* Of these three:

- *Lost updates:* The SQL implementation is required to guarantee (in all circumstances) that lost updates never occur.

- *Uncommitted dependency:* This is just another name for dirty read.

- *Inconsistent analysis:* This term covers both nonrepeatable read and phantoms.

15.10 The following brief description is taken from reference [20.15]. First of all, the system must keep:

1. For each data object, a stack of committed versions (each stack entry giving a value for the object and the ID of the transaction that established that value; i.e., each stack entry essentially consists of a pointer to the relevant entry in the log). The stack is in reverse chronological sequence, with the most recent entry being on the top.

2. A list of transaction IDs for all committed transactions (the *commit list*).

When a transaction starts executing, the system gives it a private copy of the commit list. Read operations on an object are directed to the most recent version of the object produced by a transaction on that private list. Update operations, by contrast, are directed to the actual current data object (which is why update/update conflict testing is still necessary). When the transaction commits, the system updates the commit list and the data object version stacks appropriately.

FURTHER TOPICS

We claimed in Part II of this book that the relational model is the foundation for modern database technology, and so it is. However, it is *only* the foundation: There is a lot more to database technology than just the relational model as described in Part II, and database students and professionals need to be familiar with many additional concepts and facilities in order to be fully "database-aware" (as indeed should be obvious from our discussions in Parts III and IV). We now turn our attention to a miscellaneous collection of further important topics. The topics to be covered, in sequence, are as follows:

- Security (Chapter 16)
- Optimization (Chapter 17)
- Missing information (Chapter 18)
- Type inheritance (Chapter 19)
- Distributed databases (Chapter 20)
- Decision support (Chapter 21)
- Temporal data (Chapter 22)
- Logic-based databases (Chapter 23)

Actually the foregoing sequence is a little arbitrary, but the chapters have been written on the assumption that they will be read (possibly selectively) in order as written.

CHAPTER 16

Security

16.1 INTRODUCTION

Data security issues are often lumped together with data integrity issues (at least in informal contexts), but the two concepts are really quite distinct. *Security* refers to the protection of data against unauthorized disclosure, alteration, or destruction; *integrity* refers to the accuracy or validity of that data. To put it a little glibly:

- **Security** means protecting the data against unauthorized users;
- **Integrity** means protecting it against *authorized* users.

Or even more loosely: Security means making sure users are *allowed* to do the things they are trying to do; integrity involves making sure the things they are trying to do are *correct.*

There are some similarities too, of course: In both cases, the system needs to be aware of certain *constraints* that users must not violate; in both cases those constraints must be specified (typically by the DBA) in some suitable language, and must be maintained in the system catalog; and in both cases the DBMS must monitor user operations in order to ensure that the constraints are enforced. In this chapter, we examine security in particular (integrity, of course, has already been discussed at length in Chapter 8 and elsewhere). *Note:* The main reason we so clearly separate our own discussions of the two topics is that we regard integrity as absolutely fundamental but security as more of a secondary issue.

General Considerations

There are numerous aspects to the security problem, the following among them:

- Legal, social, and ethical aspects (for example, does the person making the request, say for a customer's credit, have a legal right to the requested information?);
- Physical controls (for example, is the computer or terminal room locked or otherwise guarded?);
- Policy questions (for example, how does the enterprise owning the system decide who should be allowed access to what?);
- Operational problems (for example, if a password scheme is used, how are the passwords themselves kept secret? how often are they changed?);
- Hardware controls (for example, does the processing unit provide any security features, such as storage protection keys or a protected operation mode?);

- Operating system support (for example, does the underlying operating system erase the contents of main memory and disk files when they are finished with?);

and finally

- Issues that are the specific concern of the database system itself (for example, does the database system have a concept of data ownership?).

For obvious reasons, we limit our attention in this chapter to issues in this last category only (for the most part).

Now, modern DBMSs typically support either or both of two broad approaches to data security. The approaches are known as *discretionary* and *mandatory* control, respectively. In both cases, the unit of data or "data object" that might need to be protected can range all the way from an entire database on the one hand to a specific component within a specific tuple on the other. How the two approaches differ is indicated by the following brief outline:

- In the case of **discretionary** control, a given user will typically have different access rights (also known as **privileges**) on different objects; further, there are very few limitations—inherent limitations, that is—regarding which users can have which rights on which objects (for example, user *U1* might be able to see *A* but not *B,* while user *U2* might be able to see *B* but not *A*). Discretionary schemes are thus very flexible.

- In the case of **mandatory** control, by contrast, each data object is labeled with a certain **classification** level, and each user is given a certain **clearance** level. A given data object can then be accessed only by users with the appropriate clearance. Mandatory schemes thus tend to be hierarchic in nature and are hence comparatively rigid. (If user *U1* can see *A* but not *B,* then the classification of *B* must be higher than that of *A,* and so no user *U2* can see *B* but not *A.*)

We discuss discretionary schemes in Section 16.2 and mandatory schemes in Section 16.3.

Regardless of whether we are dealing with a discretionary scheme or a mandatory one, all decisions as to which users are allowed to perform which operations on which objects are policy decisions, not technical ones. As such, they are clearly outside the jurisdiction of the DBMS as such; all the DBMS can do is enforce those decisions once they are made. It follows that:

- The results of those policy decisions (a) must be made known to the system (this is done by means of statements in some appropriate definitional language), and (b) must be remembered by the system (this is done by saving them in the catalog).

- There must be a means of checking a given access request against the applicable security constraints in the catalog. (By "access request" here we mean the combination of *requested operation* plus *requested object* plus *requesting user,* in general.) That checking is done by the DBMS's **security subsystem,** also known as the **authorization** subsystem.

- In order to decide which security constraints are applicable to a given access request, the system must be able to recognize the *source* of that request—that is, it must be able to recognize the *requesting user*. For that reason, when users sign on to the system, they are typically required to supply, not only their user ID (to say who they are), but also a **password** (to prove they are who they say they are). The password is supposedly known only to the system and to legitimate users of the user ID concerned.*

Regarding this last point, incidentally, note that any number of distinct users might be able to share the same ID. In this way the system can support **user groups,** and can thus provide a way of allowing (say) everyone in the accounting department to share the same privileges on the same objects. The operations of adding individual users to or removing individual users from a given group can then be performed independently of the operation of specifying which privileges on which objects apply to that group. Note, however, that the obvious place to keep a record of which users are in which groups is once again the catalog (or perhaps the database itself). In this connection, we draw your attention to reference [16.9], which describes a system in which user groups can be *nested.* To quote: "The ability to classify users into a hierarchy of groups provides a powerful tool for administrating large systems with thousands of users and objects."

16.2 DISCRETIONARY ACCESS CONTROL

To repeat from the previous section, most DBMSs support either discretionary control or mandatory control or both. In fact it would be more accurate to say that most systems support discretionary control, and some systems support mandatory control as well; discretionary control is thus more likely to be encountered in practice, and so we deal with it first.

As already noted, there needs to be a language that supports the definition of (discretionary) security constraints. For fairly obvious reasons, however, it is easier to state what is *allowed* rather than what is *not* allowed; languages therefore typically support the definition, not of security constraints as such, but rather of **authorities,** which are effectively the opposite of security constraints (if something is authorized, it is not constrained). We therefore begin by briefly describing a language for defining authorities.[†] Here first is a simple example:

```
AUTHORITY SA3
   GRANT RETRIEVE ( S#, SNAME, CITY ), DELETE
   ON    S
   TO    Jim, Fred, Mary ;
```

---

*Checking that users are who they say they are is called **authentication.** We note in passing that authentication techniques are now available that are much more sophisticated than simple password checking, involving a variety of biometric devices (fingerprint readers, retinal scanners, hand geometry imagers, voice verifiers, signature recognizers, etc.). Such devices can all effectively be used to check "personal characteristics no one can steal" [16.3].

[†]**Tutorial D** as originally defined [3.3] deliberately did not include any authority definition facilities, but the hypothetical language of the present section can be regarded as being "in the spirit of" **Tutorial D.**

This example is intended to illustrate the point that (in general) authorities have *four components*, as follows:

1. A **name** (SA3—"suppliers authority three"—in the example). The authority will be registered in the catalog under this name.

2. One or more **privileges** (RETRIEVE—on certain attributes only—and DELETE, in the example), specified by means of the GRANT clause.

3. The **relvar** to which the authority applies (relvar S in the example), specified by means of the ON clause.

4. One or more **"users"** (more accurately, *user IDs*) who are to be granted the specified privileges over the specified relvar, specified by means of the TO clause.

Here then is the general syntax:

```
AUTHORITY <authority name>
   GRANT <privilege commalist>
   ON    <relvar name>
   TO    <user ID commalist> ;
```

Explanation: The *<authority name>, <relvar name>,* and *<user ID commalist>* are self-explanatory (except that we regard ALL, meaning all known users, as a legal "user ID" in this context). Each *<privilege>* is one of the following:

```
RETRIEVE [ ( <attribute name commalist> ) ]
INSERT   [ ( <attribute name commalist> ) ]
UPDATE   [ ( <attribute name commalist> ) ]
DELETE
ALL
```

RETRIEVE (unqualified), INSERT (unqualified), UPDATE (unqualified), and DELETE are self-explanatory.* If a commalist of attribute names is specified with RETRIEVE, then the privilege applies only to the attributes specified; INSERT and UPDATE with a commalist of attribute names are defined analogously. The specification ALL is shorthand for all privileges: RETRIEVE (all attributes), INSERT (all attributes), UPDATE (all attributes), and DELETE. *Note:* For simplicity, we ignore the question of whether any special privileges are required in order to perform general relational assignment operations. Also, we deliberately limit our attention to *data manipulation* operations only; in practice, of course, there are many other operations that we would want to be subject to authorization checking as well, such as the operations of defining and dropping relvars—and the operations of defining and dropping authorities themselves, come to that. We omit detailed consideration of such operations here for space reasons.

What should happen if some user attempts some operation on some object for which he or she is not authorized? The simplest option is obviously just to reject the attempt (and to provide suitable diagnostic information, of course); such a response will surely be the one

---

*Well, perhaps not quite; the RETRIEVE privilege is also needed just to *mention* the relevant object (e.g., in a view definition or an integrity constraint) as well as for retrieval *per se.*

most commonly required in practice, so we might as well make it the default. In more sensitive situations, however, some other action might be more appropriate; for example, it might be necessary to terminate the program or lock the user's keyboard. It might also be desirable to record such attempts in a special log (*threat monitoring*), in order to permit subsequent analysis of attempted security breaches and also to serve in itself as a deterrent against illegal infiltration (see the discussion of *audit trails* at the end of this section).

Of course, we also need a way of dropping authorities:

```
DROP AUTHORITY <authority name> ;
```

For example:

```
DROP AUTHORITY SA3 ;
```

For simplicity, we assume that dropping a given relvar will automatically drop any authorities that apply to that relvar.

Here are some further examples of authorities, most of them fairly self-explanatory.

1. ```
   AUTHORITY EX1
       GRANT RETRIEVE ( P#, PNAME, WEIGHT )
       ON      P
       TO      Jacques, Anne, Charley ;
   ```

   Users Jacques, Anne, and Charley can see a "vertical subset" of base relvar P. The example is thus an example of a **value-independent** authority.

2. ```
   AUTHORITY EX2
       GRANT RETRIEVE, UPDATE ( SNAME, STATUS ), DELETE
       ON      LS
       TO      Dan, Misha ;
   ```

   Relvar LS here is a view ("London suppliers"—see Fig. 9.4 in Chapter 9). Users Dan and Misha can thus see a "horizontal subset" of base relvar S. This example is an example of a **value-dependent** authority. Note too that although users Dan and Misha can DELETE certain supplier tuples (via view LS), they cannot INSERT them, and they cannot UPDATE attributes S# or CITY.

3. ```
   VAR SSPPR VIEW
      ( S JOIN SP JOIN ( P WHERE CITY = 'Rome' ) { P# } )
                                        { ALL BUT P#, QTY } ;

   AUTHORITY EX3
       GRANT RETRIEVE
       ON      SSPPR
       TO      Giovanni ;
   ```

   This is another value-dependent example: User Giovanni can retrieve supplier information, but only for suppliers who supply some part stored in Rome.
   ```

```
4.  VAR SSQ VIEW
         SUMMARIZE SP PER S { S# } ADD SUM ( QTY ) AS SQ ;

    AUTHORITY EX4
       GRANT RETRIEVE
       ON    SSQ
       TO    Fidel ;
```

User Fidel can see total shipment quantities per supplier, but not individual shipment quantities. User Fidel thus sees a **statistical summary** of the underlying base data.

```
5.  AUTHORITY EX5
       GRANT RETRIEVE, UPDATE ( STATUS )
       ON    S
       WHEN  DAY () IN ( 'Mon', 'Tue', 'Wed', 'Thu', 'Fri' )
             AND NOW () ≥ TIME '09:00:00'
             AND NOW () ≤ TIME '17:00:00'
       TO    Purchasing ;
```

Here we are extending our AUTHORITY syntax to include a WHEN clause to specify certain "context controls"; we are also assuming that the system provides two niladic operators—i.e., operators that take no operands—called DAY() and NOW(), with the obvious interpretations. Authority EX5 guarantees that supplier status values can be changed by the user "Purchasing" (presumably meaning anyone in the purchasing department) only on a weekday, and only during working hours. This is thus an example of what is sometimes called a **context-dependent** authority, because a given access request will or will not be allowed depending on the context—here the combination of day of the week and time of day—in which it is issued.

Other examples of builtin operators that the system probably ought to support anyway and could be useful for context-dependent authorities include:

```
TODAY()      — value = the current date
USER()       — value = the ID of the current user
TERMINAL()   — value = the ID of the originating terminal
                       for the current request
```

By now you have probably realized that, conceptually speaking, authorities are all "ORed" together. In other words, a given access request (meaning, to repeat, the combination of requested operation plus requested object plus requesting user) is acceptable if and only if at least one authority permits it. Note, however, that (e.g.) if (a) one authority lets user Nancy retrieve part colors and (b) another lets her retrieve part weights, it does not follow that she can retrieve part colors and weights together (a separate authority is required for the combination).

Finally, we have implied, but never quite said as much, that users can do only the things they are explicitly allowed to do by the defined authorities. Anything not explicitly authorized is implicitly outlawed!

Request Modification

In order to illustrate some of the ideas introduced above, we now briefly describe the security aspects of the University Ingres prototype and its query language QUEL, since they adopt an interesting approach to the problem. Basically, any given QUEL request is automatically modified before execution in such a way that it cannot possibly violate any specified security constraint. For example, suppose user *U* is allowed to retrieve parts stored in London only:

```
DEFINE PERMIT RETRIEVE ON P TO U
       WHERE  P.CITY = "London"
```

(see below for details of the DEFINE PERMIT operation). Now suppose user *U* issues the QUEL request:

```
RETRIEVE ( P.P#, P.WEIGHT )
WHERE       P.COLOR = "Red"
```

Using the "permit" for the combination of relvar P and user *U* as stored in the catalog, the system automatically modifies this request so that it looks like this:

```
RETRIEVE ( P.P#, P.WEIGHT )
WHERE       P.COLOR = "Red"
AND         P.CITY  = "London"
```

And of course this modified request cannot possibly violate the security constraint. Note, incidentally, that the modification process is "silent": User *U* is not informed that the system has in fact executed a statement that is somewhat different from the original request, because that fact in itself might be sensitive (user *U* might not even be allowed to know there are any nonLondon parts).

The process of *request modification* just outlined is actually identical to the technique used for the implementation of views [8.20] and also—in the case of the Ingres prototype specifically—integrity constraints [9.15]. So one advantage of the scheme is that it is very easy to implement—much of the necessary code exists in the system already. Another is that it is comparatively efficient—the security enforcement overhead occurs at compile time instead of run time, at least in part. Yet another advantage is that some of the awkwardnesses that can occur with the SQL approach when a given user needs different privileges over different portions of the same relvar (see Section 16.6) do not arise.

One *dis*advantage is that not all security constraints can be handled in this simple fashion. As a trivial counterexample, suppose user *U* is not allowed to access relvar P at all. Then no simple "modified" form of the RETRIEVE shown above can preserve the illusion that relvar P does not exist. Instead, an explicit error message along the lines of "You are not allowed to access this relvar" must necessarily be produced. (Or perhaps the system could simply *lie* and say "No such relvar exists.")

Here then is the syntax of DEFINE PERMIT:

```
DEFINE PERMIT <operation name commalist>
        ON      <relvar name> [ ( <attribute name commalist> ) ]
        TO
      [ AT      <terminal name commalist> ]
      [ FROM    <time> TO <time> ]
      [ ON      <day>  TO <day>  ]
      [ WHERE   <boolean expression> ]
```

This statement is conceptually rather similar to our AUTHORITY statement, except that it supports a WHERE clause. Here is an example:

```
DEFINE PERMIT APPEND, RETRIEVE, REPLACE
        ON      S ( S#, CITY )
        TO      Joe
        AT      TTA4
        FROM    9:00 TO 17:00
        ON      Sat TO Sun
        WHERE   S.STATUS < 50
        AND     S.S# = SP.P#
        AND     SP.P# = P.P#
        AND     P.COLOR = "Red"
```

Note: APPEND and REPLACE are the QUEL analogs of our INSERT and UPDATE, respectively.

Audit Trails

It is important not to assume that the security system is perfect. A would-be infiltrator who is sufficiently determined will usually find a way of breaking through the controls, especially if the payoff for doing so is high. In situations where the data is sufficiently sensitive, therefore, or where the processing performed on the data is sufficiently critical, an **audit trail** becomes a necessity. If, for example, data discrepancies lead to a suspicion that the database has been tampered with, the audit trail can be used to examine what has been going on and to verify that matters are under control (or to help pinpoint the wrongdoer if not).

An audit trail is essentially a special file or database in which the system automatically keeps track of all operations performed by users on the regular data. In some systems, the audit trail might be physically integrated with the recovery log (see Chapter 14), in others the two might be distinct; either way, users should be able to interrogate the audit trail using their regular query language (provided they are suitably authorized, of course!). A typical audit trail entry might contain the following information:

request (source text)

terminal from which the operation was invoked

user who invoked the operation

date and time of the operation

relvar(s), tuple(s), attribute(s) affected

old values

new values

As mentioned earlier in this section, the very fact that an audit trail is being maintained might be sufficient in itself to deter a would-be infiltrator in some situations.

16.3   MANDATORY ACCESS CONTROL

Mandatory controls are applicable to databases in which the data has a rather static and rigid classification structure, as might be the case in (e.g.) certain military or government environments. As explained briefly in Section 16.1, the basic idea is that each data object has a **classification level** (e.g., top secret, secret, confidential, etc.), and each user has a **clearance level** (with the same possibilities as for the classification levels). The levels are assumed to form a strict ordering (e.g., top secret > secret > confidential, etc.). The following simple rules, due to Bell and La Padula [16.1], are then imposed:

1. User *i* can retrieve object *j* only if the clearance level of *i* is greater than or equal to the classification level of *j* (the "simple security property");

2. User *i* can update object *j* only if the clearance level of *i* is equal to the classification level of *j* (the "star property").

The first rule here is obvious enough, but the second requires a word of explanation. Observe first that another way of stating that second rule is to say that, by definition, anything written by user *i* automatically acquires a classification level equal to *i*'s clearance level. Such a rule is necessary in order to prevent a user with, e.g., "secret" classification from copying secret data to a file of lower classification, thereby subverting the intent of the classification scheme. *Note:* From the point of view of pure "write" (INSERT) operations only, it would be sufficient for the second rule to say that the clearance level of *i* must be *less than or* equal to the classification level of *j,* and the rule is often stated in this form in the literature. But then users would be able to write things they could not read! (On second thoughts, some people do have difficulty reading their own writing . . . Perhaps the weaker rule is not so unrealistic after all.)

Mandatory controls began to receive a lot of attention in the database world in the early 1990s, because that was when the US Department of Defense (DoD) began to require any system it purchased to support such controls. As a consequence, DBMS vendors have been vying with one another to implement them. The controls in question are documented in two important DoD publications known informally as the **Orange Book** [16.19] and the **Lavender Book** [16.20], respectively; the Orange Book defines a set of security requirements for any "Trusted Computing Base" (TCB), and the Lavender Book defines an "interpretation" of the TCB requirements for database systems specifically.

The mandatory controls defined in references [16.19–16.20] in fact form part of a more general overall security classification scheme, which we summarize here for purposes of reference. First of all, the documents define four **security classes** (D, C, B, and A); broadly speaking, class D is the least secure, class C is more secure than class D, and so on. Class D is said to provide *minimal* protection, class C *discretionary* protection, class B *mandatory* protection, and class A *verified* protection.

- **Discretionary protection:** Class C is divided into two subclasses C1 and C2 (where C1 is *less* secure than C2). Each supports discretionary controls, meaning that access is subject to the discretion of the data *owner* (effectively as described in Section 16.2 above). In addition:

  1. Class C1 distinguishes between ownership and access; i.e., it supports the concept of shared data, while allowing users to have private data of their own as well.

  2. Class C2 additionally requires accountability support through sign-on procedures, auditing, and resource isolation.

- **Mandatory protection:** Class B is the class that deals with mandatory controls. It is further divided into subclasses B1, B2, and B3 (where B1 is the *least* secure of the three and B3 is the most), as follows:

  1. Class B1 requires "labeled security protection" (i.e., it requires each data object to be labeled with its classification level—secret, confidential, etc.). It also requires an informal statement of the security policy in effect.

  2. Class B2 additionally requires a *formal* statement of the same thing. It also requires that *covert channels* be identified and eliminated. Examples of covert channels might be (a) the possibility of inferring the answer to an illegal query from the answer to a legal one (see Section 16.4), or (b) the possibility of deducing sensitive information from the time it takes to perform some legal computation (see the annotation to reference [16.12]).

  3. Class B3 specifically requires audit and recovery support, as well as a designated *security administrator*.

- **Verified protection:** Class A, the most secure, requires a mathematical proof that (a) the security mechanism is consistent and that (b) it is adequate to support the specified security policy (!).

Several commercial DBMS products currently provide mandatory controls at the B1 level. They also typically provide discretionary controls at the C2 level. *Terminology:* DBMSs that support mandatory controls are sometimes called **multi-level secure** systems [16.13,16.16,16.21] (see the subsection immediately following). The term **trusted** system is also used with much the same meaning [16.17,16.19–16.20].

Multi-Level Security

Suppose we want to apply the ideas of mandatory access control to the suppliers relvar S. For definiteness and simplicity, suppose the unit of data we wish to control access to is the individual tuple within that relvar. Then each tuple needs to be labeled with its classification level, perhaps as shown in Fig. 16.1 (4 = top secret, 3 = secret, 2 = confidential, etc.).

S	S#	SNAME	STATUS	CITY	CLASS
	S1	Smith	20	London	2
	S2	Jones	10	Paris	3
	S3	Blake	30	Paris	2
	S4	Clark	20	London	4
	S5	Adams	30	Athens	3

Fig. 16.1   Relvar S with classification levels (example)

Now suppose users *U1* and *U2* have clearance levels 3 (secret) and 2 (confidential), respectively. Then *U1* and *U2* will see relvar S differently! A request to retrieve all suppliers will return four tuples—viz., those for S1, S2, S3, and S5—if issued by *U1,* but just two tuples—*viz.*, those for S1 and S3—if issued by *U2.* Moreover, *neither* user sees the tuple for S4.

One way to think about the foregoing is in terms of *request modification* once again. Consider the following query ("Get suppliers in London"):

```
S WHERE CITY = 'London'
```

The system will modify this request so that it looks like this:

```
S WHERE CITY = 'London' AND CLASS ≤ user clearance
```

Analogous considerations apply to update operations. For example, user *U1* is not aware that the tuple for S4 exists. To that user, therefore, the following INSERT seems reasonable:

```
INSERT INTO S RELATION { TUPLE { S#      S# ( 'S4' ),
                                 SNAME   NAME ( 'Baker' ),
                                 STATUS 25,
                                 CITY   'Rome' } } ;
```

The system must not reject this INSERT, because to do so would effectively tell user *U1* that supplier S4 does exist after all. So it accepts it, but modifies it to:

```
INSERT INTO S RELATION { TUPLE { S#      S# ( 'S4' ),
                                 SNAME   NAME ( 'Baker' ),
                                 STATUS 25,
                                 CITY   'Rome',
                                 CLASS  CLASS ( 3 ) } } ;
```

Observe, therefore, that the primary key for suppliers is not just {S#}, it is the combination {S#,CLASS}. *Note:* We assume for simplicity that there is just one candidate key, which we can therefore regard (harmlessly) as the *primary* key.

More terminology: The suppliers relvar is an example of a **multi-level relvar.** The fact that "the same" data looks different to different users is called **polyinstantiation.** Following the INSERT just discussed, for example, a request to retrieve supplier S4 returns one result to a user with top secret clearance, another to user *U1* (with secret clearance), and yet another to user *U2* (with confidential clearance).

UPDATE and DELETE are treated analogously (we omit the details here, but remark that several of the references at the end of the chapter discuss such issues in depth). A question: Do you think the ideas discussed above constitute a violation of *The Information Principle?* Justify your answer!

16.4 STATISTICAL DATABASES

Note: Much of the material of this section and the next originally appeared in slightly different form in reference [16.4].

A *statistical database* (in the present context) is a database that permits queries that derive aggregated information (e.g., sums, averages) but not queries that derive individual information. For example, the query "What is the average salary of programmers?" might be permitted, while the query "What is the salary of programmer Mary?" would not be.

The problem with such databases is that sometimes it is possible to make inferences from legal queries to deduce the answers to illegal ones. As reference [16.6] puts it: "Summaries contain vestiges of the original information; a snooper might be able to (re)construct this information by processing enough summaries. This is called *deduction of confidential information by inference*." We remark that this problem is likely to become more and more significant as the use of *data warehouses* increases (see Chapter 21).

Here is a detailed example. Suppose the database contains just one relvar, STATS (see Fig. 16.2). Assume for simplicity that all attributes are defined on primitive data types (basically numbers and strings). Suppose further that some user *U* is authorized to perform statistical queries (only) and is intent on discovering Alf's salary. Suppose finally

NAME	SEX	CHILDREN	OCCUPATION	SALARY	TAX	AUDITS
Alf	M	3	Programmer	50K	10K	3
Bea	F	2	Physician	130K	10K	0
Cary	F	0	Programmer	56K	18K	1
Dawn	F	2	Builder	60K	12K	1
Ed	M	2	Clerk	44K	4K	0
Fay	F	1	Artist	30K	0K	0
Guy	M	0	Lawyer	190K	0K	0
Hal	M	3	Homemaker	44K	2K	0
Ivy	F	4	Programmer	64K	10K	1
Joy	F	1	Programmer	60K	20K	1

Fig. 16.2 Relvar STATS (sample value)

that *U* knows from outside sources that Alf is a programmer and is male. Now consider queries 1 and 2 below.*

```
1. WITH ( STATS WHERE SEX = 'M' AND
          OCCUPATION = 'Programmer' ) AS X :
   COUNT ( X )
```

Result: 1.

```
2. WITH ( STATS WHERE SEX = 'M' AND
          OCCUPATION = 'Programmer' ) AS X :
   SUM ( X, SALARY )
```

Result: 50K. ■

The security of the database has clearly been compromised, even though user *U* has issued only legitimate statistical queries. As the example illustrates, if the user can find a boolean expression that identifies some individual, then information regarding that individual is no longer secure. This fact suggests that the system should refuse to respond to a query for which the cardinality of the set to be summarized is less than some lower bound *b*. It likewise suggests that the system should also refuse to respond if that cardinality is greater than the upper bound $N - b$ (where N is the cardinality of the containing relation), because the compromise above could equally well be obtained from the sequence of queries 3–6 below:

```
3. COUNT ( STATS )
```

Result: 12.

```
4. WITH ( STATS WHERE NOT ( SEX = 'M' AND
          OCCUPATION = 'Programmer' ) ) AS X :
   COUNT ( X )
```

Result: 11; $12 - 11 = 1$.

```
5. SUM ( STATS, SALARY )
```

Result: 728K.

```
6. WITH ( STATS WHERE NOT ( SEX = 'M' AND
          OCCUPATION = 'Programmer' ) ) AS X :
   SUM ( X, SALARY )
```

Result: 678K; $728K - 678K = 50K$. ■

Unfortunately, it is easy to show that simply restricting queries to those for which the set to be summarized has cardinality *c* in the range $b \leq c \leq N - b$ is inadequate to avoid compromise, in general. Consider Fig. 16.2 again, and suppose $b = 2$; queries will be answered only if *c* is in the range $2 \leq c \leq 8$. The boolean expression

```
SEX = 'M' AND OCCUPATION = 'Programmer'
```

---

*To save writing, the queries in this section are all expressed in an abbreviated form of **Tutorial D.** The expression COUNT(X) in query 1, for example, should more properly be EXTEND TABLE_DEE ADD COUNT(X) AS RESULT1 (say).

is thus no longer admissible. But consider the following sequence of queries 7–10:

```
7. WITH ( STATS WHERE SEX = 'M' ) AS X :
   COUNT ( X )
```

Result: 4.

```
8. WITH ( STATS WHERE SEX = 'M' AND NOT
                     ( OCCUPATION = 'Programmer' ) ) AS X :
      COUNT ( X )
```

Result: 3.

From queries 7 and 8, user *U* can deduce that there exists exactly one male programmer, who must therefore be Alf (since *U* already knows this description fits Alf). Alf's salary can thus be discovered as follows:

```
9. WITH ( STATS WHERE SEX = 'M' ) AS X :
   SUM ( X, SALARY )
```

Result: 328K.

```
10. WITH ( STATS WHERE SEX = 'M' AND NOT
                      ( OCCUPATION = 'Programmer' ) ) :
       SUM ( X, SALARY )
```

Result: 278K; 328K – 278K = 50K.   ■

The boolean expression SEX = 'M' AND OCCUPATION = 'Programmer' is called an **individual tracker** for Alf [16.6], because it enables the user to track down information concerning the individual Alf. In general, if the user knows a boolean expression *BE* that identifies some specific individual *I*, and if *BE* can be expressed in the form *BE1* AND *BE2*, then the boolean expression *BE1* AND NOT *BE2* is a tracker for *I* (provided that *BE1* and *BE1* AND NOT *BE2* are both admissible—that is, they both identify result sets with cardinality c in the range $b \leq c \leq N - b$). The reason is that the set identified by *BE* is identical to the difference between the set identified by *BE1* and the set identified by *BE1* AND NOT *BE2*:

```
set ( BE )  =  set ( BE1 AND BE2 )
            =  set ( BE1 ) minus set ( BE1 AND NOT BE2 )
```

See Fig. 16.3.

Reference [16.6] generalizes the foregoing ideas and shows that, for *almost any* statistical database, a **general tracker** (as opposed to a set of individual trackers) can always be found. A general tracker is a boolean expression that can be used to find the answer to *any* inadmissible query—that is, any query involving an inadmissible expression. (By contrast, an individual tracker works only for queries involving some *specific* inadmissible expression.) In fact, any expression with result set cardinality c in the range $2b \leq c \leq N - 2b$ is a general tracker (*b* must be less than *N*/4, which it typically will be in any realistic situation). Once such a tracker is found, a query involving an inadmissible expression *BE* can be answered as illustrated by the following example. (For definiteness we consider the case

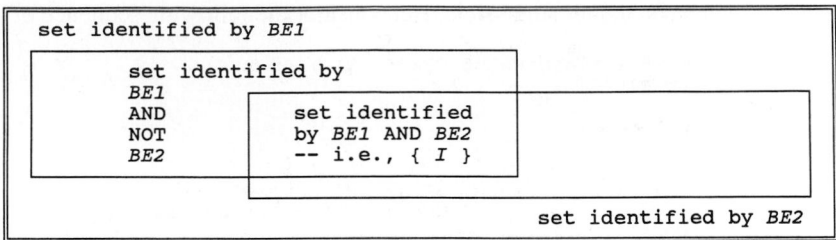

Fig. 16.3   The individual tracker *BE1* AND NOT *BE2*

where the result set cardinality corresponding to *BE* is less than *b*. The case where it is instead greater than $N - b$ is handled analogously.) Note that it follows from the definition that *T* is a general tracker if and only if NOT *T* is also a general tracker.

Example: Assume again that $b = 2$; then a general tracker is any expression with result set cardinality *c* in the range $4 \leq c \leq 6$. Suppose again that user *U* knows from outside sources that Alf is a male programmer—i.e., the inadmissible boolean expression *BE* is (as before)

```
SEX = 'M' AND OCCUPATION = 'Programmer'
```

—and suppose that *U* wishes to discover Alf's salary. We will use a general tracker twice, first to ascertain that *BE* in fact identifies Alf uniquely (Steps 2–4 below), and then to determine Alf's salary (Steps 5–7).

Step 1: Make a guess at a tracker, *T*. As our guess we choose *T* to be the expression

```
AUDITS = 0
```

Step 2: Get the total number of individuals in the database, using the expressions *T* and NOT *T*.

```
WITH ( STATS WHERE AUDITS = 0 ) AS X :
COUNT ( X )
```

Result: 5.

```
WITH ( STATS WHERE NOT ( AUDITS = 0 ) ) AS X :
COUNT ( X )
```

Result: 5; $5 + 5 = 10$.

It can now easily be seen that our guess *T* is indeed a general tracker.

Step 3: Get the result of adding (a) the number of individuals in the database plus (b) the number satisfying the inadmissible expression *BE*, using the expressions *BE* OR *T* and *BE* OR NOT *T*.

```
WITH ( STATS WHERE ( SEX = 'M' AND
                     OCCUPATION = 'Programmer' )
             OR AUDITS = 0 ) AS X :
COUNT ( X )
```

Result: 6.

```
WITH ( STATS WHERE ( SEX = 'M' AND
                     OCCUPATION = 'Programmer' )
             OR NOT ( AUDITS = 0 ) ) AS X :
COUNT ( X )
```

Result: 5; 6 + 5 = 11.

Step 4: From the results so far, we have that the number of individuals satisfying *BE* is one (result of Step 3 minus result of Step 2); that is, *BE* designates Alf uniquely.

Now we repeat (in Steps 5 and 6) the queries of Steps 2 and 3, but using SUM instead of COUNT.

Step 5: Get the total salary of individuals in the database, using the expressions *T* and NOT *T*.

```
WITH ( STATS WHERE AUDITS = 0 ) AS X :
SUM ( X, SALARY )
```

Result: 438K.

```
WITH ( STATS WHERE NOT ( AUDITS = 0 ) ) AS X :
SUM ( X, SALARY )
```

Result: 290K; 438K + 290K = 728K.

Step 6: Get the sum of Alf's salary and the total salary, using the expressions *BE* OR *T* and *BE* OR NOT *T*.

```
WITH ( STATS WHERE ( SEX = 'M' AND
                     OCCUPATION = 'Programmer' )
             OR AUDITS = 0 ) AS X :
SUM ( X, SALARY )
```

Result: 488K.

```
WITH ( STATS WHERE ( SEX = 'M' AND
                     OCCUPATION = 'Programmer' )
             OR NOT ( AUDITS = 0 ) ) AS X :
SUM ( X, SALARY )
```

Result: 290K; 488K + 290K = 778K.

Step 7: Get Alf's salary by subtracting the total salary (found in Step 5) from the result of Step 6.

Result: 50K. ∎

Fig. 16.4 illustrates the general tracker:

```
set ( BE )  =  ( set ( BE OR T ) plus set ( BE OR NOT T ) )
                                 minus set ( T OR NOT T )
```

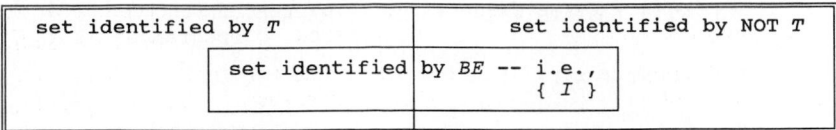

Fig. 16.4   The general tracker *T*

If the initial guess was wrong (i.e., *T* turns out not to be a general tracker), then one or both of the expressions (*BE* OR *T*) and (*BE* OR NOT *T*) might be inadmissible. For example, if the result set cardinalities for *BE* and *T* are *p* and *q*, respectively, where $p < b$ and $b \leq q \leq 2b$, then it is possible that the result set cardinality for (*BE* OR *T*), which cannot exceed $p + q$, is less than $2b$. In such a situation it is necessary to make another guess at a tracker and try again. Reference [16.6] suggests that the process of finding a general tracker is not difficult in practice. In our particular example, the initial guess *is* a general tracker (its result set cardinality is 5), and the queries in step 3 are both admissible.

To sum up: A general tracker "almost always" exists, and is usually both easy to find and easy to use; in fact, it is often possible to find a tracker quickly just by guessing [16.6]. Even in those cases where a general tracker does not exist, reference [16.6] shows that specific trackers can usually be found for specific queries. It is hard to escape the conclusion that security in a statistical database is a real problem.

So what can be done? Several suggestions have appeared in the literature, but it is not clear that any of them is totally satisfactory. For example, one possibility is "data swapping"—that is, swapping attribute values among tuples in such a way that overall statistical accuracy is maintained, so that even if a specific value (say a specific salary) is identified there is no way of knowing which particular individual that value belongs to. The difficulty with this approach lies in finding sets of entries whose values can be swapped in such a fashion. Similar limitations apply to most other suggested solutions. For the present, therefore, it seems we must agree with Denning's conclusions [16.6]: "Compromise is straightforward and cheap. The requirement of complete secrecy of confidential information is not consistent with the requirement of producing exact statistical measures for arbitrary subsets of the population. At least one of these requirements must be relaxed before assurances of secrecy can be believed."

16.5   DATA ENCRYPTION

We have assumed so far in this chapter that any would-be infiltrator will be using the normal system facilities to access the database. We now turn our attention to the case of a "user" who attempts to *bypass* the system (e.g., by physically removing part of the database, or by tapping into a communication line). The most effective countermeasure against such threats is **data encryption**—that is, storing and transmitting sensitive data in encrypted form.

In order to discuss some of the concepts of data encryption, we need to introduce some more terminology. The original (unencrypted) data is called the **plaintext.** The plaintext is **encrypted** by subjecting it to an **encryption algorithm,** whose inputs are the plaintext and an **encryption key;** the output from this algorithm—the encrypted form of the plaintext— is called the **ciphertext.** The details of the encryption algorithm are made public, or at least are not specially concealed, but the encryption key is kept secret. The ciphertext, which should be unintelligible to anyone not holding the encryption key, is what is stored in the database or transmitted down the communication line.

Example: Let the plaintext be the string

```
AS KINGFISHERS CATCH FIRE
```

(we assume for simplicity that the only data characters we have to deal with are upper case letters and blanks). Let the encryption key be the string

```
ELIOT
```

and let the encryption algorithm be as follows.

1. Divide the plaintext into blocks of length equal to that of the encryption key:

```
A S + K I    N G F I S    H E R S +    C A T C H    + F I R E
```

(blanks now shown explicitly as "+").

2. Replace each character of the plaintext by an integer in the range 00–26, using blank = 00, A = 01, ..., Z = 26:

```
0119001109   1407060919   0805181900   0301200308   0006091805
```

3. Repeat Step 2 for the encryption key:

```
0512091520
```

4. For each block of the plaintext, replace each character by the sum modulo 27 of its integer encoding and the integer encoding of the corresponding character of the encryption key:

```
0119001109   1407060919   0805181900   0301200308   0006091805
0512091520   0512091520   0512091520   0512091520   0512091520
_____   _____   _____   _____   _____
0604092602   1919152412   1317000720   0813021801   0518180625
==========   ==========   ==========   ==========   ==========
```

5. Replace each integer encoding in the result of Step 4 by its character equivalent:

```
F D I Z B    S S O X L    M Q + G T    H M B R A    E R R F Y
```

The decryption procedure for this example is straightforward, *given the key.* (*Exercise:* Decrypt the ciphertext shown above.) The question is, how difficult is it for a would-be infiltrator to determine the key without prior knowledge, given matching plaintexts and ciphertexts? In our simple example, the answer is, fairly obviously, "not very"; but, equally obviously, much more sophisticated schemes can easily be devised. Ideally the scheme employed should be such that the work involved in breaking it far outweighs any potential advantage to be gained in doing so. (In fact, a remark along the same general lines applies to all aspects of security: The aim should always be to make the cost of breaking the system significantly greater than the potential payoff.) The accepted ultimate objective for such schemes is that the *inventor* of the scheme, holding matching plaintext and ciphertext, should be unable to determine the key, and hence unable to decipher another piece of ciphertext.

The Data Encryption Standard

The example above made use of a **substitution** procedure: An encryption key was used to determine, for each character of the plaintext, a ciphertext character to be *substituted* for that character. Substitution is one of the two basic approaches to encryption as traditionally practiced; the other is **permutation,** in which plaintext characters are simply rearranged into some different sequence. Neither of these approaches is particularly secure in itself, but algorithms that combine the two can provide quite a high degree of security. One such algorithm is the **Data Encryption Standard** (DES), which was developed by IBM and adopted as a US federal standard in 1977 [16.18].

To use the DES, plaintext is divided into 64-bit blocks and each block is encrypted using a 64-bit key (actually the key consists of 56 data bits plus eight parity bits, so there are not 2^{64} but only 2^{56} possible keys). A block is encrypted by applying an initial permutation to it, then subjecting the permuted block to a sequence of 16 complex substitution steps, and finally applying another permutation, the inverse of the initial permutation, to the result of the last of those steps. The substitution at the ith step is not controlled directly by the original encryption key K but by a key Ki that is computed from the values K and i. For details, see reference [16.18].

The DES has the property that the decryption algorithm is identical to the encryption algorithm, except that the Ki's are applied in reverse order.

Public Key Encryption

Over the years, many people have suggested that the DES might not be truly secure; indeed, the advent of very fast, highly parallel processors suggests that the DES might be broken by brute force, if by no more intelligent means. Many people also feel that the more recent "public key" encryption schemes render the DES and similar traditional approaches technologically obsolete anyway. In a public key scheme, both the encryption algorithm *and the encryption key* are made freely available; thus anyone can convert plaintext into ciphertext. But the corresponding **decryption key** is kept secret (public key schemes involve *two* keys, one for encryption and one for decryption). Furthermore, the decryption key cannot feasibly be deduced from the encryption key; thus, even the person performing the original encryption cannot perform the corresponding decryption if not authorized to do so.

The original idea of public key encryption is due to Diffie and Hellman [16.7]. We describe the best-known specific approach, due to Rivest, Shamir, and Adleman [16.15], to show how such a scheme typically works in practice. Their approach (now usually referred to as *the RSA scheme,* from the initials of its inventors) is based on the following two facts:

1. There is a known fast algorithm for determining whether a given number is prime;
2. There is no known fast algorithm for finding the prime factors of a given composite (i.e., nonprime) number.

Reference [16.10] gives an example in which determining (on a given machine) whether a given number of 130 digits is prime takes about seven minutes, whereas finding the two prime factors (on the same machine) of a number obtained by multiplying together two primes of 63 digits would take about *40 quadrillion* years (one quadrillion = 1,000,000,000,000,000).*

The RSA scheme works as follows:

1. Choose, randomly, two distinct large primes p and q, and compute the product $r = p * q$.
2. Choose, randomly, a large integer e that is relatively prime to—i.e., has no factors in common with—the product $(p - 1) * (q - 1)$. The integer e is the encryption key. *Note:* Choosing e is straightforward; e.g., any prime greater than both p and q will do.
3. Take the decryption key d to be the unique "multiplicative inverse" of e modulo $(p - 1) * (q - 1)$; i.e.,

   ```
   d * e = 1 modulo (p - 1) * (q - 1)
   ```

   The algorithm for computing d given $e, p,$ and q is straightforward and is given in reference [16.15].
4. Publish the integers r and e but not d.
5. To encrypt a piece of plaintext P (which we assume for simplicity to be an integer less than r), replace it by the ciphertext C, computed as follows:

   ```
   C = Pe modulo r
   ```

6. To decrypt a piece of ciphertext C, replace it by the plaintext P, computed as follows:

   ```
   P = Cd modulo r
   ```

Reference [16.15] proves that this scheme works—i.e., that decryption of C using d does in fact recover the original P. However, computation of d knowing only r and e (and not p or q) is infeasible, as claimed earlier. Hence anyone can encrypt plaintext, but only authorized users (holding d) can decrypt ciphertext.

---

*Even so, there are some questions about the security of the RSA scheme. Reference [16.10] appeared in 1977. In 1990, Arjen Lenstra and Mark Manasse successfully factored a 155-digit number [16.22]; they estimated that the computation involved, which was spread over some 1000 computers, was equivalent to executing a million instructions a second on a single machine for a period of 273 years. The 155-digit number in question was the ninth Fermat number $2^{512} + 1$ (note that $512 = 2^9$). See also reference [16.12], which reports on a completely different—and successful!—approach to breaking RSA encryption.

We give a trivial example to illustrate the foregoing procedure. For obvious reasons we restrict ourselves to very small numbers throughout.

Example: Let $p = 3$, $q = 5$; then $r = 15$, and the product $(p-1) * (q-1) = 8$. Let $e = 11$ (a prime greater than both p and q). To compute d, we have

```
d * 11 = 1 modulo 8
```

whence $d = 3$.

Now let the plaintext P consist of the integer 13. Then the ciphertext C is given by

```
C = Pe modulo r
  = 1311 modulo 15
  = 1,792,160,394,037 modulo 15
  = 7
```

Now the original plaintext P is given by

```
P = Cd modulo r
  = 73 modulo 15
  = 343 modulo 15
  = 13  ∎
```

Because e and d are inverses of each other, public key encryption schemes also permit encrypted messages to be **"signed"** in such a way that the recipient can be certain that the message originated with the person it purports to have done (i.e., "signatures" cannot be forged). Suppose that A and B are two users who wish to communicate with each other using a public key encryption scheme. Then A and B will each publish an encryption algorithm (including in each case the corresponding encryption key), but of course will keep the decryption algorithm and key secret, even from each other. Let the encryption algorithms be ECA and ECB (for encrypting messages to be sent to A and B, respectively), and let the corresponding decryption algorithms be DCA and DCB, respectively. ECA and DCA are inverses of each other, as are ECB and DCB.

Now suppose that A wishes to send a piece of plaintext P to B. Instead of simply computing ECB(P) and transmitting the result, A first applies the *decryption* algorithm DCA to P, then encrypts the result and transmits that as the ciphertext C:

```
C = ECB ( DCA ( P ) )
```

On receipt of C, user B applies the decryption algorithm DCB and then the *encryption* algorithm ECA, producing the final result P:

```
ECA ( DCB ( C ) )
  = ECA ( DCB ( ECB ( DCA ( P ) ) ) )
  = ECA ( DCA ( P ) )          /* because DCB and ECB cancel */
  = P                          /* because ECA and DCA cancel */
```

Now B knows that the message did indeed come from A, because ECA will produce P only if the algorithm DCA was used in the encryption process, and that algorithm is known only to A. No one, *not even B*, can forge A's signature.

16.6   SQL FACILITIES

The current SQL standard supports discretionary access control only. Two more or less independent SQL features are involved—the **view mechanism,** which (as suggested in Chapter 8) can be used to hide sensitive data from unauthorized users, and the **authorization subsystem** itself, which allows users having specific privileges selectively and dynamically to grant those privileges to other users, and subsequently to revoke those privileges, if desired. Both features are discussed below.

Views and Security

To illustrate the use of views for security purposes in SQL, we first give SQL analogs of the view examples (Examples 2–4) from Section 16.2.

```
 2.  CREATE VIEW LS AS
            SELECT S.S#, S.SNAME, S.STATUS S.CITY
            FROM    S
            WHERE   S,CITY = 'London' ;
```

The view defines the data over which authorization is to be granted. The granting itself is done by means of the GRANT statement—e.g.:

```
GRANT SELECT, UPDATE ( SNAME, STATUS ), DELETE
ON     LS
TO     Dan, Misha ;
```

Note that—because they are defined by means of a special GRANT statement as shown, instead of by some hypothetical "CREATE AUTHORITY" statement—authorities are *unnamed* in SQL. (Integrity constraints, by contrast, do have names, as we saw in Chapter 8.)

```
 3.  CREATE VIEW SSPPR AS
            SELECT S.S#, S.SNAME, S.STATUS, S.CITY
            FROM    S
            WHERE   EXISTS
                ( SELECT * FROM SP
                  WHERE   EXISTS
                      ( SELECT * FROM P
                        WHERE   S.S# = SP.S#
                        AND     SP.P# = P.P#
                        AND     P.CITY = 'Rome' ) ) ;
```

Corresponding GRANT:

```
GRANT SELECT ON SSPPR TO Giovanni ;
```

```
 4.  CREATE VIEW SSQ AS
            SELECT S.S#, ( SELECT SUM ( SP.QTY )
                           FROM    SP
                           WHERE   SP.S# = S.S# ) AS SQ
            FROM    S ;
```

Corresponding GRANT:

```
GRANT SELECT ON SSQ TO Fidel ;
```

Example 5 from Section 16.2 involved a *context-dependent* authority. SQL supports a variety of niladic builtin operators—CURRENT_USER, CURRENT_DATE, CURRENT_TIME, etc.—that can be used among other things to define context-dependent views (note, however, that SQL does not support an analog of the DAY( ) operator we used in our original Example 5). Here is an example:

```
CREATE VIEW S_NINE_TO_FIVE AS
       SELECT  S.S#, S.SNAME, S.STATUS, S.CITY
       FROM    S
       WHERE   CURRENT_TIME ≥ TIME '09:00:00'
       AND     CURRENT_TIME ≤ TIME '17:00:00' ;
```

Corresponding GRANT:

```
GRANT SELECT, UPDATE ( STATUS )
ON      S_NINE_TO_FIVE
TO      Purchasing ;
```

Note, however, that S_NINE_TO_FIVE is rather an odd kind of view!—its value changes over time, even if the underlying data never changes. Furthermore, a view whose definition involves the builtin operator CURRENT_USER might even (in fact, probably will) have different values for different users. Such "views" are really different in kind from views as normally understood—in effect, they are *parameterized*. It might be preferable, at least conceptually, to allow users to define their own (potentially parameterized) relation-valued functions, and then treat "views" like S_NINE_TO_FIVE as just special cases of such functions.

Be that as it may, the foregoing examples illustrate the point that the view mechanism provides an important measure of security "for free" ("for free" because the mechanism is included in the system for other purposes anyway). What is more, many authorization checks, even value-dependent ones, can be done at compile time instead of run time, a significant performance benefit. However, the view-based approach to security does suffer from some slight awkwardness on occasion—in particular, if some particular user needs different privileges over different subsets of the same table at the same time. For example, consider the structure of an application that is allowed to scan and print all London parts and is also allowed to update some of them (just the red ones, say) during that scan.

GRANT and REVOKE

The view mechanism allows the database to be conceptually divided up into pieces in various ways so that sensitive information can be hidden from unauthorized users. However, it does not allow for the specification of the operations that *authorized* users are allowed to execute against those pieces. That task (as we have already seen in the examples above) is performed by the **GRANT** statement, which we now discuss in more detail.

Note first that the creator of any object is automatically granted all privileges that make sense for that object. For example, the creator of a base table T is automatically granted the SELECT, INSERT, UPDATE, DELETE, and REFERENCES privileges on T

(see below for an explanation of these privileges). Furthermore, these privileges are granted "with grant authority" in each case, which means that the user holding the privilege can grant it to other users.

Here then is the syntax of the GRANT statement:

```
GRANT   <privilege commalist>
        ON <object>
        TO <user ID commalist>
      [ WITH GRANT OPTION ] ;
```

Explanation:

- The legal *<privilege>*s are USAGE, SELECT, INSERT, UPDATE, DELETE, and REFERENCES.* The USAGE privilege is needed to use a specific (SQL-style) domain; the REFERENCES privilege is needed to refer to a specific named table in an integrity constraint; the other privileges should be self-explanatory. Note, however, that the INSERT, UPDATE, and REFERENCES privileges (but not the SELECT privilege, oddly enough) can be column-specific. *Note:* ALL PRIVILEGES can also be specified, but the semantics are not straightforward [4.19].

- The legal *<object>*s are DOMAIN *<domain name>* and TABLE *<table name>*. *Note:* In this context—unlike most others in SQL—the keyword "TABLE" (which is in fact optional) includes views as well as base tables.

- The *<user ID commalist>* can be replaced by the special keyword PUBLIC, meaning all users known to the system.

- WITH GRANT OPTION, if specified, means that the specified users are granted the specified privileges on the specified object **with grant authority**—meaning, as indicated above, that they can go on to grant those privileges on that object to some other user(s). Of course, WITH GRANT OPTION can be specified only if the user issuing the GRANT statement has the necessary grant authority in the first place.

Next, if user *A* grants some privilege to some other user *B,* user *A* can subsequently *revoke* that privilege from user *B*. Revoking privileges is done by means of the **REVOKE** statement—syntax:

```
REVOKE [ GRANT OPTION FOR ] <privilege commalist>
                            ON <object>
                            FROM <user ID commalist>
                            <option> ;
```

Here (a) GRANT OPTION FOR means that grant authority (only) is to be revoked; (b) *<privilege commalist>, <object>,* and *<user ID commalist>* are as for GRANT; and (c) *<option>* is either RESTRICT or CASCADE, and is discussed below. Examples:

1. `REVOKE SELECT ON S FROM Jacques, Anne, Charley RESTRICT ;`

---

*An EXECUTE privilege was added when the Persistent Stored Modules (PSM) feature was added to the standard in 1996 [4.22].

2. REVOKE SELECT, UPDATE (SNAME, STATUS), DELETE
        ON LS FROM Dan, Misha CASCADE ;

3. REVOKE SELECT ON SSPPR FROM Giovanni RESTRICT ;

4. REVOKE SELECT ON SSQ FROM Fidel RESTRICT ;

RESTRICT vs. CASCADE: Suppose *p* is some privilege on some object, and suppose user *A* grants *p* to user *B,* who in turn grants it to user *C.* What should happen if *A* now revokes *p* from *B?* Suppose for a moment that the REVOKE succeeds. Then the privilege *p* held by *C* would be "abandoned"—it would be derived from a user, namely *B,* who no longer holds it. The purpose of the RESTRICT *vs.* CASCADE option is to avoid the possibility of abandoned privileges. To be specific, RESTRICT causes the REVOKE to fail if it would lead to any abandoned privileges; CASCADE causes such privileges to be revoked as well.

Finally, dropping a domain, base table, column, or view automatically revokes all privileges on the dropped object from all users.

16.7 SUMMARY

We have discussed various aspects of the database **security** problem. We began by contrasting security and *integrity:* Security involves ensuring users are allowed to do the things they are trying to do, integrity involves ensuring the things they are trying to do are correct. Security, in other words, involves *the protection of data against unauthorized disclosure, alteration, or destruction.*

Security is enforced by the DBMS's **security subsystem,** which checks all access requests against the **security constraints** stored in the system catalog. First we considered **discretionary** schemes, in which access to a given object is at the discretion of the object's owner. Each **authority** in a discretionary scheme has a **name,** a set of **privileges** (RETRIEVE, UPDATE, etc.), a corresponding **relvar** (i.e., the data to which the constraint applies), and a set of **users.** Such authorities can be used to provide **value-dependent, value-independent, statistical summary,** and **context-dependent** controls. An **audit trail** can be used to record attempted security breaches. We took a brief look at an implementation technique for discretionary schemes known as **request modification.** This technique was pioneered by the Ingres prototype in connection with the QUEL language.

Next we discussed **mandatory** controls, in which each object has a **classification** level and each user has a **clearance** level. We explained the rules for access under such a scheme. We also summarized the security classification scheme defined by the U.S. Department of Defense in references [16.19–16.20], and briefly discussed the ideas of **multi-level relvars** and **polyinstantiation.**

Next we discussed the special problems of **statistical databases.** A statistical database is a database that contains a lot of individually sensitive items of information but is supposed to supply only statistical summary information to its users. We saw that the security of such databases is easily compromised by means of **trackers** (a fact that should be the cause for some alarm, given the increasing level of interest in data warehouse systems—see Chapter 21).

We then examined **data encryption,** touching on the basic ideas of **substitution** and **permutation,** explaining what the **Data Encryption Standard** is, and describing in outline how the **public key** schemes work. In particular, we gave a simple example of the **RSA** (prime number) scheme. We also discussed the concept of **digital signatures.**

We also briefly described the security features of SQL—in particular, the use of **views** to hide information, and the use of **GRANT** and **REVOKE** to control which users have which privileges over which objects (primarily base tables and views).

In conclusion, the point is worth emphasizing that it is no good the DBMS providing an extensive set of security controls if it is possible to bypass those controls in some way. In DB2, for example, the database is physically stored as operating system files; thus, DB2's security mechanism would be almost useless if it were possible to access those files from a conventional program via conventional operating system services. For this reason, DB2 works in harmony with its various companion systems—the underlying operating system in particular—to guarantee that the total system is secure. The details are beyond the scope of this chapter, but the message should be clear.

EXERCISES

16.1 Let base relvar STATS be as in Section 16.4:

```
STATS { NAME, SEX, CHILDREN, OCCUPATION, SALARY, TAX, AUDITS }
      PRIMARY KEY { NAME }
```

Using the hypothetical language introduced in Section 16.2, define security constraints as necessary to give:

a. User Ford RETRIEVE privileges over the entire relvar.

b. User Smith INSERT and DELETE privileges over the entire relvar.

c. Each user RETRIEVE privileges over that user's own tuple (only).

d. User Nash RETRIEVE privileges over the entire relvar and UPDATE privileges over the SALARY and TAX attributes (only).

e. User Todd RETRIEVE privileges over the NAME, SALARY, and TAX attributes (only).

f. User Ward RETRIEVE privileges as for Todd and UPDATE privileges over the SALARY and TAX attributes (only).

g. User Pope full privileges (RETRIEVE, UPDATE, INSERT, DELETE) over tuples for preachers (only).

h. User Jones DELETE privileges over tuples for people in a nonspecialist occupation, where a *nonspecialist occupation* is defined as one belonging to more than ten people.

i. User King RETRIEVE privileges for maximum and minimum salaries per occupation.

16.2 Consider what is involved in extending the syntax of AUTHORITY statements to include control over operations such as defining and dropping base relvars, defining and dropping views, defining and dropping authorities, and so on.

16.3 Consider Fig. 16.2 once again. Suppose we know from outside sources that Hal is a homemaker with at least two children. Write a sequence of statistical queries that will reveal Hal's tax figure, using an individual tracker. Assume as in Section 16.4 that the system will not respond to queries with a result set cardinality less than 2 or greater than 8.

16.4 Repeat Exercise 16.3, but using a general tracker instead of an individual tracker.

16.5 Decrypt the following ciphertext, which was produced in a manner similar to that used in the "AS KINGFISHERS CATCH FIRE" example in Section 16.5, but using a different 5-character encryption key:

```
F  N  W  A  L
J  P  V  J  C
F  P  E  X  E
A  B  W  N  E
A  Y  E  I  P
S  U  S  V  D
```

16.6 Work through the RSA public key encryption scheme with $p = 7$, $q = 5$, and $e = 17$ for plaintext $P = 3$.

16.7 Can you think of any implementation problems or other disadvantages that might be caused by encryption?

16.8 Give SQL solutions to Exercise 16.1.

16.9 Write SQL statements to drop the privileges granted in your solution to the previous exercise.

REFERENCES AND BIBLIOGRAPHY

For a broad overview of security in general, see the book by Castano *et al.* [16.2]. For a more detailed technical treatment, see the book by Denning [16.5]. The other references are mostly standards documents or technical papers (tutorials or research contributions) on various specific aspects of the security problem; there are also a few newspaper articles.

16.1 D. E. Bell and L. J. La Padula: "Secure Computer Systems: Mathematical Foundations and Model," MITRE Technical Report M74-244 (May 1974).

16.2 Silvana Castano, Mariagrazia Fugini, Giancarlo Martella, and Pierangela Samarati: *Database Security*. New York, N.Y.: ACM Press/Reading, Mass.: Addison-Wesley (1995).

16.3 James Daly: "Fingerprinting a Computer Security Code," *Computerworld* (July 27th, 1992).

16.4 C. J. Date: "Security," Chapter 4 of *An Introduction to Database Systems: Volume II*. Reading, Mass.: Addison-Wesley (1983).

16.5 Dorothy E. Denning: *Cryptography and Data Security*. Reading, Mass.: Addison-Wesley (1983).

16.6 Dorothy E. Denning and Peter J. Denning: "Data Security," *ACM Comp. Surv. 11,* No. 3 (September 1979).

A good tutorial, covering discretionary access controls, mandatory access controls (here called *flow* controls), data encryption, and *inference* controls (the special problem of statistical databases).

16.7 W. Diffie and M. E. Hellman: "New Directions in Cryptography," *IEEE Transactions on Information Theory* IT-22 (November 1976).

16.8 Ronald Fagin: "On an Authorization Mechanism," *ACM TODS 3,* No. 3 (September 1978).

An extended corrigendum to reference [16.11], *q.v.* Under certain circumstances the mechanism of reference [16.11] would revoke a privilege that ought not to be revoked. This paper corrects that flaw.

16.9 Roberto Gagliardi, George Lapis, and Bruce Lindsay: "A Flexible and Efficient Database Authorization Facility," IBM Research Report RJ6826 (May 11th, 1989).

16.10 Martin Gardner: "A New Kind of Cipher That Would Take Millions of Years to Break," *Scientific American 237,* No. 2 (August 1977).

A good informal introduction to the work on public key encryption. The title might be an overclaim [16.12, 16.22].

16.11 Patricia P. Griffiths and Bradford W. Wade: "An Authorization Mechanism for a Relational Data Base System," *ACM TODS 1,* No. 3 (September 1976).

Describes the GRANT and REVOKE mechanism originally proposed for System R. The scheme now included in the SQL standard is based on that mechanism, though significantly different in detail.

16.12 Nigel Hawkes: "Breaking into the Internet," *London Times* (March 18th, 1996).

Describes how a computer expert broke the RSA scheme by measuring how long it took for the system to decrypt messages—"the electronic equivalent of guessing the combination of a lock by watching someone turn the dials and seeing how long each took."

16.13 Sushil Jajodia and Ravi Sandhu: "Toward a Multi-Level Secure Relational Data Model," Proc. 1991 ACM SIGMOD Int. Conf. on Management of Data, Denver, Colo. (June 1991).

As explained in Section 16.3, "multi-level" in a security context refers to a system that supports mandatory access controls. This paper suggests that much of the current activity in the field is *ad hoc,* since there is very little consensus on basic concepts, and proposes a start at formalizing the principles of multi-level systems.

16.14 Abraham Lempel: "Cryptology in Transition," *ACM Comp. Surv. 11,* No. 4: Special Issue on Cryptology (December 1979).

A good tutorial on encryption and related matters.

16.15 R. L. Rivest, A. Shamir, and L. Adleman: "A Method for Obtaining Digital Signatures and Public Key Cryptosystems," *CACM 21,* No. 2 (February 1978).

16.16 Ken Smith and Marianne Winslett: "Entity Modeling in the MLS Relational Model," Proc. 18th Int. Conf. on Very Large Data Bases, Vancouver, Canada (August 1992).

"MLS" in the title of this paper stands for "multi-level secure" [16.13]. This paper focuses on the *meaning* of MLS databases, and proposes a new BELIEVED BY clause on retrieval and update operations to direct those operations to the particular state of the database understood or "believed by" a specific user. This approach is claimed to solve a number of problems with prior approaches. See also reference [16.21].

16.17 Bhavani Thuraisingham: "Current Status of R&D in Trusted Database Management Systems," *ACM SIGMOD Record 21,* No. 3 (September 1992).

A brief survey and extensive set of references on "trusted" or multi-level systems (as of the early 1990s).

16.18 U.S. Department of Commerce / National Bureau of Standards: *Data Encryption Standard.* Federal Information Processing Standards Publication 46 (1977 January 15).

Defines the official Data Encryption Standard (DES), to be used by federal agencies and anyone else who wishes to do so. The encryption/decryption algorithm (see Section 16.5) is suitable for implementation on a hardware chip, which means that devices that incorporate it can operate at a high data rate. A number of such devices are commercially available.

16.19 U.S. Department of Defense: *Trusted Computer System Evaluation Criteria* (the "Orange Book"), Document No. DoD 5200-28-STD. DoD National Computer Security Center (December 1985).

16.20 U.S. National Computer Security Center: *Trusted Database Management System Interpretation of Trusted Computer System Evaluation Criteria* (the "Lavender Book"), Document No. NCSC-TG-201, Version 1 (April 1991).

16.21 Marianne Winslett, Kenneth Smith, and Xiaolei Qian: "Formal Query Languages for Secure Relational Databases," *ACM TODS 19,* No. 4 (December 1994).

Continues the work of reference [16.16].

16.22 Ron Wolf: "How Safe Is Computer Data? A Lot of Factors Govern the Answer," *San Jose Mercury News* (July 5th, 1990).

ANSWERS TO SELECTED EXERCISES

16.1

a. ```
AUTHORITY AAA
    GRANT RETRIEVE ON STATS TO Ford ;
```

b. ```
AUTHORITY BBB
    GRANT INSERT, DELETE ON STATS TO Smith ;
```

c. ```
AUTHORITY CCC
    GRANT RETRIEVE
    ON   STATS
    WHEN   USER () = NAME
    TO   ALL ;
```

We are assuming here that users use their own name as their user ID. Note the use of a WHEN clause and the niladic builtin operator USER().

d. ```
AUTHORITY DDD
    GRANT RETRIEVE, UPDATE ( SALARY, TAX )
    ON     STATS
    TO     Nash ;
```

e. ```
AUTHORITY EEE
    GRANT RETRIEVE (NAME, SALARY, TAX)
    ON   STATS
    TO   Todd ;
```

f. ```
AUTHORITY FFF
    GRANT RETRIEVE ( NAME, SALARY, TAX ),
          UPDATE ( SALARY, TAX )
    ON     STATS
    TO     Ward ;
```

g. ```
    VAR PREACHERS VIEW
        STATS WHERE OCCUPATION = 'Preacher' ;

    AUTHORITY GGG
        GRANT ALL
        ON   PREACHERS
        TO   Pope ;
    ```

Note the need to use a view in this example.

h.  ```
    VAR NONSPECIALIST VIEW
        WITH ( STATS RENAME OCCUPATION AS X ) AS T1,
             ( EXTEND STATS
               ADD COUNT ( T1 WHERE X = OCCUPATION ) AS Y ) AS T2,
             ( T2 WHERE Y > 10 ) AS T3 :
               T3 { ALL BUT Y }

    AUTHORITY HHH
        GRANT DELETE
        ON    NONSPECIALIST
        TO    Jones ;
    ```

i. ```
    VAR JOBMAXMIN VIEW
        WITH (STATS RENAME OCCUPATION AS X) AS T1,
             (EXTEND STATS
               ADD MAX (T1 WHERE X = OCCUPATION, SALARY) AS MAXSAL,
                   MIN (T1 WHERE X = OCCUPATION, SALARY) AS MINSAL)
                                              AS T2 :
        T2 { OCCUPATION, MAXSAL, MINSAL }

    AUTHORITY III
        GRANT RETRIEVE ON JOBMAXMIN TO King ;
    ```

**16.2** We make just one observation here: A user who has the authority to create a new base relvar and in fact does so can be regarded as the **owner** of that new relvar. As in SQL, the owner of a given base relvar should automatically be granted all possible privileges on that relvar, including not only the RETRIEVE, INSERT, UPDATE, and DELETE privileges (of course), but also the privilege of defining authorities that grant privileges on that relvar to other users.

**16.3** An individual tracker for Hal is

```
CHILDREN > 1 AND NOT ( OCCUPATION = 'Homemaker' )
```

Consider the following sequence of queries:

```
COUNT ( STATS WHERE CHILDREN > 1 )
```

Result: 6.

```
COUNT ( STATS WHERE CHILDREN > 1 AND NOT
                     ( OCCUPATION = 'Homemaker' ) )
```

Result: 5.

Hence the expression

```
CHILDREN > 1 AND OCCUPATION = 'Homemaker'
```

uniquely identifies Hal.

```
SUM ( STATS WHERE CHILDREN > 1, TAX )
```
```

Result: 48K.

```
SUM ( STATS WHERE CHILDREN > 1 AND NOT
                  ( OCCUPATION = 'Homemaker' ), TAX )
```

Result: 46K.

Hence Hal's tax figure is 2K. ■

16.4 General tracker: SEX = 'F'.

```
SUM ( STATS WHERE SEX = 'F', TAX )
```

Result: 70K.

```
SUM ( STATS WHERE NOT ( SEX = 'F' ), TAX )
```

Result: 16K.

Hence the total tax is 86K.

```
SUM ( STATS WHERE ( CHILDREN > 1 AND
                    OCCUPATION = 'Homemaker' ) OR
                  SEX = 'F', TAX )
```

Result: 72K.

```
SUM ( STATS WHERE ( CHILDREN > 1 AND
                    OCCUPATION = 'Homemaker' ) OR NOT
                  ( SEX = 'F' ), TAX )
```

Result: 16K.

Adding these results and subtracting the total previously calculated, we have Hal's tax figure = 88K − 86K = 2K. ■

16.5 The plaintext is

```
EYES I DARE NOT MEET IN DREAMS
```

What is the encryption key?

16.7 One problem is that, even in a system that supports encryption, data must still be processed in its plaintext form internally (e.g., for comparisons to operate correctly), and there is thus still a risk of sensitive data being accessible to concurrently executing applications or appearing in a memory dump. Also, there are severe technical problems in indexing encrypted data and in maintaining log records for such data.

16.8

a. `GRANT SELECT ON STATS TO Ford ;`

b. `GRANT INSERT, DELETE ON STATS TO Smith ;`

c.
```
CREATE VIEW MINE AS
       SELECT STATS.*
       FROM   STATS
       WHERE  STATS.NAME = CURRENT_USER ;

GRANT SELECT ON MINE TO PUBLIC ;
```

We are assuming here that users use their own name as their user ID. Note the use of the niladic builtin operator CURRENT_USER.

d. `GRANT SELECT, UPDATE ( SALARY, TAX ) ON STATS TO Nash ;`

e.
```
CREATE VIEW UST AS
        SELECT STATS.NAME, STATS.SALARY, STATS.TAX
        FROM    STATS ;
```

```
GRANT SELECT ON UST TO Todd ;
```

SQL has to use a view here because it does not support column-specific SELECT privileges.

f. `GRANT SELECT, UPDATE ( SALARY, TAX ) ON UST TO Ward ;`

This solution uses the same view as the previous one.

g.
```
CREATE VIEW PREACHERS AS
        SELECT STATS.*
        FROM    STATS
        WHERE   STATS.OCCUPATION = 'Preacher' ;
```

```
GRANT ALL PRIVILEGES ON PREACHERS TO Pope ;
```

Observe the use of the shorthand "ALL PRIVILEGES" in this example. ALL PRIVILEGES does not literally mean all privileges, however—it means all privileges on the relevant object for which the user issuing the GRANT has grant authority.

h.
```
CREATE VIEW NONSPECIALIST AS
        SELECT STX.*
        FROM    STATS AS STX
        WHERE   ( SELECT COUNT(*)
                  FROM    STATS AS STY
                  WHERE   STY.OCCUPATION = STX.OCCUPATION ) > 10 ;
```

```
GRANT DELETE ON SPECIALISTS TO Jones ;
```

i.
```
CREATE VIEW JOBMAXMIN AS
        SELECT STATS.OCCUPATION,
               MAX ( STATS.SALARY ) AS MAXSAL,
               MIN ( STATS.SALARY ) AS MINSAL
        FROM    STATS
        GROUP   BY STATS.OCCUPATION ;
```

```
GRANT SELECT ON JOBMAXMIN TO King ;
```

16.9

a. `REVOKE SELECT ON STATS FROM Ford RESTRICT ;`

b. `REVOKE INSERT, DELETE ON STATS FROM Smith RESTRICT ;`

c. `REVOKE SELECT ON MINE FROM PUBLIC RESTRICT ;`

d.
```
REVOKE SELECT, UPDATE ( SALARY, TAX )
                    ON STATS FROM Nash RESTRICT ;
```

e. `REVOKE SELECT ON UST FROM Todd RESTRICT ;`

f. REVOKE SELECT, UPDATE (SALARY, TAX)
                        ON UST FROM Ward RESTRICT ;

g. REVOKE ALL PRIVILEGES ON PREACHERS FROM Pope RESTRICT ;

h. REVOKE DELETE ON SPECIALISTS FROM Jones RESTRICT ;

i. REVOKE SELECT ON SALS FROM King RESTRICT ;

Optimization

17.1 INTRODUCTION

Optimization represents both a challenge and an opportunity for relational systems—a challenge, because optimization is *required* in such a system if the system is ever to achieve acceptable performance; an opportunity, because it is precisely one of the strengths of the relational approach that relational expressions are at a sufficiently high semantic level that optimization is feasible in the first place. In a nonrelational system, by contrast, where user requests are expressed at a lower semantic level, any "optimization" has to be done manually by the human user ("optimization" in quotes, because the term is usually taken to mean *automatic* optimization). In such a system it is the user, not the system, who decides what low-level operations are needed and what sequence they need to be executed in—and if the user makes a bad decision, there is nothing the system can do to improve matters. Note too the implication that in such a system the user in question must have some programming expertise; this fact alone puts the system out of reach for many people who could otherwise benefit from it.

The advantage of automatic optimization is not just that users do not have to worry about how best to state their queries (i.e., how to phrase requests in order to get the best performance out of the system). The fact is, there is a real possibility that the optimizer might actually do *better* than a human user. There are several reasons for this state of affairs, the following among them:

1. A good optimizer—perhaps we should stress that "good"!—will have a wealth of information available to it that human users typically do not have. To be specific, it will know certain **statistical** information, such as:

   - The number of values in each domain;
   - The current number of tuples in each base relvar;
   - The current number of distinct values in each attribute in each base relvar;
   - The number of times each such value occurs in each such attribute;

   and so on. (All of this information will be kept in the system catalog—see Section 17.5.) As a result, the optimizer should be able to make a more accurate assessment of the efficiency of any given strategy for implementing a particular request, and thus be more likely to choose the most efficient implementation.

2. Furthermore, if the database statistics change over time, then a different choice of strategy might become desirable; in other words, *reoptimization* might be required. In a relational system, reoptimization is trivial—it simply involves a reprocessing of the original relational request by the system optimizer. In a nonrelational system, by contrast, reoptimization involves rewriting the program, and very likely will not be done at all.

3. Next, the optimizer is a *program,* and is therefore by definition much more patient than a typical human user. The optimizer is quite capable of considering literally hundreds of different implementation strategies for a given request, whereas it is extremely unlikely that a human user would ever consider more than three or four (at least in any depth).

4. Last, the optimizer can be regarded in a sense as embodying the skills and services of "the best" human programmers. As a consequence, it has the effect of making those skills and services available to *everybody*—which means, of course, that it is making an otherwise scarce set of resources available to a wide range of users, in an efficient and cost-effective manner.

All of the above should serve as evidence in support of the claim made at the beginning of this section to the effect that **optimizability**—i.e., the fact that relational requests are optimizable—is in fact a *strength* of relational systems.

The overall purpose of the optimizer, then, is to choose an efficient strategy for evaluating a given relational expression. In this chapter we describe some of the fundamental principles and techniques involved in that process. Following an introductory motivating example in Section 17.2, Section 17.3 gives an overview of how optimizers work, and Section 17.4 then elaborates on one very important aspect of the process, *viz. expression transformation* (also known as *query rewrite*). Section 17.5 briefly discusses the question of *database statistics.* Next, Section 17.6 describes one specific approach to optimization, called *query decomposition,* in some detail. Section 17.7 then addresses the question of how the relational operators (join and so on) are actually implemented, and briefly considers the use of the statistics discussed in Section 17.5 to perform cost estimation. Finally, Section 17.8 presents a summary of the entire chapter.

One final introductory remark: It is usual to refer to this subject as *query* optimization specifically. This term is slightly misleading, however, inasmuch as the expression to be optimized—the "query"—might of course have arisen in some context other than interactive interrogation of the database; in particular, it might be part of an update operation instead of a query *per se.* What is more, the term *optimization* itself is somewhat of an overclaim, since there is usually no guarantee that the implementation strategy chosen is truly *optimal* in any measurable sense; it might in fact be so, but usually all that is known for sure is that the "optimized" strategy is an *improvement* on the original unoptimized version. (In certain rather limited contexts, however, it might be possible to claim legitimately that the chosen strategy is indeed optimal in a very specific sense; see, e.g., reference [17.31].)

17.2 A MOTIVATING EXAMPLE

We begin with a simple example—an elaboration of one already discussed briefly in Chapter 6, Section 6.6—that gives an idea of the dramatic improvements that are possible. The query is "Get names of suppliers who supply part P2." An algebraic formulation of this query is:

```
( ( SP JOIN S ) WHERE P# = P# ( 'P2' ) ) { SNAME }
```

Suppose the database contains 100 suppliers and 10,000 shipments, of which only 50 are for part P2. Assume for simplicity that relvars S and SP are represented directly on the disk as two separate stored files, with one stored record per tuple. Then, if the system were simply to evaluate the expression "directly"—i.e., without any optimization at all—the sequence of events would be as follows:

1. **Join SP and S (over S#):** This step involves reading the 10,000 shipments; reading each of the 100 suppliers 10,000 times (once for each of the 10,000 shipments); constructing an intermediate result consisting of 10,000 joined tuples; and writing those 10,000 joined tuples back out to the disk (for the sake of the example, we assume there is no room for this intermediate result in main memory).

2. **Restrict the result of Step 1 to just the tuples for part P2:** This step involves reading the 10,000 joined tuples back into memory again, but produces a result consisting of only 50 tuples, which we assume is small enough to be kept in main memory.

3. **Project the result of Step 2 over SNAME:** This step produces the desired final result (50 tuples at most, which can stay in main memory).

The following procedure is equivalent to the one just described, in the sense that it necessarily produces the same final result, but is clearly much more efficient:

1. **Restrict SP to just the tuples for part P2:** This step involves reading 10,000 tuples but produces a result consisting of only 50 tuples, which we assume will be kept in main memory.

2. **Join the result of Step 1 to S (over S#):** This step involves reading the 100 suppliers (once only, not once per P2 shipment, of course) and produces a result of 50 tuples again (still in main memory).

3. **Project the result of Step 2 over SNAME** (same as Step 3 before): The desired final result (50 tuples at most) stays in main memory.

The first of these two procedures involves a total of 1,030,000 tuple I/O's, whereas the second involves only 10,100. It is clear, therefore, that if we take "number of tuple I/O's" as our performance measure, then the second procedure is a little over 100 times better than the first. (In practice, of course, it is *page* I/O's that matter, not tuple I/O's, but we can ignore this refinement for present purposes.) It is also clear that we would like the implementation to use the second procedure rather than the first!

So we see that a very simple change in the execution algorithm—doing a restriction and then a join, instead of a join and then a restriction—has produced a dramatic improvement in performance. And the improvement would be more dramatic still if shipments were **indexed** or **hashed** on P#—the number of shipment tuples read in Step 1 would be reduced from 10,000 to just 50, and the new procedure would then be nearly 7,000 times better than the original. Likewise, if suppliers were also indexed or hashed on S#, the number of supplier tuples read in Step 2 would be reduced from 100 to 50, so that the procedure would now be over 10,000 times better than the original. What this means is, if the original unoptimized query took three hours to run, the final version will run in a fraction over *one second.* And of course numerous further improvements are possible.

The foregoing example, simple though it is, should be sufficient to give some idea as to why optimization is necessary. It should also give some idea of the kinds of improvements that might be possible in practice. In the next section, we will present an overview of a systematic approach to the optimization problem; in particular, we will show how the overall problem can be divided into a series of more or less independent subproblems. That overview provides a convenient framework within which individual optimization strategies and techniques such as those discussed in later sections can be explained and understood.

17.3 AN OVERVIEW OF QUERY PROCESSING

We can identify four broad stages in query processing, as follows (refer to Fig. 17.1):

1. Cast the query into internal form
2. Convert to canonical form
3. Choose candidate low-level procedures
4. Generate query plans and choose the cheapest

We now proceed to amplify each of these four stages.

Stage 1: Cast the Query into Internal Form

The first stage involves the conversion of the original query into some internal representation that is more suitable for machine manipulation, thus eliminating purely external considerations (such as quirks of the concrete syntax of the query language under consideration) and paving the way for subsequent stages of the optimization process. *Note:* View processing—i.e., the process of replacing references to views by the applicable view-defining expressions—is also performed during this stage.

The obvious question is: What formalism should the internal representation be based on? Whatever formalism is chosen, it must of course be rich enough to represent all possible queries in the external query language. It should also be as neutral as possible, in the sense that it should not prejudice subsequent choices. The internal form typically chosen is some kind of **abstract syntax tree** or **query tree.** For example, Fig. 17.2 (opposite) shows

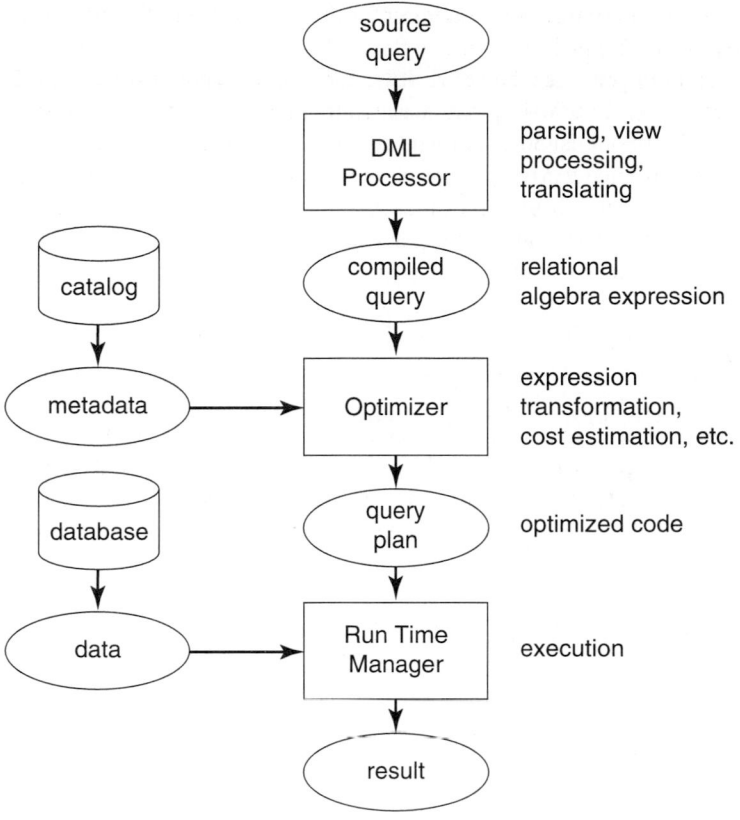

Fig. 17.1 Query processing overview

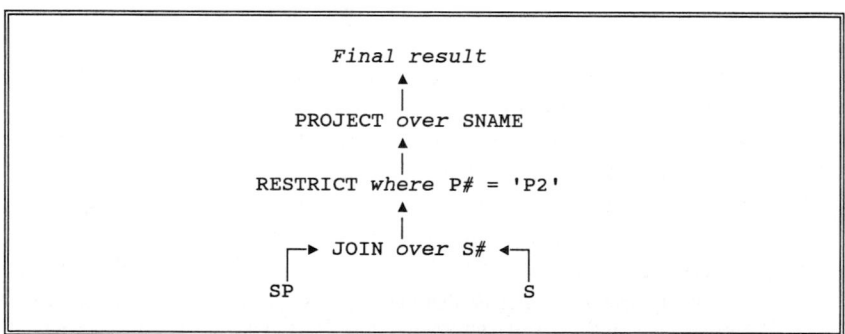

Fig. 17.2 "Get names of suppliers who supply part P2" (query tree)

a possible query tree representation for the example from Section 17.2 ("Get names of suppliers who supply part P2").

For our purposes, however, it is more convenient to assume that the internal representation is one of the formalisms we are already familiar with: namely, the relational algebra or the relational calculus. A query tree such as that of Fig. 17.2 can be regarded as just an alternative, encoded representation of some expression in one of those two formalisms. To fix our ideas, we assume here that the formalism is the algebra specifically. Thus, we will assume henceforth that the internal representation of the query of Fig. 17.2 is precisely the algebraic expression shown earlier:

```
( ( SP JOIN S ) WHERE P# = P# ( 'P2' ) ) { SNAME }
```

Stage 2: Convert to Canonical Form

In this stage, the optimizer performs a number of optimizations that are "guaranteed to be good," regardless of the actual data values and physical access paths that exist in the stored database. The point is, relational languages typically allow all but the simplest of queries to be expressed in a variety of ways that are at least superficially distinct. In SQL, for example, even a query as simple as "Get names of suppliers who supply part P2" can be expressed in literally dozens of different ways*—not counting trivial variations like replacing $A = B$ by $B = A$ or p AND q by q AND p. And the performance of a query really ought not to depend on the particular way the user chose to write it. The next step in processing the query is therefore to convert the internal representation into some equivalent **canonical form** (see below), with the objective of eliminating such superficial distinctions and—more important—finding a representation that is more efficient than the original in some way.

A note regarding "canonical form": The notion of *canonical form* is central to many branches of mathematics and related disciplines. It can be defined as follows. Given a set Q of objects (say queries) and a notion of equivalence among those objects (say the notion that queries $q1$ and $q2$ are equivalent if and only if they necessarily produce the same result), subset C of Q is said to be a **set of canonical forms** for Q under the stated definition of equivalence if and only if every object q in Q is equivalent to just one object c in C. The object c is said to be the *canonical form* for the object q. All "interesting" properties that apply to the object q also apply to its canonical form c; thus it is sufficient to study just the small set C, not the large set Q, in order to prove a variety of "interesting" results.

---

*We should point out, however, that the SQL language is exceptionally prone to this problem (see Exercise 7.12 in Chapter 7, also reference [4.18]). Other languages (e.g., the algebra or the calculus) typically do not provide quite so many different ways of doing the same thing. This unnecessary "flexibility" on the part of SQL actually makes life harder for the *implementer*—not to mention the user—because it makes the optimizer's job more difficult.

To revert to the main thread of our discussion: In order to transform the output from Stage 1 into some equivalent but more efficient form, the optimizer makes use of certain **transformation rules** or **laws.** Here is an example of such a rule: The expression

```
( A JOIN B ) WHERE restriction on A
```

can be transformed into the equivalent but more efficient expression

```
( A WHERE restriction on A ) JOIN B
```

We have already discussed this transformation briefly in Chapter 6, Section 6.6; in fact, of course, it was the one we were using in our introductory example in Section 17.2, and that example showed clearly why such a transformation is desirable. Many more transformation rules are discussed in Section 17.4 below.

Stage 3: Choose Candidate Low-Level Procedures

Having converted the internal representation of the query into some more desirable form, the optimizer must then decide how to execute the transformed query represented by that converted form. At this stage such considerations as the existence of indexes or other physical access paths, distribution of data values, physical clustering of stored data, etc., come into play. Note that we paid no heed to such matters in Stages 1 and 2 above.

The basic strategy is to consider the query expression as specifying a series of **"low-level" operations** (join, restrict, summarize, etc.), with certain interdependencies among them. An example of such an interdependency is the following: The code to perform a projection will typically require its input tuples to be sorted into some sequence, to allow it to perform duplicate elimination, which means that the immediately preceding operation in the series must produce its output tuples in that same sequence.

Now, for each possible low-level operation (and probably for various common combinations of such operations also), the optimizer will have available to it a set of predefined **implementation procedures.** For example, there will be a set of procedures for implementing the restriction operation: one for the case where the restriction is an equality test on a candidate key, one where the restriction attribute is indexed, one where it is hashed, and so on. Examples of such procedures are given in Section 17.7 (see also references [17.8–17.14]).

Each procedure will also have a (parameterized) **cost formula** associated with it, indicating the cost—typically in terms of disk I/O's, though some systems take CPU utilization and other factors into account also—of executing that procedure. These cost formulas are used in Stage 4 (see below). References [17.8–17.14] discuss and analyze the cost formulas for a number of different implementation procedures under a variety of different assumptions. See also Section 17.7, later.

Next, therefore, using information from the catalog regarding the current state of the database (existence of indexes, current cardinalities, etc.), and using also the interdependency information referred to above, the optimizer will choose one or more candidate procedures for implementing each of the low-level operations in the query expression. This process is sometimes referred to as **access path selection** (see references [17.34–17.35]).

Note: Actually, references [17.34–17.35] use the term *access path selection* to cover both Stage 3 and Stage 4, not just Stage 3. Indeed, it might be difficult in practice to make a clean separation between the two—Stage 3 does flow more or less seamlessly into Stage 4.

Stage 4: Generate Query Plans and Choose the Cheapest

The final stage in the optimization process involves the construction of a set of candidate **query plans,** followed by a choice of the best (i.e., cheapest) of those plans. Each query plan is built by combining together a set of candidate implementation procedures, one such procedure for each of the low-level operations in the query. Note that there will normally be many possible plans—probably embarrassingly many—for any given query. In fact, it might not be a good idea to generate all possible plans in practice, since there will be combinatorially many of them, and the task of choosing the cheapest might well become prohibitively expensive in itself; some heuristic technique for keeping the generated set within reasonable bounds is highly desirable, if not essential (but see reference [17.55]). "Keeping the set within bounds" is usually referred to as *reducing the search space,* because it can be regarded as reducing the range ("space") of possibilities to be examined ("searched") by the optimizer to manageable proportions.

Choosing the cheapest plan naturally requires a method for assigning a cost to any given plan. Basically, of course, the cost for a given plan is just the sum of the costs of the individual procedures that make up that plan, so what the optimizer has to do is evaluate the cost formulas for those individual procedures. The problem is, those cost formulas will depend on the size of the relation(s) to be processed; since all but the simplest queries involve the generation of intermediate results during execution, the optimizer will therefore have to estimate the size of those intermediate results in order to evaluate the formulas. Unfortunately, those sizes tend to be highly dependent on actual data values. As a consequence, accurate cost estimation can be a difficult problem. References [17.3–17.4] discuss some approaches to that problem and give references to other research in the area.

17.4 EXPRESSION TRANSFORMATION

In this section we describe some transformation rules that might be useful in Stage 2 of the optimization process. Producing examples to illustrate the rules and deciding exactly why they might be useful are both left (in part) as exercises.

Of course, you should understand that, given a particular expression to transform, the application of one rule might generate an expression that can then be transformed in accordance with some other rule. For example, it is unlikely that the original query will have been directly expressed in such a way as to require two successive projections—see the second rule in the subsection "Restrictions and Projections" immediately following—but such an expression might arise internally as the result of applying certain other transformations. (An important case in point is provided by **view processing;** consider, for example, the query "Get all cities in view V," where view V is defined as the projection of suppliers on S# and CITY.)

In other words, starting from the original expression, the optimizer will apply its transformation rules repeatedly until it finally arrives at an expression that it judges—according to some builtin set of heuristics—to be "optimal" for the query under consideration.

Restrictions and Projections

Here first are some transformations involving restrictions and projections only.

1. A sequence of restrictions on the same relation can be transformed into a single ("ANDed") restriction on that relation. E.g., the expression

   ```
   ( A WHERE restriction1 ) WHERE restriction2
   ```

   is equivalent to the expression

   ```
   A WHERE restriction1 AND restriction2
   ```

2. In a sequence of projections against the same relation, all but the last can be ignored. E.g., the expression

   ```
   ( A { attributes1 } ) { attributes2 }
   ```

   is equivalent to the expression

   ```
   A { attributes2 }
   ```

   Of course, every attribute mentioned in *attributes2* must also be mentioned in *attributes1* for the original expression to make sense in the first place.

3. A restriction of a projection can be transformed into a projection of a restriction. E.g., the expression

   ```
   ( A { attributes } ) WHERE restriction
   ```

   is equivalent to the expression

   ```
   ( A WHERE restriction ) { attributes }
   ```

   Note that it is generally a good idea to do restrictions before projections, because the effect of the restriction will be to reduce the size of the input to the projection, and hence to reduce the amount of data that might need to be sorted for duplicate elimination purposes.

Distributivity

The transformation rule used in the example in Section 17.2 (transforming a join followed by a restriction into a restriction followed by a join) is actually a special case of a more general law, called the *distributive* law. In general, the monadic operator *f* is said to **distribute** over the dyadic operator $\bigcirc$ if and only if

```
f ( A ○ B )  ≡  f ( A ) ○ f ( B )
```

for all *A* and *B*. In ordinary arithmetic, for example, SQRT (square root) distributes over multiplication, because

```
SQRT ( A * B )  ≡  SQRT ( A ) * SQRT ( B )
```

for all *A* and *B*. Therefore an arithmetic expression optimizer can always replace either of these expressions by the other when doing arithmetic expression transformation. As a counterexample, SQRT does not distribute over addition, because the square root of *A* + *B* is not equal to the sum of the square roots of *A* and *B,* in general.

In relational algebra, the **restriction** operator distributes over **union, intersection,** and **difference.** It also distributes over **join,** if and only if the restriction condition consists, at its most complex, of two separate restriction conditions ANDed together, one for each of the two join operands. In the case of the example in Section 17.2, this requirement was indeed satisfied—in fact, the condition was very simple and applied to just one of the operands—and so we could use the distributive law to replace the expression by a more efficient equivalent. The net effect was that we were able to "do the restriction early." Doing restrictions early is almost always a good idea, because it serves to reduce the number of tuples to be scanned in the next operation in sequence, and probably reduces the number of tuples in the output from that next operation too.

Here are a couple more specific cases of the distributive law, this time involving **projection.** First, the project operator distributes over **union** and **intersection** (but not **difference**):

```
( A UNION B ) { C }  ≡  A { C } UNION B { C }

( A INTERSECT B ) { C }  ≡  A { C } INTERSECT B { C }
```

A and *B* here must be of the same type, of course. Second, projection also distributes over **join**—i.e.,

```
( A JOIN B ) { C }  ≡  ( A { AC } ) JOIN ( B { BC } )
```

—if and only if:

■ *AC* is the union of (a) the attributes common to *A* and *B* and (b) those attributes of *C* that appear in *A* only, and

■ *BC* is the union of (a) the attributes common to *A* and *B* and (b) those attributes of *C* that appear in *B* only.

These laws can be used to "do projections early," which again is usually a good idea for reasons similar to those given above for restrictions.

Commutativity and Associativity

Two more important general laws are the laws of *commutativity* and *associativity.* First, the dyadic operator ○ is said to be **commutative** if and only if

```
A ○ B  ≡  B ○ A
```

for all *A* and *B*. In arithmetic, for example, multiplication and addition are commutative, but division and subtraction are not. In relational algebra, **union, intersection,** and **join** are all commutative, but **difference** and **division** are not. So, for example, if a query involves a join of two relations *A* and *B,* the commutative law means it makes no logical difference which of *A* and *B* is taken as the "outer" relation and which the "inner." The system is therefore free to choose (say) the smaller relation as the "outer" one in computing the join (see Section 17.7).

Turning to associativity: The dyadic operator $\bigcirc$ is said to be **associative** if and only if

$$A \, \bigcirc \, (\, B \, \bigcirc \, C \,) \; \equiv \; (\, A \, \bigcirc \, B \,) \, \bigcirc \, C$$

for all *A, B, C*. In arithmetic, multiplication and addition are associative, but division and subtraction are not. In relational algebra, **union, intersection,** and **join** are all associative, but **difference** and **division** are not. So, for example, if a query involves a join of three relations *A, B,* and *C,* the associative and commutative laws together mean it makes no logical difference in which order the relations are joined. The system is thus free to decide which of the various possible sequences is most efficient.

Idempotence

Another important general law is the law of *idempotence.* The dyadic operator $\bigcirc$ is said to be **idempotent** if and only if

$$A \, \bigcirc \, A \; \equiv \; A$$

for all *A*. As might be expected, the idempotence property can also be useful in expression transformation. In relational algebra, **union, intersection,** and **join** are all idempotent, but **difference** and **division** are not.

Scalar Computational Expressions

It is not just relational expressions that are subject to transformation laws. For instance, we have already indicated that certain transformations are valid for *arithmetic* expressions. Here is a specific example: The expression

$$A \, * \, B \, + \, A \, * \, C$$

can be transformed into

$$A \, * \, (\, B \, + \, C \,)$$

by virtue of the fact that "*" distributes over "+". A relational optimizer needs to know about such transformations because it will encounter such expressions in the context of the **extend** and **summarize** operators.

Note, incidentally, that this example illustrates a slightly more general form of distributivity. Earlier, we defined distributivity in terms of a *monadic* operator distributing over a *dyadic* operator; in the case at hand, however, "∗" and "+" are both *dyadic* operators. In general, the dyadic operator δ is said to **distribute** over the dyadic operator ○ if and only if

```
A δ ( B ○ C )  ≡  ( A δ B ) ○ ( A δ C )
```

for all *A, B, C* (in the arithmetic example above, take δ as "∗" and ○ as "+").

Boolean Expressions

We turn now to *boolean* (or *truth-valued* or *logical* or *conditional*) expressions. Suppose *A* and *B* are attributes of two distinct relations. Then the boolean expression

```
A > B AND B > 3
```

is clearly equivalent to—and can therefore be transformed into—the following:

```
A > B AND B > 3 AND A > 3
```

The equivalence is based on the fact that the comparison operator ">" is **transitive.** Note that this transformation is certainly worth making, because it enables the system to perform an additional restriction (on *A*) before doing the greater-than join required by the comparison "*A > B*". To repeat a point made previously, doing restrictions early is generally a good idea; having the system **infer** additional "early" restrictions, as here, is also a good idea. *Note:* This technique is implemented in several commercial products, including, e.g., DB2 (where it is called "predicate transitive closure") and Ingres.

Here is another example: The expression

```
A > B OR ( C = D AND E < F )
```

can be transformed into

```
( A > B OR C = D ) AND ( A > B OR E < F )
```

by virtue of the fact that OR distributes over AND. This example illustrates another general law, *viz.:* Any boolean expression can be transformed into an equivalent expression in what is called **conjunctive normal form** (CNF). A CNF expression is an expression of the form

```
C1 AND C2 AND ... AND Cn
```

where each of *C1, C2, ..., Cn* is, in turn, a boolean expression (called a **conjunct**) that involves no ANDs. The advantage of CNF is that a CNF expression is *true* only if every conjunct is *true;* equivalently, it is *false* if any conjunct is *false.* Since AND is commutative (*A* AND *B* is the same as *B* AND *A*), the optimizer can evaluate the individual conjuncts in any order it likes; in particular, it can do them in order of increasing difficulty (easiest first). As soon as it finds one that is *false,* the whole process can stop. Furthermore, in a parallel processing system, it might even be possible to evaluate all of the conjuncts in parallel [17.58–17.61]. Again, as soon as one conjunct yields *false,* the whole process can stop.

It follows from this subsection and its predecessor that the optimizer needs to know how general properties such as distributivity apply not only to **relational** operators such as join, but also to **comparison** operators such as ">"; **logical** operators such as AND and OR; **arithmetic** operators such as "+"; and so on.

Semantic Transformations

Consider the following expression:

```
( SP JOIN S ) { P# }
```

The join here is a *foreign-to-matching-candidate-key join;* it matches a foreign key in SP with a corresponding candidate key in S. It follows that every SP tuple does join to some S tuple, and every SP tuple therefore does contribute a P# value to the overall result. In other words, there is no need to do the join!—the expression can be simplified to just

```
SP { P# }
```

Note carefully, however, that this transformation is valid *only* because of the semantics of the situation. In general, each of the operands in a join will include some tuples that have no counterpart in the other (and hence some tuples that do not contribute to the overall result), and transformations such as the one just illustrated are not valid. In the case at hand, however, every tuple of SP does have a counterpart in S, because of the integrity constraint (actually a referential constraint) that says that every shipment must have a supplier, and so the transformation is valid after all.

A transformation that is valid only because a certain integrity constraint is in effect is called a **semantic transformation** [17.27], and the resulting optimization is called a **semantic optimization.** Semantic optimization can be defined as the process of transforming a specified query into another, qualitatively different, query that is however guaranteed to produce the same result as the original one, thanks to the fact that the data is guaranteed to satisfy a certain integrity constraint.

It is important to understand that, in principle, *any integrity constraint whatsoever* can be used in semantic optimization (the technique is not limited to referential constraints as in the example). For instance, suppose the suppliers and parts database is subject to the constraint "All red parts must be stored in London," and consider the query:

> Get suppliers who supply only red parts and are located in the same city as at least one of the parts they supply.

This is a fairly complex query! By virtue of the integrity constraint, however, it can be transformed into the much simpler form:

> Get London suppliers who supply only red parts.

Note: So far as this writer is aware, few commercial products currently do much by way of semantic optimization. In principle, however, such optimization could provide significant performance improvements—much greater improvements, very likely, than are obtained by any of today's more traditional optimization techniques. For further discussion of the semantic optimization idea, see references [17.16], [17.28–17.30], and (especially) [17.27].

Concluding Remarks

In closing this section, we emphasize the fundamental importance of the relational **closure** property to everything we have been discussing. Closure means we can write nested expressions, which means in turn that a single query can be represented by a single expression instead of a multi-statement procedure; thus, no flow analysis is necessary. Also, those nested expressions are recursively defined in terms of subexpressions, which permits the optimizer to adopt a variety of "divide and conquer" evaluation tactics (see Section 17.6 below). And, of course, the various general laws—distributivity, etc.—would not even begin to make sense in the absence of closure.

17.5   DATABASE STATISTICS

Stages 3 and 4 of the overall optimization process, the "access path selection" stages, make use of the so-called **database statistics** stored in the catalog (see Section 17.7 for more details on how those statistics are used). For purposes of illustration, we summarize below (with little further comment) some of the major statistics maintained by two commercial products, DB2 and Ingres. Here first are some of the principal statistics kept by DB2:*

- For each *base table:*
    - cardinality
    - number of pages occupied by this table
    - fraction of "table space" occupied by this table
- For each *column* of each base table:
    - number of distinct values in this column
    - second highest value in this column
    - second lowest value in this column
    - for indexed columns only, the ten most frequently occurring values in this column and the number of times they occur

---

*Since they are SQL systems, DB2 and Ingres use the terms table and column in place of relvar and attribute; in this section, therefore, so do we. Also, note that both products effectively assume that base tables map directly to *stored* tables.

- For each *index:*
    - an indication of whether this is a "clustering index" (i.e., an index that is used to cluster logically related data physically together on the disk)
    - if so, fraction of indexed table still in clustering sequence
    - number of leaf pages in this index
    - number of levels in this index

Note: The foregoing statistics are not updated every time the database is updated, because of the overhead such an approach would entail. Instead, they are updated, selectively, by means of a special system utility called RUNSTATS, which is executed on demand by the DBA (e.g., after a database reorganization). An analogous remark applies to most other commercial products (though not all), including in particular Ingres (see below), where the utility is called OPTIMIZEDB.

Here then are some of the principal Ingres statistics. *Note:* In Ingres, an index is regarded as just a special kind of stored table; thus, the statistics shown below for base tables and columns can be gathered for indexes too.

- For each *base table:*
    - cardinality
    - number of primary pages for this table
    - number of overflow pages for this table
- For each *column* of each base table:
    - number of distinct values in this column
    - maximum, minimum, and average value for this column
    - actual values in this column and the number of times they occur

17.6 A DIVIDE AND CONQUER STRATEGY

As mentioned at the end of Section 17.4, relational expressions are recursively defined in terms of subexpressions, and this fact allows the optimizer to adopt a variety of "divide and conquer" strategies. Note that such strategies are likely to be especially attractive in a parallel processing environment—in particular, in a distributed system—where different portions of the query can be executed in parallel on different processors [17.58–17.61]. In this section we examine one such strategy, called **query decomposition,** which was pioneered by the Ingres prototype [17.36–17.37]. *Note:* Further information on optimization in Ingres (more specifically in the commercial product, which is somewhat different from the prototype in this area) can be found in a paper by Kooi and Frankforth in reference [17.2]. See also reference [17.38].

The basic idea behind query decomposition is to break a query that involves many range variables* down into a sequence of smaller queries involving (typically) one or two such variables each, using *detachment* and *tuple substitution* to achieve the desired decomposition:

- **Detachment** is the process of removing a component of the query that has just one variable in common with the rest of the query.
- **Tuple substitution** is the process of substituting for one of the variables in the query a tuple at a time.

Detachment is always applied in preference to tuple substitution so long as there is a choice (see example below). Eventually, however, the query will have been decomposed via detachment into a set of components that cannot be decomposed any further using that technique, and tuple substitution must be brought into play.

We give a single example (based on an example from reference [17.36]). The query is "Get names of London suppliers who supply some red part weighing less than 25 pounds in a quantity greater than 200." Here is a QUEL formulation of this query ("query Q0"):

```
Q0:  RETRIEVE ( S.SNAME ) WHERE S.CITY   = "London"
                          AND   S.S#      = SP.S#
                          AND   SP.QTY    > 200
                          AND   SP.P#     = P.P#
                          AND   P.COLOR   = "Red"
                          AND   P.WEIGHT  < 25
```

The (implicit) range variables here are S, P, and SP, each ranging over the base relvar with the same name.

Now, if we examine this query, we can see immediately from the last two comparison terms that the only parts we are interested in are parts that are red and weigh less than 25 pounds. So we can detach the "one-variable query" (actually a projection of a restriction) involving the variable P:

```
D1:  RETRIEVE INTO P' ( P.P# ) WHERE P.COLOR  = "Red"
                               AND   P.WEIGHT < 25
```

This one-variable query is detachable because it has just one variable, namely P itself, in common with the rest of the query. Since it links up to the rest of the original query via the attribute P# (in the comparison term SP.P# = P.P#), attribute P# is what must appear in the "proto tuple" (see Chapter 7) in the detached version; that is, the detached query must retrieve exactly the part numbers of red parts weighing less than 25 pounds. We save that detached query as a query D1 that retrieves its result into a temporary relvar P′ (the effect of the INTO clause is to cause a new relvar P′, with sole attribute P#, to be defined automatically to hold the result of executing the RETRIEVE). Finally, we replace references to P in the reduced version of Q0 by references to P′. Let us refer to this new reduced version as query Q1:

```
Q1:  RETRIEVE ( S.SNAME ) WHERE S.CITY = "London"
                          AND   S.S#    = SP.S#
                          AND   SP.QTY  > 200
                          AND   SP.P#   = P'.P#
```

---

*Recall that the Ingres query language QUEL is calculus-based.

We now perform a similar process of detachment on query Q1, detaching the one-variable query involving variable SP as query D2 and leaving a modified version of Q1 (query Q2):

```
D2:   RETRIEVE INTO SP' ( SP.S#, SP.P# ) WHERE SP.QTY > 200

Q2:   RETRIEVE ( S.SNAME ) WHERE S.CITY = "London"
                     AND     S.S#    = SP'.S#
                     AND     SP'.P# = P'.P#
```

Next we detach the one-variable query involving S:

```
D3:   RETRIEVE INTO S' ( S.S#, S.SNAME ) WHERE S.CITY = "London"

Q3:   RETRIEVE ( S'.SNAME ) WHERE S'.S#  = SP'.S#
                     AND     SP'.P# = P'.P#
```

Finally we detach the two-variable query involving SP' and P':

```
D4:   RETRIEVE INTO SP'' ( SP'.S# ) WHERE SP'.P# = P'.P#

Q4:   RETRIEVE ( S'.SNAME ) WHERE S'.S# = SP''.S#
```

Thus, the original query Q0 has been decomposed into three one-variable queries D1, D2, and D3 (each of which is a projection of a restriction) and two two-variable queries D4 and Q4 (each of which is a projection of a join). We can represent the situation at this point by means of the tree structure shown in Fig. 17.3. That figure is meant to be read as follows:

- Queries D1, D2, and D3 take as input relvars P, SP, and S (more precisely, the relations that are the current values of relvars P, SP, and S), respectively, and produce as output P', SP', and S', respectively.

- Query D4 then takes as input P' and SP' and produces as output SP''.

- Finally, query Q4 takes as input S' and SP'' and produces as output the overall required result.

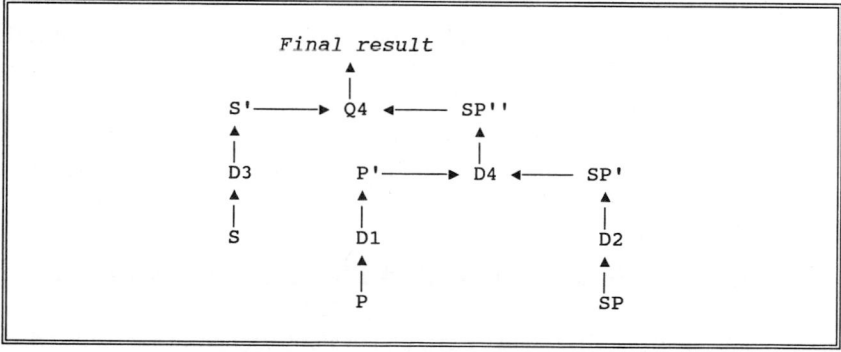

Fig. 17.3   Decomposition tree for query Q0

Observe now that queries D1, D2, and D3 are completely independent of one another and can be processed in any order (possibly even in parallel). Likewise, queries D3 and D4 can be processed in either order once queries D1 and D2 have been processed. However, queries D4 and Q4 cannot be decomposed any further and must be processed by tuple substitution (which really just means *brute force, index lookup,* or *hash lookup*—see Section 17.7). For example, consider query Q4. With our usual sample data, the set of supplier numbers in attribute SP″.S# will be the set {S1,S2,S4}. Each of these three values will be substituted for SP″.S# in turn. Q4 will therefore be evaluated as if it had been written as follows:

```
RETRIEVE ( S'.SNAME ) WHERE S'.S# = "S1"
                OR     S'.S# = "S2"
                OR     S'.S# = "S4"
```

Reference [17.36] gives algorithms for breaking the original query down into irreducible component queries and for choosing variables for tuple substitution. It is in that latter choice that much of the actual optimization resides; reference [17.36] includes heuristics for making the cost estimates that drive the choice (Ingres will usually—but not always—choose the relation with the smallest cardinality as the one to do the substitution on). The principal objectives of the optimization process as a whole are to avoid having to build Cartesian products and to keep the number of tuples to be scanned to a minimum at each stage.

Reference [17.36] does not discuss the optimization of one-variable queries. However, information regarding that level of optimization is given in the Ingres overview paper [7.11]. Basically it is similar to the analogous function in other systems, involving as it does the use of statistical information kept in the catalog and the choice of a particular access path (e.g., a hash or index) for scanning the data as stored.

Reference [17.37] presents some experimental evidence—measurements from a benchmark set of queries—that suggests that the optimization techniques described above are basically sound and in practice quite effective. Some specific conclusions from that paper are the following:

1. Detachment is the best first move.

2. If tuple substitution *must* be done first, then the best choice of variable to be substituted for is a join variable.

3. Once tuple substitution has been applied to one variable in a two-variable query, it is an excellent tactic to build an index or hash "on the fly" (if necessary) on the join attribute in the other relation. Ingres in fact often applies this tactic.

17.7 IMPLEMENTING THE RELATIONAL OPERATORS

We now present a short description of some straightforward methods for implementing certain of the relational operators, join in particular. Our primary reason for including this material is simply to remove any remaining air of mystery that might possibly still surround the optimization process. The methods to be discussed correspond to what we called "low-level implementation procedures" in Section 17.3. *Note:* Some much more sophisticated implementation techniques are described in the annotation to certain of the references at the end of the chapter.

We assume for simplicity that tuples and relations are physically stored as such. The operators we consider are project, join, and summarize—where we take "summarize" to include both of the following cases:

1. Summarize per no attributes at all

2. Summarize per at least one attribute

Case 1 is straightforward: Basically, it involves scanning the entire relation over which the summarizing is to be done—except that, if the attribute to be aggregated (e.g., averaged) happens to be indexed, it might be possible to compute the result directly from the index, without having to access the relation itself at all [17.35]. For example, the expression

```
SUMMARIZE SP ADD AVG ( QTY ) AS AQ
```

can be evaluated by scanning the QTY index (assuming such an index exists) without touching the shipments *per se* at all. An analogous remark applies if AVG is replaced by COUNT or SUM (for COUNT, any index will do). As for MAX and MIN, the result can be found in *a single access* to the last index entry (for MAX) or the first (for MIN), assuming again that an index exists for the relevant attribute.

For the rest of this section we take "summarize" to mean Case 2 specifically. Here is an example of Case 2:

```
SUMMARIZE SP PER P { P# } ADD SUM ( QTY ) AS TOTQTY
```

From the user's point of view, project, join, and Case 2 summarize are of course very different from one another. From an implementation point of view, however, they do have certain similarities, because in every case the system needs to group tuples together on the basis of common values for specified attributes. In the case of projection, such grouping allows the system to eliminate duplicates; in the case of join, it allows it to find matching tuples; and in the case of summarize, it allows it to compute the individual (i.e., per group) aggregate values. There are several techniques for performing such grouping:

1. Brute force

2. Index lookup

3. Hash lookup

4. Merge

5. Hash

6. Combinations of the above

Figs. 17.4–17.8 give pseudocode procedures for the case of join specifically (project and summarize are left as exercises). The notation used in those figures is as follows. First,

R and *S* are the relations to be joined, and *C* is their (possibly composite) common attribute. We assume that it is possible to access the tuples of each of *R* and *S* one at a time in some sequence, and we denote those tuples, in that sequence, by $R[1]$, $R[2]$, ..., $R[m]$ and $S[1]$, $S[2]$, ..., $S[n]$, respectively. We use the expression $R[i] * S[j]$ to denote the joined tuple formed from the tuples $R[i]$ and $S[j]$. Finally, we refer to *R* as the **outer** relation and *S* as the **inner** relation (because they control the outer and the inner loop, respectively).

Brute Force

Brute force is what might be termed the "plain" case, in which all possible tuple combinations are inspected (i.e., every tuple of *R* is examined in conjunction with every tuple of *S*, as indicated in Fig. 17.4). *Note:* Brute force is often referred to as "nested loops," but this name is misleading because nested loops are in fact involved in all of the algorithms.

```
do i := 1 to m ;                                /* outer loop */
   do j := 1 to n ;                             /* inner loop */
      if R[i].C = S[j].C then
         add joined tuple R[i] * S[j] to result ;
   end ;
end ;
```

Fig. 17.4   Brute force

Let us examine the costs associated with the brute force approach. *Note:* We limit our attention here to I/O costs only, although other costs (e.g., CPU costs) could also be important in practice.

First of all, the approach clearly requires a total of $m + (m * n)$ tuple read operations; but what about tuple writes?—i.e., what is the cardinality of the joined result? (The number of tuple writes will be equal to that cardinality if the result is written back out to the disk.)

- In the important special case of a many-to-one join (in particular, a foreign-to-matching-candidate-key join), the cardinality of the result is clearly equal to the cardinality— *viz.*, *m* or *n*—of whichever of *R* and *S* represents the foreign key side of the join.

- Now consider the more general case of a many-to-many join. Let *dCR* be the number of distinct values of the join attribute *C* in relation *R*, and let *dCS* be defined analogously. If we assume *uniform value distributions* (so that any given value of *C* in relation *R* is as likely to occur as any other), then for a given tuple of *R* there will be *n/dCS* tuples of *S* with the same value for *C* as that tuple; hence the total number of tuples in the join (i.e., the cardinality of the result) will be $(m * n)/dCS$. Or, if we start by considering a given tuple of *S* instead of *R*, the total number will be $(n * m)/dCR$; the two estimates will differ if $dCR \neq dCS$, i.e., if there are some values of *C* that occur in *R* but not in *S* or *vice versa*, in which case the lower estimate is the one to use.

In practice, of course, as stated in Section 17.2, it is *page* I/O's that matter, not tuple I/O's. Suppose, therefore, that the tuples of *R* and *S* are stored *pR* to a page and *pS* to a page, respectively (so that the two relations occupy m/pR pages and n/pS pages, respectively). Then it is easy to see that the procedure of Fig. 17.4 will involve $(m/pR) + (m * n)/pS$ page reads. Alternatively, if we interchange the roles of R and S (making S the outer relation and R the inner), the number of page reads will be $(n/pS) + (n * m)/pR$.

By way of example, suppose $m = 100$, $n = 10,000$, $pR = 1$, $pS = 10$. Then the two formulas evaluate to 100,100 and 1,001,000 page reads, respectively. *Conclusion:* It is desirable in the brute force approach for the smaller relation of the two to be chosen as the outer relation (where *smaller* means "smaller number of pages").

We conclude this brief discussion of the brute force technique by observing that brute force should be regarded as a worst-case procedure; it assumes that relation S is neither indexed nor hashed on the join attribute C. Experiments by Bitton *et al.* [17.7] indicate that, if that assumption is in fact valid, matters will usually be improved by constructing such an index or hash dynamically and then proceeding with an index or hash lookup join (see the next two subsections). Reference [17.37] supports this idea, as mentioned at the end of the previous section.

Index Lookup

We now consider the case in which there is an index X on attribute $S.C$ of the inner relation (refer to Fig. 17.5). The advantage of this technique over brute force is that for a given tuple of the outer relation R we can go "directly" to the matching tuples of the inner relation S. The total number of tuple reads to relations R and S is thus simply the cardinality of the joined result; making the worst-case assumption that every tuple read to S is in fact a separate page read, the total number of page reads to R and S is thus $(m/pR) + (mn/dCS)$.

```
/* assume index X on S.C */

do i := 1 to m ;                          /* outer loop */
    /* let there be k index entries X[1], ..., X[k] with    */
    /* indexed attribute value = R[i].C                     */
    do j := 1 to k ;                      /* inner loop */
        /* let tuple of S indexed by X[j] be S[j] */
        add joined tuple R[i] * S[j] to result ;
    end ;
end ;
```

Fig. 17.5 Index lookup

If relation S happens to be stored in sequence by values of the join attribute C, however, the page read figure reduces to $(m/pR) + (mn/dCS)/pS$. Taking the same sample values as before ($m = 100$, $n = 10,000$, $pR = 1$, $pS = 10$), and assuming $dCS = 100$, the two formulas evaluate to 10,100 and 1,100, respectively. The difference between these two figures clearly points up the importance of keeping stored relations in a "good" physical sequence [17.9].

However, we must of course include the overhead for accessing the index X itself. The worst-case assumption is that each tuple of R requires an "out of the blue" index lookup to find the matching tuples of *S*, which implies reading one page from each level of the index. For an index of *x* levels, this will add an extra *mx* page reads to the overall page read figure. In practice, *x* will typically be 3 or less (moreover, the top level of the index will very likely reside in a main memory buffer throughout processing, thereby reducing the page read figure still further).

Hash Lookup

Hash lookup is similar to index lookup, except that the "fast access path" to the inner relation *S* on the join attribute *S.C* is a hash instead of an index (refer to Fig. 17.6). Derivation of cost estimates for this case is left as an exercise.

```
/* assume hash table H on S.C */

do i := 1 to m ;                                /* outer loop */
   k := hash (R[i].C) ;
   /* let there be h tuples S[1], ..., S[h] stored at H[k] */
   do j := 1 to h ;                             /* inner loop */
      if S[j].C = R[i].C then
      add joined tuple R[i] * S[j] to result ;
   end ;
end ;
```

Fig. 17.6   Hash lookup

Merge

The merge technique assumes that the two relations *R* and *S* are both physically stored in sequence by values of the join attribute *C*. If such is in fact the case, the two relations can be scanned in physical sequence, the two scans can be synchronized, and the entire join can be done in a single pass over the data (at least, this claim is true if the join is one-to-many; it might not be quite true for the many-to-many case). Such a technique is unquestionably optimal, because every page is accessed just once (refer to Fig. 17.7). In other words, the number of page reads is just $(m/pR) + (n/pS)$. It follows that:

- Physical clustering of logically related data is one of the most critical performance factors of all; i.e., it is highly desirable that data be clustered in such a way as to match the joins that are most important to the enterprise [17.9].
- In the absence of such clustering, it is often a good idea to sort either or both relations at run time and then do a merge join anyway (of course, the effect of such sorting is precisely to produce the desired clustering dynamically). This technique is referred to, logically enough, as **sort/merge** [17.10].

See reference [17.35] for further discussion.

```
/* assume R and S are both sorted on attribute C ; */
/* following code assumes join is many-to-many ;   */
/* simpler many-to-one case is left as an exercise */

r := 1 ;
s := 1 ;
do while r ≤ m and s ≤ n ;                      /* outer loop */
    v := R[r].C ;
    do j := s by 1 while S[j].C < v ;
    end ;
    s := j ;
    do j := s by 1 while S[j].C = v ;    /* main inner loop */
        do i := r by 1 while R[i].C = v ;
            add joined tuple R[i] * S[j] to result ;
        end ;
    end ;
    s := j ;
    do i := r by 1 while R[i].C = v ;
    end ;
    r := i ;
end ;
```

Fig. 17.7   Merge (many-to-many case)

Hash

Like the merge technique just discussed, the hash technique requires a single pass over each of the two relations (refer to Fig. 17.8). The first pass builds a hash table for relation S on values of the join attribute $S.C;$ the entries in that table contain the join attribute value—possibly other attribute values also—and a pointer to the corresponding tuple on the disk. The second pass then scans relation R and applies the same hash function to the join attribute $R.C$. When an R tuple collides in the hash table with one or more S tuples, the algorithm checks to see that the values of $R.C$ and $S.C$ are indeed equal, and if so generates the appropriate joined tuple(s). The great advantage of this technique over the merge technique is that relations R and S do not need to be stored in any particular order, and no sorting is necessary.

```
/* build hash table H on S.C */

do j := 1 to n ;
    k := hash (S[j].C) ;
    add S[j] to hash table entry H[k] ;
end ;

/* now do hash lookup on R */
```

Fig. 17.8   Hash

As with the hash lookup technique, we leave the derivation of cost estimates for this approach as an exercise.

17.8   SUMMARY

We began by stating that optimization represents both a *challenge* and an *opportunity* for relational systems. In fact, optimizability is a **strength** of such systems, for several reasons; a relational system with a good optimizer might very well outperform a nonrelational system. Our introductory example gave some idea of the kinds of improvements that might be achievable (a factor of over 10,000 to 1 in that particular case).

The four broad stages of optimization are:

- Cast the query into some **internal form** (typically a **query tree** or **abstract syntax tree,** but such representations can be thought of as just an internalized form of the relational algebra or relational calculus);

- Convert to **canonical form,** using various **laws of transformation;**

- Choose candidate **low-level procedures** for implementing the various operations in the canonical representation of the query;

- Generate **query plans** and choose the cheapest, using **cost formulas** and knowledge of **database statistics.**

Next, we discussed the general **distributive, commutative,** and **associative** laws and their applicability to relational operators such as join (also their applicability to **arithmetic, logical,** and **comparison** operators), and we mentioned another general law, called **idempotence.** We also discussed some specific transformations for the **restriction** and **projection** operators. Then we introduced the important idea of **semantic** transformations—i.e., transformations based on the system's knowledge of **integrity constraints.**

By way of illustration, we sketched some of the statistics maintained by the **DB2** and **Ingres** products. Then we described a "divide and conquer" strategy called **query decomposition** that was introduced with the Ingres prototype, and mentioned that such strategies might be very attractive in a parallel processing or distributed environment.

Finally, we examined certain **implementation techniques** for certain of the relational operators, especially **join.** We presented pseudocode algorithms for five join techniques—**brute force, index lookup, hash lookup, merge** (including **sort/merge**), and **hash**—and briefly considered the costs associated with these techniques.

In conclusion, we should mention that many of today's products do unfortunately include certain **optimization inhibitors,** which users should at least be aware of (even though there is little they can do about them, in most cases). An optimization inhibitor is a feature of the system in question that prevents the optimizer from doing as good a job as it might otherwise do (i.e., in the absence of that feature). The inhibitors in question include *duplicate rows* (see reference [5.6]), *three-valued logic* (see Chapter 18), and *SQL's implementation of three-valued logic* (see references [18.6] and [18.10]).

EXERCISES

17.1 Some of the following pairs of expressions on the suppliers-parts-projects database are equivalent and some are not. Which pairs are indeed equivalent?

a1. `S JOIN ( ( P JOIN J ) WHERE CITY = 'London' )`

a2. `( P WHERE CITY = 'London' ) JOIN ( J JOIN S )`

b1. `( S MINUS ( ( S JOIN SPJ ) WHERE P# = P# ( 'P2' ) )`
`{ S#, SNAME, STATUS, CITY } ) { S#, CITY }`

b2. `S { S#, CITY } MINUS`
`( S { S#, CITY } JOIN`
`( SPJ WHERE P# = P# ( 'P2' ) ) ) { S#, CITY }`

c1. `( S { CITY } MINUS P { CITY } ) MINUS J { CITY }`

c2. `( S { CITY } MINUS J { CITY } )`
`MINUS ( P { CITY } MINUS J { CITY } )`

d1. `( J { CITY } INTERSECT P { CITY } ) UNION ( S { CITY } )`

d2. `J { CITY } INTERSECT S { CITY } UNION P { CITY } )`

e1. `( ( SPJ WHERE S# = S# ( 'S1' ) )`
`UNION ( SPJ WHERE P# = P# ( 'P1' ) ) )`
`INTERSECT`
`( ( SPJ WHERE J# = J# ( 'J1' ) )`
`UNION ( SPJ WHERE S# = S# ( 'S1' ) ) )`

e2. `( SPJ WHERE S# = S# ( 'S1' ) ) UNION`
`( ( SPJ WHERE P# = P# ( 'P1' ) ) INTERSECT`
`( SPJ WHERE J# = J# ( 'J1' ) ) )`

f1. `( S WHERE CITY = 'London' ) UNION ( S WHERE STATUS > 10 )`

f2. `S WHERE CITY = 'London' AND STATUS > 10`

g1. `( S { S# } INTERSECT ( SPJ WHERE J# = J# ( 'J1' ) ) { S# } )`
`UNION ( S WHERE CITY = 'London' ) { S# }`

g2. `S { S# } INTERSECT ( ( SPJ WHERE J# = J# ( 'J1' ) ) { S# }`
`UNION ( S WHERE CITY = 'London' ) { S# } )`

h1. `( SPJ WHERE J# = J# ( 'J1' ) ) { S# }`
`MINUS ( SPJ WHERE P# = P# ( 'P1' ) ) { S# }`

h2. `( ( SPJ WHERE J# = J# ( 'J1' ) )`
`MINUS ( SPJ WHERE P# = P# ( 'P1' ) ) ) { S# }`

i1. `S JOIN ( P { CITY } MINUS J { CITY } )`

i2. `( S JOIN P { CITY } ) MINUS ( S JOIN J { CITY } )`

17.2 Show that join, union, and intersection are commutative and difference is not.

17.3 Show that join, union, and intersection are associative and difference is not.

17.4 Show that:

a. Union distributes over intersection;

b. Intersection distributes over union.

17.5 Show that for all *A* and *B:*

a. `A UNION (A INTERSECT B) ≡ A;`

b. `A INTERSECT (A UNION B) ≡ A.`

Note: These two laws are called the **absorption** laws. Like the idempotence, commutative, etc., laws, they too can be useful for optimization purposes.

17.6 Show that:

a. Restriction is unconditionally distributive over union, intersection, and difference, and conditionally distributive over join;

b. Projection is unconditionally distributive over union and intersection, is conditionally distributive over join, and is not distributive over difference.

State the relevant conditions in the conditional cases.

17.7 Extend the transformation rules of Section 17.4 to take account of EXTEND and SUMMARIZE.

17.8 Can you find any useful transformation rules for the relational division operation?

17.9 Give an appropriate set of transformation rules for conditional expressions involving AND, OR, and NOT. An example of such a rule would be "commutativity of AND"—i.e., *A* AND *B* is the same as *B* AND *A*.

17.10 Extend your answer to the previous exercise to include boolean expressions involving the quantifiers EXISTS and FORALL. An example of such a rule would be the rule given in Chapter 7 (Section 7.2) that allows an expression involving a FORALL to be converted into one involving a negated EXISTS instead.

17.11 Here is a list of integrity constraints for the suppliers-parts-projects database (extracted from the exercises in Chapter 8):

- The only legal cities are London, Paris, Rome, Athens, Oslo, Stockholm, Madrid, and Amsterdam.
- No two projects can be located in the same city.
- At most one supplier can be located in Athens at any one time.
- No shipment can have a quantity more than double the average of all such quantities.
- The highest status supplier must not be located in the same city as the lowest status supplier.
- Every project must be located in a city in which there is at least one supplier of that project.
- There must exist at least one red part.
- The average supplier status must be greater than 18.
- Every London supplier must supply part P2.
- At least one red part must weigh less than 50 pounds.
- Suppliers in London must supply more different kinds of parts than suppliers in Paris.
- Suppliers in London must supply more parts in total than suppliers in Paris.

And here are some sample queries against that database:

a. Get suppliers who do not supply part P2.

b. Get suppliers who do not supply any project in the same city as the supplier.

c. Get suppliers such that no supplier supplies fewer kinds of parts.

d. Get Oslo suppliers who supply at least two distinct Paris parts to at least two distinct Stockholm projects.

e. Get pairs of colocated suppliers who supply pairs of colocated parts.

f. Get pairs of colocated suppliers who supply pairs of colocated projects.

g. Get parts supplied to at least one project only by suppliers not in the same city as that project.

h. Get suppliers such that no supplier supplies more kinds of parts.

Use the integrity constraints to transform these queries into simpler forms (still in natural language, however; you are not asked to perform this exercise *formally*).

17.12 Investigate any DBMS that might be available to you. Does that system perform any expression transformations? (Not all do.) If so, what transformations does it perform? Does it perform any *semantic* transformations?

17.13 Try the following experiment: Take a simple query, say "Get names of suppliers who supply part P2," and state that query in as many different ways as you can think of in whatever query language is available to you (probably SQL). Create and populate a suitable test database, run the different versions of the query, and measure the execution times. If those times vary significantly, you have empirical evidence that the optimizer is not doing a very good job of expression transformation. Repeat the experiment with several different queries. If possible, repeat it with several different DBMSs also.

   Note: Of course, the different versions of the query should all give the same result. If not, you have probably made a mistake—or it might be an optimizer bug; if so, report it to your vendor!

17.14 Investigate any DBMS that might be available to you. Does that system maintain any database statistics? (Not all do.) If so, what arc thcy? IIow arc thcy updatcd?—dynamically, or via somc utility? If the latter, what is the utility called? How frequently is it run? How selective is it, in terms of the specific statistics that it can update on any specific execution?

17.15 We saw in Section 17.5 that among the database statistics maintained by DB2 are the second highest and second lowest value for each column of each base table. Why the *second* highest and lowest, do you think?

17.16 Several commercial products allow the user to provide hints to the optimizer. In DB2, for example, the specification OPTIMIZE FOR n ROWS on an SQL cursor declaration means the user expects to retrieve no more than n rows via the cursor in question (i.e., to execute FETCH against that cursor no more than n times). Such a specification can sometimes cause the optimizer to choose an access path that is more efficient, at least for the case where the user does in fact execute the FETCH no more than n times. Do you think such hints are a good idea? Justify your answer.

17.17 Devise a set of implementation procedures for the restriction and projection operations (along the lines of the procedures sketched for join in Section 17.7). Derive an appropriate set of cost formulas for those procedures. Assume that page I/O's are the only quantity of interest, i.e., do not attempt to include CPU or other costs in your formulas. State and justify any other assumptions you make.

REFERENCES AND BIBLIOGRAPHY

The field of optimization is huge, and growing all the time (in fact, it is becoming more important than ever, thanks to the increasing interest in decision support systems—see Chapter 21). To take just one example, over 50 percent of the papers presented at each of the annual ACM SIGMOD conferences over the past several years have been concerned with optimization in some shape or form. The following list represents a relatively small selection from the vast literature on this subject. It is roughly divided into groups, as follows:

- References [17.1–17.7] provide introductions to, or overviews of, the general optimization problem.

- References [17.8–17.17] are concerned with the efficient implementation of specific relational operations, such as join or summarize.

- References [17.18–17.33] describe a variety of techniques based on expression transformation as discussed in Section 17.4; in particular, references [17.27–17.30] consider *semantic* transformations.

- References [17.34–17.45] discuss the techniques used in System R, DB2, and Ingres, and the general problem of optimizing queries involving SQL-style nested subqueries.

- References [17.46–17.61] address a miscellaneous set of techniques, tricks, ideas for future research, and so forth. In particular, references [17.58–17.61] consider the impact of parallel processing on the optimization issue.

Note: Publications on optimization in distributed systems are deliberately excluded. See Chapter 20.

17.1 Won Kim, David S. Reiner, and Don S. Batory (eds.): *Query Processing in Database Systems.* New York, N.Y.: Springer Verlag (1985).

This book is an anthology of papers on the general topic of query processing (not just on optimization specifically). It consists of an introductory survey paper by Jarke, Koch, and Schmidt (similar but not identical to reference [17.3]), followed by groups of papers that discuss query processing in a variety of contexts: distributed database, heterogeneous systems, view updating (reference [9.11] is the sole paper in this section), nontraditional applications (e.g., CAD/CAM), multi-statement optimization (see reference [17.49]), database machines, and physical database design.

17.2 IEEE: *Database Engineering 5,* No. 3: Special Issue on Query Optimization (September 1982).

Contains 13 short papers (from both academic and commercial environments) on various aspects of query optimization.

17.3 Matthias Jarke and Jürgen Koch: "Query Optimization in Database Systems," *ACM Comp. Surv. 16,* No. 2 (June 1984).

An excellent tutorial. The paper gives a general framework for query evaluation, much like the one in Section 17.3 of the present chapter, but based on the relational calculus rather than the algebra. It then discusses a large number of optimization techniques within that framework: syntactic and semantic transformations, low-level operation implementation, and algorithms for generating query plans and choosing among them. An extensive set of syntactic transformation rules for calculus expressions is given. A lengthy bibliography (not annotated) is also included; note, however, that the number of papers on the subject published since 1984 is probably at least an order of magnitude greater than the number prior to that time (see reference [17.4]).

The paper also briefly discusses certain other related issues: the optimization of higher-level query languages (i.e., languages that are more powerful than the algebra or calculus), optimization in a distributed database environment, and the role of database machines with respect to optimization.

17.4 Götz Graefe: "Query Evaluation Techniques for Large Databases," *ACM Comp. Surv. 25,* No. 2 (June 1993).

Another (more recent) excellent tutorial, with an extensive bibliography. To quote the abstract: "This survey provides a foundation for the design and implementation of query execution facilities . . . It describes a wide array of practical query evaluation techniques . . . including iterative execution of complex query evaluation plans, the duality of sort- and hash-based set-matching algorithms, types of parallel query execution and their implementation, and special operators for emerging database application domains." Recommended.

17.5 Frank P. Palermo: "A Data Base Search Problem," in Julius T. Tou (ed.), *Information Systems: COINS IV.* New York, N.Y.: Plenum Press (1974).

One of the very earliest papers on optimization (in fact, a classic). Starting from an arbitrary expression of the relational calculus, the paper first uses Codd's reduction algorithm to reduce that expression to an equivalent algebraic expression (see Chapter 7), and then introduces a number of improvements on that algorithm, among them the following:

- No tuple is ever retrieved more than once.

- Unnecessary values are discarded from a tuple as soon as that tuple is retrieved—"unnecessary values" being either values of attributes not referenced in the query or values used solely for restriction purposes. This process is equivalent to projecting the relation over the "necessary" attributes, and thus not only reduces the space required for each tuple but also reduces the number of tuples that need to be retained (in general).

- The method used to build up the result relation is based on a least-growth principle, so that the result tends to grow slowly. This technique has the effect of reducing both the number of comparisons involved and the amount of intermediate storage required.

- An efficient technique is employed in the construction of joins, involving (a) the dynamic factoring out of values used in join terms (such as S.S# = SP.S#) into *semijoins,* which are effectively a kind of dynamically constructed secondary index (Palermo's semijoins are not the same thing as the semijoins of Chapter 6, *q.v.*), and (b) the use of an internal representation of each join called an *indirect join,* which makes use of internal tuple IDs to identify the tuples that participate in the join. These techniques are designed to reduce the amount of scanning needed in the construction of the join, by ensuring for each join term that the tuples concerned are logically ordered on the values of the join attributes. They also permit the dynamic determination of a "best" sequence in which to access the required relations.

17.6 Jim Gray (ed.): *The Benchmark Handbook for Database and Transaction Processing Systems* (2nd edition). San Francisco, Calif.: Morgan Kaufmann (1993).

The Transaction Processing Council (TPC) is an independent body that has produced several industry-standard benchmarks over the years, and this book includes detailed information on those benchmarks in particular (as well as on several others). *TPC-A* is a benchmark that is intended to measure OLTP performance (OLTP = online transaction processing). *TPC-B* is a version of TPC-A that measures the performance of the DBMS and underlying operating system, ignoring considerations having to do with user communication and the like. *TPC-C* is modeled after an order/entry system (and in fact has largely superseded TPC-A). *TPC-D* measures decision support performance; it involves a set of 17 fairly complicated SQL queries (and is thus the only one of the four that really focuses on the quality of the optimizer as such).

Note: Vendors continually compete with each other over their performance on the TPC benchmarks. However, it is only fair to warn you to exercise caution in interpreting advertising claims in this regard; vendors can and do employ all kinds of tricks and techniques to boost their TPC numbers to the maximum possible. *Caveat emptor.*

17.7 Dina Bitton, David J. DeWitt, and Carolyn Turbyfill: "Benchmarking Database Systems: A Systematic Approach," Proc. 9th Int. Conf. on Very Large Data Bases, Florence, Italy (October/November 1983).

The first paper to describe what is now usually called "the Wisconsin benchmark" (since it was developed by the authors of the paper at the University of Wisconsin). The benchmark defines a set of relations with precisely specified attribute values, and then measures the performance of certain precisely specified algebraic operations on those relations (for example, various projections, involving different degrees of duplication in the attributes over which the projections are taken). It thus represents a systematic test of the effectiveness of the optimizer on those fundamental operations. See also reference [17.6].

17.8 S. Bing Yao: "Optimization of Query Evaluation Algorithms," *ACM TODS 4,* No. 2 (June 1979).

A general model is developed of query processing that includes many familiar algorithms as special cases. The model includes the following set of low-level operations, together with an associated set of cost formulas:

- Restriction indexing
- Join indexing
- Intersection
- Record access
- Sequential scan
- Link scan
- Restriction filter
- Join filter
- Sort
- Concatenation
- Projection

A given query processing algorithm expressed in terms of these low-level operations can be evaluated in accordance with the cost formulas. The paper identifies various classes of query processing algorithms and assigns a cost formula to each class. The problem of query optimization then becomes the problem of solving a simple set of cost equations to find a minimum cost, and then selecting the class of algorithm corresponding to that minimum cost.

17.9 M. W. Blasgen and K. P. Eswaran: "Storage and Access in Relational Databases," *IBM Sys. J. 16,* No. 4 (1977).

Several techniques for handling queries involving restriction, projection, and join operations are compared on the basis of their cost in disk I/O. The techniques in question are basically those implemented in System R [17.34].

17.10 T. H. Merrett: "Why Sort/Merge Gives the Best Implementation of the Natural Join," *ACM SIGMOD Record 13,* No. 2 (January 1983).

Presents a set of intuitive arguments to support the position statement of the title. The argument is essentially that:

a. The join operation itself will be most efficient if the two relations are each sorted on values of the join attribute (because in that case, as we saw in Section 17.7, merge is the obvious technique, and each data page will be retrieved exactly once, which is clearly optimal);

b. The cost of sorting the relations into that desired sequence, on a large enough machine, is likely to be less than the cost of any scheme for getting around the fact that they are not so sorted.

However, the author does admit that there could be some exceptions to his somewhat contentious position. For instance, one of the relations might be sufficiently small—e.g., it might be the result of a previous restriction operation—that direct access to the other relation via an index or a hash could be more efficient than sorting it. References [17.11–17.13] below give further examples of cases where sort/merge is probably not the best technique in practice.

17.11 Giovanni Maria Sacco: "Fragmentation: A Technique for Efficient Query Processing," *ACM TODS 11,* No. 2 (June 1986).

Presents a "divide and conquer" method for performing joins by recursively splitting the relations to be joined into disjoint restrictions ("fragments") and performing a series of sequential scans on those subsets. Unlike sort/merge, the technique does not require the relations to be sorted first. The paper shows that the fragmentation technique always performs better than sort/merge in the case where sort/merge requires both relations to be sorted first, and usually performs better in the case where sort/merge requires just one relation (the larger) to be sorted first. The author claims that the technique can also be applied to other operations, such as intersection and difference.

17.12 Leonard D. Shapiro: "Join Processing in Database Systems with Large Main Memories," *ACM TODS 11,* No. 3 (September 1986).

Presents three hash join algorithms, one of which is "especially efficient when the main memory available is a significant fraction of the size of one of the relations to be joined." The algorithms work by splitting the relations into disjoint partitions (i.e., restrictions) that can be processed in main memory. The author contends that hash methods are destined to become the technique of choice, given the rate at which main memory costs are decreasing.

17.13 M. Negri and G. Pelagatti: "Distributive Join: A New Algorithm for Joining Relations," *ACM TODS 16,* No. 4 (December 1991).

Another "divide and conquer" join method. "[The method] is based on the idea that . . . it is not necessary to sort both relations completely . . . It is sufficient to sort one completely and the other only partially, thus avoiding part of the sort effort." The partial sort breaks the affected relation down into a sequence of unsorted partitions $P1, P2, ..., Pn$ (somewhat as in Sacco's method [17.11], except that Sacco uses hashing instead of sorting), with the property that MAX(Pi) < MIN($P(i+1)$) for all i (1, 2, ..., n–1). The paper claims that this method performs better than sort/merge.

17.14 Götz Graefe and Richard L. Cole: "Fast Algorithms for Universal Quantification in Large Databases," *ACM TODS 20,* No. 2 (June 1995).

The universal quantifier (FORALL) is not directly supported in SQL, and hence not by current commercial DBMSs either, yet it is extremely important in formulating a wide class of queries. This paper describes and compares "three known algorithms and one recently proposed algorithm for relational division, [which is] the algebra operator that embodies universal quantification," and shows that the new algorithm runs "as fast as hash (semi-)join evaluates existential quantification over the same relations" (slightly reworded). The authors conclude among other things that FORALL should be directly supported in the user language because most optimizers "do not recognize the rather indirect formulations available in SQL."

17.15 Dina Bitton and David J. DeWitt: "Duplicate Record Elimination in Large Data Files," *ACM TODS 8,* No. 2 (June 1983).

The traditional technique for eliminating duplicates is simply to sort the records and then do a sequential scan. This paper proposes an alternative approach that has significantly better performance characteristics if the file is large.

17.16 David Simmen, Eugene Shekita, and Timothy Malkemus: "Fundamental Techniques for Order Optimization," Proc. 1996 ACM SIGMOD Int. Conf. on Management of Data, Montreal, Canada (June 1996).

Presents techniques for optimizing or avoiding sorts. The techniques, which rely in part on the work of Darwen [10.6], have been implemented in DB2.

17.17 Gurmeet Singh Manku, Sridhar Rajagopalan, and Bruce G. Lindsay: "Approximate Medians and Other Quantiles in One Pass and with Limited Memory," Proc. 1998 ACM SIGMOD Int. Conf. on Management of Data, Seattle, Wash. (June 1998).

17.18 James Miles Smith and Philip Yen-Tang Chang: "Optimizing the Performance of a Relational Algebra Database Interface," *CACM 18,* No. 10 (October 1975).

Describes the algorithms used in the "Smart Query Interface for a Relational Algebra" (SQUIRAL). The techniques used include the following:

- Transforming the original algebraic expression into an equivalent but more efficient sequence of operations, along the lines discussed in Section 17.4;

- Assigning distinct operations in the transformed expression to distinct processes and exploiting concurrency and pipelining among them;

- Coordinating the sort orders of the temporary relations passed between those processes;

- Exploiting indexes and attempting to localize page references.

This paper was one of the very first to discuss expression transformations.

17.19 P. A. V. Hall: "Optimisation of a Single Relational Expression in a Relational Data Base System," *IBM J. R&D 20,* No. 3 (May 1976).

This paper describes some of the optimizing techniques used in the system PRTV [6.9]. PRTV, like SQUIRAL [17.18], begins by transforming the given algebraic expression into some more efficient form before evaluating it (this paper was also one of the very first to discuss expression transformations). A feature of PRTV is that the system does not automatically evaluate each expression as soon as it receives it; rather, it defers actual evaluation until the last possible moment (see the discussion of step-at-a-time query formulation in Chapter 6, Section 6.5). Thus the "single relational expression" of the paper's title might actually represent an entire sequence of user operations. The optimizations described resemble those of SQUIRAL but go further in some respects; they include the following (in order of application):

- Restrictions are performed as early as possible;
- Sequences of projections are combined into a single projection;
- Redundant operations are eliminated;
- Expressions involving empty relations and trivial conditions are simplified;
- Common subexpressions are factored out.

The paper concludes with some experimental results and some suggestions for further investigations.

17.20 Matthias Jarke and Jürgen Koch: "Range Nesting: A Fast Method to Evaluate Quantified Queries," Proc. 1983 ACM SIGMOD Int. Conf. on Management of Data, San Jose, Calif. (May 1983).

Defines a variation of the relational calculus that permits some additional (and useful) syntactic transformation rules to be applied, and presents algorithms for evaluating expressions of that calculus. (The particular calculus described is actually fairly close to the tuple calculus as described in Chapter 7.) The paper describes the optimization of a particular class of expressions of the revised calculus, called "perfect nested expressions." Methods are given for converting apparently complex queries—in particular, certain queries involving FORALL—into perfect expressions. The authors show that a large subset of the queries that arise in practice correspond to perfect expressions.

17.21 Surajit Chaudhuri and Kyuseok Shim: "Including Group-By in Query Optimization," Proc. 20th Int. Conf. on Very Large Data Bases, Santiago, Chile (September 1994).

17.22 A. Makinouchi, M. Tezuka, H. Kitakami, and S. Adachi: "The Optimization Strategy for Query Evaluation in RDB/V1," Proc. 7th Int. Conf. on Very Large Data Bases, Cannes, France (September 1981).

RDB/V1 was the prototype forerunner of the Fujitsu product AIM/RDB (which is an SQL system). This paper describes the optimization techniques used in that prototype and briefly compares them with the techniques used in the Ingres and System R prototypes. One particular technique seems to be novel: the use of dynamically obtained MAX and MIN values to induce additional restrictions. This technique has the effect of simplifying the process of choosing a join order and improving the performance of the joins themselves. As a simple example of the latter point, suppose suppliers and parts are to be joined over cities. First, the suppliers are sorted on CITY; during the sort, the maximum and minimum values, HIGH and LOW say, of S.CITY are determined. Then the restriction

```
LOW ≤ P.CITY AND P.CITY ≤ HIGH
```

can be used to reduce the number of parts that need to be inspected in building the join.

17.23 Hamid Pirahesh, Joseph M. Hellerstein, and Waqar Hasan: "Extensible Rule Based Query Rewrite Optimization in Starburst," Proc. 1992 ACM SIGMOD Int. Conf. on Management of Data, San Diego, Calif. (June 1992).

As noted in Section 17.1, "query rewrite" is another name for expression transformation. The authors claim that, rather surprisingly, commercial products do little in the way of such transformations (at least as of 1992). Be that as it may, the paper describes the expression transformation mechanism of the IBM Starburst prototype (see references [17.50], [25.14], [25.17], and [25.21–25.22]). Suitably qualified users can add new transformation rules to the system at any time (hence the "extensible" of the paper's title).

17.24 Inderpal Singh Mumick, Sheldon J. Finkelstein, Hamid Pirahesh, and Raghu Ramakrishnan: "Magic is Relevant," Proc. 1990 ACM SIGMOD Int. Conf. on Management of Data, Atlantic City, N.J. (May 1990).

The infelicitous term "magic" refers to an optimization technique originally developed for use with queries—especially queries involving recursion—expressed in the "logic database" language Datalog (see Chapter 23). The present paper extends the approach to conventional relational systems, claiming on the basis of experimental measurements that it is often more effective than traditional optimization techniques (note that the query does not have to be recursive for the approach to be applicable). The basic idea is to decompose the given query into a number of smaller queries that define a set of "auxiliary relations" (somewhat as in the query decomposition approach discussed in Section 17.6), in such a way as to filter out tuples that are irrelevant to the problem at hand. The following example (expressed in relational calculus) is based on one given in the paper. The original query is:

```
R   :=   EX.ENAME WHERE EX.JOB = 'Clerk' AND EX.SAL >
              AVG ( EY WHERE EY.DEPT# = EX.DEPT#, SAL ) ;
```

("Get names of clerks whose salary is greater than the average for their department"). If this query is executed "directly"—i.e., more or less as written—the system will scan the employees tuple by tuple and hence compute the average salary for any department that employs more than one clerk several times. A traditional optimizer might therefore break the query down into the following two smaller queries:

```
T1   :=   ( EX.DEPT#,
            AVG ( EY WHERE EY.DEPT# = EX.DEPT#, SAL ) AS ASAL

T2   :=   EMP.ENAME WHERE EMP.JOB = 'Clerk' AND
              EXISTS T1 ( EMP.DEPT# = T1.DEPT# AND
                          EMP.SALARY > T1.ASAL ) ;
```

Now no department's average will be computed more than once, but some *irrelevant* averages will be computed—namely, those for departments that do not employ clerks.

The "magic" approach avoids both the repeated computations of the first approach and the irrelevant computations of the second, at the cost of generating extra "auxiliary" relations:

```
/* first auxiliary relation : name, department, and salary  */
/* for clerks                                               */
T1  :=  ( EMP.ENAME, EMP.DEPT#, EMP.SAL )
                         WHERE EMP.JOB = 'Clerk' ;

/* second auxiliary relation : departments employing clerks */
T2  :=  T1.DEPT# ;

/* third auxiliary relation : departments employing clerks  */
/* and corresponding average salaries                       */
T3  :=  ( T2.DEPT#,
          AVG ( EMP WHERE EMP.DEPT# = T2.DEPT#, SAL )
                                       AS ASAL ) ;

/* result relation */
R   :=  T1.ENAME WHERE EXISTS T3 ( T1.DEPT# = T3.DEPT# AND
                                   T1.SAL > T3.ASAL ) ;
```

The "magic" consists in determining exactly which auxiliary relations are needed.

See references [17.25–17.26] immediately following and the "References and Bibliography" section in Chapter 23 for further references to "magic."

17.25 Inderpal Singh Mumick and Hamid Pirahesh: "Implementation of Magic in Starburst," Proc. 1994 ACM SIGMOD Int. Conf. on Management of Data, Minneapolis, Minn. (May 1994).

17.26 Inderpal Singh Mumick, Sheldon J. Finkelstein, Hamid Pirahesh, and Raghu Ramakrishnan: "Magic Conditions," *ACM TODS 21,* No. 1 (March 1996).

17.27 Jonathan J. King: "QUIST: A System for Semantic Query Optimization in Relational Databases," Proc. 7th Int. Conf. on Very Large Data Bases, Cannes, France (September 1981).

The paper that introduced the idea of semantic optimization (see Section 17.4 of the present chapter). It describes an experimental system called QUIST ("QUery Improvement through Semantic Transformation") that is capable of performing such optimizations.

17.28 Sreekumar T. Shenoy and Z. Meral Ozsoyoglu: "A System for Semantic Query Optimization," Proc. 1987 ACM SIGMOD Int. Conf. on Management of Data, San Francisco, Calif. (May/June 1987).

Extends the work of King [17.27] by introducing a scheme that dynamically selects, from a potentially very large set of integrity constraints, just those that are likely to be profitable in transforming a given query. The integrity constraints considered are of two basic kinds, *implication constraints* and *subset constraints*. An example of an implication constraint is "If the shipment quantity is greater than 300 then the supplier city must be London"; an example of a subset constraint is "The set of London suppliers must be a subset of the shipment suppliers" (i.e., every London supplier must supply at least one part). Such constraints are used to transform queries by eliminating redundant restrictions and joins and introducing additional restrictions on indexed attributes. Cases in which the query can be answered from the constraints alone are also handled efficiently.

17.29 Michael Siegel, Edward Sciore, and Sharon Salveter: "A Method for Automatic Rule Derivation to Support Semantic Query Optimization," *ACM TODS 17,* No. 4 (December 1992)

As explained in Section 17.4, semantic optimization makes use of integrity constraints to transform queries. However, there are several problems associated with this idea:

- How does the optimizer know which transformations will be effective (i.e., will make the query more efficient)?

- Some integrity constraints are not very useful for optimization purposes. E.g., the constraint that part weights must be greater than zero, though important for integrity purposes, is essentially useless for optimization. How does the optimizer distinguish between useful and useless constraints?

- Some conditions might be valid for some states of the database—even for most states—and hence be useful for optimization purposes, and yet not strictly be an integrity constraint as such. An example might be the condition "employee age is less than or equal to 50"; though not an integrity constraint *per se* (employees can be older than 50), it might well be the case that no current employee is in fact older than 50.

This paper describes the architecture for a system that addresses the foregoing issues.

17.30 Upen S. Chakravarthy, John Grant, and Jack Minker: "Logic Based Approach to Semantic Query Optimization," *ACM TODS 15,* No. 2 (June 1990).

To quote from the abstract: "In several previous papers [the authors have] described and proved the correctness of a method for semantic query optimization . . . This paper consolidates the major results of those papers, emphasizing the techniques and their applicability for optimizing relational queries. Additionally, [it shows] how this method subsumes and generalizes earlier work on semantic query optimization. [It also indicates] how semantic query optimization techniques can be extended to [recursive queries] and integrity constraints that contain disjunction, negation, and recursion."

17.31 A. V. Aho, Y. Sagiv, and J. D. Ullman: "Efficient Optimization of a Class of Relational Expressions," *ACM TODS 4,* No. 4 (December 1979).

The class of relational expressions referred to in the title of this paper is those expressions that involve only equality restrictions (referred to as *selections* in the paper), projections, and natural joins—so-called *SPJ-expressions.* SPJ-expressions correspond to relational calculus queries involving only equality comparisons, ANDs, and existential quantifiers. The paper introduces **tableaus** as a means of symbolically representing SPJ-expressions. A tableau is a rectangular array, in which columns correspond to attributes and rows to conditions: specifically, to *membership conditions,* which state that a certain (sub)tuple exists in a certain relation. Rows are logically connected by the appearance of common symbols in the rows concerned. For example, the tableau

S#	STATUS	CITY	P#	COLOR		
	a1					
b1	a1	London			--	suppliers
b1			b2		--	shipments
			b2	Red	--	parts

represents the query "Get status (*a1*) of suppliers (*b1*) in London who supply some red part (*b2*)." The top row of the tableau lists all attributes mentioned in the query, the next row is the "summary" row (corresponding to the proto tuple in a calculus query or the final projection in an algebraic query), and the remaining rows (as already stated) represent membership conditions. We have tagged those rows in the example to indicate the relevant relations (or relvars, rather). Notice that the "*b*"s refer to bound variables and the "*a*"s to free variables; the summary row contains only "*a*"s.

Tableaus represent another candidate for a canonical formalism for queries (see Section 17.3), except of course that they are not general enough to represent all possible relational expressions. (In fact, they can be regarded as a syntactic variation on Query-By-Example, one that is however strictly less powerful than QBE.) The paper gives algorithms for reducing any tableau to another, semantically equivalent tableau in which the number of rows is reduced to a minimum. Since the number of rows (not counting the top two, which are special) is one more than the number of joins in the corresponding SPJ-expression, the converted tableau represents an optimal form of the query—optimal, in the very specific sense that the number of joins is minimized. (In the example above, of course, the number of joins is already the minimum possible for the query, and such optimization has no effect.) The minimal tableau can then be converted back if desired into some other representation for subsequent additional optimization.

The idea of minimizing the number of joins has applicability to queries formulated in terms of join views (in particular, queries formulated in terms of a "universal relation"—see the "References and Bibliography" section in Chapter 12). For example, suppose the user is presented with a view V that is defined as the join of suppliers and shipments over S#, and the user issues the query:

```
V { P# }
```

A straightforward view processing algorithm would convert this query into the following:

```
( SP JOIN S ) { P# }
```

As pointed out in Section 17.4, however, the following query produces the same result, and does not involve a join (i.e., the number of joins has been minimized):

```
SP { P# }
```

Note therefore that, since the algorithms for tableau reduction given in the paper take into account any explicitly stated functional dependencies among the attributes (see Chapter 10), those algorithms provide a limited example of a *semantic* optimization technique.

17.32 Y. Sagiv and M. Yannakakis: "Equivalences Among Relational Expressions with the Union and Difference Operators," *JACM 27,* No. 4 (October 1980).

Extends the ideas of reference [17.31] to include queries that make use of union and difference operations.

17.33 Alon Y. Levy, Inderpal Singh Mumick, and Yehoshua Sagiv: "Query Optimization by Predicate Move-Around," Proc. 20th Int. Conf. on Very Large Data Bases, Santiago, Chile (September 1994).

17.34 P. Griffiths Selinger *et al.*: "Access Path Selection in a Relational Database System," Proc. 1979 ACM SIGMOD Int. Conf. on Management of Data, Boston, Mass. (May/June 1979).

This seminal paper discusses some of the optimization techniques used in the System R prototype. *Note:* The System R optimizer was the forerunner of the DB2 optimizer. Reference [17.35] gives some additional information that is specific to DB2.

A query in System R is an SQL statement and thus consists of a set of "SELECT – FROM – WHERE" blocks (*query blocks*), some of which might be nested inside others. The System R optimizer first decides on an order in which to execute those query blocks; it then seeks to minimize the total cost of the query by choosing the cheapest implementation for each individual block. Note that this strategy (choosing block order first, then optimizing individual blocks) means that certain possible query plans will never be considered; in effect, it amounts to a technique for "reducing the search space" (see the remarks on this subject near the end of Section 17.3). *Note:* In the case of nested blocks, the optimizer effectively just follows the nested order as specified by the user—i.e., the innermost block will be executed first, loosely speaking. See references [17.39–17.45] for criticism and further discussion of this strategy.

For a given query block, there are basically two cases to consider (the first of which can in fact be regarded as a special case of the second):

1. For a block that involves just a restriction and/or projection of a single relation, the optimizer uses statistical information from the catalog, together with formulas (given in the paper) for intermediate result size estimates and low-level operation costs, to choose a strategy for performing that restriction and/or projection.

2. For a block that involves two or more relations to be joined together, with (probably) local restrictions and/or projections as well, the optimizer (a) treats each individual relation as in Case 1, and (b) decides on a sequence for performing the joins. The two operations (a) and (b) are not independent of one another; for example, a given strategy—say, using a certain index—for accessing an individual relation *A* might well be chosen precisely because it

produces tuples of *A* in the order in which they are needed to perform a subsequent join of *A* with some other relation *B*.

Joins are implemented by sort/merge, index lookup, or brute force. One point that is stressed in the paper is that, in evaluating (for example) the nested join (*A* JOIN *B*) JOIN *C,* it is not necessary to compute the join of *A* and *B* in its entirety before computing the join of the result and *C;* on the contrary, as soon as any tuple of *A* JOIN *B* has been produced, it can immediately be passed to the process that joins such tuples with tuples of *C.* Thus it might never be necessary to materialize the relation "*A* JOIN *B*" in its entirety at all. (This general *pipelining* idea was discussed briefly in Chapter 3, Section 3.2. See also references [17.18] and [17.60].)

The paper also includes a few observations on the cost of optimization. For a join of two relations, the cost is said to be approximately equal to the cost of between 5 and 20 database retrievals—a negligible overhead if the optimized query will subsequently be executed a large number of times. (Note that System R is a compiling system, and hence that an SQL statement might be optimized once and then executed many times, perhaps many thousands of times.) Optimization of complex queries is said to require "only a few thousand bytes of storage and a few tenths of a second" on an IBM System 370 Model 158. "Joins of eight tables have been optimized in a few seconds."

17.35 J. M. Cheng, C. R. Loosley, A. Shibamiya, and P. S. Worthington: "IBM DATABASE 2 Performance: Design, Implementation, and Tuning," *IBM Sys. J. 23,* No. 2 (1984).

Includes a brief description of optimization tactics in DB2 (as of first release): query transformation techniques, the handling of nested query blocks, join methods, access path selection, and index-only processing. *Note:* The paper also includes much interesting material concerning other performance-oriented aspects of DB2.

17.36 Eugene Wong and Karel Youssefi: "Decomposition—A Strategy for Query Processing," *ACM TODS 1,* No. 3 (September 1976).

17.37 Karel Youssefi and Eugene Wong: "Query Processing in a Relational Database Management System," Proc. 5th Int. Conf. on Very Large Data Bases, Rio de Janeiro, Brazil (September 1979).

17.38 Lawrence A. Rowe and Michael Stonebraker: "The Commercial Ingres Epilogue," in reference [7.10].

"Commercial Ingres" is the product that grew out of the "University Ingres" prototype. Some of the differences between the University and Commercial Ingres optimizers are as follows:

1. The University optimizer used "incremental planning"—i.e., it decided what to do first, did it, decided what to do next on the basis of the size of the result of the previous step, and so on. The Commercial optimizer decides on a complete plan before beginning execution, based on estimates of intermediate result sizes.

2. The University optimizer handled two-variable (i.e., join) queries by tuple substitution, as explained in Section 17.6. The Commercial optimizer supports a variety of preferred techniques for handling such queries, including in particular the sort/merge technique described in Section 17.7.

3. The Commercial optimizer uses a much more sophisticated set of statistics than the University optimizer.

4. The University optimizer did incremental planning, as noted under point 1 above. The Commercial optimizer does a more exhaustive search. However, the search process stops if the

time spent on optimization exceeds the current best estimate of the time required to execute the query (for otherwise the overhead of doing the optimization might well outweigh the advantages).

5. The Commercial optimizer considers all possible index combinations, all possible join sequences, and "all available join methods—sort/merge, partial sort/merge, hash lookup, ISAM lookup, B-tree lookup, and brute force" (see Section 17.7).

17.39 Won Kim: "On Optimizing an SQL-Like Nested Query," *ACM TODS 7,* No. 3 (September 1982).

See the annotation to reference [17.43] below.

17.40 Werner Kiessling: "On Semantic Reefs and Efficient Processing of Correlation Queries with Aggregates," Proc. 11th Int. Conf. on Very Large Data Bases, Stockholm, Sweden (August 1985).

See the annotation to reference [17.43] below.

17.41 Richard A. Ganski and Harry K. T. Wong: "Optimization of Nested SQL Queries Revisited," Proc. 1987 ACM SIGMOD Int. Conf. on Management of Data, San Francisco, Calif. (May 1987).

See the annotation to reference [17.43] below.

17.42 Günter von Bültzingsloewen: "Translating and Optimizing SQL Queries Having Aggregates," Proc. 13th Int. Conf. on Very Large Data Bases, Brighton, UK (September 1987).

See the annotation to reference [17.43] below.

17.43 M. Muralikrishna: "Improved Unnesting Algorithms for Join Aggregate SQL Queries," Proc. 18th Int. Conf. on Very Large Data Bases, Vancouver, Canada (August 1992).

The SQL language allows "nested subqueries"—i.e., a SELECT–FROM–WHERE block that is nested inside another such block, loosely speaking (see Chapter 7). This construct has caused implementers considerable grief. Consider the following SQL query ("Get names of suppliers who supply part P2"), which we will refer to as query Q1:

```
SELECT  S.SNAME
FROM    S
WHERE   S.S# IN
     ( SELECT SP.S#
       FROM    SP
       WHERE   SP.P# = 'P2' ) ;
```

In System R [17.34], this query will be implemented by evaluating the inner block first to yield a temporary table, T say, containing supplier *numbers* for the required suppliers; it will then scan table S one row at a time, and, for each such row, will scan table T to see if it contains the corresponding supplier number. This strategy is likely to be quite inefficient (especially as table T will not be indexed).

Now consider the following query (Q2):

```
SELECT  S.SNAME
FROM    S, SP
WHERE   S.S# = SP.S#
AND     SP.P# = 'P2' ;
```

This query is readily seen to be semantically identical to the previous one, but System R will now consider additional implementation strategies for it. In particular, if tables S and SP happen to be physically stored in supplier number sequence, it will use a merge join, which will be very efficient. And given that (a) the two queries are logically equivalent, but (b) the second is more immediately susceptible to efficient implementation, the possibility of transforming queries of type Q1 into queries of type Q2 seems worth exploring. That possibility is the subject of references [17.39–17.45].

Kim [17.39] was the first to address the problem. Five types of nested queries were identified and corresponding transformation algorithms described. Kim's paper included some experimental measurements that showed that the proposed algorithms improved the performance of nested queries by (typically) one to two orders of magnitude.

Subsequently, Kiessling [17.40] showed that Kim's algorithms did not work correctly if a nested subquery (at any level) included a COUNT operator in its SELECT list (it did not properly handle the case where the COUNT argument evaluated to an empty set). The "semantic reefs" of the paper's title referred to the SQL awkwardnesses and complexities that users have to navigate around in order to get consistent and correct answers to such queries. Furthermore, Kiessling also showed that Kim's algorithm was not easy to fix ("there seems to be no uniform way to do these transformations efficiently and correctly under all circumstances").

The paper by Ganski and Wong [17.41] provides a fix to the problem identified by Kiessling, by using an *outer join* (see Chapter 18) instead of the regular inner join in the transformed version of the query. (The fix is not totally satisfactory, in the present writer's opinion, because it introduces an undesirable ordering dependence among the operators in the transformed query.) The paper also identifies a further bug in Kim's original paper, which is fixed in the same way. However, the transformations in this paper contain additional bugs of their own, some having to do with the problem of duplicate rows (a notorious "semantic reef" [17.40]) and others with the flawed behavior of the SQL EXISTS quantifier [18.6].

The paper by von Bültzingsloewen [17.42] represents an attempt to put the entire topic on a theoretically sound footing (the basic problem being that, as several writers have observed, the behavior—both syntactic and semantic—of SQL-style nesting and aggregation is not well understood). It defines extended versions of both the relational calculus and the relational algebra (the extensions having to do with aggregates and nulls), and proves the equivalence of those two extended formalisms (using, incidentally, a new method of proof that seems more elegant than those previously published). It then defines the semantics of SQL by mapping SQL into the extended calculus just defined. However, it should be noted that:

1. The dialect of SQL discussed, though closer to the dialect typically supported in commercial products than that discussed in references [17.39–17.41], is still not completely orthodox: It does not include UNION, it does not directly support operators of the form "=ALL" or ">ALL" (see Appendix A), and its treatment of *unknown* truth values is different from (actually better than) that of conventional SQL.

2. The paper omits consideration of matters having to do with duplicate elimination "for technical simplification." But the implications of this omission are not clear, given that (as indicated above) the possibility of duplicates has significant consequences for the validity or otherwise of certain transformations [5.6].

Finally, Muralikrishna [17.43] claims that Kim's original algorithm [17.39], though incorrect, can still be more efficient than "the general strategy" of reference [17.41] in some cases, and therefore proposes an alternative correction to Kim's algorithm. It also provides some additional improvements.

17.44 Lars Baekgaard and Leo Mark: "Incremental Computation of Nested Relational Query Expressions," *ACM TODS 20,* No. 2 (June 1995).

Another paper on the optimization of queries involving SQL-style subqueries, especially *corre-lated* ones (the "nesting" mentioned in the paper's title refers to SQL-style nested subqueries specifically). The strategy is (1) to convert the original query into an unnested equivalent and then (2) to evaluate the unnested version incrementally. "To support step (1), we have developed a very concise algebra-to-algebra transformation algorithm . . . The [transformed] expression makes intensive use of the [MINUS] operator. To support step (2), we present and analyze an efficient algorithm for incrementally evaluating [MINUS operations]." The term *incremental computation* refers to the idea that evaluation of a given query can make use of previously computed results.

17.45 Jun Rao and Kenneth A. Ross: "Using Invariants: A New Strategy for Correlated Queries," Proc. 1998 ACM SIGMOD Int. Conf. on Management of Data, Seattle, Wash. (June 1998).

Yet another paper on the optimization of queries involving SQL-style subqueries.

17.46 David H. D. Warren: "Efficient Processing of Interactive Relational Database Queries Expressed in Logic," Proc. 7th Int. Conf. on Very Large Data Bases, Cannes, France (September 1981).

Presents a view of query optimization from a rather different perspective: namely, that of formal logic. The paper reports on techniques used in an experimental database system based on Prolog. The techniques are apparently very similar to those of System R, although they were arrived at quite independently and with somewhat different objectives. The paper suggests that, in contrast to conventional query languages such as QUEL and SQL, logic-based languages such as Prolog permit queries to be expressed in such a manner as to highlight:

- What the essential components of the query are—namely, the logic goals;
- What it is that links those components together—namely, the logic variables;
- What the crucial implementation problem is—namely, the sequence in which to try to satisfy the goals.

As a consequence, it is suggested that such a language is very convenient as a base for optimization. Indeed, it could be regarded as yet another candidate for the internal representation of queries originally expressed in some other language (see Section 17.3).

17.47 Yannis E. Ioannidis and Eugene Wong: "Query Optimization by Simulated Annealing," Proc. 1987 ACM SIGMOD Int. Conf. on Management of Data, San Francisco, Calif. (May 1987).

The number of possible query plans grows exponentially with the number of relations involved in the query. In conventional commercial applications, the number of relations in a query is usually small and so the number of candidate plans (the "search space") usually stays within reasonable bounds. In newer applications, however, the number of relations in a query can easily become quite large (see, e.g., Chapter 21). Furthermore, such applications are also likely to need "global" (i.e., multi-query) optimization [17.49] and recursive query support, both of which also have the potential for increasing the search space significantly. Exhaustive search rapidly becomes out of the question in such an environment; some effective technique of reducing the search space becomes imperative.

The present paper gives references to previous work on the problems of optimization for large numbers of relations and multi-query optimization, but claims that no previous algorithms have been published for recursive query optimization. It then presents an algorithm that it claims is suitable whenever the search space is large, and in particular shows how to apply that algorithm to the recursive query case. The algorithm (called "simulated annealing" because it models the annealing process by which crystals are grown by first heating the containing fluid and then allowing it to cool gradually) is a probabilistic, hill-climbing algorithm that has successfully been applied to optimization problems in other contexts.

See also reference [17.48] immediately following.

17.48 Arun Swami and Anoop Gupta: "Optimization of Large Join Queries," Proc. 1988 ACM SIGMOD Int. Conf. on Management of Data, Chicago, Ill. (June 1988).

The general problem of determining the optimal join order in queries involving large numbers of relations (as arise in connection with, e.g., deductive database systems—see Chapter 23) is combinatorially hard. This paper presents a comparative analysis of a number of algorithms that address this problem: perturbation walk, quasi-random sampling, iterative improvement, sequence heuristic, and simulated annealing [17.47] (the names add a pleasing element of poetry to a subject that might otherwise be thought a trifle prosaic). According to that analysis, iterative improvement is superior to all the other algorithms; in particular, simulated annealing is not useful "by itself" for large join queries.

17.49 Timos K. Sellis: "Multiple-Query Optimization," *ACM TODS 13*, No. 1 (March 1988).

Classical optimization research has focused on the problem of optimizing individual relational expressions in isolation. In future, however, the ability to optimize several distinct queries as a unit is likely to become important. One reason for this state of affairs is that what starts out as a single query at some higher level of the system might involve several queries at the relational level. For example, the natural language query "Is Mike well paid?" might conceivably lead to the execution of three separate relational queries:

- "Does Mike earn more than $75,000?"
- "Does Mike earn more than $60,000 and have less than five years of experience?"
- "Does Mike earn more than $45,000 and have less than three years of experience?"

This example illustrates the point that sets of related queries are likely to share some common subexpressions, and hence lend themselves to global optimization.

The paper considers queries involving conjunctions of restrictions and/or equijoins only. Some encouraging experimental results are included, and directions are identified for future research.

17.50 Guy M. Lohman: "Grammar-Like Functional Rules for Representing Query Optimization Alternatives," Proc. 1988 ACM SIGMOD Int. Conf. on Management of Data, Chicago, Ill. (June 1988).

In some respects, a relational optimizer can be regarded as an expert system; however, the rules that drive the optimization process have historically been embedded in procedural code, not separately and declaratively stated. As a consequence, extending the optimizer to incorporate new optimization techniques has not been easy. Future database systems (see Chapter 25) will exacerbate this problem, because there will be a clear need for individual installations to extend the optimizer to incorporate (e.g.) support for specific user-defined data types. Several researchers have therefore proposed structuring the optimizer as a conventional expert system, with explicitly stated declarative rules.

However, this idea suffers from certain performance problems. In particular, a large number of rules might be applicable at any given stage during query processing, and determining the appropriate one might involve complex computation. The present paper describes an alternative approach (implemented in the Starburst prototype—see references [25.14], [25.17], and [25.21–25.22]), in which the rules are stated by means of production rules in a grammar somewhat like the grammars used to describe formal languages. The rules, called STARs (STrategy

Alternative RuleS), permit the recursive construction of query plans from other plans and "low-level plan operators" (LOLEPOPs), which are basic operations on relations such as join, sort, etc. LOLEPOPs come in various different *flavors;* for example, the join LOLEPOP has a sort/merge flavor, a hash flavor, etc.

The paper claims that the foregoing approach has several advantages: The rules (STARs) are readily understandable by people who need to define new ones, the process of determining which rule to apply in any given situation is simpler and more efficient than the more traditional expert system approach, and the extensibility objective is met.

17.51 Ryohei Nakano: "Translation with Optimization from Relational Calculus to Relational Algebra Having Aggregate Functions," *ACM TODS 15,* No. 4 (December 1990).

As explained in Chapter 7 (Section 7.4), queries in a calculus-based language can be implemented by (a) translating the query under consideration into an equivalent algebraic expression, then (b) optimizing that algebraic expression, and finally (c) implementing that optimized expression. In this paper, Nakano proposes a scheme for combining steps (a) and (b) into a single step, thereby translating a given calculus expression directly into an *optimal* algebraic equivalent. This scheme is claimed to be "more effective and more promising . . . because it seems quite difficult to optimize complicated algebraic expressions." The translation process makes use of certain *heuristic* transformations, incorporating human knowledge regarding the equivalence of certain calculus and algebraic expressions.

17.52 Kyu-Young Whang and Ravi Krishnamurthy: "Query Optimization in a Memory-Resident Domain Relational Calculus Database System," *ACM TODS 15,* No. 1 (March 1990).

The most expensive aspect of query processing (in the main memory environment assumed by this paper) is shown to be the evaluation of boolean expressions. Optimization in that environment is thus aimed at minimizing the number of such evaluations.

17.53 Johann Christoph Freytag and Nathan Goodman: "On the Translation of Relational Queries into Iterative Programs," *ACM TODS 14,* No. 1 (March 1989).

Presents methods for compiling relational expressions directly into executable code in a language such as C or Pascal. Note that this approach differs from the approach discussed in the body of the chapter, where the optimizer effectively combines prewritten (parameterized) code fragments to build the query plan.

17.54 Kiyoshi Ono and Guy M. Lohman: "Measuring the Complexity of Join Enumeration in Query Optimization," Proc. 16th Int. Conf. on Very Large Data Bases, Brisbane, Australia (August 1990).

Given that join is basically a dyadic operation, the optimizer has to break a join involving *N* relations (*N* > 2) down into a sequence of dyadic joins. Most optimizers do this in a strictly nested fashion; that is, they choose a pair of relations to join first, then a third to join to the result of joining the first two, and so on. In other words, an expression such as *A* JOIN *B* JOIN *C* JOIN *D* might be treated as, say, ((*D* JOIN *B*) JOIN *C*) JOIN *A,* but never as, say, (*A* JOIN *D*) JOIN (*B* JOIN *C*). Further, traditional optimizers are usually designed to avoid Cartesian products if at all possible. Both of these tactics can be seen as ways of "reducing the search space" (though heuristics for choosing the sequence of joins are still needed, of course).

The present paper describes the relevant aspects of the optimizer in the IBM Starburst prototype (see references [17.50], [25.14], [25.17], and [25.21–25.22]). It argues that both of the foregoing tactics can be inappropriate in certain situations, and hence that what is needed is an *adaptable* optimizer that can be instructed to use different tactics for different queries. *Note:* Unlike the typical commercial optimizers of today, Starburst is able to treat an expression of the form $R.A = S.B + c$ as a "join" condition. It also applies "predicate transitive closure" (see Section 17.4).

17.55 Bennet Vance and David Maier: "Rapid Bushy Join-Order Optimization with Cartesian Products," *Proc. 1996 ACM SIGMOD Int. Conf. on Management of Data, Montreal, Canada (June 1996).*

As noted in the annotation to the previous reference, optimizers tend to "reduce the search space" by (among other things) avoiding plans that involve Cartesian products. This paper shows that searching the entire space "is more affordable than has been previously recognized" and that avoiding Cartesian products is not necessarily beneficial. According to the authors, the paper's main contributions are in (a) fully separating join-order enumeration from predicate analysis and (b) presenting "novel implementation techniques" for addressing the join-order enumeration problem.

17.56 Yannis E. Ioannidis, Raymond T. Ng, Kyuseok Shim, and Timos K. Sellis: "Parametric Query Optimization," *Proc. 18th Int. Conf. on Very Large Data Bases, Vancouver, Canada (August 1992).*

Consider the following query:

```
EMP WHERE SALARY > salary
```

(where *salary* is a run-time parameter). Suppose there is an index on SALARY. Then:

- If *salary* is $10,000 per month, then the best way to implement the query is to use the index (because presumably most employees will not qualify);

- If *salary* is $1,000 per month, then the best way to implement the query is by a sequential scan (because presumably most employees *will* qualify).

This example illustrates the point that some optimization decisions are best made at run time, even in a compiling system. The present paper explores the possibility of generating *sets* of query plans at compile time (each plan being "optimal" for some subset of the set of all possible values of the run-time parameters), and then choosing the appropriate plan at run time when the actual parameter values are known. In particular, it focuses on one particular parameter, namely the amount of buffer space available to the query. Experimental results show that the approach described imposes very little time overhead on the optimization process and sacrifices very little in terms of quality of the generated plans; accordingly, it is claimed that the approach can significantly improve query performance. "The savings in execution cost of using a plan that is specifically tailored to actual parameter values . . . could be enormous."

17.57 Navin Kabra and David J. DeWitt: "Efficient Mid-Query Re-Optimization of Sub-Optimal Query Execution Plans," *Proc. 1998 ACM SIGMOD Int. Conf. on Management of Data, Seattle, Wash. (June 1998).*

17.58 Jim Gray: "Parallel Database Systems 101," *Proc. 1995 ACM SIGMOD Int. Conf. on Management of Data, San Jose, Calif. (May 1995).*

This is not a research paper but an extended abstract for a tutorial presentation. The basic idea behind parallel systems in general is to break a large problem into lots of smaller ones that can be solved simultaneously, thereby improving performance. Relational database systems in particular are highly amenable to parallelization because of the nature of the relational model: It is conceptually easy (a) to break relations down into subrelations in a variety of ways, and (b) to break relational expressions down into subexpressions, again in a variety of ways. In the spirit of the title of this reference, we offer a few words on certain major parallel database system concepts.

First of all, the architecture of the underlying hardware will itself presumably involve some kind of parallelism. There are three principal architectures, each involving several processing units, several disk drives, and an interconnection network of some kind:

- *Shared memory:* The network allows all of the processors to access the same memory.

- *Shared disk:* Each processor has its own memory, but the network allows all of the processors to access all of the disks.

- *Shared nothing:* Each processor has its own memory and disks, but the network allows the processors to communicate with each other.

In practice, "shared nothing" is usually the architecture of choice, at least for large systems (the other two approaches quickly run into problems of *interference* as more and more processors are added). To be specific, shared nothing provides both linear **speed-up** (increasing hardware by a factor of N improves response time by a factor of N) and linear **scale-up** (increasing both hardware and data volume by the same factor keeps response time constant). *Note:* "Scale-up" is also known as **scalability.**

There are also several approaches to *data partitioning* (i.e., breaking a relation r into partitions or subrelations and assigning those partitions to n different processors):

- *Range partitioning:* Relation r is divided up into disjoint partitions 1, 2, …, n on the basis of values of some subset s of the attributes of r (conceptually, r is sorted on s and the result divided up into n equal-size partitions). Partition i is then assigned to processor i. This approach is good for queries involving equality or range restrictions on s.

- *Hash partitioning:* Each tuple t of r is assigned to processor $h(t)$, where h is some hash function. This approach is good for queries involving an equality restriction on the hashed attribute(s), also for queries that involve sequential access to the entire relation r.

- *Round robin partitioning:* Conceptually, r is sorted in some way; the ith tuple in the sorted result is then assigned to processor i modulo n. This approach is good for queries that involve sequential access to the entire relation r.

Parallelism can apply to the execution of an individual operation (*intraoperation* parallelism), to the execution of distinct operations within the same query (*interoperation* or *intraquery* parallelism), and to the execution of distinct queries (*interquery* parallelism). References [17.4] and [17.61] contain tutorials on all of these possibilities, and references [17.59–17.60] discuss some specific techniques and algorithms. We remark that a parallel version of *hash join* (see Section 17.7) is particularly effective and widely used in practice.

17.59 Dina Bitton, Haran Boral, David J. DeWitt, and W. Kevin Wilkinson: "Parallel Algorithms for the Execution of Relational Database Operations," *ACM TODS 8,* No. 3 (September 1983).

Presents algorithms for implementing sort, projection, join, aggregation, and update operations in a multi-processor environment. The paper gives general cost formulas that take into account I/O, message, and processor costs, and can be adjusted to different multi-processor architectures.

17.60 Waqar Hasan and Rajeev Motwani: "Optimization Algorithms for Exploiting the Parallelism-Communication Tradeoff in Pipelined Parallelism," Proc. 20th Int. Conf. on Very Large Data Bases, Santiago, Chile (September 1994).

17.61 Abraham Silberschatz, Henry F. Korth, and S. Sudarshan: *Database System Concepts* (3rd edition). New York, N.Y.: McGraw-Hill (1997).

This general textbook on database management includes a full chapter on parallel database systems, as well as one on "database system architectures" (centralized *vs.* client/server *vs.* parallel *vs.* distributed).

ANSWERS TO SELECTED EXERCISES

17.1 a. Valid. b. Valid. c. Valid. d. Not valid. e. Valid. f. Not valid (it would be valid if we replaced the AND by an OR). g. Not valid. h. Not valid. i. Valid.

17.2 By way of example, we show that join is commutative. The join A JOIN B of relations $A\{X,Y\}$ and $B\{Y,Z\}$ is a relation with heading $\{X,Y,Z\}$ and body consisting of the set of all tuples $\{X:x,Y:y,Z:z\}$ such that a tuple appears in A with X value x and Y value y and a tuple appears in B with Y value y and Z value z. This definition is clearly symmetric in A and B. Thus, A JOIN $B \equiv$ B JOIN A. ∎

17.3 By way of example, we show that union is associative. The union A UNION B of two relations A and B is a relation with the same heading as each of A and B and with a body consisting of the set of all tuples t belonging to A or B or both. Thus, if C is another relation with the same heading as A and B:

- The union $(A$ UNION $B)$ UNION C is a relation with the same heading and with a body consisting of all tuples t belonging to $(A$ UNION $B)$ or C or both;

- The union A UNION $(B$ UNION $C)$ is a relation with the same heading and with a body consisting of all tuples t belonging to A or $(B$ UNION $C)$ or both.

These two relations have the same heading, and the body in each case is the set of all tuples t such that t belongs to at least one of A, B, C. The two relations are thus identical. ∎

17.4 We show that union distributes over intersection.

- First, if $t \in A$ UNION $(B$ INTERSECT $C)$, then $t \in A$ or $t \in B$ INTERSECT C.
  - If $t \in A$, then $t \in A$ UNION B and $t \in A$ UNION C and hence $t \in (A$ UNION $B)$ INTERSECT $(A$ UNION $C)$.
  - If $t \in B$ INTERSECT C, then $t \in B$ and $t \in C$, so $t \in A$ UNION B and $t \in A$ UNION C and hence (again) $t \in (A$ UNION $B)$ INTERSECT $(A$ UNION $C)$.

- Conversely, if $t \in (A$ UNION $B)$ INTERSECT $(A$ UNION $C)$, then $t \in A$ UNION B and $t \in A$ UNION C. Hence $t \in A$ or $t \in$ both of B and C. Hence $t \in A$ UNION $(B$ INTERSECT $C)$. ∎

17.5 We show that A UNION $(A$ INTERSECT $B) \equiv A$. If $t \in A$ then clearly $t \in A$ UNION $(A$ INTERSECT $B)$. Conversely, if $t \in A$ UNION $(A$ INTERSECT $B)$, then $t \in A$ or $t \in$ both of A and B; either way, $t \in A$. ∎

17.6 The two conditional cases were covered in Section 17.4. The unconditional cases are straightforward. We show that projection does not distribute over difference by giving the following counterexample. Let $A\{X,Y\}$ and $B\{X,Y\}$ each contain just one tuple, namely the tuples $\{X:x,Y:y\}$ and $\{X:x,Y:z\}$, respectively $(y \neq z)$. Then $(A$ MINUS $B)\{X\}$ gives a relation containing just the tuple $\{X:x\}$, while $A\{X\}$ MINUS $B\{X\}$ gives an empty relation. ∎

17.9 A good set of such rules can be found in reference [17.3].

17.10 A good set of such rules can be found in reference [17.3].

17.11

a. Get "nonLondon" suppliers who do not supply part P2.

b. Get the empty set of suppliers.

c. Get "nonLondon" suppliers such that no supplier supplies fewer kinds of parts.

d. Get the empty set of suppliers.

e. No simplification possible.

f. Get the empty set of pairs of suppliers.

g. Get the empty set of parts.

h. Get "nonParis" suppliers such that no supplier supplies more kinds of parts.

Note that certain queries—to be specific, queries b., d., f., and g.—can be answered directly from the integrity constraints themselves.

17.15 For processing reasons, the true highest and/or lowest value is sometimes some kind of *dummy* value—e.g., the highest "employee name" might be a string of all Z's, the lowest might be a string of all blanks. Estimates of (e.g.) the average increment from one column value to the next in sequence would be skewed if they were based on such dummy values.

CHAPTER 18

Missing Information

18.1 INTRODUCTION

Information is often missing in the real world; examples such as "date of birth unknown," "speaker to be announced," "present address not known," and so on, are common and familiar to all of us. Thus, we clearly need some way of dealing with such missing information inside our database systems. And the approach to this problem most commonly adopted in practice—in SQL in particular, and hence in most commercial products—is based on **nulls** and **three-valued logic** (3VL). For example, we might not know the weight of some given part, say part P7, and so we might say, loosely, that the weight of that part "is null"— meaning, more precisely, that (a) we do know the part exists, and of course (b) we also know it has a weight, but (c) to repeat, we do not know what that weight is.

Let us pursue this example a little further. We obviously cannot put a genuine WEIGHT value in the tuple for part P7. What we do instead, therefore, is *mark* or *flag* the WEIGHT position in that tuple as "null," and then we interpret that mark or flag to mean, precisely, that we do not know what the genuine value is. Now, we might think, informally, of that WEIGHT position as "containing a null," or of the WEIGHT value as "being null," and indeed we often talk in such terms in practice. But it should be clear that such talk *is* only informal, and indeed not very accurate; to say that the WEIGHT component of some tuple "is null" is really to say that *the tuple contains no WEIGHT value at all.* That is why the expression "null value" (which is heard very frequently) is deprecated: The whole point about nulls is precisely that they are not values—they are, to repeat, marks or flags.

Now, we will see in the next section that any scalar comparison in which one of the comparands is null evaluates to the *unknown* truth value, instead of to *true* or *false.* The justification for this state of affairs is the intended interpretation of null as "value unknown": If the value of *A* is unknown, then obviously it is *unknown* whether, for example, *A > B,* **regardless of the value of** *B* (even—perhaps especially—if the value of *B* is unknown as well). Note in particular, therefore, that two nulls are not considered to be equal to one another; i.e., the comparison *A = B* evaluates to *unknown,* not *true,* if *A* and *B* are both null. (They are not considered to be unequal, either; i.e., the comparison *A ≠ B* evaluates to *unknown* as well.) Hence the term "three-valued logic": The concept of nulls, at least as that term is usually understood, inevitably leads us into a logic in which there are three truth values, *true, false,* and *unknown.*

Before we go any further, we should make it very clear that in our opinion (and in that of many other writers too, we hasten to add), nulls and 3VL are a serious mistake and have

584

no place in a clean formal system like the relational model.* Be that as it may, it would not be appropriate to exclude discussion of nulls and 3VL entirely from a book of this nature; hence the present chapter.

The plan of the chapter, then, is as follows. Following this introduction, in Section 18.2 we suspend disbelief for a while and describe (as best we can) the basic ideas behind nulls and 3VL, without offering much in the way of criticism of those ideas. (It is obviously not possible to criticize the ideas properly or fairly without first explaining what those ideas *are*.) Then in Section 18.3 we discuss some of the more important consequences of those ideas, in an attempt to justify our own position that nulls are a mistake. Section 18.4 considers the implications of nulls for primary and foreign keys. Section 18.5 digresses to consider an operation commonly encountered in the context of nulls and 3VL, *viz.* the *outer join* operation. Section 18.6 very briefly considers an alternative approach to missing information, using *special values.* Section 18.7 sketches the relevant aspects of SQL. Finally, Section 18.8 presents a summary.

One last preliminary remark: There are of course many reasons why we might be unable to put a genuine data value in some position within some tuple—"value unknown" is only one possible reason. Others include "value not applicable," "value does not exist," "value undefined," "value not supplied," and so on [18.5].† Indeed, in reference [5.2] Codd proposes that the relational model should be extended to include not one but two nulls, one meaning "value unknown" and the other "value not applicable"; hence, he further proposes that DBMSs should deal in terms of not three- but **four-**valued logic. We have argued against such a proposal elsewhere [18.5]; in this chapter we limit our attention to a single kind of null only, namely the "value unknown" null, which for definiteness we will henceforward often—but not invariably—refer to as **UNK** (for unknown).

18.2 AN OVERVIEW OF THE 3VL APPROACH

In this section we briefly describe the principal components of the 3VL approach to missing information. We begin by considering the effect of nulls—meaning UNKs specifically—on boolean expressions.

---

*For example, to say that a certain part tuple contains no WEIGHT value is to say—by definition—that the tuple in question is not a part tuple after all. Equivalently, it is to say that the tuple in question is not an instantiation of the applicable predicate. The truth is, the very act of trying to state precisely what the nulls scheme is all about is, or should be, sufficient to show why the idea is not very coherent. One consequence is that it is difficult to explain it coherently, too. To quote reference [18.19]: "It all makes sense if you squint a little and don't think too hard."

†We remark, however, that there is no "missing information," as such, in any of these other cases. For example, if we say that the commission for employee Joe is "not applicable," we are saying, quite explicitly, that the property of earning a commission does not apply to Joe; no information is missing here. (It is still the case, however, that if, e.g., Joe's "employee tuple" "contains" a "not applicable null" in the commission position, then that tuple is not an employee tuple—i.e., it is not an instantiation of the "employees" predicate.)

Boolean Expressions

We have already said that any scalar comparison in which either of the comparands is UNK evaluates to the *unknown* truth value, instead of *true* or *false,* and hence that we are dealing with three-valued logic (3VL). *Unknown* (which we will henceforward often—but not invariably—abbreviate to just *unk*) is "the third truth value." Here then are the 3VL truth tables for AND, OR, and NOT (*t = true, f = false, u = unk*):

```
AND | t u f        OR | t u f        NOT|
----+------        ---+------        ---+---
 t  | t u f         t | t t t         t | f
 u  | u u f         u | t u u         u | u
 f  | f f f         f | t u f         f | t
```

Suppose, for example, that A = 3, B = 4, and C is UNK. Then the following expressions have the indicated truth values:

```
A > B AND B > C  :  false
A > B OR  B > C  :  unk
A < B OR  B < C  :  true
NOT ( A = C )    :  unk
```

AND, OR, and NOT are not the only boolean operators we need, however [18.11]; another important one is MAYBE [18.5], with truth table as follows:

```
MAYBE |
------+---
  t   | f
  u   | t
  f   | f
```

To see why MAYBE is desirable, consider the query "Get employees who *may* be—but are not definitely known to be—programmers born before January 18th, 1971, with a salary less than $50,000." With the MAYBE operator, the query can be stated quite succinctly as follows:

```
EMP WHERE MAYBE ( JOB = 'Programmer' AND
                  DOB < DATE '1971-1-18' AND
                  SALARY < 50000.00 )
```

(We have assumed that attributes JOB, DOB, and SALARY of relvar EMP are of types CHAR, DATE, and RATIONAL, respectively.) Without the MAYBE operator, however, the query looks something like this:

```
EMP WHERE ( IS_UNK ( JOB ) AND
            DOB < DATE '1971-1-18' AND
            SALARY < 50000.00 )
    OR    ( JOB = 'Programmer' AND
            IS_UNK ( DOB ) AND
            SALARY < 50000.00 )
    OR    ( JOB = 'Programmer' AND
            DOB < DATE '1971-1-18' AND
            IS_UNK ( SALARY ) )
    OR    ( IS_UNK ( JOB ) AND
            IS_UNK ( DOB ) AND
            SALARY < 50000.00 )
```

```
OR     ( IS_UNK ( JOB ) AND
         DOB < DATE '1971-1-18' AND
         IS_UNK ( SALARY ) )
OR     ( JOB = 'Programmer' AND
         IS_UNK ( DOB ) AND
         IS_UNK ( SALARY ) )
OR     ( IS_UNK ( JOB ) AND
         IS_UNK ( DOB ) AND
         IS_UNK ( SALARY ) )
```

(We have assumed the existence of another truth-valued operator called **IS_UNK,** which takes a single scalar expression operand and returns *true* if that operand evaluates to UNK and *false* otherwise.)

Incidentally, the foregoing should not be construed to mean that MAYBE is the *only* new boolean operator needed for 3VL. In practice, for example, a TRUE_OR_MAYBE operator could be very useful [18.5]. See the annotation to reference [18.11] in the "References and Bibliography" section.

EXISTS and FORALL

Despite the fact that most of our examples in this book are based on the algebra rather than the calculus, we do need to consider the implications of 3VL for the calculus quantifiers EXISTS and FORALL. As explained in Chapter 7, we define EXISTS and FORALL as iterated OR and AND, respectively. In other words, if (a) *r* is a relation with tuples *t1, t2, ..., tm,* (b) *V* is a range variable that ranges over that relation, and (c) *p(V)* is a boolean expression in which *V* occurs as a free variable, then the expression

```
EXISTS V ( p ( V ) )
```

is defined to be equivalent to

```
false OR p ( t1 ) OR ... OR p ( tm )
```

Likewise, the expression

```
FORALL V ( p ( V ) )
```

is defined to be equivalent to

```
true AND p ( t1 ) AND ... AND p ( tm )
```

So what happens if *p(ti)* evaluates to *unk* for some *i?* By way of example, let relation *r* contain exactly the following tuples:

```
(   1,    2,    3   )
(   1,    2,   UNK )
( UNK,  UNK,  UNK )
```

For simplicity, assume that (a) the three attributes, in left-to-right order as shown, are called *A, B,* and *C,* respectively; (b) every attribute is of type INTEGER. Then the following expressions have the indicated values:

```
EXISTS V ( V.C > 1 )                 :  true
EXISTS V ( V.B > 2 )                 :  unk
EXISTS V ( MAYBE ( V.A > 3 ) )       :  true
EXISTS V ( IS_UNK ( V.C ) )          :  true

FORALL V ( V.A > 1 )                 :  false
FORALL V ( V.B > 1 )                 :  unk
FORALL V ( MAYBE ( V.C > 1 ) )       :  false
```

Computational Expressions

Consider the numeric expression

```
WEIGHT * 454
```

where WEIGHT represents the weight of some part, P7 say. What if the weight of part P7 happens to be UNK?—what then is the value of the expression? The answer is that it too must be considered to be UNK. In general, in fact, *any* numeric expression is considered to evaluate to UNK if any of the operands of that expression is itself UNK. Thus, e.g., if WEIGHT happens to be UNK, then all of the following expressions also evaluate to UNK:

```
WEIGHT + 454      454 + WEIGHT      + WEIGHT
WEIGHT - 454      454 - WEIGHT      - WEIGHT
WEIGHT * 454      454 * WEIGHT
WEIGHT / 454      454 / WEIGHT
```

Note: Perhaps we should point out right away that the foregoing treatment of numeric expressions does give rise to certain anomalies. For example, the expression WEIGHT – WEIGHT, which should clearly yield zero, actually yields UNK, and the expression WEIGHT/0, which should clearly raise a "zero divide" error, also yields UNK (assuming in both cases that WEIGHT is UNK in the first place, of course). We ignore such anomalies until further notice.

Analogous considerations apply to all other scalar types and operators, except for (a) the comparison operators (see the two previous subsections), (b) the operator IS_UNK discussed earlier, and (c) the operator IF_UNK discussed in the next paragraph. Thus, e.g., the character string expression *A* || *B* returns UNK if *A* is UNK or *B* is UNK or both. (Again there are certain anomalous cases, details of which we omit here.)

The **IF_UNK** operator takes two scalar expression operands and returns the value of the first operand unless that operand evaluates to UNK, in which case it returns the value of the second operand instead (in other words, the operator effectively provides a way to convert an UNK to some nonUNK value). For example, suppose UNKs are permitted for the suppliers CITY attribute. Then the expression

```
EXTEND S ADD IF_UNK ( CITY, 'City unknown' ) AS SCITY
```

yields a result in which the SCITY value is "City unknown" for any supplier whose city is given as UNK in S.

Note, incidentally, that IF_UNK can be defined in terms of IS_UNK. To be specific, the expression

```
IF_UNK ( exp1, exp2 )
```

(where expressions *exp1* and *exp2* must be of the same type) is equivalent to the expression

```
IF IS_UNK ( exp1 ) THEN exp2 ELSE exp1 END IF
```

UNK Is Not *unk*

It is important to understand that UNK (the "value unknown" null) and *unk* (the *unknown* truth value) are **not the same thing.*** Indeed, this state of affairs is an immediate consequence of the fact that *unk* is a value (a truth value, to be precise), whereas UNK is not a value at all. But let us be a little more specific. Suppose X is a variable of type BOOLEAN. Then X must have one of the values *true, false,* or *unk.* Thus, the statement "X is *unk*" means, precisely, that the value of X is **known to be** *unk.* By contrast, the statement "X is UNK" means that the value of X is **not known.**

Can a Domain Contain an UNK?

It is also an immediate consequence of the fact that UNK is not a value that UNKs cannot appear in domains (domains are sets of *values*). Indeed, if it *were* possible for a domain to contain an UNK, then type constraint checks for such a domain would never fail! However, since domains in fact *cannot* contain UNKs, a "relation" that includes an UNK—whatever else it might be—is actually **not a relation at all,** neither by the definition we gave in Chapter 5, nor by Codd's original definition as given in reference [5.1]. We will return to this important point in Section 18.6, later.

Relational Expressions

Now we turn our attention to the effect of UNKs on the operators of the relational algebra. For simplicity we limit ourselves to the operators product, restrict, project, union, and difference (the effect of UNKs on the other operators can be determined from their effect on these five).

First of all, **product** is unaffected.

Second, the **restriction** operation is (slightly) redefined to return a relation whose body contains only those tuples for which the restriction condition evaluates to *true,* i.e., not to *false* and not to *unk. Note:* We were tacitly assuming this redefinition in our MAYBE example in the subsection "Boolean Expressions," earlier.

Next, **projection.** Projection of course involves the elimination of redundant duplicate tuples. Now, in conventional *two*-valued logic (2VL), two tuples are duplicates of one another if and only if they have the same attributes and corresponding attributes have equal

---

*SQL3 thinks they are, however (see Appendix B).

values. In 3VL, however, some of those attribute values might be UNK, and UNK (as we have seen) is not equal to *anything,* not even itself. Are we then forced to conclude that a tuple that contains an UNK can never be a duplicate of anything, not even of itself?

According to Codd, the answer to this question is *no:* Two UNKs, even though they are not equal to one another, are still considered to be "duplicates" of one another for purposes of duplicate tuple elimination [13.6].* The apparent contradiction is explained away as follows:

> [Equality testing] for duplicate removal is . . . at a lower level of detail than equality testing in the evaluation of retrieval conditions. Hence, it is possible to adopt a different rule.

We leave it to you to judge whether this rationale is reasonable or not. Anyway, let us accept it for now, and hence accept the following definition:

- Two tuples are **duplicates** of one another if and only if (a) they have the same attributes, and (b) for each such attribute, either the two tuples both have the same value, or they both have an UNK, in that attribute position.

With this extended definition of "duplicate tuples," the original definition of projection now applies unchanged.

Union likewise involves the elimination of redundant duplicate tuples, and the same definition of duplicate tuples applies. Thus, we define the union of two relations *r1* and *r2* (of the same type) to be that relation *r* (again of the same type) whose body consists of all possible tuples *t* such that *t* is a duplicate of some tuple of *r1* or of some tuple of *r2* (or both).

Finally—even though it does not involve any duplicate elimination as such—**difference** is defined analogously; i.e., a tuple *t* appears in *r1* MINUS *r2* if and only if it is a duplicate of some tuple of *r1* and not a duplicate of any tuple of *r2*. (As for **intersect,** of course it is not primitive, but for completeness we note that it too is defined analogously; i.e., a tuple *t* appears in *r1* INTERSECT *r2* if and only if it is a duplicate of some tuple of *r1* and of some tuple of *r2*.)

Update Operations

There are two general points to make under this heading:

1. If attribute *A* of relvar *R* permits UNKs, and if a tuple is inserted into *R* and no value is provided for *A,* the system will automatically place an UNK in the *A* position in that tuple. If attribute *A* of relvar *R* does not permit UNKs, an attempt to create a tuple in *R* via either INSERT or UPDATE in which the *A* position is UNK is an error. (Of course, we are assuming in both cases that no nonUNK default value has been defined for *A*.)

---

*Reference [13.6] was the first of Codd's papers to discuss the missing information problem (although that problem was not the paper's primary focus—see Chapter 13). Among other things, the paper proposes "maybe" versions of the Θ-join, Θ-select (i.e., restrict), and divide operators (see Exercise 18.4), and "outer" versions of the union, intersection, difference, Θ-join, and natural join operators (see Section 18.5).

2. An attempt via either INSERT or UPDATE to create a duplicate tuple in *R* is an error, as usual. The definition of "duplicate tuples" here is as in the previous subsection.

Integrity Constraints

As explained in Chapter 8, an integrity constraint is basically a boolean expression that must not evaluate to *false.* Note, therefore, that the constraint is not considered to be violated if it evaluates to *unk* (in fact, we were tacitly assuming as much in our remarks earlier in this section regarding type constraints). Technically, of course, we should say in such a case that it is *not known* whether the constraint is violated, but, just as *unk* is regarded as *false* for the purposes of a WHERE clause, so it is regarded as *true* for the purposes of an integrity constraint (speaking a trifle loosely).

18.3   SOME CONSEQUENCES OF THE FOREGOING SCHEME

The 3VL approach as described in the previous section has a number of logical consequences, not all of which are immediately obvious. We discuss some of those consequences, and their significance, in this section.

Expression Transformations

First, we observe that several expressions that always evaluate to *true* in 2VL do not necessarily always evaluate to *true* in 3VL. Here are some examples, with commentary. Please note that the list is nowhere near exhaustive.

- *The comparison* x = x *does not necessarily give* true

  In 2VL, any value *x* is always equal to itself. In 3VL, however, *x* is not equal to itself if it happens to be UNK.

- *The boolean expression* p *OR NOT (*p*) does not necessarily give* true

  Here *p* is a boolean expression in turn. Now, in 2VL, the expression *p* OR NOT(*p*) necessarily evaluates to *true,* regardless of the value of *p.* In 3VL, however, if *p* happens to evaluate to *unk,* the overall expression evaluates to *unk* OR NOT(*unk*), i.e., to *unk* OR *unk,* which reduces to *unk,* not *true.*

  This particular example accounts for a well-known counterintuitive property of 3VL, which we illustrate as follows: If we issue the query "Get all suppliers in London," followed by the query "Get all suppliers not in London," and take the union of the two results, we do *not* necessarily get all suppliers. Instead, we need to include "all suppliers who *may be* in London."*

---

*As this discussion suggests, an expression that does always evaluate to *true* in 3VL—i.e., the 3VL analog of the 2VL expression *p* OR NOT(*p*)—is *p* OR NOT(*p*) OR MAYBE(*p*).

The point about this example is, of course, that while the two cases "city is London" and "city is not London" are mutually exclusive and exhaust the full range of possibilities in the real world, the database does *not* contain the real world—instead, it contains only **knowledge about** the real world. And there are three possible cases, not two, concerning knowledge about the real world; in the example, the three cases are "city is known to be London," "city is known not to be London," and "city is not known." Furthermore, of course (as reference [18.6] puts it), we obviously cannot ask the system questions about the real world, we can only ask it questions about its *knowledge* of the real world as represented by the data in the database. The counterintuitive nature of the example thus derives from a confusion over realms: The user is thinking in terms of the realm that is the real world, but the system is operating in terms of the realm that is *its knowledge about* that real world.

Note: It seems to this writer, however, that such a confusion over realms is a trap very easily fallen into. Note that *every single query* mentioned in previous chapters in this book (examples, exercises, etc.) has been stated in "real world" terms, not "knowledge about the real world" terms—and this book is certainly not unusual in this regard.

- *The expression* r *JOIN* r *does not necessarily give* r

  In 2VL, forming the join of a relation *r* with itself always yields the original relation *r* (i.e., join is *idempotent*). In 3VL, however, a tuple with an UNK in any position will not join to itself, because join, unlike union, is based on "retrieval-type" equality testing, not "duplicate-type" equality testing.

- *INTERSECT is no longer a special case of JOIN*

  This fact is a consequence of the fact that (again) join is based on retrieval-type equality testing, while intersection is based on duplicate-type equality testing.

- A = B *and* B = C *together do not imply* A = C

  An extended illustration of this particular point is given below in the subsection "The Departments and Employees Example."

To sum up, many equivalences that are valid in 2VL break down in 3VL. One very serious consequence of such breakdowns is as follows. In general, simple equivalences such as *r* JOIN *r* ≡ *r* lie at the heart of the various **laws of transformation** that are used to convert queries into some more efficient form, as explained in Chapter 17. Furthermore, those laws are used not only by the *system* (when doing optimization), but also by *users* (when trying to decide the "best" way to state a given query). And if the equivalences are not valid, then the laws are not valid. And if the laws are not valid, then the transformations are not valid. And if the transformations are not valid, then we will get **wrong answers** out of the system.

The Departments and Employees Example

In order to illustrate the problem of incorrect transformations, we discuss a specific example in some detail. (The example is taken from reference [18.9]; for reasons that are unimportant here, it is based on relational calculus instead of relational algebra.) Suppose

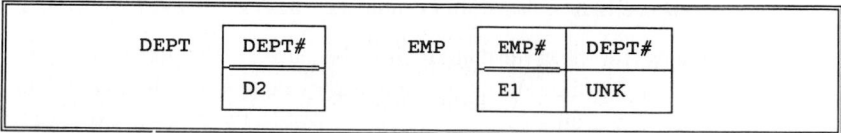

Fig. 18.1   The departments and employees database

we are given the simple departments and employees database shown in Fig. 18.1. Consider the expression

```
DEPT.DEPT# = EMP.DEPT# AND EMP.DEPT# = DEPT# ( 'D1' )
```

(which might be part of a query, of course); DEPT and EMP here are implicit range variables. For the only tuples that exist in the database, this expression evaluates to *unk* AND *unk,* i.e., to *unk.* However, a "good" optimizer will observe that the expression is of the form $a = b$ AND $b = c$, will therefore infer that $a = c$, and hence will append an additional restriction term $a = c$ to the original expression (as discussed in Chapter 17, Section 17.4), yielding

```
DEPT.DEPT# = EMP.DEPT# AND EMP.DEPT# = DEPT# ( 'D1' )
                 AND DEPT.DEPT# = DEPT# ( 'D1' )
```

This modified expression now evaluates to *unk* AND *unk* AND *false,* i.e., to *false* (for the only two tuples in the database). It follows, therefore, that the query (e.g.)

```
EMP.EMP# WHERE EXISTS DEPT ( NOT
( DEPT.DEPT# = EMP.DEPT# AND EMP.DEPT# = DEPT# ( 'D1' ) ) )
```

will return employee E1 if "optimized" in the foregoing sense and will not do so otherwise. In other words, of course, the "optimization" is in fact not valid. Thus we see that certain optimizations that are perfectly valid—and useful—under conventional 2VL are no longer valid under 3VL.

Note the implications of the foregoing for extending a 2VL system to support 3VL. At best, such an extension is likely to require some reengineering of the existing system, since portions of the existing optimizer code are likely to be invalidated; at worst, it will introduce bugs. More generally, note the implications for extending a system that supports *n*-valued logic to one that supports (*n*+1)-valued logic, for any *n* greater than one; analogous difficulties will arise for every discrete value of *n.*

The Interpretation Issue

Now let us examine the departments and employees example a little more carefully. Since employee E1 does have some corresponding department in the real world, the UNK does stand for some real value, say *d.* Now, either *d* is D1 or it is not. If it is, then the original expression

```
DEPT.DEPT# = EMP.DEPT# AND EMP.DEPT# = DEPT# ( 'D1' )
```

evaluates (for the given data) to *false,* because the first term evaluates to *false.* Alternatively, if *d* is not D1, then the expression also evaluates (for the given data) to *false,* because the second term evaluates to *false.* In other words, the original expression is always *false* in the real world, **regardless of what real value the UNK stands for.** Thus, the result that is correct according to three-valued logic and the result that is correct in the real world are not the same thing! In other words, three-valued logic does not behave in accordance with the way the real world behaves; i.e., 3VL does not seem to have a sensible **interpretation** in terms of how the real world works.

Note: This question of interpretation is very far from being the only problem arising from nulls and 3VL (see references [18.1–18.11] for an extensive discussion of several others). It is not even the most fundamental (see the next subsection). However, it is perhaps the one of greatest pragmatic significance; in this writer's opinion, in fact, it is a showstopper.

Predicates Again

Suppose the relation that is the current value of the EMP relvar contains just two tuples, (E2,D2) and (E1,UNK). The first corresponds to the proposition "There is an employee identified as E2 in the department identified as D2." The second corresponds to the proposition "There is an employee identified as E1." (Remember that to say that a tuple "contains an UNK" is really to say that the tuple actually contains nothing at all in the applicable position; thus, the "tuple" (E1,UNK)—if it is a tuple at all, in itself a dubious notion—should really be considered as being of the form just (E1).) In other words, the two tuples are instantiations of *two different predicates,* and the "relation" is not a relation at all but instead (loosely) a kind of union of two different relations with, in particular, two different headings.

Now, it might be suggested that the situation can be rescued by asserting that there really is just one predicate after all, one that involves an OR:

> There is an employee identified as E# in the department identified as D# **OR** there is an employee identified as E#.

Observe, however, that now—thanks to the Closed World Assumption—the relation will have to contain a "tuple" of the form (E*i*,UNK) for all employees E*i*! Generalizing this rescue attempt to a "relation" that "contains UNKs" in several different "attributes" is almost too horrible to contemplate. (And in any case the "relation" that results will still not be a relation—see the next paragraph.)

To put the foregoing another way: If the value of a given attribute within a given tuple within a given relation "is UNK," then (to repeat) that attribute position actually contains **nothing at all** . . . which implies that the "attribute" is not an attribute, the "tuple" is not a tuple, the "relation" is not a relation, and the foundation for what we are doing (whatever else it might be) is no longer mathematical relation theory. In other words, UNKs and 3VL *undermine the entire foundation of the relational model.*

18.4   NULLS AND KEYS

Note: We now drop the term UNK (for the most part) and revert for historical reasons to the more traditional terminology of "nulls."

Despite the message of the previous section, the fact is that nulls and 3VL are supported in most products at the time of writing. Furthermore, such support has important implications for keys in particular. In this section, therefore, we explore those implications briefly.

Primary Keys

As explained in Section 8.8, the relational model has historically required that (in the case of base relvars, at least) exactly one candidate key be chosen as the *primary* key for the relvar in question. The remaining candidate keys, if any, are then said to be *alternate* keys. And then, along with the primary key concept, the model has historically included the following "metaconstraint" or rule (the *entity integrity* rule):

- **Entity integrity:** No component of the primary key of any base relvar is allowed to accept nulls.

The rationale for this rule goes something like this: (a) Tuples in base relations represent entities in the real world; (b) entities in the real world are identifiable by definition; (c) therefore their counterparts in the database must be identifiable too; (d) primary key values serve as those identifiers in the database; (e) therefore primary key values must not be "missing."

Points arising:

1. First of all, it is often thought that the entity integrity rule says something along the lines of "Primary key values must be unique," but it does not. (It is true that primary key values must be unique, of course, but that requirement is implied by the basic definition of the primary key concept *per se.*)

2. Next, note that the rule applies only to *primary* keys; *alternate* keys can apparently have nulls allowed. But if *AK* is an alternate key that has nulls allowed, then *AK* could not have been chosen as the primary key, because of the entity integrity rule; so in what sense exactly was *AK* a "candidate" key in the first place? Alternatively, if we have to say that alternate keys cannot have nulls allowed either, then the entity integrity rule applies to *all candidate keys,* not just to the primary key. Either way, there seems to be something wrong with the rule as stated.

3. Finally, note that the entity integrity rule applies only to *base relvars;* other relvars can apparently have a primary key for which nulls are allowed. As a trivial and obvious example, consider the projection of a relvar *R* over any attribute *A* that has nulls allowed. The rule thus violates *The Principle of Interchangeability* (of base and derived relvars). In our opinion, this would be a strong argument for rejecting it (even if it did not involve nulls, a concept we reject anyway).

Note: Suppose we agreed to drop the whole idea of nulls, and used *special values* instead to represent missing information (just as we do in the real world, in fact—see Section 18.6, later). Then we might want to retain a modified version of the entity integrity rule—"No component of the primary key of any base relvar is allowed to accept such special values"—as a *guideline,* but *not* as an inviolable law (much as the ideas of further normalization serve as guidelines, but not as inviolable laws). Fig. 18.2 gives an example (taken from reference [5.7]) of a base relvar called SURVEY for which we might want to violate that guideline; it represents the results of a salary survey, showing the average, maximum, and minimum salary by birth year for a certain sample population (BIRTHYEAR is the primary key). And the tuple with the special BIRTHYEAR value "????" represents people who declined to answer the question "When were you born?"

SURVEY	BIRTHYEAR	AVGSAL	MAXSAL	MINSAL
	1960	85K	130K	33K
	1961	82K	125K	32K
	1962	77K	99K	32K
	1963	78K	97K	35K
	....	...	...	...
	1970	29K	35K	12K
	????	56K	117K	20K

Fig. 18.2   Base relvar SURVEY (sample value)

Foreign Keys

Consider the departments and employees database of Fig. 18.1 once again. You might not have noticed at the time, but we deliberately did not say that attribute DEPT# of relvar EMP in that figure was a foreign key. But now suppose it is. Then it is clear that the referential integrity rule needs some refinement, because foreign keys must now apparently be allowed to accept nulls, and null foreign key values obviously violate the rule as originally stated in Chapter 8:

■ **Referential integrity** *(original version):* The database must not contain any unmatched foreign key values.

Actually, we can keep the rule as stated, so long as we extend the definition of the term "unmatched foreign key value" appropriately. To be specific, we now define an unmatched foreign key value to be a **nonnull** foreign key value in some referencing relvar for which there does not exist a matching value of the relevant candidate key in the relevant referenced relvar.

Points arising:

1. Whether or not any given foreign key is allowed to accept nulls will have to be specified as part of the database definition. (In fact, of course, the same is true for attributes in general, regardless of whether they are part of some foreign key.)

2. The possibility that foreign keys might accept nulls raises the possibility of another referential action, SET NULL, that might be specified in a foreign key DELETE or UPDATE rule. For example:

```
VAR SP BASE RELATION { ... } ...
    FOREIGN KEY { S# } REFERENCES S
                       ON DELETE SET NULL
                       ON UPDATE SET NULL ;
```

With these specifications, a DELETE operation on the suppliers relvar will set the foreign key to null in all matching shipments and then delete the applicable suppliers; likewise, an UPDATE operation on attribute S# in the suppliers relvar will set the foreign key to null in all matching shipments and then update the applicable suppliers. *Note:* SET NULL can be specified only for a foreign key that accepts nulls in the first place, of course.

3. Last, we observe that the apparent "need" to permit nulls in foreign keys can be avoided by appropriate database design [18.20]. Consider departments and employees once again, for example. If it is really possible for the department number to be unknown for certain employees, then (as suggested near the end of the previous section) it would clearly be better not to include DEPT# in the EMP relvar at all, but rather to have a separate relvar ED (say), with attributes EMP# and DEPT#, to represent the fact that a specified employee is in a specified department. Then the fact that a certain employee has an unknown department can be represented by the *omission* of a tuple for that employee from relvar ED.

18.5   OUTER JOIN (A DIGRESSION)

In this section we digress briefly to discuss an operation known as **outer join** (see references [18.3–18.4], [18.7], and [18.14–18.16]). Outer join is an extended form of the regular or *inner* join operation. It differs from the inner join in that tuples in one relation having no counterpart in the other appear in the result with nulls in the other attribute positions, instead of simply being ignored as they normally are. It is not a primitive operation; for example, the following expression could be used to construct the outer join of suppliers and shipments on supplier numbers (assuming for the sake of the example that "NULL" is a legal scalar expression):

```
( S JOIN SP )
  UNION
( EXTEND ( ( S { S# } MINUS SP { S# } ) JOIN S )
                         ADD NULL AS P#, NULL AS QTY )
```

The result includes tuples for suppliers who supply no parts, extended with nulls in the P# and QTY positions.

Let us examine this example a little more closely. Refer to Fig. 18.3. In that figure, the top portion shows some sample data values, the middle portion shows the corresponding inner join, and the bottom portion shows the corresponding outer join. As the figure indicates, the inner join "loses information"—speaking *very* loosely—for suppliers

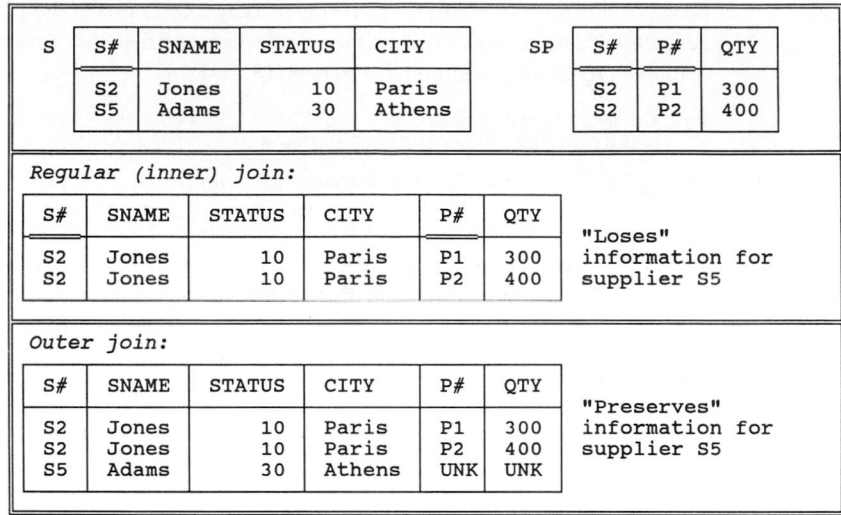

Fig. 18.3   Inner *vs.* outer join (example)

who supply no parts (supplier S5, in the example), whereas the outer join "preserves" such information. Indeed, this distinction is the whole point of outer join.

Now, the problem that outer join is intended to solve—*viz.,* the fact that inner join sometimes "loses information"—is certainly an important problem. Some writers would therefore argue that the system should provide direct, explicit support for outer join, instead of requiring the user to indulge in circumlocutions to achieve the desired effect. Codd in particular now considers outer join to be an intrinsic part of the relational model [5.2]. However, we do not endorse this position ourselves, for the following reasons among others:

- First of all, of course, the operation involves nulls, and we are opposed to nulls anyway for numerous good reasons.

- Second, note that there exist several different varieties of outer join—left, right, and full outer Θ-*join,* and left, right, and full outer *natural* join. (The "left" joins preserve information from the first operand, the "right" joins preserve information from the second operand, and the "full" joins do both; the example of Fig. 18.3 is a left join—a left outer natural join, to be precise.) Note further that there is no very straightforward way of deriving the outer natural joins from the outer Θ-joins [18.7]. As a result, it is unclear as to exactly which outer joins need to be explicitly supported.

- Next, the outer join question is far from being as trivial as the simple example of Fig. 18.3 might suggest. In fact, as reference [18.7] puts it, outer join suffers from a number of *Nasty Properties* that together imply that adding outer join support to existing languages—in particular, to SQL—is difficult to do gracefully. Several DBMS products have tried to solve this problem and dismally failed (i.e., they have tripped over those Nasty Properties). See reference [18.7] for an extensive discussion of this issue.

- Finally, *relation-valued attributes* provide an alternative approach to the problem anyway—an approach that does not involve nulls and does not involve outer join either and is in fact (in this writer's opinion) an altogether more elegant solution. Given the sample data values from the top of Fig. 18.3, for example, the expression

```
WITH ( S RENAME S# AS X ) AS Y :
EXTEND Y ADD ( SP WHERE S# = X ) AS PQ
```

yields the result shown in Fig. 18.4.

S#	SNAME	STATUS	CITY	PQ	
S2	Jones	10	Paris	P#	QTY
				P1	300
				P2	400
S5	Adams	30	Athens	P#	QTY

Fig. 18.4   Preserving information for supplier S5 (a better way)

Observe in particular that in Fig. 18.4 the empty set of parts supplied by supplier S5 is represented by an empty set, not (as in Fig. 18.3) by some weird "null." To represent an empty set by an empty set seems like an obviously good idea. In fact, *there would be no need for outer join at all* if relation-valued attributes were properly supported.

To pursue the point just a moment longer: How are we supposed to *interpret* the nulls that appear in the result of an outer join, anyway? What do they mean in the example of Fig. 18.3, for instance? They certainly do not mean either "value unknown" or "value does not apply"; in fact, the only interpretation that does make any logical sense is, precisely, "value is the empty set." See reference [18.7] for further discussion of this issue as well.

We close this section by remarking that it is also possible to define "outer" versions of certain other operations of the relational algebra—specifically, the union, intersection, and difference operations [13.6]—and again Codd now regards at least one of these, namely *outer union,* as part of the relational model [5.2]. Such operations permit unions (etc.) to be performed between two relations even if those relations are not of the same type; they basically work by extending each operand to include those attributes that are peculiar to the other (so that the operands are now of the same type), putting nulls in every tuple for all such added attributes, and then performing a normal union or intersection or difference, as applicable.* We do not discuss these operations in detail, however, for the following reasons:

- Outer intersection is guaranteed to return an empty relation, except in the special case in which the original relations are of the same type in the first place, in which case it degenerates to the normal intersection.

- Outer difference is guaranteed to return its first operand, except in the special case in which the original relations are of the same type in the first place, in which case it degenerates to the normal difference.

- Outer union has *major* problems of interpretation (they are much worse than those arising with outer join). See reference [18.2] for further discussion.

18.6   SPECIAL VALUES

We have seen that nulls wreck the relational model. In fact, it is worth pointing out that the relational model managed perfectly well without nulls for ten years!—the model was first defined in 1969 [5.1], nulls were not added until 1979 [13.1].

Suppose, therefore, that—as suggested in Section 18.4—we agree to drop the whole idea of nulls, and use *special values* instead to represent missing information. Note that using special values is exactly what we do in the real world. In the real world, for example, we might use the special value "?" to denote the hours worked by a certain employee if the actual value is unknown for some reason.[†] Thus, the general idea is simply to use an appropriate special value, distinct from all regular values of the attribute in question, when no regular value can be used. Note that the special value must be a value from the applicable domain; in the "hours worked" example, therefore, the type of the HOURS_WORKED attribute is not just integers, but integers plus whatever the special value is.

Now, we would be the first to admit that the foregoing scheme is not very elegant, but it does have the overwhelming advantage of *not undermining the logical foundations of the relational model.* For the remainder of this book, therefore, we will simply ignore the possibility of null support (except in certain SQL-specific contexts, where occasional references to nulls are unavoidable). See reference [18.12] for a detailed description of the special values scheme.

---

*This explanation refers to the operations as originally defined [13.6]. Reference [5.2] changed the definitions somewhat; you are referred to that book for the specifics (if you care).

†Observe that the one thing we do *not* do is use a null for this purpose. There is no such thing as a null in the real world.

18.7   SQL FACILITIES

SQL's support for nulls and 3VL follows the broad outlines of the approach described in Sections 18.1–18.5 above. Thus, for example, when SQL applies a WHERE clause to some table *T,* it eliminates all rows of *T* for which the expression in that WHERE clause evaluates to *false* or to *unk* (i.e., not to *true*). Likewise, when it applies a HAVING clause to some "grouped table" *G* (see Appendix A), it eliminates all groups of *G* for which the expression in that HAVING clause evaluates to *false* or to *unk* (i.e., not to *true*). In what follows, therefore, we merely draw your attention to certain 3VL features that are specific to SQL *per se,* instead of being an intrinsic part of the 3VL approach as previously discussed.

Note: The full implications and ramifications of SQL's null support are very complex. For additional information, we refer you to the official standard document [4.22] or the detailed tutorial treatment in reference [4.19].

Data Definition

As explained in Chapter 5, Section 5.5, columns in base tables usually have an associated *default* value, and that default value is often defined, explicitly or implicitly, to be null. Furthermore, columns in base tables always *permit* nulls, unless there is an integrity constraint—probably just NOT NULL—for the column in question that expressly prohibits them. The representation of nulls is implementation-dependent; however, it must be such that the system can distinguish nulls from all possible nonnull values (even though the comparison "null $\neq x$" does not give *true!*).

Table Expressions

Recall from Chapter 7, Section 7.7, that explicit JOIN support was added to SQL with the SQL/92 standard. If the keyword JOIN is prefixed with LEFT, RIGHT, or FULL (optionally followed by the noiseword OUTER in each case), then the join in question is an *outer* join. Here are some examples:

```
S LEFT JOIN SP ON S.S# = SP.S#

S LEFT JOIN SP USING ( S# )

S LEFT NATURAL JOIN SP
```

These three expressions are effectively all equivalent, except that the first produces a table with two identical columns (both called S#) and the second and third produce a table with just one such column.

SQL also supports an approximation to outer union, which it calls *union join.* The details are beyond the scope of this book.

Conditional Expressions

As noted in Chapter 8, conditional expressions are the SQL analog of what we have else-where been calling *boolean* expressions (they are explained in detail in Appendix A). Not surprisingly, such expressions are the part of SQL most dramatically affected by nulls and 3VL. We content ourselves here with a few pertinent remarks.

■ *Tests for null:* SQL provides two special comparison operators, IS NULL and IS NOT NULL, to test for the presence or absence of nulls. The syntax is:

```
<row constructor> IS [ NOT ] NULL
```

(see Appendix A for the details of *<row constructor>*). There is one trap for the un-wary: The two expressions *r* IS NOT NULL and NOT (*r* IS NULL) are *not* equivalent. For explanation, see reference [4.19].

■ *Tests for* true, false, unknown: If *p* is a conditional expression in parentheses, then the following are also conditional expressions:

```
p IS [ NOT ] TRUE
p IS [ NOT ] FALSE
p IS [ NOT ] UNKNOWN
```

The meanings of these expressions are as indicated by the following truth table:

p	*true*	*false*	*unk*
p IS TRUE	*true*	*false*	*false*
p IS NOT TRUE	*false*	*true*	*true*
p IS FALSE	*false*	*true*	*false*
p IS NOT FALSE	*true*	*false*	*true*
p IS UNKNOWN	*false*	*false*	*true*
p IS NOT UNKNOWN	*true*	*true*	*false*

Observe, therefore, that the expressions *p* IS NOT TRUE and NOT *p* are not equiva-lent. *Note:* The expression *p* IS UNKNOWN corresponds to our MAYBE(*p*).

■ *MATCH conditions:* The syntax of *<match condition>*s—see Appendix A—includes a PARTIAL *vs.* FULL option (not shown and not discussed in Appendix A) that can affect the result if nulls are present:

```
<row constructor> MATCH [ UNIQUE ]
                [ PARTIAL | FULL ] ( <table expression> )
```

There are thus six different cases, depending on (a) whether the UNIQUE option is specified or not and (b) whether the PARTIAL *vs.* FULL option is specified or not (and if it is, which it is). The details are complex, however, and beyond the scope of this book. See reference [4.19] for further discussion.

■ *EXISTS conditions:* See the annotation to reference [18.6].

Scalar Expressions

■ *"Literals":* The keyword NULL can be used as a kind of literal representation of null (e.g., in an INSERT statement). Note, however, that this keyword cannot appear in all contexts in which literals can appear; as the standard puts it, "there is no *<literal>* for a null value, although the key word NULL is used in some places to indicate that a null value is desired" [4.22]. Thus, for example, it is not possible to specify NULL explicitly as an operand of a simple comparison—e.g., "WHERE X = NULL" is illegal. (The correct form is "WHERE X IS NULL," of course.)

■ *COALESCE:* COALESCE is the SQL analog of our IF_UNK operator (see Section 18.2).

■ *Aggregate operators:* The SQL aggregate operators SUM, AVG, etc. do *not* behave in accordance with the rules for scalar operators explained in Section 18.2, but instead simply ignore any nulls in their argument (except for COUNT(*), where nulls are treated just as if they were regular values). Also, if the argument to such an operator happens to evaluate to an empty set, COUNT returns zero; the other operators all return null. (As noted in Chapter 7, this latter behavior is logically incorrect, but it is the way SQL is defined.)

■ *"Scalar subqueries":* If a scalar expression is in fact a table expression enclosed in parentheses—for example, (SELECT S.CITY FROM S WHERE S.S# = 'S1')—then normally that table expression is required to evaluate to a table containing exactly one column and exactly one row. The value of the scalar expression is then taken to be, precisely, the single scalar value contained within that table. But if the table expression evaluates to a one-column table that contains no rows at all, then SQL defines the value of the scalar expression to be null.

Keys

The interactions between nulls and keys in SQL can be summarized as follows:

■ *Candidate keys:* Let *C* be a column that is a component of some candidate key *K* of some base table. If *K* is a primary key, SQL will not permit *C* to contain any nulls (in other words, it enforces the entity integrity rule). If *K* is not a primary key, however, SQL will permit *C* to contain *any number* of nulls (together with any number of distinct nonnull values, of course).

■ *Foreign keys:* The rules defining what it means (in the presence of nulls) for a given foreign key value to match some value of the corresponding candidate key are fairly complex; we omit the details here, except to say that they are basically the same as the details of the MATCH condition (see earlier).

Nulls also have implications for the referential actions—CASCADE, SET NULL, etc.—specified in the ON DELETE and ON UPDATE clauses. (SET DEFAULT is also supported, with the obvious interpretation.) Once again, the details are quite complex, and beyond the scope of the present text; see reference [4.19] for the specifics.

Embedded SQL

- *Indicator variables:* Consider the following example of an embedded SQL "singleton SELECT" (a repeat of the example from Chapter 4):

```
EXEC SQL SELECT  STATUS, CITY
         INTO    :RANK, :CITY
         FROM    S
         WHERE   S# = :GIVENS# ;
```

Suppose there is a possibility that the value of STATUS might be null for some supplier. Then the SELECT statement shown above will fail if the STATUS selected is null (SQLSTATE will be set to the exception value 22002). In general, if it is possible that a value to be retrieved might be null, the user should specify an *indicator variable* in addition to the ordinary target variable, as here:

```
EXEC SQL SELECT  STATUS, CITY
         INTO    :RANK INDICATOR :RANKIND, :CITY
         FROM    S
         WHERE   S# = :GIVENS# ;
IF RANKIND = -1 THEN /* STATUS was null */ ... ; END IF ;
```

If the value to be retrieved is null and an indicator variable has been specified, then that indicator variable will be set to the value –1. The effect on the ordinary target variable is implementation-dependent.

- *Ordering:* The ORDER BY clause is used to impose an ordering on the rows resulting from the evaluation of the table expression in a cursor definition. (It can also be used in interactive queries, of course.) The question arises: What is the relative ordering for two scalar values *A* and *B* if *A* is null or *B* is null (or both)? The SQL answer is as follows:

1. For ordering purposes, all nulls are considered to be equal to one another.

2. For ordering purposes, all nulls are considered *either* to be greater than all nonnull values or less than all nonnull values (which of the two possibilities applies is implementation-defined).

18.8   SUMMARY

We have discussed the problem of **missing information** and a currently fashionable—though very bad—approach to that problem based on **nulls** and **three-valued logic** (3VL). We stressed the point that null is not a value, though it is common to speak as if it were (saying, e.g., that some particular attribute value within some particular tuple "is null"). Any comparison in which a comparand is null evaluates to "the third truth value" *unknown* (abbreviated *unk*), which is why the logic is three-valued. We also mentioned that, at least conceptually, there can be many different kinds of nulls, and introduced **UNK** as a convenient (and explicit) shorthand for the "value unknown" kind.

We then explored the implications of UNKs and 3VL for **boolean expressions,** the quantifiers **EXISTS** and **FORALL, computational expressions,** and the **relational operators** product, restrict, project, union, intersection, and difference, also the update operators INSERT and UPDATE. We introduced the operators **IS_UNK** (which tests for UNK), **IF_UNK** (which converts UNK into a nonUNK value), and **MAYBE** (which converts *unk* into *true*). We discussed the question of **duplicates** in the presence of UNKs, and pointed out also that UNK and *unk* are not the same thing.

Next, we examined some consequences of the foregoing ideas. First, we explained that **certain equivalences break down** in 3VL—equivalences, that is, that are valid in 2VL but not in 3VL. As a result, both users and optimizers are likely to make **mistakes in transforming expressions.** And even if such mistakes are not made, 3VL suffers from the very serious ("showstopper") problem that **it does not match reality**—that is, results that are correct according to 3VL are sometimes incorrect in the real world.

We then went on to describe the implications of nulls for **primary** and **foreign keys** (mentioning the **entity** integrity rule and the revised **referential** integrity rule in particular). Then we digressed to explain **outer join.** We do not advocate direct support for that operation ourselves (at least, not as it is usually understood), because we believe there are better solutions to the problem that outer join is intended to solve—in particular, we prefer a solution that makes use of *relation-valued attributes.* We briefly mentioned the possibility of other "outer" operations, in particular **outer union.**

Next we examined the **SQL support** for the foregoing ideas. SQL's treatment of missing information is broadly based on 3VL, but it does manage to include a large number of additional complications, most of them beyond the scope of the present book. Indeed, SQL manages to introduce a number of **additional flaws,** over and above the flaws that are inherent to 3VL *per se* [18.6,18.10]. What is more, those additional flaws serve as an additional **inhibitor to optimization** (as mentioned at the very end of the main text in Chapter 17).

We close with the following observations.

- You will appreciate that we have merely scratched the surface of the problems that can arise from nulls and 3VL. However, we have tried to cover enough ground to make it clear that the "benefits" of the 3VL approach are more than a little doubtful.

- We should also make it clear that, even if you are not convinced regarding the problems of 3VL *per se,* it would still be advisable to avoid the corresponding features of SQL, because of the "additional flaws" referred to above.

- Our recommendation to DBMS users would thus be to ignore the vendor's 3VL support entirely, and to use a disciplined "special values" scheme instead (thereby staying firmly in two-valued logic). Such a scheme is described in detail in reference [18.12].

- Finally, we repeat the following fundamental point from Section 18.6: If—speaking *very* loosely—the value of a given attribute within a given tuple within a given relation "is null," then that attribute position actually contains nothing at all . . . which implies that the "attribute" is not an attribute, the "tuple" is not a tuple, the "relation" is not a relation, and the foundation for what we are doing (whatever else it might be) is no longer mathematical relation theory.

EXERCISES

18.1 If A = 6, B = 5, C = 4, and D is UNK, state the truth values of the following expressions:

a. `A = B OR ( B > C AND A > D )`

b. `A > B AND ( B < C OR IS_UNK ( A - D ) )`

c. `A < C OR B < C OR NOT ( A = C )`

d. `B < D OR B = D OR B > D`

e. `MAYBE ( A > B AND B > C )`

f. `MAYBE ( IS_UNK ( D ) )`

g. `MAYBE ( IS_UNK ( A + B ) )`

h. `IF_UNK ( D, A ) > B AND IF_UNK ( C, D ) < B`

18.2 Let relation *r* contain exactly the following tuples:

```
( 6,    5,    4  )
( UNK,  5,    4  )
( 6,    UNK,  4  )
( UNK,  UNK,  4  )
( UNK,  UNK,  UNK )
```

As in the body of the chapter, assume that (a) the three attributes, in left-to-right order as shown, are called *A, B,* and *C,* respectively, and (b) every attribute is of type INTEGER. If *V* is a range variable that ranges over *r,* state the truth values of the following expressions:

a. `EXISTS V ( V.B > 5 )`

b. `EXISTS V ( V.B > 2 AND V.C > 5 )`

c. `EXISTS V ( MAYBE ( V.C > 3 ) )`

d. `EXISTS V ( MAYBE ( IS_UNK ( V.C ) ) )`

e. `FORALL V ( V.A > 1 )`

f. `FORALL V ( V.B > 1 OR IS_UNK ( V.B ) )`

g. `FORALL V ( MAYBE ( V.A > V.B ) )`

18.3 Strictly speaking, the IS_UNK operator is unnecessary. Why?

18.4 In reference [13.6], Codd proposes "maybe" versions of some (not all) of the relational algebra operators. For example, *maybe-restrict* differs from the normal restrict in that it returns a relation whose body contains just those tuples for which the restriction condition evaluates to *unk* instead of *true*. However, such operators are strictly unnecessary. Why?

18.5 In two-valued logic (2VL), there are exactly two truth values, *true* and *false*. As a consequence, there are exactly four possible *monadic* (single-operand) logical operators—one that maps both *true* and *false* into *true*, one that maps them both into *false*, one that maps *true* into *false* and vice versa (this one is NOT, of course), and one that leaves them both unchanged. And there are exactly 16 possible dyadic (two-operand) operators, as indicated by the following table:

A	B	
t	t	t t t t t t t t f f f f f f f f
t	f	t t t t f f f f t t t t f f f f
t	t	t t f f t t f f t t f f t t f f
t	f	t f t f t f t f t f t f t f t f

Prove that in 2VL all four monadic operators and all 16 dyadic operators can be formulated in terms of suitable combinations of NOT and either AND or OR (and hence that it is not necessary to support all 20 operators explicitly).

18.6 How many logical operators are there in 3VL? What about 4VL? More generally, what about *n*VL?

18.7 (Taken from reference [18.5].) Fig. 18.5 represents some sample values for a slight variation on the usual suppliers and parts database (the variation is that relvar SP includes a new *shipment number* attribute SHIP#, and attribute P# in that relvar now has "UNKs allowed"; relvar P is irrelevant to the exercise and has been omitted). Consider the relational calculus query

```
S WHERE NOT EXISTS SP ( SP.S# = S.S# AND
                        SP.P# = P# ( 'P2' ) )
```

(where S and SP are implicit range variables). Which of the following (if any) is a correct interpretation of this query?

  a. Get suppliers who do not supply P2.

  b. Get suppliers who are not known to supply P2.

  c. Get suppliers who are known not to supply P2.

  d. Get suppliers who are either known not or not known to supply P2.

18.8 Design a physical representation scheme for SQL base tables in which columns are permitted to contain nulls.

S

S#	SNAME	STATUS	CITY
S1	Smith	20	London
S2	Jones	10	Paris
S3	Blake	30	Paris
S4	Clark	20	London

SP

SHIP#	S#	P#	QTY
SHIP1	S1	P1	300
SHIP2	S2	P2	200
SHIP3	S3	UNK	400

Fig. 18.5 A variation on suppliers and parts

REFERENCES AND BIBLIOGRAPHY

18.1 E. F. Codd and C. J. Date: "Much Ado about Nothing," in C. J. Date, *Relational Database Writings 1991–1994*. Reading, Mass.: Addison-Wesley (1995).

Codd is probably the foremost advocate of nulls and 3VL as a basis for dealing with missing information. This article contains the text of a debate between Codd and the present writer on the subject. It includes the following delightful remark: "Database management would be easier if missing values didn't exist" (Codd).

18.2 Hugh Darwen: "Into the Unknown," in C. J. Date, *Relational Database Writings 1985–1989*. Reading, Mass.: Addison-Wesley (1990).

Raises a number of additional questions concerning nulls and 3VL, of which the following is perhaps the most searching: If (as stated in the answer to Exercise 5.9 in Chapter 5) TABLE_DEE corresponds to *true* and TABLE_DUM corresponds to *false,* and TABLE_DEE and TABLE_DUM are the only possible relations of degree zero, then **what corresponds to *unk?***

18.3 Hugh Darwen: "Outer Join with No Nulls and Fewer Tears," in C. J. Date and Hugh Darwen, *Relational Database Writings 1989–1991*. Reading, Mass.: Addison-Wesley (1992).

Proposes a simple variant of "outer join" that does not involve nulls and does solve many of the problems that outer join is supposed to solve.

18.4 C. J. Date: "The Outer Join," in *Relational Database: Selected Writings*. Reading, Mass.: Addison-Wesley (1986).

Analyzes the outer join problem in depth and presents a proposal for supporting the operation in a language like SQL.

18.5 C. J. Date: "NOT Is Not "Not"! (Notes on Three-Valued Logic and Related Matters)," in *Relational Database Writings 1985–1989*. Reading, Mass: Addison-Wesley (1990).

Suppose X is a variable of type BOOLEAN. Then X must have one of the values *true, false,* or *unk*. Thus, the statement "X is not *true*" means that the value of X is either *unk* or *false*. By contrast, the statement "X is NOT *true*" means that the value of X is *false* (see the truth table for NOT). Thus the NOT of 3VL is not the not of natural language . . . This fact has already caused several people (including the designers of the SQL standard) to stumble, and will doubtless do so again.

18.6 C. J. Date: "EXISTS Is Not "Exists"! (Some Logical Flaws in SQL)," in *Relational Database Writings 1985–1989*. Reading, Mass: Addison-Wesley (1990).

Shows that the SQL EXISTS operator is not the same thing as the existential quantifier of 3VL, because it always evaluates to *true* or *false,* never to *unk,* even when *unk* is the logically correct answer.

18.7 C. J. Date: "Watch Out for Outer Join," in C. J. Date and Hugh Darwen, *Relational Database Writings 1989–1991*. Reading, Mass.: Addison-Wesley (1992).

Section 18.5 of the present chapter mentioned the fact that outer join suffers from a number of "Nasty Properties." This paper summarizes those properties as follows:

1. Outer Θ-join is not a restriction of Cartesian product.

2. Restriction does not distribute over outer Θ-join.

3. "$A \leq B$" is not the same as "$A < B$ OR $A = B$" (in 3VL).

4. The Θ-comparison operators are not transitive (in 3VL).

5. Outer natural join is not a projection of outer equijoin.

The paper goes on to consider what is involved in adding outer join support to the SQL SELECT–FROM–WHERE construct. It shows that the foregoing Nasty Properties imply that:

1. Extending the WHERE clause does not work.

2. ANDing outer joins and restrictions does not work.

3. Expressing the join condition in the WHERE clause does not work.

4. Outer joins of more than two relations cannot be formulated without nested expressions.

5. Extending the SELECT clause (alone) does not work.

The paper also shows that many existing products have fallen foul of such considerations.

18.8 C. J. Date: "Composite Foreign Keys and Nulls," in C. J. Date and Hugh Darwen, *Relational Database Writings 1989–1991*. Reading, Mass.: Addison-Wesley (1992).

Should composite foreign key values be allowed to be wholly or partly null? This paper discusses this question.

18.9 C. J. Date: "Three-Valued Logic and the Real World," in C. J. Date and Hugh Darwen, *Relational Database Writings 1989–1991*. Reading, Mass.: Addison-Wesley (1992).

18.10 C. J. Date: "Oh No Not Nulls Again," in C. J. Date and Hugh Darwen, *Relational Database Writings 1989–1991*. Reading, Mass.: Addison-Wesley (1992).

This paper tells you more than you probably wanted to know about nulls.

18.11 C. J. Date: "A Note on the Logical Operators of SQL," in *Relational Database Writings 1991–1994*. Reading, Mass.: Addison-Wesley (1995).

Since 3VL has three truth values *true, false,* and *unk* (here abbreviated to *t, f,* and *u,* respectively), there are $3 * 3 * 3 = 27$ possible monadic 3VL operators, because each of the three possible inputs *t, f,* and *u* can map to each of the three possible outputs *t, f,* and *u.* And there are $3^9 = 19,683$ possible dyadic 3VL operators, as the following table suggests:

```
      t       u       f
t   t/u/f   t/u/f   t/u/f
u   t/u/f   t/u/f   t/u/f
f   t/u/f   t/u/f   t/u/f
```

More generally, in fact, *n*-valued logic involves *n* to the power *n* monadic operators and *n* to the power n^2 dyadic operators:

	monadic operators	dyadic operators
2VL	4	16
3VL	27	19,683
4VL	256	4,294,967,296
...	....	....
nVL	$(n)**(n)$	$(n)**(n^2)$

For any *n*VL with $n > 2$, then, the following questions arise:

- What is a suitable set of *primitive* operators? (E.g., either of the sets {NOT,AND} or {NOT,OR} is a suitable primitive set for 2VL.)

■ What is a suitable set of *useful* operators? (E.g., the set {NOT,AND,OR} is a suitable useful set for 2VL.)

The present paper shows that the SQL standard (under a *very* charitable interpretation) does at least support, directly or indirectly, all of the 19,710 3VL operators. However, the point should be made that in logic the operators operate on *predicates* as well as on propositions, whereas in SQL (even under the aforementioned charitable interpretation) the operators operate on propositions only.

18.12 C. J. Date: "Faults and Defaults" (in five parts), in C. J. Date, Hugh Darwen, and David Mc-Goveran, *Relational Database Writings 1994–1997.* Reading, Mass.: Addison-Wesley (1998).

Describes a systematic approach to the missing information problem that is based on special values and 2VL instead of nulls and 3VL. The paper argues strongly that special values are what we use in the real world—"there is no such thing as a null in the real world"—and hence that it would be desirable for our database systems to behave in this respect in the same way as the real world does.

18.13 Debabrata Dey and Sumit Sarkar: "A Probabilistic Relational Model and Algebra," *ACM TODS 21,* No. 3 (September 1996).

Proposes an approach to "uncertainty in data values" based on probability theory instead of nulls and 3VL. The "probabilistic relational model" is a compatible extension of the conventional relational model.

18.14 César A. Galindo-Legaria: "Outerjoins as Disjunctions," Proc. 1994 ACM SIGMOD Int. Conf. on Management of Data, Minneapolis, Minn. (May 1994).

Outer join is not in general an associative operator [18.4]. This paper characterizes precisely those outer joins that are and are not associative and proposes implementation strategies for each case.

18.15 César Galindo-Legaria and Arnon Rosenthal: "Outerjoin Simplification and Reordering for Query Optimization," *ACM TODS 22,* No. 1 (March 1997).

Presents "a complete set of transformation rules" for expressions involving outer joins.

18.16 Piyush Goel and Bala Iyer: "SQL Query Optimization: Reordering for a General Class of Queries," Proc. 1996 ACM SIGMOD Int. Conf. on Management of Data, Montreal, Canada (June 1996).

Like reference [18.15], this paper is concerned with transforming expressions involving outer joins: "[We] propose a method to reorder [an] SQL query containing joins, outer joins, and . . . aggregations . . . [We] identify a powerful primitive needed [to assist in such reordering, which we call] *generalized selection.*"

18.17 I. J. Heath: IBM internal memo (April 1971).

The paper that introduced the term (and the concept) "outer join."

18.18 Ken-Chih Liu and Rajshekhar Sunderraman: "Indefinite and Maybe Information in Relational Databases," *ACM TODS 15,* No. 1 (March 1990).

Contains a set of formal proposals for extending the relational model to deal with *maybe information* (e.g., "part P7 may be black") and *indefinite* or *disjunctive information* (e.g., "part P8 or part P9 is red"). *I-tables* are introduced as a means of representing normal (definite) information, maybe information, and indefinite information. The restrict, project, product, union, intersect, and difference operators are extended to operate on I-tables.

18.19 David Maier: *The Theory of Relational Databases.* Rockville, Md.: Computer Science Press (1983).

18.20 David McGoveran: "Nothing from Nothing" (in four parts), in C. J. Date, Hugh Darwen, and David McGoveran, *Relational Database Writings 1994–1997.* Reading, Mass.: Addison-Wesley (1998).

> Part I of this four-part paper explains the crucial role of logic in database systems. Part II shows why that logic must be two-valued logic (2VL) specifically, and why attempts to use three-valued logic (3VL) are misguided. Part III examines the problems that three-valued logic (3VL) is supposed to "solve." Finally, Part IV describes a set of pragmatic solutions to those problems that do not involve 3VL.

18.21 Nicholas Rescher: *Many-Valued Logic.* New York, N.Y.: McGraw-Hill (1969).

> The standard text.

ANSWERS TO SELECTED EXERCISES

18.1 a. *unk*. b. *true*. c. *true*. d. *unk* (note the counterintuitive nature of this one). e. *false*. f. *false* (note that IS_UNK never returns *unk*). g. *false*. h. *true*.

18.2 a. *unk*. b. *unk*. c. *true*. d. *false*. e. *unk*. f. *true*. g. *false*.

18.3 Because of the following identity:

```
IS_UNK ( x )  ≡  MAYBE ( x = x )
```

18.4 Because (e.g.) "MAYBE_RESTRICT *r* WHERE *p*" is the same as "*r* WHERE MAYBE(*p*)."

18.5 The four monadic operators can be defined as follows (*A* is the single operand):

```
A
NOT(A)
A OR NOT(A)
A AND NOT(A)
```

The 16 dyadic operators can be defined as follows (*A* and *B* are the two operands):

```
A OR NOT(A) OR B OR NOT(B)
A AND NOT(A) AND B AND NOT(B)
A
NOT(A)
B
NOT(B)
A OR B
A AND B
A OR NOT(B)
A AND NOT(B)
NOT(A) OR B
NOT(A) AND B
NOT(A) OR NOT(B)
NOT(A) AND NOT(B)
(NOT(A) OR B) AND (NOT(B) OR A)
(NOT(A) AND B) OR (NOT(B) AND A)
```

Incidentally, to see that we do not need both AND and OR, observe that, e.g.,

```
A OR B  ≡  NOT ( NOT ( A ) AND NOT ( B ) )
```

18.6 See the annotation to reference [18.11].

18.7 c. For further discussion, see reference [18.5]. *Subsidiary exercise:* Give a relational calculus formulation for interpretation b.

18.8 We briefly describe the representation used in DB2. In DB2, a column that can accept nulls is physically represented in the stored database by two columns, the data column itself and a hidden indicator column, one byte wide, that is stored as a prefix to the actual data column. An indicator column value of binary ones indicates that the corresponding data column value is to be ignored (i.e., taken as null); an indicator column value of binary zeros indicates that the corresponding data column value is to be taken as genuine. But the indicator column is always (of course) hidden from the user.

CHAPTER **19**

Type Inheritance

19.1 INTRODUCTION

We touched on the idea of subtypes and supertypes—more specifically, *entity* subtypes and supertypes—in Chapter 13, where we observed that (e.g.) if some employees are programmers and all programmers are employees, then we might regard entity type PROGRAMMER as a *subtype* of entity type EMPLOYEE and entity type EMPLOYEE as a *supertype* of entity type PROGRAMMER. However, we did also say in that chapter that an "entity type" was not a type in any very formal sense of that term (partly because the term "entity" itself is not very formally defined). In this chapter, we will examine subtypes and supertypes in depth, but we will use the term "type" in the more formal and precise sense of Chapter 5. Let us begin, therefore, by defining the term carefully:

- A **type** is *a named set of values* (i.e., all possible values of the type in question), along with an associated set of *operators* that can be applied to values and variables of the type in question.

Furthermore:

- Any given type can be either system- or user-defined.
- Part of the definition of any given type is a specification of the set of all legal values of that type (that specification is the applicable *type constraint,* of course, as described in Chapter 8).
- Such values can be of arbitrary complexity.
- The actual or physical representation of such values is always hidden from the user; i.e., *types* are distinguished from (actual) *representations.* However, each type has at least one *possible* representation that is explicitly exposed to the user by means of suitable THE_ operators (or something logically equivalent).
- Values and variables of a given type can be operated upon *solely* by means of the operators defined for the type in question.
- In addition to the THE_ operators already mentioned, those operators include:
  a. At least one *selector* operator (more precisely, one such operator for each exposed possible representation), which allows every value of the type in question to be "selected" or specified via an appropriate selector invocation;
  b. An *equality* operator, which allows two values of the type in question to be tested to see if they are in fact the same value;

613

  c. An *assignment* operator, which allows a value of the type in question to be assigned to a variable that has been declared to be of the type in question;

  d. Certain *type testing* operators, to be discussed in Section 19.6. *Note:* These operators might be unnecessary in the absence of inheritance support.

And to the foregoing we now add:

- Some types are **subtypes** of other **supertypes.** If *B* is a subtype of *A,* then all operators and type constraints that apply to *A* apply to *B* also (**inheritance**), but *B* has operators and type constraints of its own that do not apply to *A.*

For example, suppose we have two types ELLIPSE and CIRCLE, with the obvious interpretations. Then we might say that type CIRCLE is a subtype of type ELLIPSE (and type ELLIPSE is a supertype of type CIRCLE), by which we mean that:

- Every circle is an ellipse (i.e., the set of all circles is a subset of the set of all ellipses), but the converse is not true.

- Therefore, every operator that applies to ellipses in general applies to circles in particular (because circles *are* ellipses), but the converse is not true. For example, the operator THE_CTR ("the center of") might apply to ellipses and therefore to circles too, but the operator THE_R ("the radius of") might apply to circles only.

- Moreover, any constraint that applies to ellipses in general applies to circles in particular (again, because circles *are* ellipses), but the converse is not true. For example, if ellipses are subject to the constraint $a \geq b$ (where a and b are the major and minor semiaxes, respectively), then this same constraint must be satisfied by circles too. For circles, of course, a and b coincide in the radius $r,$ and the constraint is satisfied trivially; in fact, the constraint $a = b$ is, precisely, a constraint that applies to circles in particular but not to ellipses in general. *Note:* Throughout this chapter, we use the unqualified term "constraint" to mean a type constraint specifically. We also use the terms "radius" and "semiaxis" to mean what would more properly be referred to as the corresponding radius or semiaxis *length.*

In sum: Type CIRCLE inherits operators and constraints from type ELLIPSE, loosely speaking, but also has operators and constraints of its own that do not apply to type ELLIPSE. Observe, therefore, that the subtype has a *subset* of the values but a *superset* of the properties—a fact that can sometimes cause confusion! *Note:* Here and throughout this chapter, we use the term "properties" as a convenient shorthand for "operators and constraints."

Why Type Inheritance?

Why is this topic worth investigating? There seem to be at least two answers to this question:

- The ideas of subtyping and inheritance do seem to arise naturally in the real world. That is, it is not at all unusual to encounter situations in which all values of a given type have certain properties in common, while some subset of those values have additional special properties of their own. Thus, subtyping and inheritance look as if they might be useful tools for "modeling reality" (or *semantic modeling,* as we called it in Chapter 13).

■ Second, if we can recognize such patterns—patterns of subtyping and inheritance, that is—and build intelligence regarding them into our application and system software, we might be able to achieve certain practical economies. For example, a program that works for ellipses might work for circles too, even if it was originally written with no thought for circles at all (perhaps type CIRCLE had not been defined at the time the program was written): the so-called **code reuse** benefit.

Despite these potential advantages, however, we now observe that there does not seem to be any consensus on a formal, rigorous, and abstract **model** of type inheritance. To quote reference [19.10]:

> The basic idea of inheritance is quite simple . . . [and yet, despite] its central role in current . . . systems, inheritance is still quite a controversial mechanism . . . [A] comprehensive view of inheritance is still missing.

The discussions in this chapter are based on a model developed by the present writer in conjunction with Hugh Darwen and described in detail in reference [3.3]. Be aware, therefore, that other writers and other texts sometimes use terms such as "subtype" and "inheritance" in ways that differ from ours. *Caveat lector.*

Some Preliminaries

There are a number of preliminaries we need to get out of the way before we can get down to a proper discussion of inheritance *per se.* Those preliminaries are the principal subject of the present subsection.

■ *Values are typed*

To repeat from Chapter 5, if *v* is a value, then *v* can be thought of as carrying around with it a kind of flag that announces "I am an integer" or "I am a supplier number" or "I am a circle" (etc., etc.). Now, without inheritance, every value is of exactly one type. With inheritance, however, a value can be of several types simultaneously; e.g., a given value might be of types ELLIPSE and CIRCLE at the same time.

■ *Variables are typed*

Every variable has exactly one **declared** type. For example, we might declare a variable as follows:

```
VAR E ELLIPSE ;
```

The declared type of variable E here is ELLIPSE. Now, without inheritance, all possible values of a given variable are of exactly one type, namely the applicable declared type. With inheritance, however, a given variable might have a value that is of several types simultaneously; e.g., the current value of variable E might be an ellipse that is in fact a circle, and hence be of types ELLIPSE and CIRCLE at the same time.

■ *Single vs. multiple inheritance*

There are two broad "flavors" of type inheritance, single and multiple. Loosely speaking, **single inheritance** means each subtype has just one supertype and inherits properties from just that one type; **multiple inheritance** means a subtype can have any number of supertypes and inherits properties from all of them. Obviously, the former is a special case of the latter. Even single inheritance is fairly complicated, however (surprisingly so, in fact); in this chapter, therefore, we limit our attention to single inheritance only, and we take the unqualified term *inheritance* to mean *single* inheritance specifically. See reference [3.3] for a detailed treatment of both kinds of inheritance, multiple as well as single.

■ *Scalar, tuple, and relation inheritance*

Clearly, inheritance has implications for nonscalar values as well as scalar values,* since ultimately those nonscalar values are built up out of scalar values. In particular, of course, it has implications for tuple and relation values specifically. Even scalar inheritance is fairly complicated, however (again, surprisingly so); in this chapter, therefore, we limit our attention to scalar inheritance only, and we take the unqualified terms *type* and *value* and *variable* to mean **scalar** types and values and variables specifically. See reference [3.3] for a detailed treatment of all kinds of inheritance, tuple and relation as well as scalar.

■ *Structural vs. behavioral inheritance*

Recall that scalar values can have an internal (physical) structure or representation of arbitrary complexity; e.g., ellipses and circles can both legitimately be regarded as scalar values in suitable circumstances (as we already know), even though their internal structure might be quite complex. However, that internal structure is always *hidden from the user*. It follows that when we talk of inheritance (at least so far as our model is concerned), we do *not* mean inheritance of structure, because from the user's point of view there *is* no structure to inherit! In other words, we are interested in what is sometimes called **behavioral** inheritance, not **structural** inheritance (where "behavior" refers to operators—though we remind you that in our model, at least, constraints are inherited too). *Note:* We do not preclude structural inheritance, of course; it is just that we see it as an implementation issue merely, not relevant to the model.

■ *"Subtables and supertables"*

By now it should be clear to you that our inheritance model is concerned with what in relational terms might be called *domain* inheritance (recall that domains and types are the same thing). When asked about the possibility of inheritance in a relational context, however, most people instantly assume it is some kind of *table* inheritance that is

---

*Recall that a scalar type is one with no user-visible components. Do not be misled by the fact that scalar types have *possible representations* that in turn do have user-visible components, as explained in Chapter 5; those components are components of the possible representation, not components of the type—despite the fact that we do sometimes refer to them, sloppily, as if they were indeed components of the type.

under discussion. For example, SQL3 includes support for something it calls "subtables and supertables," according to which some table *B* might inherit all of the columns of some other table *A* and then add some more of its own (see Appendix B). However, it is our position that the "subtables and supertables" idea is a totally separate phenomenon, one that might possibly be interesting—though we are skeptical [13.12]—but has nothing to do with type inheritance *per se.*

One last preliminary remark: The subject of type inheritance really has to do with *data in general*—it is not limited to just *database* data in particular. For simplicity, therefore, most examples in this chapter are expressed in terms of local data (ordinary program variables, etc.) rather than database data.

19.2   TYPE HIERARCHIES

We now introduce a running example that we will use throughout the rest of the chapter. The example involves a set of geometric types—PLANE_FIGURE, ELLIPSE, CIRCLE, POLYGON, and so on—arranged into what is called a **type hierarchy** or, more generally, a **type graph** (see Fig. 19.1). Here in outline are **Tutorial D** definitions for some of those geometric types (note the type constraints in particular):

```
TYPE PLANE_FIGURE ... ;

TYPE ELLIPSE POSSREP ( A LENGTH, B LENGTH, CTR POINT )
     SUBTYPE OF ( PLANE_FIGURE )
     CONSTRAINT ( THE_A ( ELLIPSE ) ≥ THE_B ( ELLIPSE ) ) ;

TYPE CIRCLE POSSREP ( R LENGTH, CTR POINT )
     SUBTYPE_OF ( ELLIPSE )
     CONSTRAINT ( THE_A ( CIRCLE ) = THE_B ( CIRCLE ) ) ;
```

Now the system knows, for example, that CIRCLE is a subtype of ELLIPSE, and hence that operators and constraints that apply to ellipses in general apply to circles in particular.

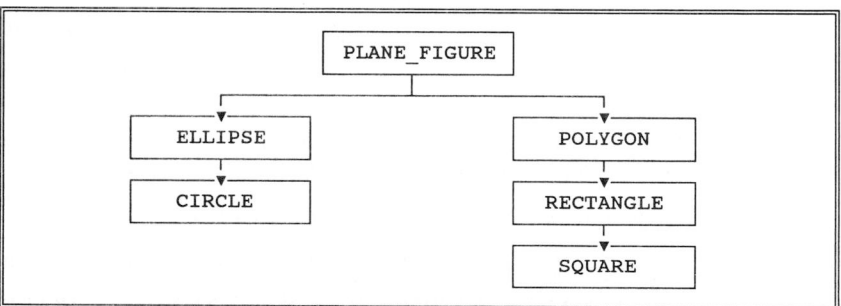

Fig. 19.1   A sample type hierarchy

We should elaborate briefly on the POSSREP specifications for types ELLIPSE and CIRCLE. Basically, we are assuming for simplicity that ellipses are always oriented such that their major axis is horizontal and their minor axis vertical; thus, ellipses might possibly be represented by their semiaxes a and b (and their center). By contrast, circles might possibly be represented by their radius r (and their center). We are also assuming—as we did in Chapter 8—that all ellipses are such that their major semiaxis a is always greater than or equal to their minor semiaxis b (i.e., they are "short and fat," not "tall and thin").

Here now in outline are definitions for some of the operators associated with the foregoing types:

```
OPERATOR AREA ( E ELLIPSE ) RETURNS ( AREA ) ;
   /* "area of" -- note that AREA is the name of both */
   /* the operator per se and the type of the result  */ ... ;
END OPERATOR ;

OPERATOR THE_A ( E ELLIPSE ) RETURNS ( LENGTH ) ;
   /* "the a semiaxis of" */ ... ;
END OPERATOR ;

OPERATOR THE_B ( E ELLIPSE ) RETURNS ( LENGTH ) ;
   /* "the b semiaxis of" */ ... ;
END OPERATOR ;

OPERATOR THE_CTR ( E ELLIPSE ) RETURNS ( POINT ) ;
   /* "the center of" */ ... ;
END OPERATOR ;

OPERATOR THE_R ( C CIRCLE ) RETURNS ( LENGTH ) ;
   /* "the radius of" */ ... ;
END OPERATOR ;
```

All of these operators except THE_R apply to values of type ELLIPSE and hence *a fortiori* to values of type CIRCLE as well; THE_R, by contrast, applies to values of type CIRCLE only.

Terminology

There are unfortunately several more definitions and terms we need to introduce before we can proceed much further. The concepts are mostly straightforward, however.

1. A supertype of a supertype is itself a supertype; e.g., POLYGON is a supertype of SQUARE.

2. Every type is a supertype of itself; e.g., ELLIPSE is a supertype of ELLIPSE.

3. If A is a supertype of B and A and B are distinct, then A is a **proper** supertype of B; e.g., POLYGON is a proper supertype of SQUARE.

Analogous remarks apply to subtypes, of course. Thus:

4. A subtype of a subtype is itself a subtype; e.g., SQUARE is a subtype of POLYGON.

5. Every type is a subtype of itself; e.g., ELLIPSE is a subtype of ELLIPSE.

6. If B is a subtype of A and B and A are distinct, then B is a **proper** subtype of A; e.g., SQUARE is a proper subtype of POLYGON.

Moreover:

7. If *A* is a supertype of *B* and there is no type *C* that is both a proper subtype of *A* and a proper supertype of *B*, then *A* is an **immediate** supertype of *B* and *B* is an **immediate** subtype of *A*. E.g., RECTANGLE is an immediate supertype of SQUARE, and SQUARE is an immediate subtype of RECTANGLE. (Note, therefore, that in our **Tutorial D** syntax the keyword SUBTYPE_OF means, quite specifically, "*immediate* subtype of.")

8. A **root** type is a type with no proper supertype; e.g., PLANE_FIGURE is a root *type*. *Note:* We do not assume there is just one root type. If there are two or more, however, we can always invent some kind of "system" type that is an immediate supertype for all of them, so there is no loss of generality in assuming just one.

9. A **leaf** type is a type with no proper subtype; e.g., CIRCLE is a leaf type. *Note:* This definition is slightly simplified, but it is adequate for present purposes (it needs a tiny extension to deal properly with multiple inheritance [3.3]).

10. Every proper subtype has exactly one immediate supertype. *Note:* Here we are just making explicit our assumption that we are dealing with single inheritance only. As already noted, the effects of relaxing this assumption are explored in detail in reference [3.3].

11. So long as (a) there is at least one type and (b) there are no *cycles*—i.e., there is no sequence of types *T1, T2, T3, ..., Tn* such that *T1* is an immediate subtype of *T2, T2* is an immediate subtype of *T3, ...,* and *Tn* is an immediate subtype of *T1*—then at least one type *must* be a root type. *Note:* In fact, there *cannot* be any cycles (why not?).

The Disjointness Assumption

We make one further simplifying assumption, as follows: If *T1* and *T2* are distinct root types or distinct immediate subtypes of the same supertype (implying in particular that neither is a subtype of the other), then we assume they are **disjoint**—i.e., no value is of both type *T1* and type *T2*. For example, no value is both an ellipse and a polygon.

The following further points are immediate consequences of this assumption:

12. Distinct type hierarchies are disjoint.

13. Distinct leaf types are disjoint.

14. Every value has exactly one **most specific** type. For example, a given value might be "just an ellipse" and not a circle, meaning its most specific type is ELLIPSE (in the real world, some ellipses are not circles). In fact, to say that the most specific type of some value *v* is *T* is to say, precisely, that the set of types possessed by *v* is the set of all supertypes of *T* (a set that includes *T* itself, of course).

One reason the disjointness assumption is desirable is that it avoids certain ambiguities that could otherwise occur. For suppose some value *v* could be of two types *T1* and *T2*, neither of which is a subtype of the other. Suppose further that an operator named *Op* has been defined for type *T1* and another operator with the same name *Op* has been defined for type *T2*.* Then an invocation of *Op* with argument *v* would be ambiguous.

Note: The disjointness assumption is reasonable so long as we limit our attention to single inheritance only, but it does need to be relaxed for multiple inheritance. See reference [3.3] for a detailed discussion.

A Note on Physical Representation

Although we are primarily concerned with a *model* of inheritance, not with implementation matters, there are certain implementation issues that you do need to understand to some extent in order to understand the overall concept of inheritance properly—and now we come to one such:

15. The fact that *B* is a subtype of *A* does not imply that the actual (hidden) representation of *B* values is the same as that of *A* values.† For example, ellipses might actually be represented by their center and semiaxes, while circles might actually be represented by their center and radius (though there is no requirement, in general, that an actual representation be the same as any of the declared possible ones).

    This point will turn out to be important in several of the sections that follow.

19.3   POLYMORPHISM AND SUBSTITUTABILITY

In this section we consider two crucial concepts, *polymorphism* and *substitutability,* that together provide the basis for achieving the code reuse benefit mentioned briefly in Section 19.1. We should say immediately that these two concepts are really just different ways of looking at the same thing. Be that as it may, let us begin by taking a look at polymorphism.

Polymorphism

The very notion of inheritance implies that if *T'* is a subtype of *T,* then all operators that apply to values of type *T* apply to values of type *T'* as well. For example, if AREA(*e*) is legal, where *e* is an ellipse, then AREA(*c*), where *c* is a circle, must be legal as well. Note, therefore, that we need to be very careful over the difference between the *parameters* in terms of which a given operator is defined, with their *declared* types, and the corresponding *arguments* to a

---

*In other words, *Op* is a *polymorphic* operator. What is more, the polymorphism in question could be either *overloading* or *inclusion* polymorphism. See Section 19.3 for further explanation

† In fact, there is no logical reason why all values of the *same* type have to have the same actual representation. For example, some points might be represented by Cartesian coordinates and some by polar coordinates; some temperatures might be represented in Celsius and some in Fahrenheit; some integers might be represented in decimal and some in binary; and so on. (Of course, the system will have to know how to convert between actual representations in all such cases, in order to be able to implement assignments, comparisons, etc., properly.)

given invocation of that operator, with their *actual* (most specific) types. For example, the operator AREA is defined in terms of a parameter of declared type ELLIPSE—see Section 19.2—but the actual (most specific) type of the argument in the invocation AREA(*c*) is CIRCLE.

Recall now that ellipses and circles, at least as we defined them in Section 19.2, have different possible representations:

```
TYPE ELLIPSE POSSREP ( A LENGTH, B LENGTH, CTR POINT ) ... ;

TYPE CIRCLE POSSREP ( R LENGTH, CTR POINT ) ... ;
```

It is conceivable, therefore, that two different versions of the AREA operator might exist under the covers, one that makes use of the ELLIPSE possible representation and one that makes use of the CIRCLE possible representation. To repeat, it is *conceivable*—but it might not be *necessary*. For example, the ELLIPSE code might look like this:

```
OPERATOR AREA ( E ELLIPSE ) RETURNS ( AREA ) ;
    RETURN ( 3.14159 * THE_A ( E ) * THE_B ( E ) ) ;
END OPERATOR ;
```

(the area of an ellipse is πab). And this code obviously works correctly if it is invoked with a circle instead of a more general ellipse since, for a circle, THE_A and THE_B both return the radius *r*. However, the person responsible for defining type CIRCLE might prefer, for a variety of reasons, to implement a distinct version of AREA that is specific to circles and invokes THE_R instead of THE_A and THE_B. *Note:* In fact, it might be desirable to implement two versions of the operator anyway, even if the possible representations are the same, for reasons of efficiency. Consider polygons and rectangles, for example. The algorithm that computes the area of a general polygon will certainly work for a rectangle, but for rectangles a more efficient algorithm—multiply the height by the width—is available.

Note, however, that the ELLIPSE code will certainly not work for circles if it is written in terms of the *actual* ELLIPSE representation instead of a possible one and the actual representations for types ELLIPSE and CIRCLE differ. The practice of implementing operators in terms of actual representations is generally not a good idea. Code defensively!

Anyway, if AREA is *not* reimplemented for type CIRCLE, then we get *code reuse* (for the AREA implementation code, that is). *Note:* We will encounter a more important kind of reuse in the next subsection.

From the point of view of the model, of course, it makes no difference how many versions of AREA exist under the covers (as far as the user is concerned, there is just one AREA operator, which works for ellipses and therefore for circles too, by definition). From the point of view of the model, in other words, AREA is **polymorphic:** It can take arguments of different types on different invocations. Note carefully, therefore, that such polymorphism is a logical consequence of inheritance: If we have inheritance, we *must* have polymorphism, otherwise we do not have inheritance!

Now, polymorphism *per se* is not a new idea, as you might have already realized. SQL, for example, already has polymorphic operators ("=", "+", "||", and many others), and in fact so do most other programming languages. Some languages even permit users to define their own polymorphic operators; PL/I provides such a facility, for example, under the name "GENERIC functions." However, there is no inheritance, as such, involved in any of these examples; they are all examples of what is sometimes called *overloading* polymorphism. The kind of polymorphism exhibited by the AREA operator, by contrast, is called *inclusion* polymorphism, on the grounds that the relationship between (say) circles and ellipses is basically that of set inclusion [19.3]. For obvious reasons, we take the unqualified term "polymorphism" in the remainder of this chapter to mean inclusion polymorphism specifically, barring explicit statements to the contrary.

Note: A helpful way of thinking about the difference between overloading and inclusion polymorphism is as follows:

- *Overloading* polymorphism means there are several distinct operators with the same name (and the user does need to know that the operators in question are in fact distinct, with distinct—though preferably similar—semantics). For example, "+" is overloaded in most languages (there is one "+" operator for adding integers, another "+" operator for adding rationals, and so on).

- *Inclusion* polymorphism means there is just one operator, with possibly several distinct implementation versions under the covers (but the user does not need to know whether or not there are in fact several implementation versions—to the user, to repeat, there is just one operator).

Programming with Polymorphism

Consider the following example. Suppose we need to write a program to display some diagram, made up of squares, circles, ellipses, and so on. Without polymorphism, the code will look something like the following pseudocode:

```
FOR EACH x IN DIAGRAM
    CASE ;
        WHEN IS_SQUARE ( x ) THEN CALL DISPLAY_SQUARE ... ;
        WHEN IS_CIRCLE ( x ) THEN CALL DISPLAY_CIRCLE ... ;
        .....
    END CASE ;
```

(We are assuming the existence of operators IS_SQUARE, IS_CIRCLE, and so forth, which can be used to test whether a given value is of the specified type.) With polymorphism, by contrast, the code is much simpler and much more succinct:

```
FOR EACH x IN DIAGRAM CALL DISPLAY ( x ) ;
```

Explanation: DISPLAY here is a polymorphic operator. The implementation version of DISPLAY that works for values of type T will be defined (typically) when type T is defined and will be made known to the system at that time. At run time, then, when the system encounters the DISPLAY invocation with argument x, it will have to determine the most specific type of x and then invoke the version of DISPLAY appropriate to that type—

a process known as **run-time binding.*** In other words, polymorphism effectively means that CASE expressions and CASE statements that otherwise would have had to appear in the user's source code are *moved under the covers:* The system effectively performs those CASE operations in the user's behalf.

Note the implications of the foregoing for program maintenance in particular. Suppose, for example, that a new type TRIANGLE is defined as another immediate subtype of POLYGON, and hence that the diagram to be displayed can now additionally include triangles. Without polymorphism, every program that contains a CASE expression or statement like the one shown above will now have to be modified to include code of the form

```
WHEN IS_TRIANGLE ( x ) THEN CALL DISPLAY_TRIANGLE ... ;
```

With polymorphism, however, no such source code modifications are necessary.

Because of examples like the foregoing, polymorphism is sometimes characterized, a little colorfully, as "allowing old code to invoke new code"; i.e., a program *P* can effectively invoke some version of some operator that did not even exist (the version, that is) at the time *P* was written. So here we have another—and more important—example of *code reuse:* The very same program *P* might be usable on data that is of a type *T* that, to repeat, did not even exist at the time *P* was written.

Substitutability

As mentioned earlier, the concept of substitutability is really just the concept of polymorphism looked at from a slightly different point of view. We have seen, for example, that if AREA(*e*) is legal, where *e* is an ellipse, then AREA(*c*), where *c* is a circle, must be legal too. In other words, wherever the system expects an ellipse, we can always substitute a circle instead. More generally, wherever the system expects a value of type *T,* we can always substitute a value of type *T'* instead, where *T'* is a subtype of *T*—*The Principle of Value Substitutability.*

Note in particular that this principle implies that if some relation *r* has an attribute *A* of declared type ELLIPSE, some of the *A* values in *r* might be of type CIRCLE instead of just type ELLIPSE. Likewise, if some type *T* has a possible representation that involves a component *C* of declared type ELLIPSE, then for some values *v* of type *T* the operator invocation THE_*C*(*v*) might return a value of type CIRCLE instead of just type ELLIPSE.

Finally, we observe that, since it is really just polymorphism in another guise, substitutability too is a logical consequence of inheritance: If we have inheritance, we *must* have substitutability, otherwise we do not have inheritance.

---

*Run-time binding is an implementation issue, of course, not a model issue. It is another of those implementation issues that you do have to appreciate to some extent in order to understand the overall concept of inheritance properly.

19.4 VARIABLES AND ASSIGNMENTS

Suppose we have two variables E and C, of declared types ELLIPSE and CIRCLE respectively:

```
VAR E ELLIPSE ;
VAR C CIRCLE ;
```

First we initialize C to some circle—say (just to be definite) the circle with radius three and center the origin:

```
C   :=   CIRCLE ( LENGTH ( 3.0 ), POINT ( 0.0, 0.0 ) ) ;
```

The right-hand side here is a selector invocation for type CIRCLE. (Recall from Chapter 5 that for every declared possible representation there is a corresponding selector operator with the same name and with parameters corresponding to the components of the possible representation in question. The purpose of a selector is to allow the user to specify or "select" a value of the type in question by supplying a value for each component of the possible representation in question.)

Now consider the following assignment:

```
E   :=   C ;
```

Normally—i.e., in the absence of subtyping and inheritance—the assignment operation requires the variable specified on the left-hand side and the value denoted by the expression on the right-hand side to be of the same type (the same *declared* type, that is, in the case of the variable). However, *The Principle of Value Substitutability* implies that wherever the system expects a value of type ELLIPSE we can always substitute a value of type CIRCLE, so the assignment is legal as shown (in fact, assignment is a polymorphic operator). And the effect is to copy the circle value from variable C to variable E; in particular, the value of variable E after the assignment is of type CIRCLE, not just type ELLIPSE. In other words:

- **Values retain their most specific type on assignment to variables of less specific declared type**. Type conversion does *not* occur on such assignment (in the example, the circle is *not* converted to become "just an ellipse"). Note that we do not want any such conversion, because it would cause the value's most specific behavior to be lost; in the case at hand, for example, it would mean that after the assignment we would not be able to obtain the radius of the circle value in variable E. *Note:* See the subsection "TREAT DOWN" later in this section for a discussion of what is involved in obtaining that radius.

- It follows that *substitutability implies that a variable of declared type T can have a value whose most specific type is **any subtype** of T*. Note, therefore, that we must now be very careful over the difference between the *declared* type of a given variable and the *actual*—i.e., most specific—type of (the current value of) that variable. We will come back to this important point in the next subsection.

To continue with the example, suppose we now have another variable A, of declared type AREA:

```
VAR A AREA ;
```

Consider the following assignment:

```
A  :=  AREA ( E ) :
```

What happens here is the following:

- First, the system performs compile-time type checking on the expression AREA(E). That check succeeds, because E is of declared type ELLIPSE and the single parameter to the AREA operator is of declared type ELLIPSE also (see Section 19.2).

- Second, the system discovers at run time that the current most specific type of E is CIRCLE, and therefore invokes the version of AREA that applies to circles (in other words, it performs the run-time binding process discussed in the previous section).

Of course, the fact that it is the circle version of AREA that is invoked, not the ELLIPSE version, should be of no concern to the user—to the user, to repeat, there is just one AREA operator.

Scalar Variables

We have seen that the current value v of a scalar variable V of declared type T can have any subtype of T as its most specific type. It follows that we can (and do) model V as an *ordered triple* of the form $<DT,MST,v>$, where:

- DT is the declared type for variable V.
- MST is the current most specific type for variable V.
- v is a value of most specific type MST—namely, the current value of variable V.

We use the notation $DT(V)$, $MST(V)$, and $v(V)$ to refer to the DT, MST, and v components, respectively, of this model of scalar variable V. Note that (a) $MST(V)$ is always a subtype— not necessarily a *proper* subtype, of course—of $DT(V)$; (b) $MST(V)$ and $v(V)$ change with time, in general; (c) in fact, $MST(V)$ is implied by $v(V)$, because every value is of exactly one most specific type.

This model of a scalar variable is useful in pinning down the precise semantics of various operations, including assignment operations in particular. Before we can elaborate on this point, however, we must explain that, of course, the notions of declared type and current most specific type can be extended in an obvious way to apply to arbitrary scalar expressions as well as to scalar variables specifically. Let X be such an expression. Then:

- X has a *declared type, $DT(X)$*—more precisely, the result of evaluating X has such a type—derived in the obvious way from the declared types of the operands of X (including the declared types of the results of any operator invocations contained within X), and *known at compile time;*

■ *X* also has a *current most specific type, MST(X)*—more precisely, the result of evalu-ating *X* has such a type—derived in the obvious way from the current values of the operands of *X* (including the current values of the results of any operator invocations contained within *X*), and *not known until run time* (in general).

Now we can explain assignment properly. Consider the assignment

```
V  :=  X ;
```

(where *V* is a scalar variable and *X* is a scalar expression). *DT(X)* must be a subtype of *DT(V)*, otherwise the assignment is illegal (this is a compile-time check). If the assignment is legal, its effect is to set *MST(V)* equal to *MST(X)* and *v(V)* equal to *v(X)*.

Incidentally, note that if the current most specific type of variable *V* is *T*, then every proper supertype of type *T* is also a "current type" of variable *V*. For example, if vari-able E (of declared type ELLIPSE) has a current value of most specific type CIRCLE, then CIRCLE, ELLIPSE, and PLANE_FIGURE are all "current types" of E. However, the phrase "current type of *X*" is usually taken, at least informally, to mean *MST(X)* specifically.

Substitutability Revisited

Consider the following operator definition:

```
OPERATOR COPY ( E ELLIPSE ) RETURNS ( ELLIPSE ) ;
   RETURN ( E ) ;
END OPERATOR ;
```

Because of substitutability, the COPY operator can obviously be invoked with an argu-ment of most specific type either ELLIPSE or CIRCLE—and whichever it is, it will clearly return a result of that same most specific type. It follows that the notion of substitutability has the further implication that *if operator Op is defined to have a result of declared type T, then the actual result of an invocation of Op can be of **any subtype** of type T* (in general). In other words, just as (a) a reference to a variable of declared type *T* can in fact denote a value of any subtype of *T* (in general), so (b) an invocation of an operator with declared re-sult type *T* can in fact return a value of any subtype of *T* (again, in general).

TREAT DOWN

Here again is the example from the beginning of this section:

```
VAR E ELLIPSE ;
VAR C CIRCLE ;

C  :=  CIRCLE ( LENGTH ( 3.0 ), POINT ( 0.0, 0.0 ) ) ;
E  :=  C ;
```

MST(E) is now CIRCLE. Now suppose we want to get the radius of the circle in ques-tion and assign it to some variable L. We might try the following:

```
VAR L LENGTH ;

L  :=  THE_R ( E ) ;            /* compile-time type error !!! */
```

As the comment indicates, however, this code fails on a compile-time type error. To be specific, it fails because the operator THE_R ("the radius of") on the right-hand side of the assignment requires an argument of type CIRCLE and the declared type of the argument E is ELLIPSE, not CIRCLE. *Note:* If the compile-time type check were not done, we would get a *run-time* type error instead—which is worse—if the current value of E at run time were only an ellipse and not a circle. In the case at hand, of course, we do know that the value at run time will be a circle; the trouble is, we know this, but the compiler does not.

To address such problems, we introduce a new operator, which we refer to informally as *TREAT DOWN.* The correct way to obtain the radius in the example is as follows:

```
L  :=  THE_R ( TREAT_DOWN_AS_CIRCLE ( E ) ) ;
```

The expression TREAT_DOWN_AS_CIRCLE(E) is defined to have declared type CIRCLE, so the compile-time type checking now succeeds. Then at run time:

- If the current value of E is indeed of type CIRCLE, then the overall expression does correctly return the radius of that circle. More precisely, the TREAT DOWN invocation yields a result, Z say, with (a) declared type $DT(Z)$ equal to CIRCLE, because of the "..._AS_CIRCLE" specification, (b) current most specific type $MST(Z)$ equal to MST(E), which is CIRCLE also in the example, and (c) current value $v(Z)$ equal to v(E); then (d) the expression "THE_R(Z)" is evaluated, to give the desired radius (which can then be assigned to L).

- However, if the current value of E is only of type ELLIPSE, not CIRCLE, then the TREAT DOWN fails on a *run-time* type error.

The general intent of TREAT DOWN is to ensure that run-time type errors can occur only in the context of a TREAT DOWN invocation.

Note: Suppose CIRCLE in turn has a proper subtype, O_CIRCLE say (where an "O-circle" is a circle that is centered on the origin):

```
TYPE O_CIRCLE POSSREP ( R LENGTH )
   SUBTYPE_OF ( CIRCLE )
   CONSTRAINT ( THE_CTR ( O_CIRCLE ) = POINT ( 0.0, 0.0 ) ) ;
```

Then the current value of variable E at some given time might be of most specific type O_CIRCLE instead of just CIRCLE. If it is, then the TREAT DOWN invocation

```
TREAT_DOWN_AS_CIRCLE ( E )
```

will succeed, and will yield a result, Z say, with (a) $DT(Z)$ equal to CIRCLE, because of the "..._AS_CIRCLE" specification, (b) $MST(Z)$ equal to O_CIRCLE, because O_CIRCLE is the most specific type of E, and (c) $v(Z)$ equal to v(E). In other words (loosely): TREAT DOWN always leaves the most specific type alone, it never "pushes it up" to make it less specific than it was before.

Here for future reference is a more formal statement of the semantics of the operator invocation TREAT_DOWN_AS_T(X), where X is some scalar expression. First of all, T must be a subtype of $DT(X)$ (this is a compile-time check). Second, $MST(X)$ must be a subtype of T (this is a run-time check). Assuming these conditions are satisfied, the invocation returns a result Z with $DT(Z)$ equal to T, $MST(Z)$ equal to $MST(X)$, and $v(Z)$ equal to $v(X)$. *Note:* Reference [3.3] also defines a generalized form of TREAT DOWN that allows one operand to be "treated down" to the type of another, instead of to some explicitly named type.

19.5   SPECIALIZATION BY CONSTRAINT

Consider the following example of a selector invocation for type ELLIPSE:

```
ELLIPSE ( LENGTH ( 5.0 ), LENGTH ( 5.0 ), POINT ( ... ) )
```

This expression returns an ellipse with equal semiaxes. But in the real world an ellipse with equal semiaxes is in fact a circle—so does this expression return a result of most specific type CIRCLE, rather than most specific type ELLIPSE?

Much controversy has raged in the literature (and in fact still does) over questions such as this one. In our own model, we decided, after much careful thought, that it is better to insist that the expression does indeed return a result of most specific type CIRCLE. More generally, if type T' is a subtype of type T, and a selector invocation for type T returns a value that satisfies the type constraint for type T', then (in our model) the result of that selector invocation is of type T'.* *Note:* You are cautioned that few if any of today's commercial implementations actually behave this way in practice, but we regard this fact as a failing on the part of those systems. Reference [3.3] shows that, as a consequence of this failing, those systems are forced to support "noncircular circles," "nonsquare squares," and similar nonsenses—a criticism that does not apply to our approach.

It follows from the foregoing that (at least in our model) no value of most specific type ELLIPSE ever has $a = b$; in other words, values of most specific type ELLIPSE correspond precisely to real-world ellipses that are not circles. By contrast, values of most specific type ELLIPSE in other inheritance models correspond to real-world ellipses that *might or might not* be circles. We thus feel our model is a little more acceptable as "a model of reality."

The idea that (e.g.) an ellipse with $a = b$ must be of type CIRCLE is known as **specialization by constraint** [3.3]—though we should warn you that other writers use this term to mean something completely different (see, e.g., references [19.7] and [19.11]).

---

*Reference [3.3] suggests that this effect be achieved by means of a SPECIALIZE clause on the definition of type T. However, we have subsequently come to the conclusion that no special syntax is needed in order to achieve the effect we desire.

THE_ Pseudovariables Revisited

Recall from Chapter 5 that THE_ pseudovariables provide a way of updating one component of a variable while leaving the other components unchanged ("components" here referring to components of some *possible* representation, of course, not necessarily an *actual* representation). For example, let variable E be of declared type ELLIPSE, and let the current value of E be an ellipse with (say) *a* five and *b* three. Then the assignment

```
THE_B ( E )  :=  LENGTH ( 4.0 ) ;
```

updates the *b* semiaxis of E to four without changing its a semiaxis or its center.

Now, as noted in Chapter 8, Section 8.2, THE_ pseudovariables are logically unnecessary—they are really just shorthand. For example, the assignment just shown, which uses a THE_ pseudovariable, is shorthand for the following one which does not:*

```
E  :=  ELLIPSE ( THE_A ( E ), LENGTH ( 4.0 ), THE_CTR ( E ) ) ;
```

So consider the following assignment:

```
THE_B ( E )  :=  LENGTH ( 5.0 ) ;
```

By definition, this assignment is equivalent to the following one:

```
E  :=  ELLIPSE ( THE_A ( E ), LENGTH ( 5.0 ), THE_CTR ( E ) ) ;
```

Specialization by constraint therefore comes into play (because the expression on the right-hand side returns an ellipse with $a = b$), and the net effect is that after the assignment MST(E) is CIRCLE, not ELLIPSE.

Next, consider the assignment:

```
THE_B ( E )  :=  LENGTH ( 4.0 ) ;
```

Now E contains an ellipse with *a* five and *b* four (as previously) and MST(E) becomes ELLIPSE once again—an effect that we refer to as **generalization** by constraint.

Note: Suppose (as we did near the end of Section 19.4) that type CIRCLE has a proper subtype O_CIRCLE (where an "O-circle" is a circle with center the origin):

```
TYPE O_CIRCLE POSSREP ( R LENGTH )
   SUBTYPE_OF ( CIRCLE )
   CONSTRAINT ( THE_CTR ( O_CIRCLE ) = POINT ( 0.0, 0.0 ) ) ;
```

Then the current value of variable E at some given time might be of most specific type O_CIRCLE instead of just CIRCLE. Suppose it is, and consider the following sequence of assignments:†

---

*We note in passing that TREAT DOWN can be used as a pseudovariable too [3.3], but again it is effectively just shorthand.

†As noted in Chapter 8, reference [3.3] proposes a *multiple* form of assignment that would allow the sequence of assignments to be executed as a single operation.

```
THE_A ( E )  :=  LENGTH ( 7.0 ) ;
THE_B ( E )  :=  LENGTH ( 7.0 ) ;
```

After the first of these assignments, E will contain "just an ellipse," thanks to generalization by constraint. After the second, however, it will contain a circle again—but will it be an O-circle specifically or "just a circle"? Obviously, we would like it to be an O-circle specifically. And indeed so it is, precisely because it satisfies the constraint for type O-CIRCLE (including the constraint inherited by that type from type CIRCLE).

Changing Types Sideways

Once again, let E be a variable of declared type ELLIPSE. We have seen how to change the type of E "down" (e.g., if its current most specific type is ELLIPSE, we have seen how to update it so that its current most specific type becomes CIRCLE); we have also seen how to change the type of E "up" (e.g., if its current most specific type is CIRCLE, we have seen how to update it so that its current most specific type becomes ELLIPSE). But what about changing type "sideways"? Suppose we extend our running example such that type ELLIPSE has two immediate subtypes, CIRCLE and NONCIRCLE (with the obvious meanings).* Without going into too much detail, it should be clear that:

- If the current value of E is of type CIRCLE (so $a = b$), updating E such that $a > b$ will cause MST(E) to become NONCIRCLE;
- If the current value of E is of type NONCIRCLE (so $a > b$), updating E such that $a = b$ will cause MST(E) to become CIRCLE.

Thus, specialization by constraint takes care of "sideways" type changes too. *Note:* In case you were wondering, updating E such that $a < b$ is impossible (it violates the constraint on type ELLIPSE).

19.6 COMPARISONS

Suppose we have our usual two variables E and C of declared types ELLIPSE and CIRCLE, respectively, and suppose we assign the current value of C to E:

```
E := C ;
```

Then it is surely obvious that if we now perform the equality comparison

```
E = C
```

we ought to get the result *true*—and so indeed we do. The general rule is as follows. Consider the comparison $X = Y$ (where X and Y are scalar expressions). The declared type $DT(X)$ must be a subtype of the declared type $DT(Y)$ or the other way around, otherwise the

---

*ELLIPSE now becomes a *dummy* type, incidentally (see Section 19.7).

comparison is illegal (this is a compile-time check). If the comparison is legal, its effect is to return *true* if the most specific type $MST(X)$ is equal to the most specific type $MST(Y)$ and the value $v(X)$ is equal to the value $v(Y)$, and *false* otherwise. Note in particular that two values cannot possibly "compare equal" if their most specific types are different.

Effect on the Relational Algebra

Equality comparisons are involved, implicitly or explicitly, in many of the operations of the relational algebra. And when supertypes and subtypes are involved, it turns out that certain of those operations exhibit behavior that might be thought (at least at first blush) a little counterintuitive. Consider the relations RX and RY shown in Fig. 19.2. Observe that the sole attribute A in RX is of declared type ELLIPSE and its counterpart A in RY is of declared type CIRCLE. We adopt the convention in the figure that values of the form E*i* are ellipses that are not circles and values of the form C*i* are circles. Most specific types are shown in lower case italics.

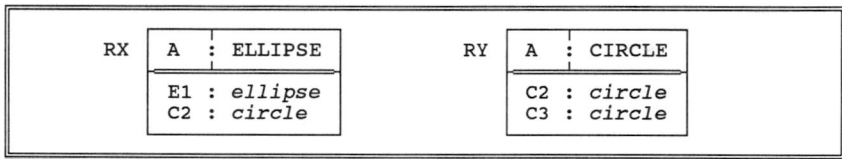

Fig. 19.2   Relations RX and RY

Now consider the join of RX and RY, RJ say (see Fig. 19.3). Clearly, every A value in RJ will necessarily be of type CIRCLE (because any A value in RX whose most specific type is merely ELLIPSE cannot possibly "compare equal" to any A value in RY). Thus, it might be thought that the declared type of attribute A in RJ should be CIRCLE, not ELLIPSE. But consider the following:

- Since RX and RY each have A as their sole attribute, RX JOIN RY reduces to RX INTERSECT RY. In such circumstances, therefore, the rule regarding the declared type of the result attribute for JOIN must obviously reduce to the analogous rule for INTERSECT.

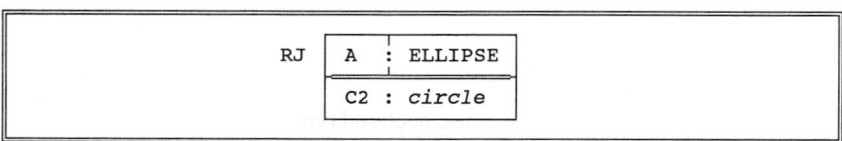

Fig. 19.3   The join RJ of relations RX and RY

- RX INTERSECT RY in turn is logically equivalent to RX MINUS (RX MINUS RY). Let the result of the second operand here—i.e., RX MINUS RY—be RZ. Then it should be clear that:

  a. RZ will include some A values of most specific type ELLIPSE, in general, and so the declared type of attribute A in RZ must be ELLIPSE.

  b. The original expression thus reduces to RX MINUS RZ, where the declared type of attribute A in both RX and RZ is ELLIPSE, and hence yields a final result in which the declared type of attribute A must obviously be ELLIPSE once again.

- It follows that the declared type of the result attribute for INTERSECT, and therefore for JOIN as well, must be ELLIPSE, not CIRCLE—even though (to repeat) every *value* of that attribute must in fact be of type CIRCLE!

Now we turn to the relational difference operator, MINUS. First, consider RX MINUS RY. It should be clear that some A values in the result of this operation will be of type ELLIPSE, not CIRCLE, and so the declared type of A in that result *must* be of type ELLIPSE. But what about RY MINUS RX? Clearly, every A value in the result of this latter operation will be of type CIRCLE, and so again it might be thought that the declared type of A in that result should be CIRCLE, not ELLIPSE. However, observe that RX INTERSECT RY is logically equivalent, not only to RX MINUS (RX MINUS RY) as already discussed, but also to RY MINUS (RY MINUS RX); given this fact, it is easy to see that specifying the declared type of A in the result of RY MINUS RX to be CIRCLE leads to a contradiction. It follows that the declared type of the result attribute for MINUS too must be ELLIPSE, not CIRCLE, even in the case of RY MINUS RX where every *value* of that attribute must in fact be of type CIRCLE.

Finally, consider RX UNION RY. In this case it should be obvious that the result will include some A values of most specific type ELLIPSE, in general, and so the declared type of attribute A in that result must necessarily be ELLIPSE. Thus, the declared type of the result attribute for UNION too must be ELLIPSE (but this particular case, unlike the JOIN, INTERSECT, and MINUS cases, can hardly be said to be counterintuitive).

Here then is the general rule:

- Let *rx* and *ry* be relations with a common attribute *A,* and let the declared types of *A* in *rx* and *ry* be $DT(Ax)$ and $DT(Ay)$, respectively. Consider the join of *rx* and *ry* (necessarily over *A,* at least in part). $DT(Ax)$ must be a subtype of $DT(Ay)$ or *vice versa*, otherwise the join is illegal (this is a compile-time check). If the join is legal, assume without loss of generality that $DT(Ay)$ is a subtype of $DT(Ax)$. Then the declared type of *A* in the result is $DT(Ax)$.

- Analogous remarks apply to union, intersection, and difference: In every case, (a) corresponding attributes of the operands must be such that the declared type of one is a subtype of the declared type of the other, and (b) the declared type of the corresponding attribute in the result is the less specific of the two (where by the **less specific** of two types T and T', one of which is a subtype of the other, we mean whichever is the supertype).

Type Testing

In an earlier section, we showed a code fragment that made use of operators of the form IS_SQUARE, IS_CIRCLE, and so on, for testing whether a specified value was of some specified type. It is time to take a closer look at such operators. First of all, we assume that defining a given type T causes automatic definition of a truth-valued operator of the form

```
IS_T ( X )
```

where X is a scalar expression such that $DT(X)$ is a supertype of T (this is a compile-time check). The overall expression gives *true* if X is of type T, *false* otherwise. Note that (to repeat) the declared type of the specified argument X must be a supertype of the specified type T. Thus, for example, if C is a variable of declared type CIRCLE, the expression

```
IS_SQUARE ( C )
```

is illegal (it fails on a compile-time type error). On the other hand, both of the following are legal, and they both give *true:*

```
IS_CIRCLE ( C )
IS_ELLIPSE ( C )
```

And if E is a variable of declared type ELLIPSE but current most specific type some subtype of CIRCLE, the expression

```
IS_CIRCLE ( E )
```

gives *true* also.*

We also assume that defining a given type T causes automatic definition of an operator of the form

```
IS_MS_T ( X )
```

where X is a scalar expression and $DT(X)$ is a supertype of T (again this is a compile-time check). The overall expression gives *true* if X is of most specific type T, *false* otherwise. *Note:* It might help to observe that whereas, e.g., the operator IS_ELLIPSE is best rendered into natural language as "is an ellipse," the operator IS_MS_ELLIPSE is better rendered as "is *most specifically* an ellipse."

Here is an example involving rectangles, squares, and IS_MS_RECTANGLE:

```
VAR R RECTANGLE ;

IF IS_MS_RECTANGLE ( R )
   THEN CALL ROTATE ( R ) ;
END IF ;
```

---

*Reference [3.3] defines generalized forms of all of the "type testing" operators introduced in this subsection—for example, a generalized form of IS_T that tests whether one operand is of the same type as another, instead of just testing whether it is of some explicitly named type.

The intuition behind this example is that (a) ROTATE is an operator that rotates its rectangle argument through 90° about its center and (b) there is no point in rotating a rectangle in this way if the rectangle in question happens to be a square.

Type testing has implications for the relational operators, too. Consider the following example. Let relvar R have an attribute A of declared type ELLIPSE, and suppose we want to get those tuples of R where the A value is in fact a circle and the radius of that circle is greater than two. We might try the following:

```
R WHERE THE_R ( A ) > LENGTH ( 2.0 )
```

However, this expression will fail on a compile-time type error, because THE_R requires an argument of type CIRCLE and the declared type of A is ELLIPSE, not CIRCLE. (Of course, if the compile-time type check were not done, we would get a *run-time* type error instead as soon as we encountered a tuple in which the A value was just an ellipse and not a circle.)

Clearly, what we need to do is filter out the tuples in which the A value is just an ellipse before we even attempt to check the radius. And that is exactly what happens with the following formulation:

```
R : IS_CIRCLE ( A ) WHERE THE_R ( A ) > LENGTH ( 2.0 )
```

This expression is defined (loosely) to return those tuples in which the A value is a circle with radius greater than two. More precisely, it returns a relation with

a. The same heading as R, except that the declared type of attribute A in that result is CIRCLE instead of ELLIPSE;

b. A body consisting of just those tuples from R in which the A value is of type CIRCLE and the radius for the circle in question is greater than two.

In other words, what we are talking about is a new relational operator of the form

```
R : IS_T ( A )
```

where R is a relational expression and A is an attribute of the relation—r, say—denoted by that expression. The declared type $DT(A)$ of A must be a supertype of T (this is a compile-time check). The value of the overall expression is defined to be a relation with:

a. A heading the same as that of r, except that the declared type of attribute A in that heading is T;

b. A body consisting of those tuples of r in which attribute A contains a value of type T, except that the declared type of attribute A in each of those tuples is T.

We also define another new relational operator of the form

```
R : IS_MS_T ( A )
```

in an analogous manner.

19.7   OPERATORS, VERSIONS, AND SIGNATURES

Recall from Section 19.3 that a given operator can have many different *implementation ver-sions* (also known as **explicit specializations**) under the covers. That is, as we travel down the path from some supertype *T* to some subtype *T'* in the type hierarchy, we must at least (for a variety of reasons) be *allowed* to reimplement type *T* operators for type *T'*. By way of example, consider the following MOVE operator:

```
OPERATOR MOVE ( E ELLIPSE, R RECTANGLE ) RETURNS ( ELLIPSE )
   VERSION ER_MOVE ;
   RETURN ( ELLIPSE ( THE_A ( E ), THE_B ( E ), R_CTR ( R ) ) ) ;
END OPERATOR ;
```

Operator MOVE "moves" ellipse E, loosely speaking, so that it is centered on the center of rectangle R—or, more precisely, it returns an ellipse just like the argument ellipse corre-sponding to parameter E, except that it is centered on the center of the argument rectangle corresponding to parameter R. Note the VERSION clause in the second line, which intro-duces a distinguishing name, ER_MOVE, for this particular version of MOVE (see the next paragraph). Note too that we have assumed the availability of an operator R_CTR that re-turns the center point of a specified rectangle.

Now let us assume an explicit specialization—that is, another version—of MOVE has been defined that moves circles instead of ellipses:*

```
OPERATOR MOVE ( C CIRCLE, R RECTANGLE ) RETURNS ( CIRCLE )
   VERSION CR_MOVE ;
   RETURN ( CIRCLE ( THE_R ( C ), R_CTR ( R ) ) ) ;
END OPERATOR ;
```

In a similar manner, we might also have an explicit specialization for the case where the arguments are of most specific types ELLIPSE and SQUARE, respectively (ES_MOVE, say), and another for the case where the arguments are of most specific types CIRCLE and SQUARE, respectively (CS_MOVE, say).

Signatures

The term **signature** means, loosely, the combination of the *name* of some operator and the *types of the operands* to the operator in question. (We note in passing, however, that dif-ferent writers and different languages ascribe slightly different meanings to the term. For example, the *result* type is sometimes regarded as part of the signature, and so too are operand and result *names*.) However, we have to be very careful once again over:

  a. The distinction between arguments and parameters;

  b. The distinction between declared types and actual (most specific) types; and

---

*Actually there is little point in defining such an explicit specialization in this particular example (why, exactly?).

c. The distinction between operators as seen by the user and operators as seen by the system (meaning in the latter case explicit specializations or versions of those operators that exist under the covers, as described above).

In fact, we can distinguish—though the literature often does not!—at least three different kinds of signatures that are associated with any given operator *Op:*

- A single **specification signature,** which consists of the operator name *Op* together with the declared types, in order, of the parameters to *Op* as specified to the user by the *Op* definer. This signature corresponds to operator *Op* as understood by the user. The specification signature for MOVE, for example, is just MOVE (ELLIPSE, RECTANGLE).*

- A set of **version signatures,** one for each explicit specialization or implementation version of *Op,* each consisting of the operator name *Op* together with the declared types, in order, of the parameters defined for that version. These signatures correspond to the various pieces of implementation code that implement *Op* under the covers. The version signature for the CR_MOVE version of MOVE, for example, is MOVE (CIRCLE, RECTANGLE).

- A set of **invocation signatures,** one for each possible combination of most specific argument types, each consisting of the operator name *Op* together with the corresponding combination of most specific argument types, in order. These signatures correspond to various possible invocations of *Op* (the correspondence is one-to-many, of course—that is, one invocation signature can correspond to many distinct invocations). For example, let E and R have most specific types CIRCLE and SQUARE, respectively. Then the invocation signature for the MOVE invocation MOVE(E,R) is MOVE (CIRCLE, SQUARE).

    Different invocation signatures involving the same operator thus correspond, at least potentially, to different implemented versions of the operator in question (i.e., to different specializations under the covers). Thus, if several versions of "the same" operator do in fact exist under the covers, then which version is invoked on any given occasion will depend on which version signature is "the best match" for the applicable invocation signature. The process of deciding that best match—that is, the process of deciding which version to invoke—is, of course, the *run-time binding* process already discussed in Section 19.3.

---

*Reference [3.3] proposes that it be possible to separate the definition of the specification signature for a given operator from the definitions of *all* of the implementations (versions) of that operator. The basic idea is to support *dummy* types (also known as "abstract" or "noninstantiable" types, or sometimes just as "interfaces")—i.e., types that are not the most specific type of any value at all. Such a type provides a way of specifying operators that apply to several different regular types, all of them proper subtypes of the dummy type in question. Such an operator can then be explicitly specialized—i.e., an appropriate version of the operator can be explicitly defined—for each of those regular subtypes. In terms of our running example, PLANE_FIGURE might well be a dummy type in this sense; the AREA operator specification signature might then be defined at the PLANE_FIGURE level, and explicit implementation code (versions) then defined for type ELLIPSE, type POLYGON, and so on.

Note, incidentally, that (a) *specification* signatures are truly a model concept; (b) *version* signatures are merely an implementation concept; (c) *invocation* signatures, though a model concept in a way, are really—like the concept of substitutability—just a direct logical consequence of the basic idea of type inheritance in the first place. Indeed, the fact that different invocation signatures are possible is really just part of the concept of substitutability.

Read-Only *vs.* Update Operators

Up to this point, we have been making a tacit assumption that MOVE is a read-only operator. But suppose we were to make it an update operator instead:

```
OPERATOR MOVE ( E ELLIPSE, R RECTANGLE ) UPDATES ( E )
   VERSION ER_MOVE ;
   BEGIN ;
      THE_CTR ( E )   :=   R_CTR ( R ) ;
      RETURN ;
   END ;
END OPERATOR ;
```

(We remind you that read-only and update operators are sometimes referred to as *observers* and *mutators,* respectively. Refer to Chapter 5 if you need to refresh your memory on the difference between them.)

Observe now that an invocation of this version of MOVE *updates its first argument* (loosely, it "changes the center" of that argument). Observe further that the update works regardless of whether that first argument is of most specific type ELLIPSE or most specific type CIRCLE; in other words, explicit specializations for circles are not needed.* Thus, one advantage of update operators in general is that they might save us from having to write out certain operator specializations explicitly. Note the implications for program maintenance in particular; for example, what happens if we subsequently introduce O_CIRCLE as a sub type of CIRCLE?

Changing Operator Semantics

The fact that it is always at least legal to reimplement operators as we go down the type hierarchy has one very important consequence: It opens up the possibility of *changing the semantics* of the operator in question. In the case of AREA, for example, it might be the case that the implementation for type CIRCLE actually returns the circumference of the circle in question, say, instead of the area. (Careful type design can help to alleviate this problem somewhat; for example, if operator AREA is defined to return a result of type AREA, obviously the implementation cannot return a result of type LENGTH instead. It can, however, still return the *wrong* area!)

---

*In fact they might not be needed anyway, if specialization by constraint is supported.

What is more (surprising as it might seem), it can even be claimed—in fact, it *has* been claimed—that changing semantics in this way can be desirable. For example, let type TOLL_HIGHWAY be a proper subtype of type HIGHWAY, and let TRAVEL_TIME be an operator that computes the time it takes to travel between two specified points on a specified highway. For a toll highway, the formula is $(d/s) + (n*t)$, where d = distance, s = speed, n = number of tollbooths, and t = time spent at each tollbooth. For a nontoll highway, by contrast, the formula is just d/s.

By way of a counterexample—that is, an example of a situation in which a semantic change is surely *un*desirable—consider ellipses and circles once again. Presumably we would like the AREA operator to be defined in such a way that a given circle has the same area, regardless of whether we consider it as a circle specifically or just as an ellipse. In other words, suppose the following events occur in sequence as shown:

1. We define type ELLIPSE and a corresponding version of the AREA operator. Assume for simplicity that the AREA code does not make use of the *actual* representation for ellipses.

2. We define type CIRCLE as a subtype of ELLIPSE but do not (yet) define a separate implementation version of AREA for circles.

3. We invoke AREA on some specific circle *c* to obtain a result, *area1* say. That invocation makes use of the ELLIPSE version of AREA, of course.

4. We now define a separate implementation version of AREA for circles.

5. We invoke AREA again on the same specific circle *c* as before to obtain a result, *area2* say (and this time it is the CIRCLE version of AREA that is invoked).

Then we would surely like to insist that *area1* = *area2*. However, this would-be requirement is not enforceable; that is, there is, as already noted, always the possibility that the version of AREA implemented for circles might return (say) the circumference instead of the area, or simply the wrong area.

Let us return to the TRAVEL_TIME example. The fact is, we find that example, and others like it, extremely unconvincing—unconvincing, that is, as an example of a situation in which changing the semantics of an operator might be thought desirable. For consider:

- If TOLL_HIGHWAY is truly a subtype of HIGHWAY, it means by definition that every individual toll highway is in fact a highway.

- Therefore, some highways (i.e., some values of type HIGHWAY) are indeed toll highways—they do indeed have tollbooths. So type HIGHWAY is not "highways with no tollbooths," it is "highways with *n* tollbooths" (where *n* might be zero).

- So the operator TRAVEL_TIME for type HIGHWAY is not "compute the travel time for a highway *with no* tollbooths," it is "compute the travel time d/s for a highway *ignoring* tollbooths."

- The operator TRAVEL_TIME for type TOLL_HIGHWAY, by contrast, is "compute the travel time $(d/s) + (n*t)$ for a highway not ignoring tollbooths." So in fact the two

TRAVEL_TIMEs are logically different operators. Confusion arises because those two different operators have been given the same name; in fact, what we have here is overloading polymorphism, not inclusion polymorphism.

(As an aside, we remark that further confusion arises in practice because, regrettably, many writers actually use the term *overloading* to refer to inclusion polymorphism anyway.)

To sum up: We still do not believe that changing operator semantics is ever a good idea. As we have seen, this requirement is not enforceable; however, we can certainly define our inheritance model—and we do—to say that if the semantics *are* changed, then **the implementation is in violation** (i.e., it is not an implementation of the model, and the implications are unpredictable). Observe that our position on this matter (i.e., our position that such changes are illegal) does have the advantage that, regardless of whether any explicit specializations of a given operator *Op* are defined, the user perception remains the same: namely, that (a) there exists an operator—a *single* operator—called *Op,* and (b) that operator *Op* applies to argument values of some specified type *T* and hence, by definition, to argument values of any proper subtype of *T*.

19.8   IS A CIRCLE AN ELLIPSE?

Are circles really ellipses? We have been assuming throughout this chapter so far—reasonably enough!—that they are, but we must now face up to the fact there is much debate in the literature on this apparently obvious point. Consider our usual variables E and C of declared types ELLIPSE and CIRCLE, respectively. Suppose these variables have been initialized as follows:

```
E   :=   ELLIPSE ( LENGTH ( 5.0 ), LENGTH ( 3.0 ),
                            POINT ( 0.0, 0.0 ) ) ;
C   :=   CIRCLE  ( LENGTH ( 5.0 ), POINT ( 0.0, 0.0 ) ) ;
```

Note in particular that THE_A(C) and THE_B(C) both now have the value five.

Now, one operation we can certainly perform on E is "update the *a* semiaxis"—for example:

```
THE_A ( E )  :=  LENGTH ( 6.0 ) ;
```

But if we try to perform the analogous operation on C—

```
THE_A ( C )  :=  LENGTH ( 6.0 ) ;
```

—we get an error! What kind of error, exactly? Well, if the update did in fact occur, variable C would wind up containing a "circle" that violates the constraint on circles to the effect that $a = b$ (*a* would now be six, while *b* would presumably still be five, since we have not changed it). In other words, C would now contain a "noncircular circle," thereby violating the type constraint on type CIRCLE.

Since "noncircular circles" are an affront to logic and common sense, it seems reasonable to suggest that the update not be allowed in the first place. And the obvious way to achieve this effect is to reject such operations at compile time, by defining update of—that is, assignment to—the *a* or *b* semiaxis of a circle to be *syntactically* illegal. In other words, assignment to THE_A or THE_B does not apply to type CIRCLE, and the attempted update fails on *a compile-time type error.*

Note: In fact, it is "obvious" that such assignments must be syntactically illegal. Recall that assignment to a THE_ pseudovariable is really just shorthand. Thus, for example, the attempted assignment to THE_A(C) shown above, if it were legal, would have to be shorthand for something like this:

```
C  :=  CIRCLE ( ... ) ;
```

And the CIRCLE selector invocation on the right hand side here would have to include a THE_A argument of LENGTH(6.0). But the CIRCLE selector does not take a THE_A argument!—it takes a THE_R argument and a THE_CTR argument. So the original assignment must clearly be illegal.

What about Changing the Semantics?

Let us immediately head off a suggestion that is sometimes made in an attempt to rescue the idea that assignment to THE_A or THE_B should be legal for circles after all. The suggestion is that assignment to (e.g.) THE_A should be *redefined*—in other words, *explicitly specialized*—for a circle in such a way as to have the side effect of assignment to THE_B too, so that the circle still satisfies the constraint *a* = *b* after the update. We reject this suggestion for at least the following three reasons:

- First, the semantics of assignment to THE_A and THE_B are—very deliberately!— prescribed by our inheritance model and must *not* be changed in the manner suggested.

- Second, even if those semantics were not prescribed by the model, we have already argued that (a) changing the semantics of an operator in arbitrary ways is a bad idea in general, and (b) changing the semantics of an operator in such a way as to cause side effects is an even worse one. It is a good general principle to insist that operators have exactly the requested effect, no more and no less.

- Third, and most important, the option of changing the semantics in the manner suggested is not always available, anyway. For example, let type ELLIPSE have another immediate subtype NONCIRCLE; let the constraint *a* > *b* apply to noncircles; and consider an assignment to THE_A for a noncircle that, if accepted, would set *a* equal to *b*. What would be an appropriate semantic redefinition for that assignment? Exactly what side effect would be appropriate?

Does a Sensible Model Even Exist?

So we are left with the situation that assignment to THE_A or THE_B is an operation that applies to ellipses in general but not to circles in particular. But:

a. Type CIRCLE is supposed to be a subtype of type ELLIPSE;

b. To say that type CIRCLE is a subtype of type ELLIPSE is supposed to mean that operations that apply to ellipses in general apply to—in other words, are *inherited by*—circles in particular;

c. But now we are saying that the operation of assignment to THE_A or THE_B is *not* inherited after all.

So do we not have a contradiction on our hands? What is going on?

Before trying to answer these questions, we need to stress the seriousness of the problem. The foregoing argument looks like a real threadpuller. For if certain operators are *not* inherited by type CIRCLE from type ELLIPSE, in what sense exactly can we say that a circle "is a" ellipse? What does "inheritance" mean if some operators are in fact not inherited after all? Does a sensible inheritance model even exist? Are we chasing a chimera in trying to find one?

Note: Some writers have even suggested—*seriously* suggested—that assignment to THE_A should work for both circles and ellipses (for a circle, it updates the radius), while assignment to THE_B should work for ellipses only, and so ELLIPSE should really be a subtype of CIRCLE! In other words, we have the type hierarchy upside down. However, a moment's thought suffices to show that this idea is a nonstarter; in particular, substitutability would break down (what is the radius of a general ellipse?).

It is precisely considerations such as the foregoing that have led some writers to conclude that there really is no such thing as a sensible inheritance model (see the annotation to reference [19.1] in the "References and Bibliography" section at the end of the chapter). Other writers have proposed inheritance models with features that are counterintuitive or clearly undesirable. For example, SQL3 permits "noncircular circles" and other such nonsenses; like SQL/92, in fact, it does not support type constraints at all, and it is that omission that allows such nonsenses to arise in the first place (see Appendix B).

The Solution

To summarize the situation so far, we find ourselves faced with the following dilemma:

■ If circles inherit the operators "assignment to THE_A and THE_B" from ellipses, then we get noncircular circles.

■ The way to prevent noncircular circles is to support type constraints.

■ But if we support type constraints, then the operators cannot be inherited.

■ So there is no inheritance after all!

How do we resolve this dilemma?

The way out is—as so often—to recognize (and act upon) the fact that there is a major logical difference between **values** and **variables.** When we say "every circle is an ellipse," what we mean, more precisely, is that every circle *value* is an ellipse *value*. We certainly do not mean that every circle *variable* is an ellipse *variable* (a variable of declared type CIRCLE is *not* a variable of declared type ELLIPSE, and it cannot contain a value of most specific type ELLIPSE). In other words, **inheritance applies to values, not variables.** In the case of ellipses and circles, for example:

- As just noted, every circle value is an ellipse value.
- Therefore, all operations that apply to ellipse values apply to circle values too.
- But the one thing we cannot do to any value is **change** it!—if we could, it would be that value no longer. (Of course, we can "change the current value of" a variable, by updating that variable, but—to repeat—we cannot change the value as such.)

Now, the operations that apply to ellipse values are precisely all of the *read-only* operators defined for type ELLIPSE, while the operations that update ELLIPSE variables are, of course, the *update* operators defined for that type. Hence, our dictum that "inheritance applies to values, not variables" can be stated more precisely as follows:

- **Read-only operators are inherited by values, and hence *a fortiori* by current values of variables** (since, of course, read-only operators can be applied—harmlessly— to those values that happen to be the current values of variables).

This more precise statement also serves to explain why the concepts of polymorphism and substitutability refer very specifically to *values,* not variables. For example (and just to remind you), substitutability says that wherever the system expects a **value** of type *T,* we can always substitute a **value** of type *T'* instead, where *T'* is a subtype of *T* (boldface added for emphasis). In fact, we specifically referred to this principle when we first introduced it as *The Principle of **Value** Substitutability* (again, note the emphasis).

What about update operators, then? By definition, such operators apply to variables, not values. So can we say that update operators that apply to variables of type ELLIPSE are inherited by variables of type CIRCLE?

Well, no, we cannot—not quite. For example, assignment to THE_CTR does apply to variables of both declared types, but (as we have seen) assignment to THE_A does not. Thus, inheritance of update operators has to be *conditional;* in fact, precisely which update operators are inherited must be specified explicitly. For example:

- Variables of declared type ELLIPSE have update operators MOVE (update version) and assignment to THE_A, THE_B, and THE_CTR;
- Variables of declared type CIRCLE have update operators MOVE (update version) and assignment to THE_CTR and THE_R but *not* to THE_A or THE_B.

Note: The MOVE operator was discussed in the previous section.

Of course, if an update operator *is* inherited, then we do have a kind of polymorphism and a kind of substitutability that apply to variables instead of just to values. For example, the update version of MOVE expects an argument that is a variable of declared type ELLIPSE, but we can invoke it with an argument that is a variable of declared type CIRCLE instead. Thus, we can (and do) talk sensibly about a *Principle of **Variable**

Substitutability—but that principle is more restrictive than the *Principle of Value Substitutability* discussed above.

19.9 SPECIALIZATION BY CONSTRAINT REVISITED

There is a small but significant postscript that needs to be added to the discussions of the foregoing sections. It has to do with examples like this one: "Let type CIRCLE have a proper subtype called COLORED_CIRCLE" (meaning that "colored circles" are supposed to be a special case of circles in general). Examples of this general nature are commonly quoted in the literature. Yet we have to say that we find such examples extremely unconvincing—even misleading, in certain important respects. To be more specific, we suggest in the case at hand that it really does not make sense to think of colored circles being somehow a special case of circles in general. After all, "colored circles" must by definition be *images,* on a display screen perhaps, whereas circles in general are not images but *geometric figures.* Thus, it seems more reasonable to regard COLORED_CIRCLE not as a subtype of CIRCLE, but rather as *a completely separate type.* That separate type might well have a **possible representation** in which one component is of type CIRCLE and another is of type COLOR, but it is not—to repeat—a subtype of type CIRCLE.

Inheriting Possible Representations

A strong argument in support of the foregoing position runs as follows. First, let us switch back for a moment to our more usual example of ellipses and circles. Here once again are the type definitions (in part):

```
TYPE ELLIPSE POSSREP ( A LENGTH, B LENGTH, CTR POINT ) ... ;

TYPE CIRCLE POSSREP ( R LENGTH, CTR POINT ) ... ;
```

Note in particular that ellipses and circles have different declared possible representations. However, the possible representation for ellipses is—*necessarily,* albeit implicitly—a possible representation for circles too, because circles *are* ellipses. That is, circles can certainly be "possibly represented" by their *a* and *b* semiaxes (and their center), even though in fact their *a* and *b* semiaxes are both the same. Of course, the converse is not true—that is, a possible representation for circles is *not* necessarily a possible representation for ellipses.

It follows that we could regard possible representations, like operators and constraints, as further "properties" that are inherited by circles from ellipses, or more generally by subtypes from supertypes.* But (reverting now to the case of circles and colored circles) it

---

*We do not regard them in this way in our formal model—i.e., we do not regard such inherited possible representations as *declared* ones—because to say they were declared ones would lead to a contradiction. To be specific, if we said that type CIRCLE inherits a possible representation from type ELLIPSE, then reference [3.3] would require assignment to THE_A or THE_B for a variable of declared type CIRCLE to be legal, and of course we know it is not. Thus, to say that type CIRCLE inherits a possible representation from type ELLIPSE is only a *façon de parler*—it carries no formal weight.

should be clear that the declared possible representation for type CIRCLE is *not* a possible representation for type COLORED_CIRCLE, because there is nothing in it that is capable of representing the color! This fact strongly suggests that colored circles are *not* circles in the same sense that, for example, circles are ellipses.

So What Do Subtypes Really Mean?

The next argument is related (somewhat) to the previous one, but is in fact stronger (*logically* stronger, that is). Here it is: *There is no way to obtain a colored circle from a circle via specialization by constraint.*

In order to explain this point, we go back for a moment to the case of ellipses and circles. Here once again are the type definitions:

```
TYPE ELLIPSE POSSREP ( A LENGTH, B LENGTH, CTR POINT ) ...
    CONSTRAINT ( THE_A ( ELLIPSE ) ≥ THE_B ( ELLIPSE ) ) ;

TYPE CIRCLE POSSREP ( R LENGTH, CTR POINT )
    SUBTYPE_OF ( ELLIPSE )
    CONSTRAINT ( THE_A ( CIRCLE ) = THE_B ( CIRCLE ) ) ;
```

As we saw earlier, the CONSTRAINT clause for type CIRCLE guarantees that an ellipse with $a = b$ will automatically be specialized to type CIRCLE. But—now switching back to circles and colored circles—there is no CONSTRAINT clause we can write for type COLORED_CIRCLE that will analogously cause a circle to be specialized to type COLORED_CIRCLE; i.e., there is no type constraint we can write such that if it is satisfied by some given circle, it means the circle in question is really a colored circle.

Again, therefore, it seems more reasonable to regard COLORED_CIRCLE and CIRCLE as completely different types, and to regard type COLORED_CIRCLE in particular as having a possible representation in which one component is of type CIRCLE and another is of type COLOR, thus:

```
TYPE COLORED_CIRCLE POSSREP ( CIR CIRCLE, COL COLOR ) ... ;
```

In fact, we are touching here on a much larger issue. The fact is, we believe that subtyping should *always* be via specialization by constraint! That is, we suggest that **if *T'* is a subtype of *T*, there should *always* be a type constraint such that, if it is satisfied by some given value of type *T*, then the value in question is really a value of type *T'*** (and should automatically be specialized to type *T'*). For let *T* and *T'* be types, and let *T'* be a subtype of *T* (in fact, we can assume without loss of generality that *T'* is an *immediate* subtype of *T*). Then:

- *T* and *T'* are both basically *sets* (named sets of values), and *T'* is a subset of *T*.
- Thus, *T* and *T'* both have *membership predicates*—predicates, that is, such that a value is a member of the set in question (and hence a value of the type in question) if and only if it satisfies the predicate in question. Let those predicates be *P* and *P'*, respectively.
- Observe now that predicate *P'* is, by definition, a predicate that can evaluate to *true* only for certain values that are in fact values of type *T*. Thus, it can in fact be formulated in terms of values of type *T* (rather than in terms of values of type *T'*).

- And that predicate *P'*, formulated in terms of values of type *T,* is precisely the type constraint that values of type *T* have to satisfy in order to be values of type *T'*. In other words, a value of type *T* is specialized to type *T'* precisely if it satisfies the constraint *P'*.

Thus, we claim that specialization by constraint is the *only* conceptually valid means of defining subtypes. As a consequence, we reject examples like the one suggesting that COLORED_CIRCLE might be a subtype of CIRCLE.

19.10 SUMMARY

We have sketched the basic concepts of a **type inheritance model.** If type *B* is a subtype of type *A* (equivalently, type *A* is a supertype of type *B*), then every value of type *B* is also a value of type *A,* and hence operators and constraints that apply to values of type *A* apply to values of type *B* also (but there will also be operators and constraints that apply to values of type *B* that do not apply to values that are only of type *A*). We distinguished **single *vs*. multiple** inheritance (but discussed single inheritance only) and **scalar *vs*. tuple *vs*. relation** inheritance (but discussed scalar inheritance only), and we introduced the concept of a **type hierarchy.** We also defined the terms **proper** subtype and supertype, **immediate** subtype and supertype, and **root** type and **leaf** type, and we stated a **disjointness assumption:** Types *T1* and *T2* are disjoint unless one is a subtype of the other. As a consequence of this assumption, every value has a unique **most specific** type (not necessarily a leaf type).

Next, we discussed the concepts of (inclusion) **polymorphism** and (value) **substitutability,** both of which are logical consequences of the basic notion of inheritance. We distinguished between **inclusion** polymorphism (which has to do with inheritance) and **overloading** polymorphism (which does not). And we showed how—thanks to **run-time binding**—inclusion polymorphism could lead to **code reuse.**

We then moved on to consider the effects of inheritance on **assignment** operations. The basic point is that type conversions do *not* occur—values retain their most specific type on assignment to variables of less specific declared type—and hence a variable of declared type *T* can have a value whose most specific type is any subtype of *T*. (Likewise, if operator *Op* is defined to have a result of declared type *T,* the actual result of an invocation of *Op* can be a value whose most specific type is any subtype of type *T*.) We therefore model a scalar variable *V*—or, more generally, an arbitrary scalar expression—as an ordered triple of the form *<DT,MST,v>*, where *DT* is the declared type, *MST* is the current most specific type, and *v* is the current value. We introduced the **TREAT DOWN** operator to allow us to operate—in ways that would otherwise give rise to a compile-time type error—on expressions whose most specific type at run time is some proper subtype of their declared type. (Run-time type errors can occur, but only within the context of TREAT DOWN.)

Next we took a closer look at **selectors.** We saw that invoking a selector for type *T* will sometimes yield a result of some proper subtype of *T* (at least in our model, though not—typically—in today's commercial products): **specialization by constraint.** We then took a closer look at **THE_ pseudovariables;** since they are really just shorthand, both specialization and **generalization** by constraint can occur on assignment to a THE_ pseudovariable.

We then went on to discuss the effects of subtypes and supertypes on **equality comparisons** and certain relational operations (**join, union, intersection,** and **difference**). We also introduced a number of **type testing** operators: **IS_T, IS_MS_T,** and so on. Then we considered the question of **read-only** *vs.* **update operators,** operator **versions,** and operator **signatures,** pointing out that the ability to define different versions of an operator opens up the door to **changing the semantics** of the operator in question (but our model prohibits such changes).

Finally, we examined the question "Are circles really ellipses?" That examination led us to the position that **inheritance applies to values, not variables.** More precisely, read-only operators (which apply to values) can be inherited 100 percent without any problem, but update operators (which apply to variables) can be inherited only **conditionally.** (Our model is at odds with most other approaches here. Those other approaches typically require update operators to be inherited unconditionally, but they then suffer from a variety of problems having to do with "noncircular circles" and the like.) And we concluded by observing that—in our opinion—specialization by constraint is the *only* logically valid way of defining subtypes.

EXERCISES

19.1 Define the following terms:

code reuse	proper subtype
dummy type	root type
generalization by constraint	run-time binding
immediate subtype	scalar type
leaf type	signature
nonscalar type	specialization by constraint
polymorphism	substitutability

19.2 Explain the TREAT DOWN operator.

19.3 Distinguish:

a. argument   *vs.*   parameter
b. declared type   *vs.*   current most specific type
c. inclusion polymorphism   *vs.*   overloading polymorphism
d. invocation signature   *vs.*   specification signature   *vs.*   version signature
e. read-only operator   *vs.*   update operator
f. value   *vs.*   variable

19.4 With reference to the type hierarchy of Fig. 19.1, consider a value *e* of type ELLIPSE. The most specific type of *e* is either ELLIPSE or CIRCLE. What is the *least* specific type of *e?*

19.5 Any given type hierarchy includes several subhierarchies that can be regarded as type hierarchies in their own right. For example, the hierarchy obtained from that of Fig. 19.1 by deleting types PLANE_FIGURE, ELLIPSE, and CIRCLE (only) can be regarded as a type hierarchy in its own right, and so can the one obtained by deleting types CIRCLE, SQUARE, and RECTANGLE (only). On the other hand, the hierarchy obtained by deleting ELLIPSE (only) *cannot* be regarded as a type hierarchy in its own right (at least, not one that can be derived from that of Fig. 19.1), because type CIRCLE "loses some of its inheritance," as it were, in that hierarchy. So how many distinct type hierarchies are there altogether in Fig. 19.1?

19.6 Using the syntax sketched in the body of the chapter, give type definitions for types RECTANGLE and SQUARE (assume for simplicity that all rectangles are centered on the origin, but do not assume that all sides are either vertical or horizontal).

19.7 Given your answer to Exercise 19.6, define an operator to rotate a specified rectangle through 90° about its center. Also give an explicit specialization of that operator for squares.

19.8 Here is a repeat of an example from Section 19.6: "Relvar R has an attribute A of declared type ELLIPSE, and we want to query R to get those tuples where the A value is in fact a circle and the radius of that circle is greater than two." We gave the following formulation of this query in Section 19.6:

```
R : IS_CIRCLE ( A ) WHERE THE_R ( A ) > LENGTH ( 2.0 )
```

a. Why could we not simply express the type test in the WHERE clause?—for example:

```
R WHERE IS_CIRCLE ( A ) AND THE_R ( A ) > LENGTH ( 2.0 )
```

b. Another candidate formulation is:

```
R WHERE CASE
          WHEN IS_CIRCLE ( A ) THEN
               THE_R ( TREAT_DOWN_AS_CIRCLE ( A ) )
                                 > LENGTH ( 2.0 )
          WHEN NOT ( IS_CIRCLE ( A ) ) THEN FALSE
        END CASE
```

Is this one valid? If not, why not?

19.9 Reference [3.3] proposes support for relational expressions of the form

```
R TREAT_DOWN_AS_T ( A )
```

Here *R* is a relational expression, *A* is an attribute of the relation—*r,* say—denoted by that expression, and *T* is a type. The declared type $DT(A)$ of *A* must be a supertype of *T* (this is a compile-time check). The value of the overall expression is defined to be a relation with:

a. A heading the same as that of *r,* except that the declared type of attribute *A* in that heading is *T;*

b. A body containing the same tuples as *r,* except that the *A* value in each of those tuples has been treated down to type *T*.

Once again, however, this operator is just a shorthand—for what, exactly?

19.10 Expressions of the form $R:IS\_T(A)$ are also shorthand—for what, exactly?

REFERENCES AND BIBLIOGRAPHY

19.1 Malcolm Atkinson *et al.:* "The Object-Oriented Database System Manifesto," Proc. First International Conference on Deductive and Object-Oriented Databases, Kyoto, Japan (1989). New York, N.Y.: Elsevier Science (1990).

Regarding the lack of consensus (noted in Section 19.1) on a good inheritance model, the authors of the present paper have this to say: "[There] are at least four types of inheritance: *substitution* inheritance, *inclusion* inheritance, *constraint* inheritance, and *specialization* inheritance . . . Various degrees of these four types of inheritance are provided by existing systems and prototypes, and we do not prescribe a specific style of inheritance."

Here are some more quotes that illustrate the same general point:

- Cleaveland [19.4] says: "[Inheritance can be] based on [a variety of] different criteria and there is no commonly accepted standard definition"—and proceeds to give eight possible interpretations. (Meyer [19.8] gives twelve.)

- Baclawski and Indurkhya [19.2] say: "[A] programming language [merely] provides a set of [inheritance] mechanisms. While these mechanisms certainly restrict what one can do in that language and what views of inheritance can be implemented . . . they do not by themselves validate some view of inheritance or other. Classes, specializations, generalizations, and inheritance are only concepts, and . . . they do not have a universal objective meaning . . . This [fact] implies that how inheritance is to be incorporated into a specific system is up to the designers of [that] system, and it constitutes a policy decision that must be implemented with the available mechanisms." In other words, there is no model!

19.2 Kenneth Baclawski and Bipin Indurkhya: Technical Correspondence, *CACM 37,* No. 9 (September 1994).

19.3 Luca Cardelli and Peter Wegner: "On Understanding Types, Data Abstraction, and Polymorphism," *ACM Comp. Surv. 17,* No. 4 (December 1985).

19.4 J. Craig Cleaveland: *An Introduction to Data Types.* Reading, Mass.: Addison-Wesley (1986).

19.5 C. J. Date: Series of articles on type inheritance on the *DBP&D* website *www.dbpd.com* (first installment February 1999).

An extended tutorial treatment (with historical notes) of the inheritance model described in the present chapter and defined more formally in reference [3.3].

19.6 C. J. Date and Hugh Darwen: "Toward a Model of Type Inheritance," *CACM 41,* No. 12 (December 1998).

This short note includes a summary of the major features of our inheritance model.

19.7 Nelson Mattos and Linda G. DeMichiel: "Recent Design Trade-Offs in SQL3," *ACM SIGMOD Record 23,* No. 4 (December 1994).

This paper gives the rationale for the decision on the part of the SQL3 designers not to support type constraints (it is based on an argument given earlier by Zdonik and Maier in reference [19.11]). We disagree with that rationale, however. The fundamental problem with it is that it fails to distinguish properly between values and variables (see Exercise 19.3).

19.8 Bertrand Meyer: "The Many Faces of Inheritance: A Taxonomy of Taxonomy," *IEEE Computer 29,* No. 5 (May 1996).

19.9 James Rumbaugh: "A Matter of Intent: How to Define Subclasses," *Journal of Object-Oriented Programming* (September 1996).

> As noted in Section 19.9, we take the view that specialization by constraint is the only logically valid way of defining subtypes. It is interesting to observe, therefore, that the object world takes exactly the opposite position!—or, at least, some denizens of that world do. To quote Rumbaugh: "Is SQUARE a subclass of RECTANGLE? . . . Stretching the *x*-dimension of a rectangle is a perfectly reasonable thing to do. But if you do it to a square, then the object is no longer a square. This is not necessarily a bad thing conceptually. When you stretch a square you *do* get a rectangle . . . But . . . most object-oriented languages do not want objects to change class . . . All of this suggests [a] design principle for classification systems: *A subclass should not be defined by constraining a superclass*" (italics in the original). *Note:* As explained in Chapter 24, the object world often uses the term *class* to mean what we mean by the term *type*.

> We find it striking that Rumbaugh apparently takes the position he does simply because object-oriented languages "do not want objects to change class." We would rather get the *model* right first before worrying about implementations.

19.10 Andrew Taivalsaari: "On the Notion of Inheritance," *ACM Comp. Surv. 28,* No. 3 (September 1996).

19.11 Stanley B. Zdonik and David Maier: "Fundamentals of Object-Oriented Databases," in reference [24.52].

ANSWERS TO SELECTED EXERCISES

19.3 We consider Case f. (value *vs.* variable) only, since it is fundamental and yet not explicitly discussed elsewhere in this book. (The following definitions are taken from reference [3.3].)

- A **value** is an "individual constant" (for example, the individual constant "3"). A value has *no location in time or space.* However, values can be represented in memory by some *encoding,* and of course such encodings do have locations in time and space (see the next paragraph). Note that, by definition, *a value cannot be updated;* for if it could, then after such an update it would not be that value any longer (in general).

- A **variable** is a holder for an encoding of a value. A variable does have a location in time and space. Also, of course, variables, unlike values, can be updated; that is, the current value of the variable in question can be replaced by another value, probably different from the previous one. (Of course, the variable in question is still the same variable after the update.)

By the way, it is important to understand that it is not just simple things like the integer "3" that are legitimate values. On the contrary, values can be arbitrarily complex; for example, a value might be an array, or a stack, or a list, or a relation, or a geometric point, or an ellipse, or an X-ray, or a document, or a fingerprint (and so on). Analogous remarks apply to variables too, of course.

19.4 The least specific type of any value of *any* of the types shown in Fig. 19.1 is PLANE_FIGURE, of course.

19.5 22 (this count includes the empty hierarchy).

19.6 Given that all rectangles are centered on the origin, a given rectangle ABCD can be uniquely identified by any two adjacent vertices, say A and B, and a given square can be uniquely identified by any single vertex, say A. To pin matters down more precisely, we take A to be the vertex in the top right quadrant of the plane ($x \geq 0$, $y \geq 0$) and B to be the vertex in the bottom right quadrant ($x \geq 0$, $y \leq 0$). Then we can define types RECTANGLE and SQUARE as follows:

```
TYPE RECTANGLE POSSREP ( A POINT, B POINT ) ... ;

TYPE SQUARE POSSREP ( A POINT )
     CONSTRAINT ( THE_X ( THE_A ( SQUARE ) ) =
                - THE_Y ( THE_B ( SQUARE ) ) AND
                  THE_Y ( THE_A ( SQUARE ) ) =
                  THE_X ( THE_B ( SQUARE ) ) ) ;
```

19.7 The operators defined below are update operators specifically. As a subsidiary exercise, define some read-only analogs of those operators.

```
OPERATOR ROTATE ( R RECTANGLE ) UPDATES ( R )
     VERSION ROTATE_RECTANGLE ;
     BEGIN ;
        VAR P POINT ;
        VAR Q POINT ;
        P   :=  THE_A ( R ) ;
        Q   :=  THE_B ( R ) ;
        THE_X ( THE_A ( R ) )  :=  - THE_Y ( Q ) ;
        THE_Y ( THE_A ( R ) )  :=    THE_X ( Q ) ;
        THE_X ( THE_B ( R ) )  :=    THE_Y ( P ) ;
        THE_Y ( THE_B ( R ) )  :=  - THE_X ( P ) ;
        RETURN ;
     END ;
END OPERATOR ;

OPERATOR ROTATE ( S SQUARE ) UPDATES ( S )
     VERSION ROTATE_SQUARE ;
     RETURN ;
END OPERATOR ;
```

19.8

a. The specified expression will fail on a compile-time type error, because THE_R requires an argument of type CIRCLE and the declared type of A is ELLIPSE, not CIRCLE. (Of course, if the compile-time type check were not done, we would get a *run-time* type error instead as soon as we encountered a tuple in which the A value was just an ellipse and not a circle.)

b. The specified expression is valid, but it yields a relation with the same heading as R, not one in which the declared type of attribute A is CIRCLE instead of ELLIPSE.

19.9 The expression is shorthand for an expression of the form

```
( ( EXTEND ( R ) ADD ( TREAT_DOWN_AS_T ( A ) ) AS A' )
                         { ALL BUT A } ) RENAME A' AS A
```

(where *A'* is an arbitrary name not already appearing as an attribute name in the result of evaluating *R*).

19.10 The expression is shorthand for an expression of the form

```
( R WHERE IS_T ( A ) ) TREAT_DOWN_AS_T ( A )
```

Moreover, this latter expression is itself shorthand for a longer one, as we saw in the answer to Exercise 19.9.

Distributed Databases

20.1 INTRODUCTION

We touched on the subject of **distributed databases** at the end of Chapter 2, where we said that (to quote) "full support for distributed database implies that a single application should be able to operate transparently on data that is spread across a variety of different databases, managed by a variety of different DBMSs, running on a variety of different machines, supported by a variety of different operating systems, and connected together by a variety of different communication networks—where the term *transparently* means that the application operates from a logical point of view as if the data were all managed by a single DBMS running on a single machine." We are now in a position to examine these ideas in some detail. To be specific, in this chapter we will explain exactly what a distributed database is, why such databases are becoming increasingly important, and what some of the technical problems are in the distributed database field.

Chapter 2 also briefly discussed **client/server** systems, which can be regarded as a simple special case of distributed systems in general. We will consider client/server systems specifically in Section 20.5.

The overall plan of the chapter is explained at the end of the next section.

20.2 SOME PRELIMINARIES

We begin with a working definition (necessarily a little imprecise at this stage):

- A distributed database system consists of a collection of **sites,** connected together via some kind of communications network, in which

    a. Each site is a full database system site in its own right, but

    b. The sites have agreed to work together so that a user at any site can access data anywhere in the network exactly as if the data were all stored at the user's own site.

It follows that the so-called "distributed database" is really a kind of *virtual* database, whose component parts are physically stored in a number of distinct "real" databases at a number of distinct sites (in effect, it is the logical union of those real databases). An example is shown in Fig. 20.1.

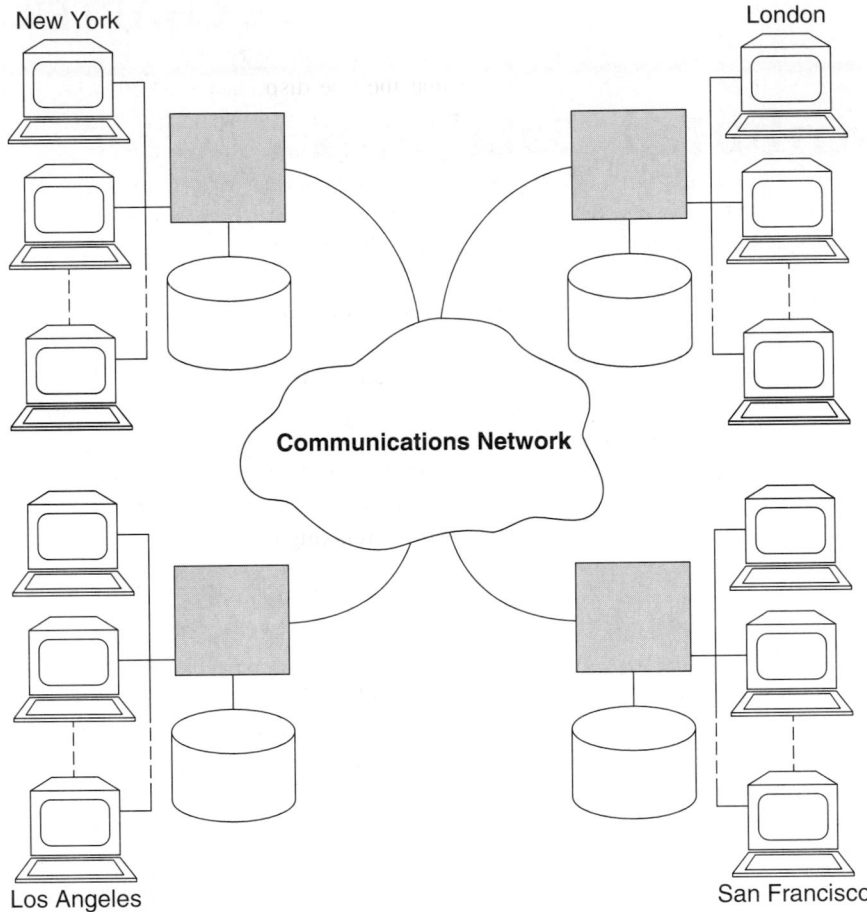

Fig. 20.1   A typical distributed database system

Note that, to repeat, **each site is a database system site in its own right.** In other words, each site has its own local "real" databases, its own local users, its own local DBMS and transaction management software (including its own local locking, logging, recovery, etc., software), and its own local data communications manager (DC manager). In particular, a given user can perform operations on data at that user's own local site exactly as if that site did not participate in the distributed system at all (at least, this is an objective). The distributed database system can thus be regarded as a kind of **partnership** among the individual local DBMSs at the individual local sites; a new software component at each site—logically an extension of the local DBMS—provides the necessary partnership functionality, and it is the combination of this new component together with the existing DBMS that constitutes what is usually called the **distributed database management system.**

Incidentally, it is common to assume that the component sites are physically dispersed—possibly in fact geographically dispersed also, as suggested by Fig. 20.1—although actually it is sufficient that they be dispersed *logically*. Two "sites" might even coexist on the same physical machine (especially during the period of initial system testing). In fact, the emphasis in distributed systems has shifted back and forth over time; the earliest research tended to assume geographic distribution, but most of the first few commercial installations involved *local* distribution instead, with (e.g.) several "sites" all in the same building and connected together by means of a local area network (LAN). More recently, however, the dramatic proliferation of wide area networks (WANs) has revived interest in the possibility of geographic distribution again. In any case, it makes little difference from a database perspective—essentially the same (database) technical problems have to be solved—and so we can reasonably regard Fig. 20.1 as representing a typical system for the purposes of this chapter.

Note: In order to simplify the exposition, we will assume until further notice that the system is *homogeneous,* in the sense that each site is running a copy of the same DBMS. We will refer to this as the **strict homogeneity** assumption. We will explore the possibility—and some of the implications—of relaxing this assumption in Section 20.6.

Advantages

Why are distributed databases desirable? The basic answer to this question is that enterprises are usually distributed already, at least logically (into divisions, departments, workgroups, etc.), and very likely physically too (into plants, factories, laboratories, etc.) from which it follows that data is usually distributed already as well, because each organizational unit within the enterprise will naturally maintain data that is relevant to its own operation. The total information asset of the enterprise is thus splintered into what are sometimes called *islands of information.* And what a distributed system does is provide the necessary *bridges* to connect those islands together. In other words, it enables the structure of the database to mirror the structure of the enterprise—local data can be kept locally, where it most logically belongs—while at the same time remote data can be accessed when necessary.

An example will help to clarify the foregoing. Consider Fig. 20.1 once again. For simplicity, suppose there are only two sites, Los Angeles and San Francisco, and suppose the system is a banking system, with account data for Los Angeles accounts kept in Los Angeles and account data for San Francisco accounts kept in San Francisco. Then the advantages are surely obvious: The distributed arrangement combines **efficiency of processing** (the data is kept close to the point where it is most frequently used) with **increased accessibility** (it is possible to access a Los Angeles account from San Francisco and *vice versa,* via the communications network).

Allowing the structure of the database to mirror the structure of the enterprise is (as just explained) probably the major benefit of distributed systems. Numerous additional benefits do also accrue, of course, but we will defer discussion of such additional benefits to appropriate points later in the chapter. However, we should mention that there are some disadvantages too, of which the biggest is the fact that distributed systems are *complex,* at least from a technical point of view. Ideally, of course, that complexity should be the implementer's problem, not the user's, but it is likely—to be pragmatic—that some aspects of it will show through to users, unless very careful precautions are taken.

Sample Systems

For purposes of subsequent reference, we briefly mention some of the better known distributed system implementations. First, prototypes. Out of numerous research systems, three of the best known are (a) *SDD-1,* which was built in the research division of Computer Corporation of America in the late 1970s and early 1980s [20.34]; (b) R^* ("R star"), a distributed version of the System R prototype, built at IBM Research in the early 1980s [20.39]; and (c) *Distributed Ingres,* a distributed version of the Ingres prototype, also built in the early 1980s at the University of California at Berkeley [20.36].

As for commercial implementations, most of today's SQL products offer some kind of distributed database support (with varying degrees of functionality, of course). Some of the best known include (a) *Ingres/Star,* the distributed database component of Ingres; (b) the *distributed database option* of Oracle; and (c) the *distributed data facility* of DB2. *Note:* These two lists of systems are obviously not meant to be exhaustive—they are just meant to identify certain systems that either have been or are being particularly influential for one reason or another, or else have some special intrinsic interest.

It is worth pointing out that the systems listed above, both prototypes and products, are all relational (at least, they all support SQL). Indeed, there are several reasons why, for a distributed system to be successful, that system *must* be relational; relational technology is a prerequisite to (effective) distributed technology [20.15]. We will see some of the reasons for this state of affairs as we proceed through the chapter.

A Fundamental Principle

Now we can state what might be regarded as **the fundamental principle of distributed database** [20.14]:

■ *To the user, a distributed system should look exactly like a **non**distributed system.*

In other words, users in a distributed system should be able to behave exactly as if the system were *not* distributed. All of the problems of distributed systems are—or should be—internal or implementation-level problems, not external or user-level problems.

Note: The term "users" in the foregoing paragraph refers specifically to users (end users or application programmers) who are performing *data manipulation* operations. All data manipulation operations should remain logically unchanged. Data *definition* operations, by contrast, will require some extension in a distributed system—for example, so that a user at site X can specify that a given relvar be divided into "fragments" that are to be stored at sites Y and Z (see the discussion of fragmentation in the next section).

The fundamental principle identified above leads to certain subsidiary rules or objectives,* twelve in number, which will be discussed in the next section. For reference, we list those objectives here:

1. Local autonomy
2. No reliance on a central site
3. Continuous operation
4. Location independence
5. Fragmentation independence
6. Replication independence
7. Distributed query processing
8. Distributed transaction management
9. Hardware independence
10. Operating system independence
11. Network independence
12. DBMS independence

Please understand that these objectives are *not* all independent of one another, nor are they necessarily exhaustive, nor are they all equally significant (different users will attach different degrees of importance to different objectives in different environments; indeed, some of them might be totally inapplicable in some situations). However, the objectives are useful as a basis for understanding distributed technology and as a framework for characterizing the functionality of specific distributed systems. We will therefore use them as an organizing principle for the bulk of the chapter. Section 20.3 presents a brief discussion of each objective; Section 20.4 then homes in on certain specific issues in more detail. Section 20.5 (as previously mentioned) discusses client/server systems. Section 20.6 examines the specific objective of DBMS independence in depth. Finally, Section 20.7 addresses the question of SQL support, and Section 20.8 offers a summary and a few concluding remarks.

One final introductory point: It is important to distinguish true, generalized, distributed *database* systems from systems that merely provide some kind of *remote data access* (which is all that client/server systems really do, incidentally). In a remote data access system, the user might be able to operate on data at a remote site, or even on data at several remote sites simultaneously, but "the seams show"; the user is definitely aware—to a greater or lesser extent—that the data is remote, and has to behave accordingly. In a true distributed database system, by contrast, the seams are hidden. (Much of the rest of this chapter

---

*"Rules" was the term used in the paper in which they were first introduced [20.14] (and the "fundamental principle" was referred to as *Rule Zero*). However, "objectives" is really a better term—"rules" sounds much too dogmatic. We will stay with the milder term "objectives" in the present chapter.

is concerned with what it means in this context to say that the seams are hidden.) Throughout what follows, we will use the term "distributed system" to refer to a true, generalized, distributed database system specifically (as opposed to a simple remote data access system), barring explicit statements to the contrary.

20.3   THE TWELVE OBJECTIVES

1. Local Autonomy

The sites in a distributed system should be **autonomous.** Local autonomy means that all operations at a given site are controlled by that site; no site X should depend on some other site Y for its successful operation (for otherwise the fact that site Y is down might mean that site X is unable to run, even if there is nothing wrong with site X itself—obviously an undesirable state of affairs). Local autonomy also implies that local data is locally owned and managed, with local accountability: All data "really" belongs to some local database, even if it is accessible from other, remote sites. Such matters as security, integrity, and storage representation of local data thus remain under the control and jurisdiction of the local site.

Actually, the local autonomy objective is not wholly achievable—there are a number of situations in which a given site X *must* relinquish a certain degree of control to some other site Y. The autonomy objective would thus more accurately be stated: Sites should be autonomous **to the maximum extent possible.** See the annotation to reference [20.14] for more details.

2. No Reliance on a Central Site

Local autonomy implies that **all sites must be treated as equals.** In particular, therefore, there must not be any reliance on a central "master" site for some central service—e.g., centralized query processing, centralized transaction management, or centralized naming services—such that the entire system is dependent on that central site. This second objective is thus in fact a corollary of the first (if the first is achieved, the second follows *a fortiori*). But "no reliance on a central site" is desirable in its own right, even if full local autonomy is not achieved. It is therefore worth spelling out as a separate objective.

Reliance on a central site would be undesirable for at least the following two reasons: First, that central site might be a bottleneck; second, and more important, the system would be *vulnerable*—if the central site went down, the whole system would be down (the "single point of failure" problem).

3. Continuous Operation

An advantage of distributed systems in general is that they should provide greater *reliability* and greater *availability:*

- **Reliability** (i.e., the probability that the system is up and running at any given moment) is improved because distributed systems are not an all or nothing proposition—they can continue to operate (at a reduced level) in the face of failure of some individual component, such as an individual site.

- **Availability** (i.e., the probability that the system is up and running continuously throughout a specified period) is improved also, partly for the same reason and partly because of the possibility of data replication (see further discussion under No. 6 below).

The foregoing discussions apply to the case where an **unplanned shutdown** (i.e., a failure of some kind) has occurred at some point within the system. Unplanned shutdowns are obviously undesirable, but hard to prohibit! **Planned** shutdowns, by contrast, should *never* be required; that is, it should never be necessary to shut the system down in order to perform some task, such as adding a new site or upgrading the DBMS at an existing site to a new release level.

4. Location Independence

The basic idea of **location independence** (also known as location **transparency**) is simple: Users should not have to know where data is physically stored, but rather should be able to behave—at least from a logical standpoint—as if the data were all stored at their own local site. Location independence is desirable because it simplifies user programs and terminal activities. In particular, it allows data to migrate from site to site without invalidating any of those programs or activities. Such migratability is desirable because it allows data to be moved around the network in response to changing performance requirements.

Note: You will doubtless realize that location independence is just an extension to the distributed case of the familiar concept of (physical) *data* independence. In fact—to jump ahead of ourselves for a moment—every objective in our list that has "independence" in its name can be regarded as an extension of data independence, as we will see. We will have a little more to say regarding location independence specifically in Section 20.4 (in our discussion of *object naming* in the subsection entitled "Catalog Management").

5. Fragmentation Independence

A system supports **data fragmentation** if a given relvar can be divided up into pieces or *fragments* for physical storage purposes. Fragmentation is desirable for performance reasons: Data can be stored at the location where it is most frequently used, so that most operations are local and network traffic is reduced. For example, consider an employees relvar EMP, with sample value as shown at the top of Fig. 20.2 (overleaf). In a system that supports fragmentation, we might define two fragments as follows:

```
FRAGMENT EMP AS
   N_EMP AT SITE 'New York'  WHERE DEPT# = 'D1'
                             OR    DEPT# = 'D3',
        L_EMP AT SITE 'London'    WHERE DEPT# = 'D2' ;
```

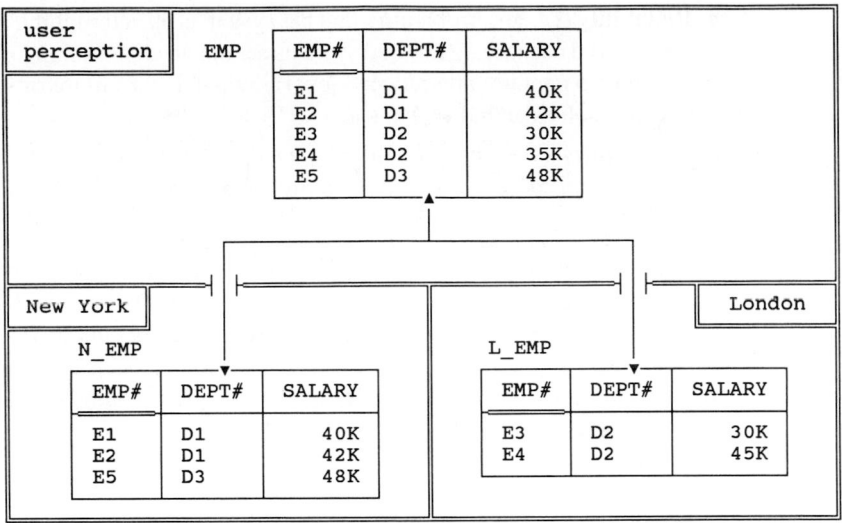

Fig. 20.2   An example of fragmentation

(refer to the lower portion of Fig. 20.2). *Note:* We are assuming that (a) employee tuples map to physical storage in some fairly direct manner; (b) employee numbers and department numbers are just character strings and salaries are just numbers; (c) D1 and D3 are New York departments and D2 is a London department. Hence, tuples for New York employees are stored at the New York site and tuples for London employees are stored at the London site. Note the system's internal fragment names N_EMP and L_EMP.

There are basically two kinds of fragmentation, *horizontal* and *vertical,* corresponding to the relational operations of restriction and projection, respectively (Fig. 20.2 shows a horizontal fragmentation). More generally, a fragment can be derived by any arbitrary combination of restrictions and projections—arbitrary, that is, except that:

- In the case of restriction, the restrictions must constitute an *orthogonal* decomposition in the sense of Chapter 12 (Section 12.6);

- In the case of projection, the projections must constitute a *nonloss* decomposition in the sense of Chapters 11 and 12.

The net effect of these two rules is that all fragments of a given relvar will be *independent,* in the sense that none of them can be derived from the others or has a restriction or a projection that can be derived from the others. (If we really do want to store the same piece of information in several different places, we can use the system's *replication* mechanism—see the next subsection.)

Reconstructing the original relvar from the fragments is done via suitable join and union operations (join for vertical fragments, union for horizontal ones). In the case of union, incidentally, observe that no duplicate elimination will be required, thanks to the first of the two rules above.

Note: We should elaborate slightly on the question of vertical fragmentation. It is true that, as stated above, such a fragmentation must be nonloss, and hence that fragmenting the EMP relvar into its projections on, say, {EMP#,DEPT#} and {SALARY} would not be valid. In some systems, however, stored relvars are regarded as having a hidden, system-provided "tuple ID" or TID attribute, where the TID for a given stored tuple is, loosely, the *address* of the tuple in question. That TID attribute is clearly a candidate key for the applicable relvar; thus, for example, if the EMP relvar included such an attribute, the relvar *could* validly be fragmented into its projections on {TID,EMP#,DEPT#} and {TID,SALARY}, since this fragmentation is clearly nonloss. Note too that the fact that the TID attributes are hidden does not violate *The Information Principle,* since fragmentation independence, *q.v.,* means the user is not aware of the fragmentation anyway.

Observe, incidentally, that ease of fragmentation and ease of reconstruction are two of the many reasons why distributed systems are relational; the relational model provides exactly the operations that are needed for these tasks [20.15].

Now we come to the main point: A system that supports data fragmentation should also support **fragmentation independence** (also known as fragmentation **transparency**)—i.e., users should be able to behave, at least from a logical standpoint, as if the data were in fact not fragmented at all. Fragmentation independence (like location independence) is desirable because it simplifies user programs and terminal activities. In particular, it allows the data to be refragmented at any time (and fragments to be redistributed at any time) in response to changing performance requirements, without invalidating any of those user programs or activities.

Fragmentation independence implies that users will be presented with a view of the data in which the fragments are logically recombined by means of suitable joins and unions. It is the responsibility of the *system optimizer* to determine which fragments need to be physically accessed in order to satisfy any given user request. Given the fragmentation shown in Fig. 20.2, for example, if the user issues the request

```
EMP WHERE SALARY > 40K AND DEPT# = 'D1'
```

the optimizer will know from the fragment definitions (which are stored in the catalog, of course) that the entire result can be obtained from the New York site—there is no need to access the London site at all.

Let us examine this example a little more closely. The EMP relvar as perceived by the user might be regarded (loosely) as a **view** of the underlying fragments N_EMP and L_EMP:

```
VAR EMP VIEW
    N_EMP UNION L_EMP ;
```

The optimizer thus transforms the user's original request into the following:

```
( N_EMP UNION L_EMP ) WHERE SALARY > 40K AND DEPT# = 'D1'
```

This expression can then be transformed further into:

```
( N_EMP WHERE SALARY > 40K AND DEPT# = 'D1' )
   UNION
( L_EMP WHERE SALARY > 40K AND DEPT# = 'D1' )
```

(because restriction distributes over union). From the definition of fragment L_EMP in the catalog, the optimizer knows that the second of these two UNION operands evaluates to an empty relation (the restriction condition DEPT# = 'D1' AND DEPT# = 'D2' can never evaluate to *true*). The overall expression can thus be simplified to just

```
N_EMP WHERE SALARY > 40K AND DEPT# = 'D1'
```

Now the optimizer knows that it need access only the New York site. *Exercise:* Consider what is involved on the part of the optimizer in dealing with the request

```
EMP WHERE SALARY > 40K
```

As the foregoing discussion suggests, the problem of supporting operations on fragmented relvars has certain points in common with the problem of supporting operations on join and union views (in fact, the two problems are one and the same—they just manifest themselves at different points in the overall system architecture). In particular, the problem of *updating* fragmented relvars is the same as the problem of updating join and union views (see Chapter 9). It follows too that updating a given tuple—loosely speaking once again!— might cause that tuple to migrate from one fragment to another, if the updated tuple no longer satisfies the predicate for the fragment it previously belonged to.

6. Replication Independence

A system supports **data replication** if a given stored relvar—or, more generally, a given *fragment* of a given stored relvar—can be represented by many distinct copies or *replicas,* stored at many distinct sites. For example:

```
REPLICATE N_EMP AS
   LN_EMP AT SITE 'London' ;

REPLICATE L_EMP AS
   NL_EMP AT SITE 'New York' ;
```

(see Fig. 20.3). Note the system's internal replica names NL_EMP and LN_EMP.

Replication is desirable for at least two reasons: First, it can mean better performance (applications can operate on local copies instead of having to communicate with remote sites); second, it can also mean better availability (a given replicated object remains available for processing—at least for retrieval—so long as at least one copy remains available). The major *dis*advantage of replication, of course, is that when a given replicated object is updated, *all copies* of that object must be updated: the **update propagation** problem. We will have more to say regarding this problem in Section 20.4.

We remark in passing that replication in a distributed system represents a specific application of the idea of *controlled redundancy* as discussed in Chapter 1.

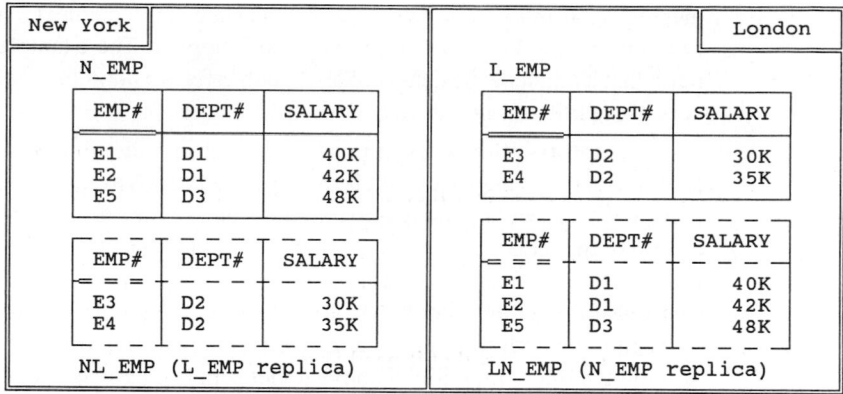

Fig. 20.3 An example of replication

Now, replication, like fragmentation, ideally should be "transparent to the user." In other words, a system that supports data replication should also support **replication independence** (also known as replication **transparency**)—i.e., users should be able to behave, at least from a logical standpoint, as if the data were in fact not replicated at all. Replication independence (like location independence and fragmentation independence) is desirable because it simplifies user programs and terminal activities; in particular, it allows replicas to be created and destroyed at any time in response to changing requirements, without invalidating any of those user programs or activities.

Replication independence implies that it is the responsibility of the system optimizer to determine which replicas physically need to be accessed in order to satisfy any given user request. We omit the specifics of this issue here.

We close this subsection by mentioning that many commercial products currently support a form of replication that does *not* include full replication independence (i.e., is *not* entirely "transparent to the user"). See the further remarks on this topic in Section 20.4, in the subsection on update propagation.

7. Distributed Query Processing

There are two broad points to be made under this heading.

- First, consider the query "Get London suppliers of red parts." Suppose the user is at the New York site and the data is at the London site. Suppose too that there are n suppliers that satisfy the request. If the system is relational, the query will basically involve two messages—one to send the request from New York to London, and one to return the result set of n tuples from London to New York. If, on the other hand, the system is not relational but a record-at-a-time system, the query will basically involve $2n$

messages—*n* from New York to London requesting "the next" supplier, and *n* from London to New York to return that "next" supplier. The example thus illustrates the point that a relational system is likely to outperform a nonrelational one by possibly orders of magnitude.

■ Second, **optimization** is even more important in a distributed system than it is in a centralized one. The basic point is that, in a query such as the one above involving several sites, there will be many possible ways of moving data around the system in order to satisfy the request, and it is crucially important that an efficient strategy be found. For instance, a request for (say) the union of a relation *Rx* stored at site *X* and a relation *Ry* stored at site *Y* could be carried out by moving *Rx* to *Y* or by moving *Ry* to *X* or by moving both to a third site *Z* (etc.). A compelling illustration of this point, involving the query mentioned above ("Get supplier numbers for London suppliers of red parts"), is presented in Section 20.4. To summarize the example briefly, six different strategies for processing the query are analyzed under a certain set of plausible assumptions, and the response time is shown to vary from a minimum of one-tenth of a second to a maximum of nearly *six hours!* Optimization is thus clearly crucial, and this fact in turn can be seen as yet another reason why distributed systems are always relational (the point being that relational requests are optimizable, while nonrelational ones are not).

8. Distributed Transaction Management

As you know, there are two major aspects to transaction management, recovery control and concurrency control. Both require extended treatment in the distributed environment. In order to explain that extended treatment, it is first necessary to introduce a new term, *agent.* In a distributed system, a single transaction can involve the execution of code at many sites; in particular, it can involve updates at many sites. Each transaction is therefore said to consist of several **agents,** where an agent is the process performed in behalf of a given transaction at a given site. And the system needs to know when two agents are part of the same transaction—for example, two agents that are part of the same transaction must obviously not be allowed to deadlock with each other.

Turning now to recovery control specifically: In order to ensure that a given transaction is atomic (all or nothing) in the distributed environment, therefore, the system must ensure that the set of agents for that transaction either all commit in unison or all roll back in unison. This effect can be achieved by means of the **two-phase commit** protocol, already discussed (although not in the distributed context) in Chapter 14. We will have more to say regarding two-phase commit for a distributed system in Section 20.4.

As for concurrency control: Concurrency control in most distributed systems is typically based on **locking,** just as it is in nondistributed systems. (Several more recent products have begun to implement *multi-version controls* [15.1]; in practice, however, conventional locking still seems to be the technique of choice for most systems.) Again, we will discuss this topic in a little more detail in Section 20.4.

9. Hardware Independence

There is actually not much to be said on this topic—the heading says it all. Real-world computer installations typically involve a multiplicity of different machines—IBM machines, ICL machines, HP machines, PCs and workstations of various kinds, etc., etc.—and there is a real need to be able to integrate the data on all of those systems and present the user with a "single-system image." Thus, it is desirable to be able to run the same DBMS on different hardware platforms, and furthermore to have those different machines all participate as equal partners in a distributed system.

10. Operating System Independence

This objective is partly a corollary of the previous one, and also does not really require much discussion here. It is obviously desirable, not only to be able to run the same DBMS on different hardware platforms, but also to be able to run it on different operating system platforms as well—including different operating systems on the same hardware—and have (e.g.) an MVS version and a UNIX version and an NT version all participate in the same distributed system.

11. Network Independence

Once again there is not much to say; if the system is to be able to support many disparate sites, with disparate hardware and disparate operating systems, it is obviously desirable to be able to support a variety of disparate communication networks also.

12. DBMS Independence

Under this heading, we consider what is involved in relaxing the strict homogeneity assumption. That assumption is arguably a little too strong: All that is really needed is that the DBMS instances at different sites **all support the same interface**—they do not necessarily all have to be copies of the same DBMS software. For example, if Ingres and Oracle both supported the official SQL standard, then it might be possible to get an Ingres site and an Oracle site to talk to each other in the context of a distributed system. In other words, it might be possible for the distributed system to be *heterogeneous,* at least to some degree.

Support for heterogeneity is definitely desirable. The fact is, real-world computer installations typically run not only many different machines and many different operating systems, they very often run different DBMSs as well; and it would be nice if those different DBMSs could all participate somehow in a distributed system. In other words, the ideal distributed system should provide **DBMS independence.**

This is such a large topic, however (and such an important one in practice), that we devote a separate section to it. See Section 20.6, later.

20.4 PROBLEMS OF DISTRIBUTED SYSTEMS

In this section, we elaborate a little on some of the problems that were mentioned only briefly in Section 20.3. The overriding problem is that communication networks—at least, "long haul" or wide area networks (WANs)—are *slow*. A typical WAN might have an effective data rate of around 5 to 10 thousand bytes per second; the typical disk drive, by contrast, has a data rate of around 5 to 10 *million* bytes per second. (Some local area networks, on the other hand, do support data rates of the same order of magnitude as disk drives.) As a consequence, an overriding objective in distributed systems (at least in the WAN case, and to some extent in the LAN case also) is **to minimize network utilization**—i.e., to minimize the number and volume of messages. This objective in turn gives rise to problems in a number of subsidiary areas, the following among them (this list is not meant to be exhaustive):

- Query processing
- Catalog management
- Update propagation
- Recovery control
- Concurrency control

Query Processing

The objective of minimizing network utilization implies that the query optimization process itself needs to be distributed, as well as the query execution process. In other words, the overall optimization process will typically consist of a **global optimization** step, followed by **local optimization** steps at each affected site. For example, suppose a query Q is submitted at site X, and suppose Q involves a union of a relation Ry of a hundred tuples at site Y with a relation Rz of a million tuples at site Z. The optimizer at site X will choose the global strategy for executing Q; and it is clearly desirable that it decide to move Ry to Z and not Rz to Y (and certainly not Ry and Rz both to X). Then, once it has decided to move Ry to Z, the strategy for performing the actual union at site Z will be decided by the local optimizer at Z.

The following more detailed illustration of the foregoing point is based on an example given in reference [20.13], which adopted it in turn from an early paper by Rothnie and Goodman [20.33].

- *Database* (suppliers and parts, simplified):

```
S   { S#, CITY }                10,000 stored tuples at site A
P   { P#, COLOR }              100,000 stored tuples at site B
SP  { S#, P# }               1,000,000 stored tuples at site A
```

Assume that every stored tuple is 25 bytes (200 bits) long.

- *Query* ("Get supplier numbers for London suppliers of red parts"):

```
( ( S JOIN SP JOIN P ) WHERE CITY = 'London' AND
                             COLOR = COLOR ('Red') ) { S# }
```

- *Estimated cardinalities of certain intermediate results:*

  Number of red parts   = 10
  Number of shipments by London suppliers   = 100,000

- *Communication assumptions:*

  Data rate   = 50,000 bits per second
  Access delay = 0.1 second

We now briefly examine six possible strategies for processing this query, and for each strategy *i* calculate the total communication time $T[i]$ from the formula

```
( total access delay ) + ( total data volume / data rate )
```

which becomes (in seconds)

```
( number of messages / 10 ) + ( number of bits / 50000 )
```

1. Move parts to site A and process the query at A.

```
T[1]  =   0.1 + ( 100000 * 200 ) / 50000
      =   400 seconds approx. (6.67 minutes)
```

2. Move suppliers and shipments to site B and process the query at B.

```
T[2]  =   0.2 + ( ( 10000 + 1000000 ) * 200 ) / 50000
      =   4040 seconds approx. (1.12 hours)
```

3. Join suppliers and shipments at site A, restrict the result to London suppliers, and then, for each of those suppliers in turn, check site B to see whether the corresponding part is red. Each of these checks will involve two messages, a query and a response. The transmission time for these messages will be small compared with the access delay.

```
T[3]  =   20000 seconds approx. (5.56 hours)
```

4. Restrict parts at site B to those that are red, and then, for each of those parts in turn, check site A to see whether there exists a shipment relating the part to a London supplier. Each of these checks will involve two messages; again, the transmission time for these messages will be small compared with the access delay.

```
T[4]  =   2 seconds approx.
```

5. Join suppliers and shipments at site A, restrict the result to London suppliers, project the result over S# and P#, and move the result to site B. Complete the processing at site B.

```
T[5]  =   0.1 + ( 100000 * 200 ) / 50000
      =   400 seconds approx. (6.67 minutes)
```

6. Restrict parts at site B to those that are red and move the result to site A. Complete the processing at site A.

```
T[6]  =  0.1 + ( 10 * 200 ) / 50000
      =  0.1 second approx.
```

Fig. 20.4 summarizes the foregoing results. Points arising:

Strategy	Technique	Communication time
1	Move P to A	6.67 mins
2	Move S and SP to B	1.12 hrs
3	For each London shipment, check if part is red	5.56 hrs
4	For each red part, check if a London supplier exists	2.00 secs
5	Move London shipments to B	6.67 mins
6	**Move red parts to A**	**0.10 secs** (best)

Fig. 20.4 Distributed query processing strategies (summary)

- Each of the six strategies represents a plausible approach to the problem, yet the variation in communication time is enormous (the slowest is *two million* times slower than the fastest).

- Data rate and access delay are both important factors in choosing a strategy.

- Computation and I/O times are likely to be negligible compared with communication time for the poor strategies. (For the better strategies, on the other hand, this might or might not be the case [20.35]. It also might not be the case on a fast LAN.)

In addition, some strategies permit parallel processing at the two sites; thus, the response time to the user might actually be less than in a centralized system. Note, however, that we have ignored the question of which site is to receive the final result.

Catalog Management

In a distributed system, the system catalog will include not only the usual catalog data regarding base relvars, views, authorizations, etc., but also all the necessary control information to enable the system to provide the desired location, fragmentation, and replication independence. The question arises: Where and how should the catalog itself be stored? Here are some possibilities:

1. *Centralized:* The total catalog is stored exactly once, at a single central site.

2. *Fully replicated:* The total catalog is stored in its entirety at every site.

3. *Partitioned:* Each site maintains its own catalog for objects stored at that site. The total catalog is the union of all of those disjoint local catalogs.

4. *Combination of 1 and 3:* Each site maintains its own local catalog, as in paragraph 3; in addition, a single central site maintains a unified copy of all of those local catalogs, as in paragraph 1.

Each of these approaches has its problems. Approach 1 obviously violates the "no reliance on a central site" objective. Approach 2 suffers from a severe loss of autonomy, in that every catalog update has to be propagated to every site. Approach 3 makes nonlocal operations very expensive (finding a remote object will require access to half the sites, on average). Approach 4 is more efficient than Approach 3 (finding a remote object requires only one remote catalog access), but violates the "no reliance on a central site" objective again. In practice, therefore, systems typically do not use *any* of these four approaches! By way of example, we describe the approach used in R* [20.39].

In order to explain how the R* catalog is structured, it is first necessary to say something about R* **object naming**. Now, object naming is a significant issue for distributed systems in general; the possibility that two distinct sites *X* and *Y* might both have an object, say a base relvar, called *A* implies that some mechanism—typically qualification by site name—will be required in order to "disambiguate" (i.e., to guarantee system-wide name uniqueness). If qualified names such as *X.A* and *Y.A* are exposed to the user, however, the location independence objective will clearly be violated. What is needed, therefore, is a means of mapping the names known to users to their corresponding system-known names.

Here then is the R* approach to this problem. First, R* distinguishes between an object's **printname,** which is the name by which the object is normally referenced by users (e.g., in an SQL SELECT statement), and its **system-wide name,** which is a globally unique internal identifier for the object. System-wide names have four components:

- *Creator ID* (the ID of the user who created the object);
- *Creator site ID* (the ID of the site at which the CREATE operation is entered);
- *Local name* (the unqualified name of the object);
- *Birth site ID* (the ID of the site at which the object is initially stored).

(User IDs are unique within site and site IDs are globally unique.) Thus, for example, the system-wide name

```
MARILYN @ NEWYORK . STATS @ LONDON
```

denotes an object, perhaps a base relvar, with local name STATS, created by the user called Marilyn at the New York site and initially stored* at the London site. This name is **guaranteed never to change**—not even if the object migrates to another site (see below).

As already indicated, users normally refer to objects by their *printname.* A printname consists of a simple unqualified name—either the "local name" component of the system-wide name (STATS in the example above), or a **synonym** for that system-wide name, defined by means of the special R* SQL statement CREATE SYNONYM. Here is an example:

```
CREATE SYNONYM MSTATS FOR MARILYN @ NEWYORK . STATS @ LONDON ;
```

Base relvars are physically stored in R, as indeed they are in just about every system known to this writer.

Now the user can say either (e.g.)

```
SELECT ... FROM STATS ... ;
```

or

```
SELECT ... FROM MSTATS ... ;
```

In the first case (using the local name), the system infers the system-wide name by assuming all the obvious defaults—namely, that the object was created by this user, it was created at this site, and it was initially stored at this site. Incidentally, one consequence of these default assumptions is that old System R applications will run unchanged on R^* (once the System R data has been redefined to R^*, that is; recall that System R was the prototype predecessor to R^*).

In the second case (using the synonym), the system determines the system-wide name by interrogating the relevant **synonym table.** Synonym tables can be thought of as the first component of the catalog; each site maintains a set of such tables for each user known at that site, mapping the synonyms known to that user to their corresponding system-wide names.

In addition to the synonym tables, each site maintains:

1. A catalog entry for every object **born** at that site;
2. A catalog entry for every object **currently stored** at that site.

Suppose the user now issues a request referring to the synonym MSTATS. First, the system looks up the corresponding system-wide name in the appropriate synonym table (a purely local lookup). Now it knows the birthsite, namely London in the example, and it can interrogate the London catalog (which we assume for generality to be a remote lookup—first remote access). The London catalog will contain an entry for the object, by virtue of point 1 above. If the object is still at London, it has now been found. However, if the object has migrated to (say) Los Angeles, then the catalog entry in London will say as much, and so the system can now interrogate the Los Angeles catalog (second remote access). And the Los Angeles catalog will contain an entry for the object, by virtue of point 2 above. So the object has been found in at most two remote accesses.

Furthermore, if the object migrates again, say to San Francisco, then the system will:

- Insert a San Francisco catalog entry;
- Delete the Los Angeles catalog entry;
- Update the London catalog entry to point to San Francisco instead of Los Angeles.

The net effect is that the object can still be found in at most two remote accesses. And this is a completely distributed scheme—there is no central catalog site, and no single point of failure within the system.

We remark that the object naming scheme used in the DB2 distributed data facility is similar but not identical to the one described above.

Update Propagation

The basic problem with data replication, as pointed out in Section 20.3, is that an update to any given logical object must be propagated to all stored copies of that object. A difficulty that arises immediately is that some site holding a copy of the object might be unavailable (because of a site or network failure) at the time of the update. The obvious strategy of propagating updates immediately to all copies is thus probably unacceptable, because it implies that the update—and therefore the transaction—will fail if any one of those copies is currently unavailable. In a sense, in fact, data is *less* available under this strategy than it would be in the nonreplicated case, thereby undermining one of the advantages claimed for replication in the previous section.

A common scheme for dealing with this problem (not the only one possible) is the so-called **primary copy** scheme, which works as follows:

- One copy of each replicated object is designated as the *primary* copy. The remainder are all secondary copies.

- Primary copies of different objects are at different sites (so this is a distributed scheme once again).

- Update operations are deemed to be logically complete as soon as the primary copy has been updated. The site holding that copy is then responsible for propagating the update to the secondary copies at some subsequent time. (That "subsequent time" must be prior to COMMIT, however, if the ACID properties of the transaction are to be preserved. See the further remarks on this subject below.)

Of course, this scheme leads to several additional problems of its own, most of them beyond the scope of this book. Note too that it does represent a violation of the local autonomy objective, because a transaction might now fail because a remote (primary) copy of some object is unavailable—even if a local copy is available.

Note: As mentioned above, the ACID requirements of transaction processing imply that all update propagation must be completed before the relevant transaction can complete ("synchronous replication"). However, several commercial products currently support a less ambitious form of replication, in which update propagation is done at some later time (possibly at some user-specified time), *not* necessarily within the scope of the relevant transaction ("asynchronous replication"). Indeed, the term *replication* has unfortunately been more or less usurped by those products, with the result that—in the commercial marketplace, at least—it is almost always taken to imply that update propagation is delayed past the commit point of the relevant transaction (see, e.g., references [20.1], [20.18], and [20.21]). The problem with this delayed propagation approach, of course, is that the database can no longer be guaranteed to be consistent at all times; indeed, the user might not even know whether it is consistent or not.

We close this subsection with a couple of additional observations on the delayed propagation approach:

1. The concept of replication in a system with delayed update propagation can be thought of as an application of the idea of *snapshots* as discussed in Chapter 9.* Indeed, it would have been better to use a different term for this kind of replication; then we could have kept the term "replica" to mean what it is usually understood to mean in ordinary discourse (namely, an exact copy). *Note:* We do not mean to suggest that delayed propagation is a bad idea—it is clearly the right thing to do in appropriate circumstances, as we will see in Chapter 21, for example. The point is, however, that delayed propagation means that the "replicas" are not true replicas and the system is not a true distributed database system.

2. One reason (perhaps the major reason) why products are implementing replication with delayed propagation is that the alternative—i.e., updating all replicas prior to COMMIT—requires two-phase commit support (see below), which can be costly in performance. This state of affairs explains the articles sometimes encountered in the trade press with mystifying titles like "Replication *vs.* Two-Phase Commit"—mystifying, because on the surface they appear to be comparing the merits of two totally different things.

Recovery Control

As explained in Section 20.3, recovery control in distributed systems is typically based on the **two-phase commit** protocol (or some variant thereof). Two-phase commit is required in *any* environment in which a single transaction can interact with several autonomous resource managers; however, it is particularly important in a distributed system, because the resource managers in question—i.e., the local DBMSs—are operating at distinct sites and hence are *very* autonomous. Points arising:

1. The "no reliance on a central site" objective dictates that the coordinator function must not be assigned to one distinguished site in the network, but instead must be performed by different sites for different transactions. Typically it is handled by the site at which the transaction in question is initiated; thus, each site must be capable of acting as the coordinator site for some transactions and as a participant site for others (in general).

2. The two-phase commit process requires the coordinator to communicate with every participant site—which means more messages and more overhead.

3. If site *Y* acts as a participant in a two-phase commit process coordinated by site *X*, then site *Y must* do what it is told by site *X* (commit or rollback, whichever applies)—a (perhaps minor) loss of local autonomy.

Let us review the basic two-phase commit process as described in Chapter 14. Refer to Fig. 20.5, which shows the interactions that take place between the coordinator and a typical participant (which we assume for simplicity to be at a remote site). Time in that figure

---

*Except that snapshots are supposed to be read-only (apart from the periodic refreshing), whereas some systems do allow users to update "replicas" directly—see, e.g., reference [20.21]. Of course, this latter capability constitutes a violation of replication independence.

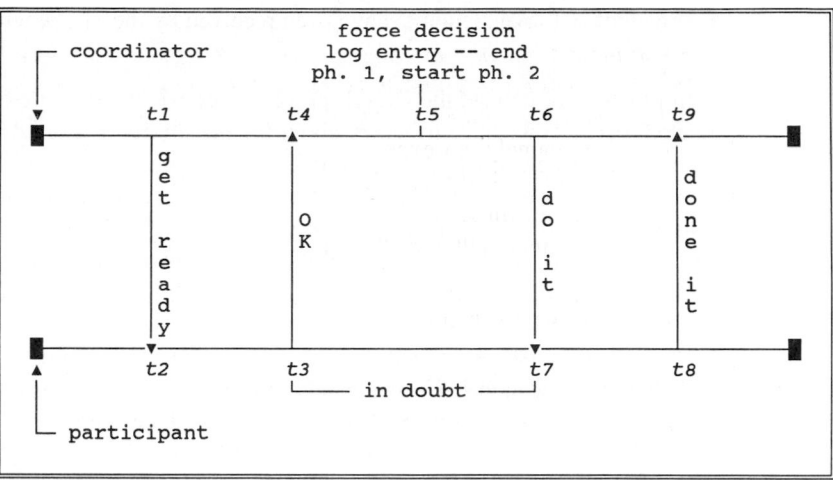

Fig. 20.5 Two-phase commit

runs from left to right (more or less!). We assume for simplicity that the transaction has requested a COMMIT, not a ROLLBACK. On receiving that COMMIT request, the coordinator goes through the following two-phase process:

- It instructs each participant to "get ready to go either way" on the transaction. Fig. 20.5 shows the "get ready" message being sent at time *t1* and being received by the participant at time *t2*. The participant now forces a log entry for the local agent out to its own physical log, and then replies "OK" to the coordinator (of course, if anything has gone wrong—in particular, if the local agent has failed), it replies "Not OK" instead. In the figure, that reply—which we assume for simplicity to be "OK"—is sent at time *t3* and is received by the coordinator at time *t4*. Note that (as already indicated) the participant now suffers a loss of autonomy: It *must* do what it is subsequently told to do by the coordinator. Furthermore, any resources locked by the local agent *must remain locked* until the participant receives and acts on that decision from the coordinator.

- When the coordinator has received replies from all participants, it makes its decision (which will be *commit* if all replies were "OK" and *rollback* otherwise). It then forces an entry to its own physical log, recording that decision, at time *t5*. That time *t5* marks the transition from Phase 1 to Phase 2.

- We assume the decision was *commit.* The coordinator therefore instructs each participant to "do it" (i.e., perform commit processing for the local agent); Fig. 20.5 shows the "do it" message being sent at time *t6* and being received by the participant at time *t7*. The participant commits the local agent and sends an acknowledgment ("done it") back to the coordinator. In the figure, that acknowledgment is sent at time *t8* and is received by the coordinator at time *t9*.

- When all acknowledgments have been received by the coordinator, the entire process is complete.

In practice, of course, the overall process is considerably more complicated than just indicated, because we have to worry about the possibility of site or network failures. For example, suppose the coordinator site fails at some time t between times $t5$ and $t6$. When the site recovers, then, the restart procedure will discover from the log that a certain transaction was in phase two of the two-phase commit process and will continue the process of sending the "do it" messages to the participants. (Note that the participant is "in doubt" on the transaction in the period from $t3$ to $t7$; if the coordinator does fail at time t as suggested, that "in doubt" period might be quite lengthy.)

Ideally, of course, we would like the two-phase commit process to be resilient to *any conceivable* kind of failure. Unfortunately, it is easy to see that this objective is fundamentally unachievable—that is, there does not exist any finite protocol that will *guarantee* that all participants will commit a successful transaction in unison, or roll back an unsuccessful one in unison, in the face of arbitrary failures. For suppose, conversely, that such a protocol does exist. Let N be the minimum number of messages required by such a protocol. Suppose now that the last of these N messages is lost because of some failure. Then either that message was unnecessary, which is contrary to the assumption that N was minimal, or the protocol now does not work. Either way there is a contradiction, from which we deduce that no such protocol exists.

Despite this depressing fact, there are at least various enhancements that can be made to the basic algorithm with a view to improving performance:

- First of all, if the agent at some particular participant site is read-only, that participant can reply "ignore me" in phase one, and the coordinator can indeed ignore that participant in phase two.

- Second, if *all* participants reply "ignore me" in phase one, phase two can be skipped entirely.

- Third, there are two important variants on the basic scheme called *presumed commit* and *presumed rollback* [20.15], which we describe in more detail in the paragraphs immediately following.

In general, the presumed commit and presumed rollback schemes have the effect of reducing the number of messages involved in the success case (for presumed commit) or the failure case (for presumed rollback). In order to explain the two schemes, we note first that the basic mechanism as described above requires the coordinator to remember its decision until it has received an acknowledgment from every participant. The reason is, of course, that if a participant crashes while it is "in doubt," it will have to interrogate the coordinator on restart in order to discover what the coordinator's decision was. Once all acknowledgments have been received, however, the coordinator knows that all participants have done what they were told, and so it can "forget" the transaction.

We focus now on **presumed commit.** Under this scheme, participants are required to acknowledge "rollback" ("undo it") messages but not "commit" ("do it") messages, and the coordinator can forget the transaction as soon as it has broadcast its decision, *provided* that decision is "commit." If an in-doubt participant crashes, then on restart it will (as always) interrogate the coordinator. If the coordinator still remembers the transaction (i.e., the coordinator is still waiting for the participant's acknowledgment), then the decision must have been "rollback," otherwise it must have been "commit."

Presumed rollback is the opposite, of course: Participants are required to acknowledge "commit" messages but not "rollback" messages, and the coordinator can forget the transaction as soon as it has broadcast its decision, so long as that decision is "rollback." If an in-doubt participant crashes, then on restart it will interrogate the coordinator. If the coordinator still remembers the transaction (i.e., the coordinator is still waiting for the participant's acknowledgment), then the decision was "commit," otherwise it was "rollback."

Interestingly (and somewhat counterintuitively), presumed rollback seems to be preferable to presumed commit (we say "counterintuitively," because surely most transactions succeed, and presumed commit reduces the number of messages in the success case). The problem with presumed commit is as follows. Suppose the coordinator crashes in phase one (i.e., before it has made its decision). On restart at the coordinator site, then, the transaction will be rolled back (since it did not complete). Subsequently, some participant interrogates the coordinator, asking for its decision with respect to this transaction. The coordinator does not remember the transaction, and so presumes "commit"—which is incorrect, of course.

In order to avoid such "false commits," the coordinator (if it is following presumed commit) must force a log entry to its own physical log at the start of phase one, giving a list of all participants in the transaction. (If the coordinator now crashes in phase one, then on restart it can broadcast "rollback" to all participants.) And this physical I/O to the coordinator log is on the critical path for *every transaction.* Thus, presumed commit is not quite so attractive as it might appear at first sight. In fact, it is probably fair to say that presumed rollback is the *de facto* standard in implemented systems at the time of writing.

Concurrency Control

As explained in Section 20.3, concurrency control in most distributed systems is based on locking, just as it is in most nondistributed systems. In a distributed system, however, requests to test, set, and release locks become *messages* (assuming that the object under consideration is at a remote site), and messages mean overhead. For example, consider a transaction T that needs to update an object for which there exist replicas at n remote sites. If each site is responsible for locks on objects stored at that site (as it will be under the local autonomy assumption), then a straightforward implementation will require at least $5n$ messages:

- n lock requests
- n lock grants
- n update messages
- n acknowledgments
- n unlock requests

Of course, we can easily improve on the foregoing by "piggybacking" messages—for example, the lock request and update messages can be combined, and so can the lock grant and acknowledgment messages—but even so, the total time for the update could still be orders of magnitude greater than it would be in a centralized system.

The usual approach to this problem is to adopt the **primary copy** strategy outlined in the subsection on "Update Propagation" above. For a given object *A,* the site holding the primary copy of *A* will handle all locking operations involving *A* (remember that the primary copies of different objects will be at different sites, in general). Under this strategy the set of all copies of an object can be considered as a single object for locking purposes, and the total number of messages will be reduced from $5n$ to $2n + 3$ (one lock request, one lock grant, n updates, n acknowledgments, and one unlock request). But notice once again that this solution entails a (severe) loss of autonomy—a transaction can now fail if a primary copy is unavailable, even if the transaction is read-only and a local copy is available. (Note that not only update operations, but also retrieval operations, need to lock the primary copy [20.15]. Thus, an unpleasant side effect of the primary copy strategy is to reduce performance and availability for retrievals as well as for updates.)

Another problem with locking in a distributed system is that it can lead to **global deadlock.** A global deadlock is a deadlock involving two or more sites. For example (refer to Fig. 20.6):

1. The agent of transaction *T2* at site *X* is waiting for the agent of transaction *T1* at site *X* to release a lock;

2. The agent of transaction *T1* at site *X* is waiting for the agent of transaction *T1* at site *Y* to complete;

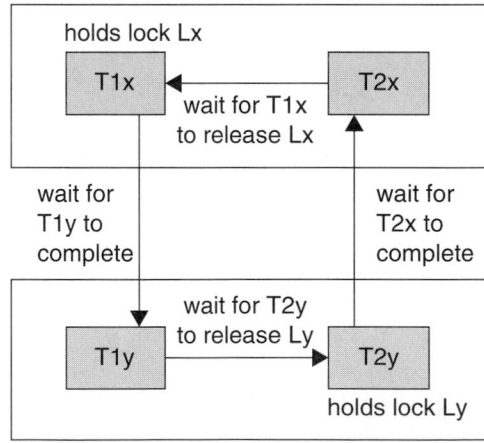

Fig. 20.6 An example of global deadlock

3. The agent of transaction *T1* at site *Y* is waiting for the agent of transaction *T2* at site *Y* to release a lock;

4. The agent of transaction *T2* at site *Y* is waiting for the agent of transaction *T2* at site *X* to complete: *Deadlock!*

The problem with a deadlock such as this one is that *neither site can detect it using only information that is internal to that site.* In other words, there are no cycles in the local Wait-For Graphs, but a cycle will appear if those two local graphs are combined to form a global graph. It follows that global deadlock detection incurs further communication overhead, because it requires individual local graphs to be brought together somehow.

An elegant (and distributed) scheme for detecting global deadlocks is described in the R* papers (see, e.g., reference [20.39]). *Note:* As pointed out in Chapter 15, not all systems do in fact detect deadlocks in practice—some just use a timeout mechanism instead. For reasons that should be obvious, this remark is particularly true of distributed systems.

20.5   CLIENT/SERVER SYSTEMS

As mentioned in Section 20.1, **client/server** systems can be regarded as a special case of distributed systems in general. More precisely, a client/server system is a distributed system in which (a) some sites are *client* sites and some are *server* sites, (b) all data resides at the server sites, (c) all applications execute at the client sites, and (d) "the seams show" (full location independence is not provided). Refer to Fig. 20.7 (a repeat of Fig. 2.5 from Chapter 2).

At the time of writing, there is a great deal of commercial interest in client/server systems, and comparatively little in true general-purpose distributed systems (though this picture is beginning to change somewhat, as we will see in the next section). We continue to believe that true distributed systems represent an important long-term trend, which is why we concentrate on such systems in the present chapter; however, it is clearly appropriate to say something regarding client/server systems specifically.

Recall from Chapter 2 that the term "client/server" refers primarily to an *architecture*, or logical division of responsibilities; the **client** is the application (also known as the *frontend*), and the **server** is the DBMS (also known as the *backend*). Precisely because the overall system can be so neatly divided into two parts, however, the possibility arises of running the two on different machines. And this latter possibility is so attractive (for so many reasons—see Chapter 2) that the term "client/server" has come to apply almost exclusively to the case where client and server are indeed on different machines.* This usage is sloppy but common, and we adopt it ourselves in what follows.

We remind you also that several variations on the basic theme are possible:

- Several clients might be able to share the same server (indeed, this is the normal case).
- A single client might be able to access several servers. This latter possibility divides in turn into two cases:

---

*The term "two-tier system" is also used (for obvious reasons) with essentially the same meaning.

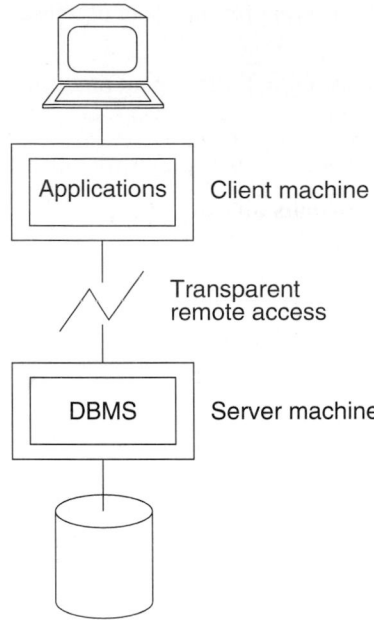

Fig. 20.7   A client/server system

a. The client is limited to accessing just one server at a time—i.e., each individual database request must be directed to just one server; it is not possible, within a single request, to combine data from two or more different servers. Furthermore, the user has to know which particular server stores which pieces of data.

b. The client can access many servers simultaneously—i.e., a single database request can combine data from several servers, which means that the servers look to the client as if they were really just one server, and the user does not have to know which servers store which pieces of data.

But Case b. here is effectively a true distributed database system ("the seams are hidden"); it is not what is usually meant by the term "client/server," and we ignore it in what follows.

Client/Server Standards

There are several standards that are applicable to the world of client/server processing:

- First of all, certain client/server features are included in the **SQL** standard, SQL/92 [4.22]. We defer discussion of these features to Section 20.7.

■ Next, there is the ISO **Remote Data Access** standard, RDA [20.26–20.27]. One reason RDA is important is that something very close to it has already been implemented by members of the **SQL Access Group** (SAG), which is a consortium of database software vendors committed to open systems and interoperability. *Note:* For our purposes it is not worth bothering to distinguish between the ISO and SAG versions of RDA; we will simply use the name "RDA" to refer to them both generically.

The intent of RDA is to define **formats and protocols** for client/server communication. It assumes that (a) the client expresses database requests in a standard form of SQL (basically a subset of the SQL/92 standard), also that (b) the server supports a standard catalog (also basically as defined in the SQL/92 standard). It then defines specific representation formats for passing messages (SQL requests, data and results, and diagnostic information) between the client and the server.

■ The third and last standard we mention here is IBM's **Distributed Relational Database Architecture** (DRDA) standard [20.25] (which is a *de facto* standard, not a *de jure* one). DRDA and RDA have similar objectives; however, DRDA differs from RDA in several important respects—in particular, it tends to reflect its IBM origins. For example, DRDA does not assume that the client is using a standard version of SQL, but instead allows for any dialect of SQL whatsoever. One consequence is (possibly) better performance, since the client might be able to exploit certain server-specific features; on the other hand, portability suffers, precisely because those server-specific features are exposed to the client (i.e., the client has to know what kind of server it is talking to). In a similar vein, DRDA does not assume any particular catalog structure at the server. The DRDA formats and protocols are quite different from those of RDA (essentially, DRDA is based on IBM's own architectures and standards, while RDA is based on international, non-vendor-specific standards).

Further details of RDA and DRDA are beyond the scope of this book; see references [20.23] and [20.30] for some analysis and comparisons.

Client/Server Application Programming

We have said that a client/server system is a special case of distributed systems in general. As suggested in the introduction to this section, a client/server system can be thought of as a distributed system in which all requests originate at one site and all processing is performed at another (assuming for simplicity that there is just one client site and just one server site). *Note:* Under this simple definition, of course, the client site is not really "a database system site in its own right" at all, and the system thus contravenes the definition of a general-purpose distributed database system given in Section 20.2. (The client site might well have its own local databases, but those databases will not play a direct part in the client/server arrangement as such.)

Be that as it may, the client/server approach does have certain implications for application programming (as indeed do distributed systems in general). One of the most important points has already been touched on in our discussion of Objective No. 7 (distributed query processing) in Section 20.3: namely, the fact that relational systems are, by definition and design, **set-level** systems. In a client/server system (and indeed in distributed systems in general), it is more important than ever that the application programmer *not* just "use the server like an access method" and write record-level code. Instead, as much functionality as possible should be bundled up into set-level requests—for otherwise performance will suffer, because of the number of messages involved. (In SQL terms, the foregoing implies *avoiding cursors* as much as possible—i.e., avoiding FETCH loops and the CURRENT forms of UPDATE and DELETE. See Chapter 4.)

The number of messages between client and server can be reduced still further if the system provides some kind of **stored procedure** mechanism. A stored procedure is basically a precompiled program that is *stored at the server site* (and is known to the server). It is invoked from the client by a **remote procedure call** (RPC). In particular, therefore, the performance penalty associated with record-level processing can be partly offset by creating a suitable stored procedure to do that processing directly at the server site.

Note: Although it is somewhat tangential to the topic of client/server processing as such, we should point out that improved performance is not the only advantage of stored procedures. Others include:

- Such procedures can be used to conceal a variety of DBMS- and/or database-specific details from the user, thereby providing a greater degree of data independence than might otherwise be the case.

- One stored procedure can be shared by many clients.

- Optimization can be done at the time the stored procedure is created instead of at run time. (This advantage applies only to systems that normally do optimization at run time, of course.)

- Stored procedures can provide better security. For example, a given user might be authorized to invoke a given procedure but not to operate directly on the data accessed by that procedure.

One disadvantage is that different vendors provide very different facilities in this area, despite the fact that—as mentioned in Chapter 4—the SQL standard was extended in 1996 to include some stored procedure support (under the name of the *Persistent Stored Modules* feature, PSM).

20.6 DBMS INDEPENDENCE

Now we return to our discussion of the twelve objectives for distributed database systems in general. The last of those objectives, you will recall, was *DBMS independence*. As explained in the brief discussion of this objective in Section 20.3, the strict homogeneity assumption is arguably too strong; all that is really needed is that the DBMSs at different sites support the same interface. As we put it in that section: If, e.g., Ingres and Oracle both supported the official SQL standard—no more and no less!—then it might be possible to get them to behave as equal partners in a heterogeneous distributed system (indeed, such a possibility is one of the arguments usually advanced in favor of the SQL standard in the first place). We begin by considering this possibility in detail. *Note:* We base our discussion on Ingres and Oracle specifically merely to make matters a little more concrete. The concepts are generally applicable, of course.

Gateways

Suppose we have two sites *X* and *Y* running Ingres and Oracle respectively, and suppose some user *U* at site *X* wishes to see a single distributed database that includes data from the Ingres database at site *X* and data from the Oracle database at site *Y*. By definition, user *U* is an Ingres user, and the distributed database must therefore be an Ingres database so far as that user is concerned. The onus is thus on Ingres, not Oracle, to provide the necessary support. What must that support consist of?

In principle, it is quite straightforward: Ingres must provide a special program—usually called a **gateway**—whose effect is "to make Oracle look like Ingres." Refer to Fig. 20.8.* The gateway might run at the Ingres site or the Oracle site or (as the figure suggests) at some special site of its own between the other two; no matter where it runs, however, it must clearly provide at least all of the functions in the following list. (Observe that several of those functions present implementation problems of a very nontrivial nature. However, the RDA and DRDA standards discussed in Section 20.5 do address some of those problems.)

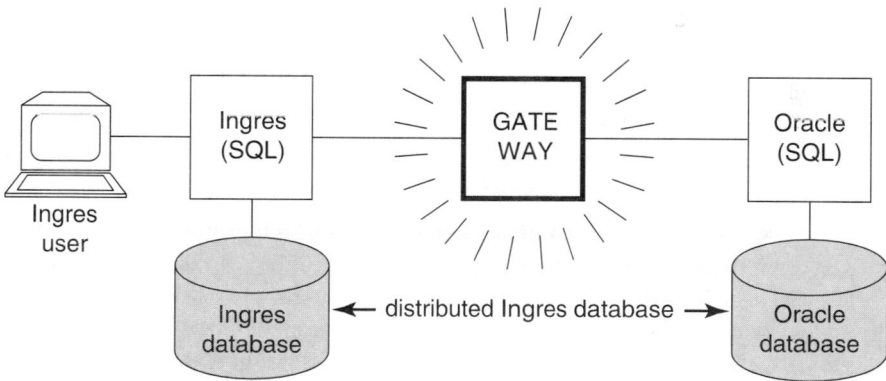

Fig. 20.8   A hypothetical Ingres-provided gateway to Oracle

---

*The term "three-tier system" is sometimes used (for obvious reasons) to refer to the kind of arrangement illustrated in the figure, as well as to other software configurations similarly involving three components (see in particular the discussion of "middleware" in the next subsection).

- Implementing protocols for the exchange of information between Ingres and Oracle—which involves (among other things) mapping the message format in which SQL source statements are sent from Ingres to the format expected by Oracle, and mapping the message format in which results are sent from Oracle into the format expected by Ingres.

- Providing a "relational server" capability for Oracle (analogous to the interactive SQL processor found in most SQL products already). In other words, the gateway must be able to execute arbitrary unplanned SQL statements on the Oracle database. In order to be able to provide this function, the gateway will have to make use of the **dynamic SQL** support or (more likely) a call-level interface such as **SQL/CLI** or **ODBC** at the Oracle site (see Chapter 4). *Note:* Alternatively, the gateway might be able to make direct use of the interactive SQL processor already provided by Oracle.

- Mapping between the Oracle and Ingres data types. This problem includes a variety of subproblems having to do with such matters as processor differences (e.g., different machine word lengths), character code differences (character string comparisons and ORDER BY requests can give unexpected results), floating point format differences (a notorious problem area), differences in date and time support (no two DBMSs known to this writer currently provide identical support in this area), etc., etc. See reference [20.15] for further discussion of these issues.

- Mapping the Ingres dialect of SQL to the Oracle dialect—for in fact neither Ingres nor Oracle does support exactly the SQL standard, "no more and no less"; in fact, both support certain features that the other does not, and there are also some features that have identical syntax in the two products but different semantics. *Note:* In this connection, we should mention that some gateway products do provide a *passthrough* mechanism by which the user can formulate (e.g.) a query in the dialect of the target system and have it passed through the gateway unmodified for execution by that target system.

- Mapping Oracle feedback information (return codes, etc.) to Ingres format.

- Mapping the Oracle catalog to Ingres format, so that the Ingres site, and users at the Ingres site, can find out what the Oracle database contains.

- Dealing with a variety of **semantic mismatch** problems that are likely to occur across disparate systems (see, e.g., references [20.9], [20.11], [20.16], and [20.38]). Examples include differences in naming (Ingres might use EMP# where Oracle uses EMPNO); differences in data type (Ingres might use character strings where Oracle uses numbers); differences in units (Ingres might use centimeters where Oracle uses inches); differences in the logical representation of information (Ingres might omit tuples where Oracle uses nulls); and much, much more.

- Serving as a participant in (the Ingres variant of) the two-phase commit protocol (assuming that Ingres transactions are to be allowed to perform updates on the Oracle database). Whether the gateway will actually be able to perform this function will depend on the facilities provided by the transaction manager at the Oracle site. It is worth pointing out that, at the time of writing, commercial transaction managers (with certain exceptions) typically do *not* provide what is necessary in this respect—namely, the ability for an application program to instruct the transaction manager to "get ready to terminate" (as opposed to instructing it to terminate, i.e., commit or rollback, unconditionally).

- Ensuring that data at the Oracle site that Ingres requires to be locked is in fact locked as and when Ingres needs it to be. Again, whether the gateway will actually be able to perform this function will presumably depend on whether the locking architecture of Oracle matches that of Ingres or not.

So far we have discussed DBMS independence in the context of relational systems only. What about nonrelational systems?—i.e., what about the possibility of including a nonrelational site in an otherwise relational distributed system? For example, would it be possible to provide access to an IMS site from an Ingres or Oracle site? Again, such a feature would be very desirable in practice, given the enormous quantity of data that currently resides in IMS and other prerelational systems.* But can it be done?

If the question means "Can it be done at the 100 percent level?"—meaning "Can all nonrelational data be made accessible from a relational interface, and can all relational operations be performed on that data?"—then the answer is quite categorically *no,* for reasons explained in detail in reference [20.16]. But if the question means "Can some useful level of functionality be provided?", then the answer is obviously *yes.* This is not the place to go into details; see references [20.14–20.16] for further discussion.

Data Access Middleware

Gateways as described in the previous subsection (sometimes called, more specifically, *point-to-point* gateways) do suffer from a number of obvious limitations. One is that they provide little location independence. Another is that the very same application might need to make use of several distinct gateways—say one for DB2, one for Oracle, and one for Informix—without any support for (e.g.) joins that span sites and so forth. As a consequence (and despite the technical difficulties mentioned in the previous subsection), gateway-style products with ever more sophisticated functionality have appeared at frequent intervals over the past few years. In fact, the whole business of what has come to be called *middleware* (also known as *mediators*) is now a significant industry in its own right. Perhaps unsurprisingly, the term "middleware" is not very precisely defined; any piece of software whose general purpose is to paper over the differences among distinct systems that are supposed to work together somehow—for example, a TP monitor—might reasonably be regarded as "middleware" [20.3]. However, we focus here on what might be termed *data access* middleware. Examples of such products include Cohera from Cohera Inc.; DataJoiner from IBM Corp.; and OmniConnect and InfoHub from Sybase Inc. By way of illustration, we briefly describe the DataJoiner product [20.7].

---

*The conventional wisdom is that some 85 percent of business data still resides in such systems (i.e., prerelational database systems and even file systems), and there is little indication that customers will move that data into newer systems any time soon.

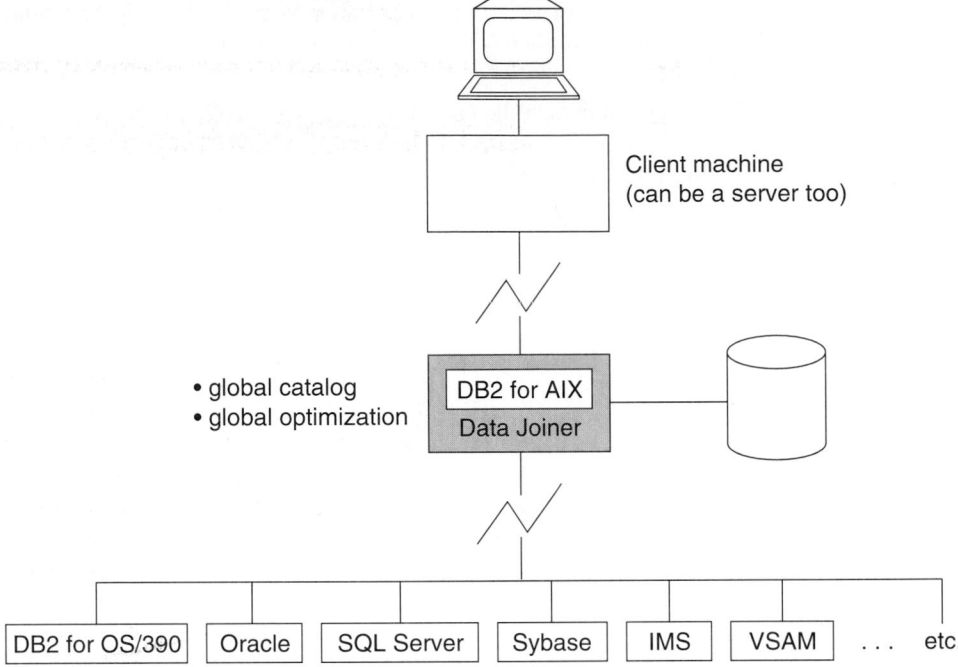

Fig. 20.9   DataJoiner as data access middleware

There are several different ways to characterize DataJoiner (see Fig. 20.9). From the point of view of an individual client, it looks like a regular database server (i.e., a DBMS); it stores data, supports (DB2-style) SQL queries, provides a catalog, does query optimization, and so forth (in fact, the heart of DataJoiner is the AIX version of IBM's DBMS product DB2). However, the data is stored, mostly, not at the DataJoiner site (though that capability is available), but rather at any number of other sites behind the scenes, under the control of a variety of other DBMSs (or even file managers such as VSAM). DataJoiner thus effectively provides the user with a virtual database that is the union of all of those "behind the scenes" data stores; it allows queries* to span those data stores, and uses its knowledge of the capabilities of the systems behind the scenes (and of network characteristics) to decide on "globally optimal" query plans.

---

*Emphasis on "queries"; update capabilities are necessarily somewhat limited, especially (but not solely) when the system behind the scenes is, say, IMS or some other nonSQL system (again, see reference [20.16]). At the time of writing, in fact, DataJoiner supports update transactions (with two-phase commit) across DB2, Oracle, Sybase, and Informix sites only.

Note: DataJoiner also includes the ability to emulate certain DB2 SQL features on systems that do not support those features directly. An example might be the WITH HOLD option on a cursor declaration (see Chapter 14).

Now, the system as described thus far is still not a full distributed database system, because the various sites behind the scenes are unaware of each other's existence (i.e., they cannot be considered equal partners in a cooperative venture). However, when any new "behind the scenes" site is added, that new site can also behave as a client site and hence issue queries via DataJoiner that access any or all of the other sites. The overall system thus constitutes what is sometimes called a **federated** system, also known as a **multi-database** system [20.19]. A federated system is a distributed system, usually heterogeneous, with close to full local autonomy; in such a system, purely local transactions are managed by the local DBMSs, but global transactions are a different matter [20.8].

Internally, DataJoiner includes a *driver* component—in effect a point-to-point gateway in the sense of the previous subsection—for each of the "behind the scenes" systems. (Those drivers typically make use of ODBC to access the remote system.) It also maintains a *global catalog,* which is used (among other things) to tell it what to do when it encounters semantic mismatches among those systems.

We note that products like DataJoiner can be useful to third-party software vendors, who can develop generic tools (e.g., report writers, statistical packages, and so on) without having to worry too much about the differences among the different DBMS products against which those tools are supposed to run.

A Final Word

There are clearly significant problems in trying to provide full DBMS independence, even when all of the participating DBMSs are SQL systems specifically. However, the potential payoff is huge, even if the solutions are less than perfect; for this reason, several data access middleware products are already available, and more are certain to appear in the near future. But you are warned that the solutions will necessarily be less than perfect—vendor claims to the contrary notwithstanding. *Caveat emptor.*

20.7   SQL FACILITIES

SQL currently provides no support at all for true distributed database systems. Of course, no support is *required* in the area of data manipulation—the whole point of a distributed database (so far as the user is concerned) is that data manipulation capabilities should remain unchanged. However, data definition operations such as FRAGMENT, REPLICATE, etc., *are* required [20.15] but are currently not provided.

On the other hand, SQL does support certain client/server capabilities, including in particular **CONNECT** and **DISCONNECT** operations for making and breaking client/server connections. In fact, an SQL application *must* execute a CONNECT operation to connect to the server before it can issue any database requests at all (though that CONNECT might be implicit). Once the connection has been established, the application—i.e., the client—can issue SQL requests in the usual way, and the necessary database processing will be carried out by the server.

SQL also allows a client that is already connected to one server to connect to another. Establishing that second connection causes the first to become **dormant;** subsequent SQL requests are processed by the second server, until such time as the client either (a) switches back to the previous server (via another new operation, **SET CONNECTION**) or (b) connects to yet another server, which causes the second connection to become dormant as well (and so on). At any given time, in other words, a given client can have one **active** connection and any number of **dormant** connections, and all database requests from that client are directed to, and processed by, the server on the active connection.

Note: The SQL standard also permits (but does not require) the implementation to support *multi-server transactions.* That is, the client might be able to switch from one server to another in the middle of a transaction, so that part of the transaction is executed on one server and part on another. Note in particular that if *update* transactions are permitted to span servers in this way, the implementation must presumably support some kind of two-phase commit in order to provide the transaction atomicity that the standard requires.

Finally, every connection established by a given client (whether currently active or currently dormant) must eventually be broken via an appropriate DISCONNECT operation (though that DISCONNECT, like the corresponding CONNECT, might be implicit in simple cases).

For additional information, refer to the SQL standard itself [4.22] or the tutorial treatment in reference [4.19].

20.8   SUMMARY

In this chapter, we have presented a brief discussion of distributed database systems. We used the **"twelve objectives"** for distributed database systems [20.14] as a basis for structuring the discussion, though we stress the point once again that not all of those objectives will be relevant in all situations. We also briefly examined certain technical problems arising in the areas of **query processing, catalog management, update propagation, recovery control,** and **concurrency control.** In particular, we discussed what is involved in trying to satisfy the **DBMS independence** objective (the discussion of **gateways** and **data access middleware** in Section 20.6). We also took a closer look at **client/server** processing, which can be regarded as a special case of distributed processing in general, one that is currently popular in the marketplace. In particular, we summarized those aspects of SQL that are relevant to client/server processing, and we stressed the point that users should **avoid record-level code** (cursor operations, in SQL terms). We also briefly described the concept of **stored procedures** and **remote procedure calls.**

Note: One problem we did not discuss at all is the (physical) **database design** problem for distributed systems. In fact, even if we ignore the possibility of fragmentation and/or replication, the problem of deciding which data should be stored at which sites—the so-called **allocation problem**—is a notoriously difficult one [20.33]. Fragmentation and replication support only serve to complicate matters further.

Another point that is worthy of mention is that certain so-called *massively parallel* computer systems are beginning to make their presence felt in the marketplace (see the annotation to reference [17.58] in Chapter 17). Such systems typically consist of a large number of separate processors connected together by means of a high-speed bus; each processor has its own main memory and its own disk drives and runs its own copy of the DBMS software, and the complete database is spread across the complete set of disk drives. In other words, such a system essentially consists of a distributed database system "in a box"!—and all of the issues we have been discussing in the present chapter regarding (e.g.) query processing strategies, two-phase commit, global deadlock, etc., are relevant.

By way of conclusion, we remark that the "twelve objectives" of distributed database (or possibly some subset of them that includes at least Nos. 4, 5, 6, and 8), taken together, seem to be equivalent to Codd's "distribution independence" rule for relational DBMSs [9.5]. For reference, we state that rule here:

- *Distribution independence* (Codd): "A relational DBMS has distribution independence . . . [meaning that the] DBMS has a data sublanguage that enables application programs and terminal activities to remain logically unimpaired:
  1. When data distribution is first introduced (if the originally installed DBMS manages nondistributed data only);
  2. When data is redistributed (if the DBMS manages distributed data)."

Note finally that (as mentioned earlier in the chapter) objectives 4–6 and 9–12—that is, all of the objectives that include the word "independence" in their name—can be regarded as extensions of the familiar notion of data independence, as that concept applies to the distributed environment. As such, they all translate into **protection for the application investment.**

EXERCISES

20.1 Define location independence, fragmentation independence, and replication independence.

20.2 Why are distributed database systems almost invariably relational?

20.3 What are the advantages of distributed systems? What are the disadvantages?

20.4 Explain the following terms:

primary copy update strategy
primary copy locking strategy
global deadlock
two-phase commit
global optimization

20.5 Describe the R* object naming scheme.

20.6 Successful implementation of a point-to-point gateway depends on reconciling the interface differences between the two DBMSs involved (among many other things). Take any two SQL systems you might be familiar with and identify as many interface differences between them as you can. Consider both syntactic and semantic differences.

20.7 Investigate any client/server system that might be available to you. Does that system support explicit CONNECT and DISCONNECT operations? Does it support SET CONNECTION or any other "connection-type" operations? Does it support multi-server transactions? Does it support two-phase commit? What formats and protocols does it use for client/server communication? What network environments does it support? What client and server hardware platforms does it support? What software platforms (operating systems, DBMSs) does it support?

20.8 Investigate any SQL DBMS that might be available to you. Does that DBMS support stored procedures? If so, how are they created? How are they invoked? What language are they written in? Do they support the whole of SQL? Do they support conditional branching (IF–THEN–ELSE)? Do they support loops? How do they return results to the client? Can one stored procedure invoke another? At a different site? Does the stored procedure execute as part of the invoking transaction?

REFERENCES AND BIBLIOGRAPHY

20.1 Todd Anderson, Yuri Breitbart, Henry F. Korth, and Avishai Wool: "Replication, Consistency, and Practicality: Are These Mutually Exclusive?", Proc. 1998 ACM SIGMOD Int. Conf. on Management of Data, Seattle, Wash. (June 1998).

>   This paper describes three schemes for asynchronous (here called *lazy*) replication schemes that guarantee transaction atomicity and global serializability without using two-phase commit, and reports on a simulation study of their comparative performance. Global locking as proposed in reference [20.21] is the first scheme; the other two—one of which is pessimistic and the other optimistic—make use of a *replication graph*. The paper concludes that the replication graph schemes typically outperform the locking scheme "usually by a huge margin."

20.2 David Bell and Jane Grimson: *Distributed Database Systems.* Reading, Mass.: Addison-Wesley (1992).

>   One of several textbooks on distributed systems (two others are references [20.10] and [20.31]). A notable feature of this particular book is the inclusion of an extended case study involving a health-care network. It is also a little more pragmatic in tone than the other two.

20.3 Philip A. Bernstein: "Middleware: A Model for Distributed System Services," *CACM 39,* No. 2 (February 1996).

>   "Various types of middleware are classified, their properties described, and their evolution explained, providing a conceptual model for understanding today's and tomorrow's distributed system software" (from the abstract).

20.4 Philip A. Bernstein, James B. Rothnie, Jr., and David W. Shipman (eds.): *Tutorial: Distributed Data Base Management.* IEEE Computer Society, 5855 Naples Plaza, Suite 301, Long Beach, Calif. 90803 (1978).

A collection of papers from various sources, grouped under the following headings:

1. Overview of relational database management
2. Distributed database management overview
3. Approaches to distributed query processing
4. Approaches to distributed concurrency control
5. Approaches to distributed database reliability

20.5 Philip A. Bernstein *et al.:* "Query Processing in a System for Distributed Databases (SDD-1)," *ACM TODS 6,* No. 4 (December 1981).

See the annotation to reference [20.34].

20.6 Philip A. Bernstein, David W. Shipman, and James B. Rothnie, Jr: "Concurrency Control in a System for Distributed Databases (SDD-1)," *ACM TODS 5,* No. 1 (March 1980).

See the annotation to reference [20.34].

20.7 Charles J. Bontempo and C. M. Saracco: "Data Access Middleware: Seeking out the Middle Ground," *InfoDB 9,* No. 4 (August 1995).

A useful tutorial, with the emphasis on IBM's DataJoiner (though other products are also mentioned).

20.8 Yuri Breitbart, Hector Garcia-Molina, and Avi Silberschatz: "Overview of Multi-Database Transaction Management," *The VLDB Journal 1,* No. 2 (October 1992).

20.9 M. W. Bright, A. R. Hurson, and S. Pakzad: "Automated Resolution of Semantic Heterogeneity in Multi-Databases," *ACM TODS 19,* No. 2 (June 1994).

20.10 Stefano Ceri and Giuseppe Pelagatti: *Distributed Databases: Principles and Systems.* New York, N.Y.: McGraw-Hill (1984).

20.11 William W. Cohen: "Integration of Heterogeneous Databases without Common Domains Using Queries Based on Textual Similarity," Proc. 1998 ACM SIGMOD Int. Conf. on Management of Data, Seattle, Wash. (June 1998).

Describes an approach to what is sometimes called "the junk mail problem"—that is, recognizing when two distinct text strings, say "AT&T Bell Labs" and "AT&T Research," refer to the same object (a particular kind of semantic mismatch, of course). The approach involves reasoning about the *similarity* of such strings "as measured using the vector space model commonly adopted in statistical information retrieval." According to the paper, the approach is much faster than "naive inference methods" and in fact surprisingly accurate.

20.12 D. Daniels *et al.:* "An Introduction to Distributed Query Compilation in R*," in H.-J. Schneider (ed.), *Distributed Data Bases:* Proc. 2nd Int. Symposium on Distributed Data Bases (September 1982). New York, N.Y.: North-Holland (1982).

See the annotation to reference [20.39].

20.13 C. J. Date: "Distributed Databases," Chapter 7 of *An Introduction to Database Systems: Volume II.* Reading, Mass.: Addison-Wesley (1983).

Portions of the present chapter are based on this earlier publication.

20.14 C. J. Date: "What Is a Distributed Database System?", in *Relational Database Writings 1985–1989.* Reading, Mass.: Addison-Wesley (1990).

The paper that introduced the "twelve objectives" for distributed systems (Section 20.3 is modeled fairly directly on this paper). As mentioned in the body of the chapter, the objective of *local autonomy* is not 100 percent achievable; there are certain situations that necessarily involve compromising on that objective somewhat. We summarize those situations here for purposes of reference:

- Individual fragments of a fragmented relvar cannot normally be accessed directly, not even from the site at which they are stored.

- Individual copies of a replicated relvar (or fragment) cannot normally be accessed directly, not even from the site at which they are stored.

- Let *P* be the primary copy of some replicated relvar (or fragment) *R,* and let *P* be stored at site *X.* Then every site that accesses *R* is dependent on site *X,* even if another copy of *R* is in fact stored at the site in question.

- A relvar that participates in a multi-site integrity constraint cannot be accessed for update purposes within the local context of the site at which it is stored, but only within the context of the distributed database in which the constraint is defined.

- A site that is acting as a participant in a two-phase commit process must abide by the decision (i.e., commit or rollback) of the corresponding coordinator site.

20.15 C. J. Date: "Distributed Database: A Closer Look," in C. J. Date and Hugh Darwen, *Relational Database Writings 1989–1991.* Reading, Mass.: Addison-Wesley (1992).

A sequel to reference [20.14], discussing most of the twelve objectives in considerably more depth (albeit still in tutorial style).

20.16 C. J. Date: "Why Is It So Difficult to Provide a Relational Interface to IMS?", in *Relational Database: Selected Writings.* Reading, Mass.: Addison-Wesley (1986).

20.17 R. Epstein, M. Stonebraker, and E. Wong: "Distributed Query Processing in a Relational Data Base System," Proc. 1978 ACM SIGMOD Int. Conf. on Management of Data, Austin, Tx. (May/June 1978).

See the annotation to reference [20.36].

20.18 Rob Goldring: "A Discussion of Relational Database Replication Technology," *InfoDB 8,* No. 1 (Spring 1994).

A good overview of asynchronous replication.

20.19 John Grant, Witold Litwin, Nick Roussopoulos, and Timos Sellis: "Query Languages for Relational Multi-Databases," *The VLDB Journal 2,* No. 2 (April 1993).

Proposes extensions to the relational algebra and relational calculus for dealing with multi-database systems. Issues of optimization are discussed, and it is shown that every multi-relational algebraic expression has a multi-relational calculus equivalent ("the converse of this theorem is an interesting research problem").

20.20 J. N. Gray: "A Discussion of Distributed Systems," Proc. Congresso AICA 79, Bari, Italy (October 1979). Also available as IBM Research Report RJ2699 (September 1979).

A sketchy but good overview and tutorial.

20.21 Jim Gray, Pat Helland, Patrick O'Neil, and Dennis Shasha: "The Dangers of Replication and a Solution," Proc. 1996 ACM SIGMOD Int. Conf. on Management of Data, Montreal, Canada (June 1996).

"Update anywhere-anytime-anyway transactional replication has unstable behavior as the workload scales up . . . A new algorithm is proposed that allows mobile (disconnected) applications to propose tentative update transactions that are later applied to a master copy" (from the abstract, slightly reworded).

20.22 Ramesh Gupta, Jayant Haritsa, and Krithi Ramamritham: "Revisiting Commit Processing in Distributed Database Systems," Proc. 1997 ACM SIGMOD Int. Conf. on Management of Data, Tucson, Ariz. (May 1997).

Proposes a new distributed commit protocol called OPT that (a) is easy to implement, (b) can coexist with traditional protocols, and (c) "provides the best transaction throughput performance for a variety of workloads and system configurations."

20.23 Richard D. Hackathorn: "Interoperability: DRDA or RDA?", *InfoDB 6,* No. 2 (Fall 1991).

20.24 Michael Hammer and David Shipman: "Reliability Mechanisms for SDD-1: A System for Distributed Databases," *ACM TODS 5,* No. 4 (December 1980).

See the annotation to reference [20.34].

20.25 IBM Corporation: *Distributed Relational Database Architecture Reference.* IBM Form No. SC26-4651.

IBM's DRDA defines four levels of distributed database functionality, as follows:

1. Remote request
2. Remote unit of work
3. Distributed unit of work
4. Distributed request

Since these terms have become *de facto* standards in the industry (in some portions of it, at least), we briefly explain them here. *Note:* "Request" and "unit of work" are IBM's terms for *SQL statement* and *transaction,* respectively.

1. **Remote request** means that an application at one site X can send an individual SQL statement to some remote site Y for execution. That request is executed *and committed* (or rolled back) entirely at site Y. The original application at site X can subsequently send another request to site Y (or possibly to another site Z), regardless of whether the first request was successful or unsuccessful.

2. **Remote unit of work** (abbreviated RUW) means that an application at one site X can send all of the database requests in a given "unit of work" (i.e., transaction) to some remote site Y for execution. The database processing for the transaction is thus executed in its entirety at the remote site $Y;$ however, the local site X decides whether the transaction is to be committed or rolled back. *Note:* RUW is effectively client/server processing with a single server.

3. **Distributed unit of work** (abbreviated DUW) means that an application at one site X can send some or all of the database requests in a given unit of work (transaction) to one or more remote sites $Y, Z, \ldots,$ for execution. The database processing for the transaction is thus spread across several sites, in general; each individual request is still executed in its entirety at a single site, but different requests can be executed at different sites. However, site X is still the coordinating site, i.e., the site that decides whether the transaction is to be committed or rolled back. *Note:* DUW is effectively client/server processing with many servers.

4. **Distributed request** is the only one of the four levels that approaches what is commonly regarded as true distributed database support. Distributed request means everything that

distributed unit of work means, *plus* it permits individual database requests (SQL statements) to span several sites—for example, a request originating from site *X* might ask for a join or union to be performed between a table at site *Y* and a table at site *Z.* Note that it is only at this level that the system can be said to be providing genuine location independence; in all three previous cases, users do have to have some knowledge regarding the physical location of data.

20.26 International Organization for Standardization (ISO): *Information Processing Systems, Open Systems Interconnection, Remote Data Access Part 1: Generic Model, Service, and Protocol (Draft International Standard).* Document ISO DIS 9579-1 (March 1990).

20.27 International Organization for Standardization (ISO): *Information Processing Systems, Open Systems Interconnection, Remote Data Access Part 2: SQL Specialization (Draft International Standard).* Document ISO DIS 9579-2 (February 1990).

20.28 B. G. Lindsay *et al.:* "Notes on Distributed Databases," IBM Research Report RJ2571 (July 1979).

This paper (by some of the original members of the R^* team) is divided into five chapters:

1. Replicated data
2. Authorization and views
3. Introduction to distributed transaction management
4. Recovery facilities
5. Transaction initiation, migration, and termination

Chapter 1 discusses the update propagation problem. Chapter 2 is almost totally concerned with authorization in a *non*distributed system (in the style of System R), except for a few remarks at the end. Chapter 3 considers transaction initiation and termination, concurrency control, and recovery control, all rather briefly. Chapter 4 is devoted to the topic of recovery in the *non*distributed case (again). Finally, Chapter 5 discusses distributed transaction management in some detail; in particular, it gives a very careful presentation of two-phase commit.

20.29 C. Mohan and B. G. Lindsay: "Efficient Commit Protocols for the Tree of Processes Model of Distributed Transactions," Proc. 2nd ACM SIGACT-SIGOPS Symposium on Principles of Distributed Computing (1983).

See the annotation to reference [20.39].

20.30 Scott Newman and Jim Gray: "Which Way to Remote SQL?", *DBP&D 4,* No. 12 (December 1991).

20.31 M. Tamer Özsu and Patrick Valduriez: *Principles of Distributed Database Systems* (2nd edition). Englewood Cliffs, N.J.: Prentice-Hall (1999).

20.32 Martin Rennhackkamp: "Mobile Database Replication," *DBMS 10,* No. 11 (October 1997).

The combination of cheap, highly portable computers and wireless communication makes possible a new kind of distributed database system with its own special benefits but also (of course) its own special problems. In particular, data in such a system can be replicated at literally thousands of "sites"—but those sites are mobile, they are frequently offline, their operational characteristics are very different from those of more conventional sites (e.g., communication costs must take battery usage and connection time into account), etc., etc. Research into such systems is comparatively new (references [20.1] and [20.21] are relevant); this short article highlights some of the principal concepts and concerns.

20.33 James B. Rothnie, Jr., and Nathan Goodman: "A Survey of Research and Development in Distributed Database Management," Proc. 3rd Int. Conf. on Very Large Data Bases, Tokyo, Japan (October 1977). Also published in reference [20.4].

A very useful early survey. The field is discussed under the following headings:

1. Synchronizing update transactions
2. Distributed query processing
3. Handling component failures
4. Directory management
5. Database design

The last of these refers to the *physical* design problem—what we called the *allocation* problem in Section 20.8.

20.34 J. B. Rothnie, Jr., *et al.:* "Introduction to a System for Distributed Databases (SDD-1)," *ACM TODS 5,* No. 1 (March 1980).

References [20.5–20.6], [20.24], [20.34], and [20.40] are all concerned with the early distributed prototype SDD-1, which ran on a collection of DEC PDP-10s interconnected via the Arpanet. It provided full location, fragmentation, and replication independence. We offer a few comments here on selected aspects of the system.

Query processing: The SDD-1 query optimizer (see references [20.5] and [20.40]) made extensive use of the *semijoin* operator as described in Chapter 6. The advantage of using semijoins in distributed query processing is that they can have the effect of reducing the amount of data shipped across the network. For example, suppose the suppliers relvar S is stored at site A and the shipments relvar SP is stored at site B, and the query is just "Join suppliers and shipments." Instead of shipping the whole of S to B (say), we can do the following:

- Compute the projection (TEMP1) of SP over S# at B.
- Ship TEMP1 to A.
- Compute the semijoin (TEMP2) of TEMP1 and S over S# at A.
- Ship TEMP2 to B.
- Compute the semijoin of TEMP2 and SP over S# at B. The result is the answer to the original query.

This procedure will obviously reduce the total amount of data movement across the network if and only if

```
size (TEMP1) + size (TEMP2) < size (S)
```

where the "size" of a relation is the cardinality of that relation multiplied by the width of an individual tuple (in bits, say). The optimizer thus clearly needs to be able to estimate the size of intermediate results such as TEMP1 and TEMP2.

Update propagation: The SDD-1 update propagation algorithm is "propagate immediately" (there is no notion of a primary copy).

Concurrency control: Concurrency control is based on a technique called **timestamping,** instead of on locking; the objective is to avoid the message overhead associated with locking, but the price seems to be that there is not in fact very much concurrency! The details are beyond the scope of this book (though the annotation to reference [15.3] does describe the basic idea very briefly); see reference [20.6] or reference [20.13] for more information.

Recovery control: Recovery is based on a *four*-phase commit protocol; the intent is to make the process more resilient than the conventional two-phase commit protocol to a failure at the coordinator site, but unfortunately it also makes the process considerably more complex. The details are (again) beyond the scope of this book.

Catalog: The catalog is managed by treating it as if it were ordinary user data—it can be arbitrarily fragmented, and the fragments can be arbitrarily replicated and distributed, just like any other data. The advantages of this approach are obvious. The disadvantage is, of course, that since the system has no *a priori* knowledge of the location of any given piece of the catalog, it is necessary to maintain a higher-level catalog—the **directory locator**—to provide exactly that information! The directory locator is fully replicated (i.e., a copy is stored at every site).

20.35 P. G. Selinger and M. E. Adiba: "Access Path Selection in Distributed Data Base Management Systems," in S. M. Deen and P. Hammersley (eds.), Proc. Int. Conf. on Data Bases, Aberdeen, Scotland (July 1980). London, England: Heyden and Sons Ltd. (1980).

See the annotation to reference [20.39].

20.36 M. R. Stonebraker and E. J. Neuhold: "A Distributed Data Base Version of Ingres," Proc. 2nd Berkeley Conf. on Distributed Data Management and Computer Networks, Lawrence Berkeley Laboratory (May 1977).

References [20.17] and [20.36–20.37] are all concerned with the Distributed Ingres prototype. Distributed Ingres consists of several copies of University Ingres, running on several interconnected DEC PDP-11s. It supports location independence (like SDD-1 and R*); it also supports data fragmentation (via restriction but not projection), with fragmentation independence, and data replication for such fragments, with replication independence. Unlike SDD-1 and R*, Distributed Ingres does not necessarily assume that the communication network is slow; on the contrary, it is designed to handle both "slow" (long-haul) networks and local (i.e., comparatively fast) networks (the optimizer understands the difference between the two cases). The query optimization algorithm is basically an extension of the Ingres decomposition strategy described in Chapter 17 of this book; it is described in detail in reference [20.17].

Distributed Ingres provides two update propagation algorithms: a "performance" algorithm, which works by updating a primary copy and then returning control to the transaction (leaving the propagated updates to be performed in parallel by a set of slave processes); and a "reliable" algorithm, which updates all copies immediately (see reference [20.37]). Concurrency control is based on locking in both cases. Recovery is based on two-phase commit, with improvements.

As for the catalog, Distributed Ingres uses a combination of full replication for certain portions of the catalog—basically the portions containing a logical description of the relvars visible to the user and a description of how those relvars are fragmented—together with purely local catalog entries for other portions, such as the portions describing local physical storage structures, local database statistics (used by the optimizer), and security and integrity constraints.

20.37 M. R. Stonebraker: "Concurrency Control and Consistency of Multiple Copies in Distributed Ingres," *IEEE Transactions on Software Engineering 5,* No. 3 (May 1979).

See the annotation to reference [20.36].

20.38 Wen-Syan Li and Chris Clifton: "Semantic Integration in Heterogeneous Databases Using Neural Networks," Proc. 20th Int. Conf. on Very Large Data Bases, Santiago, Chile (September 1994).

20.39 R. Williams *et al.:* "R*: An Overview of the Architecture," in P. Scheuermann (ed.), *Improving Database Usability and Responsiveness.* New York, N.Y.: Academic Press (1982). Also available as IBM Research Report RJ3325 (December 1981).

References [20.12], [20.29], [20.35], and [20.39] are all concerned with R*, the distributed version of the original System R prototype. R* provides location independence, but no fragmentation and no replication, and therefore no fragmentation or replication independence either. The question of update propagation does not arise, for the same reason. Concurrency control is based on locking (note that there is only one copy of any object to be locked; the question of a primary copy also does not arise). Recovery is based on two-phase commit, with improvements.

20.40 Eugene Wong: "Retrieving Dispersed Data from SDD-1: A System for Distributed Databases," in reference [20.4].

See the annotation to reference [20.34].

20.41 C. T. Yu and C. C. Chang: "Distributed Query Processing," *ACM Comp. Surv. 16,* No. 4 (December 1984).

A tutorial survey of techniques for query optimization in distributed systems. Includes an extensive bibliography.

CHAPTER 21

Decision Support

21.1 INTRODUCTION

Note: David McGoveran was the original author of this chapter.

Decision support systems are systems that help in the analysis of business information. Their aim is to help management "spot trends, pinpoint problems, and make . . . intelligent decisions" [21.7]. The roots of such systems—operations research, behavioral and scientific theories of management, and statistical process control—can be traced back to the late 1940s and 1950s, well before computers became generally available. The basic idea was, and of course still is, to collect business *operational* data (see Chapter 1) and reduce it to a form that could be used to analyze the behavior of the business and modify that behavior in an intelligent manner. For fairly obvious reasons the extent to which the data was reduced in those early days was pretty minimal, of course, typically involving little more than the generation of simple summary reports.

In the late 1960s and early 1970s, researchers at Harvard and MIT began promoting the use of computers to help in the decision-making process [21.23]. At first, such use was limited (mostly) to automating the task of report generation, although rudimentary analytical capabilities were sometimes provided as well [21.2–21.3,21.6,21.26]. Those early computer systems were initially known as **management decision systems;** later they also became known as **management information systems.** We prefer the more modern term *decision support system,* however, since a good case can be made that *all* information systems—including, e.g., OLTP systems (OLTP = online transaction processing)—can or should be regarded as "management information systems" (after all, they are all involved in, and affect, the management of the business). We will stay with the more modern term in what follows.

The 1970s also saw the development of several **query languages,** and a number of custom (inhouse) decision support systems were built around such languages. They were implemented using report generators such as RPG or data retrieval products such as Focus, Datatrieve, and NOMAD. Those systems were the first to allow suitably skilled end users to access computer data stores directly; i.e., they allowed such users to formulate business-related queries against those data stores and execute those queries directly, without having to wait for assistance from the IT department.

Of course, the data stores just referred to were mostly just simple files—most business data at the time was kept in such files, or possibly in nonrelational databases (relational systems still lay in the realms of research). Even in the latter case, the data usually had to be

694

extracted from the database and copied to files before it could be accessed by a decision support system. It was not until the early 1980s that relational databases began to be used in place of simple files for decision support purposes. In fact, decision support, *ad hoc* query, and reporting were among the earliest commercial uses of relational technology.

Even though SQL products are now widely available, the idea of **extract processing**—i.e., copying data from the operational environment to some other environment—continues to be very important; it allows users to operate on the extracted data in whatever manner they desire, without interfering further with the operational environment. And, of course, the reason for performing such extracts is very often decision support.

It should be clear from the foregoing brief history that decision support is not really part of database technology *per se*. Rather, it is a *use* of that technology (albeit an important one)—or, to be more precise, it is several such uses, distinct but intertwined. The uses in question go by the names of *data warehouse, data mart, operational data store, online analytical processing (OLAP), multi-dimensional databases,* and *data mining* (among others). We will discuss all of these topics in the sections that follow.

Caveat: We remark immediately that one thing these areas all have in common is that good logical design principles are rarely followed in any of them! The practice of decision support is, regrettably, not as scientific as it might be; often, in fact, it is quite *ad hoc*. In particular, it tends to be driven much more by physical considerations than by logical ones (indeed, the distinction between physical and logical matters is often very blurred in the decision support environment). Partly for these reasons, in this chapter we use SQL, not **Tutorial D,** as the basis for our examples, and we use the "fuzzier" SQL terminology of rows, columns, and tables in place of our preferred terminology of tuples, attributes, and relation values and variables (relvars). Also, we use the terms *logical schema* and *physical schema* as synonyms for what in Chapter 2 we called the *conceptual* schema and the *internal* schema, respectively.

The plan of the chapter, then, is as follows. In Section 21.2 we discuss certain aspects of decision support that have motivated certain design practices that we believe are somewhat misguided. Section 21.3 describes our own preferred approach to dealing with those aspects. Section 21.4 then examines the issue of data preparation (i.e., the process of getting operational data into a form in which it can be useful for decision support purposes); it also briefly considers "operational data stores." Section 21.5 discusses data warehouses, data marts, and "dimensional schemas." Section 21.6 explores online analytical processing (OLAP) and multi-dimensional databases. Section 21.7 discusses data mining. Section 21.8 presents a summary.

21.2 ASPECTS OF DECISION SUPPORT

Decision support databases display certain special characteristics, of which the overriding one is this: **The database is primarily** (though not totally) **read-only.** What updating there is is limited, typically, to periodic *load* or *refresh* operations (and those operations in turn are dominated by INSERTs—DELETEs are done only very occasionally, UPDATEs almost never). *Note:* Sometimes updating is done on certain auxiliary work tables, but normal decision support processes as such almost never update the decision support database itself.

The following further characteristics of decision support databases are also worthy of note (we will come back to elaborate on them in Section 21.3). Note that the first three are logical in nature while the last three are physical.

- Columns tend to be used in combination.

- Integrity in general is not a concern (the data is assumed to be correct when first loaded and is not subsequently updated).

- Keys often include a temporal component (see Chapter 22).

- The database tends to be large (especially where—as is often the case—business transaction* details are accumulated over time).

- The database tends to be heavily indexed.

- The database often involves various kinds of *controlled redundancy* (see Chapter 1).

Decision support queries display special characteristics, too; in particular, they tend to be quite *complex*. Here are some of the kinds of complexities that can arise:

- *Boolean expression complexity:* Decision support queries often involve complex expressions in the WHERE clause—expressions that are hard to write, hard to understand, and hard for the system to deal with adequately. (In particular, classical optimizers tend to be inadequate, because they are designed to evaluate only a limited number of access strategies.) A common problem is queries involving *time;* current systems typically do not provide good support for, e.g., queries asking for rows with a maximum timestamp value in a specified time period (again, see Chapter 22). If any joins are involved, such queries quickly become very complex indeed. The net result in all such cases is, of course, poor performance.

- *Join complexity:* Decision support queries often require access to many kinds of facts. As a consequence, in a properly designed—i.e., fully normalized—database, such queries typically involve many joins. Unfortunately, join processing technology has never managed to keep up with the ever-growing demands of decision support queries.[†] Often, therefore, designers decide to *denormalize* the database by "prejoining" certain tables. As we saw in Chapter 12, however (in Section 12.5), this approach is rarely suc-

---

*Here and throughout this chapter we distinguish business transactions (e.g., sale of a product) from transactions in the sense of Part IV of this book by always using the "business" qualifier when it is a business transaction that we mean (unless the context makes the meaning obvious).

[†]The writer (McGoveran), working on early decision support systems in 1981, observed that a three-table join of tables of even moderate size could easily take many hours. Joins of four to six tables were generally considered too costly. Today, joins of six to ten very large tables are common, and the technology usually does well. However, it is still easy (and not unusual) to generate queries that join more tables than the technology can reasonably handle. Queries joining more than twelve tables can rapidly become an adventure— and yet the requirement for such queries is common!

cessful, usually causing as many problems as it solves. What is more, the desire to avoid joins can also lead to inefficient use of relational operations, with large amounts of data being retrieved and join processing being done inside the application instead of the DBMS.

■ *Function complexity:* Decision support queries often involve statistical and other mathematical functions. Few products support such functions. As a result, it is often necessary to break a query into a sequence of smaller ones, which are then executed interleaved with user-written procedures that compute the desired functions. This approach has the unfortunate consequence that large amounts of data might need to be retrieved; also, of course, it makes the overall query much harder to write and understand.

■ *Analytical complexity:* Business questions are rarely answered in a single query. Not only is it difficult for users to write queries of extreme complexity, but limitations of SQL implementations can prevent such a query from being processed. One way to reduce the complexity of such queries is (again) to break them into a series of smaller ones, keeping intermediate results in auxiliary tables.

All of the foregoing characteristics, both those of decision support databases and those of decision support queries, lead to a strong emphasis on *designing for performance*—especially batch insert and *ad hoc* retrieval performance. It is our position, however (elaborated in the next section), that this state of affairs should affect only the physical design of the database, not the logical design. Unfortunately, however, as noted in Section 21.1, vendors and users of decision support systems often fail to distinguish adequately between logical and physical issues;* in fact, they often forgo logical design entirely. As a consequence, attempts to deal with the various characteristics discussed above tend to be *ad hoc* and often lead to insurmountable difficulties in trying to balance correctness, maintainability, performance, scalability, and usability requirements.

21.3   DATABASE DESIGN FOR DECISION SUPPORT

As stated earlier in this book (in the introduction to Part III in particular), it is our position that database design should always be done in at least two stages, logical then physical:

a. The logical design should be done first. In this stage, the focus is on *relational correctness:* Tables must represent proper relations, thereby guaranteeing that relational operations work as advertised and do not produce surprising results. Domains (types) are specified, columns defined on them, and dependencies among columns (FDs, etc.) identified. From this information, normalization can proceed and integrity constraints defined.

---

*Data warehouse and OLAP specialists tend to be especially guilty on this count; they often argue that relational design is simply "wrong" for decision support, claiming that the relational model is incapable of representing the data and must be circumvented. Such arguments almost always hinge on a failure to distinguish the relational model from its physical implementation.

b. Second, the physical design should be derived from the logical design. In this stage, of course, the focus is on *storage efficiency and performance*. In principle, any physical arrangement of the data is permissible, so long as there exists an information-preserving transformation, expressible in the relational algebra [2.5], between the logical and physical schemas. Note in particular that the existence of such a transformation implies that there exist relational views of the physical schema that make it look like the logical schema and *vice versa*.

Of course, the logical schema might subsequently change (e.g., to accommodate new kinds of data or new—or newly discovered—dependencies), and such a change will naturally require a corresponding change to the physical schema as well. Such a possibility does not concern us here. What does concern us is the possibility that the physical schema might change while the logical schema does not change. For example, suppose joining tables SP (shipments) and P (parts) is by far the dominant access pattern. Then we might wish to "prejoin" the SP and P tables at the physical level, thereby reducing I/O and join costs. However, *the logical schema must remain unchanged* if physical data independence is to be achieved. (Of course, the query optimizer will need to be aware of the existence of the stored "prejoin," and use it appropriately, if we are to obtain the desired performance benefits.) Furthermore, if the access pattern subsequently changes to one dominated by individual table accesses instead of joins, we should be able change the physical schema again so that the SP and P tables are physically separated, again without any impact at the logical level.

It should be clear from the foregoing that the problem of providing physical data independence is basically the problem of supporting view updating (except that, as with the fragment update problem discussed in Chapter 20, it manifests itself at a different point in the overall system architecture). Now, we saw in Chapter 9 that, in theory, *all* relational views are updatable. In theory, therefore, if the physical schema is derived from the logical schema in the manner described above, maximum physical data independence will be achieved: Any update expressed in terms of the logical schema will be automatically translatable into one expressed in terms of the physical schema and *vice versa*, and changes to the physical schema will not in and of themselves require changes to the logical schema. *Note:* We remark in passing that the *only* reason for making such changes to the physical schema should be to improve storage efficiency or performance.

Unfortunately, however, today's SQL products do not support view updating properly. As a consequence, the set of permissible physical schemas is considerably (and unnecessarily) limited in those products. To be specific, if (a) we think of the base tables at the logical level as views and the stored versions of those "views" at the physical level as base tables, then (b) the physical schema must be such that the product in question can implement all logically possible updates on those "views" in terms of those "base tables." *Note:* In practice, it might be possible to simulate the proper view updating mechanism by means of stored procedures, triggered procedures, middleware, or some combination thereof. Such techniques are beyond the scope of the present chapter, however.

Logical Design

The rules of logical design do not depend on the intended use of the database—the same rules apply, regardless of the kinds of applications intended. In particular, therefore, it should make no difference whether those applications are operational (OLTP) or decision support applications: Either way, the same design procedure should be followed. So let us revisit the three *logical* characteristics of decision support databases identified near the beginning of Section 21.2 and consider their implications for logical design.

■ *Column combinations and fewer dependencies*

Decision support queries—and updates, when applicable—often treat combinations of columns as a unit, meaning the component columns are never accessed individually (ADDRESS is an obvious example). Let us agree to refer to such a column combination as a *composite column.* From a logical design point of view, then, such composite columns behave as if they were in fact *not* composite! To be more specific, let CC be a composite column and let C be some other column of the same table. Then dependencies involving C and component(s) of CC reduce to dependencies involving C and CC *per se.* What is more, dependencies involving components of CC and no other columns are irrelevant and can simply be ignored. The net effect is that the total number of dependencies is reduced and the logical design becomes simpler, with fewer columns and possibly even fewer tables.

Note: It is only fair to mention that complete and proper support for composite columns is nontrivial, however, relying as it does on support for *user-defined types.* See reference [21.11] and Chapters 5 and 25 for further discussion.

■ *Integrity constraints in general*

Since as already explained (a) decision support databases are primarily read-only and (b) data integrity is checked when the database is loaded (or refreshed), it is often assumed that there is no point in declaring integrity constraints in the logical schema. Such is not the case, however. While it is true (if the database genuinely is read-only) that the constraints can never be violated, the *semantic value* of those constraints should not be overlooked. As we saw in Chapter 8 (Section 8.10), constraints serve to define the meaning of the tables and the meaning of the overall database. Declaring the constraints thus provides a means of telling users what the data means, thereby helping them in their task of formulating queries. What is more, declaring the constraints can also provide crucial information to the optimizer (see the discussion of *semantic optimization* in Chapter 17, Section 17.4).

Note: Declaring certain constraints in certain SQL products causes the automatic creation of certain indexes and other enforcement mechanisms, a fact that can significantly increase the cost of load and refresh operations. This fact in turn can serve to encourage designers to avoid constraint declarations. Once again, however, the problem derives from a confusion over logical *vs.* physical issues; it should be possible to specify integrity constraints declaratively at the *logical* level and to specify the corresponding enforcement mechanisms separately at the *physical* level. Unfortunately, however, today's SQL products do not adequately differentiate between the two levels (moreover, they scarcely recognize the semantic value of constraints at all).

■ *Temporal keys*

Operational databases usually involve current data only. Decision support databases, by contrast, usually involve historical data and therefore tend to *timestamp* most or all of that data. As a result, keys in such databases often include timestamp columns. Consider our usual suppliers and parts database, for example. Suppose we need to extend that database to show, for each shipment, the particular month (1 to 12) in which that shipment occurred. Then the shipments table SP might look as shown in Fig. 21.1. Observe that the additional column MID ("month ID") is indeed part of the key of this extended version of table SP. Observe too that queries involving SP must now be formulated very carefully in order to avoid accessing data with different timestamps (unless such access is exactly what is desired, of course). We touched on such issues briefly in Section 21.2; Chapter 22 discusses them in depth.

Note: Adding timestamp columns to a key might lead to the need for some redesign. For example, suppose, somewhat artificially, that the quantity of each shipment is determined by the month in which the shipment occurs (the sample data of Fig. 21.1 is consistent with this constraint). Then the revised version of table SP satisfies the functional dependency MID $\rightarrow$ QTY and is thus not in fifth—or even third—normal form; it should therefore be further normalized as indicated in Fig. 21.2. Unfortunately, decision support designers rarely bother to take such *induced dependencies* into account.

SP	S#	P#	MID	QTY
	S1	P1	3	300
	S1	P1	5	100
	S1	P2	1	200
	S1	P3	7	400
	S1	P4	1	200
	S1	P5	5	100
	S1	P6	4	100
	S2	P1	3	300
	S2	P2	9	400
	S3	P2	6	200
	S3	P2	8	200
	S4	P2	1	200
	S4	P4	8	200
	S4	P5	7	400
	S4	P5	11	400

Fig. 21.1   Sample value for table SP, including month IDs

SP	S#	P#	MID	MONTH_QTY	MID	QTY
	S1	P1	3		1	200
	S1	P1	5		2	600
	S1	P2	1		3	300
	S1	P3	7		4	100
	S1	P4	1		5	100
	S1	P5	5		6	200
	S1	P6	4		7	400
	S2	P1	3		8	200
	S2	P2	9		9	400
	S3	P2	6		10	100
	S3	P2	8		11	400
	S4	P2	1		12	50
	S4	P4	8			
	S4	P5	7			
	S4	P5	11			

Fig. 21.2   Normalized counterpart of Fig. 21.1

Physical Design

We said in Section 21.2 that decision support databases tend to be *large* and *heavily indexed* and to involve various kinds of *controlled redundancy*. In this subsection we briefly elaborate on these physical design issues.

First we consider **partitioning** (also known as *fragmentation*). Partitioning represents an attack on the "large database" problem; it divides a given table into a set of disjoint *partitions* or *fragments* for physical storage purposes (see the discussion of fragmentation in Chapter 20). Such partitioning can significantly improve the manageability and accessibility of the table in question. Typically, each partition is assigned certain more or less dedicated hardware resources (e.g., disk, CPU), thereby minimizing competition for such resources among partitions. Tables are partitioned horizontally* by means of a *partitioning function,* which takes values of selected columns (the *partition key*) as arguments and returns a partition number or address. Such functions typically support range, hash, and round robin partitioning, among other kinds (see the annotation to reference [17.58] in Chapter 17).

Now we turn to **indexing.** Of course, it is well known that using the right kind of index can dramatically reduce I/O. Most early SQL products provided just one kind of index, the B-tree, but several other kinds have become available over the years, especially in connection with decision support databases; they include *bitmap, hash, multi-table, boolean,* and *functional* indexes, as well as B-tree indexes *per se.* We comment briefly on each kind.

- *B-tree indexes:* B-tree indexes provide efficient access for range queries (unless the number of rows accessed becomes too large). Update of B-trees is relatively efficient.

---

*Vertical partitioning, though possibly advantageous, is not much used since most products do not support it.

- *Bitmap indexes:* Suppose the indexed table T contains *n* rows. Then a bitmap index on column C of table T keeps a vector of *n* bits for each value in the domain of C, setting the bit corresponding to row R if row R contains the applicable value in column C. Such indexes are efficient for queries involving sets of values, though they become less efficient when the sets become too large. Observe in particular that several relational operations (joins, unions, equality restrictions, etc.) can be performed entirely within the index(es) by means of simple boolean operations (AND, OR, NOT) on the bit vectors; access to the actual data is not needed at all until the final result set has to be retrieved. Update of bitmap indexes is relatively inefficient.

- *Hash indexes* (also known as *hash addressing* or just *hashing*): Hash indexes are efficient for accessing specific rows (not ranges). The computational cost is linear with the number of rows, so long as the hash function does not need to be extended to accommodate additional key values. Hashing can also be used to implement joins efficiently, as described in Chapter 17.

- *Multi-table indexes* (also known as *join indexes*): Essentially, a multi-table index entry contains pointers to rows in several tables instead of just to rows in one table. Such indexes can improve the performance of joins and the checking of multi-table (i.e., database) integrity constraints.

- *Boolean indexes* (more usually known as *expression* indexes): A boolean index indicates for which rows of a specified table a specified boolean expression (involving columns of the table in question) evaluates to *true*. Such indexes are particularly valuable when the relevant boolean expression is a common component of restriction conditions.

- *Functional indexes:* A functional index indexes the rows of a table not on the basis of values in those rows, but rather on the basis of the result of invoking some specified function on those values.

In addition to all of the foregoing, various kinds of *hybrid* indexes (combinations of those listed above) have been proposed. The value of such hybrids is hard to characterize in general terms. A huge number of *specialized* kinds of indexes have also been proposed (e.g., *R-trees,* which are intended for dealing with geometric data). We do not attempt the daunting task of describing all of these kinds of indexes in this book; see, e.g., reference [25.27] for a comprehensive discussion.

Last, we turn to the issue of **controlled redundancy.** Controlled redundancy is an important tool for reducing I/O and minimizing contention. As explained in Chapter 1, redundancy is controlled when it is managed by the DBMS and hidden from users. (Note that, by definition, redundancy that is properly controlled at the physical level is invisible at the logical level, so it has no effect on the correctness of that logical level.) There are two broad kinds of such redundancy:

- The first involves maintaining exact copies or *replicas* of the base data. *Note:* What might be regarded as a less ambitious form of replication, *copy management,* is also widely supported (see below).

■ The second involves maintaining *derived data* in addition to the base data, most often in the form of *summary tables* and/or *calculated—*or *computed* or *derived—columns.*

We discuss each in turn.

The basic concepts of **replication** were explained in Chapter 20, in Sections 20.3 and 20.4 (see especially the subsection "Update Propagation" in Section 20.4); here we just repeat a few salient points from those discussions and make a few additional remarks. Recall first that replication can be either *synchronous* or *asynchronous:*

■ In the *synchronous* case, if a given replica is updated, then all other replicas of the same piece of data are also updated within the same transaction, implying that (logically speaking) just one version of the data exists. Most products implement synchronous replication via (possibly hidden, system-managed) triggered procedures. However, synchronous replication has the disadvantage that it imposes an overhead on all transactions that update any replica (there might be availability problems, too).

■ In the *asynchronous* case, updates to one replica are propagated to the others at some later time, *not* within the same transaction. Asynchronous replication thus introduces a *time delay* or *latency* during which the replicas might not in fact be identical (and so the term "replicas" is no longer very appropriate, since we are no longer talking about exact copies). Most products implement asynchronous replication by reading the transaction log or a stable queue of updates that need to be propagated.

The advantage of asynchronous replication is that the replication overhead is uncoupled from the updating transaction, which might be "mission-critical" and highly performance-sensitive. The disadvantage is that the data can become inconsistent (inconsistent as seen by the user, that is); i.e., the redundancy can show through to the logical level—meaning, strictly speaking, that the term "controlled redundancy" is no longer very appropriate.*

We remark that, at least in the commercial world, the term "replication" has come to mean, primarily (indeed, almost exclusively), *asynchronous* replication specifically (as noted in Chapter 20).

The basic difference between replication and **copy management** is as follows. With replication, updates to one replica are (eventually) propagated to all others in an "automatic" fashion. With copy management, by contrast, there is no such automatic propagation; instead, data copies are created and maintained by means of some batch or background process that is uncoupled in time from the updating transactions. Copy management is gen-

---

*Note too that replicas can become inconsistent in ways that are hard to avoid and hard to fix. In particular, conflicts can arise over the order in which updates are applied. For example, let transaction T1 insert a row into replica RX and let transaction T2 then delete that row, and let RY be a replica of RX. If the updates are propagated to RY but arrive at RY in reverse order (e.g., because of routing delays), T2 finds no row to delete and T1 then inserts the row. The net effect is that RY contains the row while RX does not. Conflict management and consistency enforcement across replicas are difficult problems, beyond the scope of this book.

erally more efficient than replication, since large amounts of data can be copied at one time. The disadvantage is that most of the time the copies are not identical to the base data; indeed, users must generally be aware of when they have been synchronized. Copy management is usually simplified by requiring that updates be applied in accordance with some kind of "primary copy" scheme (see Chapter 20).

The other kind of redundancy we consider here is **calculated columns** and **summary tables.** These constructs are particularly important in the decision support context; they are used to hold precomputed data values (i.e., values that are computed from other data kept somewhere else in the database). Clearly, such constructs avoid the need to recompute such values each time they are needed in some query. A *calculated column* is one whose value in any given row is derived in some way from other values in the same row.* A *summary table* is a table that holds aggregations (sums, averages, counts, etc.) of values in other tables. Such aggregations are often precalculated for several different groupings of the same detail data (see Section 21.6). *Note:* If calculated columns and summary tables are truly to be instances of controlled redundancy, they need to be completely hidden from users; in today's products, however, they usually are not.

Summary tables and calculated columns are most often implemented via system-managed triggered procedures, though they can also be implemented via user-written procedural code. The former approach allows consistency to be maintained between the base and derived data (so long as both are updated in the same transaction, which might or might not be the case; even if it is, note that a high isolation level might be crucial to obtaining that consistency). The latter approach is more likely to expose inconsistencies to the user.

Common Design Errors

In this subsection, we comment briefly on some design practices that are common in the decision support environment and yet we feel are not a good idea:

- *Duplicate rows:* Decision support designers often claim that their data simply has no unique identifier and that they therefore have to permit duplicates. References [5.3] and [5.6] explain in detail why duplicates are a mistake; here we just remark that the "requirement" typically arises because the physical schema is not derived from a logical schema (which was probably never created in the first place). We note too that in such a design, the rows often have nonuniform meanings (especially if any nulls are present)—i.e., they are not all instantiations of the same predicate (see Chapter 3, Section 3.4, also Chapter 18). *Note:* Duplicates are sometimes even deliberately permitted, especially if the designer has an object-oriented background (see the very last paragraph of Section 24.2 in Chapter 24).

---

*Alternatively, the calculated value might be derived from values in several rows, in the same table or in some other table(s). However, such an approach implies that updating one row could require many other rows to be updated as well; in particular, it can have a very negative effect on load and refresh operations.

- *Denormalization and related practices:* In a misguided effort to eliminate joins and reduce I/O, designers often prejoin tables, introduce derived columns of various kinds, etc., etc. Such practices might be acceptable at the physical level, but not if they are detectable at the logical level.

- *Star schemas:* "Star schemas" (also known as *dimensional* schemas) are most often the result of an attempt to "short-circuit" proper design technique. There is little to be gained from such short cuts. Often both performance and flexibility suffer as the database grows, and resolving such difficulties via physical redesign forces changes in applications as well (because star schemas are really *physical* schemas, even though they are exposed to applications). The overall problem lies in the *ad hoc* nature of the design. *Note:* We will discuss star schemas in more detail in Section 21.5 below.

- *Nulls:* Designers often attempt to save space by permitting nulls in columns (this trick *might* work if the column in question is of some variable-length data type and the product in question represents nulls in such columns by empty strings at the physical level). Such attempts are generally misguided, however. Not only is it possible (and desirable) to design in such a way as to avoid nulls in the first place [18.20], but the resulting schemas often provide better storage efficiency and better I/O performance.

- *Design of summary tables:* The question of logical design for summary tables is often ignored, leading to uncontrolled redundancy and difficulties in maintaining consistency. As a consequence, users can become confused as to the meaning of summary data and how to formulate queries involving it. To avoid such problems, all summary tables at the same level of aggregation (see Section 21.6) should be designed as if they formed a database in their own right. Certain *cyclic update* problems can then be avoided by (a) prohibiting updates from spanning aggregation levels and (b) synchronizing the summary tables by always aggregating from the detail level up.

- *"Multiple navigation paths":* Decision support designers and users often speak (incorrectly) of there being a "multiplicity of navigational paths" to some desired data, meaning the same data can be reached via several different relational expressions. Sometimes the expressions in question are truly equivalent, as in the case of, e.g., A JOIN (B JOIN C) and (A JOIN B) JOIN C (see Chapter 17); sometimes they are equivalent only because there is some integrity constraint in effect that makes them so (again, see Chapter 17); and sometimes they are not equivalent at all! As an example of the last case, suppose tables A, B, and C all have a common column K; then "following the K path from A to B and thence to C" is certainly *not* the same (in general) as "following the K path direct from A to C."

  It is clear that users can become confused in such cases and be unsure as to which expression to use and whether or not there will be any difference in the result. Part of this problem can only be solved by proper user education, of course. Another part can be solved if the optimizer does its job properly. However, yet another part is due to designers allowing redundancies in the logical schema and/or letting users access the physical schema directly, and *that* part of the problem can only be solved by proper design practice.

In sum, we believe that many of the design difficulties allegedly arising from decision support requirements can be addressed by following a disciplined approach. Indeed, many of those difficulties are *caused* by not following such an approach (though it is only fair to add that they are often aggravated by problems with SQL).

21.4 DATA PREPARATION

Many of the issues surrounding decision support concern the tasks of obtaining and preparing the data in the first place. The data must be *extracted* from various sources, *cleansed, transformed* and *consolidated, loaded* into the decision support database, and then periodically *refreshed*. Each of these operations involves its own special considerations.* We examine each in turn, then wrap up the section with a brief discussion of *operational data stores*.

Extract

Extract is the process of capturing data from operational databases and other sources. Many tools are available to help in this task, including system-provided utilities, custom extract programs, and commercial (general-purpose) extract products. The extract process tends to be I/O-intensive and thus can interfere with mission-critical operations; for this reason, it is often performed in parallel (i.e., as a set of parallel subprocesses) and at a physical level. Such "physical extracts" can cause problems for subsequent processing, however, because they can lose information—especially relationship information—that is represented in some physical manner (e.g., by pointers or physical contiguity). For this reason, extract programs sometimes provide a means of preserving such information by introducing sequential record numbers and by replacing pointers by what are in effect foreign key values.

Cleansing

Few data sources control data quality adequately. As a result, data often requires **cleansing** (usually in batch) before it can be entered into the decision support database. Typical cleansing operations include filling in missing values, correcting typographical and other data entry errors, establishing standard abbreviations and formats, replacing synonyms by standard identifiers, and so on. Data that is known to be in error and cannot be cleansed is rejected. *Note:* Information obtained during the cleansing process can sometimes be used to identify the cause of errors at the source and hence to improve data quality over time.

---

*We remark in passing that these operations could often benefit from the set-level capabilities of relational systems, though in practice they rarely do.

Transformation and Consolidation

Even after it has been cleansed, the data will probably still not be in the form the decision support system requires, and so will need to be **transformed** appropriately. Usually the required form will be a set of files, one for each table identified in the physical schema; as a result, transforming the data might involve splitting and/or combining source records along the lines discussed in Chapter 1 (Section 1.5). *Note:* Data errors that were not corrected during cleansing are sometimes found during the transformation process. As before, any such incorrect data is generally rejected. (Also as before, information obtained as part of this process can sometimes be used to improve the quality of the data source.)

Transformation is particularly important when several data sources need to be merged, a process called **consolidation.** In such a case, any implicit relationships among data from distinct sources need to be made explicit (by introducing explicit data values). In addition, dates and times associated with the business meaning of the data need to be maintained and correlated among sources, a process called "time synchronization" [*sic!*].

For performance reasons, transformation operations are often performed in parallel. They can be both I/O- and CPU-intensive.

Note: Time synchronization can be a difficult problem. For example, suppose we want to find average customer revenue per salesperson per quarter. Suppose customer *vs.* revenue data is maintained by fiscal quarter in an accounting database, while salesperson *vs.* customer data is maintained by calendar quarter in a sales database. Clearly, we need to merge data from the two databases. Consolidating the customer data is easy—it simply involves matching customer IDs. However, the time synchronization issue is much more difficult; we can find customer revenues per *fiscal* quarter (from the accounting database), but we cannot tell which salespersons were responsible for which customers at that time, and we cannot find customer revenues per *calendar* quarter at all.

Load

DBMS vendors have placed considerable importance on the efficiency of **load** operations. For present purposes, we consider "load operations" to include (a) moving the transformed and consolidated data into the decision support database; (b) checking it for consistency (i.e., integrity checking); and (c) building any necessary indexes. We comment briefly on each step:

a. *Moving the data:* Modern systems usually provide parallel load utilities. Sometimes they will preformat the data to the internal physical format required by the target DBMS prior to the actual load. (An alternative technique that delivers much of the efficiency of preformatted loads is to load the data into work tables that mirror the target schema. The necessary integrity checking can be done on those work tables—see paragraph b.—and set-level INSERTs then used to move the data from the work tables to the target tables.)

b. *Integrity checking:* Most integrity checking on the data to be loaded can be done prior to the actual load without reference to data already in the database. However, certain constraints cannot be checked without examining the existing database; for example, a uniqueness constraint will generally have to be checked during the actual load (or in batch after the load is completed).

c. *Building indexes:* The presence of indexes can slow the load process dramatically, since most products update indexes as each row is inserted into the underlying table. For this reason, it is sometimes a good idea to drop indexes before the load and then to create them again subsequently. However, this approach is not worthwhile when the ratio of new data to existing data is small, because the cost of creating an index does not scale with the size of the table to be indexed. Also, creating a large index can be subject to unrecoverable allocation errors, such errors becoming more probable the larger the index. *Note:* Most DBMS products support parallel index creation in an effort to speed the load and index build processes.

Refresh

Most decision support databases (not all) require periodic **refreshing** of the data in order to keep it reasonably current. Refresh generally involves a partial load, although some decision support applications require dropping everything in the database and completely reloading it. Refresh involves all the problems associated with load, but might also need to be performed while users are accessing the database. See Chapter 9, Section 9.5, also references [9.2] and [9.6].

Operational Data Stores

An **operational data store** (ODS) is a "subject-oriented, integrated, volatile (i.e., updatable), current or near current collection of data" [21.19]. In other words, it is a special kind of database. The term *subject-oriented* means the data in question has to do with some specific subject area (e.g., customers, products). An operational data store can be used (a) as a staging area for the physical reorganization of extracted operational data, (b) to provide operational reports, and (c) to support operational decisions. It can also serve (d) as a point of consolidation, if operational data comes from several sources. ODSs thus serve many purposes. *Note:* Since they do not accumulate historical data, they do not grow very large (usually); on the other hand, they are typically subject to very frequent or even continuous refresh from operational data sources.* Time synchronization problems (see the subsection "Transformation and Consolidation" above) can be successfully addressed within an ODS, if refresh is frequent enough.

---

*Asynchronous replication from the operational data sources to the ODS is sometimes used for this purpose. In this way, the data can often be kept current to within a few minutes.

21.5   DATA WAREHOUSES AND DATA MARTS

Operational systems usually have strict performance requirements, predictable workloads, small units of work, and high utilization. By contrast, decision support systems typically have varying performance requirements, unpredictable workloads, large units of work, and erratic utilization. These differences can make it very difficult to combine operational and decision support processing within a single system, especially with respect to capacity planning, resource management, and system performance tuning. For these reasons, operational system administrators are usually reluctant to allow decision support activities on their systems; hence the familiar dual-system approach.

Note: We remark as an aside that matters were not always thus; early decision support systems were indeed run on operational systems, but at low priority or during the so-called "batch window." Given sufficient computing resources, there are several advantages to this arrangement, perhaps the most obvious of which is that it avoids all of the possibly expensive data copying, reformatting, and transfer (etc.) operations required by the dual-system approach. In fact, the value of integrating operational and decision support activities is becoming increasingly recognized. Further details of such integration are beyond the scope of this chapter, however.

The previous paragraph notwithstanding, the fact remains that, at least at the time of writing, decision support data usually needs to be collected from a variety of operational systems (often disparate systems) and kept in a data store of its own on a separate platform. That separate data store is a *data warehouse.*

Data Warehouses

Like an operational data store (and like a data mart—see the next subsection), a **data warehouse** is a special kind of database. The term seems to have originated in the late 1980s [21.13,21.17], though the concept is somewhat older. Reference [21.18] defines a data warehouse as "a subject-oriented, integrated, nonvolatile, time-variant data store in support of management's decisions" (where the term *nonvolatile* means that, once inserted, data cannot be changed, though it might be deleted). Data warehouses arose for two reasons: first, the need to provide a single, clean, consistent source of data for decision support purposes; second, the need to do so without impacting operational systems.

By definition, data warehouse workloads are decision support workloads and hence query-intensive (with occasional intensive batch insert activities); also, data warehouses themselves tend to be quite large (often over 500GB, and growing by as much as 50 percent a year). As a result, performance tuning is hard, though not impossible. Scalability can be a problem, though. Contributors to that problem include (a) database design errors (discussed in the final subsection of Section 21.3); (b) inefficient use of relational operations (mentioned briefly in Section 21.2); (c) weaknesses in the DBMS implementation of the relational model; (d) a lack of scalability in the DBMS itself; and (e) architectural design errors that limit capacity and preclude platform scalability. Points (d) and (e) are beyond the scope of this book; by contrast, points (a) and (b) have already been discussed in this chapter, and point (c) is discussed at length in other parts of the book.

Data Marts

Data warehouses are generally intended to provide a single source of data for all decision support activities. However, when data warehouses became popular in the early 1990s, it was soon realized that users often carried out extensive reporting and data analysis operations on a relatively small subset of the complete warehouse. Indeed, users were likely to repeat the same operations on the same subset of the data every time it was refreshed. Moreover, some of those activities—e.g., predictive analysis (forecasting), simulation, "what if" modeling of business data—involved the creation of new schemas and data, with subsequent updates to that new data.

Repeatedly executing such operations on the same subset of the complete warehouse is obviously not very efficient; the idea of building some kind of limited, special-purpose "warehouse" that is tailored to the purpose at hand thus seems like an obviously good idea. In some cases, moreover, it might be possible to extract and prepare the required data directly from local sources, providing access to the data more quickly than if it had to be synchronized with all of the other data to be loaded into the full warehouse. Such considerations led to the concept of **data marts.**

Actually there is some controversy over the precise definition of the term *data mart*. For our purposes, we can define it as "a specialized, subject-oriented, integrated, volatile, time-variant data store in support of a specific subset of management's decisions." As you can see, the primary distinctions between a data mart and a data warehouse are that a data mart is *specialized* and *volatile*. By *specialized,* we mean it contains data to support a specific area (only) of business analysis; by *volatile,* we mean users can update the data, possibly even create new data (i.e., new tables) for some purpose.

There are three main approaches to creating a data mart:

- The data can simply be extracted from the data warehouse—in effect following a "divide and conquer" approach to the overall decision support workload, in order to achieve better performance and scalability. Usually the extracted data is loaded into a database with a physical schema that closely resembles the applicable subset of that for the data warehouse; however, it might be possible to simplify it somewhat, thanks to the specialized nature of the data mart.

- Despite the fact that the data warehouse is meant to provide a "single point of control," a data mart might still be created independently (i.e., *not* via extract from the warehouse). Such an approach might be appropriate if the warehouse is inaccessible for some reason, say for financial, operational, or even political reasons (or the data warehouse might not even exist yet—see the point immediately following).

- Some installations have followed a "data mart first" approach, in which data marts are created as needed, with the overall data warehouse eventually being created as a consolidation of the various data marts.

The last two approaches both suffer from possible semantic mismatch problems. Independent data marts are particularly susceptible to such problems, since there is no obvious way to check for semantic mismatches when databases are designed independently. Consolidation of data marts into a data warehouse generally fails unless (a) a single logical schema for the data warehouse is constructed first and (b) the schemas for the individual data marts are then derived from that warehouse schema. (Of course, the warehouse schema can evolve—assuming good design practice is followed—to include the subject matter of each new data mart as it is needed.)

A note on data mart design: An important decision to be made in the design of any decision support database is the database **granularity.** The term *granularity* here refers to the lowest level of data aggregation that will be kept in the database. Now, most decision support applications require access to detail data sooner or later, so for the data warehouse the decision is easy. For a data mart, it can be more difficult. Extracting large amounts of detail data from the data warehouse and storing it in the data mart can be very inefficient if that level of detail is not needed very often. On the other hand, it is sometimes hard to state definitively just what the lowest level of aggregation needed actually is. In such cases, detail data can be accessed directly from the data warehouse if and when needed, with data that is somewhat aggregated being maintained in the data mart. At the same time, full aggregation of the data is generally not done, because the very many ways in which the data can be aggregated will generate very large amounts of summary data. This point is discussed in more detail in Section 21.6, later.

One further point: Because data mart users often employ certain analytical tools, the physical design is often dictated, in part, by the specific tool(s) to be used (see the discussion of "ROLAP *vs.* MOLAP" in Section 21.6). This unfortunate circumstance can lead to "dimensional schemas" (discussed next), which do not abide by good relational design practice.

Dimensional Schemas

Suppose we wish to collect a history of business transactions for analysis purposes. As noted in Section 21.1, early decision support systems would typically keep that history as a simple file, which would then be accessed via sequential scan. As the data volume increases, however, it becomes more and more desirable to support direct access lookup to the file from a number of different perspectives. For example, it might be useful to be able to find all business transactions involving a particular product, or all business transactions occurring within a particular time period, or all business transactions pertaining to a particular customer.

One method of organization that supports this type of access was called a "multi-catalog" database.* Continuing with our example, such a database would consist of a large central data file containing the business transaction data, together with three individual

---

*Nothing to do with catalogs in the modern database sense of the term.

"catalog" files for products, time periods, and customers, respectively. Such catalog files resemble indexes in that they contain pointers to records in the data file, but (a) entries can be placed in them explicitly by the user ("catalog maintenance"), and (b) they can contain supplemental information (e.g., customer address) that can then be removed from the data file. Note that the catalog files are usually small compared to the data file.

This organization is more efficient in terms of both space and I/O than the original design (involving just a single data file). Note in particular that the product, time period, and customer information in the central data file now reduces to just product, time period, and customer *identifiers.*

When this approach is mimicked in a relational database, the data file and catalog files become tables (images of the corresponding files), the pointers in the catalog files become primary keys in the catalog file image tables, and the identifiers in the data file become foreign keys in the data file image table. Typically, those primary and foreign keys are all indexed. In such an arrangement, the data file image is called a **fact table** and the catalog file images are called **dimension tables.** The overall design is referred to as a **dimensional** or **star schema,** because of the way it looks when drawn as an entity/relationship diagram (the fact table being surrounded by and connected to the dimension tables). *Note:* The reason for the "dimension" terminology is explained in Section 21.6.

By way of illustration, let us modify the suppliers and parts database once again, this time to show for each shipment the particular time period in which that shipment occurred. We identify time periods by a time period identifier (TP#), and we introduce another table TP to relate those identifiers to the corresponding time periods *per se.* Then the revised shipments table SP and the new time periods table TP might look as shown in Fig. 21.3.* In star schema terminology, table SP is the fact table and table TP is a dimension table (so too are the suppliers table S and the parts table P—see Fig. 21.4). *Note:* We remind you once again that the general question of handling time period data will be discussed in detail in Chapter 22.

Querying a star schema database typically involves using the dimension tables to find all foreign key combinations of interest, and then using those combinations to access the fact table. Assuming the dimension table accesses and subsequent fact table access are all bundled up into a single query, the best way to implement that query is usually by means of what is called a *star join.* "Star join" is a specific join implementation strategy; it differs from the usual strategies in that it deliberately begins by computing a Cartesian product, namely the Cartesian product of the dimension tables. As we saw in Chapter 17, query optimizers usually try to avoid computing Cartesian products [17.54–17.55]; in the case at hand, however, forming the product of the much smaller dimension tables first and then using the result to perform index-based lookups on the fact table is almost always more efficient that any other strategy. It follows that traditional optimizers require some reengineering in order to deal with star schema queries efficiently.

---

*The FROM and TO columns in table TP contain data of type timestamp. For simplicity, we do not show actual timestamp values in the figure, but instead represent them symbolically.

SP	S#	P#	TP#	QTY		TP	TP#	FROM	TO
	S1	P1	TP3	300			TP1	ta	tb
	S1	P1	TP5	100			TP2	tc	td
	S1	P2	TP1	200			TP3	te	tf
	S1	P3	TP2	400			TP4	tg	th
	S1	P4	TP1	200			TP5	ti	tj
	S1	P5	TP5	100					
	S1	P6	TP4	100					
	S2	P1	TP3	300					
	S2	P2	TP4	400					
	S3	P2	TP1	200					
	S3	P2	TP3	200					
	S4	P2	TP1	200					
	S4	P4	TP3	200					
	S4	P5	TP2	400					
	S4	P5	TP1	400					

Fig. 21.3 Sample fact table (SP) and dimension table (TP)

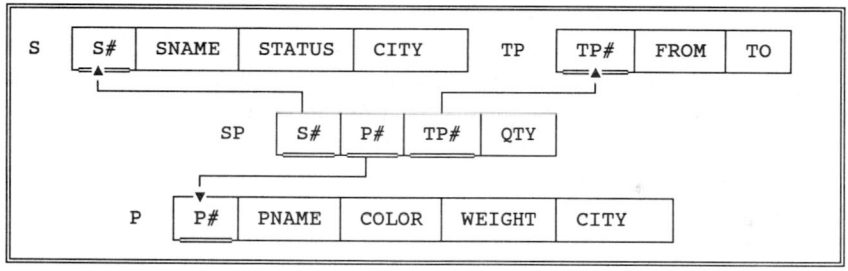

Fig. 21.4 Star schema for suppliers and parts (with time periods)

Now, at this point you might be wondering what the difference is between a star schema and what we would regard as a proper relational design. In fact, a *simple* star schema like the one discussed above can look very similar (even identical) to a good relational design. Unfortunately, however, there are several problems with the star schema approach in general:

1. First of all, it is *ad hoc* (it is based on intuition rather than principle). This lack of discipline makes it difficult to change the schema in a proper fashion when (for example) new types of data are added to the database or when dependencies change. In fact, star schemas are often constructed by simply editing a previous design, and that previous design in turn is often constructed by trial and error.

2. Star schemas are really physical, not logical, though they are talked about as if they were logical. The problem is that there is really no concept of logical design, as distinct from physical design, in the star schema approach.

3. The star schema approach does not always result in a legitimate physical design (i.e., one that preserves all of the information in a relationally correct logical design). This shortcoming becomes more apparent the more complex the schema becomes.

4. Because there is little discipline, designers often include several different types of facts in the fact table. As a consequence, the rows and columns of the fact table typically do not have a uniform interpretation. What is more, certain columns then typically apply only to certain types of facts, implying that the columns in question must permit nulls. As more and more types of facts are included, so the table becomes more and more difficult to maintain and understand, and access becomes less and less efficient. For example, we might decide to modify the shipments table to track part purchases as well as part shipments. We will then need some kind of "flag" column to show which rows correspond to purchases and which to shipments. A proper design, by contrast, would create a distinct fact table for each distinct type of fact.

5. Again because of the lack of discipline, the dimension tables too can become nonuniform. This error typically occurs when the fact table is used to maintain data pertaining to differing levels of aggregation. For example, we might (mistakenly) add rows to the shipments table that show the total part quantities for each day, each month, each quarter, each year, and even the grand total to date. Notice first that this change causes the time period identifier (TP#) and quantity (QTY) columns in table SP to have nonuniform meanings. Suppose now that the FROM and TO columns in the dimension table TP are each replaced by a combination of YEAR, MONTH, DAY, etc., columns. Then those YEAR, MONTH, DAY, etc., columns must now all permit nulls. Also, a flag column will probably be needed too, in order to indicate the type of the applicable time period.

6. The dimension tables are often less than fully normalized.* The desire to avoid joins often leads designers to bundle distinct information together in those tables that would better be kept separate. In the extreme case, columns that simply happen to be accessed together are kept together in the same dimension table. It should be clear that following such an extreme, and nonrelational, "discipline" will almost certainly lead to uncontrolled—and probably uncontrollable—redundancy.

We remark finally that a variant of the star schema is the **snowflake schema,** which normalizes the dimension tables. Again, the name is derived from the way the schema

---

*Here is some advice from a book on data warehouses: "[Resist] normalization . . . Efforts to normalize any of the tables in a dimensional database solely in order to save disk space [*sic*] are a waste of time . . . The dimension tables must not be normalized . . . Normalized dimension tables destroy the ability to browse" [21.21].

looks when drawn as an entity/relationship diagram. The terms *constellation schema* and *blizzard* (or *snowstorm*) *schema* have also been heard recently, with the obvious (?) meanings.

21.6 ONLINE ANALYTICAL PROCESSING

The term **OLAP** ("online analytical processing") was coined in a white paper written for Arbor Software Corp. in 1993 [21.10], though (as with the term "data warehouse") the concept is much older. It can be defined as "the interactive process of creating, managing, analyzing, and reporting on data"—and it is usual to add that the data in question is perceived and manipulated as though it were stored in a "multi-dimensional array." However, we choose to explain the ideas in terms of conventional SQL-style tables first, before getting into the issue of multi-dimensional representation *per se*.

The first point is that analytical processing invariably requires some kind of *data aggregation,* usually in many different ways (i.e., according to many different groupings). In fact, one of the fundamental problems of analytical processing is that the number of possible groupings becomes very large very quickly, and yet users need to consider all or most of them. Now, relational languages do support such aggregation, of course, but each individual query in such a language produces just one table as its result (and all rows in that table are of the same form and have the same kind of interpretation). Thus, to obtain *n* distinct groupings requires *n* distinct queries and produces *n* distinct result tables. For example, consider the following queries on the usual suppliers and parts database:

1. Get the total shipment quantity.
2. Get total shipment quantities by supplier.
3. Get total shipment quantities by part.
4. Get total shipment quantities by supplier and part. *Note:* Of course, the "total" quantity for a given supplier and given part is just the actual quantity for that supplier and part. The example would be more realistic if we used the suppliers-parts-projects database instead. However, we stay with suppliers and parts for simplicity.

Suppose there are just two parts, P1 and P2, and the shipments table looks like this:

SP	S#	P#	QTY
	S1	P1	300
	S1	P2	200
	S2	P1	300
	S2	P2	400
	S3	P2	200
	S4	P2	200

Here then are SQL formulations* of the four queries and the corresponding results:

1. ```
SELECT SUM(QTY) AS TOTQTY
FROM   SP
GROUP   BY () ;
```

| TOTQTY |
|--------|
| 1600   |

2. ```
SELECT  S#,
        SUM(QTY) AS TOTQTY
FROM    SP
GROUP   BY (S#) ;
```

S#	TOTQTY
S1	500
S2	700
S3	200
S4	200

3. ```
SELECT P#,
        SUM(QTY) AS TOTQTY
FROM   SP
GROUP   BY (P#) ;
```

| P# | TOTQTY |
|----|--------|
| P1 | 600    |
| P2 | 1000   |

4. ```
SELECT  S#, P#,
        SUM(QTY) AS TOTQTY
FROM    SP
GROUP   BY (S#,P#) ;
```

S#	P#	TOTQTY
S1	P1	300
S1	P2	200
S2	P1	300
S2	P2	400
S3	P2	200
S4	P2	200

The drawbacks to this approach are obvious: Formulating so many similar but distinct queries is tedious for the user, and executing all of those queries—passing over the same data over and over again—is likely to be quite expensive in execution time. It thus seems worthwhile to try to find a way (a) of requesting several levels of aggregation in a single query and thereby (b) offering the implementation the opportunity to compute all of those aggregations more efficiently (i.e., in a single pass). Such considerations are the motivation behind the *GROUPING SETS, ROLLUP,* and *CUBE* options on the GROUP BY clause. *Note:* Such options are already supported in several commercial products. They are also included in SQL3 (see Appendix B).

The **GROUPING SETS** option allows the user to specify exactly which particular groupings are to be performed. For example, the following SQL statement represents a combination of Queries 2 and 3:

```
SELECT  S#, P#, SUM(QTY) AS TOTQTY
FROM    SP
GROUP   BY GROUPING SETS ( (S#), (P#) ) ;
```

The GROUP BY clause here is effectively asking the system to execute two queries, one in which the grouping is by S# and one in which it is by P#. *Note:* The inner parentheses

---

*Perhaps we should say "*pseudo*SQL formulations," because SQL/92 does not permit GROUP BY operands to be enclosed in parentheses, nor does it permit a GROUP BY with no operands at all (though omitting the GROUP BY clause entirely is logically equivalent to specifying one with no operands).

are not actually required in this example, since each of the "grouping sets" involves just one column; however, we show those parentheses for clarity.

Now, the idea of bundling several distinct queries into a single statement in such a manner might be unobjectionable in itself (though we have to say that we would prefer to see this very general issue attacked in a more general, systematic, and orthogonal way). Unfortunately, however, SQL goes on to bundle the *results* of those logically distinct queries into a single result table!* In the example, that result table looks something like this:

S#	P#	TOTQTY
S1	*null*	500
S2	*null*	700
S3	*null*	200
S4	*null*	200
null	P1	600
null	P2	1000

Now, this result might indeed be thought of as a *table* (an SQL-style table, at any rate), but it is hardly a *relation*. Note that the supplier rows (those with nulls in the P# position) and the part rows (those with nulls in the S# position) have very different interpretations, and the meaning of TOTQTY values varies according to whether they appear in a supplier row or a part row. So what is the predicate for this "relation"?

We remark too that the nulls in this result constitute yet another kind of "missing information." They certainly do not mean either "value unknown" or "value not applicable," but exactly what they do mean is very unclear. *Note:* SQL does at least provide a way of distinguishing those new nulls from other kinds, but the details are tedious and effectively force the user into a kind of row-at-a-time thinking. We omit those details here, but you can obtain some idea of what is involved from the following example (which indicates what the GROUPING SETS example shown earlier might actually have to look like in practice):

```
SELECT CASE GROUPING (S#)              -- see Appendix A re CASE
            WHEN 1 THEN '?????'
            ELSE S#
       AS S#,
       CASE GROUPING (P#)              -- see Appendix A re CASE
            WHEN 1 THEN '!!!!!!'
            ELSE P#
       AS P#,
       SUM(QTY) AS TOTQTY
FROM   SP
GROUP  BY GROUPING SETS ( (S#), (P#) ) ;
```

Back to GROUP BY specifically. The other two GROUP BY options, ROLLUP and CUBE, are both shorthands for certain GROUPING SETS combinations. First, **ROLLUP.** Consider the following query:

---

*That single table can be regarded as an "outer union"—an extremely bizarre form of outer union, too—of those results. It should be clear from Chapter 18 that, even in its least bizarre form, "outer union" is *not* a respectable relational operation.

```
SELECT S#, P#, SUM(QTY) AS TOTQTY
FROM   SP
GROUP  BY ROLLUP ( S#, P# ) ;
```

The GROUP BY clause here is logically equivalent to the following one:

```
GROUP  BY GROUPING SETS ( (S#,P#), (S#), () )
```

In other words, the query is a bundled SQL formulation of Queries 4, 2, and 1. The result looks like this:

S#	P#	TOTQTY
S1	P1	300
S1	P2	200
S2	P1	300
S2	P2	400
S3	P2	200
S4	P2	200
S1	*null*	500
S2	*null*	700
S3	*null*	200
S4	*null*	200
null	*null*	1600

The term ROLLUP derives from the fact that (in the example) the quantities have been "rolled up" for each supplier (i.e., rolled up "along the supplier dimension"—see the subsection "Multi-Dimensional Databases" below). In general, GROUP BY ROLLUP (A, B, ..., Z)—loosely, "roll up along the A dimension"—means "group by all of the following combinations":

```
( A, B, ..., Z )
( A, B, ... )
.....
( A, B )
( A )
( )
```

Note that there are many distinct "rollups along the A dimension," in general (it depends what other columns are mentioned in the ROLLUP commalist). Note too that GROUP BY ROLLUP (A, B) and GROUP BY ROLLUP (B, A) have different meanings—i.e., GROUP BY ROLLUP (A, B) is *not* symmetric in A and B.

Now we turn to **CUBE.** Consider the following query:

```
SELECT S#, P#, SUM(QTY) AS TOTQTY
FROM   SP
GROUP  BY CUBE ( S#, P# ) ;
```

The GROUP BY clause here is logically equivalent to the following one:

```
GROUP  BY GROUPING SETS ( (S#,P#), (S#), (P#), () )
```

In other words, the query is a bundled SQL formulation of all four of our original Queries 4, 3, 2, and 1. The result looks like this:

S#	P#	TOTQTY
S1	P1	300
S1	P2	200
S2	P1	300
S2	P2	400
S3	P2	200
S4	P2	200
S1	*null*	500
S2	*null*	700
S3	*null*	200
S4	*null*	200
null	P1	600
null	P2	1000
null	*null*	1600

The unhelpful term CUBE derives from the fact that in OLAP (or at least multi-dimensional) terminology, data values can be perceived as being stored in the cells of a multi-dimensional array or *hypercube*. In the case at hand, (a) the data values are quantities; (b) the "cube" has just two dimensions, a suppliers dimension and a parts dimension (and so the "cube" is rather flat!); and of course (c) those two dimensions are of unequal sizes (so the "cube" is not even a square but rather a general rectangle). Anyway, GROUP BY CUBE (*A, B, ..., Z*) means "group by all possible subsets of the set { *A, B, ..., Z* } ."

A given GROUP BY clause can include any mixture of GROUPING SETS, ROLLUP, and CUBE specifications.

Cross Tabulations

OLAP products often display query results not as SQL-style tables but as **cross tabulations** ("crosstabs" for short). Consider Query 4 once again ("Get total shipment quantities by supplier and part"). Here is a crosstab representation of the result of that query. Incidentally, note that we show the quantities of part P1 for suppliers S3 and S4 (correctly) as zero; SQL, by contrast, would say those quantities should be *null* (see Chapter 18). In fact, the *table* that SQL produces in response to Query 4 contains no rows for (S3,P1) or (S4,P1)!—as a consequence of which, producing the crosstab from that table is not entirely trivial.

	P1	P2
S1	300	200
S2	300	400
S3	0	200
S4	0	200

This crosstab is arguably a more compact and readable way of representing the Query 4 result. What is more, it does look a little like a relational table. However, observe that *the number of columns in that "table" depends on the actual data;* to be specific, there is one column for each kind of part (and so the structure of the crosstab and the meaning of the rows both depend on the actual data). Thus, a crosstab is not a relation but a *report:* to be more specific, a report that is formatted as a simple array. (Relations have a predicate that can be deduced from the predicate(s) for the relation(s) from which they are derived; by contrast, the "predicate" for a crosstab—if such a thing can even be said to exist, in general—cannot be derived from the predicate(s) for the relation(s) from which it is derived, since as have just seen it depends on data *values.*)

Crosstabs like the one just shown are often said to have two *dimensions,* in this case suppliers and parts. Dimensions are treated as though they were *independent variables;* the intersection "cells" then contain values of the corresponding *dependent* variable(s). See the subsection "Multi-Dimensional Databases" below for further explanation.

Here is another crosstab example, representing the result from the CUBE example earlier:

	P1	P2	total
S1	300	200	500
S2	300	400	700
S3	0	200	200
S4	0	200	200
total	600	1000	1600

The rightmost column contains row totals (i.e., totals for the indicated supplier across all parts), and the bottom row contains column totals (i.e., totals for the indicated part across all suppliers). The bottom right cell contains the grand total, which is the row total of all column totals and the column total of all row totals.

Multi-Dimensional Databases

So far, we have been assuming that our OLAP data is stored in a conventional SQL database (although we have touched on the terminology and concepts of "multi-dimensional" databases a couple of times). In fact, we have tacitly been describing what is sometimes called *ROLAP* ("relational OLAP"). However, many people believe that *MOLAP* ("multi-dimensional OLAP") is a better way to go. In this subsection we take a closer look at MOLAP.

MOLAP involves a **multi-dimensional database,** which is a database in which the data is conceptually stored in the cells of a multi-dimensional array. (*Note:* We say "conceptually" stored, but in fact the physical organization in MOLAP tends to be very similar to the logical organization.) The supporting DBMS is called a *multi-dimensional DBMS.* As a simple example, the data might be represented as an array of three dimensions, corresponding to products, customers, and time periods, respectively; each individual cell value might then represent the total quantity of the indicated product sold to the indicated customer in the indicated time period. As already noted, the crosstabs of the previous subsection can also be regarded as such arrays.

Now, in a well-understood body of data, all relationships would be known, and the "variables" involved (not variables in the usual programming language sense) could then be classified, loosely, as either **dependent** or **independent.** In terms of the foregoing example, for instance, *product, customer,* and *time period* would be the independent variables and *quantity* the sole dependent variable. More generally, independent variables are variables whose values together determine the values of dependent variables (much as, in relational terms, a candidate key is a set of columns whose values determine the values of other columns). The independent variables thus form the dimensions of the array by which the data is organized and form an *addressing scheme* for that array,* and dependent variable values—which constitute the actual data—can then be stored in the cells of that array. *Note:* The distinction between values of independent or "dimensional" variables and values of dependent or "nondimensional" variables is sometimes characterized as *location vs. content.*

Unfortunately, the foregoing characterization of multi-dimensional databases is somewhat too simplistic, because most bodies of data are *not* well understood. Indeed, it is for this very reason that we want to analyze the data in the first place: to obtain a better understanding. Often the lack of understanding is severe enough that we do not know ahead of time which variables are independent and which dependent—independent variables are often chosen based on current belief (i.e., *hypothesis*) and the resulting array then tested to see how well it works (see Section 21.7). Such an approach is clearly going to involve a lot of iteration and trial and error. For such reasons, the system will typically permit dimensional and nondimensional variables to be swapped, an operation known as *pivoting.* Other operations supported will include *array transpose* and *dimensional reordering.* There will also be a way to add dimensions.

By the way, it should be clear from the foregoing description that array cells will often be empty, and arrays will thus often be *sparse.* For example, suppose product *p* was not sold to customer *c* at all in time period *t;* then cell *(c,p,t)* will be empty (or, at best, contain a zero). Multi-dimensional DBMSs support various techniques for storing sparse arrays in some more efficient (compressed) form.[†] More to the point, those empty cells correspond to "missing information," and systems therefore need to provide some computational support for them—and they do so, typically, in a manner similar to SQL (unfortunately). Note that the fact that a given cell is empty might mean the information is unknown, or has not been captured, or is not applicable, or a whole host of other things (see Chapter 18 once again).

The independent variables are often related in *hierarchies,* which determine ways in which dependent data can be aggregated. For example, there is a temporal hierarchy relating seconds to minutes to hours to days to weeks to months to years. As another example, there might be a hierarchy relating parts to assembly kits to components to boards to products. Often

---

*Array cells are thus addressed symbolically instead of by the numeric subscripts more conventionally associated with arrays.

[†]Observe the contrast here with relational systems. In a proper relational analog of the example, we would not have a *(c,p,t)* row with an empty quantity "cell," we would simply not have a *(c,p,t)* row. The concept of "sparse arrays"—or "sparse tables," rather—thus does not arise, and there is no need for clever compression techniques to deal with them.

the same data can be aggregated in many different ways (i.e., the same independent variable can belong to many different hierarchies). The system will provide operators to "drill up" and "drill down" in such hierarchies; *drill up* means going from a lower level of aggregation to a higher and *drill down* means the opposite. Numerous other operations are also available for dealing with such hierarchies (e.g., an operation to rearrange the hierarchic levels).

Note: There is a subtle difference between "drill up" and "roll up," as follows: "Roll up" is the operation of *creating* the desired groupings and aggregations; "drill up" is the operation of *accessing* those aggregations. As for "drill down," an example might be: *Given the total shipment quantity, get the total quantities for each individual supplier.* Of course, the more detailed data must be available (or computable) in order to be able to respond to such a request.

Multi-dimensional products generally also provide a variety of statistical and other mathematical functions to help in formulating and testing hypotheses (i.e., hypothesized relationships). Visualization and reporting tools are also provided to help in these tasks. Unfortunately, however, there is as yet no standard multi-dimensional query language, although research is under way to develop a calculus on which such a standard might be based [21.27]. There is also nothing analogous to normalization theory that could serve as a scientific basis for the design of multi-dimensional databases.

We close this section by noting that some products combine the ROLAP and MOLAP approaches: *HOLAP* ("hybrid OLAP"). There is considerable controversy over which of the three approaches is "best," and little can be said here to help resolve that controversy.* Generally speaking, however, MOLAP products provide faster computation but support smaller amounts of data than ROLAP products (becoming less efficient as the amount of data increases), while ROLAP products provide scalability, concurrency, and management features that are more mature than those of MOLAP products.

21.7   DATA MINING

Data mining can be described as "exploratory data analysis." The aim is to look for interesting patterns in the data, patterns that can be used to set business strategy or to identify unusual behavior (for example, a sudden increase in credit card activity could mean a card has been stolen). Data mining tools apply statistical techniques to large quantities of stored data in order to look for such patterns. *Note:* The word **large** needs to be emphasized here. Data mining databases are often *extremely* large, and it is important that algorithms be scalable.

---

*There is one thing that does need to be said, however, and that is as follows. It is often claimed that "tables are flat" (i.e., two-dimensional) while "real data is multi-dimensional," and hence that relations are inadequate as a basis for OLAP. But to argue thus is to confuse tables and relations! As we saw in Chapter 5, tables are only *pictures* of relations, not relations as such. And while it is true that those pictures are two-dimensional, relations are not: Rather, they are *n*-dimensional, where *n* is the degree. To be more precise, each tuple in a relation with *n* attributes represents a point in *n*-dimensional space, and the relation as a whole represents a set of such points.

SALES	TX#	CUST#	TIMESTAMP	PRODUCT
	TX1	C1	d1	Shoes
	TX1	C1	d1	Socks
	TX1	C1	d1	Tie
	TX2	C2	d2	Shoes
	TX2	C2	d2	Socks
	TX2	C2	d2	Tie
	TX2	C2	d2	Belt
	TX2	C2	d2	Shirt
	TX3	C3	d2	Shoes
	TX3	C3	d2	Tie
	TX4	C2	d3	Shoes
	TX4	C2	d3	Socks
	TX4	C2	d3	Belt

Fig. 21.5 The SALES table

Consider the (*not* very large!) SALES table shown in Fig. 21.5, which gives information regarding a certain retail business's sales transactions.* The business would like to perform *market basket analysis* on this data (where the term "market basket" refers to the set of products purchased in a single transaction), thereby discovering, e.g., that a customer who buys shoes is likely to buy socks as well as part of the same transaction. This correlation between shoes and socks is an example of an **association rule;** it can be expressed (a little loosely) as follows:

```
FORALL tx ( Shoes ∈ tx ⇒ Socks ∈ tx )
```

(where "Shoes ∈ *tx*" is the *rule antecedent,* "Socks ∈ *tx*" is the *rule consequent,* and *tx* ranges over all sales transactions).

We introduce some terminology. The set of all sales transactions in the example is called the **population.** Any given association rule has a *support* level and a *confidence* level. The **support** is the fraction of the population that happens to satisfy the rule. The **confidence** is the fraction of that portion of the population in which the antecedent is satisfied in which the consequent is also satisfied. (Note that the antecedent and consequent can each involve any number of different products, not necessarily just one.) By way of example, consider this rule:

```
FORALL tx ( Socks ∈ tx ⇒ Tie ∈ tx )
```

Given the sample data of Fig. 21.5, the population is 4, the support is 50 percent, and the confidence is 66.67 percent.

---

*Note that (a) the key is {TX#,PRODUCT} ; (b) the table satisfies the FDs TX# → CUST# and TX# → TIMESTAMP and is thus not in BCNF; (c) a version of the table in which column PRODUCT is relation-valued (and TX# is the key) *would* be in BCNF and might well be better suited to the kind of exploration involved in the case at hand (but it would probably not be suitable for other kinds).

More general association rules might be discovered from appropriate aggregations of the given data. For example, grouping by customer would enable us to test the validity of rules such as "If a customer buys shoes, he or she is likely to buy socks as well, though not necessarily in the same transaction."

Other kinds of rules can also be defined. For example, a **sequence correlation** rule might be used to identify buying patterns over time ("If a customer buys shoes today, he or she is likely to buy socks within five days"). A **classification** rule might be used to help decide whether to grant a credit application ("If a customer has income over $75,000 a year, he or she is likely to be a good credit risk"); and so on. Like association rules, sequence correlation and classification rules also have a support level and a confidence level.

Data mining is a huge subject in its own right [21.1], and it is clearly not possible to go into very much detail here. We therefore content ourselves by concluding with a brief description of how data mining techniques might apply to an extended version of suppliers and parts. First (in the absence of other sources for the information), we might use *neural induction* to classify suppliers by their specialty (e.g., fasteners *vs.* engine parts), and *value prediction* to predict which suppliers are most likely to be able to supply which parts. We might then use *demographic clustering* to associate shipping charges with geographic location, thereby assigning suppliers to shipping regions. *Association discovery* might then be used to discover that certain parts are generally obtained together in a single shipment; *sequential pattern discovery* to discover that shipments of fasteners are generally followed by shipments of engine parts; and *similar time sequence discovery* to discover that there are seasonal quantity changes in shipments of certain parts (some of those changes occurring in the fall and some in the spring).

21.8   SUMMARY

We have examined the use of database technology for the purpose of **decision support.** The basic idea is to collect operational data and reduce it to a form that can be used to help management understand and modify the behavior of the enterprise.

First we identified certain aspects of decision support systems that set them apart from operational systems. The key point is that the database is primarily (though not totally) **read-only.** Decision support databases tend to be very **large** and **heavily indexed** and to involve a lot of **controlled redundancy** (especially in the form of *replication* and precomputed *aggregations*), keys tend to involve a **temporal** component, and queries tend to be **complex.** As a consequence of such considerations, there is an emphasis on **designing for performance;** we agree with the emphasis, but believe it should not be allowed to interfere with good design practice. The problem is that, in practice, decision support systems usually do not distinguish adequately between **logical** and **physical** considerations.

Next, we discussed what is involved in preparing operational data for decision support. We looked at the tasks of **extraction, cleansing, transformation and consolidation, load,** and **refresh.** We also briefly mentioned **operational data stores,** which can be used (among other things) as a staging area during the data preparation process. They can also be used to provide decision support services on current data.

We then considered **data warehouses** and **data marts;** a data mart can be regarded as a specialized data warehouse. We explained the basic idea of **star schemas,** in which data is organized as a large central **fact table** and several much smaller **dimension tables.** In simple situations a star schema is indistinguishable from a classical normalized schema; in practice, however, star schemas depart from classical design principles in a variety of ways, always for performance reasons. (The problem, again, is that star schemas are really more physical than logical in nature.) We also mentioned the join implementation strategy known as *star join* and a variant of the star schema called the **snowflake** schema.

Next we turned our attention to **OLAP.** We discussed the SQL **GROUPING SETS, ROLLUP,** and **CUBE** features (all of which are options on the GROUP BY clause and provide ways of requesting several distinct aggregations within a single SQL query). We noted that SQL (unfortunately, in our opinion) bundled the results of those distinct aggregations into a single "table" containing lots of nulls. We also suggested that, in practice, OLAP products might convert such "tables" into **crosstabs** (simple arrays) for display purposes. Then we took a look at **multi-dimensional databases,** in which the data is conceptually stored not in tables but in a multi-dimensional array or *hypercube*. The dimensions of such an array represent **independent variables** and the cells contain values of the corresponding **dependent variables.** The independent variables are usually related in various **hierarchies,** which determine the ways in which the dependent data can sensibly be grouped and aggregated.

Finally we considered **data mining.** The basic idea here is that since decision support data is often not well understood, we can use the power of the computer to help us discover patterns in that data. We briefly considered various kinds of *rules*—**association, classification,** and **sequence correlation** rules—and discussed the associated notions of **support** and **confidence** levels.

EXERCISES

21.1 What are some of the major points of difference between decision support and operational databases? Why do decision support and operational applications typically use different data stores?

21.2 Summarize the steps involved in preparing operational data for decision support.

21.3 Distinguish between *controlled* and *uncontrolled* redundancy. Give some examples. Why is controlled redundancy important in the context of decision support? What happens if the redundancy is uncontrolled instead?

21.4 Distinguish between *data warehouses* and *data marts.*

21.5 What do you understand by the term *star schema?*

21.6 Star schemas are usually not fully normalized. What is the justification for this state of affairs? Explain the methodology by which such schemas are designed.

21.7 Explain the difference between ROLAP and MOLAP.

21.8 How many ways could data be summarized if it is characterized by four dimensions, each of which belongs to a three-level aggregation hierarchy (e.g., city, county, state)?

21.9 Using the suppliers-parts-projects database (see Exercise 4.1 in Chapter 4), express the following as SQL queries:

   a. Get the number of shipments and average shipment quantities for suppliers, parts, and projects considered pairwise (i.e., for each S#-P# pair, each P#-J# pair, and each J#-S# pair).

   b. Get the maximum and minimum shipment quantities for each project, each project/part combination, and overall.

   c. Get total shipment quantities rolled up "along the supplier dimension" and "along the part dimension." *Warning:* There is a trap here.

   d. Get average shipment quantities by supplier, by part, by supplier/part combinations, and overall.

In each case, show the result SQL would produce given the sample data of Fig. 4.5 (or some sample data of your own). Also show those results as crosstabs.

21.10 Near the beginning of Section 21.6, we showed a simple version of table SP containing just six rows. Suppose that table additionally included the following row (meaning—perhaps!—that supplier S5 exists but currently supplies no parts):

S5	*null*	*null*

Discuss the implications for all of the various SQL queries shown in Section 21.6.

21.11 Does the term *dimensional* mean the same thing in the phrases "dimensional schema" and "multi-dimensional database"? Explain your answer.

21.12 Consider the market basket analysis problem. Sketch an algorithm by which association rules having support and confidence levels greater than specified thresholds might be discovered. *Hint:* If some combination of products is "uninteresting" because it occurs in too few sales transactions, the same is true for all supersets of that combination of products.

REFERENCES AND BIBLIOGRAPHY

21.1 Pieter Adriaans and Dolf Zantinge: *Data Mining.* Reading, Mass.: Addison-Wesley (1996).

Although described as an executive-level overview, this book is actually a fairly detailed (and good) introduction to the subject.

21.2 S. Alter: *Decision Support Systems: Current Practice and Continuing Challenges.* Reading, Mass.: Addison-Wesley (1980).

21.3 J. L. Bennett (ed.): *Building Decision Support Systems.* Reading, Mass.: Addison-Wesley (1981).

21.4 M. J. A. Berry and G. Linoff: *Data Mining Techniques for Marketing, QTY, and Customer Support.* New York, N.Y.: McGraw-Hill (1997).

A good explanation of data mining methods and their value for selected aspects of business.

21.5 J. B. Boulden: *Computer-Assisted Planning Systems.* New York, N.Y.: McGraw-Hill (1975).

This early text addresses many of the concerns that later came to be lumped together under the heading of decision support. As indicated by the title, the emphasis is on management planning in the classic sense.

21.6 R. H. Bonczek, C. W. Holsapple, and A. Whinston: *Foundations of Decision Support Systems.* Orlando, Fla.: Academic Press (1981).

> One of the first texts to promote a disciplined approach to decision support systems. The roles of modeling (in the general sense of empirical and mathematical modeling) and management science are emphasized.

21.7 Charles J. Bontempo and Cynthia Maro Saracco: *Database Management: Principles and Products.* Upper Saddle River, N.J.: Prentice-Hall (1996).

21.8 P. Cabena, P. Hadjinian, R. Stadler, J. Verhees, and A. Zanasi: *Discovering Data Mining: From Concept to Implementation.* Upper Saddle River, N.J.: Prentice-Hall (1998).

21.9 C. L. Chang: "DEDUCE—A Deductive Query Language for Relational Data Bases," in C. H. Chen (ed.), *Pattern Recognition and Artificial Intelligence.* New York, N.Y.: Academic Press (1976).

21.10 E. F. Codd, S. B. Codd, and C. T. Salley: "Providing OLAP (Online Analytical Processing) to User-Analysts: An IT Mandate," available from Arbor Software Corp. (1993).

> As noted in the body of the chapter, this paper is the source of the term "OLAP" (though not the concept). It is interesting to note that near the beginning the paper states categorically that "The need which exists is NOT for yet another database technology, but rather for robust . . . analysis tools." It then goes on to describe and argue for yet another database technology!—with a new conceptual data representation, new operators (for update as well as retrieval), multi-user support (including security and concurrency features), new storage structures, and new optimization features; in other words, a new data model, and a new DBMS.

21.11 C. J. Date: "We Don't Need Composite Columns," in C. J. Date, Hugh Darwen, and David McGoveran, *Relational Database Writings 1994–1997.* Reading, Mass.: Addison-Wesley (1998).

> The title of this paper refers to the fact that (flawed) attempts have been made in the past to introduce composite column support without basing it on user-defined type support. If proper user-defined type support is provided, composite columns "come out in the wash."

21.12 Barry Devlin: *Data Warehouse from Architecture to Implementation.* Reading, Mass.: Addison-Wesley (1997).

21.13 B. A. Devlin and P. T. Murphy: "An Architecture for a Business and Information System," *IBM Sys. J. 27,* No. 1 (1988).

> The first published article to define and use the term "information warehouse."

21.14 Herb Edelstein: *Data Mining: Products and Markets.* Potomac, Md.: Two Crows Corp. (1997).

21.15 T. P. Gerrity, Jr.: "The Design of Man-Machine Decision Systems: An Application to Portfolio Management," *Sloan Management Review 12,* No. 2 (Winter 1971).

> One of the earliest articles on decision support systems. It describes a system to support investment managers in stock portfolio administration.

21.16 Jim Gray, Adam Bosworth, Andrew Layman, and Hamid Pirahesh: "Data Cube: A Relational Aggregation Operator Generalizing Group-By, Cross-Tab, and Sub-Totals," Proc. 12th IEEE Int. Conf. on Data Engineering, New Orleans, La. (February 1996).

> The paper that first suggested adding options such as CUBE to the SQL GROUP BY clause.

21.17 W. H. Inmon: *Data Architecture: The Information Paradigm.* Wellesley, Mass.: QED Information Sciences (1988).

> Discusses the genesis of the data warehouse concept and what a data warehouse would look like in practice. The term "data warehouse" first appeared in this book.

21.18 W. H. Inmon: *Building the Data Warehouse.* New York, N.Y.: Wiley (1992).

The first book devoted to data warehouses. It defines the term and discusses the key problems involved in developing a data warehouse. It is concerned primarily with justifying the concept and with operational and physical design issues.

21.19 W. H. Inmon and R. D. Hackathorn: *Using the Data Warehouse.* New York, N.Y.: Wiley (1994).

A discussion for users and administrators of the data warehouse. Like other books on the topic, it concentrates on physical issues. The operational data store concept is discussed in some detail.

21.20 P. G. W. Keen and M. S. Scott Morton: *Decision Support Systems: An Organizational Perspective.* Reading, Mass.: Addison-Wesley (1978).

This classic text is one of the earliest—if not *the* earliest—to address decision support explicitly. The orientation is behavioral and covers analysis, design, implementation, evaluation, and development of decision support systems.

21.21 Ralph Kimball: *The Data Warehouse Toolkit.* New York, N.Y.: John Wiley & Sons (1996).

A how-to book. As the subtitle "Practical Techniques for Building Dimensional Data Warehouses" suggests, the emphasis is on pragmatic issues, not theoretical ones. The tacit assumption throughout is that there is essentially no difference between the logical and physical levels of the system. This assumption is all too valid for today's products, of course; however, we feel it would be better to try to improve the situation instead of effectively just endorsing it.

21.22 J. D. C. Little: "Models and Managers: The Concept of a Decision Calculus," *Management Science 16,* No. 8 (April 1970).

This paper introduces a system (Brandaid) designed to support product, promotion, pricing, and advertising decisions. The author identifies four criteria for designing models to support management decision-making: robustness, ease of control, simplicity, and completeness of relevant detail.

21.23 M. S. Scott Morton: "Management Decision Systems: Computer-Based Support for Decision Making," Harvard University, Division of Research, Graduate School of Business Administration (1971).

This is the classic article that introduced the concept of management decision systems, bringing decision support clearly into the realm of computer-based systems. A specific "management decision system" was built to coordinate production planning for laundry equipment. It was then subjected to scientific test, with marketing and production managers as users.

21.24 K. Parsaye and M. Chignell: *Intelligent Database Tools and Applications.* New York, N.Y.: Wiley (1993).

This book appears to be the first to be devoted to the principles and techniques of data mining (though it refers to the subject as "intelligent databases").

21.25 A. Pirotte and P. Wodon: "A Comprehensive Formal Query Language for a Relational Data Base," *R.A.I.R.O. Informatique/Computer Science 11,* No. 2 (1977).

21.26 R. H. Sprague and E. D. Carlson: *Building Effective Decision Support Systems.* Englewood Cliffs, N.J.: Prentice-Hall (1982).

Another classic text.

21.27 Erik Thomsen: *OLAP Solutions: Building Multi-Dimensional Information Systems*. New York, N.Y.: Wiley (1997).

One of the first books on OLAP and perhaps the most comprehensive. The focus is on understanding the concepts and methods of analysis using multi-dimensional systems. A serious attempt to inject some discipline into a confused subject.

21.28 R. Uthurusamy: "From Data Mining to Knowledge Discovery: Current Challenges and Future Directions," in U. M. Fayyad, G. Piatetsky-Shapiro, P. Smyth, and R. Uthurusamy (eds.): *Advances in Knowledge Discovery and Data Mining*. Cambridge, Mass.: AAAI Press/MIT Press (1996).

ANSWERS TO SELECTED EXERCISES

21.8 There are eight ($= 2^3$) possible groupings for each hierarchy, so the total number of possibilities is $8^4 = 4{,}096$. As a subsidiary exercise, you might like to consider what is involved in using SQL to obtain all of these summarizations.

21.9 With respect to the SQL queries, we show the GROUP BY clauses only:

a. `GROUP BY GROUPING SETS ( (S#,P#), (P#,J#), (J#,S#) )`

b. `GROUP BY GROUPING SETS ( J#, (J#,P#), () )`

c. The trap is that the query is ambiguous—the term (e.g.) "rolled up along the supplier dimension" has many possible meanings. However, one possible interpretation of the requirement will lead to a GROUP BY clause looking like this:

`GROUP BY ROLLUP (S#), ROLLUP (P#)`

d. `GROUP BY CUBE ( S#, P# )`

We omit the SQL result tables. As for the crosstabs, it should be clear that crosstabs are not a very good way to display a result that involves more than two dimensions (and the more dimensions there are, the worse it gets). For example, one such crosstab—corresponding to GROUP BY S#, P#, J#—might look like this (in part):

	P1				P2				...
	J1	J2	J3	...	J1	J2	J3	...	...
S1	200	0	0	...	0	0	0	...	...
S2	0	0	0	...	0	0	0	...	...
S3	0	0	0	...	0	0	0	...	...
S4	0	0	0	...	0	0	0	...	...
S5	0	200	0	...	0	0	0	...	...
..	...	...	...	...	...	...	...	...	...

In a nutshell: The headings are clumsy, and the arrays are sparse.

CHAPTER **22**

Temporal Databases

22.1 INTRODUCTION

Note: Hugh Darwen was the original author of this chapter.

Loosely speaking, a **temporal database** is one that contains historical data instead of, or as well as, current data. Such databases have been under active investigation since the mid 1970s. Some of those investigations adopt the extreme position that data in such a database is only inserted, never deleted or updated (see the discussion of *data warehouses* in the previous chapter), in which case the database contains historical data *only*. The other extreme is a **snapshot** database,* which contains current data only, and data is deleted or updated when the facts represented by that data cease to be true (in other words, a snapshot database is just a database as usually understood, not a temporal database at all).

By way of example, consider the suppliers and parts database of Fig. 3.8 once again. That database is, of course, a snapshot database, and it shows among other things that the status of supplier S1 is currently 20. A temporal version of that database, by contrast, might show not only that the status is currently 20, but also that it has been 20 ever since July 1st, and perhaps that it was 15 from April 5th to June 30th, and so on.

In a snapshot database, the time of the snapshot is usually taken to be "now" (i.e., the time at which the database is actually inspected). Even if the time of the snapshot happens to be some time other than "now," it makes no material difference to the way the data is managed and used. As we will see, however, how the data is managed and used in a temporal database differs in a variety of important ways from how it is managed and used in a snapshot database; hence the present chapter.

The distinguishing feature of a temporal database is, of course, time itself. Temporal database research has therefore involved much investigation into the nature of time itself. Here are some of the issues that have been explored:

- The philosophical issue as to whether time has a beginning and/or end;
- The scientific issue as to whether time is a continuum or occurs in discrete quanta;
- The psychological issue of how best to characterize the important concept *now* (often referred to as "the *moving point* now");

---

*Nothing to do with snapshots in the sense of Chapter 9.

and so on. But these issues, interesting though they might be in themselves, are not especially *database* issues, and we therefore do not delve into them in this chapter; instead, we simply make what we hope are reasonable assumptions at appropriate places. This approach allows us to concentrate on matters that are more directly relevant to our overall aim. However, we do note that some of that temporal research has led to interesting generalizations, strongly suggesting that ideas developed to support temporal data could have application in other areas as well. (This last point notwithstanding, however, we follow convention in referring throughout this chapter to "temporal" keys, "temporal" operators, "temporal" relations, and so forth, even though the concepts in question are often not exclusive to temporal data as such.)

Caveat lector! We concentrate in what follows on what seem to us to be the most interesting and important of the various research ideas (in other words, the chapter is our attempt to distil out and explain "the good parts" of that research, though we do depart from the literature here and there over questions of nomenclature and other small matters). Be aware, however, that little if any of the technology we describe has yet shown up in any commercial DBMS. Possible reasons for this state of affairs include the following:

- It is only recently that disk storage has become cheap enough to make the storage of large volumes of historical data a practical proposition. As we saw in Chapter 21, however, "data warehouses" are now becoming a widespread reality; as a result, users will increasingly find themselves faced with temporal database problems and will start wanting solutions to those problems.

- Although most if not all of the features we describe have been implemented in prototype form, their incorporation into existing products—especially SQL products, where SQL's departures from the relational model will have to be catered for—could be a daunting prospect. Besides, most vendors currently have their hands full with attempts to provide *object/relational* support (see Chapter 25).

- The research community is still somewhat divided over the best way to approach the problem (and this lack of consensus might have carried over to the vendors). Some researchers favor a very specialized approach—one involving some departure from relational principles—that caters for temporal data specifically and leaves certain other problems unsolved (see, e.g., reference [22.4]). Others favor the provision of more general-purpose operators that could provide a basis for developing a specialized approach if desired, while not departing from the relational framework (see, e.g., reference [22.3]). Needless to say, we favor the latter approach.

We defer an explanation of the structure of the chapter to the section immediately following.

22.2 TEMPORAL DATA

If data is an encoded representation of facts, then temporal data is an encoded representation of **timestamped** facts. In a temporal database, according to the extreme interpretation of that term, *all* of the data is temporal, meaning every recorded fact is timestamped. It follows that a *temporal relation* is one in which each tuple includes at least one timestamp (i.e., the heading includes at least one attribute of some timestamp type). It further follows that a *temporal relvar* is one whose heading is that of a temporal relation, and a (relational) *temporal database* is one in which all of the relvars are temporal ones. *Note:* We are being deliberately vague here as to what data "of some timestamp type" might look like. We will take up this issue in Sections 22.3–22.5.

Having just offered a reasonably precise definition of the concept "temporal database" (in its extreme form), we now dismiss that concept as not very useful! We dismiss it because even if the original relvars in the database are all temporal, many relations that can be derived from that database (e.g., as query results) are *not* temporal. For example, the answer to the query "Get the names of all persons we have ever employed" might be obtained from some temporal database, but is not itself a temporal relation. And it would be a strange DBMS indeed—certainly not a relational one—that would let us obtain results that could not themselves be kept in the database.

In this chapter, therefore, we take a temporal database to be a database that does include some temporal data but is not limited to temporal data only. The rest of the chapter discusses such databases in detail. The plan for the chapter, then, is as follows:

- The remainder of the present section and Section 22.3 set the scene for subsequent sections; in particular, Section 22.3 shows why temporal data seems to require special treatment.

- Sections 22.4 and 22.5 introduce *intervals* as a convenient way of timestamping data. Sections 22.6 and 22.7 then discuss a variety of scalar and aggregate operators for dealing with such intervals.

- Section 22.8 introduces some important new relational operators for operating on temporal relations.

- Section 22.9 examines the question of integrity constraints for temporal data. Section 22.10 discusses the special problems of updating such data.

- Finally, Section 22.11 proposes some relevant (and possibly novel) database design ideas, and Section 22.12 presents a summary.

Note: It is important to understand that—with just one exception, the *interval type generator* introduced in Section 22.5—all of the new operators and other constructs to be discussed in what follows are only shorthand. That is, they can all be expressed (albeit only very longwindedly, sometimes) in terms of features already available in a complete relational language such as **Tutorial D.** We will justify this claim as we proceed (in some cases but not all).

Some Basic Concepts and Questions

We begin by appealing to the way people express what might be called "timestamped statements" in natural language. Here are three examples:

1. Supplier S1 was appointed (i.e., placed under contract) **on** July 1st, 1999.
2. Supplier S1 has been a contracted supplier **since** July 1st, 1999.
3. Supplier S1 was a contracted supplier **during** the period from July 1st, 1999, to the present day.

Each of these statements is a possible interpretation of a 2-tuple containing the supplier number "S1" and the timestamp "July 1st, 1999," and each of them might be appropriate of that 2-tuple if it appears in a snapshot database representing the current state of affairs in some enterprise. The **boldface** prepositions **on, since,** and **during** characterize the different interpretations. *Note:* Throughout this chapter we use "since" and "during" in the strong senses of "**ever** since" and "**throughout**" (the period in question), respectively, barring explicit statements to the contrary.

Now, although we have just referred to *three* possible interpretations, it might be argued that Statements 1, 2, and 3 are really all saying the same thing in slightly different ways. In fact, we do take Statements 2 and 3 to be equivalent, but not Statements 1 and 2 (or 1 and 3). For consider:

- Statement 1 clearly asserts that S1 was not a contracted supplier on the date (June 30th, 1999) immediately preceding the specified appointment date; Statement 2 neither states that fact nor implies it.

- Suppose today ("the present day") is September 25th, 2000. Then Statement 2 clearly states that S1 was a contracted supplier on every day from July 1st, 1999 to September 25th, 2000, inclusive; Statement 1 neither states *that* fact, nor implies it.

Thus, Statements 1 and 2 are not equivalent, and neither one implies the other.

That said, tuples in snapshot databases often do include things like "date of appointment," and statements like Statement 2 (or 3) often are the intended interpretation. If such is the case here, then Statement 1 in its present form is not a fully accurate interpretation of the tuple in question. We can make it more accurate by rephrasing it thus: "Supplier S1 was *most recently* appointed on July 1st, 1999." What is more, if this version of Statement 1 really is what our hypothetical 2-tuple is supposed to mean, then Statement 2 in its present form is not a fully accurate interpretation either—it needs to be rephrased thus: "Supplier S1 was not a contracted supplier on June 30th, 1999, but has been one since July 1st, 1999."

Observe now that Statement 1 expresses a time **at** which a certain **event** took place, while Statements 2 and 3 express an interval in time **during** which a certain **state** persisted. We have deliberately chosen an example in which a certain *state* might be inferred from information regarding a certain *event:* Since S1 was most recently appointed on July 1st, 1999, that supplier has been in the state of being under contract from that date to the present day. Classical database technology can handle *time instants* (times at which events occur) reasonably well; however, it does not handle *time intervals* (periods of time during which states persist) very well at all, as we will see in Section 22.3.

Observe next that although Statements 2 and 3 are logically equivalent, their form is significantly different. To be specific, the form of Statement 2 cannot be used for historical records, while that of Statement 3 can—provided we replace the phrase "the present day" in that statement by some explicit date, say September 25th, 2000. (Of course, the statement would then correspond to a 3-tuple, not a 2-tuple.) We conclude that the concept of "during" is very important for historical records, at least for state data if not for event data.*

Terminology: The time(s) at which a certain event occurred or the interval(s) during which a certain state persisted are sometimes referred to as *valid time.* More precisely, the **valid time** of a proposition *p* is the set of times at which *p* is believed to be *true.* It is distinguished from **transaction time,** which is the set of times at which *p* was actually represented in the database as being *true.* Valid times can be updated to reflect changing beliefs, but transaction times cannot; i.e., transaction times are maintained entirely by the system, and no user is allowed to change them (typically, of course, they are recorded, explicitly or implicitly, in the transaction log).

Note: The references in the foregoing paragraph to *intervals* and *sets of times* tacitly introduce a simple but fundamental idea—namely, that an interval with start time *s* and end time *e* actually denotes the set of all times *t* such that $s \leq t \leq e$ (where "<" means "earlier than," of course). Though "obvious," this simple notion has far-reaching consequences, as we will see in the sections to come.

Now, much of the foregoing discussion was deliberately meant to raise certain questions in your mind. Regardless of whether we succeeded in that aim, we now raise those questions explicitly and try to answer them.

1. Does not the expression "all times *t* such that $s \leq t \leq e$" raise the specter of infinite sets and the conceptual and computational difficulties such sets suffer from?

   Answer: Well, yes, it does appear to, but we dismiss the specter and circumvent the difficulties by adopting the assumption that the "timeline" consists of a finite sequence of discrete, indivisible *time quanta.* The interval with start time *s* and end time *e* thus involves a finite number of such quanta, *a fortiori.*

   Note: Much of the literature refers to a time quantum as a *chronon.* However, it then goes on to define a chronon as an *interval* (see, e.g., the glossary in reference [22.2]), implying that it has a start point and an end point, and perhaps further points in between, and so is not indivisible after all. (What exactly are those points? What else can they be but chronons?) We find some confusion here and hence choose to avoid the term.

2. Statements 1, 2, and 3 seem to assume that time quanta are *days,* but surely the system supports time precisions down to tiny fractions of a second. If S1 was a supplier on July 1st, 1999, but not on June 30th, 1999, what is to be done about the presumed period of time from the start of July 1st up to the very instant of appointment, during which S1 was still not officially under contract?

   Answer: We need to distinguish carefully between time quanta as such, which are the smallest time units the system can possibly represent, and the time units that are useful for some particular purpose, which might be years or months or days or weeks,

---

*Here is as good a place as any to note that, despite our repeated use of terms such as "historical records," temporal databases might well contain information concerning the future also. For example, we might wish to record the fact that supplier S1 will be a contracted supplier during the period from *a* to *b*, where *a* and *b* are both dates in the future.

etc., etc. We call such units **timepoints** (*points* for short) in order to stress the fact that *for the purpose at hand* they too are considered to be indivisible. Now, we might say, *informally,* that a timepoint is "a section of the timeline"—i.e., the set of time quanta—that stretches from one "boundary" quantum to the next (e.g., from midnight on one day to midnight on the next). We might therefore say, again informally, that timepoints have a duration—one day, in our example. *Formally,* however, timepoints are (to repeat) indivisible, and the concept of duration strictly does not apply.

Note: Much of the literature uses the term *granule* to refer to something like a timepoint as just defined. As with the term *chronon,* however, it unfortunately then goes on to say that a granule is an *interval.* We therefore choose to avoid the term *granule* also.* We do, however, make use of the (informal) term **granularity,** which we define (again informally) as the duration of the applicable timepoint. Thus, we might say in our example that the granularity is one day, meaning that we are casting aside—in this context—our usual notion of a day being made up of hours, which are made up of minutes, etc. (such notions can be expressed only by recourse to finer levels of granularity).

3. Given, then, that the timeline is basically a sequence of timepoints (of some granularity), we can refer unambiguously to "the time immediately succeeding" (or preceding) any given point. Is that right?

   Answer: Yes, up to a point—the point in question being, of course, the end of time! And down to a point, too—the beginning of time. As far as we are concerned, the beginning of time is a timepoint that has no predecessor (it might perhaps correspond to cosmologists' best estimate of the very moment of the putative Big Bang); the end of time is a timepoint that has no successor.

4. If some relation includes a 3-tuple representing the fact that supplier S1 was under contract from July 1st, 1999 to September 25th, 2000, does not the Closed World Assumption (see Chapter 5) demand that the same relation also include, for example, a 3-tuple representing the fact that S1 was under contract from July 2nd, 1999, until September 24th, 2000, and a host of other 3-tuples representing other trivial consequences of the original 3-tuple?

   Answer: Good point! Clearly, we need a more constraining predicate as our general interpretation of such 3-tuples: "Supplier S*x* was under contract on every day from date *s* to date *e,* but not on the day immediately preceding *s,* nor on the day immediately following *e.*"[†] This more constraining interpretation, in its general form,

---

*It seems to us that the confusion over whether chronons and granules are intervals stems from a confusion over intuition *vs.* formalism. An intuitive belief about the way the world works is one thing; a formal model is something else entirely. In particular, we might *believe* the timeline is continuous and infinite, but we *model* it—for the purposes of computing in particular—as discrete and finite. *Note:* While we are on this subject, we should say too that while the concept "time quantum" (or "chronon") is useful as a basis for explaining the formal model at an intuitive level, it is not in itself part of that model at all and has no part to play in it.

[†]Throughout this chapter we use the unqualified term "predicate" to refer to what in Chapter 8 we called the *external* or user-understood predicate, not the *internal* or system-understood predicate (this latter is, of course, the *relvar* predicate). Moreover, we ignore aspects of such external predicates that are either "obvious" or not germane to the subject under discussion.

provides the motivation and basis for many of the operators we describe in this chapter, in Sections 22.8 and 22.10 in particular.

22.3 WHAT IS THE PROBLEM?

We continue to use suppliers and parts as the basis for our examples in the rest of this chapter, but we clearly need to make some revisions to the database in order for it to serve the purpose adequately. We make those revisions piecemeal. First of all, we drop the parts relvar P, for simplicity. Second, we modify the shipments relvar SP by discarding the QTY attribute (leaving just S# and P#), and we interpret that revised SP relvar thus: "Supplier S# is *currently able* to supply part P#" (in other words, rather than referring to *actual* shipments of parts by suppliers, the relvar now refers just to *potential* shipments—i.e., to the *ability* of suppliers to supply parts). Fig. 22.1, a revised version of Fig. 3.8 from Chapter 3, shows a set of sample data values for this revised database. Note carefully that the database is still a snapshot database—it still does not include any temporal aspects.

S	S#	SNAME	STATUS	CITY	SP	S#	P#
	S1	Smith	20	London		S1	P1
	S2	Jones	10	Paris		S1	P2
	S3	Blake	30	Paris		S1	P3
	S4	Clark	20	London		S1	P4
	S5	Adams	30	Athens		S1	P5
						S1	P6
						S2	P1
						S2	P2
						S3	P2
						S4	P2
						S4	P4
						S4	P5

Fig. 22.1 The suppliers and shipments database (sample values)—current snapshot version

We now proceed to discuss some simple constraints and queries for this database. Later we will consider what happens to those constraints and queries when the database is extended to include various temporal features.

Constraints (current snapshot database): The only constraints we want to consider are the various *key* constraints. Just to remind you, {S#} and {S#,P#} are the primary keys of S and SP, respectively, and {S#} is a foreign key in SP referencing the primary key of S (we ignore the foreign key {P#} , of course).

Queries (current snapshot database): We consider just two queries, both of them very simple:

- *Query 1.1:* Get supplier numbers of suppliers who are currently able to supply some part.

```
SP { S# }
```

- *Query 1.2:* Get supplier numbers of suppliers who are currently unable to supply any part at all.

```
S { S# } MINUS SP { S# }
```

Observe that *Query 1.1* involves a simple **projection** and *Query 1.2* involves the **difference** between two such projections. Later, when we consider temporal analogs of these two queries, we will find that they involve temporal analogs of these two operators (see Section 22.8). *Note:* You will probably not be surprised to learn that temporal analogs of other relational operators can be defined also (see Exercise 22.8).

"Semitemporalizing" Suppliers and Shipments

In order to proceed gently, our next step is to "semitemporalize" (so to speak) relvars S and SP by adding a timestamp attribute, SINCE, to each and renaming them accordingly. See Fig. 22.2.

S_SINCE						SP_SINCE		
S#	SNAME	STATUS	CITY	SINCE		S#	P#	SINCE
S1	Smith	20	London	*d04*		S1	P1	*d04*
S2	Jones	10	Paris	*d07*		S1	P2	*d05*
S3	Blake	30	Paris	*d03*		S1	P3	*d09*
S4	Clark	20	London	*d04*		S1	P4	*d05*
S5	Adams	30	Athens	*d02*		S1	P5	*d04*
						S1	P6	*d06*
						S2	P1	*d08*
						S2	P2	*d09*
						S3	P2	*d08*
						S4	P2	*d06*
						S4	P4	*d04*
						S4	P5	*d05*

Fig. 22.2   The suppliers and shipments database (sample values)—semitemporal version

For simplicity, we do not show real timestamps in Fig. 22.2; instead, we use symbols of the form *d01, d02,* etc., where the "*d*" can conveniently be pronounced "day," a convention to which we adhere throughout this chapter. (Our examples thus all make use of timepoints that are, specifically, *days.*) We assume that day 1 immediately precedes day 2, day 2 immediately precedes day 3, and so on; also, we drop insignificant leading zeros from expressions such as "day 1" (as you can see).

The predicate for S_SINCE is "Supplier S# has been named SNAME, has had status STATUS, has been located in city CITY, and has been under contract, since day SINCE." The predicate for SP_SINCE is "Supplier S# has been able to supply part P# since day SINCE."

Constraints (semitemporal database): The primary and foreign keys for this "semitemporalized" database are the same as before. However, we need an additional constraint—one that might be thought of as *augmenting* the foreign key constraint from SP_SINCE to S_SINCE—to express the fact that no supplier can supply any part before that supplier is placed under contract. In other words, if tuple *sp* in SP_SINCE references tuple *s* in S_SINCE, the SINCE value in *sp* must not be less than that in *s:*

```
CONSTRAINT AUG_SP_TO_S_FK
   IS_EMPTY ( ( ( S_SINCE RENAME SINCE AS SS ) JOIN
                ( SP_SINCE RENAME SINCE AS SPS ) )
              WHERE SPS < SS ) ;
```

With this example we begin to see the problem. Given a "semitemporal" database like that of Fig. 22.2, we will probably have to state many "augmented foreign key" constraints like this one, and we will soon begin to wish we had some convenient shorthand for the purpose.

Queries (semitemporal database): We now consider "semitemporal" versions of *Queries 1.1 and 1.2.*

- *Query 2.1:* Get supplier numbers of suppliers who are currently able to supply some part, showing in each case the date since when they have been able to do so.

If supplier S*x* is currently able to supply several parts, then S*x* has been able to supply *some* part since the earliest SINCE date shown for S*x* in SP_SINCE (e.g., if S*x* is S1, that earliest SINCE date is *d04*). Hence:

```
SUMMARIZE SP PER SP { S# } ADD MIN ( SINCE ) AS SINCE
```

Result:

S#	SINCE
S1	*d04*
S2	*d08*
S3	*d08*
S4	*d04*

- *Query 2.2:* Get supplier numbers of suppliers who are currently unable to supply any part at all, showing in each case the date since when they have been unable to do so.

In our sample data there is just one supplier who is currently unable to supply any parts at all, supplier S5. However, we cannot deduce the date since when S5 has been under contract but unable to supply any parts, because there is insufficient information in the database—the database is still only "*semi*temporalized." For example, suppose *d10* is the current day. Then it might be that S5 was able to supply at least one part from as early as *d02,* when S5 was first appointed, up to as late as *d09;* or, going to the other extreme, it might be that S5 has never been able to supply anything at all.

To have any hope of answering *Query 2.2,* we must complete the "temporalizing" of our database, or at least the SP portion of it. To be more precise, we must keep historical records in the database showing which suppliers were able to supply which parts when, as in the subsection immediately following.

Fully Temporalizing Suppliers and Shipments

Fig. 22.3 shows a fully temporalized version of suppliers and shipments. Observe that the SINCE attributes have become FROM attributes, and each relvar has acquired an additional timestamp attribute called TO. The FROM and TO attributes together express the notion of an interval in time during which something is true; for that reason, we replace SINCE by FROM_TO in the relvar names. Because we are now keeping historical records, there are more tuples in this database than there were in either of its predecessors, as you can see. We assume for definiteness that the current date is *d10*, and so *d10* shows as the TO value for each tuple that pertains to the current state of affairs. *Note:* You might be wondering what mechanism could cause all of those *d10*'s to be replaced by *d11*'s on the stroke of midnight. Unfortunately, we have to set this issue aside for the moment; we will return to it in Section 22.11.

Note that the temporal database of Fig. 22.3 includes all of the information from the semitemporal one of Fig. 22.2, together with historical information concerning a previous period (from *d02* to *d04*) during which supplier S2 was under contract. The predicate for S_FROM_TO is "Supplier S# was named SNAME, had status STATUS, was located in city CITY, and was under contract, from day FROM (and not on the day immediately before FROM) to day TO (and not on the day immediately after TO)." The predicate for SP_FROM_TO is analogous.

S_FROM_TO	S#	SNAME	STATUS	CITY	FROM	TO
	S1	Smith	20	London	*d04*	*d10*
	S2	Jones	10	Paris	*d07*	*d10*
	S2	Jones	10	Paris	*d02*	*d04*
	S3	Blake	30	Paris	*d03*	*d10*
	S4	Clark	20	London	*d04*	*d10*
	S5	Adams	30	Athens	*d02*	*d10*

SP_FROM_TO	S#	P#	FROM	TO
	S1	P1	*d04*	*d10*
	S1	P2	*d05*	*d10*
	S1	P3	*d09*	*d10*
	S1	P4	*d05*	*d10*
	S1	P5	*d04*	*d10*
	S1	P6	*d06*	*d10*
	S2	P1	*d02*	*d04*
	S2	P2	*d03*	*d03*
	S2	P1	*d08*	*d10*
	S2	P2	*d09*	*d10*
	S3	P2	*d08*	*d10*
	S4	P2	*d06*	*d09*
	S4	P4	*d04*	*d08*
	S4	P5	*d05*	*d10*

Fig. 22.3 The suppliers and shipments database (sample values)—first fully temporal version, using timestamps

Constraints (first temporal database): First of all, we need to guard against the absurdity of a FROM-TO pair appearing in which the TO timepoint precedes the FROM timepoint:

```
CONSTRAINT S_FROM_TO_OK
   IS_EMPTY ( S_FROM_TO WHERE TO < FROM ) ;

CONSTRAINT SP_FROM_TO_OK
   IS_EMPTY ( SP_FROM_TO WHERE TO < FROM ) ;
```

Next, observe from the double underlining in Fig. 22.3 that we have included the FROM attribute in the primary key for both SP_FROM_TO and SP_FROM_TO; for example, the primary key of S_FROM_TO obviously cannot be just {S#} , for then we could not have the same supplier under contract for more than one continuous period. A similar observation applies to SP_FROM_TO. *Note:* We could have used the TO attributes instead of the FROM attributes; in fact, SP_FROM_TO and SP_FROM_TO both have two candidate keys and are good examples of relvars for which there is no obvious reason to choose one of those keys as "primary" [8.13]. We make the choices we do purely for definiteness.

However, these primary keys do not of themselves capture all of the constraints we would like them to. Consider relvar SP_FROM_TO, for example. It should be clear that if there is a tuple for supplier Sx in that relvar with FROM value f and TO value t, then we want there *not* to be a tuple for supplier Sx in that relvar indicating that Sx was under contract on the day immediately before f or the day immediately after t. E.g., consider supplier S1, for whom we have just one SP_FROM_TO tuple, with FROM = *d04* and TO = *d10*. The mere fact that {S#,FROM} is the primary key for this relvar is clearly insufficient to prevent the appearance of an additional "overlapping" S1 tuple with (say) FROM = *d02* and TO = *d06,* indicating among other things that S1 *was* under contract on the day immediately before *d04*. Clearly, what we would like is for these two S1 tuples to be coalesced into a single tuple with FROM = *d02* and TO = *d10.**

The fact that {S#,FROM} is the primary key for SP_FROM_TO is also insufficient to prevent the appearance of an "abutting" S1 tuple with (say) FROM = *d02* and TO = *d03,* indicating again that S1 was under contract on the day immediately before *d04*. As before, what we would like is for the tuples to be coalesced into a single tuple.

Here then is a constraint that does prohibit such overlapping and abutting:

```
CONSTRAINT AUG_S_FROM_TO_PK
   IS_EMPTY ( ( ( S_FROM_TO RENAME FROM AS F1, TO AS T1 ) JOIN
                ( S_FROM_TO RENAME FROM AS F2, TO AS T2 ) )
              WHERE ( T1 ≥ F2 AND T2 ≥ F1 ) ) OR
                    ( F2 = T1+1 OR F1 = T2+1 ) ) ) ;
```

This expression is quite complicated!—not to mention that we have taken the gross liberty of writing (e.g.) "T1+1" to designate the immediate successor of the day denoted by T1, a point we will come back to in Section 22.5. *Note:* Assuming this constraint is indeed

---

*Observe that *not* coalescing such tuples would be almost as bad as permitting duplicates! Duplicates amount to "saying the same thing twice." And those two tuples for S1 with overlapping time intervals do indeed "say the same thing twice"; to be specific, they both say that S1 was under contract on days 4, 5, and 6.

stated (and enforced, of course), some writers would refer to the attribute combination {S#,FROM,TO} as a *temporal candidate key* (in fact, a temporal *primary* key). The term is not very good, however, because the "temporal" candidate key is not in fact a *candidate* key in the first place!—of the relvar that contains it, that is. (In Section 22.9, by contrast, we will encounter "temporal candidate keys" that genuinely are candidate keys in the classical sense.)

Next, note carefully that the attribute combination {S#,FROM} in relvar SP_FROM_TO is *not* a foreign key from SP_FROM_TO to S_FROM_TO (even though it does involve the same attributes as the primary key of S_FROM_TO). However, we do need to ensure that if a certain supplier appears in SP_FROM_TO, then that same supplier appears in S_FROM_TO as well:

```
CONSTRAINT AUG_SP_TO_S_FK_AGAIN1
   SP_FROM_TO { S# } ≤ S_FROM_TO { S# } ;
```

(using "≤" to mean "is a subset of").

But constraint AUG_SP_TO_S_FK_AGAIN1 is not enough by itself; we also need to ensure that—even if all desired coalescing of tuples has been done—if SP_FROM_TO shows some supplier as being able to supply some part during some interval of time, then S_FROM_TO shows that same supplier as being under contract during that same interval of time. We might try the following:

```
CONSTRAINT AUG_SP_TO_S_FK_AGAIN2   /* Warning -- incorrect! */
   IS_EMPTY ( ( S_FROM_TO RENAME FROM AS SF, TO AS ST ) JOIN
               ( SP_FROM_TO RENAME FROM AS SPF, TO AS SPT ) )
             WHERE SPF < SF OR SPT > ST ) ;
```

As the comment indicates, however, this specification is in fact incorrect. To see why, let S_FROM_TO be as shown in Fig. 22.3, and let SP_FROM_TO include a tuple for supplier S2 with (say) FROM = *d03* and TO = *d04*. Such an arrangement is clearly consistent, and yet constraint AUG_SP_TO_S_FK_AGAIN2 as stated actually prohibits it.

We will not try to fix this problem here, deferring it instead to a later section (Section 22.9). However, we remark as a matter of terminology that if, as noted earlier, attribute combination {S#,FROM,TO} in relvar S_FROM_TO is regarded as a "temporal candidate key," then attribute combination {S#,FROM,TO} in relvar SP_FROM_TO might be regarded as a "temporal *foreign* key" (though it is not in fact a foreign key as such). Again, see Section 22.9 for further discussion.

Queries (first temporal database): Here now are fully temporal versions of *Queries 1.1 and 1.2:*

- *Query 3.1:* Get S#-FROM-TO triples for suppliers who have been able to supply some part at some time, where FROM and TO together designate a maximal continuous period during which supplier S# was in fact able to supply some part. *Note:* We use the term "maximal" here as a convenient shorthand to mean (in the case at hand) that supplier S# was unable to supply any part on the day immediately before FROM or after TO.

■ *Query 3.2:* Get S#-FROM-TO triples for suppliers who have been unable to supply any parts at all at some time, where FROM and TO together designate a maximal continuous period during which supplier S# was in fact unable to supply any part.

Well, you might like to take a little time to convince yourself that, like us, you would really prefer not even to attempt these queries! If you do make the attempt, however, the fact that they *can* be expressed, albeit exceedingly laboriously, will eventually emerge, but it will surely be obvious that some kind of shorthand is very desirable.

In a nutshell, therefore, the problem of temporal data is that it leads to constraints and queries that are unreasonably complex to state—unless the system provides some well-designed shorthands, of course, which (as we know) today's commercial DBMSs do not.

22.4   INTERVALS

We now embark on our development of such an appropriate set of shorthands. The first and most fundamental step is to recognize the need to deal with intervals as such in their own right, instead of having to treat them as pairs of separate values as we have been doing up to this point.

What exactly is an interval? According to Fig. 22.3, supplier S1 was able to supply part P1 during the interval from day 4 to day 10. But what does "from day 4 to day 10" mean? It is clear that days 5, 6, 7, 8, and 9 are included—but what about the start and end points, days 4 and 10? It turns out that, given some specific interval, we sometimes want to regard the specified start and end points as included in the interval and sometimes not. If the interval from day 4 to day 10 does include day 4, we say it is **closed** with respect to its start point; otherwise we say it is **open** with respect to that point. Likewise, if it includes day 10, we say it is closed with respect to its end point, otherwise we say it is open with respect to that point.

Conventionally, therefore, we denote an interval by its start point and its end point (in that order), preceded by either an opening bracket or an opening parenthesis and followed by either a closing bracket or a closing parenthesis. Brackets are used where the interval is closed, parentheses where it is open. Thus, for example, there are four distinct ways to denote the specific interval that runs from day 4 to day 10 inclusive:

```
[d04,d10]
[d04,d11)
(d03,d10]
(d03,d11)
```

Note: You might think it odd to use (e.g.) an opening bracket but a closing parenthesis; the fact is, however, there are good reasons to allow all four styles. Indeed, the so-called "closed-open" style (opening bracket, closing parenthesis) is the one most used in practice.*

---

*To see why the closed-open style might be advantageous, consider the operation of splitting the interval [*d04,d10*] immediately before, say, day *d07*. The result is the immediately adjacent intervals [*d04,d07*) and [*d07,d10*].

However, the "closed-closed" style (opening bracket, closing bracket) is surely the most intuitive, and we will favor it in what follows.

Given that intervals such as [*d04,d10*] are values in their own right, it makes sense to combine the FROM and TO attributes of, say, SP_FROM_TO (see Fig. 22.3) into a single attribute, DURING, whose values are drawn from some **interval type** (see the next section). One immediate advantage of this idea is that it avoids the need to make the arbitrary choice as to which of the two candidate keys {S#,FROM} and {S#,TO} should be primary. Another is that it also avoids the need to decide whether the FROM-TO intervals of Fig. 22.3 are to be interpreted as closed or open with respect to each of FROM and TO; in fact, [*d04,d10*], [*d04,d11*), (*d03,d10*], and (*d03,d11*) now become four distinct possible representations of the same interval, and we have no need to know which (if any) is the actual representation. Yet another advantage is that relvar constraints "to guard against the absurdity of a FROM-TO pair appearing in which the TO timepoint precedes the FROM timepoint" (as we put it in Section 22.3) are no longer necessary, because the constraint "FROM ≤ TO" is implicit in the very notion of an interval type (loosely speaking). Still another advantage is that there is now no need to talk of "temporal keys" that are not really keys at all in the classical sense (see Section 22.9). Other constraints might also be simplified (again, see Section 22.9).

Fig. 22.4 shows what happens to our example database if we adopt this approach.

S_DURING

S#	SNAME	STATUS	CITY	DURING
S1	Smith	20	London	[*d04,d10*]
S2	Jones	10	Paris	[*d07,d10*]
S2	Jones	10	Paris	[*d02,d04*]
S3	Blake	30	Paris	[*d03,d10*]
S4	Clark	20	London	[*d04,d10*]
S5	Adams	30	Athens	[*d02,d10*]

SP_DURING

S#	P#	DURING
S1	P1	[*d04,d10*]
S1	P2	[*d05,d10*]
S1	P3	[*d09,d10*]
S1	P4	[*d05,d10*]
S1	P5	[*d04,d10*]
S1	P6	[*d06,d10*]
S2	P1	[*d02,d04*]
S2	P2	[*d03,d03*]
S2	P1	[*d08,d10*]
S2	P2	[*d09,d10*]
S3	P2	[*d08,d10*]
S4	P2	[*d06,d09*]
S4	P4	[*d04,d08*]
S4	P5	[*d05,d10*]

Fig. 22.4   The suppliers and shipments database (sample values)—final fully temporal version, using intervals

22.5   INTERVAL TYPES

Our discussion of intervals in the previous section was mostly intuitive in nature; now we need to approach the issue more formally. First of all, observe that the granularity of the interval value [*d04,d10*] is "days." More precisely, we could say it is *type DATE,* by which term we mean that specific member of the usual family of "datetime" data types whose precision is "day" (as opposed to, say, "hour" or "millisecond" or "month"). This observation allows us to pin down the exact type of the interval value [*d04,d10*], as follows:

- First and foremost, of course, it is some **interval** type; this fact by itself is sufficient to determine the *operators* that are applicable to the interval value in question (just as to say that, e.g., a value *r* is of some *relation* type is sufficient to determine the operators—JOIN, etc.—that are applicable to that value *r*).

- Second, the interval value in question is, very specifically, an interval from one **date** to another, and *this* fact is sufficient to determine the set of *interval values* that constitute the interval type in question.

The specific type of [*d04,d10*] is thus INTERVAL(DATE), where:

a. INTERVAL is a **type generator** (like RELATION in **Tutorial D**—see Chapter 5—or "array" in conventional programming languages) that allows us to define a variety of specific interval types (see further discussion below), and

b. DATE is the **point type** of this specific interval type,

Note carefully that, in general, point type *PT* determines both the type *and the precision* of the start and end points—and all points in between—of values of type INTERVAL(*PT*). (In the case of type DATE, of course, the precision is implicit.)

Note: We said in Chapter 4 that precision is not part of the applicable type but rather should be seen as an *integrity constraint.* Given the declarations DECLARE X TIMESTAMP(3) and DECLARE Y TIMESTAMP(6), for example, X and Y are of the same type but are subject to different constraints (X is constrained to hold millisecond values and Y is constrained to hold microsecond values). Strictly speaking, therefore, to say that, e.g., TIMESTAMP(3)—or DATE—is a legal point type is to bundle together two concepts that would better be kept separate. Instead, it would be preferable to define two types T1 and T2, both with a TIMESTAMP possible representation but with different "precision constraints," and then say that T1 and T2 (not, e.g., TIMESTAMP(3) and TIMESTAMP(6)) are legal point types. For simplicity, however, we follow conventional usage in this chapter and pretend (for the most part) that precision is indeed part of the type.

What properties must a type possess if it is to be legal as a point type? Well, we have seen that an interval is denoted by its start and end points; we have also seen that (at least informally) an interval consists of a set of points. If we are to be able to determine the complete set of points, given just the start point *s* and the end point *e,* we must first be able to determine the point that immediately follows (in some agreed ordering) the point *s.* We call that immediately following point the **successor** of *s;* for simplicity, let us agree to refer to it as *s*+1. Then the function by which *s*+1 is determined from *s* is the **successor function** for the point type (and precision) in question. That successor function must be defined for every value of the point type, except the one designated as "last." (There will also be one point designated as "first," which is not the successor of anything.)

Having determined that *s*+1 is the successor of *s,* we must next determine whether or not *s*+1 comes after *e,* according to the same agreed ordering for the point type in question. If it does not, then *s*+1 is indeed a point in [*s,e*], and we must now consider the next point, *s*+2. Continuing this process until we come to the first point *s*+*n* that comes after *e,* we will discover every point of [*s,e*].

Noting that *s*+*n* is in fact the successor of *e* (i.e., it actually comes *immediately* after *e*), we can now safely say that the only property a type *PT* must have to be legal as a point type is that a successor function must be defined for it. In brief, there must be a **total ordering** for the values in *PT* (and we can therefore assume the usual comparison operators— "<", "≥", etc.—are available and defined for all pairs of *PT* values).

By the way, you will surely have noticed by now that we are no longer talking about temporal data specifically. Indeed, most of the rest of this chapter is about intervals in general rather than time intervals in particular, though we will consider certain specifically temporal issues in Section 22.11.

Here then (at last) is a precise definition:

- Let *PT* be a point type. Then an **interval** (or **interval value**) *i* of type INTERVAL(*PT*) is a scalar value for which two monadic scalar operators (START and END) and one dyadic operator (IN) are defined, such that:

    a. START(*i*) and END(*i*) each return a value of type *PT;*

    b. START(*i*) ≤ END(*i*);

    c. Let *p* be a value of type *PT.* Then *p* IN *i* is *true* if and only if START(*i*) ≤ *p* and *p* ≤ END(*i*) are both *true.*

Note the appeals in this definition to the defined successor function for type *PT.* Note too that the start and end points constitute a *possible representation*—in the sense of (e.g.) Chapter 5—for values of type INTERVAL(*PT*) (and hence that in **Tutorial D** we would probably refer to START and END as THE_START and THE_END, respectively). Note finally that, by definition, intervals are always nonempty (i.e., there is always at least one point "IN" any given interval).

Observe very carefully that a value of type INTERVAL(*PT*) is a **scalar** value—i.e., it has no user-visible components. It is true that it does have a possible representation—in fact, several possible representations, as we saw in the previous section—and those possible representations in turn do have user-visible components, but the interval value *per se* does not. Another way of saying the same thing is to say that intervals are *encapsulated.*

22.6   SCALAR OPERATORS ON INTERVALS

In this section we define some useful scalar operators (most of them more or less self-explanatory) that apply to interval values. Consider the interval type INTERVAL(*PT*). Let *p* be a value of type *PT*. We will continue to use the notation *p*+1, *p*+2, etc., to denote the successor of *p*, the successor of *p*+1, and so on (a real language might provide some kind of NEXT operator). Similarly, we will use the notation *p*-1, *p*-2, etc., to denote the value whose successor is *p*, the value whose successor is *p*-1, and so on (a real language might provide some kind of PRIOR operator).

Let *p1* and *p2* be values in *PT*. Then we define MAX(*p1,p2*) to return *p2* if *p1 < p2* is *true* and *p1* otherwise, and MIN(*p1,p2*) to return *p1* if *p1 < p2* is *true* and *p2* otherwise.

Notation we have already been using will do for interval **selectors** (at least in informal contexts). For example, the selector invocations [3,5] and [3,6] both yield that value of type INTERVAL(INTEGER) whose contained points are 3, 4, and 5. (A real language would probably require some more explicit syntax, as in, e.g., INTERVAL([3,5]).)

Let *i1* be the interval [*s1,e1*] of type INTERVAL(*PT*). As we have already seen, START(*i1*) returns *s1* and END(*i1*) returns *e1;* we additionally define STOP(*i1*), which returns *e1*+1. Also, let *i2* be the interval [*s2,e2*], also of type INTERVAL(*PT*). Then we define the following more or less self-explanatory interval **comparison** operators. *Note:* These operators are often known as *Allen's operators,* having first been proposed by Allen in reference [22.1].As an exercise, you might like to try drawing some simple pictures to illustrate them.

- *i1* = *i2* is *true* if and only if *s1* = *s2* and *e1* = *e2* are both *true*.
- *i1* BEFORE *i2* is *true* if and only if *e1 < s2* is *true*.
- *i1* MEETS *i2* is *true* if and only if *s2* = *e1*+1 is *true* or *s1* = *e2*+1 is *true*.
- *i1* OVERLAPS *i2* is *true* if and only if *s1* ≤ *e2* and *s2* ≤ *e1* are both *true*.
- *i1* DURING *i2* is *true* if and only if *s2* ≤ *s1* and *e2* ≥ *e1* are both *true*.*
- *i1* STARTS *i2* is *true* if and only if *s1* = *s2* and *e1* ≤ *e2* are both *true*.
- *i1* FINISHES *i2* is *true* if and only if *e1* = *e2* and *s1* ≥ *s2* are both *true*.

Note: Definitions of these operators can also be given in terms of *points* (of the applicable point type). For example, we could say that *i1* OVERLAPS *i2* is *true* if and only if there exists a value *p* of type *PT* such that *p* IN *i1* and *p* IN *i2* are both *true*.

Following reference [22.3], we can also define the following useful additions to Allen's operators:

- *i1* MERGES *i2* is *true* if and only if *i1* MEETS *i2* is *true* or *i1* OVERLAPS *i2* is *true*.
- *i1* CONTAINS *i2* is *true* if and only if *i2* DURING *i1* is *true*.[†]

---

*Observe that here (for once) DURING does *not* mean "throughout the interval in question."

[†]INCLUDES might be a better keyword than CONTAINS here; then we could use CONTAINS as the inverse of IN, defining *i* CONTAINS *p* to be equivalent to *p* IN *i*.

To obtain the length, so to speak, of an interval, we have DURATION(i), which returns the number of points in i. For example, DURATION($[d03,d07]$) = 5.

Finally, we define some useful dyadic operators on intervals that return intervals:

- $i1$ UNION $i2$ yields [MIN($s1,s2$),MAX($e1,e2$)] if $i1$ MERGES $i2$ is *true* and is otherwise undefined.

- $i1$ INTERSECT $i2$ yields [MAX($s1,s2$),MIN($e1,e2$)] if $i1$ OVERLAPS $i2$ is *true* and is otherwise undefined.

Note: UNION and INTERSECT here are the general set operators, not their special relational counterparts. Reference [22.3] calls them MERGE and INTERVSECT, respectively.

22.7 AGGREGATE OPERATORS ON INTERVALS

In this section we introduce two extremely important operators, *UNFOLD* and *COALESCE*. Each of these operators takes a set of intervals all of the same type as its single operand and returns another such set. The result in both cases can be regarded as a particular *canonical form* for the original set (refer to Chapter 17, Section 17.3, if you need to refresh your memory regarding the term *canonical form*).

The discussion that follows is motivated by observations such as the following. Let *X1* and *X2* be the sets

    { [d01,d01], [d03,d05], [d04,d06] }

and

    { [d01,d01], [d03,d04], [d05,d05], [d05,d06] }

(respectively). It is easy to see that *X1* is not the same set as *X2*. It is almost as easy to see that (a) the set of all points p such that p is contained in some interval in *X1* is the same as (b) the set of all points p such that p is contained in some interval in *X2* (the points in question are *d01, d03, d04, d05,* and *d06*). For reasons that will soon become clear, however, we are interested not so much in that set of points as such, but rather in the corresponding set of **unit intervals** (let us call it *X3*):

    { [d01,d01], [d03,d03], [d04,d04], [d05,d05], [d06,d06] }

X3 is said to be the *unfolded form* of *X1* (and *X2*). In general, if X is a set of intervals all of the same type, then the **unfolded form** of X is the set of all intervals of the form $[p,p]$ where p is a point in some interval in X.

Note that *X1, X2,* and *X3* differ in cardinality. Now, it so happens in our example that *X3* (the unfolded form) is the one whose cardinality is the greatest, but it is easy to find a set *X4* that has the same unfolded form as *X1* and has cardinality greater than that of *X3* (exercise for the reader). It is also easy to find the much more interesting—and necessarily unique—set *X5* that has the same unfolded form and the *minimum possible* cardinality:

```
{ [d01,d01], [d03,d06] }
```

X5 is said to be the **coalesced form** of *X1* (and also of *X2, X3,* and *X4*). In general, if *X* is a set of intervals all of the same type, then the **coalesced form** of *X* is the set *Y* of intervals of the same type such that (a) *X* and *Y* have the same unfolded form and (b) no two distinct members *i1* and *i2* of *Y* are such that *i1* MERGES *i2* is *true*. Note that (as we have already seen) many distinct sets can have the same coalesced form. Note too that the definition of *coalesced form* relies—as the definition of *unfolded form* does not—on the definition of the successor function for the underlying point type.

We can now define the operators **UNFOLD** and **COALESCE.** Let *X* be a set of intervals of type INTERVAL(*PT*). Then UNFOLD(*X*) returns the unfolded form of *X,* while COALESCE(*X*) returns the coalesced form of *X. Note:* We should say that *unfolded form* and *coalesced form* are not standard terms; in fact, there do not appear to be any standard terms for these concepts, even though the concepts as such are certainly discussed in the literature.

These two canonical forms both have an important part to play in the solutions we are at last beginning to approach to the problems discussed in Section 22.3. However, the UNFOLD and COALESCE operators are still not quite what we need (they are still just a step on the way); rather, what we need is certain *relational counterparts* of these operators, and we will define such counterparts in the section immediately following.

22.8   RELATIONAL OPERATORS INVOLVING INTERVALS

The scalar operators on intervals described in Section 22.6 are of course available for use in scalar expressions in the usual places within relational expressions. In **Tutorial D,** for example, those places are basically WHERE clauses on restrict and ADD clauses on EXTEND and SUMMARIZE. Using the database of Fig. 22.4, therefore, the query "Get supplier numbers for suppliers who were able to supply part P2 on day 8" might be expressed as follows:

```
( SP_DURING WHERE P# = P# ('P2') AND d08 IN DURING ) { S# }
```

Note: In practice, the expression "*d08*" here would have to be replaced by an appropriate literal of type DAY.

As another example, the following expression yields a relation showing which pairs of suppliers were located in the same city at the same time, together with the cities and times in question:

```
EXTEND
   ( ( ( ( S_DURING RENAME S# AS XS#,
                             DURING AS XD ) { XS#, CITY, XD }
          JOIN
          ( S_DURING RENAME S# AS YS#,
                             DURING AS YD ) { YS#, CITY, YD } )
       WHERE XD OVERLAPS YD )
  ADD ( XD INTERSECT YD ) AS DURING ) { XS#, YS#, CITY, DURING }
```

Explanation: The JOIN finds pairs of suppliers located in the same city. The WHERE restricts that result to pairs that were in the same city at the same time. The EXTEND ... ADD computes the relevant intervals. The final projection gives the desired result.

We now return to *Queries 3.1 and 3.2* from the very end of Section 22.3. We concentrate first on *Query 3.1*. *Query 4.1* is a restatement of that query in terms of the database of Fig. 22.4:

- *Query 4.1:* Get S#-DURING pairs for suppliers who have been able to supply some part at some time, where DURING designates a maximal continuous period during which supplier S# was in fact able to supply some part.

You will recall that an earlier version of this query, *Query 2.1,* required the use of grouping and aggregation (more specifically, it involved a SUMMARIZE operation). You will probably not be surprised to learn, therefore, that *Query 4.1* is also going to require certain operations of a grouping and aggregating nature. However, we will formulate the query one small step at a time. The first step is:

```
WITH SP_DURING { S#, DURING } AS T1 :
```

(there is more of this expression to come, as the colon suggests). This step merely discards part numbers. T1 thus looks like this:

S#	DURING
S1	[d04,d10]
S1	[d05,d10]
S1	[d09,d10]
S1	[d06,d10]
S2	[d02,d04]
S2	[d03,d03]
S2	[d08,d10]
S2	[d09,d10]
S3	[d08,d10]
S4	[d06,d09]
S4	[d04,d08]
S4	[d05,d10]

Note that this relation contains redundant information; for example, we are told no less than three times that supplier S1 was able to supply something on day 6. The desired result, eliminating all such redundancy, is clearly as follows (let us call it RESULT):

S#	DURING
S1	[d04,d10]
S2	[d02,d04]
S2	[d08,d10]
S3	[d08,d10]
S4	[d04,d10]

We call this result the **coalesced form** of T1 **on** DURING. Note carefully that a DURING value for a given supplier in this coalesced form does not necessarily exist as an explicit DURING value for that supplier in the relation T1 from which the coalesced form is derived; in our example, this remark applies to supplier S4 in particular.

Now, we will eventually reach a point where we can obtain this coalesced form by means of a simple expression of the form

```
T1 COALESCE DURING
```

However, we need to build up to that point gradually.

Observe first of all that we were using the term "coalesced form" in the previous two paragraphs in a sense slightly different from that in which we used it in Section 22.7. The COALESCE operator as defined in Section 22.7 took a set of intervals as input and produced a set of intervals as output. Here, however, we are talking about a different version—in fact, an *overloading* (see Chapter 19)—of that operator that takes a *unary relation* as input and produces another such relation (with the same heading) as output, and it is the tuples in those relations that contain the actual intervals.

Here, then, are the steps to take us from T1 to RESULT:

```
WITH ( T1 GROUP ( DURING ) AS X ) AS T2 :
```

(refer to Chapter 6 if you need to refresh your memory regarding the GROUP operator). T2 looks like this:

S#	X
S1	**DURING** [d04,d10] [d05,d10] [d09,d10] [d06,d10]
S2	**DURING** [d02,d04] [d03,d03] [d08,d10] [d09,d10]
S3	**DURING** [d08,d10]
S4	**DURING** [d06,d09] [d04,d08] [d05,d10]

Now we apply the new version of COALESCE to the relations that are values of the relation-valued attribute X:

```
WITH ( EXTEND T2 ADD COALESCE ( X ) AS Y )
                        { ALL BUT X } AS T3 :
```

T3 looks like this:

S#	Y
S1	DURING [d04,d10]
S2	DURING [d02,d04] [d08,d10]
S3	DURING [d08,d10]
S4	DURING [d04,d10]

Finally, we ungroup (again, see Chapter 6 if necessary):

```
T3 UNGROUP Y
```

This expression yields the relation we earlier called RESULT. In other words, now showing all the steps together (and simplifying slightly), RESULT is the result of evaluating the following overall expression:

```
WITH SP_DURING { S#, DURING } AS T1,
     ( T1 GROUP ( DURING ) AS X ) AS T2,
     ( EXTEND T2 ADD COALESCE ( X ) AS Y ) { ALL BUT X } AS T3 :
T3 UNGROUP Y
```

Obviously it would be desirable to be able to get from T1 to RESULT in a single operation. To that end, we invent a new "relation coalesce" operator, with syntax as follows:

```
R COALESCE A
```

(where *R* is a relational expression and *A* is an attribute—of some interval type—of the relation denoted by that expression).* The semantics of this operator are defined by obvious generalization of the grouping, extension, projection, and ungrouping operations by which

---

*The *A* operand could be extended to permit a commalist of attribute names, if desired. An analogous remark applies to the "relation unfold" operator also (see later). For the semantics, see Exercise 22.8.

we obtained RESULT from T1. *Note:* It might help to observe that coalescing *R* on *A* involves grouping *R* by all of the attributes of *R* apart from *A* (recall from Chapter 6 that, e.g., the expression "T1 GROUP (DURING) ..." can be read as "group T1 by S#," S# being the sole attribute of T1 *not* mentioned in the GROUP clause).

Putting all of the foregoing together, we can now offer the following as a reasonably straightforward formulation of *Query 4.1:*

```
SP_DURING { S#, DURING } COALESCE DURING
```

The overall operation denoted by this expression is an example of what some writers call **temporal projection.** To be more specific, it is a "temporal projection" of SP_DURING over S# and DURING. (Recall that the original version of this query, *Query 1.1,* involved the ordinary projection of SP over S#.) Observe that temporal projection is not exactly a projection as such but is, rather, a "temporal analog" of an ordinary projection.

We now move on to *Query 3.2. Query 4.2* is a restatement of that query in terms of the database of Fig. 22.4:

- *Query 4.2:* Get S#-DURING pairs for suppliers who have been unable to supply any parts at all at some time, where DURING designates a maximal continuous period during which supplier S# was in fact unable to supply any part.

Recall that the original version of this query, *Query 1.2,* involved a relational difference operation. Thus, if you are expecting to see something that might be called *temporal difference,* then of course you are right. As you might also be expecting, while "temporal projection" requires "relation coalesce," "temporal difference" requires "relation unfold."

"Temporal difference" (like the ordinary difference operation) involves two relation operands. We concentrate on the left operand first. If we unfold the result of the (regular) projection S_DURING {S#,DURING} over DURING, we obtain a relation—let us call it T1—that looks something like this:

S#	DURING
S1	[d04,d04]
S1	[d05,d05]
S1	[d06,d06]
S1	[d07,d07]
S1	[d08,d08]
S1	[d09,d09]
S1	[d10,d10]
S2	[d07,d07]
S2	[d08,d08]
S2	[d09,d09]
S2	[d10,d10]
S2	[d02,d02]
S2	[d03,d03]
S2	[d04,d04]
S3	[d03,d03]
..	....

Given the sample data of Fig. 22.4, T1 actually contains a total of 23 tuples. (*Exercise:* Check this claim.)

If we define a "unary relation" version of UNFOLD (analogous to the "unary relation" version of COALESCE), then we can obtain T1 as follows:

```
( EXTEND ( S_DURING { S#, DURING } GROUP ( DURING ) AS X )
  ADD UNFOLD ( X ) AS Y ) { ALL BUT X } UNGROUP Y
```

As already suggested, however, we can simplify matters by inventing a "relation unfold" operator with syntax as follows (and straightforward semantics):

```
R UNFOLD A
```

Now we can write

```
WITH ( S_DURING { S#, DURING } UNFOLD DURING ) AS T1 :
```

We treat the right "temporal difference" operand in like fashion:

```
WITH ( SP_DURING { S#, DURING } UNFOLD DURING ) AS T2 :
```

Now we can apply (regular) relation difference:

```
WITH ( T1 MINUS T2 ) AS T3 :
```

T3 looks like this:

S#	DURING
S2	[d07,d07]
S3	[d03,d03]
S3	[d04,d04]
S3	[d05,d05]
S3	[d06,d06]
S3	[d07,d07]
S5	[d02,d02]
S5	[d03,d03]
S5	[d04,d04]
S5	[d05,d05]
S5	[d06,d06]
S5	[d07,d07]
S5	[d08,d08]
S5	[d09,d09]
S5	[d10,d10]

Finally, we coalesce T3 on DURING to obtain the desired result:

```
T3 COALESCE DURING
```

The result looks like this:

S#	DURING
S2	[d07,d07]
S3	[d03,d07]
S5	[d02,d10]

Here then is a formulation of *Query 4.2* as a single nested expression:

```
( ( S_DURING { S#, DURING } UNFOLD DURING )
  MINUS
  ( SP_DURING { S#, DURING } UNFOLD DURING ) )
COALESCE DURING
```

As already indicated, the overall operation denoted by this expression is an example of what some writers call **temporal difference.** More precisely, it is a "temporal difference" between the projections of S_DURING and SP_DURING (in that order) over S# and DURING. *Note:* Like temporal projection, temporal difference is not exactly a difference as such but is, rather, a "temporal analog" of an ordinary difference.

We are not quite done here, however. "Temporal difference" expressions like the one shown in the example are required so frequently in practice that it seems worthwhile defining a still further shorthand for them.* To be specific, it seems worth capturing as a single operation the sequence (a) unfold both operands, (b) take the difference, and then (c) coalesce. As a bonus, moreover, such a shorthand offers the opportunity of *better performance.* When long intervals of fine granularity are involved, the result of a relation unfold can be very large in comparison to its operand; if the system actually materialized both unfoldings, computed the difference, and then coalesced the result, such queries might execute "forever" or run out of disk space. Expressing temporal difference as a single operation could help the optimizer recognize what was going on and perhaps avoid actually doing any unfolding. Here then is our proposed further shorthand:

R1 I_MINUS *R2* ON *A*

Here *R1* and *R2* are relational expressions denoting relations *r1* and *r2* of the same type and *A* is an attribute of some interval type that is common to those two relations (and the prefix "I_" stands for "interval," of course). As we have more or less seen already, this expression is defined to be semantically equivalent to the following:

((*R1* UNFOLD *A*) MINUS (*R2* UNFOLD *A*)) COALESCE *A*

See Exercise 22.2 for further discussion of "I_" operators like I_MINUS.

22.9   CONSTRAINTS INVOLVING INTERVALS

It is clear that attribute combination {S#,DURING} is a candidate key for relvar S_DURING; in Fig. 22.4, in fact, we used our double underlining convention to show it as the *primary* key specifically. (Observe that {S#} by itself is not a candidate key, because it is possible for a supplier's contract to be terminated and then reinstated at a later date—see, e.g., supplier S2 in Fig. 22.4.) Relvar S_DURING might thus be defined as follows:

```
VAR S_DURING BASE RELATION
  { S# S#, SNAME NAME, STATUS INTEGER, CITY CHAR,
    DURING INTERVAL ( DATE ) }
  KEY { S#, DURING } ;              /* Warning -- inadequate! */
```

---

*Note that (by contrast) we did *not* define an explicit shorthand for temporal projection.

However, the KEY specification as shown here (though it *is* logically correct) is also inadequate, in a sense, for it fails to prevent relvar S_DURING from containing, e.g., both of the following tuples:

S2	Jones	10	Paris	[*d02,d06*]
S2	Jones	10	Paris	[*d07,d10*]

As you can see, these two tuples display a certain *redundancy,* inasmuch as the information pertaining to supplier S2 on days 7 and 8 is recorded twice.

The KEY specification is inadequate in another way also. To be specific, it fails to prevent relvar S_DURING from containing, e.g., both of the following tuples:

S2	Jones	10	Paris	[*d02,d06*]
S2	Jones	10	Paris	[*d07,d10*]

Here there is no redundancy, but there is a certain *circumlocution,* inasmuch as we are taking two tuples to say what could be said better with one:

S2	Jones	10	Paris	[*d02,d10*]

It should be clear that, in order to prevent such redundancies and circumlocutions, what we need to do is enforce a relvar constraint—let us call it *constraint C1*—along the following lines:

If two distinct S_DURING tuples are identical except for their DURING values *i1* and *i2,* then *i1* MERGES *i2* must be *false.*

(Recall that MERGES is the OR of OVERLAPS and MEETS, loosely speaking; replacing MERGES by OVERLAPS in constraint C1 gives the constraint we need to enforce to prevent redundancy, replacing it by MEETS gives the constraint we need to enforce to prevent circumlocution.) It should also be clear that there is a very simple way to enforce constraint C1: namely, by keeping relvar S_DURING **coalesced** at all times on attribute DURING. Let us therefore define a new COALESCED clause that can optionally appear in a relvar definition, as here:

```
VAR S_DURING BASE RELATION
  { S# S#, SNAME NAME, STATUS INTEGER, CITY CHAR,
    DURING INTERVAL ( DATE ) }
  KEY { S#, DURING }         /* Warning -- still inadequate! */
  COALESCED DURING ;
```

The specification COALESCED DURING here means that relvar S_DURING must at all times be identical to the result of the expression S_DURING COALESCE DURING (implying that coalescing S_DURING on DURING never has any effect). This special syntax thus suffices to solve the redundancy and circumlocution problems.* *Note:* We assume for

---

*We note that an argument might be made for providing similar special-case syntax to avoid just the redundancy problem and not the circumlocution problem.

the time being that any attempt to update S_DURING in such a way as to leave it less than fully coalesced on DURING will simply be rejected. However, see Section 22.10 for further discussion of this point.

Unfortunately, the KEY and COALESCED specifications together are still not quite adequate, for they fail to prevent relvar S_DURING from containing, e.g., both of the following tuples:

S2	Jones	10	Paris	[*d02,d08*]
S2	Jones	20	Paris	[*d07,d10*]

Here supplier S2 is shown as having a status of both 10 and 20 on days 7 and 8—clearly an impossible state of affairs. In other words, we have a *contradiction* on our hands.

It should be clear that, in order to prevent such contradictions, what we need to do is enforce a relvar constraint—let us call it *constraint C2*—along the following lines:

> If two distinct S_DURING tuples with the same S# value have DURING values *i1* and *i2,* and *i1* OVERLAPS *i2* is *true,* then those two tuples must be identical except possibly for their DURING values.

Note carefully that constraint C2 is *not* enforced by keeping S_DURING coalesced on DURING (and it is obviously not enforced by the fact that {S#,DURING} is a candidate key). But suppose relvar S_DURING were kept **unfolded** at all times on attribute DURING. Then:

- The sole candidate key for that unfolded form S_DURING UNFOLD DURING would again be the attribute combination {S#,DURING} (because, at any given time, any given supplier currently under contract has just one name, one status, and one city).

- Hence, no two distinct tuples could possibly have the same S# value and "overlapping" DURING values (because all DURING values are unit intervals in S_DURING UNFOLD DURING, and two tuples with the same S# value and "overlapping" DURING values would thus be duplicates of each other—in fact, they would be the same tuple).

It follows that if we enforce the constraint that {S#,DURING} is a candidate key for S_DURING UNFOLD DURING, we enforce constraint C2 "automatically." Let us therefore define a new I_KEY clause ("I_" for interval) that can optionally appear in place of the usual KEY clause in a relvar definition, as here:

```
VAR S_DURING BASE RELATION
  { S# S#, SNAME NAME, STATUS INTEGER, CITY CHAR,
    DURING INTERVAL ( DATE ) }
  I_KEY { S#, DURING UNFOLDED }
  COALESCED DURING ;
```

(meaning, precisely, that {S#,DURING} is a candidate key for S_DURING UNFOLD DURING).* This special syntax thus suffices to solve the contradiction problem.

---

*Some writers define the semantics of I_KEY in such a way as to take care of the redundancy problem also. We find this approach a trifle illogical and do not adopt it ourselves (in any case it is unnecessary, since COALESCED is clearly sufficient to deal with the redundancy problem).

Note carefully that if {S#,DURING} is a candidate key for S_DURING UNFOLD DURING, it is certainly a candidate key for S_DURING; it is this fact that allows us to drop the original KEY specification for S_DURING in favor of the I_KEY specification. Note further that {S#,DURING} can be regarded as a **temporal candidate key** in the sense of Section 22.3. As we have just seen, moreover, this temporal candidate key is indeed a true candidate key for its containing relvar (unlike the "temporal candidate keys" discussed in Section 22.3).

Of course, if such "I_KEY" syntax is supported for candidate keys, we can expect it to be supported for foreign keys as well. Thus, e.g., the definition of SP_DURING might include the following:

```
FOREIGN I_KEY { S#, DURING UNFOLDED } REFERENCES S_DURING ...
```

The intent here is that if SP_DURING shows supplier S*x* was able to supply some part during interval *i*, then S_DURING must show that S*x* was under contract throughout interval *i*. If this constraint is satisfied, then attribute combination {S#,DURING} in relvar SP_DURING can be regarded as a **temporal foreign key** in the sense of Section 22.3. (It is still not a true foreign key in the classical sense, however.)

There is one more point to be made regarding relvar S_DURING. Suppose we do indeed keep that relvar coalesced on DURING at all times. Suppose too that from time to time we run a procedure that recomputes the status of suppliers currently under contract. Of course, the procedure is careful to record previous status values in S_DURING. Now, sometimes the recomputation results in no change of status. In such a case, if the procedure blindly tries to insert a record of the previous status into S_DURING, it will violate the COALESCED constraint! In order to avoid such violations, the procedure will have to make a special test for "no change in status" and perform an appropriate UPDATE instead of the INSERT that does the job when the status *does* change (see Exercise 22.3 at the end of the chapter). Alternatively, of course, we could decide not to keep S_DURING coalesced on DURING after all—a solution that is probably not appropriate in this particular case, but might be so in other cases.

22.10 UPDATE OPERATORS INVOLVING INTERVALS

In this section we consider some problems that arise with the use of the usual update operators INSERT, UPDATE, and DELETE on a temporal relvar. Consider S_DURING once again; assume the definition of that relvar includes the I_KEY and COALESCED specifications as suggested in the previous section. Assume too (as usual) that the current value of S_DURING is as shown in Fig. 22.4. Now consider the following scenarios:

- *INSERT:* Suppose we discover that supplier S2 was additionally under contract during the period from day 5 to day 6 (but still was named Jones, had status 10, and was located in Paris, throughout that time). We cannot simply insert a tuple to that effect, for if we did so the result would violate the COALESCED constraint (twice!). In fact, what we have to do is delete one of the existing S2 tuples and update the other to set the DURING value to [d02,d10].

- *UPDATE:* Suppose we discover that S2's status was temporarily increased on day 9 to 20. It is quite difficult to make the required change, even though it sounds very like a simple UPDATE. Basically, we have to split S2's [d07,d10] tuple into three, with DURING values [d07,d08], [d09,d09], and [d10,d10], respectively, and with other values unchanged, and then replace the STATUS value in the [d09,d09] tuple by the value 20.

- *DELETE:* Suppose we discover that supplier S3's contract was terminated on day 6 but reinstated on day 9. Again, the required update is nontrivial, requiring the single tuple for S3 to be split into two, with DURING values of [d03,d05] and [d09,d10], respectively.

Observe now that the solutions we have just outlined to these three problems are *specific to the current value* of relvar S_DURING (as well as to the particular updates desired)! Consider the insert problem, for example; in general, a tuple considered for insertion might just be insertable "as is," or it might need to be coalesced with a "preceding" tuple, a "following" tuple, or (as in our example) both. Analogously, updates and deletions in general might or might not require the "splitting" of existing tuples.

It is clear that life will be unbearably complicated for users if they are limited to the conventional INSERT, UPDATE, and DELETE operations; some extensions are clearly desirable. Here then are some possibilities:

- *INSERT:* Actually, the INSERT problem can be solved by simply extending the semantics of the COALESCED specification on the relvar definition appropriately. To be specific, we can permit the INSERT to be done in the normal way and then require the system to do any needed (re)coalescing following that INSERT. In other words, the COALESCED specification now no longer merely defines a constraint, it also specifies certain implicit *compensating actions* (analogous, somewhat, to referential actions on foreign key specifications).

    Unfortunately, however, extending the semantics of COALESCED in this way is not sufficient in itself to solve the UPDATE and DELETE problems (why not?).

- *UPDATE:* The UPDATE problem can be addressed by extending the UPDATE operator as suggested by the following example:*

```
UPDATE S_DURING
      WHERE S# = S# ('S2')
      DURING INTERVAL ( [d09,d09] )
      STATUS := 20 ;
```

The third line here—the syntax of which is basically *<attribute name> <interval expression>*—specifies the interval attribute to which the COALESCED specification

---

*Our syntax is similar but not identical to syntax proposed in reference [22.3].

applies (DURING in the example) and the relevant interval value ([*d09,d09*] in the example). The overall UPDATE can be understood as follows:

a. First, identify tuples for supplier S2.

b. Next, out of those tuples, identify those where the DURING value includes the interval [*d09,d09*] (of course, there should be at most one such tuple).

c. If no tuple is identified, no updating is done; otherwise, the system splits the tuple as necessary and performs the required update.

■ *DELETE:* The DELETE problem can be addressed by extending the DELETE operator analogously. Our example becomes:

```
DELETE S_DURING
       WHERE S# = S# ('S3')
       DURING INTERVAL ( [d06,d08] ) ;
```

22.11 DATABASE DESIGN CONSIDERATIONS

Our sample relvars S_DURING and SP_DURING have so far served us well, clearly illustrating the need for interval types and the desirability of defining special operators to deal with interval data. Now, those two relvars were originally "designed" by simply adding interval attributes to their snapshot counterparts. In this section, we question whether such an approach to design is really a good one. More specifically, we suggest some *further decomposition* of certain temporal relvars (where by "further decomposition" we mean decomposition beyond what classical normalization would require). In fact, we suggest both *horizontal* decomposition and *vertical* decomposition, in appropriate circumstances.

Horizontal Decomposition

Our running example assumes, reasonably enough, that the database contains historical information up to and including the present time; however, it also assumes that the present time is recorded as some specific date (*viz.,* day 10), and that assumption is not reasonable at all. In particular, such an approach suggests that whenever time marches on, so to speak, the database is somehow updated accordingly (in our example, it suggests that every such appearance of *d10* is somehow replaced by *d11* at midnight on day 10). A different example, involving intervals of finer granularity, might require such updates to occur as often as, say, every millisecond!

Some authorities have advocated the use of a special marker—we will call it *now*—to be permitted wherever a point value is permitted. Under this proposal, the interval [*d04,d10*], for example, shown in Fig. 22.4 as the DURING value for supplier S1 in S_DURING, would become [*d04,now*]. The actual value of such an interval depends, of course, on when you look at it, so to speak; on day 14 it would be [*d04,d14*].

Other authorities regard the introduction of *now* as an incautious departure from the concepts on which relational systems are based. Note that *now* is really a *variable;* the proposal therefore leads to the strange—we would say logically indefensible—notion of *values* containing *variables*. Here are some examples of questions arising from that notion that you might care to ponder over:

- What happens to the interval [*now,d14*] at midnight on day 14?
- What is the value of END([*d04,now*]) on day 14?—is it *d14* or is it *now?*

We believe it is hard to give coherent answers to questions of this nature. Thus, we prefer to look for an approach that stays with widely understood concepts.

Now, sometimes a "DURING attribute" will be used to record information regarding the future as well as (or instead of) the past. For example, we might want to record the date in the future at which a supplier's contract is to be terminated or considered for renewal. If such is the case, then the S_DURING design of Fig. 22.4 could be used. However, this approach will obviously not always be acceptable. In particular, it will not be acceptable if DURING is to carry the *transaction* time interpretation (see Section 22.2)—transaction times cannot refer to the future!

The general problem is that there is an important difference between (a) historical information and (b) information regarding the current state of affairs. The difference is this: For historical information, the start and end times are both known; for current information, by contrast, the start time is known but the end time is not (usually). This difference strongly suggests that there should be two different relvars, one for the current state of affairs and one for the history (after all, there are certainly two different *predicates*). In the case of suppliers, the "current" relvar is S_SINCE as shown in Fig. 22.2, while the "history" relvar is S_DURING as shown in Fig. 22.4 (except that tuples whose DURING values have end times of *d10* are omitted, the relevant information being recorded in S_SINCE instead).

This example thus illustrates the suggested horizontal decomposition: a relvar with a point-valued "since" attribute for the current state of affairs, and a relvar with an interval-valued "during" attribute for the history. We remark in passing that *triggered procedures* might be used to populate the history relvar; e.g., deleting a tuple from S_SINCE might "automatically" trigger the insertion of a tuple into S_DURING.

The relational UNION operator can be used to combine history and current data into a single relation—for example:

```
S_DURING UNION ( EXTEND S_SINCE
                 ADD INTERVAL [ SINCE, TODAY() ]
                 AS DURING ) { ALL BUT SINCE }
```

A possible disadvantage with horizontal decomposition arises if DURING has the *valid time* interpretation rather than the transaction time one. In that case, history is updatable! The update operators described in Section 20.10 would be helpful here, but there will be some occasions when a desired revision has to affect both relvars. Suppose, for example, that the most recent change in some supplier's status is discovered to have been a mistake. Then we might need not only to delete a tuple from S_DURING but also to update one in S_SINCE. As another example, if that most recent change in status was correct but made on the wrong day, then again the necessary revision will involve updates to both relvars.

If SP_DURING is similarly decomposed into SP_SINCE and SP_DURING, we need to take another look at the foreign key constraints. In the case of SP_DURING, we have already seen (in Section 22.9) that the relvar definition might include the following:

```
FOREIGN I_KEY { S#, DURING UNFOLDED } REFERENCES S_DURING ...
```

As we said in Section 22.9, the intent of this specification is that if supplier S*x* is shown as able to supply some part during interval *i,* then S_DURING must show that S*x* was under contract throughout interval *i*. And we went on to say that {S#,DURING} in relvar SP_DURING might now be regarded as a temporal foreign key.

In the case of SP_SINCE, however, the corresponding foreign key is only "semi-temporal"; thus, we are still faced with the problem of having to deal with the cumbersome constraint we showed in Section 22.3:

```
CONSTRAINT AUG_SP_TO_S_FK
    IS_EMPTY ( ( ( S_SINCE RENAME SINCE AS SS ) JOIN
                 ( SP_SINCE RENAME SINCE AS SPS ) )
               WHERE SPS < SS ) ;
```

Thus, horizontal decomposition does arguably lead to certain problems—the problem of cumbersome constraints, and the problem of updating current and history relvars "simultaneously" (as it were). At the time of writing, we have not seen any specific proposals for shorthands to help with either of these problems. Perhaps further research is needed. We note that the problems in question do not arise if we allow the "DURING" relvar to include information about the future as well as the past and present (because the "SINCE" relvar can then be dropped); however, this approach does require us to predict future ending times. The problems in question also do not arise in the approach proposed in reference [22.4].

Vertical Decomposition

Even before temporal data was studied—and before SQL was invented, for that matter—some writers argued in favor of decomposing relvars as far as possible, instead of just as far as classical normalization would require. Some of those writers unfortunately damaged their cause by proposing database designs consisting entirely of *binary* relvars. One criticism of this idea was that sometimes unary relvars are needed. Another was that some relvars of degree three or more really are nondecomposable (consider relvar SPJ from the suppliers-parts-projects database, for example).

Our usual (nontemporal) relvar S, on the other hand, certainly can be further decomposed. Given the truth of the sentences "S1's name is Smith," "S1's status is 20," and "S1 is located in London," we can safely conclude the truth of the statement implied by the first tuple shown for S in Fig. 22.1. We can therefore decompose S into three binary relvars, each with S# as primary key.

The idea of decomposing all the way (as it were) is motivated by a desire for reduction to the simplest possible terms. Now, the case for such decomposition is perhaps not very strong in the case of relvar S; however, it is significantly stronger in the case of relvar

S_DURING. A supplier's name, status, and city vary independently over time. Moreover, they probably vary with different frequency, too. For example, it might be that a supplier's name hardly ever changes, while that same supplier's location changes occasionally and the corresponding status changes quite often—and it might well be a nuisance to have to repeat the name and location every time the status changes. Besides, the name history, status history, and city history of a supplier are probably each more interesting and more digestible concepts than the concept of a combined name-status-city history. We therefore propose decomposing S_DURING into three historical relvars that look like this (in outline):

```
S_NAME_DURING   { S#, SNAME, DURING }
S_STATUS_DURING { S#, STATUS, DURING }
S_CITY_DURING   { S#, CITY, DURING }
```

The specifications I_KEY {S#, DURING UNFOLDED} and COALESCED DURING would apply to each of these three relvars. *Note:* We would probably want to include the following "master" suppliers relvar as well:

```
S#_DURING { S#, DURING }
```

This relvar would indicate which suppliers were under contract when. Again the specifications I_KEY {S#, DURING UNFOLDED} and COALESCED DURING would apply. In addition, the combination {S#,DURING} would serve as a temporal foreign key in each of S_NAME_DURING, S_STATUS_DURING, and S_CITY_DURING (and also SP_DURING), corresponding to the temporal candidate key {S#,DURING} in relvar S_DURING.

There is another point to be made here, too. With S_DURING as originally defined, we have to use a fairly nontrivial expression in order to obtain the status history:

```
S_DURING { S#, STATUS, DURING } COALESCE DURING
```

At the same time, the expression to give the much less interesting combined history is just a simple relvar reference! In a sense, therefore, the suggested decomposition "levels the playing field" for queries—or, rather, it makes it easier to express the more interesting ones and harder to express the less interesting ones.

The need to decompose S_SINCE is not so compelling. Note in particular that while (again) triggered procedures might be used to populate the three historical relvars—e.g., deleting a tuple from S_SINCE might "automatically" trigger updates to S#_DURING, S_NAME_DURING, S_STATUS_DURING, and S_CITY_DURING—there is no need to decompose S_SINCE in order to achieve such effects.

22.12 SUMMARY

We began this chapter with reference to the growing requirement for databases to contain **historical** as well as current data. We showed that representing historical data using only **timestamps** leads to severe difficulties—in particular, it makes certain constraints and certain queries very hard to deal with—and we discussed the use of scalar ("encapsulated") **in-**

tervals as a better approach. To be specific, we discussed an INTERVAL **type generator,** together with several new **operators** for dealing with interval data (though we remind you that almost all of those operators are really just shorthand). Intervals and their related operators are useful for more than just temporal data *per se*—despite the fact that our running example was based specifically on the type INTERVAL(DATE). We showed examples of **temporal relations** (and discussed **temporal relvars**) with attributes of this particular type.

An interval type must be defined over an underlying **point type,** and an associated **precision** must be specified (somehow) for that point type. A **successor function** must be defined for that point type and that precision.

The operators we described include operators on intervals *per se,* operators on sets of intervals, and operators on temporal relations. Operators on intervals *per se* include START, END, and **Allen's operators.** Operators on sets of intervals include **UNFOLD** and **COALESCE** (see the next paragraph). Operators on temporal relations include **relational versions** of UNFOLD and COALESCE (again, see the next paragraph). We also discussed certain specialized **update** operators and certain specialized **constraints** for temporal relvars ("temporal keys"). We showed that most of those new operators and constraints could effectively be regarded as temporal counterparts of familiar constructs.

We discussed two important *canonical forms* for sets of intervals of the same type, the **unfolded** form and the **coalesced** form. A set of intervals of type INTERVAL(*PT*) is in unfolded form if every interval in the set is a *unit interval*—i.e., an interval containing just one *point,* where a point is a value of the underlying point type *PT*. A set of intervals of type INTERVAL(*PT*) is in coalesced form if no two distinct intervals in the set *overlap* or *meet*. Both canonical forms have the advantage of avoiding certain kinds of redundancy; the coalesced form maximizes conciseness and has very pressing psychological advantages, while the unfolded form is the easiest to operate on (obviating the need for the special constraints and update operators discussed in Sections 22.9 and 22.10). We showed how the concept of these canonical forms is extended to relations with interval attributes, leading to the important new relational operators, **UNFOLD** and **COALESCE.** We used these operators to define temporal analogs of the familiar relational operators projection and difference.

Finally, we drew attention to certain **database design** issues, having to do with **horizontal** and **vertical decomposition** of certain temporal relvars.

EXERCISES

22.1

a. The SQL data type VARCHAR(3) consists of all strings of up to three characters from the *default character set,* which we will assume is ASCII. Do you think INTERVAL (VARCHAR(3)) would be an acceptable interval type?

b. If your answer to a. is yes, express the closed-open interval ['p','q') of this type in closed-closed notation.

22.2 In Section 22.8, we defined the *temporal difference* operator I_MINUS. Temporal union (I_UNION) and temporal intersect (I_INTERSECT) operators can be defined analogously. Give appropriate definitions.

22.3 Suppose relvar S_DURING is constrained to be coalesced on DURING, and suppose it needs to be updated to reflect the fact that supplier S1 had a status of 20 from day 11 to day 15. Give a statement that will have the desired effect. Do not assume that the update operators are extended as suggested in Section 22.10. However, do assume that S_DURING contains information about supplier S1 on day 10 and not after day 10. Do not make any assumption as to what S1's recorded status on day 10 might be.

22.4 In this chapter we have shown how certain operators that apply to intervals in general can be especially useful for time intervals in particular. Suggest some other possible applications of these operators, involving intervals that are not intervals in time.

22.5 Suggest some realistic examples of relations with more than one interval attribute, temporal or otherwise.

22.6 Consider relvar S_DURING once again. At any given time, if there are any suppliers at all at that time, then there is some status *smax* such that no supplier has status at that same time higher than *smax*. Use the operators discussed in this chapter to obtain the coalesced relation in which each status value that has ever been an *smax* value is paired with the interval(s) during which it was that *smax* value.

22.7 HW is a relation with attributes NAME, HEIGHT, and WEIGHT, giving the height and weight of certain persons. Write a query that shows, for each recorded weight, every range of heights such that for each height in that range there is at least one person of that height and that weight.

22.8 Consider a relation R with two distinct interval attributes $I1$ and $I2$. Prove or disprove the following assertions:

    a. `(R UNFOLD I1) UNFOLD I2`   ≡   `(R UNFOLD I2) UNFOLD I1`

    b. `(R COALESCE I1) COALESCE I2` ≡   `(R COALESCE I2) COALESCE I1`

22.9 Can you think of an example of a relvar with an interval attribute that you would *not* want to keep in coalesced form?

2.10 Investigate the possibility of extending the "temporal foreign key" concept to include referential actions such as cascade delete.

REFERENCES AND BIBLIOGRAPHY

Rather than giving what could easily be a very lengthy list of references here, we simply draw your attention to the comprehensive bibliography in reference [22.2], *q.v.*

22.1 J. F. Allen: "Maintaining Knowledge about Temporal Intervals," *CACM 16,* No. 11 (November 1983).

22.2 Opher Etzion, Sushil Jajodia, and Suryanaryan Sripada (eds.): *Temporal Databases: Research and Practice.* New York, N.Y.: Springer Verlag (1998).

An anthology giving the state of the art as of 1997, and an excellent primary reference for further study. *Part 4: General Reference* includes a comprehensive bibliography and the February 1998 version of *The Consensus Glossary of Temporal Database Concepts. Part 2: Temporal Query Languages* includes a paper entitled "Valid Time and Transaction Time Proposals: Language Design Aspects," in which the original author of the present chapter (Hugh Darwen) argues against the approach taken in TSQL2 and claims to find significant flaws in the TSQL2 specification [22.4]. It also includes a paper by David Toman entitled "Point-Based Temporal

Extensions of SQL and Their Efficient Implementation," which proposes an extension to SQL based on points instead of intervals. This idea raises some interesting questions concerning implementation. Answers to those questions could be relevant to interval-based languages too, because the *unit intervals* resulting from UNFOLD are "almost" points (indeed, they *are* points in IXSQL—see the annotation to reference [22.3]).

22.3 Nikos A. Lorentzos and Yannis G. Mitsopoulos: "SQL Extension for Interval Data," *IEEE Transactions on Knowledge and Data Engineering 9,* No. 3 (May/June 1997).

Many of the ideas discussed in the present chapter are based on the work reported in this paper. Like reference [22.2], the paper also includes many useful further references.

Before presenting their proposed SQL extension, the authors define an *Interval-Extended Relational Algebra.* The proposed SQL extension is called IXSQL (sometimes pronounced "nine SQL") and is not specifically for time intervals. Because the keywords INTERVAL and COALESCE are already used in SQL for purposes other than those at hand, the authors propose PERIOD (even for nontemporal intervals) and NORMALISE (note the spelling) in their place. As noted in the annotation to reference [22.2], the IXSQL UNFOLD differs from ours in that it yields points instead of unit intervals. As a consequence, Lorentzos and Mitsopoulos propose an inverse FOLD operator, which converts points to unit intervals, then coalesces. UNFOLD, FOLD, and NORMALISE are proposed in the form of additional clauses on the familiar SELECT–FROM–WHERE construct. It is interesting to note that the proposed NORMALISE ON clause is not only written last but—in what is a departure for SQL (see Appendix B)—is also executed last; that is, the output of the SELECT clause is input to the NORMALISE ON clause (for good reasons).

22.4 Richard T. Snodgrass (ed.): *The Temporal Query Language TSQL2.* Dordrecht, Netherlands: Kluwer Academic Pub. (1995).

TSQL2 is a set of proposed temporal extensions to SQL. To a significant extent, the TSQL2 committee spurned the general approach of scalar and relational operators on intervals in favor of something that is more convenient in certain special cases. Instead of simply supporting an interval type generator and associated operators, therefore, they propose various special kinds of tables: *snapshot tables, valid time state tables, valid time event tables, transaction time tables, bitemporal state tables,* and *bitemporal event tables.*

- A *snapshot table* is an old-fashioned SQL table, possibly including columns of data type PERIOD (as in IXSQL [22.3], this keyword is used instead of INTERVAL because SQL already uses INTERVAL for another purpose).

- The other kinds of tables are all said to have *temporal support;* temporal support implies the existence, alongside each row, of either one or two *temporal elements.* A temporal element is a set of *timestamps,* where a timestamp is either a PERIOD value or a value of some datetime data type. (Note, therefore, that the term "timestamp" is not being used here in its conventional SQL/92 sense.)

Temporal elements consisting of PERIOD values are specified to be coalesced.* Temporal elements do not appear as regular columns but instead are accessed by means of special-purpose operators.

---

*The version of TSQL2 that was proposed to ISO (but not accepted) in 1996 for inclusion in the SQL standard differed from the version described in reference [22.4], in that tables with temporal support were always "unnested" (meaning each temporal element was a single timestamp, not a set of timestamps). Whether coalescing also took place was not specified.

Here is a quick survey of the various kinds of tables "with temporal support":

- In *valid time state tables* and *transaction time tables,* each timestamp is a PERIOD value.
- In *valid time event tables,* each timestamp is a value of some datetime data type.
- A *bitemporal table* is one that is both (a) a transaction time table and (b) either a valid time state table or a valid time event table. Each row in a bitemporal table has two temporal elements, one for the transaction time and one for the valid time. A bitemporal table can therefore be operated on either as a transaction time table or as a valid time table.

TSQL2 is strongly motivated by a notion it calls *temporal upward compatibility.* The idea is to be able to add "temporal support" to an existing base table, thus converting that base table from a snapshot table to a temporal table of some kind. From then on, all regular SQL operations on that base table are interpreted as operations on the current snapshot version of that table,* but now they might have new side effects. In particular, updates and deletes on the current snapshot version result in retention of the old versions of those rows as rows with temporal elements.

The big advantage of the TSQL2 approach accrues in connection with what are called *sequenced* operations. A sequenced operation is one that is expressed as an operation on a snapshot of the database, typically the current snapshot, but is executed, as it were, on *every* snapshot. The result of a sequenced query on valid time tables, for example, is a valid time table. The query itself is expressed just as if it were a query against a current snapshot database, with the addition of a single keyword to indicate that it is a sequenced query. The application program giving such a query has to make special provisions to access the timestamps of the result rows.

Operations that cannot be expressed as sequenced operations sometimes require the use of rather arcane syntax. As a consequence of SQL's failure to support tables with no columns, TSQL2 carries the restriction that a table with temporal support must have at least one regular column in addition to its temporal element(s). Thus, queries such as the one to show periods during which at least one supplier in Paris was under contract cannot be expressed in sequenced form.

ANSWERS TO SELECTED EXERCISES

22.1 a. Probably not (though it *could* be). b. The character string immediately preceding 'q' depends on which particular character comes last in the collating sequence in use (see reference [4.19] for an explanation of SQL collating sequences). If that last character is 'Z', then the answer is ['p','pZZ']. *Note:* We remind you that, strictly speaking, the "(3)" in VARCHAR(3) is best regarded not as part of the type as such, but rather as an *integrity constraint.*

22.2 First, *R1* I_UNION *R2* ON *A* is equivalent to

```
( R1 UNION R2 )  COALESCE A
```

---

*Actually, there is another difference here between TSQL2 as defined in reference [22.4] and the version proposed to ISO. Reference [22.4] requires the keyword SNAPSHOT after SELECT to indicate that a query is against the current state of each of the tables it references; the version proposed to ISO does not.

Observe that there is no need to unfold *R1* and *R2* on *A* before forming the union (why not?). Second, *R1* I_INTERSECT *R2* ON *A* is equivalent to

```
( ( EXTEND ( ( R1 RENAME A AS A1 ) JOIN
              ( R2 RENAME A AS A2 )
              WHERE A1 OVERLAPS A2 )
      ADD ( A1 INTERSECT A2 ) AS A ) { ALL BUT A1, A2 } )
COALESCE A
```

Again there is no need to unfold *R1* and *R2* on *A*. What is more, if *R1* and *R2* are in fact coalesced on *A*, there is no need for the final coalesce step either (why not?).

Temporal versions of other relational operators (e.g., I_JOIN) can be defined analogously. In particular, the special versions of UPDATE and DELETE described in Section 22.10 made tacit use of a temporal version of restrict. *Note:* Perhaps we should explain why we emphasized the I_MINUS shorthand specifically in the body of the chapter. The point is that I_MINUS involves unfolding, whereas (as we have just seen) the other temporal relational operators typically do not,* and it is desirable to be able to avoid having to request or perform such unfoldings where possible.

22.3 Here is one possible solution:

```
IF IS_EMPTY ( S_DURING WHERE S# = S# ('S1')
                       AND STATUS = 20
                       AND END ( DURING ) = d10 )
THEN INSERT INTO S_DURING
          ( EXTEND ( S_DURING WHERE S# = S# ('S1')
                              AND END ( DURING ) = d10 )
                              { ALL BUT DURING }
            ADD INTERVAL ( [ d11, d15 ] ) AS DURING ;
ELSE UPDATE S_DURING WHERE S# = S# ('S1')
                     AND END ( DURING ) = d10
          DURING := INTERVAL ( [ START ( DURING ), d15 ] ) ;
```

22.4 Animals vary according to the range of *frequencies* of light and sound waves to which their eyes and ears are receptive. Various natural phenomena occur and can be measured in ranges in *depth* of soil or sea or *height* above sea level. The fact that tea is taken between the hours of 4:00 and 5:00 in the afternoon is a temporal observation, but one that is significantly different in kind from the examples in the body of the chapter (how, exactly?). No doubt you have been able to think of many similar examples on which interesting database applications might be based.

22.5 Animals vary according to the range of frequencies of light *and* sound waves to which their eyes and ears are receptive! Besides, as soon as we join two temporal relations *R1{A,B}* and *R2{A,C}*, where *B* and *C* are interval attributes, we obtain a result, albeit just an intermediate one, that has more than one interval attribute.

22.6
```
     WITH SP_DURING UNFOLD DURING AS SP_UNFOLDED :
    ( SUMMARIZE SP_UNFOLDED PER SP_UNFOLDED { DURING }
               ADD MAX ( STATUS ) AS SMAX ) COALESCE DURING
```

22.7
```
    (( EXTEND HW { HEIGHT, WEIGHT }
       ADD INTERVAL ( [ HEIGHT, HEIGHT ] ) AS HR )
                                     { WEIGHT, HR } ) COALESCE HR
```

---

*SUMMARIZE is an exception. See the answer to Exercise 22.6.

22.8 Assertion a. is easily seen to be valid. Assertion b. is not, however, as we now show. Let R be as follows:

I1	I2
[d01,d01]	[d08,d09]
[d01,d02]	[d08,d09]
[d03,d04]	[d08,d08]
[d04,d04]	[d08,d08]

Then the result, U, of both (R UNFOLD I1) UNFOLD I2 and (R UNFOLD I2) UNFOLD I1 is:

I1	I2
[d01,d01]	[d08,d08]
[d01,d01]	[d09,d09]
[d02,d02]	[d08,d08]
[d02,d02]	[d09,d09]
[d03,d03]	[d08,d08]
[d04,d04]	[d08,d08]

However, the result of (U COALESCE I1) COALESCE I2 is:

I1	I2
[d01,d02]	[d09,d09]
[d03,d04]	[d08,d08]

whereas the result of (U COALESCE I2) COALESCE I1 is:

I1	I2
[d01,d02]	[d08,d09]
[d03,d04]	[d08,d08]

We suggest you check these results, by writing down the results of U COALESCE I1 and U COALESCE I2, then coalescing those intermediate results on I2 and I1, respectively. We also suggest the following shorthands:

- R UNFOLD I1,I2   ≡   (R UNFOLD I1) UNFOLD I2

- R COALESCE I1,I2   ≡   (R COALESCE I1) COALESCE I2

CHAPTER 23

Logic-Based Databases

23.1 INTRODUCTION

In the mid 1980s or so, a significant trend began to emerge in the database research community toward **database systems that are based on logic.** Expressions such as *logic database, inferential DBMS, expert DBMS, deductive DBMS, knowledge base, knowledge base management system (KBMS), logic as a data model, recursive query processing,* etc., etc., began to appear in the research literature. However, it is not always easy to relate such terms and the ideas they represent to familiar database terms and concepts, nor to understand the motivation underlying the research from a traditional database perspective. There is a clear need for an explanation of all of this activity in terms of conventional database ideas and principles. This chapter is an attempt to meet that need.

Our aim is thus to explain what logic-based systems are all about from the viewpoint of someone who is familiar with traditional database technology but perhaps not so much with logic as such. As each new idea from logic is introduced, therefore, we will explain it in conventional database terms, where possible or appropriate. (Of course, we have discussed certain ideas from logic in this book already, especially in our description of relational calculus in Chapter 7. Relational calculus is directly based on logic. However, there is more to logic-based systems than just the relational calculus, as we will see.)

The structure of the chapter is as follows. Following this introductory section, Section 23.2 provides a brief overview of the subject, with a little history. Sections 23.3 and 23.4 then provide an elementary (and very much simplified) treatment of *propositional calculus* and *predicate calculus,* respectively. Next, Section 23.5 introduces the so-called *proof-theoretic* view of a database, and Section 23.6 builds on the ideas of that section to explain what is meant by the term *deductive DBMS.* Section 23.7 then discusses some approaches to the problem of *recursive query processing.* Finally, Section 23.8 offers a summary and a few concluding remarks.

23.2 OVERVIEW

Research on the relationship between database theory and logic goes back at least to the late 1970s, if not earlier—see, for example, references [23.5], [23.7], and [23.13]. However, the principal stimulus for the recent considerable expansion of interest in the subject seems to have been the publication in 1984 of a landmark paper by Reiter [23.15]. In that paper,

Reiter characterized the traditional perception of database systems as **model-theoretic**—by which he meant, loosely, that:

a. The database at any given time can be seen as a set of explicit (i.e., base) relations, each containing a set of explicit tuples, and

b. Executing a query can be regarded as evaluating some specified formula (i.e., truth-valued expression) over those explicit relations and tuples.

Note: We will define the term "model-theoretic" more precisely in Section 23.5.

Reiter then went on to argue that an alternative **proof-theoretic** view was possible, and indeed preferable in certain respects. In that alternative view (again loosely speaking):

a. The database at any given time is seen as a set of **axioms** ("ground" axioms, corresponding to values in domains and tuples in base relations, plus certain "deductive" axioms, to be discussed), and

b. Executing a query is regarded as proving that some specified formula is a logical consequence of those axioms—in other words, proving that it is a **theorem**.

Note: We will define the term "proof-theoretic" more precisely in Section 23.5 also—though it might help to point out right away that the proof-theoretic view is very close to our characterization of a database in Chapter 1, Section 1.3 (subsection "Data and Data Models"), as *a collection of true propositions* [1.2].

An example is in order. Consider the following relational calculus query against the usual suppliers and parts database:

```
SPX WHERE SPX.QTY > 250
```

(SPX here is a range variable ranging over shipments, of course). In the traditional—i.e., model-theoretic—interpretation, we examine the shipment tuples one by one, evaluating the formula "QTY > 250" for each in turn; the query result then consists of just those shipment tuples for which the formula evaluates to *true*. In the proof-theoretic interpretation, by contrast, we consider the shipment tuples (plus certain other items) as *axioms* of a certain **"logical theory"**; we then apply theorem-proving techniques to determine for which possible values of the range variable SPX the formula "SPX.QTY > 250" is a logical consequence of those axioms within that theory. The query result then consists of just those particular values of SPX.

Of course, this example is extremely simple—so simple, in fact, that you might be having difficulty in seeing what the difference between the two interpretations really is. The point is, however, that the reasoning mechanism employed in the attempted proof (in the proof-theoretic interpretation) can of course be much more sophisticated than our simple example is able to convey; indeed, it can handle certain problems that are beyond the capabilities of classical relational systems, as we will see. Furthermore, the proof-theoretic interpretation carries with it an attractive set of additional features [23.15]:

■ **Representational uniformity:** It lets us define a database language in which values in domains, tuples in base relations, "deductive axioms," queries, and integrity constraints are all represented in essentially the same uniform way.

- **Operational uniformity:** It provides a basis for a unified attack on a variety of apparently distinct problems, including query optimization (especially semantic optimization), integrity constraint enforcement, database design (dependency theory), program correctness proofs, and other problems.

- **Semantic modeling:** It offers a solid foundation on which to build a variety of "semantic" extensions to the basic model.

- **Extended application:** Finally, it provides a basis for dealing with certain issues that classical approaches have traditionally had difficulty with—for example, *disjunctive information* (e.g., "Supplier S5 supplies either part P1 or part P2, but it is not known which").

Deductive Axioms

We offer a brief and preliminary explanation of the concept, already mentioned a couple of times, of a **deductive axiom** (also known as a **rule of inference**). Basically, a deductive axiom is a rule by which, given certain facts, we are able to deduce additional facts. For example, given the facts "Anne is the mother of Betty" and "Betty is the mother of Celia," there is an obvious deductive axiom that allows us to deduce that Anne is the grandmother of Celia. To jump ahead of ourselves for a moment, therefore, we might imagine a *deductive DBMS* in which the two given facts are represented as tuples in a relation, thus:

MOTHER_OF

MOTHER	DAUGHTER
Anne	Betty
Betty	Celia

These two facts represent **ground axioms** for the system. Let us suppose also that the deductive axiom has been formally stated to the system somehow, e.g., as follows:

```
IF    MOTHER_OF      ( x, y )
AND   MOTHER_OF      ( y, z )
THEN  GRANDMOTHER_OF ( x, z ) ;
```

(hypothetical and simplified syntax). Now the system can apply the rule expressed in the deductive axiom to the data represented by the ground axioms, in a manner to be explained in Section 23.4, to deduce the result GRANDMOTHER_OF (Anne,Celia). Thus, users can ask queries such as "Who is the grandmother of Celia?" or "Who are the granddaughters of Anne?" (or, more precisely, "Who is Anne the grandmother of?").

Let us now try to relate the foregoing ideas to traditional database concepts. In traditional terms, the deductive axiom can be thought of as a *view definition*—for example:

```
VAR GRANDMOTHER_OF VIEW
  ( MX.MOTHER AS GRANDMOTHER, MY.DAUGHTER AS GRANDDAUGHTER )
    WHERE MX.DAUGHTER = MY.MOTHER ;
```

(we deliberately use a relational calculus style here; MX and MY are range variables ranging over MOTHER_OF). Queries such as the ones mentioned above can now be framed in terms of this view:

```
GX.GRANDMOTHER WHERE GX.GRANDDAUGHTER = NAME ( 'Celia' )

GX.GRANDDAUGHTER WHERE GX.GRANDMOTHER = NAME ( 'Anne' )
```

(GX is a range variable ranging over GRANDMOTHER_OF).

So far, therefore, all we have really done is presented a different syntax and different interpretation for material that is already familiar. However, we will see in later sections that there are in fact some significant differences, not illustrated by these simple examples, between logic-based systems and more traditional DBMSs.

23.3   PROPOSITIONAL CALCULUS

In this section and the next, we present a very brief introduction to some of the basic ideas of logic. The present section considers *propositional calculus* and the next considers *predicate* calculus. We remark immediately, however, that so far as we are concerned, propositional calculus is not all that important as an end in itself; the major aim of the present section is really just to pave the way for an understanding of the next one. The aim of the two sections taken together is to provide a basis on which to build in the rest of the chapter.

You are assumed to be familiar with the basic concepts of boolean algebra. For purposes of reference, we state certain laws of boolean algebra that we will be needing later on:

- *Distributive laws:*

```
f AND ( g OR  h )  ≡  ( f AND g ) OR  ( f AND h )
f OR  ( g AND h )  ≡  ( f OR  g ) AND ( f OR  h )
```

- *De Morgan's laws:*

```
NOT ( f AND g )  ≡  NOT f OR  NOT g
NOT ( f OR  g )  ≡  NOT f AND NOT g
```

Here *f, g,* and *h* are arbitrary boolean (truth-valued) expressions.

Now we turn to logic *per se.* Logic can be defined as **a formal method of reasoning.** Because it is formal, it can be used to perform formal tasks, such as testing the validity of an argument by examining just the structure of that argument as a sequence of steps (i.e., without paying any attention to the meaning of those steps). In particular, of course, because it is formal, it can be *mechanized*—i.e., it can be programmed, and thus applied by the machine.

Propositional calculus and predicate calculus are two special cases of logic in general (in fact, the former is a subset of the latter). The term "calculus," in turn, is just a general term that refers to any system of symbolic computation; in the particular cases at hand, the kind of computation involved is the computation of the truth value—*true* or *false*—of certain formulas or expressions.

Terms

We begin by assuming that we have some collection of objects, called **constants,** about which we can make statements of various kinds. In database parlance, the *constants* are the values in the underlying domains, and a *statement* might be, e.g., a conditional expression such as "3 > 2". We define a **term** as a statement that involves such constants and:

a. Either does not involve any logical connectives (see below) or is enclosed in parentheses, and

b. Evaluates unequivocally to either *true* or *false.*

For example, "Supplier S1 is located in London" and "Supplier S2 is located in London" and "Supplier S1 supplies part P1" are all terms (they evaluate to *true, false,* and *true* respectively, given our usual sample data values). By contrast, "Supplier S1 supplies part *p*" (where *p* is a variable) and "Supplier S5 will supply part P1 at some time in the future" are not terms, because they do not evaluate to either *true* or *false* unequivocally.

Formulas

Next, we define the concept of a **formula.** Formulas of the propositional calculus—and, more generally, of the *predicate* calculus—are used in database systems in the formulation of queries (among many other things).

```
<formula>
    ::=     <term>
          | NOT <term>
          | <term> AND <formula>
          | <term> OR <formula>
          | <term> => <formula>

<term>
    ::=     <atomic formula>
          | ( <formula> )
```

Formulas are evaluated in accordance with the truth values of their constituent terms and the usual truth tables for the connectives. Points arising:

1. An < *atomic formula* > is a truth-valued expression that involves no connectives and is not contained in parentheses.

2. The symbol "=►" represents the *logical implication* connective. The expression f =► g is defined to be logically equivalent to the expression NOT f OR g. *Note:* We used "IF ... THEN ..." for this connective in Chapter 7 and other earlier chapters.

3. We adopt the usual precedence rules for the connectives (NOT, then AND, then OR, then =►) in order to reduce the number of parentheses needed to express a desired order of evaluation.

4. A **proposition** is just a < *formula* > as defined above (we use the term "formula" for consistency with the next section).

Rules of Inference

Now we come to the **rules of inference** for the propositional calculus. Many such rules exist. Each is a statement of the form

$$\models \quad f \Rightarrow g$$

(where the symbol $\models$ can be read as **"It is always the case that"**; note that we do need some such symbol in order to be able to make *metastatements*, i.e., statements about statements). Here are some examples of inference rules:

1. $\models$ (f AND g) $\Rightarrow$ f

2. $\models$ f $\Rightarrow$ (f OR g)

3. $\models$ ((f $\Rightarrow$ g) AND (g $\Rightarrow$ h)) $\Rightarrow$ (f $\Rightarrow$ h)

4. $\models$ (f AND (f $\Rightarrow$ g)) $\Rightarrow$ g

   Note: This one is particularly important. It is called the **modus ponens** rule. Informally, it says that if *f* is *true* and *f* implies *g*, then *g* must be *true* as well. For example, given the fact that a. and b. below are both *true*—

   a. I have no money;

   b. If I have no money then I will have to wash dishes;

   —then we can infer that c. is *true* as well:

   c. I will have to wash dishes.

To continue with the inference rules:

5. $\models$ (f $\Rightarrow$ (g $\Rightarrow$ h)) $\Rightarrow$ ((f AND g) $\Rightarrow$ h)

6. $\models$ ((f OR g) AND (NOT g OR h)) $\Rightarrow$ (f OR h)

   Note: This is another particularly important one. It is called the **resolution** rule. We will have more to say about it under "Proofs" below and again in Section 23.4.

Proofs

We now have the necessary apparatus for dealing with formal proofs (in the context of the propositional calculus). The problem of proof is the problem of determining whether some given formula *g* (the **conclusion**) is a logical consequence of some given set of formulas *f1, f2, ..., fn* (the **premises***)—in symbols:

$$f1, \quad f2, \quad ..., \quad fn \quad \models \quad g$$

———————————

*Also spelled **premisses** (singular *premiss*).

(read as "*g* **is deducible from** *f1, f2, ..., fn*"; observe the use of another metalinguistic symbol, ⊢). The basic method of proceeding is known as **forward chaining**. Forward chaining consists of applying the rules of inference repeatedly to the premises, and to formulas deduced from those premises, and to formulas deduced from those formulas, etc., etc., until the conclusion is deduced; in other words, the process "chains forward" from the premises to the conclusion. However, there are several variations on this basic theme:

1. **Adopting a premise:** If *g* is of the form $p \Rightarrow q$, adopt *p* as an additional premise and show that *q* is deducible from the given premises plus *p*.

2. **Backward chaining:** Instead of trying to prove $p \Rightarrow q$, prove the **contrapositive** NOT $q \Rightarrow$ NOT *p*.

3. *Reductio ad absurdum:* Instead of trying to prove $p \Rightarrow q$ directly, assume that *p* and NOT *q* are both *true* and derive a contradiction.

4. **Resolution:** This method uses the resolution inference rule (No. 6 in the list given earlier).

We discuss the resolution technique in some detail, since it is of wide applicability (in particular, it generalizes to the case of predicate calculus also, as we will see in Section 23.4).

Note first that the resolution rule is effectively a rule that allows us to *cancel subformulas;* that is, given the two formulas

```
f OR g          and        NOT g OR h
```

we can cancel *g* and NOT *g* to derive the simplified formula

```
f OR h
```

In particular, given *f* OR *g* and NOT *g* (i.e., taking *h* as *true*), we can derive *f.*

Observe, therefore, that the rule applies in general to a *conjunction* (AND) of two formulas, each of which is a *disjunction* (OR) of two formulas. In order to apply the resolution rule, therefore, we proceed as follows. (To make our discussion a little more concrete, we explain the process in terms of a specific example.) Suppose we wish to determine whether the following putative proof is in fact valid:

```
A ⇒ ( B ⇒ C ), NOT D OR A, B ⊢ D ⇒ C
```

(where *A, B, C,* and *D* are formulas). We start by adopting the negation of the conclusion as an additional premise and then writing each premise on a separate line, as follows:

```
A ⇒ ( B ⇒ C )
NOT D OR A
B
NOT ( D ⇒ C )
```

These four lines are implicitly all "ANDed" together.

We now convert each individual line to **conjunctive normal form,** i.e., a form consisting of one or more formulas all ANDed together, each individual formula containing (possibly) NOTs and ORs but no ANDs (see Chapter 17). Of course, the second and third lines are already in this form. In order to convert the other two lines, we first eliminate all appearances of "➡" (using the definition of that connective in terms of NOT and OR); we then apply the distributive laws and De Morgan's laws as necessary (see the beginning of this section). We also drop redundant parentheses and pairs of adjacent NOTs (which cancel out). The four lines become

```
NOT A OR NOT B OR C
NOT D OR A
B
D AND NOT C
```

Next, any line that includes any explicit ANDs we replace by a set of separate lines, one for each of the individual formulas ANDed together (dropping the ANDs in the process). In the example, this step applies to the fourth line only. The premises now look like this:

```
NOT A OR NOT B OR C
NOT D OR A
B
D
NOT C
```

Now we can start to apply the resolution rule. We choose a pair of lines that can be *resolved,* i.e., a pair that contain (respectively) some particular formula and the negation of that formula. Let us choose the first two lines, which contain NOT *A* and *A* respectively, and resolve them, giving

```
NOT D OR NOT B OR C
B
D
NOT C
```

(*Note:* In general we also need to keep the two original lines, but in this particular example they will not be needed any more.) Now we apply the rule again, again choosing the first two lines (resolving NOT *B* and *B*), giving

```
NOT D OR C
D
NOT C
```

We choose the first two lines again (NOT *D* and *D*):

```
C
NOT C
```

And once again (*C* and NOT *C*); the final result is the empty set of propositions (usually represented thus: []), which is interpreted as a contradiction. By *reductio ad absurdum,* therefore, the desired result is proved. ∎

23.4 PREDICATE CALCULUS

We now turn our attention to the *predicate* calculus. The big difference between propositional calculus and predicate calculus is that the latter allows formulas to contain variables* and quantifiers, which makes it much more powerful and of much wider applicability. For example, the statement "Supplier S1 supplies part *p*" and "Some supplier *s* supplies part *p*" are not legal formulas of the propositional calculus, but they are legal formulas of the predicate calculus. Hence predicate calculus provides us with a basis for expressing queries such as "Which parts are supplied by supplier S1?" or "Get suppliers who supply some part" or even "Get suppliers who do not supply any parts at all."

Predicates

As explained in Chapter 3, a **predicate** is a *truth-valued function*, i.e., a function that, given appropriate arguments for its parameters, returns either *true* or *false*. For example, "$>(x,y)$"—more conventionally written "$x > y$"—is a predicate with two parameters, x and $y;$ it returns *true* if the argument corresponding to x is greater than the argument corresponding to y and *false* otherwise. A predicate that takes n arguments (i.e., equivalently, one that is defined in terms of n parameters) is called an n-place predicate. A proposition (i.e., a formula in the sense of Section 23.3) can be regarded as a zero-place predicate—it has no parameters and evaluates to *true* or *false,* unequivocally.

It is convenient to assume that predicates corresponding to "=", ">", "≥", etc., are builtin (i.e., they are part of the formal system we are defining) and that expressions using them can be written in the conventional manner. However, users should be able to define their own predicates as well, of course. Indeed, that is the whole point: The fact is, in database terms, a user-defined predicate corresponds to a user-defined *relvar* (as we already know from earlier chapters). The suppliers relvar S, for example, can be regarded as a predicate with four parameters, namely S#, SNAME, STATUS, and CITY. Furthermore, the expressions S (S1,Smith,20,London) and S (S6,White,45,Rome) represent "instances" or "instantiations" or "invocations" of that predicate that (given our usual sample set of values) evaluate to *true* and *false,* respectively. Informally, we can regard such predicates—together with any applicable *integrity constraints,* which are also predicates—as defining what the database "means," as explained in earlier parts of this book (Chapter 8 in particular).

Well-Formed Formulas

The next step is to extend the definition of "formula." In order to avoid confusion with the formulas of the previous section (which are actually a special case), we will now switch to

---

*The variables in question are *logic* variables, not programming language variables. For our purposes, we can think of them as range variables in the sense of Chapter 7.

the term **well-formed formula** (WFF, pronounced "weff") from Chapter 7. Here is a simplified syntax for WFFs:

```
<wff>  ::=   <term>
           | NOT ( <wff> )
           | ( <wff> ) AND ( <wff> )
           | ( <wff> ) OR ( <wff> )
           | ( <wff> ) => ( <wff> )
           | EXISTS <var name> ( <wff> )
           | FORALL <var name> ( <wff> )

<term> ::= [ NOT ] <pred name> [ ( <argument commalist> ) ]
```

Points arising:

1. A *<term>* is simply a possibly negated "predicate instance" (if we think of a predicate as a truth-valued function, then a predicate instance is an invocation of that function). Each *<argument>* must be a constant, a variable name, or a function invocation, where each argument to a function invocation in turn is a constant or variable name or function invocation. The *<argument commalist>* and (optionally) the corresponding parentheses are omitted for a zero-place predicate. *Note:* Functions (over and above the truth-valued functions that are the predicates, that is) are permitted in order to allow WFFs to include computational expressions such as "$+(x,y)$"—more conventionally written "$x + y$"—and so forth.

2. As in Section 23.3, we adopt the usual precedence rules for the connectives (NOT, then AND, then OR, then =>) in order to reduce the number of parentheses needed to express a desired order of evaluation.

3. You are assumed to be familiar with the quantifiers EXISTS and FORALL. *Note:* We are concerned here only with the *first-order* predicate calculus, which basically means that (a) there are no "predicate variables" (i.e., variables whose permitted values are predicates), and hence that (b) predicates cannot themselves be subjected to quantification. See Exercise 7.9 in Chapter 7.

4. De Morgan's laws can be generalized to apply to quantified WFFs, as follows:

```
NOT ( FORALL x ( f ) )  ≡  EXISTS x ( NOT ( f ) )
NOT ( EXISTS x ( f ) )  ≡  FORALL x ( NOT ( f ) )
```

This point was also discussed in Chapter 7.

5. To repeat yet another point from Chapter 7: Within a given WFF, each reference to a variable is either **free** or **bound.** A reference is bound if (a) it appears immediately following a quantifier (i.e., it denotes the *quantified variable*) or (b) it lies within the scope of a quantifier and refers to the applicable quantified variable. A variable reference is free if and only if it is not bound.

6. A **closed WFF** is one that contains no free variable references (in fact, it is a proposition). An **open WFF** is a WFF that is not closed.

Interpretations and Models

What do WFFs *mean?* In order to provide a formal answer to this question, we introduce the notion of an **interpretation.** An interpretation of a set of WFFs is defined as follows:

- First, we specify a **universe of discourse** over which those WFFs are to be interpreted. In other words, we specify a *mapping* between (a) the permitted constants of the formal system (the domain values, in database terms) and (b) objects in "the real world." Each individual constant corresponds to precisely one object in the universe of discourse.

- Second, we specify a meaning for each predicate in terms of objects in the universe of discourse.

- Third, we also specify a meaning for each function in terms of objects in the universe of discourse.

Then the interpretation consists of the combination of the universe of discourse, plus the mapping of individual constants to objects in that universe, plus the defined meanings for the predicates and functions with respect to that universe.

By way of example, let the universe of discourse be the set of integers $\{0,1,2,3,4,5\}$; let constants such as "2" correspond to objects in that universe in the obvious way; and let the predicate "$x > y$" be defined to have the usual meaning. (We could also define functions such as "+", "-", etc., if desired.) Now we can assign truth values to WFFs such as the following, as indicated:

```
2 > 1                    :  true
2 > 3                    :  false
EXISTS x ( x > 2 )       :  true
FORALL x ( x > 2 )       :  false
```

Note, however, that other interpretations are possible. For example, we might specify the universe of discourse to be a set of security classification levels, as follows:

```
destroy before reading  (level 5)
destroy after reading   (level 4)
top secret               (level 3)
secret                   (level 2)
confidential             (level 1)
unclassified             (level 0)
```

The predicate ">" could now mean "more secure (i.e., higher classification) than."

Now, you will probably realize that the two possible interpretations just given are *isomorphic*—i.e., it is possible to set up a one-to-one correspondence between them, and hence at a deep level the two interpretations are really one and the same. But it must be clearly understood that interpretations can exist that are genuinely different in kind. For example, we might once again take the universe of discourse to be the integers 0 to 5, but define the predicate ">" to mean *equality*. (Of course, we would probably cause a lot of confusion that way, but at least we would be within our rights to do so.) Now the first WFF in the list above would evaluate to *false* instead of *true*.

Another point that must be clearly understood is that two interpretations might be genuinely different in the foregoing sense and yet give the same truth values for the given set of WFFs. This would be the case with the two different definitions of ">" in our example if the WFF "2 > 1" were omitted.

Note, incidentally, that all of the WFFs we have been discussing in this subsection so far have been *closed* WFFs. The reason is that, given an interpretation, it is always possible to assign a truth value unambiguously to a closed WFF, but the truth value of an open WFF will depend on the values assigned to the free variables. For example, the open WFF

```
x > 3
```

is (obviously) *true* if the value of *x* is greater than 3 and *false* otherwise (whatever "greater than" and "3" mean in the interpretation).

Now we define a **model** of a set of (necessarily closed) WFFs to be an interpretation for which all WFFs in the set are *true*. The two interpretations given above for the four WFFs

```
2 > 1
2 > 3
EXISTS x ( x > 2 )
FORALL x ( x > 2 )
```

in terms of the integers 0 to 5 were not models for those WFFs, because some of the WFFs evaluated to *false* under that interpretation. By contrast, the first interpretation (in which ">" was defined "properly") *would* have been a model for the set of WFFs

```
2 > 1
3 > 2
EXISTS x ( x > 2 )
FORALL x ( x > 2 OR NOT ( x > 2 ) )
```

Note finally that, since a given set of WFFs can admit of several interpretations in which all of the WFFs evaluate to *true,* it can therefore have several *models* (in general). Thus, a database can have several models (in general), since—in the model-theoretic view—a database *is* just a set of WFFs. See Section 23.5.

Clausal Form

Just as any propositional calculus formula can be converted to conjunctive normal form, so any predicate calculus WFF can be converted to **clausal form,** which can be regarded as an extended version of conjunctive normal form. One motivation for making such a conversion is that (again) it allows us to apply the resolution rule in constructing or verifying proofs, as we will see.

The conversion process proceeds as follows (in outline; for more details, see reference [23.10]). We illustrate the steps by applying them to a sample WFF, namely

```
FORALL x ( p ( x ) AND EXISTS y ( FORALL z ( q ( y, z ) ) ) )
```

Here *p* and *q* are predicates and *x, y,* and *z* are variables.

1. Eliminate "➡" symbols as in Section 23.3. In our example, this first transformation has no effect.

2. Use De Morgan's laws, plus the fact that two adjacent NOTs cancel out, to move NOTs so that they apply only to terms, not to general WFFs. (Again this particular transformation has no effect in our particular example.)

3. Convert the WFF to **prenex normal form** by moving all quantifiers to the front (systematically renaming variables if necessary):

   `FORALL x ( EXISTS y ( FORALL z ( p ( x ) AND q ( y, z ) ) ) )`

4. Note that an existentially quantified WFF such as

   `EXISTS v ( r ( v ) )`

   is equivalent to the WFF

   `r ( a )`

   for some unknown constant *a;* that is, the original WFF asserts that some such *a* does exist, we just do not know its value. Likewise, a WFF such as

   `FORALL u ( EXISTS v ( s ( u, v ) ) )`

   is equivalent to the WFF

   `FORALL u ( s ( u, f ( u ) ) )`

   for some unknown function *f* of the universally quantified variable *u*. The constant *a* and the function *f* in these examples are known, respectively, as a **Skolem constant** and a **Skolem function,** after the logician T. A. Skolem. (*Note:* A Skolem constant is really just a Skolem function with no arguments.) So the next step is to eliminate existential quantifiers by replacing the corresponding quantified variables by (arbitrary) Skolem functions of all universally quantified variables that precede the quantifier in question in the WFF:

   `FORALL x ( FORALL z ( p ( x ) AND q ( f ( x ), z ) ) )`

5. All variables are now universally quantified. We can therefore adopt a convention by which all variables are *implicitly* universally quantified and so drop the explicit quantifiers:

   `p ( x ) AND q ( f ( x ), z )`

6. Convert the WFF to conjunctive normal form, i.e., to a set of clauses all ANDed together, each clause involving possibly NOTs and ORs but no ANDs. In our example, the WFF is already in this form.

7. Write each clause on a separate line and drop the ANDs:

```
p ( x )
q ( f ( x ), z )
```

This is the clausal form equivalent of the original WFF.

Note: It follows from the foregoing procedure that the general form of a WFF in clausal form is a set of clauses, each on a line of its own, and each of the form

```
NOT A1 OR NOT A2 OR ... OR NOT Am OR B1 OR B2 OR ... OR Bn
```

where the *A*'s and *B*'s are all nonnegated terms. We can rewrite such a clause, if we like, as

```
A1 AND A2 AND ... AND Am  =►  B1 OR B2 OR ... OR Bn
```

If there is at most one *B* (*n* = 0 or 1), the clause is called a **Horn clause,** after the logician Alfred Horn.

Using the Resolution Rule

Now we are in a position to see how a logic-based database system can deal with queries. We use the example from the end of Section 23.2. First, we have a predicate MOTHER_OF, which involves two parameters representing mother and daughter, respectively, and we are given the following two terms (predicate instances):

1. MOTHER_OF (Anne, Betty)

2. MOTHER_OF (Betty, Celia)

We are also given the following WFF (the "deductive axiom"):

3. MOTHER_OF (x, y) AND MOTHER_OF (y, z) =►
                              GRANDMOTHER_OF (x, z)

(note that this is a Horn clause). In order to simplify the application of the resolution rule, let us rewrite the clause to eliminate the "=►" symbol:

4. NOT MOTHER_OF (x, y) OR NOT MOTHER_OF (y, z) OR
                              GRANDMOTHER_OF (x, z)

We now proceed to prove that Anne is the grandmother of Celia—i.e., we show how to answer the query "Is Anne Celia's grandmother?" We begin by negating the conclusion that is to be proved and adopting it as an additional premise:

5. NOT GRANDMOTHER_OF (Anne, Celia)

Now, to apply the resolution rule, we must systematically substitute values for variables in such a way that we can find two clauses that contain, respectively, a WFF and its negation. Such substitution is legitimate because the variables are all implicitly universally quantified, and hence individual (nonnegated) WFFs must be *true* for each and every legal combinations of values of their variables. *Note:* The process of finding a set of substitutions that make two clauses resolvable in this manner is known as **unification.**

To see how the foregoing works in the case at hand, note first that lines 4 and 5 contain the terms GRANDMOTHER_OF (x,z) and NOT GRANDMOTHER_OF (Anne,Celia), respectively. So we substitute Anne for x and Celia for z in line 4 and resolve, to obtain

6. `NOT MOTHER_OF ( Anne, y ) OR NOT MOTHER_OF ( y, Celia )`

Line 2 contains MOTHER_OF (Betty,Celia). So we substitute Betty for y in line 6 and resolve, to obtain

7. `NOT MOTHER_OF ( Anne, Betty )`

Resolving line 7 and line 1, we obtain the empty set of clauses []: *Contradiction.* Hence the answer to the original query is "Yes, Anne is Celia's grandmother." ∎

What about the query "Who are the granddaughters of Anne?" Observe first of all that the system does not know about granddaughters, it only knows about grandmothers. We could add another deductive axiom to the effect that z is the granddaughter of x if and only if x is the grandmother of z (no males are allowed in this database). Alternatively, of course, we could rephrase the question as "Who is Anne the grandmother of?" Let us consider this latter formulation. The premises are (to repeat)

1. `MOTHER_OF ( Anne,  Betty )`

2. `MOTHER_OF ( Betty, Celia )`

3. `NOT MOTHER_OF ( x, y ) OR NOT MOTHER_OF ( y, z ) OR`
   `                        GRANDMOTHER_OF ( x, z )`

We introduce a fourth premise, as follows:

4. `NOT GRANDMOTHER_OF ( Anne, r ) OR RESULT ( r )`

Intuitively, this new premise states that either Anne is not the grandmother of anyone, or alternatively there is some person r who belongs in the result (because she *is* the grandmother of that person r). We wish to discover the identity of all such persons r. We proceed as follows.

First, substitute Anne for x and r for z and resolve lines 4 and 3, to obtain

5. `NOT MOTHER_OF ( Anne, y ) OR NOT MOTHER_OF ( y, z )`
   `                        OR RESULT ( z )`

Next, substitute Betty for y and resolve lines 5 and 1, to obtain

6. `NOT MOTHER_OF ( Betty, z ) OR RESULT ( z )`

Now substitute Celia for z and resolve lines 6 and 2, to obtain

7. `RESULT ( Celia )`

Hence Anne is the grandmother of Celia. ∎

Note: If we had been given an additional term, as follows—

`MOTHER_OF ( Betty, Delia )`

—then we could have substituted Delia for *z* in the final step (instead of Celia) and obtained

```
RESULT ( Delia )
```

The user expects to see both names in the result, of course. Thus, the system needs to apply the unification and resolution process exhaustively to generate all *possible* result values. Details of this refinement are beyond the scope of the present discussion.

23.5   A PROOF-THEORETIC VIEW OF DATABASES

As explained in Section 23.4, a *clause* is an expression of the form

```
A1 AND A2 AND ... AND Am  ⇒  B1 OR B2 OR ... OR Bn
```

where the *A*'s and *B*'s are all terms of the form

```
r ( x1, x2, ..., xt )
```

(here *r* is a predicate and *x1, x2, ..., xt* are the arguments to that predicate). Following reference [23.12], we now consider two important special cases of this general construct:

- *Case 1: m = 0, n = 1*

  In this case the clause can be simplified to just

  ```
  ⇒  B1
  ```

  or in other words (dropping the implication symbol) to just

  ```
  r ( x1, x2, ..., xt )
  ```

  for some predicate *r* and some set of arguments *x1, x2, ..., xt.* If the *x*'s are all constants, the clause represents a **ground axiom**—i.e., it is a statement that is unequivocally *true.* In database terms, such a statement corresponds to a tuple of some relvar *R.** The predicate *r* corresponds to the "meaning" of relvar *R,* as explained elsewhere in this book. For example, in the suppliers and parts database, there is a relvar called SP, the meaning of which is that the indicated supplier (S#) supplies the indicated part (P#) in the indicated quantity (QTY). Note that this meaning corresponds to an **open WFF,** since it includes references to free variables (S#, P#, and QTY). By contrast, the tuple (S1,P1,300)—in which the arguments are all constants—is a ground axiom or **closed WFF** that asserts unequivocally that supplier S1 supplies part P1 in a quantity of 300.

- *Case 2: m > 0, n = 1*

  In this case the clause takes the form

  ```
  A1 AND A2 AND ... AND Am  ⇒  B
  ```

---

*Or to a value in some domain.

which can be regarded as a **deductive axiom;** it gives a (possibly incomplete) definition of the predicate on the right-hand side of the implication symbol in terms of those on the left-hand side (see the definition of the GRANDMOTHER_OF predicate earlier for an example).

Alternatively, such a clause might be regarded as defining an **integrity constraint**—a *relvar* constraint, as it happens, to use the terminology of Chapter 8. Suppose for the sake of the example that the suppliers relvar S has just two attributes, S# and CITY. Then the clause

```
S ( s, c1 ) AND S ( s, c2 )  =►  c1 = c2
```

expresses the constraint that CITY is functionally dependent on S#. Note the use of the builtin predicate "=" in this example.

As the foregoing discussions demonstrate, tuples in relations ("ground axioms"), derived relations ("deductive axioms"), and integrity constraints can all be regarded as special cases of the general *clause* construct. Let us now try to see how these ideas can lead to the "proof-theoretic" view of a database mentioned in Section 23.2.

First, the traditional view of a database can be regarded as **model**-theoretic. By "traditional view" here, we simply mean a view in which the database is perceived as consisting of a collection of explicitly named relvars, each consisting of a set of explicit tuples, together with an explicit set of integrity constraints. It is this perception that can be characterized as *model-theoretic,* as we now explain.

- The underlying domains contain values or constants that are supposed to stand for certain objects in the "real world" (more precisely, in some **interpretation,** in the sense of Section 23.4). They thus correspond to the universe of discourse.

- The relvars (more precisely, the relvar *headings*) represent a set of predicates or open WFFs that are to be interpreted over that universe. For example, the heading of relvar SP represents the predicate "Supplier S# supplies part P# in quantity QTY."

- Each tuple in a given relvar represents an instantiation of the corresponding predicate; i.e., it represents a proposition (a closed WFF—it contains no variables) that is unequivocally *true* in the universe of discourse.

- The integrity constraints are also closed WFFs, and they are interpreted over the same universe. Since the data does not (i.e., *must* not!) violate the constraints, these constraints necessarily evaluate to *true* as well.

- The tuples and the integrity constraints can together be regarded as the set of axioms defining a certain **logical theory** (loosely speaking, a "theory" in logic *is* a set of axioms). Since those axioms are all *true* in the interpretation, then by definition that interpretation is a **model** of that logical theory, in the sense of Section 23.4. Note that, as pointed out in that section, the model might not be unique—that is, a given database might have several possible interpretations, all of them equally valid from a logical standpoint.

In the model-theoretic view, therefore, the "meaning" of the database *is* the model, in the foregoing sense of the term "model." And since there are many possible models, there are many possible meanings, at least in principle.* Furthermore, query processing in the model-theoretic view is essentially a process of evaluating a certain open WFF to discover which values of the free variables in that WFF cause the WFF to evaluate to *true* within the model.

So much for the model-theoretic view. However, in order to be able to apply the rules of inference described in Sections 23.3 and 23.4, it is necessary to adopt a different perspective, one in which the database is explicitly regarded as a certain logical theory, i.e., as a set of axioms. The "meaning" of the database then becomes, precisely, the collection of all *true* statements that can be deduced from those axioms—i.e., it is the set of **theorems** that can be proved from those axioms. This is the **proof-theoretic** view. In this view, query evaluation becomes a theorem-proving process (conceptually speaking, at any rate; in the interests of efficiency, however, the system is likely to use more conventional query processing techniques, as we will see in Section 23.7).

Note: It follows from the foregoing paragraph that one difference between the model- and proof-theoretic views (intuitively speaking) is that, whereas a database can have many "meanings" in the model-theoretic view, it typically has precisely one "meaning" in the proof-theoretic view—except that (a) as pointed out earlier, that one meaning is really *the* canonical meaning in the model-theoretic case, and in any case (b) the remark to the effect that there is only one meaning in the proof-theoretic case ceases to be true, in general, if the database includes any negative axioms [23.9–23.10].

The axioms for a given database (proof-theoretic view) can be informally summarized as follows [23.15]:

1. Ground axioms, corresponding to the values in the domains and the tuples in the base relvars. These axioms constitute what is sometimes called the **extensional database** (as opposed to the *intensional* database—see the next section).

2. A "completion axiom" for each relvar, which states that failure of an otherwise valid tuple to appear in the relvar in question can be interpreted as meaning that the proposition corresponding to that tuple is *false*. (In fact, of course, these completion axioms taken together constitute the **Closed World Assumption,** already discussed in Chapter 7.) For example, the fact that the suppliers relvar S does not include the tuple (S6,White,45,Rome) means the proposition "There exists a supplier S6 named White with status 45 located in Rome" is *false*.

3. The "unique name" axiom, which states that every constant is distinguishable from all of the others (i.e., it has a unique name).

4. The "domain closure" axiom, which states that no constants exist other than those in the database domains.

5. A set of axioms (essentially standard) to define the builtin *equality* predicate. These axioms are needed because the axioms in Nos. 2, 3, and 4 above all make use of the equality predicate.

---

*However, if we assume that the database does not explicitly contain any negative information (e.g., a proposition of the form "NOT S#(S9)," meaning that S9 is not a supplier number), there will also be a "minimal" or *canonical* meaning, which is the intersection of all possible models [23.10]. In this case, moreover, that canonical meaning will be the same as the meaning ascribed to the database under the proof-theoretic view, to be explained in a few moments.

We conclude this section with a brief summary of the principal differences between the two perceptions (model-theoretic and proof-theoretic). First of all, it has to be said that from a purely pragmatic standpoint there might not be very much difference at all!—at least in terms of the DBMSs of today. However:

- Nos. 2–5 in the list of axioms for the proof-theoretic view make explicit certain assumptions that are implicit in the notion of interpretation in the model-theoretic view [23.15]. Stating assumptions explicitly is generally a good idea; furthermore, it is necessary to specify those additional axioms explicitly in order to be able to apply general proof techniques, such as the resolution method described in Sections 23.3 and 23.4.

- Note that the list of axioms makes no mention of integrity constraints. The reason for that omission is that (in the proof-theoretic view) adding such constraints converts the system into a **deductive** DBMS. See Section 23.6.

- The proof-theoretic view does enjoy a certain elegance that the model-theoretic view does not, inasmuch as it provides a uniform perception of several constructs that are usually thought of as more or less distinct: base data, queries, integrity constraints (the previous point notwithstanding), virtual data (etc.). As a consequence, the possibility arises of more uniform interfaces and more uniform implementations.

- The proof-theoretic view also provides a natural basis for treating certain problems that relational systems have traditionally always had difficulty with—**disjunctive information** (e.g., "Supplier S6 is located in either Paris or Rome"), the derivation of **negative information** (e.g., "Who is not a supplier?"), and **recursive queries** (see the next section)—though in this last case, at least, there is no reason in principle why a classical relational system could not be extended appropriately to deal with such queries, and several commercial products already have been (see also Appendix B). We will have more to say regarding such matters in Sections 23.6 and 23.7.

- Finally, to quote Reiter [23.15], the proof-theoretic view "provides a correct treatment of [extensions to] the relational model to incorporate more real-world semantics" (as noted in Section 23.2).

23.6   DEDUCTIVE DATABASE SYSTEMS

A **deductive DBMS** is a DBMS that supports the proof-theoretic view of a database, and in particular is capable of deducing or inferring additional facts from the given facts in the extensional database by applying specified **deductive axioms** or **rules of inference** to those given facts.* The deductive axioms, together with the integrity constraints (discussed below), form what is sometimes called the **intensional database,** and the extensional database and the intensional database together constitute what is usually called the *deductive database* (not a very good term, since it is the DBMS, not the database, that carries out the deductions).

---

*In this connection, it is worth noting that Codd was claiming as far back as 1974 that one of the objectives of the relational model was precisely "to merge the fact retrieval and file management fields in preparation for the addition at a later time of inferential services in the commercial world" [11.2,25.8].

As just indicated, the deductive axioms form one part of the intensional database. The other part consists of additional axioms that represent integrity constraints (i.e., rules whose primary purpose is to constrain updates, though actually such rules can also be used in the process of deducing additional facts from the given ones).

Let us see what the suppliers and parts database of Fig. 3.8 would look like in "deductive DBMS" form. First, there will be a set of ground axioms defining the legal domain values. *Note:* In what follows, for readability reasons, we adopt essentially the same conventions regarding the representation of values as we did in (e.g.) Fig. 3.8, thereby writing 300 as a convenient shorthand for QTY(300), etc.

```
S# ( S1 )     NAME ( Smith )   STATUS (  5 )   CITY ( London )
S# ( S2 )     NAME ( Jones )   STATUS ( 10 )   CITY ( Paris  )
S# ( S3 )     NAME ( Blake )   STATUS ( 15 )   CITY ( Rome   )
S# ( S4 )     NAME ( Clark )   etc.            CITY ( Athens )
S# ( S5 )     NAME ( Adams )                   etc.
S# ( S6 )     NAME ( White )
S# ( S7 )     NAME ( Nut   )
etc.          NAME ( Bolt  )
              NAME ( Screw )
              etc.
```

etc., etc., etc.

Next, there will be ground axioms for the tuples in the base relations:

```
S ( S1, Smith, 20, London )
S ( S2, Jones, 10, Paris  )
etc.

P ( P1, Nut, Red, 12, London )
etc.

SP ( S1, P1, 300 )
etc.
```

Note: We are not seriously suggesting that the extensional database will be created by explicitly listing all of the ground axioms as indicated above; rather, of course, traditional data definition and data entry methods will be used. In other words, deductive DBMSs will typically apply their deductions to conventional databases that already exist and have been constructed in the conventional manner. Note, however, that it now becomes more important than ever that the extensional database not violate any of the declared integrity constraints!—because a database that does violate any such constraints represents (in logical terms) an inconsistent set of axioms, and it is well known that *absolutely any proposition whatsoever* can be proved to be "true" from such a starting point (in other words, contradictions can be derived). For exactly the same reason, it is also important that the stated set of integrity constraints be consistent.

Now for the intensional database. Here are the attribute constraints:

```
S ( s, sn, st, sc )  ⇒  S# ( s ) AND
                        NAME ( sn ) AND
                        STATUS ( st ) AND
                        CITY ( sc )
```

```
P ( p, pn, pl, pw, pc )  ⇒  P# ( p ) AND
                             NAME ( pn ) AND
                             COLOR ( pl ) AND
                             WEIGHT ( pw ) AND
                             CITY ( pc )
etc.
```

Candidate key constraints:

```
S ( s, sn1, st1, sc1 ) AND S ( s, sn2, st2, sc2 )
               ⇒  sn1 = sn2 AND
                   st1 = st2 AND
                   sc1 = sc2
etc.
```

Foreign key constraints:

```
SP ( s, p, q )  ⇒  S ( s, sn, st, sc ) AND
                   P ( p, pn, pl, pw, pc )
```

And so on. *Note:* We assume for the sake of the exposition that variables appearing on the right-hand side of the implication symbol and not on the left-hand side (*sn, st,* etc., in the example) are existentially quantified. (All others are universally quantified, as explained in Section 23.4.) Technically, we need some Skolem functions; *sn,* for example, should really be replaced by (say) SN(s), where SN is a Skolem function.

Notice, incidentally, that most of the constraints shown above are not pure clauses in the sense of Section 23.5, because the right-hand side is not just a disjunction of simple terms.

Now let us add some more deductive axioms:

```
S ( s, sn, st, sc ) AND st > 15
               ⇒  GOOD_SUPPLIER ( s, st, sc )
```

(compare the GOOD_SUPPLIER view definition in Chapter 9, Section 9.1).

```
S ( sx, sxn, sxt, sc ) AND S ( sy, syn, syt, sc )
                    ⇒  SS_COLOCATED ( sx, sy )

S ( s, sn, st, c ) AND P ( p, pn, pl, pw, c )
                    ⇒  SP_COLOCATED ( s, p )
```

And so on.

In order to make the example a little more interesting, let us now extend the database to include a "part structure" relvar, showing which parts *px* contain which parts *py* as immediate (i.e. first-level) components. First a constraint to show that *px* and *py* must both identify existing parts:

```
PART_STRUCTURE ( px, py )  ⇒  P ( px, xn, xl, xw, xc ) AND
                              P ( py, yn, yl, yw, yc )
```

Some data values:

```
PART_STRUCTURE ( P1, P2 )
PART_STRUCTURE ( P1, P3 )
PART_STRUCTURE ( P2, P3 )
PART_STRUCTURE ( P2, P4 )
etc.
```

(In practice PART_STRUCTURE would probably also have a "quantity" argument, showing how many *py*'s it takes to make a *px,* but we omit this refinement for simplicity.)

Now we add a pair of deductive axioms to explain what it means for part *px* to contain part *py* as a component (at any level):

```
PART_STRUCTURE ( px, py )  ⇒  COMPONENT_OF ( px, py )

PART_STRUCTURE ( px, pz )  AND COMPONENT_OF ( pz, py )
                        ⇒  COMPONENT_OF ( px, py )
```

In other words, part *py* is a component of part *px* (at some level) if it is either an immediate component of part *px* or an immediate component of some part *pz* that is in turn a component (at some level) of part *px*. Note that the second axiom here is recursive—it defines the COMPONENT_OF predicate in terms of itself.* By contrast, relational systems have historically not permitted view definitions (or queries or integrity constraints or . . .) to be recursive in such a manner. This ability to support recursion is one of the most immediately obvious distinctions between deductive DBMSs and their classical relational counterparts—although, as mentioned in Section 23.5 (and saw in Chapter 6), there is no fundamental reason why classical relational systems should not be extended to support such recursion, and some already have been.

We will have more to say regarding recursion in Section 23.7.

Datalog

From the foregoing discussion, it should be clear that one of the most directly visible portions of a deductive DBMS will be a language in which the deductive axioms (usually called **rules**) can be formulated. The best-known example of such a language is called (by analogy with Prolog) **Datalog** [23.9]. We present a brief discussion of Datalog in this subsection. *Note:* The emphasis in Datalog is on its descriptive power, not its computational power (as in fact was also the case with the original relational model [5.1]). The objective is to define a language that ultimately will have greater expressive power than conventional relational languages [23.9]. As a consequence, the stress in Datalog—indeed, the stress throughout logic-based systems in general—is very heavily on query, not update, though it is possible, and desirable, to extend the language to support update also (see later).

In its simplest form, Datalog supports the formulation of rules as simple Horn clauses without functions. In Section 23.4, we defined a Horn clause to be a WFF of either of the following two forms:

```
A1 AND A2 AND ... AND An

A1 AND A2 AND ... AND An  ⇒  B
```

---

*In fact, of course, we have defined a *transitive closure*—at any given time, the relation corresponding to COMPONENT_OF is the transitive closure of the relation corresponding to PART_STRUCTURE (see Chapter 6).

(where the *A*'s and *B* are nonnegated predicate instances involving only constants and variables). Following the style of Prolog, however, Datalog actually writes the second of these the other way around:

```
B  ⇐  A1 AND A2 AND ... AND An
```

For consistency with other publications in this area, therefore, we will do the same in what follows.

In such a clause, *B* is the **rule head** (or conclusion) and the *A*'s are the **rule body** (or premises or **goal;** each individual *A* is a **subgoal**). For brevity, the ANDs are often replaced by commas. A **Datalog program** is a set of such clauses separated in some conventional manner—e.g., by semicolons (in this book, however, we will not use semicolons but instead will simply start each new clause on a new line). No meaning attaches to the order of the clauses within such a program.

Note that *the entire "deductive database"* can be regarded as a Datalog program in the foregoing sense. For example, we could take all of the axioms stated above for suppliers and parts (the ground axioms, the integrity constraints, and the deductive axioms), write them all in Datalog style, separate them by semicolons or by writing them on separate lines, and the result would be a Datalog program. As noted earlier, however, the extensional part of the database will typically *not* be specified in such a fashion, but rather in some more conventional manner. Thus, the primary aim of Datalog is to support the formulation of deductive axioms specifically. As already pointed out, that function can be regarded as an extension of the view definition mechanism found in conventional relational DBMSs today.

Datalog can also be used as a query language (again, much like Prolog). For example, suppose we have been given the following Datalog definition of GOOD_SUPPLIER:

```
GOOD_SUPPLIER ( s, st, sc )  ⇐  S ( s, sn, st, sc )
                                 AND st > 15
```

Here then are some typical queries against GOOD_SUPPLIER:

1. Get all good suppliers:

```
?  ⇐  GOOD_SUPPLIER ( s, st, sc )
```

2. Get good suppliers in Paris:

```
?  ⇐  GOOD_SUPPLIER ( s, st, Paris )
```

3. Is supplier S1 a good supplier?

```
?  ⇐  GOOD_SUPPLIER ( S1, st, sc )
```

And so on. In other words, a query in Datalog consists of a special rule with a head of "?" and a body consisting of a single term that denotes the query result; the head "?" means (by convention) "Display."

It should be pointed out that, despite the fact that it does support recursion, there are quite a few features of conventional relational languages that Datalog as originally defined did *not* support: scalar operators ("+", "*", etc.), aggregate operators (COUNT, SUM, etc.), set difference (because clauses cannot be negated), grouping and ungrouping, etc. It also did not support attribute naming (the significance of a predicate argument depended on its ordinal position), nor did it provide full domain support (i.e., user-defined types in the sense of Chapter 5). As indicated earlier in this section, it also did not provide any update operations, nor (as a consequence of this latter fact) did it support the declarative specification of foreign key delete and update rules (ON DELETE CASCADE, etc.).

In order to address some of the foregoing shortcomings, a variety of extensions to basic Datalog have been proposed. Those extensions are intended to provide the following features, among others:

- *Negative premises*—for example:

```
SS_COLOCATED ( sx, sy )   ⬅= S ( sx, sxn, sxt, sc ) AND
                            S ( sy, syn, syt, sc ) AND
                            NOT ( sx = sy )
```

- *Scalar operators* (builtin and user-defined)—for example:

```
P_WT_IN_GRAMS ( p, pn, pl, pg, pc )   ⬅=
                P ( p, pn, pl, pw, pc ) AND pg = pw * 454
```

In this example we have assumed that the builtin function "*" can be written using conventional infix notation. A more orthodox logic representation of the term following the AND would be "$=(pg,*(pw,454))$".

- *Grouping and aggregate operators* (somewhat along the lines of our relational SUMMARIZE operator—see Chapter 6): Such operators are necessary in order to address (for example) what is sometimes called the *gross requirements* problem, which is the problem of finding, not only which parts *py* are components of some part *px* at any level, but also *how many py*'s (at all levels) it takes to make a *px*. (Naturally we are assuming here that relvar PART_STRUCTURE includes a QTY attribute.)

- *Update operations:* One approach to meeting this obvious requirement—not the only one—is based on the observations that in basic Datalog, (a) any predicate in a rule head must be nonnegated and (b) every tuple generated by the rule can be regarded as being "inserted" into the result. A possible extension would thus be to allow negated predicates in a rule head and to treat the negation as requesting the *deletion* (of pertinent tuples).

- *NonHorn clauses in the rule body*—in other words, allow completely general WFFs in the definition of rules.

A survey of the foregoing extensions, with examples, can be found in the book by Gardarin and Valduriez [23.10], which also discusses a variety of Datalog implementation techniques.

23.7 RECURSIVE QUERY PROCESSING

As indicated in the previous section, one of the most notable features of deductive database systems is their support for recursion (recursive rule definitions, and hence recursive queries also). As a consequence of this fact, the past few years have seen a great deal of research into techniques for implementing such recursion—indeed, just about every database conference since 1986 or so has included at least one paper on the subject (see the "References and Bibliography" section at the end of this chapter). Since recursive query support represents a problem that has historically not existed in classical DBMSs, we discuss it briefly in the present section.

By way of example, we repeat from Section 23.6 the recursive definition of the COMPONENT_OF in terms of PART_STRUCTURE (for brevity, however, we now abbreviate PART_STRUCTURE to PS and COMPONENT_OF to COMP; we also convert the definition to Datalog form):

```
COMP ( px, py )  ⇐  PS ( px, py )

COMP ( px, py )  ⇐  PS ( px, pz ) AND COMP ( pz, py )
```

Here is a typical recursive query against this database ("Explode part P1"):

```
?  ⇐  COMP ( P1, py )
```

To return to the definition for a moment: The second rule in that definition—i.e., the recursive rule—is said to be **linearly** recursive, because the predicate in the rule head appears just once in the rule body. Here by contrast is a definition for COMP in which the second (recursive) rule is not linearly recursive in the same sense:

```
COMP ( px, py )  ⇐  PS ( px, py )

COMP ( px, py )  ⇐  COMP ( px, pz ) AND COMP ( pz, py )
```

However, there is a general feeling that linear recursion represents "the interesting case," in the sense that most recursions that arise in practice are naturally linear, and furthermore there are known efficient techniques for dealing with the linear case [23.16]. We therefore restrict our attention to linear recursion for the remainder of this section.

Note: For completeness, we should point out that it is necessary to generalize the definition of "recursive rule" (and of linear recursion) to deal with more complex cases such as the following:

```
P ( x, y )  ⇐  Q ( x, z ) AND R ( z, y )

Q ( x, y )  ⇐  P ( x, z ) AND S ( z, y )
```

For brevity, we ignore such refinements here; see reference [23.16] for a more detailed discussion.

As in classical (i.e., nonrecursive) query processing, the overall problem of implementing a given recursive query can be divided into two subproblems, namely (a) transforming the original query into some equivalent but more efficient form and then (b) actually executing the result of that transformation. The literature contains descriptions of a variety of attacks on both of these problems (again, see the "References and Bibliography" section). In the present section, we briefly discuss some of the simpler techniques, showing their application to the query "Explode part P1" on the following sample data:

PS	PX	PY
	P1	P2
	P1	P3
	P2	P3
	P2	P4
	P3	P5
	P4	P5
	P5	P6

Unification and Resolution

One possible approach, of course, is to use the standard Prolog techniques of **unification and resolution** as described in Section 23.4. In the example, this approach works as follows. The first premises are the deductive axioms, which look like this (in conjunctive normal form):

1. NOT PS (*px, py*) OR COMP (*px, py*)

2. NOT PS (*px, pz*) OR NOT COMP (*pz, py*) OR COMP (*px, py*)

We construct another premise from the desired conclusion:

3. NOT COMP (P1, *py*) OR RESULT (*py*)

The ground axioms form the remaining premises. Consider, for example, the ground axiom

4. PS (P1, P2)

Substituting P1 for *px* and P2 for *py* in line 1, we can resolve lines 1 and 4 to yield

5. COMP (P1, P2)

Now substituting P2 for *py* in line 3 and resolving lines 3 and 5, we obtain

6. RESULT (P2)

So P2 is a component of P1. An exactly analogous argument will show that P3 is also a component of P1. Now, of course, we have the additional axioms COMP(P1,P2) and COMP(P1,P3); we can now apply the foregoing process recursively to determine the complete explosion. The details are left as an exercise.

In practice, however, unification and resolution can be quite costly in performance. It will thus often be desirable to find some more efficient strategy. The remaining subsections below discuss some possible approaches to this problem.

Naive Evaluation

Naive evaluation [23.25] is probably the simplest approach of all. As the name suggests, the algorithm is very simple-minded; it can most easily be explained (for our sample query) in terms of the following pseudocode:

```
COMP := PS ;
do until COMP reaches a "fixpoint" ;
  COMP := COMP UNION ( COMP * PS ) ;
end ;
DISPLAY := COMP WHERE PX = P# ('P1') ;
```

Relvars COMP and DISPLAY (like relvar PS) each have two attributes, PX and PY. Loosely speaking, the algorithm works by repeatedly forming an intermediate result consisting of the union of the join of PS and the previous intermediate result, until that intermediate result reaches a **fixpoint**—i.e., until it ceases to grow. *Note:* The expression "COMP * PS" is shorthand for "join COMP and PS over COMP.PY and PS.PX and project the result over COMP.PX and PS.PY"; for brevity, we ignore the attribute renaming operations that our dialect of the algebra would require to make this operation work (see Chapter 6).

Let us step through the algorithm with our sample data. After the first iteration of the loop, the value of the expression COMP * PS is as shown below on the left and the resulting value of COMP is as shown below on the right (with tuples added on this iteration flagged with an asterisk):

COMP * PS

PX	PY
P1	P3
P1	P4
P1	P5
P2	P5
P3	P6
P4	P6

COMP

PX	PY	
P1	P2	
P1	P3	
P2	P3	
P2	P4	
P3	P5	
P4	P5	
P5	P6	
P1	P4	*
P1	P5	*
P2	P5	*
P3	P6	*
P4	P6	*

After the second iteration, they look like this:

COMP * PS

PX	PY
P1	P3
P1	P4
P1	P5
P2	P5
P3	P6
P4	P6
P1	P6
P2	P6

COMP

PX	PY	
P1	P2	
P1	P3	
P2	P3	
P2	P4	
P3	P5	
P4	P5	
P5	P6	
P1	P4	
P1	P5	
P2	P5	
P3	P6	
P4	P6	
P1	P6	*
P2	P6	*

Note carefully that the computation of COMP * PS in this second step repeats the entire computation of COMP * PS from the first step but additionally computes some extra tuples (actually two extra tuples—(P1,P6) and (P2,P6)—in the case at hand). This is one reason why the naive evaluation algorithm is not very intelligent.

After the third iteration, the value of COMP ⋇ PS (after more repeated computation) turns out to be the same as on the previous iteration; COMP has thus reached a fixpoint, and we exit from the loop. The final result is then computed as a restriction of COMP:

COMP	PX	PY
	P1	P2
	P1	P3
	P1	P4
	P1	P5
	P1	P6

Another glaring inefficiency is now apparent: The algorithm has effectively computed the explosion for *every* part—in fact, it has computed the entire transitive closure of relation PS—and has then thrown everything away again except for the tuples actually wanted; in other words, again, a great deal of unnecessary work has been done.

We close this subsection by pointing out that the naive evaluation technique can be regarded as an application of forward chaining: Starting from the extensional database (i.e., the actual data values), it applies the premises of the definition (i.e., the rule body) repeatedly until the desired result is obtained. In fact, the algorithm actually computes the *minimal model* for the Datalog program (see Sections 23.5–23.6).

Seminaive Evaluation

The first obvious improvement to the naive evaluation algorithm is to avoid repeating the computations of each step in the next step: **semi**naive evaluation [23.28]. In other words, in each step we compute just the new tuples that need to be appended on this particular iteration. Again we explain the idea in terms of the "Explode part P1" example. Pseudocode:

```
NEW  := PS ;
COMP := NEW ;
do until NEW is empty ;
   NEW  := ( NEW ⋇ PS ) MINUS COMP ;
   COMP := COMP UNION NEW ;
end ;
DISPLAY := COMP WHERE PX = P# ('P1') ;
```

Let us again step through the algorithm. On initial entry into the loop, NEW and COMP are both identical to PS:

NEW	PX	PY		COMP	PX	PY
	P1	P2			P1	P2
	P1	P3			P1	P3
	P2	P3			P2	P3
	P2	P4			P2	P4
	P3	P5			P3	P5
	P4	P5			P4	P5
	P5	P6			P5	P6

At the end of the first iteration, they look like this:

NEW	PX	PY
	P1	P4
	P1	P5
	P2	P5
	P3	P6
	P4	P6

COMP	PX	PY	
	P1	P2	
	P1	P3	
	P2	P3	
	P2	P4	
	P3	P5	
	P4	P5	
	P5	P6	
	P1	P4	*
	P1	P5	*
	P2	P5	*
	P3	P6	*
	P4	P6	*

COMP is the same as it was at this stage under naive evaluation, and NEW is just the new tuples that were added to COMP on this iteration; note in particular that NEW does *not* include the tuple (P1,P3) (compare the naive evaluation counterpart).

At the end of the next iteration we have:

NEW	PX	PY
	P1	P6
	P2	P6

COMP	PX	PY	
	P1	P2	
	P1	P3	
	P2	P3	
	P2	P4	
	P3	P5	
	P4	P5	
	P5	P6	
	P1	P4	
	P1	P5	
	P2	P5	
	P3	P6	
	P4	P6	
	P1	P6	*
	P2	P6	*

The next iteration makes NEW empty, and so we leave the loop.

Static Filtering

Static filtering is a refinement on the basic idea from classical optimization theory of performing restrictions as early as possible. It can be regarded as an application of backward chaining, in that it effectively uses information from the query (the conclusion) to modify the rules (the premises). It is also referred to as *reducing the set of relevant facts,* in that it (again) uses information from the query to eliminate useless tuples in the extensional database right at the outset [23.29]. The effect in terms of our example can be explained in terms of the following pseudocode:

```
NEW   := PS WHERE PX = P# ('P1') ;
COMP := NEW ;
do until NEW is empty ;
   NEW   := ( NEW ⋈ PS ) MINUS COMP ;
   COMP := COMP UNION NEW ;
end ;
DISPLAY := COMP ;
```

Once again we step through the algorithm. On initial entry into the loop, NEW and COMP both look like this:

NEW	PX	PY
	P1	P2
	P1	P3

COMP	PX	PY
	P1	P2
	P1	P3

At the end of the first iteration, they look like this:

NEW	PX	PY
	P1	P4
	P1	P5

COMP	PX	PY	
	P1	P2	
	P1	P3	
	P1	P4	*
	P1	P5	*

At the end of the next iteration we have:

NEW	PX	PY
	P1	P6

COMP	PX	PY	
	P1	P2	
	P1	P3	
	P1	P4	
	P1	P5	
	P1	P6	*

The next iteration makes NEW empty, and so we leave the loop.

This concludes our brief introduction to recursive query processing strategies. Of course, many other approaches have been proposed in the literature, most of them much more sophisticated than the simple ones discussed above; however, there is insufficient space in a book of this nature to cover all of the background material that is needed for a proper understanding of those approaches. See, e.g., references [23.16–23.43] for further discussion.

23.8 SUMMARY

This brings us to the end of our short introduction to the topic of databases that are based on logic. Although the ideas are still restricted for the most part to the research world, a few of them have begun to find their way into commercial relational products (this remark is especially true of some of the optimization techniques). Overall, the concept of logic-based databases does look interesting; several potential advantages were identified at various points in the preceding sections. One further advantage, not mentioned explicitly in the body of the chapter, is that logic could form the basis of a genuinely seamless integration between general-purpose programming languages and the database. In other words, instead of the "embedded data sublanguage" approach supported by SQL products today—an approach that is not particularly elegant, to say the least—the system could provide a single logic-based language in which "data is data," regardless of whether it is kept in a shared database or is local to the application. (Of course, there are a number of obstacles to be overcome before such a goal can be achieved, not the least of which is to demonstrate to the satisfaction of the IT community at large that logic is a suitable basis for a general-purpose programming language in the first place.)

Let us quickly review the major points of the material we have covered. We began with a brief tutorial on **propositional** and **predicate calculus,** introducing the following concepts among others:

- An **interpretation** of a set of WFFs is the combination of (a) a universe of discourse, (b) a mapping from individual constants appearing in those WFFs to objects in that universe, and (c) a set of defined meanings for the predicates and functions appearing in those WFFs.

- A **model** for a set of WFFs is an interpretation for which all WFFs in the set evaluate to *true.* A given set of WFFs can have any number of models (in general).

- A **proof** is the process of showing that some given WFF g (the **conclusion**) is a logical consequence of some given set of WFFs $f1, f2, ..., fn$ (the **premises**). We discussed one proof method, known as **resolution and unification,** in some detail.

We then examined the **proof-theoretic** view of databases. In such a view, the database is regarded as consisting of the combination of an **extensional** database and an **intensional** database. The extensional database contains **ground axioms,** i.e., the base data (loosely speaking); the intensional database contains integrity constraints and **deductive axioms,** i.e., views (again, loosely speaking). The "meaning" of the database then consists of the set of **theorems** that can be deduced from the axioms; executing a query becomes (at least conceptually) a **theorem-proving** process. A **deductive DBMS** is a DBMS that supports this proof-theoretic view. We briefly described **Datalog,** a user language for such a DBMS.

One immediately obvious distinction between Datalog and traditional relational languages is that Datalog supports **recursive** axioms, and hence recursive queries—though there is no reason why the traditional relational algebra and calculus should not be extended to do likewise (see the discussion of the TCLOSE operator in Chapter 6).* We discussed some simple techniques for evaluating such queries.

In conclusion: We opened this chapter by mentioning a number of terms—"logic database," "inferential DBMS," "deductive DBMS," etc., etc.—that are often met with in the research literature (and even in vendor advertising, to some extent). Let us therefore close

---

*It is interesting to observe in this connection that relational DBMSs need to be able to perform recursive processing under the covers anyway, because the catalog will contain certain recursively structured information (view definitions expressed in terms of other view definitions are a case in point).

it by providing some definitions for those terms. We warn you, however, that there is not always consensus on these matters, and different definitions can probably be found in the literature. The following definitions are the ones preferred by the present writer:

- *Recursive query processing:* This is an easy one. Recursive query processing refers to the evaluation, and in particular optimization, of queries whose definition is intrinsically recursive (see Section 23.7).

- *Knowledge base:* This term is sometimes used to mean what we called the intensional database in Section 23.6—i.e., it consists of the *rules* (the integrity constraints and deductive axioms), as opposed to the base data, which constitutes the extensional database. But then other writers use "knowledge base" to mean the combination of both the intensional and extensional databases (see "deductive database" below)—except that, as reference [23.10] puts it, "a knowledge base often includes complex objects [as well as] classical relations" (see Part VI of this book for a discussion of "complex objects"). Then again, the term has another, more specific meaning altogether in natural-language systems. It is probably best to avoid the term entirely.

- *Knowledge:* Another easy one! Knowledge is what is in the knowledge base . . . This definition thus reduces the problem of defining "knowledge" to a previously unsolved problem.

- *Knowledge base management system (KBMS):* The software that manages the knowledge base. The term is typically used as a synonym for deductive DBMS (see the next paragraph).

- *Deductive DBMS:* A DBMS that supports the proof-theoretic view of databases, and in particular is capable of deducing additional information from the extensional database by applying inferential (i.e., deductive) rules that are stored in the intensional database. A deductive DBMS will almost certainly support recursive rules and so perform recursive query processing.

- *Deductive database* (deprecated term): A database that is managed by a deductive DBMS.

- *Expert DBMS:* Synonym for deductive DBMS.

- *Expert database* (deprecated term): A database that is managed by an expert DBMS.

- *Inferential DBMS:* Synonym for deductive DBMS.

- *Logic-based system:* Synonym for deductive DBMS.

- *Logic database* (deprecated term): Synonym for deductive database.

- *Logic as a data model:* A data model consists of (at least) objects, integrity rules, and operators. In a deductive DBMS, the objects, integrity rules, and operators are all represented in the same uniform way, namely as axioms in a logic language such as Datalog; indeed, as explained in Section 23.6, a database in such a system can be regarded, precisely, as a logic program containing axioms of all three kinds. In such a system, therefore, we might legitimately say that the abstract data model for the system *is* logic itself.

EXERCISES

23.1 Use the resolution method to see whether the following metastatements constitute valid proofs in the propositional calculus:

a. $A \Rightarrow B, \ C \Rightarrow B, \ D \Rightarrow (A \ \text{OR} \ C), \ D \ \vdash \ B$

b. $(A \Rightarrow B) \ \text{AND} \ (C \Rightarrow D), \ (B \Rightarrow E \ \text{AND} \ D \Rightarrow F),$
$\text{NOT} \ (E \ \text{AND} \ F), \ A \Rightarrow C \ \vdash \ \text{NOT} \ A$

c. $(A \ \text{OR} \ B) \ \Rightarrow D, \ D \Rightarrow \text{NOT} \ (E \ \text{OR} \ F), \ \text{NOT} \ (B \ \text{AND} \ C \ \text{AND} \ E)$
$\vdash \ \text{NOT} \ (G \Rightarrow \text{NOT} \ (C \ \text{AND} \ H))$

23.2 Convert the following WFFs to clausal form:

a. FORALL x (FORALL y
$(p (x, y) \Rightarrow$ EXISTS z ($q (x, z)$)))

b. EXISTS x (EXISTS y
$(p (x, y) \Rightarrow$ FORALL z ($q (x, z)$)))

c. EXISTS x (EXISTS y
$(p (x, y) \Rightarrow$ EXISTS z ($q (x, z)$)))

23.3 The following is a fairly standard example of a logic database:

```
MAN     ( Adam )
WOMAN   ( Eve )
MAN     ( Cain )
MAN     ( Abel )
MAN     ( Enoch )

PARENT ( Adam, Cain )
PARENT ( Adam, Abel )
PARENT ( Eve, Cain )
PARENT ( Eve, Abel )
PARENT ( Cain, Enoch )

FATHER ( x, y )   <=  PARENT ( x, y ) AND MAN ( x )
MOTHER ( x, y )   <=  PARENT ( x, y ) AND WOMAN ( x )

SIBLING ( x, y )  <=  PARENT ( z, x ) AND PARENT ( z, y )

BROTHER ( x, y )  <=  SIBLING ( x, y ) AND MAN ( x )

SISTER ( x, y )   <=  SIBLING ( x, y ) AND WOMAN ( x )

ANCESTOR ( x, y ) <=  PARENT ( x, y )
ANCESTOR ( x, y ) <=  PARENT ( x, z ) AND ANCESTOR ( z, y )
```

Use the resolution method to answer the following queries:

a. Who is the mother of Cain?

b. Who are Cain's siblings?

c. Who are Cain's brothers?

d. Who are Cain's sisters?

e. Who are Enoch's ancestors?

23.4 Define the terms *interpretation* and *model*.

23.5 Write a set of Datalog axioms for the definitional portion (only) of the suppliers-parts-projects database.

23.6 Give Datalog solutions, where possible, to Exercises 6.13–6.50.

23.7 Give Datalog solutions, where possible, to Exercise 8.1.

23.8 Complete to your own satisfaction the explanation given in Section 23.7 of the unification and resolution implementation of the "Explode part P1" query.

REFERENCES AND BIBLIOGRAPHY

The field of logic-based systems has mushroomed over the past few years; the following list represents a tiny fraction of the literature currently available. It is partially arranged into groups, as follows:

- References [23.1–23.9] are books that either are devoted to the subject of logic in general (particularly in a computing and/or database context) or are collections of papers on logic-based databases specifically.

- References [23.10–23.12] are tutorials, as are the books by Ceri *et al.* [23.46] and Das [23.47].

- References [23.14], [23.17–23.20], [23.30], and [23.49–23.50] are concerned with the transitive closure operation and its implementation.

- References [23.21–23.24] describe an important recursive query processing technique called *magic sets* (and variations thereon). *Note:* In this connection, see also references [17.24–17.26].

The remaining references are included principally to show just how much investigation is going on in this field; they address a variety of aspects of the subject and are presented for the most part without further comment.

23.1 Robert R. Stoll: *Sets, Logic, and Axiomatic Theories.* San Francisco, Calif.: W. H. Freeman and Company (1961).

A good introduction to logic in general.

23.2 Zohar Manna and Richard Waldinger: *The Logical Basis for Computer Programming—Volume I: Deductive Reasoning* (1985); *Volume II: Deductive Techniques* (1990). Reading, Mass.: Addison-Wesley (1985, 1990).

23.3 Peter M. D. Gray: *Logic, Algebra and Databases.* Chichester, England: Ellis Horwood Ltd. (1984).

Contains a good gentle introduction to propositional calculus and predicate calculus (among a number of other relevant topics) from a database point of view.

23.4 Adrian Walker, Michael McCord, John F. Sowa, and Walter G. Wilson: *Knowledge Systems and Prolog* (2nd edition). Reading, Mass.: Addison-Wesley (1990).

This book is about logic programming in general, not logic-based databases specifically, but it contains a great deal that is relevant to the latter topic.

23.5 Hervé Gallaire and Jack Minker: *Logic and Data Bases.* New York, N.Y.: Plenum Publishing Corp. (1978).

One of the first, if not *the* first, collections of papers in the field.

23.6 Larry Kershberg (ed.): *Expert Database Systems* (Proc. 1st Int. Workshop on Expert Database Systems, Kiawah Island, S.C.). Menlo Park, Calif.: Benjamin/Cummings (1986).

An excellent and thought-provoking collection of papers. Not all of them are directly related to the main subject of the present chapter, however. Indeed, the titles of the sections betray a certain degree of confusion as to what the subject of "expert database systems" really is! Those titles are as follows:

1. Theory of knowledge bases
2. Logic programming and databases
3. Expert database system architectures, tools, and techniques
4. Reasoning in expert database systems
5. Intelligent database access and interaction

In addition, there is a keynote paper by John Smith on expert database systems, and reports from working groups on (1) knowledge base management systems, (2) logic programming and databases, and (3) object database systems and knowledge systems. As Kershberg remarks in his preface, the expert database system concept "connotes diverse definitions and decidedly different architectures."

23.7 Jack Minker (ed.): *Foundations of Deductive Databases and Logic Programming.* San Mateo, Calif.: Morgan Kaufmann (1988).

23.8 John Mylopoulos and Michael L. Brodie (eds.): *Readings in Artificial Intelligence and Databases.* San Mateo, Calif.: Morgan Kaufmann (1988).

23.9 Jeffrey D. Ullman: *Database and Knowledge-Base Systems* (in two volumes). Rockville, Md.: Computer Science Press (1988, 1989).

Volume I of this two-volume work includes one (long) chapter (out of a total of 10) that is entirely devoted to the logic-based approach. That chapter (which is the origin of Datalog, incidentally) includes a discussion of the relationship between logic and relational algebra, and another on relational calculus—both domain and tuple versions—as a special case of the logic approach. Volume II includes five chapters (out of seven) on various aspects of logic-based databases.

23.10 Georges Gardarin and Patrick Valduriez: *Relational Databases and Knowledge Bases.* Reading, Mass.: Addison-Wesley (1989).

Contains a chapter on deductive systems that (although tutorial in nature) goes into the underlying theory, optimization algorithms, etc., in much more detail than the present chapter does.

23.11 Michael Stonebraker: *Introduction to* "Integration of Knowledge and Data Management," in Michael Stonebraker (ed.), *Readings in Database Systems.* San Mateo, Calif.: Morgan Kaufmann (1988).

23.12 Hervé Gallaire, Jack Minker, and Jean-Marie Nicolas: "Logic and Databases: A Deductive Approach," *ACM Comp. Surv. 16,* No. 2 (June 1984).

23.13 Veronica Dahl: "On Database Systems Development through Logic," *ACM TODS 7,* No. 1 (March 1982).

A good and clear description of the basic ideas underlying logic-based databases, with examples taken from a Prolog-based prototype implemented by Dahl in 1977.

23.14 Rakesh Agrawal: "Alpha: An Extension of Relational Algebra to Express a Class of Recursive Queries," *IEEE Transactions on Software Engineering 14,* No. 7 (July 1988).

Proposes a new operator called *alpha* that supports the formulation of "a large class of recursive queries" (actually a superset of linear recursive queries) while staying within the framework of conventional relational algebra. The contention is that the *alpha* operator is sufficiently powerful to deal with most practical problems involving recursion, while at the same time being easier to implement efficiently than any completely general recursion mechanism would be. The paper gives several examples of the use of the proposed operator; in particular, it shows how the transitive closure and "gross requirements" problems (see reference [23.17] and Section 23.6, respectively) can both easily be handled.

Reference [23.19] describes some related work on implementation. Reference [23.18] is also relevant.

23.15 Raymond Reiter: "Towards a Logical Reconstruction of Relational Database Theory," in Michael L. Brodie, John Mylopoulos, and Joachim W. Schmidt (eds.), *On Conceptual Modelling: Perspectives from Artificial Intelligence, Databases, and Programming Languages.* New York, N.Y.: Springer Verlag (1984).

As mentioned in Section 23.2, Reiter's work was by no means the first in this area—many researchers had investigated the relationship between logic and databases before (see, e.g., references [23.5], [23.7], and [23.13])—but it seems to have been Reiter's "logical reconstruction of relational theory" that spurred much of the subsequent activity and current high degree of interest in the field.

23.16 François Bancilhon and Raghu Ramakrishnan: "An Amateur's Introduction to Recursive Query Processing Strategies," Proc. 1986 ACM SIGMOD Int. Conf. on Management of Data, Washington, DC (May 1986). Republished in revised form in Michael Stonebraker (ed.), *Readings in Database Systems.* San Mateo, Calif.: Morgan Kaufmann (1988). Also republished in reference [23.8].

An excellent overview. The paper starts by observing that there is both a positive and a negative side to all of the research on the recursive query implementation problem. The positive side is that numerous techniques have been identified that do at least solve the problem; the negative side is that it is not at all clear how to choose the technique that is most appropriate in a given situation (in particular, most of the techniques are presented in the literature with little or no discussion of performance characteristics). Then, after a section describing the basic ideas of logic databases, the paper goes on to describe a number of proposed algorithms—naive evaluation, seminaive evaluation, iterative query/subquery, recursive query/subquery, APEX, Prolog, Henschen/Naqvi, Aho-Ullman, Kifer-Lozinskii, counting, magic sets, and generalized magic sets. The paper compares these different approaches on the basis of application domain (i.e., the class of problems to which the algorithm can usefully be applied), performance, and ease of implementation. The paper also includes performance figures (with comparative analyses) from testing the various algorithms on a simple benchmark.

23.17 Yannis E. Ioannidis: "On the Computation of the Transitive Closure of Relational Operators," Proc. 12th Int. Conf. on Very Large Data Bases, Kyoto, Japan (August 1986).

Transitive closure is an operation of fundamental importance in recursive query processing [23.18]. This paper proposes a new algorithm (based on a "divide and conquer" approach) for implementing that operation. See also references [23.14], [23.18–23.20], and [23.49–23.50].

23.18 H. V. Jagadish, Rakesh Agrawal, and Linda Ness: "A Study of Transitive Closure as a Recursion Mechanism," Proc. 1987 ACM SIGMOD Int. Conf. on Management of Data, San Francisco, Calif. (May 1987).

To quote from the abstract: "[This paper shows] that every linearly recursive query can be expressed as a transitive closure possibly preceded and followed by operations already available in relational algebra." The authors therefore suggest that providing an efficient implementation of transitive closure is sufficient as a basis for providing an efficient implementation of linear recursion in general, and hence for making deductive DBMSs efficient on a large class of recursive problems.

23.19 Rakesh Agrawal and H. Jagadish: "Direct Algorithms for Computing the Transitive Closure of Database Relations," Proc. 13th Int. Conf. on Very Large Data Bases, Brighton, UK (September 1987).

Proposes a set of transitive closure algorithms that "do not view the problem as one of evaluating a recursion, but rather obtain the closure from first principles" (hence the term *direct*). The paper includes a useful summary of earlier work on other direct algorithms.

23.20 Hongjun Lu: "New Strategies for Computing the Transitive Closure of a Database Relation," Proc. 13th Int. Conf. on Very Large Data Bases, Brighton, UK (September 1987).

More algorithms for transitive closure. Like reference [23.19], the paper also includes a useful survey of earlier approaches to the problem.

23.21 François Bancilhon, David Maier, Yehoshua Sagiv, and Jeffrey D. Ullman: "Magic Sets and Other Strange Ways to Implement Logic Programs," Proc. 5th ACM SIGMOD-SIGACT Symposium on Principles of Database Systems (1986).

The basic idea of "magic sets" is to introduce new sets of rules ("magic rules") dynamically that are guaranteed to produce the same result as the original query but are more efficient, in the sense that they reduce the set of "relevant facts" (see Section 23.7). The details are a little complex, and beyond the scope of these notes; refer to the paper or to Bancilhon and Ramakrishnan's survey [23.16] or the books by Ullman [23.9] or Gardarin and Valduriez [23.10] for more explanation. We remark that numerous variations on the basic idea have subsequently been devised—see, e.g., references [23.22–23.24] below. See also references [17.24–17.26].

23.22 Catriel Beeri and Raghu Ramakrishnan: "On the Power of Magic," Proc. 6th ACM SIGMOD-SIGACT Symposium on Principles of Database Systems (1987).

23.23 Domenico Saccà and Carlo Zaniolo: "Magic Counting Methods," Proc. 1987 ACM SIGMOD Int. Conf. on Management of Data, San Francisco, Calif. (May 1987).

23.24 Georges Gardarin: "Magic Functions: A Technique to Optimize Extended Datalog Recursive Programs," Proc. 13th Int. Conf. on Very Large Data Bases, Brighton, UK (September 1987).

23.25 A. Aho and J.D. Ullman: "Universality of Data Retrieval Languages," Proc. 6th ACM Symposium on Principles of Programming Languages, San Antonio, Tx. (January 1979).

Given a sequence of relations $R, f(R), f(f(R)), \ldots$ (where f is some fixed function), the **least fixpoint** of the sequence is defined to be a relation R^* derived in accordance with the following naive evaluation algorithm (see Section 23.7):

```
R* := R ;
do until R* stops growing ;
    R* := R* UNION f(R*) ;
end ;
```

This paper proposes the addition of a least fixpoint operator to the relational algebra.

23.26 Jeffrey D. Ullman: "Implementation of Logical Query Languages for Databases," *ACM TODS 10,* No. 3 (September 1985).

Describes an important class of implementation techniques for possibly recursive queries. The techniques are defined in terms of "capture rules" on "rule/goal trees," which are graphs that represent a query strategy in terms of clauses and predicates. The paper defines several such rules—one that corresponds to the application of relational algebra operators, two more that correspond to forward and backward chaining respectively, and a "sideways" rule that allows results to be passed from one subgoal to another. Sideways information passing later became the basis for the so-called *magic set* techniques [23.21–23.24].

23.27 Shalom Tsur and Carlo Zaniolo: "LDL: A Logic-Based Data-Language," Proc. 12th Int. Conf. on Very Large Data Bases, Kyoto, Japan (August 1986).

LDL includes (1) a "set" type generator, (2) negation (based on set difference), (3) data definition operations, and (4) update operations. It is a pure logic language (there are no ordering dependencies among statements) and is compiled, not interpreted. See also the book by Naqvi and Tsur [23.45] on the same subject.

23.28 François Bancilhon: "Naive Evaluation of Recursively Defined Relations," in Michael Brodie and John Mylopoulos (eds.), *On Knowledge Base Management Systems*: *Integrating Database and AI Systems.* New York, N.Y.: Springer Verlag (1986).

23.29 Eliezer L. Lozinskii: "A Problem-Oriented Inferential Database System," *ACM TODS 11,* No. 3 (September 1986).

The source of the concept of "relevant facts." The paper describes a prototype system that makes use of the extensional database to curb the otherwise very fast expansion of the search space that inferential techniques typically give rise to.

23.30 Arnon Rosenthal *et al.:* "Traversal Recursion: A Practical Approach to Supporting Recursive Applications," Proc. 1986 ACM SIGMOD Int. Conf. on Management of Data, Washington, DC (June 1986).

23.31 Georges Gardarin and Christophe de Maindreville: "Evaluation of Database Recursive Logic Programs as Recurrent Function Series," Proc. 1986 ACM SIGMOD Int. Conf. on Management of Data, Washington, DC (June 1986).

23.32 Louiqa Raschid and Stanley Y. W. Su: "A Parallel Processing Strategy for Evaluating Recursive Queries," Proc. 12th Int. Conf. on Very Large Data Bases, Kyoto, Japan (August 1986).

23.33 Nicolas Spyratos: "The Partition Model: A Deductive Database Model," *ACM TODS 12,* No. 1 (March 1987).

23.34 Jiawei Han and Lawrence J. Henschen: "Handling Redundancy in the Processing of Recursive Queries," Proc. 1987 ACM SIGMOD Int. Conf. on Management of Data, San Francisco, Calif. (May 1987).

23.35 Weining Zhang and C. T. Yu: "A Necessary Condition for a Doubly Recursive Rule to be Equivalent to a Linear Recursive Rule," Proc. 1987 ACM SIGMOD Int. Conf. on Management of Data, San Francisco, Calif. (May 1987).

23.36 Wolfgang Nejdl: "Recursive Strategies for Answering Recursive Queries—The RQA/FQI Strategy," Proc. 13th Int. Conf. on Very Large Data Bases, Brighton, UK (September 1987).

23.37 Kyu-Young Whang and Shamkant B. Navathe: "An Extended Disjunctive Normal Form Approach for Optimizing Recursive Logic Queries in Loosely Coupled Environments," Proc. 13th Int. Conf. on Very Large Data Bases, Brighton, UK (September 1987).

23.38 Jeffrey F. Naughton: "Compiling Separable Recursions," Proc. 1988 ACM SIGMOD Int. Conf. on Management of Data, Chicago, Ill. (June 1988).

23.39 Cheong Youn, Lawrence J. Henschen, and Jiawei Han: "Classification of Recursive Formulas in Deductive Databases," Proc. 1988 ACM SIGMOD Int. Conf. on Management of Data, Chicago, Ill. (June 1988).

23.40 S. Ceri, G. Gottlob, and L. Lavazza: "Translation and Optimization of Logic Queries: The Algebraic Approach," Proc. 12th Int. Conf. on Very Large Data Bases, Kyoto, Japan (August 1986).

23.41 S. Ceri and L. Tanca: "Optimization of Systems of Algebraic Equations for Evaluating Datalog Queries," Proc. 13th Int. Conf. on Very Large Data Bases, Brighton, UK (September 1987).

23.42 Allen Van Gelder: "A Message Passing Framework for Logical Query Evaluation," Proc. 1986 ACM SIGMOD Int. Conf. on Management of Data, Washington, DC (June 1986).

23.43 Ouri Wolfson and Avi Silberschatz: "Distributed Processing of Logic Programs," Proc. 1988 ACM SIGMOD Int. Conf. on Management of Data, Chicago, Ill. (June 1988).

23.44 Jeffrey F. Naughton *et al.*: "Efficient Evaluation of Right-, Left-, and Multi-Linear Rules," Proc. 1989 ACM SIGMOD Int. Conf. on Management of Data, Portland, Ore. (June 1989).

23.45 Shamim Naqvi and Shalom Tsur: *A Logical Language for Data and Knowledge Bases.* New York, N.Y.: Computer Science Press (1989).

An indepth, book-length presentation of the language LDL [23.27].

23.46 S. Ceri, G. Gottlob, and L. Tanca: *Logic Programming and Databases.* New York, N.Y.: Springer Verlag (1990).

23.47 Subrata Kumar Das: *Deductive Databases and Logic Programming.* Reading, Mass.: Addison-Wesley (1992).

23.48 Michael Kifer and Eliezer Lozinskii: "On Compile Time Query Optimization in Deductive Databases by Means of Static Filtering," *ACM TODS 15,* No. 3 (September 1990).

23.49 Rakesh Agrawal, Shaul Dar, and H. V. Jagadish: "Direct Transitive Closure Algorithms: Design and Performance Evaluation," *ACM TODS 15,* No. 3 (September 1990).

23.50 H. V. Jagadish: "A Compression Method to Materialize Transitive Closure," *ACM TODS 15,* No. 4 (December 1990).

Proposes an indexing technique that allows the transitive closure of a given relation to be stored in compressed form, such that testing to see whether a given tuple appears in the closure can be done via a single table lookup followed by an index comparison.

23.51 Serge Abiteboul and Stéphane Grumbach: "A Rule-Based Language with Functions and Sets," *ACM TODS 16,* No. 1 (March 1991).

Describes a language called COL ("Complex Object Language")—an extension of Datalog—that integrates the ideas of deductive and object databases.

ANSWERS TO SELECTED EXERCISES

23.1 a. Valid. b. Valid. c. Not valid.

23.2 In the following, *a, b,* and *c* are Skolem constants and *f* is a Skolem function with two arguments.

a. $p (x, y) \Rightarrow q (x, f (x, y))$

b. $p (a, b) \Rightarrow q (a, z)$

c. $p (a, b) \Rightarrow q (a, c)$

23.6 In accordance with our usual practice, we have numbered the following solutions as 23.6.*n*, where 6.*n* is the number of the original exercise in Chapter 6.

23.6.13 ? ⇐ J (j, jn, jc)

23.6.14 ? ⇐ J (j, jn, London)

23.6.15 RES (s) ⇐ SPJ (s, p, J1)
      ? ⇐ RES (s)

23.6.16 ? ⇐ SPJ (s, p, j, q) AND 300 ≤ q AND q ≤ 750

23.6.17 RES (pl, pc) ⇐ P (p, pn, pl, w, pc)
      ? ⇐ RES (pl, pc)

23.6.18 RES (s, p, j) ⇐ S (s, sn, st, c) AND
                      P (p, pn, pl, w, c) AND
                      J (j, jn, c)
      ? ⇐ RES (s, p, j)

23.6.19–23.6.20 Cannot be done without negation.

23.6.21 RES (p) ⇐ SPJ (s, p, j, q) AND
                S (s, sn, st, London)
      ? ⇐ RES (p)

23.6.22 RES (p) ⇐ SPJ (s, p, j, q) AND
                S (s, sn, st, London) AND
                J (j, jn, London)
      ? ⇐ RES (p)

23.6.23 RES (c1, c2) ⇐ SPJ (s, p, j, q) AND
                    S (s, sn, st, c1) AND
                    J (j, jn, c2)
      ? ⇐ RES (c1, c2)

23.6.24 RES (p) ⇐ SPJ (s, p, j, q) AND
                S (s, sn, st, c) AND
                J (j, jn, c)
      ? ⇐ RES (p)

23.6.25 Cannot be done without negation.

23.6.26 RES (p1, p2) ⇐ SPJ (s, p1, j1, q1) AND
                    SPJ (s, p2, j2, q2)
      ? ⇐ RES (p1, p2)

23.6.27–23.6.30 Cannot be done without grouping and aggregation.

23.6.31 RES (*jn*) ◀= J (*j, jn, jc*) AND
　　　　　　　　　　SPJ (S1, *p, j, q*)
　　　　? ◀= RES (*jn*)

23.6.32 RES (*pl*) ◀= P (*p, pn, pl, w, pc*) AND
　　　　　　　　　　SPJ (S1, *p, j, q*)
　　　　? ◀= RES (*pl*)

23.6.33 RES (*p*) ◀= P (*p, pn, pl, w, pc*) AND
　　　　　　　　　SPJ (*s, p, j, q*) AND
　　　　　　　　　J (*j, jn,* London)
　　　　? ◀= RES (*p*)

23.6.34 RES (*j*) ◀= SPJ (*s, p, j, q*) AND
　　　　　　　　　SPJ (S1, *p, j2, q2*)
　　　　? ◀= RES (*j*)

23.6.35 RES (*s*) ◀= SPJ (*s, p, j, q*) AND
　　　　　　　　　SPJ (*s2, p, j2, q2*) AND
　　　　　　　　　SPJ (*s2, p2, j3, q3*) AND
　　　　　　　　　P (*p2, pn,* Red, *w, c*)
　　　　? ◀= RES (*s*)

23.6.36 RES (*s*) ◀= S (*s, sn, st, c*) AND
　　　　　　　　　S (S1, *sn1, st1, c1*) AND *st < st1*
　　　　? ◀= RES (*s*)

23.6.37–23.6.39 Cannot be done without grouping and aggregation.

23.6.40–23.6.44 Cannot be done without negation.

23.6.45 RES (*c*) ◀= S (*s, sn, st, c*)
　　　　RES (*c*) ◀= P (*p, pn, pl, w, c*)
　　　　RES (*c*) ◀= J (*j, jn, c*)
　　　　? ◀= RES (*c*)

23.6.46 RES (*p*) ◀= SPJ (*s, p, j, q*) AND
　　　　　　　　　S (*s, sn, st,* London)
　　　　RES (*p*) ◀= SPJ (*s, p, j, q*) AND
　　　　　　　　　J (*j, jn,* London)
　　　　? ◀= RES (*p*)

23.6.47–23.6.48 Cannot be done without negation.

23.6.49–23.6.50 Cannot be done without grouping.

23.7 We show the constraints as conventional implications instead of in the "backward" Datalog style.

  a. CITY (London)
　　CITY (Paris)
　　CITY (Rome)
　　CITY (Athens)
　　CITY (Oslo)
　　CITY (Stockholm)
　　CITY (Madrid)
　　CITY (Amsterdam)

　　S (*s, sn, st, c*)　　⇒ CITY (*c*)
　　P (*p, pn, pc, pw, c*) ⇒ CITY (*c*)
　　J (*j, jn, c*)　　　⇒ CITY (*c*)

b.   Cannot be done without appropriate scalar operators.

c.   `P ( p, pn, Red, pw, pc ) ⇒ pw < 50`

d.   Cannot be done without negation or aggregate operators.

e.   `S ( s1, sn1, st1, Athens ) AND`
      `S ( s2, sn2, st2, Athens ) ⇒ s1 = s2`

f.   Cannot be done without grouping and aggregation.

g.   Cannot be done without grouping and aggregation.

h.   `J ( j, jn, c ) ⇒ S ( s, sn, st, c )`

i.   `J ( j, jn, c ) ⇒ SPJ ( s, p, j, q ) AND S ( s, sn, st, c )`

j.   `P ( p1, pn1, pl1, pw1, pc1 ) ⇒ P ( p2, pn2, Red, pw2, pc2 )`

k.   Cannot be done without aggregate operators.

l.   `S ( s, sn, st, London ) ⇒ SP ( s, P2, q )`

m.   `P ( p1, pn1, pl1, pw1, pc1 ) ⇒`
      `P ( p2, pn2, Red, pw2, pc2 ) AND pw2 < 50`

n.   Cannot be done without aggregate operators.

o.   Cannot be done without aggregate operators.

p.   Cannot be done (this is a transition constraint).

q.   Cannot be done (this is a transition constraint).

OBJECT AND
OBJECT/RELATIONAL DATABASES

Object technology is an important discipline in the field of software engineering in general; it is therefore natural to ask whether it is relevant to the field of database management in particular, and if so what that relevance is. There is, however, no consensus on answers to these questions! Some authorities believe object database systems will take over the world, replacing relational systems entirely; others believe they are suited only to certain very specific problems and will never capture more than a small fraction of the overall market. More recently, systems supporting a "third way" have begun to appear: systems, that is, that integrate object and relational technologies, in an attempt to get the best of both worlds. The two chapters in this final part of the book examine such matters in depth; Chapter 24 discusses pure object systems, Chapter 25 addresses the newer "object/relational" systems.

Object Databases

24.1 INTRODUCTION

Much interest has been generated over the past decade or so in *object-oriented* database systems (**object systems** for short). Object systems are regarded by some people as serious competitors to relational systems (or SQL systems, at any rate), at least for certain kinds of applications. In this chapter, we examine object systems in detail; we introduce and explain basic object concepts, analyze those concepts in depth, and offer some opinions regarding the suitability of incorporating such concepts into the database systems of the future.

Why is there so much current interest in object systems? Well, "everyone knows" that classical SQL systems are inadequate in a variety of ways. And some people—not this writer!—would argue that the underlying theory (i.e., the relational model) is inadequate too. Be that as it may, some of the new features we seem to need in DBMSs have existed for many years in *object programming languages* such as C++ and Smalltalk, and so it is natural to investigate the idea of incorporating those features into database systems. And many researchers, and several vendors, have done exactly that.

Object systems thus have their origins in object programming languages. And the basic idea is the same in both cases—to wit: Users should not have to wrestle with machine-oriented constructs such as bits and bytes (or even fields and records), but rather should be able to deal with **objects,** and **operations** on those objects, that more closely resemble their counterparts in the real world. For example, instead of having to think in terms of a "DEPT tuple" plus a collection of corresponding "EMP tuples" that include "foreign key values" that "reference" the "primary key value" in that "DEPT tuple," the user should be able to think directly in terms of a *department object* that actually contains a corresponding set of *employee objects.* And instead of, e.g., having to "insert" a "tuple" into the "EMP relvar" with an appropriate "foreign key value" that "references" the "primary key value" of some "tuple" in the "DEPT relvar," the user should be able to *hire* an employee object directly into the relevant department object. In other words, the fundamental idea is to **raise the level of abstraction.**

Now, raising the level of abstraction is unquestionably a worthy goal, and the object paradigm has been very successful in meeting that goal in the programming languages arena [24.15]. It therefore makes sense to ask whether the same paradigm can be applied successfully in the database arena also. Indeed, the idea of dealing with a database that is made up of "complex objects" (e.g., department objects that "know what it means" to hire an employee or change their manager or cut their budget), instead of having to deal with "relvars" and "tuple inserts" and "foreign keys" (etc., etc.) is obviously more attractive from the user's point of view—at least at first sight.

A word of caution is appropriate here, however. The point is, although the programming language and database management disciplines certainly have a lot in common, they do also differ in certain important respects (of course). To be specific:

- An application program is intended—by definition—to solve some specific problem;

- By contrast, a database is intended—again by definition—to solve a variety of different problems, some of which might not even be known at the time the database is established.

In the application programming environment, therefore, embedding a lot of "intelligence" into complex objects is clearly a good idea: It reduces the amount of code that needs to be written to make use of those objects, it improves programmer productivity, it increases application maintainability, and so on. In the database environment, by contrast, embedding a lot of intelligence into the database might or might not be a good idea: It might simplify some problems, but it might at the same time make others more difficult or even impossible.

(Incidentally, exactly this same argument was made against prerelational database systems like IMS back in the 1970s. A department object that contains a set of employee objects is conceptually very similar to an IMS hierarchy in which department "parent segments" have subordinate employee "child segments." Such a hierarchy is well suited to problems like "Get employees that work in the accounting department." It is not well suited to problems like "Get departments that employ MBAs." Thus, many of the arguments that were made against the hierarchic approach in the 1970s are surfacing again, in a different guise, in the object context.)

The foregoing remarks notwithstanding, many people believe that object systems represent a great leap forward in database technology. In particular, they believe that object techniques are the approach of choice for "complex" application areas such as the following:

- Computer-aided design and manufacturing (CAD/CAM);

- Computer-integrated manufacturing (CIM);

- Computer-aided software engineering (CASE);

- Geographic information systems (GIS);

- Science and medicine;

- Document storage and retrieval;

and so forth (note that these are all areas in which classical SQL products do tend to run into trouble). Certainly there have been numerous technical papers on such matters in the literature over the years, and more recently several commercial products have entered the marketplace.

In this chapter, therefore, we take a look at what object database technology is all about. Our aim is to introduce the most important concepts of the object approach, and in particular to describe those concepts **from a database perspective** (much of the literature, by contrast, presents the ideas very much from a *programming* perspective instead). The structure of the chapter is as follows. In the next subsection, we present a motivating example— an example, that is, that traditional SQL products do not handle very well, and hence one that object technology stands a good chance of doing better on. Next, Section 24.2 presents an overview of *objects, classes, messages,* and *methods,* and Section 24.3 then focuses on certain specific aspects of these concepts and discuss them in depth. Section 24.4 presents a "cradle-to-grave" example. Section 24.5 then discusses a few miscellaneous topics, and Section 24.6 presents a summary.

One last preliminary remark: Despite the fact that object systems were originally meant for "complex" applications such as CAD/CAM, for obvious reasons we base our examples on much simpler applications (departments and employees, etc.). Of course, this simplification in no way invalidates the presentation—and in any case, object databases, if they are to be worth their salt, should be able to handle "simple" applications too.

A Motivating Example

In this subsection we present a simple example, originally due to Stonebraker and elaborated by the present writer in reference [24.17], that illustrates some of the problems with conventional SQL products. The database (which might be thought of as a grossly simplified approximation to a CAD/CAM database) concerns *rectangles,* all of which we assume for simplicity are "square on" to the X and Y axes—i.e., all of their sides are either vertical or horizontal. Any individual rectangle can thus be uniquely identified by the coordinates $(x1,y1)$ and $(x2,y2)$ of, respectively, its bottom left and top right corners (see Fig. 24.1). In SQL:

```
CREATE TABLE RECTANGLE
     ( X1 ... , Y1 ... , X2 ... , Y2 ... , ... ,
       UNIQUE ( X1, Y1, X2, Y2 ) ) ;
```

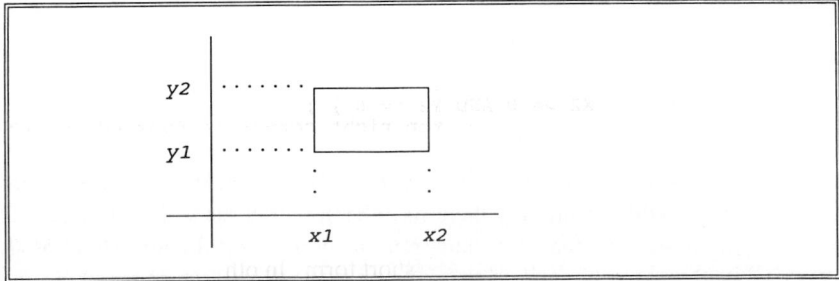

Fig. 24.1   The rectangle $(x1, y1, x2, y2)$

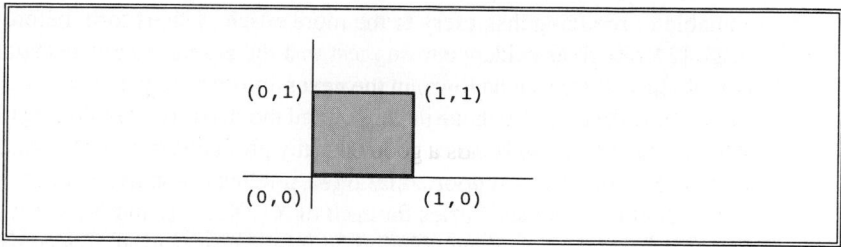

Fig. 24.2   The unit square (0,0,1,1)

Now consider the query "Get all rectangles that overlap the unit square (0,0,1,1)" (see Fig. 24.2). The "obvious" formulation of this query is:

```
SELECT  ...
FROM    RECTANGLE
WHERE   ( X1 >= 0 AND X1 <= 1 AND Y1 >= 0 AND Y1 <= 1 )
                    -- bottom left corner inside unit square
OR      ( X2 >= 0 AND X2 <= 1 AND Y2 >= 0 AND Y2 <= 1 )
                    -- top right corner inside unit square
OR      ( X1 >= 0 AND X1 <= 1 AND Y2 >= 0 AND Y2 <= 1 )
                    -- top left corner inside unit square
OR      ( X2 >= 0 AND X2 <= 1 AND Y1 >= 0 AND Y1 <= 1 )
                    -- bottom right corner inside unit square
OR      ( X1 <= 0 AND X2 >= 1 AND Y1 <= 0 AND Y2 >= 1 )
                    -- rectangle totally includes unit square
OR      ( X1 <= 0 AND X2 >= 1 AND Y1 >= 0 AND Y1 <= 1 )
                    -- bottom edge crosses unit square
OR      ( X1 >= 0 AND X1 <= 1 AND Y1 <= 0 AND Y2 >= 1 )
                    -- left edge crosses unit square
OR      ( X2 >= 0 AND X2 <= 1 AND Y1 <= 0 AND Y2 >= 1 )
                    -- right edge crosses unit square
OR      ( X1 <= 0 AND X2 >= 1 AND Y2 >= 0 AND Y2 <= 1 ) ;
                    -- top edge crosses unit square
```

(*Exercise:* Convince yourself that this formulation is correct.)

With a little further thought, however, it can be seen that the query can be expressed more simply as:

```
SELECT  ...
FROM    RECTANGLE
WHERE   ( X1 <= 1 AND Y1 <= 1
                    -- bottom left corner is "downwind" of (1,1)
AND       X2 >= 0 AND Y2 >= 0 ) ;
                    -- top right corner is "upwind" of (0,0)
```

(Exercise 24.3 at the end of the chapter asks you to convince yourself that this formulation is correct too.)

The question now is: Could the system optimizer transform the original long form of the query into the corresponding short form? In other words, suppose the user expresses the query in the "obvious"—and obviously inefficient—long form; would the optimizer be capable of reducing that query to the more efficient short form before executing it? Reference [24.17] gives evidence to suggest that the answer to this question is almost certainly *no,* at least so far as today's commercial optimizers are concerned.

In any case, although we just described the short form as "more efficient," performance on that short form will still be poor in many products, given the usual storage structures—e.g., B-tree indexes—supported by those products. (On average, the system will examine 50 percent of the index entries for each of X1, X2, Y1, and Y2.)

Thus we see that conventional SQL products are indeed inadequate in certain respects. To be specific, problems like the rectangles problem show clearly that certain "simple" user requests (a) are unreasonably difficult to express, and (b) execute with unacceptably poor performance, in those products. Such considerations provide much of the motivation behind the current interest in object systems.

Note: We will give a "good" solution to the rectangles problem in Chapter 25 (Section 25.1).

24.2   OBJECTS, CLASSES, METHODS, AND MESSAGES

In this section, we introduce some of the principal concepts of the object approach, namely *objects* themselves (of course), *object classes, methods,* and *messages.* We also relate these concepts to more familiar concepts wherever possible or appropriate. In fact, it is probably helpful to show a rough mapping of object terms to traditional terminology right at the outset (see Fig. 24.3).

Caveat: Before we get into details, we should warn you not to expect the kind of precision in the object world that you are (or should be) accustomed to in the relational world. Indeed, many object concepts—or the published definitions of those concepts, at any rate—are quite imprecise, and there is very little true consensus and much disagreement, even at the most basic level (as a careful reading of, e.g., references [24.11], [24.48], and [24.52]

Object term	Traditional term
immutable object	value
mutable object	variable
object class	type
method	operator
message	operator invocation

Fig. 24.3   Object terminology (summary)

will show). In particular, there is no abstract, formally defined "object data model," nor is there even consensus on an *in*formal model. (For such reasons we usually place phrases such as "the object model" in quotes in this chapter.) In fact, there seems, rather surprisingly, to be much confusion over levels of abstraction—specifically, over the (crucial!) distinction between **model** and **implementation.** Refer to Chapter 1 if you need to refresh your memory regarding this distinction.

You should also be warned that, as a consequence of the foregoing state of affairs, the definitions and explanations presented in this chapter are *not* universally agreed upon and do *not* necessarily correspond 100 percent to the way any given system actually works. Indeed, just about every one of those definitions and explanations could be challenged by some other writer in this field, and probably will be.

An Overview of Object Technology

Question: What is an object? *Answer:* Everything!

It is a basic tenet of the object approach that **"everything is an object"** (sometimes "everything is a **first-class** object"). Some objects are **immutable;** examples might be integers (e.g., 3, 42) and character strings (e.g., "Mozart", "Hayduke Lives!"). Other objects are **mutable;** examples might be the department and employee objects mentioned near the beginning of Section 24.1. In traditional terminology, therefore, immutable objects correspond to *values* and mutable objects to *variables**—where the values and variables in question can be of arbitrary complexity (i.e., they can make use of any or all of the usual programming language types and type generators: numbers, strings, lists, arrays, stacks, etc.). *Note:* In some systems the term *object* is reserved for the mutable case only (the term *value,* or sometimes *literal,* then being used for the immutable case). And even in those systems where the term "object" does strictly refer to both cases, you should be aware that it is common in informal contexts to take the term to mean a mutable object specifically, barring explicit statements to the contrary.

Every object has a *type* (the object term is **class**). Individual objects are sometimes referred to as object **instances** specifically, in order to distinguish them clearly from the corresponding object type or class. Also, please note that we are using the term *type* here in its usual programming language sense (as in Chapter 5); in particular, therefore, we take the term to include the set of *operators* (the object term is **methods**) that can be applied to objects of the type in question. *Note:* Actually, some object systems do distinguish between types and classes, and we will discuss such systems briefly in Section 24.3; up to that point, however, we will use the terms interchangeably.

Objects are **encapsulated.** What this means is that the physical representation—i.e., the internal structure—of such an object, say a DEPT ("department") object, is not visible to users of that object; instead, users know only that the object is capable of executing certain

---

operations (methods).* For example, the methods that apply to DEPT objects might be HIRE_EMP, FIRE_EMP, CUT_BUDGET, etc. *Note carefully that such methods constitute the ONLY operations that can be applied to the objects in question.* The code that implements those methods *is* permitted to see the internal representation of the objects—to use the jargon, that code (but only that code) is allowed to "break encapsulation"†—but of course that code is likewise not visible to users.

The advantage of encapsulation is that it allows the internal representation of objects to be changed without requiring applications that use those objects to be rewritten (provided, of course, that any such change in internal representation is accompanied by a corresponding change to the code that implements the applicable methods). In other words, encapsulation implies **physical data independence.**

Now, the foregoing characterization of encapsulation in terms of data independence makes sense from a database perspective, but it is not the way the concept is usually described in the object literature. Instead, encapsulated objects are described as having a *private memory* and a *public interface:*

- The **private memory** consists of **instance variables** (also known as *members* or *attributes*), whose values represent the internal state of the object. Now, in a "pure" system, instance variables are completely private and hidden from users, though as indicated above they are (of course) visible to the code that implements the methods. However, many systems are *not* pure in this sense but do expose instance variables to users, a point we will come back to in the next subsection.

- The **public interface** consists of interface definitions for the methods that apply to this object. Those interface definitions correspond to what in Chapter 19 we called *specification signatures*—except that (as explained in the next paragraph) object systems usually insist that such signatures be tied to just one specific "target" type or class, whereas we had no such notion in Chapter 19 (nor do we find it necessary, or even desirable [3.3]). As already noted, the code that implements those methods, like the instance variables, is hidden from the user. *Note:* It would be more accurate to say that

---

*There is much confusion in the literature surrounding the notion of encapsulation. The position that seems to make the most sense, and the one we adopt in this book, is to say that an object is encapsulated if and only if it is **scalar** in the sense of Chapter 5 (i.e., if and only if it has no user-visible components); hence, *encapsulated* and *scalar* mean exactly the same thing. Note that certain "collection" objects—see Section 24.3—are definitely not scalar, and hence (desirably) not encapsulated, by this definition. By contrast, some writers state categorically that *all* objects are encapsulated, a position that inevitably leads to certain contradictions. And others take the concept to mean that, in addition to the internal structure being hidden, *the corresponding methods are physically bundled with* (i.e., physically part of) the object or object class in question. We feel this latter interpretation mixes model and implementation considerations—indeed, that confusion is another of the reasons why, as noted in Chapter 5, we prefer not to use the term "encapsulation" at all. In the present chapter, however, we do necessarily have to use it from time to time.

†We would recommend a stronger discipline ourselves [3.3]: Only selectors and THE_ operators—see Chapter 5—should be allowed to break encapsulation in this sense; all other operators should be implemented in terms of those selectors and THE_ operators. In other words, code defensively! However, object systems typically provide, not THE_ operators as such, but rather "get and set" operators (see Section 24.4), which are *not* an exact counterpart [24.22].

the public interface is part of the **class-defining object** for the object in question, rather than part of the individual object itself. (After all, the public interface is common to all objects of the class in question, rather than being specific to some individual object.) The class-defining object or CDO is the object that defines the class of which the object in question is an instance; it is analogous to a catalog entry in a conventional relational system.

Methods are invoked by means of **messages.** A message is essentially just an *operator invocation,* in which one argument, the **target,** is distinguished and given special syntactic treatment. For example, the following might be a message to department D, asking it to hire employee E:

```
D HIRE_EMP ( E )
```

(hypothetical syntax; see the subsection "Class *vs.* Instance *vs.* Collection" in Section 24.3 for an explanation of the arguments D and E). The target here is the department object denoted by D. The analog of this message in a more conventional programming language (i.e., one that treats all arguments equally) might look like this:*

```
HIRE_EMP ( D, E )
```

In practice, an object system will come equipped with several *builtin* classes and methods. In particular, the system will almost certainly provide classes such as NUMERIC (with methods "=", "<", "+", "−", etc.), CHAR (with methods "=", "<", "||", SUBSTR, etc.), and so forth. Also, of course, the system will provide facilities for suitably skilled users to define and implement classes and methods of their own.

Instance Variables

We now take a slightly closer look at the concept of instance variables (the fact is, a certain amount of confusion does surround this subject). As stated previously, instance variables are hidden from the user in a pure system. Unfortunately, however, most systems are not pure in this sense. As a consequence, it is necessary in practice to distinguish between **public** and **private** instance variables; private ones truly are hidden, but public ones are not.

By way of example, suppose we have an object class of *line segments,* and suppose line segments are physically represented by their START and END points. Then the system will typically allow the user to write expressions of the form *ls*.START and *ls*.END to "get" the START and END points for a given line segment *ls*. Thus, START and END are *public* instance variables (note that, by definition, access to public instance variables must be via

---

*Treating one argument as special can make it easier for the system to perform the *run-time binding* process described in Chapter 19. However, it suffers from many disadvantages (see reference [3.3]), not the least of which is that it can make it harder for the method implementer to write the implementation code. Another is that which argument is chosen as the target (in cases where there is a choice—i.e., whenever there are two or more arguments) is of course arbitrary.

some special syntax—typically dot qualification, as our example suggests). And if the physical representation of line segments is now changed, say to the combination of MIDPOINT, LENGTH, and SLOPE, then any program that includes expressions such as *ls*.START and *ls*.END will now break. In other words, we have lost data independence.

Observe now that public instance variables are logically unnecessary. Suppose we define methods GET_START, GET_END, GET_MIDPOINT, GET_LENGTH, and GET_SLOPE for line segments. Then the user can "get" the start point, the end point, the midpoint, and so on, for line segment *ls* by means of appropriate *method invocations:* GET_START(*ls*), GET_END(*ls*), GET_MIDPOINT(*ls*), and so on. And now it makes no difference what the physical representation of line segments is!—just so long as the various GET_ methods are implemented appropriately, and reimplemented appropriately if that physical representation changes. Furthermore, there would be nothing wrong in allowing the user to abbreviate, e.g., GET_START(*ls*) to just *ls*.START **as a shorthand;** note that the availability of that shorthand would *not* make START into a public instance variable. Sadly, however, real systems do not usually operate in this manner; usually, public instance variables really do expose the physical representation (or part of it, at any rate, though there might be some additional instance variables that truly are private and hidden). In accordance with common practice, therefore, we will assume in what follows (until further notice) that objects typically do expose certain public instance variables, even though the concept is logically unnecessary.

There is a related point that needs to be made here, too. Suppose certain arguments—which the user might well think of, loosely, as "instance variable" arguments—happen to be required in order to create objects of some particular class.* Then it does *not* follow that those same "instance variables" can be used for arbitrary purposes. Suppose, for example, that creating a line segment requires us to specify the applicable START and END points. Then it does not follow that we can get, e.g., all line segments with a given START point; rather, such a request will be legal only if a suitable method has been defined.

Finally, note that some systems support a variation on private instance variables called **protected** instance variables. If objects of class *C* have a protected instance variable *P*, then *P* is visible to the code that implements the methods defined for class *C* (of course) *and* to the code that implements the methods defined for *any subclass* (at any level) of class *C*. See the end of Section 24.3 for a brief discussion of subclasses.

Object Identity

Every object has a unique *identifier* called its **object ID** or OID. Immutable objects like the integer 42 are *self-identifying,* i.e., they serve as their own OIDs. By contrast, mutable objects have (conceptual) *addresses* as their OIDs, and those addresses can be used elsewhere in the database as (conceptual) *pointers* to refer to the objects in question. Such addresses are not directly exposed to the user, but (for example) they can be assigned to program

---

*The objects in question must necessarily be mutable ones, by the way (why?).

variables and to instance variables within other objects. See Sections 24.3 and 24.4 for further discussion.

We remark in passing that it is sometimes claimed that it is an advantage of object systems that two distinct objects can be identical in all user-visible respects—i.e., be duplicates of one another—and yet be distinguished via their OIDs. To this writer, however, this claim seems specious. For how can the *user* distinguish between two such objects, externally? See references [5.3], [5.6], and (especially) [24.19] for further discussion of this issue.

24.3 A CLOSER LOOK

We now take a closer look at some of the ideas introduced in the previous section. Suppose we wish to define two object classes, DEPT (departments) and EMP (employees). Suppose also that the user-defined classes MONEY and JOB have already been defined and the class CHAR is builtin. Then the necessary class definitions for DEPT and EMP might look somewhat as follows (hypothetical syntax):

```
CLASS DEPT
    PUBLIC  ( DEPT#      CHAR,
              DNAME      CHAR,
              BUDGET     MONEY,
              MGR        REF ( EMP ),
              EMPS       REF ( SET ( REF ( EMP ) ) ) ) ...
    METHODS ( HIRE_EMP ( REF ( EMP ) ) ... code ... ,
              FIRE_EMP ( REF ( EMP ) ) ... code ... , ... ) ... ;

CLASS EMP
    PUBLIC  ( EMP#       CHAR,
              ENAME      CHAR,
              SALARY     MONEY,
              POSITION   REF ( JOB ) ) ...
    METHODS ( ... ) ... ;
```

Points arising:

1. We have chosen to represent departments and employees by means of a **containment hierarchy,** in which EMP objects are conceptually contained within DEPT objects. Thus, objects of class DEPT include a public instance variable called MGR, representing the given department's manager, and another one called EMPS representing the given department's employees. More precisely, objects of class DEPT include a public instance variable called MGR whose value is a *reference* ("REF") to an employee, and another one called EMPS whose value is a reference to a set of references to employees. (*Note:* "Reference to" here really means *OID of*—see further discussion below.) We will elaborate on the containment hierarchy notion in a few moments.

2. For the sake of the example, we have chosen not to include an instance variable within objects of class EMP whose value is either a department OID or a DEPT# value (a "foreign key" instance variable). This decision is consistent with our decision to represent departments and employees by means of a containment hierarchy. However, it does mean there is no direct way to get from a given EMP object to the corresponding DEPT object. See Section 24.5, subsection entitled "Relationships," for further discussion of this point.

3. Observe that each class definition includes definitions (coding details omitted) of the methods that apply to objects of the class in question. The target class for such methods is, of course, the class whose definition includes the definition of the method in question.*

Fig. 24.4 shows some sample object instances corresponding to the DEPT and EMP classes as just defined. Consider first the EMP object at the top of that figure (with OID *eee*), which contains:

- An immutable object "E001" of the builtin class CHAR in its public instance variable EMP#;
- An immutable object "Smith" of the builtin class CHAR in its public instance variable ENAME;
- An immutable object "$50,000" of the user-defined class MONEY in its public instance variable SALARY;
- **The OID of** a mutable object of the user-defined class JOB in its public instance variable POSITION.

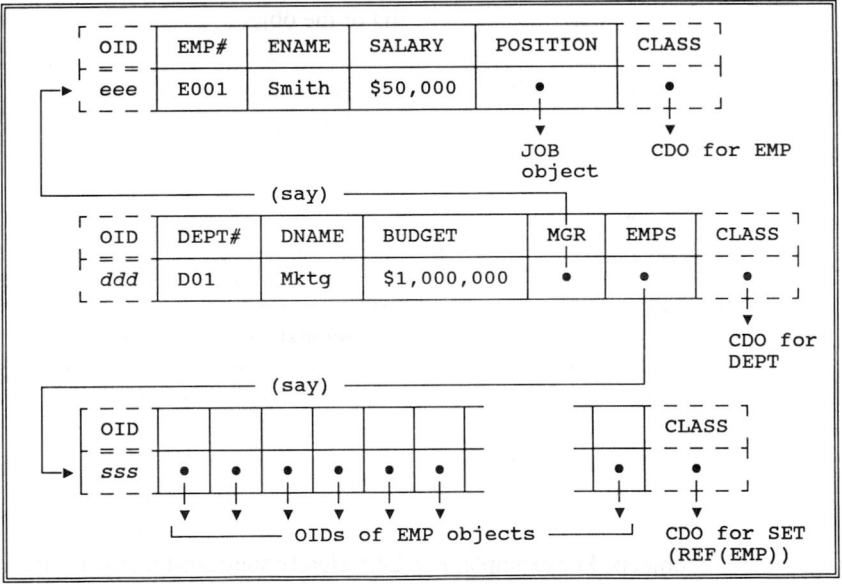

Fig. 24.4 Sample DEPT and EMP instances

---

*Note that our hypothetical syntax (undesirably, but quite typically) mixes model and implementation considerations. Note too that we have argued elsewhere [13.11] that departments and employees are bad examples of object classes anyway! Further discussion of this particular point would take us too far afield here, however.

It also contains at least two additional private instance variables, one containing the OID *eee* of the EMP object itself, and one containing the OID of the class-defining object—i.e., the CDO—for EMPs (so that the implementation can find descriptor information for this object). *Note:* These two OIDs might or might not be physically stored with the object. For instance, the value *eee* need not necessarily be stored as part of the relevant EMP object; it is necessary only that the implementation have some way of locating that EMP object given that value *eee* (i.e., some way of mapping that value *eee* to that EMP object's physical address). But conceptually the user can always think of the OID as being part of the object, as shown.

Now we turn to the DEPT object in the center of the figure, with OID *ddd*. That object contains:

- An immutable object "D01" of the builtin class CHAR in its public instance variable DEPT#;

- An immutable object "Mktg" of the builtin class CHAR in its public instance variable DNAME;

- An immutable object "$1,000,000" of the user-defined class MONEY in its public instance variable BUDGET;

- The OID *eee* of a mutable object of the user-defined class EMP in its public instance variable MGR (this is the OID of the object that represents the department manager);

- The OID *sss* of a mutable object of the user-defined class SET(REF(EMP)) in its public instance variable EMPS (see below);

- Two private instance variables containing, respectively, the OID *ddd* of the DEPT object itself and the OID of the corresponding class-defining object.

And the object with OID *sss* contains a set of OIDs of individual (mutable) EMP objects, plus the usual private instance variables.

Now, Fig. 24.4 depicts the objects "as they really are"; i.e., the figure illustrates the *data structure* component of "the object model," and such figures must thus be clearly understood by users of that model. Object texts and presentations, however, typically do not show diagrams like that of Fig. 24.4; instead, they typically represent the situation as shown in Fig. 24.5, overleaf (which might be regarded as being at a higher level of abstraction and hence easier to understand).

The representation shown in Fig. 24.5 is certainly more consistent with the containment hierarchy interpretation. However, it obscures the important fact, already stressed above, that objects often contain not other objects as such but rather **OIDs** of—i.e., pointers to—other objects. For example, Fig. 24.5 clearly suggests that the DEPT object for department D01 includes the EMP object for employee E001 *twice* (implying among other things that employee E001 might be represented, inconsistently, as having two different salaries in its two different appearances). This sleight of hand is the source of much confusion, which is why we prefer pictures like that of Fig. 24.4.

As an aside, we note that real object class definitions often increase the confusion, because they often do not define instance variables as "REFs" (as our hypothetical syntax does) but instead directly reflect the containment hierarchy interpretation. Thus, for ex-

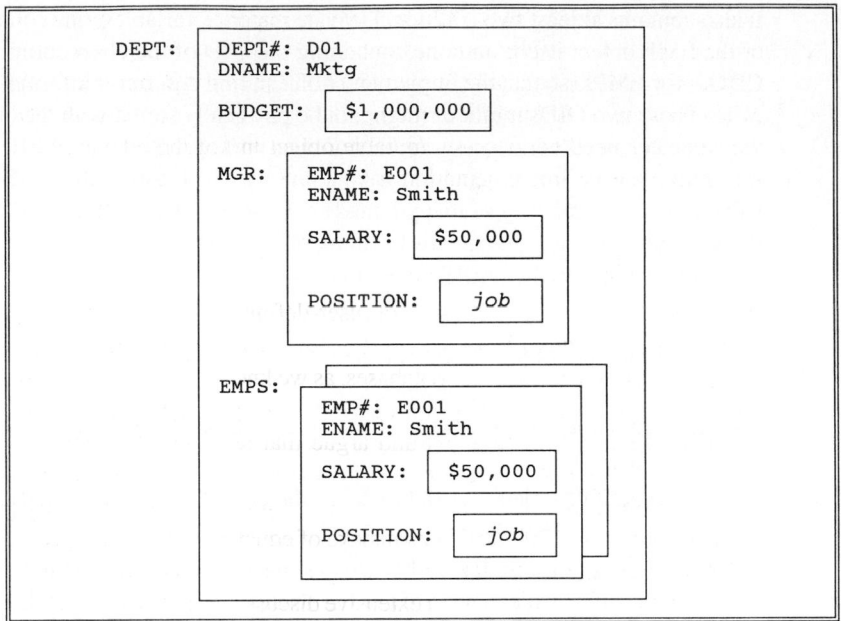

Fig. 24.5   Sample DEPT and EMP instances as a containment hierarchy

ample, instance variable EMPS in object class DEPT might be defined not as REF(SET(REF(EMP))) but just as SET(EMP). Although cumbersome, we prefer our style of definition, for clarity and accuracy.

It is worth pointing out too that all of the old criticisms of hierarchies in general as found in, e.g., IMS apply to containment hierarchies in particular. Space does not permit detailed consideration of those criticisms here; suffice it to say that the overriding issue is **lack of symmetry.** In particular, hierarchies do not lend themselves well to the representation of many-to-many relationships. Consider suppliers and parts, for instance: Do the suppliers contain the parts, or *vice versa?* Or both? What about suppliers, parts, and projects?

Actually matters are more confused than we have been suggesting so far. On the one hand, it is claimed (as previously explained) that objects are *hierarchies,* which means they are subject to the usual criticisms of hierarchies, as already noted. On the other hand, however, it is clear from figures like Fig. 24.4 that objects are not really hierarchies at all but **tuples**—where the tuple components can be any of the following:

1. Immutable "subobjects" (i.e., self-identifying values such as integers or money amounts);

2. OIDs of mutable "subobjects" (i.e., references or pointers to other, possibly shared, mutable objects);

3. Sets, lists, arrays, … of 1., 2., or 3.;

plus certain hidden OID, CDO OID, etc., components. Note point 3 in particular: Object systems typically support several "collection" **type generators**—e.g., SET, LIST, ARRAY, BAG, and so on (though usually not RELATION!)—and those generators can be combined in arbitrary ways. For example, an array of lists of bags of arrays of pointers to integer variables might constitute a single mutable object in appropriate circumstances. See the next subsection but one for further discussion.

Object IDs Revisited

Relational DBMSs typically rely on user-defined, user-controlled keys—"user keys" for short—for entity identification and referencing purposes (in fact, OID-style pointers are expressly prohibited in relational databases, as we know from Chapter 3). It is well known, however, that user keys do suffer from a number of problems; references [13.10] and [13.16] discuss such problems in detail and argue that relational DBMSs should support *system*-defined keys ("surrogates") instead, at least as an option. And the argument in favor of OIDs in object systems is similar, somewhat, to the argument in favor of surrogates in relational systems. (Do not, however, make the mistake of equating the two: Surrogates are *values* and are visible to the user, while OIDs are *addresses*—at least conceptually—and are hidden from the user. See reference [24.19] for an extensive discussion of these distinctions and related issues.)
Points and questions arising:

1. First, note that OIDs do not avoid the need for user keys, as we will see in Section 24.4. To be more precise, user keys are still needed for interaction with the outside world, even if all object cross-referencing inside the database is done via OIDs.

2. What is the OID for a *derived* object?—e.g., the "join" of a given EMP and the corresponding DEPT, or the "projection" of a given DEPT over BUDGET and MGR? (This question of *derived objects* is an important one, by the way, but we have to defer it for now. See Section 24.5.)

3. OIDs are the source of the often-heard criticisms to the effect that object systems look like "CODASYL warmed over"—where (as noted in Chapter 1) the term CODASYL refers generically to certain network (i.e., prerelational) database systems such as IDMS. Certainly OIDs tend to lead to a rather low-level, pointer-chasing style of programming (see Section 24.4) that is very reminiscent of the old CODASYL style. Also, the fact that OIDs are pointers accounts for the claims, also sometimes heard, to the effect that:
   - CODASYL systems are closer to object systems than relational systems are;
   - Relational systems are *value-based* while object systems are *identity-based*.

Class *vs.* Instance *vs.* Collection

Object systems clearly distinguish the concepts of *class, instance,* and *collection*. A **class** is (as already explained) basically a data type, possibly builtin, possibly user-defined, of arbitrary complexity.* Every class understands a **NEW** message, which causes a new (mutable) **instance** of the class to be created. (*Note:* The method invoked by the NEW message is sometimes referred to as a *constructor function.*) For example (hypothetical syntax):

```
E  :=  EMP NEW ( 'E001', 'Smith', MONEY ( 50000 ), POS ) ;
```

Here POS is a program variable that contains the OID of some JOB object. The NEW method is invoked on the object class EMP; it creates a new instance of that class, initializes it to the specified values, and returns that new instance's OID. That OID is then assigned to the program variable E.

Next, because objects can be referenced (via OIDs) by any number of other objects, they can effectively be *shared* by those other objects. In particular, they can belong to any number of **collection** objects simultaneously. To continue with the example:

```
CLASS EMP_COLL
    PUBLIC ( EMPS REF ( SET ( REF ( EMP ) ) ) ) ... ;

ALL_EMPS  :=  EMP_COLL NEW ( ) ;

ALL_EMPS ADD ( E ) ;
```

Explanation:

- An object of class EMP_COLL contains a single public instance variable, called EMPS, whose value is a pointer (OID) to a mutable object whose value is a set of pointers (OIDs) to individual EMP objects.

- ALL_EMPS is a program variable whose value is the OID of an object of class EMP_COLL. After the assignment operation, it contains the OID of such an object whose value in turn is the OID of an *empty* set of OIDs of EMP objects.

- ADD is a method that is understood by objects of class EMP_COLL. In the example, that method is applied to the object of that class whose OID is given in the program variable ALL_EMPS; its effect is to add the OID of the EMP object whose OID is given in the program variable E to the (previously empty) set of OIDs whose OID is given in the EMP_COLL object whose OID is given in the program variable ALL_EMPS.

After the foregoing sequence of operations, we can say, loosely, that the variable ALL_EMPS denotes a collection of EMPs that currently contains just one EMP, namely employee E001. (By the way, note the need to mention a user key value in this latter sentence!)

Of course, we can have any number of distinct, and possibly overlapping, "sets of employees" at any given time:

---

*As mentioned in Section 24.2, some systems use both "type" and "class," in which case "type" means *type* or *intension* and "class" means *extension* (i.e., a certain *collection*), or sometimes *implementation* (of the type in question). Then again, other systems use the terms the other way around . . . We will continue to take "class" to mean a type in the sense of Chapter 5.

```
    PROGRAMMERS   :=   EMP_COLL NEW ( ) ;

    PROGRAMMERS ADD ( E ) ;

       .....

    HIGHLY_PAID   :=   EMP_COLL NEW ( ) ;

    HIGHLY_PAID ADD ( E ) ;
```

and so on. Contrast the state of affairs in SQL systems. For example, the SQL statement

```
    CREATE TABLE EMP
        ( EMP# ... ,
          ENAME ... ,
          SALARY ... ,
          POSITION ... ) ... ;
```

creates a type *and* a collection simultaneously; the type is defined by the table heading, and the (initially empty) collection is the table body. Likewise, the SQL statement

```
    INSERT INTO EMP ( ... ) VALUES ( ... ) ;
```

creates an individual EMP row *and* adds it to the EMP collection simultaneously. In SQL, therefore:

1. There is no way for an individual EMP "object" to exist without being part of some "collection"—in fact, exactly one "collection" (but see below).

2. There is no direct way to create two distinct "collections" of the same "class" of EMP "objects" (but see below).

3. There is no direct way to share the same "object" across distinct "collections" of EMP "objects" (but see below).

At least, the foregoing are claims that are sometimes heard. In fact, however, they do not stand up to close scrutiny. First, the foreign key mechanism can be used to achieve an equivalent effect in each case; for example, we could define two more base tables called PROGRAMMERS and HIGHLY_PAID, each of them containing just the employee numbers for the relevant employees. Second (and much more important), the **view** mechanism can also be used to achieve a similar effect. For example, we could define PROGRAMMERS and HIGHLY_PAID as views of the EMP base table:

```
    CREATE VIEW PROGRAMMERS
        AS SELECT EMP#, ENAME, SALARY, POSITION
           FROM   EMP
           WHERE  POSITION = 'Programmer' ;

    CREATE VIEW HIGHLY_PAID
        AS SELECT EMP#, ENAME, SALARY, POSITION
           FROM   EMP
           WHERE  SALARY > some threshold, say 75000 ;
```

And now, of course, it is perfectly possible for the very same employee "object" to belong to two or more "collections" simultaneously. What is more, membership in those collections that happen to be views is handled automatically by the system, not manually by the programmer.

We close this discussion by mentioning an illuminating parallel between the mutable objects of object systems and the **explicit dynamic variables** of certain programming language systems (PL/I's BASED variables are a case in point). Like mutable objects of a given class, there can be any number of distinct explicit dynamic variables of a given type, the storage for which is allocated at run time by explicit program action. Furthermore, those distinct variables, again like individual mutable objects, *have no name,* and thus can be referenced only through pointers. In PL/I, for example, we might write:

```
DCL XYZ INTEGER BASED ;          /* XYZ is a BASED variable */
DCL P POINTER ;                  /* P is a pointer variable */

ALLOCATE XYZ SET ( P ) ;       /* create a new XYZ instance */
                               /* and set P to point to it  */

P -> XYZ = 3 ;              /* assign the value 3 to the XYZ */
                           /* instance pointed to by P       */
```

(and so on). This PL/I code bears a striking resemblance to the object code shown earlier; in particular, the declaration of the BASED variable is akin to the creation of an object class, and the ALLOCATE operation is akin to the creation of a NEW instance of that class. We can thus see that the reason OIDs are necessary in the object model is precisely because, in general, the objects they identify do not possess any other unique name—just like BASED variable instances in PL/I.

Class Hierarchies

No treatment of basic object concepts would be complete without some mention of **class hierarchies** (not to be confused with containment hierarchies). However, the object "class hierarchy" concept is essentially the same as the type hierarchy concept already discussed at length in Chapter 19; we therefore content ourselves here with a few brief definitions (paraphrased from Chapter 19, for the most part) and a couple of relevant observations. *Note:* We remind you that there is little consensus—in the object world or anywhere else—on an abstract inheritance *model,* and different inheritance systems therefore differ from one another considerably at the detail level.

First of all, object class Y is said to be a **subclass** of object class X—equivalently, object class X is said to be a **superclass** of object class Y—if and only if every object of class Y is necessarily an object of class X ("Y **ISA** X"). Objects of class Y then **inherit** the public instance variables and methods that apply to class X. Inheriting instance variables is referred to as **structural** inheritance, inheriting methods is referred to as **behavioral** inheritance. In a pure system, of course, there is only behavioral inheritance, no structural inheritance—at least for scalar or fully encapsulated objects—because there is no structure to inherit (no structure visible to the user, that is). In practice, however, object systems are typically not pure and do support some degree of structural inheritance (meaning, to stress the point, inheritance of public instance variables).

If class *Y* is a subclass of class *X,* the user can always use a *Y* object wherever an *X* object is permitted (e.g., as an argument to various methods)—this is the principle of **substitutability**—and thereby obtain **code reuse.** Because object systems often do not clearly distinguish between values and variables, however—i.e., between immutable and mutable objects—they tend to run into trouble over the distinction between value and variable substitutability (see Chapter 19 for further discussion). Be that as it may, the ability to apply the same method to objects of class *X* and class *Y* is referred to as (inclusion) **polymorphism.**

The system will come equipped with certain builtin class hierarchies. In OPAL, for example (see Section 24.4), every class is considered to be a subclass at some level of the builtin class OBJECT (because "everything is an object"). Builtin subclasses of OBJECT include BOOLEAN, CHAR, INTEGER, COLLECTION (etc.); COLLECTION in turn has a subclass called BAG, and BAG has another called SET (etc., etc.).

Finally, some object systems do support some form of **multiple** inheritance in addition to single inheritance. However, no system known to this writer supports tuple or relation inheritance (either single or multiple) in the sense of reference [3.3].

24.4 A CRADLE-TO-GRAVE EXAMPLE

We have now introduced the basic concepts of object systems. In this section we show how those concepts fit together by presenting a "cradle-to-grave" example—i.e., we show how an object database can be defined, how it can be populated, and how retrieval and update operations can be performed against it. Our example is based on the GemStone product (from GemStone Systems Inc.) and its data language OPAL [24.14]; OPAL in turn is based on Smalltalk [24.26], one of the purest of the object languages (which is why we use it here). *Note:* We should add that at the time of writing Smalltalk seems to be being overtaken in the marketplace by C++ and—increasingly—Java, despite the fact that these two languages are indeed less "pure" than Smalltalk.

The example involves a simplified version of the education database from Exercise 8.10 in Chapter 8. The database contains information about an inhouse company education training scheme. For each training course, the database contains details of all offerings of that course; for each offering it contains details of all student enrollments and all teachers for that offering. The database also contains information about employees. A relational version of the database looks (in outline) something like this:

```
COURSE      { COURSE#, TITLE }
OFFERING    { COURSE#, OFF#, OFFDATE, LOCATION }
TEACHER     { COURSE#, OFF#, EMP# }
ENROLLMENT  { COURSE#, OFF#, EMP#, GRADE }
EMP         { EMP#, ENAME, SALARY, POSITION }
```

Fig. 24.6 is a referential diagram for this database. Refer to the Exercises and Answers in Chapter 8 if you require further explanation.

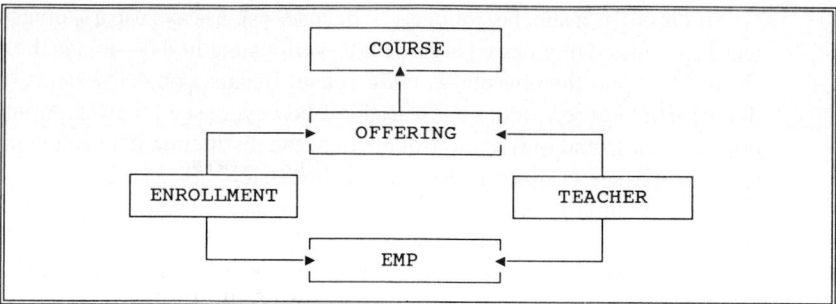

Fig. 24.6   Referential diagram for the education database

Data Definition

We now proceed to show a set of OPAL definitions for this database. Here first is the definition for an object class called EMP (the lines are numbered for purposes of subsequent reference):

```
1    OBJECT SUBCLASS : 'EMP'
2        INSTVARNAMES : #[ 'EMP#', 'ENAME', 'POSITION' ]
3        CONSTRAINTS  : #[ #[ #EMP#, STRING ] ,
4                            [ #ENAME, STRING ] ,
5                            [ #POSITION, STRING ] ] .
```

Explanation: Line 1 defines an object class called EMP, a subclass of the builtin class called OBJECT. (In OPAL terms, line 1 is *sending a message* to the OBJECT object, asking it to invoke the SUBCLASS method; INSTVARNAMES and CONSTRAINTS specify arguments to that method invocation. Defining a new class—like everything else in OPAL—is thus done by sending a message to an object.) Line 2 states that objects of class EMP have three private instance variables called EMP#, ENAME, and POSITION, respectively, and lines 3–5 constrain those instance variables each to contain objects of class STRING. *Note:* Throughout this section we omit discussion of purely syntactic details (such as the ubiquitous "#" signs above) that are essentially irrelevant to our purpose.

To repeat, instance variables EMP#, ENAME, and POSITION are *private* to class EMP; they can thus be accessed by name solely within the code that implements methods for that class. Here, for example, are definitions of methods to "get and set"—i.e., retrieve and update—employee numbers (the symbol ^ can be read as "return"):

```
METHOD : EMP
    GET_EMP#
        ^EMP#
%

METHOD : EMP
    SET_EMP# : EMP#_PARM
        EMP#  :=  EMP#_PARM
%
```

We will have more to say regarding method definition in the next subsection. Meanwhile, here is the definition of the COURSE class:

```
1   OBJECT SUBCLASS : 'COURSE'
2       INSTVARNAMES : #[ 'COURSE#', 'TITLE', 'OFFERINGS' ]
3       CONSTRAINTS  : #[ #[ #COURSE#, STRING ] ,
4                          [ #TITLE, STRING ] ,
5                          [ #OFFERINGS, OSET ] ] .
```

Explanation: Line 5 here specifies that the private instance variable OFFERINGS will contain **the OID of** an object of class OSET (a class we will define in a few moments). Informally, OFFERINGS will denote the set of all offerings for the course in question; in other words, we have chosen to model the course/offerings relationship as a containment hierarchy, in which offerings are conceptually contained within the corresponding course.

Next the OFFERING class:

```
1   OBJECT SUBCLASS : 'OFFERING'
2       INSTVARNAMES : #[ 'OFF#', 'ODATE', 'LOCATION',
3                          'ENROLLMENTS', 'TEACHERS' ]
4       CONSTRAINTS  : #[ #[ #OFF#, STRING ] ,
5                          [ #ODATE, DATETIME ] ,
6                          [ #LOCATION, STRING ] ,
7                          [ #ENROLLMENTS, NSET ] ,
8                          [ #TEACHERS, TSET ] ] .
```

Explanation: Line 7 specifies that the private instance variable ENROLLMENTS will contain the OID of an object of class NSET; informally, ENROLLMENTS will denote the set of all enrollments for the offering in question. Likewise, TEACHERS will denote the set of all teachers for the offering in question. Again, therefore, we are adopting a containment hierarchy representation. See later for the NSET and TSET definitions.

Next the ENROLLMENT class:

```
1   OBJECT SUBCLASS : 'ENROLLMENT'
2       INSTVARNAMES : #[ 'EMP', 'GRADE' ]
3       CONSTRAINTS  : #[ #[ #EMP, EMP ] ,
4                          [ #GRADE, STRING ] ] .
```

Explanation: The private instance variable EMP (line 3) will contain the OID of an object of class EMP, representing the individual employee to whom this enrollment pertains. *Note:* We have placed the EMP object "inside" the corresponding ENROLLMENT object in order to continue with the containment hierarchy representation. But notice the asymmetry: Enrollments are a many-to-many relationship, but the participants in that relationship, employees and offerings, are being treated quite differently.

Finally, teachers. For the sake of the example, we depart slightly from the original relational version of the database and treat teachers as a subclass of employees:

```
1   EMP SUBCLASS : 'TEACHER'
2       INSTVARNAMES  : #[ 'COURSES' ]
3       CONSTRAINTS   : #[ #[ #COURSES, CSET ] ] .
```

Explanation: Line 1 defines an object class called TEACHER, a subclass of the user-defined class EMP (in other words, TEACHER "ISA" EMP). Thus, each individual

TEACHER object has private instance variables EMP#, ENAME, and POSITION (all inherited from EMP*), plus COURSES, which will contain the OID of an object of class CSET; that CSET object will denote the set of all courses this teacher can teach. Each TEACHER object also inherits all EMP methods.

As already noted, the foregoing class definitions assume the existence of several collection classes (ESET, CSET, OSET, NSET, and TSET). Here now are the definitions of those classes:

```
1   SET SUBCLASS     : 'ESET'
2         CONSTRAINTS :  EMP .
```

Explanation: Line 1 defines an object class ESET, a subclass of the builtin SET class. Line 2 constrains objects of class ESET to be sets of OIDs of objects of class EMP. In general, there could be any number of objects of class ESET, but we will create just one (see the next subsection), which will be the set of OIDs of *all* EMP objects that currently exist in the database. Informally, that single ESET object can be regarded as the object analog of the EMP base relvar in the relational version of the database.

The CSET, OSET, NSET, and TSET definitions are analogous (see below). In each of these cases, however, we will definitely have to create several objects of the relevant collection class, not just one; for example, there will be a separate OSET collection object for each individual COURSE object.

```
SET SUBCLASS     : 'CSET'
      CONSTRAINTS :  COURSE .

SET SUBCLASS     : 'OSET'
      CONSTRAINTS :  OFFERING .

SET SUBCLASS     : 'NSET'
      CONSTRAINTS :  ENROLLMENT .

SET SUBCLASS     : 'TSET'
      CONSTRAINTS :  TEACHER .
```

Populating the Database

Now we consider what is involved in populating the database. We consider each of the five basic object classes (EMP, COURSE, etc.) in turn. First employees. Recall that we intend to collect together the OIDs of all currently existing EMP objects in an ESET object, so first we need to create that ESET object:

```
OID_OF_SET_OF_ALL_EMPS  :=  ESET NEW .
```

The expression on the right-hand side of this assignment returns the OID of a new, empty instance of class ESET (i.e., an empty set of EMP OIDs); the OID of that new instance is then assigned to the program variable OID_OF_SET_OF_ALL_EMPS. *Very* informally, we will say that OID_OF_SET_OF_ALL_EMPS denotes "the set of all employees."

---

*Note that it is the *private* representation (i.e., the physical implementation) that is being inherited here.

Now, every time we create a new EMP object we want the OID of that object to be inserted into the ESET object identified by the OID just saved in the variable OID_OF_SET_OF_ALL_EMPS. We therefore define a *method* for creating such an EMP object and inserting its OID into that ESET object. (Alternatively, we could write an application program to perform the same task.) Here is that method:

```
1    METHOD : ESET                              " anonymous!      "
2      ADD_EMP#  : EMP#_PARM                     " parameters      "
3      ADD_ENAME : ENAME_PARM
4      ADD_POS   : POS_PARM
5      | EMP_OID |                               " local variable "
6      EMP_OID := EMP NEW .                      " new employee   "
7      EMP_OID SET_EMP#  : EMP#_PARM ;           " initialize     "
8              SET_ENAME : ENAME_PARM ;
9              SET_POS   : POS_PARM .
10     SELF ADD: EMP_OID .                       " insert         "
11   %
```

Explanation:

- Line 1 defines the code that follows (up to the terminating percent sign in line 11) to be a method that applies to objects of class ESET. (In fact, of course, *exactly one* object of class ESET will exist in the system at run time.)

- Lines 2–4 define three parameters, with external names ADD_EMP#, ADD_ENAME, and ADD_POS. These names are used in messages that invoke the method. The corresponding internal names EMP#_PARM, ENAME_PARM, and POS_PARM are used in the code that implements the method.

- Line 5 defines EMP_OID to be a local variable, and line 6 then assigns to that variable the OID of a new, uninitialized EMP instance.

- Lines 7–9 send a message to that new EMP instance; the message specifies three methods to be invoked (SET_EMP#, SET_ENAME, and SET_POS) and passes one argument to each of them (EMP#_PARM to SET_EMP#, ENAME_PARM to SET_ENAME, and POS_PARM to SET_POS). *Note:* We are assuming here that methods SET_ENAME and SET_POS—analogous to the method SET_EMP# shown earlier—have also been defined already.

- Line 10 sends a message to SELF, which is a special symbol that denotes the object to which the method being defined is currently being applied at run time (i.e., the current *target* object). The message causes the builtin method ADD to be applied to that object (ADD is a method that is understood by all collections); the effect in the case at hand is to insert the OID of the object identified by EMP_OID into the object identified by SELF (which will be the ESET object containing the OIDs for all EMP objects that currently exist). *Note:* The reason the special variable SELF is required is that the parameter corresponding to the target object has no name of its own (see line 1).

- Note that—as pointed out in the comment in line 1—the method being defined is likewise unnamed. In general, in fact, methods do not have names in OPAL, but instead are identified by their *signature* (defined in OPAL to be the combination of the name of the class to which they apply and the external names of their parameters). This convention can lead to awkward circumlocutions, as can be seen. Note too another slightly unfortunate implication: namely, that if two methods both apply to the same class and take the same parameters, those parameters must be given arbitrarily different external names in the two methods.

Now we have a method for inserting new EMPs into the database, but we still have not actually inserted any. So let us do so:

```
OID_OF_SET_OF_ALL_EMPS ADD_EMP#  :  'E009'
                       ADD_ENAME :  'Helms'
                       ADD_POS   :  'Janitor' .
```

This statement creates an EMP object for employee E009 and adds the OID of that EMP object to the set of OIDs of all currently existing EMP objects.

Note, incidentally, that the builtin NEW method must now never be used on class EMP other than as part of the method we have just defined—for otherwise we might create some dangling EMP objects, i.e., employees who are not represented in the ESET object containing the OIDs for all EMP objects that currently exist. *Note:* We apologize for the burdensome repetition of awkward circumlocutions like "the method we have just defined" and "the ESET object containing the OIDs for all EMP objects that currently exist," but it is hard to talk about things that have no name.

Now we turn to courses. Employees really represent the simplest possible case, since they correspond to "regular entities" (to use the terminology of the E/R model), and moreover do not contain other objects embedded within themselves (apart from immutable ones). We now move on to consider the more complex case of *courses,* which—although still "regular entities"—do conceptually include other mutable objects embedded within them. In outline, the steps we must go through are as follows:

1. Apply the NEW method to class CSET to create an initially empty "set of all courses" (actually COURSE OIDs).

2. Define a method for creating a new COURSE object and adding its OID to "the set of all courses." That method will take a specified COURSE# and TITLE as arguments and will create a new COURSE object with the specified values. It will also apply the NEW method to class OSET to create an initially empty set of OFFERING OIDs, and will then place the OID of that empty set of offering OIDs into the OFFERINGS position within the new COURSE object.

3. Invoke the method just defined for each individual course in turn.

Next we turn to offerings. This time the steps are as follows:

1. Define a method for creating a new OFFERING object. That method will take a specified OFF#, ODATE, and LOCATION as arguments and create a new OFFERING object with those specified values. It will also:

   ■ Apply the NEW method to class NSET to create an initially empty set of EN-ROLLMENT OIDs, and then place the OID of that empty set into the ENROLL-MENTS position within the new OFFERING object.

- Apply the NEW method to class TSET to create an initially empty set of TEACHER OIDs, and then place the OID of that empty set into the TEACHERS position within the new OFFERING object.

2. The method will also take a COURSE# value as argument and use that COURSE# value to:

   - Locate the corresponding COURSE object for the new OFFERING object (see the next subsection for an indication of how this might be done). *Note:* Of course, the method must reject the attempt to create a new offering if the corresponding course cannot be found. We omit detailed consideration of such exception cases throughout these discussions.

   - Hence, locate "the set of all offerings" for that COURSE object.

   - Hence, add the OID of the new OFFERING object to the appropriate "set of all offerings."

   Note carefully, therefore, that (as mentioned earlier in this chapter) OIDs do not avoid the need for user keys such as COURSE#. Indeed, such keys are needed, not just to refer to objects in the outside world, but also to serve as the basis for certain lookups inside the database.

3. Finally, invoke the method just defined for each individual offering in turn.

Observe, incidentally, that (in keeping with our containment hierarchy design) we have chosen not to create a "set of *all* offerings." One implication of this omission is that any query that requires that set as its scope—e.g., "Get all offerings in New York"—will involve a certain amount of procedural workaround code (see the next subsection).

Next, enrollments. The difference in kind between the enrollments and offerings cases is that ENROLLMENT objects include an instance variable, EMP, whose value is the OID of the relevant EMP object. Hence the necessary sequence of steps is as follows:

1. Define a method for creating a new ENROLLMENT object. That method will take a specified COURSE#, OFF#, EMP#, and GRADE as arguments and create a new ENROLLMENT object with the specified GRADE value. It will then:

   - Use the COURSE# and OFF# values to locate the corresponding OFFERING object for the new ENROLLMENT object.

   - Hence, locate "the set of all enrollments" for that OFFERING object.

   - Hence, add the OID of the new ENROLLMENT object to the appropriate "set of all enrollments."

   It will also:

   - Use the EMP# value to locate the relevant EMP object.

   - Hence, place the OID of that EMP object in the EMP position within the new ENROLLMENT object.

2. Invoke the method just defined for each individual enrollment in turn.

Finally, teachers. The difference in kind between the teachers and offerings cases is that we have made TEACHER a subclass of EMP. Hence:

1. Define a method for creating a new TEACHER object. That method will take a specified COURSE#, OFF#, and EMP# as its arguments. It will then:

   ▪ Use the EMP# value to locate the relevant EMP object.

   ▪ Change the most specific class of that EMP object to TEACHER (since that employee is now additionally a teacher). Just how that change of class is done is highly dependent on the particular system under consideration (see Chapter 19); we omit further specifics here.

   It will also:

   ▪ Use the COURSE# and OFF# values to locate the corresponding OFFERING object for the new TEACHER object.

   ▪ Hence, locate "the set of all teachers" for that OFFERING object.

   ▪ Hence, add the OID of the new TEACHER object to the appropriate "set of all teachers."

2. In addition, the set of courses this teacher can teach must be specified somehow and the COURSES instance variable set appropriately in the new TEACHER object. We omit the details of this step here.

3. Invoke the method just defined for each individual teacher in turn.

Retrieval Operations

Before getting into details of retrieval operations as such, we make the point (though it should already be obvious) that OPAL—like object languages in general—is essentially a record-level (or object-level) language, not a set-level language. Hence, most problems will require some programmer to write procedural code. We consider a single example—the query "Get all New York offerings of course C001." We suppose for the sake of the example that we have a variable called OOSOAC whose value is the OID of "the set of all courses." Here then is the code:

```
1   | COURSE_C001 , C001_OFFS , C001_NY_OFFS |
2   COURSE_C001
3       :=  OOSOAC DETECT : [ :CX | ( CX GET_COURSE# ) = 'C001' ] .
4   C001_OFFS
5       :=  COURSE_C001 GET_OFFERINGS .
6   C001_NY_OFFS
7       :=  C001_OFFS SELECT :
8                  [ :OX | ( OX GET_LOCATION ) = 'New York' ] .
9   ^ C001_NY_OFFS .
```

Explanation:

▪ Line 1 declares three local variables—COURSE_C001, which will be used to hold the OID of course C001; C001_OFFS, which will be used to hold the OID of the set of

OIDs of offerings of course C001; and C001_NY_OFFS, which will be used to hold the OID of the set of OIDs of the offerings actually required (i.e., the New York ones).

- Lines 2–3 send a message to the (collection) object denoted by the variable OOSOAC. The message calls for the builtin method **DETECT** to be applied to that collection. The DETECT argument is an expression of the form

```
[ :x | p(x) ]
```

Here $p(x)$ is a conditional expression involving the variable x, and x is effectively a range variable that ranges over the members of the collection to which the DETECT is applied (i.e., the set of COURSE objects, in the example). The result of the DETECT is the OID of the first object x encountered in that set for which $p(x)$ evaluates to *true*— i.e., it is the COURSE object for course C001, in the example.* The OID of that COURSE object is then assigned to the variable COURSE_C001. *Note:* It is also possible to specify an "escape" argument to DETECT to deal with the case in which $p(x)$ never evaluates to *true*. We omit the details here.

- Lines 4–5 assign the OID of "the set of all offerings" for course C001 to the variable C001_OFFS.

- Lines 6–8 are rather similar to lines 2–3: The operation of the builtin method **SELECT** is the same as that of DETECT, except that it returns the OID of the set of OIDs of *all* objects x (instead of just the first such) for which $p(x)$ evaluates to *true*. In the example, therefore, the effect is to assign the OID of the set of OIDs of New York offerings of course C001 to the variable C001_NY_OFFS.

- Finally, line 9 returns that OID to the caller.

Points arising from this example:

1. First, note that the conditional expression $p(x)$ in SELECT and DETECT can involve (at its most complex) a set of simple scalar comparisons all ANDed together—i.e., it is not an arbitrarily complex search condition.

2. The brackets surrounding the overall argument expression in SELECT and DETECT can be replaced by braces. If braces are used, OPAL will attempt to use an index (if one exists) in applying the method. If brackets are used, it will not.

3. When we say that DETECT returns the OID of the "first" object encountered that makes $p(x)$ evaluate to *true*, we mean, of course, the first according to whatever sequence OPAL uses to search the set (sets have no intrinsic ordering of their own). In our example it makes no difference, because the "first" object that makes the condition true is in fact the only such.

---

*We assume throughout this example that methods such as GET_COURSE#—analogous to the method GET_EMP# shown earlier in this section—have already been defined.

4. As you might have noticed, we have been making considerable use of expressions such as "the DETECT method," whereas we pointed out previously that methods in OPAL have no names. Indeed, DETECT and SELECT are not method names (and phraseology such as "the DETECT method" is strictly incorrect). Rather, they are external parameter names for certain builtin, unnamed methods. For brevity and simplicity, however, we will continue to talk as if DETECT and SELECT (and other similar items) were indeed method names.

5. You might also have noticed that we have been using (many times!) the expression "the NEW method." This usage is in fact *not* incorrect: Methods that take no arguments other than a target are an exception to the general OPAL rule that methods are unnamed.

Update Operations

The object analog of the relational INSERT operation has already been discussed in the previous subsection. The object analogs of UPDATE and DELETE are discussed below.

- *Update:* Update operations are performed in essentially the same manner as retrieval operations, except that SET_ methods are used instead of GET_ methods.

- *Delete:* The builtin method REMOVE is used to delete objects (more precisely, it is used to remove the OID of a specified object from a specified collection). When an object reaches a point when there are no remaining references to it—i.e., it can no longer be accessed at all—then OPAL deletes it automatically by means of a garbage-collection process. Here is an example:

```
E001  :=  OID_OF_SET_OF_ALL_EMPS
              DETECT : [ :EX | ( EX GET_EMP# ) = 'E001' ] .
OID_OF_SET_OF_ALL_EMPS REMOVE : E001 .
```

("remove employee E001 from the set of all employees").

But what if we want to enforce (say) an ON DELETE CASCADE rule?—for example, a rule to the effect that deleting an employee is to delete all enrollments for that employee as well? The answer, of course, is that we have to implement an appropriate method once again; in other words, we have to write some more procedural code.

Incidentally, it might be thought that the garbage-collection approach to deletion does at least implement a kind of ON DELETE RESTRICT rule, inasmuch as an object is not actually deleted so long as any references to that object exist. However, such is not necessarily the case. For example, OFFERING objects do not include the OID of the corresponding COURSE object, and hence offerings do not "restrict" DELETEs on courses. (In fact, containment hierarchies tacitly imply a kind of ON DELETE CASCADE rule, unless the user chooses either

- To include the OID of the parent in the child, or
- To include the OID of the child in some other object elsewhere in the database,

in which case the containment hierarchy interpretation no longer makes sense anyway. See the discussion of *inverse variables* in the next section.)

Note finally that REMOVE can be used to emulate a relational DROP operation—e.g., to drop the ENROLLMENT class. The details are left as an exercise.

24.5   MISCELLANEOUS ISSUES

In this section we take a brief look at a somewhat mixed bag of issues—namely:

- *Ad hoc* query and related issues
- Integrity
- Relationships
- Database programming languages
- Performance considerations
- Is an object DBMS really a DBMS?

Ad Hoc Query and Related Issues

We deliberately did not stress the point earlier, but if it is really true that predefined methods are the only way to manipulate objects, then *ad hoc* query is impossible!—unless classes and methods are designed in accordance with a certain very specific discipline. For example, if the only methods defined for class DEPT are (as suggested in Section 24.2) HIRE_EMP, FIRE_EMP, and CUT_BUDGET, then even a query as simple as "Who is the manager of the programming department?" cannot be handled.

For essentially the same reason, view definitions and declarative integrity constraints on objects are also impossible, in general—again, unless a certain specific discipline is followed.

Our own recommended solution to these problems (i.e., the "specific discipline" we have in mind) is as follows:

1. Define a set of operators ("THE_ operators") that expose *some possible representation* for the objects in question, as discussed in Chapter 5.

2. Embed the objects properly in a relational framework. This part of the solution is discussed in detail in the next chapter.

However, object systems typically do *not* follow this discipline—not exactly. Instead:*

1. They typically define operators that expose, not some *possible* representation, but rather the *actual* representation (see the discussion of public instance variables in Sec-

---

*We assume here that the object system in question does in fact support *ad hoc* query, as indeed most modern ones do. Early systems sometimes did not, however, partly for reasons discussed later in this section.

tion 24.2). "All object DBMS products currently require that [instance variables] referenced in . . . queries be public" [24.38].

2. They typically support, not a relational framework, but rather a variety of other frameworks based on bags, arrays, etc. In this connection, we remind you of our contention that classes—i.e., types—plus relations are both necessary and sufficient at the logical level (see Chapter 3); as far as the core model is concerned, in fact, we believe that arrays and the rest are both unnecessary and undesirable. We conjecture that the emphasis on collections other than relations (and in fact the almost total rejection of relations) in and by object systems derives from a confusion over model *vs.* implementation issues once again.

There is another important question that arises in connection with *ad hoc* query—namely, what class is the result? For example, suppose we execute the query "Get name and salary for employees in the programming department" against the departments and employees database of Section 24.3. Presumably the result has (public) instance variables ENAME and SALARY. But there is no class in the database that has this structure. Do we therefore have to predefine such a class before we can ask the query? (Note the implications if we do: A class with n instance variables would require at least 2^n such predefined classes in order to support retrieval operations alone!) And whatever the result class is, what methods apply to it?

Analogous questions arise in connection with join operations. If we can join department and employee objects together, then again what class is the result? What methods apply?

Possibly because such questions are hard to answer in a pure object framework, some object systems support "path tracing" operations [24.25,24.47] instead of joins *per se*. Given the OPAL database of Section 24.4, for example, the following might be a valid path expression:

```
ENROLLMENT . OFFERING . COURSE
```

Meaning: "Access the unique COURSE object referenced by the unique OFFERING object referenced by this ENROLLMENT object."* A relational analog of this expression would typically involve two joins and a projection. In other words, path tracing implies access along predefined paths only (as in prerelational systems, in fact), to objects of predefined classes only (again as in prerelational systems).

Integrity

We claimed in Chapter 8 that data integrity is absolutely fundamental. However, object systems, even ones that do support *ad hoc* query, usually do not support declarative integrity constraints; instead, they require such constraints to be enforced by means of procedural

---

*Actually this example is *not* a valid path expression for the database as we have defined it, because the pointers point the wrong way! For example, OFFERINGs do not reference COURSEs but are referenced by them.

code (i.e., by methods, or possibly application programs). For example, consider the following constraint (or "business rule") from Section 8.5: "No supplier with status less than 20 can supply any part in a quantity greater than 500." Procedural code to enforce this constraint will typically have to be included in at least all of the following methods:

- Method for creating a shipment
- Method for changing a shipment quantity
- Method for changing a supplier status
- Method for assigning a shipment to a different supplier

Points and questions arising:

1. We have obviously lost the possibility of the system determining for itself when to do the integrity checking.
2. How do we ensure that all necessary methods include all necessary enforcement code?
3. How do we prevent the user from (e.g.) bypassing the "create shipment" method and using the builtin method NEW directly on the shipment object class, thereby bypassing the integrity check?
4. If the constraint changes, how do we find all methods that need to be rewritten?
5. How do we ensure that the enforcement code is correct?
6. How do we do deferred (COMMIT-time) integrity checking?
7. What about transition constraints?
8. How do we query the system to find all constraints that apply to a given object or combination of objects?
9. Will the constraints be enforced during load and other utility processing?
10. What about semantic optimization (i.e., using integrity constraints to simplify queries, as discussed in Chapter 17)?

And what are the implications of all of the above for productivity, both during application creation and subsequent application maintenance?

Relationships

Object products and the object literature typically use the term "relationships" to mean, specifically, relationships that would be represented by *foreign keys* in a relational system. And they then typically provide special-case support for this special kind of integrity constraint, as follows. Consider departments and employees once again. In a relational system, employees would normally have a foreign key referencing departments, and that would be the end of the matter. In an object system, by contrast, there are at least these three possibilities:

1. Employees can include an OID referencing departments. This possibility is similar to the relational approach but *not* identical (OIDs and foreign keys are not the same thing).

2. Departments can include a set of OIDs referencing employees. This possibility corresponds to the containment hierarchy approach as described in Section 24.3.

3. Approaches 2 and 3 can be combined as indicated here:

```
CLASS EMP ...
    ( ... DEPT REF ( DEPT ) INVERSE DEPT.EMPS ) ... ;

CLASS DEPT ...
    ( ... EMPS
            REF ( SET ( REF ( EMP ) ) ) INVERSE EMP.DEPT ) ... ;
```

Note the INVERSE specifications on the instance variables EMP.DEPT and DEPT.EMPS. These two instance variables are said to be **inverses** of each other; EMP.DEPT is a *reference* instance variable and DEPT.EMPS is a *reference-set* instance variable. (If they were both reference-set variables, the relationship would be many-to-many instead of one-to-many.)

Each of these possibilities requires some kind of referential integrity support, of course (see below). First, however, there is an obvious question that needs to be asked: How do object systems deal with relationships that involve more than two classes—say that involving suppliers, parts, and projects? The best (i.e., most symmetric) answer to this question seems to require an "SPJ" class to be created, such that each individual SPJ object has an "inverse variables" relationship with the appropriate supplier, the appropriate part, and the appropriate project. But then—given that creating a new object class is apparently the best approach for relationships of degree more than two—the obvious question arises as to why relationships of degree two are not treated in the same way.

Also, regarding inverse variables specifically, why is it necessary to introduce the asymmetry, the directionality, and two different names for what is essentially one thing? For example, the object analogs of the two relational expressions

```
SP.P# WHERE SP.S# = S#('S1')
SP.S# WHERE SP.P# = P#('P1')
```

look something like this:

```
S.PARTS.P# WHERE S.S# = S#('S1')
P.SUPPS.S# WHERE P.P# = P#('P1')
```

(hypothetical syntax, deliberately chosen to highlight essential distinctions—e.g., the use of two distinct relationship names, PARTS and SUPPS—and avoid irrelevancies).

Referential integrity: As promised, we now take a slightly closer look at object support for referential integrity (which is frequently claimed as a strength of object systems, incidentally). Various levels of support are possible. The following taxonomy is taken from Cattell [24.11]:

- *No system support:* Referential integrity is the responsibility of user-written code (as it was in the original SQL standard, incidentally).

- *Reference validation:* The system checks that all references are to existing objects of the right type; however, object deletion might not be allowed—instead, objects might be garbage-collected when there are no remaining references to them, as in OPAL. As explained in Section 24.4, this level of support is roughly equivalent (but only roughly) to (a) an ON DELETE CASCADE rule for nonshared subobjects within a containment hierarchy and (b) a kind of ON DELETE RESTRICT rule for other objects (but only if "the pointers point the right way").

- *System maintenance:* Here the system keeps all references up-to-date automatically (e.g., by setting references to deleted objects to *nil*). This level of support is somewhat akin to an ON DELETE SET NULL rule.

- *"Custom semantics":* ON DELETE CASCADE (outside of a containment hierarchy) might be an example of this case. Such possibilities are typically not supported by object systems at the time of writing but must rather be handled by user-written code.

Database Programming Languages

The OPAL examples in Section 24.4 illustrate the point that object systems typically do not employ the SQL-style "embedded data sublanguage" approach. Instead, the same **integrated language** is used for both database operations and nondatabase operations. To use the terminology of Chapter 2, the host language and the database language are *tightly coupled* in object systems (in fact, of course, they are one and the same).

Now, it is undeniable that there are advantages to such an approach.* One important one is the improved type checking that becomes possible [24.2]. And reference [24.47] argues that the following is another:

> With a single unified language, there is no *impedance mismatch* between a procedural programming language and an embedded DML with declarative semantics.

The term **impedance mismatch** here refers to the difference between the record-at-a-time level of today's typical programming languages and the set-at-a-time level of database languages such as SQL. And it is true that this difference in level does give rise to practical problems in SQL products. However, the solution to those problems is *not* to bring the database language down to the record level (which is what object systems do)!—it is to bring the programming language up to the set level instead. The fact that object languages are record-level (i.e., procedural) is a throwback to the days of prerelational systems such as IMS and IDMS.

To pursue this latter point just a moment longer: It is indeed the case that most object languages are procedural or "3GL" in nature. As a consequence, all of the relational set-level advantages are lost; in particular, the system's ability to optimize user requests is severely undermined, which means that—as in prerelational systems—performance is left in large part to human users (application programmers and/or the DBA). See the subsection immediately following.

---

*Indeed, the language **Tutorial D** used elsewhere in this book adopts the same approach, for reasons described in reference [3.3].

Performance Considerations

Raw performance is one of the biggest objectives of all for object systems. To quote Cattell again [24.11]: "An order-of-magnitude performance difference can effectively constitute a *functional* difference, because it is not possible to use the system at all if performance is too far below requirements" (slightly paraphrased).

Many factors are relevant to the performance issue. Here are a few of them:*

- *Clustering:* As we saw in Chapter 17, physical clustering of logically related data on the disk is one of the most important performance factors of all. Object systems typically use logical information from the database definition (regarding class hierarchies, containment hierarchies, or other explicitly declared interobject relationships) as a hint as to how the data should be physically clustered. Alternatively (and preferably), the DBA might be given some more explicit and direct control over the conceptual/internal mapping (to use the terminology of Chapter 2 again).

- *Caching:* Object systems are typically intended for use in a client/server environment. Fetching clustered (and hence—ideally—logically related) data as a unit from the server site and caching it for an extended period of time at the client site obviously makes sense in such an environment.

- *Swizzling:* The term "swizzling" refers to the process of replacing OID-style pointers—which are typically logical disk addresses—by main memory addresses when objects are read into memory (and *vice versa* when the objects are written back to the database, of course). The advantages for applications that process "complex objects" and thus require extensive pointer chasing are obvious.

- *Executing methods at the server:* Consider the query "Get all books with more than 20 chapters." In a traditional relational system, books might be represented as BLOBs,[†] and the client application will have to retrieve each book in turn and scan it to see if it has more than 20 chapters. In an object system, by contrast, the "get chapter count" operator will be executed by the server, and only those books actually desired will be transmitted to the client.[‡]

   Note: The foregoing is not really an argument for objects, it is an argument for *stored procedures* (see Chapters 8 and 20). A traditional SQL system with stored procedures will give the same performance benefits here as an object system with methods.

---

*In addition to the factors listed, it could be argued that object systems achieve improved performance (to the extent they actually do) by "moving users closer to the machine"—i.e., by exposing features such as pointers that ought to be hidden in the implementation.

[†]*A note regarding BLOBs:* Although no such data type is included in the SQL/92 standard, SQL products have traditionally provided "BLOBs" as a basis for dealing with "binary large objects" ("objects" here meaning objects in the generic sense, not in the special sense of object systems). A BLOB is essentially just an arbitrarily long byte string; the system provides storage and retrieval support for such strings, but not much other support. Physically, BLOBs are often stored in a special area of their own, separate from the primary storage area for the relations that logically contain them (they can and often do occupy many physical pages on the disk).

[‡]Actually this is an oversimplification: Data-intensive methods are better executed at the server, but others —e.g., display-intensive ones—might better be executed at the client.

Reference [24.13] discusses a benchmark called OO1 for measuring system performance on a bill-of-materials database. The benchmark involves:

1. Random retrieval of 1000 parts, applying a user-defined method to each;
2. Random insertion of 1000 parts, connecting each one to three others; and
3. Random part explosion (up to 7 levels), applying a user-defined method to every part encountered, together with the corresponding implosion.

According to reference [24.13], comparison of an (unspecified) object product with an (unspecified) SQL product showed a performance difference of up to two orders of magnitude in favor of the object system—especially on "warm" accesses (after the cache had been populated). However, reference [24.13] is also careful to say that:

> The differences . . . should *not* be attributed to a difference between the relational and object models . . . There is reason to believe that most of the differences can be attributed to [implementation matters].

This disclaimer is supported by the fact that the differences were much smaller when the database was "large" (i.e., when it was no longer possible to accommodate the entire database in the cache).

A similar but more extensive benchmark called OO7 is described in reference [24.10].

Is an Object DBMS Really a DBMS?

Note: The remarks in this subsection are taken for the most part from reference [24.18], which argues among other things that object and relational systems are more different than is usually realized. To quote: "Object databases grew out of a desire on the part of object application programmers—for a variety of application-specific reasons—to keep their application-specific objects in persistent memory. That persistent memory might perhaps be regarded as a database, but the important point is that *it was indeed application-specific;* it was not a shared, general-purpose database, intended to be suitable for applications that might not have been foreseen at the time the database was defined. As a consequence, many features that database professionals regard as essential were simply not requirements in the object world, at least not originally. Thus, there was little perceived need for:

1. Data sharing across applications
2. Physical data independence
3. *Ad hoc* queries
4. Views and logical data independence
5. Application-independent, declarative integrity constraints
6. Data ownership and a flexible security mechanism
7. Concurrency control
8. A general-purpose catalog
9. Application-independent database design

"These requirements all surfaced later, after the basic idea of storing objects in a database was first conceived, and thus all constitute add-on features to the original object model . . . One important consequence . . . is that there really is a **difference in kind** between an object DBMS and a relational DBMS. In fact, it could be argued that an object DBMS is not really a DBMS at all—at least, not in the same sense that a relational DBMS is a DBMS. For consider:

- A relational DBMS comes *ready* for use. In other words, as soon as the system is installed, users . . . can start building databases, writing applications, running queries, and so on.

- An object DBMS, by contrast, can be thought of as a kind of *DBMS construction kit.* When it is originally installed, it is *not* available for immediate use . . . Instead, it must first be *tailored* by suitably skilled technicians, who must define the necessary classes and methods, etc. (the system provides a set of building-blocks—class library maintenance tools, method compilers, etc.—for this purpose). Only when that tailoring activity is complete will the system be available for use by application programmers and end users; in other words, the result of that tailoring will indeed more closely resemble a DBMS in the more familiar sense of the term.

"Note further that the resultant 'tailored' DBMS will be *application-specific;* it might, for example, be suitable for CAD/CAM applications, but be essentially useless for, e.g., medical applications. In other words, it will still not be a general-purpose DBMS, in the same sense that a relational DBMS is a general-purpose DBMS."

The same paper [24.18] also argues against the idea—often referred to as **"persistence orthogonal to type"** [24.2]—according to which the database is allowed to include (mutable) objects of arbitrary complexity: "The object model requires support for [a large number of] *type generators* . . . Examples include STRUCT (or TUPLE), LIST, ARRAY, SET, BAG, and so on . . . Along with object IDs, the availability of these type generators essentially means that *any data structure that can be created in an application program can be created as an object in an object database*—and further that the structure of such objects is *visible to the user.* For example, consider the object, EX say, that is (or rather denotes) the collection of employees in a given department. Then EX might be implemented either as a linked list or as an array, and users will have to know which it is (because the access operators will differ accordingly).

"This *anything-goes* approach to what can be stored in the database is a major point of difference between the object and relational models, of course, and it deserves a little further discussion here. In essence:

- The object model says we can store anything we like—any data structure we can create with the usual programming language mechanisms.

- The relational model effectively says the same thing, but goes on to insist that whatever we do store be presented to the user in pure relational form.

"More precisely, the relational model—quite rightly—says *nothing* about what can be physically stored . . . It therefore imposes no limits on what data structures are allowed at the physical level; the only requirement is that whatever structures *are* in fact physically stored must be mapped to relations at the logical level and hence be hidden from the user. Relational systems thus make a clear distinction between logical and physical (data model *vs.* implementation), while object systems do not. One consequence is that—contrary to conventional wisdom—object systems might very well provide less data independence than relational systems. For example, suppose the implementation in some object database of the object EX mentioned above (denoting the collection of employees in a given department) is changed from an array to a linked list. What are the implications for existing code that accesses that object EX?"

24.6   SUMMARY

By way of summary, here is a list of the principal features of the object model as we have presented it, together with a subjective assessment as to which features are essential; which ones are "nice to have" but not essential; which are "nasty to have"; which are really orthogonal to the question of whether the system is an object system or some other kind; and so on. This analysis paves the way for our discussion of *object/relational* systems in Chapter 25.

- **Object classes** (i.e., *types*): Obviously essential (indeed, they are the most fundamental construct of all).

- **Objects:** Objects themselves, both "mutable" and "immutable," are clearly essential—though we would prefer to call them simply *variables* and *values,* respectively.

- **Object IDs:** Unnecessary, and in fact undesirable (at the model level, that is), because they are basically just pointers. See reference [24.19] for an extended discussion of this issue.

- **Encapsulation:** As explained in Section 24.2, "encapsulated" just means *scalar,* and we would prefer to use that term (always remembering that some "objects" are not scalar anyway).

- **Instance variables:** First, *private* (also *protected*) instance variables are by definition merely implementation matters and hence not relevant to the definition of an abstract model, which is what we are concerned with here. Second, *public* instance variables do not exist in a pure object system and are thus also not relevant. We conclude that instance variables can be ignored; "objects" should be manipulable solely by "methods."

- **Containment hierarchy:** We explained in Section 24.3 that in our opinion containment hierarchies are misleading and in fact a misnomer, since they typically contain OIDs, not "objects." *Note:* A (nonencapsulated) hierarchy that really did include objects *per se* would be permissible, however, though usually contraindicated; it would be analogous, somewhat, to a relvar with relation-valued attributes (see Parts II and III of this book).

- **Methods:** The concept is essential, of course, though we would prefer to use the more conventional term *operators*. Bundling methods with classes is *not* essential, however, and leads to several problems [3.3]; we would prefer to define "classes" (types) and "methods" (operators) separately, as we did in Chapter 5, and thereby avoid the notion of "target objects."

  There are certain operators we would insist on, too: Selectors (which among other things effectively provide a way of writing literal values of the relevant type), THE_ operators, assignment and equality comparison operators, and type testing operators (see Chapter 19). *Note:* We reject "constructor functions," however. Constructors construct *variables;* since the only variable we want in the database is, specifically, the relvar, the only "constructor" we need is an operator that creates a relvar (CREATE TABLE or CREATE VIEW, in SQL terms). Selectors, by contrast, select *values.* Also, of course, constructors return *pointers to* the constructed variables, while selectors return the selected values *per se.*

- **Messages:** Again, the concept is essential, though we would prefer to use the more conventional term *invocation* (and, again, avoid the notion that such invocations have to be directed at some "target object," but instead treat all arguments equally).

- **Class hierarchy** (and related notions—inheritance, substitutability, inclusion polymorphism, and so on): Desirable but orthogonal (we see class hierarchy support, if provided, as just part of support for classes *per se*).

- **Class *vs.* instance *vs.* collection:** The distinctions are essential, of course, but orthogonal (the *concepts* are distinct, and that is really all that needs to be said).

- **Relationships:** We have already argued in Chapter 13 (Section 13.6) that it is not a good idea to treat "relationships" as a formally distinct construct—especially if it is only binary relationships that receive such special treatment. We also do not think it is a good idea to treat the associated referential integrity constraints in some manner that is divorced from the treatment (if any) of integrity constraints in general (see below).

- **Integrated database programming language:** Nice to have, but orthogonal. However, the languages actually supported in today's object systems are typically *procedural* (3GLs) and therefore—we would argue—nasty to have (in fact, a giant step backward).

And here is a list of features that "the object model" typically does *not* support or does not support well:

- ***Ad hoc* queries:** Early object systems typically did not support *ad hoc* queries at all. More recent systems do, but they do so, typically, either by breaking encapsulation or by imposing limits on the queries that can be asked (meaning in this latter case that the queries are not really *ad hoc* after all).

- **Views:** Typically not supported (for essentially the same reasons that *ad hoc* queries are typically not supported). *Note:* Some object systems do support "derived" or "virtual" instance variables (necessarily public ones); for example, the instance variable AGE might be derived by subtracting the value of the instance variable BIRTH-DATE from the current date. However, such a capability falls far short of a full view mechanism—and in any case we have already rejected the notion of public instance variables.

- **Declarative integrity constraints:** Typically not supported (for essentially the same reasons that *ad hoc* queries and views are typically not supported). In fact, they are typically not supported even by systems that do support *ad hoc* queries.

- **Foreign keys:** The "object model" has several different mechanisms for dealing with referential integrity, none of which is quite the same as the relational model's more uniform foreign key mechanism. Such matters as ON DELETE RESTRICT and ON DELETE CASCADE are typically left to procedural code (probably methods, possibly application code).

- **Closure:** What is the object analog of the relational closure property?

- **Catalog:** Where is the catalog in an object system? What does it look like? Are there any standards? *Note:* These questions are rhetorical, of course. What actually happens is that a catalog has to be built by the professional staff whose job it is to tailor the object DBMS for whatever application it has been installed for, as discussed at the end of Section 24.5. (That catalog will then be application-specific, as will the overall tailored DBMS.)

To summarize, then, the good (essential, fundamental) features of the "object model"—i.e., the ones we would really like to support—are as shown in the following table:

Feature	Preferred term	Remarks
object class	type	scalar & nonscalar; possibly user-defined
immutable object	value	scalar & nonscalar
mutable object	variable	scalar & nonscalar
method	operator	including selectors, THE_ ops, ":=", "=", & type test operators
message	operator invocation	no "target" operand

More succinctly, we might say that the sole good idea of object systems in general is **proper data type support** (everything else—including in particular the notion of *user-defined operators*—follows from that basic idea).* But that idea is hardly new!

---

*Some might claim that type inheritance is a good idea, too. We agree, but stand by our position that support for inheritance is orthogonal to support for objects *per se*.

EXERCISES

24.1 Define the following terms:

class	message
class hierarchy	method
class-defining object	object
constructor function	object ID
containment hierarchy	private instance variable
encapsulation	protected instance variable
inverse variables	public instance variable

24.2 What are the advantages of OIDs? What are the disadvantages? How might OIDs be implemented?

24.3 In Section 24.2 we gave two SQL formulations of the query "Get all rectangles that overlap the unit square." Prove those two formulations are equivalent.

24.4 Investigate any object system that might be available to you. What programming language(s) does that system support? Does it support a query language? If so, what is it? In your opinion, is it more or less powerful than conventional SQL? What does the catalog look like? How does the user interrogate the catalog? Is there any view support? If so, how extensive is it? (e.g., what about view updating?) How is "missing information" handled?

24.5 Design an object version of the suppliers and parts database. *Note:* This design will be used as a basis for Exercises 24.6–24.8 below.

24.6 Write a set of OPAL data definition statements for your object version of suppliers and parts.

24.7 Sketch the details of the necessary "database-populating" methods for your object version of suppliers and parts.

24.8 Write OPAL code for the following queries against your object version of suppliers and parts:

a. Get all London suppliers;

b. Get all red parts.

24.9 Consider the education database once again. Show what is involved in:

a. Deleting an enrollment;

b. Deleting an employee;

c. Deleting a course;

d. Dropping the enrollments class;

e. Dropping the employees class.

You can assume that the OPAL-style garbage-collection process applies. State any assumptions you make regarding such matters as cascade delete, etc.

24.10 Suppose an object version of the suppliers-parts-projects database is to be represented by means of a single containment hierarchy. How many possible such hierarchies are there? Which one is best?

24.11 Consider a variation on the suppliers-parts-projects database in which, instead of recording that certain suppliers supply certain parts to certain projects, we wish to record only that (a) certain suppliers supply certain parts, (b) certain parts are supplied to certain projects, and (c) certain projects are supplied by certain suppliers. How many possible object designs are there now (with or without containment hierarchies)?

24.12 Consider the performance factors discussed briefly in Section 24.5. Are any of them truly object-specific? Justify your answer.

24.13 Object systems typically support integrity constraints in a *procedural* fashion, via methods; the main exception is that *referential* constraints are typically supported (at least in part) *declaratively*. What are the advantages of procedural support? Why do you think referential constraints are handled differently?

24.14 Explain the concept of *inverse variables*.

REFERENCES AND BIBLIOGRAPHY

References [24.5], [24.7], [24.11], [24.15], [24.26], [24.31], [24.38], [24.41], and [24.50] are textbooks on object topics and related matters. References [24.35–24.36] and [24.52] are collections of research papers. References [24.27–24.28], [24.44], and [24.47] are tutorials. Reference [24.4], [24.9], [24.23], and [24.37] describe specific systems.

24.1 Malcolm Atkinson *et al.:* "The Object-Oriented Database System Manifesto," Proc. 1st Int. Conf. on Deductive and Object-Oriented Databases, Kyoto, Japan (1989). New York, N.Y.: Elsevier Science (1990).

> One of the first attempts to build a consensus on what "the object model" should include. It proposes the following as mandatory features—i.e., features that (in the authors' opinion) must be supported if the DBMS in question is to deserve the label "object-oriented"):

> 1. collections
> 2. object IDs
> 3. encapsulation
> 4. types or classes
> 5. inheritance
> 6. late binding
> 7. computational completeness
> 8. user-defined types
> 9. persistence
> 10. large databases
> 11. concurrency
> 12. recovery
> 13. ad hoc query

> It also discusses certain *optional* features, including multiple inheritance and compile-time type checking; certain *open* features, including "programming paradigm"; and certain features on which the authors could reach no consensus, including—a little surprisingly, considering their importance—views and integrity constraints.

> *Note:* References [3.3] and [25.34] both comment on this paper. Regarding the comments in reference [3.3], incidentally, we should say that they are based on the premise that the aim of the paper is to define features of a good, genuine, general-purpose DBMS. We do not deny that the features listed above might be useful for a highly specialized DBMS that is tied to some specific application such as CAD/CAM, with no need for (say) integrity constraint support—but then we would question whether such a system is truly a DBMS, as that term is usually understood.

24.2 Malcolm P. Atkinson and O. Peter Buneman: "Types and Persistence in Database Programming Languages," *ACM Comp. Surv. 19,* No. 2 (June 1987).

> One of the earliest papers, if not *the* earliest, to articulate the position that persistence should be orthogonal to type. This paper is a good starting point for reading in the area of database pro-

gramming languages in general ("database programming languages" being perceived by many people as the *sine qua non* of object systems—see, for example, references [24.11–24.12]).

24.3 François Bancilhon: "A Logic-Programming/Object-Oriented Cocktail," *ACM SIGMOD Record 15,* No. 3 (September 1986).

To quote the introduction: "The object-oriented approach . . . seems to be particularly well fitted to [handling] new types of applications such as CAD, software [engineering], and [artificial intelligence]. However, the natural extension to relational database technology is . . . the logic-programming paradigm, [not] the object-oriented one. [This paper addresses the question of] whether the two paradigms are compatible." And it concludes, somewhat cautiously, that they are. *Note:* Reference [24.49] offers an opposing point of view.

24.4 J. Banerjee *et al.:* "Data Model Issues for Object-Oriented Applications," *ACM TOOIS (Transactions on Office Information Systems) 5,* No. 1 (March 1987). Republished in Michael Stonebraker (ed.), *Readings in Database Systems* (2nd edition). San Mateo, Calif.: Morgan Kaufmann (1994). Also republished in reference [24.52].

24.5 Douglas K. Barry: *The Object Database Handbook: How to Select, Implement, and Use Object-Oriented Databases.* New York, N.Y.: John Wiley and Sons (1996).

The principal thesis of this book is that we need an object system, not a relational one, if we have to deal with "complex data." Complex data is characterized as (a) ubiquitous, (b) often lacking unique identification, (c) involving numerous many-to-many relationships, and (d) often requiring the use of type codes "in the relational schema" (because of the lack of direct support for subtypes and supertypes in today's SQL products). *Note*: The author is executive director of the Object Data Management Group, ODMG [24.12].

24.6 David Beech: "A Foundation for Evolution from Relational to Object Databases," in J. W. Schmidt, S. Ceri, and M. Missikoff (eds.), *Extending Database Technology.* New York, N.Y.: Springer Verlag (1988).

This is one of several papers to discuss the possibility of extending SQL to become some kind of "Object SQL" or "OSQL" (we caution you, however, that those "Object SQLs" often do not look much like conventional SQL). Reference [24.39] gives more detail on the proposals of this particular paper.

24.7 Elisa Bertino and Lorenzo Martino: *Object-Oriented Database Systems: Concepts and Architectures.* Reading, Mass.: Addison-Wesley (1993).

24.8 Anders Björnerstedt and Christer Hultén: "Version Control in an Object-Oriented Architecture," in reference [24.36].

Many applications need the concept of distinct **versions** of a given object; examples of such applications include software development, hardware design, document creation, and so forth. And some object systems support this concept directly (though in fact it is orthogonal to the question of whether we are dealing with an object system or some other kind). Such support typically includes:

- The ability to create a new version of a given object, typically by **checking out** a copy of the object and moving it from the database to the user's private workstation, where it can be kept and modified over a possibly extended period of time (e.g., hours or days);

- The ability to establish a given object version as the current database version, typically by **checking it in** and moving it from the user's workstation back to the database (which might in turn require some kind of mechanism for **merging** distinct versions);

- The ability to **delete** (and perhaps **archive**) obsolete versions;
- The ability to interrogate the **version history** of a given object.

Note that—as Fig. 24.7 suggests—version histories are not necessarily linear (version V.2 in that figure leads to two distinct versions V.3a and V.3b, which are subsequently merged into a single version V.4).

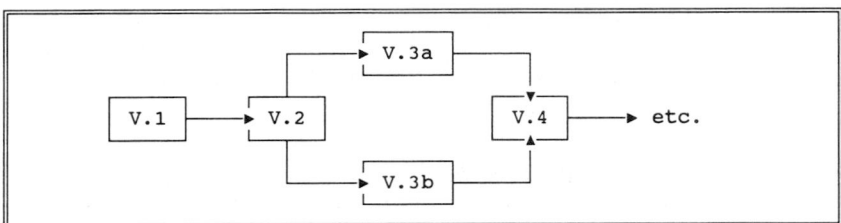

Fig. 24.7   Typical version history

Next, because objects are typically interrelated in various ways, the concept of versioning leads to the concept of *configurations*. A **configuration** is a collection of mutually consistent versions of interrelated objects. Configuration support typically includes:

- The ability to **copy** an object version from one configuration to another (e.g., from an "old" configuration to a "new" one);
- The ability to **move** an object version from one configuration to another (i.e., to add it to the "new" configuration and remove it from the "old" one).

Internally, such operations basically just involve a lot of pointer juggling—but there are major implications for language syntax and semantics in general and *ad hoc* query in particular. Most such implications are beyond the scope of this book, though the material of Chapter 22 is relevant.

24.9 Paul Butterworth, Allen Otis, and Jacob Stein: "The GemStone Object Database Management System," *CACM 34,* No. 10 (October 1991).

24.10 Michael J. Carey, David J. DeWitt, and Jeffrey F. Naughton: "The OO7 Object-Oriented Database Benchmark," Proc. 1993 ACM SIGMOD Int. Conf. on Management of Data, Washington, DC (May 1993).

24.11 R. G. G. Cattell: *Object Data Management* (revised edition). Reading, Mass.: Addison-Wesley (1994).

The first book-length tutorial on the application of object technology to databases specifically. The following edited extract suggests that the field is still a long way from any kind of consensus: "Programming languages may need new syntax . . . swizzling, replication, and new access methods also need further study . . . new end user and application development tools [are] required . . . more powerful query language features [must be] developed . . . new research in concurrency control is needed . . . timestamps and object-based concurrency semantics need more exploration . . . performance models are needed . . . new work in knowledge management needs to be integrated with object and data management capabilities . . . this [will lead to] a complex optimization problem [and] few researchers have [the necessary] expertise . . . federated [object] databases require more study."

24.12 R. G. G. Cattell and Douglas K. Barry (eds.): *The Object Database Standard: ODMG 2.0.* San Francisco, Calif.: Morgan Kaufmann (1997).

The term *ODMG* is used, loosely, to refer to the proposals of the Object Data Management Group, a consortium of representatives from "member companies [covering] almost the entire object DBMS industry." Those proposals consist of an *Object Model,* an *Object Definition Language* (ODL), an *Object Interchange Format* (OIF), an *Object Query Language* (OQL), and *bindings* of these facilities to C++, Smalltalk, and Java. (There is no "Object Manipulation Language" component; instead, object manipulation capabilities are provided by whatever language ODMG happens to be bound to.)

A detailed analysis and critique of the ODMG Object Model component can be found in reference [3.3]. See also reference [24.34].

24.13 R. G. G. Cattell and J. Skeen: "Object Operations Benchmark," *ACM TODS 17,* No. 1 (March 1992).

24.14 George Copeland and David Maier: "Making Smalltalk a Database System," Proc. 1984 ACM SIGMOD Int. Conf. on Management of Data, Boston, Mass. (June 1984). Republished in Michael Stonebraker (ed.), *Readings in Database Systems* (2nd edition). San Mateo, Calif.: Morgan Kaufmann (1994).

Describes some of the enhancements and changes that were made to Smalltalk [24.26] in order to create GemStone and OPAL.

24.15 Brad J. Cox: *Object Oriented Programming: An Evolutionary Approach.* Reading, Mass.: Addison-Wesley (1986).

A tutorial text on object ideas in the programming world, with the emphasis on the use of object techniques for software engineering.

24.16 O. J. Dahl, B. Myhrhaug, and K. Nygaard: *The SIMULA 67 Common Base Language,* Pub. S-22, Norwegian Computing Center, Oslo, Norway (1970).

SIMULA 67 was a language designed expressly for writing simulation applications. Object programming languages grew out of such languages; in fact, SIMULA 67 was really the first object language.

24.17 C. J. Date: "An Optimization Problem," in C. J. Date and Hugh Darwen, *Relational Database Writings 1989–1991.* Reading, Mass.: Addison-Wesley (1992).

24.18 C. J. Date: "Why the 'Object Model' Is Not a Data Model," in C. J. Date, Hugh Darwen, and David McGoveran, *Relational Database Writings 1994–1997.* Reading, Mass.: Addison-Wesley (1998).

24.19 C. J. Date: "Object Identifiers *vs.* Relational Keys," in C. J. Date, Hugh Darwen, and David McGoveran, *Relational Database Writings 1994–1997.* Reading, Mass.: Addison-Wesley (1998).

24.20 C. J. Date: "Encapsulation Is a Red Herring," *DBP&D 12,* No. 9 (September 1998).

In the body of this chapter, we said encapsulation implied data independence. However, we also said we would rather not use the term "encapsulation" anyway (preferring the term *scalar*). Part of the point is that "encapsulated objects" cannot provide any more data independence than *unencapsulated* relations can (at least in principle). For example, there is absolutely no reason why a base relation representing points, with Cartesian coordinate attributes X and Y, should not be stored in terms of polar coordinates R and Θ instead.

24.21 C. J. Date: "Persistence *Not* Orthogonal to Type," on the *DBP&D* website *www.dbpd.com* (October 1998).

24.22 C. J. Date: "Decent Exposure," on the *DBP&D* website *www.dbpd.com* (November 1998).

24.23 O. Deux *et al.:* "The O2 System," *CACM 34,* No. 10 (October 1991).

24.24 Fabrizio Ferrandina, Thorsten Meyer, Roberto Zicari, Guy Ferran, and Joëlle Madec: "Schema and Database Evolution in the O2 Object Database System," Proc. 21st Int. Conf. on Very Large Data Bases, Zurich, Switzerland (September 1995).

See the annotation to reference [24.43].

24.25 Jürgen Frohn, Georg Lausen, and Heinz Uphoff: "Access to Objects by Path Expressions and Rules," Proc. 20th Int. Conf. on Very Large Data Bases, Santiago, Chile (September 1994).

24.26 Adele Goldberg and David Robson: *Smalltalk-80: The Language and Its Implementation.* Reading, Mass.: Addison-Wesley (1983).

The definitive account of the pioneering efforts at the Xerox Palo Alto Research Center to design and build the Smalltalk-80 system. The first part of the book (out of four parts) is a detailed description of the Smalltalk-80 programming language, on which the OPAL language of Gem-Stone is based.

24.27 Nathan Goodman: "Object-Oriented Database Systems," *InfoDB 4,* No. 3 (Fall 1989).

Earlier editions of this book included the following quote from this paper: "At this stage it is futile to compare [the] relational and object [approaches]. We have to compare like to like: apples to apples, dreams to dreams, theory to theory, and mature products to mature products . . . [The] relational approach has been in existence for some time: It rests on a very solid theoretical foundation, and it is the basis for a large number of mature products. The object approach, by contrast, is new (at least in the database arena); it does not possess a theoretical foundation that can meaningfully be compared with the relational model, and the few products that exist can scarcely be described as mature. Thus, a great deal remains to be done before we can seriously begin to consider the question of whether object technology will ever represent a viable alternative to the relational approach."

While some of the foregoing remarks are still applicable today, matters have crystallized somewhat since those previous editions were published. In many ways, in fact, relations *vs.* objects can now be seen as something of an apples-and-oranges comparison, as we will see in Chapter 25.

24.28 Nathan Goodman: "The Object Database Debate," "The Object Data Model," and "The Object Data Model in Action," *InfoDB 5,* No. 4 (Winter 1990–91); *6,* No. 1 (Spring/Summer 1991); and *6,* No. 2 (Fall 1991).

24.29 Nathan Goodman: "An Object-Oriented DBMS War Story: Developing a Genome Mapping Database in C++," in reference [24.35].

This paper supports several of the criticisms in the body of this chapter. To quote the abstract: "Contrary to conventional wisdom, our experience suggests that it is a mistake to make the database too smart by implementing complex programs as methods inside database objects. Our experience also indicates that C++ is a poor language for implementing databases, with problems related to the mechanics of defining attributes, the mechanics of referring to objects in a systematic way, the lack of a garbage collector, and subtle traps in the inheritance model. We also found that current C++-based DBMSs lack important database functions, and to compensate for this, we were forced to provide our own simple implementations of standard DBMS functions: transaction logging for roll-forward recovery, a multi-thread transaction monitor, a query language and query processor, and storage structures. In effect, we used the C++-based DBMS as an object-oriented storage manager, and built a data management system specialized for large-scale genome mapping on top of it."

24.30 H. V. Jagadish and Xiaolei Qian: "Integrity Maintenance in an Object-Oriented Database," Proc. 18th Int. Conf. on Very Large Data Bases, Vancouver, Canada (August 1992).

Proposes a declarative integrity mechanism for object systems, showing how an integrity constraints compiler can incorporate the necessary integrity-checking code into methods for the appropriate object classes.

24.31 David Jordan: *C++ Object Databases: Programming with the ODMG Standard.* Reading, Mass.: Addison-Wesley (1997).

24.32 Michael Kifer, Won Kim, and Yehoshua Sagiv: "Querying Object-Oriented Databases." Proc. 1982 ACM SIGMOD Int. Conf. on Management of Data, San Diego, Calif. (June 1992).

Proposes another "Object SQL" called XSQL.

24.33 Won Kim: "Object-Oriented Database Systems: Promises, Reality, and the Future," Proc. 19th Int. Conf. on Very Large Data Bases, Dublin, Ireland (August 1993).

24.34 Won Kim: "Observations on the ODMG-93 Proposal for an Object-Oriented Database Language," *ACM SIGMOD Record 23,* No. 1 (March 1994).

24.35 Won Kim (ed.): *Modern Database Systems: The Object Model, Interoperability, and Beyond.* New York, N.Y.: ACM Press/Reading, Mass.: Addison-Wesley (1995).

24.36 Won Kim and Frederick H. Lochovsky: *Object-Oriented Concepts, Databases, and Applications.* Reading, Mass.: ACM Press/Addison-Wesley (1989).

24.37 Charles Lamb, Gordon Landis, Jack Orenstein, and Dan Weinreb: "The ObjectStore Database System," *CACM 34,* No. 10 (October 1991).

24.38 Mary E. S. Loomis: *Object Databases: The Essentials.* Reading, Mass.: Addison-Wesley (1995).

24.39 Peter Lyngbaek *et al.:* "OSQL: A Language for Object Databases," Technical Report HPL-DTD-91-4, Hewlett-Packard Company (January 15th, 1991).

See the annotation to reference [24.6].

24.40 Bertrand Meyer: "The Future of Object Technology," *IEEE Computer 31,* No. 1 (January 1998).

To quote: "The future of [object] databases is an interesting topic for speculation . . . Relational database vendors [have] managed since 1986 to stifle the growth of [object] databases through preemptive announcements . . . Ten years later, [object database] experts will still tell you that the offerings from the main relational vendors . . . are still far from the real thing . . . [The] market for [object] databases will continue to grow, but it will remain a fraction of the traditional database market."

24.41 Kamran Parsaye, Mark Chignell, Setrag Koshafian, and Harry Wong: *Intelligent Databases.* New York, N.Y.: John Wiley & Sons (1989).

24.42 Alexandra Poulovassilis and Carol Small: "Investigation of Algebraic Query Optimisation for Database Programming Languages," Proc. 20th Int. Conf. on Very Large Data Bases, Santiago, Chile (September 1994).

26.43 John F. Roddick: "Schema Evolution in Database Systems—An Annotated Bibliography," *ACM SIGMOD Record 21,* No. 4 (December 1992).

Traditional database products typically support only rather simple changes to an existing schema (e.g., the addition of a new attribute to an existing base relvar). However, some applications require more sophisticated schema change support, and some object prototypes have investigated this problem in depth. Note that the problem is actually more complex in an object environment, because the schema is more complex.

The following taxonomy of possible schema changes is based on one given in a paper on the object prototype ORION [24.4]. We remark that several of them (which?) seem to betray some confusion over the model *vs.* implementation distinction.

- Changes to an object class
    1. Instance variable changes
        - add instance variable
        - delete instance variable
        - rename instance variable
        - change instance variable default value
        - change instance variable data type
        - change instance variable inheritance source
    2. Method changes
        - add method
        - delete method
        - rename method
        - change method internal code
        - change method inheritance source
- Changes to the class hierarchy (assuming multiple inheritance)
    - add class A to superclass list for class B
    - delete class A from superclass list for class B
- Changes to the overall schema
    - add class (anywhere)
    - delete class (anywhere)
    - rename class
    - partition class
    - coalesce classes

It is not clear how much transparency can be achieved with respect to the foregoing changes, however, especially since views are typically not supported. In fact, the possibility of "schema evolution" implies a significant problem for object systems, owing to their 3GL nature. As reference [25.34] puts it: "If the number of indexes changes or the data is reorganized to be differently clustered, there is no way for [methods] to automatically take advantage of such changes."

Furthermore, schema evolution is also more of a *requirement* in object systems, because many of the decisions that would be DBA decisions—or even DBMS decisions!—in a relational system become application programmer decisions in an object system (see reference [24.44]). In particular, performance tuning can lead to schema redesign (again, see reference [24.44]).

24.44 C. M. Saracco: "Writing an Object DBMS Application" (in two parts), *InfoDB 7,* No. 4 (Winter 1993/94) and *InfoDB 8,* No. 1 (Spring 1994).

Gives some simple but complete (and informative) coding examples.

24.45 Gail M. Shaw and Stanley B. Zdonik: "A Query Algebra for Object-Oriented Databases," Proc. 6th IEEE Int. Conf. on Data Engineering (February 1990). Also Technical Report TR CS-89-19, Dept. of Computer Science, Brown University, Providence, R.I. (March 1989).

This paper serves to support this writer's contention that any "object algebra" will be inherently complex (because objects are complex). In particular, *equality* of arbitrarily nested hierarchic objects requires very careful treatment. The basic idea behind the specific proposals of this paper is that each query algebra operator produces a *relation,* in which each tuple contains OIDs for certain database objects. In the case of join, for example, each tuple contains OIDs of objects that match one another under the joining condition. Those tuples do not inherit any methods from the component objects.

26.46 David W. Shipman: "The Functional Data Model and the Data Language DAPLEX," *ACM TODS 6,* No. 1 (March 1981). Republished in Michael Stonebraker (ed.), *Readings in Database Systems* (2nd edition). San Mateo, Calif.: Morgan Kaufmann (1994).

There have been several attempts over the years to construct systems based on *functions* instead of relations, and DAPLEX is one of the best known. The reason we mention it here is that the functional approaches share certain ideas with the object approach, including in particular a somewhat navigational (i.e., path-tracing) style of addressing objects that are functionally related to other objects (that are functionally related to other objects, etc.). Note, however, that a function in this context is typically not a mathematical function at all; it might, for example, be multivalued. In fact, considerable violence has to be done to the function concept in order to make it capable of all the things required of it in the "functional data model" context.

24.47 Jacob Stein and David Maier: "Concepts in Object-Oriented Data Management," *DBP&D 1,* No. 4 (April 1988).

A good tutorial on object concepts, by two of the GemStone designers.

24.48 D. C. Tsichritzis and O. M. Nierstrasz: "Directions in OO Research," in reference [24.36].

This paper lends further weight to the contention of the present writer that object database technology is a long way from consensus: "There are disagreements on basic definitions; e.g., what is an object? . . . There is no reason to worry: Loose definitions are inevitable and sometimes welcome during a dynamic period of scientific discovery. They should and will become more rigorous during a period of consolidation that will inevitably follow." But object concepts have been around for well over 30 years!—in fact, they predate the relational model.

24.49 Jeffrey D. Ullman: "A Comparison between Deductive and Object-Oriented Database Systems," Proc. 2nd Int. Conf. on Deductive and Object-Oriented Databases, Munich, Germany (December 1991); C. Delobel, M. Kifer, and Y. Masunaga (eds.), *Lecture Notes in Computer Science 566.* New York, N.Y.: Springer Verlag (1992).

Although we disagree with this paper on several points of detail, we do agree with its overall conclusion, which is that "deductive" (i.e., logic-based) database systems hold more promise for the long term than object systems do. Also, the paper has an important point to make regarding *optimizability.* Suppose we were to define "an object class that behaves like binary relations, and . . . a *join* method for this class, so we can write an expression like R JOIN S JOIN T. It appears we could evaluate this expression as (R JOIN S) JOIN T or as R JOIN (S JOIN T). But can we? It was never stated what the *join* method means. Is it associative, for example? . . . The conclusion is that, if we want to program in an [object] way, and still program at the level of relations or higher, we need to give the system the information embodied in the . . . laws of relational algebra. That information cannot be deduced by the system, but must be built into it. Thus, . . . the only part of the query language that will be optimizable is the fixed set of methods for which . . . adequate semantics have been provided to the system."

24.50 Gottfried Vossen: *Data Models, Database Languages, and Database Management Systems.* Reading, Mass.: Addison-Wesley (1991).

26.51 Carlo Zaniolo: "The Database Language GEM," Proc. 1983 ACM SIGMOD Int. Conf. on Management of Data, San Jose, Calif. (May 1983). Republished in Michael Stonebraker (ed.), *Readings in Database Systems* (2nd edition). San Mateo, Calif.: Morgan Kaufmann (1994).

> GEM stands for "General Entity Manipulator." It is effectively an extension to QUEL that supports relations with set-valued attributes and relations with alternative attributes (e.g., exempt EMPs might have a SALARY attribute, while nonexempt EMPs have HOURLY_WAGE and OVERTIME attributes). It also makes use of the object idea that objects conceptually contain other objects (instead of foreign keys that reference those other objects), and extends the familiar dot qualification notation to provide a simple way of referring to attributes of such contained objects—in effect, by implicitly traversing certain predefined join paths. For example, the qualified name EMP.DEPT.BUDGET could be used to refer to the budget of the department of some given employee. Many systems have adopted and/or adapted this idea.

24.52 Stanley B. Zdonik and David Maier (eds.): *Readings in Object-Oriented Database Systems.* San Francisco, Calif.: Morgan Kaufmann (1990).

ANSWERS TO SELECTED EXERCISES

24.1 We comment here on the term *object* itself (only). Here are some "definitions" from the literature:

- "Objects are reusable modules of code that store data, information about relationships between data and applications, and processes that control data and relationships" (from a commercial product announcement).
- "An object is a chunk of private memory with a public interface" [24.47].
- "An object is an abstract machine that defines a protocol through which users of the object may interact" (introduction to reference [24.52]).
- "An object is a software structure that contains data and programs" [24.27].
- ". . . everything is an object . . . an object has a private memory and a public interface" [24.50].

Note that *none* of these "definitions" gets to what we would regard as the heart of the matter—*viz.,* that an object is essentially just a *value* (if immutable) or a *variable* (otherwise).

It is worth commenting too on the notion that "everything is an object." Here are some examples of constructs that are not objects in most object systems: *instance variables; relationships* (at least in ODMG [24.12]); *methods; OIDs; program variables.* And in some systems (again including ODMG) *values* are not objects either.

24.2 Some of the advantages of OIDs are as follows:

- They are not "intelligent." See reference [13.9] for an explanation of why this state of affairs is desirable.
- They never change so long as the object they identify remains in existence.
- They are noncomposite. See references [8.12], [13.10], and [18.8] for an explanation of why this state of affairs is desirable.
- Everything in the database is identified in the same uniform way (contrast the situation with relational databases).
- There is no need to repeat user keys in referencing objects. There is thus no need for any ON UPDATE rules.

Some of the *dis*advantages—the fact that they do not avoid the need for user keys, the fact that they lead to a low-level "pointer-chasing" style of programming, and the fact that they apply to "base" (nonderived) objects only—were discussed briefly in Sections 24.2–24.4.

Possible OID implementation techniques include:

- Physical disk addresses (fast but poor data independence);
- Logical disk addresses (i.e., page and offset addresses; fairly fast, better data independence);
- Artificial IDs (e.g., timestamps, sequence numbers; need mapping to actual addresses).

24.3 See reference [24.17].

24.5 We do not give a detailed answer to this exercise, but we do offer a few comments on the question of object database design in general. It is sometimes claimed that object systems make database design (as well as database use) easier, because they provide high-level modeling constructs and support those constructs directly in the system. (By contrast, relational systems involve an extra level of indirection: namely, the mapping process from real-world objects to relvars, attributes, foreign keys, and so on.) And there is some merit to this claim. However, it begs the larger question: How is object database design done in the first place? The fact is, "the object model" as usually understood involves far more *degrees of freedom*—in other words, more choices—than the relational model does; and this writer, at least, is unaware of the existence of any good guidelines to help in making those choices. For example, how do we decide whether to represent, say, the set of all employees as an array, or a list, or a set (etc., etc.)? "A powerful data model needs a powerful design methodology . . . and this is a *liability* of the object model" (paraphrased somewhat from reference [24.27]; we would argue that that qualifier "powerful" should really be "complicated").

24.9 We do not give a detailed answer to this exercise, but we do make one remark concerning its difficulty. First, let us agree to use the term "delete" as a shorthand to mean "make a candidate for physical deletion" (i.e., by erasing all references to the object in question). Then in order to delete an object *X,* we must first find all objects *Y* that include a reference to *X;* for each such object *Y,* we must then either delete that object *Y,* or at least erase the reference in that object *Y* to the object *X* (by setting that reference to the special value *nil*). And part of the problem is that it is not possible to tell from the data definition alone exactly which objects include a reference to *X,* nor even how many of them there are. Consider employees, for example, and the object class ESET. In principle, there could be any number of ESET instances, and any subset of those ESET instances could include a reference to some specific employee.

24.10 There are obviously six possible hierarchies:

```
S contains ( P contains ( J ) )
S contains ( J contains ( P ) )
P contains ( J contains ( S ) )
P contains ( S contains ( J ) )
J contains ( S contains ( P ) )
J contains ( P contains ( S ) )
```

"Which is best?" is unanswerable without additional information, but almost certainly *all* of them are bad.

24.11 There are at least twelve "obvious" containment hierarchy designs. Here are four of them:

```
S contains ( P contains ( J ) )
S contains ( J contains ( P ) )
S contains ( first P then J )
S contains ( first J then P )
```

There are many other candidate designs—for example, an "SP" class that shows directly which suppliers supply which parts and also includes two embedded sets of projects, one for the supplier and one for the part.

There is also a very simple design involving no (nontrivial) hierarchies at all, consisting of an "SP" class, a "PJ" class, and a "JS" class.

24.12 The performance factors discussed were *clustering, caching, pointer swizzling,* and *executing methods at the server.* All of these techniques are applicable to any system that provides a sufficient level of data independence; they are thus not truly "object-specific." In fact, the idea of using the logical database definition to decide what physical clustering to use, as some object systems do, could be seen as potentially undermining data independence. *Note:* It should be pointed out too that another very important performance factor, namely **optimization,** typically does *not* apply to object systems.

24.13 It is the opinion of this writer that declarative support, if feasible, is *always* better than procedural support (for everything, not just integrity constraints). In a nutshell, declarative support means the system does the work instead of the user. This is why relational systems support declarative queries, declarative view definitions, declarative integrity constraints, and so on.

CHAPTER 25

Object/Relational Databases

25.1 INTRODUCTION

In the five or so years since the previous edition of this book was published, several vendors have released "object/relational" DBMS products (also known, at least in the marketing world, as *universal servers*). Examples include the Universal Database version of DB2, the Universal Data Option for Informix Dynamic Server, and the Oracle 8i Universal Server, Database Server, or Enterprise Server (all three names seem to be used). The broad idea in every case is that the product should support both object and relational capabilities; in other words, the products in question are attempts at a *rapprochement* between the two technologies.

Now, it is this writer's strong opinion that any such *rapprochement* should be firmly based on the relational model (which is after all the foundation of modern database technology in general, as explained in Part II of this book). Thus, what we want is for relational systems to evolve* to incorporate the features—or, at least, the good features—of objects (we surely do not want to discard relational systems entirely, nor do we want to have to deal with two separate systems, relational and object, existing side by side). And this opinion is shared by many other writers, including in particular the authors of the Third-Generation Database System Manifesto [25.34], who state categorically that **third-generation DBMSs must subsume second-generation DBMSs**—where "first-generation DBMSs" are the prerelational ones, "second-generation DBMSs" are SQL systems, and "third-generation DBMSs" are whatever comes next. The opinion is apparently *not* shared, however, by some of the object products, nor by certain object writers. Here is a typical quote:

> Computer science has seen many generations of data management, starting with indexed files, and later, network and hierarchical DBMSs . . . [and] more recently relational DBMSs . . . Now, we are on the verge of another generation of database systems . . . [that] provide *object management*, [supporting] much more complex kinds of data [25.4].

---

*Note that we are definitely interested in evolution, not revolution. By contrast, consider this quote from the ODMG book [24.13]: "[Object DBMSs] are *a revolutionary rather than an evolutionary development*" (italics added). We do not believe the marketplace in general is ready for revolution, nor do we think it needs or ought to be—which is one reason why *The Third Manifesto* [3.3] is very specifically evolutionary, not revolutionary, in nature.

Here the writer is clearly suggesting that just as relational systems displaced the older hierarchic and network systems, so object systems will displace relational systems in turn.

The reason we disagree with this position is that *relational really is different* [25.13]. It is different because it is not *ad hoc.* The older, prerelational systems were *ad hoc;* they might have provided solutions to certain important problems of their day, but they did not rest on any solid theoretical foundation. Unfortunately, relational advocates—this writer included—did themselves a major disservice in the early days when they argued the relative merits of relational and prerelational systems; such arguments were necessary at the time, of course, but they had the unlooked-for effect of reinforcing the idea that relational and prerelational DBMSs were essentially the same kind of thing. And this mistaken idea in turn supports the position quoted above—to wit, that objects are to relations as relations were to hierarchies and networks.

So what about objects? Are they *ad hoc?* The following quote from the Object-Oriented Database System Manifesto [24.1] is revealing in this regard: "With respect to the specification of the system, we are taking a Darwinian approach: We hope that, out of the set of experimental prototypes being built, a fit [object] model will emerge." In other words, the suggestion is apparently that we should write code and build systems *without* any predefined model and see what happens!

In what follows, therefore, we take it as axiomatic—and so do most of the major DBMS vendors, by the way—that what we want to do is enhance relational systems to incorporate the good features of object technology. To repeat, we do *not* want to discard relational technology; it would be a great pity to walk away from over 30 years of solid relational research and development.

Now, we argued in Chapter 24—see also the annotation to reference [25.23]—that object-orientation involves just one good idea, namely **proper data type support** (or two good ideas, if you want to count type inheritance separately). So the question facing us becomes: How can we incorporate proper data type support into the relational model? And the answer, of course, as you have probably realized, is that the support is already there, in the shape of *domains* (which we prefer to call *types* anyway). In other words, we need do **nothing** to the relational model in order to achieve object functionality in relational systems—nothing, that is, except implement it, fully and properly, which most of today's systems have so signally failed to do.*

Thus, we believe that a relational system that supported domains properly would be able to deal with all of those "problem" kinds of data that (it is often claimed) object systems can handle and relational systems cannot: time series data, biological data, financial

---

*In particular, those systems have given rise to the all too common misconception that relational systems can support only a limited number of very simple types. The following quotes are quite typical: "Relational database systems support a small, fixed collection of data types" [25.25]; "a relational DBMS can support only . . . its builtin types [basically just numbers, strings, dates, and times]" [24.38]; "*object/relational data models* extend the relational data model by providing a richer type system" [17.61]; and so on.

data, engineering design data, office automation data, and so on. Accordingly, we also believe that a true "object/relational" system would be nothing more nor less than a true *relational* system—which is to say, a system that supports the relational model, with all that such support entails. Hence, DBMS vendors should be encouraged to do what they are in fact trying to do: namely, extend their systems to include proper type or domain support. Indeed, an argument can be made that the whole reason object systems have looked attractive is precisely because the SQL vendors have not supported the relational model adequately. But this fact should not be seen as an argument for abandoning relational systems entirely (or at all!).

By way of example, we now take care of some unfinished business from Chapter 24 (Section 24.1) and show a good *relational* solution to the rectangles problem. That solution involves, first, defining a rectangle *type* (RECT, say):

```
TYPE RECT POSSREP ( X1 RATIONAL, Y1 RATIONAL,
                    X2 RATIONAL, Y2 RATIONAL ) ... ;
```

We assume that rectangles are represented *physically* by means of one of the those storage structures that are specifically intended to support spatial data efficiently—quadtrees, R-trees, etc. [25.27].

We also define an operator to test whether two given rectangles overlap:

```
OPERATOR OVERLAP ( R1 RECT, R2 RECT )
   RETURNS ( BOOLEAN ) ;
   RETURN ( THE_X1(R1) ≤ THE_X2(R2) AND
            THE_Y1(R1) ≤ THE_Y2(R2) AND
            THE_X2(R1) ≥ THE_X1(R2) AND
            THE_Y2(R1) ≥ THE_Y1(R2) ) ;
END OPERATOR ;
```

This operator implements the *efficient* "short" form of the overlaps test (refer back to Chapter 24 if you need to refresh your memory regarding that short form) against the *efficient* (R-tree or whatever) storage structure.

Now the user can create a base relvar with an attribute of type RECT:

```
VAR RECTANGLE RELATION { R RECT, ... } KEY { R } ;
```

And the query "Get all rectangles that overlap the unit square" now becomes simply:

```
RECTANGLE WHERE OVERLAP ( R, RECT ( 0.0, 0.0, 1.0, 1.0 ) )
```

This solution overcomes *all* of the drawbacks discussed in connection with this query in Chapter 24. ■

The plan of the remainder of the chapter is as follows. Sections 25.2 and 25.3 discuss *The Two Great Blunders* (at least one of which is apparently being committed by just about every object/relational product on the market). Section 25.4 then considers certain aspects of the implementation of an object/relational system. Section 25.5 describes the benefits of a *genuine* object/relational system (i.e., one that does not commit either of the two blunders). Section 25.6 offers a summary.

25.2 THE FIRST GREAT BLUNDER

We begin with a quote from reference [3.3]:

> [Before] we can consider the question of integrating objects and relations in any detail, there is a crucial preliminary question that we need to address, and that is as follows:

> **What concept is it in the relational world that is the counterpart to the concept *object class* in the object world?**

The reason this question is so crucial is that *object class* really is the most fundamental concept of all in the object world—all other object concepts depend on it to a greater or lesser degree. And there are two equations that can be, and have been, proposed as answers to this question:

- domain = object class
- relvar = object class

We now proceed to argue, strongly, that the first of these equations is right and the second is wrong.

In fact, of course, the first equation is *obviously* right, since object classes and domains are both just types. Indeed, given that relvars are *variables* and classes are *types,* it should be immediately obvious too that the second equation is wrong (variables and types are not the same thing); for this very reason, *The Third Manifesto* [3.3] asserts categorically that **relvars are not domains.** Nevertheless, many people, and some products, have in fact embraced the second equation—a mistake that we refer to as **The Great Blunder** (or, more precisely, The *First* Great Blunder, since we will meet another one later). It is therefore instructive to take a very careful look at the second equation, and so we do. *Note:* Most of the remainder of this section is taken more or less *verbatim* from reference [3.3].

Why might anyone commit such a blunder? Well, consider the following simple class definition, expressed in a hypothetical object language that is similar but deliberately not quite identical to that of Section 24.3:

```
CREATE OBJECT CLASS EMP
     ( EMP#       CHAR(5),
       ENAME      CHAR(20),
       SAL        NUMERIC,
       HOBBY      CHAR(20),
       WORKS_FOR  CHAR(20) ) ... ;
```

(EMP#, ENAME, etc., here are *public instance variables.*) And now consider the following SQL "base relvar" definition:

```
CREATE TABLE EMP
     ( EMP#       CHAR(5),
       ENAME      CHAR(20),
       SAL        NUMERIC,
       HOBBY      CHAR(20),
       WORKS_FOR  CHAR(20) ) ... ;
```

These two definitions certainly look very similar, and the idea of equating them thus looks very tempting. And (as already indicated) certain systems, including some commercial products, have effectively done just that. So let us take a closer look. More precisely, let us take the CREATE TABLE statement just shown and consider a series of possible extensions to it that (some people would argue) serve to make it more "object-like." *Note:* The discussion that follows is based on a specific commercial product; in fact, it is based on an example in that product's own documentation. We do not identify that product here, however, since it is not our intent in this book to criticize or praise specific products. Rather, the criticisms we will be making later in this section apply, *mutatis mutandis,* to *any* system that espouses the "relvar = class" equation.

The first extension is to permit *composite* (i.e., tuple-valued) *attributes;* that is, we allow attribute values to be tuples from some other relvar (or possibly from the same relvar). In the example, we might replace the original CREATE TABLE statement by the following collection of statements (refer to Fig. 25.1):

```
CREATE TABLE EMP
     ( EMP#       CHAR(5),
       ENAME      CHAR(20),
       SAL        NUMERIC,
       HOBBY      ACTIVITY,
       WORKS_FOR  COMPANY ) ;

CREATE TABLE ACTIVITY
     ( NAME       CHAR(20),
       TEAM       INTEGER ) ;

CREATE TABLE COMPANY
     ( NAME       CHAR(20),
       LOCATION   CITYSTATE ) ;

CREATE TABLE CITYSTATE
     ( CITY       CHAR(20),
       STATE      CHAR(2) ) ;
```

Explanation: Attribute HOBBY in relvar EMP is declared to be of type ACTIVITY. ACTIVITY in turn is a relvar of two attributes, NAME and TEAM, where TEAM gives the number of players in a team corresponding to NAME; for instance, a possible "activity"

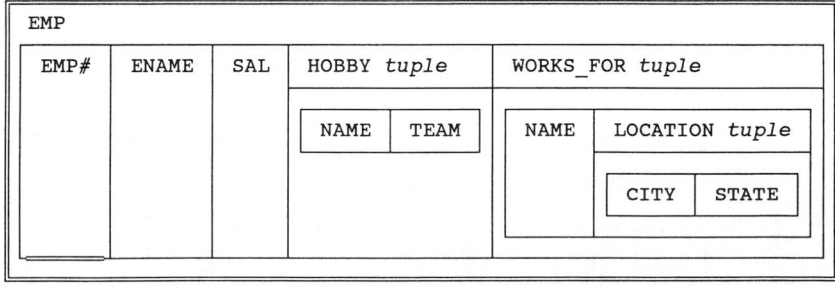

Fig. 25.1   Attributes containing (pointers to) tuples—deprecated

might be (Soccer,11). Each HOBBY value is thus actually a *pair* of values, a NAME value and a TEAM value (more precisely, it is a pair of values that currently appear as a tuple in relvar ACTIVITY). *Note:* Observe that we have already violated the *Third Manifesto* dictum that relvars are not domains—the "domain" for attribute HOBBY is defined to be the *relvar* ACTIVITY. See later in this section for further discussion of this point.

Similarly, attribute WORKS_FOR in relvar EMP is declared to be of type COMPANY, and COMPANY is also a relvar of two attributes, one of which is defined to be of type CITYSTATE, which is another two-attribute relvar, and so on. In other words, relvars ACTIVITY, COMPANY, and CITYSTATE are all considered to be *types* (or domains) as well as relvars. The same is true for relvar EMP itself, of course.

This first extension is thus roughly analogous to allowing objects to contain other objects, thereby supporting the *containment hierarchy* concept (see Chapter 24).

As an aside, we remark that we have characterized this first extension as "attributes containing tuples" because that is the way advocates of the "relvar = class" equation themselves characterize it (see, e.g., reference [24.33]). It would be more accurate, however, to characterize it as "attributes containing *pointers to* tuples"—an issue that we will be examining in a few moments. (In Fig. 25.1, therefore, we should really replace each of the three occurrences of the term *tuple* by the term *pointer to tuple.*)

Remarks analogous to those of the previous paragraph apply to the second extension also, which is to allow *relation-valued attributes;* that is, attribute values are allowed to be *sets* of tuples from some other relvar (or possibly from the same relvar). For example, suppose employees can have an arbitrary number of hobbies, instead of just one (refer to Fig. 25.2):

```
CREATE TABLE EMP
     ( EMP#        CHAR(5),
       ENAME       CHAR(20),
       SAL         NUMERIC,
       HOBBIES     SET OF ( ACTIVITY ),
       WORKS_FOR   COMPANY ) ;
```

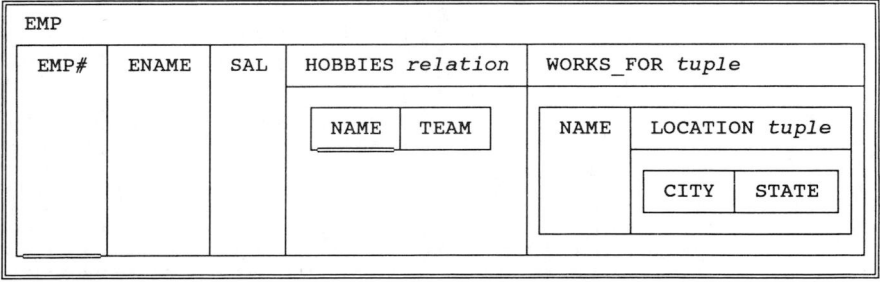

Fig. 25.2 Attributes containing sets of (pointers to) tuples—deprecated

Explanation: The HOBBIES value within any given tuple of relvar EMP is now (conceptually) a set of zero or more (NAME,TEAM) pairs—i.e., tuples—from relvar ACTIV-ITY. This second extension is thus roughly analogous to allowing objects to contain "collection" objects: a more complex version of the containment hierarchy. *Note:* We remark in passing that in the particular product on which our example is based, those collection objects can be *sequences* or *bags* as well as sets *per se*.

The third extension is to permit relvars to have associated *methods*. For example:

```
CREATE TABLE EMP
     ( EMP#        CHAR(5),
       ENAME       CHAR(20),
       SAL         NUMERIC,
       HOBBIES     SET OF ( ACTIVITY ),
       WORKS_FOR   COMPANY )
METHOD RETIREMENT_BENEFITS ( ) : NUMERIC ;
```

Explanation: RETIREMENT_BENEFITS is a method that takes a given EMP tuple as its argument and produces a result of type NUMERIC.

The final definitional extension is to permit *subclasses*. For example (refer to Fig. 25.3):

```
CREATE TABLE PERSON
     ( SS#         CHAR(9),
       BIRTHDATE   DATE,
       ADDRESS     CHAR(50) ) ;

CREATE TABLE EMP
    AS SUBCLASS OF PERSON
     ( EMP#        CHAR(5),
       ENAME       CHAR(20),
       SAL         NUMERIC,
       HOBBIES     SET OF ( ACTIVITY ),
       WORKS_FOR   COMPANY )
METHOD RETIREMENT_BENEFITS ( ) : NUMERIC ;
```

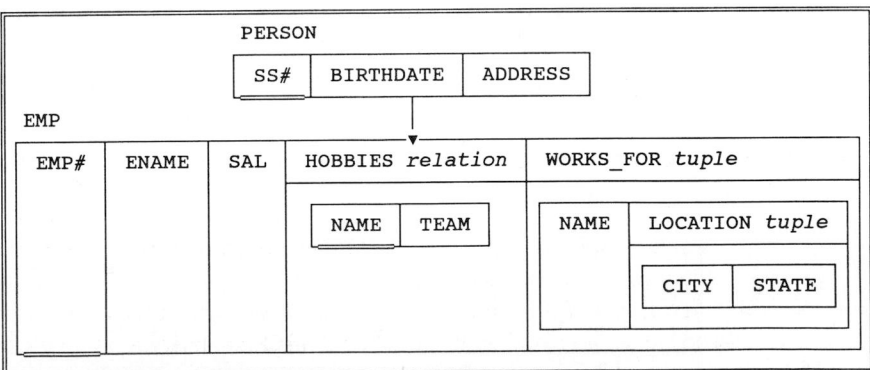

Fig. 25.3   Relvars as superclasses and subclasses—deprecated

Explanation: EMP now has three additional attributes (SS#, BIRTHDATE, and AD-DRESS) inherited from PERSON (because each EMP instance "ISA" PERSON instance as well, loosely speaking). If PERSON had any methods, it would inherit those too. *Note:* PERSON and EMP here are examples of what are sometimes called *supertables* and *subtables,* respectively. See reference [13.12], also Appendix B, for further discussion—and criticism—of these concepts.

Along with the definitional extensions sketched above, certain manipulative extensions are required too, of course—for instance:

- Path expressions—e.g., EMP.WORKS_FOR.LOCATION.STATE. Note that such expressions can return scalars or tuples or relations, in general. Note further that in the latter two cases the components of those tuples or relations might themselves be tuples or relations in turn (and so on); for example, the expression EMP.HOBBIES.NAME returns a relation. Incidentally, note that these path expressions go *down* the containment hierarchy, whereas the path expressions discussed in Chapter 24 go *up.*

- Tuple and relation literals (possibly nested)—e.g.,

```
( 'E001', 'Smith', $50000,
      ( ( 'Soccer', 11 ), ( 'Baseball', 9 ) ),
                       ( 'IBM', ( 'San Jose', 'CA' ) ) )
```

(not meant to be actual syntax).

- Relational comparison operators—e.g., SUBSET, SUBSETEQ, and so on. (The particular operators mentioned are taken from the particular product under discussion. In that product, SUBSET really means "*proper* subset," and SUBSETEQ means "subset" (!).)

- Operators for traversing the class hierarchy. *Note:* Care is needed here, too. It might well be the case that a request to retrieve PERSON information together with associated EMP information yields a result that is not a relation—meaning that the vital relational property of *closure* has been violated, with potentially disastrous implications. (In this connection, reference [25.31]—which refers to such a result as a "jagged return"—merely observes blithely that "the client program must be prepared to deal with the complexity of a jagged return"!)

- The ability to invoke methods within, e.g., SELECT and WHERE clauses (in SQL terms).

- The ability to access individual components within attribute values that happen to be tuples or relations.

So much for a quick overview of how the "relvar = class" equation is realized in practice. So what is wrong with it?

Well, note first of all that (as stated earlier) a relvar is a *variable* and a class is a *type.* So how can they possibly be the same? This first observation should be logically sufficient to stop the "relvar = class" idea dead in its tracks. However, there is more that can usefully be said, so let us agree to suspend disbelief a little longer . . . Here are some additional points to consider:

- The equation "relvar = class" implies the further equations "tuple = object" and "attribute = (public) instance variable." Thus, whereas (as we saw in Chapter 24) a true object class—at least, a scalar or "encapsulated" object class—has methods and no public instance variables, a relvar "object class" has public instance variables and only optionally has methods (it is definitely not "encapsulated"). So, again, how can the two notions possibly be the same?

- There is a major difference between the attribute definitions (e.g.) "SAL NUMERIC" and "WORKS_FOR COMPANY." NUMERIC is a true data type (equivalently, a true, albeit primitive, domain); it places a time-independent constraint on the values that can legally appear in attribute SAL. By contrast, COMPANY is *not* a true data type; the constraint it places on the values that can appear in attribute WORKS_FOR is *time-dependent* (it depends, obviously, on the current value of relvar COMPANY). In fact, as pointed out earlier, the relvar *vs.* domain distinction—or, if you prefer object terminology, the collection *vs.* class distinction—has been muddied here.

- We have seen that tuple "objects" are apparently allowed to contain other such "objects"; for example, EMP "objects" apparently contain COMPANY "objects." But they do not—not really; instead, they contain *pointers* to those "contained objects," and users must be absolutely clear on this point. For example, suppose the user updates some particular COMPANY tuple in some way (refer back to Fig. 25.1). Then that update will immediately be visible in all EMP tuples that "contain" that COMPANY tuple. *Note:* We are not saying this effect is undesirable, we are only saying it has to be explained to the user. But explaining it to the user amounts to telling the user that the "model" as shown in Fig. 25.1 is incorrect—EMP tuples do not contain COMPANY tuples, they contain *pointers to* COMPANY tuples instead (as already stated).

  Here are some further implications and questions arising from this same point:

  a. Can we insert an EMP tuple and specify a value for the "contained" COMPANY tuple that does not currently exist in the COMPANY relvar? If the answer is *yes,* the fact that attribute WORKS_FOR is defined as being of type COMPANY does not mean very much, since it does not significantly constrain the INSERT operation in any way. If the answer is *no,* the INSERT operation becomes unnecessarily complex—the user has to specify, not just an existing company name (i.e., a foreign key value) as would be required in the analogous relational situation, but an entire existing COMPANY tuple. Moreover, specifying an entire COMPANY tuple means, at best, telling the system something it already knows; at worst, it means that if the user makes a mistake, the INSERT will fail when it could perfectly well have succeeded.

  b. Suppose we want an ON DELETE RESTRICT rule for companies (i.e., an attempt to delete a company must fail if the company has any employees). Presumably this rule must be enforced by procedural code, say by some method *M* (note that relvar EMP has no foreign key to which a declarative version of the rule might be attached). Furthermore, regular SQL DELETE operations must now not be performed on relvar COMPANY other than within the code that implements that method *M*.

How is this requirement enforced? Analogous remarks and questions apply to other foreign key rules, of course, such as ON DELETE CASCADE.

   c. Note too that deleting an EMP tuple presumably will *not* "cascade" to delete the corresponding COMPANY tuple, despite the pretense that the EMP tuple contains that COMPANY tuple.

   It follows from all of the above that we are not exactly talking about the relational model any more. The fundamental data object is no longer a relation containing values, it is a "relation"—actually not a proper relation at all, so far as the relational model is concerned—containing values *and pointers.* In other words, **we have undermined the conceptual integrity of the relational model.***

- Suppose we define view V to be the projection of EMP over (say) just the attribute HOBBIES. V is a relvar too, of course, but a derived relvar instead of a base one. So if "relvar = class" is a correct equation, V is also a class. *What class is it?* Also, classes have methods; *what methods apply to V?*

   Well, "class" EMP has just one method, RETIREMENT_BENEFITS, and that method clearly does not apply to "class" V. In fact, it hardly seems reasonable that *any* methods that applied to "class" EMP would apply to "class" V—and there certainly are no others. So it looks as if (in general) *no methods at all* apply to the result of a projection; i.e., the result, whatever it is, is not really a class at all. (We might *say* it is a class, but that does not make it one!—it will have public instance variables and no methods, whereas we have already observed that a true "encapsulated" class has methods and no public instance variables.)

   In fact, it is quite clear that when people equate relvars and classes, it is specifically base relvars they have in mind—they are forgetting about the derived ones. (Certainly the pointers discussed above are pointers to tuples in base relvars, not derived ones.) But to distinguish between base and derived relvars in this way is a mistake of the highest order, because the question as to which relvars are base and which are derived is, in a very important sense, arbitrary (recall the discussion of *The Principle of Interchangeability* in Chapter 9).

- Finally, *what domains are supported?* Those who advocate the "relvar = class" equation never seem to have much to say about domains, presumably because they cannot see how domains as such fit into their overall scheme. And yet, of course, domains are essential, as we know from many of our earlier discussions (see, e.g., Chapter 3).

---

*The term *conceptual integrity* is due to Fred Brooks, who has this to say about it [25.1]: "[Conceptual] integrity is *the* most important consideration in system design. It is better to have a system omit certain anomalous features [and] to reflect one set of design ideas, than to have one that contains many good but independent and uncoordinated ideas" (italics in the original). And writing 20 years later, he adds: "A clean, elegant programming product must present . . . a coherent mental model . . . [Conceptual] integrity . . . is the most important factor in ease of use . . . **Today I am more convinced than ever**. Conceptual integrity is central to product quality" (boldface and italics in the original).

The overall message of the foregoing can be summarized as follows. Obviously, systems can be built that are based on the wrong equation "relvar = class"; indeed, some such systems already exist. Equally obviously, those systems (like a car with no oil in its engine, or a house that is built on sand) might even provide useful service, for a while—but they are doomed to eventual failure.

Where Did The First Great Blunder Come From?

It is interesting to speculate on the source of The First Great Blunder. It seems to us that it has its roots in the lack of consensus, noted in Chapter 24, on the meaning of terms in the object world. In particular, the term *object* itself does not have a universally accepted and agreed-upon meaning—which is precisely why we prefer not to use it much ourselves.

The foregoing remarks notwithstanding, it is at least fairly clear that in object programming language circles, at any rate, the term *object* refers to what more traditionally would be called either a *value* or a *variable* (or possibly both). Unfortunately, however, the term is used in other circles as well; in particular, it is used in certain *semantic modeling* circles, as part of various "object analysis and design" or "object modeling" techniques and methodologies (see, e.g., reference [13.3]). And in those circles, it seems clear that the term does *not* mean a value or a variable, but rather what the database community would more usually call an *entity* (implying among other things, incidentally, that—unlike programming language objects—such objects are definitely not encapsulated). In other words, "object modeling" is really just "entity/relationship modeling" by another name; indeed, reference [13.3] more or less admits as much. As a consequence, things that are identified as "objects" in such methodologies are then (correctly) mapped to tuples in relvars instead of to values in domains. Hey presto!

25.3   THE SECOND GREAT BLUNDER

In this section, we examine **The Second Great Blunder;** as we will see, that second blunder seems to be a logical consequence of the first, but it is also significant in its own right (moreover, it can be committed in its own right, too, even if The First Great Blunder is avoided). The blunder consists of **mixing pointers and relations.** We begin by revisiting the major features of the "relvar = class" approach, as identified in the previous section. Some people might possibly have found that section a little confusing, since some of the features we seemed to be objecting to were features we have argued in favor of at earlier points in the book (tuple- and relation-valued attributes might be a case in point). So here goes:

- *Tuple- and relation-valued attributes:* Indeed, we do not object to such attributes (how could we?). What we do object to is (a) the idea that such attributes must have, very specifically, values that currently appear in some other (base) relvar, and (b) the idea that such attributes really have values that are not tuples or relations *per se* but are, rather, **pointers** to tuples or relations—which means, of course, that we are not really talking about tuple- or relation-valued attributes at all. *Note:* In fact, the idea of pointers pointing to "tuples or relations"—meaning, specifically, tuple or relation *values*—makes no sense anyway. We will be discussing this point in detail in a few moments.

■ *Associating operators ("methods") with relvars:* We have no objections to this idea, either—it is basically just the notion of stored or triggered procedures under another guise. But we do object to the idea that such operators must be associated with relvars (and only relvars) and not with domains or types. We also object to the idea that they must be associated with *one specific* relvar (the notion of target operands under another guise).

■ *Subclasses and superclasses:* Now here we do object . . . In a system that equates relvars and classes, subclasses and superclasses become sub*tables* and super*tables*—and this notion is one we are highly skeptical of [13.12]. We want proper inheritance support as described in Chapter 19.

■ *Path expressions:* We would have no objections to path expressions that were merely syntactic shorthand for following certain associative references—e.g., from a foreign key to a matching candidate key, as proposed in reference [25.11]. However, path expressions as discussed in Section 25.2 are, rather, shorthand for following certain *pointer chains,* and these we do object to (because we object to pointers in the first place).

■ *Tuple and relation literals:* These are essential—though they need to be generalized into tuple and relation *selectors* [3.3].

■ *Relational comparison operators:* Also essential (though they ought to be done right).

■ *Operators for traversing the class hierarchy:* If "class hierarchy" really means "relvar hierarchy," then (as noted in the previous section) we have major objections, because of the probable violation of the relational closure property (see, e.g., reference [25.31]). If it means "type hierarchy" in the sense of Chapter 19, then we have no objections (but it does not).

■ *Invoking methods in, e.g., SELECT and WHERE clauses:* Of course.

■ *Accessing individual components within attribute values that happen to be tuples or relations:* Of course.

So now let us focus on the business of mixing pointers and relations. The crux of the argument is very simple. By definition, pointers point to *variables,* not *values* (because variables have addresses and values do not). By definition, therefore, if relvar R1 is allowed to have an attribute whose values are pointers "into" relvar *R2,* then those pointers point to tuple *variables,* not to tuple *values.* **But there is no such thing as a tuple variable in the relational model.** The relational model deals with relation values, which are (loosely speaking) sets of tuple values, which are in turn (again loosely speaking) sets of scalar values. It also deals with relation variables, which are variables whose values are relations. However, it does *not* deal with tuple variables (which are variables whose values are tuples) or scalar variables (which are variables whose values are scalars). The *only* kind of variable included in the relational model (and the only kind of variable permitted in a relational database) is, very specifically, the *relation* variable. *It follows that the idea of mixing pointers and relations constitutes a MAJOR departure from the relational model, introducing as it does an entirely new kind of variable.* As noted in the previous section, in fact, we would argue that it seriously undermines the conceptual integrity of the relational model.

More detailed arguments in support of this position can be found in references [24.21] and [25.11]. See also references [25.8–25.10] and [25.13], which discuss the related—and important—notion of *essentiality* (of data constructs within a data model).

Given the foregoing argument, therefore, it is sad to see that most (possibly all) of the current crop of object/relational products—even those that do avoid The First Great Blunder—nevertheless seem to be mixing pointers and relations in exactly the manner discussed, and objected to, above. When Codd first defined the relational model, he very deliberately excluded pointers. To quote reference [5.2]:

> It is safe to assume that all kinds of users [including end users in particular] understand the act of comparing values, but that relatively few understand the complexities of pointers. The relational model is based on this fundamental principle . . . [The] manipulation of pointers is more bug-prone than is the act of comparing values, even if the user happens to understand the complexities of pointers.

To be specific, pointers lead to pointer-chasing, and pointer-chasing is notoriously error-prone. As noted in Chapter 24, it is precisely this aspect of object systems that gives rise to the criticisms, sometimes heard, to the effect that such systems "look like CODASYL warmed over."

Where Did The Second Great Blunder Come From?

It is hard to find any real justification in the literature for The Second Great Blunder (any technical justification, that is—but there is evidence that the justification is not technical at all but political). Of course, given the fact that object systems and languages do all include pointers (in the form of object IDs), the idea of mixing pointers and relations almost certainly arises from a desire to make relational systems more "object-like," but this "justification" merely pushes the problem off to another level; we have already made it abundantly clear that (in our opinion) object systems expose pointers to the user precisely because they fail to distinguish properly between model and implementation.

We can only conjecture, therefore, that the reason why the idea of mixing pointers and relations is being so widely promulgated is because too few people understand why pointers were excluded from relations in the first place. As Santayana has it: *Those who cannot remember the past are condemned to repeat it* (usually quoted in the form "Those who don't know history are doomed to repeat it"). On such matters we agree strongly with Maurice Wilkes, when he writes [25.35]:

> I would like to see computer science teaching set deliberately in a historical framework . . . Students need to understand how the present situation has come about, what was tried, what worked and what did not, and how improvements in hardware made progress possible. The absence of this element in their training causes people to approach every problem from first

principles. They are apt to propose solutions that have been found wanting in the past. Instead of standing on the shoulders of their precursors, they try to go it alone.

25.4 IMPLEMENTATION ISSUES

One important implication of proper data type support is that it allows third-party vendors (as well as DBMS vendors themselves) to build and sell separate "data type" packages that can effectively be plugged into the DBMS. Examples include packages to support sophisticated text handling; financial time series processing; geospatial (cartographic) data analysis; and so on. Such packages are variously referred to as "data blades" (Informix); "data cartridges" (Oracle); "relational extenders" (IBM);* and so on. In what follows, we will stay with the term *type packages*.

Adding a new type package to the system is a nontrivial undertaking, however, and the ability to do so has significant implications for the design and structure of the DBMS itself. To see why in both cases, consider what happens if. e.g., some query includes references to data of some user-defined type or invocations of some user-defined operator (or both):

- First of all, the query language compiler has to be able to parse and type-check that request, so it has to know something about those user-defined types and operators.

- Second, the optimizer has to be able to decide on an appropriate query plan for that request, so it too has to be aware of certain properties of those user-defined types and operators. In particular, it has to know how the data is physically stored (see the next paragraph).

- Third, the component that manages physical storage has to support the newer storage structures ("quadtrees, R-trees, etc.") mentioned in our discussion of the rectangles problem in Section 25.1. It might even have to support the ability for suitably skilled users to introduce new storage structures and access methods of their own [25.21,25.33].

The net of all of the foregoing is that the system needs to be *extensible*—extensible at several levels, in fact. We discuss each level briefly.

Parsing and Type Checking

In a conventional system, since the only available types and operators are all builtin, information regarding them can be (and typically is) "hardwired" into the query language compiler. In a system in which users can define their own types and operators, by contrast, this "hardwired" approach is clearly not going to work. Instead, therefore, what has to happen is this:

---

*An *exceedingly* inappropriate term, in our opinion.

1. Information regarding user-defined types and operators—and possibly builtin types and operators as well—is kept in the system catalog. This fact implies that the catalog itself needs to be redesigned (or at least extended); it also implies that introducing a new type package involves a lot of catalog updating. (In **Tutorial D** terms, of course, that updating is performed under the covers as part of the process of executing the applicable TYPE and OPERATOR definitional statements.)

2. The compiler itself needs to be rewritten in order to access the catalog to obtain the necessary type and operator information. It can then use that information to carry out all of the compile-time type checking as described in Chapters 5, 8, and 19.

Optimization

There are many, many issues involved here, and we can only scratch the surface of the problem in this book. However, we can at least point out what a few of those issues are:

- *Expression transformation ("query rewrite"):* A conventional optimizer applies certain laws of transformation to rewrite queries, as we saw in Chapter 17. Historically, however, those laws of transformation have all been "hardwired" into the optimizer (because, again, the available data types and operators have all been builtin). In an object/relational system, by contrast, the relevant knowledge (at least insofar as it applies to user-defined types and operators specifically) needs to be kept in the catalog—implying more extensions to the catalog, and implying too that the optimizer itself needs to be rewritten. Here are some illustrations:

  a. Given an expression such as NOT (QTY > 500), a good conventional optimizer will transform it into QTY ≤ 500 (because the second version can make use of an index on QTY while the first cannot). For analogous reasons, there needs to be a way of informing the optimizer when one user-defined operator is the negation of another.

  b. A good conventional optimizer will also know that, e.g., the expressions QTY > 500 and 500 < QTY are logically equivalent. There needs to be a way of informing the optimizer when two user-defined operators are opposites in this sense.

  c. A good conventional optimizer will also know that, e.g., the operators "+" and "−" cancel out (i.e., are inverses); for example, the expression QTY + 500 − 500 reduces to just QTY. There needs to be a way of informing the optimizer when two user-defined operators are inverses in this sense.

- *Selectivity:* Given a boolean expression such as QTY > 500, optimizers typically make a guess at the *selectivity* of that expression (i.e., the percentage of tuples that make it *true*). For builtin data types and operators, again, that selectivity information can be "hardwired" into the optimizer; for user-defined types and operators, by contrast, there needs to be a way of providing the optimizer with some user-defined code to invoke in order to guess selectivities.

- *Cost formulas:* The optimizer needs to know how much it costs to execute a given user-defined operator. Given an expression such as *p* AND *q,* for example, where *p* is (say) an invocation of the AREA operator on some complicated polygon and q is a simple comparison like QTY > 500, we would probably prefer the system to execute q first, so that p is executed only on tuples for which q evaluates to *true*. Indeed, some of the classical expression transformation heuristics, such as always doing restrictions before joins, are not necessarily valid for user-defined types and operators [25.7,25.18].

- *Storage structures and access methods:* The optimizer clearly needs to be aware of the storage structures and access methods in effect (see the next subsection).

Storage Structures

It should be obvious that object/relational systems are going to need more ways—possibly many more ways—of storing and accessing data at the physical level than (e.g.) SQL systems have traditionally provided. Here are some relevant considerations:

- *New storage structures:* As already noted, the system will probably need to support new "hardwired" storage structures (R-trees, etc.), and there might even need to be a way for suitably skilled users to introduce additional storage structures and access methods of their own.

- *Indexes on data of a user-defined type:* Traditional indexes are based on data of some builtin type and a builtin understanding of what the "<" operator means. In an object/relational system, it must be possible to build indexes on data of a user-defined type, based on the semantics of the applicable user-defined "<" operator (assuming that such an operator has been defined in the first place, of course).

- *Indexes on operator results:* There would probably be little point in building an index directly over a set of data values of type POLYGON; most likely, all such an index would do would be to order the polygons by their internal byte string encodings.* However, an index based on the *areas* of those polygons could be very useful. *Note:* We referred to such indexes as *functional* indexes in Chapter 21.

25.5 BENEFITS OF TRUE *RAPPROCHEMENT*

In reference [25.31], Stonebraker presents a "classification matrix" for DBMSs (see Fig. 25.4). **Quadrant 1** of that matrix represents applications that deal only with rather simple data and have no requirement for *ad hoc* query (a traditional word processor is a good example). Such applications are not really database applications at all, in the classical sense of that term; the "DBMS" that best serves their needs is just the builtin file system provided as part of the underlying operating system.

---

*Recall from Chapter 24 that systems traditionally provide a BLOB data type for dealing with "binary large objects." In an object/relational system, data values of certain user-defined types might well be physically stored as BLOBs.

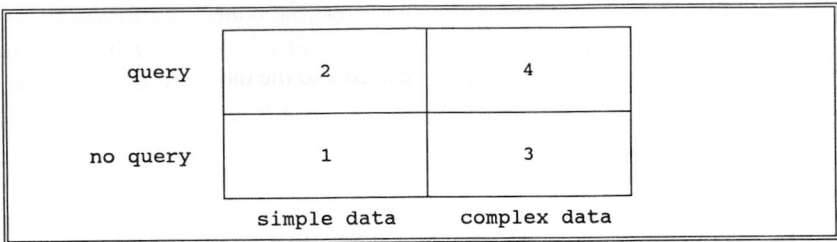

Fig. 25.4   Stonebraker's DBMS classification matrix

Quadrant 2 represents applications that do have an *ad hoc* query requirement but still deal only with rather simple data. Most of today's business applications fall into this quadrant, and they are fairly well supported by traditional relational (or at least SQL) DBMSs.

Quadrant 3 represents applications with complex data and processing requirements but no *ad hoc* query requirement. For example, CAD/CAM applications might fall into this quadrant. Current object DBMSs are primarily aimed at this segment of the market (traditional SQL products tend not to do a very good job on Quadrant 3 applications).

Finally, **Quadrant 4** represents applications with a need for both complex data and *ad hoc* queries against that data. Stonebraker gives an example of a database containing digitized 35mm slides, with a typical query being "Get pictures of sunsets taken within 20 miles of Sacramento, California." He then goes on to give arguments in support of his position that (a) an object/relational DBMS is required for applications that fall into this quadrant, and (b) over the next few years, the majority of applications will fall or move over into this quadrant. For example, even a simple human resources application might expand to include employee photographs, sound recordings (spoken messages), and the like.

In sum, Stonebraker is arguing (and we agree) that "object/relational systems are in everyone's future"; they are not just a passing fad, soon to be replaced by some other briefly fashionable idea. However, we should perhaps remind you that, so far as we are concerned, a true object/relational system is just a true *relational* system. In particular, it is a system that does not commit either of the two Great Blunders! Stonebraker does not quite seem to agree with our position here—at least, reference [25.31] never quite says as much, and indeed it implies that mixing pointers and relations is not only acceptable but desirable (in fact, required).

Be that as it may, we would argue that a *genuine* object/relational system would solve all of the problems that (we claimed in the previous chapter) are indeed problems of systems that are just plain object systems, not object/relational ones. To be specific, such a system should be able to support all of the following without undue difficulty:

- *Ad hoc* query, view definition, and declarative integrity constraints;
- Methods that span classes (there is no need for a distinguished "target" operand);
- Dynamically defined classes (for *ad hoc* query results);

- Dual mode access (we did not stress the point in Chapter 24, but object systems typically do not support the dual mode principle—instead, they use different languages for programmed and interactive access to the database);
- Deferred (COMMIT-time) integrity checking;
- Transition constraints;
- Semantic optimization;
- Relationships of degree greater than two;
- Foreign key rules (ON DELETE CASCADE, etc.);
- Optimizability;

and so on. In addition:

- OIDs and pointer chasing are now totally "under the covers" and hidden from the user;
- "Difficult" object questions (e.g., what does it mean to join two objects?) go away;
- The benefits of encapsulation, such as they are, still apply, but to scalar values within relations, not to relations *per se;*
- Relational systems can now handle "complex" application areas such as CAD/CAM, as previously discussed.

And the approach is conceptually clean.

25.6 SUMMARY

We have briefly examined the field of **object/relational** systems. Such systems are (or should be) basically just *relational* systems that support the relational **domain** concept (i.e., types) properly—meaning in particular that users are (or should be) able to define their own types. We need do nothing to the relational model in order to achieve the object functionality we want (except implement it).

We then examined the two **Great Blunders.** The first is to equate object classes and relvars (an equation that is unfortunately all too attractive, at least on the surface). We speculated that the blunder arises from a confusion over two quite distinct interpretations of the term *object.* We discussed an example (in detail) showing what a system might look like that commits The First Great Blunder, and we explained some of the consequences of that mistake. One major consequence is that it seems to lead directly to committing The Second Great Blunder as well!—namely, mixing pointers and relations (though in fact this second blunder can be committed without the first, and just about every system on the market unfortunately seems to be committing it). It is our position that The Second Great Blunder **undermines the conceptual integrity of the relational model** in numerous ways. In particular, it violates *The Principle of Interchangeability* of base and derived relations.

Next, we briefly examined a few implementation issues. The overriding point is that adding a new "type package" affects at least the compiler, optimizer, and storage manager components of the system. As a consequence, an object/relational system cannot be implemented—at least, not well—by simply imposing a new layer of code over an existing relational system; rather, the system needs to be rebuilt from the ground up, in order to make each component individually extensible as needed.

Finally, we took a look at Stonebraker's *DBMS classification matrix,* and we briefly discussed the benefits that could accrue from a true *rapproachement* between object and relational technologies (where by "true" we mean in particular that the system in question does not commit either of the two Great Blunders).

REFERENCES AND BIBLIOGRAPHY

Several object/relational prototypes have been built over the past few years. Two of the best known, and most influential, are **Postgres** from the University of California at Berkeley [25.26,25.30,25.32] and **Starburst** from IBM Research [25.14,25.17,25.21–25.22]. We remark that (at least in their original form) neither of these systems adhered to the "obviously correct" equation *domain = class.*

We should mention too that SQL3 includes a number of features that are specifically aimed at supporting object/relational systems (see Appendix B).

25.1 Frederick P. Brooks, Jr.: *The Mythical Man-Month* (20th anniversary edition). Reading, Mass.: Addison-Wesley (1995).

25.2 Michael J. Carey, Nelson M. Mattos, and Anil K. Nori: "Object/Relational Database Systems: Principles, Products, and Challenges," Proc. 1997 ACM SIGMOD Int. Conf. on Management of Data, Tucson, Ariz. (May 1997).

> To quote: "Abstract data types, user-defined functions, row types, references, inheritance, subtables, collections, triggers—just what is all this stuff, anyway?" A good question! There are eight features in the list (and there is a tacit assumption that they are all SQL3 features specifically). Of those eight, we would argue that at least four are undesirable, two others are part of the same thing, and the other two are orthogonal to the question of whether or not the system is object/relational. See Appendix B.

25.3 Michael J. Carey *et al.:* "The BUCKY Object/Relational Benchmark," Proc. 1997 ACM SIGMOD Int. Conf. on Management of Data, Tucson, Ariz. (May 1997).

> From the abstract: "BUCKY (Benchmark of Universal or Complex Kwery Ynterfaces [*sic*]) is a query-oriented benchmark that tests many of the key features offered by object/relational systems, including row types and inheritance, references and path expressions, sets of atomic values and of references, methods and late binding, and user-defined abstract data types and their methods."

25.4 R. G. G. Cattell: "What Are Next-Generation DB Systems?", *CACM 34,* No. 10 (October 1991).

25.5 Donald D. Chamberlin: "Relations and References—Another Point of View," *InfoDB 10,* No. 6 (April 1997).

> See the annotation to reference [25.11].

25.6 Surajit Chaudhuri and Luis Gravano: "Optimizing Queries over Multi-Media Repositories," Proc. 1996 ACM SIGMOD Int. Conf. on Management of Data, Montreal, Canada (June 1996).

Object/relational databases might well be used as "multi-media repositories." Queries against multimedia data typically yield not just a set of resultant objects, but also a *grade of match* for each such object that indicates how well it satisfies the search condition (e.g., the "degree of redness" of an image). Such queries can specify a threshold on the grade of match and can also specify a *quota* [6.4]. This paper considers the optimization of such queries.

25.7 Surajit Chaudhuri and Kyuseok Shim: "Optimization of Queries with User-Defined Predicates," Proc. 22nd Int. Conf. on Very Large Data Bases, Mumbai (Bombay), India (September 1996).

25.8 E. F. Codd and C. J. Date: "Interactive Support for Nonprogrammers: The Relational and Network Approaches," in C. J. Date, *Relational Database: Selected Writings*. Reading, Mass.: Addison-Wesley (1986).

The paper that introduced the notion of *essentiality,* a concept that is critical to a proper understanding of data models (in both senses of that term!—see Chapter 1, Section 1.3). The relational model basically has just one essential data construct, the relation itself. The object model, by contrast, has many: sets, bags, lists, arrays, and so forth (not to mention object IDs). See references [25.9–25.10] and [25.13] for further explanation.

25.9 C. J. Date: "Support for the Conceptual Schema: The Relational and Network approaches," in *Relational Database Writings 1985–1989*. Reading, Mass.: Addison-Wesley (1990).

One argument against mixing pointers and relations [25.11] is the complexity that pointers cause. This paper includes an example that illustrates the point very clearly (see Figs. 25.5 and 25.6, overleaf).

25.10 C. J. Date: "Essentiality," in *Relational Database Writings 1991–1994*. Reading, Mass.: Addison-Wesley (1995).

25.11 C. J. Date: "Don't Mix Pointers and Relations!" and "Don't Mix Pointers and Relations *Please!*", both in C. J. Date, Hugh Darwen, and David McGoveran, *Relational Database Writings 1994–1997*. Reading, Mass.: Addison-Wesley (1998).

The first of these two papers argues strongly against The Second Great Blunder. In reference [25.5], Chamberlin offers a rebuttal to some of the arguments of that first paper. The second paper was written as a direct response to Chamberlin's rebuttal.

25.12 C. J. Date: "Objects and Relations: Forty-Seven Points of Light," in C. J. Date, Hugh Darwen, and David McGoveran, *Relational Database Writings 1994–1997*. Reading, Mass.: Addison-Wesley (1998).

A blow-by-blow response to reference [25.19].

25.13 C. J. Date: "Relational Really Is Different," installment no. 10 of reference [5.9]. *www.intelligententerprise.com.*

25.14 Linda G. DeMichiel, Donald D. Chamberlin, Bruce G. Lindsay, Rakesh Agrawal, and Manish Arya: "Polyglot: Extensions to Relational Databases for Sharable Types and Functions in a Multi-Language Environment," IBM Research Report RJ8888 (July 1992).

To quote from the abstract: "Polyglot is an extensible relational database type system that supports inheritance, encapsulation, and dynamic method dispatch." (*Dynamic method dispatch* is another term for run-time binding. To continue:) "[Polyglot] allows use from multiple application languages and permits objects to retain their behavior as they cross the boundary between database and application program. This paper describes the design of Polyglot, extensions to the SQL language to support the use of Polyglot types and methods, and the implementation of Polyglot in the Starburst relational [prototype]."

MAJOR_P#	MINOR_P#	QTY
P1	P2	2
P1	P4	4
P5	P3	1
P3	P6	3
P6	P1	9
P5	P6	8
P2	P4	3

Fig. 25.5   A bill-of-materials relation

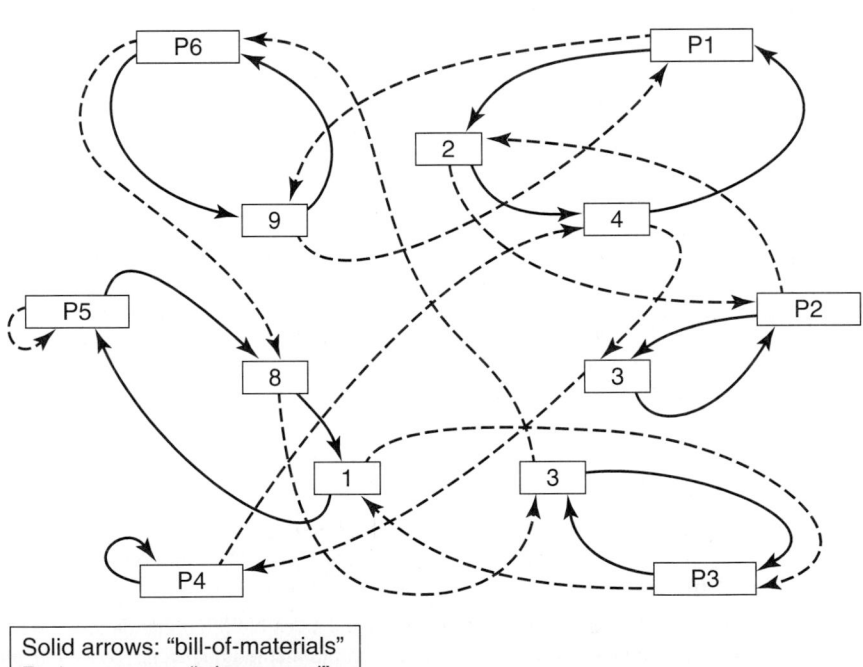

Solid arrows: "bill-of-materials"
Broken arrows: "where-used"

Fig. 25.6   Pointer-based analog of Fig. 25.5

Polyglot is clearly addressing the kinds of issues that are the subject of the present chapter (as well as Chapters 5, 19, and 24). A couple of comments are relevant, however. First, the relational term **domain** is (surprisingly) never mentioned. Second, Polyglot provides the builtin type generators (the Polyglot term is *metatypes*) **base-type, tuple-type, rename-type, array-type,** and **language-type,** but (again surprisingly) not **relation-type.** However, the system is designed to allow the introduction of additional type generators.

25.15 David J. DeWitt, Navin Kabra, Jun Luo, Jignesh M. Patel, and Jie-Bing Yu: "Client-Server Paradise," Proc. 20th Int. Conf. on Very Large Data Bases, Santiago, Chile (September 1994).

Paradise—"Parallel Data Information System"—is an object/relational (originally "extended relational") prototype from the University of Wisconsin, "designed for handling GIS applications" (GIS = Geographic Information System). This paper describes the Paradise design and implementation.

25.16 Michael Godfrey, Tobias Mayr, Praveen Seshadri, and Thorsten von Eichen: "Secure and Portable Database Extensibility," Proc. 1998 ACM SIGMOD Int. Conf. on Management of Data, Seattle, Wash. (June 1998).

"Since user-defined operators are supplied by unknown or untrusted clients, the DBMS must be wary of operators that might crash the system, or modify its files or memory directly (circumventing the authorization mechanisms), or monopolize CPU, memory, or disk resources" (slightly reworded). Controls are obviously needed. This paper reports on investigations into this issue, using Java and the object/relational prototype PREDATOR [25.24]. It concludes, encouragingly, that a database system "can support secure and portable extensibility using Java, without unduly sacrificing performance."

25.17 Laura M. Haas, J. C. Freytag, G. M. Lohman, and Hamid Pirahesh: "Extensible Query Processing in Starburst," Proc. 1989 ACM SIGMOD Int. Conf. on Management of Data, Portland, Ore. (June 1989).

The aims of the Starburst project expanded somewhat after the original paper [25.21] was first written: "Starburst provides support for adding new storage methods for tables, new types of access methods and integrity constraints, new data types, functions, and new operations on tables." The system is divided into two major components, Core and Corona, corresponding respectively to the RSS and RDS in the original System R prototype (see reference [4.2] for an explanation of these two System R components). Core supports the extensibility functions described in reference [25.21]. Corona supports the Starburst query language Hydrogen, which is a dialect of SQL that (a) eliminates most of the implementation restrictions of System R SQL, (b) is much more orthogonal than System R SQL, (c) supports recursive queries, and (d) is user-extensible. The paper includes an interesting discussion of "query rewrite"—i.e., expression transformation rules (see Chapter 17). See also reference [17.50].

25.18 Joseph M. Hellerstein and Jeffrey F. Naughton: "Query Execution Techniques for Caching Expensive Methods," Proc. 1996 ACM SIGMOD Int. Conf. on Management of Data, Montreal, Canada (June 1996).

25.19 Won Kim: "On Marrying Relations and Objects: Relation-Centric and Object-Centric Perspectives," *Data Base Newsletter 22,* No. 6 (November/December 1994).

This paper argues *against* the position that equating relvars and classes is a serious mistake ("The First Great Blunder"). Reference [25.12] is a response to this paper.

25.20 Won Kim: "Bringing Object/Relational Down to Earth," *DBP&D 10,* No. 7 (July 1997).

In this article, Kim claims that "confusion is sure to reign" in the object/relational marketplace because, first, "an inordinate weight has been placed on the role of data type extensibility," and, second, "the measure of a product's object/relational completeness . . . is a potentially serious area of perplexity." He goes on to propose "a practical metric for object/relational completeness that can be used as a guideline for determining whether a product is truly [object/relational]." His scheme involves the following criteria:

1. data model
2. query language
3. mission-critical services
4. computational model
5. performance and scalability
6. database tools
7. harnessing the power

With respect to the first of these criteria (the crucial one!), Kim takes the position—very different from that of *The Third Manifesto* [3.3]—that the data model must be "the Core Object Model defined by the Object Management Group" (OMG), which "comprises the relational data model as well as the core object-oriented modeling concepts of object-oriented programming languages." According to Kim, it thus includes all of the following concepts: *class* (Kim adds "or type"), *instance, attribute, integrity constraints, object IDs, encapsulation, (multiple) class inheritance, (multiple) ADT inheritance, data of type reference, set-valued attributes, class attributes, class methods,* and more besides. Note that relations—which of course we regard as both crucial and fundamental—are never explicitly mentioned; Kim claims that the OMG Core Object Model includes the entire relational model in addition to everything in the foregoing list, but in fact it does not.

25.21 Bruce Lindsay, John McPherson, and Hamid Pirahesh: "A Data Management Extension Architecture," Proc. 1987 ACM SIGMOD Int. Conf. on Management of Data, San Francisco, Calif. (May 1987).

Describes the overall architecture of the Starburst prototype. Starburst "facilitates the implementation of data management extensions for relational database systems." Two kinds of extensions are described in this paper, user-defined storage structures and access methods, and user-defined integrity constraints (but surely *all* integrity constraints are user-defined?) and triggered procedures. However (to quote the paper), "there are, of course, other directions in which it is important to be able to extend [DBMSs, including] user-defined . . . data types [and] query evaluation techniques."

25.22 Guy M. Lohman *et al.:* "Extensions to Starburst: Objects, Types, Functions, and Rules," *CACM 34,* No. 10 (October 1991).

25.23 David Maier: "Comments on the Third-Generation Database System Manifesto," Tech. Report No. CS/E 91-012, Oregon Graduate Center, Beaverton, Ore. (April 1991).

Maier is highly critical of just about everything in reference [25.34]. We agree with some of his criticisms and disagree with others. However, we do find the following remarks interesting (they bear out our contention that objects involve just one good idea, namely *proper data type support*): "Many of us in the object-oriented database field have struggled to distill out the essence of 'object-orientedness' for a database system . . . My own thinking about what was [*sic*] the most important features of OODBs has changed over time. At first I thought it was inheritance and the message model. Later I came to think that object identity, support for complex state, and encapsulation of behavior were more important. Recently, after starting to hear from users of OODBMSs about what they most value about those systems, I think that *type extensibility* is the key. Identity, complex state, and encapsulation are still important, but [only] insomuch as they support the creation of new data types."

25.24 Jignesh Patel *et al.:* "Building a Scalable Geo-Spatial DBMS: Technology, Implementation, and Evaluation," Proc. 1997 ACM SIGMOD Int. Conf. on Management of Data, Tucson, Ariz. (May 1997).

To quote the abstract: "This paper presents a number of new techniques for parallelizing geospatial database systems and discusses their implementation in the Paradise object/relational database system" [25.15].

25.25 Raghu Ramakrishnan: *Database Management Systems.* Boston, Mass.: McGraw-Hill (1998).

25.26 Lawrence A. Rowe and Michael R. Stonebraker: "The Postgres Data Model," Proc. 13th Int. Conf. on Very Large Data Bases, Brighton, UK (September 1987).

25.27 Hanan Samet: *The Design and Analysis of Spatial Data Structures.* Reading, Mass.: Addison-Wesley (1990).

25.28 Cynthia Maro Saracco: *Universal Database Management: A Guide to Object/Relational Technology.* San Francisco, Calif.: Morgan Kaufmann (1999).

A readable high-level overview. However, we note that Saracco embraces (as does Stonebraker, incidentally, in reference [25.31], *q.v.*) a very suspect form of inheritance, involving a version of the subtables and supertables idea—which we are skeptical about to begin with [13.12]—that is significantly different from the version included in SQL3. To be specific, suppose table PGMR ("programmers") is defined to be a subtable of table EMP ("employees"). Then Saracco and Stonebraker regard EMP as containing rows only for employees who are not programmers, whereas SQL3 would regard it as containing rows for *all* employees (see Appendix B).

25.29 Praveen Seshadri and Mark Paskin: "PREDATOR: An OR-DBMS with Enhanced Data Types," Proc. 1997 ACM SIGMOD Int. Conf. on Management of Data, Tucson, Ariz. (May 1997).

"The basic idea in PREDATOR is to provide mechanisms for each data type to specify the semantics of its methods; these semantics are then used for query optimization."

25.30 Michael Stonebraker: "The Design of the Postgres Storage System," Proc. 13th Int. Conf. on Very Large Data Bases, Brighton, UK (September 1987).

25.31 Michael Stonebraker and Paul Brown (with Dorothy Moore): *Object/Relational DBMSs: Tracking the Next Great Wave* (2nd edition). San Francisco, Calif.: Morgan Kaufmann (1999).

This book is a tutorial on object/relational systems. It is heavily—in fact, almost exclusively—based on the Universal Data Option for Informix's Dynamic Server product. That Universal Data Option was based on an earlier system called Illustra (a commercial product that Stonebraker himself was instrumental in developing). See reference [3.3] for an extended analysis and critique of this book; see also the annotation to reference [25.28].

25.32 Michael Stonebraker and Greg Kemnitz: "The Postgres Next Generation Database Management System," *CACM 34,* No. 10 (October 1991).

25.33 Michael Stonebraker and Lawrence A. Rowe: "The Design of Postgres," Proc. 1986 ACM SIGMOD Int. Conf. on Management of Data, Washington, DC (June 1986).

The stated objectives of Postgres are:

1. To provide better support for complex objects;
2. To provide user extensibility for data types, operators, and access methods;
3. To provide active database facilities (alerters and triggers) and inferencing support;
4. To simplify the DBMS code for crash recovery;

5. To produce a design that can take advantage of optical disks, multiprocessor workstations, and custom designed VLSI chips;

6. To make as few changes as possible (preferably none) to the relational model.

25.34 Michael Stonebraker *et al.:* "Third-Generation Database System Manifesto," *ACM SIGMOD Record 19,* No. 3 (September 1990).

In part, this paper is a response to—i.e., counterproposal to—the Object-Oriented Database System Manifesto [24.1], which (among other things) essentially ignores the relational model entirely (!). A quote: "Second generation systems made a major contribution in two areas, nonprocedural data access and data independence, and these advances must not be compromised by third generation systems." The following features are claimed as essential requirements of a third generation DBMS (we have paraphrased the original somewhat):

1. Provide traditional database services plus richer object structures and rules

   - Rich type system
   - Inheritance
   - Functions and encapsulation
   - Optional system-assigned tuple IDs
   - Rules (e.g., integrity rules), not tied to specific objects

2. Subsume second generation DBMSs

   - Navigation only as a last resort
   - Intensional and extensional set definitions (meaning collections that are maintained automatically by the system and collections that are maintained manually by the user)
   - Updatable views
   - Clustering, indexes, etc., hidden from the user

3. Support open systems

   - Multiple language support
   - Persistence orthogonal to type
   - SQL (characterized as "intergalactic dataspeak")
   - Queries and results must be the lowest level of client/server communication

   See reference [3.3] for an extended analysis and critique of this paper, also reference [25.23]. *Note:* By the way, we can now explain why *The Third Manifesto* is called "third" . . . It was specifically written to follow (and, we hope, supersede) the two previous manifestos, references [24.1] and [25.34].

25.35 Maurice V. Wilkes: "Software and the Programmer," *CACM 34,* No. 5 (May 1991).

APPENDIXES

Appendix A gives further details (for reference purposes) of the syntax and semantics of SQL/92 expressions. Appendix B gives an overview of the major features—especially the "object" or "object/relational" features—of SQL3. Appendix C presents a list of the more important abbreviations and acronyms introduced in the body of the text, together with their meanings.

APPENDIX A

SQL Expressions

A.1 INTRODUCTION

SQL expressions—to be more specific, SQL **table, conditional,** and **scalar** expressions—are the heart of the SQL language. In this appendix we present a detailed description of the syntax and semantics of such expressions (as of SQL/92). We should immediately say, however, that the names we use for syntactic categories and SQL language constructs are mostly different from those used in the standard itself [4.22], because the standard terms are often not very apt; in fact, the very terms *table expression, conditional expression,* and *scalar expression* are not standard terms.

A.2 TABLE EXPRESSIONS

Here first is a BNF grammar for *<table expression>*s. The grammar is complete except for a few options having to do with nulls (see Chapter 18, Section 18.7). Note that we make heavy use of the commalist convention introduced in Chapter 4, Section 4.6.

```
<table expression>
    ::=   <join table expression>
        | <nonjoin table expression>

<join table expression>
    ::=   <table reference> [ NATURAL ] JOIN <table reference>
                        [ ON <conditional expression>
                        | USING ( <column name commalist> ) ]
        | <table reference> CROSS JOIN <table reference>
        | ( <join table expression> )

<table reference>
    ::=   <table name> [ [ AS ] <range variable name>
                        [ ( <column name commalist> ) ] ]
        | ( <table expression> ) [ AS ] <range variable name>
                                [ ( <column name commalist> ) ]
        | <join table expression>

<nonjoin table expression>
    ::=   <nonjoin table term>
        | <table expression> UNION [ ALL ]
          [ CORRESPONDING [ BY ( <column name commalist> ) ] ]
                        <table term>
```

```
          | <table expression> EXCEPT [ ALL ]
            [ CORRESPONDING [ BY ( <column name commalist> ) ] ]
                      <table term>

<nonjoin table term>
    ::=    <nonjoin table primary>
         | <table term> INTERSECT [ ALL ]
           [ CORRESPONDING [ BY ( <column name commalist> ) ] ]
                      <table primary>

<table term>
    ::=    <nonjoin table term>
         | <join table expression>

<table primary>
    ::=    <nonjoin table primary>
         | <join table expression>

<nonjoin table primary>
    ::=    TABLE <table name>
         | <table constructor>
         | <select expression>
         | ( <nonjoin table expression> )

<table constructor>
    ::=    VALUES <row constructor commalist>

<row constructor>
    ::=    <scalar expression>
         | ( <scalar expression commalist> )
         | ( <table expression> )

<select expression>
    ::=    SELECT [ ALL | DISTINCT ] <select item commalist>
             FROM <table reference commalist>
               [ WHERE <conditional expression> ]
                 [ GROUP BY <column name commalist> ]
                   [ HAVING <conditional expression> ]

<select item>
    ::=    <scalar expression> [ [ AS ] <column name> ]
         | [ <range variable name>. ] *
```

We now elaborate on one special case (arguably the most important in practice): namely, *<select expression>*s. A *<select expression>* can be thought of, loosely, as a *<table expression>* that involves no JOINs, UNIONs, EXCEPTs, or INTERSECTs— "loosely," because, of course, such operators might be involved in expressions that are nested inside the *<select expression>* in question. For a discussion of JOIN, UNION, EXCEPT, and INTERSECT, see Chapter 7, Section 7.7.

As the foregoing grammar indicates, a *<select expression>* involves, in sequence, a SELECT clause, a FROM clause, and optionally a WHERE clause, a GROUP BY clause, and a HAVING clause. We consider each clause in turn.

The SELECT Clause

The SELECT clause takes the form

```
SELECT [ ALL | DISTINCT ] <select item commalist>
```

Explanation:

1. The *<select item commalist>* must not be empty (see below for a detailed discussion of *<select item>*s).

2. If neither ALL nor DISTINCT is specified, ALL is assumed.

3. Assume for the moment that the FROM, WHERE, GROUP BY, and HAVING clauses have already been evaluated. No matter which of those clauses are specified and which omitted, the conceptual result of evaluating them is always a table (possibly a "grouped" table—see later), which we will refer to as table *T1* (though that conceptual result is in fact unnamed).

4. Let *T2* be the table that is derived from *T1* by evaluating the specified *<select item>*s against *T1* (see below).

5. Let *T3* be the table that is derived from *T2* by eliminating redundant duplicate rows from *T2* if DISTINCT is specified, or a table that is identical to *T2* otherwise.

6. *T3* is the final result.

We turn now to an explanation of *<select item>*s. There are two cases to consider, of which the second is just shorthand for a commalist of *<select item>*s of the first form; thus, the first case is really the more fundamental.

Case 1: The *<select item>* takes the form

```
<scalar expression> [ [ AS ] <column name> ]
```

The *<scalar expression>* will typically (but not necessarily) involve one or more columns of *T1* (see paragraph 3 above). For each row of *T1*, the *<scalar expression>* is evaluated, to yield a scalar result. The commalist of such results (corresponding to evaluation of all *<select item>*s in the SELECT clause against a single row of *T1*) constitutes a single row of *T2* (see paragraph 4 above). If the *<select item>* includes an AS clause, the unqualified *<column name>* from that clause is assigned as the name of the corresponding column of *T2* (the optional keyword AS is just noise and can be omitted without affecting the meaning). If the *<select item>* does not include an AS clause, then (a) if it consists simply of a (possibly qualified) *<column name>*, then that *<column name>* is assigned as the name of the corresponding column of *T2;* (b) otherwise the corresponding column of *T2* effectively has no name (actually it is given an "implementation-dependent" name [4.19,4.22]).

Points arising:

- Because it is, specifically, the name of a column of *T2,* not *T1,* a name introduced by an AS clause cannot be used in the WHERE, GROUP BY, and HAVING clauses (if any) directly involved in the construction of *T1.* It can, however, be referenced in an associated ORDER BY clause if any (in particular, in DECLARE CURSOR), and also in an "outer" *<table expression>* that contains the *<select expression>* under discussion nested within it.

- If a *<select item>* includes an aggregate operator invocation *and* the *<select expression>* does not include a GROUP BY clause (see below), then no *<select item>*

in the SELECT clause can include any reference to a column of *T1* unless that column reference is the argument (or part of the argument) to an aggregate operator invocation.

Case 2: The <select item> takes the form

```
[ <range variable name> . ] *
```

If the qualifier is omitted (i.e., the <*select item*> is just an unqualified asterisk), then this <*select item*> must be the only <*select item*> in the SELECT clause. This form is shorthand for a commalist of all of the <*column name*>s for *T1*, in left-to-right column order. If the qualifier is included (i.e., the <*select item*> consists of an asterisk qualified by a range variable name *R*, thus: "*R.**"), then the <*select item*> represents a commalist of <*column name*>s for all of the columns of the table associated with range variable *R*, in left-to-right order. (Recall from Section 7.7 that a table name can and often will be used as an implicit range variable. Thus, the <*select item*> will frequently be of the form "*T.**" rather than "*R.**".)

The FROM Clause

The FROM clause takes the form

```
FROM <table reference commalist>
```

The <*table reference commalist*> must not be empty. Let the specified <*table reference*>s evaluate to tables *A, B, ..., C,* respectively. Then the result of evaluating the FROM clause is a table that is equal to the Cartesian product of *A, B, ..., C. Note:* Recall that the Cartesian product of a single table *T* is defined to be equal to *T* (see the answer to Exercise 6.12 in Chapter 6); in other words, it is (of course) legal for the FROM clause to contain just a single <*table reference*>.

The WHERE Clause

The WHERE clause takes the form

```
WHERE <conditional expression>
```

Let *T* be the result of evaluating the immediately preceding FROM clause. Then the result of the WHERE clause is a table that is derived from *T* by eliminating all rows for which the <*conditional expression*> does not evaluate to *true.* If the WHERE clause is omitted, the result is simply *T.*

The GROUP BY Clause

The GROUP BY clause takes the form

```
GROUP BY <column name commalist>
```

The <*column name commalist*> must not be empty. Let *T* be the result of evaluating the immediately preceding FROM clause and WHERE clause (if any). Each <*column name*>

mentioned in the GROUP BY clause must be the optionally qualified name of a column of *T*. The result of the GROUP BY clause is a **grouped table**—i.e., a set of groups of rows, derived from *T* by conceptually rearranging it into the minimum number of groups such that within any one group all rows have the same value for the combination of columns identified by the GROUP BY clause. Note carefully, therefore, that the result is thus "not a proper table" (it is, to repeat, a table of groups, not a table of rows). However, a GROUP BY clause never appears without a corresponding SELECT clause whose effect is to derive a proper table (i.e., a table of rows) from that table of groups, so little harm is done by this temporary departure from the relational framework.

If a *<select expression>* includes a GROUP BY clause, then there are restrictions on the form that the corresponding SELECT clause can take. To be specific, each *<select item>* in the SELECT clause (including any that are implied by an asterisk shorthand) must be **single-valued per group.** Thus, such *<select item>*s must not include any reference to any column of table *T* that is not mentioned in the GROUP BY clause itself—*unless* that reference is the argument, or part of the argument, to some aggregate operator invocation (the effect of such an invocation is, of course, to reduce some collection of scalar values from a group to a single scalar value).

The HAVING Clause

The HAVING clause takes the form

```
HAVING <conditional expression>
```

Let *G* be the grouped table resulting from the evaluation of the immediately preceding FROM clause, WHERE clause (if any), and GROUP BY clause (if any). If there is no GROUP BY clause, then *G* is taken to be the result of evaluating the FROM and WHERE clauses alone, considered as a grouped table that contains exactly one group;* in other words, there is an implicit, conceptual GROUP BY clause in this case that specifies *no grouping columns at all.* The result of the HAVING clause is a grouped table that is derived from *G* by eliminating all groups for which the *<conditional expression>* does not evaluate to *true.*

Points arising:

- If the HAVING clause is omitted but the GROUP BY clause is included, the result of the HAVING clause is simply *G*. If the HAVING and GROUP BY clauses are both omitted, the result is simply the "proper"—i.e., nongrouped—table *T* resulting from the FROM and WHERE clauses.

- Any *<scalar expression>*s in a HAVING clause must be single-valued per group (like *<scalar expression>*s in the SELECT clause if there is a GROUP BY clause, as discussed above).

---

*This is what the standard says, though logically it should say at *most* one group (there should be no group at all if the FROM and WHERE clauses yield an empty table).

A Comprehensive Example

We conclude our discussion of *<select expression>*s with a reasonably complex example that illustrates some (by no means all) of the points explained above. The query is as follows: *For all red and blue parts such that the total quantity supplied is greater than 350 (excluding from the total all shipments for which the quantity is less than or equal to 200), get the part number, the weight in grams, the color, and the maximum quantity supplied of that part.* Here is a possible SQL formulation of this query:

```
SELECT  P.P#,
        'Weight in grams =' AS TEXT1,
        P.WEIGHT * 454 AS GMWT,
        P.COLOR,
        'Max quantity =' AS TEXT2,
        MAX ( SP.QTY ) AS MXQTY
FROM    P, SP
WHERE   P.P# = SP.P#
AND     ( P.COLOR = 'Red' OR P.COLOR = 'Blue')
AND     SP.QTY > 200
GROUP   BY P.P#, P.WEIGHT, P.COLOR
HAVING  SUM ( SP.QTY ) > 350 ;
```

Explanation: First, note that (as explained in the foregoing subsections) the clauses of a *<select expression>* are conceptually evaluated in the order in which they are written—with the sole exception of the SELECT clause itself, which is evaluated last. In the example, therefore, we can imagine the result being constructed as follows:

1. **FROM:** The FROM clause is evaluated to yield a new table that is the Cartesian product of tables P and SP.

2. **WHERE:** The result of Step 1 is reduced by the elimination of all rows that do not satisfy the WHERE clause. In the example, therefore, rows not satisfying the *<conditional expression>*

```
        P.P# = SP.P#
AND     ( P.COLOR = 'Red' OR P.COLOR = 'Blue')
AND     SP.QTY > 200
```

3. **GROUP BY:** The result of Step 2 is grouped by values of the column(s) named in the GROUP BY clause. In the example, those columns are P.P#, P.WEIGHT, and P.COLOR. *Note:* In theory P.P# alone would be sufficient as the grouping column here, since P.WEIGHT and P.COLOR are themselves single-valued per part number (i.e., they are functionally dependent on part number). However, SQL is not aware of this latter fact, and will raise an error if P.WEIGHT and P.COLOR are omitted from the GROUP BY clause, because they *are* mentioned in the SELECT clause. See reference [10.6] for a discussion of this point.

4. **HAVING:** Groups not satisfying the *<conditional expression>*

```
SUM ( SP.QTY ) > 350
```

are eliminated from the result of Step 3.

5. **SELECT:** Each group in the result of Step 4 generates a single result row, as follows. First, the part number, weight, color, and maximum quantity are extracted from the

group. Second, the weight is converted to grams. Third, the two character strings "Weight in grams =" and "Max quantity =" are inserted at the appropriate points in the row. Note, incidentally, that—as the phrase "appropriate points in the row" suggests—we are relying here on the fact that columns of tables have a left-to-right ordering in SQL; the strings would not make much sense if they did not appear at those "appropriate points."

The final result looks like this:

P#	TEXT1	GMWT	COLOR	TEXT2	MXQTY
P1	Weight in grams =	5448	Red	Max quantity =	300
P5	Weight in grams =	5448	Blue	Max quantity =	400
P3	Weight in grams =	7718	Blue	Max quantity =	400

Please understand that the algorithm just described is intended purely as a **conceptual** explanation of how a *<select expression>* is evaluated. The algorithm is certainly correct, in the sense that it is guaranteed to produce the correct result. However, it would probably be rather inefficient if actually executed. For example, it would be very unfortunate if the system were actually to construct the Cartesian product in Step 1. Considerations such as these are exactly the reason why relational systems require an optimizer, as discussed in Chapter 17. Indeed, the task of the optimizer in an SQL system can be characterized as that of finding an implementation procedure that will produce the same result as the conceptual algorithm sketched above but is more efficient than that algorithm.

A.3   CONDITIONAL EXPRESSIONS

Like *<table expression>*s, *<conditional expression>*s appear in numerous contexts throughout the SQL language; in particular, of course, they are used in WHERE clauses to qualify or disqualify rows for subsequent processing.* In this section we discuss some of the most important features of such expressions. Please note, however, that our treatment is definitely *not* meant to be exhaustive. In particular, we ignore everything to do with nulls once again; as we saw in Chapter 18, *<conditional expression>*s require significantly extended treatment when the implications and complications of nulls are taken into account, and certain *<conditional expression>* formats, not covered in this appendix, are provided solely to deal with certain aspects of null support. These matters are, however, all described in Chapter 18.

As in the previous section, we begin with a BNF grammar. We then go on to discuss certain specific cases, namely *<like condition>*s, *<match condition>*s, *<all or any condition>*s, and *<unique condition>*s, in a little more detail (all other cases either have already been illustrated in the body of the book or else are self-explanatory, or both).

---

*We remind you that (as noted in Chapter 8) conditional expressions are the SQL analog of what we have been calling *boolean* expressions in the body of the book.

```
<conditional expression>
    ::=   <conditional term>
        | <conditional expression> OR <conditional term>

<conditional term>
    ::=   <conditional factor>
        | <conditional term> AND <conditional factor>

<conditional factor>
    ::=   [ NOT ] <conditional primary>

<conditional primary>
    ::=   <simple condition> | ( <conditional expression> )

<simple condition>
    ::=   <comparison condition>
        | <in condition>
        | <like condition>
        | <match condition>
        | <all or any condition>
        | <exists condition>
        | <unique condition>

<comparison condition>
    ::=   <row constructor>
                <comparison operator> <row constructor>

<comparison operator>
    ::=   =  |  <  |  <=  |  >  |  >=  |  <>

<in condition>
    ::=   <row constructor> [ NOT ] IN ( <table expression> )
        | <scalar expression> [ NOT ] IN
                        ( <scalar expression commalist> )

<like condition>
    ::=   <character string expression> [ NOT ] LIKE <pattern>
                                    [ ESCAPE <escape> ]

<match condition>
    ::=   <row constructor> MATCH UNIQUE ( <table expression> )

<all or any condition>
    ::=   <row constructor>
                <comparison operator> ALL ( <table expression> )
        | <row constructor>
                <comparison operator> ANY ( <table expression> )

<exists condition>
    ::=   EXISTS ( <table expression> )

<unique condition>
    ::=   UNIQUE ( <table expression> )
```

LIKE Conditions

LIKE conditions are intended for simple pattern-matching on character strings—i.e., testing a given character string to see whether it conforms to some prescribed pattern. The syntax (to repeat) is:

```
<character string expression> [ NOT ] LIKE <pattern>
                                 [ ESCAPE <escape> ]
```

Here *<pattern>* is an arbitrary character string expression, and *<escape>* (if specified) is a character string expression that evaluates to a single character. Here is an example:

```
SELECT P.P#, P.PNAME
FROM    P
WHERE   P.PNAME LIKE 'C%';
```

("Get part numbers and names for parts whose names begin with the letter C"). *Result:*

P#	PNAME
P5	Cam
P6	Cog

So long as no ESCAPE clause is specified, characters within *<pattern>* are interpreted as follows:

- The underscore character "_" stands for *any single character.*
- The percent character "%" stands for *any sequence of n characters* (where *n* can be zero).
- All other characters stand for themselves.

In the example, therefore, the query returns rows from table P for which the PNAME value begins with an upper case C and has any sequence of zero or more characters following that C.

Here are some more examples:

`ADDRESS LIKE '%Berkeley%'`	— evaluates to *true* if ADDRESS contains the string "Berkeley" anywhere inside it
`S# LIKE 'S__'`	— evalutes to *true* if S# is exactly 3 characters long and the first is "S"
`PNAME LIKE '%c___'`	— evaluates to *true* if PNAME is 4 characters long or more and the last but three is "C"
`MYTEXT LIKE '=_%'` `       ESCAPE '='`	— evaluates to *true* if MYTEXT begins with an underscore character (see below)

In this last example, the character "=" has been specified as the escape character, which means that the special interpretation given to the characters "_" and "%" can be disabled, if desired, by preceding such characters with an "=" character.

Finally, the *<like condition>*

```
x NOT LIKE y [ ESCAPE z ]
```

is defined to be semantically equivalent to

```
NOT ( x LIKE y [ ESCAPE z ] )
```

MATCH Conditions

A *<match condition>* takes the form

```
<row constructor> MATCH UNIQUE ( <table expression> )
```

Let *r1* be the row that results from evaluating the *<row constructor>* and let *T* be the table that results from evaluating the *<table expression>*. Then the *<match condition>* evaluates to *true* if and only if *T* contains exactly one row, *r2* say, such that the comparison

```
r1 = r2
```

evaluates to *true.* Here is an example:

```
SELECT SP.*
FROM   SP
WHERE  NOT ( SP.S# MATCH UNIQUE ( SELECT S.S# FROM S ) ) ;
```

("Get shipments that do not have exactly one matching supplier in the suppliers table"). Such a query might be useful in checking the integrity of the database, because, of course, there should not *be* any such shipments if the database is correct. Note, however, that an *<in condition>* could be used to perform exactly that same check.

Incidentally, the UNIQUE can be omitted from MATCH UNIQUE, but then MATCH becomes synonymous with IN (at least in the absence of nulls).

All-or-Any Conditions

An *<all or any condition>* has the general form

```
<row constructor> <comparison operator> <qualifier>
                                 ( <table expression> )
```

where the *<comparison operator>* is any of the usual set (=, <>, etc.), and the *<qualifier>* is ALL or ANY. In general, an *<all or any condition>* evaluates to *true* if and only if the corresponding comparison without the ALL (respectively ANY) evaluates to *true* for all (respectively any) of the rows in the table represented by the *<table expression>*. (If that table is empty, the ALL conditions evaluate to *true,* the ANY conditions evaluate to *false.*) Here is an example ("Get part names for parts whose weight is greater than that of every blue part"):

```
SELECT DISTINCT PX.PNAME
FROM    P AS PX
WHERE   PX.WEIGHT >ALL ( SELECT PY.WEIGHT
                         FROM    P AS PY
                         WHERE   PY.COLOR = 'Blue' ) ;
```

Given our usual sample data, the result looks like this:

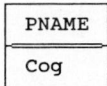

PNAME
Cog

Explanation: The nested *<table expression>* returns the set of weights for blue parts. The outer SELECT then returns the name of those parts whose weight is greater than every value in that set. In general, of course, the final result might contain any number of part names (including zero).

Note: A word of caution is appropriate here, at least for native English speakers. The fact is, *<all or any condition>*s are seriously error-prone. A very natural English formulation of the foregoing query would use the word "any" in place of "every," which could easily lead to the (incorrect) use of >ANY instead of >ALL. Analogous criticisms apply to every one of the ANY and ALL operators.

UNIQUE Conditions

A *<unique condition>* is used to test that every row within some table is unique (i.e., there are no duplicates). The syntax is:

```
UNIQUE ( <table expression> )
```

The condition evaluates to *true* if the *<table expression>* evaluates to a table in which the rows are all distinct, to *false* otherwise.

A.4   SCALAR EXPRESSIONS

SQL's *<scalar expression>*s are essentially straightforward. We content ourselves here with a list of some of the most important operators that can be used in the construction of such expressions, offering just a few comments on a couple of those operators (CASE and CAST) whose meaning is perhaps not immediately apparent. In alphabetic order, the operators are:

```
arithmetic operators (+, -, *, /)    OCTET_LENGTH
BIT_LENGTH                           POSITION
CASE                                 SESSION_USER
CAST                                 SUBSTRING
CHARACTER_LENGTH                     SYSTEM_USER
concatenation (||)                   TRIM
CURRENT_USER                         UPPER
LOWER                                USER
```

Note that aggregate operator invocations can also appear within *<scalar expression>*s, since they return a scalar result. Furthermore, a *<table expression>* enclosed in parentheses can also be treated as a scalar value, so long as it evaluates to a table of exactly one row and one column.

We now elaborate slightly on the operators CASE and CAST.

CASE Operations

A CASE operation returns one of a specified set of values, depending on a specified condition. For example:

```
CASE
    WHEN S.STATUS <  5 THEN 'Last resort'
    WHEN S.STATUS < 10 THEN 'Dubious'
    WHEN S.STATUS < 15 THEN 'Not too good'
    WHEN S.STATUS < 20 THEN 'Mediocre'
    WHEN S.STATUS < 25 THEN 'Acceptable'
    ELSE                   'Fine'
END
```

CAST Operations

CAST converts a specified scalar value to a specified scalar data type. For example:

```
CAST ( P.WEIGHT AS FLOAT )
```

Not all pairs of data types are mutually convertible; for example, conversions between numbers and bit strings are not supported. See reference [4.22] for details of precisely which data types can be converted to which.

An Overview of SQL3

B.1 INTRODUCTION

SQL3 will probably be ratified as a standard ("SQL/99") round about the time this book appears in print. We did not want to base our earlier SQL discussions on SQL3, however, partly for reasons explained in Chapter 4 and partly because—to say the least—we find SQL3 somewhat confused anyway. On the other hand, we did feel an overview, at least, of the major SQL3 features should be included somewhere; hence this appendix.

SQL3 includes the whole of SQL/92, of course, except for a few minor features (none of them discussed in this book) that have deliberately been dropped: SQLCODE, unsigned integers instead of column names in ORDER BY, "introducers" on identifiers, certain user-defined character sets and collations and translations, and a few other things. For obvious reasons, however, we concentrate here on those features that have been added since 1992, and we use the name "SQL3" for convenience to refer to those features specifically. Of those new features, easily the most significant are the ones having to do with user-defined data types and related matters, which we discuss in Sections B.2–B.5. The most important of the other features are surveyed briefly in Section B.6. *Note:* A detailed analysis and critique of the subject matter of Sections B.2–B.5 can be found in reference [3.3].

Before getting into details of SQL3 as such, we should say a word regarding **SQLJ** [4.6]. The name "SQLJ" refers informally to a project to consider possible degrees of integration between SQL and Java (the project is a joint effort involving some of the best-known SQL DBMS vendors). Part 0 of that project deals with embedded SQL in Java programs; Part 1 is concerned with the idea of invoking Java from SQL (e.g., calling a stored procedure that is written in Java); and Part 2 addresses the possibility of using Java classes as SQL data types (e.g., as a basis for defining columns in SQL tables). None of this activity is technically part of SQL3 as such, but SQLJ Part 0 has already been published (at least in the US) as the first component of a new *Part 10* of the draft SQL standard [4.22], and it is likely that SQLJ Parts 1 and 2 will follow soon, possibly around the time SQL3 is formally published.

It is also likely that a new version of **SQL/CLI** (see Chapter 4) will appear at round about the same time.

A few editorial comments regarding what follows: First, we often use the "#" character in column names in our examples (as we did in the body of the book), even though "#" is in fact not a valid SQL3 character; we also use the semicolon ";" as a statement terminator (again as in earlier examples). Second, we should make it clear that the discussions that follow are nowhere near exhaustive. Finally, of course, it is in the nature of things that some details might have changed by the time SQL3 is ratified. *Caveat lector.*

B.2 NEW DATA TYPES

As suggested in the previous section, the most immediately visible aspects of SQL3 all have to do with data types.* There are new **builtin** types (new builtin *scalar* types, to be precise); there are new builtin **type generators** (SQL3 calls them type *constructors*); and there is a **CREATE TYPE** statement that allows users to define their own types (and a corresponding DROP TYPE statement also, of course). We consider each of these features in turn.

Builtin Scalar Types

Three new builtin scalar types are supported:

- **BOOLEAN:** BOOLEAN is, of course, a *truth value* type; the usual boolean operators (NOT, AND, OR) are supported, and a boolean expression can appear in all the places where scalar expressions can usually appear (loosely speaking). Note, however, that SQL considers there to be *three* truth values, not two, as we saw in Chapter 18; the corresponding literals are TRUE, FALSE, and UNKNOWN. This fact notwithstanding, the type BOOLEAN includes only two values, not three; the *unknown* truth value is represented—quite incorrectly!—by *null* (for example, assigning UNKNOWN to a variable of type BOOLEAN will actually set that variable to null). To understand the seriousness of this flaw, you might care to meditate on the analogy of a numeric type that used null instead of zero to represent zero.

  Another oddity is that SQL3 (strangely) does not regard a simple boolean variable reference as an instance of what in Appendix A we called a *<conditional primary>*. Thus, e.g., if B is of type BOOLEAN, a WHERE clause of the form WHERE B is illegal!

  Along with the BOOLEAN type, SQL3 introduces two new *aggregate operators,* EVERY—not ALL, for some reason—and ANY. The argument in both cases is a column of BOOLEAN values (almost certainly a derived column, as in, e.g., the WHERE clause WHERE ANY (QTY > 200)). If the column is empty, both operators return *unknown* (or, rather, *null*);[†] if the column is nonempty, EVERY returns *true* if every value in the column is *true* and *false* otherwise, and ANY returns *false* if every value in the column is *false* and *true* otherwise. As with other SQL aggregate operators, nulls are eliminated before the aggregation is done.

- **CLOB** ("character large object"): This type represents variable-length character strings of essentially unlimited size. An associated *locator* mechanism, analogous (somewhat)

---

*It is tempting to add that one of the most immediately *in*visible parts is SQL-style "domains" (see Chapters 4 and 5), which seem to be quietly being ignored.

[†]Contrast the behavior of the all-or-any conditions in this respect (see Appendix A).

to the familiar cursor mechanism, allows such strings to be accessed piecemeal. Many of the usual character string operators are not supported for such strings; among those that *are* supported are "=" and LIKE.

- **BLOB** ("binary large object"): Analogous, except that the strings are strings of "octets"—i.e., bytes, in effect—instead of characters.

Generated Types

The SQL3 type generators are REF, ARRAY, and ROW. However, the only way to define a "REF type" is *implicitly,* as a side effect of defining a "structured type" via CREATE TYPE (see later in this section); we therefore ignore REF for now. As for ARRAY and ROW types, they cannot really be *defined,* as such, at all (there are no separate CREATE ARRAY TYPE or CREATE ROW TYPE statements); they can only be *used,* by invoking the relevant type generator "inline" in (e.g.) a CREATE TABLE statement. Here, for example, is an illustration of the use of an **ARRAY type:**

```
CREATE TABLE SALES
     ( ITEM# CHAR(5),
       QTY   INTEGER ARRAY [12],
     PRIMARY KEY ( ITEM# ) ) ;
```

Column QTY here is array-valued; a QTY value consists of an array of 12 elements, each of type INTEGER. *Note:* SQL arrays are limited to one dimension, and the elements are not allowed to be arrays in turn.

Here is an example of a query against SALES:

```
SELECT  ITEM#
FROM    SALES
WHERE   QTY [3] > 100 ;
```

("Get item numbers for items whose March sales exceeded 100"; note the subscripted reference). And here is an example of inserting a row:

```
INSERT INTO SALES ( ITEM#, QTY )
VALUES ( 'X4320',
         ARRAY [ 0, 0, 0, 0, 0, 0, 0, 0, 0, 0, 0, 0 ] ) ;
```

(note the array literal).

ROW types are similar. For example:

```
CREATE TABLE CUST
    ( CUST# CHAR(3),
      ADDR  ROW ( STREET CHAR(50),
                  CITY    CHAR(25),
                  STATE   CHAR(2),
                  ZIP     CHAR(5) )
    PRIMARY KEY ( CUST# ) ) ;
```

Sample query:

```
SELECT  CUST#
FROM    CUST
WHERE   ADDR.STATE = 'CA' ;
```

Sample insertion:

```
INSERT INTO CUST ( CUST#, ADDR )
VALUES ( '001', ROW ( '1600 Pennsylvania Ave.',
                      'Washington', 'DC', '20500' ) ) ;
```

DISTINCT Types

The new CREATE TYPE statement creates a **user-defined type:** either a *DISTINCT* type or a *"structured"* type (observe in passing that *generated* types—see the previous subsection—are not regarded as "user-defined" types in the same sense). In this subsection, we discuss DISTINCT types only. A DISTINCT type (we set "DISTINCT" in upper case to stress the point that the word is not being used in its usual natural language sense) is a limited special case of a user-defined type. In particular, its physical implementation must involve exactly one of the builtin scalar types. Here is the syntax for defining a **DISTINCT type:**

```
CREATE TYPE <type name>
    AS <builtin scalar type name> FINAL
    [ <cast options> ]
    [ <method specification commalist> ] ;
```

Here is an example:

```
CREATE TYPE WEIGHT AS NUMERIC (5,1) FINAL ;
```

Explanation:

1. Type WEIGHT inherits the comparison operators that apply to the underlying type (i.e., type NUMERIC). Note, however, that WEIGHT values are comparable with each other *and nothing else.* Thus, for example, if WT is an SQL variable of type WEIGHT, the following comparison is not legal:

```
WT > 14.7
```

   Assuming appropriate *<cast options>* have been specified, however (we omit the details here), the following comparisons, by contrast, would both be legal:

```
WT > CAST ( 14.7 AS WEIGHT )

CAST ( WT AS NUMERIC ) > 14.7
```

   Moreover, the two CAST invocations shown could be abbreviated to WEIGHT(14.7) and NUMERIC(WT), respectively. *Note:* The function names WEIGHT and NUMERIC here are specified by the type definer (in the *<cast options>*)—they are *not* implied by the name of the type being defined or the name of its underlying type.

2. Analogous remarks apply to assignment—i.e., a WEIGHT value can be assigned only to a target of type WEIGHT (and nothing else can be assigned to such a target).

3. Type WEIGHT does not automatically inherit other operators from the underlying type. However, the *<method specification>*s (none shown in the example) allow the type definer to specify "methods"—see the next subsection—that apply to values and

variables of type WEIGHT. Regular SQL procedures and functions can also be defined that operate on values and variables of type WEIGHT. We might, for example, define a function called ADDW that adds two weights to obtain a third, thereby allowing the user to write expressions such as the following:

```
ADDW ( WT1, WT2 )

ADDW ( WT1, WEIGHT ( 14.7 ) )
```

4. The specification FINAL must appear. See the subsection immediately following.

Structured Types

The other kind of user-defined type is a **structured type.** Here are a couple of examples:*

```
CREATE TYPE POINT AS ( X FLOAT, Y FLOAT ) FINAL ;

CREATE TYPE LINESEG AS ( BEGIN POINT, END POINT ) FINAL ;
```

Explanation:

1. Type POINT is said to have *attributes* X and Y (not to be confused with tuple and relation attributes as defined in Part II of this book); likewise, type LINESEG is said to have attributes BEGIN and END. An attribute can be of any known type.

2. Unfortunately, the attributes mentioned in the definition of a structured type constitute the *physical implementation* of values of the type in question, not a "possible representation" in the sense of Chapter 5. Thus, e.g., points in the example are physically implemented in terms of their Cartesian coordinates.

3. Each attribute definition automatically causes definition of one *observer* (loosely, "get") operator and one *mutator* (loosely, "set") operator, for which dot qualification syntax is used.† For example, let Z, P, and LS be SQL variables of types FLOAT, POINT, and LINESEG, respectively. Then the following are all legal:

```
P.X            /* gets the value of the X component of point P */

LS.BEGIN.X             /* gets the value of the X component of */
                       /* the BEGIN point of line segment LS   */

SET P.X = Z ;          /* sets the X component of point P to */
                       /* the value of Z                     */

SET LS.BEGIN.X = Z ;   /* sets the X component of the BEGIN */
                       /* point of line segment LS to the   */
                       /* value of Z                        */
```

---

*Actually the second example fails, because BEGIN and END are reserved words.

†It should be noted that the "mutator" is not truly a mutator in the sense of Chapter 5—i.e., an update operator—because it is defined to return a value. The (unpleasant) consequences of this fact are unfortunately beyond the scope of this brief appendix. See reference [3.3] for a detailed discussion.

4. The only other operators available for these types—because we have not defined any additional ones—are equality comparison and assignment operators, which are available for *every* type. Note in particular that POINT and LINESEG "selectors" (in the sense of Chapter 5) are not defined automatically, and hence that there are no POINT and LINESEG literals.

5. The specification FINAL means that any attempt to define another type as a proper subtype of either of these types will fail (see Section B.3); i.e., these types are both leaf types, and will remain so.

6. Are types POINT and LINESEG (or structured types in general) "encapsulated"? Sadly, the answer to this question seems to depend on context. For example, when a structured type is used as the type of some *column,* the answer is *yes* (sort of). However, when it is used as the type of some *table*—see Section B.4—then the answer is definitely *no.*

   Note: The reason we say "sort of" in the first case is that, even in that case, the "get and set" operators effectively expose the attributes of the type (as already noted), and those operators cannot be overridden. Perhaps we should use the term "*pseudoencapsulated*"—or perhaps **pseudoscalar**—to refer to the first case.

Here then is the general syntax for defining a structured type that is not a proper subtype (see Section B.3 for a discussion of the proper subtype case):

```
CREATE TYPE <type name>
    AS ( <attribute definition commalist> )
      [ <ref type implementation> ]
    [ [ NOT ] INSTANTIABLE ]
    [ NOT ] FINAL
    [ <method specification commalist> ] ;
```

Explanation:

1. The <attribute definition commalist> must not be empty.

2. The optional <*ref type implementation*> is discussed in Section B.4.

3. NOT INSTANTIABLE means the type is a *dummy* type in the sense of Chapter 19. The default is INSTANTIABLE.

4. NOT FINAL means the type can have proper subtypes, FINAL means it cannot.

5. The operators that apply to values and variables of a given structured type *T* are:

   a. The attribute observers and mutators described above;

   b. Assignment, "=", and possibly "<" (the last two of these are both defined by means of a separate statement, CREATE ORDERING FOR *T,* though why an ordering should have to be created just to define "=" is not very clear);

   c. Those procedures and functions that are defined to take a parameter of type *T* (or any proper supertype thereof—see Section B.3);

   d. Those *methods* that are defined to take a special "target" parameter of type *T* or any proper supertype thereof (again, see Section B.3). *Note:* "Methods" here are methods in the traditional object sense (see Chapter 24)—i.e., they are operators that treat one parameter as special. If method *M* is defined for type *T* and *X* is an expression of type *T*, then the special dot qualification syntax *X.M* is used to invoke *M* on *X*. (We assume here for simplicity that *M* takes no other parameters.)

The <*method specification*>s define method "specification signatures" in the sense of Chapters 19 and 24. However, they also include a great deal of other material, much of it of an implementation nature and (in this writer's opinion) misplaced. The actual code that implements the methods is defined elsewhere.

B.3 TYPE INHERITANCE

SQL3's support for type inheritance is not very orthogonal, since it applies only to structured types; i.e., it does not support type inheritance for builtin, generated,* or DISTINCT types. Furthermore, it does not support multiple inheritance at all. In this section, we consider type inheritance for "pseudoscalar" structured types only (which might be regarded as the respectable case, more or less); we leave the case of *unencapsulated* structured types to Section B.5, later.

The biggest logical differences between the type inheritance model presented in Chapter 19 and SQL3's "pseudoscalar" type inheritance are as follows:

- SQL3 supports structural as well as behavioral inheritance.
- SQL3 does not adequately distinguish between values and variables; in particular, therefore, it does not distinguish between value substitutability and variable substitutability.
- SQL3 has no support for type constraints, and hence no support for specialization by constraint either.
- SQL3 requires update operators ("mutators") to be inherited unconditionally.

One consequence of these differences is that SQL3 permits "noncircular circles" and similar nonsenses, as noted in Chapter 19. Another is that certain SQL3 comparisons will give *false* when they ought to give *true* (because, e.g., a value of most specific type ELLIPSE can have equal semiaxes, and therefore correspond to a circle in the real world, in SQL3).

Here is what our usual ellipses and circles example might look like in SQL3:

```
CREATE TYPE ELLIPSE
   AS ( A LENGTH, B LENGTH, CTR POINT )
      NOT FINAL ;

CREATE TYPE CIRCLE UNDER ELLIPSE
   AS ( R LENGTH )                    -- unrealistic! (see below)
      NOT FINAL ;
```

---

*Except possibly row types. There are some puzzles in connection with row type inheritance, however, the details of which are beyond the scope of this appendix.

Note, however, that with these definitions the physical implementation of type CIRCLE will involve four components—A, B, and CTR (inherited from type ELLIPSE), and R (specified for type CIRCLE only). For any given circle, of course, three of those components will have the same value. Alternatively, we might define a *method* R for type CIRCLE (instead of the R attribute); type CIRCLE would then have the same physical implementation as type ELLIPSE, and that implementation would thus involve less redundancy. On the other hand, if C is a variable of declared type CIRCLE, then assignment to C.R will be legal with the first of these designs but not with the second. Then again, assignment to C.R, if supported, will—in general—produce a "circle" such that C.R ≠ C.A!

Here are a few more points of difference between the type inheritance model described in Chapter 19 and type inheritance as supported in SQL3:

- SQL3 uses the term "direct" (as in *direct subtype*) in place of the more apt "immediate."

- SQL3 uses the term "maximal supertype" in place of "root type."

- SQL3 supports an operator called TREAT (analogous to TREAT DOWN). For example, the SQL3 analog of the expression TREAT_DOWN_AS_CIRCLE(E) is TREAT E AS CIRCLE.

- SQL3 also supports an operator that might be thought of (loosely) as "TREAT UP." For example, consider the following operator invocation:

```
AREA ( C AS ELLIPSE )
```

The specification "AS ELLIPSE" forces the *ELLIPSE* version of the AREA operator to be invoked, even if the declared type of variable C is CIRCLE. *Note:* This operator can be used only in certain contexts; to be specific, it can be used only to "treat up" an argument to an invocation of some user-defined operator, as in the example. We remark that the provision of this functionality seems to suggest some confusion over model *vs.* implementation issues—after all, users should not even have to know there are two versions of AREA.

- SQL3 also supports a method of the form *X*.SPECIFICTYPE, which returns the most specific type of its argument *X* as a character string.

- The SQL3 analogs of IS_*T*(*X*) and IS_MS_*T*(*X*) look like this:

```
X IS OF ( T )

X IS OF ( ONLY T )
```

B.4 REFERENCE TYPES

Recall our claim in Chapter 24 that object systems involve just one good idea, namely *proper data type support* (or two good ideas, if we count type inheritance separately). As we have seen, SQL3 does include some of this "good" functionality (though its support is far from ideal). Unfortunately, however, it also includes some related functionality that is—in our opinion—very bad. In fact, SQL3 comes very close to committing both *The First*

Great Blunder (equating tables and classes) and *The Second Great Blunder* (mixing pointers and tables) as well. And it has to be said that the "justification" for doing so is very unclear, at least to this writer; it seems to be little more than a vague idea that the features in question somehow make SQL3 more "object-like."

Be that as it may, let us now try to explain what the relevant features actually are. First of all, SQL3 allows a base table to be defined, not just in terms of an explicit set of named typed columns in the usual way, but also in terms of a *user-defined structured type*. For example:

```
CREATE TYPE DEPT_TYPE
    AS ( DEPT#  CHAR(3),
         DNAME  CHAR(25),
         BUDGET MONEY )
       REF IS SYSTEM GENERATED ... ;

CREATE TABLE DEPT OF DEPT_TYPE
      ( REF IS DEPT_ID SYSTEM GENERATED,
        PRIMARY KEY ( DEPT# ),
        UNIQUE ( DEPT_ID ) ) ... ;
```

Explanation:

1. Given the definition of a structured type *T,* the system automatically generates an associated *reference type* ("REF type") called REF(*T*). Values of type REF(*T*) are "references" to rows of type *T* within some base table* that has been defined to be "OF" type *T* (see point 3 below). *Note: T* can be used in other contexts, of course—for example, as the declared type for some variable *V* or some column *C*. However, no REF(*T*) values are associated with those other uses.

2. REF IS SYSTEM GENERATED in a CREATE TYPE statement means the actual values of the associated REF type are provided by the system (other options—for example, REF IS USER GENERATED—are available, but we omit the details here). REF IS SYSTEM GENERATED is the default.

3. A base table can be defined (via CREATE TABLE) to be "OF" some structured type. The keyword OF here is not really very appropriate, however, because the table is *not* actually "of" the type in question, and neither are its rows.[†] In particular, additional columns, over and above the "columns" (or attributes, rather) of the structured type itself, can be specified for the table. In fact, at least one such additional column *must* be specified—namely, a column of the applicable REF type—though the syntax for defining that column is not the usual column definition syntax but instead looks like this:

```
REF IS <column name> SYSTEM GENERATED
```

This extra column is used to contain unique IDs ("references") for the rows of the base table in question (the specification UNIQUE (<*column name*>) is implied, though it can also be stated explicitly as in our example). The ID for a given row is assigned

---

*Or possibly some view. Details of the view case are beyond the scope of this appendix.

[†]Note in particular, therefore, that if the declared type of some parameter *P* to some operator *Op* is some structured type *T,* a row from a base table that has been defined to be "OF" type *T* cannot be passed as a corresponding argument to an invocation of that operator *Op*.

when the row is inserted and remains associated with that row* until it is deleted. *Note:* The repetition of the specification SYSTEM GENERATED is apparently required. (Perhaps surprisingly, a SYSTEM GENERATED column *can* be a target column in an INSERT or UPDATE operation, though special considerations apply; we omit the details here.) More to the point, it is not clear why it should be necessary to define the table to be "OF" some structured type in the first place—instead of just defining an appropriate column in the usual way—in order to obtain the "unique ID" functionality,

4. As indicated in Section B.2, a structured type such as DEPT_TYPE is not regarded as encapsulated when it is used as the basis for defining a base table, although it *is* so regarded (more or less) in other contexts. In the example, therefore, base table DEPT has four columns, not just two as it would if DEPT_TYPE were encapsulated.

5. We have shown DEPT# as the primary key for table DEPT. Given that DEPT rows have unique IDs ("references"), however, we could use those IDs as primary key values instead, if we wanted to, thus:

```
CREATE TABLE DEPT OF DEPT_TYPE
      ( REF IS DEPT_ID SYSTEM GENERATED,
        PRIMARY KEY ( DEPT_ID ),
        UNIQUE ( DEPT# ) ) ... ;
```

Let us now extend the example to introduce an EMP base table, thus:

```
CREATE TABLE EMP
      ( EMP#    CHAR(5),
        ENAME   CHAR(25),
        SALARY  MONEY,
        DEPT_ID REF ( DEPT_TYPE ) SCOPE DEPT
                REFERENCES ARE CHECKED
                ON DELETE CASCADE,
      PRIMARY KEY ( EMP# ) ) ... ;
```

Normally, base table EMP would include a foreign key column DEPT# that refers to departments by department number. Here, however, we have a "reference" column DEPT_ID—not explicitly declared to be a foreign key column as such—that refers to departments by their "references" instead. SCOPE DEPT specifies the applicable referenced table. REFERENCES ARE CHECKED means referential integrity is to be maintained (REFERENCES ARE NOT CHECKED would permit "dangling references"; it is not clear why it would ever be desirable to specify this option). ON DELETE . . . specifies a delete rule, analogous to the usual foreign key delete rules (the same options are supported); note, however, that if it is in fact the case that column DEPT_ID in base table DEPT cannot be updated (see point 3 above), then no corresponding ON UPDATE rule is needed.

We now consider some sample queries involving this database. Here first is an SQL3 formulation of "Get department number for employee E1":

```
SELECT EX.DEPT_ID -> DEPT# AS DEPT#
FROM   EMP EX
WHERE  EX.EMP# = 'E1' ;
```

---

*There is some circularity here: "That row" can only mean "the row that has the particular ID in question." Note the value *vs.* variable confusion!

Note the **dereferencing** operation* in the SELECT clause (the expression EX.DEPT_ID → DEPT# returns the DEPT# value from the DEPT row that the DEPT_ID value in question points to). Note too that the AS specification in that clause is more or less required (if it were omitted, the result column would be given an "implementation-dependent" name). Note finally the counterintuitive nature of the FROM clause—the DEPT# value to be retrieved comes from DEPT, not EMP, but DEPT_ID values come from EMP, not DEPT. *Note:* It is hard to resist the temptation to point out that this query will probably perform *worse* than its conventional SQL counterpart (which would access just one table, not two). We make this observation because the usual argument in favor of "references" is that they are supposed to improve performance.

By the way, if the query had been "Get the *department* (instead of just the department number) for employee E1," the dereferencing operation would have been rather different:

```
SELECT DEREF ( EX.DEPT_ID ) AS DEPT
FROM   EMP EX
WHERE  EX.EMP# = 'E1' ;
```

Furthermore, the DEREF invocation shown would return, not a *row* value, but an "encapsulated" (scalar) value.

Here is another example—"Get employee numbers for employees in department D1" (note the dereferencing in the WHERE clause):

```
SELECT EX.EMP#
FROM   EMP EX
WHERE  EX.DEPT_ID -> DEPT# = 'D1' ;
```

And here is an INSERT example (insertion of an employee):

```
INSERT INTO EMP ( EMP#, DEPT_ID )
       VALUES ( 'E5', ( SELECT DX.DEPT_ID
                        FROM   DEPT DX
                        WHERE  DX.DEPT# = 'D2' ) ) ;
```

B.5 SUBTABLES AND SUPERTABLES

Consider the following structured types:

```
CREATE TYPE EMP_TYPE
  AS ( EMP# ..., DEPT# ... )
     REF IS SYSTEM GENERATED
     NOT FINAL ... ;

CREATE TYPE PGMR_TYPE UNDER EMP_TYPE
  AS ( LANG ... )
     NOT FINAL ... ;
```

Note, incidentally, that PGMR_TYPE has no REF IS … clause; instead, it effectively inherits such a clause from its immediate ("direct") supertype EMP_TYPE.

---

*Most languages that support dereferencing support a *referencing* operation as well, but SQL3 does not.

Now consider the following base table definitions:

```
CREATE TABLE EMP OF EMP_TYPE
    ( REF IS EMP_ID SYSTEM GENERATED,
      PRIMARY KEY ( EMP# ),
      UNIQUE ( EMP_ID ) ) ;

CREATE TABLE PGMR OF PGMR_TYPE UNDER EMP ;
```

Note the specification UNDER EMP on the definition of base table PGMR (note also the omission of the REF IS ..., PRIMARY KEY, and UNIQUE specifications for that base table). Base tables PGMR and EMP are said to be a **subtable** and the corresponding immediate ("direct") **supertable,** respectively; PGMR inherits the columns (etc.) of EMP and adds one column, LANG, of its own. The intuition behind the example is that nonprogrammers have a row in table EMP only, while programmers have a row in both tables—so every row in PGMR has a counterpart in EMP, but the converse is not true.

Data manipulation operations on these tables behave as follows:

- *SELECT:* SELECT on EMP behaves normally. SELECT on PGMR behaves as if PGMR actually contained the columns of EMP, as well as the column LANG. *Note:* The qualifier ONLY can be used in a *<table reference>* to exclude rows that have counterparts in some subtable of the table in question. Thus, e.g., the operation SELECT ... FROM ONLY EMP behaves as if EMP included only rows with no counterpart in PGMR.

- *INSERT:* INSERT into EMP behaves normally. INSERT into PGMR effectively causes new rows to appear in both EMP and PGMR.

- *DELETE:* DELETE from EMP causes rows to disappear from EMP and (when the rows in question happen to correspond to programmers) from PGMR too. DELETE from PGMR causes rows to disappear from both EMP and PGMR.

- *UPDATE:* Updating LANG, necessarily via PGMR, updates PGMR only; updating other columns, via either EMP or PGMR, updates both tables (conceptually).

Note the following implications of the foregoing:

- Suppose employee Joe becomes a programmer. If we simply try to insert a row for Joe into PGMR, the system will attempt to insert a row for Joe into EMP as well—an attempt that will fail, of course. Instead, we have to delete Joe's row from EMP and then insert an appropriate row into PGMR.

- Conversely, suppose employee Joe ceases to be a programmer. This time, we have to delete Joe's row from either EMP or PGMR (whichever table we specify, the effect will be to delete it from both) and then insert an appropriate row into EMP.

What does all of this have to do with type inheritance? As far as we can see, the answer is *nothing*—nothing, that is, except that (for reasons that are unclear, to say the least) SQL3 requires a subtable and its immediate ("direct") supertable to be defined over structured types that are, respectively, a subtype and its immediate ("direct") supertype. Observe that there is no substitutability involved in this arrangement; observe too that the types involved are very definitely not "encapsulated."

So what do subtables and supertables buy us? The answer seems to be "very little," at least at the level of the *model*.* It is true that certain *implementation* economies might be realized, if the subtable and its supertable are physically stored as a single table on the disk; but, of course, such considerations should not be allowed to have any effect on the model as such. In other words, not only is it unclear, as noted in the previous paragraph, as to why "sub and super" tables have to rely on "sub and super" structured types, it is also very unclear as to why the feature is supported *at all*.

B.6   OTHER FEATURES

CREATE TABLE

SQL3 supports a **LIKE option** on CREATE TABLE, permitting some or all of the column definitions of a new base table to be copied from some existing named table (note that *named*—it is not possible to specify an arbitrary table expression in place of the table name).

Table Expressions

In Chapter 5 we described a **WITH** clause, the purpose of which is to introduce shorthand names for certain expressions. SQL3 includes a similar construct, but its use is limited to *table* expressions only. Here is an example:

```
WITH LONG_TERM_EMPS AS
    ( SELECT *
      FROM   EMP
      WHERE  DATE_HIRED < DATE '1980-01-01' )
SELECT EMP#, ( LONG_TERM_CT - 1 ) AS #_OF_FELLOW_LONG_TERM_EMPS
FROM   LONG_TERM_EMPS AS L1,
      ( SELECT DEPT#, COUNT(*) AS LONG_TERM_CT
        FROM   LONG_TERM_EMPS
        GROUP  BY DEPT# ) AS L2
WHERE  L1.DEPT# = L2.DEPT# ;
```

("For each employee who has been with the company since 1979 or earlier, get the employee number and a count of other such employees in the same department.")

The SQL3 WITH clause can be used in particular to formulate certain **recursive** queries. For example, given the table PARENT_OF (PARENT, CHILD), the following recursive query returns all pairs of people (*a,b*) such that *a* is an ancestor of *b*. Observe that the definition of the introduced name ANCESTOR_OF includes a reference to ANCESTOR_OF itself.

---

*Perhaps we should remind you of our own preferred approach to this issue—if issue it truly is—which makes use of *views* (see the example at the very end of Section 13.5).

```
WITH RECURSIVE ANCESTOR_OF ( ANCESTOR, DESCENDANT )
AS ( SELECT PARENT, CHILD
     FROM   PARENT_OF
     UNION
     SELECT A.PARENT, P.CHILD
     FROM   ANCESTOR_OF AS A, PARENT_OF AS P
     WHERE  A.CHILD = P.PARENT )

SELECT *
FROM   ANCESTOR_OF ;
```

Conditional Expressions

SQL3 provides a new **DISTINCT** condition (not to be confused with the existing UNIQUE condition—see Appendix A) for testing whether two rows are "distinct." Let the rows in question be *Left* and *Right; Left* and *Right* must contain the same number, *n* say, of components each. Let the *i*th components of *Left* and *Right* be *Li* and *Ri,* respectively (*i* = 1, 2, …, *n*). The type of *Li* must be compatible with the type of *Ri.* Then the expression

   Left IS DISTINCT FROM *Right*

returns *false* if and only if, for all *i,* either (a) "*Li = Ri*" is *true,* or (b) *Li* and *Ri* are both null; otherwise it returns *true.* (In other words, *Left* and *Right* are "distinct" if and only if they are not "duplicates" of one another in the sense of Chapter 18.) Note that a DISTINCT condition never evaluates to *unknown.*

SQL3 also provides a new **SIMILAR** condition, which (like LIKE) is intended for character string pattern-matching—i.e., testing a given character string to see whether it conforms to some prescribed pattern. The difference is that SIMILAR supports a much more extensive range of possibilities ("wild cards," etc.) than LIKE does. The syntax is:

   <character string expression> [NOT] SIMILAR TO <pattern>
                                         [ESCAPE <escape>]

The *<pattern>* and *<escape>* specifications are essentially as for LIKE, except that *<pattern>* can involve additional special characters—not just "_" and "%" as in LIKE, but also "∗", "+", "−", and many others. The general intent seems to be to support the parsing of expressions written in some formal language. *Note:* It is worth mentioning that the rules for SIMILAR were copied from the similar operator in POSIX.

In closing this subsection, we remark that, given the existence of the new builtin type BOOLEAN, conditional expressions are now really just a special kind of scalar expression (as indeed they should have been all along).

Integrity

SQL3 supports the **RESTRICT** *<referential action>,* which is similar but not identical to NO ACTION (see Chapter 8 for an explanation of the difference). It also includes some support for **triggered procedures** ("triggers"); in particular, it includes a CREATE TRIGGER statement, which defines a *trigger*—i.e., a combination of an *event* specification and an *action* specification, where:

- An *event* is an INSERT, UPDATE (optionally of specified columns), or DELETE against a specified named table;
- The *action* is an action (in effect, a procedure) to be performed AFTER or BEFORE the specified event occurs.

More precisely, the *action* consists of an optional conditional expression (defaulting to TRUE), plus an SQL procedure that will be executed if and only if the condition is *true* when the *event* occurs. The user can specify whether the action is to take place just once per occurrence of the event or once FOR EACH ROW of the table with which the event is associated. Furthermore, the action specification can refer to "before" and "after" values in the table associated with the specified event, thus providing a primitive level of support for (among other things) *transition constraints.*

View Updating

SQL3 extends SQL's support for **view updating** to include "UNION ALL" views and one-to-one and one-to-many join views. Analogous extensions apply to cursors also.

Transaction Management

SQL3 includes several new transaction management features:

- An explicit **START TRANSACTION** statement (with the same operands as SET TRANSACTION—see Chapter 14);
- A **WITH HOLD** option on DECLARE CURSOR (again, see Chapter 14);
- Support for **savepoints** (see the annotation to reference [14.11]).

Security

SQL3 supports **column-specific SELECT privileges** (the "SELECT(x)" privilege allows the holder to reference a specific column x of a specific named table within a *<table expression>*). It also supports user-defined **roles;** an example might be ACCG, meaning everyone in the accounting department. Once created, a role can be granted privileges, just as if it were a user ID. Furthermore, roles can be granted, like privileges, and, like all privileges, they can be granted either to a user ID or to another role.

Missing Information

We make just one observation under this heading: namely, that SQL3's new type facilities are (predictably enough) complicated by the presence of nulls. For example, let V be a variable of some structured type T. Then it is possible that some component of V might be null (in which case the conditional expression $V = V$ will give *unknown*), and yet the conditional expression V IS NULL will give *false!* In fact, we can say in general that if $((V = V)$ IS NOT TRUE) IS TRUE is *true,* then V is either null or includes a null component.

Decision Support

SQL3 includes support for the **GROUPING SETS, ROLLUP,** and **CUBE** options on GROUP BY as described in Chapter 21.

Abbreviations, Acronyms, and Symbols

ACID	atomicity/consistency/isolation/durability
ACM	Association for Computing Machinery
ADT	abstract data type
ANSI	American National Standards Institute
ANSI/SPARC	literally, ANSI/Systems Planning and Requirements Committee; used to refer to the three-level database system architecture described in Chapter 2
ARIES	algorithm for recovery and isolation exploiting semantics
BB	same as GB
BCNF	Boyce/Codd normal form
BCS	British Computer Society
BLOB	binary large object
BNF	Backus-Naur form or Backus normal form
CACM	*Communications of the ACM* (ACM publication)
CAD/CAM	computer-aided design/computer-aided manufacturing
CASE	computer-aided software engineering
CDO	class-defining object
CIM	computer-integrated manufacturing
CLI	Call-Level Interface (part of the SQL standard)
CLOB	character large object
CNF	conjunctive normal form
CODASYL	literally, Conference on Data Systems Languages; used to refer to certain prerelational (network) systems such as IDMS
CPU	central processing unit
CS	cursor stability (DB2)
CWA	Closed World Assumption

DA	data administrator
DB/DC	database/data communications
DBA	database administrator
DBMS	database management system
DBP&D	*Database Programming & Design* (magazine, now online)
DBTG	literally, Data Base Task Group; used interchangeably with CODASYL (in database contexts)
DC	data communications
DCO	"domain check override"
DDB	distributed database
DDBMS	distributed DBMS
DDL	data definition language
DES	Data Encryption Standard
DK/NF	domain-key normal form
DML	data manipulation language
DNF	disjunctive normal form
DRDA	Distributed Relational Database Architecture (IBM)
DSL	data sublanguage
DSS	decision support system
DUW	distributed unit of work
E/R	entity/relationship
EB	exabyte (1024PB)
EDB	extensional database
EKNF	elementary key normal form
EMVD	embedded MVD
FD	functional dependence
GB	gigabyte (1024MB)
GIS	geographic information system
HOLAP	hybrid OLAP
I/O	input/output
IDB	intensional database
IDMS	Integrated Database Management System
IEEE	Institute for Electrical and Electronics Engineers
IMS	Information Management System
IND	inclusion dependence

IS	intent shared (lock); information systems
ISBL	Information System Base Language
ISO	International Organization for Standardization
IT	information technology
IX	intent exclusive (lock)
JACM	*Journal of the ACM* (ACM publication)
JD	join dependence
JDBC	Java Database Connectivity
K	1024 (sometimes 1000)
KB	kilobyte (1024 bytes)
LAN	local area network
LOB	large object
MB	megabyte (1024KB)
MLS	multi-level secure
MOLAP	multi-dimensional OLAP
MVD	multi-valued dependence
NCITS	National Committee on Information Technology Standards (previously known as X3)
NCITS/H2	NCITS database committee (previously known as X3H2)
NF^2	"NF squared" = NFNF = non first normal form (?)
ODBC	Open Database Connectivity
ODMG	Object Data Management Group
ODS	operational data store
OID	object ID
OLAP	online analytic processing
OLCP	online complex processing
OLDM	online decision management
OLTP	online transaction processing
OMG	Object Management Group
OO	object-oriented; object orientation
OODB	object-oriented database
OOPL	object-oriented programming language
OQL	Object Query Language (part of ODMG)
OSI	Open Systems Interconnection
OSQL	"Object SQL"

PB	petabyte (1024TB)
PC	personal computer
PJ/NF	projection-join normal form
PODS	Principles of Database Systems (ACM conference)
PRTV	Peterlee Relational Test Vehicle
PSM	Persistent Stored Modules (part of the SQL standard)
QBE	Query-By-Example
QUEL	Query Language
RAID	redundant array of inexpensive disks
RDA	Remote Data Access
RDB	relational database
RDBMS	relational DBMS
RID	(stored) record ID or row ID
ROLAP	relational OLAP
RM/T	relational model/Tasmania
RM/V1	relational model/Version 1
RM/V2	relational model/Version 2
RPC	remote procedure call
RR	repeatable read (DB2)
RUW	remote unit of work
RVA	relation-valued attribute
S	shared (lock)
SIGMOD	Special Interest Group on Management of Data (ACM special interest group)
SIX	shared intent exclusive (lock)
SPARC	*see* ANSI/SPARC
SQL	(originally) Structured Query Language; sometimes Standard Query Language
TB	terabyte (1024GB)
TCB	Trusted Computing Base
TCP/IP	Transmission Control Protocol/Internet Protocol
TID	(stored) tuple ID
TODS	*Transactions on Database Systems* (ACM publication)
TPC	Transaction Processing Council
U	update (lock)

UDT	user-defined type
UML	Unified Modeling Language
unk	*unknown* (truth value)
UNK	unknown (null)
UOW	unit of work
VLDB	very large database; Very Large Data Bases (annual conference)
VSAM	Virtual Storage Access Method (IBM)
WAL	write-ahead log
WAN	wide area network
WFF	well-formed formula
WORM	write once/read many times
WYSIWYG	what you see is what you get
X	exclusive (lock)
X3	*see* NCITS
X3H2	*see* NCITS/H2
1NF	first normal form
2NF	second normal form
2PC	two-phase commit
2PL	two-phase locking
2VL	two-valued logic
2øC	same as 2PC
2øL	same as 2PL
3GL	third generation language
3VL	three-valued logic
3NF	third normal form
4GL	fourth generation language
4NF	fourth normal form
4VL	four-valued logic
5NF	fifth normal form (same as PJ/NF)
$\in$	belongs to
Θ	comparison operator (=, <, etc.)
$\emptyset$	the empty set
$\rightarrow$	functionally determines

$\twoheadrightarrow$	multi-determines
$\equiv$	is equivalent to
$\Rightarrow$	implies (logical connective)
$\vdash$	implies (metalinguistic symbol)
$\vDash$	it is always the case that (metalinguistic symbol)
■	end (of proof, example, etc.)

Index

GROUP (**Tutorial D**), *see* grouping and ungrouping
GROUP BY clause (SQL), 223, 891–892
grouped table (SQL), 892
grouping and ungrouping, 179ff
reversibility, 181
GROUPING SETS, 716
growth in the database, 293
Grumbach, Stéphane, 807
Gupta, Anoop, 578
Gupta, Ramesh, 689

Haas, Laura M., 883
Hackathorn, Richard D., 689, 728
Haderle, Don, 470
Hadjinian, P., 727
Hadzilacos, Vassos, 466
Hall, Patrick A. V., 153, 187, 189, 443, 568
Halpin, Terry, 444, 445
Hammer, Joachim, 321
Hammer, Michael M., 277, 446, 447, 689
Han, Jiawei, 806, 807
Härder, Theo, 469, 497
Haritsa, Jayant, 689
Hasan, Waqar, 569, 581
hash join, *see* join implementation
hash lookup, *see* join implementation
HAVING clause (SQL), 224, 892
Hawkes, Nigel, 531
heading
relation, 65, 123
relvar, 131
Heath, Ian J., 354, 366, 379, 610
Heath's theorem, 354, 379, 393
Held, Gerald D., 231, 232
Helland, Pat, 688
Heller, M., 493
Hellerstein, Joseph M., 274, 569, 883
Hellman, M. E., 522, 530
Henschen, Lawrence J., 806, 807
hidden data, 292
hierarchic system, 25–26
Hitchcock, Peter, 187, 189
HOLAP, 722

Holsapple, C. W., 727
Hopewell, Paul, 30
Horn, Alfred, 782
Horn clause, 782
Horowitz, Bruce M., 277
host language, 37
Howard, J. H., 410
Hull, Richard, 447
Hultén, Christer, 852
Hurson, A. R., 687
hybrid OLAP, *see* HOLAP

I_KEY, 756
I_MINUS, *see* temporal difference
IDB, 787
idempotence, 547
IF ... THEN..., *see* logical implication
IF_UNK, 588
impedance mismatch, 843
implementation *vs.* model, *see* data model
implication, *see* logical implication
implication problem, 410
IN
SQL, 106, 218, 219, 224
Tutorial D, 183
in doubt, 672
inclusion dependency, *see* IND
inclusion polymorphism, *see* polymorphism
inconsistent analysis, 476, 480
IND, 342
independent projections, 364–365, 384
index lookup, *see* join implementation
indicator variable (SQL), 604
individual tracker, 517
Indurkhya, Bipin, 648
inference controls, 530
inferential DBMS, 800
inflight checking, 277
Information Principle, 61, 221
Information Schema (SQL), 87
Informix Universal Data Option, 862
Ingres, 231, 232, 279, 510–511, 574
Ingres/Star, 654

inheritance
effect on relational algebra, 631, 632
scalar *vs.* tuple *vs.* relation, 616
single *vs.* multiple, 616
SQL3, 906ff
structural *vs.* behavioral, 616
type 613ff
see also subtype
Inmon, William H., 727, 728
INSERT
embedded (SQL), 93
SQL, 4, 87
Tutorial D, 132
instance, *see* object
instance variable, 818, 819–820
inverse, 842
private, 819
protected, 820
public, 819
virtual, 849
integrated (database), *see* data integration
integrity, 249ff
OO, 840–841
SQL, 267–271
see also candidate key; dependency; foreign key; integrity constraint; predicate; referential integrity
integrity constraint, 18
attribute, *see* attribute constraint
classification scheme, 251
database, *see* database constraint
immediate *vs.* deferred, 251–254
relvar, *see* relvar constraint
SQL, 267–271
state *vs.* transition, 256–257
type, *see* type constraint
intension (relation heading), 123
intensional database, *see* IDB
intent locking, 486–488, 496
Interchangeability Principle, 263, 295
internal DDL, 40
internal level, 33, 40
internal record, 40
see also stored record

ADDISON-WESLEY
INTERACTIVE TEXTBOOKS

Powered By Versabook Version 3.53

If the text runs off the side of your screen, select Word Wrap from the Edit menu. All the text will now fit on your screen.

SETTING UP

Take note of the minimum system requirements and follow the installation instructions.

RECOMMENDED SYSTEM REQUIREMENTS

- Pentium CPU (minimum 133 mhz)
- Windows 95 OSR2, 98, 2000, NT or ME
- 32 MB RAM
- 100 MB free hard disk space
- 800 x 600 monitor resolution
- 16 bit high-color
- 12X CD-ROM drive (recommended) or DVD-ROM drive
- 28.8K modem to connect to the Versabook eBookstore and other online components
- Windows compatible sound card

(please see other side for installation instructions)

```
<table expression>
   ::=    <join table expression>
        | <nonjoin table expression>

<join table expression>
   ::=    <table reference>
                [ NATURAL ] JOIN <table reference>
                [ ON <conditional expression>
                | USING ( <column name commalist> ) ]
        | <table reference> CROSS JOIN <table reference>
        | ( <join table expression> )

<table reference>
   ::=    <table name> [ [ AS ] <range variable name>
                        [ ( <column name commalist> ) ] ]
        | ( <table expression> ) [ AS ] <range variable name>
                        [ ( <column name commalist> ) ]
        | <join table expression>

<nonjoin table expression>
   ::=    <nonjoin table term>
        | <table expression> UNION [ ALL ] [ CORRESPONDING
                        [ BY ( <column name commalist> ) ] ]
                        <table term>
        | <table expression> EXCEPT [ ALL ] [ CORRESPONDING
                        [ BY ( <column name commalist> ) ] ]
                        <table term>

<nonjoin table term>
   ::=    <nonjoin table primary>
        | <table term> INTERSECT [ ALL ] [ CORRESPONDING
                        [ BY ( <column name commalist> ) ] ]
                        <table primary>

<table term>
   ::=    <nonjoin table term>
        | <join table expression>

<table primary>
   ::=    <nonjoin table primary>
        | <join table expression>

<nonjoin table primary>
   ::=    TABLE <table name>
        | <table constructor>
        | <select expression>
        | ( <nonjoin table expression> )

<table constructor>
   ::=    VALUES <row constructor commalist>

<row constructor>
   ::=    <scalar expression>
        | ( <scalar expression commalist> )
        | ( <table expression> )

<select expression>
   ::=    SELECT [ ALL | DISTINCT ] <select item commalist>
             FROM <table reference commalist>
                [ WHERE <conditional expression> ]
                   [ GROUP BY <column name commalist> ]
                      [ HAVING <conditional expression> ]

<select item>
   ::=    <scalar expression> [ [ AS ] <column name> ]
        | [ <range variable name>. ] *
```

The syntax of SQL *table expression*s